# Proof, Language, and Interaction

**Foundations of Computing (selected titles)**

Michael Garey and Albert Meyer, editors

*Algebraic Theory of Processes*
Matthew Hennessy, 1988

*PX: A Computational Logic*
Susumu Hayashi and Hiroshi Nakano, 1989

*The Stable Marriage Problem: Structure and Algorithms*
Dan Gusfield and Robert Irving, 1989

*Realistic Compiler Generation*
Peter Lee, 1989

*Basic Category Theory for Computer Scientists*
Benjamin C. Pierce, 1991

*Categories, Types, and Structures: An Introduction to Category Theory for the Working Computer Scientist*
Andrea Asperti and Giuseppe Longo, 1991

*Semantics of Programming Languages: Structures and Techniques*
Carl A. Gunter, 1992

*The Formal Semantics of Programming Languages: An Introduction*
Glynn Winskel, 1993

*Hilbert's Tenth Problem*
Yuri V. Matiyasevich, 1993

*Exploring Interior-Point Linear Programming: Algorithms and Software*
Ami Arbel, 1993

*Theoretical Aspects of Object-Oriented Programming: Types, Semantics, and Language Design*
edited by Carl A. Gunter and John C. Mitchell, 1994

*From Logic to Logic Programming*
Kees Doets, 1994

*The Structure of Typed Programming Languages*
David A. Schmidt, 1994

*Logic and Information Flow*
edited by Jan van Eijck and Albert Visser, 1994

*Circuit Complexity and Neural Networks*
Ian Parberry, 1994

*Control Flow Semantics*
Jaco de Bakker and Erik de Vink, 1996

*Algebraic Semantics of Imperative Programs*
Joseph A. Goguen and Grant Malcolm, 1996

*Algorithmic Number Theory, Volume I: Efficient Algorithms*
Eric Bach and Jeffrey Shallit, 1996

*Foundations for Programming Languages*
John C. Mitchell, 1996

*Computability and Complexity: From a Programming Perspective*
Neil D. Jones, 1997

*Proof, Language, and Interaction: Essays in Honour of Robin Milner*
edited by Gordon Plotkin, Colin Stirling, and Mads Tofte, 2000

# Proof, Language, and Interaction
# Essays in Honour of Robin Milner

Edited by Gordon Plotkin, Colin Stirling, and Mads Tofte

The MIT Press
Cambridge, Massachusetts
London, England

This book was set in Times Roman by LaTeX and was printed and bound in the United States of America.

Library of Congress Cataloging-in-Publication Data

Proof, language, and interaction : essays in honour of Robin Milner

edited by Gordon Plotkin, Colin Stirling, and Mads Tofte.

p. cm. — (Foundation of computing)

Includes bibliographical references (p. ).

ISBN 0-262-16188-5 (hc : alk. paper)

1. Computer science. 2. Milner, R. (Robin), 1934– .

I. Plotkin, G. (Gordon), 1946– . II. Stirling, Colin

III. Tofte, Mads. IV. Milner, R. (Robin), 1934– . V. Series.

QA76.P699 2000

004—dc21 99-27800

CIP

# Contents

## Series Foreword

Theoretical computer science has now undergone several decades of development. The "classical" topics of automata theory, formal languages, and computational complexity have become firmly established, and their importance to other theoretical work and to practice is widely recognized. Stimulated by technological advances, theoreticians have been rapidly expanding the areas under study, and the time delay between theoretical progress and its practical impact has been decreasing dramatically. Much publicity has been given recently to breakthroughs in cryptography and linear programming, and steady progress is being made on programming language semantics, computational geometry, and efficient data structures. Newer, more speculative, areas of study include relational databases, VLSI theory, and parallel and distributed computation. As this list of topics continues expanding, it is becoming more and more difficult to stay abreast of the progress that is being made and increasingly important that the most significant work be distilled and communicated in a manner that will facilitate further research and application of this work. By publishing comprehensive books and specialized monographs on the theoretical aspects of computer science, the series on Foundations of Computing provides a forum in which important research topics can be presented in their entirety and placed in perspective for researchers, students, and practitioners alike.

Michael R. Garey
Albert R. Meyer

# Preface

This volume is a Festschrift to honour the scientific life and achievement of Robin Milner. Robin's contributions have been both profound and varied, over a period, now, of some thirty years. They range through the semantic foundations of programming languages, computer-assisted theorem-proving, programming language design, and the theory of concurrency. Throughout this work Robin has combined taste and elegance with a well-judged concern for applicability. Indeed, the relation between theory and practice has been a major source of concern and inspiration, not only in his scientific work but also in his contribution to the social fabric of our subject, both as a founder and first director of the Laboratory for Foundations of Computer Science at Edinburgh University, and, more recently, as head of department at Cambridge. His work continues to have a strong and wide influence, and we feel it will have a permanent place in the history of our subject.

When we first began the Festschrift project we did not anticipate how long it would take nor how large was the task. We therefore particularly appreciate the generous help we have been given by many people, whether as referees, giving technical advice, offering encouragement, or being a (very) patient editor. We therefore thank: Samson Abramsky, Peter Aczel, Jos Baeten, Gérard Berry, Gérard Boudol, Julian Bradfield, Pierre-Louis Curien, Edmund Clarke, Gianluigi Ferrari, Andrzej Filinski, Mike Fourman, Healfdene Goguen, Mike Gordon, Matthew Hennessy, Robert Harper, Tony Hoare, Gérard Huet, Hans Huttel, Paul Jackson, Cliff Jones, David Matthews, Pepe Meseguer, Albert Meyer, Eugenio Moggi, Faron Moller, Mogens Nielsen, Luke Ong, Joachim Parrow, Lawrence Paulson, Benjamin Pierce, Randy Pollack, John Power, Bob Prior, Jon Riecke, Giuseppe Rosolini, Davide Sangiorgi, Vladimiro Sassone, Scott Smolka, David N. Turner, David Walker, and Glynn Winskel.

Gordon Plotkin
Colin Stirling
Mads Tofte

Robin Milner

# Introduction

We have included here papers representing all areas of Robin's contribution. They have been written by a range of his collaborators and also of those colleagues whose work is closely related. As well as being a tribute to Robin, we hope that readers will take away an impression of a seamless whole, ranging from quite abstract considerations to systems of great utility. That is, there is a certain semantically oriented approach to (a part of) the foundations of computer science that helps understand a wide range of hardware and software systems and applications, and moreover guides their construction and analysis. This is a point that is not, perhaps, as widely appreciated as it should be. That it holds, is in great part due to Robin's pioneering effort.

The volume begins with a brief scientific biography to give the reader some appreciation of the scope of his scientific contribution and an impression of its evolution over the years. Other papers are also of a historical nature: Gordon's contribution tells of the history of the HOL system, and its roots in Robin's LCF; Engberg and Nielsen recount their early work on name-passing calculi, comparing it to Robin's later $\pi$-calculus.

There are five sections: Semantic Foundations, Programming Logic, Programming Languages, Concurrency, and Mobility. To an extent this reflects the development of Robin's interests. However, some papers that might have been included under one of the last two headings in fact appear elsewhere. We feel that this not only results in a better balance, but also makes a point about the ultimate unity of our subject.

The section on Semantic Foundations begins with two papers about full abstraction. That by Curien et al. is in a tradition of exploring mathematical structures that may eventually lead to a direct construction of a fully abstract model for PCF; that by Abramsky is in the more recent game-theoretic tradition, and aims at an axiomatic account of such intensional models. The last three papers concern the semantics of programming languages more broadly, whether operational, denotational or given more indirectly by axioms. The paper by Hoare et al. relates the operational semantics to algebraic laws; that by de Bakker and van Brueghel relates operational semantics to a denotational semantics using metric spaces; that by Gadducci and Montanari presents an abstract categorical framework for operational semantics well adapted to process calculi, and bearing some relation to Robin's work on action structures.

The section on Programming Logic begins with two papers concerning systems for computer-aided proof. They are within a type-theoretic approach, as was Milner's LCF. Paulson considers the implementation of proof systems for recursive types, that is types defined in terms of themselves; these include inductively defined sets and with types with infinite objects. Constable et al. present a formalization of computational mathematics within a constructive type theory: an interesting juxtaposition. Huet and Saïbi present a formalization of category theory, a project that makes full use of the resources of type theory.

The last two papers rather concern the logic of programs. The one by Collette and Jones is on the logic of parallel programs; the difficulty here stems from the fact that processes sharing a common store may interfere with each other. That of Berezin et al. considers how to check that a formula of a certain logic is true (in a given interpretation); the logic here is the propositional modal $\mu$-calculus; it is of great interest as it can be used to efficiently encode and decide temporal properties of a wide range of concurrent systems.

The section on Programming Languages begins with two papers about Robin's ML language. Harper and Stone explore the significant thesis that programming languages (here ML) bear a very close relationship to type theories (if not identity!). Tofte and Birkedal show how properties of ML-style type checking can be extended to region inference, a compile-time analysis for memory management. The last two papers here have roots in Robin's work on process calculi. That of Berry relates to Robin's synchronous process calculus, SCCS; he gives an overview of his Esterel language, which has had multiple use, for example in real-time process control. Pierce and Turner's paper is based on Robin's more recent $\pi$-calculus; they propose a high-level typed concurrent language, Pict, that permits experimentation with a variety of notions of concurrent object.

The section on Concurrency begins with two papers concerning Robin's original process calculus, CCS. The first, by Hirshfeld and Moller, solves an open problem concerning the star height of regular expressions with respect to bisimulation (a finer relation than language equivalence). Ferreira et al. consider a combination of CCS with a type-theory—here a call-by-value $\lambda$-calculus—to produce what they term a communicate-by-value concurrent language. The next two papers are in the tradition of exploring variations rather than extensions of process calculus, but still more or less following the original CCS paradigm. That by Baeten et al. considers discrete time; that of Stark and Smolka considers making the choice operator of CCS probabilistic. Both papers present new sound and complete axiomatisations. Baeten et al. use branching bisimulation, which is a refinement of weak bisimulation, and Stark and Smolka use probabilistic bisimulation, which is a refinement of strong bisimulation.

The last section, on Mobility, is really part of the story of concurrency. However, with the current increasing importance of mobile computing it takes on a special interest of its own. Robin's contribution to this area was the $\pi$-calculus. An issue in concurrency is which criteria to use when comparing the expressiveness of calculi and Parrow considers this for a fully expressive fragment of $\pi$-calculus. A major strength of $\pi$-calculus is its ability to model both object-oriented and functional programming styles. The final three papers explore the technical underpinning of this modeling. Liu and Walker's paper models concurrent object-oriented programs within an extension of $\pi$-calculus. The papers by Boudol and Laneve and by Sangiorgi explore encodings of $\lambda$-calculus in $\pi$-calculus and the equivalences thereby induced on $\lambda$-terms.

# A Brief Scientific Biography of Robin Milner

**Gordon Plotkin, Colin Stirling, and Mads Tofte**

Robin Milner was born in 1934 to John Theodore Milner and Muriel Emily Milner. His father was an infantry officer and at one time commanded the Worcestershire Regiment. During the second world war the family led a nomadic existence in Scotland and Wales while his father was posted to different parts of the British Isles. In 1942 Robin went to Selwyn House, a boarding Preparatory School that is normally based in Broadstairs, Kent but was evacuated to Wales until the end of the war in 1945.

In 1947 Robin won a scholarship to Eton College, a public school whose fees were a long way beyond the family's means; fortunately scholars only paid what they could afford. While there he learned how to stay awake all night solving mathematics problems. (Scholars who specialised in maths were expected to score 100 percent on the weekly set of problems, which were tough.)

In 1952 he won a major scholarship to King's College, Cambridge, sitting the exam in the Examinations Hall, which is 100 yards from his present office. However, before going to Cambridge he did two years' national military service in the Royal Engineers, gaining a commission as a second lieutenant (which relieved his father, who rightly suspected that Robin might not be cut out to be an army officer).

By the time he went to Cambridge in 1954 Robin had forgotten a lot of mathematics; but nevertheless he gained a first-class degree after two years (by omitting Part I of the Tripos). In 1956 he took a short computing course on the EDSAC; he then deserted numerate study for a while to take Part II of the moral sciences Tripos ("moral sciences" was then Cambridge's name for philosophy).

For some reason, academic life did not appeal and he went to London in 1958, wondering whether to take up music seriously, having done a lot of singing and oboe playing, some cello, and some composition while at Cambridge. He decided otherwise, and instead taught mathematics for a year at Marylebone Grammar School.

In 1960 Robin took a programming job at Ferranti, in London. He looked after the program library of a small decimal computer called Sirius, and even helped to sell some of the twenty-odd sold altogether. Then in 1963 he moved to a lectureship in mathematics and computer science at The City University. In the same year he married Lucy. During the next five years while they lived in London their children Gabriel, Barney, and Chloë were born.

It was at City that he became interested in artificial intelligence, the semantics of programs, and mathematical logic. His interest in the theory of computing was further inspired by Christopher Strachey, Rod Burstall, Peter Landin, David Park, Michael Paterson, and Dana Scott.

Moving towards a life in research, he took a position as senior research assistant in the Computer and Logic group of David Cooper at Swansea University in 1968, working on program correctness. He wrote two papers on program schemata (1969, 1970) and one on program simulation (1971). The former was inspired by the work of Michael Paterson; the latter used an algebraic approach, under the influence of Peter Landin. The algebraic orientation continued in later research, providing a valuable means of modelling structure in computing systems and linking up with later interest in process calculi. While at Swansea he learnt of Dana Scott's work with Christopher Strachey on the foundations of programming languages. In particular, in 1969, Dana Scott wrote a celebrated article proposing the use of a hierarchy of continuous partial functions and giving a typed $\lambda$-calculus and logic for it; this would prove very influential.

In 1971 Robin moved to Stanford University as a research associate, joining John McCarthy's group at the Artificial Intelligence Project. Robin took up Scott's ideas as the basis of a system for computer-assisted theorem proving, the Stanford LCF system (1972a, b, c)—LCF stands for "Logic of Computable Functions," referring to Scott's logic. He also began his work on concurrency, again in the tradition of Scott and Strachey, formulating a domain-based notion of process to model the behaviour of computing agents.

In 1973, he was appointed to a lectureship at Edinburgh University, and obtained a Personal Chair in 1984. Edinburgh LCF (1979) was a development of the Stanford work, but now with a specially designed programming language, Edinburgh ML, to serve for finding and constructing proofs—ML stands for "Metalanguage." He also worked on the semantic foundations of LCF; see, especially, his (1977). Next, the language ML itself became of independent interest, with its many novel features, such as implicit typing. A new research effort, with Burstall and others, finally led to the development of Standard ML (1990, 1991).

Perhaps, though, his greatest effort at Edinburgh was devoted to concurrency, starting with the invention of CCS—his Calculus for Communicating Systems (1980, 1989). Its semantics went through an interesting development, beginning with a domain-theoretic approach, but ultimately emphasizing a novel operational approach to the equality of processes, employing the important notion of bisimulation. This in turn led to the development of other calculi, such as the $\pi$-calculus for mobile computing and, most recently, to action structures and calculi, intended to provide a framework for comparing process and other calculi, with a view also towards unifying sequential and concurrent computation.

Robin's research forms a coherent body of work, with one idea or system or calculus, leading to another in what seems to be an entirely natural, if miraculous, progression. His research has had great influence on others, both direct and indirect, and he has received well-deserved recognition. In 1987 he and his collaborators won the British Computer Society Technical Award for the development of Standard ML. In one year, 1988, he became a founder member of Academia Europaea, a Distinguished Fellow of the British Computer

Society and a Fellow of the Royal Society. In 1991 he was accorded the ultimate accolade of the Turing Award.

The coherence and strength of Robin's research can in part be attributed to a clear philosophical position: that computer science, like other sciences, has both an experimental and a theoretical aspect. The experimental one resides in computing systems (whether hardware or software, and including applications); these have a rich behaviour, demonstrate interesting and practically important phenomena, and provide the experiments at hand. The theoretical aspect is the provision of mathematical models to ease the construction, and permit the analysis of such systems; the concepts and structures arising in these models originate in the understanding of the systems to which they apply. This view of the subject is exemplified in Robin's work on, say, LCF, ML, and CCS: each is rooted in application and all are characterized by an economy of concept that yet permits great elasticity of expression.

Robin has also carried these ideas forward in his social contribution to our subject. In 1986 he was one of the founding members and the first director of the Laboratory for Foundations of Computer Science—a happy outcome of the UK Alvey Programme. Robin's philosophy, expounded in his founding lecture (1987b), is pervasive, whether in the title of the Laboratory or in its research. In 1995, he left Edinburgh to take up a Chair at Cambridge (in fact the first established chair in Computer Science at Cambridge) becoming Head of Department a year later. There he continues energetically promoting the integration of advanced application with applicable theory.

## Semantics and Domain Theory

Milner's work at Stanford and at Edinburgh (at least, until around 1978) was within the Scott-Strachey paradigm. Here one considers the semantics of programming languages as being given compositionally by denotation functions that ascribe meanings to programs. These meanings are elements of Scott domains or related kinds of complete partial order. The notation used to write the meanings is one or another $\lambda$-calculus. Scott's LCF was based on one such, later called PCF; it is simply typed with two base types, natural numbers and booleans, with arithmetic and boolean primitives, and with recursive definitions at all types. Milner's LCF system employed a more elaborate typed calculus, PP$\lambda$, with a signature of a finite set of base types and constants, with sum, product, and recursively defined types, and with a simple kind of polymorphism.

His other (perhaps less official) strand of work at Stanford was on concurrency, introducing recursively defined domains of processes—later termed *resumptions* by Plotkin—to provide abstract models of the behaviour of transducers or other types of computing agents (1973, 1975a). An example of such a domain equation is:

$$P \cong V \to (L \times V \times P)$$

These resumptions are used to model deterministic agents that input values from $V$ and output them to locations in $L$. Nondeterminism (used to account for parallelism) is dealt with by means of oracles, raising the issue of an adequate treatment of nondeterministic relations within the domain-theoretic framework; this inspired later work on powerdomains. Algebraic ideas occur here with the presentation of semantics using "combinators," the means for combining programs. The most important one is that for the parallel composition of programs. Milner had an idea of his agents as automata whose only means of communication was via a collection of lines, though that was not strongly emphasized in his writing. Perhaps this and the algebra helped inspire the later invention of CCS.

A notable point was the discussion at a general level of full abstraction. The idea of full abstraction is that two terms are to have the same denotation if—and only if—they are contextually equivalent in a sense determined by an operational semantics (for example, one given via an abstract machine). It is precisely the difficulty of providing such a fully abstract domain-theoretic treatment of concurrency that led Milner to his later operational treatment. The question also arises as to the full abstraction of Scott's standard model for PCF. After it was shown that this semantics is not fully abstract, Milner gave a fully abstract domain-theoretic model by means of an ingenious syntactic, or "term model," construction (1977).

The subject was developed much further by many people over the following years, searching for the proper notion of model; they were generally looking for an extensional notion of sequentiality at higher types. Notable further contributions included the introduction of stable functions (stability is an approximation to the desired notion of sequentiality) and of game-theoretic models (games provide an intensional characterization of sequentiality). It was recently shown that the operational equivalence relation is undecidable even for PCF restricted so that the only base type is the booleans. It follows that there can be no "finitary" extensional mathematical account of sequentiality, thereby providing a fundamental reason previous attempts failed.

Beyond PCF, full abstraction studies have been undertaken for a wide variety of languages. However, it is fair to say that for the case of concurrency, the one of original interest to Milner, there is as yet no satisfactory widely applicable treatment within the domain-theoretic paradigm.

## Computer Assisted Theorem Proving

Milner's LCF system enables one to carry out proofs on a machine, where the structure of the proof is largely known in advance. This was a considerable, if not entirely novel, departure from the contemporary emphasis on theorem proving systems in Artificial Intelligence. Systems such as De Bruijn's Automath and Hewitt's PLANNER were forerunners; the former enabled one to write down and check large proofs and the latter permitted the design of proof strategies.

The need for proof-checking systems resides in their intended application. The proofs needed to show computer systems correct are, in a way, tedious. While their structure is generally fairly clear (say a large induction), they can be very large, not least since computer systems are. One is therefore liable to make mistakes in such proofs when working "by hand," and machine help is much to be desired to provide the security of an assurance that no such mistakes have occurred.

With LCF, Milner, and his colleagues, firmly established the field of large-scale computer-assisted theorem proving. In doing so, they made several important contributions: tactics (subgoaling strategies for finding proofs) and tacticals (for their combination); a specially designed typed programming language for writing tactics and tacticals; and a means to achieve security against faulty deduction.

The programming language was ML, and was designed by Milner and his colleagues at Edinburgh. The features of ML are well adapted to the application of computer-assisted theorem-proving. Its higher-order and exception features are used to write tactics and tacticals. Its type discipline provides the desired security, achieved through an abstract recursively defined data type of proofs whose elements can only be constructed by means of the inference steps of the underlying logic of LCF. The inclusion of assignment, pattern matching, polymorphism and call-by-value were motivated by related practical concerns.

The article by Gordon in this volume provides much further detail on the development of Stanford and Edinburgh LCF and later projects. In particular, projects such as LCF require the efforts of many people: Gordon gives a good account of their contribution. Milner's own work on computer-assisted theorem proving effectively came to an end in 1978, but the subject had been established. It was pursued further at Cambridge and INRIA with the development of Cambridge LCF, HOL, and Isabelle, as well as the further development of ML. Other systems arose: some incorporate various constructive type theories, notable here are Coq and LEGO (both based on the Calculus of Constructions) and NuPrl and ALF (based on Martin-Löf's type theory); others such as Mizar, PVS, or (for example) Larch arose from different research traditions.

What started out as a mechanization of one particular logic has evolved into a field of wider scope. Experience shows that one naturally wishes to conduct proofs in a variety of logics, with the particular one being chosen by the user of a system rather than its designer. A subject of logical frameworks has arisen to accommodate such variety, and systems such as Isabelle and ELF are designed for just this task. Finally, the size of the proofs that can be performed has risen substantially. It is now possible to tackle large systems of commercial interest.

## Standard ML

As explained above, the design of ML was strongly influenced by the needs of theorem proving. But it was equally shaped by Milner's approach to language design in general. Two objectives stand out in this approach: first, the language should solve the practical problems that motivated its existence; second, it should do so with an absolute minimum of concepts, all of which should be rigorously defined and analysed. It should also be remarked that ML falls within the wider tradition of functional programming languages. Several such languages were influential in the design of ML: Burstall and Popplestone's POP-2, Evan's PAL, Landin's ISWIM, McCarthy's LISP, and Reynold's GEDANKEN.

The detailed story of the evolution of ML is complex; an account of the period from 1974 to 1996 can be found in (1997). Here we rather discuss some highlights of that evolution, with emphasis on Milner's contribution. The first, practical, design objective was addressed through implementation work and experiments. Milner was involved with several people working on early implementations of ML: Malcolm Newey, Lockwood Morris, Michael Gordon, Christopher Wadsworth, Luca Cardelli, Alan Mycroft, Kevin Mitchell, and John Scott.

The technical vehicle that guided the design of ML was language semantics. This provided a framework that permitted economy of design, the second objective. In particular Milner's paper on ML's polymorphic type discipline (1978a) was seminal in several ways. Besides presenting the ML type discipline (described below), it provided a strong indication that formal semantics could play a central rôle in the design of nontrivial programming languages.

The ML type discipline possesses several properties that distinguished it from contemporary languages. First, it is provably sound: If an expression of the type system has a type, then its value (the result of its evaluation) has the same type; or, as Milner put it, "well-typed expressions do not go wrong." Second, some expressions are allowed to have more than one type, that is, to be "polymorphic." For example, the polymorphic list reverse function can reverse all lists, irrespective of the type of the elements of the list. Third, types can be inferred automatically from programs by an algorithm, called $W$. As shown in the later paper with Damas (1982b), $W$ always terminates, either by failing (when the expression cannot be typed) or with a most general, also called *principal*, type of the expression.

Although discovered independently, Milner's type discipline has much in common with Curry, Hindley, and others' earlier work on principal type schemes in Combinatory Logic. In particular, both he and Hindley use Robinson's unification algorithm for type checking. The main difference between the two is that Milner's type discipline allows type schemes with quantification in the typing of declarations. For example, consider the Standard ML program declaring a function length:

```
fun length [] = 0
  | length (_::xs) = 1 + length xs
  val n = length [1,2,3] + length [true, false];
```

The function `length` is given the type scheme

$\texttt{length} : \forall\alpha.\alpha\,\texttt{list} \rightarrow \texttt{int}$

which can be instantiated to both $\texttt{int list} \rightarrow \texttt{int}$ and $\texttt{bool list} \rightarrow \texttt{int}$.

By 1985, several dialects and implementations of ML existed. Further, new ideas had emerged both within the immediate ML community and also from Burstall and his group who had developed influential languages: CLEAR, a specification language designed with Goguen, and HOPE, a functional programming language. It was evident that standardization was necessary. A number of design meetings were held, leading to a technical report consisting of Milner's description of the Core Language, MacQueen's module system and Harper's I/O primitives. Around the same time, operational semantics was gaining momentum, through work by Plotkin, Milner, and Kahn. Milner's description of the dynamic semantics of the Core was essentially a natural language formulation of an operational semantics.

In 1985, Milner, Tofte, and Harper began working on an operational semantics of full Standard ML, including static and dynamic semantics of both Core and Modules. Every construct of the language was described by a very small number of rules, typically one defining the static semantics (elaboration) and one defining the dynamic semantics (evaluation) of the construct. For example, the elaboration rule for recursive value bindings is

$$\frac{C + VE \vdash \ valbind \Rightarrow VE}{C \vdash \texttt{rec}\ valbind \Rightarrow VE}$$

where $C$ is a context mapping free identifiers of *valbind* to their static meaning, and $VE$ is a static value environment mapping the identifiers defined by *valbind* to their types. The evaluation rule for recursive value bindings is

$$\frac{E \vdash valbind \Rightarrow VE}{E \vdash \texttt{rec}\ valbind \Rightarrow \mathrm{Rec}\ VE}$$

where $VE$ is a dynamic value environment (a finite map from variables to values) and Rec $VE$ is a finite value environment that represents one unfolding of the recursively defined values.

More difficult was the handling of Modules, owing to novel concepts such as structure sharing and functors. New theory had to be invented for dealing with these constructs (1987c). A key idea was that type checking of structure sharing could be done using a nonstandard form of unification, related to unification in record calculi. The work eventually led to the Definition of Standard ML (1990) and the Commentary on Standard ML (1991). Some years later, in 1996, when a clearer understanding of the semantics and pragmatics of the language had emerged, Milner, Tofte, Harper, and MacQueen revised and simplified the language, leading to a new Definition (1997). Structure sharing was abandoned and type abbreviations in signatures were added. The resulting static semantics of Modules is a mere eight pages long and fulfils a longstanding desire to obtain a simple operational semantics for ML Modules.

On the theoretical side, ML's type discipline gave rise to a considerable body of theoretical work. Particularly interesting was the result that deciding ML typability is complete for deterministic exponential time, contrasting with the observation that ML type inference works well in practice. Another important result is that type checking polymorphic recursion is equivalent to the (undecidable) semi-unification problem. There has also been work extending the ML type discipline with higher ranks of polymorphism, subtyping, object types and overloading—much more than can be described here. The ML type system appears to be a local optimum in the design space. Subtyping is a case in point: while there has been some success in extending the notion of principal type to a notion of principal solution of constraint sets, it seems to be very hard to find a notion of "most general type" which coincides with "most readable type."

Standard ML has developed in other ways, for example through work on implementations. Implementation technology was developed in the context of Standard ML of New Jersey, Edinburgh ML, and Poly/ML. Other Standard ML implementations have emerged: Moscow ML, The ML Kit and, most recently, MLWorks, a commercial implementation developed by Harlequin. Good textbooks on programming with Standard ML have been written and the language has become quite widely used for teaching and research.

Variants of ML have emerged, notably Caml Light and Objective Caml, both developed at INRIA. Objective Caml extends ML with facilities for object-oriented programming. Several researchers, including Berry, Milner, and Turner (1992b), have explored the combination of ML and concurrency, leading to Concurrent ML, FACILE, Distributed Poly/ML and LCS. Finally, there is a new design effort underway, known as the ML2000 project; this involves researchers from France and several sites in the United States.

**Concurrency**

As outlined above, Milner's initial work (1973, 1975a) on concurrency was carried out within the Scott-Strachey approach to semantics. The intention was to extend the scope of denotational semantics beyond sequential input/output programs. Difficulties arise from non-terminating programs with side-effects, nondeterministic programs and parallel programs. Milner showed that these computational features can be modelled operationally using (deterministic) transducers. The notion of name or location was important here. It was given as an address at which communication takes place (which later turned into the notion of a port): in a given state with a given input value the output function of a transducer determines both the output communication line and the value to be transmitted on that line.

Transducers are intensional objects whose extensional behaviour as processes he wished to capture mathematically. Such processes were modelled by means of the domain of resumptions given by the recursive domain equation presented above. The domain was intended to play the same rôle for nonsequential programs as the domain of continuous functions for sequential programs. This was before the invention of powerdomains, and so for nondeterminism oracles were employed. A semantics for a programming language with these nonsequential features was presented in (1973). Notable here was the global recursive definition of a combinator for the parallel composition of processes, a definition made possible by the use of the domain of resumptions. The analysis of assignment as a complex action involving communication with registers was also important.

In (1975a) he discussed this model further, including a general discussion of criteria for denotational semantics. Compositionality can be achieved by regarding syntax as a word algebra and semantics as the (unique) homomorphism to an algebra of operators on processes (or other suitable mathematical entities). The semantics should be justified by its relationship to an operational semantics for the language; in particular it should be *adequate* or, and much better, *fully abstract*, as described above.

The work of the later 1970s has a stronger algebraic flavour. Flowgraphs were introduced in the two papers (1979b, d), both written in 1977, the second jointly with Milne. Communication plays a central rôle, and is to be understood as exchange of values at explicitly named ports. A flowgraph is a (pictorial) representation of the potential flow of information through ports in a system. Just as with Scott's flow diagrams, flowgraphs provide an intermediary between a program and its meaning. Combinators for combining flowgraphs were introduced; these became the static operators of CCS: binary parallel composition, renaming and restriction. Various laws of flow were presented (such as the commutativity and associativity of parallel composition), and in (1979b) Milner showed that flowgraphs form the free such algebra, thereby justifying the laws. Flowgraphs can be viewed as an expression of *heterarchy*, where one and the same system can be viewed as built up from subsystems in distinct ways. The contrast is with a *hierarchical* view, where systems can be uniquely analysed into subsystems and so have a tree-like form rather than a graphical one.

Meanings of concurrent programs, the processes, are elements of a powerdomain of resumptions: this is where the dynamics of a system are described. The domain of processes is also a flow algebra. The domain equation for processes is

$$P_L \cong \mathcal{P}\left(\sum_{\mu \in L}(U_\mu \times (V_\mu \to P_L))\right)$$

where $L$ is the set of ports, $U_\mu$ and $V_\mu$ are, respectively, domains of input and output values at port $\mu$, and $\mathcal{P}$ is a powerdomain operator (for nondeterminism). Milner had in mind the Smyth powerdomain with an added empty set (for termination), although he was unhappy with this account as it identifies too many processes.

Further developments culminated in CCS. In (1978b) Milner recounted the definition of a flow algebra, and introduced, as one particular instance, synchronization trees (without the presence of value-passing). The dynamic operators of CCS, prefixing and summation, were then introduced as combinators on these trees. The prefixing operator provides a facility for value-passing *actions*, whether for input or output. The silent $\tau$ action also appeared as the result of synchronization. Later that year in (1978c), written while visiting Aarhus, these dynamic operators were explicitly included alongside the static operators as part of the definition of an algebra for modelling communicating systems. The notion of a single observer was used to justify interleaving (instead of a partial order approach as in the case of Petri nets). This was exemplified in the equational law relating parallel composition with nondeterminism, which later became the expansion theorem. With these two papers the general conception of CCS was in place: concurrent systems can be modelled by behaviour expressions, and equational reasoning provides a mechanism for showing properties of systems. By way of an example, Milner showed the possibility of deadlock for a description of the dining philosophers. However, one ingredient was still missing: a justification for the equational laws.

The next crucial step was the paper (1980a) written with Hennessy. This paper isolated basic CCS where there is no value-passing, only synchronization. Basic CCS bears much the same relation to full CCS as propositional logic does to predicate logic. Observational equivalence of synchronization trees was introduced both in a strong form, and in a weak form where $\tau$ actions are abstracted away. At this stage equivalences were defined iteratively instead of using greatest fixed points; they arose from the simple idea that an observer can repeatedly interact with an agent by choosing an available transition from it. The equivalence of processes was then defined in terms of the ability of these observers to continually match each other's choices of transition by one labelled with the same action. Hennessy-Milner logic (with strong and weak modalities) was also introduced in order to provide a logical account of the equivalences. Equational axiomatizations of the associated congruences were presented for finitary terms (here, those built from prefixing, binary summation, and nil). As a result there was an intended model for process expressions, given by synchronization trees quotiented by observational congruence.

One additional ingredient needed to define observational equivalence directly on process expressions was their structural operational semantics using transition systems labelled by actions. The combination of structure and labelling has since proved a very adaptable specification method and is now standard. These ideas were presented in the influential CCS book (1980) written in Aarhus, and presented as lectures. The book inspired the whole field of process calculus in the same way that Milner's paper (1978a) inspired that of (polymorphic) type theoretic work in programming languages. The two paradigms reflect his principled approach to theoretical computer science, with its concern for applicability and the use of a small number of primitives. As Milner says (1979a) about his approach to concurrency

> The broad aim of the approach is to be able to write and manipulate expressions which not only denote ... the behaviour of composite communicating systems, but may reveal in their form the physical structure of such systems.

The accessibility of the material is also most important. Parts of the book (1980) can be taught as an undergraduate course. Indeed Milner's later more polished book (1989) is a distillation of the ideas arising from teaching CCS to final year undergraduates at Edinburgh. Both books give interesting accounts of the evolution of CCS, as does (1990b).

Further developments of the theory of CCS occurred through the 1980s. In 1981 Park gave a notion of bisimulation leading to a somewhat different, but more satisfactory notion of observational equivalence (for both the strong and weak forms); it also has an interesting and useful characterization as a greatest fixed point. Milner used bisimulations in the paper (1983a) which, further, introduced SCCS, a synchronous version of CCS (and, in a way, more basic). Mathematically SCCS is very elegant, and its model turns out to provide a canonical model for non-well-founded set theory. Variations on the notion of observational equivalence were considered. For example, in (1981) Milner defined an observational preorder for processes that is sensitive to divergence. Again, an alternative framework for defining equivalences using testing was introduced: the resulting equivalences are very closely related to the failures model for Hoare's CSP.

Milner extended the finitary axiomatizations of strong and weak bisimulation to finite terms that permit guarded recursion (1984a, 1989a). The axiomatization in the first of these papers was based on Salomaa's axiomatization of language equivalence for regular expressions, except for the axiom $a(X+Y) = aX + aY$. However, the theory is subtly different. Indeed automata theory from the perspective of bisimulation equivalence, as opposed to language equivalence, contains surprises. One example is that bisimulation equivalence is decidable for context-free grammars. In another direction, some recent work has concentrated on value-passing, providing complete equational theories for regular value-passing process expressions, for both testing and bisimulation congruences. Again, Hennessy-Milner logic is not very expressive, and is unable to capture liveness and safety properties of processes. Various extensions have been proposed, such as modal $\mu$-calculus, for describing temporal properties of processes: these extensions have the feature that two bisimulation equivalent systems have the same temporal properties.

The theory of CCS has inspired tools such as AUTO/GRAPH and the Concurrency Workbench for analysing concurrent systems. These tools allow automatic checking of equivalences and preorders between finite-state processes. The Concurrency Workbench, written in ML and developed jointly in Edinburgh and Sussex, also permits model checking temporal properties of processes. Notions of simulation and bisimulation have also found their way into model-checking tools.

Since the mid-1980s various extensions to process calculi have been presented, for example for modelling time, probability, location, and priority. The CCS paradigm has motivated various results about these extensions, including definitions of equivalence, characteristic modal logics and temporal extensions, and connections with automata theory.

Operational semantics are paramount in the theory of CCS and related calculi; indeed Milner has never returned to a denotational theory of processes. However, a denotational account of strong bisimulation is possible. Semantics fully abstract with respect to strong bisimulation have been given within a variety of mathematical frameworks: non-well-founded sets, domains, and metric spaces. In all cases appropriate "domain equations" are employed, giving a suitable notion of resumption. It should be emphasized that, to date, no corresponding treatment of weak bisimulation is available.

Milner was dissatisfied with CCS for two reasons. The first originated in a particular practical problem presented in the CCS book (1980). There the meanings of parallel imperative programs were given by translation into value-passing CCS. Program variables were modelled using explicit registers which appeared in parallel with the translation of the programs themselves. However, when the programming language permits recursive procedures, the modelling suffered because concurrent calls of the same procedure were interleaved. Milner remarked that a more natural modelling would include a return link for each call of a procedure, and this would require passing ports as values, which is impossible in CCS. The second concern resulted from the notable success of process calculi, as inspired by Milner's work. Numerous process calculi have flourished over the years, and many different equivalences have been defined. But there are too many apparently different calculi, with none accepted as canonical, and too many equivalences. Recent work on rule formats for defining process operators has offered some insights into the dynamics of some classes of calculi, but that can only be part of the story.

Both these concerns have underpinned Milner's later work in concurrency. An important development was a tractable calculus for passing ports, thereby allowing dynamic communication topologies to be modelled. Early discussions with Nielsen in 1981, while in Aarhus, had failed to produce such a calculus. Then, in 1986, Engberg and Nielsen made an important breakthrough, finding such a calculus. Following this, Milner jointly with Parrow and Walker, beginning in 1987, produced a simpler approach, the $\pi$-calculus (1992d, e; see also the paper by Engberg and Nielsen in this volume). This calculus contains fewer primitives than value-passing CCS, being based only on names. There is also a subtle mechanism for dynamically changing the scope of static name bindings. A fundamental point is that the $\lambda$-calculus can be encoded within $\pi$-calculus.

The combination of names and binding causes difficulties when giving an operational semantics for the calculus. Transition system models are not entirely natural as actions are unexpectedly complex: both bound and free output actions are required. This induces corresponding complexity in the definition of both strong and weak bisimulation and their characteristic Hennessy-Milner logics (1992d, e, 1993f). The calculus does, however, highlight an interesting difference between early and late bisimulation, which also applies to value-passing CCS (1993f).

In order to resolve these problems, Milner introduced a change in the style of semantics. Instead of transition systems, he used reductions, based on Berry and Boudol's elegant Chemical Abstract Machine approach. With Sangiorgi, Milner could then define bisimulation congruence using reductions and barbs (1993e). The calculus presented there was also more refined than the original one, incorporating sorts (analogous to types) and the communication of tuples. An interesting question for reduction-based approaches is how to define temporal logics for $\pi$-calculus agents.

The $\pi$-calculus has had a strong impact. In part this is because process calculi, $\lambda$-calculi, and concurrent object-oriented programs can all be modelled within it. This yields a relationship with functional programming and a fundamental model of "mobile" objects providing a framework for understanding contemporary programming disciplines. Other developments include higher-order process calculi, and experimental programming languages such as Pict and the join calculus.

Milner's most recent work in concurrency is on action structures and calculi, and is intended to address the second concern. The aim is to find mathematical structures that can underlie concrete models of computation and which are free from ad hoc details. Again the motivations reflect basic concerns (1994a), for we "lack a canonical structure which is combinational i.e. which explains how processes are synthesized, and which embodies the dynamics of interaction among processes." Action structures are categories with extra structure, including certain "controls"; actions are modelled as morphisms and the controls allow complex actions to be built from simple ones. They also possess an ordering on the actions, used to specify (reduction) dynamics. The categorical structure has been shown to link up with (categorical models of) Girard's linear logic, a topic of independent computational interest. The controls allow an analysis of the structural aspects of such process calculi as the $\pi$-calculus; however it is still not clear how to give a uniform analysis of such aspects of their dynamics as observational equivalence. These issues remain an active concern of Milner's.

## Doctoral Students

**Before 1980** R. Aubin (1976); G. Milne (1978).

**From 1980 to 1989** A. Cohn (1980); A. Mycroft, M. Sanderson (1982); L. Damas, B. Monahan (1985); K. Larsen, K. Mitchell (1986); K. V. S. Prasad, M. Tofte (1988); F. Moller (1989).

**After 1990** D. Berry, C. Tofts (1990); D. Sangiorgi (1993); P. E. Sewell (1995); D. N. Turner (1996); A. Mifsud (1996).

**Current** J. Leifer, M. Sawle, A. Unyapoth.

## Publications

### Books

[1976] (Edited with S. Michaelson) *Proc. 3rd. Int. Coll. on Automata, Languages and Programming*, Edinburgh, Edinburgh University Press.

[1979] (With M. J. Gordon & C. P. Wadsworth) *Edinburgh LCF; a Mechanized Logic of Computation*, Lecture Notes in Computer Science, Vol. 78, Berlin, Springer-Verlag.

[1980] *A Calculus of Communicating Systems*, Lecture Notes in Computer Science, Vol. 92, Berlin, Springer-Verlag.

[1989] *Communication and Concurrency*, New York, Prentice-Hall.

[1990] (With M. Tofte & R. Harper) *The Definition of Standard ML*, Cambridge, MIT Press.

[1991] (With M. Tofte) *Commentary on Standard ML*, Cambridge, MIT Press.

[1996] (Edited with I. Wand) *Computing Tomorrow*, Cambridge, Cambridge University Press.

[1997] (With M. Tofte & R. Harper & D. MacQueen) *The Definition of Standard ML (Revised)*, Cambridge, MIT Press.

[1999] *Communicating and Mobile Systems: the Pi-Calculus*, Cambridge, Cambridge University Press.

### Articles

[1968] *String handling in ALGOL*, British Computer Journal, Vol. 10, pp. 321–324.

[1969] *Program schemes and recursive function theory*. In Machine Intelligence 5 (eds. B. Meltzer and D. Michie), pp. 39–58, Edinburgh, Edinburgh University Press.

[1970] *Equivalences on program schemes*, Journal of Computer and Systems Sciences, Vol. 4, No. 2, pp. 205–219.

[1971] *An algebraic notion of simulation between programs.* In Proc. 2nd Int. Joint Conf. on Artificial Intelligence, London, pp. 481–49, London, British Computer Society.

[1972a] *Implementation and applications of Scott's logic for computable functions.* In Proc. ACM Conf. on Proving Assertions about Programs, New Mexico State University, pp. 1–6, New York, ACM.

[1972b] (With R. W. Weyhrauch) *Program semantics and correctness in a mechanized logic.* In Proc. USA–Japan Computer Conf., Tokyo, pp. 384–392.

[1972c] (With R. W. Weyhrauch) *Proving compiler correctness in a mechanized logic.* In Machine Intelligence 7 (eds. B. Meltzer and D. Michie), pp. 51–70, Edinburgh, Edinburgh University Press.

[1973] *An approach to the semantics of parallel programs.* In Proc. Convegno di Informatica Teoretica, pp. 285–301. Pisa, Instituto di Elaborazione della Informazione.

[1974] *A calculus for the mathematical theory of computation*, Int. Symp. on Theoretical Programming (eds. A. Ershov and V. A. Nepomniaschy), Novosibirsk, USSR, August 1972, Lecture Notes in Computer Science, Vol. 5, pp. 332–343, Berlin, Springer-Verlag.

[1975a] *Processes: A mathematical model of computing agents*, In Proc. Logic Colloquium (eds. H. E. Rose and J. C. Shepherdson), Bristol, July 1973, Studies in Logic and the Foundations of Mathematics, Vol. 80, pp. 157–174, Amsterdam, North-Holland.

[b] (With L. Morris and M. Newey) *A logic for computable functions with reflexive and polymorphic types*, Conf. on Proving and Improving Programs, Arc-et-Senans, July 1975, pp. 371–394, Colloques IRIA, Rocquencourt, IRIA-Laboria.

[1976a] *LCF: A methodology for performing rigorous proofs about programs.* In Proc. 1st. IBM Symp. on Mathematical Foundations of Computer Science, Amagi, Japan.

[b] *Models of LCF.* In Foundations of Computer Science II, Part 2 (eds. K. Apt and J. W. de Bakker), Mathematical Centre Tracts 82, pp. 49–63, Amsterdam, Mathematisch Centrum.

[c] *Program semantics and mechanized proof.* In Foundations of Computer Science II, Part 2 (eds. K. Apt and J. W. de Bakker), Mathematical Centre Tracts 82, pp. 3–44, Amsterdam, Mathematisch Centrum.

[1977] *Fully abstract models of typed λ-calculi*, Theoretical Computer Science, Vol. 4, pp. 1–22.

[1978a] *A theory of type polymorphism in programming*, Journal of Computer and Systems Sciences, Vol. 17, No. 3, pp. 348–375.

[b] *Algebras for communicating systems.* In Proc. AFCET/S.M.F. joint colloquium in Applied Mathematics, Paris.

[c] *Synthesis of communicating behaviour.* In Proc. 7th. Int. Symp. on Foundations of Computer Science (ed. J. Winkowski), Zakopane, Lecture Notes in Computer Science, Vol. 64, pp. 71–83, Berlin, Springer-Verlag.

[d] (With M. Gordon, L. Morris, M. Newey, and C. Wadsworth) *A metalanguage for interactive proof in LCF.* In Proc. 5th. Annual ACM Symp. on Principles of Programming Languages, New York, ACM.

[1979a] *An algebraic theory for synchronization.* In Proc. 4th. G.I. Conf. on Theoretical Computer Science (ed. K. Weihrauch), Aachen, Lecture Notes in Computer Science, Vol. 67, pp. 27–35, Berlin, Springer-Verlag.

[1979b] *Flowgraphs and Flow Algebras*, Journal of the ACM, Vol. 26, No. 4, pp. 794–818.

[1979c] *LCF: a way of doing proofs with a machine.* In Proc. 8th. Int. Symp. on Foundations of Computer Science (ed. J. Bečvář), Olomouc, Lecture Notes in Computer Science, Vol. 74, pp. 146–159, Berlin, Springer-Verlag.

[1979d] (With G. Milne) *Concurrent processes and their syntax*, Journal of the ACM, Vol. 26, No. 2, pp. 302–321.

[1980a] (With M. Hennessy) *On observing nondeterminism and concurrency.* In Proc. 7th. Coll. on Automata Languages and Programming (eds. J. de Bakker and J. van Leeuwen), Lecture Notes in Computer Science, Vol. 85, pp. 299–309, Berlin, Springer-Verlag.

[1981] *A modal characterisation of observable machine-behaviour.* In Proc. 6th. Colloquium on Trees in Algebra and Programming (eds. E. Astesiano and C. Böhm), Genoa, Lecture Notes in Computer Science, Vol. 112, pp. 25–34, Berlin, Springer-Verlag.

[1982a] *Four combinators for concurrency.* In Proc. 9th. ACM Symp. on Principles of Distributed Computing, Ottawa, pp. 104–110, New York, ACM.

[b] (With L. Damas) *Principal type schemes for functional programs.* In Proc. 9th. Annual ACM Symp. on Principles of Programming Languages, Albuquerque, pp. 207–212, New York, ACM.

[1983a] *Calculi for synchrony and asynchrony*, Journal of Theoretical Computer Science, Vol. 25, pp. 267–310.

[b] *How ML Evolved*, Polymorphism—The ML/LCF/Hope Newsletter, Vol. 1, No. 1.

[1984a] *A complete inference system for a class of regular behaviours*, Journal of Computer and Systems Sciences, Vol. 28, No. 2, pp. 439–466.

[b] *The use of machines to assist in rigorous proof*, Phil. Trans. Roy. Soc. London, Ser. A, Vol. 312, pp. 411–422.

[c] *Using Algebra for Concurrency.* In Chapter 21, Distributed Computing (eds. F. B. Chambers, D. A. Duce, and G. P. Jones), pp. 291–305, London, Academic Press.

[1985] (With M. Hennessy) *Algebraic laws for nondeterminism and concurrency*, Journal of the ACM, Vol. 32, No. 1, pp. 137–161.

[1986a] *Lectures on a calculus for communicating systems.* In Control Flow and Data Flow: Concepts of Distributed Programming (ed. M. Broy), Proc. Int. Summer School at Marktoberdorf, pp. 205–228, Springer Study Edition, Berlin, Springer-Verlag.

[b] *Process constructors and interpretations.* In Proc. 10th. IFIP World Computer Congress (ed. H.-J. Kugler), Dublin, pp. 507–514, Amsterdam, North-Holland.

[1987a] *Dialogue with a proof system.* In Proc. TAPSOFT '87, Vol. 1 (eds. H. Ehrig, R. Kowalski, G. Levi, and U. Montanari), Pisa, Lecture Notes in Computer Science, Vol. 249, pp. 271–275, Berlin, Springer-Verlag.

[b] *Is computing an experimental science?* Journal of Information Technology, Vol. 2, No. 2, pp. 60–66.

[c] (With R. Harper and M. Tofte) *A type discipline for program modules.* In Proc. TAPSOFT '87, Vol. 2 (eds. H. Ehrig, R. Kowalski, G. Levi and U. Montanari), Pisa, Lecture Notes in Computer Science, Vol. 250, pp. 308–319, Berlin, Springer-Verlag.

[d] (With K. G. Larsen) *Verifying a protocol using relativized bisimulation.* In Proc. 14th. ICALP (ed. Th. Ottman), Lecture Notes in Computer Science, Vol. 267, pp. 126–135, Berlin, Springer-Verlag.

[1988a] *Interpreting one concurrent calculus in another.* In Proc. Int. Conf. on Fifth Generation Computer Systems, Tokyo, Vol. 2, pp. 321–326.

[b] *Some directions in concurrency theory*, Statement for panel on "Theory and Practice in Concurrency." In Proc. Int. Conf. on Fifth Generation Computer Systems (edited by the Institute for New Generation Computer Technology), Tokyo, Vol. 1, pp. 163–164.

[1989a] *A complete axiomatisation for observational congruence of finite-state behaviours*, Journal of Information and Computation, Vol. 81, No. 2, pp. 227–247.

[1990a] *Functions as processes.* In Proc. 17th. Int. Conf. on Automata, Languages and Programming (ed. M. S. Paterson), University of Warwick, Lecture Notes in Computer Science, Vol. 443, pp. 167–180, Berlin, Springer-Verlag.

[b] *Operational and algebraic semantics of concurrent processes.* In Handbook of Theoretical Computer Science (ed. J. van Leeuwen), Vol. B: Formal Models and Semantics, Chapter 19, pp. 1201–1242, Amsterdam, Elsevier.

[1991a] (With M. Tofte) *Co-induction in relational semantics*, Theoretical Computer Science, Vol. 87, No. 1, pp. 209–220.

[1992a] *Functions as processes*, Mathematical Structures in Computer Science, Vol. 2, No. 2, pp. 119–141.

[b] (With D. Berry and D. N. Turner) *A semantics for Standard ML concurrency primitives.* In Proc. 17th. Annual ACM Symposium on Principles of Programming Languages, San Francisco, pp. 119–129, New York, ACM.

[c] (With K. G. Larsen) *A compositional protocol verification using relativized bisimulation*, Information and Computation, Vol. 99, No. 1, pp. 80–108.

[d] (With J. Parrow and D. Walker) *A calculus of mobile processes, I*, Information and Computation, Vol. 100, No. 1, pp. 1–40.

[e] (With J. Parrow and D. Walker) *A calculus of mobile processes, II*, Information and Computation, Vol. 100, No. 1, pp. 41–77.

[f] (With D. Sangiorgi) *Barbed bisimulation*. In Proc. 19th. Int. Conf. on Automata, Languages and Programming (ed. W. Kuich), Wien, Lecture Notes in Computer Science, Vol. 623, pp. 685–695, Berlin, Springer-Verlag.

[g] (With D. Sangiorgi) *The problem of "weak bisimulation up to."* In Proc. CONCUR'92: Third International Conference on Concurrency Theory (ed. W. R. Cleveland), Stony Brook, Lecture Notes in Computer Science, Vol. 630, pp. 32–46, Berlin, Springer-Verlag.

[1993a] *Action calculi, or syntactic action structures*. In Proc. 18th. MFCS Conf. (eds. A. M. Borzyszkowski and S. Sokolowski), Gdańsk, Lecture Notes in Computer Science, Vol. 711, pp. 105–121, Berlin, Springer-Verlag.

[b] *An action structure for synchronous $\pi$-calculus*. In Proc. 9th. FCT Conf. (ed. Z. Ésic), Szeged, Lecture Notes in Computer Science, Vol. 710, pp. 87–105, Berlin, Springer-Verlag.

[c] *Elements of interaction*, Communications of the ACM, Vol. 36, No. 1, pp. 78–89.

[d] *Higher-order action calculi*. In Proc. 9th. CSL Conf. (eds. E. Börger, Y. Gurevich, and K. Meinke), Swansea, Lecture Notes in Computer Science, Vol. 832, pp. 238–260, Berlin, Springer-Verlag.

[e] *The polyadic $\pi$-calculus: A tutorial*. In Logic and Algebra of Specification (eds. F. L. Bauer, W. Brauer, and H. Schwichtenberg), pp. 203–246, Berlin, Springer-Verlag.

[f] (With J. Parrow and D. Walker) *Modal logics for mobile processes*, Theoretical Computer Science, Vol. 114, pp. 149–171.

[1994a] *Action structures and the $\pi$-calculus*. In Proof and Computation (ed. H. Schwichtenberg), pp. 317–378, Series F: Computer and Systems Sciences, Vol. 139, NATO Advanced Study Institute, Proc. Int. Summer School held in Marktoberdorf, Germany, 1993, Berlin, Springer-Verlag.

[b] *Computing is interaction* (abstract). In Proc. 13th. IFIP World Computer Congress (eds. B. Pehrson and I. Simon), Hamburg, Vol. 1, pp. 232–233, Amsterdam, North-Holland.

[1995] (With A. Mifsud and J. Power) *Control structures*. In Proc. Tenth Symposium on Logic in Computer Science, San Diego, pp. 188–198, Washington, IEEE Computer Press.

[1996a] *Calculi for interaction*. In Acta Informatica, Vol. 33, No. 8, pp. 707–737.

[b] *Semantic ideas in computing*. In Computing Tomorrow (eds. I. Wand and R. Milner), Cambridge, pp. 246–283, Cambridge University Press.

[1997a] *Strong normalisation in higher-order action calculi*. In Proc. 3rd. TACS Symp. (eds. M. Abadi and T. Ito), Lecture Notes in Computer Science, Vol. 1281, pp. 1–19, Berlin, Springer Verlag.

[b] *Graphical calculi for interaction* (Abstract). In Proc. 24th. ICALP Coll. (eds. P. Degano, R. Gorrieri, and A. Marchetti-Spaccamela), Lecture Notes in Computer Science, Vol. 1256, p. 1, Berlin, Springer Verlag.

[1998] *The pi-calculus and its applications*. In Proc. 1998 Joint Int. Symp. and Conf. on Logic Programming (ed. J. Jaffar), pp. 3–4, Cambridge, MIT Press.

# I Semantic Foundations

# 1 Bistructures, Bidomains, and Linear Logic

**Pierre-Louis Curien, Gordon Plotkin, and Glynn Winskel**

## 1 Introduction

In this paper we link Winskel's bistructures [25], Girard's linear logic [10] and Berry's bidomains [25]. We show how bistructures provide a model of classical linear logic extending Girard's web model [10, 11]; we show too that a certain class of bistructures represent bidomains. We hope that the structures isolated here will help in the search for a direct, extensional and "mathematically natural" account of sequentiality and thereby of Milner's fully abstract model of PCF [20].

Girard has given an analysis of intuitionistic logic in terms of his more primitive linear logic. When we consider models, this is reflected in the fact that cartesian closed categories (categorical models of intuitionistic logic) arise as the co-Kleisli categories associated with categorical models of linear logic. In particular, linear logic yields refined analyses of the categories of domains used in denotational semantics. For instance, Berry and Curien's category of concrete data structures and sequential algorithms [5] may be obtained as the co-Kleisli category of a games model [6, 16]. The connection between games and sequentiality has in turn informed recent work on intensional models of PCF and their fully abstract extensional collapse [1, 12].

After Berry isolated the mathematically natural notion of stability [3], it was soon realized that sequential functions are stable. While there is a cartesian closed category of stable functions, at higher orders the extensional ordering is not respected. It was therefore natural for Berry to introduce bidomains. These are *biorders*—that is, sets equipped with two partial orders. One is an intensional stable ordering, based on the method of computation; the other is an extensional ordering, inherited from Scott's domain theory. Models of this kind can be viewed as mathematically tractable "approximations" to the desired sequential structures.

Event structures are partial orders of events equipped with a conflict relation and obeying an axiom of finite causes. They were introduced in [21] as a model of concurrency, and turned out to have close connections with concrete domains [14] and hence sequentiality [5]; they are also a natural generalisation of Girard's webs. Winskel introduced bistructures (of events) in [25], representing a full sub-cartesian closed category of bidomains. They are biorders equipped with a binary consistency relation; the two orders are obtained by decomposing the event structure order into left and right (input and output) components.

The main idea of this paper is that the inherent symmetry of bistructures enables one to obtain a model of classical linear logic, generalising the web model. The model is obtained by modifying the original definition—retaining its axiom of finite causes, but with all axioms symmetric. The configurations of a bistructure can be equipped with both a stable and an extensional ordering, that is they are biorders; further, the morphisms of the category of bistructures yield linear functions of the biorders (in a certain sense). Unfortunately, not all biorders obtained in this way are bidomains; further, not all linear functions come from morphisms of bistructures.

However, by considering the co-Kleisli category and then restricting the allowed bistructures, one obtains a category equivalent to a full sub-cartesian closed category of Berry's category of bidomains and which provides a model of PCF. It has to be admitted that the situation here is not entirely as one would like: perhaps the notions of bistructures and bidomains should be adjusted. Ideal would be to have a bidomain model of classical linear logic, with a co-Kleisli category equivalent to that of stable continuous functions, and containing a (full) submodel equivalent to one of bistructures; further, there should be a representation theorem, that the bidomains corresponding to bistructures are precisely those satisfying suitable axioms.

It may be that a natural extensional account of sequentiality can be given within a "bistructural" framework. One can imagine replacing the stable ordering by a structure for sequentiality. If one does not know the right axioms, one could instead look for suitable variants of bistructures of events.

However, Loader's undecidability result [19] for the finitary fragment of PCF shows that there is a major obstacle to finding a category of structured sets providing a fully abstract model of PCF. We would expect that such structures would not be "finitary" in the sense that, say, partial orders and topological spaces are, but that measure spaces are not (note that the definition of measure spaces refers to the "external" notion of the natural numbers).[1] It may nonetheless be possible to find suitable infinitary structure. The work in this paper suggests that one might do well to seek linear models whose co-Kleisli categories correspond to the sequential functions. There may even be enough symmetry that one has a model of classical linear logic.

In Sections 2 and 3 we give two approaches to bistructures; these represent two independent developments of the ideas of this paper [23, 7]. Section 2 starts from the world of webs and stable domain theory; Section 3 proceeds from that of event structures and continuous domain theory. We introduce bistructures in Section 4, and bistructure morphisms in Section 5. In Section 6 we show (Theorem 1) that bistructures provide a model of classical linear logic. In Section 7 we consider bidomains, establishing the connection with bistructures (Theorem 2). In Section 8 we discuss possible variations and connections

[1] In fact, a notion of finitary category of structured sets can be formalised; one requires that the structures and morphisms are specified by formulas of higher-order logic referring only to the carrier sets. Then Loader's result implies that such a category cannot provide a fully abstract model of PCF, assuming that it is finitarily cartesian closed (in a suitable sense) and that the structured set corresponding to the Booleans has finite carrier.

with other work; in particular we consider strengthenings of bistructures incorporating Ehrhard's hypercoherences (see [8]) thereby accounting for strong stability within our approach.

In this paper, cpos are partial orders with a least element and lubs of all directed sets; continuous functions between cpos are those monotonic functions preserving all the directed lubs. For other domain-theoretic terminology see, for example, [28].

## 2 Motivation from Stability

We recall the basics of Girard's stable model of classical linear logic [10, 11]. A *web* is a structure $(E, \smile)$, where:

- $E$ is a set of *events* (or tokens), and
- $\smile$ is a binary irreflexive symmetric relation of *conflict* (called strict incoherence in [10]).

Throughout this paper we use Girard's notation: $\mathrel{\substack{\smile\\\frown}}$ is the reflexive closure of the irreflexive relation $\smile$, and $\mathrel{\substack{\frown\\\smile}}$, the complement of $\smile$, is the reflexive closure of the irreflexive relation $\frown$. It is clear that specifying one relation determines all the others.

The *configurations* (called cliques in [10]) of $(E, \smile)$ are the subsets $x \subseteq E$ which are

- *consistent*: $\forall\, e, e' \in x \;\; e \mathrel{\substack{\frown\\\smile}} e'$.

Ordered by inclusion, the configurations of $E$ form a cpo $(\Gamma(E), \subseteq)$; as a collection of sets, $\Gamma(E)$ is a *coherence space* in the sense of [10, 11]. The webs form a category, taking the morphisms from $E_0$ to $E_1$ to be the stable functions from $\Gamma(E_0)$ to $\Gamma(E_1)$, *i.e.*, those continuous functions $f$ such that whenever $e_1 \in f(x)$ there is a minimum finite $x_0 \subseteq x$ such that $e_1 \in f(x_0)$. In this setting, the stable functions coincide with the conditionally multiplicative functions, *i.e.*, the continuous functions that preserve binary compatible glbs (which are, categorically speaking, pullbacks).

The category is cartesian closed: the function space $E_0 \to E_1$ has as events the pairs $(x, e_1)$ of a finite configuration of $E_0$ and an event of $E_1$, with incoherence defined by:

$$(x, e_1) \mathrel{\substack{\smile\\\frown}} (y, e_1') \Leftrightarrow (x \uparrow y) \text{ and } (e_1 \mathrel{\substack{\smile\\\frown}} e_1')$$

where $x \uparrow y$ means $\exists\, z \;\; x, y \subseteq z$. The configurations of $E_0 \to E_1$ are in 1-1 correspondence with the morphisms from $E_0$ to $E_1$, associating to each stable function $f$ its *trace* $\mathrm{tr}(f)$, consisting of those pairs $(x, e_1)$ such that $e_1 \in f(x)$ and $e_1 \notin f(y)$ if $y \subset x$. The inclusion of configurations determines an ordering on stable functions, refining the pointwise ordering and called the *stable ordering* [2].

The definition of $E_0 \to E_1$ is asymmetric in that configurations are paired with events, rather than events with events. This led Girard to two successive decompositions, each of which turned out to have deep logical significance.

• First, $E_0 \to E_1$ can be obtained as $(!E_0) \multimap E_1$, where, for any $E$, the web $!E$ (the *exponential* of $E$, pronounced "bang $E$") has as events the finite configurations of $E$ (with $\overset{\frown}{\smile} = \uparrow$), and where, for any $E_0$, $E_1$, the web $E_0 \multimap E_1$, the *linear function space*, has as events pairs $(e_0, e_1)$ of events of $E_0$ and events of $E_1$, with incoherence defined by:

$$(e_0, e_1) \overset{\smile}{\frown} (e_0', e_1') \Leftrightarrow (e_0 \overset{\frown}{\smile} e_0') \text{ and } (e_1 \overset{\smile}{\frown} e_1')$$

• Second, the remarkable symmetry between $\overset{\frown}{\smile}$ and $\overset{\smile}{\frown}$ in the definition of $E_0 \multimap E_1$ leads to the decomposition $E_0 \multimap E_1 = (E_0^{\perp}) \wp E_1$, where, for any $E$, the web $E^{\perp}$, the *linear negation* of $E$, has the same events as $E$, but has as coherence the incoherence of $E$, and where, for any $E_0$, $E_1$, the web $E_0 \wp E_1$ (the "*par*" of $E_0$ and $E_1$) has as events the pairs $(e_0, e_1)$ of an event of $E_0$ and an event of $E_1$, with incoherence defined by:

$$(e_0, e_1) \overset{\smile}{\frown} (e_0', e_1') \Leftrightarrow (e_0 \overset{\smile}{\frown} e_0') \text{ and } (e_1 \overset{\smile}{\frown} e_1')$$

Returning to the consideration of stable functions, let us see how to describe the pointwise order between stable functions at the level of traces. In $E_0 \to E_1$ there arises a natural ordering between events $(x, e_1)$ if we vary only the input $x$ (whence the superscript $^L$, for "left"):

$$(x, e_1) \leq^L (y, e_1') \Leftrightarrow (y \subseteq x \text{ and } e_1 = e_1')$$

Now define a partial order $\sqsubseteq$ on $\Gamma(E_0 \to E_1)$ by:

$$\phi \sqsubseteq \psi \Leftrightarrow \forall (x, e_1) \in \phi \ \exists y \subseteq x \ \ (y, e_1) \in \psi$$

or, equivalently:

$$\phi \sqsubseteq \psi \Leftrightarrow \forall e \in \phi \ \exists e' \in \psi \ \ e \leq^L e'$$

Then it is easy to see that for any two stable functions $f, g$:

$$(\forall x \ \ f(x) \subseteq g(x)) \Leftrightarrow \mathrm{tr}(f) \sqsubseteq \mathrm{tr}(g)$$

Since the stable ordering is a refinement of the pointwise ordering, it makes sense to ask whether there exists a sensible "complement" of the stable ordering. Indeed we shall see in Proposition 1 that we can always factor $\phi \sqsubseteq \psi$ uniquely as $\phi \sqsubseteq^L \chi \subseteq \psi$. Here $\phi \sqsubseteq^L \chi$ means that $\phi \sqsubseteq \chi$ and $\chi$ is minimal with respect to inclusion (*i.e.*, the stable ordering) among all $\chi'$ such that $\phi \sqsubseteq \chi'$; in other words, $\chi$ is "the part of $\psi$ showing that $\phi \sqsubseteq \psi$" (notice that, given $(x, e_1)$, the $y$ in the definition of $\phi \sqsubseteq \psi$ is unique).

So far, our discussion has been implicitly carried at first-order types, where we have stable functions that can be ordered in two ways ($\subseteq$ and $\sqsubseteq$). If we next consider second-order types, or functionals, the explicit consideration of both the pointwise and the stable orderings at first-order types leads us to focus on functionals that are not only stable with respect to the stable ordering, but also monotonic with respect to the pointwise ordering. That is, we want to retain only those stable functionals $H$ from $\Gamma(E_0 \to E_1)$ to $\Gamma(E_2)$ such that:

$$\forall \phi, \psi \ \ (\phi \sqsubseteq \psi \Rightarrow H(\phi) \subseteq H(\psi))$$

(where we now freely confuse functions with their traces), which, by the $\subseteq$-monotonicity of $H$ and the definition of $\sqsubseteq^L$, can be rephrased as:

$$\forall \phi, \psi \ \ (\phi \sqsubseteq^L \psi \Rightarrow H(\phi) \subseteq H(\psi))$$

Now, specialising to finite $\phi$ and $\psi$, suppose that $(\phi, e_2) \in H$. Then we must have that $e_2 \in H(\psi)$, *i.e.*, there must exist $(\psi_0, e_2)$ in $H$ such that $\psi_0 \subseteq \psi$. Therefore we ask for the following condition, called the *securedness* condition:

$$\forall e \in H \ \ \forall e' \ \ (e' \leq^R e \Rightarrow \exists e'' \in H \ \ e' \leq^L e'')$$

where the order $\leq^R$ is defined by

$$(\psi, e_2') \leq^R (\phi, e_2) \Leftrightarrow (\phi \sqsubseteq^L \psi \text{ and } e_2' = e_2)$$

To summarise, by going from base types successively to first-order and then to second-order types, we have identified two orderings on events.

- The $\leq^L$ ordering allows us to describe the extensional ordering between traces.
- The securedness condition, which involves both orderings $\leq^L$ and $\leq^R$, allows us to capture the preservation of this extensional ordering by functionals.

This suggests that we consider structures $(E, \leq^L, \leq^R, \frown)$, where $(E, \frown)$ is a web, with the aim of building a cartesian closed category of biordered domains (cf. the introduction), and, as it turns out, a model of classical linear logic.

## 3 Motivation from Continuity

In event structures (which predate Girard's webs), a causal dependency relation inspired from Petri net theory is considered in addition to the conflict relation [21]. In full, an event structure is a structure $(E, \leq, \smile)$ where[2]:

- $E$ is a set of *events*,
- $\leq$ is a partial order of *causal dependency*, and
- $\smile$ is a binary, irreflexive, symmetric relation of *conflict*.

The *configurations* (or *states*) of such an event structure are those subsets $x \subseteq E$ which are:

- *consistent*: $\forall\, e, e' \in x \;\; e \frown e'$, and
- *left closed*: $\forall\, e, e' \in E \;\; e' \leq e \in x \Rightarrow e' \in x$.

Ordered by inclusion, the configurations form a coherent prime algebraic domain $(\Gamma(E), \subseteq)$ [21]; such domains are precisely the infinitely distributive, coherent Scott domains [27]. An instance of the causal dependency ordering $e' \leq e$ when $e$ and $e'$ are distinct, is understood as meaning that the event $e$ causally depends on the event $e'$, in that the event $e$ can only occur after $e'$ has occurred. Given this understanding it is reasonable to impose a finiteness axiom, expressing that an event has finite causes:

$\{e' \mid e' \leq e\}$ is finite, for all events $e$.

The event structures satisfying this axiom yield the dI-domains [2] which are coherent, and therefore lead to a cartesian closed category of stably ordered stable functions. (See [26] where an alternative description of event structures using an enabling relation instead of an ordering on events is used to give a simple description of the function space construction.)

But event structures can also be used to describe a continuous model of intuitionistic linear logic, equivalent to the category of coherent prime algebraic domains, with completely additive functions (*i.e.*, functions preserving arbitrary lubs—just called "additive" below). We take as objects event structures (but without the axiom of finite causes: this is the price to pay), and as morphisms configurations of a "function space" of event structures. Let $E_i = (E_i, \leq_i, \smile_i)$, $i = 0, 1$, be event structures. Define:

$$E_0 \multimap E_1 = (E_0 \times E_1, \leq, \smile)$$

where $(e_0, e_1) \leq (e_0', e_1') \Leftrightarrow e_0' \leq_0 e_0$ and $e_1 \leq_1 e_1'$,

and $(e_0, e_1) \smile (e_0', e_1') \Leftrightarrow e_0 \frown_0 e_0'$ and $e_1 \smile_1 e_1'$.

The configurations of $E_0 \multimap E_1$ are in 1-1 correspondence with the additive functions from $\Gamma(E_0)$ to $\Gamma(E_1)$—additive functions are determined by their action on complete

[2] In [21], an axiom relating causal dependency and conflict is imposed; however, it is inessential in that it does not affect the class of domains represented.

primes[3] that correspond to events. The configuration associated with an additive function $f$ is its *graph*, consisting of those pairs $(e_0, e_1)$ such that $e_1 \in f(\{e'_0 \mid e'_0 \leq e_0\})$.

The inclusion ordering on configurations reflects the pointwise ordering on functions; in particular, the function events $(e_0, e_1)$ correspond to the prime additive one step functions (see [31]); and the order $\leq$ to the pointwise order between them.

A morphism $E_0 \rightarrow E_1$ is defined to be a configuration of $E_0 \multimap E_1$. As such it is a relation between the events of $E_0$ and $E_1$. Composition in the category is that of relations. The category is a model of intuitionistic linear logic, as defined in [24, 4]. For instance, its tensor is given in a coordinatewise fashion. For event structures $E_i = (E_i, \leq_i, \smile_i)$, for $i = 0, 1$, define:

$$E_0 \otimes E_1 = (E_0 \times E_1, \leq, \smile)$$

where $(e_0, e_1) \leq (e'_0, e'_1) \Leftrightarrow e_0 \leq_0 e'_0$ and $e_1 \leq_1 e'_1$,

and $(e_0, e_1) \frown\!\!\!\!\smile (e'_0, e'_1) \Leftrightarrow e_0 \frown\!\!\!\!\smile_0 e'_0$ and $e_1 \frown\!\!\!\!\smile_1 e'_1$.

Monoidal-closure follows from the isomorphism

$$(E_0 \otimes E_1 \multimap E_2) \cong (E_0 \multimap (E_1 \multimap E_2))$$

natural in $E_0$ and $E_2$. Product and coproduct are obtained by disjoint juxtaposition of event structures, extending conflict across the two event sets in the case of coproduct. The comonad operation is:

$$!E = (\Gamma(E)^0, \subseteq, \smile)$$

for an event structure $E$, with events the *compact* configurations $\Gamma(E)^0$, and where $\smile$ stands for incompatibility with respect to inclusion. The continuous functions $\Gamma(E_0) \rightarrow \Gamma(E_1)$, between configurations of event structures $E_0, E_1$, are in 1-1 correspondence with the configurations of $!E_0 \multimap E_1$.

Notice that this does not yield a model of classical linear logic. The reader should compare the asymmetric definition of conflict in $E_0 \multimap E_1$ given above to capture continuity with the symmetric definition of incoherence in the stable framework (cf. Section 2).

Moreover, in this model of intuitionistic linear logic, all hope of considering the order $\leq$ as causal dependency is lost. The difficulty stems from the definition of the order $\leq$ for $(E_0 \multimap E_1)$. Its events are ordered by:

$$(e_0, e_1) \leq (e'_0, e'_1) \Leftrightarrow e'_0 \leq_0 e_0 \text{ and } e_1 \leq_1 e'_1$$

[3] A complete prime of a Scott domain $(D, \sqsubseteq)$ is an element $p$ for which whenever $X$ is bounded above and $p \sqsubseteq \sqcup X$ then $p \sqsubseteq x$ for some $x$ in $X$. Complete primes are *a fortiori* compact, where the definition of compact is obtained by replacing "$X$ is bounded above" by "$X$ is directed."

The reversal in the $\leq_0$ order can lead to $\leq$ violating the axiom of finite causes, even though $\leq_0$ and $\leq_1$ do not: an infinite, ascending chain of events in $E_0$ can give rise to an infinite, *descending* chain in $E_0 \multimap E_1$. Of course, there is no reason the extensional ordering on functions should be a relation of causal dependency, so it was not to be expected that its restriction to step functions should be finitary.

However, if we factor $\leq$ into two orderings, one associated with input (on the left) and one with output (on the right), we can expose two finitary orderings. Define

$$(e_0, e_1) \leq^L (e_0', e_1') \Leftrightarrow e_0' \leq_0 e_0 \text{ and } e_1 = e_1',$$

$$(e_0, e_1) \leq^R (e_0', e_1') \Leftrightarrow e_0' = e_0 \text{ and } e_1 \leq_1 e_1'.$$

Then, it is clear that $\leq$ factors as

$$(e_0, e_1) \leq (e_0', e_1') \Leftrightarrow (e_0, e_1) \leq^L (e_0', e_1) \text{ and } (e_0', e_1) \leq^R (e_0', e_1'),$$

and that this factorisation is unique. Provided the orderings of $E_0$ and $E_1$ are finitary, then so are $\leq^R$ and $\geq^L$. This factorisation is the first step towards the definition of bistructures. To indicate its potential, and to further motivate bistructures, we study a simple example.

Let $E_0$ and $E_1$ be the event structures shown below. Both have empty conflict relations. Taking advantage of the factorisation we have drawn them alongside the additive function space $E_0 \multimap E_1$.

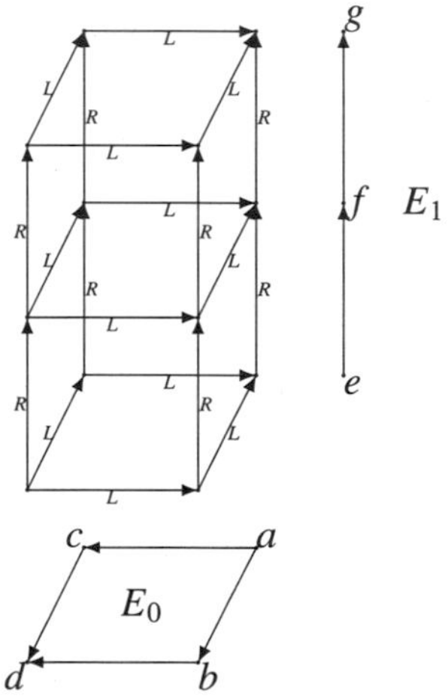


The conflict relation of $E_0 \multimap E_1$ is empty. So here an additive function from $\Gamma(E_0)$ to $\Gamma(E_1)$ is represented by a $\leq$-downwards-closed subset of events of $E_0 \multimap E_1$. For instance, the events in the diagram (below left) are associated with the function that outputs $e$ on getting input event $a$, outputs $f$ for input $b$ or $c$, and outputs $g$ for input $d$. The extensional ordering on functions corresponds to inclusion on $\leq$-downwards-closed subsets of events. It is clear that such a function is determined by specifying the minimal input events which yield some specific output (shown in the diagram below right). This amounts to the subset of $\leq^L$-maximal events of the function, and we can call this subset the *trace* of the function. Notice, though, that this particular function is not stable; output $f$ can be obtained for two non-conflicting but distinct events $b$ and $c$. A stable function should not have $\leq^L$-downwards compatible distinct events in its trace.

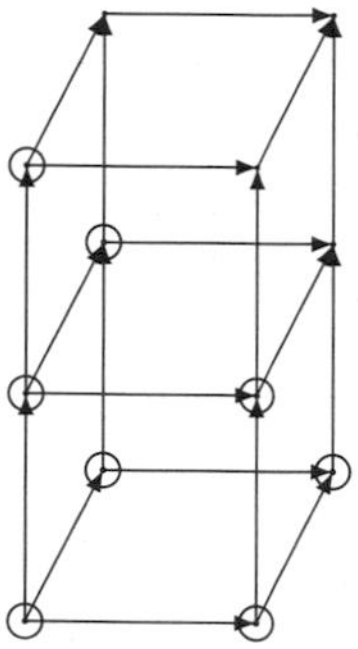

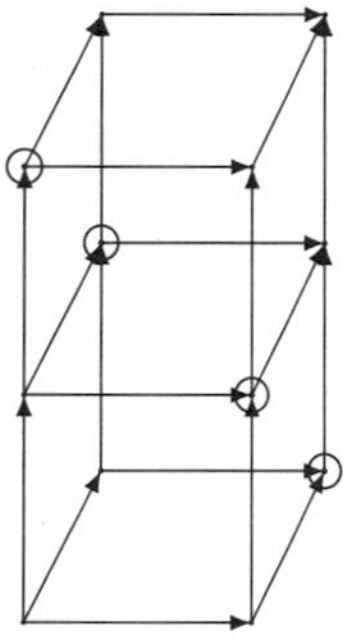

For stable functions, the stable ordering is obtained as inclusion of traces. For example:

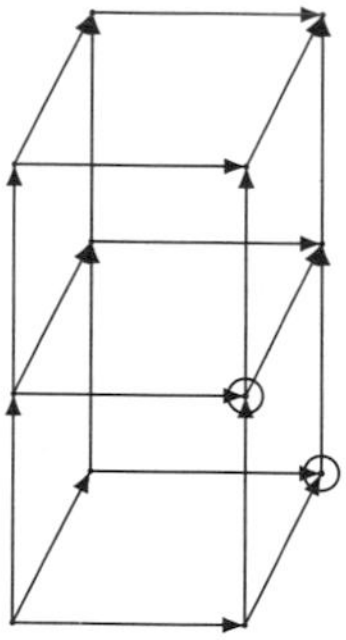

is stable below

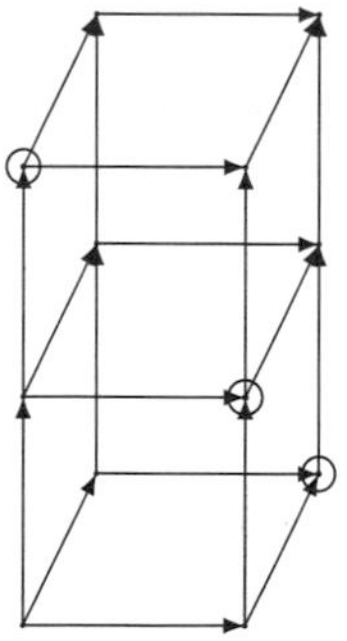

Notice that traces $\phi$ of additive functions from from $\Gamma(E_0)$ to $\Gamma(E_1)$ are secured, in the sense that:

$(e \in \phi \text{ and } e' \leq^R e) \Rightarrow (\exists e'' \in \phi \;\; e' \leq^L e'')$

or more concretely:

$((e_0, e_1) \in \phi \text{ and } e_1' \leq e_1) \Rightarrow (\exists e_0' \ (e_0', e_1') \in \phi \text{ and } e_0' \leq e_0)$

This is the same securedness condition that appeared in Section 2. Here we can understand the condition as saying that for any output, lesser output must arise through the same or lesser input.

Let us summarise this discussion.

- The graphs of additive functions are the $\leq$-downwards-closed, consistent subsets of events.
- The extensional order corresponds to inclusion of graphs.
- The traces of functions are the sets of $\leq^L$-maximal events of their graphs.
- The stable order corresponds to inclusion of traces.

These observations, based on the continuous model construction, will, as it turns out, also make sense in a biordered framework. They encourage us to consider bistructures $(E, \leq^L, \leq^R, \smile)$ and provide guidance as to which axioms we should impose on $\leq^L$,$\leq^R$, and $\smile$. One expects a function-space construction that maintains both stable and extensional orderings, corresponding to taking as morphisms those functions which are continuous with respect to the extensional ordering and stable with respect to the stable ordering.

We end the section with a remark. One might wonder why we have explicitly considered an ordering $\leq$ on events to describe a cartesian closed category of continuous functions, while webs suffice for the purpose of building a cartesian closed category of stable functions. The reason is that the treatment of stability is based on traces of functions, while the treatment of continuity is based on their graphs. Graphs of continuous functions[4] are upwards closed in their first component, even if the underlying event structure has a trivial partial order, and we need an order relation on events to capture that fact.

## 4 Bistructures

The following definition of bistructures allows us to fulfill the hopes expressed in the previous sections.

DEFINITION 1 A *(countable) bistructure* is a structure $(E, \leq^L, \leq^R, \smile)$ where $E$ is a countable set of *events*, $\leq^L, \leq^R$ are partial orders on $E$ and $\smile$ is a binary reflexive, symmetric relation on $E$ such that:

[4] The *graph* of a continuous function $f$ from $\Gamma(E_0)$ to $\Gamma(E_1)$ consists of all pairs $(x, e_1)$ with $x$ compact such that $e_1 \in f(x)$.

1. defining $\leq = (\leq^L \cup \leq^R)^\star$, we have the following factorisation property:

$e \leq e' \Rightarrow \exists\, e'' \;\; e \leq^L e'' \leq^R e'$

2. defining $\preceq = (\geq^L \cup \leq^R)^\star$,

(a) $\preceq$ is finitary, *i.e.*, $\{e' \mid e' \preceq e\}$ is finite, for all $e$,

(b) $\preceq$ is a partial order;

3. (a) $\downarrow^L \subseteq \asymp$ (b) $\uparrow^R \subseteq \stackrel{\frown}{\smile}$

The two compatibility relations are defined by:

$e \downarrow^L e' \Leftrightarrow \exists\, e'' \;\; e'' \leq^L e \;$ and $e'' \leq^L e'$,

$e \uparrow^R e' \Leftrightarrow \exists\, e'' \;\; e \leq^R e'' \;$ and $e' \leq^R e''$.

Notice the symmetry of the axioms. They are invariant under the "duality":

$\leq^L \mapsto \geq^R$,

$\leq^R \mapsto \geq^L$,

$\stackrel{\frown}{\smile} \;\mapsto\; \stackrel{\smile}{\frown}$

which is why we obtain a model of the *classical* logic. Bistructures of the form $(E,\ id_E, \leq, \stackrel{\frown}{\smile})$, *i.e.*, such that the $\leq^L$ order is degenerate, are essentially the ordinary, countable event structures, $(E, \leq, \smile)$, satisfying the axiom of finite causes. We say "essentially" because Axiom 3(b) is not part of the above definition of event structure, but does not restrict the class of domains represented.

*Remark 1* In the presence of Axiom 2(a), Axiom 2(b) is equivalent to requiring that $e \prec e'$ is well founded, where $e \prec e'$ means $e \preceq e'$ and $e \neq e'$. (A fortiori, $<^R$ and $>^L$ are well founded.)

The axioms of bistructures are strong enough to imply the uniqueness of the decomposition of $\leq = (\leq^L \cup \leq^R)^\star$, and also that $\leq$ is a partial order.

LEMMA 1 Let $E$ be a bistructure. The following properties hold, for all $e, e'$ in $E$:

(1) ($e \downarrow^L e'$ and $e \stackrel{\frown}{\smile} e'$) $\Rightarrow e = e'$,

(2) ($e \downarrow^L e'$ and $e \uparrow^R e'$) $\Rightarrow e = e'$,

(3) $e \leq e'$ $\qquad\qquad \Rightarrow \exists\,!e'' \;\; e \leq^L e'' \leq^R e'$

*Proof* (1) If $e \downarrow^L e'$, then $e \stackrel{\smile}{\frown} e'$, which together with $e \stackrel{\frown}{\smile} e'$ implies $e = e'$ by definition of $\stackrel{\smile}{\frown}$.

(2) Immediate consequence of (1) since $e \uparrow^R e'$ implies $e \frown e'$.

(3) Suppose that $e \leq^L e'' \leq^R e'$ and $e \leq^L e''' \leq^R e'$. Then $e'' \downarrow^L e'''$ and $e'' \uparrow^R e'''$, therefore $e'' = e'''$ by (1). □

The unique factorisation property enables a diagrammatic style of proof.

LEMMA 2 The relation $\leq$ defined in Axiom 1 of bistructures is a partial order.

*Proof* The relation $\leq$ is certainly reflexive and transitive. With the aim of proving anti-symmetry, suppose $e \leq e'$ and $e' \leq e$. Then pictorially by factorising $\leq$, for some events $\varepsilon$ and $\varepsilon'$, we have:

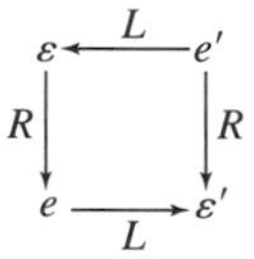


So $e \leq \varepsilon$, and factorising this we get $e \leq^L \varepsilon'' \leq^R \varepsilon \leq^R e$, for some $\varepsilon''$. But $e \leq^L e \leq^R e$ so the uniqueness of factorisation gives $e = \varepsilon''$. Then as $\leq^R$ is a partial order $e = \varepsilon$. Therefore, the above picture collapses to:

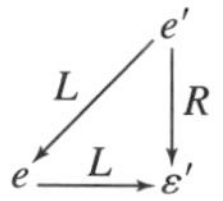


The uniqueness of the factorisation of $e' \leq e'$ gives $\varepsilon' = e'$, so as $\leq^L$ is a partial order, $e = e'$, as required. □

As with Girard's webs, bistructures provide a concrete level of description of abstract points, or configurations, which we define next.

DEFINITION 2 A *configuration* of a bistructure $(E, \leq^L, \leq^R, \frown)$ is a subset $x \subseteq E$ which is:

- *consistent*: $\forall\, e, e' \in x \;\; e \frown e'$, and
- *secured*: $\forall\, e \in x \;\; \forall e' \leq^R e \;\; \exists e'' \in x \;\; e' \leq^L e''$.

[Notice that $e''$ is unique in any consistent set because of Axiom 3(a) on bistructures.] Write $\Gamma(E)$ for the set of configurations of a bistructure $E$, and $\Gamma(E)^0$ for the set of finite configurations (see Proposition 2).

When $\leq^L = id$, the securedness condition amounts to $\leq^R$-downwards-closure, hence in that case configurations are just the configurations of the underlying event structure $(F, \leq^R, \smile)$.

We next define order relations on configurations.

DEFINITION 3 Let $E$ be a bistructure. We define the *stable* ordering $\sqsubseteq^R$ and the *extensional* ordering $\sqsubseteq$ on configurations by:

$\sqsubseteq^R$ is set-theoretic inclusion,
$x \sqsubseteq y \Leftrightarrow \forall e \in x \ \exists e' \in y \ e \leq^L e'$

It follows from these definitions and from the reflexivity of $\leq^L$ that $\sqsubseteq^R$ is included in $\sqsubseteq$. We define a third relation $\sqsubseteq^L$ as follows:

$$x \sqsubseteq^L y \Leftrightarrow x \sqsubseteq y \text{ and } (\forall z \in \Gamma(E)\ (x \sqsubseteq z \text{ and } z \sqsubseteq^R y) \Rightarrow y = z)$$

Thus, $x \sqsubseteq^L y$ means that $y$ is a $\sqsubseteq^R$-minimal configuration such that $x \sqsubseteq y$. Write $x \uparrow^R y$ for $(\exists z \in \Gamma(E)\ \ x, y \sqsubseteq^R z)$.

Some elementary properties of configurations are given in the following lemmas.

LEMMA 3 Let $E$ be a bistructure, and suppose that $x \in \Gamma(E)$. If $e$ is in the $\leq$-downwards-closure of $x$, then it is in the $\leq^L$-downwards-closure of $x$.

*Proof* Let $e'$ in $x$ be such that $e \leq e'$:

$\exists e''\ \ e \leq^L e'' \leq^R e'$ by factorisation,
$\exists e''' \in x\ \ e'' \leq^L e'''$ by securedness

Then $e \leq^L e'''$, which completes the proof. □

It follows from Lemma 3 that $x \sqsubseteq y$ is equivalently defined by stating that the $\leq$-downwards-closure of $x$ is included in the $\leq$-downwards-closure of $y$. This characterisation is in accordance with the discussion in Section 3: compare $\sqsubseteq^R$ and $\sqsubseteq$ with graph and trace inclusion, respectively.

LEMMA 4 Let $E$ be a bistructure, and suppose that $x, y$ are in $\Gamma(E)$. If $x \uparrow^R y$, $e \in x$, $e' \in y$, and $e \downarrow^L e'$, then $e = e'$.

*Proof* Let $z \in \Gamma(E)$ be such that $x \sqsubseteq^R z$ and $y \sqsubseteq^R z$. We have $e \in z$ and $e' \in z$, hence $e \frown e'$. On the other hand, by Axiom 3(a) we find that $e \asymp e'$, hence $e = e'$. □

*Remark 2* Lemma 4 has two interesting consequences.

• If $x$ is a configuration and $e \in x$, then $e$ is $\leq^L$-maximal in $x$. In turn, this implies the antisymmetry of $\sqsubseteq$, which is thus a partial order (reflexivity and transitivity are immediate). In turn, the antisymmetry of $\sqsubseteq$ entails the reflexivity of $\sqsubseteq^L$.

- If $x \uparrow^R y$, then the set intersection $x \cap y$ is the glb of $x$ and $y$ with respect to both $\sqsubseteq^R$ and $\sqsubseteq$.

DEFINITION 4 For $x$ in $\Gamma(E)$, we define the relativised relation $\preceq_x$ as the reflexive, transitive closure of $\preceq_x^1$ where:

$$e \preceq_x^1 e' \Leftrightarrow_{def} e \in x \text{ and } e' \in x \text{ and } \exists e'' \ e \geq^L e'' \leq^R e'.$$

LEMMA 5 Let $E$ be a bistructure. The following property holds, for all $x$, $y$ in $\Gamma(E)$ and $e$ in $E$:

$$(x \uparrow^R y \text{ and } e \in x \cap y) \Rightarrow (\forall e' \in E \ e' \preceq_x e \Leftrightarrow e' \preceq_y e)$$

(or, equivalently, in asymmetric form: $(x \uparrow^R y, e \in x \cap y \text{ and } e' \preceq_x e) \Rightarrow e' \in y)$.

*Proof* It is clearly enough to show this for the one step relations $\preceq_x^1$ and $\preceq_y^1$. Suppose $e' \preceq_x^1 e$, and let $e''$ be such that $e' \geq^L e'' \leq^R e$. Since $y$ is secured, and since $e \in y$, there exists $e'''$ in $y$ such that $e'' \leq^L e'''$. By Lemma 4 applied to $x$, $y$, $e'$, and $e'''$, we get $e' = e''' \in y$. □

In the rest of this section, we examine some of the properties of the relations $\sqsubseteq^R$, $\sqsubseteq$, and $\sqsubseteq^L$: Proposition 1 concerns factorisation—preparing the ground for the definition of exponentials in Section 6, while Propositions 2 and 3 concern completeness properties.

DEFINITION 5 For $x$ in $\Gamma(E)$ and a subset $z \subseteq x$, define

$$[z]_x = \{e_0 \in x \mid \exists e \in z \ e_0 \preceq_x e\}$$

If $z$ is a singleton $\{e\}$, we write simply $[e]_x$.

LEMMA 6 Let $E$ be a bistructure, and suppose that $x \in \Gamma(E)$ and $z \subseteq x$. Then $[z]_x$ is a configuration which is finite if $z$ is finite and such that:

$$z \subseteq [z]_x \sqsubseteq^R x \quad \text{and} \quad (\forall y \in \Gamma(E) \ (z \subseteq y \uparrow^R x) \Rightarrow ([z]_x \sqsubseteq^R y))$$

*Proof* We show that $[z]_x$ is a configuration. It is clearly consistent, as it is a subset of $x$. If $e \in [z]_x$ and $e_1 \leq^R e$, since $x$ is secured, there exists $e_2$ in $x$ such that $e_1 \leq^L e_2$, and then $e_2 \in [z]_x$ by the construction of $[z]_x$. Thus $[z]_x$ is a configuration. The finiteness property follows from Axiom 2(a). The rest of the statement is an immediate consequence of Lemma 5. □

*Remark 3* For any $e$ the following "canonical" set

$$[e] = \{e' \mid e' \leq^R e\}$$

is a configuration containing $e$, and if $x$ is any other such, then $[e] \sqsubseteq x$. In contrast, there need be no $\subseteq$-least configuration containing a given $e$ (cf. Lemma 6).

PROPOSITION 1 Let $\sqsubseteq^R$, $\sqsubseteq$, and $\sqsubseteq^L$ be the relations on configurations defined above. The following properties hold:

1. $\sqsubseteq$ is $(\sqsubseteq^L \cup \sqsubseteq^R)^\star$, and satisfies Axiom 1,
2. for all configurations $x, y$:

$$x \sqsubseteq^L y \Leftrightarrow (x \sqsubseteq y \text{ and } \forall e \in y\ \exists e_0 \in x, e_1 \in y\ \ e \preceq_y e_1 \geq^L e_0)$$

3. $\sqsubseteq^L$ is a partial order, and
4. for all configurations $x, y$ with $x \sqsubseteq y$ there is a unique $z$ such that $x \sqsubseteq^L z \sqsubseteq^R y$.

*Proof* (1) Suppose $x \sqsubseteq y$. The subset $z = \{e_1 \in y \mid \exists e_0 \in x\ \ e_0 \leq^L e_1\}$ represents the part of $y$ actually used to check $x \sqsubseteq y$. But we have to close this subset to make it secured. Thus we consider $z_1 = [z]_y$, which is a configuration by Lemma 6. We show $x \sqsubseteq^L z_1$. Suppose that $x \sqsubseteq z_1' \sqsubseteq^R z_1$, and let $e$ be an element of $z_1$. By the construction of $z_1$, there are $e_0$ in $x$ and $e_1$ in $y$ such that $e \preceq_y e_1 \geq^L e_0$. Since $x \sqsubseteq z_1'$, $e_0 \leq^L e_1'$ for some $e_1'$ in $z_1'$. Applying Lemma 4 to $y, z_1', e_1$, and $e_1'$, we get $e_1 = e_1'$, hence $e_1 \in z_1'$, which implies $e \in z_1'$ by Lemma 5. Therefore $z_1 \sqsubseteq^R z_1'$, which completes the proof that $x \sqsubseteq^L z_1$. The decomposition $x \sqsubseteq^L z_1 \sqsubseteq^R y$ shows that $\sqsubseteq$ is contained in $(\sqsubseteq^L \cup \sqsubseteq^R)^\star$. The converse inclusion is obvious.

(2) follows immediately from the proof of (1), observing that, in full:

$$z_1 = \{e \in y \mid \exists e_0 \in x, e_1 \in y\ \ e \preceq_y e_1 \geq^L e_0\}$$

(3) The antisymmetry follows from the inclusion of $\sqsubseteq^L$ in $\sqsubseteq$. The reflexivity of $\sqsubseteq^L$ has been already pointed out in remark 2. Suppose that $x \sqsubseteq^L y' \sqsubseteq^L y$. Clearly $x \sqsubseteq y$, so with an eye to using (2) to show $x \sqsubseteq^L y$ suppose $e \in y$. By (2), there exist $e_0$ in $y'$, $e_1$ in $y$, $e_0'$ in $x$ and $e_1'$ in $y'$ such that

$e_0 \leq^L e_1$ and $e \preceq_y e_1$,

$e_0' \leq^L e_1'$ and $e_0 \preceq_{y'} e_1'$.

Or in full:

$$e_0 \leq^L e_1 \geq^R e_2 \cdots \leq^L e_{2i+1} = e \qquad \text{with } e_{2j+1} \in y \text{ for all } 0 \leq j \leq i,$$

$$e_0' \leq^L e_1' \geq^R e_2' \cdots \leq^L e_{2i'+1}' = e_0 \qquad \text{with } e_{2j+1}' \in y' \text{ for all } 0 \leq j \leq i'$$

Since $y' \sqsubseteq y$ and $e'_1 \in y'$, there exists $e''_1$ such that $e'_1 \leq^L e''_1$ and $e''_1 \in y$. Since $e'_2 \leq^R e'_1 \leq^L e''_1$, there exists $e''_2$ such that $e'_2 \leq^L e''_2 \leq^R e''_1$, by factorisation. Since $y$ is secured, there exists $e''_3$ in $y$ such that $e''_2 \leq^L e''_3$. In order to continue this lifting of the $e'_i$ relative to $y'$ to a sequence of the $e''_i$ relative to $y$, we have to make sure that $e'_3 \leq^L e''_3$: But

$e'_3 \leq^L e'''_3 \in y$ for some $e'''_3 \in y$ since $y' \sqsubseteq y$, and

$e'''_3 = e''_3$ since $e'_2 \leq^L e''_3, e'_2 \leq^L e'''_3$, and $e''_3, e'''_3 \in y$

Continuing in this way, we get:

$$e'_0 \leq^L e''_1 \geq^R e''_2 \cdots \leq^L e''_{2i'+1} = e_1 \geq^R e_2 \cdots \leq^L e_{2i+1} = e$$

where $e''_{2i'+1} = e_1$ follows from Lemma 4 applied to $y$, $y$, $e''_{2i'+1}$, and $e_1$. Since $e_{2j+1} \in y$ for all $0 \leq j \leq i$ and $e''_{2j+1} \in y$ for all $0 \leq j \leq i'$, by (2), we conclude that $x \sqsubseteq^L y$.

(4) Only the uniqueness of $z$ is in question, so suppose that $x \sqsubseteq^L z \sqsubseteq^R y$ and $x \sqsubseteq^L z' \sqsubseteq^R y$. By symmetry, it is enough to show that $z \subseteq z'$. So suppose that $e \in z$. Then by (2) there are $e_0$ in $x$ and $e_1$ in $z$ such that $e \preceq_z e_1 \geq^L e_0$. We begin by showing that $e_1 \in z'$. Since $e_0 \in x \sqsubseteq z'$ there is an $e'_1$ in $z'$ such that $e_0 \sqsubseteq^L e'_1$. So $e_1 \downarrow^L e'_1$ and therefore, by Lemma 4 applied to $z, z', e_1$ and $e'_1$, we have $e_1 = e'_1 \in z'$. Now by Lemma 5 applied to $z, z', e_1$, and $e$ we have $e \preceq_{z'} e_1$ and so $e \in z'$, concluding the proof. □

PROPOSITION 2 Let $E$ be a bistructure. The following properties hold of the associated biorder:

1. all $\sqsubseteq$-directed lubs and $\sqsubseteq^R$-bounded lubs exist,
2. all $\sqsubseteq^R$-lubs of $\sqsubseteq^R$-directed sets exist, coinciding with their $\sqsubseteq$-lubs, and
3. a configuration is $\sqsubseteq$-compact iff it is $\sqsubseteq^R$-compact iff it is finite.

It follows that $(\Gamma(E), \sqsubseteq^R)$ and $(\Gamma(E), \sqsubseteq)$ are $\omega$-algebraic cpos (with common least element $\emptyset$), and that, moreover, $(\Gamma(E), \sqsubseteq^R)$ is bounded complete, *i.e.*, is a Scott domain.

*Proof* (1) Let $\Delta$ be $\sqsubseteq$-directed. We show:

$$z = \left\{ e \in \bigcup \Delta e \text{ is } \leq^L \text{-maximal in } \bigcup \Delta \right\} \text{ is the } \sqsubseteq\text{-lub of } \Delta$$

We first check that $z$ is a configuration. If $e_1, e_2 \in z$, then $e_1 \in \delta_1$ and $e_2 \in \delta_2$ for some $\delta_1, \delta_2$ in $\Delta$. Let $\delta$ in $\Delta$ be such that $\delta_1, \delta_2 \sqsubseteq \delta$. Then by definition of $z$ and $\sqsubseteq$, it follows that $e_1, e_2 \in \delta$. Therefore $e_1 \smile e_2$. If $e \in z$ and $e_1 \leq^R e$, let $\delta$ in $\Delta$ be such that $e \in \delta$. Since $\delta$ is secured, there exists $e_2$ in $\delta$ such that $e_1 \leq^L e_2$. By definition of $z$ and by Axiom 2 (cf. Remark 1), we can find $e_3$ in $z$ such that $e_2 \leq^L e_3$. Hence $z$ is indeed a configuration.

It is obvious from the definition of $z$ that $\delta \sqsubseteq z$ holds for any $\delta$ in $\Delta$, and that if $z_1$ is an $\sqsubseteq$-upper bound of $\Delta$ then $z \sqsubseteq z_1$.

The $\sqsubseteq^R$-bounded lubs exist: if $X \subseteq \Gamma(E)$ and if $x$ is an $\sqsubseteq^R$-upper bound of $X$, then $\bigcup X$ is consistent as a subset of $x$ and secured as a union of secured sets of events.

(2) Let $\Delta$ be $\sqsubseteq^R$-directed (and hence *a fortiori* $\sqsubseteq$-directed). Clearly $\bigsqcup^R \Delta$ exists and is $\bigcup \Delta$; we prove that $\bigsqcup \Delta = \bigcup \Delta$ (where $\bigsqcup^R$ and $\bigsqcup$ are relative to $\sqsubseteq^R$ and $\sqsubseteq$, respectively). We have to show that any $e$ in $\bigcup \Delta$ is $\leq^L$-maximal. Suppose there exists $e_1$ in $\bigcup \Delta$ such that $e \leq^L e_1$. Then, applying Lemma 4 to $\bigcup \Delta$, $\bigcup \Delta$, $e$, and $e_1$, we get $e = e_1$.

(3) We prove three implications.

- $x$ finite $\Rightarrow$ $x$ $\sqsubseteq$-compact: Let $\{e_1, \ldots, e_n\} \sqsubseteq \bigsqcup \Delta$. There exist $e'_1, \ldots, e'_n$ in $\bigsqcup \Delta$ such that $e_i \leq^L e'_i$ for all $i$. Let $\delta_1, \ldots \delta_n$ in $\Delta$ be such that $e'_i \in \delta_i$ for all $i$, and let $\delta$ in $\Delta$ be such that $\delta_i \sqsubseteq \delta$ for all $i$. Then by the $\leq^L$-maximality of $e'_1, \ldots, e'_n$ we get that $e'_i \in \delta$ for all $i$. Hence $\{e_1, \ldots, e_n\} \sqsubseteq \delta$.
- $x$ $\sqsubseteq$-compact $\Rightarrow$ $x$ $\sqsubseteq^R$-compact: If $x \sqsubseteq^R \bigsqcup^R \Delta$, then, *a fortiori*, $x \sqsubseteq \bigsqcup \Delta$, therefore $x \sqsubseteq \delta$ for some $\delta$ in $\Delta$. We show that actually $x \sqsubseteq^R \delta$ holds. Suppose $e \in x$ and let $e_1$ in $\delta$ be such that $e \leq^L e_1$. Then we get $e = e_1$ by Lemma 4 applied to $x$, $\delta$, $e$, and $e_1$.
- $x$ $\sqsubseteq^R$-compact $\Rightarrow$ $x$ finite: We claim that, for any $z$:

$\{y \mid y$ finite configuration and $y \sqsubseteq^R z\}$

is $\sqsubseteq^R$-directed and has $z$ as lub. The directedness is obvious. We have to check that $z \sqsubseteq^R \bigsqcup^R \{y \mid y$ finite and $y \sqsubseteq^R z\}$, *i.e.*, for all $e$ in $z$, there exists a finite $y$ such that $y \sqsubseteq^R z$ and $e \in y$. The configuration $[e]_z$ (cf. Lemma 6) does the job. □

PROPOSITION 3 Let $E$ be a bistructure. Then the following properties hold:

1. the complete primes of $(\Gamma(E), \sqsubseteq^R)$ are the configurations of the form $[e]_x$, and
2. $(\Gamma(E), \sqsubseteq^R)$ is a dI-domain.

*Proof* (1) Consider a configuration $[e]_x$. We show it is a complete prime. If $Y$ is bounded above and $[e]_x \sqsubseteq^R \bigsqcup^R Y = \bigcup Y$, then $e \in y$ for some $y$ in $Y$. Since $[e]_x \uparrow^R y$, we infer that $[e]_x \subseteq y$, by Lemma 5. Conversely, every complete prime is of this form, since for any configuration $x$ we have $x = \bigcup\{[e]_x \mid e \in x\}$.

(2) A dI-domain is a Scott domain which is distributive (see Definition 7) and satisfies Axiom I, which states that a compact element dominates finitely many elements. Axiom I follows from the finiteness of compacts, proved in Proposition 2. Distributivity is then equivalent to prime-algebraicity, *i.e.*, the property that any element is the lub of the complete

primes that it dominates. (We refer to [31, 27] for a proof.) Prime-algebraicity is an immediate consequence of (1). □

The properties proved in Proposition 2 and Proposition 3 correspond to the most interesting structure of Berry's bidomains. However, to show its configurations form a bidomain we will require a bistructure to fulfill extra axioms; these assure the existence of enough meets. We pursue these matters in Section 7.

## 5 A Category of Bistructures

Morphisms between bistructures correspond to configurations of the function-space construction given below. They determine (certain—see Remark 4) extensional, linear (= stable and additive) functions on domains of configurations. Given bistructures $E_i = (E_i, \leq_i^L, \leq_i^R, \smile_i)$, for $i = 0, 1$, their *linear function space* is defined by:

$$E_0 \multimap E_1 = (E_0 \times E_1, \leq^L, \leq^R, \smile)$$

where $(e_0, e_1) \leq^L (e_0', e_1') \Leftrightarrow e_0' \leq^R e_0$ and $e_1 \leq^L e_1'$,

$(e_0, e_1) \leq^R (e_0', e_1') \Leftrightarrow e_0' \leq^L e_0$ and $e_1 \leq_1^R e_1'$

and $(e_0, e_1) \asymp (e_0', e_1') \Leftrightarrow e_0 \smile_0 e_0'$ and $e_1 \asymp_1 e_1'$.

It is straightforward to show that this is a bistructure. We define the category of bistructures **BS** by taking the morphisms from $E_0$ to $E_1$ to be configurations of $E_0 \multimap E_1$, with composition being that of relations. We must show that this composition is well defined and has identities.

PROPOSITION 4 Let $\alpha$ be a configuration of $E \multimap E'$ and $\beta$ be a configuration of $E' \multimap E''$. Then their relational composition $\beta \circ \alpha$ is a configuration of $E \multimap E''$. Also the identity relation on a bistructure $E$ is a configuration of $E \multimap E$.

*Proof* That identity relations are configurations relies, for securedness, on the factorisation property (1) of bistructures: if $(e_1, e_2) \leq_R (e, e)$, then $(e_1, e_2) \leq_L (e_3, e_3)$ where $e_3$ is obtained by factorisation of $e_2 \leq e_1$. For the relational composition $\beta \circ \alpha$ to be a configuration we require it to be consistent and secured.

*Consistency*: From the definition of $\asymp$ on function space we require that for $(e_1, e_1'')$, $(e_2, e_2'')$ in $\beta \circ \alpha$ that

(*i*) $e_1 \smile e_2 \Rightarrow e_1'' \smile e_2''$ and (*ii*) $e_1'' \asymp e_2'' \Rightarrow e_1 \asymp e_2$,

facts which hold of the composition $\beta \circ \alpha$ because they hold of $\alpha$ and $\beta$.

*Securedness*: Suppose $(e, e'') \in \beta \circ \alpha$ and that

$(e_0, e''_0) \leq^R (e, e'')$,

*i.e.*, $e \leq^L e_0$ and $e''_0 \leq^R e''$. It is required that there is

$(e^\star, e''^\star) \in \beta \circ \alpha$

such that

$(e_0, e''_0) \leq^L (e^\star, e''^\star)$,

*i.e.*, $e^\star \leq^R e_0$ and $e''_0 \leq^L e''^\star$. [In the following argument, it is helpful to refer to the diagram below.]

As $(e, e'') \in \beta \circ \alpha$ there is $e'^\star_0$ such that $(e, e'^\star_0) \in \alpha$ and $(e'^\star_0, e'') \in \beta$. Because $e''_0 \leq^R e''$, we obtain that

$(e'^\star_0, e''_0) \leq^R (e'^\star_0, e'')$

As $\beta$ is secured there is $(e'_1, e''_1)$ in $\beta$ for which $(e'^\star_0, e''_0) \leq^L (e'_1, e''_1)$, *i.e.*,

$$(e'_1, e''_1) \in \beta \text{ and } e'_1 \leq^R e'^\star_0 \text{ and } e''_0 \leq^L e''_1. \tag{1$\beta$}$$

As $e \leq^L e_0$ and $e'_1 \leq^R e'^\star_0$, we have $(e_0, e'_1) \leq^R (e, e'^\star_0)$. But $\alpha$ is secured, so there is $(e_1, e'^\star_1)$ in $\alpha$ for which $(e_0, e'_1) \leq^L (e_1, e'^\star_1)$, *i.e.*,

$$(e_1, e'^\star_1) \in \alpha \text{ and } e_1 \leq^R e_0 \text{ and } e'_1 \leq^L e'^\star_1. \tag{1$\alpha$}$$

From $(1\alpha)$ and $(1\beta)$ we obtain:

$$e_0 \geq^R e_1 \quad (e_1, e'^\star_1) \in \alpha \quad e'^\star_1 \geq_L e'_1 \quad (e'_1, e''_1) \in \beta \quad e''_1 \geq^L e''_0 \tag{1}$$

We now show that this pattern in $e_1, e'^\star_1, e'_1, e''_1$, relative to $e_0$ and $e''_0$, must repeat.

It follows from $e'_1 \leq^L e'^\star_1$ that $(e'^\star_1, e''_1) \leq^R (e'_1, e''_1) \in \beta$. As $\beta$ is secured, there is an $(e'_2, e''_2)$ in $\beta$ for which $(e'^\star_1, e''_1) \leq^L (e'_2, e''_2)$, *i.e.*,

$$(e'_2, e''_2) \in \beta \text{ and } e'_2 \leq^R e'^\star_1 \text{ and } e''_1 \leq^L e''_2 \tag{2$\beta$}$$

As $e'_2 \leq^R e'^\star_1$, we have $(e_1, e'_2) \leq^R (e_1, e'^\star_1) \in \alpha$. But $\alpha$ is secured, so there is an $(e_2, e'^\star_2)$ in $\alpha$ for which $(e_1, e'_2) \leq^L (e_2, e'^\star_2)$, *i.e.*,

$$(e_2, e'^\star_2) \in \alpha \text{ and } e_2 \leq^R e_1 \text{ and } e'_2 \leq^L e'^\star_2 \tag{2$\alpha$}$$

and the pattern in (1) repeats in (2) below—obtained directly from $(2\alpha)$ and $(2\beta)$:

$$e_0 \geq^R e_2 \quad (e_2, e'^\star_2) \in \alpha \quad e'^\star_2 \geq_L e'_2 \quad (e'_2, e''_2) \in \beta \quad e''_2 \geq^L e''_0 \tag{2}$$

where $e'_2 \leq^R e'^{\star}_1$. This can be repeated infinitely. Diagrammatically:

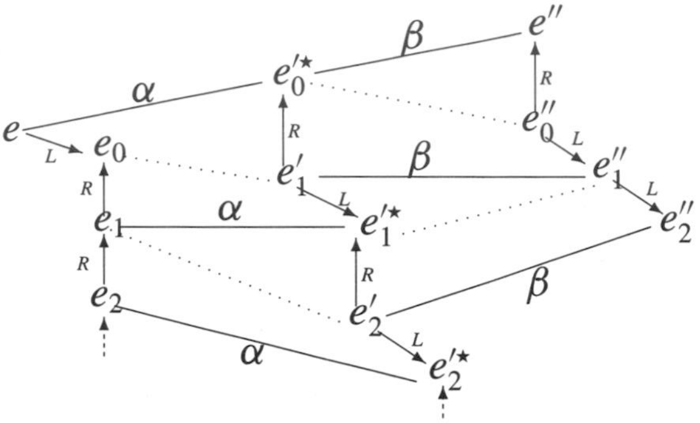

The chain

$$e'^{\star}_0 \geq^R e'_1 \leq^L e'^{\star}_1 \geq^R e'_2 \leq^L e'^{\star}_2 \geq^R \cdots$$

must eventually be constant by Axiom 2(a) on bistructures. Hence we obtain

$$(e_n, e'^{\star}_n) \in \alpha \ \text{ and } \ e'_n = e'^{\star}_n \ \text{ and } \ (e'_n, e''_n) \in \beta$$

yielding $(e_n, e''_n)$ in $\beta \circ \alpha$ with $e_n \leq^R e_0$ and $e''_0 \leq^L e''_n$, *i.e.*, $(e_0, e''_0) \leq^L (e_n, e''_n)$; so $(e_n, e''_n)$ fulfills the requirements we seek for $(e^\star, e''^\star)$. □

PROPOSITION 5 Let $F$ be a configuration of $E \multimap E'$ and let $x$ be a configuration of $E$. Defining

$$F \cdot x = \{e' \mid \exists e \in x \ \ (e, e') \in F\}$$

yields a configuration of $E'$. The function $x \mapsto F \cdot x \ : \Gamma(E) \to \Gamma(E')$ is linear with respect to $\sqsubseteq^R$ and continuous with respect to $\sqsubseteq$.

*Proof* The first part of the statement is a consequence of Proposition 4, since $F \cdot x$ can be read as $F \circ x$ if $x$ is viewed as a configuration from $I$ (the tensor unit, defined at the beginning of the next section) to $E$. The verification that $x \mapsto F \cdot x$ is linear is easy. We check only that it preserves compatible binary lubs. Suppose that $e' \in F \cdot (x \sqcup^R y)$, *i.e.*, $(e, e') \in F$ for some $e$ in $x \sqcup^R y$. Then $e \in x$ or $e \in y$, hence $e' \in (F \cdot x) \sqcup^R (F \cdot y)$.

For continuity, by Lemma 7 below, it is enough to check $\sqsubseteq$-monotonicity, which is proved using a "staircase argument" similar to that of the previous proof: if $x \sqsubseteq y$ and $e' \in F \cdot x$, let $e$ in $x$ be such that $(e, e') \in F \cdot x$, and let $e_1$ in $y$ be such that $e \leq^L e_1$. Since $(e_1, e') \leq^R (e, e')$, there exists $(e_2, e'_1)$ in $F$ such that $e' \leq^L e'_1$ and $e_2 \leq^R e_1$. From there we find an $e_3$ such that $e_3 \in y$ and $e_2 \leq^L e_3$, which leads to an $(e_4, e'_2)$ in $F$ such that $(e_3, e'_1) \leq^L (e_4, e'_2)$.

In this way, we construct $e' \leq^L e'_1 \leq^L e'_2 \cdots$, where the $e'_i$ are in $y$. The sequence eventually ends, yielding an $e'_i$ that fits. □

LEMMA 7 Let $E$ and $E'$ be bistructures. Suppose that $f : \Gamma(E) \to \Gamma(E')$ is $\sqsubseteq^R$-continuous and $\sqsubseteq$-monotonic. Then it is also $\sqsubseteq$-continuous.

*Proof* Suppose $\{e_1, \ldots, e_n\} \sqsubseteq f(x)$. Then there exist $e'_1, \ldots, e'_n$ in $f(x)$ such that $e_i \leq^L e'_i$ for all $i$. By $\sqsubseteq^R$-continuity, there exists a finite $x_1 \sqsubseteq^R x$ such that $e'_1, \ldots, e'_n \in f(x_1)$, hence $\{e_1, \ldots, e_n\} \sqsubseteq f(x_1)$. □

*Remark 4* Not all $\sqsubseteq^R$-linear and $\sqsubseteq$-continuous functions are represented by a morphism. The represented functions also satisfy a uniformity requirement, where a $\sqsubseteq^R$-stable and $\sqsubseteq$-continuous function $f$ from $\Gamma(E)$ to $\Gamma(E')$ is *uniform* iff for all $e$ in $E$ and configurations $x$ containing $e$ and for all $e'$ in $E'$ we have that $([e]_x, e') \in \mathrm{tr}(f)$ implies $([e], e') \in \mathrm{tr}(f)$ (see Definition 6 below, and cf. Remark 3); unfortunately, even this condition is not sufficient for representability. On a more positive note, one can show that the assignment of functions to configurations is 1-1.

## 6 A model of Classical Linear Logic

Here we give the constructions showing that **BS** is a (non-compactly closed) model of classical linear logic. The constructions extend those of Girard (recalled in Section 2). Define *linear negation*, the involution of linear logic, by

$$E^\perp = (E, \geq^R, \geq^L, \asymp)$$

where $E = (E, \leq^L, \leq^R, \smile)$. Clearly $(E^\perp)^\perp = E$. The remaining multiplicatives, $\wp$ (*par*) and $\otimes$ (*tensor*), are determined by the usual isomorphisms of classical linear logic:

$$E_0 \wp E_1 \cong (E_0^\perp \multimap E_1),$$
$$E_0 \otimes E_1 \cong (E_0 \multimap E_1^\perp)^\perp$$

In more detail, the tensor product is defined as follows:

$$E_0 \otimes E_1 = (E_0 \times E_1, \leq^L, \leq^R, \smile)$$

where $(e_0, e_1) \leq^L (e'_0, e'_1) \Leftrightarrow e_0 \leq^L e'_0$ and $e_1 \leq^L e'_1$,

$(e_0, e_1) \leq^R (e'_0, e'_1) \Leftrightarrow e_0 \leq^R e'_0$ and $e_1 \leq^R_1 e'_1$

and $(e_0, e_1) \smile (e'_0, e'_1) \Leftrightarrow e_0 \smile_0 e'_0$ and $e_1 \smile_1 e'_1$.

The construction $E^\perp$ is isomorphic to $(E \multimap I)$ where $I = (\{\bullet\},\ id,\ id,\ id)$ is the unit of $\otimes$. *Product* and *coproduct* in the category **BS** are (again) obtained by disjoint juxtaposition (now of bistructures), extending conflict across the two event sets in the case of coproduct. The terminal object is $1 = (\emptyset, \emptyset, \emptyset, \emptyset)$.

We define the *exponential* $!E$ of a bistructure $E$ by:

$$!E = (\Gamma(E)^0, \sqsubseteq^L, \sqsubseteq^R, \uparrow^R)$$

(recall $\sqsubseteq^L$ and $\sqsubseteq^R$, and $\uparrow^R$ from Definition 3).

LEMMA 8 $!E$ is a bistructure.

*Proof* Obviously, $\sqsubseteq^R$ is a partial order. By Proposition 1, $\sqsubseteq^L$ is a partial order and so Axiom 1 is verified. Given the definition of $\frown_!$, Axiom 3(b) holds *a fortiori*, and we can rephrase Axiom 3(a) as:

$$(x_1 \downarrow^L x_2 \text{ and } x_1 \uparrow^R x_2) \Rightarrow x_1 = x_2$$

which is an immediate consequence of Proposition 1.4.

The main difficulty in the proof is in showing Axiom 2(b), *i.e.*, that the relation $\preceq_! = (\sqsupseteq^L \cup \sqsubseteq^R)^\star$ of $!E$ is a partial order. We need only show antisymmetry. Thus suppose for $x_i, x_i'$ in $\Gamma(E)^0$ we have:

$$x_0 \sqsubseteq^R x_0' \sqsupseteq^L x_1 \sqsubseteq^R x_1' \sqsupseteq^L \cdots \sqsupseteq^L x_n \sqsubseteq^R x_n' \tag{1}$$

with $x_n = x_0$ and $x_n' = x_0'$. We shall show $x_i = x_i' = x_j = x_j'$ for all $i, j$. Then by the definition of $\preceq_!$ on $!E$ it follows that $\preceq_!$ is antisymmetric.

Define $\mathit{fix} = \bigcap_i x_i$. We first show $\mathit{fix} \in \Gamma(E)$. Consistency is obvious. Suppose $e \in \mathit{fix}$ and $e_1 \leq^R e$. Since $e \in x_i$, there exist $e_1^i$ in $x_i$ such that $e_1 \leq^L e_1^i$, for all $i \geq 1$. Since $x_i \sqsubseteq x_{i-1}'$, there exist $e_1'^i$ in $x_{i-1}'$ such that $e_1^i \leq^L e_1'^i$, for all $i \geq 1$. We now apply Lemma 4 twice.

- From $e_1 \leq^L e_1'^i$, $e_1 \leq^L e_1^{i-1}$ and $x_{i-1} \sqsubseteq^R x_{i-1}'$ we conclude $e_1'^i = e_1^{i-1}$, therefore $e_1^{i-1} \geq^L e_1^i$.
- From $e_1 \leq^L e_1^0$, $e_1 \leq^L e_1^n$ and $x_0 = x_n$, we obtain $e_1^0 = e_1^n$.

Since $\leq^L$ is a partial order, we get: $e_1^0 = \cdots = e_1^i = \cdots = e_1^n$, hence $e_1^0 \in \mathit{fix}$, which shows that $\mathit{fix}$ is secured. Consequently $\mathit{fix} \in \Gamma(E)$ and clearly $\mathit{fix} \sqsubseteq^R x_i, x_i'$ for all $i$. It remains to show $\mathit{fix} = x_i = x_i'$ for all $i$. Notice that in chain (1) we can bring any index $i$ to the head position, by a circular permutation. Thus, it suffices to show $x_0 = x_0' = \mathit{fix}$.

Take $e$ in $x'_0$. Then by repeated use of Proposition 1, we deduce from (1) that

$$e = e_0 \preceq_{x'_0} e'_0 \geq^L e_1 \preceq_{x'_1} e'_1 \geq^L e_2 \cdots \geq^L e_m \preceq_{x'_{[m]_n}} e'_m \geq^L e_{m+1} \cdots \quad (2)$$

for some $e_i$ in $x_{[i]_n}$ and $e'_i$ in $x'_{[i]_n}$ where $i \in \omega$ (here $[m]_n$ is $m$ modulo $n$).

The sequence has been continued infinitely by going around and around the loop (1). As $x'_0$ is finite and the sequence (2) visits $x'_0$ infinitely often there must be $e_m$, $e_q$ in $x'_0$ such that $m < q$ and $[m]_n = [q]_n = 0$ and $e_m = e_q$. Then as $\preceq$ is a partial order, $e_m = e'_m = e_{m+1} = \cdots = e_q$. Thus $e_m \in \mathit{fix}$ so the sequence (2) eventually contains an element of $\mathit{fix}$. We know $\mathit{fix} \sqsubseteq^R x_i, x'_i$, for all $i$. Now, working backwards along the chain (2), starting at $e_m$, we show that all elements of the chain are in $\mathit{fix}$.

- From $e_{i+1}$ to $e'_i$: this follows from Lemma 4 applied to $\mathit{fix}$, $x'_i$, $e_{i+1}$, and $e'_i$.
- From $e'_i$ to $e_i$: by Lemma 5.

In particular, $e_0$ $(= e) \in \mathit{fix}$. We have proved $x'_0 \sqsubseteq^R \mathit{fix}$, which together with $\mathit{fix} \sqsubseteq^R x_0 \sqsubseteq^R x'_0$ implies $x_0 = x'_0 = \mathit{fix}$ as required. Thus the relation $\preceq_!$ on $!E$ is a partial order.

Finally, we prove Axiom 2(a), *i.e.*, $\{x' \in \Gamma(E)^0 \mid x' \preceq_! x\}$ is finite, for $x \in \Gamma(E)^0$. By Proposition 1 it is clear that

$$x' \preceq_! x \Rightarrow \forall e' \in x' \ \exists e \in x \ \ e' \preceq e$$

Thus:

$$x' \preceq_! x \Rightarrow x' \subseteq \bigcup \{e' \mid \exists e \in x \ \ e' \preceq e\}$$

As $x$ is finite and $\preceq$ is finitary, we have $\{x' \in \Gamma(E)^0 \mid x' \preceq_! x\}$ is finite, as required. □

The configurations of the bistructure $!E_0 \multimap E_1$ are in 1-1 correspondence with the functions from $(\Gamma(E_0), \sqsubseteq^R, \sqsubseteq)$ to $(\Gamma(E_1), \sqsubseteq^R, \sqsubseteq)$ considered by Berry in his cartesian closed category of bidomains. We need notions of trace and extensional and stable orderings for such functions (cf. Section 3):

DEFINITION 6 Let $f$ be a $\sqsubseteq$-continuous and $\sqsubseteq^R$-stable function from $\Gamma(E_0)$ to $\Gamma(E_1)$. Then:

$$\mathrm{tr}(f) = \{(x, e) \in \Gamma(E_0)^0 \times E_1 \mid x \text{ is } \sqsubseteq^R\text{-minimal such that } e \in f(x)\}$$

The *stable* ordering on such functions is defined by:

$$f \leq g \Leftrightarrow \forall x \sqsubseteq^R y \ \ f(x) = f(y) \cap g(x)$$

The *extensional* ordering on such functions is defined by:

$$f \sqsubseteq g \Leftrightarrow \forall x \;\; f(x) \sqsubseteq g(x)$$

PROPOSITION 6 Let $E_0$, $E_1$ be bistructures. For $R$ in $\Gamma(!E_0 \multimap E_1)$ and $x$ in $\Gamma(E_0)$ define

$$\bar{R}(x) = \{e \mid \exists x_0 \sqsubseteq^R x \;\; (x_0, e) \in R\}.$$

Then $\bar{R}$ is a function $\Gamma(E_0) \to \Gamma(E_1)$ which is continuous with respect to $\sqsubseteq$ and stable with respect to $\sqsubseteq^R$ on configurations. In fact, $R \mapsto \bar{R}$ is a 1-1 correspondence between configurations of $!E_0 \multimap E_1$ and such functions, with inverse $f \mapsto \mathrm{tr}(f)$. Further, for the stable ordering of functions we have:

$$f \leq g \Leftrightarrow \mathrm{tr}(f) \sqsubseteq^R \mathrm{tr}(g)$$

and for the extensional ordering we have:

$$f \sqsubseteq g \Leftrightarrow \mathrm{tr}(f) \sqsubseteq \mathrm{tr}(g)$$

*Proof* We first check that $\bar{R}(x)$ is a configuration. Consistency follows from the definition of $\frown$ in $!E_0 \multimap E_1$. Suppose $e \in \bar{R}(x)$ and $e' \leq^R e$. Choose $x_0 \sqsubseteq^R x$ such that $(x_0, e) \in R$. Then $(x_0, e') \leq^R (x_0, e)$, hence by securedness there exists $(x'', e'')$ in $R$ such that $(x_0, e') \leq^L (x'', e'')$. Then $e''$ fits since $x'' \sqsubseteq^R x_0 \sqsubseteq^R x$. Thus the function $\bar{R}$ is well defined. It is $\sqsubseteq^R$-continuous by construction and $\sqsubseteq^R$-stable by the definition of $\frown$ in $!E_0 \multimap E_1$. We next show that $\bar{R}$ is $\sqsubseteq$-monotonic, hence $\sqsubseteq$-continuous, by Lemma 7. Suppose $x \sqsubseteq y$ and $e \in \bar{R}(x)$. Choose $x_0 \sqsubseteq^R x$ such that $(x_0, e) \in R$. Let us factorise $x_0 \sqsubseteq y$ as $x_0 \sqsubseteq^L x_1 \sqsubseteq^R y$. Since $(x_1, e) \leq^R (x_0, e)$, there exists $(x_2, e_1)$ in $R$ such that $(x_1, e) \leq^L (x_2, e_1)$, by securedness. Then $e_1$ fits, since $e \leq^L e_1$ and $x_2 \sqsubseteq^R x_1 \sqsubseteq^R y$.

We now show that tr is the inverse of $R \mapsto \bar{R}$. Suppose $f : \Gamma(E_0) \to \Gamma(E_1)$ is $\sqsubseteq$-continuous and $\sqsubseteq^R$-stable. We need first that $\mathrm{tr}(f) \in \Gamma(!E_0 \multimap E_1)$, *i.e.*, that $\mathrm{tr}(f)$ is consistent and secured:

*Consistency*: Suppose $(x, e), (x', e') \in \mathrm{tr}(f)$ and that $(x, e) \asymp (x', e')$, *i.e.*, $x \uparrow^R x'$ and $e \asymp e'$. We show $(x, e) = (x', e')$. As $e, e' \in f(x \cup x')$, we must have $e \frown e'$, which combined with $e \asymp e'$, entails $e = e'$. Now, $(x, e), (x', e)$ are both in the trace of $f$. Because $x \uparrow^R x'$ and $f$ is $\sqsubseteq^R$-stable we conclude that $x = x'$.

*Securedness*: Suppose $(x', e') \leq^R (x, e) \in \mathrm{tr}(f)$. Then $x \sqsubseteq^L x'$ and $e' \leq^R e$. As $f$ is $\sqsubseteq$-monotonic, $f(x) \sqsubseteq f(x')$. Because $e' \leq^R e$ and $e \in f(x)$, we see that $e'$ is in the $\leq$-downwards-closure of $f(x')$. Thus by Lemma 3, there exists $e''$ in $f(x')$ such that:

$$e' \leq^L e'' \tag{1}$$

By the definition of $\mathrm{tr}(f)$, there is

$$x_0 \sqsubseteq^R x' \tag{2}$$

such that

$$(x_0, e'') \in \mathrm{tr}(f) \tag{3}$$

Combining (1), (2), (3) we obtain, as required

$$(x', e') \leq^L (x_0, e'') \in \mathrm{tr}(f).$$

For $f$ a $\sqsubseteq$-continuous, $\sqsubseteq^R$-stable function $\Gamma(E_0) \to \Gamma(E_1)$ its continuity with respect to $\sqsubseteq^R$ entails $\overline{\mathrm{tr}(f)} = f$. For $R$ in $\Gamma(!E_0 \multimap E_1)$ a direct translation of the definitions yields $\mathrm{tr}(\bar{R}) = R$. Thus the map $R \mapsto \bar{R} = R$ is a 1-1 correspondence.

Turning to the two orderings of functions, the claim for the stable ordering is established exactly as in the case of webs [11]. For the extensional ordering, suppose first that $f \sqsubseteq g$ and choose $(x, e)$ in $\mathrm{tr}(f)$. Then $e \in f(x) \sqsubseteq g(x)$, and so for some $e' \geq^L e$, $e' \in g(x)$. But then there is an $x_0 \sqsubseteq^R x$ such that $(x_0, e') \in \mathrm{tr}(g)$ and we have that $(x, e) \leq^L (x_0, e') \in \mathrm{tr}(g)$. Conversely, suppose that $\mathrm{tr}(f) \sqsubseteq \mathrm{tr}(g)$ and choose $e, x$ with $e \in f(x)$. Then for some subset $x_0$ of $x$, $(x_0, e) \in \mathrm{tr}(f) \sqsubseteq \mathrm{tr}(g)$, and so there is a $y \sqsubseteq^R x_0$ and an $e' \geq^L e$ such that $(y, e') \in \mathrm{tr}(g)$. Then we have $e \leq^L e' \in g(y) \sqsubseteq^R g(x)$, concluding the proof. □

This section has provided the key constructions for showing that **BS** is a model of classical linear logic, and that the associated co-Kleisli category is equivalent to one of biorders:

THEOREM 1 The category **BS** forms a linear category in the sense of [24]. The exponential! forms a comonad on the category **BS**. Together they form a model of classical linear logic (a Girard category in the sense of [24]—see also [4]).

The associated co-Kleisli category is (necessarily) cartesian closed and isomorphic to the category whose objects are the structures $(\Gamma(E), \sqsubseteq^R, \sqsubseteq)$, where $E$ is a bistructure, and whose morphisms are the $\sqsubseteq$-continuous and $\sqsubseteq^R$-stable functions.

*Proof* The proof that **BS** forms a linear category is a straightforward extension of the web case, while the facts about the co-Kleisli category largely follow from Proposition 6. For the monoidal structure, at the level of events, the canonical isomorphisms are given by:

$$((e_0, e_1), e_2) \leftrightarrow (e_0, (e_1, e_2)),$$
$$(e, \bullet) \leftrightarrow e,$$
$$(\bullet, e) \leftrightarrow e$$

The first of these correspondences also serves to establish the closed structure. For example, we have:

$$((e_0, e_1), e_2) \leq^L_{E_0 \otimes E_1 \multimap E_2} ((e'_0, e'_1), e'_2)$$
$$\Leftrightarrow e'_0 \leq^R_{E_0} e_0 \text{ and } e'_1 \leq^R_{E_1} e_1 \text{ and } e_2 \leq^L_{E_2} e'_2$$
$$\Leftrightarrow (e_0, (e_1, e_2)) \leq^L_{E_0 \multimap (E_1 \multimap E_2)} (e'_0, (e'_1, e'_2))$$

The trace of the canonical morphism from $E$ to $(E \multimap I) \multimap I$ is:

$$\{(e, ((e, \bullet), \bullet)) \mid e \in E\}$$

It is clear that it has as inverse the function whose trace is:

$$\{(((e, \bullet), \bullet), e) \mid e \in E\}$$

Turning to the comonadic structure, the counit $\varepsilon : !E \multimap E$ is given by:

$$\varepsilon = \{([e]_x, e) \mid e \in x \in \Gamma(E)\}$$

For any $\alpha : !E_0 \multimap E_1$, its *lift* $\alpha^\sharp : !E_0 \multimap !E_1$ is given by:

$$\alpha^\sharp = \left\{ \left( \bigcup_{i=1,n} x_i, \{e_1, \ldots, e_n\} \right) \in !E_0 \times !E_1 \mid (x_i, e_i) \in \alpha \text{ (for } i = 1, n) \right\}$$

(Then the comultiplication $\delta : !E \multimap !!E$ is $(id_{!E})^\sharp$ and the functorial action of ! is $f \mapsto (f \circ \varepsilon)^\sharp$.) The canonical isomorphism $!(E_0 \times E_1) \cong (!E_0) \otimes (!E_1)$ is given by:

$$x \leftrightarrow (x \cap E_0, x \cap E_1)$$

The isomorphism $!1 \cong I$ follows immediately from the observation that $\Gamma(1)$ is a singleton.

For the last part, the isomorphism is to send a bistructure $E$ to the biorder $(\Gamma(E), \sqsubseteq^R, \sqsubseteq)$, and a morphism $R : !E_0 \multimap E_1$ to the function $\overline{R} : \Gamma(E_0) \to \Gamma(E_1)$. Given the results of Proposition 6, it only remains to show functoriality, and that is automatic from the comonadicity of the exponential, once we notice that $\overline{R}(x) = R \circ x^\sharp$, identifying elements of $\Gamma(E)$ with morphisms from $!1$ to $E$. □

*A fortiori*, bistructures provide a model of simply typed λ-calculi, and of PCF in particular. One interprets base types as event structures, *i.e.*, bistructures of the form $(E, id, \leq, \smile)$. At first order, $\Gamma(!E_0 \multimap E_1)$ is up to bijection the set of stable functions from $\Gamma(E_0)$ to $\Gamma(E_1)$, represented, not as an event structure, but as a bistructure with a non-trivial $\leq^L$-order which captures the extensional order between stable functions. At higher orders, as discussed in Section 2, the model diverges from the stable model by enforcing both $\sqsubseteq^R$-stability and $\sqsubseteq$-continuity of the morphisms. In the next section we shall see that this model coincides with that obtained from Berry's category of bidomains.

## 7 Bidomains

Bidomains are not very widely known, so we present their definition here. They were introduced in Gérard Berry's Thèse de Doctorat d'Etat [2]. More details and background motivation can be obtained either from Berry's thesis or the references [3, 25].

The most general biordered domains Berry considered were the bicpos.

DEFINITION 7 A *bicpo* is a biorder $(D, \leq, \sqsubseteq)$ such that:

1. the structure $(D, \sqsubseteq)$ is a cpo with a continuous greatest-lower-bound operation $\sqcap$ (the order $\sqsubseteq$ is called the *extensional* order),

2. the structure $(D, \leq)$ is a cpo, with the same least element as $(D, \sqsubseteq)$ and the identity on $D$ is a continuous function from $(D, \leq)$ to $(D, \sqsubseteq)$ (the order $\leq$ is called the *stable* order),

3. the operation $\sqcap$ is $\leq$-continuous—in fact, $\leq$-monotonicity suffices, by 1. and 2. (it follows that the $\leq$-greatest lower bound, $x \wedge y$, of points $x, y$, bounded above in $(D, \leq)$, exists and coincides with $x \sqcap y$), and

4. for all $\sqsubseteq$-directed subsets $S, S' \subseteq D$, if for all $s$ in $S$, $s'$ in $S'$ there are $t$ in $S$, $t'$ in $S'$ such that

$s \sqsubseteq t$ and $s' \sqsubseteq t'$ and $t \leq t'$

then $\bigsqcup S \leq \bigsqcup S'$.

A bicpo is *distributive* iff

- whenever $x, y$ are bounded above in $(D, \leq)$ then their least upper bounds, $x \vee y$, in $(D, \leq)$, and $x \sqcup y$, in $(D, \sqsubseteq)$, exist and coincide, and
- the cpo $(D, \leq)$ is distributive, *i.e.*, for all $x, y, z$ in $D$, if $\{x, y, z\}$ is bounded above, then $x \wedge (y \vee z) = (x \wedge y) \vee (x \wedge z)$.

Bicpos form a category where the morphisms are taken to be those functions which are continuous with respect to the extensional order and conditionally multiplicative with respect to the stable order, *i.e.*, the functions preserve binary compatible glbs. This category is cartesian closed; products are given by cartesian products of the underlying sets, the two orders being obtained in a coordinatewise fashion; the function space $[D_0 \to D_1]$ consists of the set of morphisms from $D_0$ to $D_1$ with the extensional order $\sqsubseteq$ being the pointwise order, based on the extensional order of $D_1$, and with the order $\leq$ being the stable order of functions, based on the stable orders of $D_0$ and $D_1$.

Here are brief hints on how the axioms of Definition 7 are used. Lubs and glbs in the function spaces are defined pointwise. The continuity properties of the meet operation are put to use when proving that the pointwise lubs are conditionally multiplicative. Axiom 4 serves to establish that the pointwise extensional lubs are monotonic with respect to the stable ordering.

The smallest category of biordered domains Berry considered was that of bidomains. They are a form of distributive bicpo, satisfying a restriction which ensures that they are dI-domains with respect to the stable order.

DEFINITION 8 A *finite projection* on a bicpo $D$ is a morphism $\psi : D \rightarrow D$ such that $h \circ h = h$ and $h(x) \leq x$, for all $x$ in $D$, and which is compact with respect to the stable order on $[D \rightarrow D]$.

A bicpo $D$ is said to be a *bidomain* iff it is distributive and there is a sequence of finite projections $\psi_i$ $(i \in \omega)$ on it, increasing with respect to the stable order, whose least upper bound is the identity function $1_D : D \rightarrow D$.

The category of bidomains and of $\sqsubseteq$-continuous and $\leq$-stable functions is a full sub-cartesian closed category of that of bicpos. [In the subcategory, we have stable = conditionally multiplicative.]

We now make good our earlier claim that configurations of (suitably restricted) bistructures form a bidomain. Let $E$ be a bistructure. The problem is that the axioms of bistructures adopted here are too weak to ensure the existence of enough $\sqsubseteq$-glbs to yield a bicpo. We can prove the existence of the required glbs provided we add two further axioms on bistructures:

DEFINITION 9 A B-bistructure ("B" stands for "Bidomain") is a bistructure $(E, \leq^L, \leq^R, \smile)$ that satisfies the following two additional axioms:

4. if $e \geq^L e'$ and $e \frown e''$, then $e' \frown e''$, and
5. bounded binary $\leq^L$-lubs exist, *i.e.*, if $e_1, e_2 \leq^L e$, for some event $e$, then the lub, $e_1 \vee^L e_2$, with respect to $\leq^L$ exists.

B-bistructures are quite similar to the original version of bistructures in [25]—for example, Axioms 1, 2 and 5 are common, factorisation is unique in both, and all the other axioms relate to the interaction between coherence and the two partial orders. Axiom 3(a) is missing in [25]; instead, configurations are defined in a way equivalent to requiring for any elements $e, e'$ that not only $e \smile e'$ but also $\neg(e \downarrow^L e')$. Pleasantly, as is straightforward to show, the class of biorders obtained from the original version is included in that obtained from B-bistructures.

PROPOSITION 7 Let $E$ be a B-bistructure. Then $(\Gamma(E), \sqsubseteq^R, \sqsubseteq)$ is a bidomain.

*Proof* We must first show that $(\Gamma(E), \sqsubseteq^R, \sqsubseteq)$ is a distributive bicpo. We already know from Proposition 2 that $(\Gamma(E), \sqsubseteq)$ and $(\Gamma(E), \sqsubseteq^R)$ are cpos, and that $\sqsubseteq^R$-directed lubs are $\sqsubseteq$-lubs, which is the same as requiring that the identity function is continuous from

$(\Gamma(E), \sqsubseteq^R)$ to $(\Gamma(E), \sqsubseteq)$. We also know that $(\Gamma(E), \sqsubseteq)$ is algebraic, which is easily seen to imply the continuity of $\sqcap$, provided binary glbs exist, which we prove now, using Axioms 4 and 5. Let $x$ and $y$ be two configurations. We define $x \sqcap y$ as the set of all events $e$ such that $e$ is in the $\leq^L$-downwards-closure of both $x$ and $y$, and is $\leq^L$-maximal with that property. This is clearly the glb of $x$ and $y$ if only it is a configuration. The definition ensures securedness by construction: if $e \in x \sqcap y$ and $e' \leq^R e$, then $e'$ is in the $\leq^L$-downwards-closure of both $x$ and $y$ by Lemma 3, and by definition of $x \sqcap y$ there exists $e''$ in $x \sqcap y$ such that $e' \leq^L e''$. Suppose now that $e_1, e_2$ are in $x \sqcap y$. Let $e_1', e_2'$ in $x$ be such that $e_1 \leq^L e_1'$ and $e_2 \leq^L e_2'$, and let $e_1'', e_2''$ in $y$ be such that $e_1 \leq^L e_1''$ and $e_2 \leq^L e_2''$. Since $e_1', e_2' \in x$, we have $e_1' \smile e_2'$, and similarly $e_1'' \smile e_2''$. We distinguish several cases.

- $e_1' \neq e_2'$. Here, by two applications of Axiom 4 we get first $e_1 \frown e_2'$, then $e_1 \frown e_2$.
- $e_1'' \neq e_2''$. We obtain $e_1 \frown e_2$ similarly to the previous case.
- $e_1' = e_2'$ and $e_1'' = e_2''$. By Axiom 5, $e_1 \vee^L e_2$ exists. It is in the $\leq^L$-downwards-closure of both $x$ and $y$, which, by the definition of $x \sqcap y$, forces $e_1 = e_2 = e_1 \vee^L e_2$.

In all cases, we have $e_1 \smile e_2$. This completes the proof of Axioms 1 and 2.

We next check Axiom 3. Let $y \sqsubseteq^R z$ and $e \in x \sqcap y$. Then $e$ is in the $\leq^L$-downwards-closure of both $x$ and $z$. We show that $e$ is $\leq^L$-maximal with that property. Suppose that $e \leq^L e'$ and $e' \leq^L e_1' \in x$ and $e' \leq^L e_2' \in z$. Now, for some $e_3'$ in $y$, $e \leq^L e_3'$ and thus, by Lemma 4, we have that $e_2' = e_3' \in y$. Therefore, $e = e'$ by the maximality property of $e$ with respect to $x$ and $y$. Hence $e \in x \sqcap z$, and we have proved $x \sqcap y \sqsubseteq^R x \sqcap z$.

To check Axiom 4, let subsets $S, S'$ be $\sqsubseteq$-directed subsets of $\Gamma(E)$ such that whenever $s \in S$ and $s' \in S'$ there are $t$ in $S$ and $t'$ in $S'$ such that

$s \sqsubseteq t$ and $s' \sqsubseteq t'$ and $t \sqsubseteq^R t'$.

By the proof of Proposition 2,

$$\bigsqcup S = \left\{e \in \bigcup S \mid e \text{ is } \leq^L \text{-maximal in } \bigcup S\right\}$$

Equivalently, $\bigsqcup S$ consists of the events $e$ such that $e \in s$ for some $s$ in $S$ with the property that

$$\forall t \in S\ (s \sqsubseteq t \Rightarrow e \in t). \tag{1}$$

Indeed, suppose that $e$ and $s$ satisfy property (1), and let $e_1 \geq^L e$ be such that $e_1 \in \bigcup S$, *i.e.*, $e_1 \in t$ for some $t$ in $S$. Let $s'$ in $S$ be such that $s \sqsubseteq s'$ and $t \sqsubseteq s'$. Then $e \in s'$ and $e_1$ is in the $\leq^L$-downwards-closure of $s'$. This combined with $e \leq^L e_1$ yields $e = e_1$. Conversely, if $e \in s \in S$ and $e$ is $\leq^L$-maximal in $\bigcup S$, then $e, s$ obviously satisfy (1).

Given $e$ and $s$ satisfying (1), we wish to show $e \in \bigsqcup S'$. By assumption, taking $s'$ an arbitrary element of $S'$, we have for some $t$ in $S$ and $t'$ in $S'$ that

$$t \sqsubseteq^R t' \text{ and } s \sqsubseteq t \text{ and } s' \sqsubseteq t'.$$

By (1), we get that $e \in t'$. Suppose $t' \sqsubseteq t'' \in S'$. Replacing $s'$ by $t''$, and reasoning as above, we get that $e \in t'''$ for some $t'''$ such that $t'' \sqsubseteq t'''$. Finally, one easily derives that $e \in t''$ from $t' \sqsubseteq t'' \sqsubseteq t'''$, $e \in t'$ and $e \in t'''$. Thus $e$ and $t'$ satisfy property (1) relative to $S'$, *i.e.*, $e \in \bigsqcup S'$. We conclude that $\bigsqcup S \sqsubseteq^R \bigsqcup S'$, as required. Thus $(\Gamma(E), \sqsubseteq^R, \sqsubseteq)$ is a bicpo.

For distributivity, by Proposition 3, we know that $(\Gamma(E), \sqsubseteq^R)$ is a distributive cpo. Now remark that if $x \uparrow^R y$, $x \sqsubseteq z$ and $y \sqsubseteq z$, then also $x \cup y \sqsubseteq z$ by the definition of $\sqsubseteq$.

Finally, to show that $(\Gamma(E), \sqsubseteq^R, \sqsubseteq)$ is a bidomain we need to produce an $\omega$-chain of finite projections on it whose least upper bound is the identity on $\Gamma(E)$. Here we refer to Proposition 6, showing how continuous stable functions on $\Gamma(E)$ correspond to configurations of the bistructure $!E \multimap E$; a configuration $F$ of $!E \multimap E$ corresponds to a continuous, stable function $\overline{F} : \Gamma(E) \to \Gamma(E)$ so that inclusion of configurations corresponds to the stable ordering of functions. Let $X$ be the configuration of $!E \multimap E$ corresponding to the identity function on $\Gamma(E)$. Because the events of $!E \multimap E$ form a countable set we may enumerate them as $e_0, e_1, \ldots, e_n, \ldots$. Define $X_n$ as the configuration

$$[e_0]_X \cup \cdots \cup [e_n]_X.$$

Each $X_n$ is a finite set and so compact with respect to $\sqsubseteq^R$. By Proposition 6, we obtain a chain of functions $\overline{X}_n$, $n$ in $\omega$, compact and increasing with respect to the stable order, with least upper bound the identity function on $\Gamma(E)$. Being stably less than the identity, each function $\overline{X}_n$ must be a projection.

We conclude that $\Gamma(E)$ is a bidomain. □

PROPOSITION 8 If $E_0$ and $E_1$ are B-bistructures, then so are $E_0 \times E_1$ and $!E_0 \multimap E_1$.

*Proof* The verification for the product is immediate. We check Axioms 4 and 5 for $!E_0 \multimap E_1$. Let $(x, e_1) \geq^L (y, e_1')$ and $(x, e_1) \frown (z, e_1'')$. Then $x \subseteq y$, $e_1 \geq^L e_1'$ and either $x \smile z$ or $e_1 \frown e_1''$. If $x \smile z$ then $y \smile z$ (as $x \subseteq y$); if $e_1 \frown e_1''$ then $e_1' \frown e_1''$, by Axiom 4 for $E_1$. In either case it follows that $(y, e_1') \frown (z, e_1'')$. The verification of Axiom 5 is straightforward: $(x, e_1) \vee^L (y, e_1') = (x \sqcap^R y, e_1 \vee^L e_1')$, where we use Axiom 5 for $E_1$ and the fact that $\Gamma(E_0)$ is $\sqsubseteq^R$-bounded complete (cf. Proposition 2). [In bounded-complete cpos, all non-empty glbs exist.] □

*Remark 5* On the other hand, Axiom 4 is not preserved by any of $\otimes$, $(\cdot)^\perp$ or !. Therefore we do not see how to get a model of linear logic with B-bistructures.

THEOREM 2 The B-bistructures yield a full sub-cartesian closed category of the co-Kleisli category of the exponential comonad on **BS**. It is equivalent to a full sub-cartesian closed category of bidomains.

*Proof* The first assertion is immediate from Proposition 8. By Proposition 7 and the last part of Theorem 1, the subcategory is equivalent to a full subcategory of the category of bidomains. It remains to show that there are isomorphisms of bidomains between $\Gamma(E_0)\times\Gamma(E_1)$ and $\Gamma(E_0 \times E_1)$, and also between $\Gamma(E_0) \to \Gamma(E_1)$ and $\Gamma(!E_0 \multimap E_1)$. The first is easy to see (it is $(x, y) \mapsto x \cup y$, assuming $E_0$ and $E_1$ disjoint). The second is given by $f \mapsto \mathrm{tr}(f)$, by virtue of the remarks above on function spaces of bidomains and Proposition 6. □

Notice that if $\leq^L\ = id$, Axioms 4 and 5 hold vacuously, hence the category of B-bistructures is large enough to contain the models of typed λ-calculi where the base types are interpreted by event structures.

## 8 Discussion

In this section, we discuss possible variations and connections with other work.

**Variations** Besides coherence spaces there are a few other "web-based" models of intuitionistic linear logic or full classical linear logic. Most notably, there are Ehrhard's *hypercoherences* with a Kleisli category of *strongly stable functions*, which can be seen as an extensional (although not order-extensional) account of sequentiality. At first order, the strongly stable model contains exactly the sequential functions. At higher orders, it is the extensional collapse of the model of sequential algorithms [8, 9]. Generalisations encompassing both Girard's webs and hypercoherences have been proposed independently by Lamarche [18] (based on quantale-valued sets) and by Winskel [30] (based on a notion of indexing inspired by logical relations). We believe that our biordering treatment can be applied to all these categories. We checked this for hypercoherences. There, the binary coherence relation $\frown$ is replaced by a coherence hypergraph $\Gamma$. Thus, a hypercoherence is given by a set $E$ of events and a set $\Gamma$ of finite non-empty subsets of $E$. We axiomatise "hypercoherence-bistructures" exactly like bistructures, replacing $\frown$ by $\Gamma$, and Axiom 3 by:

3($a$) ($X \in \Gamma$ and $X$ is $\leq^L$ –lower bounded) $\Rightarrow$ $X$ is a singleton,

3($b$) $X$ is $\leq^R$ –upper bounded $\Rightarrow X \in \Gamma$

The variation works smoothly because there is very little interaction between the axiomatisation of the coherence structure and that of the orders. The two propagate smoothly in the construction of the connectives, and are related only through Axiom 3 or its variants.

Although the bidomain model incorporates both the stable and pointwise order, its PCF theory (those inequalities on terms which hold in the bidomain model) does not include that of the Scott model. The argument follows Jim and Meyer's in [13], and is based on the bidomain model failing to eliminate an "or-tester," the first of Curien's examples in [5], Proposition 4.4.2. The same argument applies to the variation sketched above, where coherence is replaced by hypercoherence. In [29] it is shown how to adjoin an additional conflict relation to bistructures to obtain a model of PCF whose theory strictly includes that of the Scott model. Several strengthenings of this idea are possible; the conflict relation can be combined with hypercoherences on bistructures, or even replaced by coherence relations of a more complex kind (akin to logical relations, as in [30]).

As remarked in the introduction, by Loader's result [19] there is no hope of finding a direct presentation of the fully abstract model for PCF in this way, adjoining a suitable coherence structure to the two orders of bistructures, unless, as in [22], this is of an infinitary nature. However, the fact that there are hypercoherence-based bistructure models refining the Scott model shows (adapting the "Definability Lemma," *e.g.*, Proposition 4.1.10 of [5], to a slightly broader setting) that there are extensions of PCF, having some claims to being sequential and functional, but which nevertheless have an effectively given fully abstract model. Such extensions to PCF escape Loader's proof. But the precise programming constructs associated with these extensions is a mystery, and would need a deeper understanding of the operational nature of bistructure models.

**Connections** Lamarche [17] (followed by Kegelmann [15]) has proposed a large cartesian closed category of "interpolative domains" encompassing, as full sub-cartesian closed categories, categories of continuous functions on one hand, and categories of stable functions on the other. Lamarche's framework has some technical similarities with ours; two orders are axiomatised, with a factorisation property. But the approach and goals are quite different. In Lamarche's setting, once the standard interpretation of the basic flat domains of, say, PCF, is fixed appropriately, the larger category induces exactly the continuous or stable model, whereas we obtain a model simultaneously refining both the stable and continuous models.

## Acknowledgements

Gordon Plotkin's research was supported by an EPSRC Senior Fellowship.

## References

[1] Abramsky, S., Jagadeesan, R., and Malacaria, P., *Games and full abstraction for PCF*, manuscript available from http://www.dcs.ed.ac.uk, 1995.

[2] Berry, G., *Modèles complètement adéquats et stables des lambda-calculs typés.* Thèse de Doctorat d'Etat, Université de Paris VII, 1979.

[3] Berry, G., Curien, P.-L. and Lévy, J.-J., The full abstraction problem: state of the art, in *Proc. French-US Seminar on the Applications of Algebra to Language Definition and Compilation*, Cambridge University Press, 1985.

[4] Bierman, G.M., What is a categorical model of intuitionistic linear logic? in *Proc. 2nd. Int. Conf. on Typed Lambda Calculi and Applications* (eds. Dezani-Ciancaglini, M. and Plotkin, G.), LNCS, Vol. 902, pp. 78–93, Springer-Verlag, 1995.

[5] Curien, P.-L., *Categorical combinators, sequential algorithms, and functional programming*. Second edition, Birkhäuser, 1993.

[6] Curien, P.-L., On the symmetry of sequentiality, in *Proc. 9th Int. Conf. on Mathematical Foundations of Programming Semantics* (eds. Brookes, S., Main, M., Melton, A., Mislove, M. and Schmidt, D.), LNCS, Vol. 802, pp. 29–71, Springer-Verlag, 1994.

[7] Curien, P.-L., *Coherence bistructures*, unpublished manuscript, Beijing, 1994.

[8] Ehrhard, T., *Hypercoherences: a strongly stable model of linear logic*. MSCS, Vol. 3, No. 4, pp. 365–385, 1993.

[9] Ehrhard, T., *A relative PCF-definability result for strongly stable functions*, available by ftp at iml.univ-mrs.fr, in directory /pub/ehrhard/rel.[dvi,ps].Z, 1996.

[10] Girard, J-Y., *Linear logic*. TCS Vol. 50, No. 1, pp. 1–102, 1987.

[11] Girard, J-Y., Lafont, Y., and Taylor, P., *Proofs and types*. Cambridge University Press, 1989.

[12] Hyland, J.M.E., and Ong, C-H.L., *On full abstraction for PCF: I, II and III*, available by ftp at ftp.comlab.ox.ac.uk, in directory /pub/Documents/techpapers/Luke.Ong/pcf.ps.gz, 1994.

[13] Jim, T., and Meyer, A., Full abstraction and the context lemma. in *Proc. 1st. Int. Conf. on Theoretical Aspects of Computer Software* (eds. Ito, T. and Meyer, A.R.), Sendai, LNCS Vol. 526, pp. 131–152, Springer-Verlag, 1991.

[14] Kahn, G. and Plotkin, G., Concrete Domains, in *A Collection of Contributions in Honour of Corrado Böhm on the Occasion of his 70th Birthday*. TCS Vol. 121, Nos. 1–2, pp. 187–278, 1993.

[15] Kegelmann, M., *Factorization systems on domains*, Technical Report, School of Computer Science, The University of Birmingham, 1996.

[16] Lamarche, F., Sequentiality, games and linear logic, in *Proc. CLICS Workshop*, Aarhus University, Aarhus University DAIMI PB-397 (II), 1992.

[17] Lamarche, F., *A large cartesian closed category of domains*, to appear in Inform. and Comp.

[18] Lamarche, F., Generalizing coherence spaces and hypercoherences, in *Proc. 11th. Int. Conf. on Mathematical Foundations of Programming Semantics* (eds. Brookes, S., Main, M., Melton, A. and Mislove, M.), Electronic Notes in Theoretical Computer Science, pp. 259–268, North Holland, 1995.

[19] Loader, R., *Finitary PCF is not decidable*. Submitted for publication, 1996.

[20] Milner, R., *Fully Abstract Models of Typed λ-calculi*, in Theoretical Comp. Sci., Vol. 4, pp. 1–22, 1977.

[21] Nielsen, M., Plotkin, G., and Winskel, G., *Petri nets, event structures and domains, part I*. TCS, Vol. 13, No. 1, pp. 85–108, 1981.

[22] O'Hearn, P.W. and Riecke, J.G., *Kripke logical relations and PCF*. Inform. and Comp., Vol. 120, No. 1, pp. 107–116, 1995.

[23] Plotkin, G., and Winskel, G., Bistructures, bidomains and linear logic, in *Proc. 21st ICALP* (eds. Abiteboul, S., and Shamir, E.), LNCS, Vol. 820, pp. 352–363, Springer-Verlag, 1994.

[24] Seely, R.A.G., Linear logic, ⋆-autonomous categories and cofree coalgebras, in *Categories in Computer Science and Logic* (eds. Gray, J.W. and Scedrov, A.), Contempory Mathematics, Vol. 92, pp. 371–382, American Mathematical Society, 1989.

[25] Winskel, G., *Events in computation*. Ph.D. thesis, University of Edinburgh, CST-10-80, 1980.

[26] Winskel, G., Event structures, in *Petri Nets: Applications and Relationships to Other Models of Concurrency, Advances in Petri Nets 1986, Part II; Proceedings of an Advanced Course*, (eds. Brauer, W., Reisig, W. and Rozenberg, G.), LNCS, Vol. 255, pp. 325–392, Springer-Verlag, 1987.

[27] Winskel, G., An introduction to event structures, in *REX School/Workshop on Linear Time, Branching Time and Partial Order in Logics and Models for Concurrency*, (eds. de Bakker, J.W., de Roever, W.P. and Rozenberg, G.), LNCS, Vol. 354, pp. 364–397, Springer-Verlag, 1989.

[28] Winskel, G., *The formal semantics of programming languages*, MIT Press, 1993.

[29] Winskel, G., Stable bistructure models of PCF, in *Proc. 19th Int. Conf. on Mathematical Foundations of Programming Semantics*, (eds. Prívara, I., Rovan, B., and Ružička, P.,) LNCS, Vol. 841, Springer-Verlag, 1994.

[30] Winskel, G., *Hypercoherences*, handwritten notes, 1994.

[31] Zhang, G.Q., *Logic of domains*. Birkhäuser, 1991.

# 2 Axioms for Definability and Full Completeness

**Samson Abramsky**

## 1 Introduction

The term "full abstraction" was coined by Robin Milner in [Mil75]. In 1977 two seminal papers on the programming language PCF, by Milner and Plotkin, appeared in *Theoretical Computer Science* [Mil77, Plo77]. These papers initiated an extensive body of work centering on the Full Abstraction problem for PCF (see [BCL86, Cur93, Ong95] for surveys).

The importance of full abstraction for the semantics of programming languages is that it is one of the few quality filters we have. Specifically, it provides a clear criterion for assessing how definitive a semantic analysis of some language is. It must be admitted that to date the quest for fully abstract models has not yielded many obvious applications; but it has generated much of the deepest work in semantics. Perhaps it is early days yet.

Recently, game semantics has been used to give the first syntax-independent constructions of fully abstract models for a number of programming languages, including PCF [AJM96, HO96, Nic94], richer functional languages [AM95, McC96b, McC96a, HY97], and languages with non-functional features such as reference types and non-local control constructs [AM97c, AM97b, AM97a, Lai97]. A noteworthy feature is that the key definability results for the richer languages are proved by a reduction to definability for the functional fragment, using a technique of *factorization theorems*. Thus the results originally obtained for PCF prove to be a lynch-pin in the analysis of a much wider class of languages.

When some success has been achieved with concrete constructions, it becomes important to identify the key properties of these constructions at a more abstract level; thus the trend towards axiomatic and synthetic domain theory, for example [Fio96, Hyl91]. There has also been considerable progress in axiomatizing sufficient conditions for computational adequacy [FP94, Bra97, McC96a]. In another vein, the work on action structures [MMP95] can be seen as an axiomatics for process calculi and other computational formalisms.

In the present paper we make the first contribution towards an axiomatic account of full abstraction, with specific reference to PCF. We present axioms on models of PCF from which the key results on definability and full abstraction can be proved. It should be emphasized that not only the results of [AJM96], but also the top-level structure of the actual proofs, are captured by our axiomatic account. In particular, our main axioms are abstracted from key lemmas in [AJM96]. The axioms mostly take the form of assertions that some canonical map is an isomorphism, which is quite standard in categorical axiomatizations, for example of Synthetic Differential Geometry [Koc81], distributive categories [Wal92], or dualizing objects [MOM91]. It is also noteworthy that, although our results apply to intuitionistic types, the axioms make essential use of the linear decompositions of these types [Gir87].

The present paper is only a first step. We hope that it will lead to further work in a number of directions:

- a more abstract perspective on game semantics
- a synthetic/axiomatic account of sequentiality
- general results on full abstraction
- a fine structure theory of "behavioural features" of categorical models.

## 2 Preliminaries

This section is concerned with setting up some basic language in which the substantive axioms can be expressed.

### 2.1 Affine Categories

We firstly recall the standard definition of a categorical model for the $(\otimes, \multimap, \times, \mathsf{1}, !)$ fragment of Affine logic [See87, Bie95].

An *affine category* is a symmetric monoidal closed category $\mathcal{C}$ with finite products, such that the tensor unit is the terminal object $\mathsf{1}$, together with a comonad which we write in "co-Kleisli form" [Man76] as $(\,!, \mathtt{der}, (\cdot)^{\dagger})$ where $! : \mathcal{C} \to \mathcal{C}$, $\mathtt{der}_A : !A \to A$ for all $A$, and

$$(\cdot)^{\dagger}_{A,B} : \mathcal{C}(\,!A, B) \to \mathcal{C}(\,!A,\ !B)$$

satisfy:

$$f^{\dagger}; g^{\dagger} = (f^{\dagger}; g)^{\dagger} \tag{1}$$

$$f^{\dagger}; \mathtt{der} = f \tag{2}$$

$$\mathtt{der}^{\dagger}; f = f. \tag{3}$$

There are moreover natural isomorphisms (the "exponential laws" )

$$\begin{aligned} e_{A,B} : \ & !(A \times B) \xrightarrow{\cong} !A \otimes !B \\ e_{\mathsf{1}} : \ & \qquad !\mathsf{1} \xrightarrow{\cong} \mathsf{1} \end{aligned}$$

satisfying the coherence conditions given in [Bie95]. Every object $!A$ has a cocommutative comonoid structure given by

$$\mathtt{con}_A = !A \xrightarrow{!\Delta} !(A \times A) \xrightarrow{e_{A,A}} !A \otimes !A$$

$$\mathtt{weak}_A = !A \xrightarrow{!\mathsf{t}_A} !\mathsf{1} \xrightarrow{e_{\mathsf{1}}} \mathsf{1}.$$

The co-Kleisli category $K_!(\mathcal{C})$ is cartesian closed, with products as in $\mathcal{C}$, and function space

$$A \Rightarrow B = !A \multimap B.$$

## 2.2 Partiality

Recall firstly that $\mathbf{Set}_\star$, the category of *pointed sets*, has as objects sets with a specified base point, and as morphisms functions preserving the base point. $\mathbf{Set}_\star$ is symmetric monoidal closed, with tensor given by smash product and function spaces by basepoint-preserving maps. It has products as in **Set**, and coproducts given by coalesced sums (*i.e.* disjoint unions with basepoints identified). We write $\coprod$ for disjoint union of sets, and $+$ for coproduct in $\mathbf{Set}_\star$. We write $X_\star$ for an object of $\mathbf{Set}_\star$, where $X$ is the set of elements excluding the basepoint. Thus $X_\star + Y_\star = (X \coprod Y)_\star$.

Now let $\mathcal{C}$ be a category with finite products. $\mathcal{C}$ *has* $\bot$*-maps* if for each object $A$ there is a distinguished morphism $\bot_A : 1 \to A$. We then define $\bot_{A,B}$ for all $A, B$ by

$$\bot_{A,B} = A \xrightarrow{t_A} 1 \xrightarrow{\bot_B} B.$$

We require that $\bot_{B,C} \circ f = \bot_{A,C}$ for all objects $A, B, C$ and $f : A \to B$; and that

$$\bot_{A \times B} = \langle \bot_A, \bot_B \rangle.$$

A morphism $f : A \to B$ is *strict* if $f \circ \bot_A = \bot_B$. The strict morphisms form a subcategory which we denote $\mathcal{C}_s$. Note that $\mathcal{C}_s$ is enriched over $\mathbf{Set}_\star$. Thus there is an enriched hom-functor

$$\mathcal{C}_s(-,-) : \mathcal{C}_s^{\mathrm{o}} \times \mathcal{C}_s \longrightarrow \mathbf{Set}_\star.$$

Note also that for any object $A$,

$$\mathcal{C}(A,-) : \mathcal{C}_s \longrightarrow \mathbf{Set}_\star$$

is a well-defined functor, since the basepoint of $\mathcal{C}(A, B)$ is $\bot_{A,B}$, and for any strict $f : B \to C$,

$$f \circ \bot_{A,B} = \bot_{A,C}.$$

A morphism $f : A \to B$ is *total* if it is strict and $f \neq \bot_{A,B}$. We write $\mathcal{C}_t(A, B)$ for the set of total morphisms from $A$ to $B$, so that

$$\mathcal{C}_s(A, B) = \mathcal{C}_t(A, B)_\star.$$

However, note that total morphisms need not be closed under composition.

*Examples* In the category **Cpo** of directed-complete partial orders with least elements and continuous maps, strictness has its expected meaning.

In the categories of games in [AJM96, HO96, McC96a], the $\bot$-maps are the empty strategies. The strict strategies $\sigma : A \to B$ are those which respond to the opening move by Opponent (which must be in $B$) with a move in $A$ if they have any response at all.

### 2.3 Atomic and Discrete Objects

Let $\mathcal{C}$ be a category with finite products and $\bot$-maps. An object $B$ of $\mathcal{C}$ is a *$\pi$-atom* (*cf.* [Joy95a, Joy95b]) if

$$\mathcal{C}_s(-, B) : \mathcal{C}_s^{\mathsf{O}} \longrightarrow \mathbf{Set}_\star$$

preserves coproducts, *i.e.* for each finite family $\{A_i \mid i \in I\}$ of objects in $\mathcal{C}$, the canonical map

$$\sum_{i\in I} \mathcal{C}_s(A_i, B) = \left(\coprod_{i\in I} \mathcal{C}_t(A_i, B)\right)_\star \longrightarrow \mathcal{C}_s\left(\prod_{i\in I} A_i, B\right)$$

$$\begin{cases} (i, f) \mapsto \pi_i; f \\ \quad * \quad \mapsto \bot_{\prod_{i\in I} A_i, B} \end{cases}$$

is a bijection. The motivation for this terminology comes from lattice theory (Joyal is generalizing Whitman's theorem on free lattices). A $\pi$-atom in a lattice (also often called a meet-irreducible element, *cf.* [DP90]) is an element $a$ such that

$$\bigwedge_{i=1}^{n} a_i \le a \Longrightarrow \exists i.\, a_i \le a.$$

Generalizing from posets to (enriched) categories, we get the definition given above.

An object $B$ is *discrete* if for each $A$ the canonical map

$$\mathcal{C}_s(A, B) + \mathcal{C}(1, B) \longrightarrow \mathcal{C}(A, B)$$

$$f : A \to_s B \mapsto f : A \to B, \quad x : 1 \to B \mapsto A \to 1 \xrightarrow{x} B$$

is a bijection.

The idea behind this definition is that any morphism into a discrete object is either strict or constant. It should be recalled that the coproduct on the left is the coalesced sum in $\mathbf{Set}_\star$; this allows the constant–$\bot$ morphism (which is both strict *and* constant) to be properly accounted for.

We write $\mathcal{C}^\pi$ for the full subcategory of $\mathcal{C}$ determined by the $\pi$-atomic objects.

*Examples* In the (Linear) categories of games in [AJM96, HO96, McC96a], any game $B$ with a unique initial question is $\pi$-atomic. The response to this unique initial question in $B$ made by a total strategy $\prod_{i \in I} A_i \to B$ must be in one of the games $A_i$. Making such a move entails projecting the product onto the $i$'th factor. Flat games—*i.e.*, those with a unique initial question and a set of possible answers, after which nothing more can happen—are discrete. This just says that if $A$ is discrete, then any strategy $A \to B$ is either the empty strategy, or responds to the unique initial question in $B$ with some move in $A$—and hence is strict; or responds with an answer in $B$ which completes the play, and hence is a "constant" strategy.

In **Cpo**, flat domains are discrete (any continuous function into a flat domain is either strict or constant); **Coh**, the category of coherence spaces and linear maps, is *soft* in the sense of [Joy95a, Joy95b]—see [HJ97].

### 2.4 Standard Datatypes

Let $\mathcal{C}$ be a category with $\bot$-maps as in Section 2.2. We assume given a class of objects of $\mathcal{C}$ which we will call "well opened," which forms an exponential ideal, *i.e.*, if $B$ is well opened so is $A \multimap B$, and which moreover is closed under products. We write $\mathcal{C}^{wo}$ for the sub-category of well opened objects.

We say that $\mathcal{C}$ *has standard datatypes* if:

- The total maps on $\mathcal{C}^{wo}$ form a sub-category $\mathcal{C}^{wo}_t$.
- The functor

$$\mathcal{C}(1, -) : \mathcal{C}^{wo}_t \longrightarrow \mathbf{Set}_\star$$

has a left adjoint left inverse $\widetilde{(\cdot)}$.

Unpacking this definition, for each well opened object $A$ of $\mathcal{C}$ and pointed set $X_\star$, there is an isomorphism

$$\mathcal{C}^{wo}_t(\widetilde{X_\star}, A) \cong \mathbf{Set}_\star(X_\star, \mathcal{C}(1, A))$$

natural in $X_\star$ and $A$, such that the unit

$$\eta_{X_\star} : X_\star \longrightarrow \mathcal{C}(1, \widetilde{X_\star})$$

is an isomorphism. In particular, $X_\star$ is well opened, and there are maps

$$\bar{x} : 1 \to \widetilde{X_\star} \quad (x \in X)$$

with $\bar{x} \neq \bot_{\widetilde{X_\star}}$, and for each family

$$(f_x : 1 \to A \mid x \in X)$$

a unique total morphism

$$[f_x \mid x \in X] : \widetilde{X_\star} \to A$$

such that

$$\bar{x}_0; [f_x \mid x \in X] = f_{x_0} \quad (x_0 \in X).$$

*Examples* In the categories of games in [AJM96, HO96, McC96a], $\widetilde{X_\star}$ is the "flat game" with a unique initial question, and one answer for each $x \in X$. The well opened objects in these categories are those in which any move that *can* occur as the first move in a play can *only* so occur.

In **Cpo**, a slightly different situation prevails. The functor

$$\mathbf{Cpo}(1, -) : \mathbf{Cpo}_s \longrightarrow \mathbf{Set}_\star$$

has a left adjoint left inverse, which sends $X_\star$ to the flat domain $X_\bot$.

## 3 Sequential Categories

Let $\mathcal{C}$ be an affine category with $\bot$-maps and standard datatypes. $\mathcal{C}$ is a *sequential category* if it satisfies the following axioms (A1)–(A5).

(A1) $\widetilde{X_\star}$ is discrete for each set $X$.

(A2) $\widetilde{X_\star}$ is $\pi$-atomic for each set $X$, and $\mathcal{C}^\pi$ is an exponential ideal.

(A3) **(Uniformity of threads)**. Let $A$ and $B$ be well opened objects. Then

$$\mathcal{C}(\,!A,\ !B) \cong \mathcal{C}(\,!A, B).$$

More precisely, there are canonical maps

$$\begin{array}{lll} f : !A \to !B \mapsto & f; \mathtt{der}_B & : !A \to B \\ g : !A \to B \mapsto & g^\dagger & : !A \to !B \end{array}$$

and since $(\,!, \mathtt{der}, (\cdot)^\dagger)$ is a comonad,

$$g^\dagger; \mathtt{der}_B = g.$$

The content of (A3) is that

$$(f; \mathtt{der}_B)^\dagger = f$$

*i.e.* that the two passages are mutually inverse.

This property was proved for categories of games in [AJM96] and subsequently in [McC96a], under the name of the "Bang Lemma." The idea is that morphisms $f : !A \to !B$ must display uniform behaviour in all "threads," *i.e.*, in each copy of $B$ together with its associated copies of $A$. This property holds in these categories as a consequence of *history-freeness* in [AJM96], and of *innocence* in [McC96a]. The idea in each case is that a strategy $f : !A \to !B$ can only "see" the current thread, and hence must play like the promotion of its restriction to a single thread, i.e., like $(f; \mathtt{der}_B)^{\dagger}$.

(A4) **(Linearization of Head Occurrence).**

$\mathcal{C}_s(!A, B) \cong \mathcal{C}_s(A, !A \multimap B)$.

More precisely, there is a canonical map

$$\begin{array}{c}
\mathcal{C}_s(A, !A \multimap B) \\
\Big\downarrow \Lambda^{-1} \\
\mathcal{C}(A \otimes !A, B) \\
\Big\downarrow \mathcal{C}(\mathtt{der}_A \otimes \mathtt{id}_{!A}, \mathtt{id}_B) \\
\mathcal{C}(!A \otimes !A, B) \\
\Big\downarrow \mathcal{C}(\mathtt{con}_A, \mathtt{id}_B) \\
\mathcal{C}(!A, B)
\end{array}$$

The content of (A4) is firstly that this map factors through the inclusion

$\mathcal{C}_s(!A, B) \hookrightarrow \mathcal{C}(!A, B)$

and secondly that the corestriction

$\mathcal{C}_s(A, !A \multimap B) \longrightarrow \mathcal{C}_s(!A, B)$

is a bijection.

This property was proved, under the name of "Separation of Head Occurrence," for categories of games firstly in [AJM96], and subsequently in [McC96a]. There is a suggestive analogy, at least, with operational and proof-theoretic ideas of treating head variables linearly [Gir87, DHR96]. The idea is simply that we can split the use of many copies of $A$ in $!A$ on the left into the tensor product of the *first* copy used, of type $A$, and the remaining copies, of type $!A$. In the case of strict strategies, which are either empty or use at least one copy of $A$, this correspondence is biunique.

(A5) **(Linear Function Extensionality).** There is an isomorphism

$\mathcal{C}_s(A \multimap B, !C \multimap D) \cong \mathcal{C}(!C, A)_{\star} \otimes \mathcal{C}_s(B, !C \multimap D)$

provided $B$ and $D$ are discrete. (The tensor product on the right is smash product in $\mathbf{Set}_\star$. Note that

$$\mathcal{C}(\,!C, A)_\star \otimes \mathcal{C}_s(B,\ !C \multimap D) = (\mathcal{C}(\,!C, A) \times \mathcal{C}_t(B,\ !C \multimap D))_\star.)$$

More precisely, there is a canonical map

$$\begin{array}{c}
\mathcal{C}(\,!C, A) \times \mathcal{C}_t(B,\ !C \multimap D) \\
\Big\downarrow (-) \multimap (-) \\
\mathcal{C}(A \multimap B,\ !C \multimap (\,!C \multimap D)) \\
\Big\downarrow \cong \\
\mathcal{C}(A \multimap B,\ !C \otimes !C \multimap D) \\
\Big\downarrow \mathcal{C}(\mathtt{id}, \mathtt{con}_C \multimap \mathtt{id}) \\
\mathcal{C}(A \multimap B,\ !C \multimap D)
\end{array}$$

The content of (A5) is that this map factors through the inclusion

$$\mathcal{C}_t(A \multimap B,\ !C \multimap D) \hookrightarrow \mathcal{C}(A \multimap B,\ !C \multimap D)$$

and that the corestriction

$$\mathcal{C}(!C, A) \times \mathcal{C}_t(B,\ !C \multimap D) \longrightarrow \mathcal{C}_t(A \multimap B,\ !C \multimap D)$$

and hence also the "lifted" map

$$\mathcal{C}(\,!C, A)_\star \otimes \mathcal{C}_s(B,\ !C \multimap D) \longrightarrow \mathcal{C}_s(A \multimap B,\ !C \multimap D)$$

is a bijection.

A special case of this property, under the same name, was proved for categories of games in [AJM96], and subsequently in [McC96a]. The general case was implicit in the proof of the Decomposition Theorem in [AJM96]. Intuitively, this axiom says that the only thing we can do with a linear functional parameter is to apply it to an argument, and apply some function to the result. The verification of this axiom in the categories of games considered in [AJM96, McC96a] makes essential use *both* of history-freeness/innocence, *and* of well bracketedness. The idea is that a strict strategy of the type displayed in the axiom must respond to the initial question in $D$ by "calling its function argument," i.e., by making the (unique) initital move in $B$. By the bracketing condition, the initial question in $D$ cannot be answered until the initial question in $B$ has been answered, i.e., until the play in $B$ is complete. This allows us to decompose the strategy we started with into sub-strategies, corresponding to what is done before and after the play in $B$ is completed. History-freeness/innocence then guarantess that the continuation strategy which proceeds after the play in $B$ is completed can depend *only* on the answer returned, not on the interaction which took place between the function and its arguments. This is one of the key points where essentially non-functional behaviour is being excluded.

*Examples* A minor embarassment is that neither of our two concrete examples of models for the above axioms, namely the categories of games described in [AJM96, McC96a], *quite* succeeds in being a sequential category! They *do* satisfy the key axioms (A1)–(A5). In the case of the category in [AJM96], the problem is that it fails to have products in the underlying Affine category—although the co-Kleisli category *is* cartesian closed. However, there is a "candidate" for the product in the Affine category—which turns into a real product in the co-Kleisli category—which *does* have projections, and with respect to which the required properties relating to $\pi$-atomicity do hold. This is enough for our applications to definability to follow. Similarly, in the category used in [McC96a] ! fails to be a co-monad; however, one does get a cartesian closed co-Kleisli category by restricting to the well-opened objects.

These minor mismatches are probably best taken as an indication that we do not yet have a definitive formulation of game semantics.

## 4 Decomposition

We will now prove a decomposition theorem in the sense of [AJM96] from the axioms.

Let $\mathcal{C}$ be a sequential category. Let

$$A_i = !(B_{i,1} \times \cdots \times B_{i,q_i}) \multimap \widetilde{X_\star} \quad (1 \leq i \leq k)$$

be objects of $\mathcal{C}$. We write $\vec{A} = A_1 \times \cdots \times A_k$. Consider a morphism $f : !\vec{A} \to \widetilde{X_\star}$. By (A1), $\widetilde{X_\star}$ is discrete, hence three disjoint cases apply:

- $f = \bot$.
- $f = !\vec{A} \to 1 \xrightarrow{g} \widetilde{X_\star}$. In this case, by the universal property of $\widetilde{X_\star}$, we must have $g = \bar{x}$ for some unique $x \in X$.
- $f$ is total. In this case, by (A4) $f$ is in bijective correspondence with a total morphism

$$f' : \vec{A} \to !\vec{A} \multimap \widetilde{X_\star}.$$

By (A2), $f'$ factors by a projection $\pi_i$ through

$$f_i : A_i \to_t !\vec{A} \multimap \widetilde{X_\star}$$

for a unique $i$, $1 \leq i \leq k$. By (A5), $f_i$ decomposes into

$$g : !\vec{A} \to !\vec{B}_i, \quad h : \widetilde{X_\star} \to_t (!\vec{A} \multimap \widetilde{X_\star})$$

where $\vec{B}_i = B_{i,1} \times \cdots \times B_{i,q_i}$. By (A3), $g = (g; \mathtt{der}_{\vec{B}_i})^\dagger$, and by the universal property of the product,

$$g = \langle g_1, \ldots, g_{q_i} \rangle^\dagger$$

for unique $g_j : !\vec{A} \to B_{i,j}$, $1 \leq j \leq q_i$. By the universal property of $\widetilde{X_\star}$,

$$h = [h_x : 1 \to !\vec{A} \multimap \widetilde{X_\star} \mid x \in X].$$

Thus we obtain

$$f = \mathbf{C}_i(g_1, \ldots, g_{q_i}, (h_x \mid x \in X))$$

where $\mathbf{C}_i(g_1, \ldots, g_{q_i}, (h_x \mid x \in X))$ abbreviates

$$\mathtt{con}_{\vec{A}}; (\mathtt{con}_{\vec{A}}; (\mathtt{der}_{\vec{A}}; \pi_i) \otimes \langle g_1, \ldots, g_{q_i} \rangle^\dagger; \mathtt{Ap}) \otimes \mathtt{id}_{!\vec{A}}; \Lambda^{-1}([h_x \mid x \in X]).$$

We summarise this analysis in

THEOREM 4.1 (DECOMPOSITION) With notation as above, one of the following three cases applies:

- $f = \bot$.
- $f = !\vec{A} \to 1 \xrightarrow{\bar{x}} \widetilde{X_\star}$.
- $f = \mathbf{C}_i(g_1, \ldots, g_{q_i}, (h_x \mid x \in X))$.

Moreover, this decomposition is unique.

## 5 PCF

In this section we briefly recall the language PCF, its operational semantics and observational preorder, in a streamlined version convenient for our purposes.

PCF is an applied simply typed λ-calculus with a single base type **nat**. The constants are as follows:

- recursion combinators $\mathbf{Y}_T : (T \Rightarrow T) \Rightarrow T$ for each type $T$.
- $\Omega : \mathbf{nat}$.
- $\underline{n} : \mathbf{nat}$ for each $n \in \mathbb{N}$.
- $\mathtt{case}_k : \mathbf{nat} \Rightarrow \underbrace{\mathbf{nat} \Rightarrow \cdots \Rightarrow \mathbf{nat}}_{k} \Rightarrow \mathbf{nat}$ for each $k \in \mathbb{N}$.

The main difference from PCF as originally presented by Scott and Plotkin is in the use of the $\mathtt{case}_k$ constants instead of the more familiar conditionals and arithmetic operations.

The $\mathtt{case}_k$ constants are needed for a precise correspondence at the intensional level, and as shown in detail in [AJM96], the difference is insignificant as far as observational equivalence is concerned.

The operational semantics is defined via a structural congruence $\equiv$ (*cf.* [Mil92]) and an evaluation relation $\_\Downarrow\_$. The structural congruence is the congruence on terms generated by $\beta\eta$-conversion and all instances of

$$\mathbf{Y}M \equiv M(\mathbf{Y}M).$$

The evaluation relation $P \Downarrow \underline{n}$ is defined between *programs*, *i.e.*, closed terms of type **nat**, and numerals $\underline{n}$, inductively as follows:

$$\frac{M \equiv M' \quad M' \Downarrow \underline{n}}{M \Downarrow \underline{n}} \qquad \frac{}{\underline{n} \Downarrow \underline{n}}$$

$$\frac{P \Downarrow \underline{i} \quad (i < k) \quad P_i \Downarrow \underline{n}}{\mathtt{case}_k P P_0 \cdots P_{k-1} \Downarrow \underline{n}}$$

Let $\mathsf{Trm}(\Gamma, T)$ be the set of terms $M$ such that $\Gamma \vdash M : T$ is derivable. Let $\mathsf{Ctxt}(\Gamma, T)$ be the set of contexts $C[\cdot]$ such that $C[M]$ is a program for all $M \in \mathsf{Trm}(\Gamma, T)$. The observational preorder is defined at $\Gamma, T$ by:

$$M \precsim_{\Gamma,T} N \iff \forall C[\cdot] \in \mathsf{Ctxt}(\Gamma, T).\, C[M]\Downarrow \underline{n} \implies C[N]\Downarrow \underline{n}.$$

## 6 Computational Adequacy

Let $\mathcal{C}$ be an affine category with $\bot$-maps and standard datatypes. The cartesian closed category $K_!(\mathcal{C})$ provides a model of the fragment of PCF obtained by omitting the recursion combinators $\mathbf{Y}_T$. The base type **nat** is interpreted by $\widetilde{\mathbb{N}_\star}$, the constants $\underline{n}$ by $\overline{n}$, $n \in \mathbb{N}$, and $\Omega$ by $\bot_{\widetilde{\mathbb{N}_\star}}$. The constant $\mathtt{case}_k$ is interpreted by

$$\mathtt{der}_{\widetilde{\mathbb{N}_\star}}; [f_i \mid i \in \mathbb{N}]$$

where

$$f_i = \begin{cases} \Lambda^k(\pi_i), & 0 \leq i < k \\ \bot, & i \geq k. \end{cases}$$

This interpretation is extended to all terms in the standard way [Cro94].

To accommodate recursion, we need another definition. Let $\mathcal{K}$ be a cartesian closed category. A *fixpoint operator* on $\mathcal{K}$ is a family of maps

$$(\,)^\nabla_A : \mathcal{K}(A, A) \longrightarrow \mathcal{K}(1, A)$$

satisfying

$$f \circ f^{\nabla} = f^{\nabla}.$$

Given such an operator, we can interpret the fixpoint combinator $\mathbf{Y}_A : 1 \rightarrow (A \Rightarrow A) \Rightarrow A$ by

$$[\![F : (A \Rightarrow A) \Rightarrow A \vdash \lambda f : A \Rightarrow A.\, f(Ff)]\!]^{\nabla}.$$

A model is said to be *computationally adequate* if, for all programs $P$ and $n \in \mathbb{N}$:

$$P \Downarrow \underline{n} \iff [\![P]\!] = \overline{n}.$$

Let $\mathcal{C}$ be an affine category with $\perp$-maps and standard datatypes, equipped with a fixpoint operator on $K_!(\mathcal{C})$. $\mathcal{C}$ is said to be *continuously observable* if, for all $f : A \rightarrow A$ and $g : A \rightarrow \widetilde{X_\star}$ in $K_!(\mathcal{C})$, and all $x \in X$:

$$g \circ f^{\nabla} = \overline{x} \iff \exists k \in \omega.\, g \circ f^k \circ \perp = \overline{x}.$$

Recall from [AJM96] that a *rational cartesian closed category* is a cartesian closed category enriched over pointed posets, with least upper bounds of "definable" chains, i.e., those of the form $(f^k \circ \perp \mid k \in \omega)$. This provides just enough structure to interpret the recursion combinators $\mathbf{Y}$ in terms of least fixpoints. It is shown in [AJM96] that the category of games studied there is rational; this, together with the fact that the "points" of the standard datatypes form flat domains implies that the category is continuously observable.

THEOREM 6.1 (COMPUTATIONAL ADEQUACY) If $\mathcal{C}$ is continuously observable then $K_!(\mathcal{C})$ is a computationally adequate model of PCF.

The original proof by Plotkin for the Scott continuous function model [Plo77] goes through in our axiomatic setting (*cf.* [Bra97]).

In practice, it is often more convenient to verify somewhat stronger axioms. We say that a sequential category $\mathcal{C}$ is *normed* if:

- It is enriched over algebraic cpo's, with the $\perp$-morphisms being the least elements in the partial orderings, and such that $\mathcal{C}(1, \widetilde{X_\star})$ is order-isomorphic to the flat domain $X_\perp$.
- There is a norm function $\|f\| \in \mathbb{N}$ on *compact* morphisms $f$, such that, for each PCF type $T$ and compact $f : 1 \longrightarrow [\![T]\!]$:

$$f = \mathbf{C}_i(f_1, \ldots, f_{q_i}, (g_n \mid n \in \mathbb{N})) \Longrightarrow$$

$$\sup(\{\|f_j\| \mid 1 \leq j \leq q_i\} \cup \{\|g_n\| \mid n \in \mathbb{N}\}) < \|f\|,$$

and $g_n = \perp$ for almost all $n \in \mathbb{N}$.

Note that a normed category is automatically observably continuous and hence computationally adequate.

The categories in [HO96, McC96a] are normed, with the norm of a compact innocent strategy given by the cardinality of its view function.

## 7 Definability

Let $T = T_1 \Rightarrow \cdots T_k \Rightarrow \mathbf{nat}$ be a PCF type. Note that

$$\begin{aligned} [\![T]\!] &= [\![T_1]\!] \Rightarrow \cdots [\![T_k]\!] \Rightarrow [\![\mathbf{nat}]\!] \\ &= ![\![T_1]\!] \multimap \cdots ![\![T_k]\!] \multimap \widetilde{\mathbb{N}_\star} \\ &\cong (![\![T_1]\!] \otimes \cdots \otimes ![\![T_k]\!]) \multimap \widetilde{\mathbb{N}_\star} \\ &\cong !([\![T_1]\!] \times \cdots \times [\![T_k]\!]) \multimap \widetilde{\mathbb{N}_\star}. \end{aligned}$$

To save notational overhead, we shall elide this canonical isomorphism, equating the "curried" and "uncurried" versions of types. (However, for a careful treatment in which these isomorphisms are made explicit, see [AJM96]).

Let $\mathcal{C}$ be a sequential category. For each $f : 1 \to [\![T]\!]$ in $\mathcal{C}$ and $k \in \omega$, we define $p_k(f)$ inductively as follows:

$$p_0(f) = \bot$$

$$p_{k+1}(f) = \begin{cases} \bot, & f = \bot \\ f, & f = \mathsf{t}; \overline{n} \\ f', & f = \mathbf{C}_i(f_1, \ldots, f_{q_i}, (g_n \mid n \in \mathbb{N})) \end{cases}$$

where

$$f' = \mathbf{C}_i(p_k(f_i), \ldots, p_k(f_{q_i}), (h_n \mid n \in \mathbb{N}))$$

$$h_n = \begin{cases} p_k(g_n), & 0 \le n < k \\ \bot & n \ge k. \end{cases}$$

This definition by cases is valid by the Decomposition Theorem.

THEOREM 7.1 (DEFINABILITY) For each PCF type $T$, $f : 1 \to [\![T]\!]$ and $k \in \omega$, $p_k(f)$ is definable in PCF. That is, there exists a PCF term $\vdash M : T$ such that $p_k(f) = [\![M]\!]$.

*Proof* By induction on $k$, and cases on the decomposition of $f$. We write $T = \widetilde{T} \Rightarrow \mathbf{nat}$, where $\widetilde{T} = T_1, \ldots, T_k$.

$$\begin{aligned} p_0(f) &= \bot = [\![\lambda \tilde{x} : \widetilde{T}.\, \Omega]\!] \\ p_{k+1}(\bot) &= \bot = [\![\lambda \tilde{x} : \widetilde{T}.\, \Omega]\!] \\ p_{k+1}(\mathsf{t}; \overline{n}) &= \mathsf{t}; \overline{n} = [\![\lambda \tilde{x} : \widetilde{T}.\, \underline{n}]\!] \end{aligned}$$

$$p_{k+1}(\mathbf{C}_i(p_k(f_i), \ldots . p_k(f_{q_i}), (h_n \mid n \in \mathbb{N}))) =$$

$$[\![\lambda \tilde{x} : \widetilde{T}.\,\mathtt{case}_k(x_i(M_1\tilde{x}) \cdots (M_{q_i}\tilde{x}))(P_0\tilde{x}) \cdots (P_{k-1}\tilde{x})]\!]$$

where

$$p_k(f_j) = [\![M_j]\!], \quad 1 \leq j \leq q_i,$$
$$p_k(g_n) = [\![P_n]\!], \quad 0 \leq n < k. \qquad \square$$

For normed categories, we can prove a stronger result.

THEOREM 7.2 (DEFINABILITY FOR NORMED SEQUENTIAL CATEGORIES) For each PCF type $T$ and compact $f : 1 \rightarrow [\![T]\!]$, $f$ is definable in PCF. That is, there exists a PCF term $\vdash M : T$ such that $f = [\![M]\!]$.

*Proof* By complete induction on $\|f\|$, and cases on the decomposition of $f$. We write $T = \widetilde{T} \Rightarrow$ **nat**, where $\widetilde{T} = T_1, \ldots, T_k$. If $f = \bot$, then

$$f = [\![\lambda \tilde{x} : \widetilde{T}.\,\Omega]\!].$$

If $f = \mathrm{t}; \overline{n}$, then

$$f = [\![\lambda \tilde{x} : \widetilde{T}.\,\underline{n}]\!].$$

If $f = \mathbf{C}_i(f_1, \ldots, f_{q_i}, (g_n \mid n \in \mathbb{N}))$, then

$$f = [\![\lambda \tilde{x} : \widetilde{T}.\,\mathtt{case}_l(x_i(M_1\tilde{x}) \cdots (M_{q_i}\tilde{x}))(P_0\tilde{x}) \cdots (P_{k-1}\tilde{x})]\!]$$

where by induction hypothesis

$$f_j = [\![M_j]\!], \quad 1 \leq j \leq q_i,$$
$$g_n = [\![P_n]\!], \quad 0 \leq n < l,$$

and $g_m = \bot$ for all $m \geq l$. $\square$

We note that the terms used to exhibit definability in Theorems 7.1 and 7.2 are of a special form; the *evaluation trees* of [AJM96]. These can be seen as a form of Bohm tree appropriate for PCF. These trees were in fact first identified as the right notion of normal forms for PCF terms as a consequence of the work on game semantics; this is an interesting example of feedback from semantics to syntax. In [AJM96] it is shown that there is an order-isomorphism between the (possibly infinite) evaluation trees at any PCF type, and the strategies for the game denoted by that type. A similar result can be obtained at the axiomatic level of this paper. Since it is not needed in order to obtain the full abstraction results, we will omit the details.

## 8 Full Abstraction

Let $\mathcal{C}$ be a poset-enriched model of PCF. $\mathcal{C}$ is *sound* if, for all $M, N \in \mathsf{Trm}(\Gamma, T)$,

$$[\![\Gamma \vdash M : T]\!] \leqslant [\![\Gamma \vdash N : T]\!] \Longrightarrow M \sqsubseteq_{\Gamma,T} N,$$

and *complete* if the converse holds. $\mathcal{C}$ is *fully abstract* if it is both sound and complete.

LEMMA 8.1 $\mathcal{C}$ is fully abstract iff soundness and completeness hold for all *closed* terms.

*Proof* The left-to-right implication is immediate. For the converse, we show firstly that, if $\Gamma = x_1 : T_k, \ldots, x_k : T_k$,

$$M \sqsubseteq_{\Gamma,T} N \Longleftrightarrow \lambda\tilde{x} : \tilde{T}.\, M \sqsubseteq_{\varnothing,T} \lambda\tilde{x} : \tilde{T}.\, N. \tag{4}$$

Again, the left-to-right implication is immediate. For the converse, assume that $\lambda\tilde{x} : \tilde{T}.\, M \sqsubseteq_{\Gamma,T} \lambda\tilde{x} : \tilde{T}.\, N$ and that $C[M]\Downarrow\underline{n}$. Define a new context

$$D[\cdot] = C[[\cdot]\tilde{x}].$$

Then $D[\lambda\tilde{x} : \tilde{T}.\, M] \equiv C[M]$ and hence $D[\lambda\tilde{x} : \tilde{T}.\, M]\Downarrow\underline{n}$. This implies that $D[\lambda\tilde{x} : \tilde{T}.\, N]\Downarrow\underline{n}$, but since $D[\lambda\tilde{x} : \tilde{T}.\, N] \equiv C[N]$, we conclude that $C[N]\Downarrow\underline{n}$, as required.

Furthermore, since currying $\Lambda_{A,B,C} : \mathcal{C}(A \times B, C) \longrightarrow \mathcal{C}(A, B \Rightarrow C)$ is an order-isomorphism, it is immediate that

$$[\![\Gamma \vdash M : T]\!] \leqslant [\![\Gamma \vdash N : T]\!] \Longleftrightarrow [\![\vdash \lambda\tilde{x} : \tilde{T}.\, M]\!] \leqslant [\![\vdash \lambda\tilde{x} : \tilde{T}.\, N]\!]. \tag{5}$$

By assumption,

$$\lambda\tilde{x} : \tilde{T}.\, M \sqsubseteq_{\tilde{T}\Rightarrow T} \lambda\tilde{x} : \tilde{T}.\, N \Longleftrightarrow [\![\lambda\tilde{x} : \tilde{T}.\, M]\!] \leqslant [\![\lambda\tilde{x} : \tilde{T}.\, N]\!]. \tag{6}$$

Combining (4), (5) and (6) we conclude that $\mathcal{C}$ is fully abstract. □

Now let $\mathcal{C}$ be an observably continuous sequential category. $K_!(\mathcal{C})$ is a computationally adequate model of PCF, by the Computational Adequacy Theorem. We define the *intrinsic preorder* $\lesssim_A$ on each $K_!(\mathcal{C})(1, A)$ by

$$f \lesssim_A g \Longleftrightarrow \forall \alpha : A \to \widetilde{\mathbb{N}_\star}.\, \alpha \circ f = \overline{n} \Rightarrow \alpha \circ g = \overline{n}.$$

This is extended to general homsets $K_!(\mathcal{C})(A, B)$ via the names of morphisms:

$$f \lesssim_{A,B} g \Longleftrightarrow \ulcorner f \urcorner \lesssim_{A\Rightarrow B} \ulcorner g \urcorner.$$

PROPOSITION 9 For all $A, B$ $\lesssim_{A,B}$ is a preorder, with least element $\bot_{A,B}$, and $K_!(\mathcal{C})$ is an enriched cartesian closed category with respect to this preorder. The poset reflection

$K_!(\mathcal{C})/\lesssim$ is a rational cartesian closed category, and there is a full cartesian closed functor $Q : K_!(\mathcal{C}) \to K_!(\mathcal{C})/\lesssim$ with the evident universal property which translates the interpretation of PCF in $K_!(\mathcal{C})$ to that in $K_!(\mathcal{C})/\lesssim$.

*Proof* See [HO96, McC96a, Bra97]. □

We say that $\mathcal{C}$ is *approximating* if for all PCF types $T$, $f : [\![T]\!] \to \widetilde{X_\star}$ and $\alpha : 1 \to [\![T]\!]$ in $K_!(\mathcal{C})$, and $x \in X$:

$$f \circ \alpha = \overline{x} \iff \exists k \in \omega.\, p_k(f) \circ \alpha = \overline{x}.$$

In [AJM96], Section 3.4, it is proved that the category of games considered there is approximating.

THEOREM 8.1 Let $\mathcal{C}$ be an approximating sequential category. Then $K_!(\mathcal{C})/\lesssim$ is a fully abstract model of PCF.

*Proof* By the Lemma, it suffices to show soundness and completeness for closed terms. Note that if $M$ is closed, $C[M] \equiv (\lambda x.\, C[x])M$ ($x \notin FV(M)$), and hence $C[M]{\Downarrow}\underline{n} \iff D[M]{\Downarrow}\underline{n}$, where $D[\cdot] = (\lambda x.\, C[x])[\cdot]$. Thus $T$-contexts reduce to applications of functions of type $T \Rightarrow$ **nat**.

Suppose then that $[\![M]\!] \leqslant [\![N]\!]$, and that $C[M]{\Downarrow}\underline{n}$. By computational adequacy, $[\![C[M]]\!] = \overline{n}$, *i.e.* $f \circ [\![M]\!] = \overline{n}$, where $f = [\![\lambda x.\, C[x]]\!]$. This implies that $f \circ [\![N]\!] = \overline{n}$ *i.e.* $[\![C[N]]\!] = \overline{n}$, and by computational adequacy again, $C[N]{\Downarrow}\underline{n}$. This establishes soundness.

For completeness, suppose that $[\![\vdash M : T]\!] \leqslant [\![\vdash N : T]\!]$, *i.e.* for some $f : [\![T]\!] \to \widetilde{\mathbb{N}_\star}$, $f \circ [\![M]\!] = \overline{n}$ and $f \circ [\![N]\!] \neq \overline{n}$. Since $\mathcal{C}$ is approximating, for some $k \in \omega$, $p_k(f) \circ [\![M]\!] = \overline{n}$ and $p_k(f) \circ [\![N]\!] \neq \overline{n}$. By the Definability Theorem, for some $P$, $p_k(f) = [\![P]\!]$ and hence, defining $C[\cdot] = P[\cdot]$, $[\![C[M]]\!] = p_k(f) \circ [\![M]\!] = \overline{n}$ while $[\![C[N]]\!] = p_k(f) \circ [\![N]\!] \neq \overline{n}$. By computational adequacy, $C[M]{\Downarrow}\underline{n}$ while $\neg(C[N]{\Downarrow}\underline{n})$, and hence $\neg(M \sqsubsetsim_T N)$, as required. □

We have the corresponding result for normed sequential categories.

THEOREM 8.2 Let $\mathcal{C}$ be a normed sequential category. Then $K_!(\mathcal{C})/\lesssim$ is a fully abstract model of PCF.

*Proof* The proof is almost identical to that of the preceding theorem. The only difference is in the argument for completeness. Given the separating morphism $f : [\![T]\!] \to \widetilde{\mathbb{N}_\star}$, we use the compactness of $\overline{n}$ in $\mathcal{C}(1, \widetilde{\mathbb{N}_\star})$, the algebraicity of $\mathcal{C}([\![T]\!], \widetilde{\mathbb{N}_\star})$, and the continuity of composition to obtain a *compact* $f_0 : [\![T]\!] \to \widetilde{\mathbb{N}_\star}$ such that $f_0 \circ [\![M]\!] = \overline{n}$ and $f_0 \circ [\![N]\!] \neq \overline{n}$. Then we use the Definability Theorem for normed sequential categories to obtain the separating context $C[\cdot]$. □

## 9 Full Completeness

Just as PCF is prototypical for higher-order programming languages, so is the pure simply typed $\lambda$-calculus for logical systems. (Definability results for game semantics of the pure calculus are discussed in [DHR96], and were already known to the authors of [AJM96, HO96].)

We shall indicate how our axiomatic approach can be modified (in fact: simplified) to deal with the pure calculus.

We define a *pure* sequential category to be an affine category $\mathcal{C}$ with a specified subcategory $\mathcal{C}_s$, with the same objects as $\mathcal{C}$, which has an initial object $\iota$ (initial in $\mathcal{C}_s$), satisfying the following axioms:

(a1) $\mathcal{C}(A, \iota) = \mathcal{C}_s(A, \iota)$ for all $A$.

(a2) $\iota$ is $\pi$-atomic (meaning that $\mathcal{C}_s(-, \iota) : \mathcal{C}_s^{\mathrm{o}} \longrightarrow \mathbf{Set}$ preserves finite coproducts), and the $\pi$-atomic objects form an exponential ideal.

(a3) **Uniformity of Threads**. As in Section 3.

(a4) **Linearization of Head Occurrence**. As in Section 3.

(a5) **Linear Function Extensionality**.

$\mathcal{C}_s(A \multimap \iota,\ !C \multimap \iota) \cong \mathcal{C}(!C, A)$.

More precisely, the canonical map

$(-) \multimap \mathtt{id}_\iota : \mathcal{C}(!C, A) \longrightarrow \mathcal{C}(A \multimap \iota,\ !C \multimap \iota)$

is asserted to corestrict bijectively onto $\mathcal{C}_s(A \multimap \iota,\ !C \multimap \iota)$. Note by the way that, since $\iota$ is initial in $\mathcal{C}_s$, $\mathcal{C}_s(\iota, \iota) = \{\mathtt{id}_\iota\}$.

The following decomposition theorem can then be proved for any

$$f : !\left(\prod_{i \in I} A_i\right) \longrightarrow \iota,$$

where

$$A_i = !\left(\prod_{j=1}^{q_i} B_{i,j}\right) \multimap \iota, \qquad 1 \leq i \leq k.$$

THEOREM 9.1 (DECOMPOSITION)

$$f = \mathbf{C}_i(g_1, \ldots g_{q_i}) \\ \triangleq \mathtt{con}_{\vec{A}}; (\mathtt{der}_{\vec{A}}; \pi_i) \otimes \langle g_1, \ldots, g_{q_i} \rangle^{\dagger}; \mathtt{Ap}$$

for a unique $i$, $1 \leq i \leq k$, and

$$f_j : !\left(\prod_{i=1}^{k} A_i\right) \to B_{i,j}, \qquad 1 \leq j \leq q_i.$$

*Proof* By (a1), $f$ is strict. By (a4) we obtain a strict morphism $f' : \vec{A} \to (\vec{A} \multimap \iota)$, and by (a2) this factors by a unique $\pi_i$, $1 \leq i \leq k$, through

$$f_i : A_i \to (\vec{A} \multimap \iota).$$

By (a5) we obtain $g : !\vec{A} \to \vec{B}_i$, and by (a3) and the universal property of the product we obtain

$$g = \langle g_1, \ldots, g_{q_i} \rangle^{\dagger}. \qquad \square$$

We replace the continuity postulates appropriate for PCF by a finiteness axiom. We stipulate that each morphism $f : A \to B$ in $\mathcal{C}$ has a norm $\|f\|_{A,B} \in \mathbb{N}$, such that

$$f = \mathbf{C}_i(g_1, \ldots, g_{q_i}) \Rightarrow \sup_{j=1,\ldots,q_i} \|g_j\| < \|f\|.$$

THEOREM 9.2 (DEFINABILITY) Let $T$ be a simple type built from $\iota$. Then every $f : 1 \to [\![T]\!]$ in $\mathcal{C}$ is definable, and in fact is the denotation of a unique long-$\beta\eta$-normal form.

*Proof* By complete induction on $\|f\|$. If $T = \widetilde{T} \Rightarrow \iota$ and $f = \mathbf{C}_i(g_1, \ldots, g_{q_i})$, then

$$f = [\![\lambda \tilde{x} : \widetilde{T}. x_i(M_1\tilde{x}) \cdots (M_{q_i}\tilde{x})]\!]$$

where $g_j = [\![M_j]\!]$, $1 \leq j \leq q_i$. $\square$

*Examples* The intended examples are the versions of [AJM96, HO96, McC96a] in which only total, compact strategies are included. Strictness of a strategy $\sigma : A \to B$ means that it responds to the opening move by moving in $A$. The interpretation of $\iota$ is as the game with a single move, which is an Opponent question.

The above result is essentially a characterization of the free cartesian closed category generated by the one-object one-morphism category. More general characterization results can probably be developed along similar lines.

Since under the Curry-Howard isomorphism [GLT89] the pure simply-typed λ-calculus corresponds to minimal implicational logic, this result has some relevance for Proof Theory. An interesting contrast with the full completeness results proved for Multiplicative Linear Logic in [AJ94] and a number of other subsequent works is that various notions of "uniformity," dinaturality etc. play an important role in those results, but do not arise here.

**Universality** In [AJM96, HO96] a stronger result than Full Abstraction is proved, namely *Universality*, i.e., that *all recursive strategies are definable in PCF*; or, equivalently, that the model consisting of just the recursive strategies has *all* its elements definable. This is the strongest possible definability result, and is closely related to the notion of "Logical Full Abstraction" introduced by Longley and Plotkin in [LP96], as shown *loc. cit.*

The axiomatic methods developed in the present paper can be extended to yield this stronger result. We briefly sketch the necessary extensions. Firstly, we take our sequential categories to be enriched over *enumerated sets* [AL91] rather than just pointed sets. All the isomorphisms required in the axioms have then to be given effectively. This leads to an effective version of the Decomposition Theorem as in [AJM96]. The development then proceeds exactly as in [AJM96]. That is, universal terms are defined in PCF, from which the definability of all strategies follows directly.

**Acknowledgements** The research described in this paper was supported by the U.K. EP-SRC grant "Foundational Structures for Computing Science." I am grateful to Guy McCusker and the two anonymous referees for their comments on the preliminary version of this paper.

## References

[AJ94] S. Abramsky and R. Jagadeesan. Games and full completeness for multiplicative linear logic. *Journal of Symbolic Logic*, 59(2):543–574, 1994.

[AJM96] S. Abramsky, R. Jagadeesan, and P. Malacaria. Full abstraction for PCF. To appear in *Information and Computation*.

[AL91] A. Asperti and G. Longo. *Categories, Types and Structures*. MIT Press, 1991.

[AM95] S. Abramsky and G. McCusker. Games and full abstraction for the lazy λ-calculus. In *Tenth Annual Symposium on Logic in Computer Science*, pages 234–243, 1995.

[AM97a] S. Abramsky and G. McCusker. Call-by-value games. In *Computer Science Logic: CSL '97*, pages 1–17, volume 1414 of Lecture Notes in Computer Science, Springer Verlag 1998.

[AM97b] S. Abramsky and G. McCusker. Full abstraction for Idealized Algol with passive expressions. To appear in *Theoretical Computer Science*.

[AM97c] S. Abramsky and G. McCusker. Linearity, sharing and state. In P. O'Hearn and R. D. Tennent, editors, *Algol-like Languages*, volume 2, pages 297–329. Birkhauser, 1997.

[BCL86] G. Berry, P.-L. Curien, and J.-J. Lévy. Full abstraction for sequential languages: the state of the art. In M. Nivat and J. C. Reynolds, editors, *Algebraic Semantics*, pages 89–132. Cambridge University Press, 1986.

[Bie95] G. Bierman. What is a categorical model of intuitionistic linear logic? In *International Conference on Typed Lambda Calculi and Applications*. Springer-Verlag, 1995. Lecture Notes in Computer Science.

[Bra97] T. Brauner. A simple adequate categorical model for PCF. In *Proceedings of Third International Conference on Typed Lambda Calculi and Applications*, volume 1210 of *Lecture Notes in Computer Science*. Springer-Verlag, 1997.

[Cro94] R. Crole. *Categories for Types*. Cambridge University Press, 1994.

[Cur93] P.-L. Curien. *Categorical Combinators, Sequential Algorithms and Functional Programming*. Birkhauser, 1993.

[DHR96] V. Danos, H. Herbelin, and L. Regnier. Games and abstract machines. In *International Symposium on Logic in Computer Science*, 1996.

[DP90] B. Davey and H. Priestley. *Introduction to Lattices and Order*. Cambridge University Press, 1990.

[Fio96] M. Fiore. *Axiomatic domain theory in categories of partial maps*. Cambridge University Press, 1996.

[FP94] M. Fiore and G. Plotkin. An axiomatization of computationally adequate domain theoretic models of FPC. In *Ninth Annual IEEE Symposium on Logic in Computer Science*, pages 92–102, 1994.

[Gir87] J.-Y. Girard. Linear logic. *Theoretical Computer Science*, 50:1–102, 1987.

[GLT89] J.-Y. Girard, Y. Lafont, and P. Taylor. *Proofs and Types*. Cambridge University Press, 1989.

[HJ97] H. Hu and A. Joyal. Coherence completion of categories. Submitted for publication, 1997.

[HO96] M. Hyland and C.H. L. Ong. On full abstraction for PCF. To appear in Information and Computation.

[HY97] K. Honda and N. Yoshida. Game-theoretic analysis of call-by-value computation. In *Automata, Languages and Programming: 24th International Colloquium, ICALP '97*, Lecture Notes in Computer Science, pages 225–236. Springer-Verlag, 1997.

[Hyl91] M. Hyland. First steps in synthetic domain theory. In *Category Theory*. Springer-Verlag, 1991. Lecture Notes in Mathematics vol. 1488.

[Joy95a] A. Joyal. Free bicomplete categories. *Math. Rep., Acad. Sci. Canada*, 17(5):219–225, October 1995.

[Joy95b] A. Joyal. Free lattices, communication and money games. In *Proceedings of the 10th International Congress on Logic, Methodology and Philosophy of Science*, 1995.

[Koc81] A. Kock. *Synthetic Differential Geometry*. Cambridge University Press, 1981.

[Lai97] J. G. Laird. Full abstraction for functional languages with control. In *Twelfth Annual IEEE Symposium on Logic in Computer Science*, pages 58–64, 1997.

[LP96] J. Longley and G. Plotkin. Logical full abstraction and PCF. To appear in: Proceedings of Tbilisi Symposium on Logic, Language and Computation, SiLLI/CSLI, 1996.

[Man76] E. Manes. *Algebraic Theories*. Springer-Verlag, 1976.

[McC96a] G. McCusker. *Games and Full Abstraction for a functional metalanguage with recursive types*. Springer 1998.

[McC96b] G. McCusker. Games and full abstraction for FPC. In *International Symposium on Logic in Computer Science*, 1996.

[Mil75] R. Milner. Processes: a mathematical model of computing agents. In *Logic Colloquium '73*, pages 157–173. North Holland, 1975.

[Mil77] R. Milner. Fully abstract models of typed λ-calculi. *Theoretical Computer Science*, 4:1–22, 1977.

[Mil92] R. Milner. Functions as processes. *Mathematical Structures in Computer Science*, 2(2):119–142, 1992.

[MMP95] A. Mifsud, R. Milner, and J. Power. Control structures. In *Tenth Annual Symposium on Logic in Computer Science*, pages 188–198, 1995.

[MOM91] N. Marti-Oliet and J. Meseguer. From Petri nets to linear logic via categories: a survey. *International Journal on Foundations of Computer Science*, 2(4):297–399, 1991.

[Nic94] H. Nickau. Hereditarily sequential functionals. In *Proceedings of the Symposium on Logical Foundations of Computer Science: Logic at St. Petersburg*, volume 813 of *Lecture Notes in Computer Science*. Springer-Verlag, 1994.

[Ong95] C.-H. L. Ong. Correspondence between operational and denotational semantics: the full abstraction problem for PCF. In S. Abramsky, D. Gabbay, and T. S. E. Maibaum, editors, *Handbook of Logic in Computer Science*, volume 4, pages 270–356. Oxford University Press, 1995.

[Plo77] G. Plotkin. LCF considered as a programming language. *Theoretical Computer Science*, 5:223–255, 1977.

[See87] R. A. G. Seeley. Linear logic, $*$-autonomous categories and cofree coalgebras. In *Category theory, computer science and logic*. American Mathematical Society, 1987.

[Wal92] R. Walters. *Categories and Computer Science*. Cambridge University Press, 1992.

# 3 Algebraic Derivation of an Operational Semantics

**C. A. R. Hoare, He Jifeng, and Augusto Sampaio**

## 1 Introduction

Professional practice in a mature engineering discipline is based on relevant scientific theories, usually expressed in the language of mathematics. A mathematical semantics for a programming notation aims to provide a scientific basis for specification, design and implementation of computer programs expressed in that notation. The long-term goal is to improve the cost, quality, and duration of software engineering projects. Such a goal is akin to those of applied mathematics, but the most relevant concepts are discrete rather than continuous, and are taken from branches of logic and pure mathematics.

The study of program semantics may be rationally structured into three main branches, differentiated by their style of presentation. The *denotational* style relates each program to a description of its observable properties and behaviour when executed. This style is most directly applicable to capture of requirements, and the establishment of correctness of specifications and designs, even before the program has been written. The process languages CSP [12] and occam [16] have been given a semantics in this style by Bill Roscoe and his colleagues at Oxford [4, 7, 8]. The *algebraic* style characterises a programming language by a somewhat complete collection of equations which are postulated to hold between programs. These can be used directly to reason about specifications, to transform designs, and to optimise programs for efficient execution. The process language ACP [2] has been defined primarily in algebraic style by Jan Bergstra and his colleagues in Amsterdam. The *operational* style [19] gives meaning to a program by showing how its execution can be split into a sequence of atomic steps performed by a simple abstract mechanism. This gives an essential insight into the efficiency and even the computability of the language. An operational semantics is the starting point for the process notation CCS [17, 18], designed and explored by Robin Milner and his colleagues at Edinburgh and elsewhere.

One of the main inspirations of scientific research is the pursuit of simplicity. And simple theories are also easier to use in engineering practice. So the notations selected to illustrate a given semantic style will naturally be chosen to simplify their semantic treatment in that style. The selection may be subtly or deeply different from a selection made to optimise definition in a different style. In principle a definition method should not exert unintended bias on the details of the theory being defined; and in practice such biases can lead to unnecessary controversy between the adherents of theories defined by alternative methods. In natural science, such conflicts would be subjected to the decisive test of experiment. In computing science, no such test seems possible; and to a superficial view, differences in notation are taken as a symptom of the immaturity of the subject. Meanwhile, practising software engineers continue to use notations with no semantics or underlying theory at all.

The best way to resolve conflicts which are not amenable to experimental test is to prove that they do not exist, and this has often been successful in science and mathematics. For example, the physical theory of gravitation may be presented in terms of Newtonian force acting at a distance, or in field theory, or by Einsteinian geodesics; and all of these are provably equivalent. In mathematics, a topology may be defined equivalently by a family of sets, by a neighbourhood system, or by a closure operator. Scientists and mathematicians will be equally familiar with all approaches, and will use whichever presentation is easiest for the purpose in hand. (Of course, this does not prevent arguments about teaching syllabus design.)

To follow the example of mature disciplines, any programming theory recommended for practical use should be presentable in many different styles, thereby combining their individual distinctive advantages; and the theorist should guarantee that they are equivalent. A theory presented equivalently in many differing styles is much less susceptible to bias. Ideally, all the presentations should be equally simple, and even the proof of their consistency should be accessible and elegant. An inspiring example is the computational equivalence proved between transition systems and a logical language, Hennessy–Milner logic, which characterizes it. An algebraic semantics may be derived from a denotational simply by proving the validity of all its equations. Another important linkage between definitional styles is that between operational and algebraic semantics. Again, Robin Milner has led the way, showing how the algebraic properties of CCS can be derived from its structured operational semantics, by means of various kinds of bisimulation and congruence [18]. This direction of derivation was pursued by Vaandrager and his colleagues in [1]. In this tribute to Robin Milner, we also make a connection between algebraic and operational semantics, but in the reverse direction. Given a reasonably complete set of algebraic laws, it is possible to use them to transform any program to a kind of normal form, namely a simple loop: each iteration of the loop executes a single step of the operational semantics. If the algebraic laws are proved, postulated, or even defined to be valid for the programming language, it follows that the operational semantics are a valid implementation of it.

The technique is illustrated by application to a programming notation which is simple and non-controversial. It is essentially the sequential non-deterministic language introduced by Dijkstra to explore the Discipline of Programming [5]. It already has a denotational semantics in terms of predicate transformers. It already has an algebraic semantics very similar to that of the relational calculus [13]. It is not difficult to write down the obviously intended operational semantics; the only challenge is to prove its correctness in an elegant fashion, one which may be generalised to more complex languages in due course.

In Section 2, we summarise a selection of the algebraic laws that are presented as the algebraic specification of the language. These laws support inequational reasoning, using a partial order, representing a refinement or improvement relation. In a denotational model of the algebra this would correspond to Smyth ordering [20]. The easiest way to derive an operational semantics is to show that the final state of each operational step is an improvement on its initial state. Because improvement is transitive, the final state of the whole computation will be better than its initial state, the one which contains the whole program loaded for execution. This approach is worked out in Section 3.

Unfortunately this approach guarantees only partial correctness, ignoring the dangers of both deadlock and non-termination. The solution is outlined in Section 4. This starts with a definition of the meaning of an operational semantics, written as a program which repeatedly interprets its transition relation. Like a metacircular interpreter for a functional language, this is written in the programming language itself. Then in Section 5 the interpretation of the *text* of any program is proved to be equal in meaning to the program itself. The proof is conducted exclusively at the higher conceptual level of the programming language. It uses algebraic transformations, and avoids more operational or computational inductive modes of reasoning in favour of structural induction on the text of the program. A similar technique has been applied in the ProCoS project [3] to prove the correctness of a translator to machine code [14].

## 2 The Language and Its Algebraic Semantics

The programming language contains the following primitives and operators:

| | |
|---|---|
| $\bot$ | abort (the wholly useless program) |
| $II$ | skip (do nothing) |
| $x, y, \ldots, z := e, f, \ldots, g$ | multiple assignment |
| $P; Q$ | sequential composition |
| $P \sqcap Q$ | non-determinism (either $P$ or $Q$) |
| $P \lhd b \rhd Q$ | conditional: if b then $P$ else $Q$ |
| $\mu X :: P(X)$ | recursive program $X$ with body $P$ |

The notation $\bot$ suggests the bottom of a partial order. It will stand for a program that is useless because it fails to terminate. The notation $\sqcap$ denotes the greatest lower bound in the Smyth ordering. The notation $\lhd b \rhd$ for the conditional is motivated by a simplification in the algebraic laws. The notation $\mu$ is standard for the weakest fixed point; in our case the most non-deterministic.

For simplicity we will assume throughout that all expressions ($e, f, \ldots, g, b$ above) are everywhere defined. In addition to the above, the following operators will be used for reasoning about the correctness of the operational semantics:

| | |
|---|---|
| $\top$ | miracle (the mythical top of the lattice) |
| $x :\in S$ | generalised assignment ($x$ gets a value from $S$) |
| **var** $v$ | declaration introducing variable $v$ |
| **end** $v$ | end the scope of $v$ |

The algebraic semantics of our simple programming language is given by a set of laws (equations and inequations). In the remainder of this section we present a selection of algebraic laws which will be used to prove the correctness of an operational semantics for the language. A *complete*[1] set of laws for Dijkstra's language is given in [13, 14]. To ease future reference, we associate both a number and a name with each law.

### Monoid Properties

The execution of $II$ always terminates and leaves everything unchanged; therefore to precede or follow a program by $II$ does not make any difference.

**Law 2.1** $(II;\ P) = P = (P;\ II)$ $\langle ;\!-\ II\ \text{unit}\rangle$

To precede or follow a program $P$ by the command $\bot$ results in abortion.

**Law 2.2** $(\bot;\ P) = \bot = (P;\ \bot)$ $\langle ;\!-\!\bot\ \text{zero}\rangle$

It is the law $(\bot;\ P) = \bot$ that permits an eager execution of programs, starting from the left and proceeding rightward. The second half of the law $(P;\ \bot = \bot)$ states indirectly that the language is not reactive. There are no intermediate observations that permit one to distinguish a program that ends with a non-terminating loop from one that begins with such a loop. Note that the laws are not true in a purely relational model of non-determinism, where $\bot$ is the universal relation and $\top$ is the empty relation. However, they are valid for the subset of relations that are expressible in the notations of the programming language [15], which do not include $\top$.

Sequential composition is associative.

**Law 2.3** $P;\ (Q;\ R) = (P;\ Q);\ R$ $\langle ;\ \text{assoc}\rangle$

[1] The set of laws is complete in the sense that they are sufficient to reduce any finite (non-recursive) program to a *normal form*.

### Non-determinism

The operator $\sqcap$ satisfies many useful laws: it is associative, commutative, idempotent and has $\bot$ as zero. In addition, sequential composition distributes through non-determinism.

**Law 2.4** $P;\ (Q \sqcap R);\ S = (P;\ Q;\ S) \sqcap (P;\ R;\ S)$ $\langle ;\!- \sqcap \text{ distrib}\rangle$

### The Ordering Relation

Equational reasoning is sometimes too limited for purposes of program transformation. It has become standard practice to introduce a *refinement relation*: $P \sqsubseteq Q$ means that $Q$ is at least as good as $P$ in the sense that it will meet every purpose and satisfy every specification satisfied by $P$. Furthermore, substitution of $Q$ for $P$ in any context can only be an improvement. We define $\sqsubseteq$ in terms of $\sqcap$. Informally, if $Q$ is better than $P$ in all situations, then a non-deterministic choice between $P$ and $Q$ is just as bad as $P$; and vice versa.

DEFINITION 2.1 (THE ORDERING RELATION)

$$P \sqsubseteq Q \overset{def}{=} (P \sqcap Q) = P$$ □

The relation $\sqsubseteq$ is a complete partial ordering: it is reflexive, transitive and antisymmetric. Moreover, $\sqsubseteq$ has $\bot$ as its bottom element, $\sqcap$ as the *greatest lower bound*.

**Law 2.5** $\bot \sqsubseteq P$ $\langle \sqsubseteq -\bot \text{ bottom}\rangle$

**Law 2.6** $(R \sqsubseteq P \land R \sqsubseteq Q) \equiv R \sqsubseteq (P \sqcap Q)$ $\langle \sqsubseteq - \sqcap \text{ glb}\rangle$

Let $\mathcal{SP}$ be a set of programs. The greatest lower bound of $\mathcal{SP}$, denoted by $\sqcap \mathcal{SP}$, is defined by

$$(\sqcap \mathcal{SP} \sqsupseteq R) \quad \textbf{iff} \quad (\forall X : X \in \mathcal{SP} : X \sqsupseteq R)$$

Here we use the quantifier notations introduced by Dijkstra and adopted in $Z$

$(\forall$ *bound variables* : *range* : *body*$)$

In order to use the algebraic laws to transform subcomponents of compound programs, it is crucial that $P \sqsubseteq Q$ implies $F(P) \sqsubseteq F(Q)$, for all *contexts* $F$ (functions from programs to programs). This is equivalent to saying that $F$ (and consequently, all the operators of our language) must be *monotonic* with respect to $\sqsubseteq$. For example:

**Law 2.7** If $P \sqsubseteq Q$ then

**(1)** $(P \sqcap R) \sqsubseteq (Q \sqcap R)$ $\langle \sqcap$ monotonic$\rangle$

**(2)** $(R;\ P;\ S) \sqsubseteq (R;\ Q;\ S)$ $\langle ;$ monotonic$\rangle$

### Miracle

$\top$ can be used to serve any purpose; thus it is better than any program. The only trouble with $\top$ is that it cannot be implemented.

**Law 2.8** $\top \sqsupseteq P$ $\langle \sqsubseteq - \top$ top$\rangle$

To start a program by $\top$ is already a miracle.

**Law 2.9** $(\top;\ P) = \top$ $\langle ; - \top$ left zero$\rangle$

### Conditional

The most basic property of the conditional is that its left branch is executed if the condition holds initially; otherwise its right branch is executed.

**Law 2.10** $(P \lhd \mathit{true} \rhd Q) = P = (Q \lhd \mathit{false} \rhd P)$ $\langle \mathit{cond}$ unit$\rangle$

Sequential composition distributes leftward through a conditional.

**Law 2.11** $(P \lhd b \rhd Q);\ R = (P;\ R) \lhd b \rhd (Q;\ R)$ $\langle ; - \mathit{cond}$ left distrib$\rangle$

Conditional is idempotent and obeys a kind of associative law.

**Law 2.12** $(P \lhd b \rhd P) = P$ $\langle \mathit{cond}$ idemp$\rangle$

**Law 2.13** $(P \lhd b \rhd Q) \lhd c \rhd R = P \lhd b \wedge c \rhd (Q \lhd c \rhd R)$ $\langle \mathit{cond}$ assoc$\rangle$

We will use the notation $b_\perp$ to stand for an *assertion*, which may be written at any point in the program [6]. It behaves like $II$ if $b$ is true; otherwise it behaves like $\perp$. The following definition enables us to combine assertional reasoning with algebraic.

DEFINITION 2.2 (ASSERTION)

$$b_\perp \stackrel{\mathit{def}}{=} (II \lhd b \rhd \perp)$$ □

The *assumption* of a condition $b$, designated as $b^\top$, can be regarded as a miraculous test: it leaves the state unchanged (behaving like $II$) if $b$ is true; otherwise it behaves like $\top$.

DEFINITION 2.3 (ASSUMPTION)

$$b^{\top} \stackrel{def}{=} (\,II \lhd b \rhd \top) \qquad \square$$

The intended purpose of assertions and assumptions is to give to *pre-* and *postconditions* the status of programs. For example

$$a^{\top};\ P;\ b_{\bot}$$

represents the fact that $a$ is an obligation placed on the environment of program $P$: if the environment fails to provide a state satisfying $a$, $a^{\top}$ behaves like $\top$, which (from law $\langle ;-\top$ leftzero$\rangle$) makes the whole program behaves miraculously. On the other hand, an assertion is an obligation placed on the program itself. If $P$ fails to make $b$ true on its completion, it ends up behaving like $\bot$. The total correctness of the program $P$ with respect to these assertions may be established by proof of the algebraic inequation

$$P \sqsubseteq a^{\top};\ P;\ b_{\bot}$$

## Assignment

Obviously, the assignment of the value of a variable to itself does not change anything.

**Law 2.14** $(x := x) = II$ $\langle$Skip$\rangle$

In fact, such a vacuous assignment can be added to any other assignment without changing its effect.

**Law 2.15** $(x, y := e, y) = (x := e)$ $\langle$assignment identity$\rangle$

The list of variables and expressions may be subjected to the same permutation without changing the effect of the assignment.

**Law 2.16** $(x, y, z := e, f, g) = (y, x, z := f, e, g)$ $\langle$assignment symm$\rangle$

The sequential composition of two assignments to the same variable is easily combined to a single assignment.

**Law 2.17** $(x := e; x := f(x)) = (x := ((x := e);\ f(x))) = (x := f(e))$
$\langle$combine assignments$\rangle$

Here the expressions $(x := e);\ f(x)$ and $f(e)$ mean the same thing; they are easily calculated by substituting the expression $e$ for the variable $x$ in the expression $f(x)$. A similar law holds for multiple assignments, where $x$, $e$ and $f$ are lists of the same length.

From a strictly formal point of view, the substitution in law 2.17 may be confusing. Substitution of $e$ for $x$ in $f(x)$ is a syntactic operation on texts, whereas the $=$ in the middle of the law asserts equality of the *meaning* of the texts. To resolve the confusion, 2.17 may be understood as a pattern for generating an infinite collection of laws, each with different actual program variables in place of $x$, and different program expressions in place of $e$, $f(x)$ and $f(e)$, provided that $f(x)$ and $f(e)$ are related by the intended substitution. In future we shall rely on the reader's good will to make such interpretations as seem desirable.

Assignment distributes rightward through a conditional, replacing occurrences of the assigned variables in the condition by the corresponding expressions.

**Law 2.18** $x := e;\ (P \lhd b \rhd Q) = (x := e;\ P) \lhd ((x := e);\ b) \rhd (x := e;\ Q)$
$\langle := -cond$ right distrib$\rangle$

An assignment of a value to $x$ can be eliminated if $x$ has that value initially.

**Law 2.19** $((x = e)_\bot;\ (x := e)) = (x = e)_\bot$ ⟨void assignment⟩

### Recursion and Iteration

A recursive program $\mu X :: P(X)$ is defined as the least (weakest) fixed point of the equation

$X = P(X)$

Algebraically, recursion can be characterised by the following well-known fixed point laws.

**Law 2.20** $\mu X :: P(X) = P(\mu X :: P(X))$ ⟨$\mu$ fixed point⟩

**Law 2.21** $P(Y) \sqsubseteq Y \Rightarrow (\mu X :: P(X)) \sqsubseteq Y$ ⟨$\mu$ least fixed point⟩

Iteration can be defined as a special case of recursion:

DEFINITION 2.4 (ITERATION)

$$(b * P) \stackrel{def}{=} \mu\, X :: ((P;\ X) \lhd b \rhd II)$$ □

Therefore it is possible to prove (rather than just postulate) the properties of iteration given below. They are all special cases of more general theorems stated and proved in [14]. The first law shows how to transform a tail recursion into an iteration or vice versa.

THEOREM 2.1 $\mu X :: ((P;\ X) \lhd b \rhd Q) = (b * P);\ Q$ ⟨tail recursion⟩

The following non-trivial law allows the combination of loops with the same body if the condition of the first is stronger.

THEOREM 2.2 $((b \wedge c) * P);\ (b * P) = (b * P)$ ⟨$*$ combination⟩

### Variable Declaration

The declaration **var** $x, y, \ldots, z$ introduces the variables $x, y, \ldots, z$ for use in the program which follows. The undeclaration **end** $x, y, \ldots, z$ ends the scope of the variables $x, y, \ldots, z$ in the program that precedes it. In a reasonably implementable language, **var** $x$ and **end** $x$ have to be properly nested; and we will use them only in contexts which are properly nested. But for theoretical calculation it is convenient to relax the restriction that prohibits

**var** $x$; ... **var** $y$; ... **end** $x$; ... **end** $y$

It does not matter if variables are declared in one list or singly; nor does it matter in which order they are declared.

**Law 2.22** ⟨**dec** comm⟩

**(1)** (**var** $x$; **var** $y$) $=$ **var** $x, y$ $=$ (**var** $y$; **var** $x$)

**(2)** (**end** $x$; **end** $y$) $=$ **end** $x, y$ $=$ (**end** $y$; **end** $x$)

The scope of a variable may be increased (or reduced) without effect, provided that this does not interfere with other variables with the same name.

**Law 2.23** If $x$ does not occur in $P$ ⟨**dec** change scope⟩

**(1)** $P$; **var** $x$ $=$ **var** $x$; $P$

**(2)** **end** $x$; $P = P$; **end** $x$

Declaration distributes through a conditional, as long as the condition does not depend on the declared variable.

**Law 2.24** If $x$ does not occur in $b$

**var** $x$; $(P \lhd b \rhd Q) =$ (**var** $x$; $P) \lhd b \rhd$ (**var** $x$; $Q$) ⟨**dec** – *cond* distrib⟩

The corresponding law for **end** is already available (2.11).
**var** $x$ followed by **end** $x$ has no effect whatsoever.

**Law 2.25** (**var** $x$; **end** $x$) $= II$ ⟨**var** – **end** skip⟩

The next law postulates that (**end** $x$; **var** $x$) has the effect of undefining the value of $x$; a new value may be restored to $x$ by an assignment to $x$ that does not rely on its previous value.

**Law 2.26** If $x$ does not appear in $e$

(**end** $x$; **var** $x$; $x := e) = (x := e)$ ⟨**end** – **var** skip⟩

An assignment to a variable just before the end of its scope is irrelevant.

**Law 2.27** $(x := e;\ \mathbf{end}\, x) = \mathbf{end}\, x$ $\langle \mathbf{end} - := \text{ final value}\rangle$

### Generalised Assignment

Let $S$ be a set of expressions. The notation $x :\in S$ stands for a *generalised assignment command*, which assigns the value of any member of the set $S$ to $x$. Here the choice made by $x :\in S$ among the possible final values of $x$ is arbitrary. When the set $S$ is empty, $x :\in S$ behaves like $\top$.

**Law 2.28** $x :\in (S \cup T) = (x :\in S) \sqcap (x :\in T)$ $\langle :\in\ \sqcap\rangle$

**Law 2.29** $x :\in \emptyset = \top$ $\langle :\in\ \emptyset\rangle$

An assignment $x := e$ can be written as a generalised assignment.

**Law 2.30** $(x := e) = (x :\in \{e\})$ $\langle :\in \text{ intro}\rangle$

## 3 Derivation of the Step Relation

It is the purpose of an operational semantics to define the relationship between a program and its possible executions by machine. For this we need a concept of execution and a design of machine which are sufficiently realistic to provide guidance for practical implementation, but sufficiently abstract for application to the hardware of a variety of real computers. Furthermore it is the major aim of this paper to show that it is possible to derive this kind of semantics in such a way to guarantee its correctness (with respect to the algebraic semantics presented in the previous section). In this section, we take a very simplistic approach [10], leading to problems which will be solved in a later section.

In the most abstract view, a computation consists of a sequence of individual *steps*. Each step takes the machine from one state $m$ to a closely similar one $m'$; the transition is often denoted $m \longrightarrow m'$. Each step is drawn from a very limited repertoire, within the capabilities of a simple machine. A definition of the set of all possible single steps simultaneously defines the machine and all possible execution sequences that it can give rise to in the execution of a program.

The step can be defined as a relation between the machine state before the step and the machine state after. In the case of a stored program computer, the states are identified as pairs $(\mathtt{s}, \mathtt{P})$, where

- $\mathtt{s}$ is a *text*, defining the data state as an assignment of constants to all the variables.

• P is a *program text*, representing the rest of the program that remains to be executed. When this is II, there is no more program to be executed; the state (s, II) is the last state of any execution sequence that contains it, and s defines the final values of the variables.

Here we have to make the vital distinction between two natures of a program: *syntactic* (its textual representation) and *semantic* (its meaning, of which we assume only that it satisfies all the algebraic laws). In future, we use typewriter font to distinguish text from meaning: P is the text of a program whose meaning is $P$ and s is the text of the assignment $s$. This convention may presume upon the good will of the reader. A more familiar presentation [21] would make a clearer distinction between syntax and semantics, and use syntactic brackets ⟦P⟧ to stand for the semantic function which maps a text to its meaning. The important point is that the step relation $\longrightarrow$ is defined between the texts, rather than the meanings.

It is convenient to represent the data part s of the state by the text of an assignment

$$\texttt{x, y, \ldots, z := k, l, \ldots, m}$$

where k, l, ..., m are *constant* values, which the state ascribes to the variables x, y, ..., z respectively; and these are the entire collection of global variables of the program. Such an assignment is called *total*, and will be written v := e, where v stands for a list of all current variables, and e stands for a list of expressions of the same length. The convenience of this representation is that it permits the semantics of the machine state to be represented simply as the composition of the data state and the program state.

Suppose that $(s;\ P) \sqsubseteq t$, where s and t range over data states as represented above. This means that an implementation which is required to execute P in initial state s is permitted to execute the much shorter program $t$, and this immediately defines the final state t. Similarly, $(s;\ P) \sqsubseteq (t;\ Q)$ means that an implementation of the program $(s;\ P)$ is permitted instead to execute $(t;\ Q)$, and the result can only be an improvement of the original. This suggests a criterion for valid stepwise execution of a program. Each step merely replaces the current machine state (s, P) with a new machine state (t, Q), which is known from the algebraic laws to be an improvement of it. This account does not yet give a fully sufficient condition for total correctness of execution, but it explains the preliminary definition of the step relation given below.

DEFINITION 3.1 (STEP RELATION)

$$(\texttt{s, P}) \longrightarrow (\texttt{t, Q}) \stackrel{def}{=} (s;\ P) \sqsubseteq (t;\ Q) \qquad \Box$$

This definition allows the following transition rules numbered (1) to (7) to be derived as theorems, rather than being presented as postulates or definitions; they are easily proved from the algebraic laws of the programming language.

The effect of a total assignment $\mathtt{v} := \mathtt{e}$ starting on an initial state s is to end in a final state in which the variables of the program have constant values $(\mathtt{s};\ \mathtt{e})$, by which we mean the result of evaluating the list of expressions e with all variables in it replaced by their initial values in the data state s. Here we recall the simplifying assumption that expressions are everywhere defined.

(1) $(\mathtt{s}, \mathtt{v} := \mathtt{e}) \longrightarrow (\mathtt{v} := (\mathtt{s};\ \mathtt{e}), \mathtt{II})$

*Proof* from laws 2.1 ⟨;– *II* unit⟩ and 2.17 ⟨combine assignments⟩. □

A II in front of a program Q is immediately discarded.

(2) $(\mathtt{s}, (\mathtt{II};\ \mathtt{Q})) \longrightarrow (\mathtt{s}, \mathtt{Q})$

*Proof* from law 2.1 ⟨;– *II* unit⟩. □

The first step of the program (P; R) is the same as the first step of P, with R saved up for execution (by the preceding rule) when P has terminated.

(3) $(\mathtt{s}, (\mathtt{P};\ \mathtt{R})) \longrightarrow (\mathtt{t}, (\mathtt{Q};\ \mathtt{R}))$ whenever $(\mathtt{s}, \mathtt{P}) \longrightarrow (\mathtt{t}, \mathtt{Q})$

*Proof* from laws 2.3 ⟨; assoc⟩ and 2.7 ⟨; monotonic⟩. □

The first step of the program $(\mathtt{P} \sqcap \mathtt{Q})$ is to discard either one of the components P or Q. The criterion for making the choice is completely undetermined.

(4) $(\mathtt{s}, \mathtt{P} \sqcap \mathtt{Q}) \longrightarrow (\mathtt{s}, \mathtt{P})$
$(\mathtt{s}, \mathtt{P} \sqcap \mathtt{Q}) \longrightarrow (\mathtt{s}, \mathtt{Q})$

*Proof* from law 2.6 ⟨$\sqsubseteq - \sqcap$ glb⟩. □

The first step of the program $(\mathtt{P} \lhd \mathtt{b} \rhd \mathtt{Q})$ is also a choice, but unlike in the previous rule the choice is made in accordance with the truth or falsity of $(\mathtt{s};\ \mathtt{b})$, that is, the result of evaluating b with all free variables replaced by their initial values in the data state s.

(5) $(\mathtt{s}, \mathtt{P} \lhd \mathtt{b} \rhd \mathtt{Q}) \longrightarrow (\mathtt{s}, \mathtt{P})$ whenever $s;\ b$
$(\mathtt{s}, \mathtt{P} \lhd \mathtt{b} \rhd \mathtt{Q}) \longrightarrow (\mathtt{s}, \mathtt{Q})$ whenever $s;\ \neg b$

*Proof* from laws 2.18 ⟨:= −*cond* right distrib⟩ and 2.10 ⟨*cond* unit⟩. □

Recursion is implemented by the copy rule, whereby each recursive call within the procedure body is replaced by the whole recursive procedure.

(6) $(\mathtt{s}, \mu\mathtt{X} :: \mathtt{P}(\mathtt{X})) \longrightarrow (\mathtt{s}, \ \mathtt{P}(\mu\mathtt{X} :: \mathtt{P}(\mathtt{X})))$

*Proof* from law 2.20 $\langle \mu$ fixed point$\rangle$. □

The worst program $\perp$ engages in an infinite repetition of vacuous steps.

(7) $(\mathtt{s}, \perp) \longrightarrow (\mathtt{s}, \perp)$

*Proof* $\sqsubseteq$ is reflexive. □

The correctness of each of these transition rules has been proved simply and separately from the algebraic laws. But the main motive for formulating and proving these particular laws was to give a complete recipe for executing arbitrary programs expressed in the language, and for reasoning about such executions. In effect, the laws constitute an operational semantics whose step is *defined* as the *least* relation satisfying the transition rules (1) to (7). This is the view that underlies all presentations of operational semantics, and it is the view that we will take in the remainder of this paper. But our main goal is to show that, as so often in mathematics, the theorems of one branch become the axioms or the definitions of some apparently distinct branch; and it is these relationships that clearly illuminate the structure of mathematics as a coherent intellectual discipline.

## 4 An Interpreter

In the previous section, we used the refinement relation $\sqsubseteq$ to justify the seven clauses of the operational semantics of the language. The intention was to guarantee the consistency of the operational semantics, in the sense that every final state of an execution satisfies the predicate associated with the program. This is certainly a necessary condition for correctness. But it is not a sufficient condition. There are two kinds of error that it does not guard against:

(i) There may be too few transitions (or even none at all!). An omitted transition would introduce a new and unintended class of terminal state. A more subtle error would be omission of the second of the two laws (4) for $(\mathtt{P} \sqcap \mathtt{Q})$, thereby eliminating non-determinism from the language.

(ii) There may be too many transitions. For example, the transition

$(\mathtt{s}, \mathtt{Q}) \rightarrow (\mathtt{s}, \mathtt{Q})$

is entirely consistent with the approach of the previous section, since it just expresses reflexivity of implication. But its inclusion in the operational definition of the language would mean that every execution of every program could result in an infinite iteration of this dumb step.

Nevertheless, it is fairly obvious that the operational semantics derived in the previous section is the one that we want. The only program with no transition is `II`; the only program with more than one transition is $\mathtt{P} \sqcap \mathtt{Q}$; and the only way that an infinite sequence can arise is by recursion; and in this case the resulting non-termination is decreed to be the fault of the programmer rather than the implementor. It is the task of this section to formalise the statement of what we want of an operational semantics, so that it applies to more general languages, and can be subjected to rigorous proof.

The purpose of an operational semantics is to define the "machine code" of an abstract machine. One of the best and most common ways of defining a machine code is to write an interpreter for it in a high level programming language, whose meaning is already known; and a language immediately available for this purpose is the one whose algebraic properties have been given in Section 2. The criterion of total correctness of such an interpreter is that its application to a textual representation of any program can be proved to be equal to the meaning of the program itself. That is the nub of the theorem that will be formalised in this section and proved in the next.

But what does a program mean? Fortunately, we do not need to give a definitive answer to this question: we will accept *any* meaning which is consistent with the algebraic laws listed in Section 2. If our proof of correctness uses only these laws, it will be valid for any possible meaning that may be proposed now or later. We avoid the charge of circularity of definition by abandoning the claim to have defined the language, either by the algebraic or by the operational presentation of its semantics.

The alphabet of global variables of our interpreter will be

$s$ to hold the data state (as text)

$p$ to hold the program state (as text).

They will be updated on each step of the interpreter by selecting one of the possible transitions from the operational semantics

$$next =_{df} \{(\mathtt{t},\, \mathtt{q}) \mid (\mathtt{s},\, \mathtt{p}) \rightarrow (\mathtt{t},\, \mathtt{q})\}$$

$$(s,\, p) :\in next \qquad \ldots STEP$$

Note that the $(\mathtt{s},\, \mathtt{p})$ occurring in the right hand side of this assignment refers as usual to the current *textual values* of the interpreter's variables $(s,\, p)$.

This step is repeated until reaching a state in which there is no further transition

$$(next \neq \emptyset) * STEP \qquad \ldots LOOP$$

where the Boolean condition $next \neq \emptyset$ of the program *LOOP* can be replaced by the equivalent one $p \neq \mathtt{II}$, since the only program with no transitions is `II`.

The original program $P$ uses and updates the global variables $v$. But the interpreter does not change or even access these variables. It operates solely on the variables $s$ and $p$, containing textual representations of the values of the program variables and of the program remaining to be executed. In principle, two programs that operate on different collections of global variables cannot be compared at all. In order to compare the interpreter of P with the program $P$, the interpreter variables must obviously be declared local to the interpreter. Furthermore, the variable $s$ must be initialised to the current values of $v$ before the interpreter starts; and the final value of $s$ must be used at the end to define the final value of $v$.

The required effect is achieved with the aid of two auxiliary functions:

- $dump(v)$ yields a text of an assignment which assigns to the variables $v$ a list of constants equal to the current values of these variables, just like a symbolic dump from a debugging compiler.
- $v := undump(s)$ assigns to $v$ the values of the constants appearing on the right hand side of $s$, which is the text of an assignment.

The important property of these functions is that they are mutual inverses:

$$s = dump(undump(s))$$
$$v = undump(dump(v))$$

The following laws are restatements of the inverse property.

**Law 4.1** $(s := dump(v);\ v := undump(s)) = (s := dump(v))$.

**Law 4.2** $(v := undump(s);\ s := dump(v)) = (v := undump(s))$.

DEFINITION 4.1 (INTERPRETER) The full interpreter is defined to operate on the original program variables $v$ as follows, where the parameter $X$ ranges over program texts.

$\mathcal{I}(X) =_{df}$ **var** $s, p;\ (s, p := dump(v), X);$

$LOOP;$

$v := undump(s);$ **end** $s, p$ □

The interpreter is *correct* if $\mathcal{I}(\mathrm{P})$ describes exactly the same range of effects as are described by the program $P$ corresponding to the program text P

$\mathcal{I}(\mathrm{P}) = P$ for all programs P

The proof is outlined in the next section.

## 5 Correctness of the Interpreter

In section 3, each transition rule of the operational semantics was accompanied by proof of the corresponding algebraic inequation. But $\rightarrow$ has now been defined inductively as a relation between machine states, so we have to adapt the definition of section 3 as merely a definition of the *consistency* of an operational semantics (with the algebraic).

DEFINITION 5.1 (CONSISTENCY) A transition relation $\rightarrow$ is *consistent* with a semantical relation $\sqsubseteq$ if

$$(\mathtt{s}, \mathtt{P}) \rightarrow (\mathtt{t}, \mathtt{Q}) \Rightarrow (s;\ P) \sqsubseteq (t;\ Q) \qquad \square$$

A simple structural induction (based on the proofs of section 3) shows that any relation defined by (1) to (7) will be consistent. But this is not enough. Obviously, an empty transition relation is always consistent. We therefore need a criterion which will make the transition relation large enough. That criterion will be called *completeness*. It means that the non-deterministic union of all possible steps is an exhaustive description of the entire range of possible behaviours of the program.

DEFINITION 5.2 (COMPLETENESS) A transition relation $\rightarrow$ is *complete* if for any program $\mathtt{P} \neq \mathtt{II}$

$$s;\ P = \sqcap \{t;\ Q \mid (\mathtt{s}, \mathtt{P}) \rightarrow (\mathtt{t}, \mathtt{Q})\} \qquad \square$$

THEOREM 5.3 The operational semantics of section 3 is complete.

*Proof* When there is only one transition possible, the definition of completeness simplifies to

$$(\mathtt{s}, \mathtt{P}) \rightarrow (\mathtt{t}, \mathtt{Q}) \Rightarrow s;\ P = t;\ Q$$

This holds for all our transitions except for non-determinism. Here there are exactly two transitions, and we use the trivial fact $s;\ (P \sqcap Q) = (s;\ P) \sqcap (s;\ Q)$ $\square$

THEOREM 5.4 For any complete transition relation

$$\mathcal{I}(\mathtt{P}) \sqsubseteq P \qquad \text{for all programs } \mathtt{P}$$

*Proof* Define

$$T(\mathtt{P}) =_{df} (p = \mathtt{P})^{\top};\ (v := \mathit{undump}(s));\ P;\ \mathbf{end}\ s, p$$
$$T =_{df} \sqcap \{T(\mathtt{P}) \mid \mathtt{P}\ \mathit{is\ a\ program}\}$$

The execution of $T$ at the initial state where $p = \mathtt{P}$ behaves like the program $(s;\ P)$ except that the final values of the variables $s$ and $p$ are hidden at the end. Since the transition relation is complete one has

$$(\heartsuit) \qquad [(p \neq \mathtt{II})^{\top};\ T] = (p \neq \mathtt{II})^{\top};\ (STEP;\ T)$$

First we want to show

$$(*) \qquad (LOOP;\ v := undump(s);\ \mathbf{end}\ s,\ p) \sqsubseteq T.$$

$$\begin{aligned}
& T && \{\text{law } 2.12\} \\
&= T \lhd p \neq \mathtt{II} \rhd T && \{\text{def of } T \text{ and law } 2.1\} \\
&= T \lhd p \neq \mathtt{II} \rhd (v := undump(s);\ \mathbf{end}\ s,\ p) && \{\text{property } (\heartsuit)\} \\
&= (STEP;\ T) \lhd p \neq \mathtt{II} \rhd (v := undump(s);\ \mathbf{end}\ s,\ p) && \{(next = \emptyset) \equiv (p = \mathtt{II})\} \\
&= (STEP;\ T) \lhd next \neq \emptyset \rhd (v := undump(s);\ \mathbf{end}\ s,\ p)
\end{aligned}$$

The conclusion $(*)$ follows from laws 2.21 $\langle\mu$ least fixed point$\rangle$ and theorem 2.1 $\langle$tail recursion$\rangle$. Finally we have

$$\begin{aligned}
& \mathcal{I}(\mathtt{P}) && \{\text{def of } \mathcal{I} \text{ and } (*)\} \\
\sqsubseteq\ & \mathbf{var}\ s,\ p;\ (s,\ p := dump(v),\ \mathtt{P});\ T && \{\text{def of } T \text{ and law } 4.1\} \\
=\ & \mathbf{var}\ s,\ p;\ (s,\ p := dump(v),\ \mathtt{P});\ P;\ \mathbf{end}\ s,\ p && \{\text{laws } 2.23,\ 2.25 \text{ and } 2.27\} \\
=\ & P && \Box
\end{aligned}$$

Theorem 5.4 reflects the fact that the interpreter is *partially* correct, in the sense that whenever it terminates, any of its possible results is *consistent* with the meaning of the program. Unfortunately the inequation of Theorem 5.4 is in the wrong direction for *total* correctness. For this we need to show that the interpretation is an *improvement* on the meaning of the program

$$P \sqsubseteq \mathcal{I}(\mathtt{P}) \qquad \text{for all programs } \mathtt{P}$$

The proof in this direction seems to be considerably more difficult.

In fact, what we will prove is a much stronger property of the interpreter: it is a *homomorphism* from the algebra of program texts (the initial or term algebra) to the algebra of program meanings. This requires proof of the usual set of distribution properties through all operators in the signature of the language; but since we need a proof only in one direction, the equations can be replaced by inequations, giving what we will call a *directed* homomorphism.

$$\begin{aligned}
\mathcal{I}(\mathtt{II}) &\sqsupseteq \mathit{II}\\
\mathcal{I}(\mathtt{v := e}) &\sqsupseteq (v := e)\\
\mathcal{I}(\bot) &\sqsupseteq \bot\\
\mathcal{I}(\mathtt{P} \sqcap \mathtt{Q}) &\sqsupseteq \mathcal{I}(\mathtt{P}) \sqcap \mathcal{I}(\mathtt{Q})\\
\mathcal{I}(\mathtt{P} \lhd \mathtt{b} \rhd \mathtt{Q}) &\sqsupseteq \mathcal{I}(\mathtt{P}) \lhd b \rhd \mathcal{I}(\mathtt{Q})\\
\mathcal{I}(\mathtt{P;\ Q}) &\sqsupseteq \mathcal{I}(\mathtt{P})\,;\ \mathcal{I}(\mathtt{Q})\\
\mathcal{I}(\mu \mathtt{X} :: \mathtt{P(X)}) &\sqsupseteq \mu X :: P(X)
\end{aligned}$$

All of these can be proved by algebraic calculation, although the case of sequential composition seems much harder than the others. We give the proof only in the case of sequential composition and recursion.

The proof of the distributivity of $\mathcal{I}$ over sequential composition is based on the fact that the interpretation of $\mathtt{P;\ Q}$ does not depend on the nature or even the existence of $\mathtt{Q}$ until $\mathtt{P}$ is $\mathtt{II}$.

LEMMA 5.5 $(p \neq \mathtt{II})^{\top}; (p := p; \mathtt{Q}); \mathit{STEP} = (p \neq \mathtt{II})^{\top}; \mathit{STEP}; (p := p; \mathtt{Q})$

*Proof* By calculation of the *STEP*. □

Note that the assignment $p := p; \mathtt{Q}$ is one that appends the text of $\mathtt{Q}$ as a constant to the current textual value of the interpreter's variable $p$.

LEMMA 5.6 $(p := p; \mathtt{Q});\ (p \neq \mathtt{II} \wedge p \neq \mathtt{II; Q}) * \mathit{STEP} \sqsupseteq \mathit{LOOP};\ (p := p; \mathtt{Q})$

*Proof* Let $\mathit{LOOP}1 \stackrel{def}{=} (p \neq \mathtt{II} \wedge p \neq \mathtt{II; Q}) * \mathit{STEP}$.

$\quad \mathit{LHS}$ {law 2.20}

$= (p := p; \mathtt{Q}); ((\mathit{STEP}; \mathit{LOOP}1) \lhd\ p \neq \mathtt{II} \wedge p \neq \mathtt{II; Q} \rhd \mathit{II})$ {law 2.18}

$= ((p := p; \mathtt{Q}); \mathit{STEP}; \mathit{LOOP}1) \lhd\ p \neq \mathtt{II} \rhd (p := p; \mathtt{Q})$ {lemma 5.5}

$= (\mathit{STEP}; \mathit{LHS}) \lhd\ p \neq \mathtt{II} \rhd (p := p; \mathtt{Q})$ {laws 2.19 and 2.17}

$= (\mathit{STEP}; \mathit{LHS}) \lhd\ p \neq \mathtt{II} \rhd (p := \mathtt{II; Q})$

from which and law 2.21 $\langle \mu$ least fixed point$\rangle$ it follows that

$\quad \mathit{LHS}$

$\sqsupseteq \mu X :: ((\mathit{STEP};\ X) \lhd\ p \neq \mathtt{II} \rhd (p := \mathtt{II; Q}))$ {theorem 2.1}

$= \mathit{RHS}$ □

Now we can prove that $\mathcal{I}$ distributes through sequential composition.

THEOREM 5.7 $\mathcal{I}(\mathtt{P;\ Q}) \sqsupseteq \mathcal{I}(\mathtt{P}); \mathcal{I}(\mathtt{Q})$.

*Proof*

$$
\begin{array}{ll}
\quad \mathcal{I}(\mathtt{P};\, \mathtt{Q}) & \{\text{theorem 2.2}\} \\
= \mathbf{var}\ s, p;\ (s, p := dump(v), \mathtt{P}); & \\
\quad (p := p;\, \mathtt{Q});\ ((p \neq \mathtt{II} \wedge p \neq (\mathtt{II};\, \mathtt{Q})) * STEP); & \\
\quad LOOP;\ v := undump(s);\ \mathbf{end}\ s, p & \{\text{lemma 5.6}\} \\
\sqsupseteq \mathbf{var}\ s, p;\ (s, p := dump(v), \mathtt{P});\ LOOP; & \\
\quad (p := \mathtt{II};\, \mathtt{Q});\ LOOP;\ v := undump(s);\ \mathbf{end}\ s, p & \{\text{laws 2.26 and 2.23}\} \\
= \mathbf{var}\ s, p;\ (s, p := dump(v), \mathtt{P});\ LOOP;\ \mathbf{end}\ v;\ \mathbf{var}\ v; & \\
\quad (p := \mathtt{II};\, \mathtt{Q});\ LOOP;\ v := undump(s);\ \mathbf{end}\ s, p & \{\text{laws 2.27 and 4.2}\} \\
= \mathbf{var}\ s, p;\ (s, p := dump(v), \mathtt{P});\ LOOP; & \\
\quad v := undump(s);\ s := dump(v);\ \mathbf{end}\ v;\ \mathbf{var}\ v; & \\
\quad (p := \mathtt{II};\, \mathtt{Q});\ LOOP;\ v := undump(s);\ \mathbf{end}\ s, p & \{\text{def of } next(s, \mathtt{II};\, \mathtt{Q})\} \\
= \mathbf{var}\ s, p;\ (s, p := dump(v), \mathtt{P});\ LOOP; & \\
\quad v := undump(s);\ s := dump(v);\ \mathbf{end}\ v;\ \mathbf{var}\ v; & \\
\quad (p := \mathtt{Q});\ LOOP;\ v := undump(s);\ \mathbf{end}\ s, p & \{\text{laws 2.23 and 2.26}\} \\
= \mathcal{I}(\mathtt{P});\, \mathcal{I}(\mathtt{Q}) & \square
\end{array}
$$

The following theorem shows that any directed homomorphism on the non-recursive operators of the language can be lifted neatly to the recursive case.

THEOREM 5.8 $\mathcal{I}(\mu \mathtt{X} :: \mathtt{P(X)}) \sqsupseteq \mu X :: P(X)$.

*Proof*

$$
\begin{array}{ll}
\quad \mathcal{I}(\mu \mathtt{X} :: \mathtt{P(X)}) & \{\text{laws 2.20, 2.18 and 2.10}\} \\
= \mathbf{var}\ s, p;\ (s, p := dump(v), \mu \mathtt{X} :: \mathtt{P(X)}); & \\
\quad STEP;\ LOOP;\ v := undump(s);\ \mathbf{end}\ s, p & \{\text{def of } next\} \\
= \mathbf{var}\ s, p;\ (s, p := dump(v), \mathtt{P}(\mu \mathtt{X} :: \mathtt{P(X)})); & \\
\quad LOOP;\ v := undump(s);\ \mathbf{end}\ s, p & \{\text{def of } \mathcal{I}\} \\
= \mathcal{I}(\mathtt{P}(\mu \mathtt{X} :: \mathtt{P(X)})) & \{\text{distributivity of } \mathcal{I}\} \\
\sqsupseteq P(\mathcal{I}(\mu \mathtt{X} :: \mathtt{P(X)})) &
\end{array}
$$

The conclusion follows by law 2.21 $\langle \mu$ least fixed point$\rangle$. □

These theorems provide all the cases needed to prove the main theorem of this paper.

THEOREM 5.9 $\mathcal{I}(\mathrm{P}) = P$ for any program P.

*Proof* Using structural induction on the text of the program P. □

Normally, in proving the correctness of an implementation, it is sufficient to show that it is an improvement on its specification

$$P \sqsubseteq \mathcal{I}(\mathrm{P})$$

Our stronger equation is required to show that the interpreter also preserves incorrectness of programs.

The homomorphism property of the interpreter makes precise the condition under which an operational semantics can claim to be *structured*. It would be nice to formulate some general conditions, like the tyxt-tyft format for structural operational semantics [9], and so obtain a guarantee that an operational semantics will give an interpreter which is a homomorphism. We leave this as a challenge for the interested reader.

## 6 Conclusion

This paper has presented an approach to deriving an operational from an algebraic semantics of a programming language. A weak form of *consistency* of the operational semantics has been easily proved by the algebraic laws, showing how each step replaces its state by a better one. A complementary task was to prove that the rules are complete (not in the logical sense, but) in the sense that there are no omitted transitions which would introduce a new and unintended class of terminal states. Furthermore, our approach also prevents the inclusion of unnecessary transitions which could, for example, lead to non-termination. That is established by the equation displayed as Theorem 5.9. The approach has been illustrated by application to a very simple programming language for expression of sequential algorithms with possible non-determinism. It is our hope that it will generalise to more complex languages, perhaps those which combine communication and concurrency with sequential updating of state. In [10] we give an indication how this may be done for a *labelled* transition relation like that of the structural operational semantics. It shows how the external choice operator (+ of CCS) has to be factored into the definition of the *STEP*. But [10] stops short of the complexities of Section 5.

The validity of the theorem depends utterly on the validity of the algebraic laws which are needed to prove it. These may be proved as theorems from some suitable model, like those used in a traditional denotational semantics, as suggested in [15]. Or they may just be postulated as axioms, like those of group theory; they then constitute an axiomatic semantics of the language. Or they may be derived by one of the many kinds of bisimulation [18] from an operational semantics; in this case Theorem 5.9 is still a useful check of the completeness of the laws and the appropriateness of the choice of the bisimulation. It is a sign of the maturity of a mathematical theory that it is founded on cyclic proofs of interderivability of alternative presentations.

There is no unique starting point, fixed a priori for development of a theory of programming; and the choice between them could depend on the overall goal of the study. If the area of study is defined by a set of operational steps, this is because the goal is to explore a range of alternative bisimulation relations leading to a variety of algebras; the operational definition of CCS [17] has been an inspirational example of this approach. An alternative goal is to define a programming language at the highest level of abstraction, so that it can be implemented, with equivalent logical effect but with differing efficiency, in a number of radically different ways. A good example is the parallelism and communication of occam [16], which has a distributed implementation on multiprocessors, and a timeshared implementation on a single processor; or it can even be implemented by transformation to a single sequential program. That is why CSP starts with a denotational and algebraic presentation rather than an operational one. An additional advantage of starting with algebra is that widely different languages often share a large collection of the same laws; and proofs based on these laws can be widely reused. But no matter what the starting point, the essential goal is the same: a consistent unified theory about programming [15], which can combine the merits of many styles of presentation, without being unduly influenced by any one of them.

**Acknowledgements** We gratefully acknowledge the support of the European Community under ESPRIT Basic Research Action **ProCoS** and **Concur**. Augusto Sampaio acknowledges the financial support provided by the Brazilian Research Council (CNPq). He Jifeng acknowledges support provided by the EPSRC on grant number GR/K58708. We wish to thank F.M. Vaandrager for his comments on earlier version of this paper. The material of the paper was presented at the Newton Institute Symposium in the summer of 1995.

## References

[1] L. Aceto, B. Bloom and F. W. Vaandrager *Turning SOS rules into equations. Information and Computation* 111(1), 1–52, 1994.

[2] J. A. Bergstra and J. W. Klop. *Algebra of Communicating Processes with Abstraction. Theoretical Computer Science*, 37(1): 77–121, 1985.

[3] D. Bjorner. *A ProCoS project description.* In I. Plander, editor, Proc. of International Conference on AI and Robotics, North-Holland, 1989.

[4] S. D. Brookes, C. A. R. Hoare and A. W. Roscoe. *A theory of communicating sequential processes. Journal of the ACM*, 31: 560–599, 1984.

[5] E. W. Dijkstra. *A Discipline of Programming*. Prentice-Hall, Englewood Cliffs, 1976.

[6] R. Floyd. *Assigning meaning to programs.* In *Mathematical Aspect of Computer Science*, XIX: 19–32, 1967.

[7] M. Goldsmith, A. W. Roscoe and B. G. O. Scott. *Denotational Semantics for occam2. Transputer Communications: Part 1*, 1(2): 65–91, 1993.

[8] M. Goldsmith, A. W. Roscoe and B. G. O. Scott. *Denotational Semantics for occam2. Transputer Communications: Part 2*, 2(1): 25–67, 1993.

[9] J. F. Groote, F. W. Vaandrager. *Structural operational semantics and bisimulation as a congruence.* Springer-Verlag, Lecture Notes in Computer Science 372, 423–438, 1989.

[10] He Jifeng and C. A. R. Hoare. *From Algebra to operational semantics. Information Processing Letters*, 45: 75–80, 1993.

[11] M. C. Hennessy and R. Milner. *Algebraic Laws for Nondeterminism and Concurrency. Journal of ACM*, 32(1): 137–161, 1985.

[12] C. A. R. Hoare. *Communicating Sequential Processes.* Prentice-Hall International Series in Computer Science. Prentive Hall, 1985.

[13] C. A. R. Hoare *et al. Laws of Programming. Communications of the ACM*, 30(8): 672–686, August 1987.

[14] C. A. R. Hoare, He Jifeng and A. Sampaio. *Normal Form Approach to Compiler Design. Acta Informatica*, 30: 701–739, 1993.

[15] C. A. R. Hoare and He Jifeng. *Unifying Theories of Programming.* Prentice-Hall International Series in Computer Science. Prentice Hall, 1998.

[16] INMOS Ltd. *occam 2 Reference Manual.* Prentice-Hall International Series in Computer Science. Prentice Hall, 1988.

[17] R. Milner. *A Calculus of Communicating Systems*. Springer-Verlag, Lecture Notes in Computer Science 92, 1980.

[18] R. Milner. *Communication and Concurrency*. Prentice-Hall International Series in Computer Science, Prentice Hall, 1989.

[19] G. D. Plotkin. *A Structural Approach to Operational Semantics.* Technical report, DAIMI-FN-19, Aarhus University, Denmark, 1981.

[20] M. B. Smyth. *Power domain and predicate transformers: a topological view.* Springer-Verlag, Lecture Notes in Computer Science 154, 662–675, 1983.

[21] C. Strachey. *Fundamental Concepts in Programming Languages.* Technical Report of Programming Research Group, Oxford University, 1968.

# 4 From Banach to Milner: Metric Semantics for Second Order Communication and Concurrency

**Jaco de Bakker and Franck van Breugel**

## Introduction

In recent years the study of higher order programming notions has become a central topic in the field of semantics. Seminal in this development have been two schools of research, viz that of typed $\lambda$-calculi in the area of functional programming (see, e.g., Barendregt's survey [Bar92]), and that of higher order processes in the theory of concurrency (see, e.g., the theses by Sangiorgi [San92] and Thomsen [Tho90]). The aim of the present paper is to provide another perspective on this problem area by studying higher order notions embedded in the traditional setting of imperative languages.

The higher order notion we study is *second order communication.*[1] It differs from ordinary—what is also called first order—communication in the following way. First order communication arises when one process sends a value along a channel to another process. For example, in Milner's CCS [Mil80] this is expressed by the two actions send $(c, e)$ and receive $(c, v)$ occurring in two parallel processes.[2] Synchronised execution of these actions results in the transmission of the current value of the expression $e$ along the channel $c$ from the one process to the other. The latter assigns the received value to the variable $v$. In second order communication, statements rather than values are transmitted. At the moment of synchronised execution of the actions send $(c, s)$ and receive $(c, x)$ the statement $s$ is passed along the channel $c$. The sent statement is stored in the statement variable $x$. The stored statement can be called by call $(x)$. Second order communication provides the programmer with a powerful and elegant abstraction mechanism. One encounters this higher order phenomenon in, e.g., $\gamma$-calculus [Bou89], CHOCS [Tho95], Concurrent ML [Rep92], Facile [TLK96], and higher order $\pi$-calculus [San93].

In Section 12.2 of [BV96] (see also [BM88, KR90]), De Bakker and De Vink present an operational and a denotational semantics for a simple imperative language with first order communication. Here, we study its second order variant.[3] Though this higher order notion is, we hope, conceptually quite simple, a not so simple arsenal of semantic tools is necessary to adapt De Bakker and De Vink's models, and to obtain a full picture of the relationship between them.

The definition of the *operational semantics* is given in terms of a *labelled transition system*, as advocated by Plotkin [Plo81]. In the configurations of the labelled transition

[1] For a discussion why it is called second order we refer the reader to Section 7.4 of Milner's tutorial [Mil91].

[2] In [Mil80] the notation $\bar{c}e$ and $cv$ is used.

[3] For simplicity we have left out the recursive while statement. However, we can add this construct without too much difficulty (see Chapter 8 of [Bre97]).

system we encounter *syntactic stores*, a second order variant of ordinary states. A state assigns to each variable its value. A syntactic store assigns to each statement variable a statement. The transitions are labelled by pairs of states and syntactic stores. For example, for a state $\sigma$ and a syntactic store $\theta$ we have the transition

$$[\mathsf{call}\,(x),\ \sigma, \theta] \xrightarrow{(\sigma,\theta)} [\theta(x),\ \sigma, \theta].$$

Second order communication is modelled operationally by assigning the statement $s$ to the statement variable $x$ in the syntactic store. The labelled transition system is *finitely branching*: each configuration has only finitely many outgoing transitions. We exploit this fact when relating the operational and denotational semantics.

The *denotational semantics* employs a *complete 1-bounded ultrametric space*. This space is defined as the solution of a recursive equation. In the equation we use *semantic stores*. A semantic store assigns to each statement variable the denotation of a statement. Denotationally, second order communication is modelled by passing the denotation of the statement $s$ along the channel $c$ and storing it in statement variable $x$ in the semantic store.

To link the operational and denotational semantics we introduce an *intermediate semantics*. Like the operational semantics the intermediate model is defined by means of a labelled transition system. In the configurations of the system we use the (denotational) semantic stores rather than the (operational) syntactic stores. Because we use semantic stores in the intermediate semantics, we have for a state $\sigma$ and a semantic store $\vartheta$ the transition

$$[\mathsf{call}\,(x),\ \sigma, \vartheta] \xrightarrow{(\sigma,\vartheta)} [\vartheta(x),\ \sigma, \vartheta].$$

As a consequence, denotations of statements like $\vartheta(x)$ appear in the configurations of the labelled transition system. This phenomenon is known as *processes as terms* (see Rutten's [Rut92]). The presence of these denotations causes that the system is not finitely branching—a property which is usually exploited in relating different semantic models. By providing metrics to the configurations and labels we obtain a *metric labelled transition system* (see [Bre94]). This metric labelled transition system is *compactly branching*: each configuration has a compact set of outgoing transitions. This fact is used in relating the operational and denotational semantics via the intermediate model.

*Banach's fixed point theorem* [Ban22] plays a crucial role in the present paper. It is used to define the metric space employed in the denotational semantics, various operators on this space, and the intermediate semantics. Furthermore, the operational, intermediate, and denotational semantic models are related by means of this theorem.

In Section 1 we introduce a simple imperative language with second order communication. The operational and denotational semantics are presented in Section 2 and 3 and are related in Section 4. In the concluding section we discuss some related issues including bisimulation and full abstractness. Appendix A contains some notions from metric topology and Banach's theorem.

**Acknowledgements** The authors have benefited from discussions with Marcello Bonsangue, Michele Boreale, Uffe Engberg, Furio Honsell, Marina Lenisa, Vincent van Oostrom, Prakash Panangaden, Jan Rutten, and Davide Sangiorgi, and the constructive comments of the referees.

## 1 Language Definition

We present a simple imperative language with assignment, send, and receive statements, statement calls, conditional statements, sequential composition, and parallel composition. The syntax of the language is given in BNF. The basic components are a set $(v \in)$ *Var*[4] of *variables*, a set $(e \in)$ *Exp* of *expressions*, a set $(b \in)$ *BExp* of *Boolean expressions*, a set $(c \in)$ *Chan* of *channels*, and a set of $(x \in)$ *SVar* of *statement variables*. We assume a simple syntax for the sets of expressions and Boolean expressions.

DEFINITION 1.1 The set $(s \in)$ *Stat* of *statements* is defined by

$$s ::= v := e \mid \mathsf{send}\,(c, s) \mid \mathsf{receive}\,(c, x) \mid \mathsf{call}\,(x) \mid \mathsf{if}\; b\; \mathsf{then}\; s\; \mathsf{else}\; s\; \mathsf{fi} \mid s\,;\, s \mid s \parallel s.$$

For this language we present an operational and a denotational semantics in the following two sections.

## 2 Operational Semantics

The operational semantics is defined by means of a labelled transition system. In the configurations of the labelled transition system we encounter statements, states, and syntactic stores.[5]

To the set of statements we add the *empty statement* E. We use this statement in the labelled transition system to signal successful termination.

DEFINITION 2.1 The set $(\bar{s} \in)$ $Stat_{\mathrm{E}}$ is defined by

$$\bar{s} ::= \mathrm{E} \mid s.$$

[4] Throughout this paper we use the notation $(x \in)$ $X$ for the introduction of a set or space $X$ with typical elements $x, x', x_1, \ldots$

[5] In Section 3 we introduce *semantic* stores.

Let ($\alpha \in$) *Val* be a set of *values*. A state is used to store and retrieve the values of the variables. It assigns to each variable its value.

DEFINITION 2.2 The set ($\sigma \in$) *State* of *states* is defined by

$$State = Var \to Val.$$

Storing the value $\alpha$ for the variable $v$ in the state $\sigma$ gives rise to the state $\sigma\{\alpha/v\}$ defined by

$$\sigma\{\alpha/v\}(w) = \begin{cases} \alpha & \text{if } v = w \\ \sigma(w) & \text{if } v \neq w \end{cases}$$

We use a syntactic store to administrate which statements the statement variables are assigned to.

DEFINITION 2.3 The set ($\theta \in$) *SynStore* of *syntactic stores* is defined by

$$SynStore = SVar \to Stat.$$

Assigning the statement $s$ to the statement variable $x$ in the syntactic store $\theta$ gives rise to the syntactic store $\theta\{s/x\}$ defined by

$$\theta\{s/x\}(y) = \begin{cases} s & \text{if } x = y \\ \theta(y) & \text{if } x \neq y \end{cases}$$

In the configurations of the labelled transition system a statement is accompanied by a state and a syntactic store. The labels are syntactic actions: pairs of states and syntactic stores, or syntactic communications. A syntactic communication $c\,!\,s$ is used to model the willingness to send the statement $s$ along the channel $c$. To model the willingness to receive a statement along the channel $c$ and store it in the statement variable $x$ we use the syntactic communication $c\,?\,x$.

DEFINITION 2.4 The set ($\pi \in$) *SynCom* of *syntactic communications* is defined by

$$\pi ::= c\,!\,s \mid c\,?\,x.$$

DEFINITION 2.5 The set ($\rho \in$) *SynAct* of *syntactic actions* is defined by

$$\rho ::= (\sigma, \theta) \mid \pi.$$

We assume that the evaluation of a (Boolean) expression always terminates and delivers a value (*true* or *false*). These evaluations are modelled by the given semantic functions

$$\mathcal{E} : Exp \to State \to Val$$

and

$\mathcal{B}\colon \mathit{BExp} \to \mathit{State} \to \{\mathit{true},\ \mathit{false}\}.$

With $\mathcal{E}[\![e]\!](\sigma)$ we denote the value of the expression $e$ in the state $\sigma$. The value of the Boolean expression $b$ in the state $\sigma$ is indicated by $\mathcal{B}[\![b]\!](\sigma)$.

For succinctness we use $;_\mathrm{E}$ and $\|_\mathrm{E}$ defined by

$$\bar{s}_1 ;_\mathrm{E} \bar{s}_2 = \begin{cases} \bar{s}_2 & \text{if } \bar{s}_1 = \mathrm{E} \\ \bar{s}_1 ; \bar{s}_2 & \text{otherwise} \end{cases}$$

and

$$\bar{s}_1 \|_\mathrm{E} \bar{s}_2 = \begin{cases} \mathrm{E} & \text{if } \bar{s}_1 = \mathrm{E} \text{ and } \bar{s}_2 = \mathrm{E} \\ \bar{s}_2 & \text{if } \bar{s}_1 = \mathrm{E} \text{ and } \bar{s}_2 \neq \mathrm{E} \\ \bar{s}_1 & \text{if } \bar{s}_1 \neq \mathrm{E} \text{ and } \bar{s}_2 = \mathrm{E} \\ \bar{s}_1 \parallel \bar{s}_2 & \text{otherwise} \end{cases}$$

The transition relation is presented in

DEFINITION 2.6 The transition relation $\to$ is defined as the smallest subset of

$$(\mathit{Stat}_\mathrm{E} \times \mathit{State} \times \mathit{SynStore}) \times \mathit{SynAct} \times (\mathit{Stat}_\mathrm{E} \times \mathit{State} \times \mathit{SynStore})$$

satisfying the following axioms and rules.

(1) $[v := e,\ \sigma, \theta] \xrightarrow{(\sigma\{\alpha/v\},\theta)} [\mathrm{E},\ \sigma\{\alpha/v\}, \theta]$, where $\alpha = \mathcal{E}[\![e]\!](\sigma)$

(2) $[\mathsf{send}\,(c, s),\ \sigma, \theta] \xrightarrow{c!s} [\mathrm{E},\ \sigma, \theta]$

(3) $[\mathsf{receive}\,(c, x),\ \sigma, \theta] \xrightarrow{c?x} [\mathrm{E},\ \sigma, \theta]$

(4) $[\mathsf{call}\,(x),\ \sigma, \theta] \xrightarrow{(\sigma,\theta)} [\theta(x),\ \sigma, \theta]$

(5) $$\frac{[s_1,\ \sigma, \theta] \xrightarrow{\rho} [\bar{s}_1,\ \sigma', \theta']}{[\mathsf{if}\ b\ \mathsf{then}\ s_1\ \mathsf{else}\ s_2\ \mathsf{fi},\ \sigma, \theta] \xrightarrow{\rho} [\bar{s}_1,\ \sigma', \theta']}, \text{ if } \mathcal{B}[\![b]\!](\sigma) = \mathit{true}$$

(6) $$\frac{[s_2,\ \sigma, \theta] \xrightarrow{\rho} [\bar{s}_2,\ \sigma', \theta']}{[\mathsf{if}\ b\ \mathsf{then}\ s_1\ \mathsf{else}\ s_2\ \mathsf{fi},\ \sigma, \theta] \xrightarrow{\rho} [\bar{s}_2,\ \sigma', \theta']}, \text{ if } \mathcal{B}[\![b]\!](\sigma) = \mathit{false}$$

(7) $$\frac{[s_1,\ \sigma, \theta] \xrightarrow{\rho} [\bar{s}_1,\ \sigma', \theta']}{[s_1\ ;\ s_2,\ \sigma, \theta] \xrightarrow{\rho} [\bar{s}_1\ ;_{\mathrm{E}}\ s_2,\ \sigma', \theta']}$$

(8) $$\frac{[s_1,\ \sigma, \theta] \xrightarrow{\rho} [\bar{s}_1,\ \sigma', \theta']}{[s_1 \parallel s_2,\ \sigma, \theta] \xrightarrow{\rho} [\bar{s}_1 \parallel_{\mathrm{E}} s_2,\ \sigma', \theta']}$$

(9) $$\frac{[s_1,\ \sigma, \theta] \xrightarrow{c!s} [\bar{s}_1,\ \sigma', \theta'] \qquad [s_2,\ \sigma, \theta] \xrightarrow{c?x} [\bar{s}_2,\ \sigma'', \theta'']}{[s_1 \parallel s_2,\ \sigma, \theta] \xrightarrow{(\sigma, \theta\{s/x\})} [\bar{s}_1 \parallel_{\mathrm{E}} \bar{s}_2,\ \sigma,\ \theta\{s/x\}]}$$

We have omitted the symmetric versions of the rules (8) and (9).

A transition

$$[s,\ \sigma,\ \theta] \xrightarrow{(\sigma', \theta')} [\bar{s},\ \sigma',\ \theta']$$

denotes that the statement $s$ in the (current) state $\sigma$ and syntactic store $\theta$ can perform a computation step resulting in the statement $\bar{s}$ and the (possibly updated) state $\sigma'$ and syntactic store $\theta'$. Note that transitions of the form

$$[s,\ \sigma,\ \theta] \xrightarrow{(\sigma', \theta')} [\bar{s},\ \sigma'',\ \theta''],$$

with $\sigma' \neq \sigma''$ or $\theta' \neq \theta''$, are not provable. A transition

$$[s_1,\ \sigma,\ \theta] \xrightarrow{c!s} [\bar{s}_1,\ \sigma,\ \theta]$$

denotes that the statement $s_1$ in the state $\sigma$ and syntactic store $\theta$ is willing to send the statement $s$ along the channel $c$. Note that the state and syntactic store do not change. Since communication is synchronous, the statement $s$ can only be sent if there is a statement $s_2$ in parallel with $s_1$ in the same state and syntactic store willing to receive a statement along the channel $c$ (and store it in some statement variable $x$) denoted by

$$[s_2,\ \sigma,\ \theta] \xrightarrow{c?x} [\bar{s}_2,\ \sigma,\ \theta].$$

Also in this case the state and syntactic store stay the same.

The labelled transition system is *finitely branching*: every configuration has only finitely many outgoing transitions, i.e., for all $\bar{s} \in \mathit{Stat}_{\mathrm{E}}$, $\sigma \in \mathit{State}$, and $\theta \in \mathit{SynStore}$, the set

$$\mathcal{FB}([\bar{s},\ \sigma,\ \theta]) = \{(\rho, [\bar{s}',\ \sigma',\ \theta']) \mid [\bar{s},\ \sigma,\ \theta] \xrightarrow{\rho} [\bar{s}',\ \sigma',\ \theta']\}$$

is finite. This property is one of the ingredients of the proof relating the operational and denotational semantics (see Property 4.17 and 4.19). An alternative formulation[6] is presented in

PROPERTY 2.7 The function $\mathcal{FB} : (\mathit{Stat}_{\mathrm{E}} \times \mathit{State} \times \mathit{SynStore}) \to \mathcal{P}(\mathit{SynAct} \times (\mathit{Stat}_{\mathrm{E}} \times \mathit{State} \times \mathit{SynStore}))$ defined by

$$\mathcal{FB}([\bar{s}, \sigma, \theta]) = \{(\rho, [\bar{s}', \sigma', \theta']) \mid [\bar{s}, \sigma, \theta] \xrightarrow{\rho} [\bar{s}', \sigma', \theta']\}$$

is an element of $(\mathit{Stat}_{\mathrm{E}} \times \mathit{State} \times \mathit{SynStore}) \to \mathcal{P}_f\,(\mathit{SynAct} \times (\mathit{Stat}_{\mathrm{E}} \times \mathit{State} \times \mathit{SynStore}))$.

*Proof* By structural induction on $\bar{s}$. □

In the operational semantics we collect the labels of successive transitions. We do not consider transitions modelling (unsuccessful) communication attempts, i.e., transitions labelled by syntactic communications. In this way we obtain sequences of pairs, each pair consisting of a state and a syntactic store. We distinguish three types of sequences:

- finite sequences modelling successfully terminating computations (the final configuration is of the form $[\mathrm{E}, \sigma, \theta]$),
- finite sequences followed by a $\delta$ modelling deadlocking computations (the final configuration is of the form $[s, \sigma, \theta]$ and can only make unsuccessful communication attempts), and
- infinite sequences modelling nonterminating computations.

DEFINITION 2.8 The set $(\mathit{State} \times \mathit{SynStore})^{\infty}_{\delta}$ is defined by

$$\begin{aligned}&(\mathit{State} \times \mathit{SynStore})^{\infty}_{\delta}\\ &\quad = (\mathit{State} \times \mathit{SynStore})^{*} \cup (\mathit{State} \times \mathit{SynStore})^{*} \cdot \{\delta\} \cup (\mathit{State} \times \mathit{SynStore})^{\omega}.\end{aligned}$$

Given a statement $s$ and a state $\sigma$ and syntactic store $\theta$, the (linear) operational semantics $\mathcal{O}_{\mathrm{L}}$ gives us the set $\mathcal{O}_{\mathrm{L}}\,[\![s]\!](\sigma, \theta)$ of sequences modelling all possible computations of $s$ started in $\sigma$ and $\theta$.

DEFINITION 2.9 The *operational semantics*

$$\mathcal{O}_{\mathrm{L}} : \mathit{Stat} \to (\mathit{State} \times \mathit{SynStore}) \to \mathcal{P}\big((\mathit{State} \times \mathit{SynStore})^{\infty}_{\delta}\big)$$

[6] We present this alternative formulation as it can be generalised more conveniently (see Property 4.7).

is defined by

$$\mathcal{O}_{\mathrm{L}}[\![s]\!](\sigma,\theta) =$$

$$\{(\sigma_1,\theta_1)(\sigma_2,\theta_2)\cdots(\sigma_n,\theta_n) \mid [s,\ \sigma,\ \theta] \xrightarrow{(\sigma_1,\theta_1)} [s_1,\ \sigma_1,\ \theta_1] \xrightarrow{(\sigma_2,\theta_2)} \cdots \xrightarrow{(\sigma_n,\theta_n)} [\mathrm{E},\ \sigma_n,\ \theta_n]\} \cup$$

$$\{(\sigma_1,\theta_1)(\sigma_2,\theta_2)\cdots(\sigma_n,\theta_n)\delta \mid [s,\ \sigma,\ \theta] \xrightarrow{(\sigma_1,\theta_1)} [s_1,\ \sigma_1,\ \theta_1] \xrightarrow{(\sigma_2,\theta_2)} \cdots \xrightarrow{(\sigma_n,\theta_n)} [s_n,\ \sigma_n,\ \theta_n] \text{ deadlocks}\} \cup$$

$$\{(\sigma_1,\theta_1)(\sigma_2,\theta_2)\cdots \mid [s,\ \sigma,\ \theta] \xrightarrow{(\sigma_1,\theta_1)} [s_1,\ \sigma_1,\ \theta_1] \xrightarrow{(\sigma_2,\theta_2)} \cdots\},$$

where $[s,\ \sigma,\ \theta]$ *deadlocks* if $[s,\ \sigma,\ \theta] \xrightarrow{(\sigma',\theta')}$ for no $\sigma' \in \mathit{State}$ and $\theta' \in \mathit{SynStore}$.

The operational semantics is not compositional with respect to parallel composition as is shown in the following example (cf. [Mil93]). The operational semantics is compositional with respect to all the other operators.

EXAMPLE 2.10 We have that

$$\mathcal{O}_{\mathrm{L}}[\![v := 1\ ;\ v := 2]\!] = \mathcal{O}_{\mathrm{L}}[\![v := 1\ ;\ v := v + 1]\!]$$

but

$$\mathcal{O}_{\mathrm{L}}[\![(v := 1\ ;\ v := 2) \parallel v := 3]\!] \neq \mathcal{O}_{\mathrm{L}}[\![(v := 1\ ;\ v := v + 1) \parallel v := 3]\!].$$

Also

$$\mathcal{O}_{\mathrm{L}}[\![\mathsf{receive}\,(c, x)]\!] = \mathcal{O}_{\mathrm{L}}[\![\mathsf{send}\,(c, s)]\!]$$

but

$$\mathcal{O}_{\mathrm{L}}[\![\mathsf{receive}\,(c, x) \parallel \mathsf{send}\,(c, s)]\!] \neq \mathcal{O}_{\mathrm{L}}[\![\mathsf{send}\,(c, s) \parallel \mathsf{send}\,(c, s)]\!].$$

Furthermore,

$$\mathcal{O}_{\mathrm{L}}[\![\mathsf{send}\,(c_1, x) \parallel (\mathsf{send}\,(c_1, x)\ ;\ \mathsf{send}\,(c_2, x))]\!]$$
$$= \mathcal{O}_{\mathrm{L}}[\![\mathsf{send}\,(c_1, x)\ ;\ (\mathsf{send}\,(c_1, x) \parallel \mathsf{send}\,(c_2, x))]\!].$$

Note that the former statement can make a $c_1\ !\ x$-transition to the statement send $(c_1, x)$ ; send $(c_2, x)$ which can only make a $c_1\ !\ x$-transition. The latter statement can only make a $c_1\ !\ x$-transition to the statement send $(c_1, x) \parallel$ send $(c_2, x)$ which can make both a $c_1\ !\ x$-

and a $c_2\ !\ x$-transition. As a consequence,

$$\mathcal{O}_L [\![ (\mathsf{send}\ (c_1, x) \parallel (\mathsf{send}\ (c_1, x)\ ;\ \mathsf{send}\ (c_2, x))) \parallel (\mathsf{receive}\ (c_1, x)\ ;\ \mathsf{receive}\ (c_2, x)) ]\!]$$
$$\neq \mathcal{O}_L [\![ (\mathsf{send}\ (c_1, x)\ ;\ (\mathsf{send}\ (c_1, x) \parallel \mathsf{send}\ (c_2, x))) \parallel (\mathsf{receive}\ (c_1, x)\ ;\ \mathsf{receive}\ (c_2, x)) ]\!].$$

## 3 Denotational Semantics

We need a space containing more structure than the sets of sequences used in the operational semantics to give a denotational semantics (cf. Example 2.10). In Definition 3.4 below we introduce the complete (1-bounded ultrametric) space $\mathbb{P}$ (see Definition A.1 and A.5). The elements of this (branching) space can be viewed as tree like objects. It will turn out that this space is rich enough to model parallel composition (and all other constructs) compositionally.

In the definition of the space $\mathbb{P}$ we encounter the spaces *SemStore*, *SemCom*, and *SemAct*—the semantic counterparts of the sets *SynStore*, *SynCom*, and *SynAct*, respectively. Before defining these spaces we first turn the sets *State*, *SVar*, and *Chan* into spaces by endowing them with the discrete metric (see Definition A.2). Below, we employ various operations on spaces which are defined in the appendix.

A semantic store assigns to each statement variable the denotation of a statement rather than a statement as a syntactic store does.

DEFINITION 3.1 The space ($\vartheta \in$) *SemStore* of *semantic stores* is defined by

$$\mathit{SemStore} = \mathit{SVar} \to \tfrac{1}{2} \cdot \mathbb{P}.$$

The role of the $\frac{1}{2}\cdot$ in the above definition is discussed later. It will turn out that the $\frac{1}{2}\cdot$ is essential both in the definition of the space $\mathbb{P}$ and the (branching) denotational semantics $\mathcal{D}_B$.

Instead of sending statements as we did operationally, denotationally we send denotations of statements.

DEFINITION 3.2 The space ($\varpi \in$) *SemCom* of *semantic communications* is defined by

$$\mathit{SemCom} = \left(\mathit{Chan} \times \tfrac{1}{2} \cdot \mathbb{P}\right) + (\mathit{Chan} \times \mathit{SVar}).$$

In Definition 2.5 we defined the set of syntactic actions. Its semantic counterpart is presented in the following definition.

DEFINITION 3.3 The space ($\varrho \in$) *SemAct* of *semantic actions* is defined by

$$SemAct = (State \times SemStore) + SemCom.$$

Note that we use $\rho$ to range over syntactic actions and $\varrho$ to range over semantic actions. Similarly, $\theta$ and $\pi$ range over syntactic stores and syntactic communications and $\vartheta$ and $\varpi$ range over semantic stores and semantic communications.

DEFINITION 3.4 The space ($\bar{p} \in$) $\mathbb{P}$ is defined by the equation

$$\mathbb{P} \cong \{\mathrm{E}\} + \left(State \times SemStore \to^1 \mathcal{P}_{nc}\left(SemAct \times \tfrac{1}{2} \cdot \mathbb{P}\right)\right).$$

The elements of the space $\mathbb{P}$ can be viewed as tree like objects. We distinguish the following two subspaces of $\mathbb{P}$.

- $\{\mathrm{E}\}$: Like in the operational semantics, also in the denotational semantics we use E to model successful termination. It can be seen as the empty tree consisting of one node and no edges.
- $(p \in)\mathbb{P}\backslash\{\mathrm{E}\}$: Let, for $\sigma, \sigma' \in State$ and $\vartheta, \vartheta' \in SemStore$,

$$p(\sigma, \vartheta) = \{\langle \varrho_1, \bar{p}_1 \rangle, \ldots, \langle \varrho_m, \bar{p}_m \rangle\}$$
$$p(\sigma', \vartheta') = \{\langle \varrho'_1, \bar{p}'_1 \rangle, \ldots, \langle \varrho'_n, \bar{p}'_n \rangle, \ldots\}$$

The semantic entity $p$ can be viewed as the labelled tree

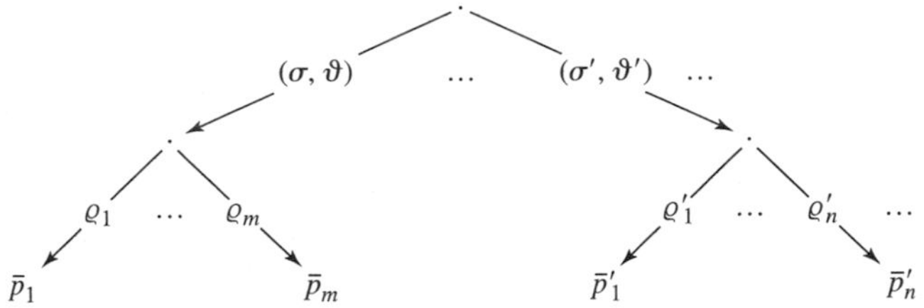


In the above picture the upper level of branching is due to the functional nature of $p$. It records the change of the state and semantic store caused by the environment (a process in parallel). The lower level of branching stems from the set structure of $p(\sigma, \vartheta)$ and $p(\sigma', \vartheta')$. It records the nondeterminism caused by the parallel composition. The labels at the lower level are semantic actions. This allows us to model communication attempts. For example, if the environment changes the state to $\sigma$ and the semantic store to $\vartheta$, then the semantic actions $\varrho_1, \ldots, \varrho_m$ are possible followed by $\bar{p}_1, \ldots, \bar{p}_m$, respectively.

Note that we use the convention that $p$ ranges over $\mathbb{P}\backslash\{\mathrm{E}\}$ and $\bar{p}$ ranges over $\mathbb{P}$.

Let us explain how to solve the above equation. (Patience, the development of the denotational semantics resumes shortly.) The equation is of the form

$$\mathbb{P} \cong F(\mathbb{P})$$

with $F$ being an operation assigning to each (nonempty complete) space another (nonempty complete) space. A solution of the equation is a (nonempty complete) space being isometric (see Definition A.11) to its $F$-image. We shall treat the isometries as identities and thus elide their use. They can be put in without any difficulties, but will clutter up the presentation. To conclude that the equation has a (unique) solution (up to isometry) we exploit the theory developed by America and Rutten in [AR89]. As is shown in that paper, the operation $F$ can be extended to a functor $F$ on a suitable category of spaces. Since the equation is of the form

$$\mathbb{P} \cong \cdots \mathbb{P} \cdots \to^1 \cdots \mathbb{P} \cdots,$$

i.e., there are both positive and negative[7] occurrences of $\mathbb{P}$ in the equation, nonexpansive embedding-projection pairs are used as arrows in the category. The arrows are such that the equation has a (unique) solution if and only if the functor has a (unique) fixed point. In Theorem 4.4 of [AR89] it is shown that a (locally contractive[8] and) contractive functor has a (unique) fixed point. The proof of this theorem relies on Banach's theorem (see Theorem A.13). The functor $F$ satisfies both conditions. If we had left out one of the $\frac{1}{2}\cdot$'s in the above definitions, the functor obtained would have been neither locally contractive nor contractive.

To define the denotational semantics we have to introduce for each syntactic operator a semantic counterpart. Apart from the semantic sequential composition and parallel composition, the semantic operators are defined straightforwardly (see Definition 3.6). The semantic sequential composition and parallel composition are defined as the unique fixed point (Banach's theorem) of a contractive function (see Definition A.12) from the nonempty complete space $\mathbb{P} \times \mathbb{P} \to^1 \mathbb{P}$ to itself. We only give the equations characterising the semantic operators. For the details we refer the reader to [BV96, KR90] where various related semantic operators are defined in this way.

DEFINITION 3.5 The operator ; is the unique function $; : \mathbb{P} \times \mathbb{P} \to^1 \mathbb{P}$ satisfying

$$\bar{p}_1 ; \bar{p}_2 = \begin{cases} \bar{p}_2 & \text{if } \bar{p}_1 = \mathrm{E} \\ \lambda(\sigma, \vartheta) \cdot \{\langle \varrho, \bar{p}'_1 ; \bar{p}_2 \rangle \mid \langle \varrho, \bar{p}'_1 \rangle \in \bar{p}_1(\sigma, \vartheta)\} & \text{if } \bar{p}_1 \neq \mathrm{E} \end{cases}$$

[7] An occurrence of $\mathbb{P}$ is negative if it is to the left, hereditarily, of an odd number of $\to^1$'s.

[8] This terminology is taken from [RT92]. In [AR89] hom-contractive is used instead. The conditions hom-contractive and contractive can be found in Definition 4.3 and 3.12 of [AR89].

The operator $\|$ is the unique function $\| : \mathbb{P} \times \mathbb{P} \to^1 \mathbb{P}$ satisfying

$$\bar{p}_1 \parallel \bar{p}_2 = \begin{cases} \mathrm{E} & \text{if } \bar{p}_1 = \mathrm{E} \text{ and } \bar{p}_2 = \mathrm{E} \\ \bar{p}_2 & \text{if } \bar{p}_1 = \mathrm{E} \text{ and } \bar{p}_2 \neq \mathrm{E} \\ \bar{p}_1 & \text{if } \bar{p}_1 \neq \mathrm{E} \text{ and } \bar{p}_2 = \mathrm{E} \\ \bar{p}_1 \mathbin{\|\!\lfloor} \bar{p}_2 \cup \bar{p}_2 \mathbin{\|\!\lfloor} \bar{p}_1 \cup \bar{p}_1 \lfloor \bar{p}_2 \cup \bar{p}_2 \lfloor \bar{p}_1 & \text{if } \bar{p}_1 \neq \mathrm{E} \text{ and } \bar{p}_2 \neq \mathrm{E} \end{cases}$$

where

$$p_1 \mathbin{\|\!\lfloor} p_2 = \lambda(\sigma, \vartheta) \cdot \{\langle \varrho, \bar{p}_1 \parallel p_2 \rangle \mid \langle \varrho, \bar{p}_1 \rangle \in p_1(\sigma, \vartheta)\}$$

and

$$p_1 \lfloor p_2 = \lambda(\sigma, \vartheta) \cdot \{\langle (\sigma, \vartheta\{\bar{p}/x\}), \bar{p}_1 \parallel \bar{p}_2 \rangle \mid \langle (c, \bar{p}), \bar{p}_1 \rangle \\ \in p_1(\sigma, \vartheta) \wedge \langle (c, x), \bar{p}_2 \rangle \in p_2(\sigma, \vartheta)\}$$

and

$$p_1 \cup p_2 = \lambda(\sigma, \vartheta) \cdot p_1(\sigma, \vartheta) \cup p_2(\sigma, \vartheta).$$

Having introduced the space $\mathbb{P}$ and the (nontrivial) semantic operators we are ready to give the denotational semantics.

DEFINITION 3.6 The *denotational semantics* $\mathcal{D}_{\mathrm{B}} : \mathit{Stat} \to \mathbb{P}$ is defined by

$$\begin{aligned}
\mathcal{D}_{\mathrm{B}} [\![ v := e ]\!] &= \lambda(\sigma, \vartheta) \cdot \{\langle (\sigma\{\alpha/v\}, \vartheta), \mathrm{E} \rangle\}, \text{ where } \alpha = \mathcal{E} [\![ e ]\!](\sigma) \\
\mathcal{D}_{\mathrm{B}} [\![ \mathsf{send}\,(c, s) ]\!] &= \lambda(\sigma, \vartheta) \cdot \{\langle (c, \mathcal{D}_{\mathrm{B}} [\![ s ]\!]), \mathrm{E} \rangle\} \\
\mathcal{D}_{\mathrm{B}} [\![ \mathsf{receive}\,(c, x) ]\!] &= \lambda(\sigma, \vartheta) \cdot \{\langle (c, x), \mathrm{E} \rangle\} \\
\mathcal{D}_{\mathrm{B}} [\![ \mathsf{call}\,(x) ]\!] &= \lambda(\sigma, \vartheta) \cdot \{\langle (\sigma, \vartheta), \vartheta(x) \rangle\} \\
\mathcal{D}_{\mathrm{B}} [\![ \mathsf{if}\ b\ \mathsf{then}\ s_1\ \mathsf{else}\ s_2\ \mathsf{fi} ]\!] & \\
&= \lambda(\sigma, \vartheta) \cdot \begin{cases} \mathcal{D}_{\mathrm{B}} [\![ s_1 ]\!](\sigma, \vartheta) \text{ if } \mathcal{B} [\![ b ]\!](\sigma) = \mathit{true} \\ \mathcal{D}_{\mathrm{B}} [\![ s_2 ]\!](\sigma, \vartheta) \text{ if } \mathcal{B} [\![ b ]\!](\sigma) = \mathit{false} \end{cases} \\
\mathcal{D}_{\mathrm{B}} [\![ s_1 \,;\, s_2 ]\!] &= \mathcal{D}_{\mathrm{B}} [\![ s_1 ]\!] \,;\, \mathcal{D}_{\mathrm{B}} [\![ s_2 ]\!] \\
\mathcal{D}_{\mathrm{B}} [\![ s_1 \parallel s_2 ]\!] &= \mathcal{D}_{\mathrm{B}} [\![ s_1 ]\!] \parallel \mathcal{D}_{\mathrm{B}} [\![ s_2 ]\!]
\end{aligned}$$

Of course one has to check that, for all $s \in \mathit{Stat}$, $\mathcal{D}_{\mathrm{B}} [\![ s ]\!] \in \mathbb{P}$. This can be verified by structural induction on $s$. We only consider the case $s = \mathsf{call}\,(x)$ as it shows us the importance of the positioning of the $\frac{1}{2}\cdot$'s in the above definitions. Obviously, for all $\sigma \in \mathit{State}$ and $\vartheta \in \mathit{SemStore}$, the set $\{\langle (\sigma, \vartheta), \vartheta(x) \rangle\}$ is compact. Let $\sigma, \sigma' \in \mathit{State}$ and $\vartheta, \vartheta' \in \mathit{SemStore}$.

We have that

$$
\begin{aligned}
& d(\{\langle(\sigma, \vartheta), \vartheta(x)\rangle\}, \{\langle(\sigma', \vartheta'), \vartheta'(x)\rangle\}) \\
&\quad = d(\langle(\sigma, \vartheta), \vartheta(x)\rangle, \langle(\sigma', \vartheta'), \vartheta'(x)\rangle) \\
&\quad = \max\{d((\sigma, \vartheta), (\sigma', \vartheta')), \tfrac{1}{2} \cdot d(\vartheta(x), \vartheta'(x))\} \\
&\quad \leq \max\{d((\sigma, \vartheta), (\sigma', \vartheta')), d(\vartheta, \vartheta')\} \quad \text{[see below]} \\
&\quad = d\,((\sigma, \vartheta), (\sigma', \vartheta')).
\end{aligned}
$$

The $\frac{1}{2}\cdot$ in Definition 3.1 is essential, since

$$
\begin{aligned}
& d_{SemStore}(\vartheta, \vartheta') \\
&\quad = \sup_{x \in SVar} d_{\frac{1}{2}\cdot\mathbb{P}}(\vartheta(x), \vartheta'(x)) \\
&\quad = \sup_{x \in SVar} \tfrac{1}{2} \cdot d_{\mathbb{P}}\,(\vartheta(x), \vartheta'(x)) \\
&\quad \geq \tfrac{1}{2} \cdot d_{\mathbb{P}}(\vartheta(x), \vartheta'(x)).
\end{aligned}
$$

## 4 Relating Operational and Denotational Semantics

The operational and denotational semantics differ in various aspects:

- the operational semantics is defined in terms of transitions,
- the denotational semantics is compositional,
- the operational semantics uses syntactic stores whereas the denotational semantics employs semantic stores,
- the denotational semantics records communication attempts in contrast to the operational semantics, which only models deadlock, and
- the operational semantics is a linear model—it uses sets of sequences—whereas the denotational semantics is a branching model—it utilises tree like objects.

Relating the operational and denotational semantics we use the following three operators. The linearise operator *LIN* abstracts from some of the structure of the branching space arriving at a linear space. It removes (unsuccessful) communication attempts and extracts deadlock information. The semantify operator *sem* assigns to each syntactic store (action) a corresponding semantic store (action). The semantify operator *SEM* is an obvious extension of *sem* from a syntactic linear space to a semantic linear space.

In the rest of this section we prove

THEOREM 4.1 For all $s \in Stat$, $\sigma \in State$, and $\theta \in SynStore$, $SEM(\mathcal{O}_{\mathrm{L}}[\![s]\!](\sigma, \theta)) = LIN(\mathcal{D}_{\mathrm{B}}[\![s]\!])(\sigma, sem(\theta))$.

To prove the above theorem, the operational semantics $\mathcal{O}_{\mathrm{L}}$ suggests the use of induction on transitions whereas the denotational semantics $\mathcal{D}_{\mathrm{B}}$ hints at using structural induction. We introduce a (branching) intermediate semantics $\mathcal{I}_{\mathrm{B}}$ which is defined in terms of transitions and is compositional, allowing us to use both proof principles. The proof is divided into two parts. First, an extension of the denotational semantics is shown to be equal to the intermediate semantics. Second, the intermediate semantics is related to the operational semantics by means of the linearise and semantify operators. Both parts are proved by uniqueness of fixed point. This proof technique is due to Kok and Rutten [KR90]. Numerous applications of this technique can be found in [BV96]. To prove the semantic models $\mathcal{S}_1$ and $\mathcal{S}_2$ equal by uniqueness of fixed point, we introduce a semantics transformation $\mathcal{T}$. This transformation is a contractive function from a nonempty complete space of semantic models to itself. According to Banach's theorem, $\mathcal{T}$ has a unique fixed point. By showing that both $\mathcal{S}_1$ and $\mathcal{S}_2$ are a fixed point of $\mathcal{T}$, we can conclude that the models are equal.

## 4.1 Intermediate Semantics

Like the denotational semantics, the intermediate semantics assigns to each statement an element of the space $\mathbb{P}$. This requires that the labelled transition system employs semantic stores and semantic actions rather than their syntactic counterparts. Clause (4) of Definition 2.6 then obtains the form

$$[\mathsf{call}\,(x),\ \sigma,\ \vartheta] \xrightarrow{(\sigma,\vartheta)} [\vartheta\,(x),\ \sigma,\ \vartheta].$$

As a consequence, denotations of statements like $\vartheta\,(x)$ appear in the configurations. Besides elements of $\mathbb{P}$ we also encounter mixed terms like $p\,;\,s$. We extend the set *Stat* of statements and the set $\mathbb{P} \setminus \{\mathrm{E}\}$ (forgetting about the metric for a moment) with a restricted set of mixed terms in

DEFINITION 4.2 The set $(r \in)$ $Stat^{+}$ is defined by

$$r ::= s \mid p \mid r\,;\,s \mid r \parallel r.$$

Note that we do not consider E nor mixed terms built from E in the set $Stat^{+}$ of extended statements. We comment on this choice later. Like in the operational semantics we use the empty statement E to signal successful termination. For technical convenience all the semantic models introduced in this section will also assign a meaning to the empty statement. We add E in

DEFINITION 4.3 The set $(\bar{r} \in)$ $Stat_{\mathrm{E}}^{+}$ is defined by

$\bar{r} ::= \mathrm{E} \mid r.$

The configurations of the labelled transition system consist of an extended statement, a state, and a semantic store. The labels are semantic actions. We introduce two axioms such that the configuration $[p, \sigma, \vartheta]$, with $p(\sigma, \vartheta) = \{\langle \varrho_1, \bar{p}_1 \rangle, \ldots, \langle \varrho_n, \bar{p}_n \rangle, \ldots\}$, can make the following transitions:

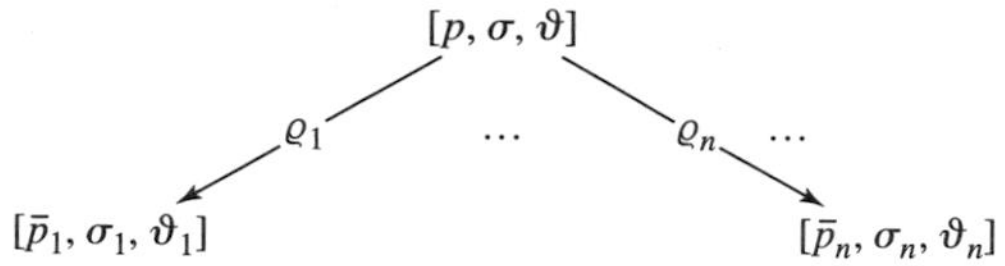


where

$$(\sigma_i, \vartheta_i) = \begin{cases} (\sigma, \vartheta) & \text{if } \varrho_i \in SemCom \\ \varrho_i & \text{if } \varrho_i \in State \times SemStore \end{cases}$$

The other axioms and rules are straightforward modifications of the ones of Definition 2.6.

DEFINITION 4.4 The transition relation $\rightarrow$ is defined as the smallest subset of

$(Stat_{\mathrm{E}}^{+} \times State \times SemStore) \times SemAct \times (Stat_{\mathrm{E}}^{+} \times State \times SemStore)$

satisfying the following axioms and rules.

(1) $[v := e, \sigma, \vartheta] \xrightarrow{(\sigma\{\alpha/v\}, \vartheta)} [\mathrm{E}, \sigma\{\alpha/v\}, \vartheta]$, where $\alpha = \mathcal{E}[\![e]\!](\sigma)$

(2) $[\mathsf{send}\,(c, s), \sigma, \vartheta] \xrightarrow{(c, \mathcal{D}[\![s]\!])} [\mathrm{E}, \sigma, \vartheta]$

(3) $[\mathsf{receive}\,(c, x), \sigma, \vartheta] \xrightarrow{(c, x)} [\mathrm{E}, \sigma, \vartheta]$

(4) $[\mathsf{call}\,(x), \sigma, \vartheta] \xrightarrow{(\sigma, \vartheta)} [\vartheta(x), \sigma, \vartheta]$

(5) $[p, \sigma, \vartheta] \xrightarrow{(\sigma', \vartheta')} [\bar{p}, \sigma', \vartheta']$, if $\langle (\sigma', \vartheta'), \bar{p} \rangle \in p(\sigma, \vartheta)$

(6) $[p, \sigma, \vartheta] \xrightarrow{\varpi} [\bar{p}, \sigma, \vartheta]$, if $\langle \varpi, \bar{p} \rangle \in p(\sigma, \vartheta)$

$$(7)\quad \frac{[s_1,\ \sigma,\ \vartheta] \xrightarrow{\varrho} [\bar{s}_1,\ \sigma',\ \vartheta']}{[\mathsf{if}\ b\ \mathsf{then}\ s_1\ \mathsf{else}\ s_2\ \mathsf{fi},\ \sigma,\ \vartheta] \xrightarrow{\varrho} [\bar{s}_1,\ \sigma',\ \vartheta']},\ \text{if}\ \mathcal{B}[\![b]\!](\sigma) = \mathit{true}$$

$$(8)\quad \frac{[s_2,\ \sigma,\ \vartheta] \xrightarrow{\varrho} [\bar{s}_2,\ \sigma',\ \vartheta']}{[\mathsf{if}\ b\ \mathsf{then}\ s_1\ \mathsf{else}\ s_2\ \mathsf{fi},\ \sigma,\ \vartheta] \xrightarrow{\varrho} [\bar{s}_2,\ \sigma',\ \vartheta']},\ \text{if}\ \mathcal{B}[\![b]\!](\sigma) = \mathit{false}$$

$$(9)\quad \frac{[r,\ \sigma,\ \vartheta] \xrightarrow{\varrho} [\bar{r},\ \sigma',\ \vartheta']}{[r\ ;\ s,\ \sigma,\ \vartheta] \xrightarrow{\varrho} [\bar{r}\ ;_{\mathrm{E}}\ s,\ \sigma',\ \vartheta']}$$

$$(10)\quad \frac{[r_1,\ \sigma,\ \vartheta] \xrightarrow{\varrho} [\bar{r}_1,\ \sigma',\ \vartheta']}{[r_1 \parallel r_2,\ \sigma,\ \vartheta] \xrightarrow{\varrho} [\bar{r}_1 \parallel_{\mathrm{E}} r_2,\ \sigma',\ \vartheta']}$$

$$(11)\quad \frac{[r_1,\ \sigma,\ \vartheta] \xrightarrow{(c,p)} [\bar{r}_1,\ \sigma',\ \vartheta'] \qquad [r_2,\ \sigma,\ \vartheta] \xrightarrow{(c,x)} [\bar{r}_2,\ \sigma'',\ \vartheta'']}{[r_1 \parallel r_2,\ \sigma,\ \vartheta] \xrightarrow{(\sigma,\ \vartheta\,\{p/x\})} [\bar{r}_1 \parallel_{\mathrm{E}} \bar{r}_2,\ \sigma,\ \vartheta\,\{p/x\}]}$$

The symmetric versions of the rules (10) and (11) have been omitted.

Note that if we had considered E in Definition 4.2 then we should have changed, e.g., rule (9) in order to deal with configurations like $[\mathrm{E}\ ;\ s,\ \sigma,\ \vartheta]$.

From the above introduced labelled transition system we derive an intermediate semantics

$$\mathcal{I}_{\mathrm{B}} : \mathit{Stat}_{\mathrm{E}}^{+} \to \mathbb{P}$$

satisfying

$$\mathcal{I}_{\mathrm{B}}\,(\mathrm{E}) = \mathrm{E}$$
$$\mathcal{I}_{\mathrm{B}}\,(r) = \lambda(\sigma,\vartheta)\cdot\{\langle\varrho, \mathcal{I}_{\mathrm{B}}\,(\bar{r})\rangle \mid [r,\ \sigma,\ \vartheta] \xrightarrow{\varrho} [\bar{r},\ \sigma',\ \vartheta']\}$$

To conclude that, for all $\bar{r} \in \mathit{Stat}_{\mathrm{E}}^{+}$, $\mathcal{I}_{\mathrm{B}}\,(\bar{r}) \in \mathbb{P}$, we have to check that, for all $r \in \mathit{Stat}^{+}$, $\sigma \in \mathit{State}$, and $\vartheta \in \mathit{SemStore}$, the set $\mathcal{I}_{\mathrm{B}}\,(r)(\sigma,\vartheta)$ is compact. Usually, the compactness is derived from the fact that the labelled transition system is finitely branching. However, the system at hand is not finitely branching.

EXAMPLE 4.5 Consider

$$p = \lambda(\sigma,\vartheta)\cdot\{\langle(\sigma,\vartheta),\ \bar{p}_n\rangle \mid n \in \mathbb{N} \cup \{\omega\}\},$$

where

$$\bar{p}_n = \begin{cases} \mathrm{E} & \text{if } n = 1 \\ \lambda(\sigma, \vartheta) \cdot \{\langle(\sigma, \vartheta), \bar{p}_{n-1}\rangle\} & \text{if } n > 1 \end{cases}$$

and $\bar{p}_\omega$ is the unique element of $\mathbb{P}$ satisfying

$$\bar{p}_\omega = \lambda(\sigma, \vartheta) \cdot \{\langle(\sigma, \vartheta), \bar{p}_\omega\rangle\}.$$

We have, for all $n \in \mathbb{N} \cup \{\omega\}$,

$$[p, \sigma, \vartheta] \xrightarrow{(\sigma,\vartheta)} [\bar{p}_n, \sigma, \vartheta].$$

Consequently, the set $\mathcal{FB}([p, \sigma, \vartheta])$ is infinite.

By endowing the configurations and the labels of the labelled transition system with suitable complete metrics, we are able to show that the obtained *metric labelled transition system* is *compactly branching* (see Property 4.7): every configuration has a compact set of outgoing transitions and transitioning is nonexpansive, i.e., for all $\bar{r}_1, \bar{r}_2, \bar{r}_1' \in \mathit{Stat}_{\mathrm{E}}^+$, $\sigma_1, \sigma_2, \sigma_1' \in \mathit{State}$, $\vartheta_1, \vartheta_2, \vartheta_1' \in \mathit{SemStore}$, and $\varrho_1 \in \mathit{SemAct}$, if

$$[\bar{r}_1, \sigma_1, \vartheta_1] \xrightarrow{\varrho_1} [\bar{r}_1', \sigma_1', \vartheta_1']$$

then there exist $\varrho_2 \in \mathit{SemAct}$, $\bar{r}_2' \in \mathit{Stat}_{\mathrm{E}}^+$, $\sigma_2' \in \mathit{State}$ and $\vartheta_2' \in \mathit{SemStore}$ such that

$$[\bar{r}_2, \sigma_2, \vartheta_2] \xrightarrow{\varrho_2} [\bar{r}_2', \sigma_2', \vartheta_2']$$

and

$$d(\varrho_1, \varrho_2) \leq d([\bar{r}_1, \sigma_1, \vartheta_1], [\bar{r}_2, \sigma_2, \vartheta_2])$$

and

$$d([\bar{r}_1', \sigma_1', \vartheta_1'], [\bar{r}_2', \sigma_2', \vartheta_2']) \leq \tfrac{1}{2} \cdot d([\bar{r}_1, \sigma_1, \vartheta_1], [\bar{r}_2, \sigma_2, \vartheta_2]).$$

This will turn out to be sufficient to prove that the intermediate semantics assigns to each extended statement an element of $\mathbb{P}$. The set of extended statements is turned into a complete space by the metric introduced in

DEFINITION 4.6 The metric $d : \mathit{Stat}_{\mathrm{E}}^+ \times \mathit{Stat}_{\mathrm{E}}^+ \to [0, 1]$ is defined by

$$d(\bar{r}_1, \bar{r}_2) = 0$$

if $\bar{r}_1 = \bar{r}_2$, otherwise

$$d(\bar{r}_1, \bar{r}_2) = \begin{cases} d_{\mathbb{P}}(p_1, p_2) & \text{if } \bar{r}_1 = p_1 \text{ and } \bar{r}_2 = p_2 \\ d(r_1, r_2) & \text{if } \bar{r}_1 = r_1 \,;\, s \text{ and } \bar{r}_2 = r_2 \,;\, s \\ \max\{d(r_1, r_2), d(r_1', r_2')\} & \text{if } \bar{r}_1 = r_1 \parallel r_1' \text{ and } \bar{r}_2 = r_2 \parallel r_2' \\ 1 & \text{otherwise} \end{cases}$$

The metric on $Stat_{\mathrm{E}}^{+}$ is designed in such a way that the metric labelled transition system is compactly branching. The other components of the configurations, the states and the semantic stores, are endowed with the discrete metric and the metric introduced in Definition 3.1. The labels, the semantic actions, are provided with the metric presented in Definition 3.3.

Now we are ready to prove that the metric labelled transition system, the labelled transition system the configurations and labels of which are endowed with the above mentioned complete metrics, is compactly branching.

PROPERTY 4.7 The function $\mathcal{CB} : Stat_{\mathrm{E}}^{+} \times State \times SemStore \rightarrow \mathcal{P}(SemAct \times (Stat_{\mathrm{E}}^{+} \times State \times SemStore))$ defined by

$$\mathcal{CB}([\bar{r}, \sigma, \vartheta]) = \{(\varrho, [\bar{r}', \sigma', \vartheta']) \mid [\bar{r}, \sigma, \vartheta] \xrightarrow{\varrho} [\bar{r}', \sigma', \vartheta']\}$$

is an element of $Stat_{\mathrm{E}}^{+} \times State \times SemStore \rightarrow^{1} \mathcal{P}_c(SemAct \times \frac{1}{2} \cdot (Stat_{\mathrm{E}}^{+} \times State \times SemStore))$.

*Proof* First, we prove that, for all $\bar{r} \in Stat_{\mathrm{E}}^{+}$, $\sigma \in State$, and $\vartheta \in SemStore$, the set $\mathcal{CB}([\bar{r}, \sigma, \vartheta])$ is compact by structural induction on $\bar{r}$. We only consider the following two cases.

1. Let $\bar{r} = p$. Since

$$\begin{aligned} \mathcal{CB}([p, \sigma, \vartheta]) = {} & \{((\sigma', \vartheta'), [\bar{p}, \sigma', \vartheta']) \mid \langle(\sigma', \vartheta'), \bar{p}\rangle \in p(\sigma, \vartheta)\} \cup \\ & \{(\varpi, [\bar{p}, \sigma, \vartheta]) \mid \langle\varpi, \bar{p}\rangle \in p(\sigma, \vartheta)\} \end{aligned}$$

and the set $p(\sigma, \vartheta)$ is compact, also the set $\mathcal{CB}([p, \sigma, \vartheta])$ is compact.

2. Let $\bar{r} = r \,;\, s$. We have that

$$\mathcal{CB}([r \,;\, s, \sigma, \vartheta]) = \{(\varrho, [\bar{r} \,;_{\mathrm{E}}\, s, \sigma', \vartheta']) \mid (\varrho, [\bar{r}, \sigma', \vartheta']) \in \mathcal{CB}([r, \sigma, \vartheta])\}.$$

By induction, the set $\mathcal{CB}([r, \sigma, \vartheta])$ is compact. One can easily verify that the extended operator $;_{\mathrm{E}}$ is nonexpansive. Because the nonexpansive image of a compact set is compact (a consequence of Theorem III of [Ale27]), we can conclude that the set $\mathcal{CB}([r \,;\, s, \sigma, \vartheta])$ is compact.

Second, we prove that, for all $\bar{r}_1, \bar{r}_2 \in Stat_{\mathrm{E}}^{+}$, $\sigma_1, \sigma_2 \in State$, and $\vartheta_1, \vartheta_2 \in SemStore$,

$$d(\mathcal{CB}([\bar{r}_1, \sigma_1, \vartheta_1]), \mathcal{CB}([\bar{r}_2, \sigma_2, \vartheta_2])) \le d([\bar{r}_1, \sigma_1, \vartheta_1], [\bar{r}_2, \sigma_1, \vartheta_1])$$

by structural induction on $\bar{r}_1$ and $\bar{r}_2$. We only consider those $\bar{r}_1$ and $\bar{r}_2$ satisfying $0 < d(\bar{r}_1, \bar{r}_2) < 1$, since for all other $\bar{r}_1$ and $\bar{r}_2$ the above equation is vacuously true. Only two cases are elaborated on.

1. Let $\bar{r}_1 = p_1$ and $\bar{r}_2 = p_2$.

$$\begin{aligned}
&d(\mathcal{CB}([p_1, \sigma_1, \vartheta_2]), \mathcal{CB}([p_2, \sigma_2, \vartheta_2])) \\
&\quad = d(\{((\sigma_1', \vartheta_1'), [\bar{p}_1, \sigma_1', \vartheta_1']) \mid \langle(\sigma_1', \vartheta_1'), \bar{p}_1\rangle \in p_1(\sigma_1, \vartheta_1)\} \cup \\
&\qquad \{(\varpi_1, [\bar{p}_1, \sigma_1, \vartheta_1]) \mid \langle\varpi_1, \bar{p}_1\rangle \in p_1(\sigma_1, \vartheta_1)\}, \\
&\qquad \{((\sigma_2', \vartheta_2'), [\bar{p}_2, \sigma_2', \vartheta_2']) \mid \langle(\sigma_2', \vartheta_2'), \bar{p}_2\rangle \in p_2(\sigma_2, \vartheta_2)\} \cup \\
&\qquad \{(\varpi_2, [\bar{p}_2, \sigma_2, \vartheta_2]) \mid \langle\varpi_2, \bar{p}_2\rangle \in p_2(\sigma_2, \vartheta_2)\}) \\
&\quad = d(p_1(\sigma_1, \vartheta_1), p_2(\sigma_2, \vartheta_2)) \\
&\quad \leq \max\{d(p_1(\sigma_1, \vartheta_1), p_2(\sigma_1, \vartheta_1)), d(p_2(\sigma_1, \vartheta_1), p_2(\sigma_2, \vartheta_2))\} \quad \text{[ultrametricity]} \\
&\quad \leq \max\{d(p_1, p_2), d((\sigma_1, \vartheta_1), (\sigma_2, \vartheta_2))\} \quad [p_2 \text{ is nonexpansive}] \\
&\quad = d([p_1, \sigma_1, \vartheta_1], [p_2, \sigma_2, \vartheta_2]).
\end{aligned}$$

2. Let $\bar{r}_1 = r_1 \,;\, s$ and $\bar{r}_2 = r_2 \,;\, s$.

$$\begin{aligned}
&d(\mathcal{CB}([r_1 ; s, \sigma_1, \vartheta_1]), \mathcal{CB}([r_2 ; s, \sigma_2, \vartheta_2])) \\
&\quad = d(\{(\varrho_1, [\bar{r}_1 ;_{\mathrm{E}} s, \sigma_1', \vartheta_1']) \mid (\varrho_1, [\bar{r}_1, \sigma_1', \vartheta_1']) \in \mathcal{CB}([r_1, \sigma_1, \vartheta_1])\}, \\
&\qquad \{(\varrho_2, [\bar{r}_2 ;_{\mathrm{E}} s, \sigma_2', \vartheta_2']) \mid (\varrho_2, [\bar{r}_2, \sigma_2', \vartheta_2']) \in \mathcal{CB}([r_2, \sigma_2, \vartheta_2])\}) \\
&\quad \leq d(\mathcal{CB}([r_1, \sigma_1, \vartheta_1]), \mathcal{CB}([r_2, \sigma_2, \vartheta_2])) \quad [;_{\mathrm{E}} \text{ is nonexpansive}] \\
&\quad \leq d([r_1, \sigma_1, \vartheta_1], [r_2, \sigma_2, \vartheta_2]) \quad \text{[induction]} \\
&\quad = d([r_1 ; s, \sigma_1, \vartheta_1], [r_2 ; s, \sigma_2, \vartheta_2]).
\end{aligned}$$

□

If we were to leave out the $\frac{1}{2}\cdot$ then we would obtain a more restrictive condition which the metric labelled transition system does not satisfy (consider, e.g., the extended statements $\bar{p}_1$ and $\bar{p}_2$ of Example 4.5).

The branching intermediate semantics $\mathcal{I}_{\mathrm{B}}$ is defined as the unique fixed point of $\mathcal{T}_{\mathrm{B}}$ introduced in

PROPERTY 4.8 The compactly branching metric labelled transition system of Definition 4.4 induces the *branching semantics transformation*

$$\mathcal{T}_{\mathrm{B}} : (Stat_{\mathrm{E}}^{+} \to^{1} \mathbb{P}) \to (Stat_{\mathrm{E}}^{+} \to^{1} \mathbb{P})$$

defined by

$$\mathcal{T}_B(\mathcal{S})(E) = E$$

$$\mathcal{T}_B(\mathcal{S})(r) = \lambda(\sigma, \vartheta) \cdot \{\langle \varrho, \mathcal{S}(\bar{r})\rangle \mid [r, \sigma, \vartheta] \xrightarrow{\varrho} [\bar{r}, \sigma', \vartheta']\}$$

*Proof* We prove that

1. for all $\mathcal{S} \in Stat^+_E \to^1 \mathbb{P}$, $r \in Stat^+$, $\sigma \in State$, and $\vartheta \in SemStore$, the set $\mathcal{T}_B(\mathcal{S})(r)(\sigma, \vartheta)$ is nonempty and compact,
2. for all $\mathcal{S} \in Stat^+_E \to^1 \mathbb{P}$ and $r \in Stat^+$, the function $\mathcal{T}_B(\mathcal{S})(r)$ is nonexpansive, and
3. for all $\mathcal{S} \in Stat^+_E \to^1 \mathbb{P}$, the function $\mathcal{T}_B(\mathcal{S})$ is nonexpansive.

In this proof we frequently use the fact that

$$\mathcal{T}_B(\mathcal{S})(r)(\sigma, \vartheta) = \{\langle \varrho, \mathcal{S}(\bar{r})\rangle \mid (\varrho, [\bar{r}, \sigma', \vartheta']) \in \mathcal{CB}([r, \sigma, \vartheta])\}.$$

We start with 1. Since the set $\mathcal{CB}([r, \sigma, \vartheta])$ is nonempty (as can easily be verified), we can conclude that the set $\mathcal{T}_B(\mathcal{S})(r)(\sigma, \vartheta)$ is also nonempty. According to Property 4.7, the set $\mathcal{CB}([r, \sigma, \vartheta])$ is compact. Because $\mathcal{S}$ is nonexpansive and the nonexpansive image of a compact set is compact, the set $\mathcal{T}_B(\mathcal{S})(r)(\sigma, \vartheta)$ is compact. We continue with 2. For all $\sigma_1, \sigma_2 \in State$ and $\vartheta_1, \vartheta_2 \in SemStore$,

$$\begin{aligned}
&d(\mathcal{T}_B(\mathcal{S})(r)(\sigma_1, \vartheta_1), \mathcal{T}_B(\mathcal{S})(r)(\sigma_2, \vartheta_2))\\
&\quad = d(\{\langle \varrho_1, \mathcal{S}(\bar{r}_1)\rangle \mid (\varrho_1, [\bar{r}_1, \sigma_1', \vartheta_1']) \in \mathcal{CB}([r, \sigma_1, \vartheta_1])\},\\
&\qquad \{\langle \varrho_2, \mathcal{S}(\bar{r}_2)\rangle \mid (\varrho_2, [\bar{r}_2, \sigma_2', \vartheta_2']) \in \mathcal{CB}([r, \sigma_2, \vartheta_2])\})\\
&\quad \le d(\mathcal{CB}([r, \sigma_1, \vartheta_1]), \mathcal{CB}([r, \sigma_2, \vartheta_2])) \quad [\mathcal{S} \text{ is nonexpansive}]\\
&\quad \le d([r, \sigma_1, \vartheta_1], [r, \sigma_2, \vartheta_2]) \quad [\text{Property 4.7}]\\
&\quad = d((\sigma_1, \vartheta_1), (\sigma_2, \vartheta_2)).
\end{aligned}$$

We conclude with 3. For all $r_1, r_2 \in Stat^+$, $\sigma \in State$, and $\vartheta \in SemStore$,

$$\begin{aligned}
&d(\mathcal{T}_B(\mathcal{S})(r_1)(\sigma, \vartheta), \mathcal{T}_B(\mathcal{S})(r_2)(\sigma, \vartheta))\\
&\quad \le d([r_1, \sigma, \vartheta], [r_2, \sigma, \vartheta]) \quad [\text{as in the proof of 2.}]\\
&\quad = d(r_1, r_2).
\end{aligned}$$

□

In the above property we restricted ourselves to nonexpansive functions from $Stat^+_E$ to $\mathbb{P}$. Without this restriction the property is not valid (consider, e.g., $p$ of Example 4.5 and $\mathcal{S}$ satisfying, for all $n \in \mathbb{N}$, $\mathcal{S}(\bar{p}_n) = \bar{p}_n$ and $\mathcal{S}(\bar{p}_\omega) = E$).

The branching semantics transformation $\mathcal{T}_B$ is a function from the nonempty complete space $\mathit{Stat}_E^+ \to^1 \mathbb{P}$ to itself. The fact that $\mathcal{T}_B$ is a contraction can be easily proved. According to Banach's theorem, $\mathcal{T}_B$ has a unique fixed point.

DEFINITION 4.9 The *branching intermediate semantics* $\mathcal{I}_B : \mathit{Stat}_E^+ \to^1 \mathbb{P}$ is defined by

$\mathcal{I}_B = \mathit{fix}\,(\mathcal{T}_B).$

## 4.2 Relating Intermediate and Denotational Semantics

The intermediate semantics $\mathcal{I}_B$ is shown to be equal to the extended denotational semantics $\mathcal{D}_B^+$. This model is a natural extension of $\mathcal{D}_B$.

DEFINITION 4.10 The *extended denotational semantics* $\mathcal{D}_B^+ : \mathit{Stat}_E^+ \to \mathbb{P}$ is defined by

$$
\begin{aligned}
\mathcal{D}_B^+\,(\mathrm{E}) &= \mathrm{E} \\
\mathcal{D}_B^+\,(s) &= \mathcal{D}_B\,[\![s]\!] \\
\mathcal{D}_B^+\,(p) &= p \\
\mathcal{D}_B^+\,(r\,;\,s) &= \mathcal{D}_B^+\,(r)\,;\,\mathcal{D}_B^+\,(s) \\
\mathcal{D}_B^+\,(r_1 \parallel r_2) &= \mathcal{D}_B^+\,(r_1) \parallel \mathcal{D}_B^+\,(r_2)
\end{aligned}
$$

The semantic models $\mathcal{I}_B$ and $\mathcal{D}_B^+$ are shown to be equal by uniqueness of fixed point, viz we show that $\mathcal{D}_B^+$ is a fixed point of $\mathcal{T}_B$.

PROPERTY 4.11 $\mathcal{T}_B\,(\mathcal{D}_B^+) = \mathcal{D}_B^+.$

*Proof* First, we should check that $\mathcal{D}_B^+$ is nonexpansive, which can be verified by structural induction. Second, we should show that $\mathcal{D}_B^+$ is a fixed point of $\mathcal{T}_B$, which can also be proved by structural induction. □

By uniqueness of fixed point we can conclude

LEMMA 4.12 $\mathcal{I}_B = \mathcal{D}_B^+.$

*Proof* Immediate consequence of Definition 4.9, Property 4.11, and Banach's theorem. □

## 4.3 Relating Intermediate and Operational Semantics

Next, we relate the branching intermediate semantics and the linear operational semantics. For that purpose we introduce the already mentioned linearise and semantify operators.

The linearise operator abstracts from some of the structure of the branching space $\mathbb{P}$ arriving at the linear space

$$State \times SemStore \to^1 \mathcal{P}_{nc}((State \times SemStore)^{\infty}_{\delta})$$

where the space $(State \times SemStore)^{\infty}_{\delta}$ is an instance of

DEFINITION 4.13 Let $(x \in) X$ be a nonempty complete space. The space $(w \in) X^{\infty}_{\delta}$ is defined by the equation

$$X^{\infty}_{\delta} \cong \{\varepsilon\} + \{\delta\} + \left(X \times \tfrac{1}{2} \cdot X^{\infty}_{\delta}\right).$$

The elements of the space $X^{\infty}_{\delta}$ are finite sequences over $X$, finite sequences over $X$ followed by $\delta$, and infinite sequences over $X$. Instead of $(x_1, (x_2, \ldots, (x_n, \varepsilon)\ldots))$, $(x_1, (x_2, \ldots, (x_n, \delta)\ldots))$, and $(x_1, (x_2, \ldots))$ we write $x_1 x_2 \ldots x_n$, $x_1 x_2 \ldots x_n \delta$, and $x_1 x_2 \ldots$, respectively.

If we endow *State* $\times$ *SynStore* with the discrete metric, the above definition gives us the set introduced in Definition 2.8 endowed with a Baire-like [Bai09] metric as presented in, e.g., [Niv79].

The linearise operator *LIN* removes (unsuccessful) communication attempts, extracts deadlock information, removes the changes caused by the environment, and collapses the branching structure. Like the semantic sequential composition and parallel composition, *LIN* is defined as the unique fixed point of a contractive function from a nonempty complete space to itself.

DEFINITION 4.14 The function *LIN* is the unique function

$$LIN : \mathbb{P} \to^1 (State \times SemStore) \to^1 \mathcal{P}_{nc}((State \times SemStore)^{\infty}_{\delta})$$

satisfying

$$LIN(\mathrm{E})(\sigma, \vartheta) = \{\varepsilon\}$$

$$LIN(p)(\sigma, \vartheta) = \begin{cases} \{\delta\} & \text{if } p(\sigma, \vartheta) \subseteq SemCom \times \mathbb{P} \\ \{(\sigma', \vartheta')\, w \mid \langle(\sigma', \vartheta'), \bar{p}\rangle \in \\ \quad p(\sigma, \vartheta) \wedge w \in LIN(\bar{p})(\sigma', \vartheta')\} & \text{otherwise} \end{cases}$$

The condition $p(\sigma, \vartheta) \subseteq SemCom \times \mathbb{P}$ is the semantic counterpart of the syntactic deadlocking condition introduced in Definition 2.9. More precisely, from Theorem 4.1 we can derive that, for all $s \in Stat$, $\sigma \in State$, and $\theta \in SynStore$,

$[s, \sigma, \theta]$ deadlocks if and only if $\mathcal{D}_{\mathrm{B}}[\![s]\!](\sigma, sem(\theta)) \subseteq SemCom \times \mathbb{P}$.

The semantify operator *sem* assigns to each syntactic store and syntactic action a corresponding semantic one. This operator is defined in terms of the denotational semantics $\mathcal{D}_{\mathrm{B}}$.

The semantify operator *SEM* is the obvious extension of *sem* from the syntactic linear space $\mathcal{P}_{nc}((State \times SynStore)^{\infty}_{\delta})$ to the semantic linear space $\mathcal{P}_{nc}((State \times SemStore)^{\infty}_{\delta})$.

DEFINITION 4.15 The function $sem : SynStore \to SemStore$ is defined by

$$sem(\theta) = \lambda x \cdot \mathcal{D}_{\mathrm{B}}[\![\theta(x)]\!].$$

The function $sem : SynAct \to SemAct$ is defined by

$$\begin{aligned} sem(\sigma, \theta) &= (\sigma, sem(\theta)) \\ sem(c\ !\ s) &= (c, \mathcal{D}_{\mathrm{B}}[\![s]\!]) \\ sem(c\ ?\ x) &= (c, x) \end{aligned}$$

The function *Sem* is the unique function

$$Sem : (State \times SynStore)^{\infty}_{\delta} \to^{1} (State \times SemStore)^{\infty}_{\delta}$$

satisfying

$$\begin{aligned} Sem(\varepsilon) &= \varepsilon \\ Sem(\delta) &= \delta \\ Sem((\sigma, \theta)\, w) &= sem(\sigma, \theta)\ Sem(w) \end{aligned}$$

The function $SEM : \mathcal{P}_{nc}((State \times SynStore)^{\infty}_{\delta}) \to^{1} \mathcal{P}_{nc}((State \times SemStore)^{\infty}_{\delta})$ is defined by

$$SEM(W) = \{Sem(w) \mid w \in W\}.$$

To relate the linear operational semantics $\mathcal{O}_{\mathrm{L}}$ and the branching intermediate semantics $\mathcal{I}_{\mathrm{B}}$, we link the linear models $\mathcal{O}^{*}_{\mathrm{L}}$ and $\mathcal{I}_{\mathrm{L}}$ introduced below.

DEFINITION 4.16 The function

$$\mathcal{O}^{*}_{\mathrm{L}} : State_{\mathrm{E}} \times State \times SynStore \to \mathcal{P}\big((State \times SynStore)^{\infty}_{\delta}\big)$$

is defined by

$$\begin{aligned} \mathcal{O}^{*}_{\mathrm{L}}([\mathrm{E}, \sigma, \theta]) &= \{\varepsilon\} \\ \mathcal{O}^{*}_{\mathrm{L}}([s, \sigma, \theta]) &= \mathcal{O}_{\mathrm{L}}[\![s]\!](\sigma, \theta) \end{aligned}$$

The function

$$\mathcal{I}_{\mathrm{L}} : State_{\mathrm{E}} \times State \times SynStore \to \mathcal{P}_{nc}\big((State \times SemStore)^{\infty}_{\delta}\big)$$

is defined by

$$\mathcal{I}_{\mathrm{L}}([\bar{s}, \sigma, \theta]) = LIN(\mathcal{I}_{\mathrm{B}}(\bar{s}))(\sigma, sem(\theta)).$$

The equivalence of $\mathcal{I}_{\mathrm{L}}$ and $SEM \circ \mathcal{O}^*_{\mathrm{L}}$ is proved by uniqueness of fixed point. We show that $\mathcal{I}_{\mathrm{L}}$ and $SEM \circ \mathcal{O}^*_{\mathrm{L}}$ are both a fixed point of $\mathcal{T}_{\mathrm{L}}$.

PROPERTY 4.17 The finitely branching labelled transition system of Definition 2.6 induces the *linear semantics transformation*

$$\mathcal{T}_{\mathrm{L}} : \big(Stat_{\mathrm{E}} \times State \times SynStore \to \mathcal{P}_{nc}\big((State \times SemStore)^{\infty}_{\delta}\big)\big)$$
$$\to \big(Stat_{\mathrm{E}} \times State \times SynStore \to \mathcal{P}_{nc}\big((State \times SemStore)^{\infty}_{\delta}\big)\big)$$

defined by

$$\mathcal{T}_{\mathrm{L}}(\mathcal{S})([\mathrm{E},\ \sigma,\ \theta]) = \{\varepsilon\}$$
$$\mathcal{T}_{\mathrm{L}}(\mathcal{S})([s,\ \sigma,\ \theta]) = \begin{cases} \{\delta\} & \text{if } [s,\ \sigma,\ \theta] \text{ deadlocks} \\ \{sem\,(\sigma',\theta')\,w \mid [s,\ \sigma,\ \theta] \xrightarrow{(\sigma',\theta')} & \\ \quad [\bar{s},\ \sigma',\ \theta'] \wedge w \in \mathcal{S}\,([\bar{s},\ \sigma',\ \theta'])\} & \text{otherwise} \end{cases}$$

*Proof* Similar to the proof of Property 4.8 using Property 2.7. □

The space $Stat_{\mathrm{E}} \times State \times SynStore \to \mathcal{P}_{nc}\,((State \times SemStore)^{\infty}_{\delta})$ is nonempty and complete. We leave it to the reader to verify that $\mathcal{T}_{\mathrm{L}}$ is contractive. We have left to show that both $\mathcal{I}_{\mathrm{L}}$ and $SEM \circ \mathcal{O}^*_{\mathrm{L}}$ are a fixed point of $\mathcal{T}_{\mathrm{L}}$.

PROPERTY 4.18 $\mathcal{T}_{\mathrm{L}}\,(\mathcal{I}_{\mathrm{L}}) = \mathcal{I}_{\mathrm{L}}$.

*Proof* First, we relate the transition relations of Definition 2.6 and 4.4.

1. For all $\bar{s}, \bar{s}' \in Stat_{\mathrm{E}}$, $\sigma, \sigma' \in State$, $\theta, \theta' \in SynStore$, and $\rho \in SynAct$, if

$$[\bar{s},\ \sigma,\ \theta] \xrightarrow{\rho} [\bar{s}',\ \sigma',\ \theta']$$

then there exists a $\bar{r} \in Stat^{+}_{\mathrm{E}}$ such that

$$[\bar{s},\ \sigma,\ sem\,(\theta)] \xrightarrow{sem\,(\rho)} [\bar{r},\ \sigma',\ sem\,(\theta')]$$

and $\mathcal{I}_{\mathrm{B}}(\bar{s}') = \mathcal{I}_{\mathrm{B}}(\bar{r})$.

2. For all $\bar{s} \in Stat_{\mathrm{E}}$, $\sigma, \sigma' \in State$, $\theta \in SynStore$, $\varrho \in SemAct$, $\bar{r} \in Stat^{+}_{\mathrm{E}}$, and $\vartheta' \in SemStore$, if

$$[\bar{s},\ \sigma,\ sem\,(\theta)] \xrightarrow{\varrho} [\bar{r},\ \sigma',\ \vartheta']$$

then there exist $\rho \in \mathit{SynAct}$, $\bar{s}' \in \mathit{Stat}_{\mathrm{E}}$, and $\theta' \in \mathit{SynStore}$ such that

$$[\bar{s},\ \sigma,\ \theta] \xrightarrow{\rho} [\bar{s}',\ \sigma',\ \theta'],$$

$$\mathit{sem}\,(\rho) = \varrho, \mathcal{I}_{\mathrm{B}}\,(\bar{r}) = \mathcal{I}_{\mathrm{B}}\,(\bar{s}'), \text{ and } \mathit{sem}\,(\theta') = \vartheta'.$$

Both 1. and 2. can be proved by structural induction on $\bar{s}$ (cf. Lemma 4.15 of [BB93]).

Second, we show that, for all $\bar{s} \in \mathit{Stat}_{\mathrm{E}}$, $\sigma \in \mathit{State}$, and $\theta \in \mathit{SynStore}$,

$$\mathcal{T}_{\mathrm{L}}(\mathcal{I}_{\mathrm{L}})([\bar{s},\ \sigma,\ \theta]) = \mathcal{I}_{\mathrm{L}}\,([\bar{s},\ \sigma,\ \theta]).$$

We only consider the case that $\bar{s} \not\equiv \mathrm{E}$ and $[\bar{s},\ \sigma,\ \theta]$ does not deadlock. The other two cases are much simpler and left to the reader.

$$\begin{aligned}
&\mathcal{T}_{\mathrm{L}}\,(\mathcal{I}_{\mathrm{L}})([\bar{s},\ \sigma,\ \theta])\\
&\quad = \{\mathit{sem}\,(\sigma', \theta')\,w \mid [\bar{s},\ \sigma,\ \theta] \xrightarrow{(\sigma',\theta')} [\bar{s}',\ \sigma',\ \theta'] \wedge w \in \mathcal{I}_{\mathrm{L}}\,([\bar{s}',\ \sigma',\ \theta'])\}\\
&\quad = \{\mathit{sem}\,(\sigma', \theta')\,w \mid [\bar{s},\ \sigma,\ \theta] \xrightarrow{(\sigma',\theta')} [\bar{s}',\ \sigma',\ \theta'] \wedge w \in \mathit{LIN}\,(\mathcal{I}_{\mathrm{B}}\,(\bar{s}'))(\sigma',\ \mathit{sem}\,(\theta'))\}\\
&\quad = \{(\sigma', \vartheta')\,v \mid [\bar{s},\ \sigma,\ \mathit{sem}\,(\theta)] \xrightarrow{(\sigma',\vartheta')} [\bar{r},\ \sigma',\ \vartheta'] \wedge v \in \mathit{LIN}\,(\mathcal{I}_{\mathrm{B}}\,(\bar{r}))(\sigma', \vartheta')\}\\
&\qquad\qquad [\text{1. and 2.}]\\
&\quad = \{(\sigma', \vartheta')\,v \mid \langle(\sigma', \vartheta'), \bar{p}\rangle \in \mathcal{I}_{\mathrm{B}}\,(\bar{s})(\sigma,\ \mathit{sem}\,(\theta)) \wedge v \in \mathit{LIN}\,(\bar{p})(\sigma', \vartheta')\}\\
&\quad = \mathit{LIN}\,(\mathcal{I}_{\mathrm{B}}\,(\bar{s}))(\sigma,\ \mathit{sem}\,(\theta))\\
&\quad = \mathcal{I}_{\mathrm{L}}\,([\bar{s},\ \sigma,\ \theta]).
\end{aligned}$$

□

Since $\mathcal{I}_{\mathrm{L}}$ is a fixed point of $\mathcal{T}_{\mathrm{L}}$ and $\mathcal{I}_{\mathrm{B}} = \mathcal{D}_{\mathrm{B}}^{+}$ (Lemma 4.12), we can conclude that

$$\lambda[\bar{s},\ \sigma,\ \theta].\begin{cases}\{\varepsilon\} & \text{if } \bar{s} \equiv \mathrm{E}\\ \mathit{LIN}\,(\mathcal{D}_{\mathrm{B}}\,(\bar{s}))(\sigma,\ \mathit{sem}\,(\theta)) & \text{otherwise}\end{cases} \tag{1}$$

is also a fixed point of $\mathcal{T}_{\mathrm{L}}$. Because the semantic function described in (1) is not compositional, we cannot prove that it is a fixed point of $\mathcal{T}_{\mathrm{L}}$ in the way we can show that $\mathcal{D}_{\mathrm{B}}^{+}$ is a fixed point of $\mathcal{T}_{\mathrm{B}}$ (Property 4.11). This motivates the introduction of the intermediate semantics $\mathcal{I}_{\mathrm{B}}$.

PROPERTY 4.19 $\mathcal{T}_{\mathrm{L}}(\mathit{SEM} \circ \mathcal{O}_{\mathrm{L}}^{*}) = \mathit{SEM} \circ \mathcal{O}_{\mathrm{L}}^{*}$.

*Proof* First, we have to check that, for all $\bar{s} \in \mathit{Stat}_{\mathrm{E}}$, $\sigma \in \mathit{State}$, and $\theta \in \mathit{SynStore}$, the set $\mathcal{O}_{\mathrm{L}}^{*}\,([\bar{s},\ \sigma,\ \theta])$ is nonempty and compact. This can be proved using Property 2.7 (cf., e.g., the proof of Theorem 4.2.7 of [Bre94]).

Second, we show that, for all $\bar{s} \in Stat_{\mathrm{E}}$, $\sigma \in State$, and $\theta \in SynStore$,

$$\mathcal{T}_{\mathrm{L}}\,(SEM \circ \mathcal{O}^*_{\mathrm{L}})([\bar{s},\, \sigma,\, \theta]) = (SEM \circ \mathcal{O}^*_{\mathrm{L}})\,([\bar{s},\, \sigma,\, \theta]).$$

Again we only consider the case that $\bar{s} \neq \mathrm{E}$ and $[\bar{s},\, \sigma,\, \theta]$ does not deadlock.

$$\begin{aligned}
&\mathcal{T}_{\mathrm{L}}\,(SEM \circ \mathcal{O}^*_{\mathrm{L}})([\bar{s},\, \sigma,\, \theta]) \\
&\quad = \{sem\,(\sigma', \theta')\, w \mid [\bar{s},\, \sigma,\, \theta] \xrightarrow{(\sigma',\theta')} [\bar{s}',\, \sigma',\, \theta'] \wedge w \in (SEM \circ \mathcal{O}^*_{\mathrm{L}})\,([\bar{s}',\, \sigma',\, \theta'])\} \\
&\quad = SEM\,(\{(\sigma', \theta')\, v \mid [\bar{s},\, \sigma,\, \theta] \xrightarrow{(\sigma',\theta')} [\bar{s}',\, \sigma',\, \theta'] \wedge v \in \mathcal{O}^*_{\mathrm{L}}\,([\bar{s}',\, \sigma',\, \theta'])\}) \\
&\quad = (SEM \circ \mathcal{O}^*_{\mathrm{L}})([\bar{s},\, \sigma,\, \theta]).
\end{aligned}$$

□

By uniqueness of fixed point we can conclude

LEMMA 4.20 $SEM \circ \mathcal{O}^*_{\mathrm{L}} = \mathcal{I}_{\mathrm{L}}$.

*Proof* Immediate consequence of Property 4.18 and 4.19 and Banach's theorem. □

Combining Lemma 4.12 and 4.20 we arrive at

*Proof of Theorem 4.1*

$$\begin{aligned}
&SEM\,(\mathcal{O}_{\mathrm{L}}\,[\![s]\!](\sigma, \theta)) \\
&\quad = (SEM \circ \mathcal{O}^*_{\mathrm{L}})([s,\, \sigma,\, \theta]) \\
&\quad = \mathcal{I}_{\mathrm{L}}([s,\, \sigma,\, \theta]) \quad \text{[Lemma 4.20]} \\
&\quad = LIN\,(\mathcal{I}_{\mathrm{B}}\,(s))(\sigma,\, sem\,(\theta)) \\
&\quad = LIN\,(\mathcal{D}^+_{\mathrm{B}}\,(s))(\sigma,\, sem\,(\theta)) \quad \text{[Lemma 4.12]} \\
&\quad = LIN\,(\mathcal{D}_{\mathrm{B}}\,[\![s]\!])(\sigma,\, sem\,(\theta)).
\end{aligned}$$

□

## Conclusion

In the preceding four sections we introduced a simple imperative language with second order communication, presented an operational and a denotational semantics, and linked the two models. From a semantical point of view, higher order notions like second order communication can be nicely embedded in the traditional setting of imperative languages, as we have shown that the results for the first order case reported in [BV96] can be extended to the second order case using known techniques. These techniques could be used to provide similar links between many variations of both the operational and denotation semantics.

Bisimulation, a notion due to Milner and Park [Mil80, Par81, Mil94], plays an important role in the theory of concurrency. Various notions of *higher order bisimulation* have been introduced (see, e.g., [AGR92, MS92]). By means of the theory developed by Rutten and Turi in [RT92] we can define two notions of second order bisimulation. The first one is given for statements in terms of the transition relation of Definition 2.6. An equivalence relation $\mathcal{R}$ on $Stat_{\mathrm{E}}$ is called a *second order bisimulation* if, for all $\bar{s}_1, \bar{s}_2 \in Stat_{\mathrm{E}}$, $\bar{s}_1 \mathrel{\mathcal{R}} \bar{s}_2$ implies that

- for all $\bar{s}'_1 \in Stat_{\mathrm{E}}$, $\sigma, \sigma' \in State$, and $\theta, \theta_1 \in SynStore$, if

$$[\bar{s}_1, \sigma, \theta] \xrightarrow{(\sigma', \theta_1)} [\bar{s}'_1, \sigma', \theta_1]$$

then there exist $\bar{s}'_2 \in Stat_{\mathrm{E}}$ and $\theta_2 \in SynStore$ such that

$$[\bar{s}_2, \sigma, \theta] \xrightarrow{(\sigma', \theta_2)} [\bar{s}'_2, \sigma', \theta_2],$$

$\bar{s}'_1 \mathrel{\mathcal{R}} \bar{s}'_2$, and $\theta_1(x) \mathrel{\mathcal{R}} \theta_2(x)$ for all $x \in SVar$,

- for all $\bar{s}'_1 \in Stat_{\mathrm{E}}$, $\sigma \in State$, $\theta \in SynStore$, and $c\,!\,s_1 \in SynCom$, if

$$[\bar{s}_1, \sigma, \theta] \xrightarrow{c!s_1} [\bar{s}'_1, \sigma, \theta]$$

then there exist $\bar{s}'_2 \in Stat_{\mathrm{E}}$ and $c\,!\,s_2 \in SynCom$ such that

$$[\bar{s}_2, \sigma, \theta] \xrightarrow{c!s_2} [\bar{s}'_2, \sigma, \theta],$$

$\bar{s}'_1 \mathrel{\mathcal{R}} \bar{s}'_2$ and $s_1 \mathrel{\mathcal{R}} s_2$, and

- for all $\bar{s}'_1 \in Stat_{\mathrm{E}}$, $\sigma \in State$, $\theta \in SynStore$, and $c\,?\,x \in SynCom$, if

$$[\bar{s}_1, \sigma, \theta] \xrightarrow{c?x} [\bar{s}'_1, \sigma, \theta]$$

then there exists a $\bar{s}'_2 \in Stat_{\mathrm{E}}$ such that

$$[\bar{s}_2, \sigma, \theta] \xrightarrow{c?x} [\bar{s}'_2, \sigma, \theta]$$

and $\bar{s}'_1 \mathrel{\mathcal{R}} \bar{s}'_2$.

As usual, two statements $\bar{s}_1$ and $\bar{s}_2$ are called *second order bisimilar*, denoted by $\bar{s}_1 \sim \bar{s}_2$, if there exists a second order bisimulation $\mathcal{R}$ with $\bar{s}_1 \mathrel{\mathcal{R}} \bar{s}_2$. This second order bisimilarity characterises the equivalence induced by the intermediate semantics $\mathcal{I}_{\mathrm{B}}$ restricted to (the *sem*-image of) the syntactic stores: for all $\bar{s}_1, \bar{s}_2 \in Stat_{\mathrm{E}}$,

$$\bar{s}_1 \sim \bar{s}_2 \text{ if and only if, for all } \sigma \in State \text{ and } \theta \in SynStore,\ \mathcal{I}_{\mathrm{B}}(\bar{s}_1)(\sigma, sem(\theta)) = \mathcal{I}_{\mathrm{B}}(\bar{s}_2)(\sigma, sem(\theta)).$$

The second notion is defined for extended statements in terms of the transition relation of Definition 4.4. An equivalence relation $\mathcal{R}$ on $Stat^{+}_{\mathrm{E}}$ is called a *second order bisimulation* if, for all $\bar{r}_1, \bar{r}_2 \in Stat_E^+$, $\bar{r}_1 \mathcal{R} \bar{r}_2$ implies that, for all $\bar{r}_1' \in Stat_E^+$, $\sigma, \sigma' \in State$, $\vartheta, \vartheta' \in SemStore$, and $\varrho \in SemAct$, if

$$[\bar{r}_1, \sigma, \vartheta] \xrightarrow{\varrho} [\bar{r}_1', \sigma', \vartheta']$$

then there exists a $\bar{r}_2' \in Stat_E^+$ such that

$$[\bar{r}_2, \sigma, \vartheta] \xrightarrow{\varrho} [\bar{r}_2', \sigma', \vartheta']$$

and $\bar{r}_1' \mathcal{R} \bar{r}_2'$.

Two extended statements $\bar{r}_1$ and $\bar{r}_2$ are called *second order bisimilar*, denoted by $\bar{r}_1 \approx \bar{r}_2$, if there exists a second order bisimulation $\mathcal{R}$ with $\bar{r}_1 \mathcal{R} \bar{r}_2$. This notion characterises the equivalence induced by the intermediate semantics $\mathcal{I}_B$: for all $\bar{r}_1, \bar{r}_2 \in Stat_E^+$,

$$\bar{r}_1 \approx \bar{r}_2 \text{ if and only if } \mathcal{I}_B(\bar{r}_1) = \mathcal{I}_B(\bar{r}_2). \tag{2}$$

From (2) and Lemma 4.12 we can deduce that, for all $s_1, s_2 \in Stat$,

$$s_1 \approx s_2 \text{ if and only if } \mathcal{D}_B [\![s_1]\!] = \mathcal{D}_B [\![s_2]\!]. \tag{3}$$

We have that $\sim$ is an extension of $\approx$: for all $\bar{s}_1, \bar{s}_2 \in Stat_E$,

$$\text{if } \bar{s}_1 \approx \bar{s}_2 \text{ then } \bar{s}_1 \sim \bar{s}_2.$$

Whether the implication in the other direction also holds we don't know. This might be proved exploiting the techniques developed by Lenisa in [Len96].

The denotational semantics $\mathcal{D}_B$ is not *fully abstract*—the full abstractness problem for programming languages was first raised by Milner [Mil73, Mil77]—with respect to the operational semantics $\mathcal{O}_L$. For example, the statements send $(c, v := 2)$ and send $(c, v := 1 + 1)$ are identified by the denotational semantics but not by the operational model. More abstract denotational models might be obtained by adapting the ones given by Brookes [Bro96] and Hennessy [Hen94]. However, $\mathcal{D}_B$ is fully abstract with respect to $\approx$ according to (3). Since the elements of $\mathbb{P}$ are extended statements, $\approx$ defines second order bisimilarity on $\mathbb{P}$. From (2) and

$$\begin{aligned} &\mathcal{I}_B(\bar{p}) \\ &\quad = \mathcal{D}_B^+(\bar{p}) \quad \text{[Lemma 4.12]} \\ &\quad = \bar{p} \end{aligned}$$

we can conclude that the space $\mathbb{P}$ is internally fully abstract: for all $\bar{p}_1, \bar{p}_2 \in \mathbb{P}$,

$$\bar{p}_1 \approx \bar{p}_2 \text{ if and only if } p_1 = p_2.$$

A simplification with respect to the usual languages of this kind is that we assume one global state and store, rather than a distribution of *local* states and stores over the various parallel components. The design of a mechanism for local states and stores can be found in the work on the semantics of Philips's parallel object oriented language POOL [ABKR86, ABKR89].

In a setting with local states and stores arbitrary combinations of sequential and parallel compositions might give rise to statements which are of very little significance. These combinations can be ruled out by replacing the language construct parallel composition by *process creation*. For metric semantic models of process creation we refer the reader to America and De Bakker's [AB88].

In a distributed setting it would be meaningful to transmit a *closure*, a pair consisting of a statement and a local store, rather than just a statement as we do here. This seems to be related to the explicit substitution in the $\lambda\rho$- and $\lambda\sigma$-calculus of Curien et al. [Cur88, ACCL91].

In our setting receive $(c, x)$ is not a *binder* (binding $x$) as it is in, e.g., ECCS [EN86], and $\pi$-calculus [MPW92]. Consider the following statement:

$$(\mathsf{send}\,(c, s_1)\,;\,\mathsf{send}\,(c, s_2)) \parallel \mathsf{receive}\,(c, x) \parallel (\mathsf{receive}\,(c, x)\,;\,\mathsf{call}\,(x)).$$

Which statement is stored for the statement variable $x$ upon the execution of call $(x)$ is dependent on the order the communications take place. This is a consequence of considering one global store. If we were to consider local stores receive $(c, x)$ would become a binder.

## References

[AB88] P. America and J.W. de Bakker. Designing Equivalent Models for Process Creation. *Theoretical Computer Science*, 60(2):109–176, September 1988.

[ABKR86] P. America, J.W. de Bakker, J.N. Kok, and J.J.M.M. Rutten. Operational Semantics of a Parallel Object-Oriented Language. In *Proceedings of the 13th Annual ACM Symposium on Principles of Programming Languages*, pages 194–208, St. Petersburg Beach, January 1986. ACM.

[ABKR89] P. America, J.W. de Bakker, J.N. Kok, and J.J.M.M. Rutten. Denotational Semantics of a Parallel Object-Oriented Language. *Information and Computation*, 83(2):152–205, November 1989.

[ACCL91] M. Abadi, L. Cardelli, P.-L. Curien, and J.-J. Lévy. Explicit Substitutions. *Journal of Functional Programming*, 1(4):375–416, 1991.

[AGR92] E. Astesiano, A. Giovini, and G. Reggio. Observational Structures and their Logics. *Theoretical Computer Science*, 96(1):249–283, April 1992.

[Ale27] P. Alexandroff. Über stetige Abbildungen kompakter Räume. *Mathematische Annalen*, 96:555–571, 1927.

[AR89] P. America and J.J.M.M. Rutten. Solving Reflexive Domain Equations in a Category of Complete Metric Spaces. *Journal of Computer and System Sciences*, 39(3):343–375, December 1989.

[Bai09] R. Baire. Sur la Représentation des Fonctions Discontinues. *Acta Mathematica*, 32(1):97–176, 1909.

[Ban22] S. Banach. Sur les Opérations dans les Ensembles Abstraits et leurs Applications aux Equations Intégrales. *Fundamenta Mathematicae*, 3:133–181, 1922.

[Bar92] H.P. Barendregt. Lambda Calculi with Types. In S. Abramsky, Dov M. Gabbay, and T.S.E. Maibaum, editors, *Handbook of Logic in Computer Science*, volume 2, Background: Computational Structures, chapter 2, pages 117–309. Clarendon Press, Oxford, 1992.

[BB93] J.W. de Bakker and F. van Breugel. Topological Models for Higher Order Control Flow. In S. Brookes, M. Main, A. Melton, M. Mislove, and D. Schmidt, editors, *Proceedings of the 9th International Conference on Mathematical Foundations of Programming Semantics*, volume 802 of *Lecture Notes in Computer Science*, pages 122–142, New Orleans, April 1993. Springer-Verlag.

[BM88] J.W. de Bakker and J.-J.Ch. Meyer. Metric Semantics for Concurrency. *BIT*, 28(3):504–529, 1988.

[Bou89] G. Boudol. Towards a Lambda-Calculus for Concurrent and Communicating Systems. In J. Diaz and F. Orejas, editors, *Proceedings of the International Joint Conference on Theory and Practice of Software Development*, volume 351 of *Lecture Notes in Computer Science*, pages 149–162, Barcelona, March 1989. Springer-Verlag.

[Bre94] F. van Breugel. *Topological Models in Comparative Semantics*. PhD thesis, Vrije Universiteit, Amsterdam, September 1994.

[Bre97] F. van Breugel. *Comparative Metric Semantics of Programming Languages: nondeterminism and recursion*. Progress in Theoretical Computer Science. 1997. Birkhäuser Boston, Cambridge.

[Bro96] S. Brookes. Full Abstraction for a Shared-Variable Parallel Language. *Information and Computation*, 127(2):145–163, June 1996.

[BV96] J.W. de Bakker and E.P. de Vink. *Control Flow Semantics*. Foundations of Computing Series. The MIT Press, Cambridge, 1996.

[Cur88] P.-L. Curien. The $\lambda\rho$-calculus: an abstract framework for environment machines. Report, LIENS, Paris, October 1988.

[EN86] U. Engberg and M. Nielsen. A Calculus of Communicating Systems with Label Passing. Report DAIMI PB-208, Aarhus University, Aarhus, May 1986.

[Eng89] R. Engelking. *General Topology*, volume 6 of *Sigma Series in Pure Mathematics*. Heldermann Verlag, Berlin, revised and completed edition, 1989.

[Hau14] F. Hausdorff. *Grundzüge der Mengenlehre*. Leipzig, 1914.

[Hen94] M. Hennessy. A Fully Abstract Denotational Model for Higher-Order Processes. *Information and Computation*, 112(1):55–95, July 1994.

[KR90] J.N. Kok and J.J.M.M. Rutten. Contractions in Comparing Concurrency Semantics. *Theoretical Computer Science*, 76(2/3):179–222, November 1990.

[Kur56] K. Kuratowski. Sur une Méthode de Métrisation Complète des Certains Espaces d'Ensembles Compacts. *Fundamenta Mathematicae*, 43(1):114–138, 1956.

[Len96] M. Lenisa. Final Semantics for a Higher Order Concurrent Language. In H. Kirchner, editor, *Proceedings of the 21st International Colloquium on Trees in Algebra and Programming*, volume 1059 of *Lecture Notes in Computer Science*, pages 102–118, Linköping, April 1996. Springer-Verlag.

[Mil73] R. Milner. Processes: a Mathematical Model of Computing Agents. In H.E. Rose and J.C. Shepherdson, editors, *Proceedings of the Logic Colloquium*, volume 80 of *Studies in Logic and the Foundations of Mathematics*, pages 157–173, Bristol, July 1973. North-Holland.

[Mil77] R. Milner. Fully Abstract Models of Typed $\lambda$-Calculi. *Theoretical Computer Science*, 4(1):1–22, February 1977.

[Mil80] R. Milner. *A Calculus of Communicating Systems*, volume 92 of *Lecture Notes in Computer Science*. Springer-Verlag, Berlin, 1980.

[Mil91] R. Milner. The Polyadic $\pi$-Calculus: a tutorial. Report ECS-LFCS-91-180, University of Edinburgh, Edinburgh, October 1991.

[Mil93] R. Milner. Elements of Interaction. *Communications of the ACM*, 36(1):78–89, January 1993. Turing Award Lecture.

[Mil94] R. Milner. David Michael Ritchie Park (1935–1990) in memoriam. *Theoretical Computer Science*, 133(2):187–200, October 1994.

[MPW92] R. Milner, J. Parrow, and D. Walker. A Calculus of Mobile Processes, I and II. *Information and Computation*, 100(1):1–40 and 41–77, September 1992.

[MS92] R. Milner and D. Sangiorgi. Barbed Bisimulation. In W. Kuich, editor, *Proceedings of the 19th International Colloquium on Automata, Languages and Programming*, volume 623 of *Lecture Notes in Computer Science*, pages 685–695, Vienna, July 1992. Springer-Verlag.

[Niv79] M. Nivat. Infinite Words, Infinite Trees, Infinite Computations. In J.W. de Bakker and J. van Leeuwen, editors, *Foundations of Computer Science III*, part 2: Languages, Logic, Semantics, volume 109 of *Mathematical Centre Tracts*, pages 3–52. Mathematical Centre, Amsterdam, 1979.

[Par81] D. Park. Concurrency and Automata on Infinite Sequences. In P. Deussen, editor, *Proceedings of 5th GI-Conference on Theoretical Computer Science*, volume 104 of *Lecture Notes in Computer Science*, pages 167–183, Karlsruhe, March 1981. Springer-Verlag.

[Plo81] G.D. Plotkin. A Structural Approach to Operational Semantics. Report DAIMI FN-19, Aarhus University, Aarhus, September 1981.

[Rep92] J.H. Reppy. *Higher-Order Concurrency*. PhD thesis, Cornell University, Ithaca, January 1992.

[RT92] J.J.M.M. Rutten and D. Turi. On the Foundations of Final Semantics: non-standard sets, metric spaces, partial orders. In J.W. de Bakker, W.-P. de Roever, and G. Rozenberg, editors, *Proceedings of the REX Workshop on Semantics: Foundations and Applications*, volume 666 of *Lecture Notes in Computer Science*, pages 477–530, Beekbergen, June 1992. Springer-Verlag.

[Rut92] J.J.M.M. Rutten. Processes as Terms: Non-Well-Founded Models for Bisimulation. *Mathematical Structures in Computer Science*, 2(3):257–275, September 1992.

[San92] D. Sangiorgi. *Expressing Mobility in Process Algebras: first-order and higher-order paradigms*. PhD thesis, University of Edinburgh, Edinburgh, 1992.

[San93] D. Sangiorgi. From $\pi$-Calculus to Higher-Order $\pi$-Calculus—and back. In M.-C. Gaudel and J.-P. Jouannaud, editors, *Proceedings of the 5th International Conference on Theory and Practice of Software Development*, volume 668 of *Lecture Notes in Computer Science*, pages 151–166, Orsay, April 1993. Springer-Verlag.

[Tho90] B. Thomsen. *Calculi for Higher Order Communicating Systems*. PhD thesis, Imperial College, London, September 1990.

[Tho95] B. Thomsen. A Theory of Higher Order Communicating Systems. *Information and Computation*, 116(1):38–57, January 1995.

[TLK96] B. Thomsen, L. Leth, and T.-M. Kuo. A Facile Tutorial. In U. Montanari and V. Sassone, editors, *Proceedings of CONCUR'96*, volume 1119 of *Lecture Notes in Computer Science*, pages 278–298, Pisa, August 1996. Springer-Verlag.

## A Ultrametric Spaces

We present some notions from metric topology and Banach's fixed point theorem. For further details on (metric) topology we refer the reader to Engelking's standard work [Eng89].

We start with the definition of a basic notion: a 1-bounded ultrametric space.

DEFINITION A.1 A *(1-bounded ultrametric) space* is a pair $(X, d_X)$ consisting of

- a set $X$ and

- a function $d_X : X \times X \to [0, 1]$, called *(ultra-) metric*, satisfying, for all $x, y, z \in X$,

$*$ $d_X(x, y) = 0$ if and only if $x = y$,
$*$ $d_X(x, y) = d_X(y, x)$, and
$*$ $d_X(x, z) \leq \max\{d_X(x, y), d_X(y, z)\}$.

To simplify notations we shall usually write $X$ instead of $(X, d_X)$ and denote the metric of a space $X$ by $d_X$.

An example of a metric is presented in

DEFINITION A.2 Let $X$ be a set. The *discrete* metric $d_X : X \times X \to [0, 1]$ is defined by

$$d_X(x, y) = \begin{cases} 0 & \text{if } x = y \\ 1 & \text{if } x \neq y \end{cases}$$

From spaces one can build new spaces by means of operations like the shrinking operation $\frac{1}{2}\cdot$, the Cartesian product $\times$ and the disjoint union $+$.

DEFINITION A.3 Let $X$ and $Y$ be spaces.

- The metric $d_{\frac{1}{2}\cdot X} : X \times X \to [0, 1]$ is defined by

$$d_{\frac{1}{2}\cdot X}(x, y) = \frac{1}{2} \cdot d_X(x, y).$$

- The metric $d_{X \times Y} : (X \times Y) \times (X \times Y) \to [0, 1]$ is defined by

$$d_{X \times Y}((v, w), (x, y)) = \max\{d_X(v, x), d_Y(w, y)\}.$$

- The metric $d_{X+Y} : (X + Y) \times (X + Y) \to [0, 1]$ is defined by

$$d_{X+Y}(v, w) = \begin{cases} d_X(v, w) & \text{if } v \in X \text{ and } w \in X \\ d_Y(v, w) & \text{if } v \in Y \text{ and } w \in Y \\ 1 & \text{otherwise} \end{cases}$$

Below we will encounter some other operations on spaces.

The completeness of a space is essential in Banach's theorem. Before we introduce this notion we first present the definitions of converging and Cauchy sequence.

DEFINITION A.4 Let $X$ be a space. Let $(x_n)_n$ be a sequence in $X$ and $x$ an element of $X$.

- The sequence $(x_n)_n$ is said to *converge* to the element $x$ if

$$\forall \epsilon > 0 : \exists N \in \mathbb{N} : \forall n \geq N : d_X(x_n, x) \leq \epsilon.$$

- The sequence $(x_n)_n$ is called *Cauchy* if

$$\forall \epsilon > 0 : \exists N \in \mathbb{N} : \forall m, n \geq N : d_X(x_m, x_n) \leq \epsilon.$$

As can be easily seen, every convergent sequence is Cauchy.

DEFINITION A.5 A space is called *complete* if every Cauchy sequence in the space is convergent.

As one can easily verify, the operations $\frac{1}{2}\cdot$, $\times$, and $+$ preserve completeness.
Compactness, a generalisation of finiteness, is introduced in

DEFINITION A.6 A subset of a space is called *compact* if every sequence in the set has a converging subsequence.

The set $\mathcal{P}_{nc}(X)$ of nonempty and compact subsets of the space $X$ is turned into a space by endowing it with the Hausdorff metric (see Chapter VIII of [Hau14]) introduced in

DEFINITION A.7 Let $X$ be a space. The *Hausdorff* metric $d_{\mathcal{P}_{nc}(X)} : \mathcal{P}_{nc}(X) \times \mathcal{P}_{nc}(X) \to [0, 1]$ is defined by

$$d_{\mathcal{P}_{nc}(X)}(A, B) = \max \{\max_{a \in A} \min_{b \in B} d_X(a, b), \max_{b \in B} \min_{a \in A} d_X(b, a)\}.$$

The operation $\mathcal{P}_{nc}$ preserves completeness (Lemma 3 of [Kur56]). The space $\mathcal{P}_c(X)$ of compact subsets of the space $X$ is defined by

$$\mathcal{P}_c(X) = \mathcal{P}_{nc}(X) + \{\emptyset\}.$$

The set $X \to Y$ of functions from the space $X$ to the space $Y$ is turned into a space by endowing it with the metric introduced in

DEFINITION A.8 Let $X$ and $Y$ be spaces. The metric $d_{X \to Y} : (X \to Y) \times (X \to Y) \to [0, 1]$ is defined by

$$d_{X \to Y}(f, g) = \sup_{x \in X} d_Y(f(x), g(x)).$$

Frequently we restrict ourselves to the subspace of nonexpansive functions.

DEFINITION A.9 Let $X$ and $Y$ be spaces. A function $f : X \to Y$ is called *nonexpansive* if, for all $x, y \in X$,

$$d_Y(f(x), f(y)) \leq d_X(x, y).$$

We denote the space of nonexpansive functions from the space $X$ to the space $Y$ by $X \to^1 Y$. The operations $\to$ and $\to^1$ preserve completeness as can easily be verified.

Next we will introduce an equivalence notion on spaces.

DEFINITION A.10 Let $X$ and $Y$ be spaces. A function $f : X \to Y$ is called *isometric* if, for all $x, y \in X$,

$$d_Y(f(x), f(y)) = d_X(x, y).$$

Note that an isometric function is injective.

DEFINITION A.11 The spaces $X$ and $Y$ are called *isometric*, denoted by $X \cong Y$, if there exists an isometric function from $X$ to $Y$ which is surjective.

Besides the completeness of the space, the contractiveness of the function is another essential ingredient of Banach's theorem.

DEFINITION A.12 Let $X$ and $Y$ be spaces. A function $f : X \to Y$ is called *contractive* if there exists an $\epsilon$, with $0 \leq \epsilon < 1$, such that, for all $x, y \in X$,

$$d_Y(f(x), f(y)) \leq \epsilon \cdot d_X(x, y).$$

We conclude with Banach's fixed point theorem.

THEOREM A.13 (BANACH) Let $X$ be a nonempty complete space. If the function $f : X \to X$ is contractive then it has a unique fixed point *fix* $(f)$.

*Proof* See Theorem II.6 of [Ban22]. □

# 5 The Tile Model

**Fabio Gadducci and Ugo Montanari**

## 1 Introduction

It is not an overstatement to say that, in the latest years, there has been an unprecedented flow of proposals, aiming at methodologies that could offer a flexible framework (intended as a meta-formalism) for specifying the behaviour of rule-based computational systems. Widely spread in the field of concurrency theory, *transition systems* [24] offers a useful tool: They are roughly defined as a set of *states*, representing the possible *configurations* (e.g., memory contents, data structures, etc.) of an abstract machine; and a *transition relation* over states, where each element $\langle s, t \rangle$ denotes the evolution from state $s$ to state $t$. Due to its simplicity, however, this view is clearly no more adequate when we consider formalisms with a compositional structure over states, and the transition relation needs to be inductively defined according to that structure. This is the case for example of *Petri nets* [42], where a state is a multi-set of atomic components, and disjoint subsets may evolve simultaneously (i.e., *in parallel*); of *term rewriting systems* [26], where states are terms of an algebra, and rewriting steps are obtained by closure under substitution and contextualisation from a set of rewrite rules; or, in general, of those formalisms that rely on the use of *synchronisation* and *side-effects* in determining the actual behaviour of a given system.

We consider as a major breakthrough the introduction of the *structural operational semantics* (SOS) approach [40]: States are terms of an algebra, whose operators express basic features of a system, and the transition relation is defined by means of inference rules, guided by the structure of the states. Some of the extensions to this approach that proved fruitful for our view are *context systems* [30], where the transition relation is defined on *open* terms (that is, terms that may contain free variables), describing partially unspecified component of a system; and *structured transition systems* [9, 15], where, in order to account for the spatial distribution of a system, transitions are equipped with an algebraic structure, too. The first approach generalises observational semantics to partially specified behaviours, while the latter characterises equationally those (sequences of) transitions that identify "computationally equivalent" behaviours.

To equip transitions (actually, rewriting steps) with an algebraic structure is also a key point of the *rewriting logic* approach [33]: A system is considered as a logical theory, and any sequence of transitions as a *sequent* entailed by the theory. The entailment relation is defined by means of a suitable calculus, whose inference rules are driven by the structure of terms,

Research partially supported by MURST Project *Tecniche Formali per Sistemi Software*, by CNR Integrated Project *Metodi per Sistemi Connessi mediante Reti*, and by ESPRIT Working Group *CONFER2*.

and are intended to express some basic feature of the system. Computing is then identified with deduction, and equivalent computations correspond to proofs with the same structure.

Trying to summarise, we could say that our *tile model* combines the SOS idea of a structure-driven set of inference rules with the use of an incremental format (analogous to context systems, but more general) that allows us to build new rules from old ones. Furthermore, from structured transition systems and rewriting logic the framework retains the idea of an explicit representation of transitions as an algebra, where certain basic structural axioms describe the concurrency properties of the model.

In our logic, a sequent is then a tuple $\alpha : s \xrightarrow[b]{a} t$, where $s \to t$ is a rewriting step from term $s$ to $t$, $\alpha$ is the *proof term* associated to the step, $a$ is the *trigger* of the step, and $b$ is its *effect*. Graphically, this is represented as a *tile*

$$\begin{array}{ccc} n & \xrightarrow{s} & m \\ {\scriptstyle a}\downarrow & \alpha & \downarrow{\scriptstyle b} \\ p & \xrightarrow[t]{} & q \end{array}$$

stating that the *initial configuration* $s$ of the system evolves to the *final configuration* $t$ producing an effect $b$. However, $s$ may be an open term, and the rewriting step is possible only if the sub-components of $s$ may evolve producing a cumulative effect $a$, that serves as the trigger for $\alpha$. Both trigger and effect are called *observations*, and model the interaction, during a computation, of the system with its environment. More precisely, both system configurations are equipped with an *input interface* and an *output interface*, and the trigger just describes the evolution of the input interface from its initial to its final configuration. Similarly for the effect. So, it is natural to visualise a tile as a two-dimensional structure, where the horizontal dimension corresponds to the extension of the system, while the vertical dimension corresponds to the extension of the computation. Actually, we should also imagine a third dimension (the *thickness* of the tile), which models parallelism: Configurations, observations, interfaces and tiles themselves are all supposed to consist of several components in parallel.

This spatial structure is reflected by the inference rules of the calculus, in particular, by the three composition rules. Two sequents $\alpha, \beta$ can be composed in parallel ($\alpha \otimes \beta$), coordinated ($\alpha * \beta$) or composed sequentially ($\alpha \cdot \beta$), varying accordingly the corresponding source, target, trigger and effect. The first operator allows for different components of a system to act simultaneously, explicitly describing parallelism by a *monoidal* structure over transitions. Together with the second, they offer the possibility for different sub-components to synchronise, according to the information carried by their effects, and the presence of an eventual coordinator with an adequate trigger. The third expresses the execution of a sequence of transitions. Proof terms allow us to equip each rewriting step with a suitable encoding of its causes, and a suitable equivalence relation over proof terms will then provide a concurrent semantics for the systems that are under examination.

Space limitations prevent us from dealing with the full range of applications of the framework, or to give a full account of the expressive power that the use of a three-dimensional structure can give in capturing also higher-order formalisms, despite the simple term structure we chose for configurations. In fact, tiles have been used for coordination formalisms equipped with flexible synchronisation primitives [6, 37] and for calculi for mobile processes, like the asynchronous $\pi$-calculus [16]. Tiles are also convenient for handling concurrent process calculi [17]. These results are then strengthened by the tight relationship between the categorical models of sharing graphs (as introduced in [18]) and gs-monoidal theories (see Section 2), a framework used to accommodate the behaviour of e.g. Milner's *action calculus* [36].

As far as categorical models are concerned, *2-categories* [25] are the best-known cat-enriched structure in computer science: They are categories such that each hom-set (the set of arrows with same source and target) is the object-set of another category, whose arrows (called *cells*) are closed under certain composition operators, and are subject to suitable coherence axioms. A more refined enrichment is present in *double categories* [3], whose structure can be informally described as the superposition of a vertical and a horizontal category of cells. It is well-known that 2-categories represent a faithful model for term rewriting systems [8, 41, 43]: The arrows of the underlying category denote terms, and cells denote (equivalence classes of) rewrites. In the paper we show that a similar adequacy result holds for our tile model, if we consider double categories instead. Thus, the generality of our tile model is further confirmed by the richer structure of double categories with respect to 2-categories.

The paper has the following structure. In Section 2 we generalise the usual notion of term over a signature, providing three concrete descriptions which formalise the assumptions implicitly made in the ordinary term algebra construction. In Section 3 we introduce our rewriting systems, providing them with a suitable logic that describes the classes of derivations entailed by a system. In Section 4 we deal with our case study, showing how the standard observational semantics of many process algebras (and context systems) can be recovered in our framework. Finally, in Section 5 we provide a sound and complete categorical model for our logic by means of double categories.

## 2 Building States

We open this section recalling some basic definitions from graph theory, used to recast in a more general fashion the usual notion of term over a signature.

DEFINITION 1 (GRAPHS) A *graph* $G$ is a 4-tuple $\langle O_G, A_G, \delta_0, \delta_1\rangle$: $O_G$, $A_G$ are sets whose elements are called respectively *objects* and *arrows*, and $\delta_0, \delta_1 : A_G \to O_G$ are functions, called respectively *source* and *target*. A graph $G$ is *reflexive* if there exists an *identity* function $id : O_G \to A_G$ such that $\delta_0(id(a)) = \delta_1(id(a)) = a$ for all $a \in O_G$; it is *with pairing* if its class of objects forms as monoid; it is *monoidal* if reflexive and both its classes of objects and arrows form a monoid, and the functions preserve the monoidal operator and the neutral element. □

We can think of an ordinary, one-sorted signature $\Sigma$ of operators as a graph with pairing: Its nodes are elements of the monoid $\mathbb{N}_c$ of (underlined) natural numbers, where sum is defined as $\underline{n} \otimes \underline{m} = \underline{n+m}$, and $\underline{0}$ is the neutral element; its arcs are operators, such that $f : \underline{n} \to \underline{1}$ iff $f \in \Sigma_n$. This view allows for an inductive, step-by-step account of the usual algebraic notion of term, by means of a chain of structures of increasing complexity.

DEFINITION 2 (GRAPH THEORIES) Given a signature $\Sigma$, the associated *graph theory* $G(\Sigma)$ is the monoidal graph with objects the elements of the monoid $\mathbb{N}_c$, and arrows those generated by the following inference rules

$$(generators)\ \frac{f \in \Sigma_n}{f : \underline{n} \to \underline{1} \in G(\Sigma)} \qquad (pairing)\ \frac{s : \underline{n} \to \underline{m},\ t : \underline{n'} \to \underline{m'}}{s \otimes t : \underline{n} \otimes \underline{n'} \to \underline{m} \otimes \underline{m'}}$$

$$(identities)\ \frac{\underline{n} \in \mathbb{N}_c}{id_{\underline{n}} : \underline{n} \to \underline{n}}$$

Monoidality implies that $id_{\underline{0}}$ is the neutral object of the monoid of arrows, and that the *monoidality* axiom $id_{\underline{n}\otimes\underline{m}} = id_{\underline{n}} \otimes id_{\underline{m}}$ holds for all $\underline{n}, \underline{m} \in \mathbb{N}$. □

Graph theories simply equip a signature with an explicit notion of pairing: Each arrow then denotes an array of operators and identities. This theory is rather expressiveless, per se: We will use it only in conjunction with the rewriting mechanism to be introduced later on.

DEFINITION 3 (MONOIDAL THEORIES) Given a signature $\Sigma$, the associated *monoidal theory* $\mathbf{M}(\Sigma)$ is the monoidal graph with objects the elements of the monoid $\mathbb{N}_c$, and arrows those generated by the following inference rules

$$(generators)\ \frac{f \in \Sigma_n}{f : \underline{n} \to \underline{1} \in \mathbf{M}(\Sigma)} \qquad (pairing)\ \frac{s : \underline{n} \to \underline{m},\ t : \underline{n'} \to \underline{m'}}{s \otimes t : \underline{n} \otimes \underline{n'} \to \underline{m} \otimes \underline{m'}}$$

$$(identities)\ \frac{\underline{n} \in \mathbb{N}_c}{id_{\underline{n}} : \underline{n} \to \underline{n}} \qquad (composition)\ \frac{s : \underline{n} \to \underline{m},\ t : \underline{m} \to \underline{k}}{s; t : \underline{n} \to \underline{k}}$$

Moreover, the composition operator is associative, and the monoid of arrows satisfies the *functoriality* axiom

$$(s \otimes t); (s' \otimes t') = (s; s') \otimes (t, t')$$

(whenever both sides are defined) and the *identity* axiom $id_{\underline{n}}; s = s = s; id_{\underline{m}}$ for all $s : \underline{n} \to \underline{m}$. □

Monoidal theories add composition: In fact, any arrow in $\mathbf{M}(\Sigma)$ can be written in a normal form as a sequence of concrete arrows already "appearing" in the underlying graph theory. Thanks to the functoriality axiom, it is easy to show that each term can be decomposed in a tree-like fashion: A monoidal theory is just an example of a so-called *strict monoidal category* [32], for which many representation results are well-known. Now we introduce the more expressive kind of theories we deal with in our paper, *gs-monoidal theories*.

DEFINITION 4 (GS-MONOIDAL THEORIES) Given a signature $\Sigma$, the associated *gs-monoidal theory* $\mathbf{GS}(\Sigma)$ is the monoidal graph with objects the elements of the monoid $\mathbb{N}_c$, and arrows those generated by the following inference rules

$$(generators)\ \frac{f \in \Sigma_n}{f : \underline{n} \to \underline{1} \in \mathbf{GS}(\Sigma)} \qquad (pairing)\ \frac{s : \underline{n} \to \underline{m},\ t : \underline{n'} \to \underline{m'}}{s \otimes t : \underline{n} \otimes \underline{n'} \to \underline{m} \otimes \underline{m'}}$$

$$(identities)\ \frac{\underline{n} \in \mathbb{N}_c}{id_{\underline{n}} : \underline{n} \to \underline{n}} \qquad (composition)\ \frac{s : \underline{n} \to \underline{m},\ t : \underline{m} \to \underline{k}}{s; t : \underline{n} \to \underline{k}}$$

$$(duplicators)\ \frac{\underline{n} \in \mathbb{N}_c}{\nabla_{\underline{n}} : \underline{n} \to \underline{n} \otimes \underline{n}} \qquad (dischargers)\ \frac{\underline{n} \in \mathbb{N}_c}{!_{\underline{n}} : \underline{n} \to \underline{0}}$$

$$(permutation)\ \frac{\underline{n}, \underline{m} \in \mathbb{N}_c}{\rho_{\underline{n},\underline{m}} : \underline{n} \otimes \underline{m} \to \underline{m} \otimes \underline{n}}$$

Moreover, the composition operator is associative, and the monoid of arrows satisfies the functoriality axiom

$$(s \otimes t); (s' \otimes t') = (s; s') \otimes (t; t')$$

(whenever both sides are defined); the identity axiom $id_{\underline{n}}; s = s = s; id_{\underline{m}}$ for all $s : \underline{n} \to \underline{m}$; the *monoidality* axioms

$$\rho_{\underline{n} \otimes \underline{m}, \underline{p}} = (id_{\underline{n}} \otimes \rho_{\underline{m},\underline{p}}); (\rho_{\underline{n},\underline{p}} \otimes id_{\underline{m}})$$

$$!_{\underline{n} \otimes \underline{m}} = !_{\underline{n}} \otimes !_{\underline{m}} \qquad \nabla_{\underline{n} \otimes \underline{m}} = (\nabla_{\underline{n}} \otimes \nabla_{\underline{m}}); (id_{\underline{n}} \otimes \rho_{\underline{n},\underline{m}} \otimes id_{\underline{n}})$$

$$!_{\underline{0}} = \nabla_{\underline{0}} = \rho_{\underline{0},\underline{0}} = id_{\underline{0}}$$

for all $\underline{n}, \underline{m}, \underline{p} \in \mathbb{N}_c$; the *coherence* axioms

$$\nabla_{\underline{n}}; (id_{\underline{n}} \otimes \nabla_{\underline{n}}) = \nabla_{\underline{n}}; (\nabla_{\underline{n}} \otimes id_{\underline{n}}) \qquad \nabla_{\underline{n}}; \rho_{\underline{n},\underline{n}} = \nabla_{\underline{n}}$$

$$\nabla_{\underline{n}}; (id_{\underline{n}} \otimes !_{\underline{n}}) = id_{\underline{n}} \qquad \rho_{\underline{n},\underline{m}}; \rho_{\underline{m},\underline{n}} = id_{\underline{n}} \otimes id_{\underline{m}}$$

for all $\underline{n}, \underline{m} \in \mathbb{N}_c$; and the *naturality* axiom

$$(s \otimes t); \rho_{\underline{m},\underline{q}} = \rho_{\underline{n},\underline{p}}; (t \otimes s)$$

for all $s : \underline{n} \to \underline{m}, t : \underline{p} \to \underline{q} \in S$. □

Intuitively, a gs-monoidal theory is a symmetric strict monoidal category enriched with additional structure, namely the operators $\nabla$ and !, allowing for a (controlled) form of *duplication* and *discharge* of data. This structure falls short of the usual definition of cartesian category only for two axioms, imposing the satisfaction of naturality also for these operators.

DEFINITION 5 (ALGEBRAIC THEORIES) Given a signature $\Sigma$, the associated *algebraic theory* $\mathbf{A}(\Sigma)$ is the monoidal graph with objects the elements of the monoid $\mathbb{N}_c$, and arrows those generated by the same inference rules given for gs-monoidal theories. Moreover, besides the set of axioms already valid for these theories, also a naturality axiom for both dischargers and duplicators holds, namely

$$s; !_{\underline{m}} = !_{\underline{n}} \qquad s; \nabla_{\underline{m}} = \nabla_{\underline{n}}; (s \otimes s)$$

for all $s : \underline{n} \to \underline{m} \in S$. □

It can be considered categorical folklore that a cartesian category can be decomposed into a symmetric monoidal category, together with a family of suitable natural transformations, usually denoted as *diagonals* and *projections* (related papers range from [20, 39] to the more recent [22, 28]). Then, our notion of algebraic theory can be proved equivalent to the classical definition, dating back to the early work of Lawvere [27, 31]: Hence, a classical result states the equivalence of these theories with the usual term algebras.

PROPOSITION 1 (ALGEBRAIC THEORIES AND TERM ALGEBRAS) Let $\Sigma$ be a signature. Then for all $\underline{n}, \underline{m} \in \mathbb{N}_c$ there exists a one-to-one correspondence between the set of arrows from $\underline{n}$ to $\underline{m}$ of $\mathbf{A}(\Sigma)$ and the $m$-tuples of elements of the term algebra —over a set of $n$ variables— associated to $\Sigma$. □

In other words, each arrow $\underline{n} \to \underline{1}$ uniquely identifies an element $t$ of the term algebra over the set $\{x_1, \ldots, x_n\}$: An arrow $\underline{n} \to \underline{m}$ is an $m$-tuple of such elements, and arrow composition is term substitution. Note that this correspondence *requires* that both $\nabla$ and

! are natural: That is, gs-monoidal theories are too concrete, distinguishing elements that intuitively represent the same term. A fundamental property of correspondence can be shown between gs-monoidal theories and *term graphs* (roughly, graphs whose nodes are labeled by operators, as defined e.g. in the introductory chapter of [44]): Each arrow $\underline{n} \to \underline{m}$ identifies a term graph $t$ over $\Sigma$ with a specified $m$-tuple of roots and a specified $n$-tuple of variables nodes, and arrow composition is graph replacement [7]. This correspondence motivates the acronym, where *gs* stands for *graph substitution*.

EXAMPLE 1 (TERMS AND THEORIES) Let us consider the signature $\Sigma_\epsilon = \bigcup_{i=0}^{2} \Sigma_i$, where $\Sigma_0 = \{a, b\}$, $\Sigma_1 = \{f, g\}$ and $\Sigma_2 = \{h\}$ (that same signature is often used in the next sections). Some of the elements in $\mathbf{GS}(\Sigma_\epsilon)$ are $a; f : \underline{0} \to \underline{1}$, $f; g : \underline{1} \to \underline{1}$ and $a; \nabla_{\underline{1}}; (f \otimes id_{\underline{1}}); h : \underline{0} \to \underline{1}$: They correspond to terms $f(a)$, $g(f(x))$ and $h(f(a), a)$, respectively, for a given variable $x$. Let us consider instead the elements $a; \nabla_{\underline{1}}; h$ and $(a \otimes a); h$: They correspond to the same term $h(a, a)$, but they are different as elements of $\mathbf{GS}(\Sigma_\epsilon)$, while they are identified by the naturality axiom for $\nabla$ in $\mathbf{A}(\Sigma_\epsilon)$. □

We believe that the incremental description of these theories, and in particular the relevance of the computational interpretation of (the different presentations of) gs-monoidal theories, has not received enough attention in the literature, despite a few notable exceptions (see e.g. [10, 23, 28]). In fact, the main point for our discussion is that, although their definition is more involved than the classical, set-theoretical ones, algebraic (and *a fortiori* gs-monoidal) theories allow a description of terms which is far more general, and at the same time more concrete, than the one allowed by the ordinary descriptions as elements of a term algebra, separating in a better way the "$\Sigma$-structure" from the additional algebraic structure that the *meta-operators* used in the set-theoretical presentation of term algebras (like *substitution*) implicitly enjoy.[1] In particular, they will allow for an easy graphical depiction of our *rewriting systems*.

## 3 Describing Systems

In this section we propose a general framework for describing the behaviour of rule-based systems, in the vein of both the *rewriting logic* formalism of Meseguer [33] and the SOS approach of Plotkin [40]. Intuitively, what we are seeking is a suitable definition of *rewriting system*: Each rule should be considered as a *module* (kind of basic component of a system) carrying information (equivalently, expressing a few restrictions) on the possible behaviour of its sub-components (that is, of the terms to which it can be applied).

[1] In this view, ! and $\nabla$ describe respectively *garbage collection* and *sharing* [7, 8].

DEFINITION 6 (ALGEBRAIC REWRITING SYSTEMS) An *algebraic rewriting system* (ARS) $\mathcal{R}$ is a four-tuple $\langle \Sigma_\sigma, \Sigma_\tau, N, R \rangle$, where $\Sigma_\sigma$, $\Sigma_\tau$ are signatures, $N$ is a set of (rule) names and $R$ is a function $R : N \to \mathbf{A}(\Sigma_\sigma) \times G(\Sigma_\tau) \times G(\Sigma_\tau) \times \mathbf{A}(\Sigma_\sigma)$ such that for all $d \in N$, with $R(d) = \langle l, a, b, r \rangle$, we have $l : \underline{n} \to \underline{m}, r : \underline{p} \to \underline{q}$ iff $a : \underline{n} \to \underline{p}, b : \underline{m} \to \underline{q}$. $\square$

With an abuse of notation, in the previous definition we denote the set of arrows of a theory by the theory itself. In the following, we usually write a *rule* as $d : l \xrightarrow[b]{a} r$ or, graphically, as a *tile*

$$\begin{array}{ccc} n & \xrightarrow{l} & m \\ {\scriptstyle a}\downarrow & d & \downarrow{\scriptstyle b} \\ p & \xrightarrow[r]{} & q \end{array}$$

making explicit source and target of the operators.

A rewriting system is *gs-monoidal* (*monoidal*, *graph*) if, in defining $R$, $l$ and $r$ are elements of $\mathbf{GS}(\Sigma_\sigma)$ ($\mathbf{M}(\Sigma_\sigma)$ and $G(\Sigma_\sigma)$, respectively): The choice depends on *how expressive* we need our system to be. For example, a *context system*, introduced in [30] in order to generalise SOS rules to deal with process contexts, is just a graph system, where $R : N \to \Sigma_\sigma \times G(\Sigma_\tau) \times \Sigma_\tau \times \Sigma_\sigma$, with the further restriction that $a : \underline{1} \to \underline{1}$ for all $a \in \Sigma_\tau$ (hence, for all $d \in N$, if $R(d) = \langle l, a, b, r \rangle$ then $l, r$ have the same source and target). A *term rewriting system* [26], instead, is given by a pair $\langle \Sigma, R \rangle$ where $\Sigma$ is an ordinary signature, and $R$ is a set of *rules*, i.e., of pairs $\langle l, r \rangle$ for $l, r$ elements of the term algebra over $\Sigma$; thanks to Proposition 1, it is just an algebraic rewriting system, where $\Sigma_\tau$ is empty.

EXAMPLE 2 (AN ALGEBRAIC REWRITING SYSTEM) Let us consider the signatures $\Sigma_\epsilon$ (already introduced) and $\Sigma_\eta = \Sigma_1 = \{u, v, w\}$. Our running example will be the algebraic rewriting system $\mathcal{R}_e = \langle \Sigma_\epsilon, \Sigma_\eta, N_e, R_e \rangle$, such that

$$R_e = \left\{ d : a \xrightarrow[u]{id} b, d_1 : f \xrightarrow[v]{u} g, d_2 : f \xrightarrow[w]{v} f, d_3 : h \xrightarrow[w]{u \otimes v} !_{\underline{1}} \otimes g \right\},$$

(where $id$ is shorthand for $id_{\underline{0}}$) described, in pictorial form, by the tiles

$$\begin{array}{ccc} 0 & \xrightarrow{a} & 1 \\ {\scriptstyle id}\downarrow & d & \downarrow{\scriptstyle u} \\ 0 & \xrightarrow[b]{} & 1 \end{array} \qquad \begin{array}{ccc} 1 & \xrightarrow{f} & 1 \\ {\scriptstyle u}\downarrow & d_1 & \downarrow{\scriptstyle v} \\ 1 & \xrightarrow[g]{} & 1 \end{array} \qquad \begin{array}{ccc} 1 & \xrightarrow{f} & 1 \\ {\scriptstyle v}\downarrow & d_2 & \downarrow{\scriptstyle w} \\ 1 & \xrightarrow[f]{} & 1 \end{array} \qquad \begin{array}{ccc} 2 & \xrightarrow{h} & 1 \\ {\scriptstyle u \otimes v}\downarrow & d_3 & \downarrow{\scriptstyle w} \\ 2 & \xrightarrow[!_{\underline{1}} \otimes g]{} & 1 \end{array}$$

The intuitive meaning of rule $d$ is that the element $a$ can be rewritten to $b$, producing an effect $u$; of $d_1$, that $f$ can be rewritten to $g$, producing an effect $v$, whenever there exists a suitable rewrite with an effect $u$. Or, in the ordinary term rewriting view: The term $f(x)$ is rewritten to $g(x)$, producing an effect $v$, but the rule can be applied only if the eventual sub-term associated to $x$ is rewritten with an effect $u$; and so on for the other rules. □

How to recover the actual behaviour of a large system, from the behaviours of its basic components? We consider a rewriting system $\mathcal{R}$ as a logical theory, and any rewrite—using rules in $\mathcal{R}$—as a *sequent* entailed by that theory. A sequent is therefore a five-tuple $\langle \alpha, s, a, b, t \rangle$, where $s \to t$ is a rewriting step, $\alpha$ is a *proof term* (an encoding of the causes of the step), $a$ and $b$ are respectively the input and output conditions, the *observations* associated to the rewrite. In the following, we say that *s rewrites to t via* $\alpha$ (using a *trigger* $a$ and producing an *effect* $b$) if the sequent $\alpha : s \xrightarrow[b]{a} t$ can be obtained by finitely many applications of the set of *inference rules* described below.[2]

DEFINITION 7 (THE TILE LOGIC) Let $\mathcal{R} = \langle \Sigma_\sigma, \Sigma_\tau, N, R \rangle$ be an ARS. We say that $\mathcal{R}$ *entails* the set $T(\mathcal{R})$ of *algebraic sequents* $\alpha : s \xrightarrow[b]{a} t$ obtained by a finite number of applications of the following set of *inference rules*: The *basic rules*

$$(gen)\ \frac{d : s \xrightarrow[b]{a} t \in R}{d : s \xrightarrow[b]{a} t \in T(\mathcal{R})}$$

$$(h\text{-}refl)\ \frac{s : \underline{n} \to \underline{m} \in \mathbf{A}(\Sigma_\sigma)}{id^s : s \xrightarrow[id]{id} s \in T(\mathcal{R})} \qquad (v\text{-}refl)\ \frac{a : \underline{n} \to \underline{m} \in \mathbf{M}(\Sigma_\tau)}{id_a : id \xrightarrow[a]{a} id \in T(\mathcal{R})}$$

(where $id$ is shorthand for both $id_{\underline{n}}$ and $id_{\underline{m}}$); the *composition rules*

$$(par)\ \frac{\alpha : s \xrightarrow[b]{a} t,\ \beta : u \xrightarrow[d]{c} v \in T(\mathcal{R})}{\alpha \otimes \beta : s \otimes u \xrightarrow[b \otimes d]{a \otimes c} t \otimes v \in T(\mathcal{R})}$$

$$(hor)\ \frac{\alpha : s \xrightarrow[c]{a} t,\ \beta : u \xrightarrow[b]{c} v \in T(\mathcal{R})}{\alpha * \beta : s; u \xrightarrow[b]{a} t; v \in T(\mathcal{R})}$$

$$(vert)\ \frac{\alpha : s \xrightarrow[b]{a} u,\ \beta : u \xrightarrow[d]{c} t \in T(\mathcal{R})}{\alpha \cdot \beta : s \xrightarrow[b; d]{a; c} t \in T(\mathcal{R})};$$

[2] Note that, from the point of view of the inference system, there was no need to restrict our attention to rules whose effect and trigger are just elements of a graph theory. The reason for this choice lies in the simpler characterisation of both the algebraic and the categorical semantics (respectively in Section 3.2 and Section 5) of the logic, yet obtaining at the same time a device that is powerful enough for our main case study in Section 4.

and finally, the *auxiliary rules*

$$(perm)\ \frac{a : \underline{n} \to \underline{m},\ b : \underline{n'} \to \underline{m'} \in \mathbf{M}(\Sigma_\tau)}{\rho_{a,b} : \rho_{\underline{n},\underline{n'}} \xrightarrow[b \otimes a]{a \otimes b} \rho_{\underline{m},\underline{m'}} \in T(\mathcal{R})}$$

$$(dupl)\ \frac{a : \underline{n} \to \underline{m} \in \mathbf{M}(\Sigma_\tau)}{\nabla_a : \nabla_{\underline{n}} \xrightarrow[a \otimes a]{a} \nabla_{\underline{m}} \in T(\mathcal{R})} \qquad (dis)\ \frac{a : \underline{n} \to \underline{m} \in \mathbf{M}(\Sigma_\tau)}{!_a : !_{\underline{n}} \xrightarrow[id]{a} !_{\underline{m}} \in T(\mathcal{R})}$$

(where $id$ is shorthand for $id_{\underline{0}}$). □

The basic rules provide the generators of the sequents, together with suitable identity arrows, whose intuitive meaning is that an element of $\mathbf{A}(\Sigma_\sigma)$ or $\mathbf{M}(\Sigma_\tau)$ stays idle during a rewrite (that is, it rewrites to itself) showing no effect and using no trigger. The composition rules express the way in which sequents can be combined, either sequentially (*vert*), or executing them in parallel (*par*) or nesting one inside the other (*hor*). The auxiliary rules are the counterpart of the auxiliary operators in Definition 4: They provide a way of permutating (*perm*) two sequents, duplicating (*dupl*) (or better, making a copy of the associated pointer, so to say) or discharging (*dis*) a sequent (making it inaccessible from the outside), as we discussed referring to the underlying structure of algebraic theories. In fact, we could denote a sequent as *gs-monoidal* if the underlying system is gs-monoidal; or *monoidal*, if the underlying rewriting system is monoidal, and the sequents are generated using basic and composition rules only.

EXAMPLE 3 (REWRITES AS SEQUENTS) Let us consider now the ARS $\mathcal{R}_e$ we previously defined. As an example, it entails the sequent

$$\frac{\dfrac{\dfrac{}{d : a \xrightarrow[u]{id} b} \quad \dfrac{}{d_1 : f \xrightarrow[v]{u} g}}{d * d_1 : a; f \xrightarrow[v]{id} b; g}\ (hor) \qquad \dfrac{}{d_2 : f \xrightarrow[w]{v} f}}{(d * d_1) * d_2 : a; f; f \xrightarrow[w]{id} b; g; f}\ (hor)$$

(with $id$ shorthand for $id_{\underline{0}}$), where the derivation is described in a natural deduction style. Both $d$ and $d_1$ are axioms: They are combined through a *horizontal* composition, obtaining the sequent $d * d_1$, that expresses the simultaneous execution of two rewrites on nested sub-terms of $a;\ f$ (that is, of the term $f(a)$). Then, the resulting sequent is, again horizontally, composed with $d_2$.

Another example is represented by the sequent

$$\dfrac{\dfrac{\dfrac{}{d : a \xrightarrow[u]{id} b} \qquad \dfrac{\dfrac{}{d : a \xrightarrow[u]{id} b} \quad \dfrac{}{d_1 : f \xrightarrow[v]{u} g}}{d * d_1 : a; f \xrightarrow[v]{id} b; g}\,(hor)}{d \otimes (d * d_1) : a \otimes (a; f) \xrightarrow[u \otimes v]{id} b \otimes (b; g)}\,(par) \qquad \dfrac{}{d_3 : h \xrightarrow[w]{u \otimes v} !_{\underline{1}} \otimes g}}{(d \otimes (d * d_1)) * d_3 : (a \otimes (a; f)); h \xrightarrow[w]{id} b; g; g}\,(hor)$$

At first, the sequent $d$ is combined in parallel with $d * d_1$, so that they act simultaneously on disjoint parts of $a \otimes (a; f)$, corresponding to the ordered pair of terms $\langle a, f(a) \rangle$. Then, the resulting sequent $d \otimes (d * d_1)$ is nested inside $d_3$. A different sequent entailed by the system, yet with the same source and target of $d \otimes (d * d_1)$, is obtained through the following derivation

$$\dfrac{\dfrac{\dfrac{}{d : a \xrightarrow[u]{id} b} \quad \dfrac{}{d : a \xrightarrow[u]{id} b}}{d \otimes d : a \otimes a \xrightarrow[u \otimes u]{id} b \otimes b}\,(par) \qquad \dfrac{\dfrac{}{id_u : id_{\underline{1}} \xrightarrow[u]{u} id_{\underline{1}}} \quad \dfrac{}{d_1 : f \xrightarrow[v]{u} g}}{id_u \otimes d_1 : id_{\underline{1}} \otimes f \xrightarrow[u \otimes v]{u \otimes u} id_{\underline{1}} \otimes g}\,(par)}{(d \otimes d) * (id_u \otimes d_1) : (a \otimes a); (id_{\underline{1}} \otimes f) \xrightarrow[u \otimes v]{id} (b \otimes b); (id_{\underline{1}} \otimes g)}\,(hor)$$

since $(a \otimes a); (id_{\underline{1}} \otimes f) = a \otimes (a; f)$ and $(b \otimes b); (id_{\underline{1}} \otimes g) = b \otimes (b; g)$ by the functoriality and identity axioms. □

## 3.1 An Operational Semantics

The set $T(\mathcal{R})$ we just defined can be regarded as too concrete, in the sense (as we argued on a different level about gs-monoidal and algebraic theories) that sequents that intuitively represent the same rewrite may have different representations. An equivalence over sequents can then be considered as an abstraction from implementation details, identifying *computationally* equivalent derivations.

DEFINITION 8 (ABSTRACT ALGEBRAIC SEQUENTS) Let $\mathcal{R} = \langle \Sigma_\sigma, \Sigma_\tau, N, R \rangle$ be an ARS. We say that it entails the set $T(\mathcal{R})_E$ of *abstract algebraic sequents*, whose elements are the equivalence classes of the algebraic sequents entailed by $\mathcal{R}$ modulo a set $E$ of axioms, which are intended to apply to the corresponding proof terms. The set $E$ contains three *associativity* axioms, stating that all the composition operators are associative; the *functoriality* axioms

$$(\alpha \otimes \beta) \cdot (\gamma \otimes \delta) = (\alpha \cdot \gamma) \otimes (\beta \cdot \delta) \qquad (\alpha \otimes \beta) * (\gamma \otimes \delta) = (\alpha * \gamma) \otimes (\beta * \delta)$$
$$(\alpha \cdot \beta) * (\gamma \cdot \delta) = (\alpha * \gamma) \cdot (\beta * \delta)$$

(satisfied whenever both sides are defined); the *identity* axioms $id_{id_{\underline{n}}} = id^{id_{\underline{n}}}$, $id^s \cdot \alpha = \alpha = \alpha \cdot id^t$ and $id_a * \alpha = \alpha = \alpha * id_b$ for all $\alpha : s \xrightarrow[b]{a} t$; the *monoidality* axioms

$$id^{s \otimes t} = id^s \otimes id^t \qquad id_{a \otimes b} = id_a \otimes id_b$$

$$id^{s;t} = id^s * id^t \qquad id_{a;b} = id_a \cdot id_b$$

$$\alpha \otimes id_{id_{\underline{0}}} = \alpha = id_{id_{\underline{0}}} \otimes \alpha \qquad \rho_{a \otimes b, c} = (id_a \otimes \rho_{b,c}) * (\rho_{a,c} \otimes id_b)$$

$$!_{a \otimes b} = !_a \otimes !_b \qquad \nabla_{a \otimes b} = (\nabla_a \otimes \nabla_b) * (id_a \otimes \rho_{a,b} \otimes id_b)$$

$$!_{id_{\underline{0}}} = \nabla_{id_{\underline{0}}} = \rho_{id_{\underline{0}}, id_{\underline{0}}} = id_{id_{\underline{0}}}$$

for all $\alpha \in T(\mathcal{R})$, $s, t \in \mathbf{A}(\Sigma_\sigma)$ and $a, b, c \in \mathbf{M}(\Sigma_\tau)$; the *coherence* axioms

$$\nabla_a * (id_a \otimes \nabla_a) = \nabla_a * (\nabla_a \otimes id_a) \qquad \nabla_a * \rho_{a,a} = \nabla_a$$

$$\nabla_a * (id_a \otimes !_a) = id_a \qquad \rho_{a,b} * \rho_{b,a} = id_a \otimes id_b$$

for all $a, b \in \mathbf{M}(\Sigma_\tau)$; the *composition* axioms

$$\nabla_{a;b} = \nabla_a \cdot \nabla_b \qquad !_{a;b} = !_a \cdot !_b \qquad \rho_{a;b,c;d} = \rho_{a,c} \cdot \rho_{b,d}$$

for all $a; b, c; d \in \mathbf{M}(\Sigma_\tau)$; and the *naturality* axioms

$$(\alpha \otimes \beta) * \rho_{b,d} = \rho_{a,c} * (\beta \otimes \alpha)$$

$$\alpha * !_b = !_a \qquad \alpha * \nabla_b = \nabla_a * (\alpha \otimes \alpha)$$

for all $\alpha : s \xrightarrow[b]{a} t$, $\beta : u \xrightarrow[d]{c} v \in T(\mathcal{R})$. □

It can be easily checked that the previous axioms preserve the "borderline" of sequents: For any rewriting system $\mathcal{R}$ entailing the sequents $\alpha : s \xrightarrow[b]{a} t$ and $\beta : u \xrightarrow[d]{c} v$, whenever the proof terms $\alpha, \beta$ are equivalent, also their source and target (and trigger and effect) are equivalent as elements of the associated algebraic (monoidal, respectively) theory.

The axiomatisation we propose properly extends the one given for rewriting logic [33]. It could then be argued that this axiomatisation is able to capture the *concurrent behaviour* of a system: Each equivalence class of sequents should intuitively describe the same set of *causally unrelated computations*. This is not so different in spirit from the well-known *permutation equivalence* [5, 21], and there exists in fact a tight correspondence between the two notions [29]. For a few initial considerations about the actual degree of concurrency expressed by the axioms, we refer to [8].

EXAMPLE 4 (EQUATING SEQUENTS) Let us consider again the ARS $\mathcal{V}$. As shown in Example 3, the system entails the sequents $d \otimes (d * d_1)$ and $(d \otimes d) * (id_u \otimes d_1)$. Their respective source and target are equivalent as elements of the algebraic theory over $\Sigma_\epsilon$; and also the two sequents coincide as abstract sequents, since their proof terms are identified by functoriality and identity axioms, even though they have different derivations. □

## 3.2 An Observational Semantics

We already noted that the abstract semantics we defined in the previous section preserves the "along the border" structure of sequents: That is, to equivalent proof terms correspond sequents whose source and target (and trigger and effect) coincide as elements of the algebraic (monoidal, respectively) theory. Such a semantics can then be considered as operational in flavour, since it does correspond to a certain extent to proof normalisation, reflecting more what we could call the degree of abstraction of a system as a computational device, that is, the way in which the deduction process is actually implemented.

Nevertheless, we should remark that the two spatial dimensions of a sequent —horizontal for source and target, vertical for effect and trigger— hardly play the same role. In fact, when we introduced pictorially the system $\mathcal{R}_e$ in Example 2, we explicitly referred to source and target as *states* of our system, and to trigger and effect as *conditions* to be verified, before applying a given rule. It seems then rather perspicuous to introduce a semantics over states, which is only observational: That is, identifying states that show the same behaviour on the input (trigger) and output (effect) components. To this end, we simplify the structure of sequents, dropping the proof term, thus recovering a generalised notion of *transition system* [24].

DEFINITION 9 (TILE TRANSITION SYSTEM) Let $\mathcal{R} = \langle \Sigma_\sigma, \Sigma_\tau, N, R \rangle$ be an ARS. The associated *tile transition system* is the relation $Tr(\mathcal{R}) \subseteq \mathbf{A}(\Sigma_\sigma) \times \mathbf{M}(\Sigma_\tau) \times \mathbf{M}(\Sigma_\tau) \times \mathbf{A}(\Sigma_\sigma)$ obtained dropping the first component from relation $T(\mathcal{R})$. □

In the following, with an abuse of notation, we will refer to a four-tuple $\langle s, a, b, t \rangle$ as a sequent entailed by an ARS. This is justified by the fact that an equivalent relation is obtained adding to the set $E$ of Definition 8 the axiom

$$\frac{\alpha : s \xrightarrow[b]{a} t,\ \beta : s \xrightarrow[b]{a} t}{\alpha = \beta}.$$

intuitively equating those five-tuples with the same border. Restricting our attention to a transition system allows us to define a suitable notion of behavioural equivalence by the well-known technique of *bisimulation* [38].

DEFINITION 10 (TILE BISIMULATIONS) Let $\mathcal{R} = \langle \Sigma_\sigma, \Sigma_\tau, N, R \rangle$ be an ARS. An equivalence relation $\equiv_b \subseteq \mathbf{A}(\Sigma_\sigma) \times \mathbf{A}(\Sigma_\sigma)$ is a *tile bisimulation* for $\mathcal{R}$ if, whenever $s \equiv_b t$ for $s, t$ elements of $\mathbf{A}(\Sigma_\sigma)$, then for any sequent $s \xrightarrow[b]{a} s'$ entailed by $\mathcal{R}$ a corresponding sequent $t \xrightarrow[b]{a} t'$ is entailed by $\mathcal{R}$ with $s' \equiv_b t'$. □

PROPOSITION 2 (STRONG TILE BISIMULATION) Tile bisimulations are closed under union. Hence there exists a maximal tile bisimulation: It is called *strong tile bisimulation*, and denoted by $\equiv$. □

A fundamental requirement for any behavioural equivalence is *congruence*: This allows for an inductive account of a system, where equivalent sub-terms can be interchanged, without modifying the overall behaviour. In the framework of universal algebra, an equivalence is a congruence whenever it preserves the operators. In our case, this "operator preserving" property can be restated in terms of parallel and horizontal composition.

DEFINITION 11 (TILE FUNCTORIALITY AND ALGEBRAICITY) Let $\mathcal{R} = \langle \Sigma_\sigma, \Sigma_\tau, N, R \rangle$ be an ARS. An equivalence relation $\cong_f \subseteq \mathbf{A}(\Sigma_\sigma) \times \mathbf{A}(\Sigma_\sigma)$ is *functorial* for $\mathcal{R}$ if for $s, s', t, t'$ elements of $\mathbf{A}(\Sigma_\sigma)$, whenever $s \cong_f t$ and $s' \cong_f t'$, then $s; s' \cong_f t; t'$ (whenever defined) and $s \otimes s' \cong_f t \otimes t'$. It is *algebraic* for $\mathcal{R}$ if for $s_i, t_i : \underline{0} \to \underline{1}$, $i = 1 \ldots n$, elements of $\mathbf{A}(\Sigma_\sigma)$, whenever $s_i \cong_f t_i$, then $(s_1 \otimes \ldots \otimes s_n); f \cong_f (t_1 \otimes \ldots \otimes t_n); f$ for each $n$-ary operator $f \in \Sigma_\sigma$. □

In other words, functoriality requires that the *quotient category* $\mathbf{A}(\Sigma_\sigma)/\cong_f$ is well-defined, and it is cartesian; hence, it can be considered as some kind of congruence with respect to parallel and sequential composition. Instead, algebraicity is a weaker property, and it simply requires that the equivalence on (tuples of) *closed* terms (that is, terms with source $\underline{0}$ and target $\underline{1}$) is preserved under composition with an operator; it is indeed reminiscent of the usual notion of algebraic congruence, as it will be clarified by the results of next section.

In general, a tile bisimulation is neither functorial nor algebraic: A characterisation of the former property can be given in terms of *tile decomposition*.

DEFINITION 12 (TILE DECOMPOSITION) Let $\mathcal{R}$ be an ARS. We say that it is *decomposable* if for $s, t$ elements of $\mathbf{A}(\Sigma_\sigma)$

1. whenever it entails a sequent $s; t \xrightarrow[b]{a} u$, then it entails also $s \xrightarrow[c]{a} s'$ and $t \xrightarrow[b]{c} t'$ with $u = s'; t'$;
2. whenever it entails a sequent $s \otimes t \xrightarrow[b]{a} u$, then it entails also $s \xrightarrow[b_1]{a_1} s'$ and $t \xrightarrow[b_2]{a_2} t'$ with $u = s' \otimes t'$, $a = a_1 \otimes a_2$ and $b = b_1 \otimes b_2$. □

A very simple system that is not decomposable is given by $\mathcal{R}_\alpha = \langle \Sigma_\alpha, \Sigma_a, N_a, R_a \rangle$, where $\Sigma_\alpha = \{nil : 0 \to 1, a : 1 \to 1\}$, $\Sigma_a = \{a_1 : 1 \to 1, a_2 : 1 \to 1\}$ and

$$R_a = \left\{ act : nil; a \xrightarrow[a_1]{id} nil, cons : a \xrightarrow[a_1]{u_1} id_{\underline{1}} \right\}.$$

The basic sequent *act* cannot be decomposed, while its source obviously can.

PROPOSITION 3 (DECOMPOSITION AND FUNCTORIALITY) Let $\mathcal{R}$ be an ARS. If it is decomposable, then the associated strong tile bisimulation is functorial. □

The converse is not true. In fact, the strong tile bisimulation associated to $\mathcal{R}_a$ is functorial, and it is generated from the basic classes $\{nil\}$, $\{id_{\underline{0}}\}$, $\{id_{\underline{1}}\}$ and $\{a, a; a, \ldots\} = \{a^n | n \geq 1\}$, but the system does not verify the decomposition property. Note also the importance of $a_2 \in \Sigma_a$, which is responsible for the non-equivalence of $id_{\underline{1}}$ and $a$: Without, functoriality would not hold.

Also algebraicity may be characterized in a syntactical way, by requiring that the rules verify a very simple format.

THEOREM 1 (BASIC COMPONENTS AND ALGEBRAICITY) Let $\mathcal{R} = \langle \Sigma_\sigma, \Sigma_\tau, N, R \rangle$ be an ARS. If $\Sigma_\tau$ contains only unary operators, and for all rules $\alpha : s \xrightarrow[b]{a} t \in R$ we have that $s \in \Sigma_\sigma$, then the strong tile bisimulation associated to $\mathcal{R}$ is algebraic.

*Proof Sketch* Let us make explicit some of the properties of the theories. General results ensure us that each arrow $s : \underline{m} \to \underline{n} \in \mathbf{A}(\Sigma_\sigma)$ is factored as $d_s; (s_1 \otimes \ldots \otimes s_n)$, for $s_i : \underline{m_i} \to \underline{1} \in \mathbf{M}(\Sigma_\sigma)$ and $d_s : \underline{m} \to \underline{m_1} \otimes \ldots \otimes \underline{m_n}$ a *functional* (namely, an arrow obtained composing only identities, duplicators, dischargers and permutations). In addition, since all operators of $\Sigma_\tau$ are unary, the source and target of any arrow $b \in \mathbf{M}(\Sigma_\tau)$ coincide, and the arrow can then be factored as $b_1 \otimes \ldots \otimes b_p$ for $b_i : \underline{1} \to \underline{1}$ and $p \in \mathbb{N}$.

Algebraicity says that, given closed terms $s_i \cong_{\mathtt{f}} t_i$ and operator $f \in \Sigma_\sigma$, then $(s_1 \otimes \ldots \otimes s_n); f \cong_{\mathtt{f}} (t_1 \otimes t_n); f$. In order to prove that, for any sequent $\beta$ entailed by $\mathcal{R}$ with source $(s_1 \otimes \ldots \otimes s_n); f$, a corresponding one with source $(t_1 \otimes \ldots \otimes t_n); f$ must also be entailed. Our proof will proceed in three steps, presenting a factorisation property for sequents verifying a suitable format.

At first, we need to prove that any sequent $\gamma : u \xrightarrow[c]{id} v$, with $u, v : \underline{0} \to \underline{n} \in \mathbf{M}(\Sigma_\sigma)$ and $c : \underline{n} \to \underline{n}$, can be factored as $\gamma_1 \otimes \ldots \otimes \gamma_n$ for $\gamma_i : u_i \xrightarrow[c_i]{id} v_i$ with $u_i, v_i : \underline{0} \to \underline{1} \in \mathbf{M}(\Sigma_\sigma)$ and $c_i : \underline{1} \to \underline{1}$; basically, the proof uses the fact that the effect of any rule is an operator of $\Sigma_\tau$, and it is unary.

The second step is to prove that each sequent $\delta : w \xrightarrow[d]{id} z$, with $w, z : \underline{0} \rightarrow \underline{1} \in \mathbf{M}(\Sigma_\sigma)$ and $d : \underline{1} \rightarrow \underline{1}$, can be factored as $\delta_1 \cdot \ldots \cdot \delta_k$, for $\delta_i : w_{i-1} \xrightarrow[d_i]{id} w_i$ with $w_0 = w$, $w_k = z$ and any $\delta_i$ can be entailed without using the (*vert*) rule; basically, the proof uses the previous factorisation result, and the fact that the source of any rule is just an operator.

The third step proves that for any sequent $\xi$ entailed by $\mathcal{R}$ without using the (*vert*) rule and with initial configuration $x : \underline{0} \rightarrow \underline{1}$, and for any factorisation $(x_1 \otimes \ldots \otimes x_l); g$ of $x$, then $\xi$ can be decomposed as $(\xi_1 \otimes \ldots \otimes \xi_l) * \xi'$ for $\xi_i : x_i \xrightarrow[e_i]{id} x'_i$ and $\xi' : g \xrightarrow[e]{e_1 \otimes \ldots \otimes e_l} x'$ rule.

Let us then consider again our closed terms $s_i \cong_{\mathtt{f}} t_i$ and operator $f \in \Sigma_\sigma$, and let $\beta : (s_1 \otimes \ldots \otimes s_n); f \xrightarrow[b]{id} t$ be a sequent entailed by $\mathcal{R}$ without using the (*vert*) rule. Then $\beta$ can be decomposed as $(\beta_1 \otimes \ldots \otimes \beta_n) * \alpha$ for $\beta_i : s_i \xrightarrow[b_i]{id} s'_i$ and $\alpha : f \xrightarrow[b]{b_1 \otimes \ldots \otimes b_n} t'$ rule. By induction hypothesis, $\mathcal{R}$ must entails also $\beta'_1, \ldots, \beta'_n$ with $\beta'_i : t_i \xrightarrow[b_i]{id} t'_i$ and $s'_i \cong_{\mathtt{f}} t'_i$. Now, note that $t' = \delta_{t'}; t''$ for functional $\delta_{t'}$ and that the application of the functional simply results in some possible duplication and/or deletion (plus a reshuffling) of terms $s'_i$'s and $t'_i$'s. Then $(s'_1 \otimes \ldots \otimes s'_n); \delta_{t'}; t''$ can be factored as $(s'_{i_1} \otimes \ldots \otimes s'_{i_m}); t''$ for $i_j \in \{1 \ldots n\}$, and similarly $(t'_1 \otimes \ldots \otimes t'_n); \delta_{t'}; t''$ can be factored as $(t'_{i_1} \otimes \ldots \otimes t'_{i_m}); t''$. Since $t'' \in \mathbf{M}(\Sigma_\sigma)$ can be factored as $(u_1 \otimes \ldots u_p); h$ for $u_i \in \mathbf{M}(\Sigma_\sigma)$, the theorem holds by coinductive hypothesis. □

In fact, $\mathcal{R}_a$ verifies the conditions of Theorem 1, hence the associated (and rather dull) strong tile bisimulation is algebraic.

## 4 A Case Study on Process Algebras

In this section we show how to recast *process algebras* and their well-known operational semantics by suitable rewriting systems. In particular, we first introduce CCS [35], maybe the best known example of these formalisms; and then we define an algebraic rewriting system $\mathcal{R}_{ccs}$ which faithfully corresponds to the CCS transition system. Furthermore, we show that, when applied to the sequents entailed by $\mathcal{R}_{ccs}$, tile bisimulation provides a recasting of bisimilarity for CCS processes.

### 4.1 Operational Semantics of CCS

In *concurrency theory* it is quite common to deal with formalisms relying on the notions of *side-effect* and *synchronisation* in determining the actual behaviour of a system. *Process (Description) Algebras* [4, 19, 35] offer a constructive way to describe *concurrent systems*, considered as structured entities (the *agents*) interacting by means of some synchronisation mechanism. A system is then a term of an algebra over a set of process constructors, on the assumption that algebraic operators represent basic concurrency features. We present here one of the best known examples of process algebra, the *Calculus of Communicating Systems* (CCS), introduced by Milner in the early Eighties (see [35] for an up-to-date presentation), restricting our attention to *finite* CCS.

DEFINITION 13 (THE CALCULUS OF COMMUNICATING SYSTEMS) Let *Act* be a set of atomic *actions*, ranged over by $\mu$, with a distinguished symbol $\tau$ and equipped with an involutive function $\bar{\cdot}$ : Act $\rightarrow$ Act preserving $\tau$. Moreover, let $\alpha, \overline{\alpha}, \ldots$ range over $Act \backslash \{\tau\}$. A CCS *process* (also *agent*) is a term generated by the following syntax

$$P ::= nil,\ \mu.P,\ P\backslash_\alpha,\ P[\Phi],\ P_1 + P_2,\ P_1 || P_2$$

where $\Phi : Act \rightarrow Act$ is a *relabeling* (that is, a bijective function preserving involution and $\tau$). We let $P, Q, R, \ldots$ range over the set *Proc* of processes. □

In the following, we indicate as $\Sigma_{ccs}$ the signature associated with CCS processes (for example, *nil* is a constant, $\mu$ stands for a unary operator, one for each element in *Act*, and so on). Given a process $P$, its dynamic behaviour can be described by a suitable transition system, along the lines of the SOS approach, where the transition relation is freely generated by a set of inference rules.

DEFINITION 14 (OPERATIONAL SEMANTICS OF CCS) The CCS *transition system* is the relation $T_{ccs} \subseteq Proc \times Act \times Proc$ inductively generated by the following set of axioms and inference rules

$$\frac{}{\mu.P \xrightarrow{\mu} P} \text{ for } \mu \in Act \qquad \frac{P \xrightarrow{\mu} Q}{P[\Phi] \xrightarrow{\Phi(\mu)} Q[\Phi]} \text{ for } \Phi \text{ a relabeling}$$

$$\frac{P \xrightarrow{\mu} Q}{P\backslash_\alpha \xrightarrow{\mu} Q\backslash_\alpha} \text{ for } \mu \notin \{\alpha, \overline{\alpha}\}$$

$$\frac{P \xrightarrow{\mu} Q}{P + R \xrightarrow{\mu} Q} \qquad \frac{P \xrightarrow{\mu} Q}{R + P \xrightarrow{\mu} Q}$$

$$\frac{P \xrightarrow{\mu} Q}{P||R \xrightarrow{\mu} Q||R} \qquad \frac{P \xrightarrow{\alpha} Q,\ P' \xrightarrow{\overline{\alpha}} Q'}{P||P' \xrightarrow{\tau} Q||Q'} \qquad \frac{P \xrightarrow{\mu} Q}{R||P \xrightarrow{\mu} R||Q}$$

where $P \xrightarrow{\mu} Q$ means that $\langle P, \mu, Q \rangle \in T_{ccs}$. □

A process $P$ may execute an action $\mu$ and become $Q$ if (we can *inductively* construct a sequence of rule applications, such that) the *transition* $\langle P, \mu, Q \rangle \in T_{ccs}$. As an example, to infer that $P = (\alpha.nil + \beta.nil)||\overline{\alpha}.nil$ may evolve into $P \xrightarrow{\alpha} Q = nil||\overline{\alpha}.nil$, three different rules must be applied. A *computation* from $P$ to $Q$ is a chain $P = P_0 \xrightarrow{\mu_1} P_1 \dots P_{n-1} \xrightarrow{\mu_n} P_n = Q$ of one-step transitions.

The operational semantics we just defined is however too intensional, and more abstract semantics have been introduced by defining suitable *behavioural equivalences*, which identify processes exhibiting the same *observational behaviour*. Most of them are defined on the basic notion of *bisimulation*: Two processes $P, Q$ are *bisimilar* if, whenever $P$ performs an action $\mu$ evolving to $P'$, then also $Q$ may execute that same action, evolving to $Q'$ bisimilar to $P'$.

DEFINITION 15 (BISIMULATIONS) An equivalence relation $\sim_b \subseteq Proc \times Proc$ is a *bisimulation* if, whenever $P \sim_b Q$ for $P, Q$ processes, then for any transition $P \xrightarrow{\mu} P'$ there exists a corresponding transition $Q \xrightarrow{\mu} Q'$ with $Q \sim_b Q'$. □

PROPOSITION 4 (STRONG BISIMULATION) Bisimulations are closed under union. Hence there exists a maximal bisimulation: It is called *strong bisimulation*, and denoted by $\sim$. □

## 4.2 Using Tiles for CCS

From an operational point of view a process algebra can be faithfully described by a triple $\langle \Sigma, A, R \rangle$, where $\Sigma$ is the signature of the algebra of agents, $A$ is the set of actions, and $R$ is the set of deduction rules. Note that these rules are *conditional*: You need information on the *actions* performed by the transitions in the premise before applying a rule. Moreover, the rewriting steps are always performed *on top*: The order in which the rewrites are actually executed is important since, as an example, the correct operational behaviour of the agent $P = \alpha.\beta.nil$ is expressed saying that it executes first $\alpha$ and then $\beta$. If we let $A_{ccs}$ be the signature containing all the atomic actions of $Act$ (i.e., $A_{ccs} = \{\mu : \underline{1} \to \underline{1} \mid \mu \in Act\}$), then both those features are easily described using tile logic.

DEFINITION 16 (THE CCS REWRITING SYSTEM) The ARS $\mathcal{R}_{ccs}$ associated with CCS is the tuple $\langle \Sigma_{ccs}, A_{ccs}, N, R \rangle$, with the following set of rules

$$act_\mu : \mu \xrightarrow[\mu]{id} id_{\underline{1}} \qquad rel_\Phi : \Phi \xrightarrow[\Phi(\mu)]{\mu} \Phi$$

$$res_\alpha : \backslash_\alpha \xrightarrow[\mu]{\mu} \backslash_\alpha \qquad \text{for} \quad \mu \notin \{\alpha, \overline{\alpha}\}$$

$$\langle + : + \xrightarrow[\mu]{\mu \otimes id} id_{\underline{1}} \otimes !_{\underline{1}} \qquad +\rangle : + \xrightarrow[\mu]{id \otimes \mu} !_{\underline{1}} \otimes id_{\underline{1}}$$

$$\xi_l : \| \xrightarrow[\mu]{\mu \otimes id} \| \qquad \xi_r : \| \xrightarrow[\mu]{id \otimes \mu} \| \qquad \xi_s : \| \xrightarrow[\tau]{\alpha \otimes \overline{\alpha}} \|$$

(where $id$ is shorthand for $id_{\underline{1}}$). □

Note that there is exactly one basic rule for each operational rule of CCS; some of them (such as $act_\mu$ and $rel_\Phi$) are parametric with respect to the set of actions or to the set of relabelings, since the corresponding rules are so. The effect $\mu$ indicates that the process is actually "running", outputting the action $\mu$. For example, the rule $act_\mu$ prefixes an idle process with the action $\mu$, and then starts the execution, consuming that same action. There are also three rules dealing with the parallel operator: $\xi_s$ synchronises two running processes, while $\xi_l$ and $\xi_r$ perform an asynchronous move, taking a running and an idle process.

EXAMPLE 5 (THREE PROCESSES) Let us consider again the process $P = \alpha.\beta.nil$, executing sequentially first the action $\alpha$, then the action $\beta$. It is not easy to model even such a simple agent in term rewriting, since the execution ordering, that is fundamental for expressing its behaviour correctly, is difficult to model in that setting. The operational behaviour is described by the sequent

$$(id^{nil;\beta} * act_\alpha) \cdot (id^{nil} * act_\beta) : nil;\, \beta;\, \alpha \xrightarrow[\alpha;\beta]{id} nil$$

whose two-steps entailment is the following

$$\frac{\dfrac{}{id^{nil;\beta} : nil;\, \beta \xrightarrow[id]{id} nil;\, \beta} \quad \dfrac{}{act_\alpha : \alpha \xrightarrow[\alpha]{id} id_{\underline{1}}}}{id^{nil;\beta} * act_\alpha : nil;\, \beta;\, \alpha \xrightarrow[\alpha]{id} nil;\, \beta}\ (hor)$$

$$\frac{\dfrac{}{id^{nil} : nil \xrightarrow[id]{id} nil} \quad \dfrac{}{act_\beta : \beta \xrightarrow[\beta]{id} id_{\underline{1}}}}{id^{nil} * act_\beta : nil;\, \beta \xrightarrow[\beta]{id} nil}\ (hor)$$

(where $id$ is shorthand for both $id_{\underline{0}}$ and $id_{\underline{1}}$), showing the importance of effects in expressing the ordering constraints: $P$ can execute $\alpha$ only if the underlying process $P' = \beta.nil$ is actually idle.

For the agent $P = (\alpha.nil)\backslash_\beta$, instead, the execution of the action $\alpha$ is represented by the sequent $(id^{nil} * act_\alpha) * res_\beta$

$$\dfrac{\dfrac{\dfrac{}{id^{nil} : nil \xrightarrow[id]{id} nil} \quad \dfrac{}{act_\alpha : \alpha \xrightarrow[\alpha]{id} id_{\underline{1}}}}{id^{nil} * act_\alpha : nil;\alpha \xrightarrow[\alpha]{id} nil}\,(hor) \qquad \dfrac{}{res_\beta : \backslash_\beta \xrightarrow[\alpha]{\alpha} \backslash_\beta}}{(id^{nil} * act_\alpha) * res_\beta : nil;\alpha;\backslash_\beta \xrightarrow[\alpha]{id} nil;\backslash_\beta}\,(hor)$$

Nesting $act_\alpha$ into $res_\beta$ is possible since $res_\beta$ can be applied to any sequent whose effect is different from either $\beta$ or $\bar{\beta}$.

Finally, the agent $P = \alpha.nil + \alpha.nil$ can execute $\alpha$ in two different ways, namely with the sequent $(id^{nil;\alpha} \otimes (id^{nil} * act_\alpha)) * +\rangle$

$$\dfrac{\dfrac{\dfrac{}{id^{nil;\alpha} : nil;\alpha \xrightarrow[id]{id} nil;\alpha} \quad \dfrac{}{id^{nil} * act_\alpha : nil;\alpha \xrightarrow[\alpha]{id} nil}}{id^{nil;\alpha} \otimes (id^{nil} * act_\alpha) : (nil;\alpha) \otimes (nil;\alpha) \xrightarrow[id\otimes\alpha]{id} (nil;\alpha) \otimes nil}\,(par) \qquad \dfrac{}{+\rangle : + \xrightarrow[\alpha]{id\otimes\alpha} !_{\underline{1}} \otimes id_{\underline{1}}}}{(id^{nil;\alpha} \otimes (id^{nil} * act_\alpha)) * +\rangle : ((nil;\alpha) \otimes (nil;\alpha)); + \xrightarrow[\alpha]{id} nil}\,(hor)$$

and the symmetric, yet computationally unrelated, $((id^{nil} * act_\alpha) \otimes id^{nil;\alpha}) * \langle +$ (belonging to the same equivalence class of $(id^{nil;\alpha} \otimes (id^{nil} * act_\alpha)) * \rho_{id,\alpha} * \langle +)$. □

The abstract sequents entailed by $\mathcal{R}_{ccs}$ offer a description where many derivations are identified, corresponding to "essentially" equivalent CCS computations. This description is still more concrete than the one given by the set–theoretic relation entailed by the CCS transition system: It suffices to consider the process $P = \alpha.nil + \alpha.nil$ in Example 5. However, if we restrict ourselves to the tile transition system $Tr(\mathcal{R}_{ccs})$, an obvious adequacy result can be proved.

PROPOSITION 5 (INTERLEAVING CORRESPONDENCE) Let $P$, $Q$ be CCS agents, and $P_a$, $Q_a$ the associated elements of $\mathbf{A}(\Sigma_{ccs})$. Then the transition $P \xrightarrow{\mu} Q$ is entailed by the CCS transition system $T_{ccs}$ iff the sequent $P_a \xrightarrow[\mu]{id} Q_a$ is entailed by the tile transition system $Tr(\mathcal{R}_{ccs})$. □

There are however many more "transitions" in $Tr(\mathcal{R}_{ccs})$ than in $T_{ccs}$: In fact, the last result simply states that the two transition systems coincide when we restrict our attention to so-called *closed* processes, terms with source $\underline{0}$ and target $\underline{1}$. Then there is a complete coincidence between bisimilarity over CCS processes and tile bisimilarity over the corresponding elements of $\mathbf{A}(\Sigma_{ccs})$.

PROPOSITION 6 (BISIMULATION CORRESPONDENCE) Let $P$, $Q$ be CCS agents, and $P_a$, $Q_a$ the associated elements of $\mathbf{A}(\Sigma_{ccs})$. Then $P \sim Q$ iff $P_a \equiv Q_a$. □

Moreover, $\mathcal{R}_{ccs}$ verifies the conditions of Theorem 1, hence the following corollary holds.

COROLLARY 1 (STRONG BISIMULATION IS ALGEBRAIC) The strong tile bisimulation $\equiv$ associated to $\mathcal{R}_{ccs}$ is algebraic. □

Thanks to Proposition 6, this result implies that strong bisimilarity for CCS processes is also a congruence. As an example, let $P$, $Q$ be CCS agents, $P_a$, $Q_a$ the associated elements of $\mathbf{A}(\Sigma_{ccs})$, and let us assume that $P \sim Q$. Hence $P_a \equiv Q_a$ and, by algebraicity, $P_a; \alpha \equiv Q_a; \alpha$, so that $\alpha.P \sim \alpha.Q$. And since also $Q_a \equiv P_a$ by symmetry, so then $(P_a \otimes Q_a); || \equiv (Q_a \otimes P_a); ||$, and $P||Q \sim Q||P$ holds.

### 4.3 On Formats and Expressiveness

In the previous section we have taken into account the classical operational semantics of CCS, and proved a correspondence theorem with our model. However, one of the claims of the paper is that tile logic represents a generalisation of SOS specifications. This is obviously true to a certain extent, since we are able to take into account contexts (that is, partially unspecified processes): A useful device both in verification [30] and truly concurrent analysis of systems [1]. Nevertheless, a natural question to be asked is if, for a given SOS specification, there exists a suitable rewriting system preserving its operational behaviour. In a first approximation, this obviously depends on which kind of system we consider. As an example, we already noted that graph systems generalise context systems [30]; moreover, they are fully adequate for those algebras in *basic deSimone format* [1], i.e., where all the rules are of the form

$$\frac{P_i \xrightarrow{a_i} Q_i \text{ for } i \in I}{f(P_1, \ldots, P_n) \xrightarrow{a} g(Q_1, \ldots, Q_n)}$$

where $f, g \in \Sigma_{\mathcal{P}}$, $a_i, a \in A_{\mathcal{P}}$ and $I \subseteq \{1 \ldots n\}$. Moreover, all the $P_i$'s, $Q_j$'s are different, except for $P_k = Q_k$ with $k \notin I$.

Actually, algebraic rewriting systems allow for dealing also with process algebras in *deSimone format* [12], i.e., such that all their rules have the form

$$\frac{P_i \xrightarrow{a_i} Q_i \text{ for } i \in I}{f(P_1, \ldots, P_n) \xrightarrow{a} D[Q_1 \ldots Q_n]} \text{ for } Pr(a_1, \ldots, a_n, a)$$

where $f \in \Sigma_{\mathcal{P}}$, $I \subseteq \{1 \ldots n\}$ and all the $P_i$'s, $Q_j$'s are different, except for $P_k = Q_k$ with $k \notin I$, as before. Moreover, each process variable appears *at most once* in the process context $D$ (i.e., a term with undefined sub-terms, indicated by the occurrence of process variables), $a_i$, *a range over* $A_{\mathcal{P}}$ and $Pr$ is an $n+1$-ary relation over $A_{\mathcal{P}}$. Equivalently, this means that each rule actually is just a schema, corresponding to a possibly infinite set of rules: A typical example is the rule for the restriction operator $\backslash_\alpha$ of CCS we gave in the previous section.

Note that rewriting systems satisfying the "basic components" requirement of Theorem 1 are more general than SOS specifications in the deSimone format. We are then able to recast the most important result for this format, namely, that for all SOS specifications satisfying it, strong bisimulation is actually a congruence.

Thanks to their expressiveness, ARS's are able to characterise those specifications whose rules are in what we called the *algebraic format*.

DEFINITION 17 (RULES IN ALGEBRAIC FORMAT) A process algebra $\mathcal{P}$ is in the *algebraic format* iff all its deduction rules have the form

$$\frac{P_i \xrightarrow{a_i} Q_i \text{ for } i \in I}{C[P_1 \dots P_n] \xrightarrow{a} D[Q_1 \dots Q_n]} \text{ for } Pr(a_1, \dots, a_n, a)$$

where $I \subseteq \{1 \dots n\}$, $a_i$, $a$ range over $A_{\mathcal{P}}$ and $Pr$ is an $n+1$-ary relation over $A_{\mathcal{P}}$. $C$, $D$ are process contexts, containing *any number of times* each process variable, and all the $P_i$'s, $Q_j$'s are different, except for $P_k = Q_k$ with $k \notin I$. □

For instance, an axiom such as

$$\frac{}{\delta P \xrightarrow{\tau} \delta P || P} \quad \dagger$$

(which represents the spawning with replication of a process) is in the algebraic format, but not in the deSimone one. Actually, this format is maybe too expressive: A meaningful restriction would be to assume that, whenever a variable $P_k$, $k \notin I$, appears in $D[Q_1 \dots Q_n]$, then it must appear also in $C[P_1 \dots P_n]$. For term rewriting, this restriction is analogous to assuming that for each rule $l \to r$ the set of free variables of $r$ is contained in that of $l$.

DEFINITION 18 (FROM PROCESS ALGEBRAS TO REWRITING SYSTEMS) Let $\mathcal{P}$ be a process algebra $\langle \Sigma, A, R \rangle$ in the algebraic format. Then the associated ARS is the tuple $\langle \Sigma_{\mathcal{P}}, A_{\mathcal{P}}, N, R_{\mathcal{P}} \rangle$, where $N$ is an arbitrary set of names, and $R_{\mathcal{P}}$ is the set of rules such that

$$C \xrightarrow[a]{b} D \in R_{\mathcal{P}} \qquad \text{iff} \qquad \frac{P_i \xrightarrow{a_i} Q_i \text{ for } i \in I}{C[P_1 \dots P_n] \xrightarrow{a} D[Q_1 \dots Q_n]} \in R$$

where $b = a_1 \otimes \dots \otimes a_n$ and $a_k = id_{\underline{1}}$ for $k \notin I$. □

In the previous definition we assumed that the conditions on actions are explicitly provided, dealing in this way with a possibly infinite set of rules. This is meaningful thanks to Proposition 1, which implies that, for a given process algebra $\mathcal{P}$ in the algebraic format, any process context appearing in a rule can be uniquely described by an element of the algebraic theory associated with $\Sigma_{\mathcal{P}}$. For example, the axiom † is described by

$$d_\dagger : \delta \xrightarrow[\tau]{id} \nabla_{\underline{1}}; (\delta \otimes id); ||$$

PROPOSITION 7 (PROCESS ALGEBRAS AND SEQUENTS) Let $P$, $Q$ be terms of a process algebra $\mathcal{P} = \langle \Sigma, A, R \rangle$ in the algebraic format, and $P_{\mathcal{P}}$, $Q_{\mathcal{P}}$ the associated elements of $\mathbf{A}(\Sigma_{\mathcal{P}})$. Then, the transition $P \xrightarrow{a} Q$ belongs to the transition system associated to $\mathcal{P}$ iff the sequent $P_{\mathcal{P}} \xrightarrow[a]{id} Q_{\mathcal{P}}$ is entailed by $\mathcal{R}_{\mathcal{P}}$. □

## 5 A Categorical Semantics for Rewriting Systems

The aim of this section is to provide an alternative characterisation for the notion of abstract sequent given in Definition 8. First, we sketch a categorical description for the theories presented in Section 2. Then, we introduce *double categories* and, starting from there, we characterise a rewriting system as a suitable finitary structure, a *computad*, able to generate by a free construction the different classes of abstract sequents. For the sake of space, a few categorical definitions are assumed to be known by the reader: We refer for details to [32].

### 5.1 Theories as Free Categories

The relevance of *monoidal categories* in computer science as a suitable framework for expressing basic properties of computing devices has been shown by a large amount of work in recent years. In this vein, we could consider the categorical description of Petri nets [42] proposed in [34] as one of the starting point for our work, and *gs-monoidal* categories [7] as a further enrichment, in order to deal with specific problems involving duplication and erasing of data.

DEFINITION 19 (GS-MONOIDAL CATEGORIES) A *gs-monoidal category* $\mathbf{C}$ is a six-tuple $\langle \mathbf{C}_0, \otimes, e, \rho, \nabla, ! \rangle$, where $\langle \mathbf{C}_0, \otimes, e, \rho \rangle$ is a symmetric strict monoidal category and $! : Id_{\mathbf{C}_0} \Rightarrow e : \mathbf{C}_0 \to \mathbf{C}_0$, $\nabla : Id_{\underline{\mathbf{C}}_0} \Rightarrow \otimes \circ \Delta : \mathbf{C}_0 \to \mathbf{C}_0$ are two transformations ($\Delta$ is the diagonal functor), such that $!_e = \nabla_e = id_e$ and satisfying the *coherence* axioms

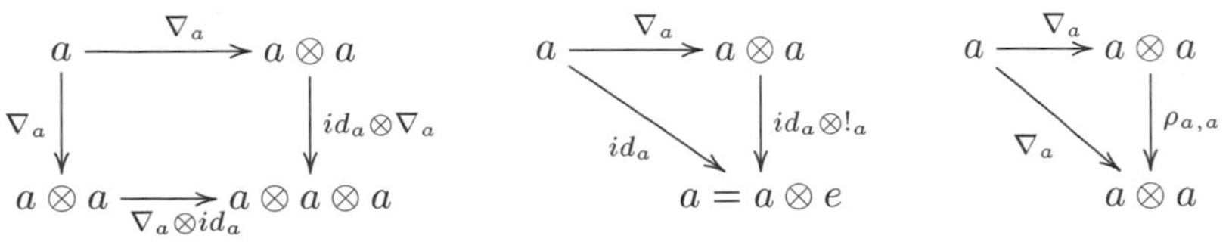

and the *monoidality* axioms

$$\begin{array}{ccc} a \otimes b & \xrightarrow{\nabla_{a \otimes b}} & a \otimes b \otimes a \otimes b \\ & \searrow^{\nabla_a \otimes \nabla_b} & \downarrow^{id_a \otimes \rho_{b,a} \otimes id_b} \\ & & a \otimes a \otimes b \otimes b \end{array} \qquad \begin{array}{ccc} e & \xleftarrow{!_{a \otimes b}} & a \otimes b \\ & \searrow^{id_e} & \downarrow^{!_a \otimes !_b} \\ & & e = e \otimes e \end{array}$$

A *gs-monoidal functor* $F : \mathbf{C} \to \mathbf{C}'$ is a symmetric monoidal functor such that $F(!_a) = !'_{F(a)}$ and $F(\nabla_a) = \nabla'_{F(a)}$. The category of small gs-monoidal categories and gs-monoidal functors is denoted by **GSM-Cat**. □

The monoidality axioms could be rephrased stating that the two transformations are actually *symmetric monoidal*. The relevant point however is that they are *not* natural: Such a requirement would change dramatically their properties, as stated by the following result, that seems to have become part of the categorical folklore in recent years (see e.g. [7, 22, 28]).

PROPOSITION 8 (CARTESIANNESS AS ENRICHED MONOIDALITY) Let $\mathbf{C}$ be a gs-monoidal category $\langle \mathbf{C}_0, \otimes, e, \rho, \nabla, ! \rangle$ such that $\nabla$ and $!$ are *natural* transformations. Then $\mathbf{C}$ is cartesian. □

Hence, a gs-monoidal category such that both $\nabla$ and $!$ are natural is a category with *finite products*, and a gs-monoidal functor between such cartesian categories also preserve products. Then, we have a chain of adjunctions

$$\mathbf{GR}_p \overset{F_1}{\rightleftarrows} \mathbf{GR}_m \overset{F_2}{\rightleftarrows} \mathbf{M\text{-}Cat} \overset{F_3}{\rightleftarrows} \mathbf{GSM\text{-}Cat} \overset{F_4}{\rightleftarrows} \mathbf{FC\text{-}Cat}$$

relating the category $\mathbf{GR}_p$ of graphs with pairing (that is, whose set of objects forms a monoid) and graph morphisms preserving the monoidal structure; the category $\mathbf{GR}_m$ of monoidal graphs and monoidal graph morphisms; and the category **M-Cat** (**GSM-Cat**, **FC-Cat**) of monoidal (gs-monoidal, with finite products) categories and monoidal (gs-monoidal) functors.

Although space limitations prevent us to provide further details, the previous chain basically means that the theories we introduced in Section 2 can actually be characterised as suitable free constructions, starting from the graph with pairing $G_\Sigma$ associated to a signature $\Sigma$.

PROPOSITION 9 (THEORIES AS FREE CATEGORIES) Let $\Sigma$ be a signature. Then the following categorical isomorphisms hold

$$F_1(G_\Sigma) = G(\Sigma) \qquad F_2(G(\Sigma)) = \mathbf{M}(\Sigma)$$
$$F_3(\mathbf{M}(\Sigma)) = \mathbf{GS}(\Sigma) \qquad F_4(\mathbf{GS}(\Sigma)) = \mathbf{A}(\Sigma)$$

where $G_\Sigma$ is a graph with pairing, with objects the elements of $\mathbb{N}_c$, and arrows $f : \underline{n} \to \underline{1}$ for each $f \in \Sigma_n$. □

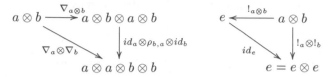

## 5.2 Some Categorical Notions

Introduced in [13, 14], *double categories* roughly are *category objects* in **Cat**, that is, categories whose classes of objects and arrows actually form categories, and the source, target and identity functions are actually functors (see [3] for a survey, or [11] for some recent results on *pasting*). They represent an intuitive generalisation of the better known *2-categories*, and admit the following *naïve* presentation, adapted from [25].

DEFINITION 20 (DOUBLE CATEGORIES)  A double category $\underline{C}$ consists of a collection $\{a, b, c, \ldots\}$ of *objects*, a collection $\{f, g, h, \ldots\}$ of *horizontal arrows*, a collection $\{x, y, z, \ldots\}$ of *vertical arrows*, and a collection $\{\alpha, \beta, \gamma, \ldots\}$ of *cells*. Objects and horizontal arrows form a category, the *horizontal 1-category* $\mathbf{C}_h$, with identity $id_a$ for each object $a$; objects and vertical arrows also form a category, the *vertical 1-category* $\mathbf{C}_v$, with identity $id^a$ for each object $a$. Cells are assigned *horizontal source* and *target* (which are vertical arrows), written as $\alpha : x \Rightarrow_h y$, and *vertical source* and *target* (which are horizontal arrows), written as $\alpha : f \Rightarrow_v g$. Furthermore, these arrows must be *compatible*, i.e., they satisfy particular requirements on their source and target. In graphical terms,

$$
\begin{array}{ccc}
a & \xrightarrow{\ f\ } & b \\
x\downarrow & \alpha & \downarrow y \\
c & \xrightarrow[g]{} & d
\end{array}
$$

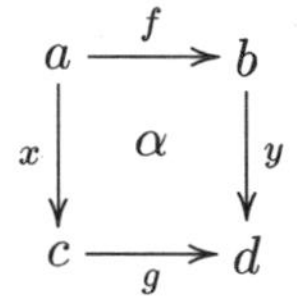

In addition, cells can be composed both horizontally ($\alpha *_h \beta$) and vertically ($\gamma *_v \delta$)

$$
\begin{array}{ccc}
a \xrightarrow{f;h} e \\
x\downarrow\ \alpha *_h \beta\ \downarrow z \\
c \xrightarrow[g;i]{} m
\end{array}
\quad = \quad
\begin{array}{ccc}
a \xrightarrow{\ f\ } b \xrightarrow{\ h\ } e \\
x\downarrow\ \alpha\ \downarrow y\ \beta\ \downarrow z \\
c \xrightarrow[g]{} d \xrightarrow[i]{} m
\end{array}
$$

$$
\begin{array}{ccc}
a \xrightarrow{\ f\ } b \\
x;w\downarrow\ \gamma *_v \delta\ \downarrow y;z \\
e \xrightarrow[h]{} m
\end{array}
\quad = \quad
\begin{array}{ccc}
a \xrightarrow{\ f\ } b \\
x\downarrow\ \gamma\ \downarrow y \\
c \xrightarrow{g} d \\
w\downarrow\ \delta\ \downarrow z \\
e \xrightarrow[h]{} m
\end{array}
$$

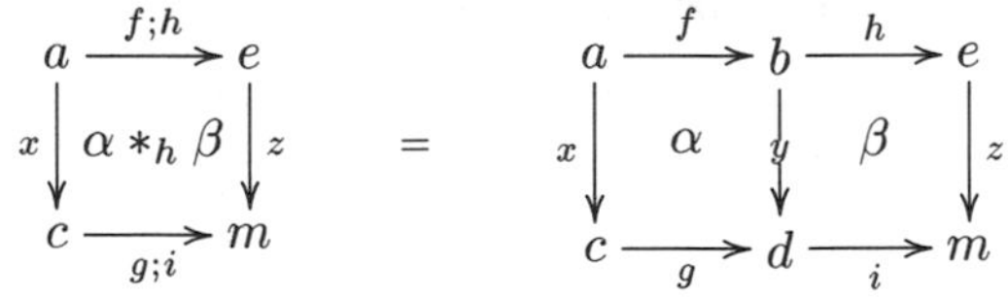

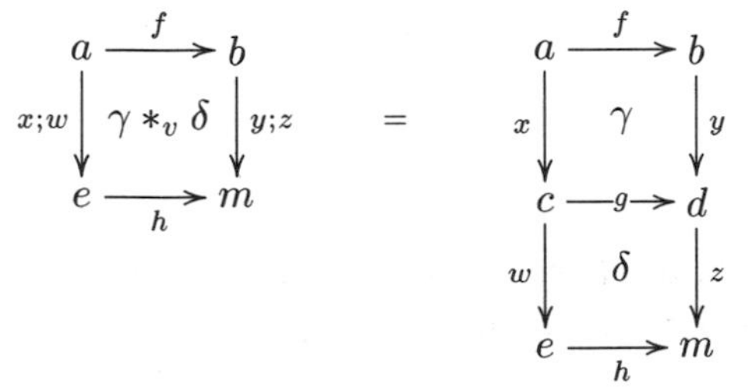

Under each of these laws cells form a category, the *horizontal category* $\mathbf{C}_H$ and the *vertical category* $\mathbf{C}_V$ respectively, with identities

$$
\begin{array}{ccc}
a & \xrightarrow{id_a} & a \\
x \downarrow & 1_x & \downarrow x \\
b & \xrightarrow[id_b]{} & b
\end{array}
\qquad\qquad
\begin{array}{ccc}
a & \xrightarrow{f} & b \\
id^a \downarrow & 1^f & \downarrow id^b \\
a & \xrightarrow[f]{} & b
\end{array}
$$

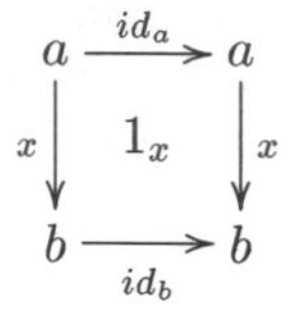

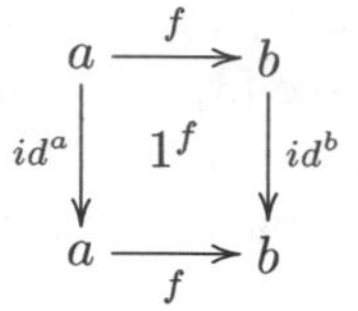

Moreover, the following equations must hold

1. whenever the composite

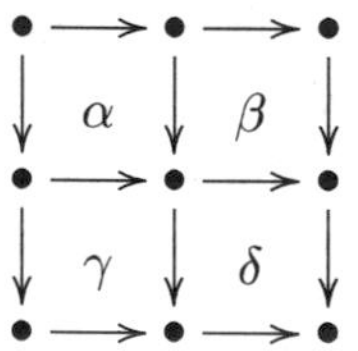

is well-defined, it is unique, namely $(\alpha *_v \gamma) *_h (\beta *_v \delta) = (\alpha *_h \beta) *_v (\gamma *_h \delta)$;

2. the composite

$$
\begin{array}{ccccc}
a & \xrightarrow{f} & b & \xrightarrow{g} & c \\
id^a \downarrow & 1^f & id^b \downarrow \quad 1^g & & \downarrow id^c \\
a & \xrightarrow[f]{} & b & \xrightarrow[g]{} & c
\end{array}
$$

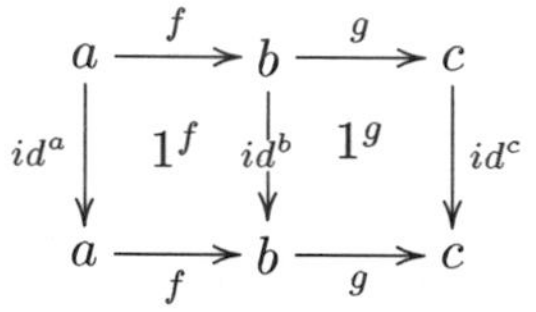

has to be $1^{f;g}$, and similarly for vertical composition of horizontal identities;

3. finally, the horizontal and vertical identities

$$
\begin{array}{ccc}
a & \xrightarrow{id_a} & a \\
id^a \downarrow & 1_{id_a} & \downarrow id^a \\
a & \xrightarrow[id_a]{} & a
\end{array}
\qquad\qquad
\begin{array}{ccc}
a & \xrightarrow{id_a} & a \\
id^a \downarrow & 1^{id_a} & \downarrow id^a \\
a & \xrightarrow[id_a]{} & a
\end{array}
$$

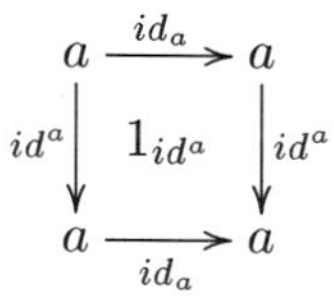

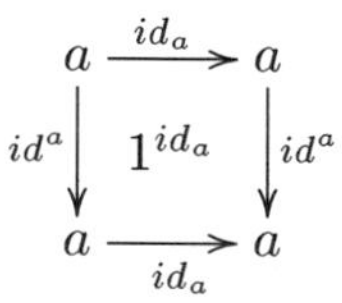

must coincide.

A *double functor* $F : \underline{\mathbf{C}} \to \underline{\mathbf{D}}$ is a four-tuple of functions mapping objects to objects, horizontal (vertical) arrows to horizontal (vertical) arrows and cells to cells, preserving identities and compositions of all kinds. We denote by **D-Cat** the category of double categories and double functors. □

In the "internal category" view, we may simply consider $\mathbf{C}_h$ and $\mathbf{C}_H$ as the categories of objects and arrows of the (double) category $\underline{\mathbf{C}}$. Vertical source and target functions are then functors between these categories, and the components are the structures forming the vertical categories: For example, the set of objects of $\mathbf{C}_h$ and $\mathbf{C}_H$ forms respectively the set of objects and arrows of $\mathbf{C}_v$, and so on; while, at the same time, horizontal source and target become functors between these categories. Since we need double categories with additional structure, this is intuitively obtained enriching the underlying horizontal categories, corresponding to internalising over richer categorical universes. Notationally, we denote this structure by prefixing an adjective which indicates which category we are internalising into.

DEFINITION 21 (MONOIDAL DOUBLE CATEGORIES) Let $\underline{\mathbf{C}}$ be a double category. We say that it is *monoidal* if both $\mathbf{C}_h$ and $\mathbf{C}_H$ are monoidal, vertical source and target are monoidal functors, and the monoidal structure preserves composition in the vertical categories. A double functor is *monoidal* if it preserves the additional structure. □

The preservation requirement is equivalent to imposing the functoriality of horizontal product with respect to vertical composition: That is, whenever the composite is well-defined, then $(\alpha *_v \beta) \otimes (\gamma *_v \delta) = (\alpha \otimes \gamma) *_v (\beta \otimes \delta)$. This implies then that both $\mathbf{C}_v$ and $\mathbf{C}_V$ are monoidal: In fact, given any two cells

$$\begin{array}{ccc} a & \xrightarrow{f} & b \\ {\scriptstyle x}\downarrow & \alpha & \downarrow{\scriptstyle y} \\ c & \xrightarrow[g]{} & d \end{array} \qquad\qquad \begin{array}{ccc} m & \xrightarrow{h} & n \\ {\scriptstyle w}\downarrow & \beta & \downarrow{\scriptstyle z} \\ p & \xrightarrow[i]{} & q \end{array}$$

then their composition is given by the cell $\gamma = \alpha \otimes \beta$, such that

$$\begin{array}{ccc} a \otimes m & \xrightarrow{f \otimes h} & b \otimes n \\ {\scriptstyle x \otimes w}\downarrow & \gamma & \downarrow{\scriptstyle y \otimes z} \\ c \otimes p & \xrightarrow[g \otimes i]{} & d \otimes q \end{array}$$

Equivalently, we could say that a monoidal double category is a category object in **M-Cat**. And, analogously, a *gs-monoidal* double category is a category object in **GSM-Cat**.

DEFINITION 22 (GS-MONOIDAL DOUBLE CATEGORIES) Let $\underline{\mathbf{C}}$ be a double category. We say that it is *gs-monoidal* if both $\mathbf{C}_h$ and $\mathbf{C}_H$ are gs-monoidal, vertical source and target are gs-monoidal functors, and the auxiliary operators preserves composition in the vertical categories. A double functor is *gs-monoidal* if it preserves the additional structure. □

Hence, gs-monoidality implies the existence of three kind of cells

$$\begin{array}{ccc} a\otimes b & \xrightarrow{\rho_{a,b}} & b\otimes a \\ {\scriptstyle x\otimes y}\downarrow & \rho_{x,y} & \downarrow{\scriptstyle y\otimes x} \\ c\otimes d & \xrightarrow[\rho_{c,d}]{} & d\otimes c \end{array} \qquad \begin{array}{ccc} a & \xrightarrow{\nabla_a} & a\otimes a \\ {\scriptstyle x}\downarrow & \nabla_x & \downarrow{\scriptstyle x\otimes x} \\ b & \xrightarrow[\nabla_b]{} & b\otimes b \end{array} \qquad \begin{array}{ccc} a & \xrightarrow{!_a} & e \\ {\scriptstyle x}\downarrow & !_x & \downarrow{\scriptstyle id_e} \\ b & \xrightarrow[!_b]{} & e \end{array}$$

which satisfies a few additional axioms on $\mathbf{C}_H$, making it gs-monoidal, like the naturality axioms for $\rho_{x,y}$: Given the cell $\alpha \otimes \beta$, then $(\alpha \otimes \beta) *_h \rho_{y,z} = \rho_{x,w} *_h (\beta \otimes \alpha)$. Graphically, the two cells

$$\begin{array}{ccccc} a\otimes m & \xrightarrow{f\otimes h} & b\otimes n & \xrightarrow{\rho_{b,n}} & n\otimes b \\ {\scriptstyle x\otimes w}\downarrow & \alpha\otimes\beta & \downarrow{\scriptstyle y\otimes z} & \rho_{y,z} & \downarrow{\scriptstyle z\otimes y} \\ c\otimes p & \xrightarrow[g\otimes i]{} & d\otimes q & \xrightarrow[\rho_{d,q}]{} & q\otimes d \end{array} \qquad \begin{array}{ccccc} a\otimes m & \xrightarrow{\rho_{a,m}} & m\otimes a & \xrightarrow{h\otimes f} & n\otimes b \\ {\scriptstyle x\otimes w}\downarrow & \rho_{x,w} & \downarrow{\scriptstyle w\otimes x} & \beta\otimes\alpha & \downarrow{\scriptstyle z\otimes y} \\ c\otimes p & \xrightarrow[\rho_{c,p}]{} & p\otimes c & \xrightarrow[i\otimes g]{} & q\otimes d \end{array}$$

must coincide. We say that a double category has *finite products* if it is a cat-object in **FC-Cat**: That is, if it is gs-monoidal, and also $\nabla$ and ! satisfy the naturality axiom on $\mathbf{C}_H$. In the following, we will denote with **DFC-Cat** the category of double categories with finite products, and gs-monoidal double functors.

We want now to introduce a finitary structure, which is able to generate a double category with a free construction, starting from a given set of cells. We then present the notion of *computad* [45, 46].

DEFINITION 23 (COMPUTADS) A *computad* is a triple $\langle \mathbf{C}, D, S\rangle$, where $\mathbf{C}$ is a category, $D$ is a graph (whose set of objects coincides with the set of objects of $\mathbf{C}$) and $S$ is a set of cells, each of which has assigned two pairs of compatible arrows in $\mathbf{C}$ and $D$ as *horizontal* and *vertical source* and *target*, respectively. A *computad morphism* $\langle F, G, h\rangle : \langle \mathbf{C}, D, S\rangle \to \langle \mathbf{C}', D', S'\rangle$ is a triple such that $F : \mathbf{C} \to \mathbf{C}'$ is a functor, $G : D \to D'$ is a graph morphism, and $h : S \to S'$ is a function preserving identities and compositions of all kinds. □

If we then define **Comp** as the category of computads, general results (see e.g. [2], and [9] for an applications of these results in the structured transition system approach) state the existence of an adjoint pair $\langle U_d, F_d \rangle$ between **Comp** and **D-Cat**, where $U_d$ is the forgetful component and $F_d$ the left adjoint. This adjoint composes the cells of a computad in all the possible ways, both horizontally and vertically, imposing further equalities in order to satisfy the axioms of a double category. Analogous adjoints exist also when computads have a more enriched structure. As an example, we indicate with **DFC-Comp** the category of computads $\langle \mathbf{C}, D, S \rangle$ such that $\mathbf{C}$ has finite products and $D$ is monoidal: There exists a forgetful functor $U_{df}$ : **DFC-Cat** → **DFC-Comp**, with left-adjoint $F_{df}$.

## 5.3 Sequents as Cells

From the point of view of entailment, the key component in the definition of a rewriting system $\langle \Sigma_\sigma, \Sigma_\tau, N, R \rangle$ is the relation $R$, which basically describes the building blocks to be used in the inductive construction of the sequents. Such a relation has its counterpart in the basic cells of a computad, which can then be used to freely generate the double category associated to the system.

DEFINITION 24 (FROM REWRITING SYSTEMS TO COMPUTADS) Let $\mathcal{R} = \langle \Sigma_\sigma, \Sigma_\tau, N, R \rangle$ be an ARS. The associated computad $\mathbf{C}(\mathcal{R})$ is the tuple $\langle \mathbf{A}(\Sigma_\sigma), G(\Sigma_\tau), S_R \rangle$, where $S_R$ is the set of cells such that

$$\begin{array}{ccc} n & \xrightarrow{s} & m \\ {\scriptstyle a}\downarrow & d & \downarrow{\scriptstyle b} \\ p & \xrightarrow[t]{} & q \end{array} \in S_R \qquad \textit{iff} \qquad d : s \xrightarrow[b]{a} t \in R.$$

□

Of course, different kinds of computads (monoidal, algebraic, etc.) could be used, according to which underlying theories we consider. Nevertheless, whatever computad we have, the adjunction with the corresponding double category is pivotal in defining a model for rewriting theories: A double category is freely generated from a computad, such that its cells represent (abstract) sequents.

DEFINITION 25 (SPACES OF COMPUTATIONS) Let $\mathcal{R}$ be an ARS, and let $\mathbf{C}(\mathcal{R})$ be its associated computad. Then the associated *algebraic double theory* $\underline{\mathbf{A}(\mathcal{R})}$ is the double category $F_{df}(\mathbf{C}(\mathcal{R}))$ with finite products. □

The algebraic double theory truly represents a "space of computations", intended as a set of rewrites, equipped with an equivalence relation. If we consider our running example

$\mathcal{R}_e$, the computad $\mathbf{C}(\mathcal{R}_e)$ has the following set of cells

$$\begin{array}{ccc} 0 & \xrightarrow{a} & 1 \\ {\scriptstyle id}\downarrow & d & \downarrow{\scriptstyle u} \\ 0 & \xrightarrow[b]{} & 1 \end{array} \qquad \begin{array}{ccc} 1 & \xrightarrow{f} & 1 \\ {\scriptstyle u}\downarrow & d_1 & \downarrow{\scriptstyle v} \\ 1 & \xrightarrow[g]{} & 1 \end{array} \qquad \begin{array}{ccc} 1 & \xrightarrow{f} & 1 \\ {\scriptstyle v}\downarrow & d_2 & \downarrow{\scriptstyle w} \\ 1 & \xrightarrow[f]{} & 1 \end{array} \qquad \begin{array}{ccc} 2 & \xrightarrow{h} & 1 \\ {\scriptstyle u\otimes v}\downarrow & d_3 & \downarrow{\scriptstyle w} \\ 2 & \xrightarrow[!_{\underline{1}}\otimes g]{} & 1 \end{array}$$

which are by no chance coincidental to the pictorial form for those same rules we used in Example 2. Some of the cells in $\underline{\mathbf{A}(\mathcal{R}_e)}$ are

$$\begin{array}{ccccc} 0 & \xrightarrow{a} & 1 & \xrightarrow{f} & 1 \\ {\scriptstyle id}\downarrow & d & \downarrow{\scriptstyle u} & d_1 & \downarrow{\scriptstyle v} \\ 0 & \xrightarrow[b]{} & 1 & \xrightarrow[g]{} & 1 \end{array} \qquad \begin{array}{ccccccc} 0 & \xrightarrow{a} & 1 & \xrightarrow{f} & 1 & \xrightarrow{f} & 1 \\ {\scriptstyle id}\downarrow & d & \downarrow{\scriptstyle u} & d_1 & \downarrow{\scriptstyle v} & d_2 & \downarrow{\scriptstyle w} \\ 0 & \xrightarrow[b]{} & 1 & \xrightarrow[g]{} & 1 & \xrightarrow[f]{} & 1 \end{array}$$

$$\begin{array}{ccccc} 0 & \xrightarrow{a\otimes(a;f)} & 2 & \xrightarrow{h} & 1 \\ {\scriptstyle id}\downarrow & d\otimes(d*d_1) & \downarrow{\scriptstyle u\otimes v} & d_3 & \downarrow{\scriptstyle w} \\ 0 & \xrightarrow[b\otimes(b;g)]{} & 2 & \xrightarrow[!_{\underline{1}}\otimes g]{} & 1 \end{array}$$

Next theorem states the correspondence, for a given ARS $\mathcal{R}$, between the cells of the associated algebraic double theory, and the families of abstract sequents.

THEOREM 2 (CORRESPONDENCE BETWEEN MODELS) Let $\mathcal{R}$ be an ARS. Then there exists a bijective, operator-preserving function $\phi : T(\mathcal{R})_E \to \underline{\mathbf{A}(\mathcal{R})}$ between the class of abstract algebraic sequents entailed by $\mathcal{R}$ and the cells of the associated algebraic double theory, such that

$$\begin{array}{ccc} n & \xrightarrow{s} & m \\ {\scriptstyle a}\downarrow & \phi(\alpha) & \downarrow{\scriptstyle b} \\ p & \xrightarrow[t]{} & q \end{array} \in \underline{\mathbf{A}(\mathcal{R})} \qquad \textit{iff} \qquad \alpha : s \xrightarrow[b]{a} t \in T(\mathcal{R})_E$$

*Proof Sketch* We inductively define $\phi$ over the structure of proof terms. First, note that cells are obtained simply closing with respect to the monoidal operation and the vertical and horizontal composition; moreover, the axioms of double categories with finite products are in a one-to-one correspondence with those of the abstract algebraic sequents. Hence, the intuitive function mapping each generator sequent to the corresponding generator cell, each horizontal composition of sequents to the horizontal composition of the associated cells, and so on, preserves the axioms and it is also a bijection. □

We close the section by explicitly providing the computad associated to CCS, since we feel that the geometrical intuition may ease the grasp of the rewriting system construction.

DEFINITION 26 (THE CCS COMPUTAD) The computad $\mathbf{C}(\mathcal{R}_{ccs})$ associated to CCS is the tuple $\langle \mathbf{A}(\Sigma_{ccs}), G(A_{ccs}), S_{ccs}\rangle$, where $S_{ccs}$ is the set of cells

$$\begin{array}{ccc} 1 & \xrightarrow{\mu} & 1 \\ {\scriptstyle id}\downarrow & \mathrm{act}_\mu & \downarrow{\scriptstyle \mu} \\ 1 & \xrightarrow[id]{} & 1 \end{array} \qquad \begin{array}{ccc} 1 & \xrightarrow{\Phi} & 1 \\ {\scriptstyle \mu}\downarrow & \mathrm{rel}_\Phi & \downarrow{\scriptstyle \Phi(\mu)} \\ 1 & \xrightarrow[\Phi]{} & 1 \end{array}$$

$$\begin{array}{ccc} 1 & \xrightarrow{\backslash\alpha} & 1 \\ {\scriptstyle \mu}\downarrow & \mathrm{res}_\alpha & \downarrow{\scriptstyle \mu} \\ 1 & \xrightarrow[\backslash\alpha]{} & 1 \end{array} \qquad \mathit{for} \quad \mu \notin \{\alpha, \overline{\alpha}\}$$

$$\begin{array}{ccc} 2 & \xrightarrow{+} & 1 \\ {\scriptstyle \mu\otimes id}\downarrow & \langle + & \downarrow{\scriptstyle \mu} \\ 2 & \xrightarrow[id\otimes !]{} & 1 \end{array} \qquad \begin{array}{ccc} 2 & \xrightarrow{+} & 1 \\ {\scriptstyle id\otimes\mu}\downarrow & +\rangle & \downarrow{\scriptstyle \mu} \\ 2 & \xrightarrow[!\otimes id]{} & 1 \end{array}$$

$$\begin{array}{ccc} 2 & \xrightarrow{\|} & 1 \\ {\scriptstyle \mu\otimes id}\downarrow & \xi_l & \downarrow{\scriptstyle \mu} \\ 2 & \xrightarrow[\|]{} & 1 \end{array} \qquad \begin{array}{ccc} 2 & \xrightarrow{\|} & 1 \\ {\scriptstyle id\otimes\mu}\downarrow & \xi_r & \downarrow{\scriptstyle \mu} \\ 2 & \xrightarrow[\|]{} & 1 \end{array} \qquad \begin{array}{ccc} 2 & \xrightarrow{\|} & 1 \\ {\scriptstyle \alpha\otimes\overline{\alpha}}\downarrow & \xi_s & \downarrow{\scriptstyle \tau} \\ 2 & \xrightarrow[\|]{} & 1 \end{array}$$

(where $id$ is a shorthand for $id_{\underline{1}}$). □

There is one cell for each rule, horizontal arrows are used to describe processes, vertical ones actions. As an example, a cell associated to the process $P = \alpha.\beta.nil$ is

$$\begin{array}{ccccccc}
0 & \xrightarrow{nil} & 1 & \xrightarrow{\beta} & 1 & \xrightarrow{\alpha} & 1 \\
{\scriptstyle id}\downarrow & & \downarrow{\scriptstyle id} & & \downarrow{\scriptstyle id} & & \downarrow{\scriptstyle \alpha} \\
0 & \xrightarrow{nil} & 1 & \xrightarrow{\beta} & 1 & \xrightarrow{id} & 1 \\
{\scriptstyle id}\downarrow & & \downarrow{\scriptstyle id} & & \downarrow{\scriptstyle \beta} & & \downarrow{\scriptstyle \beta} \\
0 & \xrightarrow[nil]{} & 1 & \xrightarrow[id]{} & 1 & \xrightarrow[id]{} & 1
\end{array}$$

showing the importance of the vertical arrows in expressing the ordering constraints: The process can execute $\alpha$ only if the underlying process is actually idle (i.e., the corresponding vertical arrow is $id_{\underline{1}}$).

PROPOSITION 10 (REPHRASING INTERLEAVING CORRESPONDENCE) Let $P, Q$ be CCS agents, and $P_a$, $Q_a$ the associated elements of $\mathbf{A}(\Sigma_{ccs})$. Then the transition $P \xrightarrow{\mu} Q$ is entailed by the CCS transition system $T_{ccs}$ iff there exists a cell $d$ in $F_{df}(\mathbf{C}(\mathcal{R}_{ccs}))$ such that

$$\begin{array}{ccc}
0 & \xrightarrow{P_a} & 1 \\
{\scriptstyle id}\downarrow & d & \downarrow{\scriptstyle \mu} \\
0 & \xrightarrow[Q_a]{} & 1
\end{array}$$

□

**Acknowledgements**. We would like to thank Roberto Bruni, Andrea Corradini, Gianluigi Ferrari, Reiko Heckel, Wolfram Kahl, Narciso Martí-Oliet and José Meseguer for the interesting discussions and the careful reading of the paper.

## References

[1] E. Badouel and P. Darondeau. Trace nets and process automata. *Acta Informatica*, 32:647–679, 1995.

[2] M. Barr and C. Wells. *Category Theory for Computing Science*. Prentice Hall, 1990.

[3] A. Bastiani and C. Ehresmann. Multiple functors I: Limits relative to double categories. *Cahiers de Topologie et Géométrie Différentielle*, 15:545–621, 1974.

[4] J.A. Bergstra and J.W. Klop. Process algebra for synchronous communication. *Information and Computation*, 60:109–137, 1984.

[5] G. Boudol. Computational semantics of term rewriting systems. In M. Nivat and J. Reynolds, editors, *Algebraic Methods in Semantics*, pages 170–235. Cambridge University Press, 1985.

[6] R. Bruni and U. Montanari. Zero-safe nets, or transition synchronization made simple. In C. Palamidessi and J. Parrow, editors, *Expressiveness in Concurrency*, volume 7 of *Electronic Notes in Computer Science*. Elsevier, 1997.

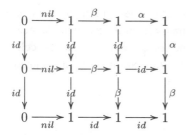

[7] A. Corradini and F. Gadducci. A 2-categorical presentation of term graph rewriting. In E. Moggi and G. Rosolini, editors, *Category Theory and Computer Science*, volume 1290 of *LNCS*, pages 87–105. Springer Verlag, 1997.

[8] A. Corradini, F. Gadducci, and U. Montanari. Relating two categorical models of term rewriting. In J. Hsiang, editor, *Rewriting Techniques and Applications*, volume 914 of *LNCS*, pages 225–240. Springer Verlag, 1995.

[9] A. Corradini and U. Montanari. An algebraic semantics for structured transition systems and its application to logic programs. *Theoret. Comput. Sci.*, 103:51–106, 1992.

[10] V.-E. Căzănescu and Gh. Ştefănescu. Towards a new algebraic foundation of flowchart scheme theory. *Fundamenta Informaticae*, 13:171–210, 1990.

[11] R. Dawson and R. Paré. General associativity and general composition for double categories. *Cahiers de Topologie ed Géométrie Différentielle Catégoriques*, 34:57–79, 1993.

[12] R. De Simone. Higher level synchronizing devices in MEIJE–SCCS. *Theoret. Comput. Sci.*, 37:245–267, 1985.

[13] E. Ehresmann. Catégories structurèes: I–II. *Annales École Normal Superieur*, 80:349–426, 1963.

[14] E. Ehresmann. Catégories structurèes: III. *Cahiers de Topologie et Géométrie Différentielle*, 5, 1963.

[15] G. Ferrari and U. Montanari. Towards the unification of models for concurrency. In A. Arnold, editor, *Trees in Algebra and Programming*, volume 431 of *LNCS*, pages 162–176. Springer Verlag, 1990.

[16] G. Ferrari and U. Montanari. A tile-based coordination view of the asynchronous $\pi$-calculus. In I. Prívara and P. Ružička, editors, *Mathematical Foundations of Computer Science*, volume 1295 of *LNCS*, pages 52–70. Springer Verlag, 1997.

[17] G. Ferrari and U. Montanari. Tiles for concurrent and located calculi. In C. Palamidessi and J. Parrow, editors, *Expressiveness in Concurrency*, volume 7 of *Electronic Notes in Computer Science*. Elsevier, 1997.

[18] M. Hasegawa. *Models of Sharing Graphs*. PhD thesis, University of Edinburgh, Department of Computer Science, 1997.

[19] C.A.R. Hoare. *Communicating Sequential Processes*. Prentice Hall, 1985.

[20] H.-J. Hoenke. On partial recursive definitions and programs. In M. Karpiński, editor, *Fundamentals of Computation Theory*, volume 56 of *LNCS*, pages 260–274. Springer Verlag, 1977.

[21] G. Huet and J.-J. Lévy. Computations in orthogonal rewriting systems, I. In J.-L. Lassez and G. Plotkin, editors, *Computational Logic: Essays in honour of Alan Robinson*, pages 395–414. MIT Press, 1991.

[22] B. Jacobs. Semantics of weakening and contraction. *Annals of Pure and Applied Logic*, 69:73–106, 1994.

[23] P. Katis, N. Sabadini, and R.F.C. Walters. Bicategories of processes. *Journal of Pure and Applied Algebra*, 115:141–178, 1997.

[24] R. Keller. Formal verifications of parallel programs. *Communications of the ACM*, 7:371–384, 1976.

[25] G.M. Kelly and R.H. Street. Review of the elements of 2-categories. In G.M. Kelly, editor, *Sydney Category Seminar*, volume 420 of *Lecture Notes in Mathematics*, pages 75–103. Springer Verlag, 1974.

[26] J.W. Klop. Term rewriting systems. In S. Abramsky, D. Gabbay, and T. Maibaum, editors, *Handbook of Logic in Computer Science*, volume 1, pages 1–116. Oxford University Press, 1992.

[27] A. Kock and G.E. Reyes. Doctrines in categorical logic. In J. Barwise, editor, *Handbook of Mathematical Logic*, pages 283–313. North Holland, 1977.

[28] Y. Lafont. Equational reasoning with 2–dimensional diagrams. In H. Comon and J.-P. Jouannaud, editors, *Term Rewriting*, volume 909 of *LNCS*, pages 170–195. Springer Verlag, 1995.

[29] C. Laneve and U. Montanari. Axiomatizing permutation equivalence in the $\lambda$-calculus. In H. Kirchner and G. Levi, editors, *Algebraic and Logic Programming*, volume 632 of *LNCS*, pages 350–363. Springer Verlag, 1992.

[30] K.G. Larsen and L. Xinxin. Compositionality through an operational semantics of contexts. In M.S. Paterson, editor, *Automata, Languages and Programming*, volume 443 of *LNCS*, pages 526–539. Springer Verlag, 1990.

[31] F.W. Lawvere. Functorial semantics of algebraic theories. *Proc. National Academy of Science*, 50:869–872, 1963.

[32] S. Mac Lane. *Categories for the working mathematician*. Springer Verlag, 1971.

[33] J. Meseguer. Conditional rewriting logic as a unified model of concurrency. *Theoret. Comput. Sci.*, 96:73–155, 1992.

[34] J. Meseguer and U. Montanari. Petri nets are monoids. *Information and Computation*, 88:105–155, 1990.

[35] R. Milner. *Communication and Concurrency*. Prentice Hall, 1989.

[36] R. Milner. Calculi for interaction. *Acta Informatica*, 33:707–737, 1996.

[37] U. Montanari and F. Rossi. Graph rewriting and constraint solving for modelling distributed systems with synchronization. In P. Ciancarini and C. Hankin, editors, *Coordination Languages and Models*, volume 1061 of *LNCS*, pages 12–27. Springer Verlag, 1996.

[38] D. Park. Concurrency and automata on infinite sequences. In P. Deussen, editor, *Theoretical Computer Science*, volume 104 of *LNCS*, pages 167–183. Springer Verlag, 1981.

[39] M. Pfender. Universal algebra in s-monoidal categories. Technical Report 95–22, University of Munich, Department of Mathematics, 1974.

[40] G. Plotkin. A structural approach to operational semantics. Technical Report DAIMI FN-19, Aarhus University, Computer Science Department, 1981.

[41] A.J. Power. An abstract formulation for rewrite systems. In D.H. Pitt, D.E. Rydehard, P. Dybjer, A.M. Pitts, and A. Poigné, editors, *Category Theory and Computer Science*, volume 389 of *LNCS*, pages 300–312. Springer Verlag, 1989.

[42] W. Reisig. *Petri Nets: An Introduction*. EACTS Monographs on Theoretical Computer Science. Springer Verlag, 1985.

[43] D.E. Rydehard and E.G. Stell. Foundations of equational deductions: A categorical treatment of equational proofs and unification algorithms. In D.H. Pitt, A. Poigné, and D.E. Rydehard, editors, *Category Theory and Computer Science*, volume 283 of *LNCS*, pages 114–139. Springer Verlag, 1987.

[44] M.R. Sleep, M.J. Plasmeijer, and M.C. van Eekelen, editors. *Term Graph Rewriting: Theory and Practice*. Wiley, 1993.

[45] R.H. Street. Higher categories, strings, cubes and simplex equations. *Applied Categorical Structures*, 3:29–77, 1995.

[46] R.H. Street. Categorical structures. In M. Hazewinkel, editor, *Handbook of Algebra*, pages 529–577. Elsevier, 1996.

# II PROGRAMMING LOGIC

# 6 From LCF to HOL: A Short History

**Mike Gordon**

## 1 Introduction

The original LCF system was a proof-checking program developed at Stanford University by Robin Milner in 1972. Descendents of LCF now form a thriving paradigm in computer assisted reasoning. Many of the developments of the last 25 years have been due to Robin Milner, whose influence on the field of automated reasoning has been diverse and profound. One of the descendents of LCF is HOL, a proof assistant for higher order logic originally developed for reasoning about hardware.[1] The multifaceted contribution of Robin Milner to the development of HOL is remarkable. Not only did he invent the LCF-approach to theorem proving, but he also designed the ML programming language underlying it and the innovative polymorphic type system used both by ML and the LCF and HOL logics. Code Milner wrote is still in use today, and the design of the hardware verification system LCF_LSM (a now obsolete stepping stone from LCF to HOL) was inspired by Milner's Calculus of Communicating Systems (CCS).

## 2 Stanford LCF

"LCF" abbreviates "Logic for Computable Functions," Milner's name for a logic devised by Dana Scott in 1969, but not published until 1993 [46]. The LCF logic has terms from the typed λ-calculus and formulae from predicate calculus. Types are interpreted as Scott domains (CPOs) and the logic is intended for reasoning, using fixed-point induction, about recursively defined functions of the sort used in denotational semantic definitions.

The original LCF team at Stanford consisted of Robin Milner, assisted by Whitfield Diffie (from whom Milner learnt Lisp). Diffie subsequently became interested in cryptography, where he became well known. A bit later Richard Weyhrauch joined the team, soon followed by Malcolm Newey. All these people collaborated on designing, implementing and using the original LCF system, now known as Stanford LCF. The resulting system is a proof checker for Scott's logic and is described by Milner as follows [34]:

> The proof-checking program is designed to allow the user interactively to generate formal proofs about computable functions and functionals over a variety of domains, including those of interest to the computer scientist—for example, integers, lists and computer programs and their semantics. The user's task is alleviated by two features: a subgoaling facility and a powerful simplification mechanism.

[1] "HOL" abbreviates "Higher Order Logic."

Proofs are conducted by declaring a main goal (a formula in Scott's logic) and then splitting it into subgoals using a fixed set of subgoaling commands (such as induction to generate the basis and step). Subgoals are either solved using a simplifier or split into simpler subgoals until they can be solved directly. Data structures representing formal proofs in Scott's logic are created when proof commands are interpreted. These can consume a lot of memory.

Stanford LCF was used for a number of case studies. Weyhrauch worked on the proof of correctness of a compiling algorithm for a simple imperative language to a stack-based target language [36] and Newey on the generation of equational theories of integers and lists.

## 3 Edinburgh LCF

Around 1973 Milner moved to Edinburgh University and established a project to build a successor to Stanford LCF, which was subsequently dubbed Edinburgh LCF. He initially hired Lockwood Morris and Malcolm Newey (both recent PhD graduates from Stanford) as research assistants. Two problems with Stanford LCF were (i) that the size of proofs was limited by available memory and (ii) the fixed set of proof commands could not be easily extended. Milner set out to correct these deficiencies in Edinburgh LCF. For (i) he had the idea that instead of saving whole proofs, the system should just remember the results of proofs, namely theorems. The steps of a proof would be performed but not recorded, like a mathematics lecturer using a small blackboard who rubs out earlier parts of proofs to make space for later ones. To ensure that theorems could only be created by proof, Milner had the brilliant idea of using an abstract data type whose predefined values were instances of axioms and whose operations were inference rules. Strict typechecking then ensured that the only values that could be created were those that could be obtained from axioms by applying a sequence of inference rules—namely theorems. To enable the set of proof commands to be extended and customised—(ii) above—Milner, ably assisted by Morris and Newey, designed the programming language ML (an abbreviation for "Meta Language"). This was strictly typed to support the abstract type mechanism needed to ensure theorem security [35].

In Stanford LCF, the axioms and rules of inference of Scott's logic were directly encoded in the implementation of the simplification and subgoaling mechanism. The user could only construct proofs "backwards" from goals. In Scott's unpublished paper, his logic was presented in the conventional way by giving axiom schemes and rules of inference. The direct notion of formal proof suggested by this is a sequence, each member of which is either an axiom or follows from an earlier member via a rule of inference (this notion of proof is sometimes called "forward"). By encoding the logic as an abstract type, Edinburgh

LCF directly supported forward proof. The design goal was to implement goal directed proof tools by programs in ML. To make ML convenient for this, the language was made functional so that subgoaling strategies could be represented as functions (called "tactics" by Milner) and operations for combining strategies could be programmed as higher-order functions taking strategies as arguments and returning them as results (called "tacticals"). It was anticipated that strategies might fail (e.g., by being applied to inappropriate goals) so an exception handling mechanism was included in ML. The needs of theorem proving very strongly influenced the design of the first version of ML. Many design details were resolved by considering alternatives in the light of their use for programming proof tools. This narrow design focus resulted in a simple and coherent language.

In 1975, Morris and Newey took up faculty positions at Syracuse University and the Australian National University, respectively, and were replaced by Chris Wadsworth and myself. The design and implementation of ML and Edinburgh LCF was finalised and the book "Edinburgh LCF" [15] was written and published.[2] In 1978, the first LCF project finished, Chris Wadsworth went off trekking in the Andes (returning to a permanent position at the Rutherford Appleton Laboratory) and I remained at Edinburgh supported by a postdoctoral fellowship and with a new research interest: hardware verification. After the first LCF project finished, application studies using Edinburgh LCF continued. Milner's student Avra Cohn did a PhD on verifying programming language implementations with LCF and Brian Monahan did a PhD on the theory and mechanisation (using LCF) of datatypes. Researchers who worked with LCF included Jacek Leszczylowski and Stefan Sokolowski.

## 4 Cambridge LCF

In 1981, I moved to a permanent position as Lecturer at the University of Cambridge Computer Laboratory. Another LCF project was funded by SERC, split between Edinburgh and Cambridge, with one research assistant at each site. Larry Paulson, recently graduated with a PhD from Stanford, was hired at Cambridge and David Schmidt followed by Lincoln Wallen at Edinburgh.[3] About this time, and in parallel, Gérard Huet ported the Edinburgh LCF code to Lelisp and MacLisp.[4] Paulson and Huet then established a collaboration and did a lot of joint development of LCF by sending each other magnetic tapes in the post. Huet improved and extended ML (his group subsequently developed Caml) and optimised

[2] The author "Arthur J. Milner" of this book was the result of a bug in the way Springer-Verlag created title pages: they asked for the author's full name on a form and then used it without properly checking its appropriateness.

[3] In the 1980s work at Edinburgh broadened its emphasis from LCF to generic logical frameworks, and then to constructive type theory.

[4] Edinburgh LCF, including the ML interpreter, was implemented in Lisp.

the implementation of LCF's theory files. Paulson improved and simplified much of the Lisp code, and removed some space optimisations that had been necessary to get Edinburgh LCF to run in the limited amount of memory available on the Edinburgh DEC-10 system. Edinburgh LCF ran interpretively, but during Paulson and Huet's collaboration an ML compiler was implemented that provided a speedup by a factor of about twenty.

As part of his LCF work at Cambridge, Paulson made dramatic improvements both to our understanding of how to design and program proof tools and (in collaboration with Gérard Huet) to the implementation of LCF. The now-standard techniques of conversions [39] and theorem continuations [40, Section 8.7.2] were devised by him and then used to implement a large collection of tools. Edinburgh LCF had a monolithic simplifier provided as a primitive. Paulson redesigned and reprogrammed this as a simple and clean derived rule. Inspired by an algorithm from the book *Artificial Intelligence Programming* [3], he implemented a data structure (discrimination nets) for efficiently indexing sets of equations used in rewriting. This became an essential tool for efficiently handling large sets of rules.

Paulson also upgraded the LCF logic to include all the standard constructs of predicate calculus (Scott's logic didn't have disjunction or existential quantification). He also implemented a simple package for managing subgoals on a stack (users of Edinburgh LCF typically managed subgoals by hand by explicitly binding them to ML variables with cumbersome names like g_2_1_3). These developments were driven and tested by a number of major case studies, including the formalisation and checking, by Paulson [42], of a proof of correctness of the unification algorithm. The resulting new LCF system was named "Cambridge LCF" and completed around 1985. Paulson did little work on it after that. Mikael Hedlund (of the Rutherford Appleton Laboratory) then ported Cambridge LCF to Standard ML (using a new implementation of ML that he created). The resulting Standard ML based version of Cambridge LCF is documented (with supporting case studies and a tutorial of underlying theory) in Paulson's 1987 book *Logic and Computation* [40].

## 5 From LCF to HOL

Whilst Paulson was designing and implementing Cambridge LCF, I was mainly concerned with hardware verification. I had been impressed by how the Expansion Theorem of Milner's Calculus of Communicating Systems (CCS) [37] enabled a direct description of the behaviour of a composite agent to be calculated from the parallel composition of its individual components. This seemed like a good paradigm for deriving the behaviour of a digital system from its structural description. I invented a rather *ad hoc* notation (called "LSM" for Logic of Sequential Machines) for denoting sequential machine behaviour, together with a law manipulatively similar to CCS's Expansion Theorem. To provide a proof assistant for LSM, I lashed up a version of Cambridge LCF (called LCF_LSM) that added parsing and pretty-printer support for LSM and provided the expansion-law as an additional axiom scheme [11]. This lash-up worked quite well and even got used outside Cambridge. I used it to verify a toy microprocessor [12], subsequently called Tamarack[5] and the LSM notation was used by a group in the Royal Signals and Radar Establishment (RSRE) to specify the ill-fated Viper processor [5]. During this time Ben Moskowski, who had recently graduated from Stanford, was doing a postdoc at Cambridge. He showed me how the terms of LSM could be encoded in predicate calculus in such a way that the LSM expansion-law just becomes a derived rule (i.e., corresponds to a sequence of standard predicate calculus inferences). This approach is both more elegant and rests on a firmer logical foundation, so I switched to it and HOL was born. Incidently, not only was CCS's Expansion Theorem an inspirational stepping stone from LCF via LSM to HOL, but recently things have come "full circle" and Monica Nesi has used HOL to provide proof support for CCS, including the mechanisation of the Expansion Theorem [38]!

The logic supported by Cambridge LCF has the usual formula structure of predicate calculus, and the term structure of the typed $\lambda$-calculus. The type system, due to Milner, is essentially Church's original one [4], but with type variables moved from the meta-language to the object language (in Church's system, a term with type variables is actually a meta-notation—a term-schema—denoting a family of terms, whereas in LCF it is a single polymorphic term). LCF's interpretation of terms as denoting members of Scott domains is overkill for hardware verification where the recursion that arises is normally just primitive recursion. For hardware verification, there is rarely the need for the extra sophistication of fixed-point (Scott) induction; ordinary mathematical induction suffices. The HOL system retains the syntax of LCF, but reinterprets types as ordinary sets, rather than Scott domains.

To enable existing LCF code to be reused, the axioms and rules of inference of HOL were not taken to be the standard ones due to Church. For example, the LCF logic has parallel substitution as a primitive rule of inference (a decision taken after experimentation when Edinburgh LCF was designed), but Church's logic has a different primitive. HOL employs the LCF substitution because I wanted to use the existing efficient code. As a result the HOL logic ended up with a rather *ad hoc* formal basis. Another inheritance from LCF is the use of a natural deduction logic (Church used a Hilbert-style formal system). However, this inheritance is, in my opinion, entirely good.

[5] The name "Tamarack" is due to Jeff Joyce, who reverified it in HOL [27] and fabricated a chip based on it whilst visiting Xerox Parc as a summer student.

### 5.1 The Development of HOL

Originally HOL was created for hardware verification at the register transfer level. The modelling technique to be supported represents hardware devices as relations between input and output signals, with internal signals hidden by existential quantification. Signals are represented by functions from time to values (wire states), so that higher-order relations and quantification are necessary. This immediately suggests higher-order logic as an appropriate formalism [13] (the same idea occurred earlier to Keith Hanna [19], the designer of the Veritas hardware verification system). The design of HOL was largely taken "off the shelf," the theory being classical higher order logic and the implementation being LCF. The development of the system was, at first, primarily driven by hardware verification case studies.

The first version of the HOL system was created by modifying the Cambridge LCF parser and pretty-printer to support higher order logic concrete syntax. HOL terms were encoded as LCF constructs in a way designed to support maximum reuse of LCF code (the encoding did not represent any coherent domain-theoretic semantics). Many aspects of LCF, e.g., typechecking and theory management, were carried over unchanged to HOL. The LCF primitive axioms and inference rules were modified to be correct for higher order logic, and then the higher level theorem proving infrastructure (conversions, tactics, tacticals, subgoal package, etc.) was modified to work correctly.

### 5.2 Primitive Definitional Principles

The HOL system, unlike LCF, emphasises definition rather than axiom postulation as the primary method of developing theories. Higher order logic makes possible a purely definitional development of many mathematical objects (numbers, lists, trees, etc.) and this is supported and encouraged.[6]

The definitional principles provided by HOL evolved during the 1980s. Initially, constants could only be defined via equations of the form $\mathsf{c} = t$, where $\mathsf{c}$ was a new name and $t$ a closed term. Types could be defined by a scheme, devised by Mike Fourman, in which new types could be introduced as names for non-empty subsets (specified by a predicate) of existing types. Somewhat later, HOL users at ICL (Roger Jones *et al.*) proposed that "loose specifications" of constants be allowed. This was implemented by a definitional principle that allowed constants $\mathsf{c}_1, \ldots, \mathsf{c}_n$ to be introduced satisfying a property $P(\mathsf{c}_1, \ldots, \mathsf{c}_n)$, as long as $\exists x_1 \cdots x_n \cdot P(x_1, \ldots, x_n)$ could be proved. This principle is called "constant specification" in HOL.

[6] Axiomatic developments, like group theory, have been attempted with some success [18] (though the LCF/HOL theory mechanism is not ideal for it and various improvements have been proposed). The facilities inherited from LCF for declaring axioms are still available in HOL.

The first versions of the definitional principles seemed "obviously correct," but Mark Saaltink and Roger Jones independently noticed that in fact they were unsound in the sense that making a definition did not necessarily preserve consistency.[7] It is easy to fix the problems by adding side conditions to the definitional principles. With the support of DSTO Australia, Dr Andrew Pitts was commissioned to validate HOL's definitional principles. He produced informal proofs that they could not introduce inconsistency [14, Chapter 16].

### 5.3 Derived Definitional Principles

The primitive built-in definitional principles are low-level, but high-level derived principles can be programmed in ML. These take a property one wants a new constant or type to have and then automatically define constants and/or types that have the property. For example, one early derived constant-definition principle defined arithmetical functions to satisfy any user-supplied primitive recursive equation by instantiating the primitive recursion theorem (which was previously proved from the definition of numbers).

Building on ideas originally developed by Milner, Monahan and Paulson for LCF, Melham implemented a derived type-definition principle that converts descriptions of recursive datatypes into primitive definitions and then automatically derives the natural induction and primitive recursion principles for the datatype [29].[8]

It was probably this tool that was most responsible for changing the perception of HOL from being purely a hardware verification system to being a general purpose proof assistant. For example, it became dramatically easier to embed languages inside HOL, by defining a recursive type of abstract syntax trees and a primitive recursive semantic function. Another derived definitional principle, also due to Melham [30], allows inductively defined relations to be specified by a transition system, and then a rule-induction tactic to be automatically generated. This enables operational semantics to be easily defined inside HOL.

[7] The problem was HOL's treatment of type variables. In the HOL logic, constants can have polymorphic types—i.e., types containing type variables. For example, the identity function I has type $\alpha\to\alpha$, where $\alpha$ is a type variable. Polymorphic constants are not explicitly parameterised on type variables, so a constant definition $\mathsf{c} = t$ in which there is a free type variable in the type of $t$ but not in the type of c might lead to inconsistency. For example, it is easy to devise [14, page 221] a closed boolean term (i.e., formula), $t$ say, that contains a type variable, $\alpha$ say, and is such that $t$ is true for some instances of $\alpha$, and false for others. A constant definition $\mathsf{c} = t$ will then be inconsistent, because it will be possible to prove c equals both true and false, by type-instantiating the definition with the two instances. In future versions of HOL it is expected that there will be explicit type variable quantification [31], i.e., terms of the form $\forall\alpha \cdot t$ (where $\alpha$ is a type variable). The right hand side of definitions will be required to be closed with respect to both term and type variables. Melham has shown that this will make defining mechanisms much cleaner and also permit an elegant treatment of type specifications.

[8] The various datatype packages in LCF were not definitional—LCF did not distinguish definitions from arbitary axioms. In LCF, new constants and types were characterised by asserting new axioms. Melham's package for HOL automatically generates constant and type definitions and then proves theorems corresponding to the characterising axioms used in LCF.

Other derived definitional principles have also been implemented, including a powerful tool by Konrad Slind for making general recursive definitions of functions [47] (which also runs in Isabelle/HOL) and at least two independent packages for creating quotient types.

### 5.4 Simplification

Cambridge LCF had a powerful simplifier that dealt separately with term rewriting and formula simplification. In HOL, boolean terms played the role of formulae, so a separate syntactic class of formulae was not needed and hence separate sets of tools for formula and term simplification were no longer necessary. Unfortunately, when I modified Paulson's simplifier for use in HOL, I never got around to making the condition-handling (backchaining) parts of his code work, so HOL ended up without conditional simplification. At the time I justified my laziness with the thought that this would not be important, because in LCF conditional simplification had mainly been used to manage definedness and strictness assumptions arising from the bottom element ($\perp$) of domain theory. Such assumptions do not arise in HOL. However, with hindsight, it is clear that Paulson's superior simplifier would have been very useful for HOL applications, and would have saved many people much low-level proof hacking. Over the years several people have contributed conditional simplification packages as optional add-ons to HOL, but only recently has conditional simplification been added to the core of the system. It is now part of a new simplifier that integrates rewriting, conversions and decision procedures into a single tool.[9]

## 6 Versions of HOL

The HOL system has always been very open and many people have contributed to its development. Several groups have built their own versions of the system, essentially starting from scratch. This has good and bad aspects: perhaps some effort has been wasted through duplication and there may be a bit of confusion about which version to use, but on the other hand poor design decisions have been rectified and new ideas (e.g., Mizar mode—see 7.3) have had an opportunity to get incorporated. The latest versions of HOL incorporate ideas from other successful systems, like Isabelle, PVS and Mizar.

### 6.1 HOL88

The core HOL system became stable in about 1988. A new release that consolidated various changes and enhancements called HOL88 was issued then.[10] We were fortunate to receive

[9] HOL's new simplifier uses ideas from Isabelle and is being developed by Donald Syme.

[10] The release was prepared by Tom Melham and paid for by ICL.

support from DSTO Australia to document HOL[11] and from Hewlett Packard to port it from Franz Lisp to Common Lisp (a job very ably done by John Carroll). The current versions of HOL and its documentation are public domain[12] and available on the Internet.[13]

### 6.2 HOL90

In the late 1980s Graham Birtwistle of the University of Calgary started a project to reimplement HOL in Standard ML. The work was done by Konrad Slind, under Birtwistle's direction and with the collaboration of the HOL group at Cambridge. The resulting system, called HOL90, was first released around 1990. It introduced much rationalisation to the legacy-code-based HOL88, and provided a significant performance improvement. During the 1990s Slind continued to develop HOL90 in collaboration with Elsa Gunter of AT&T Bell Laboratories (which has recently become Bell Labs Innovations, Lucent Technologies). HOL90 is now the main version of HOL in use around the world, though users of HOL88 still linger on.

### 6.3 ProofPower

In parallel with the development of HOL90, ICL created their own commercial version of HOL, now called ProofPower.[14] This was targetted at in-house and commercial use, especially for security applications. ProofPower supports exactly the same logic as the other HOL systems, but has different proof infrastructure that evolved to meet the needs of the targetted applications (e.g., customised theorem-proving support for the Z notation and a verification condition generator for the Z-(SPARK) Ada compliance notation).

### 6.4 Isabelle/HOL

Besides HOL, several other LCF-style proof assistants were developed with ML as their metalanguage (in some cases code from LCF was used as the starting point). These include a proof system for the Calculus of Contructions [10, 9], Nuprl [8], and a proof system for Martin Löf type theory [44]. These applied Milner's LCF methodology to widely different logics. To try to provide a systematic implementation methodology for "LCF-style" systems,

[11] A documentation standard was designed and then each of the several hundred ML functions comprising HOL was priced at £5 or £10. Members of the Cambridge HOL users community were then invited to write documentation for money. The whole job was done painlessly in a few weeks.

[12] A licence agreement for HOL is available, but signing it is optional.

[13] `http://lal.cs.byu.edu/lal/hol-documentation.html`

[14] `http://www.to.icl.fi/ICLE/ProofPower/index.html`

Paulson developed the generic prover Isabelle [41, 43]. This provided a metalogic in which the proof rules of object logics can be described declaratively (in LCF and HOL, rules are represented as ML programs—i.e., they are implemented rather than specified). At first sight Isabelle seems to provide a similar collection of proof tools as HOL, but the way they work is quite different. Metalogic rules are composed using a meta-inference rule based on higher order unification (resolution).[15] Forward and backward proof in HOL corresponds to special cases of rule composition in Isabelle. However, Milner's key idea of using ML's abstract types to ensure that theorems can only be obtained by allowable combinations of allowable rules is retained, and lifted to the metalogic level. One of the object logics developed for Isabelle by Paulson was the HOL logic. The resulting Isabelle/HOL system has a somewhat different 'look and feel' to the original HOL system, due to Isabelle's different proof infrastructure. It provides better general logic automation than HOL (via its customisable simplifier and first-order theorem proving tools)[16] and some HOL users have migrated to it.

### 6.5 HOL Light

Recently John Harrison and Konrad Slind have entirely reworked the design of HOL to, among other things, rationalise the primitive constants, axioms and rules of inference. For example, the logic is initially taken to be constructive, and only after considerable proof infrastructure has been defined are non-constructive principles added. This new version of HOL is called "HOL Light." It is implemented in Caml Light and runs on modest platforms (e.g., standard PCs). It is faster than the Lisp-based HOL88, but a bit slower than HOL90 running in modern implementations of Standard ML. HOL Light contains many new facilities, including automatic provers that separate proof search from checking. It also provides "Mizar mode" (see 7.3) as well as the normal goal-oriented proof styles.

## 7 Features of HOL

HOL is characterised by a number of key features: a simple core logic, LCF-style "full expansiveness," support for a growing diversity of proof styles and a large corpus of user-supplied theories and proof tools.

[15] Higher order unification is built into Isabelle, thus Isabelle's "trusted core" is considerably more complex than HOL's.

[16] Tools based on the Isabelle simplifier, and others comparable to its first order automation facilities, are now part of HOL90 and HOL Light.

## 7.1 The Core Logic

There are only four separate kinds of primitive terms: variables, constants, function applications and λ-abstractions. Using standard techniques, other useful notations are supported on top of these by the parser and pretty-printer. For example, quantifications $Qx \cdot t$ (where $Q$ is $\forall$ or $\exists$) are encoded (following Church) as the application of a constant to an abstraction—i.e., as $Q(\lambda x \cdot t)$, and local variable binding `let` $x = t_1$ `in` $t_2$ is equivalent (following Landin) to $(\lambda x \cdot t_2)t_1$. Thus all variable binding is reduced to λ-binding.

Notations including infixes, conditional terms, set abstractions, restricted quantifications (i.e., quantification over predicate subtypes), tuple notation, and tupled variable binding (e.g., $\lambda(x, y) \cdot t$) are considered to be derived forms (i.e., "syntactic sugar"). This strategy of translating away complex notations has worked pretty well. It means that procedures designed to process all terms need often only consider four cases (variables, constants, applications and abstractions) and so can be short and semantically transparent.[17] On the other hand, the encoding of everything into just variables, constants, applications and abstractions makes the computation of the natural constituents of constructs expensive. This makes writing interfaces (e.g., pretty printing) quite complex.[18] A particular danger with reducing complex notations to a simple core is that what the user sees printed can be remote from what thc inference mechanisms actually process. Errors in the parsing and pretty printing interface can be just as dangerous as errors in the infererence rules (e.g., consider an interface that translated *true* to *false* with a pretty-printer that inverted this translation). This problem has been worried about a lot. One approach to minimising the dangers is to use trustworthy tools that generate parsers and pretty printers from a declarative input. A recent example of such tool is CLaReT, due to Richard Boulton.

## 7.2 Full Expansiveness

The LCF approach to theorem proving is "fully expansive" in that all proofs are expanded into sequences of primitive inferences. At first sight this seems to be very inefficient and it has been argued that it is incompatible with acceptable performance. However, a whole

17 An example of this is Grundy's window inference system for hierarchical transformational reasoning (e.g., program refinement) [17]. This provides an environment on top of HOL for pointing at subterms and then transforming them "in place" (subject, of course, to context-dependent side-conditions). Grundy was able to base his system on three primitives (one each for the function and argument constituents of applications and one for the bodies of λ-abstractions) and then have ML programs automatically compose guaranteed-sound window rules for transforming arbitrarily complex terms as syntax-directed compositions of the three primitives. If HOL had had different primitive terms for each user-level notation, then Grundy would have had to hand-build a primitive window-rule for each of them.

18 For example, it is more work than it looks to extract the constituents $x$, $y$, $t_1$ and $t_2$ from `let` $(x, y) = t_1$ `in` $t_2$, which is actually parsed to $\mathrm{LET}(\mathrm{UNCURRY}(\lambda x \cdot \mathrm{UNCURRY}(\lambda y \cdot \lambda z \cdot t_2)))t_1$.

programming methodology has evolved for programming efficient derived rules and tactics. For example, decision procedures for particular classes of problems have been developed. Although these expand out to primitive inferences, they are surprisingly efficient. HOL has such decision procedures for tautology checking (based on BDDs and due to John Harrison) and for a subset of arithmetic (due to Richard Boulton) which users find adequately fast and powerful for many applications. An important efficiency improving technique is to exploit the expressive power of higher order logic by encoding as single theorems facts that would have to be derived rules of inference (e.g., theorem schemas) in first order logic. Thus time-consuming repetitions of sequences of proof steps can often be avoided by proving a general theorem once and then instantiating it many times. Another programming technique is to separate out proof search from proof checking. An ML program, or even an external oracle (like a C-coded tautology checker or an algebra system [22]), can be used to find a proof. The result is validated by formal inference inside the HOL logic. One way of packaging (and automating) this separation is Boulton's technique of lazy theorems [2].[19]

There have been many developments in the implementation and use of tactics over the last twenty years. It is remarkable that Milner's original concept has turned out to be sufficiently general to support them.

### 7.3 A diversity of proof styles

Current releases of HOL support forward proof and goal directed proof. The latter via a stack-based subgoal package provided for Cambridge LCF by Paulson. Other styles are available as libraries (e.g., window inference and tree based subgoal package due to Sara Kalvala). One way that HOL is expected to evolve is as a tool with a fixed logic but with an ever growing variety of built-in proof styles. For example, recently a lot of excitement has been generated by the remarkable Mizar system[20] in which proofs are constructed by refining arguments expressed in a natural-language-like textbook style. It seems that this forward style is better for some things and a goal-oriented style for others. In particular, a goal-oriented style works well for verifying complex artifacts (e.g., microprocessors) where the proof can be generated via specialised algorithms, whereas the forward Mizar style seems better for developing general mathematical theories (e.g., algebra, functional

[19] A lazy theorem is a pair consisting of a term, together with a procedure for proving it. Lazy theorems can be created using a (fast) non-expansive decision procedure, and supplying a (slow) expansive procedure as the proof function. Such lazy theorems can be manipulated (with some additional effort) much like proper theorems, by composing the proof functions. At some point they need to be coerced into proper theorems (by running the proof part), but this can be postponed to a convenient moment—e.g., coffee time. With lazy theorems one gets the interactive speed of conventional decision procedures with the security of full-expansiveness.

[20] `http://web.cs.ualberta.ca:80/~piotr/Mizar/`

analysis, topology). Many applications (e.g., floating point verification, cryptography, signal processing) require a general mathematical infrastructure to be brought to bear via problem-specific algorithms [20]. It is thus useful to provide the option of using a Mizar style for developing theories and a goal oriented style for deploying them. To this end, John Harrison has recently added support for "Mizar mode" in HOL [21].

## 7.4 Libraries and Other User Supplied Contributions

To enable theories (and other utility code) to be shared, HOL has a rudimentary library facility. This provides a file structure and documentation format for self contained HOL developments (usually a combination of theories and theorem proving tools). Over the years many libraries were supplied by users from around the world. Although the core HOL system remained fairly stable, the set of libraries grew. Libraries currently distributed with HOL include arithmetic and tautology decision procedures, a development of group theory, a package to support inductively defined relations, theories of integers and reals (only natural numbers are predefined in the core system) theories of $n$-bit words, character strings, general lists and sets, well-ordered sets (transfinite induction, etc.), support for UNITY and Hoare-style programming logics, tools for hardware verification and program refinement (window inference).

Libraries are intended to be fairly polished and documented to a high standard. Also distributed with HOL are "contributions," which are subject to minimal quality control. Currently distributed contributions include: CSP trace theory, proof tools for associative-commutative unification, tactics implementing Boyer and Moore's automatic proof heuristics (as described in the book *A Computational Logic*), the proof of a sequential multiplier (used as a benchmark for HOL), theories of infinite state automata, rules for simplifying conditional expressions, the definition of fixedpoints and the derivation of Scott induction, tools to support language embedding in higher order logic, Knuth-Bendix completion as a derived rule, various enhancements to the recursive types package (e.g., for nested and mutual recursion), the formalisation of a significant part of the definition of Standard ML, the application of a database query language to HOL, a compiler for generating efficient conversions from sets of equations, theories supporting partial functions and a hyperlinked guide to HOL theories. Considering the way it was built, there have been relatively few bugs in HOL. Because the system is completely open, early bug-fixes were often done by intrepid users[21] and then mailed to me for inclusion in future releases.

[21] Subtle Lisp bugs in early versions of HOL were fixed by David Shepherd of Inmos and Ton Kalker of Philips.

## 8 Conclusions

Over the last ten years the scale of what can be proved with HOL (as with other provers) has increased dramatically. In the early 1980's the verification of simple systems with a few registers and gates was considered significant. By the late 1980s simple microprocessors [6, 7, 16, 49] and networking hardware [23] was being verified and by the mid 1990s complex hardware structures (e.g., pipelines) were being analysed and many non-hardware applications were being attempted, including program and algorithm verification, support for process algebras and the mechanisation of classical mathematical analysis (i.e., the theory of limits, differentiation and integration). There are nearly 400 publications and 30 dissertations listed in Tom Melham's HOL bibliography[22]. There is no space to summarise all the work that has been done with HOL here, but recent work can be found in the proceedings of the conference now called[23] *Theorem Proving in Higher Order Logics* [28, 32, 45, 48] or in special issues of *The Computer Journal* [26] and *Formal Methods in System Design* [24, 25].

One noteworthy niche has been the embedding of programming and hardware description languages in HOL.[24] This was opened up by Melham's packages for recursive types and inductive relations (and enhancements to these by David Shepherd, Elsa Gunter, and John Harrison). One result of this particular focus of activity has been the accumulation of wisdom (and jargon) concerning language embeddings and the development of syntax directed support tools. These tools both automate the construction of embeddings and help reduce the dangers discussed at the end of 7.1. An embedding that previously might have taken weeks/months can now often be done in hours/days.

For a proof assistant, HOL has a large user community. There have been nine HOL Users Workshops, which have gradually evolved from informal gettogethers to elaborate international meetings with refereed papers. In the future, these conferences will be targetted at the whole higher order logic theorem proving community, rather than just HOL users.

[22] `http://www.dcs.glasgow.ac.uk/~tfm/hol-bib.html`

[23] Previous names include *International Conference on Higher Order Logic Theorem Proving and Its Applications*.

[24] The embedding of Standard ML has been extensively studied by Elsa Gunter, Myra Van-Inwegen and Donald Syme, the embedding of a large subset of C is currently being undertaken by Michael Norrish at Cambridge. Embeddings of subsets of the hardware description languages ELLA, NODEN, Silage, VHDL and Verilog have been done (or are in progress). Steve Brackin has embedded a language of security assertions and provided a GUI that hides HOL, all input and output being in terms of the security language. Flemming Andersen (partly supported by the Technical University at Lyngby in Denmark and partly by TFL) has embedded the UNITY language and provided theorem proving support for it. Joakim Von Wright and Thomas Långbacka have embedded Lamport's Temporal Logic of Actions (TLA).

To harvest the accumulated wisdom of the whole proof assistant community and to position HOL for the results of ML2000,[25] a public initiative called "HOL2000" has been launched.[26] Only time will tell how this evolves. The end of the century should be an exciting time for HOL—and all thanks to Robin Milner.

## 9 Acknowledgements

Richard Boulton, Paul Curzon, Jim Grundy, John Harrison, Tom Melham, Robin Milner, Larry Paulson and Konrad Slind provided help in writing this paper and/or suggestions for improving it. An anonymous referee suggested several substantial improvements and clarifications.

## References

[1] Graham Birtwistle and P. A. Subrahmanyam, editors. *Current Trends in Hardware Verification and Automated Theorem Proving*. Springer, 1989.

[2] R. J. Boulton. Lazy techniques for fully expansive theorem proving. *Formal Methods in System Design*, 3(1/2): 25–47, August 1993.

[3] E. Charniak, C. K. Riesbeck, and D. V. McDermott. *Artificial Intelligence Programming*. Lawrence Erlbaum Associates, 1980.

[4] A. Church. A formulation of the simple theory of types. *The Journal of Symbolic Logic*, 5: 56–68, 1940.

[5] Avra Cohn. A proof of correctness of the VIPER microprocessor: The first level. In Graham Birtwistle and P. A. Subrahmanyam, editors, *VLSI Specification, Verification and Synthesis*, pages 27–71. Kluwer Academic Publishers, 1988.

[6] Avra Cohn. Correctness properties of the Viper block model: The second level. In Birtwistle and Subrahmanyam [1], pages 1–91.

[7] Avra Cohn. The notion of proof in hardware verification. *Journal of Automated Reasoning*, 5(2): 127–139, 1989.

[8] R. L. Constable et al. *Implementing Mathematics with the Nuprl Proof Development System*. Prentice-Hall, 1986.

[9] Thierry Coquand and Gérard Huet. Constructions: A higher order proof system for mechanizing mathematics. In Bruno Buchberger, editor, *EUROCAL '85*, volume 203 of *Lecture Notes in Computer Science*, pages 151–184, Berlin, 1985. Springer-Verlag.

[10] Thierry Coquand and Gérard Huet. The calculus of constructions. *Information and Computation*, 76: 95–120, 1988.

25 Under the slogan "ML2000," a cabal from the ML community have started investigating ideas for a major revision of ML. Their aim is to design a language in the ML tradition that builds on current experience with Standard ML and Caml as well as recent theoretical work on language design and semantics (such as type systems for object oriented programming).

26 `http://lal.cs.byu.edu/lal/hol2000/hol2000.html`

[11] M. J. C. Gordon. LCF_LSM: A system for specifying and verifying hardware. Technical Report 41, University of Cambridge Computer Laboratory, 1983.

[12] M. J. C. Gordon. Proving a computer correct. Technical Report 42, University of Cambridge Computer Laboratory, 1983.

[13] M. J. C. Gordon. Why higher-order logic is a good formalism for specifying and verifying hardware. In Milne and Subrahmanyam [33], pages 153–177.

[14] M. J. C. Gordon and T. F. Melham, editors. *Introduction to HOL: a theorem-proving environment for higher-order logic*. Cambridge University Press, 1993.

[15] M. J. C. Gordon, R. Milner, and C. P. Wadsworth. *Edinburgh LCF: A Mechanised Logic of Computation*, volume 78 of *Lecture Notes in Computer Science*. Springer-Verlag, 1979.

[16] B. T. Graham. *The SECD Microprocessor: A Verification Case Study*. Kluwer, 1992.

[17] Jim Grundy. A window inference tool for refinement. In Clifford Bryn Jones, B. Tim Denvir, and Roger C. F. Shaw, editors, *Proceedings of the 5th Refinement Workshop*, Workshops in Computing, pages 230–254, Lloyd's Register, London, January 1992. BCS FACS, Springer-Verlag.

[18] E. L. Gunter. Doing algebra in simple type theory. Technical Report MS-CIS-89-38, Dept. of Computer and Information Science, Moore School of Engineering, University of Pennsylvania, June 1989.

[19] F. K. Hanna and N. Daeche. Specification and verification using higher-order logic: a case study. In Milne and Subrahmanyam [33], pages 179–213.

[20] John Harrison. Constructing the real numbers in HOL. *Formal Methods in System Design*, 5: 35–59, 1994.

[21] John Harrison. A mizar mode for HOL. In Joakim von Wright, Jim Grundy, and John Harrison, editors, *Theorem Proving in Higher Order Logics: 9th International Conference, TPHOLs'96*, volume 1125 of *Lecture Notes in Computer Science*, pages 203–220, Turku, Finland, 1996. Springer-Verlag.

[22] John Harrison and Laurent Théry. Extending the HOL theorem prover with a computer algebra system to reason about the reals. In Joyce and Seger [28], pages 174–184.

[23] J. Herbert. Case study of the Cambridge Fast Ring ECL chip using HOL. Technical Report 123, Computer Laboratory, University of Cambridge, UK, 1988.

[24] *Formal Methods in System Design*, volume 3, number 1/2. Special issue on Higher Order Logic Theorem Proving and its Applications, August 1993.

[25] *Formal Methods in System Design*, volume 5, number 1/2. Special issue on Higher Order Logic Theorem Proving and its Applications, July/August 1993.

[26] *The Computer Journal*, volume 38, number 2. Special issue on Higher Order Logic Theorem Proving and its Applications, 1995.

[27] G. Birtwistle J. Joyce and M. J. C. Gordon. Proving a computer correct in higher order logic. Technical Report 100, University of Cambridge Computer Laboratory, 1986.

[28] Jeffrey J. Joyce and Carl Seger, editors. volume 780 of *Lecture Notes in Computer Science*, UBC, Vancouver, Canada, 1993. Springer-Verlag.

[29] T. F. Melham. Automating recursive type definitions in higher order logic. In Birtwistle and Subrahmanyam [1], pages 341–386.

[30] T. F. Melham. A package for inductive relation definitions in hol. In *Proceedings of the 1991 International Workshop on the HOL Theorem Proving System and its Applications*, pages 32–37. IEEE Computer Society Press, August 1991.

[31] T. F. Melham. The HOL logic extended with quantification over type variables. *Formal Methods in System Design*, 3(1/2): 7–24, August 1993.

[32] Thomas F. Melham and Juanito Camilleri, editors. *Higher Order Logic Theorem Proving and Its Applications: 7th International Workshop*, LNCS 859. Springer, September 1994.

[33] G. Milne and P. A. Subrahmanyam, editors. *Formal Aspects of VLSI Design*. North-Holland, 1986.

[34] R. Milner. Logic for computable functions; description of a machine implementation. Technical Report STAN-CS-72-288, A.I. Memo 169, Stanford University, 1972.

[35] R. Milner. A theory of type polymorphism in programming. *Journal of Computer and System Sciences*, 17(3): 348–375, December 1978.

[36] R. Milner and R. Weyhrauch. Proving compiler correctness in a mechanized logic. In Bernard Meltzer and Donald Michie, editors, *Machine Intelligence 7*, pages 51–70. Edinburgh University Press, 1972.

[37] Robin Milner. *Communication and Concurrency*. Prentice-Hall, 1989.

[38] Monica Nesi. A formalization of the process algebra CCS in higher order logic. Technical Report 278, University of Cambridge, Computer Laboratory, December 1992.

[39] L. C. Paulson. A higher-order implementation of rewriting. *Science of Computer Programming*, 3: 119–149, 1983.

[40] L. C. Paulson. *Logic and Computation: Interactive Proof with Cambridge LCF*, volume 2 of *Cambridge Tracts in Theoretical Computer Science*. Cambridge University Press, 1987.

[41] L. C. Paulson. Isabelle: The next 700 theorem provers. In P. Odifreddi, editor, *Logic and Computer Science*, pages 361–386. Academic Press, 1990.

[42] Lawrence C. Paulson. Verifying the unification algorithm in LCF. *Science of Computer Programming*, 5: 143–170, 1985.

[43] Lawrence C. Paulson. *Isabelle: A Generic Theorem Prover*. Springer, 1994. LNCS 828.

[44] K. Petersson. A programming system for type theory. Technical Report 21, Department of Computer Science, Chalmers University, Göteborg, Sweden, 1982.

[45] E. Thomas Schubert, Phillip J. Windley, and James Alves-Foss, editors. *Higher Order Logic Theorem Proving and Its Applications 8th International Workshop*, LNCS 971. Springer, September 1995.

[46] Dana S. Scott. A type-theoretical alternative to ISWIM, CUCH, OWHY. *Theoretical Computer Science*, 121: 411–440, 1993. Annotated version of the 1969 manuscript.

[47] Konrad Slind. Function definition in higher order logic. In *Theorem Proving in Higher Order Logics, 9th International Conference, TPHOLs'96*, number 1125 in Lecture Notes in Computer Science, Turku, Finland, August 1996. Springer Verlag.

[48] Joakim von Wright, Jim Grundy, and John Harrison, editors. Volume 1125 of *Lecture Notes in Computer Science*, Turku, Finland, 1996. Springer-Verlag.

[49] P. J. Windley. The practical verification of microprocessor designs. In *Proceedings of the 1991 International Workshop on the HOL Theorem Proving System and its Applications*, pages 32–37. IEEE Computer Society Press, August 1991.

# 7 A Fixedpoint Approach to (Co)Inductive and (Co)Datatype Definitions

**Lawrence C. Paulson**

## 1 Introduction

Several theorem provers provide commands for formalizing recursive data structures, like lists and trees. Robin Milner implemented one of the first of these, for Edinburgh LCF [16]. Given a description of the desired data structure, Milner's package formulated appropriate definitions and proved the characteristic theorems. Similar is Melham's recursive type package for the Cambridge HOL system [15]. Such data structures are called **datatypes** below, by analogy with datatype declarations in Standard ML. Some logics take datatypes as primitive; consider Boyer and Moore's shell principle [4] and the Coq type theory [22].

A datatype is but one example of an **inductive definition**. Such a definition [2] specifies the least set $R$ **closed under** given rules: applying a rule to elements of $R$ yields a result within $R$. Inductive definitions have many applications. The collection of theorems in a logic is inductively defined. A structural operational semantics [13] is an inductive definition of a reduction or evaluation relation on programs. A few theorem provers provide commands for formalizing inductive definitions; these include Coq [22] and again the HOL system [5].

The dual notion is that of a **coinductive definition**. Such a definition specifies the greatest set $R$ **consistent with** given rules: every element of $R$ can be seen as arising by applying a rule to elements of $R$. Important examples include using bisimulation relations to formalize equivalence of processes [17] or lazy functional programs [1]. Other examples include lazy lists and other infinite data structures; these are called **codatatypes** below.

Not all inductive definitions are meaningful. **Monotone** inductive definitions are a large, well-behaved class. Monotonicity can be enforced by syntactic conditions such as "strictly positive," but this could lead to monotone definitions being rejected on the grounds of their syntactic form. More flexible is to formalize monotonicity within the logic and allow users to prove it.

This paper describes a package based on a fixedpoint approach. Least fixedpoints yield inductive definitions; greatest fixedpoints yield coinductive definitions. Most of the discussion below applies equally to inductive and coinductive definitions, and most of the code is shared.

The package supports mutual recursion and infinitely branching datatypes and codatatypes. It allows use of any operators that have been proved monotone, thus accepting all provably monotone inductive definitions, including iterated definitions.

J. Grundy and S. Thompson made detailed comments. Mads Tofte and the referees were also helpful. The research was funded by the SERC grants GR/G53279, GR/H40570 and by the ESPRIT Project 6453 "Types."

The package has been implemented in Isabelle [25, 29] using ZF set theory [24, 26]; part of it has since been ported to Isabelle/HOL (higher-order logic). The recursion equations are specified as introduction rules for the mutually recursive sets. The package transforms these rules into a mapping over sets, and attempts to prove that the mapping is monotonic and well typed. If successful, the package makes fixed point definitions and proves the introduction, elimination and (co)induction rules. Users invoke the package by making simple declarations in Isabelle theory files.

Most datatype packages equip the new datatype with some means of expressing recursive functions. My package is no exception: it provides structural recursion for the datatype. The Isabelle/ZF theory provides well-founded recursion [26], which is harder to use than structural recursion but considerably more general. Slind [34] has written a package to automate the definition of well-founded recursive functions in Isabelle/HOL.

**Outline.** Section 2 introduces the least and greatest fixedpoint operators. Section 3 discusses the form of introduction rules, mutual recursion and other points common to inductive and coinductive definitions. Section 4 discusses induction and coinduction rules separately. Section 5 presents several examples, including a coinductive definition. Section 6 describes datatype definitions. Section 7 presents related work. Section 8 draws brief conclusions.

Most of the definitions and theorems shown below have been generated by the package. I have renamed some variables to improve readability.

## 2 Fixed Point Operators

In set theory, the least and greatest fixed point operators are defined as follows:

$$\mathtt{lfp}(D, h) \equiv \bigcap \{X \subseteq D \cdot h(X) \subseteq X\}$$

$$\mathtt{gfp}(D, h) \equiv \bigcup \{X \subseteq D \cdot X \subseteq h(X)\}$$

Let $D$ be a set. Say that $h$ is **bounded by** $D$ if $h(D) \subseteq D$, and **monotone below** $D$ if $h(A) \subseteq h(B)$ for all $A$ and $B$ such that $A \subseteq B \subseteq D$. If $h$ is bounded by $D$ and monotone then both operators yield fixed points:

$$\mathtt{lfp}(D, h) = h(\mathtt{lfp}(D, h))$$

$$\mathtt{gfp}(D, h) = h(\mathtt{gfp}(D, h))$$

These equations are instances of the Knaster-Tarski theorem, which states that every monotonic function over a complete lattice has a fixed point [6]. It is obvious from their definitions that `lfp` must be the least fixed point, and `gfp` the greatest.

This fixed point theory is simple. The Knaster-Tarski theorem is easy to prove. Showing monotonicity of $h$ is trivial, in typical cases. We must also exhibit a bounding set $D$ for $h$. Frequently this is trivial, as when a set of theorems is (co)inductively defined over some previously existing set of formulæ. Isabelle/ZF provides suitable bounding sets for infinitely branching (co)datatype definitions; see §6.1. Bounding sets are also called **domains**.

The powerset operator is monotone, but by Cantor's theorem there is no set $A$ such that $A = \mathcal{P}(A)$. We cannot put $A = \mathtt{lfp}(D, \mathcal{P})$ because there is no suitable domain $D$. But §5.5 demonstrates that $\mathcal{P}$ is still useful in inductive definitions.

## 3 Elements of an Inductive or Coinductive Definition

Consider a (co)inductive definition of the sets $R_1, \ldots, R_n$, in mutual recursion. They will be constructed from domains $D_1, \ldots, D_n$, respectively. The construction yields not $R_i \subseteq D_i$ but $R_i \subseteq D_1 + \cdots + D_n$, where $R_i$ is contained in the image of $D_i$ under an injection. Reasons for this are discussed elsewhere [26, §4.5].

The definition may involve arbitrary parameters $\vec{p} = p_1, \ldots, p_k$. Each recursive set then has the form $R_i(\vec{p})$. The parameters must be identical every time they occur within a definition. This would appear to be a serious restriction compared with other systems such as Coq [22]. For instance, we cannot define the lists of $n$ elements as the set $\mathtt{listn}(A, n)$ using rules where the parameter $n$ varies. Section 5.2 describes how to express this set using the inductive definition package.

To avoid clutter below, the recursive sets are shown as simply $R_i$ instead of $R_i(\vec{p})$.

### 3.1 The Form of the Introduction Rules

The body of the definition consists of the desired introduction rules. The conclusion of each rule must have the form $t \in R_i$, where $t$ is any term. Premises typically have the same form, but they can have the more general form $t \in M(R_i)$ or express arbitrary side-conditions.

The premise $t \in M(R_i)$ is permitted if $M$ is a monotonic operator on sets, satisfying the rule

$$\frac{A \subseteq B}{M(A) \subseteq M(B)}$$

The user must supply the package with monotonicity rules for all such premises.

The ability to introduce new monotone operators makes the approach flexible. A suitable choice of $M$ and $t$ can express a lot. The powerset operator $\mathcal{P}$ is monotone, and the premise $t \in \mathcal{P}(R)$ expresses $t \subseteq R$; see §5.5 for an example. The *list of* operator is monotone, as is easily proved by induction. The premise $t \in \mathtt{list}(R)$ avoids having to encode the effect of $\mathtt{list}(R)$ using mutual recursion; see §5.6 and also my earlier paper [26, §4.4].

Introduction rules may also contain **side-conditions**. These are premises consisting of arbitrary formulæ not mentioning the recursive sets. Side-conditions typically involve type-checking. One example is the premise $a \in A$ in the following rule from the definition of lists:

$$\frac{a \in A \quad l \in \mathtt{list}(A)}{\mathtt{Cons}(a, l) \in \mathtt{list}(A)}$$

### 3.2 The Fixed Point Definitions

The package translates the list of desired introduction rules into a fixed point definition. Consider, as a running example, the finite powerset operator $\mathtt{Fin}(A)$: the set of all finite subsets of $A$. It can be defined as the least set closed under the rules

$$\emptyset \in \mathtt{Fin}(A) \qquad \frac{a \in A \quad b \in \mathtt{Fin}(A)}{\{a\} \cup b \in \mathtt{Fin}(A)}$$

The domain in a (co)inductive definition must be some existing set closed under the rules. A suitable domain for $\mathtt{Fin}(A)$ is $\mathcal{P}(A)$, the set of all subsets of $A$. The package generates the definition

$$\begin{array}{l}\mathtt{Fin}(A) \equiv \mathtt{lfp}(\mathcal{P}(A),\ \lambda X \cdot \{z \in \mathcal{P}(A) \cdot z = \emptyset \vee \\ (\exists a\, b \cdot z = \{a\} \cup b \wedge a \in A \wedge b \in X)\})\end{array}$$

The contribution of each rule to the definition of $\mathtt{Fin}(A)$ should be obvious. A coinductive definition is similar but uses `gfp` instead of `lfp`.

The package must prove that the fixedpoint operator is applied to a monotonic function. If the introduction rules have the form described above, and if the package is supplied a monotonicity theorem for every $t \in M(R_i)$ premise, then this proof is trivial.[1]

The package returns its result as an ML structure, which consists of named components; we may regard it as a record. The result structure contains the definitions of the recursive sets as a theorem list called `defs`. It also contains some theorems; `dom_subset` is an inclusion such as $\mathtt{Fin}(A) \subseteq \mathcal{P}(A)$, while `bnd_mono` asserts that the fixedpoint definition is monotonic.

[1] Due to the presence of logical connectives in the fixedpoint's body, the monotonicity proof requires some unusual rules. These state that the connectives $\wedge$, $\vee$ and $\exists$ preserve monotonicity with respect to the partial ordering on unary predicates given by $P \sqsubseteq Q$ if and only if $\forall x \cdot P(x) \rightarrow Q(x)$.

Internally the package uses the theorem `unfold`, a fixedpoint equation such as

$$\texttt{Fin}(A) = \{z \in \mathcal{P}(A) \cdot z = \emptyset \lor \\ (\exists a\, b \cdot z = \{a\} \cup b \land a \in A \land b \in \texttt{Fin}(A))\}$$

In order to save space, this theorem is not exported.

### 3.3 Mutual Recursion

In a mutually recursive definition, the domain of the fixedpoint construction is the disjoint sum of the domain $D_i$ of each $R_i$, for $i = 1, \ldots, n$. The package uses the injections of the binary disjoint sum, typically `Inl` and `Inr`, to express injections $h_{1n}, \ldots, h_{nn}$ for the $n$-ary disjoint sum $D_1 + \cdots + D_n$.

As discussed elsewhere [26, §4.5], Isabelle/ZF defines the operator `Part` to support mutual recursion. The set $\texttt{Part}(A, h)$ contains those elements of $A$ having the form $h(z)$:

$$\texttt{Part}(A, h) \equiv \{x \in A \cdot \exists z \cdot x = h(z)\}.$$

For mutually recursive sets $R_1, \ldots, R_n$ with $n > 1$, the package makes $n + 1$ definitions. The first defines a set $R$ using a fixedpoint operator. The remaining $n$ definitions have the form

$$R_i \equiv \texttt{Part}(R, h_{in}), \qquad i = 1, \ldots, n.$$

It follows that $R = R_1 \cup \cdots \cup R_n$, where the $R_i$ are pairwise disjoint.

### 3.4 Proving the Introduction Rules

The user supplies the package with the desired form of the introduction rules. Once it has derived the theorem `unfold`, it attempts to prove those rules. From the user's point of view, this is the trickiest stage; the proofs often fail. The task is to show that the domain $D_1 + \cdots + D_n$ of the combined set $R_1 \cup \cdots \cup R_n$ is closed under all the introduction rules. This essentially involves replacing each $R_i$ by $D_1 + \cdots + D_n$ in each of the introduction rules and attempting to prove the result.

Consider the $\texttt{Fin}(A)$ example. After substituting $\mathcal{P}(A)$ for $\texttt{Fin}(A)$ in the rules, the package must prove

$$\emptyset \in \mathcal{P}(A) \qquad \frac{a \in A \quad b \in \mathcal{P}(A)}{\{a\} \cup b \in \mathcal{P}(A)}$$

Such proofs can be regarded as type-checking the definition.[2] The user supplies the package with type-checking rules to apply. Usually these are general purpose rules from the ZF theory. They could however be rules specifically proved for a particular inductive definition; sometimes this is the easiest way to get the definition through!

The result structure contains the introduction rules as the theorem list `intrs`.

### 3.5 The Case Analysis Rule

The elimination rule, called `elim`, performs case analysis. It is a simple consequence of `unfold`. There is one case for each introduction rule. If $x \in \mathtt{Fin}(A)$ then either $x = \emptyset$ or else $x = \{a\} \cup b$ for some $a \in A$ and $b \in \mathtt{Fin}(A)$. Formally, the elimination rule for $\mathtt{Fin}(A)$ is written

$$\frac{x \in \mathtt{Fin}(A) \qquad \begin{matrix} [x = \emptyset] \\ \vdots \\ Q \end{matrix} \qquad \begin{matrix} [x = \{a\} \cup b \quad a \in A \quad b \in \mathtt{Fin}(A)]_{a,b} \\ \vdots \\ Q \end{matrix}}{Q}$$

The subscripted variables $a$ and $b$ above the third premise are eigenvariables, subject to the usual "not free in ..." proviso.

## 4 Induction and Coinduction Rules

Here we must consider inductive and coinductive definitions separately. For an inductive definition, the package returns an induction rule derived directly from the properties of least fixed points, as well as a modified rule for mutual recursion. For a coinductive definition, the package returns a basic coinduction rule.

### 4.1 The Basic Induction Rule

The basic rule, called `induct`, is appropriate in most situations. For inductive definitions, it is strong rule induction [5]; for datatype definitions (see below), it is just structural induction.

The induction rule for an inductively defined set $R$ has the form described below. For the time being, assume that $R$'s domain is not a Cartesian product; inductively defined relations are treated slightly differently.

[2] The Isabelle/HOL version does not require these proofs, as HOL has implicit type-checking.

The major premise is $x \in R$. There is a minor premise for each introduction rule:

- If the introduction rule concludes $t \in R_i$, then the minor premise is $P(t)$.
- The minor premise's eigenvariables are precisely the introduction rule's free variables that are not parameters of $R$. For instance, the eigenvariables in the $\texttt{Fin}(A)$ rule below are $a$ and $b$, but not $A$.
- If the introduction rule has a premise $t \in R_i$, then the minor premise discharges the assumption $t \in R_i$ and the induction hypothesis $P(t)$. If the introduction rule has a premise $t \in M(R_i)$ then the minor premise discharges the single assumption

$t \in M(\{z \in R_i \cdot P(z)\})$.

Because $M$ is monotonic, this assumption implies $t \in M(R_i)$. The occurrence of $P$ gives the effect of an induction hypothesis, which may be exploited by appealing to properties of $M$.

The induction rule for $\texttt{Fin}(A)$ resembles the elimination rule shown above, but includes an induction hypothesis:

$$\frac{x \in \texttt{Fin}(A) \quad P(\emptyset) \quad \begin{matrix} [a \in A \quad b \in \texttt{Fin}(A) \quad P(b)]_{a,b} \\ \vdots \\ P(\{a\} \cup b) \end{matrix}}{P(x)}$$

Stronger induction rules often suggest themselves. We can derive a rule for $\texttt{Fin}(A)$ whose third premise discharges the extra assumption $a \not\in b$. The package provides rules for mutual induction and inductive relations. The Isabelle/ZF theory also supports well-founded induction and recursion over datatypes, by reasoning about the **rank** of a set [26, §3.4].

## 4.2 Modified Induction Rules

If the domain of $R$ is a Cartesian product $A_1 \times \cdots \times A_m$ (however nested), then the corresponding predicate $P_i$ takes $m$ arguments. The major premise becomes $\langle z_1, \ldots, z_m \rangle \in R$ instead of $x \in R$; the conclusion becomes $P(z_1, \ldots, z_m)$. This simplifies reasoning about inductively defined relations, eliminating the need to express properties of $z_1, \ldots, z_m$ as properties of the tuple $\langle z_1, \ldots, z_m \rangle$. Occasionally it may require you to split up the induction variable using `SigmaE` and `dom_subset`, especially if the constant `split` appears in the rule.

The mutual induction rule is called `mutual_induct`. It differs from the basic rule in two respects:

- Instead of a single predicate $P$, it uses $n$ predicates $P_1, \ldots, P_n$: one for each recursive set.
- There is no major premise such as $x \in R_i$. Instead, the conclusion refers to all the recursive sets:

$$(\forall z \cdot z \in R_1 \to P_1(z)) \wedge \cdots \wedge (\forall z \cdot z \in R_n \to P_n(z))$$

Proving the premises establishes $P_i(z)$ for $z \in R_i$ and $i = 1, \ldots, n$.

If the domain of some $R_i$ is a Cartesian product, then the mutual induction rule is modified accordingly. The predicates are made to take $m$ separate arguments instead of a tuple, and the quantification in the conclusion is over the separate variables $z_1, \ldots, z_m$.

### 4.3 Coinduction

A coinductive definition yields a primitive coinduction rule, with no refinements such as those for the induction rules. (Experience may suggest refinements later.) Consider the codatatype of lazy lists as an example. For suitable definitions of `LNil` and `LCons`, lazy lists may be defined as the greatest set consistent with the rules

$$\mathtt{LNil} \in \mathtt{llist}(A) \qquad \frac{a \in A \quad l \in \mathtt{llist}(A)}{\mathtt{LCons}(a, l) \in \mathtt{llist}(A)}(-)$$

The $(-)$ tag stresses that this is a coinductive definition. A suitable domain for $\mathtt{llist}(A)$ is $\mathtt{quniv}(A)$; this set is closed under the variant forms of sum and product that are used to represent non-well-founded data structures (see §6.1).

The package derives an `unfold` theorem similar to that for $\mathtt{Fin}(A)$. Then it proves the theorem `coinduct`, which expresses that $\mathtt{llist}(A)$ is the greatest solution to this equation contained in $\mathtt{quniv}(A)$:

$$\frac{x \in X \quad X \subseteq \mathtt{quniv}(A) \quad \begin{array}{c}[z \in X]_z \\ \vdots \\ z = \mathtt{LNil} \vee (\exists a\, l \cdot z = \mathtt{LCons}(a, l) \wedge a \in A \wedge \\ l \in X \cup \mathtt{llist}(A))\end{array}}{x \in \mathtt{llist}(A)}$$

This rule complements the introduction rules; it provides a means of showing $x \in \mathtt{llist}(A)$ when $x$ is infinite. For instance, if $x = \mathtt{LCons}(0, x)$ then applying the rule with $X = \{x\}$ proves $x \in \mathtt{llist}(\mathtt{nat})$. (Here `nat` is the set of natural numbers.)

Having $X \cup$ `llist`$(A)$ instead of simply $X$ in the third premise above represents a slight strengthening of the greatest fixedpoint property. I discuss several forms of coinduction rules elsewhere [27].

The clumsy form of the third premise makes the rule hard to use, especially in large definitions. Probably a constant should be declared to abbreviate the large disjunction, and rules derived to allow proving the separate disjuncts.

## 5 Examples of Inductive and Coinductive Definitions

This section presents several examples from the literature: the finite powerset operator, lists of $n$ elements, bisimulations on lazy lists, the well-founded part of a relation, and the primitive recursive functions.

### 5.1 The Finite Powerset Operator

This operator has been discussed extensively above. Here is the corresponding invocation in an Isabelle theory file. Note that `cons`$(a, b)$ abbreviates $\{a\} \cup b$ in Isabelle/ZF.

```
Finite = Arith +
consts        Fin :: i=>i
inductive
  domains     "Fin(A)" <= "Pow(A)"
  intrs
    emptyI    "0 : Fin(A)"
    consI     "[| a: A;   b: Fin(A) |] ==> cons(a,b)  : Fin(A)"
  type_intrs "[empty_subsetI, cons_subsetI, PowI]"
  type_elims "[make_elim PowD]"
end
```

Theory `Finite` extends the parent theory `Arith` by declaring the unary function symbol `Fin`, which is defined inductively. Its domain is specified as $\mathcal{P}(A)$, where $A$ is the parameter appearing in the introduction rules. For type-checking, we supply two introduction rules:

$$\emptyset \subseteq A \qquad \frac{a \in C \quad B \subseteq C}{\{a\} \cup B \subseteq C}$$

A further introduction rule and an elimination rule express both directions of the equivalence $A \in \mathcal{P}(B) \leftrightarrow A \subseteq B$. Type-checking involves mostly introduction rules.

Like all Isabelle theory files, this one yields a structure containing the new theory as an ML value. Structure `Finite` also has a substructure, called `Fin`. We can refer to the

`Fin`$(A)$ introduction rules as the list `Fin.intrs` or individually as `Fin.emptyI` and `Fin.consI`. The induction rule is `Fin.induct`.

### 5.2 Lists of $n$ Elements

This has become a standard example of an inductive definition. Following Paulin-Mohring [22], we could attempt to define a new datatype $\texttt{listn}(A, n)$, for lists of length $n$, as an $n$-indexed family of sets. But her introduction rules

$$\texttt{Niln} \in \texttt{listn}(A, 0) \qquad \frac{n \in \texttt{nat} \quad a \in A \quad l \in \texttt{listn}(A, n)}{\texttt{Consn}(n, a, l) \in \texttt{listn}(A, \texttt{succ}(n))}$$

are not acceptable to the inductive definition package: `listn` occurs with three different parameter lists in the definition.

The Isabelle version of this example suggests a general treatment of varying parameters. It uses the existing datatype definition of $\texttt{list}(A)$, with constructors `Nil` and `Cons`, and incorporates the parameter $n$ into the inductive set itself. It defines $\texttt{listn}(A)$ as a relation consisting of pairs $\langle n, l\rangle$ such that $n \in \texttt{nat}$ and $l \in \texttt{list}(A)$ and $l$ has length $n$. In fact, $\texttt{listn}(A)$ is the converse of the length function on $\texttt{list}(A)$. The Isabelle/ZF introduction rules are

$$\langle 0, \texttt{Nil}\rangle \in \texttt{listn}(A) \qquad \frac{a \in A \quad \langle n, l\rangle \in \texttt{listn}(A)}{\langle \texttt{succ}(n), \texttt{Cons}(a, l)\rangle \in \texttt{listn}(A)}$$

The Isabelle theory file takes, as parent, the theory `List` of lists. We declare the constant `listn` and supply an inductive definition, specifying the domain as $\texttt{nat} \times \texttt{list}(A)$:

```
ListN = List +
consts  listn :: i=>i
inductive
  domains   "listn(A)" <= "nat*list(A)"
  intrs
    NilI  "<0,Nil>: listn(A)"
    ConsI "[| a: A;  <n,l>: listn(A) |] ==> <succ(n),
     Cons(a,l)>: listn(A)"
  type_intrs "nat_typechecks @ list.intrs"
end
```

The type-checking rules include those for 0, `succ`, `Nil` and `Cons`. Because $\texttt{listn}(A)$ is a set of pairs, type-checking requires the equivalence $\langle a, b\rangle \in A \times B \leftrightarrow a \in A \wedge b \in B$. The package always includes the rules for ordered pairs.

The package returns introduction, elimination and induction rules for $\texttt{listn}$. The basic induction rule, $\texttt{listn.induct}$, is

$$\frac{\langle z_1, z_2\rangle \in \texttt{listn}(A) \quad P(0, \texttt{Nil}) \quad \begin{array}{c}[a \in A \quad \langle n, l\rangle \in \texttt{listn}(A) \quad P(n, l)]_{a,l,n} \\ \vdots \\ P(\texttt{succ}(n), \texttt{Cons}(a, l))\end{array}}{P(z_1, z_2)}$$

This rule lets the induction formula to be a binary property of pairs, $P(n, l)$. It is now a simple matter to prove theorems about $\texttt{listn}(A)$, such as

$$\forall l \in \texttt{list}(A) \cdot \langle \texttt{length}(l),\ l\rangle \in \texttt{listn}(A)$$

$$\texttt{listn}(A)``\{n\} = \{l \in \texttt{list}(A).\texttt{length}(l) = n\}$$

This latter result—here $r``X$ denotes the image of $X$ under $r$—asserts that the inductive definition agrees with the obvious notion of $n$-element list.

A "list of $n$ elements" really is a list, namely an element of $\texttt{list}(A)$. It is subject to list operators such as append (concatenation). For example, a trivial induction on $\langle m, l\rangle \in \texttt{listn}(A)$ yields

$$\frac{\langle m, l\rangle \in \texttt{listn}(A) \quad \langle m', l'\rangle \in \texttt{listn}(A)}{\langle m + m',\ l@l'\rangle \in \texttt{listn}(A)}$$

where $+$ denotes addition on the natural numbers and @ denotes append.

## 5.3 Rule Inversion: The Function mk_cases

The elimination rule, $\texttt{listn.elim}$, is cumbersome:

$$\frac{x \in \texttt{listn}(A) \quad \begin{array}{c}[x = \langle 0, \texttt{Nil}\rangle] \\ \vdots \\ Q\end{array} \quad \begin{array}{c}\left[\begin{array}{l} x = \langle \texttt{succ}(n), \texttt{Cons}(a, l)\rangle \\ a \in A \\ \langle n, l\rangle \in \texttt{listn}(A)\end{array}\right]_{a,l,n} \\ \vdots \\ Q\end{array}}{Q}$$

The ML function $\texttt{listn.mk\_cases}$ generates simplified instances of this rule. It works by freeness reasoning on the list constructors: $\texttt{Cons}(a, l)$ is injective in its two arguments and differs from $\texttt{Nil}$. If $x$ is $\langle i, \texttt{Nil}\rangle$ or $\langle i, \texttt{Cons}(a, l)\rangle$ then $\texttt{listn.mk\_cases}$ deduces the corresponding form of $i$; this is called rule inversion. Here is a sample session:

```
listn.mk_cases "<i,Nil> : listn(A)";
 "[| <?i, []> : listn(?A); ?i = 0 ==> ?Q |] ==> ?Q" : thm

listn.mk_cases "<i,Cons(a,l)> : listn(A)";
 "[| <?i, Cons(?a, ?l)> : listn(?A);
      !!n. [| ?a : ?A; <n, ?l> : listn(?A); ?i = succ(n) |]
  ==> ?Q
  |] ==> ?Q" : thm
```

Each of these rules has only two premises. In conventional notation, the second rule is

$$\dfrac{\langle i, \texttt{Cons}(a, l)\rangle \in \texttt{listn}(A) \qquad \begin{matrix} \left[\begin{matrix} a \in A \\ \langle n, l\rangle \in \texttt{listn}(A) \\ i = \texttt{succ}(n) \end{matrix}\right]_n \\ \vdots \\ Q \end{matrix}}{Q}$$

The package also has built-in rules for freeness reasoning about 0 and succ. So if $x$ is $\langle 0, l\rangle$ or $\langle \texttt{succ}(i), l\rangle$, then listn.mk_cases can deduce the corresponding form of $l$.

The function mk_cases is also useful with datatype definitions. The instance from the definition of lists, namely list.mk_cases, can prove that $\texttt{Cons}(a, l) \in \texttt{list}(A)$ implies $a \in A$ and $l \in \texttt{list}(A)$:

$$\dfrac{\texttt{Cons}(a, l) \in \texttt{list}(A) \qquad \begin{matrix} [a \in A \quad l \in \texttt{list}(A)] \\ \vdots \\ Q \end{matrix}}{Q}$$

A typical use of mk_cases concerns inductive definitions of evaluation relations. Then rule inversion yields case analysis on possible evaluations. For example, Isabelle/ZF includes a short proof of the diamond property for parallel contraction on combinators. Ole Rasmussen used mk_cases extensively in his development of the theory of residuals [32].

### 5.4 A Coinductive Definition: Bisimulations on Lazy Lists

This example anticipates the definition of the codatatype $\texttt{llist}(A)$, which consists of finite and infinite lists over $A$. Its constructors are LNil and LCons, satisfying the introduction rules shown in §4.3. Because $\texttt{llist}(A)$ is defined as a greatest fixed point and uses the variant pairing and injection operators, it contains non-well-founded elements such as solutions to $\texttt{LCons}(a, l) = l$.

The next step in the devclopment of lazy lists is to define a coinduction principle for proving equalities. This is done by showing that the equality relation on lazy lists is the greatest fixed point of some monotonic operation. The usual approach [31] is to define some notion of bisimulation for lazy lists, define equivalence to be the greatest bisimulation, and finally to prove that two lazy lists are equivalent if and only if they are equal. The coinduction rule for equivalence then yields a coinduction principle for equalities.

A binary relation $R$ on lazy lists is a **bisimulation** provided $R \subseteq R^+$, where $R^+$ is the relation

$$\{\langle \texttt{LNil}, \texttt{LNil}\rangle\} \cup \{\langle \texttt{LCons}(a, l), \texttt{LCons}(a, l')\rangle \cdot a \in A \land \langle l, l'\rangle \in R\}.$$

A pair of lazy lists are **equivalent** if they belong to some bisimulation. Equivalence can be coinductively defined as the greatest fixed point for the introduction rules

$$\langle \texttt{LNil}, \texttt{LNil}\rangle \in \texttt{lleq}(A) \qquad \frac{a \in A \quad \langle l, l'\rangle \in \texttt{lleq}(A)}{\langle \texttt{LCons}(a, l), \texttt{LCons}(a, l')\rangle \in \texttt{lleq}(A)}(-)$$

To make this coinductive definition, the theory file includes (after the declaration of $\texttt{llist}(A)$) the following lincs:

```
consts    lleq :: i=>i
coinductive
  domains "lleq(A)" <= "llist(A) * llist(A)"
  intrs
    LNil  "<LNil,LNil> : lleq(A)"
    LCons "[| a:A; <l,l'>: lleq(A) |] ==> <LCons(a,l),
      LCons(a,l')>: lleq(A)"
  type_intrs  "llist.intrs"
```

The domain of $\texttt{lleq}(A)$ is $\texttt{llist}(A) \times \texttt{llist}(A)$. The type-checking rules include the introduction rules for $\texttt{llist}(A)$, whose declaration is discussed below (§6.3).

The package returns the introduction rules and the elimination rule, as usual. But instead of induction rules, it returns a coinduction rule. The rule is too big to display in the usual notation; its conclusion is $x \in \texttt{lleq}(A)$ and its premises are $x \in X$,

$X \subseteq \texttt{llist}(A) \times \texttt{llist}(A)$ and

$$\frac{\begin{matrix}[z \in X]_z \\ \vdots \end{matrix}}{z = \langle \texttt{LNil}, \texttt{LNil} \rangle \vee (\exists a\, l\, l' \cdot z = \langle \texttt{LCons}(a, l), \texttt{LCons}(a, l') \rangle \wedge a \in A \wedge \langle l, l' \rangle \in X \cup \texttt{lleq}(A))}$$

Thus if $x \in X$, where $X$ is a bisimulation contained in the domain of $\texttt{lleq}(A)$, then $x \in \texttt{lleq}(A)$. It is easy to show that $\texttt{lleq}(A)$ is reflexive: the equality relation is a bisimulation. And $\texttt{lleq}(A)$ is symmetric: its converse is a bisimulation. But showing that $\texttt{lleq}(A)$ coincides with the equality relation takes some work.

### 5.5 The Accessible Part of a Relation

Let $\prec$ be a binary relation on $D$; in short, $(\prec) \subseteq D \times D$. The **accessible** or **well-founded** part of $\prec$, written $\texttt{acc}(\prec)$, is essentially that subset of $D$ for which $\prec$ admits no infinite decreasing chains [2]. Formally, $\texttt{acc}(\prec)$ is inductively defined to be the least set that contains $a$ if it contains all $\prec$-predecessors of $a$, for $a \in D$. Thus we need an introduction rule of the form

$$\frac{\forall y \cdot y \prec a \to y \in \texttt{acc}(\prec)}{a \in \texttt{acc}(\prec)}$$

Paulin-Mohring treats this example in Coq [22], but it causes difficulties for other systems. Its premise is not acceptable to the inductive definition package of the Cambridge HOL system [5]. It is also unacceptable to the Isabelle package (recall §3.1), but fortunately can be transformed into the acceptable form $t \in M(R)$.

The powerset operator is monotonic, and $t \in \mathcal{P}(R)$ is equivalent to $t \subseteq R$. This in turn is equivalent to $\forall y \in t \cdot y \in R$. To express $\forall y \cdot y \prec a \to y \in \texttt{acc}(\prec)$ we need only find a term $t$ such that $y \in t$ if and only if $y \prec a$. A suitable $t$ is the inverse image of $\{a\}$ under $\prec$.

The definition below follows this approach. Here $r$ is $\prec$ and $\texttt{field}(r)$ refers to $D$, the domain of $\texttt{acc}(r)$. (The field of a relation is the union of its domain and range.) Finally $r^{-}``\{a\}$ denotes the inverse image of $\{a\}$ under $r$. We supply the theorem Pow_mono, which asserts that $\mathcal{P}$ is monotonic.

```
consts     acc :: i=>i
inductive
  domains "acc(r)" <= "field(r)"
  intrs
```

```
    vimage   "[| r-"{a}: Pow(acc(r)); a: field(r) |] ==> a:
      acc(r)"
  monos       "[Pow_mono]"
```

The Isabelle theory proceeds to prove facts about $\texttt{acc}(\prec)$. For instance, $\prec$ is well founded if and only if its field is contained in $\texttt{acc}(\prec)$.

As mentioned in §4.1, a premise of the form $t \in M(R)$ gives rise to an unusual induction hypothesis. Let us examine the induction rule, `acc.induct`:

$$\frac{x \in \texttt{acc}(r) \qquad \begin{array}{c} \begin{bmatrix} r^{-}``\{a\} \in \mathcal{P}(\{z \in \texttt{acc}(r) \cdot P(z)\}) \\ a \in \texttt{field}(r) \end{bmatrix}_a \\ \vdots \\ P(a) \end{array}}{P(x)}$$

The strange induction hypothesis is equivalent to $\forall y \cdot \langle y, a\rangle \in r \rightarrow y \in \texttt{acc}(r) \wedge P(y)$. Therefore the rule expresses well-founded induction on the accessible part of $\prec$.

The use of inverse image is not essential. The Isabelle package can accept introduction rules with arbitrary premises of the form $\forall \vec{y} \cdot P(\vec{y}) \rightarrow f(\vec{y}) \in R$. The premise can be expressed equivalently as

$$\{z \in D \cdot P(\vec{y}) \wedge z = f(\vec{y})\} \in \mathcal{P}(R)$$

provided $f(\vec{y}) \in D$ for all $\vec{y}$ such that $P(\vec{y})$. The following section demonstrates another use of the premise $t \in M(R)$, where $M = \texttt{list}$.

### 5.6 The Primitive Recursive Functions

The primitive recursive functions are traditionally defined inductively, as a subset of the functions over the natural numbers. One difficulty is that functions of all arities are taken together, but this is easily circumvented by regarding them as functions on lists. Another difficulty, the notion of composition, is less easily circumvented.

Here is a more precise definition. Letting $\vec{x}$ abbreviate $x_0, \ldots, x_{n-1}$, we can write lists such as $[\vec{x}]$, $[y+1, \vec{x}]$, etc. A function is **primitive recursive** if it belongs to the least set of functions in $\texttt{list}(\texttt{nat}) \rightarrow \texttt{nat}$ containing

- The **successor** function SC, such that $\texttt{SC}[y, \vec{x}] = y + 1$.
- All **constant** functions $\texttt{CONST}(k)$, such that $\texttt{CONST}(k)[\vec{x}] = k$.
- All **projection** functions $\texttt{PROJ}(i)$, such that $\texttt{PROJ}(i)[\vec{x}] = x_i$ if $0 \le i < n$.

• All **compositions** $\texttt{COMP}(g, [f_0, \ldots, f_{m-1}])$, where $g$ and $f_0, \ldots, f_{m-1}$ are primitive recursive, such that

$$\texttt{COMP}(g, [f_0, \ldots, f_{m-1}])[\vec{x}] = g[f_0[\vec{x}], \ldots, f_{m-1}[\vec{x}]].$$

• All **recursions** $\texttt{PREC}(f, g)$, where $f$ and $g$ are primitive recursive, such that

$$\texttt{PREC}(f, g)[0, \vec{x}] = f[\vec{x}]$$

$$\texttt{PREC}(f, g)[y + 1, \vec{x}] = g[\texttt{PREC}(f, g)[y, \vec{x}],\ y,\ \vec{x}].$$

Composition is awkward because it combines not two functions, as is usual, but $m + 1$ functions. In her proof that Ackermann's function is not primitive recursive, Nora Szasz was unable to formalise this definition directly [35]. So she generalised primitive recursion to tuple-valued functions. This modified the inductive definition such that each operation on primitive recursive functions combined just two functions.

Szasz was using ALF, but Coq and HOL would also have problems accepting this definition. Isabelle's package accepts it easily since $[f_0, \ldots, f_{m-1}]$ is a list of primitive recursive functions and `list` is monotonic. There are five introduction rules, one for each of the five forms of primitive recursive function. Let us examine the one for `COMP`:

$$\frac{g \in \texttt{primrec} \qquad fs \in \texttt{list(primrec)}}{\texttt{COMP}(g,\ fs) \in \texttt{primrec}}$$

The induction rule for `primrec` has one case for each introduction rule. Due to the use of `list` as a monotone operator, the composition case has an unusual induction hypothesis:

$$\begin{array}{c} [g \in \texttt{primrec} \quad fs \in \texttt{list}(\{z \in \texttt{primrec} \cdot P(z)\})]_{fs,g} \\ \vdots \\ P(\texttt{COMP}(g,\ fs)) \end{array}$$

The hypothesis states that $fs$ is a list of primitive recursive functions, each satisfying the induction formula. Proving the `COMP` case typically requires structural induction on lists, yielding two subcases: either $fs = \texttt{Nil}$ or else $fs = \texttt{Cons}(f,\ fs')$, where $f \in \texttt{primrec}$, $P(f)$, and $fs'$ is another list of primitive recursive functions satisfying $P$.

Figure 1 presents the theory file. Theory `Primrec` defines the constants `SC`, `CONST`, etc. These are not constructors of a new datatype, but functions over lists of numbers. Their definitions, most of which are omitted, consist of routine list programming. In Isabelle/ZF, the primitive recursive functions are defined as a subset of the function set $\texttt{list(nat)} \rightarrow \texttt{nat}$.

The Isabelle theory goes on to formalize Ackermann's function and prove that it is not primitive recursive, using the induction rule `primrec.induct`. The proof follows Szasz's excellent account.

```
Primrec = List +
consts
  primrec :: i
  SC      :: i
  :
defs
  SC_def     "SC == lam l:list(nat).list_case(0, %x xs.succ(x), l)"
  :
inductive
  domains "primrec" <= "list(nat)->nat"
  intrs
    SC        "SC : primrec"
    CONST     "k: nat ==> CONST(k)  : primrec"
    PROJ      "i: nat ==> PROJ(i)  : primrec"
    COMP      "[| g: primrec; fs: list(primrec) |] ==> COMP(g,fs): primrec"
    PREC      "[| f: primrec; g: primrec |] ==> PREC(f,g): primrec"
  monos       "[list_mono]"
  con_defs    "[SC_def,CONST_def,PROJ_def,COMP_def,PREC_def]"
  type_intrs "nat_typechecks @ list.intrs @
              [lam_type, list_case_type, drop_type, map_type,
              apply_type, rec_type]"
end
```

**Figure 1**
Inductive definition of the primitive recursive functions

## 6 Datatypes and Codatatypes

A (co)datatype definition is a (co)inductive definition with automatically defined constructors and a case analysis operator. The package proves that the case operator inverts the constructors and can prove freeness theorems involving any pair of constructors.

### 6.1 Constructors and Their Domain

A (co)inductive definition selects a subset of an existing set; a (co)datatype definition creates a new set. The package reduces the latter to the former. Isabelle/ZF supplies sets having strong closure properties to serve as domains for (co)inductive definitions.

Isabelle/ZF defines the Cartesian product $A \times B$, containing ordered pairs $\langle a, b\rangle$; it also defines the disjoint sum $A+B$, containing injections $\texttt{Inl}(a) \equiv \langle 0, a\rangle$ and $\texttt{Inr}(b) \equiv \langle 1, b\rangle$.

For use below, define the $m$-tuple $\langle x_1, \ldots, x_m\rangle$ to be the empty set $\emptyset$ if $m = 0$, simply $x_1$ if $m = 1$ and $\langle x_1, \langle x_2, \ldots, x_m\rangle\rangle$ if $m \geq 2$.

A datatype constructor $\texttt{Con}(x_1, \ldots, x_m)$ is defined to be $h(\langle x_1, \ldots, x_m\rangle)$, where $h$ is composed of `Inl` and `Inr`. In a mutually recursive definition, all constructors for the set $R_i$ have the outer form $h_{in}$, where $h_{in}$ is the injection described in §3.3. Further nested injections ensure that the constructors for $R_i$ are pairwise distinct.

Isabelle/ZF defines the set $\texttt{univ}(A)$, which contains $A$ and furthermore contains $\langle a, b\rangle$, $\texttt{Inl}(a)$ and $\texttt{Inr}(b)$ for $a, b \in \texttt{univ}(A)$. In a typical datatype definition with set parameters $A_1, \ldots, A_k$, a suitable domain for all the recursive sets is $\texttt{univ}(A_1 \cup \cdots \cup A_k)$. This solves the problem for datatypes [26, §4.2].

The standard pairs and injections can only yield well-founded constructions. This eases the definition of recursive functions over datatypes. But they are unsuitable for codatatypes, which typically contain non-well-founded objects.

To support codatatypes, Isabelle/ZF defines a variant notion of ordered pair, written $\langle a; b\rangle$. It also defines the corresponding variant notion of Cartesian product $A \otimes B$, variant injections $\texttt{QInl}(a)$ and $\texttt{QInr}(b)$ and variant disjoint sum $A \oplus B$. Finally it defines the set $\texttt{quniv}(A)$, which contains $A$ and furthermore contains $\langle a; b\rangle$, $\texttt{QInl}(a)$ and $\texttt{QInr}(b)$ for $a, b \in \texttt{quniv}(A)$. In a typical codatatype definition with set parameters $A_1, \ldots, A_k$, a suitable domain is $\texttt{quniv}(A_1 \cup \cdots \cup A_k)$. Details are published elsewhere [28].

### 6.2 The Case Analysis Operator

The (co)datatype package automatically defines a case analysis operator, called $R\_\texttt{case}$. A mutually recursive definition still has only one operator, whose name combines those of the recursive sets: it is called $R_1\_\ldots\_R_n\_\texttt{case}$. The case operator is analogous to those for products and sums.

Datatype definitions employ standard products and sums, whose operators are `split` and `case` and satisfy the equations

$$\begin{aligned}\texttt{split}(f, \langle x, y\rangle) &= f(x, y)\\ \texttt{case}(f, g, \texttt{Inl}(x)) &= f(x)\\ \texttt{case}(f, g, \texttt{Inr}(y)) &= g(y)\end{aligned}$$

Suppose the datatype has $k$ constructors $\texttt{Con}_1, \ldots, \texttt{Con}_k$. Then its case operator takes $k+1$ arguments and satisfies an equation for each constructor:

$$R\_\text{case}(f_1, \ldots, f_k, \texttt{Con}_i(\vec{x})) = f_i(\vec{x}), \qquad i = 1, \ldots, k$$

The case operator's definition takes advantage of Isabelle's representation of syntax in the typed $\lambda$-calculus; it could readily be adapted to a theorem prover for higher-order logic. If $f$ and $g$ have meta-type $i \Rightarrow i$ then so do $\texttt{split}(f)$ and $\texttt{case}(f, g)$. This works because `split` and `case` operate on their last argument. They are easily combined to make complex case analysis operators. For example, $\texttt{case}(f, \texttt{case}(g, h))$ performs case analysis for $A + (B + C)$; let us verify one of the three equations:

$$\texttt{case}(f, \texttt{case}(g, h), \texttt{Inr}(\texttt{Inl}(b))) = \texttt{case}(g, h, \texttt{Inl}(b)) = g(b)$$

Codatatype definitions are treated in precisely the same way. They express case operators using those for the variant products and sums, namely `qsplit` and `qcase`.

To see how constructors and the case analysis operator are defined, let us examine some examples. Further details are available elsewhere [26].

### 6.3 Example: Lists and Lazy Lists

Here is a declaration of the datatype of lists, as it might appear in a theory file:

```
consts   list :: i=>i
datatype "list(A)" = Nil | Cons ("a:A", "l: list(A)")
```

And here is a declaration of the codatatype of lazy lists:

```
consts   llist :: i=>i
codatatype "llist(A)" = LNil | LCons ("a: A", "l: llist(A)")
```

Each form of list has two constructors, one for the empty list and one for adding an element to a list. Each takes a parameter, defining the set of lists over a given set $A$. Each is automatically given the appropriate domain: $\texttt{univ}(A)$ for $\texttt{list}(A)$ and $\texttt{quniv}(A)$ for $\texttt{llist}(A)$. The default can be overridden.

Now $\texttt{list}(A)$ is a datatype and enjoys the usual induction rule. But $\texttt{llist}(A)$ is a codatatype and has no induction rule. Instead it has the coinduction rule shown in §4.3. Since variant pairs and injections are monotonic and need not have greater rank than their components, fixedpoint operators can create cyclic constructions. For example, the definition

$$\texttt{lconst}(a) \equiv \texttt{lfp}(\texttt{univ}(a), \lambda l \cdot \texttt{LCons}(a, l))$$

yields $\texttt{lconst}(a) = \texttt{LCons}(a, \texttt{lconst}(a))$.

### 6.4 Example: A Four-Constructor Datatype

A bigger datatype will illustrate some efficiency refinements. It has four constructors $\mathtt{Con}_0$, …, $\mathtt{Con}_3$, with the corresponding arities.

```
consts     data :: [i,i] => i
datatype   "data(A,B)" = Con0
                       | Con1 ("a: A")
                       | Con2 ("a: A", "b: B")
                       | Con3 ("a: A", "b: B", "d: data(A,B)")
```

Because this datatype has two set parameters, $A$ and $B$, the package automatically supplies $\mathtt{univ}(A \cup B)$ as its domain. The structural induction rule has four minor premises, one per constructor, and only the last has an induction hypothesis. (Details are left to the reader.)

The constructors are defined by the equations

$$\begin{aligned}
\mathtt{Con}_0 &\equiv \mathtt{Inl}(\mathtt{Inl}(\emptyset)) \\
\mathtt{Con}_1(a) &\equiv \mathtt{Inl}(\mathtt{Inr}(a)) \\
\mathtt{Con}_2(a, b) &\equiv \mathtt{Inr}(\mathtt{Inl}(\langle a, b\rangle)) \\
\mathtt{Con}_3(a, b, c) &\equiv \mathtt{Inr}(\mathtt{Inr}(\langle a, b, c\rangle)).
\end{aligned}$$

The case analysis operator is

$$\begin{aligned}
\mathtt{data_case}(f_0, f_1, f_2, f_3) \equiv\; &\mathtt{case}(\mathtt{case}(\lambda u \cdot f_0,\ f_1), \\
&\mathtt{case}(\mathtt{split}(f_2),\ \mathtt{split}(\lambda v \cdot \mathtt{split}(f_3(v)))))
\end{aligned}$$

This may look cryptic, but the case equations are trivial to verify.

In the constructor definitions, the injections are balanced. A more naive approach is to define $\mathtt{Con}_3(a, b, c)$ as $\mathtt{Inr}(\mathtt{Inr}(\mathtt{Inr}(\langle a, b, c\rangle)))$; instead, each constructor has two injections. The difference here is small. But the ZF examples include a 60-element enumeration type, where each constructor has 5 or 6 injections. The naive approach would require 1 to 59 injections; the definitions would be quadratic in size. It is like the advantage of binary notation over unary.

The result structure contains the case operator and constructor definitions as the theorem list `case_eqns`. It contains the case equations, such as

$$\mathtt{data\_case}(f_0, f_1, f_2, f_3, \mathtt{Con}_3(a, b, c)) = f_3(a, b, c),$$

as the theorem list `case_eqns`.There is one equation per constructor.

## 6.5 Proving Freeness Theorems

There are two kinds of freeness theorems:

- **injectiveness** theorems, such as

$\mathtt{Con}_2(a, b) = \mathtt{Con}_2(a', b') \leftrightarrow a = a' \wedge b = b'$

- **distinctness** theorems, such as

$\mathtt{Con}_1(a) \neq \mathtt{Con}_2(a', b')$

Since the number of such theorems is quadratic in the number of constructors, the package does not attempt to prove them all. Instead it returns tools for proving desired theorems—either manually or during simplification or classical reasoning.

The theorem list `free_iffs` enables the simplifier to perform freeness reasoning. This works by incremental unfolding of constructors that appear in equations. The theorem list contains logical equivalences such as

$$\begin{aligned} \mathtt{Con}_0 = c &\leftrightarrow c = \mathtt{Inl}(\mathtt{Inl}(\emptyset)) \\ \mathtt{Con}_1(a) = c &\leftrightarrow c = \mathtt{Inl}(\mathtt{Inr}(a)) \\ &\vdots \end{aligned}$$

$$\mathtt{Inl}(a) = \mathtt{Inl}(b) \leftrightarrow a = b$$
$$\mathtt{Inl}(a) = \mathtt{Inr}(b) \leftrightarrow \mathtt{False}$$
$$\langle a, b\rangle = \langle a', b'\rangle \leftrightarrow a = a' \wedge b = b'$$

For example, these rewrite $\mathtt{Con}_1(a) = \mathtt{Con}_1(b)$ to $a = b$ in four steps.

The theorem list `free_SEs` enables the classical reasoner to perform similar replacements. It consists of elimination rules to replace $\mathtt{Con}_0 = c$ by $c = \mathtt{Inl}(\mathtt{Inl}(\emptyset))$ and so forth, in the assumptions.

Such incremental unfolding combines freeness reasoning with other proof steps. It has the unfortunate side-effect of unfolding definitions of constructors in contexts such as $\exists x \cdot \mathtt{Con}_1(a) = x$, where they should be left alone. Isabelle's simplifier performs the checks needed to prevent this.

# 7 Related Work

The use of least fixedpoints to express inductive definitions seems obvious. Why, then, has this technique so seldom been implemented?

Most automated logics can only express inductive definitions by asserting axioms. Little would be left of Boyer and Moore's logic [4] if their shell principle were removed. With ALF the situation is more complex; earlier versions of Martin-Löf's type theory could (using wellordering types) express datatype definitions, but the version underlying ALF requires new rules for each definition [7]. With Coq the situation is subtler still; its underlying Calculus of Constructions can express inductive definitions [14], but cannot quite handle datatype definitions [22]. It seems that researchers tried hard to circumvent these problems before finally extending the Calculus with rule schemes for strictly positive operators. Recently Giménez has extended the Calculus of Constructions with inductive and coinductive types [11], with mechanized support in Coq.

Higher-order logic can express inductive definitions through quantification over unary predicates. The following formula expresses that $i$ belongs to the least set containing 0 and closed under `succ`:

$$\forall P \cdot P(0) \wedge (\forall x \cdot P(x) \rightarrow P(\mathtt{succ}(x))) \rightarrow P(i)$$

This technique can be used to prove the Knaster-Tarski theorem, which (in its general form) is little used in the Cambridge HOL system. Melham [15] describes the development. The natural numbers are defined as shown above, but lists are defined as functions over the natural numbers. Unlabelled trees are defined using Gödel numbering; a labelled tree consists of an unlabelled tree paired with a list of labels. Melham's datatype package expresses the user's datatypes in terms of labelled trees. It has been highly successful, but a fixed point approach might have yielded greater power with less effort.

Elsa Gunter [12] reports an ongoing project to generalise the Cambridge HOL system with mutual recursion and infinitely branching trees. She retains many features of Melham's approach.

Melham's inductive definition package [5] also uses quantification over predicates. But instead of formalizing the notion of monotone function, it requires definitions to consist of finitary rules, a syntactic form that excludes many monotone inductive definitions.

PVS [21] is another proof assistant based on higher-order logic. It supports both inductive definitions and datatypes, apparently by asserting axioms. Datatypes may not be iterated in general, but may use recursion over the built-in `list` type.

The earliest use of least fixed points is probably Robin Milner's. Brian Monahan extended this package considerably [19], as did I in unpublished work.[3] LCF is a first-order logic of domain theory; the relevant fixed point theorem is not Knaster-Tarski but concerns fixedpoints of continuous functions over domains. LCF is too weak to express recursive predicates. The Isabelle package might be the first to be based on the Knaster-Tarski theorem.

[3] The datatype package described in my LCF book [23] does *not* make definitions, but merely asserts axioms.

## 8 Conclusions and Future Work

Higher-order logic and set theory are both powerful enough to express inductive definitions. A growing number of theorem provers implement one of these [9, 33]. The easiest sort of inductive definition package to write is one that asserts new axioms, not one that makes definitions and proves theorems about them. But asserting axioms could introduce unsoundness.

The fixedpoint approach makes it fairly easy to implement a package for (co)inductive definitions that does not assert axioms. It is efficient: it processes most definitions in seconds and even a 60-constructor datatype requires under a minute. It is also simple: The first working version took under a week to code, consisting of under 1100 lines (35K bytes) of Standard ML.

In set theory, care is needed to ensure that the inductive definition yields a set (rather than a proper class). This problem is inherent to set theory, whether or not the Knaster-Tarski theorem is employed. We must exhibit a bounding set (called a domain above). For inductive definitions, this is often trivial. For datatype definitions, I have had to formalize much set theory. To justify infinitely branching datatype definitions, I have had to develop a theory of cardinal arithmetic [30], such as the theorem that if $\kappa$ is an infinite cardinal and $|X(\alpha)| \leq \kappa$ for all $\alpha < \kappa$ then $|\bigcup_{\alpha<\kappa} X(\alpha)| \leq \kappa$. The need for such efforts is not a drawback of the fixedpoint approach, for the alternative is to take such definitions on faith.

Care is also needed to ensure that the greatest fixedpoint really yields a coinductive definition. In set theory, standard pairs admit only well-founded constructions. Aczel's anti-foundation axiom [3] could be used to get non-well-founded objects, but it does not seem easy to mechanise. Isabelle/ZF instead uses a variant notion of ordered pairing, which can be generalized to a variant notion of function. Elsewhere I have proved that this simple approach works (yielding final coalgebras) for a broad class of definitions [28].

Several large studies make heavy use of inductive definitions. Lötzbeyer and Sandner have formalized two chapters of a semantics book [37], proving the equivalence between the operational and denotational semantics of a simple imperative language. A single theory file contains three datatype definitions (of arithmetic expressions, boolean expressions and commands) and three inductive definitions (the corresponding operational rules). Using different techniques, Nipkow [20] and Rasmussen [32] have both proved the Church-Rosser theorem; inductive definitions specify several reduction relations on $\lambda$-terms. Recently, I have applied inductive definitions to the analysis of cryptographic protocols [29].

To demonstrate coinductive definitions, Frost [10] has proved the consistency of the dynamic and static semantics for a small functional language. The example is due to Milner and Tofte [18]. It concerns an extended correspondence relation, which is defined coinductively. A codatatype definition specifies values and value environments in mutual recursion. Non-well-founded values represent recursive functions. Value environments are variant functions from variables into values. This one key definition uses most of the package's novel features.

The approach is not restricted to set theory. It should be suitable for any logic that has some notion of set and the Knaster-Tarski theorem. I have ported the (co)inductive definition package from Isabelle/ZF to Isabelle/HOL (higher-order logic). Völker [36] is investigating how to port the (co)datatype package. HOL represents sets by unary predicates; defining the corresponding types may cause complications.

## References

[1] Abramsky, S., The lazy lambda calculus, In *Research Topics in Functional Programming*, D. A. Turner, Ed. Addison-Wesley, 1977, pp. 65–116.

[2] Aczel, P., An introduction to inductive definitions, In *Handbook of Mathematical Logic*, J. Barwise, Ed. North-Holland, 1977, pp. 739–782.

[3] Aczel, P., *Non-Well-Founded Sets*, CSLI, 1988.

[4] Boyer, R. S., Moore, J. S., *A Computational Logic*, Academic Press, 1979.

[5] Camilleri, J., Melham, T. F., Reasoning with inductively defined relations in the HOL theorem prover, Tech. Rep. 265, Comp. Lab., Univ. Cambridge, Aug. 1992.

[6] Davey, B. A., Priestley, H. A., *Introduction to Lattices and Order*, Cambridge Univ. Press, 1990.

[7] Dybjer, P., Inductive sets and families in Martin-Löf's type theory and their set-theoretic semantics, In *Logical Frameworks*, G. Huet G. Plotkin, Eds. Cambridge Univ. Press, 1991, pp. 280–306.

[8] Dybjer, P., Nordström, B., Smith, J., Eds., *Types for Proofs and Programs: International Workshop TYPES '94*, LNCS 996. Springer, published 1995.

[9] Farmer, W. M., Guttman, J. D., Thayer, F. J., IMPS: An interactive mathematical proof system, *J. Auto. Reas.* **11**, 2 (1993), 213–248.

[10] Frost, J., A case study of co-induction in Isabelle, Tech. Rep. 359, Comp. Lab., Univ. Cambridge, Feb. 1995.

[11] Giménez, E., Codifying guarded definitions with recursive schemes, In Dybjer et al. [8], pp. 39–59.

[12] Gunter, E. L., A broader class of trees for recursive type definitions for HOL, In *Higher Order Logic Theorem Proving and Its Applications: HUG '93* (Published 1994), J. Joyce C. Seger, Eds., LNCS 780, Springer, pp. 141–154.

[13] Hennessy, M., *The Semantics of Programming Languages: An Elementary Introduction Using Structural Operational Semantics*, Wiley, 1990.

[14] Huet, G., Induction principles formalized in the Calculus of Constructions, In *Programming of Future Generation Computers* (1988), K. Fuchi M. Nivat, Eds., Elsevier, pp. 205–216.

[15] Melham, T. F., Automating recursive type definitions in higher order logic, In *Current Trends in Hardware Verification and Automated Theorem Proving*, G. Birtwistle P. A. Subrahmanyam, Eds. Springer, 1989, pp. 341–386.

[16] Milner, R., How to derive inductions in LCF, note, Dept. Comp. Sci., Univ. Edinburgh, 1980.

[17] Milner, R., *Communication and Concurrency*, Prentice-Hall, 1989.

[18] Milner, R., Tofte, M., Co-induction in relational semantics, *Theoretical Comput. Sci.* **87** (1991), 209–220.

[19] Monahan, B. Q., *Data Type Proofs using Edinburgh LCF*, PhD thesis, University of Edinburgh, 1984.

[20] Nipkow, T., More Church-Rosser proofs (in Isabelle/HOL), In *Automated Deduction — CADE-13 International Conference* (1996), M. McRobbie J. K. Slaney, Eds., LNAI 1104, Springer, pp. 733–747.

[21] Owre, S., Shankar, N., Rushby, J. M., *The PVS specification language*, Computer Science Laboratory, SRI International, Menlo Park, CA, Apr. 1993, Beta release.

[22] Paulin-Mohring, C., Inductive definitions in the system Coq: Rules and properties, In *Typed Lambda Calculi and Applications* (1993), M. Bezem J. Groote, Eds., LNCS 664, Springer, pp. 328–345.

[23] Paulson, L. C., *Logic and Computation: Interactive proof with Cambridge LCF*, Cambridge Univ. Press, 1987.

[24] Paulson, L. C., Set theory for verification: I. From foundations to functions, *J. Auto. Reas.* **11**, 3 (1993), 353–389.

[25] Paulson, L. C., *Isabelle: A Generic Theorem Prover*, Springer, 1994, LNCS 828.

[26] Paulson, L. C., Set theory for verification: II. Induction and recursion, *J. Auto. Reas.* **15**, 2 (1995), 167–215.

[27] Paulson, L. C., Mechanizing coinduction and corecursion in higher-order logic, *J. Logic and Comput.* **7**, 2 (Mar. 1997), 175–204.

[28] Paulson, L. C., A concrete final coalgebra theorem for ZF set theory, In Dybjer et al. [8], pp. 120–139.

[29] Paulson, L. C., Tool support for logics of programs, In *Mathematical Methods in Program Development: Summer School Marktoberdorf 1996*, M. Broy, Ed., NATO ASI Series F. Springer, Published 1997, pp. 461–498.

[30] Paulson, L. C., Grąbczewski, K., Mechanizing set theory: Cardinal arithmetic and the axiom of choice, *J. Auto. Reas.* **17**, 3 (Dec. 1996), 291–323.

[31] Pitts, A. M., A co-induction principle for recursively defined domains, *Theoretical Comput. Sci.* **124** (1994), 195–219.

[32] Rasmussen, O., The Church-Rosser theorem in Isabelle: A proof porting experiment, Tech. Rep. 364, Computer Laboratory, University of Cambridge, May 1995.

[33] Saaltink, M., Kromodimoeljo, S., Pase, B., Craigen, D., Meisels, I., An EVES data abstraction example, In *FME '93: Industrial-Strength Formal Methods* (1993), J. C. P. Woodcock P. G. Larsen, Eds., LNCS 670, Springer, pp. 578–596.

[34] Slind, K., Function definition in higher-order logic, In *Theorem Proving in Higher Order Logics: TPHOLs '96* (1996), J. von Wright, J. Grundy, J. Harrison, Eds., LNCS 1125.

[35] Szasz, N., A machine checked proof that Ackermann's function is not primitive recursive, In *Logical Environments*, G. Huet G. Plotkin, Eds. Cambridge Univ. Press, 1993, pp. 317–338.

[36] Völker, N., On the representation of datatypes in Isabelle/HOL, In *Proceedings of the First Isabelle Users Workshop* (Sept. 1995), L. C. Paulson, Ed., Technical Report 379, Comp. Lab., Univ. Cambridge, pp. 206–218.

[37] Winskel, G., *The Formal Semantics of Programming Languages*, MIT Press, 1993.

# 8 Constructively Formalizing Automata Theory

**Robert L. Constable, Paul B. Jackson, Pavel Naumov, and Juan Uribe**

## 1 Introduction

### 1.1 Background

It is widely believed that we know how to formalize large tracts of *classical* mathematics—namely write in the style of Bourbaki [4] using some version of set theory and fill in all the details. Indeed, the *Journal of Formalized Mathematics* publishes results formalized in set theory and checked by the Mizar system. Despite this belief and the many formalizations accomplished, massive formalization is not a *fait accompli*; many challenges remain in such areas as the organization of large databases of mathematics and the raising of the level of automation.

In contrast, there is no general agreement on how to formalize *computational* mathematics. Even worse, few people appreciate that this is a significant new problem (see [5]). Our interest is in examining whether some kind of *constructive type theory* is an appropriate formalism.

There are two immediately-appealing aspects of constructive type theories. First, they have built-in a functional programming language in which algorithms can be expressed. Second, propositions can be read as claiming the existence of functional programs and data, and if some proof can be given of a proposition, the corresponding programs and data can be automatically synthesized (or sometimes we say *extracted*) from the proof. For example, from the proof of $\forall x \in S.\ \exists y \in T.\ P(x, y)$, we can synthesize a functional program that, when given any element $s$ of type $S$ as data, can compute some $t$ of type $T$ such that proposition $P(s, t)$ holds. We sometimes call the programs and data that can be synthesized from proofs of some proposition the *computational content* of the proposition.

There is a tradeoff in gaining this extra expressivity: fewer truths can be proven in logics based on constructive type theories than in classical logic. For example, the propositions $P \Leftrightarrow \neg\neg P$, and $P \vee \neg P$ are no longer true for arbitrary propositions $P$. For introductory material on constructive type theory, consult [30] or [10].

The particular constructive type theory we are working with is similar to one of Martin-Löf's [24], and is implemented in the Nuprl proof development system [6, 20]. Nuprl provides an environment for assembling *theories* consisting of definitions, theorems, and proofs. It also has an interpreter for executing the functional programs that users write and that are synthesized from proofs.

Supported in part by NSF grants CCR-9423687, DUE-955162, and ONR grant N00014-92-J-1764.

Previous topics we have experimented with in Nuprl include elementary number theory [17], elementary analysis [9], and the algebra of polynomials [20].

### 1.2 Choice of Topic

Automata theory is an appealing topic for formalization because of its central role in computer science. Recently, we have been considering whether we could formalize a whole book on automata theory such as Hopcroft and Ullman's *Formal Languages and their Relation to Automata* [15]. Such a formalization could have significant pedagogical value: it could serve as a novel hypertext reference for students studying automata theory, and would stand as a corpus of familiar examples for any computer scientist interested in formalization techniques.

We report in this article on a preliminary step in this direction, namely, the formalization in Nuprl of the Myhill-Nerode theorem on the existence and uniqueness of minimum finite automata. We based the formalization on the presentation in the book cited above. We chose this theorem because it is one of the first significant theorems in the book, and because it involves computationally interesting constructions.

Automata theory was previously explored in Nuprl by Christoph Kreitz in 1986 [22]. In particular, he proved the pumping lemma for finite automata. We saw that we needed this lemma for our constructivization of the Myhill-Nerode theorem, and so reproved it using Nuprl's current tactic collection. We therefore could compare the currently achievable level of automation with that achievable in 1986.

An under-explored aspect of Nuprl's type theory is its novel quotient types (see Section 4.3). Jackson, for example, had experimented with these previously [20], but we still didn't have much experience with how best to reason efficiently with them. The heart of the Myhill-Nerode theorem involves a quotient construction, and so provided a good opportunity to gain more experience.

### 1.3 Value of the Formalization

Readers can evaluate the formal text on the Web that resulted from our formalization efforts. It is possible to directly judge whether our definitions are faithful to Hopcroft and Ullman's, whether the formal definitions help clarify the concepts, whether the proofs are sufficiently readable and informative, and whether the availability of detail about all proof steps is useful. The formal material also provided the underpinning for this article in that our definitions and proof summaries refer to the complete formal library. The material can be the foundation for other documents that explain the detailed proofs. We have not yet produced such documents for the automata library. However, there are examples of this genre of writing in the Formal-Courseware section of the Nuprl home page. For example, Stuart Allen has produced a hybrid style of formal and informal proof to accompany the basic theorems about functions proved by Paul Jackson and used extensively in this formalization.

There are other aspects and by-products of our formalization that cannot be directly evaluated by reading the formal text; they require experience with the system. In this category is the experience of *confidence* in the results that comes from learning to trust Nuprl. We know that reading results checked by both a human and a machine raises confidence in their correctness, similar to the added confidence gained by having a trusted colleague check a result.

Another value of the formalization is the interactivity provided by the underlying system. For example, Nuprl can show dependencies among theorems and definitions, and it can execute algorithms extracted from proofs. Users can experiment with alternate proofs and can observe the effect on the extracted programs.

In addition to the readable and highly reliable interactive formal text, the formalization has created an interesting *digital artifact.* The formal theory becomes an object that we can manipulate, measure, transform and explore. To experience these capabilities, one must learn to use a system like Nuprl.

## 1.4 Interpretations of the Mathematics

Nuprl's type theory can be interpreted in several ways. In the semantics given by Allen [1], all functions are computable. The type theory is therefore compatible with *recursive mathematics* in which all functions are given by Turing machines. Every theorem in Nuprl can be seen as a theorem of recursive mathematics, but the converse is not true; the type theory is sufficiently weak that non-classical results in recursive mathematics, such as that every function from $\mathbb{R}$ to $\mathbb{R}$ is continuous, are not provable.

Howe has given a set-theoretic interpretation of Nuprl's type theory that shows that every theorem provable in Nuprl can be read as a theorem of classical mathematics [19]. This interpretation includes all non-computational set-theoretic functions in the denotation of function types.

Having both classical and recursive interpretations makes Nuprl a suitable tool for formalizing constructive mathematics in the style advocated by Bishop [2].

## 1.5 Electronic Access to Formalization

The key ideas of the formalization are presented in this article in a self-contained way. To find out more, the reader is invited to browse the full formalization on the World Wide Web. Start by visiting the Nuprl project's home page at URL

`http://www.cs.cornell.edu/Info/Projects/NuPrl/nuprl.html`

From there, the reader can access hypertext presentations of both the work presented in this article and other more recent work in automata theory.

Nuprl itself is free software that can be obtained from this web site. It runs on a freely-available version Allegro Common Lisp under Linux as well as free CMU Common Lisp under Unix.

### 1.6 Related Work

A non-constructive set-theoretic formalization of minimization theorems for Moore and Mealy automata has been done in the Mizar system [21]. This closely follows a presentation in Denning, Dennis, Qualitz [8].

Theorems asserting the equivalence between deterministic (DFA) and nondeterministic (NFA) finite state automata, and between NFAs with and without epsilon moves, were proven in Nqthm [31], and subsequently in PVS [28]. These formalizations were based on theorems 2.1 and 2.2 in [16]. Notably, a flaw was found in the textbook proof of theorem 2.2. The formation of DFA states from sets of NFA states was significantly more complicated in the constructive Nqthm proofs than the non-constructive PVS proofs. Part of the difficulty in the Nqthm proofs was in modeling finite sets using lists, and handling the equality of lists considered as sets. We wouldn't expect to have this difficulty in Nuprl because, as shown in [20], we can take advantage of Nuprl's quotient type to appropriately redefine the equality relation on lists.

Quotient types have been explored in the ECC constructive type theory by Hofmann [14], and probably most of the development presented in this article could be straightforwardly formalized in the LEGO mechanization of ECC [27]. One major difference between ECC and Nuprl is that, in ECC, both explicitly written and synthesized programs must be embellished with parts that are unimportant for computation, but necessary for proofs of correctness.

### 1.7 Outline

In Section 2 we present the basic ideas from Nuprl needed for this article. Section 3 defines the notion of a formal language, and Section 4 provides the preliminaries on automata. Section 5 proves the Myhill-Nerode theorem, and Section 6 presents a corollary that makes explicit the construction and properties of the minimum automaton introduced in the course of proving the Myhill-Nerode theorem. Section 7 discusses various issues that came up, Section 8 summarizes our results, and Section 9 presents our conclusions and outlines future work. Finally, Appendix A provides an index for notation.

All the material on languages and automata closely follows that in Chapter 1 and Sections 3.1 and 3.2 of Hopcroft and Ullman [15].

## 2 Type Theory Preliminaries

### 2.1 Basic Types

The integers $\mathbb{Z}$ are a primitive type of Nuprl. Defined subtypes of the integers include the bounded-below range $\{i \ldots\} == \{j : \mathbb{Z} \mid i \leq j\}$, the naturals $\mathbb{N} == \{0 \ldots\}$, and the finite types $\mathbb{N}k == \{n : \mathbb{N} \mid n < k\}$. (In Nuprl notation, we use $==$ for definitional equality).

The Booleans $\mathbb{B}$ are defined type. For the purposes of this article the exact definition is unimportant. The canonical elements of $\mathbb{B}$ are *tt* and *ff* denoting true and false respectively. As explained in Section 2.6, boolean expressions and propositions are distinct. The prefix operation $\uparrow$ converts a boolean expression to a proposition.

### 2.2 Recursive Types

The only recursive type relevant here is the *list* type. Given any type $A$, the type $A$ *list* is the type of finite sequences of elements of type $A$. The empty list is *nil*. Lists are constructed using an infix "." constructor, often referred to as "cons." Given an element $a$ of type $A$ and a list $l$ of type $A$ *list*, cons forms a new list $a.l$. The functions *hd* (head) and *tl* (tail) take lists apart.

They satisfy the equations $hd(a.l) = a$ and $tl(a.l) = l$. The boolean-valued function *null* tests whether a list is empty. The infix append operation @ joins two lists together.

### 2.3 Product Types

If $A$ and $B$ are types, then so is their *cartesian product*, $A \times B$. The elements of $A \times B$ are ordered pairs, $\langle a, b\rangle$ with $a \in A$ and $b \in B$. The product and pairing operation are assumed to associate to the right, so we write $A \times B \times C$ for $A \times (B \times C)$, and $\langle a, b, c\rangle$ for $\langle a, \langle b, c\rangle\rangle$.

The product type is a special case of a *dependent product type*, also known as a $\Sigma$ type. In this type, the type of the second component of pairs can depend on the first component of pairs.

### 2.4 Function Types

If $A$ and $B$ are types, then $A \rightarrow B$ denotes the type of all total computable functions from $A$ to $B$. The canonical elements of this type are lambda terms, $\lambda x.b$. Let $b[a/x]$ denote the substitution of the term $a$ for all free occurrences of $x$ in $b$. For $\lambda x.b$ to be a function from $A$ to $B$, its value $b[a/x]$ must be of type $B$ for all arguments $a$ of type $A$. If $f \in A \to B$ and $a \in A$, then $f\ a$ denotes the application of $f$ to argument $a$.

The function type is a special case of a *dependent function type*, also known as a $\Pi$ type. The type of an application of a function in a dependent function type can depend on the argument the function is applied to. There are no examples of dependent function types in this article.

### 2.5 Recursive Function Definitions

A recursive function definition in Nuprl is written *lhs* $==_r$ *rhs*, where *lhs* is the function being defined, and *rhs* may include instances of *lhs* as subterms. For example, the list append operation @ can be defined with

$$u@v ==_r \textit{if } null(u) \textit{ then } v \textit{ else } hd(u).(tl(u)@v).$$

Recursive functions are created using the $Y$ recursion combinator, which is definable since Nuprl's computation language is untyped. Immediately after introducing a recursive definition, we prove a well-formedness lemma showing that evaluation of the definition on arguments in specified types always terminates and gives a result in a specified type. The lemma for @ is

$$\vdash \forall A : \mathbb{U}.\ \forall u, v : A\ \textit{list}.\ u@v \in A\ \textit{list}.$$

### 2.6 Propositions and Universes

In so-called classical accounts of logic, a proposition has a truth value in $\mathbb{B}$, and propositions can be treated as boolean expressions. We are interested not only in the truth value of propositions, but also in their computational sense; how they can be seen as specifications for programs. To support this computational view, it is necessary for us to have a type $\mathbb{P}$ of propositions distinct from $\mathbb{B}$.

There are two distinguished atomic propositions, $\top$ the canonically true one and $\bot$ the canonically false one. Given propositions $P$, $Q$ we can form compounds in the usual way:

$P \wedge Q$ for "$P$ and $Q$ ",

$P \vee Q$ for "$P$ or $Q$",

$P \Rightarrow Q$ for "$P$ implies $Q$" also written "$P$ only if $Q$,"

$P \Leftrightarrow Q$ for "$P$ if and only if $Q$" also written "$P$ iff $Q$."

Negation, $\neg P$, is defined as $P \Rightarrow \perp$.

A *propositional function* on a type $T$ is any map $P \in T \to \mathbb{P}$. Given such a $P$, we can form the propositions:

$\forall x:T.\ P\ x$ "for all $x$ of type $A$, $P\ x$ holds,"

$\exists x:T.\ P\ x$ "for some $x$ of type $A$, $P\ x$ holds."

Associated with every type $T$ is the atomic equality relation $x = y$ *in* $T$. The definition of this equality is given with each type. Often, the *in* $T$ is dropped; it usually can be inferred from consideration of $x$ or $y$.

Types in Nuprl are members of *universe* types. Nuprl has a hierarchy of universe types to avoid the problem of a universe type being a member of itself. There happens also to be a corresponding hierarchy of proposition types. For the purposes of this article, it is sufficient that we use $\mathbb{U}$ to denote some typical universe type and $\mathbb{P}$ to denote some typical type of propositions. See [6] or [20] for fuller accounts of Nuprl's logic and universe types.

### 2.7 Subtypes

If $T$ is a type and $P \in T \to \mathbb{P}$ is a propositional function, then $\{x : A \mid P\ x\}$ denotes the type of all elements of $A$ satisfying $P$. Looking at this subset type from a constructive point of view, it's important to note that when we assume that we have some element $a$ in this type, we don't have any access to the computational content of the proposition $P\ x$, even though we know it to be true. Further discussion of the subset type can be found in [6, 20, 25] as well as in Section 2.8.

### 2.8 Finiteness

A predicate asserting that a type $T$ is finite is

$Fin(T) == \exists k:\mathbb{N}.\ \mathit{1\text{-}1\text{-}Corresp}(\mathbb{N}k; T)$,

where $\mathit{1\text{-}1\text{-}Corresp}(\mathbb{N}k; T)$ just when there exists functions $f$ of type $\mathbb{N}k \to T$ and $g$ of type $T \to \mathbb{N}k$ that are mutual inverses.

Constructively, if we assume $Fin(T)$, we are assuming that $T$'s cardinality and the computable functions $f$ and $g$ are available for use. Likewise, if we are proving $Fin(T)$, we have to give $T$'s cardinality and produce suitable computable functions $f$ and $g$.

Because the predicate $Fin(T)$ has significant computational content, it is not that constructively useful to form the type of all finite types $\{T : \mathbb{U} \mid Fin(T)\}$ using the subset type; if we know some type is in this collection of finite types, we still have no way of finding out its size, or enumerating its contents.

## 3 Languages and Their Representation

### 3.1 Alphabets and Languages

Hopcroft and Ullman begin their book with the question: What is a language? Their answer starts with a definition of an *alphabet*. They define an alphabet to be any finite set of *symbols*. The exact structure of symbols is unimportant, so we take an alphabet to be any type *Alph*, and we always assume $Fin(Alph)$. As noted in Section 2.8, a consequence of finiteness is that the equality relation on *Alph* is decidable.

In Hopcroft and Ullman we read that a *sentence* over an alphabet is any string of finite length composed of symbols from the alphabet. We use lists of type *Alph list* to represent strings over an alphabet *Alph*. We choose to reverse the order of alphabet symbols, so the string `abc` is represented by the list `c.b.a.`*nil*.

Hopcroft and Ullman define a *language* to be a set of sentences over an alphabet. In Nuprl's type theory, though types superficially resemble sets, they are not as versatile. For example, one cannot take the union or intersection of two arbitrary types, and a type membership predicate can be awkward to reason with. So, instead of considering a language $L$ over an alphabet *Alph* to be a subtype of *Alph list*, we consider $L$ to be a propositional function over *Alph list*, that is, a function of type *Alph list* $\rightarrow \mathbb{P}$. When sets are represented in Nuprl's type theory as propositional functions over some common domain type, common set operations and predicates are straightforward to define and use.

We let $Language(Alph)$, the type of languages over alphabet *Alph*, be an abbreviation for *Alph list* $\rightarrow \mathbb{P}$.

We define two languages to be equal, written $L = M$, just when for all $x$ in *Alph list*, $L\,x \Leftrightarrow M\,x$.

### 3.2 Representations of Languages

Our definition of a language as a propositional function $L \in$ *Alph list* $\rightarrow \mathbb{P}$ captures the intuition that to know a language is to know the criteria for saying when a sentence is in it. To say $x$ is in the language $L$ is to know how to prove $L\,x$. This agrees with Hopcroft and Ullman; they are concerned with certain special ways of knowing $L\,x$.

One especially simple kind of representation of $L$ arises when the proposition $L\ x$ is decidable, i.e., when there is a function $R_L \in$ *Alph list* $\rightarrow \mathbb{B}$ such that

$L\ x$ iff $\uparrow (R_L\ x)$.

We call the function $R_L$ a *language recognizer*, and the language in this case is said to be *decidable* or *recursive*.

## 4 Finite Automata

### 4.1 Definition

Hopcroft and Ullman define a *finite automaton M* to be a system

$\langle K,\ Alph, \delta, q_0,\ F\rangle$

where $K$ is a finite nonempty set of *states*, *Alph* is a finite *input alphabet*, $\delta$ is a mapping of $K \times$ *Alph* into $K$, $q_0$ *in* $K$ is the *initial state*, and $F \subseteq K$ is the set of *final states*.

In defining a finite automaton in Nuprl, we first assume that some type *Alph* is given for an alphabet, and some type *St* for the set of states. We assume both *Alph* and *St* are finite, though occasionally we relax these constraints when they are not necessary. An automaton $A$ is then a triple $\langle\delta(A),\ I(A),\ F(A)\rangle$, where the next state function $\delta(A)$ has type *St* $\rightarrow$ *Alph* $\rightarrow$ *St*, the initial state $I(A)$ is a member of *St*, and $F(A)$ is a function of type *St* $\rightarrow \mathbb{B}$ that returns *tt* just when applied to final states. By defining $F(A)$ as a boolean-valued function, we ensure that we can compute when an automaton is in a final state. The type of all such automata is

$Automata(Alph;\ St) == (St \rightarrow Alph \rightarrow St) \times St \times (St \rightarrow \mathbb{B})$.

See Section 7.1 for a discussion of the difference between our and Hopcroft and Ullman's definition.

### 4.2 Semantics of Automata

Hopcroft and Ullman extend the automaton transition function $\delta$ to input strings with the recursive definition:

$\hat{\delta}(q, nil) = q$

$\hat{\delta}(q, a.x) = \delta(\hat{\delta}(q, x), a)$,

where $a$ is a symbol in the alphabet *Alph* and $x$ is a string over *Alph*. They define the language accepted by the automaton as

$$\{x \mid \hat{\delta}(q_0, x) \text{ is in } F\}.$$

We make analogous definitions in Nuprl. Let $A$ be an automaton of type *Automata*(*Alph*; *St*), let $l$ be an input string in type *Alph list*, and let $s$ be a state in *St*. We define the recursive function

$$\delta'(A)(s;\ l) ==_r \mathit{if}\ \mathit{null}(l)\ \mathit{then}\ s\ \mathit{else}\ \delta(A)\ \ \delta'(A)(s;\ \mathit{tl}(l))\ \ \mathit{hd}(l),$$

which given $A$ in state $s$ to start, computes the new state of $A$ after input of $l$.

We then define $A(l)$ which computes the state of $A$ after input of $l$, starting in the initial state:

$$A(l) == \delta'(A)(I(A);\ l).$$

Using the final-state function $F(A)$, we define a language recognizer $L_b(A)$ for $A$ as

$$L_b(A) == \lambda l: \mathit{Alph\ list}.\ F(A)\ A(l).$$

The language accepted by $A$ is defined by a similar function that returns a proposition rather than a boolean. Using the $\uparrow$ function that converts a boolean to the corresponding proposition, $L(A)$, the language accepted by $A$, is defined as

$$L(A) == \lambda l: \mathit{Alph\ list}. \uparrow (L_b(A)\ l).$$

### 4.3 Equivalence Relations and Quotient Types

Prior to presenting the Myhill-Nerode theorem, Hopcroft and Ullman give a brief introduction to equivalence relations and how they partition the sets they are over into equivalence classes. They take a binary relation on a set $S$ to be a set of pairs of elements of $S$. As with representing languages (see Section 3.1), we find it more convenient to represent relations as characteristic functions: we consider a binary relation on a type $S$ to be a function of type $S \to S \to \mathbb{P}\, (= S \to (S \to \mathbb{P}))$. To express that elements $x$ and $y$ of type $S$ are related by a binary relation $R$ of type $S \to S \to \mathbb{P}$, we use both prefix application notation $R\ x\ y$ and infix notation $x\ R\ y$.

In the Myhill-Nerode theorem, an automaton is constructed that uses the equivalence classes of an equivalence relation as the states of an automaton. This is problematic constructively, because the equivalence classes in question have infinite size, and we would like to have finite representations of states on which we can define computable transition functions.

The obvious solution is to use some element of an equivalence class as a representative for the whole class. We do this with the help of Nuprl's quotient types. Given a type $S$ and an equivalence relation $E$ on $S$, the *quotient type* $S//E$ has the same members as $S$, but has as its associated equality relation the relation $E$ rather than the equality relation associated with $S$.

In Nuprl's type theory, for a function $f$ to be in a type $S \to T$, it must respect the equalities associated with $S$ and $T$. Specifically, if the equalities are $=_S$ and $=_T$ respectively, we have $f\ x =_T f\ y$ whenever $x =_S y$. If $E$ is an equivalence relation on $S$, and we want to show that $f$ also has type $S//E \to T$, we have to check that $f\ x =_T f\ y$ whenever $x\ E\ y$.

The quotient type $S//E$ behaves much like a type of the equivalence classes of $E$. Often when set-theoretically defining a function with a set of equivalence classes as domain, the function mentions representatives of equivalence classes, and it is necessary to check that the value of the function is independent of the particular choice of representatives. With the quotient type $S//E$ as domain of a function in Nuprl's type theory, the rules for function type inhabitation enforce a corresponding constraint.

In presentations of quotient types from Nuprl theories, we occasionally use the notation $x, y : S//(x\ E\ y)$ for the type $S//E$. This more verbose notation is useful when the primary notation for relation $E$ includes its arguments.

### 4.4 Finite Index Equivalence Relations

In set theory, an equivalence relation $E$ on a set $S$ is said to be of *finite index* if $E$ has a finite number of equivalence classes.

In Nuprl's type theory, we express that an equivalence relation $E$ on type $S$ has finite index by saying $Fin(S//E)$, that is, the quotient type $S//E$ is in one-one correspondence with $\{0 \ldots k-1\}$ for some non-negative number $k$. This definition works because the functions defining the bijection between $S//E$ and $\{0 \ldots k-1\}$ must respect $E$. Note that when $S$ is infinite, is possible for $S//E$ to be finite, even though $S$ and $S//E$ have the same elements.

### 4.5 Equivalence Relations on Strings

We introduce here a couple of definitions that are useful for stating the Myhill-Nerode theorem.

DEFINITION An equivalence relation $E$ on *Alph list* is called *extension invariant*[1] just when for all $x, y, z$ in *Alph list*

$x\ E\ y \Rightarrow (z@x)\ E\ (z@y)$.

[1] Hopcroft and Ullman have strings that are extended on the right and call such relations *right invariant.*

DEFINITION A language $L$ over alphabet *Alph* *induces* an equivalence relation $R(L)$ given by

$x\,R(L)\,y \Leftrightarrow (\forall z : Alph\ list.\ z@x \in L \Leftrightarrow z@y \in L).$

## 5 The Myhill-Nerode Theorem

We reproduce Hopcroft and Ullman's presentation of the Myhill-Nerode theorem in Section 5.1, and discuss its formalization in the following sections.

### 5.1 Hopcroft and Ullman Version

The statement and proof of the Myhill-Nerode theorem here is taken almost verbatim from [15]. A few changes have been made to make the notation more similar to that used in the formal development. The definitions of what it means for an equivalence relation to be *extension invariant* and of the equivalence relation *induced* by a language can be found in Section 4.5.

THEOREM 3.1 The following three statements are equivalent:

(1) The set $L \subseteq$ *Alph list* is accepted by some finite automaton.

(2) $L$ is the union of some of the equivalence classes of an extension invariant equivalence relation of finite index.

(3) The equivalence relation on *Alph list* induced by $L$ is of finite index.

*Proof*

(1) $\Rightarrow$ (2).

Assume that $L$ is accepted by $M = (K, Alph, \delta, q_0, F)$. Let $R$ be the equivalence relation $x\ R\ y$ if and only if $\delta(q_0, x) = \delta(q_0, y)$. $R$ is extension invariant since, for any $z$, if $\delta(q_0, x) = \delta(q_0, y)$, then

$\delta(q_0, z@x) = \delta(q_0, z@y).$

The index of $R$ is finite since the index is at most the number of states in $K$. Furthermore, $L$ is the union of those equivalence classes that include an element $x$ such that $\delta(q_0, x)$ is in $F$.

(2) $\Rightarrow$ (3).

We show that any equivalence relation $R$ satisfying statement (2) is a refinement of the equivalence relation $R(L)$ induced by $L$; that is, every equivalence class of $R$ is entirely contained in some equivalence class of $R(L)$. Thus the index of $R(L)$ cannot be greater than the index of $R$ and so is finite. Assume that $x\ R\ y$. Then since $R$ is extension invariant, for each $z$ in *Alph list*, $z@x\ R\ z@y$, and thus $z@y$ is in $L$ if and only if $z@x$ is in $L$. Thus $x\ R(L)\ y$, and hence, the equivalence class of $x$ in $R$ is contained in the equivalence class of $x$ in $R(L)$. We conclude that each equivalence class of $R$ is contained within some equivalence class of $R(L)$.

(3) $\Rightarrow$ (1).

Assume that $x\ R(L)\ y$. Then for each $w$ and $z$ in *Alph list*, $z@w@x$ is in $L$ if and only if $z@w@y$ is in $L$. Thus $w@x\ R(L)\ w@y$, and $R(L)$ is extension invariant. Now let $K'$ be the finite set of equivalence classes of $R(L)$ and $[x]$ the element of $K'$ containing $x$. Define $\delta([x], a) = [x.a]$. The definition is consistent, since $R(L)$ is extension invariant. Let $q_0' = [nil]$ and let $F' = \{[x] \mid x \in L\}$. The finite automaton $M' = (K', Alph, \delta', q_0', F')$ accepts $L$ since $\delta'(q_0', x) = [x]$, and thus $x$ is in $L(M')$ if and only if $[x]$ is in $F'$. **Qed**

### 5.2 Formalizing (1) $\Rightarrow$ (2)

The formal statement of the theorem in Nuprl's notation is

$$
\begin{aligned}
&\vdash \forall\, Alph : \mathbb{U}.\ \forall L : Language(Alph).\\
&\quad Fin(Alph)\\
&\quad \Rightarrow (\exists St : \mathbb{U}.\ \exists Auto : Automata(Alph; St).\ \ Fin(St) \wedge L = L(Auto))\\
&\quad \Rightarrow (\exists R : Alph\ list \rightarrow\ Alph\ list \rightarrow \mathbb{P}\\
&\qquad EquivRel(Alph\ list;\ R)\\
&\qquad \wedge \exists g : Alph\ list//R \rightarrow \mathbb{B}\\
&\qquad\quad Fin(Alph\ list//R)\\
&\qquad\quad \wedge\ (\forall l : Alph\ list.\ L\ l \Leftrightarrow\ \uparrow (g\ l))\\
&\qquad\quad \wedge\ (\forall x, y, z : Alph\ list.\ R\ x\ y \Rightarrow R\ (z@x)\ (z@y))).
\end{aligned}
$$

An English rendering of this is:

- Let *Alph*, an alphabet, be a finite type and let $L$ be a language over *Alph*,
- assume there exists a finite type of states *St* and an automaton *Auto* over *Alph* and *St* that accepts the language $L$,

- then there exists a binary relation $R$ on *Alph list* that is
  - an equivalence relation $(EquivRel(Alph\ list;\ R)\})$,
  - right invariant $(\forall x, y, z: Alph\ list.\ R\ x\ y \Rightarrow R\ (z@x)\ (z@y))$,
  - and of finite index $(Fin(Alph\ list//R))$,
- and there exists a boolean-valued function $g$ with domain $Alph\ list//R$ that returns boolean true ($tt$) exactly on strings in the language $L$

$(\exists g: Alph\ list//R \rightarrow \mathbb{B}.\ \forall l: Alph\ list.\ L\ l \Leftrightarrow \uparrow (g\ l))$.

The function $g$ here acts as the characteristic function for the set of equivalence classes of the relation $R$ whose union gives the language $L$. As remarked in Section 3.1, it is often more straightforward in Nuprl's type theory to represent sets as characteristic functions than as types. Note that the Nuprl quotient type $Alph\ list//R$ still contains elements of *Alph list* as members, so it is legitimate to pass the function $g$ an element $l$ of *Alph list* as an argument.

In requiring that $g$ be boolean ($\mathbb{B}$) valued rather than proposition ($\mathbb{P}$) valued, we are augmenting the statement (2) of the theorem with the requirement that membership in the language $L$ be decidable. This augmentation is necessary for the constructive proofs of the other parts of the theorem.

*Proof*

1. As with the Hopcroft and Ullman proof, $R\ x\ y$ is defined as $Auto(x) = Auto(y)$. Showing $R$ is an equivalence relation and is extension invariant is straightforward.
2. Finiteness of $Alph\ \ list//R$ is argued by noting that $Alph\ list//R$ is isomorphic to the set of accessible states, which is a subset of *St*.

The finiteness argument is first carried out abstractly by proving the lemma

$$\vdash \forall T, S: \mathbb{U}.\ \forall f: T \rightarrow S.\ Fin(S) \wedge (\forall s: S.\ Dec(\exists t: T.\ f t = s))$$
$$\Rightarrow Fin(x, y: T//(f x = f y))$$

which is then instantiated with $T$ being *Alph list*, $S$ being *St*, and $f$ being the function $\lambda l.\ Auto(l)$.

In using this lemma, the precondition

$$\forall s:\ St.\ Dec(\exists t: Alph\ list.\ Auto(t) = s)$$

has to be discharged. Read constructively, this precondition requires that, for any state $s$, it is possible to compute whether or not $s$ is accessible, and further, if $s$ is accessible, it must be possible to compute some string $t$ that, when input to the automaton, puts the automaton into state $s$.

The precondition is proven with the help of a corollary of the pumping lemma which states that in searching for a string that puts an automaton in a certain state, it is only necessary to try strings whose length is not greater than the number of states of the automaton.

3. We define $g$ on $Alph\ list//R$ to be $tt$ exactly when $F(Auto(x)){=}tt$, i.e., $g\ x{=}F(Auto(x))$. That $g$ is functional *wrt* $R$ follows directly from the definition of $R$. **Qed**

### 5.3 Formalizing (2) ⇒ (3)

Given a type $A$ representing an alphabet, and a language $L$ over $A$, the binary relation $R(L)$ induced by $L$ is defined as

$$R(L) == \lambda x, y. \forall z : A\ list.\ L\ z@x \Leftrightarrow L\ z@y$$

and has type $A\ list \to A\ list \to \mathbb{P}$. The display of parameter $A$ to $R(L)$ is suppressed, since $A$ can be inferred from considering the type of $L$. We establish straightforwardly that $R(L)$ is an equivalence relation.

The formal statement of (2) ⇒ (3) is:

$$\begin{aligned}
&\vdash \forall n : \{1 \ldots\}.\ \forall A : \mathbb{U}.\ \forall L :\ Language(A).\ \forall R : A\ list \to\ A\ list \to \mathbb{P}.\\
&\quad Fin(A)\\
&\quad \Rightarrow\ EquivRel(A\ list;\ R)\\
&\quad \Rightarrow\ \textit{1-1-Corresp}(\mathbb{N}n;\ A\ list//R)\\
&\quad \Rightarrow (\forall x, y, z : A\ list.\ x\ R\ y \Rightarrow (z@x)\ R\ (z@y))\\
&\quad \Rightarrow (\exists g : A\ list//R \to \mathbb{B} \cdot \forall l : A\ list.\ L\ l \Leftrightarrow\uparrow (g\ l))\\
&\quad \Rightarrow (\exists m : \mathbb{N}.\ \textit{1-1-Corresp}(\mathbb{N}m;\ A\ list//\ R(L)))\\
&\qquad \wedge(\forall l : A\ \ list.\ Dec(L\ l)).
\end{aligned}$$

An English reading is:

- Let the alphabet $A$ be a finite type,
- let R be a binary relation on $A$ *list* that is
  - an equivalence relation,
  - extensionally invariant,

– and of finite index

(*1-1-Corresp*($\mathbb{N}n$; $A$ *list*//$R$) where $n$ is a positive integer),

- let $L$ be a language over $A$,
- assume $L$ is a union of equivalence classes of $R$ and is decidable

($\exists g : A\ \ list//R \to \mathbb{B}.\ \forall l : A\ \ list\,.\ L\ l \Leftrightarrow\uparrow (g\ l)$),

- then $R(L)$ is of finite index

($\exists m : \mathbb{N}.$ *1-1-Corresp*($\mathbb{N}m$; $A$ *list*// $R(L)$)),

- and $L$ is decidable.

Note that here both statements (2) and (3) of Hopcroft and Ullman have been augmented with a requirement that membership in $L$ be decidable. The augmentation of (3) is necessary for the proof of (3) $\Rightarrow$ (1).

*Proof* The argument that $R$ is a refinement of $R(L)$ follows the Hopcroft and Ullman argument and is completely straightforward.

To show that therefore the index of $R(L)$ is no larger than the index of $R$, we could instantiate a lemma of form

**Quotient Index Lemma 1**. If $P$ and $Q$ are binary relations over a type $T$, and $P$ is a refinement of $Q$ ($x\ P\ y \Rightarrow x\ Q\ y$ for any $x$ and $y$), and the index of $T//P$ is some natural number $n$, then the index of $T//Q$ is some natural number $m$ such that $m \leq n$.

For this lemma to be constructive, a precondition requiring $S$ to be a decidable relation needs to be added.

Proving this lemma is tedious; it involves giving the explicit construction of a bijection between $\{0 \ldots m-1\}$ and $T//S$ given a bijection between $\{0 \ldots n-1\}$ and $T//R$. It turns out to be simpler to prove a lemma of form:

**Quotient Index Lemma 2**. If $Q$ is a decidable binary relation over a type $T$, and the index of $T$ is some natural number $n$, then the index of $T//Q$ is some natural number $m$ such that $m \leq n$.

We instantiate the $T$ of this lemma with the type *Alph list*//$R$ and the $Q$ of this lemma with a binary relation $R'(g)$ which is similar to $R(L)$ in definition, but is defined over *Alph list*//$R$ rather than *Alph list*. The precondition that *Alph list*//$R$ is of finite index follows by assumption, and we get the result that (*Alph list*//$R$)// $R'(g)$ is of finite index.

That $Alph\ list//\ R(L)$ is of finite index trivially follows when we use the result that there is a one-one correspondence between $(Alph\ list//R)//\ R'(g)$ and $Alph\ list//\ R(L)$.

A remaining precondition of Quotient Index Lemma 2 is to show that $R'(g)$, or equivalently $R(L)$, is a decidable relation. This is not immediately obvious: Since $x\ R(L)\ y$ iff $z@x\ R\ z@y$ for every $z$, it seems that we have to try an infinite number of $z$ to compute if $x\ R(L)\ y$ true. (Note that we can test if $z@x\ R\ z@y$ since $R$ is decidable.) Again, the pumping lemma is of help; it shows that it is sufficient to only consider every $z$ of length up to the number of states of our automata $M$ which accepts $L$. Since $Alph$ is finite, there are only a finite number of $z$ to try. **Qed**

### 5.4 Formalizing (3) ⇒ (1)

The formal statement of the theorem is:

$$\vdash \forall Alph : \mathbb{U}.\ \forall L : Language(Alph)$$

$$Fin(Alph)$$

$$\Rightarrow (Fin(Alph\ list//\ R(L)) \wedge \forall l : Alph\ list.\ Dec(L\ l))$$

$$\Rightarrow \exists St : \mathbb{U}. \exists Auto : Automata(Alph;\ St).\ Fin(St) \wedge L = L(Auto).$$

In English,

- Let the alphabet *Alph* be a finite type, and let $L$ be a language over *Alph*,
- assume the relation $R(L)$ induced by $L$ is of finite index,
- assume membership of $L$ is decidable,
- then there is a finite type of states *St*, and an automaton *Auto* over *Alph* and *St* that accepts $L$.

*Proof* Checking $R(L)$ is extension invariant is straightforward.

For the type of states *St* we take the quotient type $Alph\ list//\ R(L)$ instead of the set of equivalence classes of $R(L)$. Whereas Hopcroft and Ullman define the action of the automaton in terms of equivalence classes, writing $\delta([x], a) = [a.x]$, here we use a function that works on representatives of equivalence classes. Specifically, given an element $x$ of *Alph list* and an element $a$ of *Alph*, we define $\delta(Auto)\ x\ a$ to be the list $a.x$.

For the start state $I(Auto)$, we use the empty list *nil*, and for $F(Auto)$ we use a boolean-valued version of the characteristic function $L$ (remember that we represent languages using characteristic functions rather than subtypes). A boolean-valued version of $L$ exists because we have as an assumption that $L$ is decidable.

In type-checking each of these components of *Auto*, we check that the definition of *Auto* is consistent. For example, we check that $\delta(Auto)$ has type $Alph\ list//\ R(L) \rightarrow Alph \rightarrow Alph\ list//\ R(L)$. In checking this, we show that if $x\ R(L)\ y$, then $(\delta(Auto)\ x\ a)\ R(L)\ (\delta(Auto)\ y\ a)$. That is, $\delta(Auto)$ maps possibly-different representatives of some equivalence class of $R(L)$ to representatives of the same equivalence class of $R(L)$. **Qed**

## 6 State Minimization

We discuss in this section a corollary to the Myhill-Nerode theorem that explicitly states the existence and uniqueness of a minimum finite automaton for any language accepted by some finite automaton.

### 6.1 Textbook Proof

The presentation here is taken almost verbatim from [15, p29]. The main change is to adopt the notation for strings used in the Nuprl development.

THEOREM 3.2 The minimum state automaton accepting $L$ is unique up to an isomorphism (i.e., a renaming of the states) and is given by $M'$ of Theorem 3.1.

*Proof* In the proof of Theorem 3.1 we saw that any $M = (K, Alph, \delta, q_0, F)$ accepting $L$ defines an equivalence relation which is a refinement of $R(L)$. Thus the number of states of $M$ is greater than or equal to the number of states of $M'$ of Theorem 3.1. If equality holds, then each of the states of $M$ can be identified with one of the states of $M'$. That is, let $q$ be a state of $M$. There must be some $x$ in *Alph list*, such that $\delta(q_0, x) = q$, otherwise $q$ could be removed from $K$, and a smaller automaton found. Identify $q$ with the state $\delta'(q_0', x)$ of $M'$. This identification will be consistent. If $\delta(q_0, x) = \delta(q_0, y) = q$, then, by Theorem 3.1, $x$ and $y$ are in the same equivalence class of $R$. Thus $\delta'(q_0', x) = \delta'(q_0', y)$. **Qed**

### 6.2 Formalization of Minimization Theorem

First we make a few definitions. As earlier, let *Alph* be an alphabet, *St* be a type for states, and *Auto* be some automaton over *Alph* and *St*.

The type of states *MinSt(Auto)* of the minimum automaton for the language accepted by *Auto* is

$$MinSt(Auto) == Alph\ list//R(L(Auto))$$

and the minimum automaton itself is

$$MinAuto(Auto) == \langle(\lambda s, a.(a.s)), nil, L_b(Auto)\rangle.$$

We show that *MinAuto(Auto)* has type *Automata(Alph; MinSt(Auto))*. These definitions make explicit the constructions implicit in our proof of the Myhill-Nerode theorem.

With the help of various auxiliary lemmas from the Myhill-Nerode development, we prove such theorems as that *MinSt(Auto)* is a finite type and *MinAuto(Auto)* accepts the same language as *Auto*.

We split our statement and proof of the minimization theorem into two parts. It is important to note here that the definitions of *MinSt(Auto)* and *MinAuto(Auto)* depend only on the language accepted by *Auto*, not on any particular structure of *Auto*. Without this observation, the two main statements will not be seen to claim what we intend them to claim. The two statements are

1. The statement that the minimum automaton really has the smallest number of states of any automata accepting the same language is

$$\vdash \forall\, Alph : \mathbb{U}.\ Fin(Alph) \Rightarrow$$
$$\forall\, St : \mathbb{U}.\ Fin(St) \Rightarrow$$
$$\forall\, Auto : Automata(Alph,\ St).$$
$$|St| \geq |MinSt(Auto)|.$$

Here we use the definition

$$|S| \geq |T| == \exists f : S \rightarrow T.\, Surj(S;\, T;\, f),$$

that is, a type $S$ is at least as large as a type $T$ if there exists a surjective function from $S$ to $T$. When $S$ is non-empty and $T$ is empty, this predicate is false, whereas one would ideally want it to be true. We don't need to be concerned with this pathological case since types of states always include initial states.

*Proof* Most of the argument here is already gone over in the Myhill-Nerode proof. In a few cases we have to prove some new intermediate lemmas that make various facts more explicit. **Qed**

2. Our statement that the minimum automata is isomorphic to any other is

$$\vdash \forall\, Alph : \mathbb{U}.\ Fin(Alph) \Rightarrow$$
$$\forall\, St : \mathbb{U}.\ Fin(St) \Rightarrow$$
$$\forall\, Auto : Automata(Alph,\ St)$$
$$1\text{-}1\text{-}Corresp(St;\ MinSt(Auto)) \Rightarrow$$
$$Auto \equiv MinAuto(Auto).$$

Here we use the definition

$$
\begin{aligned}
&A1 \equiv A2 == \\
&\quad \exists f : S1 \to S2. \\
&\quad Bij(S1;\ S2;\ f) \\
&\quad \wedge (\forall s : S1. \forall a : Alph.\ f(\delta(A1)\ s\ a) = \delta(A2)(f\ s)a) \\
&\quad \wedge f I(A1) = I(A2) \\
&\quad \wedge (\forall s : S1.\ F(A1)s = F(A2)(f\ s)
\end{aligned}
$$

to say that automata $A1$ and $A2$ are isomorphic. This definition follows the pattern of definitions of isomorphisms for algebraic structures. Hopcroft and Ullman omit the definition entirely, no doubt on the grounds that it is the obvious one to use. $Bij(S1;\ S2;\ f)$ is the proposition that function $f$ from type $S1$ to type $S2$ is a bijection. The definition of $\equiv$ takes $S1$, $S2$, and *Alph* as parameters, but the display of these is suppressed because they can easily be inferred from consideration of the types of $A1$ and $A2$.

*Proof* As with the Hopcroft and Ullman proof, we argue that we can assume without loss of generality that *Auto* is connected. We then use our analogue of their construction of the identification function $f$ for the isomorphism. Hopcroft and Ullman state without proof that this identification is consistent. We need ourselves to fill in the tedious but routine steps of proof showing that the identification function has all the properties that make it an isomorphism. **Qed**

## 7 Discussion

### 7.1 Structuring the Definition of Automata

Our parameterization of the type of automata by both an alphabet and a type of states is inelegant (See Section 4.1). Parameterization by an alphabet has its merits, but it is clear that the type of states ought to be paired with the transition function, the initial state, and the set of final states. Constructively, a full specification of an automata also requires evidence that the state type is finite.

One solution is to have automata over a finite alphabet be tuples of form

$$\langle Fin\ St, \delta, I, F \rangle$$

where $\delta$, $I$, and $F$ are as before, and *Fin St* is an element of a type of "finite types," of four-tuples of form $\langle T, n, f, g \rangle$, where $T$ is a type, $n$ is the size of $T$, and $f$ and $g$ define an isomorphism between $T$ and $\mathbb{N}n$.

A similar solution involves writing the type of finite types as

$T : \mathbb{U} \times Fin(T).$

(This is the notation for Nuprl's dependent product type, sometimes called a $\Sigma$ type.) From the point of view of classical mathematics this is ill formed, a proposition $Fin(T)$ is being used in a position where a type is expected. However, in constructive type theory, this is well formed because propositions *are* types. Elements of $Fin(T)$ are tuples of form $\langle n, f, g, *\rangle$, and elements of $T : \mathbb{U} \times Fin(T)$ are tuples of form $\langle T, \langle n, f, g, *\rangle\rangle$.

The $*$ here is a term witnessing the proposition that $f$ and $g$ form an isomorphism. Such witnesses can form significant clutter, and there are standard techniques, for example using subset types, to define propositions carefully so that they have minimal or no such witnesses.

We avoided taking this approach, using $Fin(T)$ as a type, partly because of a wish to keep a straightforward classical reading. Perhaps though this is not important when so many of our concerns are with constructivity.

### 7.2 Use of Quotient Types

Due to the richness of Nuprl's type theory, type-checking is undecidable. In practice, heuristics help carry out most simpler type checking tasks completely automatically. However, Nuprl's quotient types introduce a new dimension of variability into the problem. Frequently we use a function with domain type $T$ where a function with domain type $T//E$ is expected, and we then repeatedly get proof obligations to show that the function respects $E$.

We realize that we need to introduce a discipline for use of quotient types, where, as much as possible, such problems are localized to the right-hand-side of definitions that are type-checked just once, and then always exploited in proofs with the help of characterizing lemmas, rather than definition expansion. We now have several similar proposals for such a discipline, but didn't have the time to try one in this formalization. One key aspect of these proposals is that injections into quotient types are always explicitly tagged. This helps both the type checker in its type-inference, and the reader in understanding what terms in Nuprl's computation language are denoting.

For example, if $x$ is of type $T$ and $E$ is an equivalence relation over $T$, we might have the injection of $x$ into $T//E$ written as $[x]\{T//E\}$. For projections out of quotient types, we might have a projection operator written $qproj\,\{T//E\}(f)$ that takes a function $f$ of type $T \to S$, and turns it into a function of type $T//E \to S$. The type checking conditions for *qproj* would include the requirement that $f$ be shown to respect $E$.

Using these injection and projection operators does not free us from checking that equivalence relations are respected, but it does make the location of those checks more predictable. Analogous operators are required when quotient types are implemented in strongly-typed type theories such as ECC [14], and when working with quotient structures in set theory.

### 7.3 Inadequacies in Construction of the Minimum Automaton

A hard-to-understand definition in this formalization is that of the *MinAuto* function (see Section 6.2).There, the intended meaning of the state transition function mapping equivalence classes to equivalence classes is only apparent when we look at the type the function is supposed to have. If we write the transition function definition as

$$qproj\{MinSt(Auto)\}(\lambda x : Alph\ list.\ \lambda a : Alph.\ [a.x]\{MinSt(Auto)\}),$$

instead of

$$\lambda x,\ a.\ (a.x),$$

its meaning is more immediately evident. Here we have used the quotient type injection and projection operators described in Section 7.2 as well as type annotations on the lambda terms, again to help both readability and typechecking.

Another perhaps more serious defect of our construction of *MinAuto*(*Auto*) is that it is computationally trivial. If we imagine applying *MinAuto*(*Auto*) to some input string, then it does nothing more than copy that string, and pass it to *Auto* to check if it should be accepted.

Creating a minimization function that actually does the work of computing a minimum automaton is not difficult, though we have not carried this out yet. We need to define a type of automata, *MinAuto′* say, in which automata are represented by finite data structures (integers, pairs, and lists, for example), not functions. The key is to exploit the function we can synthesize from the proof of *Fin*(*MinAuto*(*Auto*)). Given *Auto* as argument, this function can compute the size $n$ of the minimum automaton accepting the language *Auto* accepts and can provide mapping functions between *MinSt*(*Auto*) and $\mathbb{N}n$. Using these mapping functions, we can construct a function that, when evaluated on argument *MinAuto*(*Auto*), returns the finite data structures for a minimum automaton that accepts the same language as *Auto*.

### 7.4 Computational Complexity of Synthesized Algorithms

With the proofs as we initially completed them, the time complexity of several extracted functions, including the size function described in Section 7.3, was exponential in the number of states. Aleksey Nogin at Cornell has recently reworked some of the proofs and introduced alternate auxiliary functions to reduce the complexity of the size function to a low-order polynomial. His work is viewable at the Nuprl web site (see Section 1.5). Following the approach described in Section 7.3, we should be able to extend Nogin's work so that we can synthesize an automata minimization function of low polynomial time complexity.

## 8 Summary of Results

• We were successful in formalizing the Myhill-Nerode theorem in constructive type theory.

• We did not find errors in the statement or proof of the theorem in Hopcroft and Ullman. We did note Hopcroft and Ullman's elision of more-routine definitions and proofs. For example, they employ but do not define an isomorphism relation on automata, and they claim but do not prove that a mapping between the sets of states of two automata is an automata isomorphism.

• To make the Myhill-Nerode theorem constructively provable, we needed to add conditions on the decidability of language membership to two of the three equivalent propositions in its statement.

Constructivity considerations when reasoning about finiteness forced us to consider how various automata properties can be computed. For example, by a combination of explicit introduction, and synthesis from appropriate constructive proofs, we introduced functions for

- determining whether a state of an automaton is accessible, and, if so, what input string would put the automaton in that state,
- testing whether two states are equivalent.

Such functions can form the core of a function for carrying out the minimization procedure. Initially they had time complexity exponential in the number of states, but, in ongoing work, we have introduced alternate functions with low-order polynomial complexity.

## 9 Conclusions and Future Work

With this article and the accompanying online material, we have a presentation of a piece of mathematics that is completely precise and that can be viewed at differing levels of detail. We have argued that such presentations are superior to textbook only presentations, and we believe that we have begun to demonstrate this.

At Cornell we are currently experimenting with other examples of such formally-grounded explanations. We have already formalized other parts of Hopcroft and Ullman, including account of grammars and of nondeterministic automata. We judge that it would be possible to formalize Chapters 1–9 with our four person team in about eighteen months.

The collaboration methods we have learned would extend to larger teams. It would be especially interesting to collaborate with other theorem proving systems as Howe and his colleagues are doing with HOL and Nuprl [19, 18]. Much of a classical treatment of languages can easily be re-interpreted constructively. It would be especially fruitful to collaborate with teams using other constructive provers such as Alf, Coq, Lego, or Isabelle with its Martin-Löf-type-theory object logic. Although these provers are based on different formalizations of constructive mathematics, they all share the critical properties that computational notions can be expressed and that programs can be synthesized from proofs.

One weak point of our online presentation is the readability of proofs. We see no reason why online formal proofs should not be at least as clear as any informal proofs. Unlike many other provers, Nuprl maintains a proof tree datastructure that already assists us in generating comprehensible presentations of proofs. Ideas we are currently exploring to improve readability include the grouping of lower level tactic sequences under user supplied comments and the suppression of less-important proof branches. We are also following the work of the Centaur group to make proofs more readable [3, 29], and we expect to use the modularity feature of the Nuprl-Light refiner [13] to help us better structure theories.

## 10 Acknowledgments

We acknowledge the support granted by the National Science Foundation and the Office of Naval Research. We also thank Stuart Allen and Karl Crary for the discussions and input concerning this topic, Karla Consroe for help in preparing the document, and Aleksey Nogin for his work improving the efficiency of many critical proofs.

## A Index for Notation

The numbers on the right refer to pages where the notation is first introduced.

| | | |
|---|---|---|
| *nil* | empty list | 217 |
| *null*($l$) | function testing if list $l$ is empty | 217 |
| *1-1-Corresp*($S$; $T$) | 1-1 correspondence between types $S$ and $T$ | 219 |
| $R'(g)$ | like $R(L)$ but typing involves quotient type | 228 |
| $R(L)$ | relation induced by language $L$ | 224 |
| *tl*($l$) | tail of list $l$ | 217 |
| *tt* | boolean true | 217 |

## References

[1] Stuart F. Allen. A Non-type-theoretic Definition of Martin-Löf's Types. In *Proc. of Second Symp. on Logic in Comp. Sci.*, pages 215–224. IEEE, June 1987.

[2] E. Bishop. *Foundations of Constructive Analysis*. McGraw Hill, NY, 1967.

[3] P. Borras, D. Clément, T. Despeyroux, J. Incerpi, G. Kahn, B. Lang, and V. Pascual. Centaur: the system. In *Software Engineering Notes*, volume 13(5). Third Symposium on Software Development Environments, 1988.

[4] N. Bourbaki. *Elements of Mathematics, Theory of Sets*. Addison-Wesley, Reading, MA, 1968.

[5] Robert L. Constable. Experience using type theory as a foundation for computer science. In *Proceedings of the Tenth Annual IEEE Symposium on Logic in Computer Science*, pages 266–279. LICS, June 1995.

[6] Robert L. Constable, Stuart F. Allen, H. M. Bromley, W. R. Cleaveland, J. F. Cremer, R. W. Harper, Douglas J. Howe, T. B. Knoblock, N. P. Mendler, P. Panangaden, James T. Sasaki, and Scott F. Smith. *Implementing Mathematics with the Nuprl Development System*. Prentice-Hall, NJ, 1986.

[7] Thierry Coquand and G. Huet. The Calculus of Constructions. *Information and Computation*, 76:95–120, 1988.

[8] P. J. Denning, J. B. Dennis, and J. E. Qualitz. *Machines, Languages, and Computation*. Prentice-Hall, 1978.

[9] Max B. Forester. Formalizing constructive real analysis. Technical Report TR93-1382, Computer Science Dept., Cornell University, Ithaca, NY, 1993.

[10] J-Y. Girard, P. Taylor, and Y. Lafont. *Proofs and Types*. Cambridge Tracts in Computer Science, Vol. 7. Cambridge University Press, 1989.

[11] Michael Gordon and Tom Melham. *Introduction to HOL: a theorem proving environment for higher-order logic*. Cambridge University Press, 1993.

[12] Michael Gordon, Robin Milner, and Christopher Wadsworth. *Edinburgh LCF: a mechanized logic of computation,* Lecture Notes in Computer Science, Vol. 78. Springer-Verlag, NY, 1979.

[13] Jason J. Hickey. Nuprl-light: An implementation framework for higher-order logics. In *14th International Conference on Automated Deduction*, 1997.

[14] Martin Hofmann. *Extensional concepts in intensional type theory*. PhD thesis, University of Edinburgh, Laboratory for Foundations of Computer Science, 1994.

[15] John E. Hopcroft and Jeffrey D. Ullman. *Formal Languages and Their Relation to Automata*. Addison-Wesley, Reading, Massachusetts, 1969.

[16] John E. Hopcroft and Jeffrey D. Ullman. *Introduction to Automata Theory, Languages, and Computation*. Addison-Wesley, Reading, Massachusetts, 1979.

[17] Douglas J. Howe. Implementing number theory: An experiment with Nuprl. In *8th International Conference on Automated Deduction*, volume 230 of *Lecture Notes in Computer Science*, pages 404–415. Springer-Verlag, July 1987.

[18] Douglas J. Howe. Importing mathematics from HOL into Nuprl. In J. von Wright, J. Grundy, and J. Harrison, editors, *Theorem Proving in Higher Order Logics*, volume 1125, of *LNCS*, pages 267–282. Springer-Verlag, Berlin, 1996.

[19] Douglas J. Howe. Semantic foundations for embedding HOL in Nuprl. In Martin Wirsing and Maurice Nivat, editors, *Algebraic Methodology and Software Technology*, volume 1101 of *LNCS*, pages 85–101. Springer-Verlag, Berlin, 1996.

[20] Paul B. Jackson. *Enhancing the Nuprl Proof Development System and Applying it to Computational Abstract Algebra*. PhD thesis, Cornell University, Ithaca, NY, January 1995.

[21] Miroslava Kaloper and Piotr Rudnicki. FSM_1: Minimization of finite state machines. *Journal of Formalized Mathematics*, 6, 1994. Electronically accessible from
`http://www.mizar.org/JFM/` or
`http://www.cs.ualberta.ca/~piotr/Mizar/mirror/htdocs/JFM/`.

[22] C. Kreitz. Constructive automata theory implemented with the Nuprl proof development system. Technical Report 86-779, Cornell University, Ithaca, New York, September 1986.

[23] Per Martin-Löf. Constructive mathematics and computer programming. In *Sixth International Congress for Logic, Methodology, and Philosophy of Science*, pages 153–75. North-Holland, Amsterdam, 1982.

[24] Per Martin-Löf. *Intuitionistic Type Theory, Studies in Proof Theory, Lecture Notes*. Bibliopolis, Napoli, 1984.

[25] B. Nordstrom, K. Petersson, and J. Smith. *Programming in Martin-Löf's Type Theory*. Oxford Sciences Publication, Oxford, 1990.

[26] L. C. Paulson. *Isabelle: A Generic Theorem Prover*, volume 828 of *Lecture Notes in Computer Science*. Springer-Verlag, 1994.

[27] Robert Pollack. *The Theory of LEGO: A Proof Checker for the Extended Calculus of Constructions*. PhD thesis, University of Edinburgh, Dept. of Computer Science, JCMaxwell Bldg, Mayfield Rd, Edinburgh EH9 3JZ, April 1995.

[28] N. Shankar. Rabin-Scott automata equivalence/flaw in Hopcroft-Ullman proof. Posting to PVS mail-list on 3 December 1995. Posting archived at
`http://www.csl.sri.com/pvs/mail-archive/pvslist95.txt.gz`.

[29] L. Théry, Y. Bertot, and G. Kahn. Real theorem provers deserve real user-interfaces. In *Software Engineering Notes*, volume 17(5), pages 120–129. 5th Symposium on Software Development Environments, 1992.

[30] S. Thompson. *Type Theory and Functional Programming*. Addison-Wesley, 1991.

[31] Debora Weber-Wulff. *Contributions to Mechanical Proofs of Correctness for Compiler Front-Ends*. PhD thesis, Institut für Informatik und Praktische Mathematik der Christian-Albrechts-Universität zu Kiel, April 1997.

# 9 Constructive Category Theory

**Gérard Huet and Amokrane Saïbi**

## 1 Introduction

These notes are part of a preliminary attempt at developing abstract algebra in constructive type theory. The developments that follow are inspired from a previous axiomatization by P. Aczel in LEGO in Jan. 1993, as an initial step to a program of formal development of Galois Theory[1]. Our version of type theory is the Calculus of Inductive Constructions, as implemented in Coq V6.1[4]. This paper gives the full transcript of the Coq axiomatization.

In this note we develop one possible axiomatization of the notion of category by modeling objects as types and Hom-sets as Hom-setoids of arrows parameterized by their domain and codomain types. Thus we may quotient arrows, but not objects. We develop in this setting functors, as functions on objects, and extentional maps on arrows. We show that CAT is a category, and we do not need to distinguish to this effect "small" and "big" categories. We rather have implicitly categories as relatively small structures indexed by a universe. Thus we just need two instances of the same notion of category in order to define CAT.

We then construct the Functor Category, with the natural definition of natural transformations. We then show the Interchange Law, which exhibits the 2-categorical structure of the Functor Category. We end this paper by giving a corollary to Yoneda's lemma.

This incursion in Constructive Category Theory shows that Type Theory is adequate to represent faithfully categorical reasoning. Three ingredients are essential: $\Sigma$-types, to represents structures, dependent types, so that arrows are indexed with their domains and codomains, and a hierarchy of universes, in order to escape the foundational difficulties. Some amount of type reconstruction is necessary, in order to write equations between arrows without having to indicate their type other than at their binder, and notational abbreviations, allowing, e.g., infix notation, are necessary to offer the formal mathematician a language close to the ordinary informal categorical notation.

## 2 Relations

We assume a number of basic constructions, which define quantifiers and equality at the level of sort `Type`. These definitions are included in the prelude module `Logic_Type` of the Coq system.

This research was partially supported by ESPRIT Basic Research Action "TYPES."

We start with a few standard definitions pertaining to binary relations.

```
Section Orderings.

Variable U : Type.

Definition Relation :=  U -> U -> Prop.

Variable R : Relation.

Definition Reflexive :=  (x: U) (R x x).

Definition Transitive :=  (x,y,z: U) (R x y) -> (R y z)
                          -> (R x z).

Definition Symmetric :=  (x,y: U) (R x y) -> (R y x).

Structure Partial_equivalence : Prop :=
  {Prf_trans  : Transitive;
   Prf_sym    : Symmetric}.

Structure Equivalence : Prop :=
  {Prf_refl    :  Reflexive;
   Prf_pequiv :> Partial_equivalence}.

End Orderings.
```

The notations used should be familiar to the reader, once he gets used to the fact that universal quantification is denoted by parenthesised typing judgments, like `(x:T)(P x)`, standing for $\forall x : T \cdot P(x)$. Similarly, functional abstraction is denoted by square brackets, like `[x:T](f x)`, standing for $\lambda x : T \cdot f(x)$.

The "Section" mechanism of Coq allows to parameterize the notions defined in the body of the section by the variables and axioms on which they depend. In our case, all the notions defined inside section `Orderings` are parameterized by parameters `U` and `R`. Thus, for instance, the definition of `Reflexive` becomes, upon closing of this section:

```
Definition Reflexive := [U:Type][R:(Relation U)](x: U)
                        (R x x).
```

We now describe new syntactic facilities we used in the definitions above.

• To every declared object is associated the list of the positions of its *implicit arguments* [14]. These implicit arguments correspond to the arguments which can be deduced from the following ones. For instance the first argument `U` of `Reflexive` is implicit since it can be deduced from the type of `R:(Relation U)`. Thus when one applies these functions to arguments, one should omit the implicit ones. They are then automatically replaced by symbols "?" to be synthesized from the context. This way we use type synthesis to elide information which is implicit from the context. Thus it is sufficient to write `(Reflexive R)`.

The mechanism of synthesis of implicit arguments is not complete, so we have sometimes to give explicitly certain implicit arguments of an application. The syntax is *i*`!t` where *i* is the position of an implicit argument and `t` is its corresponding explicit term. We can also give all the arguments of an application, we have then to write `(!c t1...tn)`. For instance, we could write in a more explicit fashion `(Reflexive 1!U R)` or equivalently `(!Reflexive U R)`.

• Remark that in Coq $\Sigma$-types (records) are not primitive, but are built as inductive types with one constructor. The macro `Structure` constructs the corresponding inductive type and defines the projection functions for destructuring a `Partial_equivalence` into its constituent fields. It defines also a constructor `Build_Partial_equivalence` to build an object of type `Partial_equivalence` from its constituents. One can choose a different name for the constructor by putting the desired name before the opening brace of the Structure defining expression. Such specialized macros are user-definable in the same way as tactics.

• The symbol `:>` in the definition of `Equivalence`, declares the constant `Prf_pequiv` as an *implicit coercion* [15] between the *classes* `Equivalence` and `Partial_equivalence`. The declared coercions are composed to build new coercions. Appropriate coercions are automatically inserted into ill-typed terms to make them well-typed. For instance, the term `(f e)` where `f:Partial_equivalence -> nat` and `e:Equivalence`, is transformed into `(f (Prf_pequiv e))`. Coercions are not always record projections, they may be any function with an appropriate type; they are then declared using the dedicated command `Coercion`. Remark also that coercions may have parameters, like the coercion `Prf_pequiv` after the end of the section.

```
Prf_pequiv : (U:Type)(R:(Relation U))(Equivalence R)
             -> (Partial_equivalence R)
```

## 3 Setoid

We now move to the development of "Setoids." Setoids are triples composed of a Type S, a relation R over S, and a proof that R is an equivalence relation over S. Thus a Setoid is a set considered as the quotient of a Type by a congruence. Setoids were first investigated by M. Hofmann in the framework of Martin-Löf's type theory [8]. This terminology is due to R. Burstall.

### 3.1 The Setoid Structure

```
Structure Setoid : Type :=
 {Carrier   :> Type;
  Equal     :  (Relation Carrier);
  Prf_equiv :> (Equivalence Equal)}.
```

```
Coercion Build_Setoid : Equivalence >-> Setoid.
```

The constant `Carrier` is a coercion from `Setoid` to the abstract class `SORTCLASS`, the class of sorts (`Type` and `Prop`). These coercions are used in the situations where sorts are expected, like in λ-abstractions and dependent types.

To have a more pleasing notation, we first introduce a concrete syntax declaration allowing to parse `(Carrier A)` as `|A|`:

```
Grammar command command1 := [ "|" command0($s) "|"]
                            -> [$0 = <<(Carrier $s)>>].
```

Such a `Grammar` declaration may be read as follows. A grammar production for the `command` language consists of two parts. The first part represents a production which is added to the corresponding non-terminal entry; here `command1`, receives the new production `"|" command0($s) "|."` The second part is the semantic action which builds the corresponding abstract syntax tree when firing this production; here we indicate that we build an application of the constant `Carrier` to the result of parsing with entry `command0` what is enclosed in the vertical bars. The various entries `commandn` stratify the commands according to priority levels.

Given a Setoid `A`, `(Equal A)` is its associated relation. We give it the infix notation `=%S` with the precedence 2, the parameter `A` being synthesised by type-checking.

```
Infix 2 "=%S" Equal.
```

Note that `=%S` is a generic Setoid equality, since the type of its elements may in general be inferred from the context.

The last extracted field is the proof that the equality of a Setoid is an equivalence relation.

### 3.2 An Example

As example of the preceding notions, let us define the Setoid of natural numbers. The type of its elements can be directly inductively defined.

```
Inductive Nat : Type := Z : Nat | Suc : Nat -> Nat.

Definition Eq_Nat := [N1,N2:Nat] N1==N2.
```

The == symbol which appears in the body of the definition of `Eq_Nat`, is the standard polymorphic Leibniz equality defined in the `Logic_Type` module. In our case, it is instantiated over the Type `Nat`, inferred from the type of `N1`.

Right after this, we give the equivalence proof of `Eq_Nat` and build the setoid of natural numbers. We get this proof easily with the help of Coq's proof engine, driven by tactics. Here as in the rest of the document, we do not give the proof scripts, just the statements of lemmas.

```
Lemma Eq_Nat_equiv : (Equivalence Eq_Nat).

Definition Set_of_nat : Setoid := Eq_Nat_equiv.
```

In the last definition, we imposed the type of the constant. Since its inferred type (i.e., `(Equivalence Eq_Nat)`) is different from the declared one (i.e., `Setoid`), the system inserts an implicit coercion `Build_Setoid`.

### 3.3 Alternative: Partial Setoids

Alternatively, we could build Partial Setoids, where the equality equivalence is replaced by a weaker partial equivalence relation of coherence; total elements are defined as being coherent with themselves:

```
Structure PSetoid : Type :=
 {PCarrier :> Type;
  Coherence :  (Relation PCarrier);
  Prf_PER   :> (Partial_equivalence Coherence)}.

Coercion Build_PSetoid : Partial_equivalence >-> PSetoid.

Definition Total := [A:PSetoid][x:A](Coherence x x).
```

### 3.4 The Setoid of Maps between Two Setoids

We now define a Map between Setoid `A` and Setoid `B` as a function from `|A|` to `|B|` which respects equality. Thanks to implicit coercions, we can write `A->B` instead of `|A|->|B|`. Remark also the use of generic equality in `Map_law` below.

```
Section maps.

Variables A, B : Setoid.

Definition Map_law := [f:A->B]
    (x,y:A) x =%S y -> (f x) =%S (f y).

Structure Map : Type := Build_Map
 {Ap   :> A->B;
  Pres :> (Map_law Ap)}.

Coercion Build_Map : Map_law >-> Map.
```

A Map `m` over `A` and `B` is thus similar to a pair, packing a function `(Ap m)` (of type `|A|->|B|`) with the proof `(Pres m)` that this function respects equality. The constant `Ap` is also a coercion from `Map` to `FUNCLASS`, the class of functions. It allows us to write `(f x)` where `f:Map` instead of `(Ap f x)`.

Two Maps `f` and `g` are defined to be equal iff they are extensionaly equal, i.e., $\forall x \cdot f(x) = g(x)$:

```
Definition Ext := [f,g:Map](x:A) (f x) =%S (g x).

Lemma Ext_equiv : (Equivalence Ext).

Definition Map_setoid : Setoid := Ext_equiv.

End maps.
```

We write `f =%M g` for $f = g$.

```
Infix 2 "=%M" Ext.
Infix Assoc 6 "==>" Map_setoid.
```

This last command allows us to write A==>B, with appropriate precedence level, for the Setoid of Maps between Setoids A and B. It associates to the right.

A (curried) binary application Map2 between Setoids A, B and C is then simply a Map between A and B==>C. We prove that a binary function verifying the congruence laws for both arguments is equivalent to a binary application.

```
Section fun2_to_map2.

Variable A, B, C : Setoid.

Definition Map2 := (Map A (B ==> C)).

Variable f : A -> B -> C.

Definition Map2_congl_law := (b1,b2:B)(a:A)
                             (b1 =%S b2) -> (f a b1)
                             =%S  (f a b2).

Definition Map2_congr_law := (a1,a2:A)(b:B)
                             (a1 =%S a2) -> (f a1 b)
                             = %S (f a2 b).

Definition Map2_cong_law := (a1,a2:A)(b1,b2:B)
                            (a1 =%S a2) -> (b1 =%S b2)
                            ->  (f a1 b1) =%S (f a2 b2).

Hypothesis pgcl : Map2_congl_law.
Hypothesis pgcr : Map2_congr_law.

Lemma Map2_map_law1 : (a:A)(Map_law (f a)).

Definition Map2_map1 : A -> (B==>C)
                     := [a:A] (Map2_map_law1 a).

Lemma Map2_map_law2 : (Map_law Map2_map1).

Definition Build_Map2 : Map2 := (Build_Map Map2_map_law2).
```

```
End fun2_to_map2.
Section prop_map2.

Variable A, B, C : Setoid.
Variable f       : (Map2 A B C).

Definition Ap2 := [a:A][b:B] ((f a) b).

Lemma Prf_map2_congl : (Map2_congl_law Ap2).

Lemma Prf_map2_congr : (Map2_congr_law Ap2).

Lemma Prf_map2_cong : (Map2_cong_law Ap2).

End prop_map2.

Coercion Ap2 : Map2 >-> FUNCLASS.

Identity Coercion Map2_Map : Map2 >-> Map.
```

We end this section by defining a generic Ap2, denoting the application function associated with a (curried) binary application, useful for what follows. The Identity Coercion builds an identity function between the specified classes and declares it as a coercion.

## 4 Categories

### 4.1 The Category Structure

We now axiomatise a category as consisting of a Type of Objects and a family of Hom Setoids indexed by their domain and codomain types. We write Hom as infix -->.

```
Section cat.

Variable Ob  : Type.
Variable Hom : Ob -> Ob -> Setoid.

Infix 6 "-->" Hom.
```

The next component of a category is a composition operator, which for any Objects `a,b,c,` belongs to `(a --> b) ==> ((b --> c) ==> (a --> c))`. We write this operator (parameters `a,b,c,` being implicit by type synthesis) as infix `o`.

```
Variable Op_comp : (a,b,c:Ob)(Map2 a-->b b-->c a-->c).

Definition Cat_comp := [a,b,c:Ob][f:a --> b][g:b --> c]
                       ((Op_comp a b c) f g).

Infix Assoc 6 "o" Cat_comp.
```

Composition is assumed to be associative:

```
Definition Assoc_law := (a,b,c,d:Ob)(f:a --> b)(g:b --> c)
                        (h:c --> d)
                        (f o (g o h)) =%S ((f o g) o h).
```

The final component of a category is, for every object `a`, an arrow in `a --> a` which is an identity for composition:

```
Variable Id : (a:Ob) a-->a.

Definition Idl_law := (a,b:Ob)(f:a --> b)
                      ((Id ?) o f) =%S f.

Definition Idr_law := (a,b:Ob)(f:b --> a) f =%S
                      (f o (Id ?)).

End cat.
```

We are now able to define synthetically a Category:

```
Structure Category : Type :=
 {Ob      :> Type;
  Hom     :  Ob -> Ob -> Setoid;
  Op_comp :  (a,b,c:Ob)(Map2 (Hom a b) (Hom b c) (Hom a c));
  Id      :  (a:Ob)(Hom a a);
  Prf_ass :  (Assoc_law Op_comp);
  Prf_idl :  (Idl_law Op_comp Id);
  Prf_idr :  (Idr_law Op_comp Id)}.
```

We successively define the projections which extract the various components of a category.

```
Definition Comp := [C:Category](Cat_comp (!Op_comp C)).

Infix 6 "-->" Hom.
Infix Assoc 6 "o" Comp.
```

Remark that we now use the infix notation o in the context of a local Category parameter C. It must be noticed that Infix notations inside Sections disappear when their section is closed. Thus the new rule giving syntax for Comp does not conflict with the previous one giving syntax for Cat_comp.

Actually, a composition operator is nothing else than a binary function verifying the congruence laws for both arguments. Thus we provide a general method allowing the construction of a composition operator from such a function. We shall use systematically this tool in the following, for every category definition.

```
Section composition_to_operator.

Variable A    : Type.
Variable H    : A -> A -> Setoid.
Variable Cfun : (a,b,c:A)(H a b) -> (H b c) -> (H a c).

Definition Congl_law := (a,b,c:A)(f,g:(H b c))(h:(H a b))
           f =%S g -> (Cfun h f) =%S (Cfun h g).

Definition Congr_law := (a,b,c:A)(f,g:(H a b))(h:(H b c))
           f =%S g -> (Cfun f h) =%S (Cfun g h).

Definition Cong_law := (a,b,c:A)(f,f':(H a b))(g,g':(H b c))
           f =%S f' -> g =%S g' -> (Cfun f g)
           =%S (Cfun f' g').

Hypothesis pcgl : Congl_law.
Hypothesis pcgr : Congr_law.

Variable a, b, c : A.
```

```
Definition Build_Comp := (Build_Map2 (!pcgl a b c)
                          (!pcgr a b c)).

End composition_to_operator.
```

We now check that composition preserves the morphisms equalities, to the left and to the right, and prove as a corollary the congruence law for composition:

```
Section cat_cong.

Variable C : Category.

Lemma Prf_congl : (Congl_law (!Comp C)).

Lemma Prf_congr : (Congr_law (!Comp C)).

Lemma Prf_cong : (Cong_law (!Comp C)).

End cat_cong.
```

### 4.2 Hom Equality

We need for the following a technical definition: two arrows in (*Hom a b*) of category *C* are equal iff the corresponding elements of the Setoid (*Hom a b*) are equal. This is a typical example where Type Theory obliges us to make explicit an information which does not even come up in the standard mathematical discourse based on set theory. Of course we would like the standard "abus de notation" to be implemented in a more transparent way, through overloading or implicit coercions. We deal with this problem here by implicit synthesis of the category parameter and of the object parameters in order to write simply `f =%H g` for the equality of arrows `f` and `g`.

```
Inductive Equal_hom [C:Category;a,b:C;f:a --> b]
  : (c,d:C)(c --> d) -> Prop := Build_Equal_hom
  : (g:a --> b) f =%S g -> (Equal_hom C a b f a b g).

Infix Assoc 6 "=%H" Equal_hom.
```

Here the reader may be puzzled at our seemingly too general type for arrow equality: the predicate `Equal_hom` takes as arguments a Category `C`, objects `a,b,c,d` of `C`, and arrows (f:a --> b) and (g:c --> d). Since the only possible constructor for this equality is Build_Equal_hom, which requires the second arrow g to have the same type as the first one f, it might seem sufficient to restrict the type of Equal_hom accordingly. However, this generality is needed, because we want to be able to state the equality of two arrows whose respective domains are not definitionally equal, but will be equal for certain instanciations of parameters. For instance, later on, the problem will arise when defining functor equality: we want to be able to write $F(f) = G(f)$, which will force say $F(A)$ and $G(A)$ to be definitionally equal objects, but there is no way to specify $F$ and $G$ with type declarations such that $F(A) = G(A)$. This would necessitate an extension of type theory with definitional constraints, which could be problematic with respect to decidability of definitional equality. This extension is not really needed if one takes care to write dependent equalities with sufficiently general types.

```
Section equal_hom_equiv.

Variable C    : Category.
Variable a, b : C.
Variable f    : a --> b.

Lemma Equal_hom_refl : f =%H f.

Variable c, d : C.
Variable g    : c --> d.

Lemma Equal_hom_sym : f =%H g -> g =%H f.

Variable i, j : C.
Variable h    : i --> j.

Lemma Equal_hom_trans : f =%H g -> g =%H h -> f =%H h.

End equal_hom_equiv.
```

### 4.3 Dual Categories

The dual category $C^\circ$ of a category $C$ has the same objects as $C$. Its arrows, however, are the opposites of the arrows of $C$, i.e., $f^\circ : a \longrightarrow b$ is a morphism of $C^\circ$ iff $f : b \longrightarrow a$ is a morphism of $C$.

```
Section d_cat.

Variable C : Category.

Definition DHom := [a,b:C]b --> a.
```

Composition is defined as expected: $f^\circ \circ^\circ g^\circ = (g \circ f)^\circ$. Identity arrows are invariant. We then check the category laws.

```
Definition Comp_Darrow := [a,b,c:C][df:(DHom a b)]
                          [dg:(DHom b c)] dg o df.

Lemma Comp_dual_congl : (Congl_law Comp_Darrow).

Lemma Comp_dual_congr : (Congr_law Comp_Darrow).

Definition Comp_Dual
 := (Build_Comp Comp_dual_congl Comp_dual_congr).

Lemma Assoc_Dual : (Assoc_law Comp_Dual).

Lemma Idl_Dual : (Idl_law 2!DHom Comp_Dual (!Id C)).

Lemma Idr_Dual : (Idr_law 2!DHom Comp_Dual (!Id C)).
```

We write `(Dual C)` for the dual category of `C`.

```
Definition Dual
 := (Build_Category Assoc_Dual Idl_Dual Idr_Dual).

End d_cat.

Syntactic Definition DHOM := (!Hom (Dual ?)).
```

The combinator `DHOM` is defined by the `Syntactic Definition` above. This is just a macro definition facility, which will in the rest of the session replace every occurrence of `DHOM` by `(!Hom (Dual ?))`.

### 4.4 Category Exercises

We define epics, monos, and isos. As an exercise, we show that two initial objects are isomorphic.

A morphism $f : a \longrightarrow b$ is *epi* when for any two morphisms $g, h : b \longrightarrow c$, the equality $f \circ g = f \circ h$ implies $g = h$.

```
Section epic_monic_def.

Variable C     : Category.
Variable a, b : C.

Definition Epic_law := [f:a --> b](c:C)(g,h:b --> c)
                       (f o g) =%S (f o h) -> g =%S h.

Structure Epic : Type :=
 {Epic_mor    :  a --> b;
  Prf_isEpic :> (Epic_law Epic_mor)}.

Coercion Build_Epic : Epic_law >-> Epic.
```

A morphism $f : b \longrightarrow a$ is monic when for any two morphisms $g, h : c \longrightarrow b$, the equality $g \circ f = h \circ f$ implies $g = h$.

```
Definition Monic_law := [f:b --> a](c:C)(g,h:c --> b)
                        (g o f) =%S (h o f) -> g =%S h.

Structure Monic : Type :=
 {Monic_mor    :  b --> a;
  Prf_isMonic :> (Monic_law Monic_mor)}.

Coercion Build_Monic : Monic_law >-> Monic.

End epic_monic_def.
```

Two opposite morphisms $f : a \longrightarrow b$ and $f^{-1} : b \longrightarrow a$ are iso if $f^{-1} \circ f = Id_b$ and $f \circ f^{-1} = Id_a$.

```
Section iso_def.

Variable C : Category.

Definition RIso_law := [a,b:C][f:a --> b][f1:b --> a]
                       (f1 o f) =%S (Id b).

Variable a, b : C.

Definition AreIsos := [f:a --> b][f1:b --> a]
                      (RIso_law f f1)/\ (RIso_law f1 f).
```

We now say that two objects *a* and *b* are isomorphic ($a \cong b$) if they are connected by an isomorphism.

```
Structure Iso : Type :=
 {Iso_mor : a --> b;
  Inv_iso : b --> a;
  Prf_Iso :> (AreIsos Iso_mor Inv_iso)}.

Coercion Build_Iso : AreIsos >-> Iso.
```

Now we say that object *a* is *initial* in Category *C* iff for any object *b* there exists a unique arrow in (*Hom a b*). We should explicitely provide the function giving this unique morphism.

```
Section initial_def.

Variable C : Category.

Definition IsInitial := [a:C][h:(b:C) a --> b](b:C)
                        (f:a --> b) f =%S (h b).

Structure Initial : Type :=
 {Initial_ob    :  C;
  MorI          : (b:C) Initial_ob --> b;
  Prf_isInitial :> (IsInitial MorI)}.

Coercion Build_Initial : IsInitial >-> Initial.
```

As an exercise we may prove easily that any two initial objects must be isomorphic:

```
Lemma I_unic : (i1,i2:Initial)(Iso (Initial_ob i1)
                (Initial_ob i2)).
End initial_def.
```

Dually we define when an object *b* is *terminal* in Category *C*: for any object *a* there exists a unique arrow in (*Hom a b*).

```
Section terminal_def.

Variable C : Category.

Definition IsTerminal := [b:C][h:(a:C) a --> b](a:C)
                          (f:a--> b) f =%S (h a).

Structure Terminal : Type :=
 {Terminal_ob     :  C;
  MorT            :  (a:C) a --> Terminal_ob;
  Prf_isTerminal  :> (IsTerminal MorT)}.

Coercion Build_Terminal : IsTerminal >-> Terminal.

End terminal_def.
```

We also prove that the property of being terminal is dual to that of being initial: an initial object in $C$ is terminal in $C^{\circ}$.

```
Lemma Initial_dual : (C:Category)(a:C)(h:(b:C) a --> b)
                     (IsInitial h) ->
                     (IsTerminal 1!(Dual C) h).

Coercion Initial_dual : IsInitial >-> IsTerminal.
```

### 4.5 The Category of Setoids

We now define the Category of Setoids with Maps as Homs. First we have to define composition and identity of Maps. The composition of two Maps is defined from the composition of their underlying functions; we have to check extensionality of the resulting function. We use the infix notation `o%M`.

```
Section mcomp.

Variable A, B, C : Setoid.
Variable f       : A ==> B.
Variable g       : B ==> C.

Definition Comp_fun := [x:A](g (f x)).

Lemma Comp_fun_map_law : (Map_law Comp_fun).

Definition Comp_map : A ==> C := Comp_fun_map_law.

End mcomp.

Infix Assoc 6 "o%M" Comp_map.
```

The operator `Comp_map` is just a function. We shall now "mapify" it, by proving that it is extensional in its two arguments, in order to get a Map composition operator.

```
Lemma Comp_map_congl : (Congl_law Comp_map).

Lemma Comp_map_congr : (Congr_law Comp_map).

Definition Comp_SET
  := (Build_Comp Comp_map_congl Comp_map_congr).
```

After checking the associativity of our composition operation, we define the identity Map from the identity function $\lambda x \cdot x$, checking other category laws.

```
Lemma Assoc_SET : (Assoc_law Comp_SET).

Section id_map_def.

Variable A : Setoid.

Definition Id_fun := [x:A]x.

Lemma Id_fun_map_law : (Map_law Id_fun).
```

```
Definition Id_map : A ==> A := Id_fun_map_law.

End id_map_def.

Definition Id_SET := Id_map.

Lemma Idl_SET : (Idl_law Comp_SET Id_SET).

Lemma Idr_SET : (Idr_law Comp_SET Id_SET).
```

Now we have all the ingredients to form the Category of Setoids SET.

```
Definition SET := (Build_Category Assoc_SET Idl_SET
                   Idr_SET).

Syntactic Definition MAP := (!Hom SET).
```

## 5 Functors

### 5.1 Definition of Functor

Functors between categories $C$ and $D$ are defined in the usual way, with two components, a function from the objects of $C$ to the objects of $D$, and a Map from Hom-sets of $C$ to Hom-sets of $D$. Remark how type theory expresses in a natural way the type constraints of these notions, without arbitrary codings.

```
Section funct_def.

Variable C, D : Category.

Section funct_laws.

Variable FOb  : C -> D.
Variable FMap : (a,b:C)(Map (a --> b) ((FOb a)
                --> (FOb b))).
```

Functors must preserve the Category structure, and thus verify the two laws: $F(f \circ g) = F(f) \circ F(g)$ and $F(Id_a) = Id_{F(a)}$.

```
Definition Fcomp_law := (a,b,c:C)(f:a --> b)(g:b --> c)
```

```
((FMap a c) (f o g)) =%S (((FMap a b) f) o
((FMap b c) g)).

Definition Fid_law := (a:C)((FMap a a) (Id a)) =%S
                      (Id (FOb a)).

End funct_laws.

Structure Functor : Type :=
 {FOb          :> C -> D;
  FMap          :  (a,b:C)(Map (a --> b) ((FOb a)
                   -->  (FOb b)));
  Prf_Fcomp_law :  (Fcomp_law FMap);
  Prf_Fid_law   :  (Fid_law  FMap)}.
```

As usual, we define some abbreviations. Thus $F(a)$ will be written `(F a)` and $F(f)$ will be written `(FMor F f)`.

```
Definition FMor := [F:Functor][a,b:C][f:a --> b]
                   ((FMap F a b) f).
```

We now define the Setoid of Functors. The equality of Functors is extensional equality on their morphism function component, written as infix `=%F` with appropriate type synthesis:

```
Definition Equal_Functor := [F,G:Functor](a,b:C)(f:a --> b)
                            (FMor F f) =%H (FMor G f).

End funct_def.

Infix 2 "=%F" Equal_Functor.

Lemma Equal_Functor_equiv : (C,D:Category)
                            (Equivalence (!Equal_Functor C D)).
```

We now have all the ingredients to form the Functor Setoid.

```
Definition Functor_setoid
  := [C,D:Category](Build_Setoid (Equal_Functor_equiv C D)).
```

### 5.2 Hom Functors

We give in this section an example of functor construction, with the family of Hom-Functors.

Let $C$ be a category and $a$ an object of $C$. The functor $Hom(a, -) : C \longrightarrow SET$ is defined by:

- for every object $b$ of $C$, $Hom(a, -)(b) = (Hom\ a\ b)$

```
Section funset.

Variable C : Category.
Variable a : C.

Definition FunSET_ob := [b:C] a --> b.
```

- for every $f : b \longrightarrow c$, $Hom(a, -)(f) : (Hom\ a\ b) \longrightarrow (Hom\ a\ c)$ is a Map, mapping morphism $g : a \longrightarrow b$ of $C$ to morphism $g \circ f$.

```
Section funset_map_def.

Variable b, c : C.

Section funset_mor_def.

Variable f : b --> c.

Definition FunSET_mor1 := [g:a --> b] (g o f).

Lemma FunSET_map_law1 : (Map_law FunSET_mor1).

Definition FunSET_mor : (FunSET_ob b) ==> (FunSET_ob c)
                                         := FunSET_map_law1.

End funset_mor_def.

Lemma FunSET_map_law : (Map_law FunSET_mor).

Definition FunSET_map : (b --> c)
  ==> (MAP (FunSET_ob b) (FunSET_ob c)) := FunSET_map_law.
```

```
End funset_map_def.
```

We check the functorial properties for *Hom*$(a, -)$ and define it, with notation `(FunSET a)`.

```
Lemma Fun_comp_law : (Fcomp_law FunSET_map).

Lemma Fun_id_law : (Fid_law FunSET_map).

Definition FunSET := (Build_Functor Fun_comp_law Fun_id_law).

End funset.
```

## 5.3 The Category of Categories

In this section we now reflect the theory upon itself: Categories may form the type of a category of Categories CAT, the arrows being Functors. All is really needed is to define Functor composition and Identity, and to prove a few easy lemmas exhibiting the Category structure of CAT.

The first step consists in defining the composition of two functors. We compose functors $G : C \longrightarrow D$ and $H : D \longrightarrow E$ to form a functor $G \circ H : C \longrightarrow E$, by composing separately their object functions and their morphism maps. We write `o%F` for this functor composition.

```
Section Comp_F.

Variable C, D, E : Category.
Variable G       : (Functor C D).
Variable H       : (Functor D E).

Definition Comp_FOb := [a:C](H (G a)).

 Section comp_functor_map.

 Variable a, b : C.

 Definition Comp_FMor := [f:a --> b](FMor H (FMor G f)).

 Lemma Comp_FMap_law : (Map_law Comp_FMor).
```

```
 Definition Comp_FMap : (Map (a --> b) ((Comp_FOb a) -->
                        (Comp_FOb b))) := Comp_FMap_law.

 End comp_functor_map.

Lemma Comp_Functor_comp_law : (Fcomp_law Comp_FMap).

Lemma Comp_Functor_id_law : (Fid_law Comp_FMap).

Definition Comp_Functor
  := (Build_Functor Comp_Functor_comp_law
      Comp_Functor_id_law).

End Comp_F.

Infix Assoc 6 "o%F" Comp_Functor.
```

As before, we construct a composition operator after checking the Congruence laws.

```
Lemma Comp_Functor_congl
  : (Congl_law 2!Functor_setoid Comp_Functor).

Lemma Comp_Functor_congr
  : (Congr_law 2!Functor_setoid Comp_Functor).

Definition Comp_CAT
  := (Build_Comp Comp_Functor_congl Comp_Functor_congr).

Lemma Assoc_CAT : (Assoc_law Comp_CAT).
```

For every category $C$, we construct the identity functor $Id_C$ from the identity function on objects and the identity map on morphisms.

```
Section idCat.

Variable C : Category.

Definition Id_CAT_ob := [a:C]a.
```

```
Definition Id_CAT_map := [a,b:C](Id_map (a --> b)).

Lemma Id_CAT_comp_law : (Fcomp_law 3!Id_CAT_ob Id_CAT_map).

Lemma Id_CAT_id_law : (Fid_law 3!Id_CAT_ob Id_CAT_map).

Definition Id_CAT
  := (Build_Functor Id_CAT_comp_law Id_CAT_id_law).

End idCat.
```

We now have all the ingredients to recognize in CAT the structure of a Category. All we need to do is to take a second copy of the notion of Category, called Category'. The implicit universe adjustment mechanism will make sure that its Type refers to a bigger universe.

```
Structure Category' : Type :=
 {Ob'       :> Type;
  Hom'      :  Ob' -> Ob' -> Setoid;
  Opcomp'   :  (a,b,c:Ob')(Map2 (Hom' a b) (Hom' b c)
               (Hom' a c));
  Id'       :  (a:Ob')(Hom' a a);
  Prf_ass'  :  (Assoc_law Opcomp');
  Prf_idl'  :  (Idl_law Opcomp' Id');
  Prf_idr'  :  (Idr_law Opcomp' Id')}.

Definition CAT : Category' := (Build_Category'
                                Assoc_CAT Idl_CAT Idr_CAT).
```

Note that here we make an essential use of the universe's hierarchy: There is not a unique *CAT*, there is a family of $CAT_i$, and each $CAT_i$ is a $Category_j$ for $i < j$. Thus we do not have "small" and "large" categories, but "relatively small" categories. Thus the construction of CAT above is consistent with the analysis by Coquand [5] of paradoxes related to the category of categories.

It is to be remarked that this example justifies the mechanism called "universe polymorphism" defined by Harper and Pollack [7]. That is, with universe polymorphism, we could directly define CAT as a Category, without having to make an explicit copy of the notion, the copying being done implicitly for each occurrence of the name Category. Coq does not implement universe polymorphism at present, because this mechanism is rather costly in space, and seldom used in practice.

### 5.4 Functor Exercises

It is easy to check that a functor preserves the property of being iso, i.e., $a \cong b$ implies $F(a) \cong F(b)$.

```
Section functor_prop.

Variable C, D : Category.

Lemma Functor_preserves_iso : (F:(Functor C D))(a,b:C)
                              (Iso a b)->(Iso (F a)(F b)).
```

A functor $F : C \longrightarrow D$ is said to be *faithful* if for any pair $a, b$ of objects of $C$, and any pair $f, g : a \longrightarrow b$ of morphisms, we have $F(f) = F(g)$ only if $f = g$.

```
Definition Faithful_law := [F:(Functor C D)](a,b:C)
                           (f,g:a --> b)((FMor F f)
                           =%S (FMor F g)) -> (f =%S g).

Structure Faithful : Type :=
 {Faithful_functor :> (Functor C D);
  Prf_isFaithful   :> (Faithful_law Faithful_functor)}.

Coercion Build_Faithful : Faithful_law >-> Faithful.
```

A functor is said to be *full* if, for any pair $a, b$ of objects of $C$, and any morphism $h : F(a) \longrightarrow F(b)$, there exists a morphism $f : a \longrightarrow b$ such that $h = F(f)$. According to the axiom of choice, there exists a function $H$ such that for every morphism $h : F(a) \longrightarrow F(b)$, $H(h)$ corresponds to f, i.e., $h = F(H(h))$.

```
Definition Full_law := [F:(Functor C D)][H:(a,b:C)((F a)
                       --> (F b)) -> (a --> b)]
                       (a,b:C)(h:(F a) --> (F b))
                       h =%S (FMor F (H a b h)).

Structure Full : Type :=
 {Full_functor :> (Functor C D);
  Full_mor     : (a,b:C)((Full_functor a)
                 --> (Full_functor b)) -> (a --> b);
  Prf_isFull   :> (Full_law Full_mor)}.
```

```
Coercion Build_Full : Full_law >-> Full.

End functor_prop.
```

These two properties are closed by composition:

```
Section comp_functor_prop.

Variable C, D, E : Category.
Variable F       : (Functor C D).
Variable G       : (Functor D E).

Lemma IsFaithful_comp : (Faithful_law F) -> (Faithful_law G)
                        -> (Faithful_law (F o%F G)).

Variable F1      : (a,b:C)((F a) --> (F b)) -> (a --> b).
Variable G1      : (a,b:D)((G a) --> (G b)) -> (a --> b).

Lemma IsFull_comp : (Full_law F1) -> (Full_law G1) ->
                    [H1=[a,b:C][h:(G (F a))
                    --> (G (F b))](F1 (G1 h))]
                    (Full_law 3!(F o%F G) H1).

End comp_functor_prop.
```

In the definition of `IsFull_comp`, `H1` is a local constant.

## 6 The Functor Category

The type of Functors from Category $C$ to Category $D$ admits a Category structure. The corresponding arrows are called Natural Transformations.

### 6.1 Natural Transformations

We now define Natural Transformations between two Functors $F$ and $G$ from $C$ to $D$. A Natural Transformation $T$ from $F$ to $G$ maps an object $a$ of Category $C$ to an arrow $T_a$ from object $F(a)$ to object $G(a)$ in Category $D$ such that the following naturality law holds: $F(f) \circ T_b = T_a \circ G(f)$.

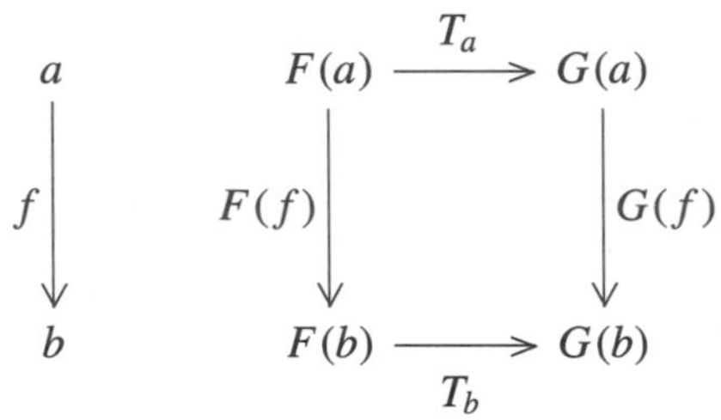


Note that Natural Transformations are defined as functions, not as Maps, since the type of objects are not given as a Setoid.

```
Section nt_def.

Variable C, D : Category.
Variable F, G : (Functor C D).

Definition NT_law := [T:(a:C)(F a) --> (G a)] (a,b:C)
                     (f:a --> b)((FMor F f) o (T b))
                     =%S ((T a) o (FMor G f)).

Structure NT : Type :=
 {ApNT        :> (a:C)(F a) --> (G a);
  Prf_NT_law :> (NT_law ApNT)}.

End nt_def.

Coercion Build_NT : NT_law >-> NT.
```

We now define the Natural Transformations Setoid between Functors $F$ and $G$. Equality of natural transformations is also extensional. Thus, two natural transformations $T$ and $T'$ are said to be equal whenever their components are equal for an arbitrary object: $\forall a \cdot T_a = T'_a$. As previously, we write `=%NT` for this equality.

```
Section setoid_nt.

Variable C, D : Category.
Variable F, G : (Functor C D).

Definition Equal_NT := [T,T':(NT F G)](a:C)(T a) =%S (T' a).
```

```
Lemma Equal_NT_equiv : (Equivalence Equal_NT).

Definition NT_setoid : Setoid := Equal_NT_equiv.

End setoid_nt.

Infix 2 "=%NT" Equal_NT.
```

## 6.2 An Example of Natural Transformation

Let $C$ be any category, and $f : a \longrightarrow a$ be a morphism of $C$. We define a natural transformation $H(f) : Hom(b, -) \longrightarrow Hom(a, -)$, called the *Yoneda map*, as follows.

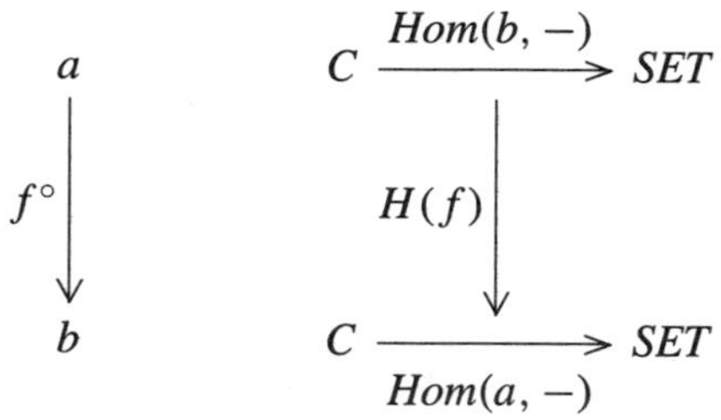


For every object $c$ of $C$, $H(f)(c)$ is a Map mapping a morphism $h : b \longrightarrow c$ of $C$ to the morphism $f \circ h$.

```
Section funset_nt.

Variable C    : Category.
Variable b, a : C.
Variable f    : a --> b.

Section nth_map_def.

Variable c : C.

Definition NtH_arrow := [h:b --> c] f o h.

Lemma NtH_map_law : (Map_law NtH_arrow).
```

```
Definition NtH_map : (MAP ((FunSET b) c) ((FunSET a) c))
                     := NtH_map_law.

End nth_map_def.
```

We check the naturality of this map and define the natural transformation $H(f)$, written as (NtH f).

```
Lemma NtH_nt_law : (NT_law 3!(FunSET b) 4!(FunSET a)
                   NtH_map).

Definition NtH : (NT (FunSET b) (FunSET a)) := NtH_nt_law.

End funset_nt.
```

### 6.3 Constructing the Category of Functors

We now have all the tools to define the category of Functors from $C$ to $D$. Objects are Functors, arrows are corresponding Natural Transformations Setoids.

We define the composition of two natural transformations $T$ and $T'$ as $(T \circ_v T')_a = T_a \circ T'_a$. The $v$ subscript stands for "vertical," since we shall define later another "horizontal" composition.

```
Section cat_functor.

Variable C, D : Category.

Section compnt.

Variable F, G, H : (Functor C D).
Variable  T      : (NT_setoid F G).
Variable T'      : (NT_setoid G H).

Definition Comp_tau := [a:C] (T a) o (T' a).

Lemma Comp_tau_nt_law : (NT_law [a:C](Comp_tau a)).

Definition CompV_NT : (NT_setoid F H) := Comp_tau_nt_law.
```

```
End compnt.

Lemma CompV_NT_congl : (Congl_law CompV_NT).

Lemma CompV_NT_congr : (Congr_law CompV_NT).

Definition Comp_CatFunct
  := (Build_Comp CompV_NT_congl CompV_NT_congr).

Lemma Assoc_CatFunct : (Assoc_law Comp_CatFunct).
```

To every functor $F$, we associate an identity natural transformation $Id_F$ defined as $\lambda a \cdot Id_{F(a)}$:

```
Section id_catfunct_def.

Variable F : (Functor C D).

Definition Id_CatFunct_tau := [a:C](Id (F a)).

Lemma Id_CatFunct_nt_law: (NT_law Id_CatFunct_tau).

Definition Id_CatFunct : (NT_setoid F F)
                        := Id_CatFunct_nt_law.

End id_catfunct_def.

Lemma Idl_CatFunct : (Idl_law Comp_CatFunct Id_CatFunct).

Lemma Idr_CatFunct : (Idr_law Comp_CatFunct Id_CatFunct).
```

Having checked that we have all categorical properties, we may now define the functor category.

```
Definition CatFunct
 :=(Build_Category Assoc_CatFunct Idl_CatFunct
    Idr_CatFunct).

End cat_functor.
```

```
Infix Assoc 6 "o%NTv" CompV_NT.

Syntactic Definition NT1 := (!Hom (CatFunct ? ?)).
```

## 7 The Interchange Law

In order to put to the test our categorical constructions, we prove the *interchange law*. This is one of the laws of 2-categories (categories whose arrows have themselves a category structure). This notion is used in theoretical computer science for the study of programming languages semantics and type theory.

Let $A$, $B$ and $C$ be categories, $F, G : A \longrightarrow B$ and $F', G' : B \longrightarrow C$ be functors. We define the *horizontal composition* of natural transformations $T : F \longrightarrow G$ and $T' : F' \longrightarrow G'$ as $(T \circ_h T')_a = T'_{F(a)} \circ G'(T_a)$. We check that $T \circ_h T'$ is indeed a natural transformation from $F \circ F'$ to $G \circ G'$.

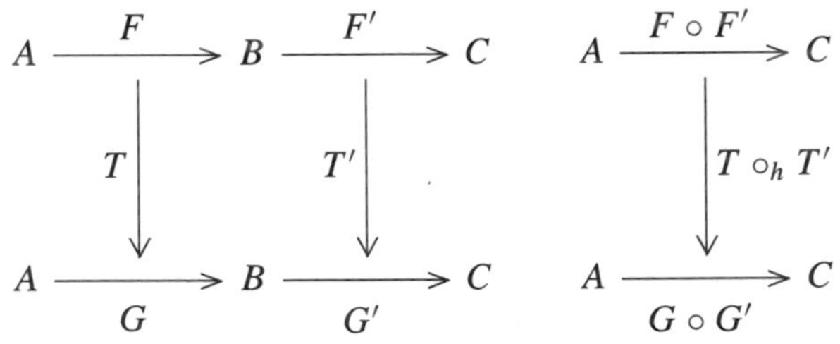


```
Section horz_comp.

Variable A, B, C : Category.
Variable F, G    : (Functor A B).
Variable F', G'  : (Functor B C).
Variable T       : (NT F G).
Variable T'      : (NT F' G').

Definition Ast : (a:A)((F o%F F') a) --> ((G o%F G') a) :=
           [a:A](T' (F a)) o (FMor G' (T a)).
```

In order to prove the naturality of $T \circ_h T'$, we use the equality:

$$(T \circ_h T')_a = T'_{F(a)} \circ G'(T_a) = F'(T_a) \circ T'_{G(a)}$$

which follows from the naturality diagram of $T'$ for the morphism $T_a$:

$$\begin{array}{ccccc}
F(a) & \quad & F'(F(a)) & \xrightarrow{T'_{F(a)}} & G'(F(a)) \\
{\scriptstyle T_a}\downarrow & & {\scriptstyle F'(T_a)}\downarrow & & \downarrow{\scriptstyle G'(T_a)} \\
G(a) & & F'(G(a)) & \xrightarrow[T'_{G(a)}]{} & G'(G(a))
\end{array}$$

```
Lemma Ast_eq : (a:A) ((FMor F' (T a)) o (T' (G a))) =%S
                     ((T' (F a)) o (FMor G' (T a))).

Lemma Ast_nt_law : (NT_law Ast).

Definition CompH_NT : (NT (F o%F F') (G o%F G'))
                       := Ast_nt_law.

End horz_comp.
```

We shall write `o%NTh` for horizontal composition.

```
Infix Assoc 6 "o%NTh" CompH_NT.
```

We shall now verify an important algebraic property, the *Interchange Law*, which links horizontal and vertical composition.

Let $A, B, C$ be categories, $F, G, H : A \longrightarrow B$, $F', G', H' : B \longrightarrow C$ be functors, and $T : F \longrightarrow G, T' : F' \longrightarrow G', U : G \longrightarrow H, U' : G' \longrightarrow H'$ be natural transformations.

$$\begin{array}{ccccc}
A & \xrightarrow{F} & B & \xrightarrow{F'} & C \\
 & {\scriptstyle T}\downarrow & & \downarrow{\scriptstyle T'} & \\
A & \xrightarrow{G} & B & \xrightarrow{G'} & C \\
 & {\scriptstyle U}\downarrow & & \downarrow{\scriptstyle U'} & \\
A & \xrightarrow[H]{} & B & \xrightarrow[H']{} & C
\end{array}$$

*Interchange Law:*

$$(T \circ_h T') \circ_v (U \circ_h U') = (T \circ_v U) \circ_h (T' \circ_v U')$$

```
Section interchangelaw.

Variable A, B, C     : Category.
Variable F, G, H     : (Functor A B).
Variable F', G', H'  : (Functor B C).
Variable T           : (NT F G).
Variable T'          : (NT F' G').
Variable U           : (NT G H).
Variable U'          : (NT G' H').

Lemma InterChange_law : ((T o%NTh T') o%NTv (U o%NTh U'))
                        =%NT
                        ((T o%NTv U) o%NTh (T' o%NTv U')).

End interchangelaw.
```

We end this section by showing that the horizontal composition of natural transformations is associative. Here lurks a small difficulty.

Given Categories $A, B, C$, Functors $F, G$ from $A$ to $B$ and Functors $F', G'$ from $B$ to $C$, the horizontal composition of Natural Transformation $T$ from $F$ to $G$ and Natural Transformation $T'$ from $F'$ to $G'$ yields a Natural Transformation $T \circ T'$ from $F \circ F'$ to $G \circ G'$. Expressing the associativity of this horizontal composition operation would need to identify, as types, say $(F \circ F') \circ F''$ and $F \circ (F' \circ F'')$. But here we run into a problem. Although these two terms are equal in the sense of Functor equality, they are *not* definitionally equal, and thus we are unable to even write the statement of associativity of horizontal composition: it does not typecheck.

In order to circumvent this problem, we need to define a less constrained equality `=%NTH` between natural transformations as follows.

```
Definition EqualH_NT := [C,D:Category][F,G,F',G':
                        (Functor C D)]
                        [T:(NT F G)]
                        [T':(NT F' G')]
                        (a:C)
                        (T a) =%H (T' a).
```

```
Infix 2 "=%NTH" EqualH_NT.

Section assoc_horz_comp.

Variable A,B,C,D : Category.
Variable F,G      : (Functor A B).
Variable F',G'    : (Functor B C).
Variable F'',G''  : (Functor C D).
Variable T        : (NT F G).
Variable T'       : (NT F' G').
Variable T''      : (NT F'' G'').

Lemma CompH_NT_assoc : ((T o%NTh T') o%NTh T'')
                          =%NTH (T o%NTh (T' o%NTh T'')).

End assoc_horz_comp.
```

## 8 Yoneda's Embedding

We now construct a functor $Y : C^\circ \longrightarrow \mathit{CatFunct}(C, \mathit{SET})$ as follows:

- for every object $a$ of $C$, $Y(a) = \mathit{Hom}(a, -)$
- for every morphism $f^\circ : b \longrightarrow a$ of $C^\circ$, $Y(f^\circ) = H(f)$

```
Section yoneda_functor.

Variable C : Category.

Section funy_map_def.

Variable a, b : C.

Lemma FunY_map_law : (Map_law 2!(NT1 (FunSET a)
                      (FunSET b)) (!NtH C a b)).

Definition FunY_map : (MAP (DHOM a b) (NT1 (FunSET a)
                        (FunSET b))) := FunY_map_law.
```

```
End funy_map_def.

Lemma FunY_comp_law : (Fcomp_law 1!(Dual C) FunY_map).

Lemma FunY_id_law : (Fid_law 1!(Dual C) FunY_map).

Definition FunY := (Build_Functor FunY_comp_law FunY_id_law).
```

Lemma : $Y$ is full and faithful.

```
Lemma Y_full : [f=[a,b:C][h:(NT1 (FunSET a) (FunSET b))]
                ((h a) (Id a))] (Full_law 3!FunY f).

Lemma Y_faithful : (Faithful_law FunY).

End yoneda_functor.
```

This result may be obtained as corollary of a more general result known as Yoneda's lemma. We give here a direct proof. Let $f, g : a \longrightarrow b$ be morphisms of $C$, $Y(f^\circ) = Y(g^\circ)$ implies that $\forall c : C, \forall k : b \longrightarrow c, f \circ k = g \circ k$. For $k = Id_b$, we obtain $f = g$ (and thus $f^\circ = g^\circ$). This shows that $Y$ is faithful.

We now must show that $Y$ is full. Let $T : Y(b) \longrightarrow Y(a)$ (i.e., $Hom(b, -) \longrightarrow Hom(a, -)$) be a natural transformation between hom-functors, we are looking for a morphism $f : a \longrightarrow b$ such that $T = Y(f^\circ)$. We know that $T_b : (Hom\ b\ b) \longrightarrow (Hom\ a\ b)$ is a Map. We define $f = T_b(Id_b)$. Let us check that $T = Y(f^\circ)$. This is equivalent to $\forall c : C, \forall k : b \longrightarrow c, T_c(k) = T_b(Id_b) \circ k$. This last assertion is a particular case of the naturality property of $T$:

$$
\begin{array}{ccccc}
b & \quad & (Hom\ b\ b) & \xrightarrow{\ T_b\ } & (Hom\ a\ b) \\
k\big\downarrow & & Hom(b,-)(k)\big\downarrow & & \big\downarrow Hom(a,-)(k) \\
c & & (Hom\ b\ c) & \xrightarrow[\ T_c\ ]{} & (Hom\ a\ c)
\end{array}
$$

Thus after simplification $\forall g : b \longrightarrow b, T_c(g \circ k) = T_b(g) \circ k$. Taking $g = Id_b$, we get $T_c(k) = T_b(Id_b) \circ k$. We conclude that $Y$ is full.

This result shows that any natural transformation between hom-functors $T : Hom(b, -) \longrightarrow Hom(a, -)$ is completely determined by a unique morphism in $a \longrightarrow b$ (which is actually $T_b(Id_b)$).

## 9 Conclusion

The development shown in this paper is but a tiny initial fragment of the theory of categories. However, it is quite promising, in that the power of dependent types and inductive types (or at least $\Sigma$-types) is put to full use; note in particular the dependent equality between morphisms of possibly non-convertible types.

We also point out that the syntactic facilities offered by the new version V6.1 of Coq are a first step in the right direction: the user may define his own notations through extensible grammars, types which are implicitly known by dependencies are synthesised automatically, the macro-definition facility (so-called `Syntactic Definition`) and the implicit coercions allow a certain amount of high-level notation. For this initial development of Category Theory, the implicit coercions are not strictly necessary, and in the initial version of this work, this facility was lacking. But further developments [14] showed that this facility was absolutely necessary for scaling up.

In order to show how crucial these tools are, we give below the statement of the interchange law without syntactic abbreviations:

```
(Equal_NT A C (Comp_Functor A B C F F')
  (Comp_Functor A B C H H')
          (CompV_NT A C (Comp_Functor A B C F F')
            (Comp_Functor A B C G G')
                    (Comp_Functor A B C H H')
                       (CompH_NT A B C F G F' G' T T')
                  (CompH_NT A B C G H G' H' U U'))
          (CompH_NT A B C F H F' H' (CompV_NT A B F G H T U)
                    (CompV_NT B C F' G' H' T' U')))
```

We are thus closing the gap with standard mathematical practice, although some supplementary overloading mechanisms are obviously still lacking in order to implement the usual "abus de notation."

From the point of view of user comfort of our proof assistant, two main difficulties have been encountered. The first one is due to the fact that Coq does very few automatic unfoldings of constants. We are too often required to make explicit manual unfoldings before being allowed to apply a lemma. The second difficulty is due to the lack of non-trivial automatic theorem proving tools. For instance, this development would benefit from efficient multi-relations rewriting tactics. These tactics ought to be extensible enough to allow the user specification of rewriting strategies, and generic enough to be usable in other developments. Such tactics have already been written for LCF [12] and NuPRL [10]. Their adaptation to Coq is currently under study.

This logical reconstruction of the basics of category theory follows initial attempts by R. Dyckhoff [6] in Martin-Löf type theory. It shows that intentional type theory is sufficient for developing this kind of mathematics, and we may thus hope to develop more sophisticated notions such as adjunction, which so far have been formally pursued only in extensional type theory [2]. Burstall and Rydeheard [13] have implemented a substantial number of concepts and constructions of category theory in SML (an ML dialect). The essential difference with our approach is that they do not include in their formalisation the properties (such as equations deriving from diagrams) of their categorical constructions. Thus they cannot mechanically check that their constructions have the intended properties. This exhibits the essential expressivity increase from a functional programming language with simple types to a type theory with dependent types, whose Curry-Howard interpretation includes the verification of predicate calculus conditions.

The above axiomatisation may indeed be pursued to include a significant segment of category theory. Thus A. Saïbi shows in [14] how to define adjunction and limits, develops standard constructions such as defining limits from equalisers and products, and shows the existence of left adjoint functors under the conditions of Freyd's theorem.

## References

[1] P. Aczel. "Galois: A Theory Development Project." Turin workshop on the representation of mathematics in Logical Frameworks, January 1993.

[2] J. A. Altucher and P. Panangaden. "A Mechanically Assisted Constructive Proof in Category Theory." In proceedings of CADE 10, LNAI 449, pp. 500–513, Springer-Verlag 1990.

[3] R. Asperti and G. Longo. "Categories, Types, and Structures." MIT Press, 1991.

[4] B. Barras and al. "The Coq Proof Assistant Reference Manual, version V6.1." Technical Report in Preparation, 1997.

[5] T. Coquand. "An analysis of Girard's paradox." Proceedings of LICS, Cambridge, Mass. July 1986, IEEE Press.

[6] R. Dyckhoff. "Category theory as an extension of Martin-Löf type theory." Internal Report CS 85/3, Dept. of Computational Science, University of St. Andrews, Scotland.

[7] R. Harper and R. Pollack. "Type checking with universes." *Theoretical Computer Science* 89, 1991.

[8] M. Hofmann. "Elimination of extensionality in Martin-Löf type theory." Proceedings of workshop TYPES'93, Nijmegen, May 1993. In "Types for Proofs and Programs," Eds. H. Barendregt and T. Nipkow, LNCS 806, Springer-Verlag 1994.

[9] G. Huet. “Initiation à la Théorie des Catégories.” Notes de Cours, DEA Paris 7, Nov. 1985.

[10] P. B. Jackson. “Enhancing the NuPRL proof development system and applying it to computational abstract algebra.” Ph.D. dissertation, Cornell University, Ithaca, NY, 1995.

[11] S. Mac Lane. “Categories for the working mathematician.” Springer-Verlag, 1971.

[12] L. C. Paulson. “A higher order implementation of rewriting.” *Science of Computer Programming,* 3:119–149, 1983.

[13] D. E. Rydeheard and R. M. Burstall. “Computational Category Theory.” Prentice Hall, 1988.

[14] A. Saïbi. “Algèbre constructive en théorie des types. Outils génériques de modélisation et de démonstration. Application à la théorie des catégories.” PhD Thesis, Université Paris VI, March 1999.

[15] A. Saïbi. “Typing algorithm in type theory with inheritance.” In Proceedings 24th POPL, pp. 292–301, ACM Press, Paris 1997.

# 10 Enhancing the Tractability of Rely/Guarantee Specifications in the Development of Interfering Operations

**Pierre Collette and Cliff B. Jones**

## 1 Introduction

Formal methods based on model-oriented specifications like VDM or B are applicable to the development of sequential operations. In such approaches, state components can be common to several operations but only one operation is executed at a time. A sequential operation can then be interpreted as a binary relation on the state space and specified with pre and post conditions; examples are given below but readers are assumed to be familiar with pre/post specifications in the style of VDM. In [12], rely and guarantee conditions are proposed as an extension to cope with the specification and development of *concurrent* operations, a situation that occurs when operations sharing state components have overlapping executions. The necessary background about rely/guarantee specifications is recalled in this paper—detailed expositions (including sound and complete proof systems) can be found in [23]. The new insights in this paper come from an emphasis on methodological issues. Theoretical aspects of rely/guarantee specifications are intentionally omitted in favour of suggestions that improve their practicability in the development of concurrent operations.

This paper is concerned with imperative programs whose meaning can be discussed with respect to a set of states—say $s_i \in \sum$. The additional complexity of concurrent versus sequential operations is due to the presence of *interference*: operations access state components that can be modified by the execution of other operations during their own execution. This difference with sequential operations can be emphasized by looking at computations. A computation of a sequential operation can be viewed as a single transition

$$s_0 \xrightarrow{\pi} s_1$$

from a starting state $s_0$ to a final state $s_1$. Of course, there might be many intermediate states between $s_0$ and $s_1$ but only the initial and final states can be accessed by other operations. The (superfluous) label $\pi$ indicates that this transition is performed by the operation. In the presence of interference, a computation not only includes steps of the operation, but also steps from its environment (other operations). If the latter are labelled with $\epsilon$, a computation can be represented by a sequence of transitions

$$s_0 \xrightarrow{l_0} s_1 \xrightarrow{l_1} s_2 \ldots$$

where each label $l_i$ is either $\pi$ or $\epsilon$; computations that terminate have a finite number of $\pi$-labelled steps.[1]

[1] Whether these are finer or coarser grained steps is a key issue that is discussed further below; meanwhile the steps are referred to as the visible steps of an operation.

Usually, termination in an acceptable state can only be ensured under assumptions about the initial state. In specifications of sequential operations, such *assumptions* are recorded in a pre condition, whereas the *commitments* of the operation (definition of acceptability) are recorded in a post condition. It is understood that the commitments are to be fulfilled only when the assumptions are satisfied. Termination of an interfering operation in an acceptable state also requires assumptions about the initial state but this is not sufficient: assumptions about the $\epsilon$-labelled steps are essential. Indeed, nothing reasonable can be expected from an operation whose environment modifies the state in an arbitrary way.

The use of assumption/commitment specifications in the development of concurrent systems is not restricted to the formalism discussed in this paper: other examples are [2, 6, 8, 14, 15, 16, 20, 22, 25]. Some of the methodological issues raised in this paper hopefully spread across examples and formalisms but the case study is only representative of one specific class of shared-state operations. In general, operations have both an *input/output* behaviour and a *reactive* behaviour. The former determines the result of an operation in terms of its inputs whereas the latter describes the way it interacts with other operations. This paper focuses on operations for which the input/output behaviour is more important than the reactive behaviour; what really matters for these operations is their final result. This can be contrasted with the development of components like schedulers or senders/receivers whose reactive behaviour is prominent and which can probably be better specified in formalisms like temporal logic. Any classification is highly debatable but a possible characterisation is that, in the absence of interference, the same operations should be specifiable with pre and post conditions. The case study illustrates this. Section 2 gives specifications for both the sequential and the interfering versions of the same operations; the latter are inevitably more sophisticated than the former but in both cases, what really matters is the input/output behaviour.

Section 2 illustrates the use of rely and guarantee conditions with top-level specifications from the case study; a brief sketch of the development is also given. No novelty appears in Section 2; in particular, the specifications are subject to substantial improvement—in accordance with the suggestions made—in the remainder of the paper. Visible steps are defined in Section 3. Next, the use of data invariants and other useful invariant properties is advocated in Section 4. Finally, recommendations on writing specifications and on the refinement of operations towards code are proposed in Sections 5 and 6 respectively.

## 2 Introduction to the Case Study

The problem of recording equivalence classes over a (finite) set $T$ of elements occurs in a variety of contexts from controlling equivalent part numbers in manufacturing applications to tracking equivalence classes in cryptography. The two basic operations are TEST$(a, b)$ that tests if $a$ and $b$ are elements of the same class and EQUATE$(a, b)$ that merges the equivalence classes of $a$ and $b$ into a single class. An efficient implementation—both in terms of space and time—can be based on a representation which records equivalence classes as trees (one tree per class); there are various proposals for keeping the path lengths short within trees, here a new operation CLEANUP$(a)$ that shortens the path from $a$ to its root in the tree is added.

The representation by trees and the introduction of the CLEANUP operation are clearly insights in the development; but this case study has been carried out without other insights than these. This deliberate ignorance of previous solutions and the hunger for interfering operations actually led to tackling a more general problem. The complexity of this problem indeed increases with the degree of concurrency. In the absence of interference, algorithms for the operations can be designed quite easily; the task becomes more complex when CLEANUP interferes with EQUATE or TEST, by modifying the inner structure of trees. This development goes further in that it also permits the concurrent execution of TEST and EQUATE, and also the concurrent execution of *several instances* thereof. Although the usefulness of such a high degree of concurrency is debatable, it provides a sufficiently complex problem to raise issues about the practicability of a development method.

In model-oriented developments, operations are first specified over an abstract state space, which is then progressively reified into more concrete ones until all operations are specified in terms of implementable data structures. This section gives specifications of TEST and EQUATE on abstract states. The unique state component is $p$: *T-partition* where

$$T\text{-}partition = \{p \in (T\text{-}\mathbf{set})\text{-}\mathbf{set} \mid is\text{-}partition(p)\}.$$

The type invariant $is\text{-}partition(p)$ indicates that the union of the sets in $p$ is $T$ and that sets are disjoint;[2] each set in $p$ records an equivalence class on $T$. VDM specifications for the sequential version of TEST and EQUATE are given first; rely and guarantee conditions are then introduced to cope with the concurrent execution of several instances of TEST with several instances of EQUATE.

### 2.1 Sequential Operations

Sequential operations can be specified by pre and post conditions; hooked variables in post conditions refer to the initial state. Those elements in the same class as $a$ in $p$ are denoted by $P\text{-}class(a, p)$; the predicate $P\text{-}equiv(a, b, p)$ stands for $P\text{-}class(a, p) = P\text{-}class(b, p)$. Specifications P-TEST$_0$ and P-EQUATE$_0$ should not require further explanation.[3]

[2] Omitted definitions can be found in the appendix.

[3] Specifications are prefixed and subscripted; undecorated names are reserved for informal references to operations; collections of states and operations could be collected into VDM modules.

P-TEST$_0$ $(a\colon T,\ b\colon T)\ t\colon \mathbb{B}$

**rd** $p$ : *T-partition*

**post** $t \Leftrightarrow$ *P-equiv*$(a, b, p)$

P-EQUATE$_0$ $(a\colon\ T,\ b\colon\ T)$

**wr** $p$ : *T-partition*

**post** $p = (\overleftarrow{p} \setminus \{P\text{-}class(a, \overleftarrow{p}),\ P\text{-}class(b, \overleftarrow{p})\}) \cup \{P\text{-}class(a, \overleftarrow{p}) \cup P\text{-}class(b, \overleftarrow{p})\}$

**Note on Data Invariants** At this abstraction level, a state *is* a partition of $T$ and thus there exists no "state" in which two sets in $p$ have a non-empty intersection. Nevertheless, this does not exclude an (inefficient) implementation of EQUATE that first copies all elements of one set into the other and then destroys the first set, thus creating intermediate sets with non-empty intersection. The correctness of this implementation can be formally justified by a reification of the state space that removes the data invariant *is-partition*$(p)$ and adds it as a conjunct to the pre and post conditions of EQUATE. A "representation" state is then just a set of sets in $T$ but those sets must form a partition when the operation terminates. Data invariants can thus be considered as pre and post conditions.

### 2.2 Interfering Operations

Because of the (potential) concurrent execution of EQUATE, equivalence classes might be merged *during* the execution of TEST, and also during the execution of another instance of EQUATE. The high degree of interference is more apparent when equivalence classes are represented by trees (roots change, the inner structure of trees change), but interference can already be specified, hence better understood, at this abstraction level.

Consider the specification P-TEST$_1$ below, where the keyword **ext** indicates that $p$ can be modified by other operations. Its *rely* condition asserts that classes only grow. This rely condition is thus an assumption about the interference of the environment (other operations) during the execution of TEST. It is interpreted as a reflexive and transitive binary relation that characterises any uninterrupted sequence of $\epsilon$-labelled steps in a computation.

$$P\text{-}grows(p_1,\ p_2) \triangleq \forall a\colon\ T \cdot P\text{-}class(a,\ p_1) \subseteq\ P\text{-}class(a,\ p_2)$$

P-TEST$_1$ $(a\colon\ T,\ b\colon\ T)\ t\colon \mathbb{B}$

**ext rd** $p$ : *T-partition*

**rely** *P-grows*$(\overleftarrow{p},\ p)$

**post** $(P\text{-}equiv(a,\ b,\ \overleftarrow{p}) \Rightarrow\ t) \wedge (\ t \Rightarrow P\text{-}equiv(a,\ b,\ p))$

An operation is only required to terminate and satisfy the post condition if the pre condition holds initially *and* the rely condition holds for all $\epsilon$-labelled steps. Interference is thus explicitly specified but, as for the specification P-TEST$_0$ (without interference), the important part is the input/output behaviour. The post condition now consists of

- a sufficient condition that forces $t$ to be **true** if $a$ and $b$ were members of the same class when the operation started; and
- a necessary condition that allows $t$ to be **true** only if $a$ and $b$ are members of the same class when the operation terminates.

The result of the operation cannot be determined in the case where the classes of $a$ and $b$ are initially disjoint and then merged by a concurrent execution of EQUATE. Note that, in the presence of arbitrary interference (i.e., no rely condition), the result would be absolutely unpredictable. In contrast, if no interference is allowed (i.e., a rely condition of $p = \overleftarrow{p}$), the post condition of P-TEST$_1$ reduces to the post condition of P-TEST$_0$.

The counterpart of the rely condition is the *guarantee* condition which specifies the interference to others caused by an operation; this is what other operations may rely upon. This guarantee condition is interpreted as a reflexive binary relation that holds for all $\pi$-labelled steps in a computation. Together with the post condition, it forms the commitments of the operation to its environment. There is no explicit guarantee condition in P-TEST$_1$ above but the mode restriction **rd** $p$ guarantees that no step of the TEST operation modifies $p$. A guarantee condition appears in P-EQUATE$_1$: it asserts that classes only grow and no other classes than those of $a$ and $b$ can be modified by steps of the operation.

P-EQUATE$_1$ $(a\colon T,\ b\colon T)$
  **ext wr** $p : T\text{-}partition$
**rely** $P\text{-}grows(\overleftarrow{p},\ p)$
**guar** $P\text{-}grows(\overleftarrow{p},\ p) \wedge$
      **let** $rest = T \setminus (P\text{-}class(a, \overleftarrow{p}) \cup P\text{-}class(b, \overleftarrow{p}))$ **in**
      $\forall e \in rest \cdot P\text{-}class(e, p) = P\text{-}class(e, \overleftarrow{p})$
**post** $P\text{-}equiv(a,\ b,\ p)$

Here again, this specification can be shown—in the absence of interference—to specialise to the non-interfering case (P-EQUATE$_0$): the argument relies on the guarantee condition as well as the post condition.

**Coexistence** Whenever two operations are intended to be executed in parallel, there is a coexistence proof obligation on their specifications by which it is verified that the interference caused by one operation is allowed by the other. In this case, several instances of TEST can be executed in parallel with several instances of EQUATE because TEST is a read-only operation and the guarantee condition of P-EQUATE$_1$ implies the rely conditions of P-EQUATE$_1$ and P-TEST$_1$.

### 2.3 Data Reification

The recording of equivalence classes in a representation based on trees is captured by the reification of partitions into forests. The concrete state contains a single component $f$: *T-forest* where[4]

$$T\text{-}forest = \{f \in T \xrightarrow{m} T \mid is\text{-}forest(f)\}.$$

The type invariant *is-forest*($f$) prevents $f$ from containing cycles; each tree in $f$ represents an equivalence class. Those elements in the same tree as $a$ are denoted by $F\text{-}class(a, f)$; $F\text{-}equiv(a, b, f)$ stands for $F\text{-}class(a, f) = F\text{-}class(b, f)$; $is\text{-}root(a, f)$ indicates that $a$ is a root in $f$; *ancestors*($a$, $f$) is the set of elements on the path from $a$ to its root ($a$ not included).

Partitions can be easily retrieved from forests:

$$p = \{F\text{-}class(a, f) \mid a \in T \wedge is\text{-}root(a, f)\}.$$

In a second stage of reification, the forest is implemented by an array $m$ from $T$ to $T$; $m(a) = a$ indicates that $a$ is a root; the set of roots in $m$ is *rts*($m$). The new data invariant is then

$$m\text{-}is\text{-}forest(m) \;\underline{\triangle}\; is\text{-}forest(rts(m) \,⩤\, m)$$

and the forest retrieved from $m$ is *fr*($m$).

$$fr : T\text{-}array \to T\text{-}forest$$

$$fr(m) \;\underline{\triangle}\; rts(m) \,⩤\, m$$

**pre** $m\text{-}is\text{-}forest(m)$

### 2.4 Operation Refinement

First, the specifications of TEST and EQUATE over partitions are refined into operations over forests and a new operation CLEANUP is added. These operations are then refined into more

[4] The VDM notation $m: A \xrightarrow{m} B$ indicates a finite map $m$ with domain type $A$ and range type $B$; $⩤$ is the operator for domain subtraction (**dom** $s ⩤ m =$ **dom** $m \setminus s$).

```
local x, y: T; t: 𝔹 in
  x, y := a, b
  repeat
    F-ROOT1(x) || F-ROOT1(y);
    protect f in F-TEST-AND-CONNECT1(x, y, t)
  until t
end
```

**Figure 10.1**
Decomposition of F-EQUATE$_1$

elementary operations. The decomposition of the EQUATE operation on the forest $f$ is shown in Figure 10.1; variables $x$, $y$, and $t$ are local. F-ROOT$_1$($z$) is an operation specified to compute the root of $z$ in $f$ (with result in $z$); F-TEST-AND-CONNECT$_1$($c$, $d$, $t$) is an operation specified to first check (with result in $t$) if $c$ and $d$ are roots *at the same time*; in case $t =$ **true** the operation connects $c$ and $d$, otherwise it does nothing; these specifications are given in detail in Section 5. The latter is embedded in a section protected from interference, otherwise trees could be merged by a concurrent instance of EQUATE between the test of *is-root*$(c, f)$ and the test of *is-root*$(d, f)$.

## 3 Visible Steps

The question of granularity arises as soon as interference is discussed; a detailed introduction to this problem with examples can be found in [18]. In this context, the question amounts to what are the $\pi$-labelled steps in a computation. This directly affects the interpretation of the guarantee condition of an operation (and of course the rely conditions of others). As discussed in next section, this also affects the interpretation of invariants.

A visible step of an operation is one that produces values relevant to other operations. These include the initial and the final values of its shared (non-local) variables (relevant for sequential composition) but must also encompass every *public* intermediate value of its shared variables. Each occurrence of a variable in the code of an operation can be classified as either *public* or *private* [18]. An occurrence of a shared variable is private if the variable cannot be accessed by a concurrently executed operation, e.g., when it appears inside mutually exclusive code sections.

In this case study, all occurrences of the array $m$ in the code are public and thus each assignment to $m$ is a visible step. This, however, does not mean that all assignment statements are executed atomically. For example, a crucial assignment statement for detecting the termination of the computation of roots is $r := (m(z) = z)$. This statement has been safely introduced in the development with the assumption that other operations may interfere (and change the truth value of $m(z) = z$) between the read and write memory accesses; $r$ and $z$ are local variables. Imposing atomicity for all assignment statements would generate a lot of synchronisation overhead to implement them (see e.g. [3]). Such overheads should only be incurred when required and specified by the designer (e.g., using atomic brackets). As discussed later in this paper, the evaluation of expressions is not assumed to be atomic either: the assignment statement $t := (m(x) = x \wedge m(y) = y)$ in the actual code of EQUATE is not supposed to be executed atomically but enough synchronisation has been introduced during the design to ensure that other operations may read but not modify $m$ when this statement is executed.

## 4 Invariants for Interfering Operations

A development method is helpful only if it helps master the inherent complexity of a problem. The use of rely and guarantee conditions favours local reasoning but the first versions of the specifications of TEST and EQUATE (exposed later in this paper) were still too complex, hence their subsequent modification. Essentially, the gratuitous complexity was due to the lack of invariant properties. This section first discusses the application of data invariants (in the style of VDM) to interfering operations; it then introduces a new kind of invariant property.

### 4.1 Data Invariants

In a first attempt, the state component was basically the array $m$ from $T$ to $T$ described in Section 2 but the predicate *m-is-forest* appeared almost everywhere in the specifications of operations and in the pre conditions of auxiliary functions (*is-root*, *ancestors*, ...). Without doubt, it is much easier to view *m-is-forest* as a data invariant. This motivates the introduction of the type *T-forest*. Data invariants are helpful in the development of sequential operations and remain so in the development of interfering operations. However, their interpretation appears to differ in the two cases. In the specification of sequential operations, data invariants can be considered as implicit pre and post conditions on all operations on the state space. Since the initial and final values are the only visible values of a sequential operation, this means that data invariants are required to hold for all visible values of an operation. Remarkably, this is conceptually the same for interfering operations. Data invariants are still required to hold for all visible values; there are just more visible values than the initial and final ones.

Preservation of an invariant by visible steps can thus be considered as an implicit guarantee condition on all operations (hence a rely condition as well). In this case study, the preservation of the invariant is ultimately verified for the assignments to $m$, one in EQUATE, and one in CLEANUP.

### 4.2 Evolution Invariant

Although helpful, data invariants are not enough. The complexity of a development can be further reduced by the use of another invariant property. It should be clear from the examples in Section 2 that the relation $P\text{-}grows(p, p')$ holds for *any* pair of states where $p'$ follows $p$ in a computation (no matter whether the intermediate steps are operation or environment steps). This relation between computation states can be recorded by an *evolution* invariant, that should appear just next to the data invariant, in the data part of a specification.

$$ev\text{-}T\text{-}partition(p_1, p_2) \triangleq P\text{-}grows(p_1, p_2)$$

This evolution invariant can be viewed as an implicit guarantee condition on all operations, and thus an implicit rely condition as well. Specifications then simplify. For instance, there is no explicit rely condition in P-EQUATE$_2$ and the guarantee condition is simpler than in P-EQUATE$_1$.

P-EQUATE$_2$ $(a\colon T,\ b\colon T)$
 **ext wr** $p\ :\ T\text{-}partition$
**guar let** $rest = T \backslash (P\text{-}class(a, \overleftarrow{p}) \cup P\text{-}class(b, \overleftarrow{p}))$ **in**
 $\forall e \in rest \cdot P\text{-}class(e, p) = P\text{-}class(e, \overleftarrow{p})$
**post** $P\text{-}equiv(a, b, p)$

At the forest representation level, the evolution invariant records the fact that not only do classes grow but also that no new root is ever created. It also prevents the situation where an ancestor of an element later becomes one of its descendants; the case $ancestors(a, f_2) \not\subseteq F\text{-}class(a, f_1)$ is due to the possible merging of trees. The proof obligation that the evolution invariant on forests implies the one on partitions is easily discharged.

$$ev\text{-}T\text{-}forest(f_1, f_2) \triangleq F\text{-}grows(f_1, f_2) \wedge no\text{-}new\text{-}roots(f_1, f_2) \wedge no\text{-}loop(f_1, f_2)$$

where

$$F\text{-}grows(f_1, f_2) \triangleq \forall a\colon T \cdot F\text{-}class(a, f_1) \subseteq F\text{-}class(a, f_2)$$
$$no\text{-}new\text{-}roots(f_1, f_2) \triangleq \forall a\colon T \cdot is\text{-}root(a, f_2) \Rightarrow is\text{-}root(a, f_1)$$
$$no\text{-}loop(f_1, f_2) \triangleq \forall a\colon T \cdot ancestors(a, f_2) \cap F\text{-}class(a, f_1) \subseteq ancestors(a, f_1)$$

With computations restricted by that evolution invariant, the three operations on forests are specified below. The guarantee condition in F-EQUATE$_1$ ensures that equivalence classes are merged only by connecting the root of a tree to another tree. The rely condition of F-CLEANUP$_1$ is not an evolution invariant because some steps of CLEANUP are obviously intended to modify the inner structure of trees. The same applies to its guarantee condition (equivalence classes are untouched and nothing but $f(a)$ changes) because $f$ can be modified by the environment in other ways.

$$bodyunch(f_1, f_2) \triangleq \forall a: T \cdot \neg\, is\text{-}root(a, f_1) \Rightarrow \neg\, is\text{-}root(a, f_2) \wedge f_2(a) = f_1(a)$$
$$rootunch(f_1, f_2) \triangleq \forall a: T \cdot is\text{-}root(a, f_2) \Leftrightarrow is\text{-}root(a, f_1)$$

F-TEST$_1$ $(a: T,\ b: T)\ t: \mathbb{B}$

**ext rd** $f$ : *T-forest*

**post** $(F\text{-}equiv(a, b, \overleftarrow{f}) \Rightarrow t) \wedge (t \Rightarrow F\text{-}equiv(a, b, f))$

F-EQUATE$_1$ $(a: T,\ b: T)$

**ext wr** $f$ : *T-forest*

**guar** $bodyunch(\overleftarrow{f}, f) \wedge$

  **let** $rest = T \setminus (F\text{-}class(a, \overleftarrow{f}) \cup F\text{-}class(b, \overleftarrow{f}))$ **in**

  $\forall e \in rest \cdot F\text{-}class(e, f) = F\text{-}class(e, \overleftarrow{f})$

**post** $F\text{-}equiv(a, b, f)$

F-CLEANUP$_1$ $(a: T)$

**ext wr** $f$: *T-forest*

**rely** $bodyunch(\overleftarrow{f}, f)$

**guar** $rootunch(\overleftarrow{f}, f) \wedge \{a\} \ntriangleleft f = \{a\} \ntriangleleft \overleftarrow{f}$

**post** $\neg\, is\text{-}root(a, \overleftarrow{f}) \wedge \neg\, is\text{-}root(\overleftarrow{f}(a), \overleftarrow{f}) \Rightarrow f(a) \neq \overleftarrow{f}(a)$

The evolution invariant at the array representation level just mimics the previous one:

$$ev\text{-}T\text{-}array(m_1, m_2) \triangleq ev\text{-}T\text{-}forest(fr(m_1), fr(m_2))$$

Evolution invariants are not a novelty *per se*. Predicates that appear in the rely and guarantee conditions of all operations were already emphasized in [23] (called there binary invariants). As explained in Section 5, there are advantages in moving them from the specifications of individual operations into the specification of the shared state. But the idea that properties of all computations can be attached to the definition of a state is not new either. The state specification modules of [17] include a dynamic constraint which is a temporal formula. Interestingly, in the detailed case study of [17], the temporal formula has precisely the form of an evolution invariant.

## 5 Writing Specifications

Based on lessons learned from the case study, this section presents a few guidelines on writing specifications. To understand their impact, there is some incentive to include a 'bad' specification, very similar to one of the very first ones written during this case study. This is a specification of the ROOT operation. The first mistake was that the level of abstraction was wrong: ROOT was immediately viewed as an operation on the array $m$.

### 5.1 Usefulness of the Invariants

Data and evolution invariants do not increase the expressive power of specifications because they can be otherwise incorporated into specifications. Indeed, the data invariant holds initially (pre condition), is preserved by visible steps (rely and guar condition) and thus holds upon termination (post condition); the evolution invariant holds for every pair of visible steps (rely and guar condition) and by transitivity holds upon termination (post condition).

Yet, data and evolution invariants are not just syntactic sugar. They both bring insight into the problem. Having those invariants in mind helps the process of writing specifications. Interesting properties can also be deduced from the invariant. A typical example is the irreversibility of the transformation of forests:

$$\frac{\begin{array}{c} f_1, f_2, f_3\colon \textit{T-forest} \\ \textit{ev-T-forest}(f_1, f_2),\ \textit{ev-T-forest}(f_2, f_3) \\ f_3 = f_1 \end{array}}{f_2 = f_1}$$

The many roles of the evolution invariant (rely, guar, and post conditions) are especially useful in proofs. The first premise of most proofs is in fact a list of state components, e.g., $f_0, f_1, f_2$: *T-forest*. The states in consideration can be the initial state, the intermediate state in a sequential composition, the states before and after a visible step of the operation (proof obligations for guarantee condition), a potential final state, and a new one due to interference. In all cases, they represent successive states in a computation and this means that

*ev-T-forest*$(f_0, f_1)$, *ev-T-forest*$(f_1, f_2)$, *ev-T-forest*$(f_0, f_2)$

can be freely used anywhere in the proof, just like

*is-forest*$(f_0)$, *is-forest*$(f_1)$, *is-forest*$(f_2)$

can be. Automatic inheritance of those predicates is convenient in proofs. A typical example from this development is when *F-equiv*$(a, b, f_1)$ holds after the execution of a suboperation and *F-equiv*$(a, b, f_2)$ is required to hold after the execution of some other suboperation which, together with the environment, transforms $f_1$ into $f_2$. This easily follows from *F-grows*$(f_1, f_2)$; another frequent case is the deduction of (*is-root*$(a, f_2) \Rightarrow t$) from (*is-root*$(a, f_1) \Rightarrow t$) which follows from *no-new-roots*$(f_1, f_2)$. Without explicit invariants, those predicates would have had to have been reconstructed separately from the guarantee conditions of the sub-operations and from the overall rely condition.

In conclusion, although data and evolution invariants could be incorporated in the individual specifications of the operations, what eases the development process is precisely *avoiding* thinking about them in terms of assumptions and commitments. Invariants should be considered as *given* and available for free use in writing and reasoning about specifications. The same philosophy is adopted in [19]: the use of invariants in the design should be separate from their ultimate verification. How the latter is carried out is addressed in Section 6.

### 5.2 Enriched Mode Restrictions

Write-mode restrictions on variables can be understood as commitments of the operation: no other variables can be modified. Read-mode can be interpreted in several ways [4]; in this paper, all variables that can be accessed but not modified by the operation are required to appear with read-mode; non-mentioned variables cannot be accessed by the operation. The mode restrictions also play a syntactic role: only the variables in write-mode can be hooked in post conditions of sequential operations. However, in the presence of interference, it makes sense to use the hooked version of read-mode variables in post conditions because these might have been modified by the environment during the execution; P-TEST$_1$ in Section 2 is a typical example. This in fact reveals an asymmetry in the use of mode restrictions: they give commitments of the operations but no assumptions on the environment. To compensate for this, the **rd** and **wr** mode restrictions are enriched with:

- the keyword **ext** (external) if the variable can be modified by the environment;
- the keyword **ptc** (protected) if the variable can be accessed but not modified by the environment;
- the keyword **prv** (private) if the variable cannot be accessed by the environment.

The result variables of an operation are implicitly of mode **prv wr**. The use of **ext** and **ptc** mode restrictions was already advocated in [23]; the novelty is the explicit distinction between protected and private variables.

The specifications F-ROOT$_1$ and F-TEST-AND-CONNECT$_1$ below illustrate the use of mode restrictions. The former must be used in a context where $z$ is private and the latter must be used in a context where $f$ is protected; the decomposition of F-EQUATE$_1$ in Figure 10.1 provides such a context. In this case, there are concurrent instances of ROOT but the variables $x$ and $y$ match a **prv** mode because each of the two concurrent instances of ROOT manipulates only one of these variables.

F-ROOT$_1$

**ext rd** $f$ : *T-forest*

**prv wr** $z$: $T$

**post** $\textit{F-equiv}(\overleftarrow{z}, z, f) \wedge \textit{is-root}(z, \overleftarrow{f})$

F-TEST-AND-CONNECT$_1$ $(c,\ d{:}\ T)\ t{:}\,\mathbb{B}$

**ptc rd** $f$: *T-forest*

**guar** $\textit{bodyunch}(\overleftarrow{f}, f) \wedge$

**let** $\textit{rest} = T \setminus (\textit{F-class}(c, \overleftarrow{f}) \cup \textit{F-class}(d, \overleftarrow{f}))$ **in**

$\forall e \in \textit{rest} \cdot \textit{F-class}(e, f) = \textit{F-class}(e, \overleftarrow{f})$

**post** $(t \Leftrightarrow \textit{is-root}(c, \overleftarrow{f}) \wedge \textit{is-root}(d, \overleftarrow{f})) \wedge (t \Rightarrow \textit{F-equiv}(c, d, f))$

With richer mode restrictions, information on interference can be better organised. First of all, only external variables have to be taken into account when the effect of environment steps has to be considered (e.g., in writing post conditions or in the proof obligations related to interference). Tool-supported proof obligations also become simpler because mode restrictions identify which variables are kept unchanged by environment and/or operation steps and automatic substitution of equals simplifies proofs significantly.

Mode restrictions also play a syntactic role by restricting the set of variables whose names may occur free in the various parts of a specification. Far from being exhaustive, it is first observed that protected variables should not appear hooked in rely conditions because none can be modified by the environment. Private variables should not appear in the rely nor the guarantee conditions because those characterise visible steps and the intermediate value of private variables are invisible to other operations. As one would hope, this implies that operations on private variables have pre and post conditions only; these are indeed sequential operations and thus sequential reasoning should be the standard.

### 5.3 Predominance of the Post Condition

Since both the guarantee and the post condition are commitments of the operations, there can be a debate about where to put some information. For the considered class of problems (when the input/output behaviour is more important than the reactive behaviour), preference should be given to the post condition. In other words, the guarantee condition should be used for what it is intended, i.e the commitments of the operation to interference, nothing else. This is partially enforced by the syntactic constraints due to mode restrictions (no private variables in the guarantee condition).

### 5.4 Interference and Post Conditions

Because of interference from other operations, the post condition of an operation which has to tolerate interference is often weaker and more sophisticated than that for the sequential version. This is illustrated by P-TEST$_1$ in Section 2. Post conditions expressed with the same pattern as in P-TEST$_1$ (necessary and sufficient conditions) often occurred in the case study. An example is F-TEST-ROOT$_1$: interfering operations that destroy roots (as allowed by the evolution invariant) influence the result of this operation.

F-TEST-ROOT$_1$ $(a: T)\ t: \mathbb{B}$

**ext rd** $f : \textit{T-forest}$

**post** $(\textit{is-root}(a, f) \Rightarrow t) \wedge (t \Rightarrow \textit{is-root}(a, \overleftarrow{f}))$

For the same reason, the ROOT operation can only "approximate" the root of an element. The post condition in F-ROOT$_1$ above only requires $z$ to be a root when the computation started. Indeed, even if the process of going up in the tree stops because $z$ is tested to be a root, it might not be a root when the operation terminates.

The preservation of the post condition by interference is probably the most important single proof obligation on specifications. Most significantly, it reveals potential errors in specifications. In the case of the ROOT operation, the failure of the proof obligation

$$\frac{\begin{array}{c} f_1: \textit{T-forest},\ f_2: \textit{T-forest} \\ \textit{ev-T-forest}(f_1, f_2) \\ \textit{is-root}(z, f_1) \end{array}}{\textit{is-root}(z, f_2)} \quad \text{(fail)}$$

reveals that the post condition *is-root*$(z, f)$ would be erroneous (in this case, there is no rely condition and interference is fully specified by the evolution invariant). Evolution invariants are thus often very helpful in writing correct specifications, and consequently in detecting wrong ones.

## 5.5 Reasoning about Specifications

The proof that the post-condition is preserved by interference creates confidence in the specification. But, as for the specifications of sequential operations, more confidence can be gained by establishing further properties of specifications. A typical check for interfering operations is to consider how the post condition simplifies in the case of less interference. For instance, the fact that $z$ is the root of $c$ in $f$ easily follows from the post condition of F-ROOT$_1$ if $f$ is not subject to interference. A less trivial example is given by the specification F-CLEANUP$_1$. In case the class of $a$ is merged with another class during its execution, CLEANUP might connect $a$ to an element in that new class. But suppose that the equivalence class of $a$ is preserved throughout the computation (*ii*); then, one may verify that the operation effectively shortens the path from $a$ to its root (*v*), if possible (*iii*). Premise (*iv*) is the post condition of F-CLEANUP$_1$. This validation thus additionally shows that the evolution invariant (*i*) can also be thought of as a post condition.

(*i*) $a\colon T;\ f_0,\ f_1\colon T,\ \textit{ev-T-forest}(f_0, f_1)$

(*ii*) $\textit{F-class}(a, f_1) = \textit{F-class}(a, f_0)$

(*iii*) $\neg\ \textit{is-root}(a, f_0) \wedge \neg\ \textit{is-root}(f_0(a), f_0)$

(*iv*) $\neg\ \textit{is-root}(a, f_0) \wedge \neg\ \textit{is-root}(f_0(a), f_0) \Rightarrow f_1(a) \neq f_0(a)$

---

(*v*) $f_1(a) \in \textit{ancestors}(f_0(a), f_0)$

The proof is as follows:

| | |
|---|---|
| (1) $\textit{ancestors}(a, f_1) \subseteq \textit{F-class}(a, f_1)$ | **by** (*i*), def(s). |
| (2) $\textit{no-loop}(f_0, f_1) \wedge \textit{no-new-roots}(f_0, f_1)$ | **by** (*i*), def(s). |
| (3) $\textit{ancestors}(a, f_1) \cap \textit{F-class}(a, f_0) \subseteq \textit{ancestors}(a, f_0)$ | **by** (2), def(s). |
| (4) $\textit{ancestors}(a, f_1) \cap \textit{F-class}(a, f_1) \subseteq \textit{ancestors}(a, f_0)$ | **by** (*ii*), (3) |
| (5) $\textit{ancestors}(a, f_1) \subseteq \textit{ancestors}(a, f_0)$ | **by** (1), (3) |
| (6) $\neg\ \textit{is-root}(a, f_1)$ | **by** (*iii*), (2) |
| (7) $f_1(a) \in \textit{ancestors}(a, f_1)$ | **by** (*i*), (6), def(s). |
| (8) $f_1(a) \in \textit{ancestors}(a, f_0)$ | **by** (5), (7) |

(9) $f_1(a) \neq f_0(a)$ **by** (*iii*), (*iv*)

(10) $ancestors(a, f_0) = \{f_0(a)\} \cup ancestors(f_0(a), f_0)$ **by** (*i*), (*iii*), def(s).

(*v*) $f_1(a) \in ancestors(f_0(a), f_0)$ **by** (8), (9), (10)

All specifications make an intensive use of auxiliary functions (*no-loop*, *ancestors*, *bodyunch*, ...). It is recommanded [11] to use them to develop a 'theory' of the data types involved. This not only simplifies proofs but also improves the designer's understanding of the problem.

### 5.6 Transitivity

The verification that the evolution invariant and the rely conditions are transitive is another useful proof obligation. An error in the development was spotted quite late because that proof obligation had been postponed. Indeed, the predicate *no-loop* prevents the situation where the computation of roots does not terminate because of interfering operations that, for example, first connect an element $a$ to an element $b$, then connect $b$ to $a$. In a first development without evolution invariants, the rely condition was

$$F\text{-}grows(\overleftarrow{f}, f) \wedge no\text{-}new\text{-}roots(\overleftarrow{f}, f) \wedge$$
$$(\forall\, a, b: T \cdot a \in ancestors(b, \overleftarrow{f}) \Rightarrow b \notin ancestors(a, f))$$

but this fails to prevent that situation because it is not transitive.

## 6 Towards Code

The previous section was devoted to guidelines on writing specifications. How a specification is written obviously influences its subsequent development in that the sub-operations are often designed from it. This section is devoted to further comments on the development of specifications toward code. This can only be subjective and incomplete, if only because comments that are not specific to the development of interfering operations are not included.

### 6.1 Control over Interference

As illustrated by the examples in previous sections, specification of interference is part of the design method. But not only can interference be specified; it can also be *controlled.* The search for the most adequate mechanisms to control interference is out of the scope of this paper but some are of course needed in the examples. This case study uses the **protect** mechanism that prevents the environment of an operation from modifying state

**protect** $m$ **in**

$t := (m(x) = x \wedge m(y) = y);$

**if** $t \wedge x \neq y$ **then** $m(x) := y$ **endIf**;

**end**

**Figure 10.2**
Pseudo-code with critical sections

components (no $\epsilon$-labelled step modifies them). This mechanism is not assumed to be part of the programming language, and the decision of how to be implement it has in fact been postponed.

The protected section of Figure 10.1 (Section 2) is developed into the pseudo-code of Figure 10.2. Protection prevents other operations from modifying $m$ and this ensures that

1. the two accesses to $m$ return the same value in the expression $m(x) = x \wedge m(y) = y$;
2. $x$ and $y$ are still roots in $m$ when the connection occurs.

Nevertheless, $m$ can still be accessed (but not modified) by other operations (e.g., TEST), even between the two accesses to $m$ in the Boolean expression. Thus, the assignment statements in Figure 10.2 are not assumed to be executed atomically.

Critical sections are well known in concurrent programming (e.g., [3]). The key issue is that such critical sections do not appear all of a sudden in the final code. They can be introduced *during the design*. This **protect** mechanism has been introduced (cf. Figure 10.1) in the early refinement of EQUATE( $a$, $b$) before the specifications F-ROOT$_1$ and F-TEST-AND-CONNECT$_1$ were further developed. This control information is recorded by the mode restrictions introduced in Section 5 and thus propagates through the design to the final code. Whether the occurrence of a variable in the code is protected or not thus follows from the design.

**Control over Granularity** The **protect** mechanism does not enforce mutual exclusion in that other operations have read-access to the shared state components. If mutual exclusion (or atomic execution of an assignment statement) was required, then this should also be introduced explicitly during the design. Such a mechanism was in fact introduced in a first attempt to implement TEST-AND-CONNECT but this appeared to be a bad design decision. Indeed, if $m$ appears in any section where read access is forbidden, implementation of that critical section will require synchronisation overhead to be added before and after *every* access to $m$, including in the much executed ROOT operation.

**Easiness versus Efficiency** Control over interference can be necessary: roots should not be connected by other operations between the "test" and "connect" parts in Figure 10.2: protecting each part separately is not sufficient. At the other extreme, the development of EQUATE would have been easier if the whole body of the operation was under the scope of a **protect** mechanism. This would, however, drastically restrict concurrency! In this development, the computation of roots, which is probably the most time consuming part of the execution of EQUATE, can be executed concurrently with any other operation.

Suppose that **protect** is implemented by a readers and writers protocol.[5] Then the only synchronisation overhead is: a reader protocol around one test in TEST (after the computation of roots), a writer protocol around the code for TEST-AND-CONNECT inside EQUATE, and a writer protocol around the only assignment statement of CLEANUP. There is no synchronisation overhead in the computation of roots.

The writer protocol around the assignment in CLEANUP is of special interest. Its presence is due to the implementation of the **protect** mechanism in other operations. This mechanism made the development of TEST-AND-CONNECT easier, but the loss of efficiency in CLEANUP is excessive. In fact, only roots need to be protected and the guarantee condition in $\text{F-CLEANUP}_1$ tells us that roots are unchanged. Thus, on the one hand, the current formal development gives enough confidence for a safe removal of the synchronisation overhead in CLEANUP. But, on the other hand, it is unclear how to do it formally, in a cost-effective way.

**Synchronisation and Compositionality** When the concurrent execution of several instances of EQUATE was first considered, it seemed that the addition of *explicit* synchronisation variables between the operations might be required. A fully compositional development indeed requires each operation to be developed independently down to machine code. But an attempt to add explicit synchronisation variables was quickly abandoned, first because it was unclear how to choose the variables, and second because this would have implied adding all "protocol information" in specifications and carry all those complications through the development. An easier development that ends up with (perhaps less efficient) pseudo-code like that in Figure 10.2 is preferred.

### 6.2 Introduction of Code

As illustrated in Figure 10.1, language constructs (loop, ";", assignment statements) appear early in the development. This of course biases the development towards imperative programming languages, but those are the target languages, at least for the code of the

[5] Details in the appendix.

individual operations. How those operations are actually activated (procedure call, message passing, etc.) is not considered in this development.

But the most interesting feature is the introduction of assignment statements. Most often, it is much easier to introduce an assignment statement than to describe it by a specification. A description of $x,\ y := a,\ b$ in Figure 10.1 with guarantee and post conditions is unnecessarily opaque. A similar remark holds for the development of the specifications M-CONNECT-TO-ANCESTOR$_1$ and M-CONNECT-ROOTS$_1$ below into the assignment statement $m(a) := b$. There is no need for any intermediate specification that would try to mimic the effect of the assignment statement in the guarantee condition. This is in accordance with the suggestion of Section 5 that the effect of an operation should be specified in the post condition rather than in the guarantee condition.

M-CONNECT-TO-ANCESTOR$_1$ $(a,\ b\colon T)$

**ext wr** $m$: *T-array*

**pre** $a \notin rts(m) \wedge b \in ancestors(a,\ fr(m))$

**rely** $bodyunch(fr(\overleftarrow{m}),\ fr(m))$

**guar** $rts(m) = rts(\overleftarrow{m}) \wedge \{a\} \lessdot m = \{a\} \lessdot \overleftarrow{m}$

**post** $m(a) = b$

M-CONNECT-ROOTS$_1$ $(a,\ b\colon T)$

**ptc** **wr** $m$: *T-array*

**pre** $a \neq b \wedge a \in rts(m) \wedge b \in rts(m)$

**guar** $bodyunch(fr(\overleftarrow{m}),\ fr(m)) \wedge$

**let** $rest = T \setminus (F\text{-}class(a,\ fr(\overleftarrow{m})) \cup F\text{-}class(b,\ fr(\overleftarrow{m})))$ **in**

$\forall e \in rest \cdot F\text{-}class(e,\ fr(m)) = F\text{-}class(e,\ fr(\overleftarrow{m}))$

**post** $m = \overleftarrow{m} \dagger \{a \mapsto b\} \vee m = \overleftarrow{m} \dagger \{b \mapsto a\}$

The proof that the implementation of those specifications by $m(a) := b$ is correct proceeds by taking into account interference from the environment before $m$ is assigned to; the interference after termination of the assignment statement has already been captured by the proof obligation on the post condition. Three values of $m$ can then be identified: the initial value $m_0$, the value $m_1$ just before $m$ is assigned to, and the value $m_2$ just after it is assigned to. The pre condition characterises $m_0$, the rely condition characterises the transitions from $m_0$ to $m_1$, and the transition from $m_1$ to $m_2$ is characterised by $m_2 = m_1 \dagger \{a \mapsto b\}$. As usual, all transitions are also characterised by the evolution invariant and $m\text{-}is\text{-}forest(m_i)$ can be assumed for each $i$.

### 6.3 Verification of the Invariants

As illustrated by M-CONNECT-TO-ANCESTOR$_2$, invariants could be expanded into the individual specifications before assignment statements are introduced.

M-CONNECT-TO-ANCESTOR$_2$ $(a,\ b\colon T)$

**ptc** **wr** $m$ : $T\text{-}array$

**pre** $m\text{-}is\text{-}forest(m) \wedge a \notin rts(m) \wedge b \in ancestors(a, fr(m))$

**rely** $m\text{-}is\text{-}forest(\overleftarrow{m}) \Rightarrow$
$m\text{-}is\text{-}forest(m) \wedge ev\text{-}T\text{-}array(\overleftarrow{m}, m) \wedge bodyunch(fr(\overleftarrow{m}), fr(m))$

**guar** $m\text{-}is\text{-}forest(\overleftarrow{m}) \Rightarrow$
$m\text{-}is\text{-}forest(m) \wedge ev\text{-}T\text{-}array(\overleftarrow{m}, m) \wedge rts(m) = rts(\overleftarrow{m}) \wedge \{a\} \Leftarrow m = \{a\} \Leftarrow m$

**post** $m(a) = b$

But this does not help. Keeping the invariants outside the individual specifications until code is introduced seems as easy. The preservation of invariants (between $m_1$ and $m_2$) by the assignment statement is then to be verified first. There are only two such proof obligations in this case study. The one for the implementation of M-CONNECT-TO-ANCESTOR$_1$ is:

$$\frac{\begin{array}{c} m_0,\ m_1,\ m_2\colon T\text{-}array \\ m\text{-}is\text{-}forest(m_0) \wedge m\text{-}is\text{-}forest(m_1) \\ ev\text{-}T\text{-}array(m_0, m_1) \\ a \notin rts(m_0) \wedge b \in ancestors(a, fr(m_0)) \\ bodyunch(fr(m_0), fr(m_1)) \\ m_2 = m_1 \dagger \{a \mapsto b\} \end{array}}{m\text{-}is\text{-}forest(m_2) \wedge ev\text{-}T\text{-}array(m_1, m_2)}$$

Once this proof obligation is discharged, the invariants can be freely used in the proof obligations for the guarantee and post conditions of M-CONNECT-TO-ANCESTOR$_1$. Notice that a common pattern to all proofs related to assignment statements is to first show that the pre condition is preserved by interference, that is to show $a \notin rts(m_1) \wedge b \in ancestors(a, fr(m_1))$ in this case.

## 7 Conclusion

Rely and guarantee conditions have been proposed to handle concurrency while preserving local reasoning in the development. Designed for the specification of interference, these conditions can also be used in an anarchic way, by encoding as much information as possible into them. This quickly leads to intractable specifications. In contrast, despite the high level of concurrency, this development makes a rather economic use of rely and guarantee conditions: out of 11 specifications at the forest level, only 5 have an explicit guarantee condition, and only 3 have an explicit rely condition. A development that tends to generate many sophisticated rely and guarantee conditions is probably poorly organised. Of course, this remark is based on a single case study but the failure to present an elegant development in other cases would probably indicate that the specified operations fall outside the considered class of problems. In particular, the specification style in this paper does not work well with operations whose reactive behaviour is the most important feature; the use of other styles of rely/guarantee specifications for the development of a non-trivial reactive system is illustrated in [15].

Although rely and guarantee conditions favour local reasoning, this paper emphasizes the role of the invariants (data invariant and evolution invariant), which by nature record global information. Therefore, local reasoning is not totally enforced because each operation is not developed independently down to code: a data reification step (with strengthening of the invariants) concern all operations. But this is already the case for data reification steps in the development of sequential operations in VDM [13] or B [1]. The methodological importance of invariants in concurrency is not new; detailed developments based on invariants can be found, for example, in [7, 10].

As mentioned in the introduction of this paper, theoretical aspects have been intentionally neglected. Expressiveness is one of them. An attentive reader should have noticed that the only restriction to concurrency in this paper is the execution of at most one instance of CLEANUP at a time. Concurrent execution of that operation not only further complicates the development but also raises expressiveness problems: it seems that the formulation of an adequate evolution invariant then requires the use of history determined auxiliary variables. Use of auxiliary variables with rely/guarantee specifications is detailed in [9, 23]. Auxiliary variables lead to clearer specifications than nested temporal operators, but inappropriate use can also lead to cumbersome specifications. At worse, rely and guarantee conditions could be reduced to an update of a history variable that records all transitions in a computation and the post condition be then expressed as a predicate on that history variable; guidelines for auxiliary variables are thus required.

The design of appropriate proof rules for data reification with rely/guarantee conditions is another theoretical aspect that deserves further work. Thanks to the evolution invariant, the problem of the appearance of new rely conditions with data reification [24] does not occur in this case study but might appear in others.

**Acknowledgements**

This work has been supported by funding from the UK EPSRC. We thank Ketil Stølen for his helpful comments on a draft of this paper.

## A Technical Summary

### Types and Auxiliary Functions

$$is\text{-}disj : T\textbf{-set} \times T\textbf{-set} \to \mathbb{B}$$

$$is\text{-}disj(s_1, s_2) \underline{\triangle}\ s_1 \cap s_2 = \{\,\}$$

$$is\text{-}partition : (T\textbf{-set})\textbf{-set} \to \mathbb{B}$$

$$is\text{-}partition(p) \underline{\triangle} \bigcup p = T \wedge \{\,\} \notin p \wedge (\forall s_1, s_2 \in p \cdot s_1 = s_2 \vee is\text{-}disj(s_1, s_2))$$

$$T\text{-}partition = \{p \in (T\textbf{-set})\textbf{-set} \mid is\text{-}partition(p)\}.$$

$$P\text{-}class : T \times T\text{-}partition \to T\textbf{-set}$$

$$P\text{-}class(a, p) \underline{\triangle}\ \iota s \in p \cdot a \in s$$

$$P\text{-}equiv : T \times T \times T\text{-}partition \to \mathbb{B}$$

$$P\text{-}equiv(a, b, p) \underline{\triangle}\ P\text{-}class(a, p) = P\text{-}class(b, p)$$

$$P\text{-}grows : T\text{-}partition \times T\text{-}partition \to \mathbb{B}$$

$$P\text{-}grows(p_1, p_2) \underline{\triangle}\ \forall a{:}\ T \cdot P\text{-}class(a, p_1) \subseteq P\text{-}class(a, p_2)$$

$$in\text{-}cycles : (T \xrightarrow{m} T) \rightarrow (T\textbf{-set})\textbf{-set}$$

$$in\text{-}cycles\,(f) \triangleq \{c \colon T\textbf{-set} \mid c \subseteq \textbf{dom}\, f \wedge \forall e \in c \cdot f(e) \in c\}$$

$$is\text{-}forest : (T \xrightarrow{m} T) \rightarrow \mathbb{B}$$

$$is\text{-}forest(f) \triangleq in\text{-}cycles(f) = \{\,\}$$

$$T\text{-}forest = \{f \in T \xrightarrow{m} T \mid is\text{-}forest(f)\}.$$

$$F\text{-}class : T \times T\text{-}forest \rightarrow T\textbf{-set}$$

$$F\text{-}class(a, f) \triangleq \{b \mid root(b, f) = root(a, f)\}$$

$$F\text{-}equiv : T \times T \times T\text{-}forest \rightarrow \mathbb{B}$$

$$F\text{-}equiv(a, b, f) \triangleq F\text{-}class(a, f) = F\text{-}class(b, f)$$

$$is\text{-}root : T \times T\text{-}forest \rightarrow \mathbb{B}$$

$$is\text{-}root(a, f) \triangleq a \notin \textbf{dom}\, f$$

$$ancestors : T \times T\text{-}forest \rightarrow T\textbf{-set}$$

$$ancestors(a, f) \triangleq \textbf{if } is\text{-}root(a, f) \textbf{ then } \{\,\} \textbf{ else } f(a) \cup ancestors(f(a), f)$$

$$F\text{-}grows : T\text{-}forest \times T\text{-}forest \rightarrow \mathbb{B}$$

$$F\text{-}grows(f_1, f_2) \triangleq \forall a \colon T \cdot F\text{-}class(a, f_1) \subseteq F\text{-}class(a, f_2)$$

$$no\text{-}new\text{-}roots : T\text{-}forest \times T\text{-}forest \rightarrow \mathbb{B}$$

$$no\text{-}new\text{-}roots(f_1, f_2) \triangleq \forall a \colon T \cdot is\text{-}root(a, f_2) \Rightarrow is\text{-}root(a, f_1)$$

$$no\text{-}loop : T\text{-}forest \times T\text{-}forest \rightarrow \mathbb{B}$$

$$no\text{-}loop(f_1, f_2) \triangleq \forall a \colon T \cdot ancestors(a, f_2) \cap F\text{-}class(a, f_1) \subseteq ancestors(a, f_1)$$

$bodyunch : T\text{-}forest \times T\text{-}forest \to \mathbb{B}$

$bodyunch(f_1, f_2) \triangleq \forall a : T \cdot \neg is\text{-}root(a, f_1) \Rightarrow \neg is\text{-}root(a, f_2) \wedge f_2(a) = f_1(a)$

$rootunch : T\text{-}forest \times T\text{-}forest \to \mathbb{B}$

$rootunch(f_1, f_2) \triangleq \forall a : T \cdot is\text{-}root(a, f_1) \Leftrightarrow is\text{-}root(a, f_2)$

$T\text{-}array = \{m \in T \xrightarrow{m} T \mid \mathbf{dom}\ m = T\}.$

$rts : T\text{-}array \to T\text{-}\mathbf{set}$

$rts(m) \triangleq \{a : T\} \mid m(a) = a$

$m\text{-}is\text{-}forest : T\text{-}array \to \mathbb{B}$

$m\text{-}is\text{-}forest(m) \triangleq is\text{-}forest(rts(m) \mathbin{\lessdot\!\!\!-} m)$

$fr : T\text{-}array \to T\text{-}forest$

$fr(m) \triangleq rts(m) \mathbin{\lessdot\!\!\!-} m$

**pre** $m\text{-}is\text{-}forest(m)$

**Specifications**

P-TEST$_2$ $(a : T,\ b : T)\ t : \mathbb{B}$
 **ext rd** $p$ : $T\text{-}partition$
**post** $(P\text{-}equiv(a, b, \overleftarrow{p}) \Rightarrow t) \wedge (t \Rightarrow P\text{-}equiv(a, b, p))$

P-EQUATE$_2$ $(a : T,\ b : T)$
 **ext wr** $p$ : $T\text{-}partition$
**guar let** $rest = T \setminus (P\text{-}class(a, \overleftarrow{p}) \cup P\text{-}class(b, \overleftarrow{p}))$ **in**
  $\forall e \in rest \cdot P\text{-}class(e, p) = P\text{-}class(e, \overleftarrow{p})$
**post** $P\text{-}equiv(a, b, p)$

F-TEST$_1$ $(a : T,\ b : T)\ t : \mathbb{B}$
 **ext rd** $f$ : $T\text{-}forest$
**post** $(F\text{-}equiv(a, b, \overleftarrow{f}) \Rightarrow t) \wedge (t \Rightarrow F\text{-}equiv(a, b, f))$

$\text{F-EQUATE}_1\ (a{:}\ T,\ b{:}\ T)$

**ext wr** $f\ :\ \textit{T-forest}$

**guar** $\textit{bodyunch}(\overleftarrow{f}, f) \wedge$

  **let** $\textit{rest} = T \setminus (\textit{F-class}(a, \overleftarrow{f}) \cup \textit{F-class}(b, \overleftarrow{f}))$ **in**

  $\forall e \in \textit{rest} \cdot \textit{F-class}(e, f) = \textit{F-class}(e, \overleftarrow{f})$

**post** $\textit{F-equiv}(a, b, f)$

$\text{F-CLEANUP}_1\ (a{:}\ T)$

**ext wr** $f\ :\ \textit{T-forest}$

**rely** $\textit{bodyunch}(\overleftarrow{f}, f)$

**guar** $\textit{rootunch}(\overleftarrow{f}, f) \wedge \{a\} \mathbin{\lhd\!\!\!-} f = \{a\} \mathbin{\lhd\!\!\!-} \overleftarrow{f}$

**post** $\neg \textit{is-root}(a, \overleftarrow{f}) \wedge \neg \textit{is-root}(\overleftarrow{f}(a), \overleftarrow{f}) \Rightarrow f(a) \neq \overleftarrow{f}(a)$

$\text{F-ROOT}_1$

**ext rd** $f\ :\ \textit{T-forest}$

**prv** **wr** $z\ :\ T$

**post** $\textit{F-equiv}(\overleftarrow{z}, z, f) \wedge \textit{is-root}(z, \overleftarrow{f})$

$\text{F-TEST-2-ROOTS}_1\ (a,\ b{:}\ T)\ t{:}\ \mathbb{B}$

**ptc** **rd** $f\ :\ \textit{T-forest}$

**post** $t \Leftrightarrow \textit{is-root}(a, f) \wedge \textit{is-root}(b, f)$

$\text{F-TEST-ROOT}_1\ (a{:}\ T)\ \ t{:}\ \mathbb{B}$

**ext rd** $f\ :\ \textit{T-forest}$

**post** $(\textit{is-root}(a, f) \Rightarrow t) \wedge (t \Rightarrow \textit{is-root}(a, \overleftarrow{f}))$

$\text{F-GO-UP}_1$

**ext rd** $f\ :\ \textit{T-forest}$

**prv** **wr** $x\ :\ T$

**pre** $\neg \textit{is-root}(x, f)$

**post** $\textit{F-equiv}(\overleftarrow{x}, x, f) \wedge (\textit{F-equiv}(\overleftarrow{x}, x, \overleftarrow{f}) \Rightarrow x \in \textit{ancestors}(\overleftarrow{x}, \overleftarrow{f}))$

F-FATHER$_1$ $(a\colon T)\ x\colon T$

**ext rd** $f\ :\ \mathit{T\text{-}forest}$

**pre** $\neg \mathit{is\text{-}root}(a,\ f)$

**rely** $\mathit{bodyunch}(\overleftarrow{f},\ f)$

**post** $x = \overleftarrow{f}(a)$

F-CONNECT-TO-ANCESTOR$_1$ $(a,\ b\colon T)$

**ext wr** $f\ :\ \mathit{T\text{-}forest}$

**pre** $\neg \mathit{is\text{-}root}(a,\ f) \wedge b \in \mathit{ancestors}(a,\ f)$

**rely** $\mathit{bodyunch}(\overleftarrow{f},\ f)$

**guar** $\mathit{rootunch}(\overleftarrow{f},\ f) \wedge \{a\} \mathbin{⩤} f = \{a\} \mathbin{⩤} \overleftarrow{f}$

**post** $f(a) = b$

F-TEST-AND-CONNECT$_1$ $(c,\ d\colon T)\ t\colon \mathbb{B}$

**ptc** **rd** $f\ :\ \mathit{T\text{-}forest}$

**guar** $\mathit{bodyunch}(\overleftarrow{f},\ f) \wedge$

$\quad$ **let** $\mathit{rest} = T \setminus (\mathit{F\text{-}class}(c,\ \overleftarrow{f}) \cup \mathit{F\text{-}class}(d,\ \overleftarrow{f}))$ **in**

$\quad$ $\forall e \in \mathit{rest} \cdot \mathit{F\text{-}class}(e,\ f) = \mathit{F\text{-}class}(e,\ \overleftarrow{f})$

**post** $(t \Leftrightarrow \mathit{is\text{-}root}(c,\ \overleftarrow{f}) \wedge \mathit{is\text{-}root}(d,\ \overleftarrow{f})) \wedge (t \Rightarrow \mathit{F\text{-}equiv}(c,\ d,\ f))$

F-CONNECT-ROOTS$_1$ $(a\colon T,\ b\colon T)$

**ptc** **wr** $f\ :\ \mathit{T\text{-}forest}$

**pre** $a \neq b \wedge \mathit{is\text{-}root}(a,\ f) \wedge \mathit{is\text{-}root}(b,\ f)$

**guar** $\mathit{bodyunch}(\overleftarrow{f},\ f) \wedge$

$\quad$ **let** $\mathit{rest} = T \setminus (\mathit{F\text{-}class}(a,\ \overleftarrow{f}) \cup \mathit{F\text{-}class}(b,\ \overleftarrow{f}))$ **in**

$\quad$ $\forall\ e \in \mathit{rest} \cdot \mathit{F\text{-}class}(e,\ f) = \mathit{F\text{-}class}(e,\ \overleftarrow{f})$

**post** $f = \overleftarrow{f} \dagger \{a \mapsto b\} \vee f = \overleftarrow{f} \dagger \{b \mapsto a\}$

**Refinements** Refinement of F-TEST$_1(a, b, t)$:

```
local x, y: T in
    x, y := a, b;
    repeat
      F-ROOT1(x) || F-ROOT1(y);
       t := (x = y)
   until t ∨ (r from (protect f in F-TEST-2-ROOTS1(x, y, r)))
end
```

Refinement of F-EQUATE$_1(a, b)$:

```
local x, y: T; t: 𝔹 in
    x, y := a, b
    repeat
      F-ROOT1(x) || F-ROOT1(y);
      protect f in F-TEST-AND-CONNECT1(x, y, t)
   until t
end
```

Refinement of F-ROOT$_1(x)$:

```
while ¬ t from F-TEST-ROOT1(x, t)
   do
   F-GO-UP1(x)
   od
```

Refinement of F-TEST-AND-CONNECT$_1(a, b, t)$:

```
F-TEST-2-ROOTS1(a, b, t);
if t ∧ a ≠ b
then F-CONNECT-ROOTS1(a, b)
```

Refinement of F-CLEANUP$_1(a)$:

```
local x: T in
  if ¬ t from F-TEST-ROOT1(a, t)
  then F-FATHER1(a, x);
     if ¬ t from F-TEST-ROOT1(x, t)
     then F-FATHER1(x, x);
           F-CONNECT-TO-ANCESTOR1(a, x)
end
```

### Specifications

M-TEST-2-ROOTS$_1$ $(a,\ b{:}\ T)\ t{:}\ \mathbb{B}$

**ptc** **rd** $m$ : *T-array*

**post** $t \Leftrightarrow a \in rts(m) \wedge\ b \in rts(m)$

M-TEST-ROOT$_1$ $(a{:}\ T)$ **wr** $t{:}\ \mathbb{B}$

**ext rd** $m$ : *T-array*

**post** $(a \in\ rts(m) \Rightarrow t) \wedge (t \Rightarrow a \in\ rts(m))$

M-GO-UP$_1$

**ext rd** $m$ : *T-array*

**prv** **wr** $x$ : $T$

**pre** $x \notin rts(m)$

**post** $F\text{-}equiv(\overleftarrow{x},\ x,\ fr(m)) \wedge (F\text{-}equiv(\overleftarrow{x},\ x,\ fr(\overleftarrow{m})) \Rightarrow x \in ancestors(\overleftarrow{x},\ fr(\overleftarrow{m})))$

M-FATHER$_1$ $(a{:}\ T)\ x{:}\ T$

**ext rd** $m$ : *T-array*

**pre** $a \notin rts(m)$

**rely** $bodyunch(fr(\overleftarrow{m}), fr(m))$

**post** $x = \overleftarrow{m}(a)$

M-CONNECT-TO-ANCESTOR$_1$ $(a,\ b{:}\ T)$

**ext wr** $m$ : *T-array*

**pre** $a \notin\ rts(m) \wedge\ b \in ancestors(a,\ fr(m))$

**rely** $bodyunch(fr(\overleftarrow{m}), fr(m))$

**guar** $rts(m) = rts(\overleftarrow{m}) \wedge \{a\} \ntriangleleft m = \{a\} \ntriangleleft \overleftarrow{m}$

**post** $m(a) =\ b$

M-CONNECT-ROOTS$_1$ $(a,\ b{:}\ T)$

**ptc** **wr** $m$ : *T-array*

**pre** $a \neq b \wedge a \in rts(m) \wedge b \in rts(m)$

**guar** $bodyunch(fr(\overleftarrow{m}), fr(m)) \wedge$
**let** $rest = T \setminus (F\text{-}class(a, fr(\overleftarrow{m})) \cup F\text{-}class(b, fr(\overleftarrow{m})))$ **in**
$\forall e \in rest \cdot F\text{-}class(e, fr(m)) = F\text{-}class(e, fr(\overleftarrow{m}))$

**post** $m = \overleftarrow{m} \dagger \{a \mapsto b\} \vee m = \overleftarrow{m} \dagger \{b \mapsto a\}$

**Refinements** Refinement of M-TEST-2-ROOT$_1$:

$t := (m(a) = a) \wedge (m(b) = b)$

Refinement of M-TEST-ROOT$_1$:

$t := m(a) = a$

Refinement of M-GO-UP$_1$:

$x := m(x)$

Refinement of M-FATHER$_1$:

$x := m(a)$

Refinement of M-CONNECT-TO-ANCESTOR$_1$:

$m(a) := b$

Refinement of M-CONNECT-ROOTS$_1$:

$m(a) := b$

### Code for the Operations

TEST$(a, b)$: $t$

**local** $x, y$: $T$, $r$: $\mathbb{B}$ **in**
$x, y := a, b$;

EQUATE$(a, b)$

**local** $x, y$: $T$; $t$: $\mathbb{B}$ **in**
$x, y := a, b$;

```
repeat
  ROOT(x) || ROOT(y);
  t := (x = y);
  reader-entry-protocol
    r := m(x) = x ∧ m(y) := y
  reader-exit-protocol
until t ∨ r
end
```

```
repeat
  ROOT(x) || ROOT(y);
  writer-entry-protocol
    t := (m(x) = x ∧ m(y) = y);
    if t ∧ x ≠ y
    then m(x) := y
  writer-exit-protocol
until t
end
```

CLEANUP($a$)

```
local x: T, t: 𝔹 in
  t := m(a) = a;
  if ¬ t
  then
    x := m(a);
    t := m(x) = x;
    if ¬ t
    then
      x := m(x);
      writer-entry-protocol
            m(a) := x
      writer-exit-protocol
end
```

ROOT(var $z$)

```
local t: 𝔹 in
  t := m(z) = z;
  while ¬ t
    do
      z := m(z);
      t := m(z) = z
    od
end
```

## References


[1] J.-R. Abrial. *The B-Book: Assigning programs to meanings.* Cambridge University Press, 1996.

[2] Martin Abadi and Leslie Lamport. Composing specifications. *ACM Transactions on Programming Languages and Systems*, 15:73–132, 1993.

[3] Gregory R. Andrews. *Concurrent Programming: Principles and Practice.* The Benjamin /Cummings Publishing Company Inc., 1991.

[4] Juan Bicarregui. Operation semantics with read and write frames. In D. Till, editor, *Proceedings of the 6th Refinement Workshop*, pages 260–278. Springer-Verlag, 1994.

[5] R. Bloomfield, R. B. Jones, and L. S. Marshall, editors. *VDM'88: VDM—The Way Ahead*, volume 328 of *Lecture Notes in Computer Science*. Springer-Verlag, 1988.

[6] Howard Barringer and Ruud Kuiper. Hierarchical development of concurrent systems in a temporal logic framework. In S. D. Brookes, A. W. Roscoe, and G. Winskel, editors, *Seminar on Concurrency*, volume 197 of *Lecture Notes in Computer Science*, pages 35–61. Springer-Verlag, 1985.

[7] K. M. Chandy and J. Misra. *Parallel Program Design: A Foundation*. Addison-Wesley, 1988.

[8] Pierre Collette. Composition of assumption-commitment specifications in a UNITY style. *Science of Computer Programming*, 23:107–126, 1994.

[9] Peter Grønning, Thomas Qvist Nielsen, and Hans Henrik Løvengreen. Refinement and composition of transition-based rely-guarantee specifications with auxiliary variables. In K. V. Nori and C. E. Veni Madhavan, editors, *Foundations of Software Technology and Theoretical Computer Science*, volume 472 of *Lecture Notes in Computer Science*, pages 332–348. Springer-Verlag, 1991.

[10] E. P. Gribomont. Concurrency without toil: a systematic method for parallel program design. *Science of Computer Programming*, 21:1–56, 1993.

[11] C. B. Jones. Constructing a theory of a data structure as an aid to program development. *Acta Informatica*, 11:119–137, 1979.

[12] C. B. Jones. *Development Methods for Computer Programs including a Notion of Interference*. PhD thesis, Oxford University, June 1981. Printed as: Programming Research Group, Technical Monograph 25.

[13] C. B. Jones. *Systematic Software Development using VDM*. Prentice Hall International, second edition, 1990.

[14] Bengt Jonsson and Yih-Kuen Tsay. Assumption/guarantee specifications in linear time temporal logic. In P. D. Mosses, M. Nielsen, and M. I. Schwartzbach, editors, *TAPSOFT'95: Theory and Practice of Software Development*, volume 915 of *Lecture Notes in Computer Science*, pages 262–276. Springer-Verlag, 1995.

[15] A. Kay and J. N. Reed. A rely and guarantee method for timed CSP: A specification and design of a telephone exchange. *IEEE, Transactions on Software Engineering*, 19(6):625–639, 1992.

[16] J. Misra and K. M. Chandy. Proofs of networks of processes. *IEEE Transactions on Software Engineering*, 7:417–426, 1981.

[17] Cornelius A. Middelburg. *Logic and Specification: Extending VDM-SL for advanced formal specification*. Chapman and Hall, 1993.

[18] Zohar Manna and Amir Pnueli. *The Temporal Logic of Reactive and Concurrent Systems: Specification*. Springer-Verlag, 1992.

[19] C. C. Morgan and T. Vickers. *On the Refinement Calculus*. Formal Approaches to Computing and Information Technology series (FACET). Springer-Verlag, 1994.

[20] Paritosh K. Pandya and Mathai Joseph. P-A logic—a compositional proof system for distributed programs. *Distributed Computing*, 5:27–54, 1991.

[21] S. Prehn and W. J. Toetenel, editors. *VDM'91—Formal Software Development Methods. Proceedings of the 4th International Symposium of VDM Europe, Noordwijkerhout, The Netherlands, October 1991. Vol. 1: Conference Contributions*, volume 551 of *Lecture Notes in Computer Science*. Springer-Verlag, 1991.

[22] Eugene W. Stark. A proof technique for rely/guarantee properties. In S. N. Maheshwari, editor, *Foundations of Software Technology and Theoretical Computer Science*, volume 206 of *Lecture Notes in Computer Science*, pages 369–391. Springer-Verlag, 1986.

[23] K. Stølen. An Attempt to Reason About Shared-State Concurrency in the Style of VDM. In [21], pages 324–342, 1991.

[24] J. C. P. Woodcock and B. Dickinson. Using VDM with rely and guarantee-conditions: Experiences of a real project. In [5], pages 434–458, 1988.

[25] Job Zwiers, Arie de Bruin, and Willem-Paul de Roever. A proof system for partial correctness of dynamic networks of processes. In E. Clarke and D. Kozen, editors, *Logics of Programs*, volume 164 of *Lecture Notes in Computer Science*, pages 513–527. Springer-Verlag, 1984.

# 11 Model Checking Algorithms for the $\mu$-Calculus

**Sergey Berezin, Edmund Clarke, Somesh Jha, and Will Marrero**

## 1 Introduction

The propositional $\mu$-calculus is a powerful language for expressing properties of transition systems by using least and greatest fixpoint operators. Recently, the $\mu$-calculus has generated much interest among researchers in computer-aided verification. This interest stems from the fact that many temporal and program logics can be encoded into the $\mu$-calculus. In addition, important relations between transition systems, such as weak and strong bisimulation equivalence, also have fixpoint characterizations [20].

Another source of interest in the $\mu$-calculus comes from the existence of efficient model checking algorithms for this formalism. As a consequence, verification procedures for many temporal and modal logics can be derived from these algorithms. Wide-spread use of binary decision diagrams has made fixpoint based algorithms even more important, since methods that require the manipulation of individual states do not take advantage of this representation.

Several versions of the propositional $\mu$-calculus have been described in the literature, and the ideas in this paper will work with any of them. For the sake of concreteness, we will use the propositional $\mu$-calculus of Kozen [15]. Closed formulas in this logic evaluate to sets of states. A considerable amount of research has focused on finding techniques for evaluating such formulas efficiently, and many algorithms have been proposed for this purpose. These algorithms generally fall into two categories, local and global.

Local procedures are designed for proving that a specific state of the transition system satisfies the given formula. Because of this, it is not always necessary to examine all the states in the transition system. However, the worst-case complexity of these approaches is generally larger than the complexity of the global methods. Tableau-based local approaches have been developed by Cleaveland [11], Stirling and Walker [22], and Winskel [24]. More recently, Andersen [1] and Larsen [16] have developed efficient local methods for a subset of the $\mu$-calculus. Mader [18] has also proposed improvements to the tableau-based method of Stirling and Walker that seem to increase its efficiency.

In this paper, we restrict ourselves to global model checking procedures. Global procedures generally work bottom-up through the formula, evaluating each subformula based on

This research was sponsored in part by the Wright Laboratory, Aeronautical Systems Center, Air Force Material Command, USAF, and the Advanced Research Projects Agency (ARPA) under grant number F33615-93-1-1330.

The views and conclusions contained in this document are those of the authors and should not be interpreted as necessarily representing the official policies or endorsements, either expressed or implied, of Wright Laboratory or the U. S. Government.

The U. S. Government is authorized to reproduce and distribute reprints for Government purposes notwithstanding any copyright notation thereon. This manuscript is submitted for publication with the understanding that the U. S. Government is authorized to reproduce and distribute reprints for Governmental purposes.

the values of its subformulas. Iteration is used to compute the fixpoints. Because of fixpoint nesting, a naive global algorithm may require about $O(n^k)$ iterations to evaluate a formula, where $n$ is the number of states in the transition system and $k$ is the depth of nesting of the fixpoints. Emerson and Lei [14] improve on this by observing that successively nested fixpoints of the same type do not increase the complexity of the computation. They formalize this observation using the notion of *alternation depth* and give an algorithm requiring only about $O(n^d)$ iterations, where $d$ is the alternation depth. In an implementation, bookkeeping and set manipulations may add another factor of $n$ or so to the time required. Subsequent work by Cleaveland, Klein, Steffen, and Andersen [1, 12, 13] has reduced this extra complexity, but the overall number of iterations has remained about $O(n^d)$. In [17] the authors have improved on this by giving an algorithm that uses only $O(n^{d/2})$ iterations to compute a formula with alternation depth $d$, thus requiring only about the square root of the time needed by earlier algorithms.

This paper describes the propositional $\mu$-calculus and general algorithms for evaluating $\mu$-calculus formulas. Examples of verification problems that can be encoded within the language of the $\mu$-calculus are also provided. The remainder of this paper is organized as follows. A formal syntax and semantics for the propositional $\mu$-calculus is given in Section 2. Section 3 discusses different algorithms for evaluation of $\mu$-calculus formulas and their complexities. A brief description of Ordered Binary Decision Diagrams (OBDDs) is given in Section 4. Section 5 presents the algorithm for encoding $\mu$-calculus formulas with OBDDs. The syntax and semantics for CTL and for CTL with fairness constraints is given in Section 6, while a translation of these logics into the $\mu$-calculus is given in Section 7. Definitions for different kinds of simulation preorders and bisimulation equivalences are given in Section 8 along with encodings for these relations in the $\mu$-calculus. Finally, Section 9 concludes the paper and discusses some open problems.

## 2 The Propositional $\mu$-Calculus

In the propositional $\mu$-calculus, formulas are constructed as follows:

- atomic propositions $AP = \{p, p_1, p_2, \ldots\}$
- relational variables $VAR = \{R, R_1, R_2, \ldots\}$
- logical connectives $\neg\cdot$, $\cdot \wedge \cdot$ and $\cdot \vee \cdot$
- modal operators $\langle a \rangle\cdot$ and $[a]\cdot$, where $a$ is an action in the set $Act = \{a, b, a_1, a_2, \ldots\}$
- fixpoint operators $\mu R_i.(\cdots)$ and $\nu R_i.(\cdots)$. Relational variables bound by the fixpoint operators must be in the scope of the even number of negations.

There is a standard notion of free and bound variables (by fixpoint operators) in the formulas. Closed formulas are the formulas without free variables. Formulas in this calculus are interpreted relative to a transition system $M = (\top, T, L)$ that consists of:

- a nonempty set of states $\top$
- a mapping $L : AP \rightarrow 2^{\top}$ that takes each atomic proposition to some subset of $\top$ (the states where the proposition is true)
- a mapping $T : Act \rightarrow 2^{\top \times \top}$ that takes each action to a binary relation over $\top$ (the state changes that can result from making an action)

The intuitive meaning of the formula $\langle a \rangle \phi$ is "it is possible to make an $a$-action and transition to a state where $\phi$ holds." $[\cdot]$ is the dual of $\langle \cdot \rangle$; for $[a]\phi$, the intended meaning is that "$\phi$ holds in all states reachable (in one step) by making an $a$-action." The $\mu$ and $\nu$ operators are used to express least and greatest fixpoints, respectively. To emphasize the duality between least and greatest fixpoints, we write the empty set of states as $\bot$. Also, in the rest of this paper, we will use the more intuitive notation $s \xrightarrow{a} s'$ to mean $(s, s') \in T(a)$.

Formally, a formula $\phi$ is interpreted as a set of states in which $\phi$ is true. We write such set of states as $[\![\phi]\!]_M\, e$, where $M$ is a transition system and $e : VAR \rightarrow 2^{\top}$ is an environment. We denote by $e\,[R \leftarrow S]$ a new environment which is the same as $e$ except that $e\,[R \leftarrow S]\,(R) = S$. The set $[\![\phi]\!]_M\, e$ is defined recursively as follows.

- $[\![p]\!]_M\, e = L(p)$
- $[\![R]\!]_M\, e = e(R)$
- $[\![\neg\phi]\!]_M\, e = \top - [\![\phi]\!]_M\, e$
- $[\![\phi \wedge \psi]\!]_M\, e = [\![\phi]\!]_M\, e \cap [\![\psi]\!]_M\, e$
- $[\![\phi \vee \psi]\!]_M\, e = [\![\phi]\!]_M\, e \cup [\![\psi]\!]_M\, e$
- $[\![\langle a \rangle \phi]\!]_M\, e = \{s \mid \exists t\, [s \xrightarrow{a} t \text{ and } t \in [\![\phi]\!]_M\, e]\}$
- $[\![[a]\, \phi]\!]_M\, e = \{s \mid \forall t\, [s \xrightarrow{a} t \text{ implies } t \in [\![\phi]\!]_M\, e]\}$
- $[\![\mu R\,.\,\phi]\!]_M\, e$ is the least fixpoint of the predicate transformer $\tau{:}\, 2^{\top} \rightarrow 2^{\top}$ defined by:

$\tau(S) = [\![\phi]\!]_M\, e\,[R \leftarrow S]$

- The interpretation of $\nu R\,.\,\phi$ is similar, except that we take the greatest fixpoint.

Within formulas, the negation is restricted in use, and so the fixpoints are guaranteed to be well-defined. Formally, every logical connective except negation is monotonic

($\phi \rightarrow \phi'$ implies $\phi \wedge \psi \rightarrow \phi' \wedge \psi$, $\phi \vee \psi \rightarrow \phi' \vee \psi$, $\langle a\rangle\phi \rightarrow \langle a\rangle\phi'$, and $[a]\phi \rightarrow [a]\phi'$), and all the negations can be pushed down to the atomic propositions using De Morgan's laws and dualities ($\neg[a]\phi \equiv \langle a\rangle\neg\phi$, $\neg\langle a\rangle\phi \equiv [a]\neg\phi$, $\neg\mu R.\phi(R) \equiv \nu R.\neg\phi(\neg R)$, $\neg\nu R.\phi(R) \equiv \mu R\,.\neg\phi(\neg R)$). Since bound variables are under even number of negations, they will be negation free after this process. Thus, each possible predicate transformer $\tau$ is monotonic ($S \subseteq S'$ implies $\tau(S) \subseteq \tau(S')$). This is enough to ensure the existence of the fixpoints [23]. Furthermore, since we will be evaluating formulas over finite transition systems, monotonicity of $\tau$ implies that $\tau$ is also $\cup$-continuous and $\cap$-continuous, and hence the least and greatest fixpoints can be computed by iterative evaluation:

$$[\![\mu R.\phi]\!]_M\, e = \bigcup_i \tau^i(\bot) \qquad [\![\nu R.\phi]\!]_M\, e = \bigcap_i \tau^i(\top).$$

($\tau^i(S)$ can be defined recursively as $\tau^0(S) = S$ and $\tau^{i+1}(S) = \tau(\tau^i(S))$). Since the domain $\top$ is finite, the iteration must stop after a finite number of steps. More precisely, for some $i \leq |\top|$, the fixpoint is equal to $\tau^i(\bot)$ (for a least fixpoint) or $\tau^i(\top)$ (for a greatest fixpoint). To find the fixpoint, we repeatedly apply $\tau$ starting from $\bot$ or from $\top$ until the result does not change.

The *alternation depth* of a formula is intuitively equal to the number of alternations in the nesting of least and greatest fixpoints, when all negations are applied only to propositions. There are other more elaborate definitions of alternation depth [1, 2, 12], that take into account the possibility that nested fixpoints may still be independent. Such fixpoints do not depend on the value of approximations to outer fixpoints. Consequently, they only need to be evaluated once. This type of nesting does not increase the effective alternation depth. However, to simplify our presentation we will use the definition of alternation depth given by Emerson and Lei [14]. Formally, the alternation depth is defined as follows:

DEFINITION 2.1

- The alternation depth of an atomic proposition or a relational variable is 0;
- The alternation depth for formulas like $\phi \wedge \psi$, $\phi \vee \psi$, $\langle a\rangle\phi$, etc., is the maximum alternation depth of the subformulas $\phi$ and $\psi$.
- The alternation depth of $\mu R.\phi$ is the maximum of: one, the alternation depth of $\phi$, and one plus the alternation depth of any top-level $\nu$-subformulas of $\phi$. A top-level $\nu$-subformula of $\phi$ is a subformula $\nu R'.\psi$ of $\phi$ that is not contained within any other fixpoint subformula of $\phi$. The *alternation depth* of $\nu R.\phi$ is similarly defined.

*Example 2.1* Consider the following formula which will be discussed in Section 7.

$\nu Y.(P \wedge \langle a\rangle\, [\mu X.(P \wedge \langle a\rangle X) \vee (h \wedge Y)])$

This formula expresses the property "*P* holds continuously along some fair *a*-path" and has an alternation depth of two. Here *h* is a fairness constraint.

Because of the duality,

$$\nu R.\phi(\ldots, R, \ldots) = \neg \mu R.\neg \phi(\ldots, \neg R, \ldots)$$

we could have defined the propositional $\mu$-calculus with just the least fixpoint operator and negation. In order to give a succinct description of certain constructions we sometimes use the dual formulation. However, the concept of alternation depth is easier to define using the formulation given earlier.

## 3   Evaluating Fixpoint Formulas

We define *model checking* as a technique for verifying that an interpretation is a model for a $\mu$-calculus specification. This is the same as evaluating a formula in a model, i.e., finding the set of states of the model where the formula is true.

1.  function eval($\phi, e$)
2.  if $\phi = p$ then return $L(p)$
3.  if $\phi = R$ then return $e(R)$
4.  if $\phi = \psi_1 \wedge \psi_2$ then
5.      return eval($\psi_1, e$) $\cap$ eval($\psi_2, e$)
6.  if $\phi = \psi_1 \vee \psi_2$ then
7.      return eval($\psi_1, e$) $\cup$ eval($\psi_2, e$)
8.  if $\phi = \langle a \rangle \psi$ then
9.      return $\{s \mid \exists t \, [s \xrightarrow{a} t$ and $t \in$ eval($\psi, e$)]$\}$
10. if $\phi = [a]\psi$ then
11.     return $\{s \mid \forall t [s \xrightarrow{a} t$ implies $t \in$ eval($\psi, e$)]$\}$
12. if $\phi = \mu R.\psi(R)$ then
13.     $R_{\text{val}} := \perp$
14.     repeat
15.         $R_{\text{old}} := R_{\text{val}}$
16.         $R_{\text{val}} :=$ eval($\psi, e[R \leftarrow R_{\text{val}}]$)
17.     until $R_{\text{val}} = R_{\text{old}}$
18.     return $R_{\text{val}}$

```
if φ = νR.ψ(R) then
    R_val := ⊤
    repeat
        R_old := R_val
        R_val := eval(ψ, e[R ← R_val])
    until R_val = R_old
    return R_val
```

The above program presents the naive, straightforward, recursive algorithm for evaluating $\mu$-calculus formulas. The time complexity of the algorithm in the above program is exponential in the length of the formula. To see this, we analyze the behavior of the algorithm when computing nested fixpoints. The algorithm computes fixpoints by iteratively computing approximations. These successive approximations form a chain ordered by inclusion. Since the number of strict inclusions in such a chain is limited by the number of possible states, the loop will execute at most $n+1$ times, where $n = |\top|$. Each iteration of the loop involves a recursive call to evaluate the body of the fixpoint with a different value for the fixpoint variable. If in turn, the subformula being evaluated contains a fixpoint, the evaluation of its body will also involve a loop containing up to $n+1$ recursive calls. Thus, the total number of recursive calls will be $O(n^2)$. In general, the body of the innermost fixpoint will be evaluated $O(n^k)$ times where $k$ is the maximum nesting depth of fixpoint operators in the formula.

Note that we have only considered the number of iterations required when evaluating fixpoints and not the number of steps required to evaluate a $\mu$-calculus formula. While each fixpoint may only take $O(n)$ iterations, each individual iteration can take up to $O(|M||\phi|)$ steps, where $M = (\top, T, L)$ is the model and $|M| = |\top| + \sum_{a \in Act} |T(a)|$. In general, then, this algorithm has time complexity $O[|M||\phi|n^k]$.

A result by Emerson and Lei demonstrates that the value of a fixpoint formula can be computed with $O((|\phi|n)^d)$ iterations, where $d$ is the alternation depth of $\phi$. Their algorithm is similar to the straightforward one described above, except when a fixpoint is nested directly within the scope of another fixpoint of the same type. In this case, the fixpoints are computed slightly differently.

A simple example will suffice to demonstrate the idea. When discussing the evaluation of fixpoint formulas, we will use $R_1, \ldots, R_k$ as the fixpoint variables, with $R_1$ being the outermost fixpoint variable and $R_k$ being the innermost. We will use the notation $R_j^{i_1 \cdots i_j}$ to denote the value of the $i_j$-th approximation for $R_j$ after having computed the $i_l$-th approximation for $R_l$ for $1 \leq l < j$. We use $i_j = \omega$ to indicate that we are considering the final approximation (the actual fixpoint value) for $R_j$. For example, $R_1^{\omega}$ is the value of the fixpoint for $R_1$ and $R_2^{30}$ is the initial approximation for $R_2$ after having computed the third approximation for $R_1$. Consider the formula

$\mu R_1.\psi_1(R_1, \mu R_2.\psi_2(R_1, R_2))$.

The subformula $\mu R_2.\psi_2(R_1, R_2)$ defines a monotonic predicate transformer $\tau$ taking one set (the value of $R_1$) to another (the value of the least fixpoint of $R_2$). When evaluating the outer fixpoint, we start with the initial approximation $R_1^0 = \bot$ and then compute $\tau(R_1^0)$. This is done by iteratively computing approximations for the inner fixpoint also starting from $R_2^{00} = \bot$ until we reach a fixpoint $R_2^{0\omega}$. Now $R_1$ is increased to $R_1^1$, the result of evaluating $\psi_1(R_1^0, R_2^{0\omega})$. We next compute the least fixpoint $\tau(R_1^1)$. Since $R_1^0 \subseteq R_1^1$, by monotonicity we know that $\tau(R_1^0) \subseteq \tau(R_1^1)$. Now note that the following lemma holds:

LEMMA 3.1 If $S \subseteq \bigcup_i \tau^i(\bot)$ then $\bigcup_i \tau^i(S) = \bigcup_i \tau^i(\bot)$.

In other words, to compute a least fixpoint, it is enough to start iterating with any approximation known to be below the fixpoint. Thus , we can start iterating with $R_2^{10} = R_2^{0\omega} = \tau(R_1^0)$ instead of $R_2^{10} = \bot$. When we compute the fixpoint $R_2^{1\omega}$, we next compute the new approximation to $R_1$, which is $R_1^2$, the result of evaluating $\psi_1(R_1^1, R_2^{1\omega})$. Again, we know that $R_1^1 \subseteq R_1^2$ which implies that $\tau(R_1^1) \subseteq \tau(R_1^2)$. But $\tau(R_1^1) = R_2^{1\omega}$, the value of the last inner fixpoint computed, and $\tau(R_1^2) = R_2^{2\omega}$ the fixpoint to be computed next. Again, we can start iterating with any approximation below the fixpoint. So to compute $R_2^{2\omega}$ we begin with $R_2^{20} = R_2^{1\omega} = \tau(R_1^1)$. In general, when computing $R_2^{i\omega}$ we always begin with $R_2^{i0} = R_2^{(i-1)\omega}$. Since we never restart the inner fixpoint computation, we can have at most $n$ increases in the value of the inner fixpoint variable. Overall, we only need $O(n)$ iterations to evaluate this expression, instead of $O(n^2)$. In general, this type of simplification leads to an algorithm that computes fixpoint formulas in time exponential in the alternation depth of the formula since we only reset an inner fixpoint computation when there is an alternation in fixpoints in the formula.

1. function eval($\phi$,$e$)
2. $N$ := The number of fixpoint operators in $\phi$
3. for $i$ := 1 to $N$ do $A[i]$ := if the $i$-th fixpoint of $\phi$ is $\mu$ then $\bot$ else $\top$
4. return evalrec($\phi$, $e$)

Where *evalrec* is defined recursively as

1. function evalrec($\phi$, $e$)
2. if $\phi = p$ then return $L(p)$
3. if $\phi = R$ then return $e(R)$
4. if $\phi = \psi_1 \wedge \psi_2$ then

    return evalrec($\psi_1, e$)$\cap$ evalrec($\psi_2, e$)
if $\phi = \psi_1 \vee \psi_2$ then
    return evalrec($\psi_1, e$)$\cup$ evalrec($\psi_2, e$)
if $\phi = \langle a \rangle \psi$ then
    return $\{s \mid \exists t[s \xrightarrow{a} t$ and $t \in$ evalrec$(\psi, e)]\}$
if $\phi = [a]\psi$ then
    return $\{s \mid \forall t[s \xrightarrow{a} t$ implies $t \in$ evalrec$(\psi, e)]\}$
if $\phi = \mu R_i.\psi(R_i)$ then
    For all top-level greatest fixpoint subformulas $\nu R_j.\psi'(R_j)$ of $\psi$
        do $A[j] := \top$
    repeat
        $R_{\text{old}} := A[i]$
        $A[i] :=$ evalrec($\psi, e[R_i \leftarrow A[i]]$)
    until $A[i] = R_{\text{old}}$
    return $A[i]$
if $\phi = \nu R_i.\psi(R_i)$ then
    For all top-level least fixpoint subformulas $\mu R_j.\psi'(R_j)$ of $\psi$
        do $A[j] := \bot$
    repeat
        $R_{\text{old}} := A[i]$
        $A[i] :=$ evalrec($\psi, e[R_i \leftarrow$ A[i]])
    until $A[i] = R_1$
    return $A[i]$

Thus, this algorithm for evaluating $\mu$-calculus formulas is identical to the naive algorithm except in the case when the main connective is a fixpoint operator. The pseudocode for this algorithm is given in the program given above. Note that unlike the naive algorithm, the approximation values $A[i]$ are not reset when evaluating the subformula $\mu R_i.\psi(R_i)(\nu R_i.\psi(R_i))$. Instead, we reset all top-level greatest (least) fixpoint variables contained in $\psi$. Recall that by the top-level fixpoints in a formula we mean all the fixpoints of the same type ($\mu$ or $\nu$) that are not in the scope of the other type of fixpoints. This guarantees that when we evaluate a top-level fixpoint subformula of the same type, we do not start the computation from $\bot$ or $\top$, but from the previously computed value as in our example.

In [17] the authors observe that by storing even more intermediate values, the time complexity for evaluating fixpoint formulas can be reduced to $O(n^{\lfloor d/2 \rfloor + 1})$ where again $d$ is the alternation depth of the formula. To simplify our discussion, we consider formulas with strict alternation of fixpoints. We present a small example to illustrate the idea behind this algorithm.

Consider the formula:

$$\mu R_1.\psi_1(R_1, \nu R_2.\psi_2(R_1, R_2, \mu R_3.\psi_3(R_1, R_2, R_3))).$$

To compute the outer fixpoint, we start with $R_1 = \bot$, $R_2 = \top$ and $R_3 = \bot$. As in the previous case, we denote these values by $R_1^0$, $R_2^{00}$, and $R_3^{000}$ respectively. The superscript on $R_k$ gives the iteration indices for the fixpoints involving $R_1, \ldots R_k$. We then iterate to compute the inner fixpoint; call the value of this fixpoint $R_3^{00\omega}$. We now compute the next approximation $R_2^{01}$ for $R_2$ by evaluating $\psi_2(R_1^0, R_2^{00}, R_3^{00\omega})$ and go back to the inner fixpoint. Eventually, we reach the fixpoint for $R_2$, having computed $R_2^{00}$, $R_3^{00\omega}$, $R_2^{01}$, $R_3^{01\omega}$, $\ldots$, $R_2^{0\omega}$, $R_3^{0\omega\omega}$. Now we proceed to $R_1^1 = \psi_1(R_1^0, R_2^{0\omega}, R_3^{0\omega\omega})$. We know that $R_1^0 \subseteq R_1^1$, and we are now going to compute $R_2^{1\omega}$. Note that the values $R_2^{0\omega}$ and $R_2^{1\omega}$ are given by

$$R_2^{0\omega} = \nu R_2.\psi_2\left(R_1^0, R_2, \mu R_3.\psi_3\left(R_1^0, R_2, R_3\right)\right)$$

and

$$R_2^{1\omega} = \nu R_2.\psi_2\left(R_1^1, R_2, \mu R_3.\psi_3\left(R_1^1, R_2, R_3\right)\right).$$

By monotonicity, we know that $R_2^{1\omega}$ will be a superset of $R_2^{0\omega}$. However, since $R_2$ is computed by a greatest fixpoint, this information does not help; we still must start computing with $R_2^{10} = \top$. At this point, we begin to compute the inner fixpoint again. But now let us look at $R_3^{00\omega}$ and $R_3^{10\omega}$. We have

$$R_3^{00\omega} = \mu R_3.\psi_3\left(R_1^0, R_2^{00}, R_3\right)$$

and

$$R_3^{10\omega} = \mu R_3.\psi_3\left(R_1^1, R_2^{10}, R_3\right).$$

Since $R_1^0 \subseteq R_1^1$ and $R_2^{00} \subseteq R_2^{10}$, monotonicity implies that $R_3^{00\omega} \subseteq R_3^{10\omega}$. Now $R_3$ is a least fixpoint, so starting the computation of $R_3^{10\omega}$ anywhere below the fixpoint value is acceptable. Thus, we can start the computation for $R_3^{10\omega}$ with $R_3^{100} = R_3^{00\omega}$. Since $R_3^{00\omega}$ is in general larger than $\bot$, we obtain faster convergence. In addition, we have

$$R_2^{01} = \psi_2\left(R_1^0, R_2^{00}, R_3^{00\omega}\right)$$

and

$$R_2^{11} = \psi_2\left(R_1^1, R_2^{10}, R_3^{10\omega}\right)$$

Since $R_1^0 \subseteq R_1^1$, $R_2^{00} \subseteq R_2^{10}$, and $R_3^{00\omega} \subseteq R_3^{10\omega}$, we will have $R_2^{01} \subseteq R_2^{11}$. This means that we can use the same trick when computing $R_3^{11\omega}$: we start the computation from $R_3^{110} = R_3^{01\omega}$. And again, since $R_1^0 \subseteq R_1^1$, $R_2^{01} \subseteq R_2^{11}$, and $R_3^{01\omega} \subseteq R_3^{11\omega}$, we will have $R_2^{02} \subseteq R_2^{12}$. In general, we will have $R_2^{0j} \subseteq R_2^{1j}$ and $R_3^{0j\omega} \subseteq R_3^{1j\omega}$ so we can start computing $R_3^{1j\omega}$ from $R_3^{1j0} = R_3^{0j\omega}$. Similarly, once we find $R_1^2$ (or in general, $R_1^{k+1}$), we can start computing the inner fixpoints from $R_3^{2m0} = R_3^{1m\omega}$ (in general $R_3^{(k+1)m0} = R_3^{km\omega}$).

The table in Figure 11.1 illustrates this by showing the relationship between all the different possible approximation values for $R_3$. Each row can have at most $n+1$ entries, one for each approximation to $\nu R_2.\psi_2$. At first glance, it seems possible that each column could have as many as $n^2$ entries. However, each chain represented by each column can have at most $n+1$ distinct values. Repeated values only appear when convergence is reached ($R_3^{ij\omega} = R_3^{ij(\omega-1)}$) and when we start a computation from a previously computed fixpoint ($R_3^{(i+1)j0} = R_3^{ij\omega}$). Convergence is reached every time the fixpoint is evaluated, and this fixpoint is evaluated once for every outer greatest fixpoint approximation of which there can be no more than $n+1$. Since there can be no more than $n+1$ evaluations, we can start from a previously computed fixpoint no more than $n$ times. So the number of repeated values is bounded by $2n+1$. Thus, the total number of entries in any column is bound by $3n+2$ and the total number of assignments to $R_3$ during the entire computation is bound by $(3n+2)(n+1)$. This means that there are at most $O(n^2)$ iterations performed to compute the innermost fixpoint.

Again, this algorithm for evaluating a $\mu$-calculus formula is identical to the naive algorithm except when the main connective is a fixpoint operator. To facilitate explanation, we consider only formulas with strict alternation of fixpoints, and in particular, with the form:

$$\begin{aligned}
F_1 &\equiv \mu R_1.\psi_1(R_1, \nu R_1'.\psi_1'(R_1, R_1', F_2))\\
F_2 &\equiv \mu R_2.\psi_2(R_1, R_1', R_2, \nu R_2'.\psi_2'(R_1, R_1', R_2, R_2', F_3))\\
&\vdots\\
F_q &\equiv \mu R_q.\psi_q(R_1, R_1', \ldots, R_q, \nu R_q'.\psi_q'(R_1, R_1', \ldots, R_q, R_q'))
\end{aligned}$$

The pseudocode for this part of the algorithm is given in Figure 11.2. For computing the outermost fixpoint (corresponding to $R_1$) we follow the naive algorithm, i.e., start with $\bot$ and iterate until convergence. The algorithm uses a table $\mathcal{T}_i$ to store the last computed fixpoint values for the $\mu$-variables $R_i$ (for $i \geq 2$). Initially, all entries in $\mathcal{T}_i$ are $\bot$. The table $\mathcal{T}_i$ is a multi-dimensional table. For the $i$-th least fixpoint (corresponding to $R_i$) we index the table $\mathcal{T}_i$ by the iteration counters $k_1, \ldots, k_{i-1}$ of the greatest fixpoints in which

$$
\begin{array}{ccccccc}
R_3^{\omega 0 \omega} & \supseteq & R_3^{\omega 1 \omega} & \supseteq & \cdots & \supseteq & R_3^{\omega \omega \omega} \\
\rotatebox{90}{$\subseteq$} & & \rotatebox{90}{$\subseteq$} & & & & \rotatebox{90}{$\subseteq$} \\
\vdots & & \vdots & & & & \vdots \\
\rotatebox{90}{$\subseteq$} & & \rotatebox{90}{$\subseteq$} & & & & \rotatebox{90}{$\subseteq$} \\
R_3^{\omega 01} & \supseteq & R_3^{\omega 11} & \supseteq & \cdots & \supseteq & R_3^{\omega \omega 1} \\
\rotatebox{90}{$\subseteq$} & & \rotatebox{90}{$\subseteq$} & & & & \rotatebox{90}{$\subseteq$} \\
R_3^{\omega 00} & \supseteq & R_3^{\omega 10} & \supseteq & \cdots & \supseteq & R_3^{\omega \omega 0} \\
\| & & \| & & & & \| \\
\vdots & & \vdots & & & & \vdots \\
\| & & \| & & & & \| \\
R_3^{10 \omega} & \supseteq & R_3^{11 \omega} & \supseteq & \cdots & \supseteq & R_3^{1 \omega \omega} \\
\rotatebox{90}{$\subseteq$} & & \rotatebox{90}{$\subseteq$} & & & & \rotatebox{90}{$\subseteq$} \\
\vdots & & \vdots & & & & \vdots \\
\rotatebox{90}{$\subseteq$} & & \rotatebox{90}{$\subseteq$} & & & & \rotatebox{90}{$\subseteq$} \\
R_3^{101} & \supseteq & R_3^{111} & \supseteq & \cdots & \supseteq & R_3^{1 \omega 1} \\
\rotatebox{90}{$\subseteq$} & & \rotatebox{90}{$\subseteq$} & & & & \rotatebox{90}{$\subseteq$} \\
R_3^{100} & \supseteq & R_3^{110} & \supseteq & \cdots & \supseteq & R_3^{1 \omega 0} \\
\| & & \| & & & & \| \\
R_3^{00 \omega} & \supseteq & R_3^{01 \omega} & \supseteq & \cdots & \supseteq & R_3^{0 \omega \omega} \\
\rotatebox{90}{$\subseteq$} & & \rotatebox{90}{$\subseteq$} & & & & \rotatebox{90}{$\subseteq$} \\
\vdots & & \vdots & & & & \vdots \\
\rotatebox{90}{$\subseteq$} & & \rotatebox{90}{$\subseteq$} & & & & \rotatebox{90}{$\subseteq$} \\
R_3^{001} & \supseteq & R_3^{011} & \supseteq & \cdots & \supseteq & R_3^{0 \omega 1} \\
\rotatebox{90}{$\subseteq$} & & \rotatebox{90}{$\subseteq$} & & & & \rotatebox{90}{$\subseteq$} \\
R_3^{000} & \supseteq & R_3^{010} & \supseteq & \cdots & \supseteq & R_3^{0 \omega 0}
\end{array}
$$

**Figure 11.1**
Monotonicity constraints on approximations to $R_3$

the $i$-th least fixpoint is nested. When evaluating $R_i$, we start with the corresponding table value and iterate until convergence. At the end of the iteration, the table holds the fixpoint value. When evaluating $R_i'$, we always begin with $\top$ and iterate until convergence. Note that this algorithm implements the ideas in the previous example.

If we use these ideas, how many steps does the computation take? To try to answer this question, we look at the number of approximations computed for the $R_i$s and $R_i'$s in the algorithm. Let $T_i$ denote the number of approximations for $R_i$, and let $T_i'$ denote the number

12.  if $\phi = \mu R_i . \psi_i(R_i)$ and $i \geq 2$ then

13.  $\qquad R_{\mathrm{val}} := T_i[k_1] \cdots [k_{i-1}]$

14.  $\qquad$ repeat

15.  $\qquad\qquad R_{\mathrm{old}} := R_{\mathrm{val}}$

16.  $\qquad\qquad R_{\mathrm{val}} := \mathrm{evalrec}(\psi_i, e\,[R_i \leftarrow R_{\mathrm{old}}])$

17.  $\qquad$ until $R_{\mathrm{val}} = R_{\mathrm{old}}$

18.  $\qquad T_i[k_1] \cdots [k_{i-1}] := R_{\mathrm{val}}$

19.  $\qquad$ return $R_{\mathrm{val}}$

20.  if $\phi = \nu R_i' . \psi_i'(R_i')$ then

21.  $\qquad k_i := 0$

22.  $\qquad R_{\mathrm{val}} := \top$

23.  $\qquad$ repeat

24.  $\qquad\qquad R_{\mathrm{val}} := \mathrm{evalrec}(\psi_i', e\,[R_i' \leftarrow R_{\mathrm{val}}])$

25.  $\qquad\qquad k_i := k_i + 1$

26.  $\qquad$ until $k_i = |\top|$

27.  $\qquad$ return $R_{\mathrm{val}}$

**Figure 11.2**
Pseudocode for the efficient algorithm

of approximations for $R_i'$. The fixpoint for $R_i'$ is evaluated at most $T_i$ times (the number of approximations to the enclosing $R_i$). Each evaluation can take at most $n + 1$ iterations for a total of $(n + 1)T_i$ approximations. Thus, $T_i' \leq (n + 1)T_i$. The fixpoint for $R_i$ has a table $T_i$ with $(n + 1)^{i-1}$ entries. Because of the monotonicity constraints, each entry can go through at most $n + 1$ distinct values. Since there are $(n + 1)^{i-1}$ entries, we have a total of $(n + 1)^i$ iterations. These iterations correspond to the case when the loop test is false. In addition, each time we evaluate the fixpoint for $R_i$ we will take one extra step to detect convergence which will not result in a new value for the corresponding table entry. We evaluate the fixpoint for $R_i$ at most $T_{i-1}'$ times. Thus we make at most $T_{i-1}'$ iterations when the loop test is true. In total, we have $T_i \leq (n + 1)^i + T_{i-1}'$. Solving this recurrence, we get:

$$T_i \leq i(n + 1)^i$$
$$T_i' \leq i(n + 1)^{i+1}$$

Summing over all fixpoints and expressing the result in terms of the alternation depth $d = 2q$, we get that the algorithm takes $O(d(n+1)^{d/2+1})$ iterations when computing the fixpoints in a formula with strict alternation. In comparison, previously known algorithms may require $O(n^d)$ iterations.

## 4 Ordered Binary Decision Diagrams (OBDDs)

In this section we give a brief description of an efficient data structure for representing boolean functions. Consider the space $\mathcal{BF}_n$ of boolean functions on $n$ variables $x_0, x_1, \ldots, x_{n-1}$. We assume that there is a total ordering on the boolean variables. The ordering is given by the index, i.e., $x_i$ is ordered before $x_j$ iff $i < j$. The symbol OBDD($f$) will denote the Ordered Binary Decision Diagram (OBDD) for the boolean function $f$ [7]. OBDDs have the following *canonicity* property:

THEOREM 4.1 (CANONICITY THEOREM) Given two boolean functions $f$ and $g$ in the space $\mathcal{BF}_n$, $\text{OBDD}(f) = \text{OBDD}(g)$ iff $f = g$.

A detailed proof is given in [7].

We will give a succinct explanation of how OBDDs work through an example. For a more thorough treatment see [7, 9]. Consider the following boolean function $f$:

$$f = x_0 \oplus x_1 \oplus x_2$$

where $\oplus$ is the exclusive "or" operator. Figure 11.3 gives the binary tree $T$ corresponding to the boolean function $f$. Notice that the binary subtree which we get by following the paths (0, 1) and (1, 0) from the root are the same. The same is true if we follow the paths (0, 0) and (1, 1). Figure 11.4 reflects this sharing. Notice that the number of nodes is reduced from 15 to 7. In general, the binary tree corresponding to the parity of $n$ bits has $2^{n+1} - 1$ nodes. The OBDD for the same function has $2n + 1$ nodes. Therefore, in some cases OBDD can be exponentially more succinct than the straightforward representation. We will use $|\text{OBDD}(f)|$ to denote the size of the OBDD for $f$, i.e., the number of nodes in OBDD($f$). In addition to being a canonical representation, OBDDs support the usual operations on boolean functions efficiently. The complexity of some of the operations is shown below:

- Given the OBDDs for $f$ and $g$, the OBDD for $f \vee g$ and $f \wedge g$ can be computed in time $O(|\text{OBDD}(f)| \cdot |\text{OBDD}(g)|)$.
- Given the OBDD for $f$, the OBDD for $\neg f$ can be computed in time $O(|\text{OBDD}(f)|)$.
- Given the OBDD for $f$, the OBDDs for $\exists x_i f$ and $\forall x_i f$ can be computed in time $O(|\text{OBDD}(f)|^2)$.

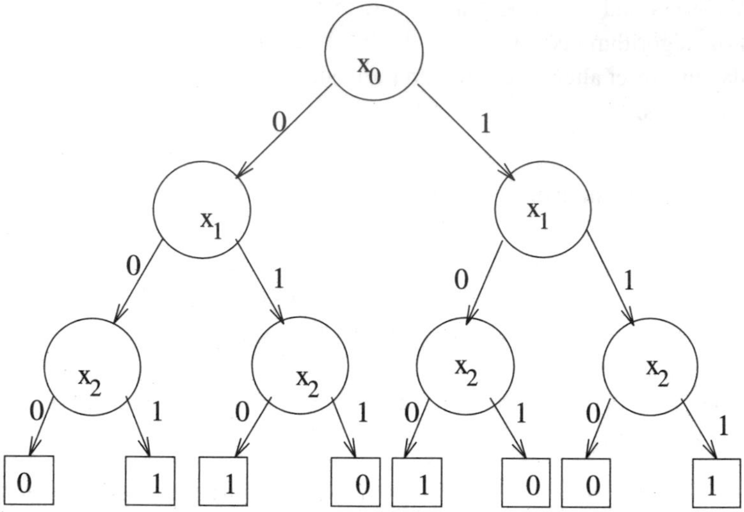


**Figure 11.3**
Tree for the 3 bit parity function

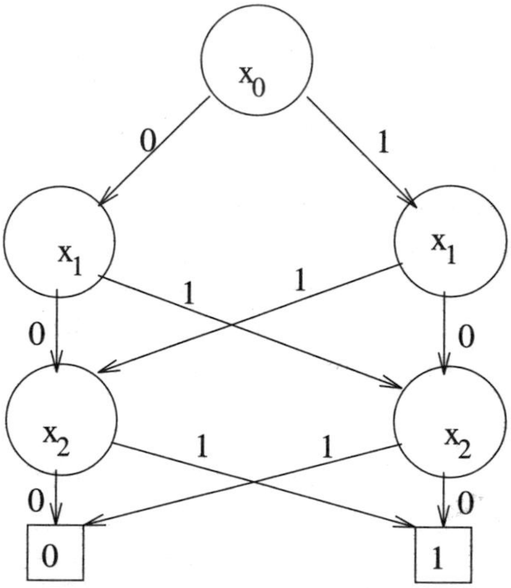


**Figure 11.4**
OBDD for the 3 bit parity function

Variable ordering is extremely important in OBDDs. For example, consider the following boolean function:

$$f(x_1, \ldots, x_n, x_1', \ldots, x_n') = \bigwedge_{i=1}^{n} (x_i = x_i')$$

The OBDD for $f$ with the variable ordering

$$x_1 < x_1' < x_2 < x_2' < \cdots x_n < x_n'$$

has size $3n + 2$. As the following lemma shows, the OBDD for $f$ can have size exponential in $n$ under some variable orderings. Moreover, there are some functions whose OBDDs have exponential size under any variable ordering [7].

LEMMA 4.1 Let $f(x_1, \ldots, x_n, x_1', \ldots, x_n')$ be the following boolean function:

$$\bigwedge_{i=1}^{n} (x_i = x_i')$$

Let $F$ be the OBDD for $f$ such that all the unprimed variables are ordered before all the primed variables. In this case $|F| \geq 2^n$.

*Proof* Consider two distinct assignments $(b_1, \ldots, b_n)$ and $(c_1, \ldots, c_n)$ to the boolean vector $(x_1, \ldots, x_n)$. These two assignments can be distinguished because of the following equation:

$$f(b_1, \ldots, b_n, b_1, \ldots, b_n) \neq f(c_1, \ldots, c_n, b_1, \ldots, b_n)$$

Let $v_1$ and $v_2$ be the nodes reached after following the path $(b_1, \ldots, b_n)$ and $(c_1, \ldots, c_n)$ from the top node. Since these two assignments can be distinguished, $v_1 \neq v_2$. There are $2^n$ different assignments to the boolean vector $(x_1, \ldots, x_n)$ and each of them corresponds to a different node (at level $n$) in the OBDD $F$. Therefore, the number of nodes at level $n$ in the OBDD $F$ is greater than or equal to $2^n$. □

## 5 Translating the $\mu$-Calculus into OBDDs

In this section we describe how to use OBDDs in the model checking algorithms described earlier. First, we show how to encode a transition system $M = (\top, T, L)$ into OBDDs. The domain $\top$ is encoded by the set of values of the $n$ boolean variables $x_1, \ldots, x_n$, i.e., $\top$ is now the space of 0-1 vectors of length $n$. Each variable $x_i$ has a corresponding primed variable $x_i'$. Instead of writing $x_1, \ldots, x_n$, we sometimes use the vector notation $\vec{x}$. For example, we write OBDD$(x_1, \ldots, x_n)$ as OBDD$(\vec{x})$. Given an interpretation we build the OBDDs corresponding to closed $\mu$-calculus formulas in the following manner.

• Each atomic proposition $p$ has an OBDD associated with it. We will denote this OBDD by $\text{OBDD}_p(\vec{x})$. $\text{OBDD}_p(\vec{x})$ has the property that $\vec{y} \in \{0, 1\}^n$ satisfies $\text{OBDD}_p$ iff $\vec{y} \in L(p)$.

• Each program letter $a$ has an ordered binary decision diagram $\text{OBDD}_a(\vec{x}, \vec{x}')$ associated with it. A 0-1 vector $(\vec{y}, \vec{z}) \in \{0, 1\}^{2n}$ satisfies $\text{OBDD}_a$ iff

$(\vec{y}, \vec{z}) \in T(a)$

Now we describe the encoding of the semantic sets of formulas into OBDDs. Assume that we are given a $\mu$-calculus formula $\phi$ with free relational variables $R_1, \ldots, R_k$. $\mathcal{A}[R_i]$ gives the OBDD corresponding to the relational variable $R_i$. $\mathcal{A}\langle R \leftarrow B_R \rangle$ creates a new association by adding a relational variable $R$ and associating an OBDD $B_R$ with $R$. In other words, $\mathcal{A}$ can be considered as an environment with OBDD representation. The procedure $B$ given below takes a $\mu$-calculus formula $\phi$ and an association list $\mathcal{A}$ ($\mathcal{A}$ assigns an OBDD to each free relational variable occuring in $\phi$) and returns an OBDD corresponding to the semantics of $\phi$.

- $B(p, \mathcal{A}) = \text{OBDD}_p(\vec{x})$.
- $B(R_i, \mathcal{A}) = \mathcal{A}[R_i]$.
- $B(\neg\phi, \mathcal{A}) = \neg B(\phi, \mathcal{A})$
- $B(\phi \wedge \psi, \mathcal{A}) = B(\phi, \mathcal{A}) \wedge B(\psi, \mathcal{A})$.
- $B(\phi \vee \psi, \mathcal{A}) = B(\phi, \mathcal{A}) \vee B(\psi, \mathcal{A})$.
- $B(\langle a \rangle\phi, \mathcal{A}) = \exists \vec{x}'(\text{OBDD}_a(\vec{x}, \vec{x}') \wedge B(\phi, \mathcal{A})(\vec{x}'))$
- $B([a]\phi, \mathcal{A}) = B(\neg\langle a \rangle\neg\phi, \mathcal{A})$.

The last equation uses the dual formulation for $[a]$.

- $B(\mu R.\phi, \mathcal{A}) = \mathit{FIX}(\phi, \mathcal{A}, \text{FALSE-BDD})$.
- $B(\nu R.\phi, \mathcal{A}) = \mathit{FIX}(\phi, \mathcal{A}, \text{TRUE-BDD})$.

The OBDDs for the boolean functions **false** and **true** are denoted by FALSE-BDD and TRUE-BDD respectively. *FIX* is described in Figure 11.5. Now we give a short example to illustrate our point.

*Example 5.1* Assume that the state space $\top$ is encoded by $n$ boolean variables $x_1, \ldots, x_n$. Consider the following formula:

$\phi = \mu Z.(q \wedge Y \vee \langle a \rangle Z)$

Notice that the variable $Y$ is free in $\phi$. Assume that the interpretation for $q$ is an OBDD $\text{OBDD}_q(\vec{x})$. Similarly, the OBDD corresponding to the program letter $a$ is $\text{OBDD}_a(\vec{x}, \vec{x}')$.

```
function FIX(φ, A, B_R)
result-bdd = B_R
do
    old-bdd = result-bdd
    result-bdd = B(φ, A⟨R ← old-bdd⟩)
while (not-equal(old-bdd, result-bdd))
return(result-bdd)
```

**Figure 11.5**
Pseudocode for the function *FIX*

Also assume that we are given an association list $\mathcal{A}$ which pairs the OBDD $B_Y(\vec{x})$ with $Y$. In the routine *FIX* the OBDD result-bdd is initially set to:

$$N^0(\vec{x}) = \text{FALSE-BDD}$$

Let $N^i$ be the value of result-bdd at the $i$-th iteration in the loop of the function *FIX*. At the end of the iteration the value of result-bdd is given by:

$$N^{i+1}(\vec{x}) = \text{OBDD}_q(\vec{x}) \wedge B_Y(\vec{x}) \vee \exists \vec{x}'(\text{OBDD}_a(\vec{x}, \vec{x}') \wedge N^i(\vec{x}'))$$

The iteration stops when $N^i(\vec{x}) = N^{i+1}(\vec{x})$.

## 6 Branching Time Temporal Logics

Let *AP* be a set of atomic propositions. A Kripke structure over *AP* is a triple $M = (S, T, L)$, where

- $S$ is a finite set of *states*,
- $T \subseteq S \times S$ is a *transition relation*, which must be total (i.e., for every state $s_1$ there exists a state $s_2$ such that $(s_1, s_2) \in T$).
- $L : S \to 2^{AP}$ is a *labeling function* which associates with each state a set of atomic propositions that are true in the state.

There are two types of formulas in the temporal logic *CTL*$^\star$: *state formulas* (which are true in a specific state) and *path formulas* (which are true along a specific path). The state operators in *CTL*$^\star$ are: **A** ("for all computation paths"), **E** ("for some computation paths"). The path operators in *CTL*$^\star$ are: **X** ("next time"), **G** ("always"), **F** ("sometimes"), **U** ("until"), and **V** ("unless"). Let *AP* be a set of atomic propositions. A state formula is either:

- $p$, if $p \in AP$;
- $\neg f$ or $f \vee g$, where $f$ and $g$ are state formulas; or
- $\mathbf{E}(f)$ where $f$ is a path formula.

Path formulas are defined as follows:

- every state formula is a path formula; and
- if $f$ and $g$ are path formulas, then $\neg f$, $f \vee g$, $\mathbf{X}\, f$, $f\, \mathbf{U}\, g$, and $f\, \mathbf{V}\, g$ are path formulas.

*CTL** is the set of state formulas generated by the above rules.

We define the semantics of *CTL** with respect to a Kripke structure $M = (S, T, L)$. A *path* in $M$ is an infinite sequence of states $\pi = s_0, s_1, \ldots$ such that, for every $i \geq 0$, $(s_i, s_{i+1}) \in T$. $\pi^i$ denotes the *suffix* of $\pi$ starting at $s_i$. $\pi[i]$ denotes the $i$-th state on the path $\pi$. The starting state of path $\pi$ is $\pi[0]$. We use the standard notation to indicate that a state formula $f$ holds in a structure. $M, s \models f$ means that $f$ holds at the state $s$ in the structure $M$. Similarly, $M, \pi \models f$ means that the path formula $f$ is true along the path $\pi$. Assume that $f_1$ and $f_2$ are state formulas and $g_1$ and $g_2$ are path formulas, then the relation $\models$ is defined inductively as follows:

1. $s \models p \Leftrightarrow p \in L(s)$
2. $s \models \neg f_1 \Leftrightarrow s \not\models f_1$
3. $s \models f_1 \vee f_2 \Leftrightarrow s \models f_1$ or $s \models f_2$
4. $s \models \mathbf{E}(g_1) \Leftrightarrow$ there exists a path $\pi$ starting with $s$ such that $\pi \models g_1$
5. $\pi \models f_1 \Leftrightarrow \pi[0] \models f_1$
6. $\pi \models \neg g_1 \Leftrightarrow \pi \not\models g_1$
7. $\pi \models g_1 \vee g_2 \Leftrightarrow \pi \models g_1$ or $\pi \models g_2$
8. $\pi \models \mathbf{X}\, g_1 \Leftrightarrow \pi^1 \models g_1$
9. $\pi \models g_1\, \mathbf{U}\, g_2 \Leftrightarrow$ there exists $k \geq 0$ such that $\pi^k \models g_2$ and for all $0 \leq j < k$, $\pi^j \models g_1$.
10. $\pi \models g_1\, \mathbf{V}\, g_2 \Leftrightarrow$ for every $k \geq 0$, if $\pi^j \not\models g_1$ for all $0 \leq j < k$, then $\pi^k \models g_2$.

*CTL* is the subset of *CTL** in which the path formulas are restricted to be:

- if $f$ and $g$ are state formulas, then $\mathbf{X}\, f$, $f\, \mathbf{U}\, g$, and $f\, \mathbf{V}\, g$ are path formulas.

The basic modalities of *CTL* are $\mathbf{EX}\, f$, $\mathbf{EG}\, f$, and $\mathbf{E}(f\, \mathbf{U}\, g)$, where $f$ and $g$ are again *CTL* formulas. The operator $\mathbf{E}(f\, \mathbf{V}\, g)$ can be expressed as follows:

$$\begin{aligned} \mathbf{E}(f\, \mathbf{V}\, g) &= \mathbf{E}((\neg f \wedge g)\, \mathbf{U}\, (f \wedge g)) \vee \mathbf{EG}(\neg f \wedge g) \\ \mathbf{EF}\, f &= \mathbf{E}(\mathit{true}\, \mathbf{U}\, f) \\ \mathbf{EG} f &= \mathbf{E}(\mathit{false} \mathbf{V}\, f) \end{aligned}$$

The operators $\mathbf{AG}\, f$, $\mathbf{AF}\, f$ and $\mathbf{A}(f\ \mathbf{U}\ g)$ can be expressed in terms of the basic modalities described above.

$$\begin{aligned} \mathbf{AG}\, f &= \neg\, \mathbf{EF} \neg f \\ \mathbf{AF}\, f &= \neg\, \mathbf{EG} \neg f \\ \mathbf{A}(f\ \mathbf{U}\ g) &= \neg\, \mathbf{E}(\neg f\ \mathbf{V}\ \neg g) \end{aligned}$$

Next, we discuss the issue of *fairness*. In many cases, we are only interested in the correctness along paths with certain conditions. For example, if we are verifying a protocol with a scheduler, we may wish to consider only executions where processes are not ignored by the scheduler, i.e., every process is given a chance to run infinitely often. This type of fairness constraint cannot be expressed in *CTL* [10]. In order to handle such properties we have to modify the semantics of *CTL*. A *fairness constraint* can be an arbitrary set of states, usually described by a *CTL* formula. Generally, there will be several fairness constraints. In this paper we will denote the set of all fairness constraints by $H = \{h_1, \ldots, h_n\}$. We have the following definition of a *fair* path.

DEFINITION 6.1 Given a Kripke Structure $M = (S, T, L)$ and a set of fairness constraints $H = \{h_1, \ldots, h_n\}$, a path $\pi$ in $M$ is called *fair* iff each *CTL* formula $h_i$ is satisfied infinitely often on the path $\pi$.

The semantics of *CTL* has to be modified to handle fairness constraints $H$. The basic idea is to restrict path quantifiers to fair paths. The formal definition is given below:

- $s \models \mathbf{EX}_H\, f$ iff there exists a fair path $\pi$ starting from the state $s$ such that $\pi[1] \models f$.
- $s \models \mathbf{E}(g_1\ \mathbf{U}_H\ g_2)$ iff there exists a fair path $\pi$ starting from the state $s$ and there exists $k \geq 0$ such that $\pi[k] \models g_2$ and for all $0 \leq j < k$, $\pi[j] \models g_1$.
- $s \models \mathbf{EG}_H\, f$ iff there exists a fair path $\pi$ starting from the state $s$ such that for all $i \geq 0$, $\pi[i] \models f$.

## 7 Translating *CTL* into the $\mu$-Calculus

In this section we give a translation of *CTL* into the propositional $\mu$-calculus [3, 9]. The algorithm *Tr* takes as its input a *CTL* formula and outputs an equivalent $\mu$-calculus formula with only one action $a$.

- $Tr(p) = p$.
- $Tr(\neg f) = \neg Tr(f)$.
- $Tr(f \wedge g) = Tr(f) \wedge Tr(g)$.
- $Tr(\mathbf{EX}\, f) = \langle a \rangle Tr(f)$.

- $Tr(\mathbf{E}(f\ \mathbf{U}\ g)) = \mu Y.(Tr(g) \vee (Tr(f) \wedge \langle a \rangle Y))$.
- $Tr(\mathbf{EG}\ f) = \nu Y.(Tr(f) \wedge \langle a \rangle Y)$.

Note that any resulting $\mu$-calculus formula is closed. Therefore, we can omit the environment in the set $[\![\phi]\!]_M$.

LEMMA 7.1 Let $M = (S, T, L)$ be a Kripke Structure, $f$ be a *CTL* formula, and $a$ be an action with interpretation $T$. Consider the predicate transformer $\tau$:

$$\begin{aligned}\tau(Z) &= f \wedge \langle a \rangle Z \\ &= \{s \in S \mid s \models f \wedge \exists s' \in S((s, s') \in T \wedge s' \in Z)\}\end{aligned}$$

$\tau$ satisfies the following conditions:

- $\tau$ is monotonic.
- Let $\tau^{i_0}(\top)$ be the limit of the sequence $\top \subseteq \tau(\top) \subseteq \ldots$. For every $s \in S$, if $s \in \tau^{i_0}(\top)$ then $s \models f$, and there is a state $s'$ such that $(s, s') \in T$ and $s' \in \tau^{i_0}(\top)$.

*Proof* Let $P_1 \subseteq P_2$. In this case $\langle a \rangle P_1 \subseteq \langle a \rangle P_2$, i.e., the successor relation is monotonic. Therefore, $\tau(P_1) \subseteq \tau(P_2)$. Since $\tau^{i_0}(\top)$ is the fixpoint of the predicate transformer $\tau$, we have the following equation:

$$\tau(\tau^{i_0}(\top)) = \tau^{i_0}(\top)$$

Let $s \in \tau^{i_0}(\top)$. Using the equation given above we get that $s \in \tau(\tau^{i_0}(\top))$. By definition of $\tau$ we get that $s \models f$ and there exists a state $s'$, such that $(s, s') \in T$ and $s' \in \tau^{i_0}(\top)$. □

The theorem given below proves the correctness of the translation algorithm *Tr*.

THEOREM 7.1 Let $M = (S, T, L)$ be the underlying Kripke Structure. Let $\phi$ be a *CTL* formula. Let the interpretation of the action $a$ be $T$. An atomic proposition $p$ in $Tr(\phi)$ has the interpretation $L(p)$. The set of states $\top$ is $S$. In this case, for all $s \in S$

$$s \models \phi \Leftrightarrow s \in [\![Tr(\phi)]\!]_M$$

*Proof* The proof is by structural induction on $\phi$.

- $\phi = p$: In this case the result is true by definition.
- $\phi = \neg f$: By definition $[\![Tr(\phi)]\!]_M = S - [\![Tr(f)]\!]_M$. The result follows by using the induction hypothesis on $f$.
- $\phi = f \wedge g$: By definition $[\![Tr(\phi)]\!]_M = [\![Tr(f)]\!]_M \cap [\![Tr(g)]\!]_M$. The result follows by using the induction hypothesis on $f$ and $g$.

• $\phi = \mathbf{EX}\, f$: Let $S_f$ be the set of states where $f$ is true. By the induction hypothesis, $[\![Tr(f)]\!]_M = S_f$. The set of states satisfying $\phi$ is the set of states $S_1$ which have a successor in $S_f$. It is clear from the semantics of $\langle a \rangle$ that $[\![Tr(\phi)]\!]_M = S_1$.

• $\phi = \mathbf{EG}\, f$: Let $Y_1$ be the set of states $s$ such that $s \models \mathbf{EG}\, f$. Let $\tau : 2^S \to 2^S$ be the following predicate transformer

$$\tau(Z) = [\![Tr(f)]\!]_M \cap ([\![\langle a \rangle X]\!]_M\, e\, [X \leftarrow Z])$$

By definition, the greatest fixpoint of $\tau$ is given by $\bigcap_i \tau^i(\top)$, where $\tau^0(\top) = \top$, and $\tau^{i+1}(\top) = \tau(\tau^i(\top))$. Using the semantics of **EG** we get that if $s \in Y_1$, then there exists a path $\pi$ starting from $s$ such that each state on the path satisfies $f$. Therefore, if $s \in Y_1$, then $s$ has a successor $s'$ such that $(s, s') \in T$, $s \models f$, and $s' \models \mathbf{EG}\, f$. Hence $Y_1$ is a fixpoint for the predicate transformer $\tau$, i.e.,

$$\tau(Y_1) = Y_1$$

Since $\bigcap_i \tau^i(\top)$ is the greatest fixpoint of $\tau$, we have the following inclusion:

$$Y_1 \subseteq \bigcap_i \tau^i(\top)$$

Now assume that $s \in \bigcap_i \tau^i(\top)$. By Lemma 7.1, $s$ is the start of an infinite path $\pi$ such that each state $s'$ on the path $\pi$ satisfies $f$. Therefore, we have the following inclusion:

$$Y_1 \supseteq \bigcap_i \tau^i(\top)$$

Using the two equations we get that $Y_1$ is the greatest fixpoint of the predicate transformer $\tau$.

• $\phi = \mathbf{E}(f\ \mathbf{U}\ g)$: Let $S_1$ be the set of states $s$ such that $s \models \mathbf{E}(f\ \mathbf{U}\ g)$. Let $\tau : 2^S \to 2^S$ be the following predicate transformer:

$$\tau(Z) = [\![Tr(g)]\!]_M \cup ([\![Tr(f)]\!]_M \cap ([\![\langle a \rangle X]\!]_M\, e\, [X \leftarrow Z]))$$

First, we will show that $S_1$ is a fixpoint of $\tau$, i.e.,

$$\tau(S_1) = S_1$$

By definition, $s \models \mathbf{E}(f\ \mathbf{U}\ g)$ iff there exists a path $\pi$ starting from $s$ such that there exists a $k \geq 0$ with the property that $\pi^k \models g$ and $\pi^i \models f$ (for $0 \leq i < k$). Equivalently, $s \models \mathbf{E}(f\ \mathbf{U}\ g)$ iff $s \models g$ or $s \models f$ and there exists a state $s_1$ such $(s, s_1) \in T$ and $s_1 \models \mathbf{E}(f\ \mathbf{U}\ g)$. From this condition it is clear that $S_1$ is a fixed point of the predicate transformer $\tau$. By definition, the least fixpoint of $\tau$ is given by

$$\bigcup_i \tau^i(\bot)$$

Since $S_1$ is a fixpoint for $\tau$, we have that

$$S_1 \supseteq \bigcup_i \tau^i(\bot)$$

Next we prove that

$$S_1 \subseteq \bigcup_i \tau^i(\bot)$$

which proves that $S_1$ is equal to the least fixpoint of the predicate transformer $\tau$. By definition, if $s \in S_1$, then there exists a path $\pi$ and a $k \geq 0$ such that $\pi^k \models g$ and $\pi^j \models f$ (for $j < k$). We will prove by induction on $k$ that $s \in \tau^k(\bot)$. The basis case is trivial. If $k = 0$, then $s \models g$ and therefore $s \in \tau(\bot)$, which is equal to $[\![Tr(g)]\!]_M \cup ([\![Tr(f)]\!]_M \cap [\![\langle a \rangle \bot]\!]_M) = [\![Tr(g)]\!]_M$.

For the inductive step, assume that the above claim holds for every $s$ and every $k \leq m$. Let $s$ be the start of a path $\pi = s_0, s_1, \ldots$ such that $s_{m+1} \models g$ and for every $i < m+1$, $s_i \models f$. By induction hypothesis $s_1 \in \tau^m(\bot)$. Notice that $s_0 = s \in [\![Tr(f)]\!]_M$ and $s \in \langle a \rangle \tau^m(\bot)$. Therefore, by definition $s \in \tau^{m+1}(\bot)$. Hence, if $s \in S_1$, then $s \in \bigcup_i \tau^i(\bot)$. □

Using Theorem 7.1 we have the following result:

THEOREM 7.2 Given a Kripke Structure $M = (S, T, L)$, an initial state $s_0 \in S$, and a *CTL* formula $f$, one can decide in $O(|S||f|)$ iterations whether $M, s_0 \models f$, where $|f|$ denotes the number of symbols in the formula $f$.

*Proof* Consider the following formula:

$$\nu Y.(\mu Z.(q \vee (p \wedge \langle a \rangle Z)) \wedge \langle a \rangle Y)$$

The formula given above is $Tr(\mathbf{EG}(\mathbf{E}(p\ \mathbf{U}\ q)))$. Since the inner least fixpoint does not use the relational variable $Y$ ( associated with the outer greatest fixpoint), we can compute it first and reuse that value in the outer fixpoint computation. Therefore, if we compute the inner fixpoint first, we can evaluate the formula given above in $O(2|S|)$ iterations. Notice that given a *CTL* formula $f$, $Tr(f)$ has the property that the inner fixpoints never use the variables associated with the outer fixpoint. By evaluating the fixpoints in the nesting order (evaluating the inner fixpoints first), we do not have to recompute the fixpoints. Therefore, the total complexity is the sum of the complexities for evaluating each fixpoint independently. This is bounded by $O(|S||f|)$.[1] □

[1] By definition of alternation depth given in [1], the formula $Tr(f)$ always has alternation depth one. Hence, the linear complexity of *CTL* model checking follows directly from the algorithm in [1].

Given fairness constraints $H = \{h_1, \ldots, h_n\}$, we extend the translation algorithm *Tr* in the following way:

- $Tr(\mathbf{EG}_H\ f) = \nu Y.\big(Tr(f) \wedge \langle a \rangle \bigwedge_{i=1}^{n} \mu X.\,[(Tr(f) \wedge \langle a \rangle X) \vee (Y \wedge Tr(h_i))]\big)$

We introduce the following formula which is satisfied at a state $s$ iff there is a fair path $\pi$ starting from $s$.

- $fair = \mathbf{EG}_H\ True$
- $Tr(\mathbf{EX}_H\ f) = \langle a \rangle (Tr(f) \wedge Tr(fair))$.
- $Tr(\mathbf{E}(f\ \mathbf{U}_H\ g)) = \mu Y.(Tr(g) \wedge Tr(fair) \vee (Tr(f) \wedge \langle a \rangle Y))$.

We will give an informal proof of correctness for the $\mathbf{EG}_H$ case. Consider the following formula:

$$\nu Y.(P \wedge \langle a \rangle \mu X.\,[(P \wedge \langle a \rangle X) \vee (Y \wedge h)])$$

This corresponds to the formula $Tr(\mathbf{EG}_H\ f)$, where $H = \{h\}$ and $P = Tr(f)$. First, note that the condition "$h$ holds infinitely often along a path" is equivalent to saying that from any point along that path in a finite number of steps we will reach a state where $h$ holds. To understand the formula given above, notice that $\mu X.((P \wedge \langle a \rangle X) \vee (Y \wedge h))$ means that "$P$ holds until $Y \wedge h$, and $Y \wedge h$ is reachable in a finite number of steps." Since the outer fixpoint $\nu Y.(P \wedge \cdots)$ indicates that this property holds globally along the path, the formula exactly corresponds to the desired property.

## 8 Simulation Preorders and Bisimulation Equivalences

### 8.1 Simulation and Bisimulation

In this section we will use essentially the same definition of a transition system that was introduced in Section 2, except for two special program letters $\varepsilon$ and $\tau$. The letter $\varepsilon$ represents the *idle* action; its interpretation is always fixed: $T(\varepsilon) = \{(s, s) \mid s \in S\}$. The program letter $\tau$ denotes the *invisible* action from CCS [19] and will be used in the definition of the weak simulation and bisimulation relations [20].

DEFINITION 8.1 A relation $\mathcal{E} \subseteq S \times S$ is called a *simulation relation*, if for every $(s, s') \in \mathcal{E}$ the following condition holds:

$$\forall a \in Act.\forall q \in S.\text{ if } s \xrightarrow{a} q \text{ then } \exists q' \in S.s' \xrightarrow{a} q' \text{ and } (q, q') \in \mathcal{E}.$$

DEFINITION 8.2 A relation $\mathcal{E} \subseteq S \times S$ is called a *bisimulation* if $\mathcal{E}$ and $\mathcal{E}^{-1}$ are both simulation relations. In other words, $\mathcal{E}$ satisfies the following conditions: $(s, s') \in \mathcal{E}$ iff

$(i)$ $\forall a \in Act.\forall q \in S.$ if $s \xrightarrow{a} q$ then $\exists q' \in S.s' \xrightarrow{a} q'$ and $(q, q') \in \mathcal{E}$;
$(ii)$ $\forall a \in Act.\forall q' \in S.$ if $s' \xrightarrow{a} q'$ then $\exists q \in S.s \xrightarrow{a} q$ and $(q, q') \in \mathcal{E}$.

We define the *simulation preorder* as follows:

$s \preceq s'$ iff there exists a simulation relation $\mathcal{E}$ such that $(s, s') \in \mathcal{E}$.

We define *bisimulation equivalence* in a similar manner:

$s \sim s'$ iff there exists a bisimulation relation $\mathcal{E}$ such that $(s, s') \in \mathcal{E}$.

It is straightforward to check that $\preceq$ is a preorder. In fact, it is the maximal simulation relation under inclusion. It is also possible to show that bisimulation equivalence $\sim$ is an equivalence relation. Moreover, it is the maximal bisimulation relation under inclusion.

## 8.2 Encoding Simulation and Bisimulation into the $\mu$-Calculus

In order to check if the initial states of two transition systems are bisimilar using the propositional $\mu$-calculus [3, 4], we first need to construct a new transition system. Given two transition systems $M = (S, T, L)$ over *Act* and $M' = (S, T', L')$ over *Act*, we define the product $\tilde{M} = M \times M'$ over $\tilde{Act}$ as follows: $\tilde{M} = (\tilde{S}, \tilde{T}, \tilde{L})$, where

- $\tilde{Act} = \{a\varepsilon,\ \varepsilon a \mid a \in Act\}$,
- $\tilde{S} = S \times S$,
- $\tilde{T}$ is defined as follows: $(s, s') \xrightarrow{a\varepsilon} (q, s')$ iff $s \xrightarrow{a} q$ and $(s, s') \xrightarrow{\varepsilon b} (s, q')$ iff $s' \xrightarrow{b} q'$
- $\tilde{L}$ may be arbitrary in this case.

We assume that $M$ and $M'$ have the same state and action sets. This is a technical issue because we can always define the transition systems on larger state and action sets.

THEOREM 8.1 Let $s$ and $s'$ be the states of the two transition systems $M$ and $M'$. Then $s \preceq s'$ iff the following formula holds in the state $(s, s')$ of the transition system $\tilde{M}$:

$$\nu X. \left( \bigwedge_{a \in Act} [a\varepsilon]\, \langle \varepsilon a \rangle X \right)$$

*Proof* Consider the definition of a simulation relation:

$(s, s') \in \mathcal{E}$ iff $\forall a \in Act.\forall q \in S.$ if $s \xrightarrow{a} q$ then $\exists q' \in S.s' \xrightarrow{a} q'$ and $(q, q') \in \mathcal{E}$.

This is the same as the equation

$$\mathcal{E} \equiv \bigwedge_{a \subset Act} [a\varepsilon] \langle \varepsilon a \rangle \mathcal{E}$$

in the transition system $\tilde{M}$ (see the semantics of modalities in Section 2, and definition of $\tilde{M}$). Therefore, $\mathcal{E}$ is a simulation relation iff it is a fixpoint of the above equation. We show that $\preceq$ is the greatest fixpoint. Let $\mathcal{Y}$ denote the set $\nu X.(\bigwedge_{a \in Act} [a\varepsilon] \langle \varepsilon a \rangle X)$.

$\subseteq$: $s \preceq s'$ implies that $(s, s') \in \mathcal{E}$ for some simulation relation $\mathcal{E}$. Since $\mathcal{E}$ is a fixpoint of the equation, we have $\mathcal{E} \subseteq \mathcal{Y}$ by definition of the greatest fixpoint, therefore $(s, s') \in \mathcal{Y}$.

$\supseteq$: Let $(s, s') \in \mathcal{Y}$. Since $\mathcal{Y}$ satisfies the fixpoint equation, it is a simulation relation, hence $s \preceq s'$. □

THEOREM 8.2 Two states $s$ and $s'$ are bisimilar ($s \sim s'$) iff the following formula holds in the state $(s, s')$ of the model $\tilde{M}$:

$$\nu X. \left( \bigwedge_{a \in Act} [a\varepsilon] \langle \varepsilon a \rangle X \wedge [\varepsilon a] \langle a\varepsilon \rangle X \right)$$

The proof of this theorem is almost identical to the proof of the previous theorem.

Obviously, the alternation depth of the formulas is one, therefore the complexity is $O(|\tilde{S}|)$ iterations, where $|\tilde{S}| = |S|^2$. The total time complexity is $O(|\tilde{S}||Act||\tilde{M}|) = O(|S|^2|Act||M||M'|)$. The size of the formula is $O(|Act|)$, and hence each iteration takes $O(|Act||\tilde{M}|)$ time (see Section 3). For bisimulation equivalence one can obtain a more efficient algorithm than the one presented here by using the first-order $\mu$-calculus [8]. The basic idea is to construct the disjoint sum $M_1$ of the two LTSs $M$ and $M'$ instead of computing the product. Notice that number of transitions in $M_1$ is $|T| + |T'|$ instead of $|T| \cdot |T'|$. An algorithm for bisimulation equivalence with time complexity $O(|Act|(|T|+|T'|)\log(|S|))$ is given in [21]. However, it is not clear if this algorithm can be modified to compute the simulation preorder or if it can be adapted to use OBDDs.

## 8.3 Weak Simulation and Bisimulation

Weak simulation preorder and weak bisimulation equivalence require a more elaborate encoding. The definition of weak (bi)simulation is similar to (bi)simulation. The difference is that each of the transition systems is allowed to perform an unbounded but finite number of invisible actions $\tau$. Formally, first define a relation $\Rightarrow$ by

$$s \overset{a}{\Rightarrow} q \text{ iff } \exists s_1, s_2 . s \overset{\tau^*}{\rightarrow} s_1 \overset{a}{\rightarrow} s_2 \overset{\tau^*}{\rightarrow} q,$$

and $s \overset{\tau^*}{\rightarrow} q$ means that $q$ is reachable from $s$ by 0 or more $\tau$-transitions.

DEFINITION 8.3 A relation $\mathcal{E} \subseteq S \times S$ is called a *weak simulation* with invisible action $\tau$, when $(s, s') \in \mathcal{E}$ iff

$\forall a \in Act.\forall q \in S.$ if $s \stackrel{a}{\Rightarrow} q$ then $\exists q' \in S.s' \stackrel{a}{\Rightarrow} q'$ and $(q, q') \in \mathcal{E}$.

DEFINITION 8.4 A relation $\mathcal{E} \subseteq S \times S$ is called a *weak bisimulation* with invisible action $\tau$, when $(s, s') \in \mathcal{E}$ iff

(*i*) $\forall a \in Act.\forall q \in S.$ if $s \stackrel{a}{\Rightarrow} q$ then $\exists q' \in S.s' \stackrel{a}{\Rightarrow} q'$ and $(q, q') \in \mathcal{E}$;
(*ii*) $\forall a \in Act.\forall q' \in S.$ if $s' \stackrel{a}{\Rightarrow} q'$ then $\exists q \in S.s \stackrel{a}{\Rightarrow} q$ and $(q, q') \in \mathcal{E}$.

As before, we introduce a preorder called *weak simulation preorder*:

$s \preceq\!\!\!\!\prec s'$ iff there exists a weak simulation relation $\mathcal{E}$ such that $(s, s') \in \mathcal{E}$,

and an equivalence called *weak bisimulation equivalence*:

$s \approx s'$ iff there exists a weak bisimulation relation $\mathcal{E}$ such that $(s, s') \in \mathcal{E}$.

To encode the weak (bi)simulation in the propositional $\mu$-calculus we use the transition system $\tilde{M}$ described earlier. Define the abbreviations:

$$\langle \tau^*; a; \tau^* \rangle \phi \equiv_{df} \mu X.(\langle \tau \rangle X \vee \langle a \rangle (\mu Y.\phi \vee \langle \tau \rangle Y))$$
$$[\tau^*; a; \tau^*]\, \phi \equiv_{df} \neg \langle \tau^*; a; \tau^* \rangle \neg \phi$$

To understand the formulas better, notice that informally they can be viewed as translations of $\mathbf{EF}(\langle a \rangle\, \mathbf{EF}\, \phi)$ and $\mathbf{AG}([a]\, \mathbf{AG}\, \phi)$, where CTL operators refer to $\tau$-paths. Now, it is straightforward to show that the following theorems hold:

THEOREM 8.3 Let $s$ and $s'$ be states of the two transition systems. Then $s \preceq\!\!\!\!\prec s'$ iff the following formula holds in the state $(s, s')$ of the transition system $\tilde{M}$:

$$\nu X. \left( \bigwedge_{a \in Act} [(\tau\varepsilon)^*; a\varepsilon; (\tau\varepsilon)^*] \langle (\varepsilon\tau)^*; \varepsilon a; (\varepsilon\tau)^* \rangle X \right)$$

THEOREM 8.4 Two states $s$ and $s'$ are weakly bisimilar ($s \approx s'$) iff the following formula holds in the state $(s, s')$ of the model $\tilde{M}$:

$$\nu X. \left( \bigwedge_{a \in Act} \begin{array}{l} [(\tau\varepsilon)^*; a\varepsilon; (\tau\varepsilon)^*]\, \langle (\varepsilon\tau)^*; \varepsilon a; (\varepsilon\tau)^* \rangle X \wedge \\ [(\varepsilon\tau)^*; \varepsilon a; (\varepsilon\tau)^*]\, \langle (\tau\varepsilon)^*; a\varepsilon; (\tau\varepsilon)^* \rangle X \end{array} \right)$$

Although there are five levels of nesting in these formulas, the alternation depth is only two. Therefore, we can compute it by the algorithm given in [14] using $O(|\tilde{S}|^2 |Act|^2)$ iterations or $O(|Act|^3 |\tilde{M}||\tilde{S}|^2)$ time, since each iteration can take upto $O(|Act||\tilde{M}|)$ time.

For weak bismulation it is again possible to use the first-order $\mu$-calculus to obtain a more efficient algorithm. There is an algorithm by H. Andersen [2] that can compute the fixpoints in $O(|Act|^2|\tilde{S}||\tilde{M}|)$ time. By using fixpoint inversion [5], it is possible to express weak bisimulation by a formula with only one alternation of fixpoints (although in a different kind of fixpoint logic), and the complexity is $O(|S|m + m_\tau \cdot min(|Act||S|, m))$, where $m = |T| + |T'|$ and $m_\tau = |T(\tau)| + |T'(\tau)|$. The algorithm in [21] can also be adapted to compute weak bisimulation equivalence by precomputing the transitive closure of the $\tau$ relation. However, the expense of this step dominates the cost of the entire computation. Again, it is not clear that OBDDs can be used in the last two algorithms.

## 9 Conclusion

In this paper, we show the importance of the propositional $\mu$-calculus by giving translations of various graph-based verification algorithms into the $\mu$-calculus. We also present an OBDD based algorithm for $\mu$-calculus model checking which has proved to be extremely efficient in practice. Finally, we give the best known algorithm for evaluating $\mu$-calculus formulas. However, there is still much work to be done in each of these areas.

Although OBDDs do not reduce the worst-case complexity of the model checking problem for the $\mu$-calculus, their use in model checking has had an enormous effect on formal verification. Before the use of OBDDs, it was only possible to verify models with at most $10^6$ states [10]. By using the OBDD techniques described in this paper, in practice, it is now possible to verify examples with up to $10^{120}$ states and several hundred state variables [8]. However, there is no theoretical framework which explains when OBDDs will work well in practice. Our algorithm does not depend on the data structure used to represent boolean functions, so it should be possible to use any better data structures that may be discovered.

In addition to the verification problems we have considered, there are other graph theoretic problems that can be encoded in the $\mu$-calculus. An important question is how useful these OBDD and fixpoint techniques are for problems like finding minimum spanning trees, determining graph isomorphism, etc. For example, let $E(u, v)$ be the edge relation for a directed graph and let each vertex $v$ be a state encoded by an assignment $\vec{v}$ to the boolean variables $\vec{x} = x_1, \ldots, x_k$. The formula

$$\phi(\vec{x}) \equiv \mu R.\vec{x} \vee \langle a \rangle R$$

computes the set of states reachable from the state encoded by the assignment to $\vec{x}$, where the interpretation for the program letter $a$ is the edge relation $E$. Then the graph satisfies the formula

$$[\vec{u} \rightarrow \phi(\vec{v})] \wedge [\vec{v} \rightarrow \phi(\vec{u})]$$

if and only if the two vertices $u$ and $v$ are in the same strongly connected component. In general, the graph is strongly connected if and only if every vertex satisfies the formula

$$\forall \vec{x}.\phi(\vec{x}).$$

Although strictly speaking this is not a $\mu$-calculus formula according to our syntax, recall that we allow quantification over boolean variables in our translation of the $\mu$-calculus into OBDDs.

We also discuss efficient evaluation algorithms, which exploit monotonicity properties when evaluating fixpoints. However, these algorithms remain exponential in the alternation depth. We conjecture that there is no polynomial-time algorithm for determining if a state satisfies a given formula. Consider an algorithm that computes least fixpoints by iterating and that guesses greatest fixpoints. The guess for a greatest fixpoint can be easily checked to see that it really is a fixpoint. Furthermore, while we cannot verify that it is the greatest fixpoint, we know that the greatest fixpoint must contain any verified guess. Then by monotonicity, the final value computed by this nondeterministic algorithm will be a subset of the real interpretation of the formula. The state in question satisfies the formula if and only if it is in the set computed by some run of the algorithm. Also note that we can negate formulas, so the complexity of determining if a state satisfies a formula is the same as the complexity of determining if a state does not satisfy the formula. Thus, the problem is in the intersection of NP and co-NP. This suggests that our conjecture will be very difficult to prove.

## References

[1] H. R. Andersen. Model checking and boolean graphs. In B. Krieg-Bruckner, editor, *Proceedings of the Fourth European Symposium on Programming, LNCS* 582. Springer-Verlag, February 1992.

[2] H. R. Andersen. Model checking and boolean graphs. *Theoretical Computer Science*, 126:3–30, 1994.

[3] Henrik R. Andersen. *Verification of Temporal Properties of Concurrent Systems*. PhD thesis, Department of Computer Science, Aarhus University, Denmark, June 1993. PB-445.

[4] Henrik R. Andersen. A polyadic modal $\mu$-calculus. Technical Report ID-TR: 1994-145, Department of Computer Science, Technical University of Denmark, August 1994.

[5] Henrik R. Andersen and Bart Vergauwen. Efficient checking of behavioural relations and modal assertions using fixed-point inversion. In *Proceedings of CAV'95, Liege, Belgium. LNCS 939,* Springer-Verlag, pages 142–154, July 1995.

[6] G. V. Bochmann and D. K. Probst, editors. *Proceedings of the Fourth Workshop on Computer-Aided Verification*, volume 663 of *Lecture Notes in Computer Science*. Springer-Verlag, July 1992.

[7] R. E. Bryant. Graph-based algorithms for boolean function manipulation. *IEEE Transactions on Computers*, C-35(8):677–691, August 1986.

[8] J. R. Burch, E. M. Clarke, D. E. Long, K. L. McMillan, and D. L. Dill. Symbolic model checking for sequential circuit verification. *IEEE Transactions on Computer-Aided Design of Integrated Circuits*, 13(4):401–424, April 1994.

[9] J. R. Burch, E. M. Clarke, K. L. McMillan, D. L. Dill, and L. J. Hwang. Symbolic model checking: $10^{20}$ states and beyond. *Information and Computation*, 98(2):142–170, June 1992.

[10] E. M. Clarke, E. A. Emerson, and A. P. Sistla. Automatic verification of finite-state concurrent systems using temporal logic specifications. *ACM Transactions on Programming Languages and Systems*, 8(2):244–263, April 1986.

[11] R. Cleaveland. Tableau-based model checking in the propositional mu-calculus. *Acta Informatica*, 27(8): 725–747, September 1990.

[12] R. Cleaveland, M. Klein, and B. Steffen. Faster model checking for the modal mu-calculus. In Bochmann and Probst [6].

[13] R. Cleaveland and B. Steffen. A linear-time model-checking algorithm for the alternation-free modal mu-calculus. *Formal Methods in System Design*, 2(2):121–147, April 1993.

[14] E. A. Emerson and C.-L. Lei. Efficient model checking in fragments of the propositional mu-calculus. In *Proceedings of the First Annual Symposium on Logic in Computer Science*. IEEE Computer Society Press, June 1986.

[15] D. Kozen. Results on the propositional mu-calculus. *Theoretical Computer Science*, 27:333–354, December 1983.

[16] K. G. Larsen. Efficient local correctness checking. In Bochmann and Probst [6].

[17] D. Long, A. Browne, E. Clarke, S. Jha, and W. Marrero. An improved algorithm for the evaluation of fixpoint expressions. In D. Dill, editor, *Proceedings of the 1995 Workshop on Computer-Aided Verification, LNCS* 818, Springer-Verlag, pages 338–350, June 1994.

[18] A. Mader. Tableau recycling. In Bochmann and Probst [6].

[19] R. Milner. *A Calculus of Communicating Systems*, volume 92 of *Lecture Notes in Computer Science*. Springer-Verlag, 1980.

[20] Robin Milner. *Communication and Concurrency*. Prentice-Hall, 1989.

[21] R. Paige and R. E. Tarjan. Three partition refinement algorithms. *SIAM Journal of Computing*, 6(16): 973–989, 1987.

[22] C. Stirling and D. J. Walker. Local model checking in the modal mu-calculus. *Theoretical Computer Science*, 89(1):161–177, October 1991.

[23] A. Tarski. A lattice-theoretic fixpoint theorem and its applications. *Pacific Journal of Mathematics*, 5:285–309, 1955.

[24] G. Winskel. Model checking in the modal $\nu$-calculus. In *Proceedings of the Sixteenth International Colloquium on Automata, Languages, and Programming, LNCS* 372, Springer-Verlag, pages 761–772, 1989.

# III PROGRAMMING LANGUAGES

# 12 A Type-Theoretic Interpretation of Standard ML

**Robert Harper and Christopher Stone**

## 1 Introduction

It has been nearly twenty years since Robin Milner introduced ML as the metalanguage of the LCF interactive theorem prover [5]. His elegant use of abstract types to ensure validity of machine-generated proofs, combined with his innovative and flexible polymorphic type discipline, and supported by his rigorous proof of soundness for the language, inspired a large body of research into the type structure of programming languages.[1] As a design tool type theory gives substance to informal ideas such as "orthogonality" and "safety" and provides a framework for evaluating and comparing languages. As an implementation tool type theory provides a framework for structuring compilers and supports the use of efficient data representations even in the presence of polymorphism [28, 27].

Milner's work on ML culminated in his ambitious proposal for Standard ML [17] that sought to extend ML to a full-scale programming language supporting functional and imperative programming and an expressive module system. Standard ML presented a serious challenge to rigorous formalization of its static and dynamic semantics. These challenges were met in *The Definition of Standard ML* (hereafter, *The Definition*), which provided a precise definition of the static and dynamic semantics in a uniform relational framework. A key difficulty in the formulation of the static semantics of Standard ML is to manage the propagation of type information in a program so as to support data abstraction while avoiding excessive notational burdens on the programmer. This is achieved in *The Definition* through the use of "generative stamps." Roughly speaking, each type is assigned a unique "stamp" that serves as proxy for the underlying representation of that type. This ensures that two abstract types with the same representation are distinguished from one another, and facilitates the use of type inference-based techniques in the semantics of modules. The stamp formalism does not inhibit the dynamic semantics of the language because types are erased prior to execution. Consequently, no management of stamps is required at run-time.

Much recent research on both the metatheory and implementation of programming languages is based on an *explicitly-typed* interpretation in which the dynamic semantics is

This research was sponsored in part by the Advanced Research Projects Agency CSTO under the title "The Fox Project: Advanced Languages for Systems Software," ARPA Order No. C533, issued by ESC/ENS under Contract No. F19628-95-C-0050, and in part by the National Science Foundation under Grant No. CCR-9502674. The second author was also partly supported by the US Army Research Office under Grant No. DAAH04-94-G-0289. The views and conclusions contained in this document are those of the authors and should not be interpreted as representing official policies, either expressed or implied, of the Advanced Research Projects Agency, the U.S. Government or the National Science Foundation.

[1] See Cardelli's overview of type systems [3] for a comprehensive survey and references to the literature.

defined on typed, rather than type-erased, programs [28, 2]. From a semantic viewpoint programs are seen as intrinsically typed, and hence fundamental relations such as operational equivalence are defined so as to limit the set of observations to those that make type sense. From an implementation viewpoint types are used to determine the behavior of primitive operations (such as array subscripting) and to perform storage management at run-time. The untyped interpretation is a special case of the typed interpretation in which we consider only one (typically recursive) type. Thus there is no loss of generality in considering the explicitly-typed case.

While there has been considerable progress in developing a type-theoretic account of programming languages, a complete treatment of fully-featured languages such as Standard ML has thus far not been achieved. One obstacle is scale: Standard ML has a rich collection of mechanisms that must be accounted for in any formal treatment. More significantly, Standard ML presents a number of challenges to a type-theoretic account, principally the module system. For example, it is not immediately clear how to extend the generative stamps formalism of *The Definition* to an explicitly-typed setting. The main difficulty is that in a typed framework the underlying representation of an abstract type must be exposed at run-time. Consequently, an explicit association between stamps and their implementation types must be maintained in a typed semantics. Other aspects of Standard ML, including recursive datatype declarations, pattern matching, polymorphic equality, and "generative" functors, also present significant challenges for a type-theoretic interpretation.

In this paper we outline an interpretation of Standard ML in a typed framework. The interpretation takes the form of a translation from Standard ML into an explicitly-typed $\lambda$-calculus. The target of the translation we call the *internal language*, or *IL*; the source language is then called the *external language*, or *EL*. The external language considered here is the 1997 dialect of Standard ML, as described in the revised *Definition* [18]. The internal language is derived from the XML language of Harper and Mitchell [9], but with a richer collection of primitive types and a more expressive module system based on the *translucent sum* [8], or *manifest type* [13], formalism. The internal language is given a type-passing dynamic semantics in the form of a transition system between states of an abstract machine.

The translation is presented by a set of inference rules reminiscent of the static semantics given in *The Definition*, with the internal language playing the role of static semantic objects. The translation rules typically define the translation of a phrase in terms of the translation of its constituent phrases, subject to context-sensitive constraints expressed by the internal language type system. Type propagation is controlled by a combination of the translucent sum formalism together with the representation of abstract types as modules with opaque type components. The internal language ensures that abstraction is respected, and, moreover, provides the requisite association of an abstract type with its underlying representation.

The interpretation may be viewed as an alternative to *The Definition* in which the "static semantic objects" have been formalized as expressions of a typed $\lambda$-calculus and in which the elaboration relation has been generalized to a translation into the internal language. From this point of view the internal language plays a role analogous to Scott's LAMBDA language for denotational semantics [25]. The meaning of a Standard ML program is defined by interpretation into the internal language, which is given meaning by some other means. In our setting the semantics of the internal language is given by a sound operational semantics, but we conjecture that it would also be feasible to give it a domain-theoretic interpretation as in denotational semantics.

The interpretation may also be viewed as a declarative specification of the elaboration rules for type-based compilers for Standard ML such as TIL [28] and SML/NJ [26]. The front-end of the TIL compiler is a "determinization" of elaboration rules described below, using standard methods such as unification to defer non-deterministic choices until the context resolves any ambiguity. Preliminary results indicate that basing a compiler on a typed interpretation has numerous advantages, both in terms of expressive power (resolving a long-standing difficulty with the compilation of functors in Standard ML) and efficiency (leading to significant improvements in space and time requirements).

The internal language is intended to capture the fundamental constructs shared by many programming languages. We conjecture that languages such as Caml, Haskell, and Scheme could be interpreted into an internal language substantially similar to the one we give here. For example, we may translate Scheme expressions into internal language expressions of a fixed recursive sum type. Correspondingly, the primitive operations dispatch on the form of values, much as actual Scheme implementations analyze tag bits at run-time. The interpretation framework neatly handles Scheme's decision to leave the evaluation order of function arguments unspecified—the translation rules can rely on the indeterminacy of the relational framework to "choose" an evaluation order at each application expression. Direct approaches to the semantics of Scheme have great difficulty accounting for this aspect of the language.

## 2 The Internal Language

The internal language is an explicitly-typed $\lambda$-calculus with two levels, a *core* level and a *module* level. The two levels are linked by the ability to declare a module within a core-level expression. The internal language is based loosely on Harper and Mitchell's XML language [9], but with a treatment of modules derived from Harper and Lillibridge's [8, 15] translucent sum formalism and Leroy's manifest type system [13].

This section consists of a brief overview of the internal language. The language is defined by a set of inference rules for deriving the judgment forms given in Figure 12.1.

| *Judgment...* | *Meaning...* |
|---|---|
| $\vdash decs$ ok | *decs* is well-formed |
| $decs \vdash dec$ ok | *dec* is well-formed |
| $decs \vdash bnd : dec$ | *bnd* has declaration *dec* |
| $decs \vdash knd : \mathsf{Kind}$ | *knd* is well-formed |
| $decs \vdash con : knd$ | *con* has kind *knd* |
| $decs \vdash con \equiv con' : knd$ | constructor equivalence at kind *knd* |
| $decs \vdash exp : con$ | *exp* has type *con* |
| $decs \vdash sdecs$ ok | *sdecs* is well-formed |
| $decs \vdash sig : \mathsf{Sig}$ | *sig* is well-formed |
| $decs \vdash sdecs \leq sdecs'$ | component-wise subtyping |
| $decs \vdash sig \leq sig' : \mathsf{Sig}$ | signature subtyping |
| $decs \vdash sdecs \equiv sdecs'$ | component-wise equivalence |
| $decs \vdash sig \equiv sig' : \mathsf{Sig}$ | signature equivalence |
| $decs \vdash sbnds : sdecs$ | *sbnds* has declaration list *sdecs* |
| $decs \vdash mod : sig$ | *mod* has signature *sig* |
| $decs \vdash exp \downarrow con$ | *exp* is valuable with type *con* |
| $decs \vdash mod \downarrow sig$ | *mod* is valuable with signature *sig* |

**Figure 12.1**
Judgments of the Internal Language Static Semantics

A selection of the rules is given in Appendix B; the remainder can be found in a companion technical report [11]. For further background and motivation the reader is urged to consult the references cited above.

## 2.1 Constructors and Kinds

The syntax of *constructors* and *kinds* is given in Figure 12.2. Kinds classify constructors. Constructors of kind $\Omega$ are called *types*. Kinds are closed under formation of record kinds and function kinds.

The internal language types include various base types, record types, sum types, partial and total function types, recursive types, reference types, tag types, and a type of tagged values. There is no subtyping at the core level, which is consistent with the lack of subtyping in the SML core language. Most of the type constructors are relatively standard, except for total function types, tag types, and the type of tagged values.

| | | | |
|---|---|---|---|
| $con ::= var$ | type variables | $rdecs ::= \cdot$ | empty |
| $\mid$ Int $\mid$ Float $\mid$ Char $\mid \cdots$ | base types | $\mid rdecs,\ rdec$ | sequence |
| $\mid \{rdecs\}$ | record type | $rdec ::= lab{:}con$ | record field type |
| $\mid con$ Ref | reference type | | |
| $\mid con \rightharpoonup con'$ | partial function type | $knd ::= \Omega$ | kind of types |
| $\mid con \rightarrow con'$ | total function type | $\mid \{lab_1{:}\,knd_1, \ldots\}$ | record kinds |
| $\mid$ Tagged | extensible sum type | $\mid knd \Rightarrow knd'$ | function kinds |
| $\mid con$ Tag | exception-tag type | | |
| $\mid \Sigma_{\langle lab\rangle}\ (lbl_1 \mapsto con_1, \ldots)$ | (labelled) sum type | | |
| $\mid\ mod_v.lab$ | module projection | | |
| $\mid \lambda var : knd.con$ | constructor function | | |
| $\mid \mu\, con$ | constructor fixed-point | | |
| $\mid con\ con'$ | constructor application | | |
| $\mid \{lab_1 = con_1, \ldots\}$ | constructor records | | |

**Figure 12.2**
Constructors and Kinds

We borrow from the computational λ-calculus [20] an abstract notion of "definedness," called *valuability*, and the closely-associated notion of "totality" for functions. Valuability of core- and module-level expressions is expressed by a judgment form expressing that the given expression may be evaluated without engendering any computational effect. For decidability reasons, the rules define a conservative approximation of valuability. The approximation is strong enough to express the "value restriction" on polymorphism [31, 12] in Standard ML, as discussed in Section 3. In particular, all canonical forms are valuable, as are all variables (the dynamic semantics is call-by-value), and any application of a total function to a valuable argument. Total functions include primitives such as record field selection and those partial functions whose bodies are deemed valuable.

The internal language type Tagged is a type of dynamically-tagged values, corresponding to the external language type `exn`. The dynamically-generated tags are similar to the "names" considered by Pitts and Stark [22], except that we associate a type with each name to ensure type safety. Tags of values of type *con* are themselves values of type *con* Tag.

## 2.2 Expressions

The syntax of internal language expressions is given in Figure 12.3. Expressions are annotated with sufficient type information to ensure that each expression has a unique type.

Most of the expression forms are familiar from the λ-calculus literature. The treatment of functions is somewhat unusual, in order to account for mutually-recursive functions in a

| | | | |
|---|---|---|---|
| $exp$ ::= $scon$ | constants | \| $\mathsf{inj}^{con}_{lab}$ $exp$ | injection into sum |
| \| $var$ | variables | \| proj $exp$ | sum projection |
| \| $loc$ | memory locations | \| case $exp$ of $exp_1, \ldots$ end | sum case analysis |
| \| $tag$ | exception tags | \| new_tag[$con$] | extend type Tagged |
| \| fix $fbnds$ end | recursive functions | \| tag($exp$, $exp$) | injection into Tagged |
| \| $exp\ exp'$ | application | \| iftagof $exp$ is $exp'$ then $exp''$ else $exp'''$ | tag analysis |
| \| {$rbnds$} | record expression | \| $exp_1 =_{\mathsf{Int}} exp_2, \ldots$ | base equalities |
| \| $\pi_{lab}$ $exp$ | record projection | \| $mod.lab$ | module projection |
| \| handle $exp$ with $exp'$ | handle exception | | |
| \| $\mathsf{raise}^{con}$ $exp$ | raise exception | | |
| \| $\mathsf{ref}^{con}$ $exp$ | new ref cell | $rbnds$ ::= $\cdot$ | empty |
| \| get $exp$ | dereference | \| $rbnds$, $rbnd$ | sequence |
| \| set ( $exp$, $exp'$) | assignment | $rbnd$ ::= $lab = exp$ | record field binding |
| \| $\mathsf{roll}^{con}$ $exp$ | coerce to $\mu$ type | | |
| \| $\mathsf{unroll}^{con}$ $exp$ | coerce from $\mu$ type | $fbnds$ ::= $\cdot$ | empty |
| \| $\partial$ $exp$ | coerce total to partial | \| $fbnds$, $fbnd$ | sequence |
| | | $fbnd$ ::= $var'(var{:}con) : con' \mapsto exp$ | function binding |
| | | $labs$ ::= $lab$ \| $labs.\ lab$ | sequence of labels |
| | | $path$ ::= $var$ \| $var.\ labs$ | qualified variable |

**Figure 12.3**
Expressions

call-by-value setting. An expression of the form

$$\begin{array}{l} \mathsf{fix}\quad var'_1(var_1 : con_1) : con'_1 \mapsto exp_1, \\ \qquad\qquad\vdots \\ \qquad var'_n(var_n : con_n) : con'_n \mapsto exp_n \\ \mathsf{end} \end{array}$$

represents a "tuple" of $n$ mutually-recursive functions. This expression, as well as any projection from it, is valuable.

New exception tags of type $con$ Tag are created using the expression form new_tag. An expression is injected into the type Tagged with a particular tag by the tag form. The corresponding "projection" iftagof checks for a specified tag and if found extracts the underlying value.

Reference types are built into the internal language to avoid unnatural encodings. The operations ref, get, and set of the internal language correspond directly to the operations `ref`, `!`, and `:=`, respectively, of SML.

For similar reasons an exception mechanism is built into the internal language. Exceptions carry values of a specific type, which is taken here to be the type Tagged to be consistent with Standard ML, but we note that there is no essential connection between the type Tagged and the exception mechanism *per se*. We could as well consider exception values of any fixed type, or even have several different exception mechanisms, each carrying values of a type specific to that form of exception.

The core and module levels of the language are linked by the expression form for module component selection *mod.lab*. Allowing *mod* to be an arbitrary module means that "let-polymorphism" is definable in our internal language. More importantly, the bindings that may occur in a such let are exactly those that may occur in a structure, and we have the ability to define modules *within* an expression. This is exploited heavily in the interpretation of Standard ML given in Section 3.

## 2.3 Modules and Signatures

The module language is based on the *translucent sum* (or *manifest type*) formalism [8, 13]. The syntax for modules and signatures is given in Figure 12.4. The basic form of module is a *structure*, which consists of a sequence of constructor, expression, and module bindings. *Structure signatures* consist of a corresponding sequence of constructor, expression, and module declarations. The module system is closed under formation of *functors*, which are functions mapping modules to modules. *Functor signatures* are dependent function types

| | | | |
|---|---|---|---|
| $mod$ ::= | $var$ | | module variable |
| | \| | $[sbnds]$ | structure |
| | \| | $\lambda var{:}sig.mod$ | functor |
| | \| | $mod\; mod'$ | functor application |
| | \| | $mod.lab$ | structure projection |
| | \| | $mod : sig$ | signature ascription |
| $sbnds$ ::= | $\cdot$ | | structure field bindings |
| | \| | $sbnds,\ sbnd$ | |
| $sbnd$ ::= | $lab{:}bnd$ | | |
| $bnd$ ::= | $var = con$ | | constructor binding |
| | \| | $var = exp$ | expression binding |
| | \| | $var = mod$ | module binding |

| | | | |
|---|---|---|---|
| $sig$ ::= | $[sdecs]$ | | structure signature |
| | \| | $(var : sig) \rightharpoonup sig'$ | partial functor signature |
| | \| | $(var : sig) \rightarrow sig'$ | total functor signature |
| $sdecs$ ::= | $\cdot$ | | structure field dec. |
| | \| | $sdecs,\ sdec$ | |
| $sdec$ ::= | $lab : dec$ | | |
| $decs$ ::= | $\cdot$ | | declaration lists |
| | \| | $decs,\ dec$ | |
| $dec$ ::= | $var : con$ | | expression variable dec. |
| | \| | $var : sig$ | module variable dec. |
| | \| | $var : knd$ | opaque type dec. |
| | \| | $var : knd = con$ | transparent type dec. |
| | \| | $loc : con$ | typed locations |
| | \| | $tag : con$ | typed exception tag |

**Figure 12.4**
Modules and Signatures

describing the result of a functor in terms of its argument. Modules are "second-class"—there are no conditional module expressions, nor may modules be stored in reference cells or returned from core-level functions.

The main characteristic of the internal language module calculus is the reliance on signatures to mediate inter-module dependencies—the formation of a module expression relies only on the interface, and not the implementation, of any modules on which it depends. Propagation of type sharing information is managed by the selective exposure of type information in a signature through the use of *transparent* and *opaque* type specifications. Translucent sums may be seen as a generalized form of existential type [19] that affords fine-grained control over the "degree" of abstractness of a type. They may also be seen as a variant of the "dependent sum" type [16], adopting the flexible "projection" notation for component selection, but avoiding implementation dependencies.

Structure signatures consist of a sequence of constructor, value, and module declarations. Constructor declarations may either be opaque (specifying only a kind) or transparent (specifying the identity of the constructor). Value declarations specify the type of a value component, and module declarations specify the signature of a module component. Each declaration specifies an *internal name* and an *external name* for that component. The internal name is used to express dependencies of one declaration on another. For example, the type of a value component may refer (via the internal name) to a type declared earlier in the signature, or the definition of a constructor may refer to previously-declared constructors. Internal names are bound variables introduced at the point of declaration; they may be freely renamed within their scope without changing the meaning of the signature. The external name of a component is a label; structure components are accessed using these labels. External names are not variables and may not be renamed without changing the meaning of the signature. For example, the signature $[T \triangleright t : \Omega, U \triangleright u : \Omega = t \times t, X \triangleright x : u]$, describes a module with two type components, with external names $T$ and $U$, and internal names $t$ and $u$, respectively, and one value component, with external name $X$ and internal name $x$. The type component $U$ is defined to be equal to the product of the $T$ component with itself, and the $X$ component has type $U$. Notice that the dependencies are expressed using the internal names.

Every module value possesses a most-specific signature in which the identity of all type components is propagated using transparent type bindings. For example, the most specific signature for the structure

$$[T \triangleright t = \mathsf{Int}, U \triangleright u = \mathsf{Int} \times \mathsf{Int}, X \triangleright x = (3, 4)]$$

is given by

$$[T \triangleright t : \Omega = \mathsf{Int}, U \triangleright u : \Omega = \mathsf{Int} \times \mathsf{Int}, X \triangleright x : \mathsf{Int} \times \mathsf{Int}].$$

Modules may be given less-specific signatures using *subsumption*—the signature of a module may be weakened to a "larger" signature in the sub-signature ordering. This ordering is a non-coercive, forgetful ordering in which signatures may be weakened by neglecting type definitions, rendering opaque one or more transparent components. For example, using subsumption we may assign the less informative signatures $[T \triangleright t : \Omega, U \triangleright u : \Omega = t \times t, X \triangleright x : u]$ and $[T \triangleright t : \Omega = \mathsf{Int}, U \triangleright u : \Omega, X \triangleright x : u]$ to the module expression given above.

A module may be "sealed" by signature *ascription*. The module expression *mod* : *sig* is well-formed if *mod* has the signature *sig* (possibly through a use of subsumption). Then *mod* : *sig* has most-specific signature *sig*. In practice we use ascription to make type components of a module abstract.

Parameterized modules, or *functors*, are written using the familiar $\lambda$-notation; there are no recursive functors. *Functor signatures* are a form of "$\Pi$ type" (dependent function type) in which the signature of the result depends on the argument to the functor. This is used to express the propagation of type sharing properties from the argument to the result, without relying on exposure of the implementation of the functor. The sub-signature relation is extended to functor signatures in the usual way, contravariantly in the domain and covariantly in the codomain [2]. Only non-dependent functors may be applied to arguments; the dependency must first be eliminated through the use of the sub-signature and signature equivalence relations. In the general translucent sum calculus this may not be possible for all arguments; however we have made syntactic restrictions in our IL so that the dependency can always be eliminated.

For example, suppose we have a functor

$$f : (u : [T \triangleright t : \Omega, X \triangleright x : t]) \rightharpoonup [T' \triangleright t' : \Omega = u.T \times u.T, X' \triangleright x' : t']$$

and we wish to apply this functor to a structure with signature $[T \triangleright t : \Omega = \mathsf{Float}, X \triangleright x : \mathsf{Float}]$. This is possible because by subsumption $f$ also satisfies the non-dependent signature:

$$u : [T \triangleright t : \Omega = \mathsf{Float}, X \triangleright x : \mathsf{Float}] \rightharpoonup$$
$$[T' \triangleright t' : \Omega = \mathsf{Float} \times \mathsf{Float}, X' \triangleright x' : \mathsf{Float} \times \mathsf{Float}].$$

Thus the application will have signature $[T' \triangleright t' : \Omega = \mathsf{Float} \times \mathsf{Float}, X' \triangleright x' : \mathsf{Float} \times \mathsf{Float}]$.

As in the core language, module expressions are categorized as valuable or non-valuable. Functors whose bodies are valuable module expressions are said to be *total*; all others are partial. Modules whose components are all valuable are themselves valuable, as are all module variables, and all selections of module components from valuable modules. An *ascription* of a signature to a module, written *mod* : *sig*, is valuable if the underlying module is valuable, but is not a value. Since type components may only be selected from module *values*, this ensures that abstraction boundaries are respected. Specifically, if a signature is ascribed to a module, then its abstract type components may only be accessed by first binding that module to a variable, then selecting from that variable. This ensures that the abstraction boundary imposed by the ascription is respected, and ascribing the same signature to the same module will yield incompatible abstract types.

## 2.4 Dynamic Semantics

The dynamic semantics of the internal language is a call-by-value operational semantics presented as a rewriting relation between states of an abstract machine. The presentation is strongly influenced by the work of Plotkin [23] and Wright and Felleisen [32], but is a departure from the framework of *The Definition of Standard ML*. The state-machine presentation avoids the need for implicit evaluation rules for handling exceptions, and supports a natural interpretation of type soundness that does not rely on artificial "wrong" transitions. We prefer to use substitution, rather than environments, because this allows us to regard values as particular forms of expression; this also simplifies the statement of soundness, particularly in the presence of references. We maintain a store for assignable cells and dynamically-generated tags, as in *The Definition*, but, in addition, we maintain an explicit store- and tag-typing context, in keeping with our explicitly-typed framework.

Each state $\Sigma$ of the abstract machine is a triple of the form $(\Delta, \sigma,\ exp)$, where

- $\Delta$ is a typing context (*decs*) for locations and tags created at run-time. This maintains a record of what exception tags and locations have already been allocated, and is also used in our soundness proofs.
- $\sigma$ is a finite mapping from locations typed in $\Delta$ to expression values ($exp_{\mathrm{v}}$). The syntax of all values appears in Figure 12.5.
- *exp* is an expression.

A state is *terminal* if it has one of the following forms:

| | |
|---|---|
| $(\Delta, \sigma, exp_{\mathrm{v}})$ | normal termination |
| $(\Delta, \sigma, \mathsf{raise}^{con}\ exp_{\mathrm{v}})$ | uncaught exception |

All other states are *nonterminal*. We let $\Sigma_t$ range over terminal states.

The dynamic semantics is a transition relation $\Sigma \hookrightarrow \Sigma'$ between states, defined by the rules given in Appendix C. As usual, we denote the reflexive, transitive closure of $\hookrightarrow$ by $\hookrightarrow^*$. The rules defining the relation have the form

$$(\Delta, \sigma,\ exp) \hookrightarrow (\Delta', \sigma',\ exp'),$$

$$
\begin{array}{rcl}
exp_{\mathrm{v}} & ::= & scon \\
& \mid & loc \\
& \mid & tag \\
& \mid & path \\
& \mid & \{rbnds_{\mathrm{v}}\} \\
& \mid & \mathsf{fix}\ fbnds\ \mathsf{end} \\
& \mid & \pi_{\overline{k}}\,\mathsf{fix}\ fbnds\ \mathsf{end} \\
& \mid & \mathsf{inj}_i^{con}\ exp_{\mathrm{v}} \\
& \mid & \mathsf{tag}(tag, exp_{\mathrm{v}}) \\
& \mid & \mathsf{roll}^{con}\ exp_{\mathrm{v}} \\
& \mid & \partial\ exp_{\mathrm{v}} \\
\\
rbnds_{\mathrm{v}} & ::= & \cdot \\
& \mid & rbnds_{\mathrm{v}},\ rbnd_{\mathrm{v}} \\
rbnd_{\mathrm{v}} & ::= & lab{=}exp_{\mathrm{v}} \\
\\
val & ::= & exp_{\mathrm{v}} \\
& \mid & mod_{\mathrm{v}} \\
& \mid & con
\end{array}
\qquad
\begin{array}{rcl}
mod_{\mathrm{v}} & ::= & path \\
& \mid & [sbnds_{\mathrm{v}}] \\
& \mid & \lambda var{:}sig.mod \\
\\
bnd_{\mathrm{v}} & ::= & var = exp_{\mathrm{v}} \\
& \mid & var = mod_{\mathrm{v}} \\
& \mid & var = con \\
\\
sbnds_{\mathrm{v}} & ::= & \cdot \\
& \mid & sbnds_{\mathrm{v}},\ sbnd_{\mathrm{v}} \\
\\
sbnd_{\mathrm{v}} & ::= & lab{:}bnd_{\mathrm{v}}
\end{array}
$$

**Figure 12.5**
Internal Language Values

possibly with some side conditions. The rules make use of the notion of an "evaluation context," an expression or module with a single "hole," written [] (see Figure 12.6). The expression $E[phrase]$ is the expression resulting from replacing the hole in $E$ by *phrase*. We use $R$ to denote an expression context constructed from the grammar in Figure 12.6 without the form handle $E$ with *exp*.

Most of the rules of the dynamic semantics are straightforward interpretations of the constructs of the internal language. Exceptions are handled using explicit "jumps" though evaluation contexts that do not involve exception handlers. This is achieved by relying on a form of pattern-matching to capture the informal idea of jumping to the nearest enclosing exception handler. Tags and reference cells are explicitly allocated during evaluation, and their types are maintained in the state. Uses of the sub-signature relation have no run-time significance; control over type sharing properties is entirely a matter of static checking.

$$
\begin{array}{rll}
E ::= & E\ exp & \mid\ \mathsf{tag}(E,\ exp) \\
\mid & exp_{\mathrm{v}}\ E & \mid\ \mathsf{tag}(exp_{\mathrm{v}},\ E) \\
\mid & \{rbnds_{\mathrm{v}},\ lab{=}E,\ rbnds\} & \mid\ \mathsf{iftagof}\ E\ \mathsf{is}\ exp\ \mathsf{then}\ exp'\ \mathsf{else}\ exp'' \\
\mid & \pi_{lab}\, E & \mid\ \mathsf{iftagof}\ exp_{\mathrm{v}}\ \mathsf{is}\ E\ \mathsf{then}\ exp'\ \mathsf{else}\ exp'' \\
\mid & \mathsf{handle}\ E\ \mathsf{with}\ exp & \mid\ E{=}_{con}\ exp \\
\mid & \mathsf{raise}^{con}\ E & \mid\ exp_{\mathrm{v}}{=}_{con}\, E \\
\mid & \mathsf{ref}^{con}\ E & \mid\ [sbnds_{\mathrm{v}},\ lab \triangleright var{=}E,\ sbnds] \\
\mid & \mathsf{get}\ E & \mid\ E\ mod \\
\mid & \mathsf{set}\,(E,\ exp) & \mid\ mod_{\mathrm{v}}\ E \\
\mid & \mathsf{set}\,(exp_{\mathrm{v}},\ E) & \mid\ E.\ lab \\
\mid & \mathsf{roll}^{con}\ E & \mid\ E : sig \\
\mid & \mathsf{unroll}^{con}\ E & \mid\ [] \\
\mid & \mathsf{inj}_i^{con}\ E & \\
\mid & \mathsf{proj}_i\ E & \\
\mid & \mathsf{case}\ E\ \mathsf{of}\ exp_1, \ldots,\ exp_n\ \mathsf{end} &
\end{array}
$$

**Figure 12.6**
Evaluation Contexts

As a technical convenience, for the purpose of the dynamic semantics we include a CHAM-like structural equivalence rule for structures, extending the standard equivalence of terms or modules up to alpha-conversion. This is generated by the schema

$$[sbnds,\ lab \triangleright var = val,\ sbnds'] \equiv [sbnds,\ lab \triangleright var = val,\ \{val/var\}sbnds']$$

which allows us to remove dependencies between fields in a structure when the dependency is on a field carrying a value. Factoring out such substitutions separately simplifies the dynamic semantics, but is not critical to the framework.

We have given a high-level operational semantics in that types are propagated, but never normalized or examined at run-time. To describe primitives which do intensional type analysis [10] we could refine the semantics to perform normalization computations at the constructor level as well.

## 2.5 Properties of the Internal Language

In order to relate the static and dynamic semantics, we must first state some technical properties of the operational semantics.

We define two states to be *equivalent*, written

$$(\Delta, \sigma,\ exp) \cong (\Delta', \sigma',\ exp'),$$

if they are component-wise equal up to consistent renaming of the locations and exception tags appearing in $\Delta$ and of bound variables in the expression component.

PROPOSITION 1 (DETERMINACY OF EVALUATION) The following properties hold:

1. If $\Sigma$ is terminal and $\Sigma \cong \Sigma'$, then $\Sigma'$ is also terminal.
2. If $\Sigma \hookrightarrow \Sigma_1$ and $\Sigma \cong \Sigma'$, then there exists a state $\Sigma_1' \cong \Sigma_1$ such that $\Sigma' \hookrightarrow \Sigma_1'$.
3. If $\Sigma_1 \hookrightarrow \Sigma_1'$, $\Sigma_2 \hookrightarrow \Sigma_2'$ and $\Sigma_1 \cong \Sigma_2$ then $\Sigma_1' \cong \Sigma_2'$.
4. If $\Sigma \hookrightarrow^* \Sigma_t$ and $\Sigma \hookrightarrow^* \Sigma_t'$ then $\Sigma_t \cong \Sigma_t'$.

The following proposition states that internal language judgments are preserved under substitution of values for free variables in a typing judgment, where a value is defined syntactically in Figure 12.5 to be a phrase in evaluated form.

PROPOSITION 2 (DECOMPOSITION AND REPLACEMENT)

1. If $decs \vdash E[exp] : con$ and $exp$ is closed, then $decs \vdash exp : con'$ for some type $con'$. Furthermore, if $decs \vdash exp' : con'$ where $exp'$ is closed, then $decs \vdash E[exp'] : con$.
2. If $decs \vdash E[mod] : con$ and $mod$ is closed, then $decs \vdash mod : sig$ for some signature $sig$ such that if $decs \vdash mod' : sig$ where $mod'$ is closed, then $decs \vdash E[mod'] : con$.

Following Harper [7] and Wright and Felleisen [32], we say that a store $\sigma$ is well-formed with respect to a context $\Delta$, written $\Delta \vdash \sigma$, if

$$\forall\, loc \in \mathrm{BV}(\Delta),\ \text{if } \Delta \vdash loc : con\ \mathsf{Ref} \text{ then } \Delta \vdash \sigma(x) : con.$$

This formulation of store typing avoids the need for complex maximal fixed point constructions [29].

Fix a base type $ans$ of *answers* to which a complete, closed program might evaluate.[2] We say that a machine state is well-formed, written

$$\vdash (\Delta, \sigma, exp),$$

if and only if $\Delta \vdash exp : ans$, $exp$ has no free (expression, constructor, or module) variables, and $\Delta \vdash \sigma$.

Well-formedness of a state is preserved by evaluation.

PROPOSITION 3 (PRESERVATION)
If $\vdash (\Delta, \sigma, exp)$ and $(\Delta, \sigma, exp) \hookrightarrow (\Delta', \sigma', exp')$ then $\vdash (\Delta', \sigma', exp')$.

[2] A reasonable choice might be String, or Unit if we model all I/O by updating the store; the particular choice does not affect our results.

Evaluation can never "get stuck": if a well-formed state is not terminal, then there is always an applicable transition to another (well-formed) state. The proof relies on a characterization of the shapes of closed values of each type.

PROPOSITION 4 (CANONICAL FORMS)

1. Assume $\Delta \vdash exp'_{\mathrm{v}} : con'$ where $exp'_{\mathrm{v}}$ is closed.

| If $con'$ is of the form... | then $exp'_{\mathrm{v}}$ is of the form... |
|---|---|
| $con_1 \rightharpoonup con_2$ | $\pi_{\overline{k}}\,\mathsf{fix}\ fbnds\ \mathsf{end}$ |
| $con_1 \rightarrow con_2$ | $\pi_{\overline{1}}\,\mathsf{fix}\ fbnd\ \mathsf{end}$ |
| $\{lab_1{:}con_1, \ldots, lab_n{:}con_n\}$ | $\begin{cases} \{lab_1 = exp_{\mathrm{v}1}, \ldots, lab_n = exp_{\mathrm{v}n}\} \\ \mathsf{fix}\ fbnds\ \mathsf{end} \end{cases}$ |
| $\Sigma_{\langle lab_i \rangle}\ (lab_1 \mapsto con_1, \ldots, lab_n \mapsto con_n)$ | $\mathsf{inj}^{con''}_{lab_i}\ exp_{\mathrm{v}}$ |
| $(\pi_i\ (\mu\ con))\ con'$ | $\mathsf{roll}^{con''}\ exp_{\mathrm{v}}$ |
| $\mathsf{Tagged}$ | $\mathsf{tag}(tag, exp_{\mathrm{v}})$ |
| $con\ \mathsf{Ref}$ | $loc$ |
| *base type* | $scon$ |

2. Assume $\Delta \vdash mod'_{\mathrm{v}} : sig'$ where $mod'_{\mathrm{v}}$ is closed.

| If $sig'$ is of the form... | then $mod'_{\mathrm{v}}$ is of the form... |
|---|---|
| $[sdecs]$ | $[sbnds_{\mathrm{v}}]$ |
| $var{:}sig \rightharpoonup sig'$ | $\lambda var{:}sig.mod$ |
| $var{:}sig \rightarrow sig'$ | $\lambda var{:}sig.mod$ |

PROPOSITION 5 (PROGRESS) Let $\Sigma = (\Delta, \sigma, exp)$. If $\vdash \Sigma$ then either $\Sigma$ is terminal or there exists a state $\Sigma'$ such that $\Sigma \hookrightarrow \Sigma'$.

## 3 Elaboration of Standard ML into the Internal Language

The type-theoretic interpretation of Standard ML takes the form of a set of inference rules for deriving *elaboration judgments* of the form

$$\Gamma \vdash \textit{EL-phrase} \leadsto phrase : class.$$

Here *EL-phrase* is a phrase of the Standard ML abstract syntax, *phrase* is its translation into the internal language, and *class* is an internal-language kind, type, or signature classifying *phrase*. The context $\Gamma$ associates external names and classifiers to internal names. A complete list of the judgment forms constituting the interpretation is given in Figure 12.7.

| *Judgment...* | *Meaning...* |
|---|---|
| $\Gamma \vdash expr \rightsquigarrow exp : con$ | expression |
| $\Gamma \vdash match \rightsquigarrow exp : con$ | pattern match |
| $\Gamma \vdash strdec \rightsquigarrow sbnds : sdecs$ | declaration |
| $\Gamma \vdash strexp \rightsquigarrow mod : sig$ | structure expression |
| $\Gamma \vdash spec \rightsquigarrow sdecs$ | signature specification |
| $\Gamma \vdash sigexp \rightsquigarrow sig : \mathsf{Sig}$ | signature expression |
| $\Gamma \vdash ty \rightsquigarrow con : \Omega$ | type expression |
| $\Gamma \vdash tybind \rightsquigarrow sbnds : sdecs$ | `type` definition |
| $\Gamma \vdash datbind \rightsquigarrow sbnds : sdecs$ | `datatype` definition |
| $\Gamma \vdash_{\text{ctx}} labs \rightsquigarrow path : class$ | lookup in $\Gamma$ |
| $decs; path{:}sig \vdash_{\text{sig}} labs \rightsquigarrow labs' : class$ | lookup in signature |
| $decs \vdash_{\text{inst}} [sbnds_{\text{v}}] : [sdecs']$ | polymorphic instantiation |
| $\Gamma \vdash pat \Longleftarrow exp : con \ \mathsf{else}\ exp' \rightsquigarrow sbnds : sbnds$ | pattern compilation |
| $decs \vdash_{\text{eq}} con \rightsquigarrow exp_{\text{v}}$ | equality compilation |
| $decs \vdash_{\text{sub}} path : sig_0 \preceq sig \rightsquigarrow mod : sig'$ | coercion compilation |
| $sig \vdash_{\text{wt}} labs := con : knd \rightsquigarrow sig' : \mathsf{Sig}$ | impose definition |
| $sig \vdash_{\text{sh}} labs := labs' : knd \rightsquigarrow sig' : \mathsf{Sig}$ | impose sharing |

**Figure 12.7**
Judgment forms for the Elaboration

The elaboration of Standard ML into the internal language involves the following major steps:

1. **Identifier resolution**. External-language identifiers are translated into internal-language paths according to the scoping rules of Standard ML. Re-defined identifiers are renamed to avoid conflicts.

2. **Type checking and type reconstruction**. The elaboration rules ensure that the translation of an external-language phrase is well-formed with a specified classifier (kind, type, or signature). Implicit type information—such as type labels on variables and polymorphic abstraction and instantiation—is made explicit. Polymorphic abstractions are represented as internal-language functors.

3. **Datatype and pattern-matching translation**. Datatype declarations are translated into modules with an opaque implementation type and operations for creating and destructuring values of this type. Patterns are compiled into uses of these operations, along with record projections and equality tests.

4. **Equality compilation**. For types that admit equality, a canonical equality operation is generated and passed as required. Equality polymorphic operations are represented as functors taking the type together with the associated equality operation. Datatypes that admit equality are equipped with an equality operation.

5. **Signature matching**. The *instantiation* ordering—arising from the presence or absence of type definitions in signatures—is managed by the sub-signature relation of the internal language. The *enrichment* ordering—arising from the ability in Standard ML to drop or re-order module components—is handled by an explicit coercion operation generated by the elaborator. Since we are working with an explicitly-typed internal language, polymorphic instantiation in signature matching is also managed by explicit coercion.

6. **Sharing expansion**. Uses of type sharing specifications are expanded into uses of type definitions in signatures [14]. The `where type` construct of Standard ML is translated by explicitly "patching" internal-language signatures.

7. **Generativity and persistence**. In Standard ML type identifiers may persist beyond their apparent scope of definition. This is managed here by the restriction to "named form" programs at the module level (according to which all modules must be bound to identifiers before use), and an explicit mechanism for retaining types through renaming when they appear to go out of scope.

The elaboration rules use a number of "derived forms" in the internal language; these are shown in Appendix D.1. Specifics of the elaboration process are discussed in more detail in the remainder of this section.

### 3.1 Identifier Resolution

A fundamental task of elaboration is associating internal-language paths to external-language identifiers. Since the external language permits shadowing of identifiers, we cannot assume a fixed correspondence between Standard ML identifiers and internal-language variables. Therefore we translate identifiers into internal-language paths, and the correspondence is maintained by an elaboration context. This context is essentially a sequence of internal-language structure field bindings, but with the possibility of duplicated labels due to shadowing. We may regard elaboration contexts as declaration lists by dropping the labels from the components (turning each *sdec* into its underlying *dec*); in this way the formation rules of the internal language determine validity of elaboration contexts.

We postulate an injection $\overline{\cdot}$ of ML identifiers into internal-language labels. The range of this mapping is assumed co-infinite in the set of labels, ensuring that we may choose arbitrarily many new labels not in the range of this mapping. We further assume that the labels "eq," "expose," "it," and "tag" are outside of the range of this mapping, and that identically-named identifiers from different external language namespaces (expression identifiers, type identifiers, signature identifiers, structure identifiers, *etc.*) are mapped to distinct labels. On the other hand, we assume a single namespace for external-language variables, datatype constructors, and exception constructors; in Standard ML these distinctions are not syntactically apparent and making this distinction falls to the elaboration itself.

The translation of an (possibly overbarred) long identifier into an path is expressed by the judgment

$$\Gamma \vdash_{\text{ctx}} labs \rightsquigarrow path : class,$$

which looks up the sequence of labels *labs* in the elaboration context $\Gamma$ and returns a path *path* with classifier *class*. The lookup rules describe a sequential search[3] from right-to-left, subject to a simple convention, called the *star convention*, for handling "open" structures. Labels marked with an asterisk are treated as names of open structures, whose bindings are implicitly available for use in a Standard ML phrase. A second set of lookup rules expresses identifier search within a structure; these rules are also used in translating Standard ML long identifiers. Thus, for example, we have the translation

$$X \triangleright x : \mathsf{Int},\ L \triangleright l : [X : \mathsf{Char}] \vdash_{\text{ctx}} X \rightsquigarrow x : \mathsf{Int},$$

but, in contrast, when $L$ is open we have

$$X \triangleright x : \mathsf{Int},\ L^* \triangleright l : [X : \mathsf{Char}] \vdash_{\text{ctx}} X \rightsquigarrow l.X : \mathsf{Char}.$$

### 3.2 Expressions and Declarations

The general form of elaboration judgment for expressions is

$$\Gamma \vdash expr \rightsquigarrow exp : con$$

where *expr* is an external-language expression, and *exp* is the corresponding internal-language expression having type *con*. These elaboration rules are shown in full in Appendix D.2. Identifiers are translated using the lookup rules mentioned above, and if found to be polymorphic are immediately instantiated (polymorphism is discussed in more detail below). Datatype constructors (functions with total types) are translated to user-level functions (with partial types) when used as values. Application translates to internal-language application, with a check to ensure that the translated application is well-formed.

[3] In our compiler implementation, a more efficient algorithm is used.

Record expressions are translated to internal-language records. Since Standard ML identifies record types under permutation of fields, the translation reorders these fields into a canonical order while preserving the order of evaluation. Explicit type constraints are verified, but do not appear in the translation. The exception expressions `raise` and `handle` translate into their internal-language equivalents. Function abstractions in the EL translate to function abstractions in the IL, wrapped to raise the `Match` exception in the case of pattern match failure. Equality comparisons invoke the equality compiler (also described below) to generate the appropriate equality operation.

An important invariant of the translation is that "syntactic values" in the Standard ML sense are translated to valuable expressions. This is necessary to enforce the value restriction on polymorphism, according to which only syntactic values may be polymorphically generalized. However, our treatment of pattern matching leads to a minor discrepancy between the interpretation given here and *The Definition of Standard ML*, as discussed in Section 3.5 below.

The general form of elaboration judgment for declarations is

$$\Gamma \vdash \mathit{strdec} \leadsto \mathit{sbnds} : \mathit{sdecs}.$$

A selection of such judgments is shown in Appendix D.5. Each external-language declaration is translated into structure field bindings. For simple bindings, there is exactly one field binding for each identifier bound. In more complex cases—such as complex patterns or `datatype` declarations—the result contains not only bindings for the identifiers explicitly involved in the declaration, but also "internal" fields used by the elaborator itself.

The `open` declaration (Rule 108) is regarded as the declaration of an "anonymous" substructure; this is implicitly opened for identifier lookup using the "star convention" discussed above. In implementation terms this means that an `open` declaration requires only constant time and space, rather than time and space proportional to the size of the opened structure. To account for shadowing, declaration sequencing goes beyond simple concatenation of bindings by renaming fields corresponding to shadowed identifiers.

### 3.3 Polymorphism

Polymorphism is interpreted by explicit type abstraction and type application [9]. However, we do not treat type abstraction and application as a primitive notion (as in the polymorphic $\lambda$-calculus [4, 24]). Instead, we represent a polymorphic value as an internal-language functor abstracted on a structure whose components are types, yielding a structure with a single component labeled "it" for the value itself. This representation is consistent with the "second class" nature of both polymorphic values and modules in Standard ML. It is especially natural in the presence of equality type variables, which we regard as structures consisting of a type and the corresponding equality operation (see Section 3.6 for further details).

For example, the polymorphic identity function is translated[4] to the functor

$$\lambda(s : [T : \Omega]).[\mathrm{it}{=}\lambda(x : s.T) \,.\, x]$$

with signature

$$(s : [T : \Omega]) \rightarrow [\mathrm{it}{:}s.T \rightharpoonup s.T].$$

Note that the functor is given a *total* functor type, expressing the fact that type instantiation does not engender an effect. This is consistent with the "value restriction" on polymorphism in Standard ML, according to which only syntactic values may be polymorphically abstracted.

### 3.4 Datatype Declarations

The treatment of datatypes is technically complex, but conceptually straightforward. A `datatype` declaration elaborates to a structure consisting of a type together with operations to create and analyze values of the type. If the datatype admits equality, then the structure contains an equality function as well. The underlying implementation type is defined to be a recursive sum type, with one summand corresponding to each constructor in the declaration. The constructors are represented by total functions that inject values into the appropriate summand of the recursive type. The analysis operation exposes values of the abstract type as values of a corresponding sum type. The structure is "sealed" with a signature derived from the `datatype` declaration in which the implementation type is held abstract, and the operations described above are declared as operations on that abstract type. Holding the implementation type abstract captures the "generativity" of `datatype` declarations in Standard ML; the declared type is "new" in the sense that it is represented by a path that is, by $\alpha$-conversion, distinct from all previous types in the program. Analogously, `datatype` specifications (which may occur in signatures) are elaborated into the same signature used to seal the structure resulting from elaboration of the corresponding `datatype` declaration.

The treatment of datatypes is best illustrated by example. Viewed as a specification, the Standard ML phrase

```
datatype 'a list = Nil | Cons of 'a * 'a list.
```

[4] We have simplified the translation slightly for the sake of readability.

$$
\begin{array}{l}
[\overline{\texttt{list}} \triangleright \texttt{list}{:}\Omega \Rightarrow \Omega, \\
\text{eq}{:}(s{:}[T^*{:}[T \triangleright t{:}\Omega,\ \text{eq}{:}t \times t \rightharpoonup \mathsf{Bool}]]) \rightarrow [\text{it}{:}\mathit{list}\,(s.T^*.T) \times \mathit{list}\,(s.T^*.T) \rightharpoonup \mathsf{Bool}] \\
\overline{\texttt{Nil}}{:}(s{:}[T{:}\Omega]) \rightarrow [\text{it}{:}\mathit{list}\,(s.T)], \\
\overline{\texttt{Cons}}{:}(s{:}[T{:}\Omega]) \rightarrow [\text{it}{:}s.T \times \mathit{list}\,(s.T) \rightarrow \mathit{list}\,(s.T)], \\
\text{expose}{:}(s{:}[T{:}\Omega]) \rightarrow [\text{it}{:}\mathit{list}\,(s.T) \rightarrow \Sigma(\mathsf{Unit},\ s.T \times \mathit{list}\,(s.T))]]
\end{array}
$$

**Figure 12.8**
The signature $sig_{\texttt{list}}$

$$
\begin{array}{l}
[\overline{\texttt{list}} \triangleright \texttt{list}{=}\mu\,\lambda l{:}\Omega \Rightarrow \Omega.\lambda\alpha{:}\Omega.\Sigma\left(\overline{\texttt{Nil}} \mapsto \mathsf{Unit},\ \overline{\texttt{Cons}} \mapsto \alpha \times l\,\alpha\right), \\
\text{eq}{=}\cdots, \\
\overline{\texttt{Nil}}{=}\lambda s{:}[T{:}\Omega].[\text{it}{=}\mathsf{roll}^{\mathit{list}\,(s.T)}\ (\mathsf{inj}^{\mathsf{Unit}+s.T \times \mathit{list}\,(s.T)}_{\overline{\texttt{Nil}}}\ \{\})], \\
\overline{\texttt{Cons}}{=}\lambda s{:}[T{:}\Omega].[\text{it}{=}\lambda(x{:}s.T \times \mathit{list}\,(s.T)).\ \mathsf{roll}^{\mathit{list}\,(s.T)}\ (\mathsf{inj}^{\mathsf{Unit}+s.T \times \mathit{list}\,(s.T)}_{\overline{\texttt{Cons}}}\ x)], \\
\text{expose}{=}\lambda s{:}[T{:}\Omega].[\text{it}{=}\lambda(x{:}\ \mathit{list}\,(s.T)).\mathsf{unroll}^{\mathit{list}\,(s.T)}\ x]
\end{array}
$$

**Figure 12.9**
The structure $mod_{\texttt{list}}$

elaborates to the signature $sig_{\texttt{list}}$ given in Figure 12.8. Viewed as a declaration, this phrase elaborates into the sealed structure $mod_{\texttt{list}} : sig_{\texttt{list}}$, where $mod_{\texttt{list}}$ is given in Figure 12.9.

The signature $sig_{\texttt{list}}$ describes a structure with five components, one corresponding to the `list` type constructor itself, one for `list` equality, two for the constructors, and one for deconstructing values of this type. The `list` type constructor is represented by a type operator of kind $\Omega \Rightarrow \Omega$. The operation eq is the equality function on lists; it takes a type $T$ and an equality for values of type $T$, and returns the equality function for values of type $\overline{\texttt{list}}\,T$. The value constructor `Nil` is the polymorphic total function that, when given a type, creates the empty list of that type. Similarly $\overline{\texttt{Cons}}$ is the polymorphic total function to add an element to the front of a list. The polymorphic function expose exposes the underlying implementation of the datatype as a sum type for the purposes of destructuring.

The structure $mod_{\texttt{list}}$ implements the signature $sig_{\texttt{list}}$. The implementation is relatively straightforward, following the informal discussion above. We have elided the definition of equality on lists, but it corresponds directly to the obvious recursive definition which can be generated mechanically.

The account of datatypes given here differs from that in Standard ML in that we do not provide an equal operation for "non-uniform" datatypes, for which we would need polymorphic recursion, which is not admitted in Standard ML or in our internal language. For example, the following declaration is legal in Standard ML, and the declared type admits equality:

```
datatype 'a t = A of 'a | B of ('a * 'a) t
```

Although this is an admissible declaration according to our elaboration rules, it does not admit equality in the translation due to the absence of polymorphic recursion.[5]

### 3.5 Pattern Compilation

Pattern compilation is the process of translating pattern-matching bindings and clausal functions into the more rudimentary mechanisms of the internal language. Given a target pattern, a candidate internal-language expression, and a failure exception, the pattern compiler generates a sequence of bindings corresponding to the result of matching the candidate against the target. The expected evaluation order is preserved, and an exception is raised if the match does not succeed; these bindings then become the fields of a structure.

Clausal functions are handled by exception propagation (see Appendix D.3). Each clause is compiled into a function that, when applied, matches the argument against the pattern of the clause, and continues with the expression part of the clause in the case that the match succeeds, and fails otherwise. Alternation is handled by generating a function that calls the compilation of the first alternative, yielding its result on success, and passing the argument to the second in the case of failure. Upon failure of the last clause, the internal failure is turned into a `Match` exception. In the case of a `val` binding there is no alternative to failure; a `Bind` exception is raised immediately.

The pattern-compiler given here is unsophisticated, doing sequential search among the patterns and within the patterns until a complete match is found. More efficient algorithms based on decision tree heuristics are routinely used in Standard ML compilers. We present a "reference" implementation of pattern compilation so as to avoid undue commitments to specific strategies, to admit generalizations of pattern matching that may engender effects (such as forcing memoized suspensions [21]), and for the sake of perspicuity of the translation.

There is a subtle, but important, interaction between pattern compilation and the value restriction on polymorphism. In the revised *Definition*, the determination of whether or not a variable is generalizable is made based only upon the syntactic form of the right-hand side of a `val` binding (the value restriction for polymorphism); it does not matter whether or not the left-hand side is a complex pattern. However, since the pattern match may not

[5] It is a questionable feature of Standard ML that such types admit equality such that the equality operation they admit is not definable in SML itself.

succeed, the "true" binding of the variable (after pattern compilation) in a pattern may involve the application of a partial destructuring operation to that value, possibly raising an exception. For example, if `y` is an EL identifier bound to a polymorphic list value (*e.g.*, `Cons(fn x => x, Nil))` then under Standard ML the binding `val (Cons (x,xs)) = y` will make the variables `x` and `xs` polymorphic since `y` is a syntactic value. In contrast we assess the valuability of the binding of an identifier *after* pattern compilation. Any variable whose "true" binding is not valuable may not be generalized. In particular, the code generated by the pattern compiler will test whether `y` really is a `Cons`, and will raise an exception otherwise. Allowing `y` to be polymorphic would delay any `Bind` exception would be delayed until one of the functors created for `x` or `xs` was instantiated. We therefore do not generalize such identifiers.

We note that due to the value restriction, and more generally the definition of total functor, we are guaranteed that a polymorphic value with a sum type has a single fixed tag. In more conventional notation, there is an isomorphism between $\forall\alpha\cdot(\tau_1+\tau_2)$ and $(\forall\alpha\cdot\tau_1)+(\forall\alpha\cdot\tau_2)$. Therefore, one could imagine handling polymorphism for refutable patterns by checking the tag once (by instantiating at some arbitrary type), and either raising a `Bind` exception or using projection from the sum as a total operation on this value thereafter. A weakness of our internal language is that this cannot be expressed; it is unclear how it might be cleanly modified to account for this anomaly.

### 3.6 Equality Compilation

Polymorphic equality, equality type variables, and `eqtype` specifications are all elaborated into explicit uses of equality functions. The idea is to define a canonical equality operation at each closed type, and to associate with each type variable or `eqtype` constructor an equality operation to be supplied by the caller. In the case of equality type variables, polymorphic instantiation provides (passes at run-time) the equality operation based on the instance. In the case of `eqtype` specifications, the signature matching generates the equality test when the signature is ascribed. There is no need for separate "equality attributes" in our IL; a type admits equality if and only if the equality compiler is able to generate an equality operation for it. Our approach is related to the compilation of overloading in Haskell [30] and to the treatment of equality proposed by Gunter, Gunter and MacQueen [6].

The judgment $\Gamma \vdash_{\text{eq}} con \rightsquigarrow exp_{\text{v}}$ expresses that $\Gamma \vdash exp_{\text{v}} : con \times con \rightharpoonup \mathsf{Bool}$ is the equality function for type *con*. These equality functions are the obvious structural equalities for immutable types (primitive equality functions at base types, component-wise equality for record types, a recursively-defined equality function for recursive types, etc.) and primitive pointer equality for reference types.

### 3.7 Signature Matching

Signature matching is divided into two relations, *instantiation*, which handles type sharing relationships between modules, and *enrichment*, which handles dropping, re-ordering, and instantiation of components of a module. The instantiation relation is captured by the sub-signature relation of the internal language. It is non-coercive in the sense that it has no significance during evaluation. The enrichment relation is handled by the elaboration rules, which introduce coercions that are executed during evaluation. These coercions drop components and introduce polymorphic instantiations to build a structure satisfying a less restrictive signature than that of a given module. Separating the coercive aspects from the internal-language subtyping relation guarantees that the number and order of components in a structure is apparent from its signature.

In one particular case, the coercion introduces, rather than eliminates, components of a structure. This arises because of `eqtype` specifications: the equality compiler must be invoked to determine the appropriate equality function for that type. For example, ascribing the opaque signature

```
sig eqtype T end
```

to a structure having EL signature

```
sig type T = int end
```

augments the structure containing the type component (equal to Int) with an equality function (on integers).

### 3.8 Type Generativity

One of the more subtle aspects of Standard ML goes under the heading of "type generativity." Roughly speaking, generativity captures the informal idea that a `datatype` declaration introduces a "new" type, distinct from all others, despite possible structural similarities. This aspect of generativity may be regarded as a form of data abstraction. Indeed, in Section 3.4 we relied on opaque signature ascription in the internal language to ensure that the implementation type of a datatype is held abstract.

This basic conception of type generativity must be extended to account for the generative behavior of functors. Datatype generativity interacts with functor instantiation in such a way that each application of a functor that declares a datatype introduces a "new copy" of that datatype, distinct from all other instances introduced by the same functor (and all types otherwise introduced). Following Leroy [14] we capture this behavior by imposing the requirement that module expressions be restricted to "named form." This means that every non-trivial module expression must be bound to a module identifier before it can be used. This restriction is reflected in the grammar by, *e.g.*, the requirement that functor arguments be structure identifiers, rather than arbitrary structure expressions. There is no loss of generality in assuming that programs are written in named form; we can make a prepass introduces bindings for non-trivial module expression [14]. The practical effect of the restriction to named form is that the result of every functor application is bound to module variable, which thereafter serves as the "unique name" of that instance of the functor application. Consequently, opaque types (including datatypes) selected from that instance are unique.

A second subtlety of the Standard ML type system is that types may escape their (apparent) scope. Provided that programs are in named form, this phenomenon can arise in only one way, through the use of `local` declarations and module-level `let` expressions. For example, the following declaration is legal in Standard ML, and results in a binding whose type involves a "hidden" type constructor:

```
local
  datatype t = A | B
in
  val x = A
end
```

The declaration of the datatype `t` is "hidden"; only the variable `x` is exported by the declaration. In our type-theoretic internal language, we clearly cannot allow the binding of `x` to escape the scope of the binding for the type `t`. Instead we export the type `t` along with `x`, but rename it to a variant that lies outside of the "overbar" mapping, ensuring that the type cannot conflict with any user-defined type in the external language.[6] Thus, the "information hiding" of the `local` construct is implemented entirely by the elaborator, and has no significance at the level of the internal language.

A closely-related phenomenon arises in connection with the transparent ascription mechanism of Standard ML, whereby signature ascriptions hide components, but not the identities, of types. By hiding a type component that is required to express the type of a value component or the type sharing properties of another type component, we encounter a situation similar to a `local` declaration. For example, in the code

[6] More precisely, the "hidden" part of a `local` declaration is represented by a substructure with an inaccessible name, and the references to hidden identifiers are replaced by accesses to the substructure. Conflicts are avoided by $\alpha$-conversion of the internal name of the structure.

```
functor F(M : sig type 'a con end) : sig type t end =
    struct
        datatype d = D
        type t = d con
    end
```

we would like to express that the type returned by `F` is the result of applying the argument type constructor to a datatype. We could then deduce solely from the functor's signature that applying it to the structure

```
struct type 'a con = int end
```

yields a structure containing the type `int`. However, since the transparent ascription "hides" the datatype `d`, we cannot refer to this in describing the returned `t` component. The behavior of this functor on types cannot be expressed in a Standard ML signature.

However, the restriction to named form entails that the ascription generate a module-level `let` expression, which is then translated into type theory by renaming, rather than dropping, the hidden component `d`. Named form and component renaming ensures that the exact behavior of all (first-order) functors is always expressible in the internal-language signature of the translated functor.

Note that the simple renaming mechanism we have outlined here is not "safe for space complexity" [1]. In particular, the elaboration given here retains not only the hidden type components that are required for subsequent specifications, but also type components that are not so required, and value components, which are never required. However, these components may be easily eliminated by a process similar to dead code elimination in a compiler. In practice we would retain only those hidden type components that are necessary to ensure that the translation is well formed.

### 3.9 Properties of the Elaborator

The minimal requirement for the elaborator is that the elaboration of external-language code yields well-formed internal-language code:

PROPOSITION 6 (WELL-FORMED TRANSLATION) If $\vdash \Gamma$ ok and $\Gamma \vdash$ *EL*-phrase $\rightsquigarrow$ phrase : class then $\Gamma \vdash$ phrase : class.

The elaboration rules in the Appendix D assume a structure variable *basis* which represents the initial basis for programs. For our purposes here, it suffices to assume a structure with signature $sig_{basis}$, given by

$[\overline{\texttt{Bind}}^{*}$ :[tag:Unit Tag, $\overline{\texttt{Bind}}$:Tagged],
$\overline{\texttt{Match}}^{*}$:[tag:Unit Tag, $\overline{\texttt{Match}}$:Tagged],
fail* :[tag:Unit Tag, fail:Tagged],
$\overline{\texttt{bool}}^{*}$ :[$\overline{\texttt{bool}} \rhd b{:}\Omega = \Sigma(\text{Unit, Unit})$,
eq:$b \times b \rightharpoonup$ Bool,
$\overline{\texttt{false}}$:$b$,
$\overline{\texttt{true}}$:$b$,
expose:$b \rightarrow \Sigma(\text{Unit, Unit})$].

The interpretation of Standard ML we have outlined above relies on a relational presentation of what is essentially a translation function. The relational framework allows us to avoid overspecifying the translation, and admits a clean separation between "algorithmic" and "definitional" considerations. However, we incur the obligation to demonstrate that the interpretation is *coherent* in the sense that all interpretations of a Standard ML program yield internal-language expressions with the same observable behavior. We conjecture that the translation we have given is coherent:

CONJECTURE 7 (COHERENCE) If

$$\text{basis}^{*} \rhd \mathit{basis} : \mathit{sig}_{\mathit{basis}} \vdash \mathit{expr} \leadsto \mathit{exp} : \mathit{ans}$$

$$\text{basis}^{*} \rhd \mathit{basis} : \mathit{sig}_{\mathit{basis}} \vdash \mathit{expr} \leadsto \mathit{exp}' : \mathit{ans}$$

$$(\cdot, \cdot, \text{let } \mathit{basis}{=}\mathit{mod}_{\mathit{basis}} \text{ in } \mathit{exp} \text{ end}) \hookrightarrow^{*} \Sigma_t$$

then for some terminal state $\Sigma_t' \cong \Sigma_t$,

$$(\cdot, \cdot, \text{let } \mathit{basis}{=}\mathit{mod}_{\mathit{basis}} \text{ in } \mathit{exp}' \text{ end}) \hookrightarrow^{*} \Sigma_t'.$$

## 4 Summary

We have given a brief overview of an interpretation of Standard ML into a typed λ-calculus. A fully detailed account of the interpretation appears in a companion technical report [11]. The complete interpretation consists of approximately 270 inference rules, of which approximately 140 form the typing rules and dynamic semantics of the internal language (120 rules and 20 rules, respectively), with the remaining 130 rules being the interpretation itself. Of these approximately 10 rules are concerned with signature matching, 8 with equality compilation, 25 with identifier lookup, and 12 with pattern compilation. By contrast *The Definition of Standard ML* consists of approximately 190 rules, of which approximately 100 are for the static semantics, the remainder being for the dynamic semantics. Note, however, that the dynamic semantics has "implicit" rules for handling exceptions, making it difficult to give a precise count.

Our internal language is formalized using relatively standard techniques. The type checking rules rely on conventions such as implicit $\alpha$-conversion of binding operators to avoid identifier conflicts, and relies on definitional equality relations and a sub-typing relations to define the type system. The operational semantics is defined by a transition relation on states of an abstract machine, and does not rely on implicit rules for exception propagation. It can be easily extended to account for control operators such as call-with-current-continuation. The internal language admits a clean formulation of the soundness theorem that does not rely on instrumentation of the rules with explicit "wrong" transitions. To state soundness in the framework of *The Definition* requires that the dynamic semantics be instrumented with such error transitions, which would significantly increase the number of rules required. Finally, we note that the internal language does not rely on any external global "admissibility" conditions as are imposed on the static semantic objects of *The Definition*.

The translation from Standard ML into the internal language is, at times, rather complex. The single most complicated rule—for handling datatype declarations—requires one page in its complete form. The complexity is easily explained: a single datatype declaration introduces $n$ mutually recursive type constructors, each with its own arity, and each introducing $k_i$ value constructors, each of which may or may not take an argument. Unravelling these complexities into the simple orthogonal mechanisms of the internal language is clearly a rather complicated affair. Other sources of complexity are the use of rules to define identifier lookup and signature patching, the introduction of coercions for signature matching, the compilation of equality types into modules consisting of a type and an equality operation, and the compilation of patterns into primitive projections.

How might the presentation be simplified? The use of rules for identifier lookup and signature specialization is a matter of presentation. We could easily have defined these at the metalevel of the semantics, rather than give explicit rules. Equality compilation introduces considerable complexity. Since we are working in an explicitly-typed framework we could have postulated in the internal language a primitive polymorphic equality operation that dispatches on types. We chose not to do so primarily because the elaborator would nevertheless have to check for admissibility of equality at compile time to ensure that invalid uses of equality are rejected during type checking. It is only marginally more complicated to equip equality types with their equality operation and eliminate equality at non-base types from the internal language entirely. We see no plausible alternative to the coercive interpretation of signature matching. One might consider enriching the internal language with a coercive pre-order on signatures corresponding to the enrichment ordering, but to do so would require unnatural, ML-specific extensions such as implicit polymorphic instantiation during signature matching. The treatment of datatypes and pattern matching appears to be essentially forced since the association between an abstract type and its representation must be made explicit in the dynamic semantics, and this is what is accomplished here. We consider it an important direction for further research to determine if a simpler treatment of datatypes can be given in an explicitly-typed framework.

The interpretation we have given here follows *The Definition* by clearly separating definitional from algorithmic issues. The rules exploit the indeterminacy of the relational framework for the sake of simplicity and concision. The internal language type system is used to express context-sensitive formation constraints. An implementation must resolve these indeterminacies and must define algorithms for the internal language type system. A thorough treatment of these matters lies beyond the scope of this work.

The type-theoretic interpretation has both advantages and disadvantages as an alternative to *The Definition*. The primary disadvantage is that the dynamic semantics of Standard ML must be understood by translation into the internal language. Since the translation rules are not fully determinate, this raises the question of coherence of the translation, which we conjecture to hold for the translation given here. There is also the psychological question of whether the kind of translation we give here can serve as a useful reference for programmers. As a tool for compiler-writers, both *The Definition* and the interpretation we propose here have contributed directly to the construction of practical implementations of Standard ML. In this regard the two accounts complement one another—different compiler technologies correspond to different interpretations of the language.

## A External Language Syntax

### A.1 Abstract Syntax

$$
\begin{array}{rl}
\mathit{expr} ::= & \mathit{scon} \\
 & \mid \mathit{longid} \\
 & \mid \{\, \mathit{lab}_1 = \mathit{expr}_1, \ldots, \mathit{lab}_n = \mathit{expr}_n \} \\
 & \mid \texttt{let}\ \mathit{strdec}\ \texttt{in}\ \mathit{expr}\ \texttt{end} \\
 & \mid \mathit{expr}\ \mathit{expr}' \\
 & \mid \mathit{expr} : \mathit{ty} \\
 & \mid \mathit{expr}\ \texttt{handle}\ \mathit{match} \\
 & \mid \texttt{raise}\ \mathit{expr} \\
 & \mid \texttt{fn}\ \mathit{match} \\
 & \mid \mathit{expr}_1 = \mathit{expr}_2
\end{array}
$$

$$
\begin{array}{rl}
\mathit{mrule} ::= & \mathit{pat} \Rightarrow \mathit{expr} \\
\mathit{match} ::= & \mathit{mrule} \\
 & \mid \mathit{mrule} \mid \mathit{match}
\end{array}
$$

```
strdec ::= ·
         | val (tyvar1, ..., tyvarn) pat = exp
         | val (tyvar1, ..., tyvarn) rec pat = exp
         | strdec1 strdec2
         | open longid1 ··· longidn
         | exception id
         | exception id of ty
         | exception id = longid
         | local strdec1 in strdec2 end
         | type tybind
         | datatype datbind
         | datatype (tyvar1, ..., tyvarn) tycon =
             datatype (tyvar1, ..., tyvarn) longtycon
         | structure strbind
         | functor funbind

 tybind ::= ⟨(tyvar1, ..., tyvarn)⟩ tycon = ty ⟨⟨and tybind⟩⟩
datbind ::= (tyvar1, ..., tyvarn) tycon = conbind
            ⟨and datbind⟩
conbind ::= id ⟨of ty⟩ ⟨⟨| conbind⟩⟩

 strexp ::= longstrid
          | struct strdec end
          | longfunid ( longstrid)
          | longstrid : sigexp
          | longstrid :> sigexp
          | let strdec in strexp end

spec ::= ·
       | val id : ty
       | type typdesc
       | eqtype etypdesc
       | datatype datbind
       | datatype (tyvar1, ..., tyvarn) tycon' =
           datatype (tyvar1, ..., tyvarn) longtycon
       | exception id
       | exception id of ty
       | structure strid : sigexp
```

$$
\begin{array}{rl}
 & \mid \texttt{functor}\ \textit{funid}\ \texttt{(}\ \textit{strid}\ \texttt{:}\ \textit{sigexp}\texttt{)}\ \texttt{:}\ \textit{sigexp}' \\
 & \mid \texttt{include}\ \textit{sigexp} \\
 & \mid \textit{spec}_1\ \textit{spec}_2 \\
 & \mid \textit{spec}\ \texttt{sharing type}\ \textit{longid}_1 = \textit{longid}_2 \\
\\
\textit{typdesc} ::= & \langle\texttt{(}\ \textit{tyvar}_1\texttt{,}\ \ldots\texttt{,}\ \textit{tyvar}_n\texttt{)}\rangle\ \textit{tycon} \\
 & \quad \langle\langle\texttt{and}\ \textit{typdesc}\rangle\rangle \\
 & \mid \langle\texttt{(}\ \textit{tyvar}_1\texttt{,}\ \ldots\texttt{,}\ \textit{tyvar}_n\texttt{)}\rangle\ \textit{tycon} = \textit{ty} \\
 & \quad \langle\langle\texttt{and}\ \textit{typdesc}\rangle\rangle \\
\\
\textit{etypdesc} ::= & \langle\texttt{(}\ \textit{tyvar}_1\texttt{,}\ \ldots\texttt{,}\ \textit{tyvar}_n\texttt{)}\rangle\ \textit{tycon} \\
 & \quad \langle\langle\texttt{and}\ \textit{etypdesc}\rangle\rangle \\
\\
\textit{sigexp} ::= & \texttt{sig}\ \textit{spec}\ \texttt{end} \\
 & \mid \textit{sigexp}\ \texttt{where type} \\
 & \quad \langle\texttt{(}\ \textit{tyvar}_1\texttt{,}\ \ldots\texttt{,}\ \textit{tyvar}_n\texttt{)}\rangle\ \textit{longtycon} = \textit{ty} \\
\\
\textit{pat} ::= & \textit{scon} \\
 & \mid \textit{longid} \\
 & \mid \texttt{\_} \\
 & \mid \textit{pat}\ \texttt{:}\ \textit{ty} \\
 & \mid \textit{longid}\ \textit{pat} \\
 & \mid \texttt{\{}\ \textit{lab}_1 = \textit{pat}_1\texttt{,}\ \ldots\texttt{,}\ \textit{lab}_n = \textit{pat}_n\langle\texttt{,}\ \texttt{...}\rangle\texttt{\}} \\
 & \mid \textit{pat}_1\ \texttt{as}\ \textit{pat}_2 \\
 & \mid \texttt{ref}\ \textit{pat} \\
\\
\textit{ty} ::= & \textit{base} \\
 & \mid \textit{tyvar} \\
 & \mid \texttt{\{}\ \textit{lab}_1\ \texttt{:}\ \textit{expr}_1\texttt{,}\ \ldots\texttt{,}\ \textit{lab}_n\ \texttt{:}\ \textit{expr}_n\texttt{\}} \\
 & \mid \langle\texttt{(}\ \textit{ty}_1\texttt{,}\ \ldots\texttt{,}\ \textit{ty}_n\texttt{)}\rangle\ \textit{longtycon} \\
 & \mid \textit{ty}\ \texttt{->}\ \textit{ty}' \\
\\
\textit{strbind} ::= & \textit{strid} = \textit{strexp}\ \langle\texttt{and}\ \textit{strbind}\rangle \\
\textit{funbind} ::= & \textit{funid}\ \texttt{(}\ \textit{strid}\ \texttt{:}\ \textit{sigexp}\texttt{)} = \textit{strexp} \\
 & \quad \langle\texttt{and}\ \textit{funbind}\rangle
\end{array}
$$

This grammar has a few minor differences from that specified in the revised *Definition*. We have simplified the grammar by removing some of the distinctions made solely for the purposes of the parser, which are inappropriate for abstract syntax. The most significant difference is the restricted form we allow for structure expressions (*strexp*); Standard ML programs can always be put into this form by a simple prepass. We also extend the grammar to allow for module definitions local to an expression, and for functor specifications in signatures. We also do not support `abstype` here; in the presence of local module definitions and the opaque (:>) signature ascription, `abstype` is redundant. For simplicity, we assume that `signature` declarations are syntactic sugar which have been "inlined away." See the *Definition* for further syntactic restrictions information on how derived forms desugar into the above grammar. As in the Definition, we use the convention that angle brackets and double angle brackets mark optional components of a rule or syntactic item.

## B Internal Language Static Semantics (excerpt)

### B.1 Constructor Equivalence

$$\frac{\vdash decs \text{ ok} \qquad decs = decs', var{:}knd = con, decs''}{decs \vdash var \equiv con : knd} \tag{1}$$

$$\frac{decs \vdash mod_{\text{v}} : [sdecs, lab : knd = con, sdecs'] \qquad \text{BV}(sdecs) \cap \text{FV}(con) = \emptyset}{decs \vdash mod_{\text{v}}.lab \equiv con : knd} \tag{2}$$

$$\frac{decs \vdash con_1 \equiv con_2 : \Omega \qquad decs \vdash con_1' \equiv con_2' : \Omega}{decs \vdash con_1 \rightharpoonup con_1' \equiv con_2 \rightharpoonup con_2' : \Omega} \tag{3}$$

$$\frac{decs \vdash con_1 \equiv con_2 : \Omega \qquad decs \vdash con_1' \equiv con_2' : \Omega}{decs \vdash con_1 \to con_1' \equiv con_2 \to con_2' : \Omega} \tag{4}$$

$$\frac{decs \vdash con \equiv con' : \Omega}{decs \vdash con\ \mathsf{Ref} \equiv con'\ \mathsf{Ref} : \Omega} \tag{5}$$

$$\frac{decs \vdash con \equiv con' : \Omega}{decs \vdash con\ \mathsf{Tag} \equiv con'\ \mathsf{Tag} : \Omega} \tag{6}$$

$$\frac{lab_1, \ldots, lab_n \text{ distinct} \qquad \forall i \in 1..n : decs \vdash con_i \equiv con_i' : \Omega}{decs \vdash \{lab_1 : con_1, \ldots, lab_n : con_n\} \equiv \{lab_1 : con_1', \ldots, lab_n : con_n'\} : \Omega} \tag{7}$$

$$\frac{decs \vdash con \equiv con' : knd \Rightarrow knd}{decs \vdash \mu\, con \equiv \mu\, con' : knd} \tag{8}$$

$$\frac{\langle i \in 1 \ldots n\rangle \qquad \forall i \in 1..n : \mathit{decs} \vdash \mathit{con}_i \equiv \mathit{con}'_i : \Omega}{\mathit{decs} \vdash \Sigma_{\langle \mathit{lab}_i \rangle}(\mathit{lab}_1 {\mapsto} \mathit{con}_1, \ldots, \mathit{lab}_n {\mapsto} \mathit{con}_n) \equiv \Sigma_{\langle \mathit{lab}_i \rangle}\left(\mathit{lab}_1 {\mapsto} \mathit{con}'_1, \ldots, \mathit{lab}_n {\mapsto} \mathit{con}'_n\right) : \Omega} \tag{9}$$

$$\frac{\mathit{decs} \vdash \mathit{con}_1 \equiv \mathit{con}_2 : \mathit{knd}' {\Rightarrow} \mathit{knd} \quad \mathit{decs} \vdash \mathit{con}'_1 \equiv \mathit{con}'_2 : \mathit{knd}'}{\mathit{decs} \vdash \mathit{con}_1\, \mathit{con}_2 \equiv \mathit{con}'_1\, \mathit{con}'_2 : \mathit{knd}} \tag{10}$$

$$\frac{\mathit{decs}, \mathit{var}{:}\mathit{knd}' \vdash \mathit{con} : \mathit{knd} \qquad \mathit{decs} \vdash \mathit{con} : \mathit{knd}'}{\mathit{decs} \vdash (\lambda \mathit{var}{:}\mathit{knd}'.\mathit{con})\, \mathit{con}' \equiv \{\mathit{con}'/\mathit{var}\}\mathit{con} : \mathit{knd}} \tag{11}$$

$$\frac{\mathit{decs} \vdash \mathit{con} : \mathit{knd}}{\mathit{decs} \vdash \mathit{con} \equiv \mathit{con} : \mathit{knd}} \tag{12}$$

$$\frac{\mathit{decs} \vdash \mathit{con}' \equiv \mathit{con} : \mathit{knd}}{\mathit{decs} \vdash \mathit{con} \equiv \mathit{con}' : \mathit{knd}} \tag{13}$$

$$\frac{\mathit{decs} \vdash \mathit{con} \equiv \mathit{con}' : \mathit{knd} \quad \mathit{decs} \vdash \mathit{con}' \equiv \mathit{con}'' : \mathit{knd}}{\mathit{decs} \vdash \mathit{con} \equiv \mathit{con}'' : \mathit{knd}} \tag{14}$$

## B.2 Well-formed Expressions

$$\frac{\vdash \mathit{decs}\ \mathrm{ok}\ \mathit{decs} = \mathit{decs}', \mathit{var}{:}\mathit{con}, \mathit{decs}''}{\mathit{decs} \vdash \mathit{var} : \mathit{con}} \tag{15}$$

$$\frac{\vdash \mathit{decs}\ \mathrm{ok}\ \mathit{decs} = \mathit{decs}', \ \mathit{loc}{:}\mathit{con}, \mathit{decs}''}{\mathit{decs} \vdash \ \mathit{loc} : \mathit{con}} \tag{16}$$

$$\frac{\vdash \mathit{decs}\ \mathrm{ok}\ \mathit{decs} = \mathit{decs}', \ \mathit{tag}{:}\mathit{con}, \mathit{decs}''}{\mathit{decs} \vdash \ \mathit{tag} : \mathit{con}} \tag{17}$$

$$\frac{\mathit{decs} \vdash \mathit{exp} : \mathit{con}' {\rightharpoonup} \mathit{con} \qquad \mathit{decs} \vdash \mathit{exp}' : \mathit{con}'}{\mathit{decs} \vdash \mathit{exp}\, \mathit{exp}' : \mathit{con}} \tag{18}$$

$$\frac{\mathit{decs} \vdash \mathit{exp} : \mathit{con}' {\rightarrow} \mathit{con} \qquad \mathit{decs} \vdash \mathit{exp}' : \mathit{con}'}{\mathit{decs} \vdash \mathit{exp}\, \mathit{exp}' : \mathit{con}} \tag{19}$$

$$\frac{\forall i \in 1..\, n : \ \mathit{decs}, (\mathit{var}'_j{:}\mathit{con}_j {\rightharpoonup} \mathit{con}'_j)_{j=1}^{n}, \mathit{var}_i{:}\mathit{con}_i \vdash \mathit{exp}_i : \mathit{con}'_i}{\mathit{decs} \vdash \mathsf{fix}\, (\mathit{var}'_i(\mathit{var}_i{:}\mathit{con}_i) : \mathit{con}'_i \mapsto \mathit{exp}_i)_{i=1}^{n}\ \mathsf{end} : \{1{:}\mathit{con}_1 {\rightharpoonup} \mathit{con}'_1, \ldots, n{:}\mathit{con}_n {\rightharpoonup} \mathit{con}'_n\}} \tag{20}$$

$$\frac{var' \notin \mathrm{FV}(exp) \quad decs, var{:}con \vdash exp \downarrow con'}{decs \vdash \mathsf{fix}\, var'(var{:}con) : con' \mapsto exp\, \mathsf{end} : \{\overline{1}{:}con \to con'\}} \tag{21}$$

$$\frac{lab_1, \cdots, lab_n \text{ distinct} \quad \forall i \in 1..n : decs \vdash exp_i : con_i}{decs \vdash \{lab_1{=}exp_1, \ldots, lab_n{=}exp_n\} : \{lab_1{:}con_1, \ldots, lab_n{:}con_n\}} \tag{22}$$

$$\frac{decs \vdash exp : \{rdecs, lab{:}con, rdecs'\}}{decs \vdash \pi_{lab}\, exp : con} \tag{23}$$

$$\frac{decs \vdash exp : con \qquad decs \vdash exp' : \mathsf{Tagged} \rightharpoonup con}{decs \vdash \mathsf{handle}\, exp\, \mathsf{with}\, exp' : con} \tag{24}$$

$$\frac{decs \vdash exp : \mathsf{Tagged} \qquad decs \vdash con : \Omega}{decs \vdash \mathsf{raise}^{con}\, exp : con} \tag{25}$$

$$\frac{decs \vdash con : \Omega}{decs \vdash \mathsf{new\_tag}[con] : con\, \mathsf{Tag}} \tag{26}$$

$$\frac{decs \vdash exp : con}{decs \vdash \mathsf{ref}^{con}\, exp : con\, \mathsf{Ref}} \tag{27}$$

$$\frac{decs \vdash exp : con\, \mathsf{Ref}}{decs \vdash \mathsf{get}\, exp : con} \tag{28}$$

$$\frac{decs \vdash exp : con\, \mathsf{Ref} \quad decs \vdash exp' : con}{decs \vdash \mathsf{set}\,(exp, exp') : \mathsf{Unit}} \tag{29}$$

$$\frac{decs \vdash con \equiv (\pi_{lab}\,(\mu\, con'))\,\langle con''\rangle : \Omega \quad decs \vdash exp : (\pi_{lab}\,(con'\,(\mu\, con')))\,\langle con''\rangle}{decs \vdash \mathsf{roll}^{con}\, exp : con} \tag{30}$$

$$\frac{decs \vdash con \equiv (\pi_{lab}\,(\mu\, con'))\,\langle con''\rangle : \Omega \quad decs \vdash exp : con}{decs \vdash \mathsf{unroll}^{con}\, exp : (\pi_{lab}\,(con'\,(\mu\, con')))\,\langle con''\rangle} \tag{31}$$

$$\frac{decs \vdash exp : con \to con'}{decs \vdash \partial\, exp : con \rightharpoonup con'} \tag{32}$$

$$\frac{i \in 1..n \quad con = \Sigma_{lab_i}\,(lab_1 \mapsto con_1, \ldots, lab_n \mapsto con_n) \qquad decs \vdash exp : con_i}{decs \vdash \mathsf{inj}^{con}_{lab_i}\; exp : con} \tag{33}$$

$$\frac{i \in 1..n \quad decs \vdash exp : \Sigma_{lab_i}\,(lab_1 \mapsto con_1, \ldots, lab_n \mapsto con_n)}{decs \vdash \mathsf{proj}\; exp : con_i} \tag{34}$$

$$\frac{\begin{array}{c} n \geq 1 \\ con = \Sigma(lab_1 \mapsto con_1, \ldots, lab_n \mapsto con_n) \\ decs \vdash exp : con \\ \forall i \in 1..n : \quad decs \vdash exp_i : \Sigma_{lab_i}\,(lab_1 \mapsto con_1, \ldots, lab_n \mapsto con_n) \rightharpoonup con' \end{array}}{decs \vdash \mathsf{case}\; exp\; \mathsf{of}\; exp_1, \ldots, exp_n\; \mathsf{end} : con'} \tag{35}$$

$$\frac{decs \vdash exp : con\,\mathsf{Tag} \qquad decs \vdash exp' : con}{decs \vdash \mathsf{tag}(exp, exp') : \mathsf{Tagged}} \tag{36}$$

$$\frac{\begin{array}{c} decs \vdash exp : \mathsf{Tagged} \qquad decs \vdash exp' : con\,\mathsf{Tag} \\ decs \vdash exp'' : con \rightharpoonup con' \qquad decs \vdash exp''' : con' \end{array}}{decs \vdash \mathsf{iftagof}\; exp\; \mathsf{is}\; exp'\; \mathsf{then}\; exp''\; \mathsf{else}\; exp''' : con'} \tag{37}$$

$$\frac{decs \vdash mod : [sdecs, lab{:}con, sdecs'] \quad \mathrm{BV}(sdecs) \cap \mathrm{FV}(con) = \emptyset}{decs \vdash mod.lab : con} \tag{38}$$

$$\frac{decs \vdash exp : con' \qquad decs \vdash con \equiv con' : \Omega}{decs \vdash exp : con} \tag{39}$$

## B.3 Signature Subtyping

$$\frac{}{decs \vdash \cdot \;\leq\; \cdot} \tag{40}$$

$$\frac{decs, var{:}knd = con \vdash sdecs \;\leq\; sdecs'}{decs \vdash lab \triangleright var{:}knd = con, sdecs \;\leq\; lab \triangleright var{:}knd, sdecs'} \tag{41}$$

$$\frac{decs \vdash sig \leq sig' : \mathsf{Sig} \quad decs, var{:}sig \vdash sdecs \;\leq\; sdecs'}{decs \vdash lab \triangleright var : sig, sdecs \;\leq\; lab \triangleright var : sig', sdecs'} \tag{42}$$

$$\frac{\mathit{decs} \vdash \mathit{lab}:\mathit{dec} \equiv \mathit{lab}:\mathit{dec}' \qquad \mathit{decs},\ \mathit{dec} \vdash \mathit{sdecs} \leq \mathit{sdecs}'}{\mathit{decs} \vdash \mathit{lab} \triangleright \mathit{dec}, \mathit{sdecs} \leq \mathit{lab} \triangleright \mathit{dec}', \mathit{sdecs}'} \tag{43}$$

$$\frac{\mathit{decs} \vdash \mathit{sdecs} \leq \mathit{sdecs}'}{\mathit{decs} \vdash [\mathit{sdecs}] \leq [\mathit{sdecs}'] : \mathsf{Sig}} \tag{44}$$

$$\frac{\mathit{decs} \vdash \mathit{sig}_2 \leq \mathit{sig}_1 : \mathsf{Sig} \qquad \mathit{decs}, \mathit{var}:\mathit{sig}_2 \vdash \mathit{sig}_1' \leq \mathit{sig}_2' : \mathsf{Sig}}{\mathit{decs} \vdash \mathit{var}:\mathit{sig}_1 \rightharpoonup \mathit{sig}_1' \leq \mathit{var}:\mathit{sig}_2 \rightharpoonup \mathit{sig}_2' : \mathsf{Sig}} \tag{45}$$

$$\frac{\mathit{decs} \vdash \mathit{sig}_2 \leq \mathit{sig}_1 : \mathsf{Sig} \qquad \mathit{decs}, \mathit{var}:\mathit{sig}_2 \vdash \mathit{sig}_1' \leq \mathit{sig}_2' : \mathsf{Sig}}{\mathit{decs} \vdash \mathit{var}:\mathit{sig}_1 \rightarrow \mathit{sig}_1' \leq \mathit{var}:\mathit{sig}_2 \rightharpoonup \mathit{sig}_2' : \mathsf{Sig}} \tag{46}$$

$$\frac{\mathit{decs} \vdash \mathit{sig}_2 \leq \mathit{sig}_1 : \mathsf{Sig} \qquad \mathit{decs}, \mathit{var}:\mathit{sig}_2 \vdash \mathit{sig}_1' \leq \mathit{sig}_2' : \mathsf{Sig}}{\mathit{decs} \vdash \mathit{var}:\mathit{sig}_1 \rightarrow \mathit{sig}_1' \leq \mathit{var}:\mathit{sig}_2 \rightarrow \mathit{sig}_2' : \mathsf{Sig}} \tag{47}$$

## B.4 Well-formed Modules

$$\frac{}{\mathit{decs} \vdash \cdot : \cdot} \tag{48}$$

$$\frac{\mathit{decs} \vdash \mathit{bnd} : \mathit{dec} \qquad \mathit{decs},\ \mathit{dec} \vdash \mathit{sbnds} : \mathit{sdecs}}{\mathit{decs} \vdash \mathit{lab} \triangleright \mathit{bnd}, \mathit{sbnds} : \mathit{lab} \triangleright \mathit{dec}, \mathit{sdecs}} \tag{49}$$

$$\frac{\vdash \mathit{decs}\ \mathrm{ok} \qquad \mathit{decs} = \mathit{decs}', \mathit{var}:\mathit{sig}, \mathit{decs}''}{\mathit{decs} \vdash \mathit{var} : \mathit{sig}} \tag{50}$$

$$\frac{\mathit{decs} \vdash \mathit{sbnds} : \mathit{sdecs}}{\mathit{decs} \vdash [\mathit{sbnds}] : [\mathit{sdecs}]} \tag{51}$$

$$\frac{\mathit{decs}, \mathit{var}:\mathit{sig} \vdash \mathit{mod} : \mathit{sig}'}{\mathit{decs} \vdash \lambda \mathit{var}:\mathit{sig}.\mathit{mod} : \mathit{var}:\mathit{sig} \rightharpoonup \mathit{sig}'} \tag{52}$$

$$\frac{\mathit{decs}, \mathit{var}:\mathit{sig} \vdash \mathit{mod} \downarrow \mathit{sig}'}{\mathit{decs} \vdash \lambda \mathit{var}:\mathit{sig}.\mathit{mod} : \mathit{var}:\mathit{sig} \rightarrow \mathit{sig}'} \tag{53}$$

$$\frac{\mathit{decs} \vdash \mathit{mod} : \mathit{sig}' \rightharpoonup \mathit{sig} \qquad \mathit{decs} \vdash \mathit{mod}' : \mathit{sig}'}{\mathit{decs} \vdash \mathit{mod}\,\mathit{mod}' : \mathit{sig}} \tag{54}$$

$$\frac{decs \vdash mod : [sdecs, lab : sig, sdecs'] \quad \mathrm{BV}(sdecs) \cap \mathrm{FV}(sig) = \emptyset}{decs \vdash mod.lab : sig} \quad (55)$$

$$\frac{decs \vdash mod : sig}{decs \vdash mod : sig : sig} \quad (56)$$

$$\frac{decs \vdash mod_{\mathrm{v}} : [sdecs, lab \rhd var{:}knd, sdecs']}{decs \vdash mod_{\mathrm{v}} : [sdecs, lab \rhd var{:}knd = mod_{\mathrm{v}}.lab, sdecs']} \quad (57)$$

$$\frac{decs \vdash mod_{\mathrm{v}} : [sdecs, lab \rhd var : sig, sdecs'] \qquad decs \vdash mod_{\mathrm{v}}.lab : sig'}{decs \vdash mod_{\mathrm{v}} : [sdecs, lab \rhd var : sig', sdecs']} \quad (58)$$

$$\frac{decs \vdash mod : sig \qquad decs \vdash sig \leq sig' : \mathsf{Sig}}{decs \vdash mod : sig'} \quad (59)$$

### B.5 Valuability Judgments

$$\frac{decs \vdash exp : con \qquad decs \vdash exp \downarrow}{decs \vdash exp \downarrow con} \quad (60)$$

$$\frac{decs \vdash mod : sig \qquad decs \vdash mod \downarrow}{decs \vdash mod \downarrow sig} \quad (61)$$

$$\frac{}{decs \vdash exp_{\mathrm{v}} \downarrow} \quad (62)$$

$$\frac{decs \vdash mod \downarrow}{decs \vdash mod.lab \downarrow} \quad (63)$$

$$\frac{decs \vdash exp_1 \downarrow con' \rightarrow con \qquad decs \vdash exp_2 \downarrow}{decs \vdash exp_1\, exp_2 \downarrow} \quad (64)$$

$$\frac{decs \vdash exp_1 \downarrow \qquad \cdots \qquad decs \vdash exp_n \downarrow}{decs \vdash \{lab_1 = exp_1, \ldots, lab_n = exp_n\} \downarrow} \quad (65)$$

$$\frac{}{decs \vdash mod_{\mathrm{v}} \downarrow} \quad (66)$$

$$\frac{decs \vdash mod \downarrow sig' \rightarrow sig \qquad decs \vdash mod' \downarrow}{decs \vdash mod\, mod' \downarrow} \quad (67)$$

$$\frac{decs \vdash mod \downarrow}{decs \vdash mod.lab \downarrow} \quad (68)$$

## C IL Dynamic Semantics

$$(\Delta, \sigma, E[(\langle\partial\rangle\pi_{\bar{k}} exp_{\mathrm{v}})exp'_{\mathrm{v}}]) \hookrightarrow$$
$$(\Delta, \sigma, E[\{\pi_{\bar{1}} exp_{\mathrm{v}}/var_1\} \cdots \{\pi_{\bar{n}} exp_{\mathrm{v}}/var_n\}\{exp'_{\mathrm{v}}/var'_k\}exp_k])$$
$$\text{where } exp_{\mathrm{v}} = \mathsf{fix}\ (var_i(var'_i{:}con_i){:}con'_i \mapsto exp_i)_{i=1}^{n}\mathsf{end} \quad (69)$$

$$(\Delta, \sigma, E[\pi_{lab}\{rbnds_{\mathrm{v}}, lab = exp_{\mathrm{v}}, rbnds'_{\mathrm{v}}\}]) \hookrightarrow (\Delta, \sigma, E[exp_{\mathrm{v}}]) \quad (70)$$

$$(\Delta, \sigma, E[\mathsf{handle}\ exp_{\mathrm{v}} \mathsf{with}\ exp]) \hookrightarrow (\Delta, \sigma, E[exp_{\mathrm{v}}]) \quad (71)$$

$$(\Delta, \sigma, E[\mathsf{ref}^{con} exp_{\mathrm{v}}]) \hookrightarrow (\Delta[loc : con], \sigma[loc \mapsto exp_{\mathrm{v}}], E[loc]) \text{ if } loc \notin \mathrm{BV}(\Delta) \quad (72)$$

$$(\Delta, \sigma, E[\mathsf{get}\ loc]) \hookrightarrow (\Delta, \sigma, E[\sigma(loc)]) \quad (73)$$

$$(\Delta, \sigma, E[\mathsf{set}(loc, exp_{\mathrm{v}})]) \hookrightarrow (\Delta, \sigma[loc \mapsto exp_{\mathrm{v}}], E[\{\}]) \quad (74)$$

$$(\Delta, \sigma, E[\mathsf{unroll}^{con}(\mathsf{roll}^{con'} exp_{\mathrm{v}})]) \hookrightarrow (\Delta, \sigma, E[exp_{\mathrm{v}}]) \quad (75)$$

$$(\Delta, \sigma, E[\mathsf{new\_tag}[con]]) \hookrightarrow (\Delta[tag : con\mathsf{Tag}], \sigma, E[tag]) \text{ if } tag \notin \mathrm{BV}(\Delta) \quad (76)$$

$$(\Delta, \sigma, E[\mathsf{proj}(\mathsf{inj}_i^{con} exp_{\mathrm{v}})]) \hookrightarrow (\Delta, \sigma, E[exp_{\mathrm{v}}]) \quad (77)$$

$$(\Delta, \sigma, E[\mathsf{iftagof\ tag}(tag, exp_{\mathrm{v}})\ \mathsf{is}\ tag\ \mathsf{then}\ exp\ \mathsf{else}\ exp']) \hookrightarrow (\Delta, \sigma, E[exp\ exp_{\mathrm{v}}]) \quad (78)$$

$$(\Delta, \sigma, E[\mathsf{iftagof\ tag}(tag', exp_{\mathrm{v}})\ \mathsf{is}\ tag\ \mathsf{then}\ exp\ \mathsf{else}\ exp']) \hookrightarrow (\Delta, \sigma, E[exp'])$$
$$\text{if } tag \neq tag' \quad (79)$$

$$(\Delta, \sigma, E[(\lambda var : sig \cdot mod)mod_{\mathrm{v}}]) \hookrightarrow (\Delta, \sigma, E[\{mod_{\mathrm{v}}/var\}mod]) \quad (80)$$

$$(\Delta, \sigma, E[(mod_{\mathrm{v}} : sig]) \hookrightarrow (\Delta, \sigma, E[mod_{\mathrm{v}}]) \quad (81)$$

$$(\Delta, \sigma, E[[sbnds_{\mathrm{v}}, lab = val, sbnds'_{\mathrm{v}}] \cdot lab]) \hookrightarrow (\Delta, \sigma, E[val])$$
$$\text{where } \mathrm{BV}(sbnds_{\mathrm{v}}) \cap \mathrm{FV}(val) = \emptyset \quad (82)$$

$$(\Delta, \sigma, E[exp_{\mathrm{v}} =_{con} exp'_{\mathrm{v}}]) \hookrightarrow (\Delta, \sigma, E[\mathsf{true}])$$
$$\text{if } exp_{\mathrm{v}} \text{ and } exp'_{\mathrm{v}} \text{ are equal at type } con \quad (83)$$

$$(\Delta, \sigma, E[exp_{\mathrm{v}} =_{con} exp'_{\mathrm{v}}]) \hookrightarrow (\Delta, \sigma, E[\mathsf{false}])$$
$$\text{if } exp_{\mathrm{v}} \text{ and } exp_{\mathrm{v}} \text{ are unequal at type } con \quad (84)$$

$$\left(\Delta, \sigma, E\left[\mathsf{case}\left(\mathsf{inj}_{lab_{\mathrm{i}}}^{\Sigma_{lab_{\mathrm{i}}}(lab_1 \mapsto con_1, \ldots)} exp_{\mathrm{v}}\right) \mathsf{of}\ exp_i, \ldots, exp_n \mathsf{end}\right]\right) \hookrightarrow$$
$$\left(\Delta, \sigma, E\left[exp_{\mathrm{i}}\left(\mathsf{inj}_{lab_{\mathrm{i}}}^{\Sigma_{lab_{\mathrm{i}}}(lab_1 \mapsto con_1, \ldots)} exp_{\mathrm{v}}\right)\right]\right)$$

$$(\Delta, \sigma, E[\text{handle } R[\text{raise}^{con} exp_v] \text{ with } exp']) \hookrightarrow (\Delta, \sigma, E[exp' exp_v]) \tag{85}$$

$$(\Delta, \sigma, R[\text{raise}^{con} exp_v]) \hookrightarrow (\Delta, \sigma, \text{raise}^{ans} exp_v) \text{ if } R \neq [] \tag{86}$$

## D Elaboration (excerpts)

### D.1 Derived Forms

$knd_1 \times \cdots \times knd_n \mapsto \{1 : knd_1, \ldots, n : knd_n\}$
$knd^n \mapsto \{1 : knd, \ldots, n : knd\}$

$\text{Unit} \mapsto \{\}$
$\text{Bool}_{\langle lab \rangle} \mapsto \Sigma_{\langle lab \rangle} \left(\overline{\text{true}} \mapsto \text{Unit}, \overline{\text{false}} \mapsto \text{Unit}\right)$
$con_1 \times \cdots \times con_n \mapsto \{\overline{1} = con_1, \ldots, \overline{n} = con_n\}$
$\lambda(var_1, \ldots, var_n) \cdot con \mapsto$
$\quad \lambda var{:}\Omega^n.(\{\pi_1\, var/var_1\} \cdots \{\pi_n\, var/var_n\}con)$
$(con_1, \ldots, con_n) \mapsto \{1 = con_1, \ldots, n = con_n\}$

$(exp_1, \ldots, exp_n) \mapsto \{\overline{1} = exp_1, \ldots, \overline{n} = exp_n\}$
$\lambda(var : con){:}con'.exp \mapsto$
$\quad \pi_{\overline{1}}\, \text{fix}\, var'(var{:}con) : con' \mapsto exp\ \text{end}$
$\qquad var' \notin \text{FV}(exp)$
$\lambda(var_1{:}con_1, \ldots, var_n{:}con_n){:}con.exp \mapsto$
$\quad \lambda(var{:}con_1 \times \cdots \times con_n){:}con.$
$\qquad \{\pi_1\, var/var_1\} \cdots \{\pi_n\, var/var_n\}exp$
$\qquad var \notin \text{FV}exp$
$\text{let}\ bnd_1, \ldots, bnd_n\ \text{in}\ exp\ \text{end} \mapsto$
$\quad [1 = bnd_1, \ldots, n = bnd_n, (n+1) = exp].(n+1)$
$\text{catch}^{con}\ exp\ \text{with}\ exp' \mapsto$
$\quad \text{handle}\ exp\ \text{with}\ (\lambda var{:}\text{Tagged}.$
$\qquad \text{iftagof}\ var\ \text{is}\ \ basis.\text{fail}^*.\text{tag}$
$\qquad\quad \text{then}\ \lambda var : \text{Unit}.exp'\ \text{else}\ \text{raise}^{con}\ var$
$\quad var \notin \text{FV}(exp')$
$\text{false} \mapsto \text{inj}^{\text{Bool}}_{\text{false}}\ \{\}$
$\text{if}\ exp_1\ \text{then}\ exp_2\ \text{else}\ exp_3 \mapsto$
$\quad \text{case}\ exp_1\ \text{of}$
$\qquad \lambda var : \text{Bool}_{\overline{\text{false}}}.exp_3, \lambda var : \text{Bool}_{\overline{\text{true}}}.exp_2$
$\qquad var \notin \text{FV}(exp_2, exp_3)\ \text{end}$
$exp_1\ \text{and}\ exp_2 \mapsto \text{if}\ exp_1\ \text{then}\ exp_2\ \text{else}\ \text{false}$

## D.2 Expressions

$$\frac{}{\Gamma \vdash \overline{scon} \rightsquigarrow scon : \mathrm{type}(\overline{scon})} \tag{87}$$

Rule 87: We assume a meta-level function type which gives the IL type of each constant.

$$\frac{\Gamma \vdash_{\mathrm{ctx}} \overline{longid} \rightsquigarrow path : con \quad \text{Rule 89 does not apply.}}{\Gamma \vdash longid \rightsquigarrow path : con} \tag{88}$$

Rule 88: Monomorphic variables.

$$\frac{\Gamma \vdash_{\mathrm{ctx}} \overline{longid} \rightsquigarrow path : con \rightarrow con'}{\Gamma \vdash longid \rightsquigarrow \partial\,(path) : con \rightharpoonup con'} \tag{89}$$

Rule 88: Monomorphic value constructors.

$$\frac{\Gamma \vdash_{\mathrm{ctx}} \overline{longid} \rightsquigarrow path : sig \rightarrow [\mathrm{it}{:}con] \quad \Gamma \vdash_{\mathrm{inst}} \rightsquigarrow mod : sig \quad \text{Rule 91 does not apply.}}{\Gamma \vdash longid \rightsquigarrow path(mod) \cdot \mathrm{it} : con} \tag{90}$$

Rule 90: Polymorphic variables. The module *mod* is the structure of types (and equality functions) that we "guess" to instantiate the polymorphism.

$$\frac{\Gamma \vdash_{\mathrm{ctx}} \overline{longid} \rightsquigarrow path : sig \rightarrow [\mathrm{it}{:}con \rightarrow con'] \qquad \Gamma \vdash_{\mathrm{inst}} \rightsquigarrow mod : sig}{\Gamma \vdash longid \rightsquigarrow \partial\,(path(mod) \cdot \mathrm{it}) : con \rightharpoonup con'} \tag{91}$$

Rule 91: Polymorphic value constructors.

$$\frac{\begin{array}{c}\sigma \text{ a permutation of } 1..n \\ var_1, \ldots, var_n \notin \mathrm{BV}(\Gamma) \\ lab_{\sigma(1)} < \cdots < lab_{\sigma(n)} \\ \forall i \in 1..n : \quad \Gamma \vdash expr_i \rightsquigarrow exp_i : con_i\end{array}}{\begin{array}{l}\Gamma \vdash \{\, lab_1 = expr_1, \ldots,\ lab_n = expr_n\} \rightsquigarrow \\ \quad \mathsf{let}\ var_1 = exp_1, \ldots, var_n = exp_n\ \mathsf{in} \\ \quad \{\, \overline{lab_{\sigma(1)}} = var_{\sigma(1)}, \ldots, \overline{var_{\sigma(n)}} = var_{\sigma(n)}\}\ \mathsf{end} : \\ \quad \{\, \overline{lab_{\sigma(1)}}{:}con_{\sigma(1)}, \ldots,\ \overline{lab_{\sigma(n)}}\,{:}con_{\sigma(n)}\}\end{array}} \tag{92}$$

Rule 92: The order in which labels appear in the record type is significant for the IL, so in the translation we normalize record types by sorting the labels with some fixed ordering <.

Note that though the order of the records fields is given by this ordering, the components are evaluated (and side-effects occur) in the order that they are listed in the EL.

$$\frac{\begin{array}{c}\Gamma \vdash \mathit{strdec} \rightsquigarrow \mathit{sbnds} : \mathit{sdecs} \\ \mathit{var} \notin \mathrm{BV}(\Gamma) \qquad \Gamma, 1^* \rhd \mathit{var} : [\mathit{sdecs}] \vdash \mathit{expr} \rightsquigarrow \mathit{exp} : \mathit{con}' \\ \Gamma, \mathit{var} : [\mathit{sdecs}] \vdash \mathit{con}' \equiv \mathit{con} : \Omega \quad \Gamma \vdash \mathit{con} : \Omega\end{array}}{\begin{array}{l}\Gamma \vdash \texttt{let } \mathit{strdec} \texttt{ in } \mathit{expr} \texttt{ end} \rightsquigarrow \\ \quad \mathsf{let}\ \mathit{var} = \mathit{mod}\ \mathsf{in}\ \mathit{exp}\ \mathsf{end} : \mathit{con}\end{array}} \tag{93}$$

Rule 93: The declarations *strdec* are translated into the components of a structure; the "starred structure" convention is used here to make these components accessible while translating *expr*. Standard ML prohibits the type of the body from depending on abstract types defined locally—in particular, values created from a datatype cannot escape the scope of that datatype.

$$\frac{\Gamma \vdash \mathit{expr} \rightsquigarrow \mathit{exp} : \mathit{con}'' \rightharpoonup \mathit{con} \quad \Gamma \vdash \mathit{expr}' \rightsquigarrow \mathit{exp}' : \mathit{con}' \quad \Gamma \vdash \mathit{con}' \equiv \mathit{con}'' : \Omega}{\Gamma \vdash \mathit{expr}\ \mathit{expr}' \rightsquigarrow \mathit{exp}\ \mathit{exp}' : \mathit{con}} \tag{94}$$

Rule 94: General application.

$$\frac{\Gamma \vdash_{\mathrm{ctx}} \mathit{longid} \rightsquigarrow \mathit{path} : \mathit{con}' \rightarrow \mathit{con} \quad \Gamma \vdash \mathit{expr}' \rightsquigarrow \mathit{exp}' : \mathit{con}'}{\Gamma \vdash \mathit{longid}\ \mathit{expr}' \rightsquigarrow \mathit{path}\ \mathit{exp}' : \mathit{con}} \tag{95}$$

Rule 95: Application of monomorphic value constructor.

$$\frac{\Gamma \vdash_{\mathrm{ctx}} \mathit{longid} \rightsquigarrow \mathit{path} : \mathit{sig} \rightarrow [\mathrm{it} : \mathit{con}' \rightarrow \mathit{con}] \quad \Gamma \vdash_{\mathrm{inst}} \mathit{mod} : \mathit{sig} \quad \Gamma \vdash \mathit{expr}' \rightsquigarrow \mathit{exp}' : \mathit{con}'}{\Gamma \vdash \mathit{longid}\ \mathit{expr}' \rightsquigarrow (\mathit{path}\,(\mathit{mod}).\mathrm{it})\ \mathit{exp}' : \mathit{con}} \tag{96}$$

Rule 96: Application of polymorphic value constructor.

$$\frac{\Gamma \vdash \mathit{expr} \rightsquigarrow \mathit{exp} : \mathit{con} \quad \Gamma \vdash \mathit{ty} \rightsquigarrow \mathit{con}' : \Omega \quad \Gamma \vdash \mathit{con} \equiv \mathit{con}' : \Omega}{\Gamma \vdash \mathit{expr} : \mathit{ty} \rightsquigarrow \mathit{exp} : \mathit{con}} \tag{97}$$

Rule 97: Type constraints on expressions are verified, but do not appear in the translation.

$$\frac{\begin{array}{c}\Gamma \vdash \mathit{expr} \rightsquigarrow \mathit{exp} : \mathit{con} \quad \Gamma \vdash \mathit{match} \rightsquigarrow \mathit{exp}' : \mathsf{Tagged} \rightharpoonup \mathit{con}' \\ \Gamma \vdash \mathit{con} \equiv \mathit{con}' : \Omega \quad \mathit{var} \notin \mathrm{BV}(\Gamma)\end{array}}{\begin{array}{l}\Gamma \vdash \mathit{expr} \texttt{ handle } \mathit{match} \rightsquigarrow \\ \mathsf{handle}\ \mathit{exp}\ \mathsf{with} \\ \quad \lambda(\mathit{var}{:}\mathsf{Tagged}){:}\mathit{con}. \\ \qquad (\mathsf{catch}^{\mathit{con}}\ \mathit{exp}'\ \mathit{var}\ \mathsf{with}\ \mathsf{raise}^{\mathit{con}}\ \mathit{var}) : \\ \mathit{con}\end{array}} \tag{98}$$

Rule 98: The handling expression *exp′ var* may fail if the handler pattern does not match the exception raised, in which case we propagate the exception.

$$\frac{\Gamma \vdash expr \leadsto exp : \mathsf{Tagged} \quad \Gamma \vdash con : \Omega}{\Gamma \vdash \texttt{raise}\ expr \leadsto \mathsf{raise}^{con}\ exp : con} \tag{99}$$

Rule 99: The translation of a `raise` expression can be given any valid type *con*.

$$\frac{\begin{array}{c} var \notin \mathrm{BV}(\Gamma) \\ \Gamma \vdash match \leadsto exp : con_1 \rightharpoonup con_2 \end{array}}{\begin{array}{l} \Gamma \vdash \texttt{fn}\ match \leadsto \\ \quad \lambda(var{:}con_1){:}con_2. \\ \quad (\mathsf{catch}^{con_2}\ exp\ var \\ \quad \mathsf{with\ raise}^{con_2}\ basis.\overline{\texttt{Match}}^{*}.\overline{\texttt{Match}}) \\ \quad con_1 \rightharpoonup con_2 \end{array} :} \tag{100}$$

Rule 100: The expression *exp var* will fail if the match fails; here we turn the *basis*.fail*.fail exception into $basis.\overline{\texttt{Match}}^{*}.\overline{\texttt{Match}}$. The resulting function has a partial type because it can (syntactically) raise an exception.

$$\frac{\begin{array}{c} \Gamma \vdash expr_1 \leadsto exp_1 : con_1 \quad \Gamma \vdash expr_2 \leadsto exp_2 : con_2 \\ \Gamma \vdash con_1 = con_2 : \Omega \quad \Gamma \vdash_{eq} con_1 \leadsto exp_v \end{array}}{\Gamma \vdash expr_1 \ = \ expr_2 \leadsto exp_v(exp_1, exp_2) : \mathsf{Bool}} \tag{101}$$

Rule 101: Translation of equality comparison; $exp_v$ is the equality function, having type $con \times con \rightharpoonup \mathsf{Bool}$.

### D.3 Matches

$$\frac{\begin{array}{c} var, var' \notin \mathrm{BV}(\Gamma) \qquad \Gamma \vdash con' : \Omega \\ \Gamma \vdash pat \Leftarrow var' : con'\ \mathsf{else}\ basis.\mathrm{fail}^{*}.\mathrm{fail} \leadsto sbnds : sdecs \\ \Gamma, 1^{*} \triangleright var : [sdecs] \vdash expr \leadsto exp : con \end{array}}{\begin{array}{l} \Gamma \vdash pat \ \texttt{=>}\ expr \leadsto \\ \quad \lambda(var'{:}con'){:}con.\mathsf{let}\ var{=}[sbnds]\ \mathsf{in}\ exp\ \mathsf{end} : con' \rightharpoonup con \end{array}} \tag{102}$$

Rule 102:
The result of translating a match is a function that may fail if the match fails.

$$\frac{\begin{array}{l} var \notin \mathrm{BV}(\Gamma) \quad \Gamma \vdash mrule \leadsto exp : con_1 \rightharpoonup con_2 \\ \qquad \Gamma \vdash match \leadsto exp' : con_1' \rightharpoonup con_2' \\ \qquad \Gamma \vdash con_1 \rightharpoonup con_2 \equiv con_1' \rightharpoonup con_2' : \Omega \end{array}}{\begin{array}{l} \Gamma \vdash mrule \mid match \leadsto \\ \quad \lambda(var{:}con_1){:}con_2. \qquad : \\ \quad \mathsf{catch}^{con}\ exp\ var\ \mathsf{with}\ exp'\ var \\ \quad con' \rightharpoonup con \end{array}} \tag{103}$$

Rule 103: The failure of pattern matching in the first clause is caught, and we try again with the next clause.

## D.4 Polymorphic Instantiation

$$\frac{\begin{array}{c} decs \vdash con : \Omega \\ \langle decs \vdash_{\mathrm{eq}} con \leadsto exp_{\mathrm{v}} \rangle \\ \langle\langle decs \vdash_{\mathrm{inst}} \leadsto [sbnds_{\mathrm{v}}] : [sdecs] \rangle\rangle \end{array}}{\begin{array}{l} decs \vdash_{\mathrm{inst}} \leadsto \\ :\ [lab'{=}[lab \triangleright var{=}con\langle, \mathrm{eq}{=}exp_{\mathrm{v}}\rangle]\langle\langle, sbnds_{\mathrm{v}}\rangle\rangle] \\ \ [lab'{:}[lab \triangleright var{:}\Omega{=}con\langle, \mathrm{eq}{:}var \times var \rightharpoonup \mathsf{Bool}\rangle]]\langle\langle, sdecs\rangle\rangle \end{array}} \tag{104}$$

Rule 104 Nondeterministically choose types and the corresponding equality functions so as to match a fully-transparent signature.

## D.5 Declarations

$$\frac{\begin{array}{c} var \notin \mathrm{BV}(\Gamma) \\ \Gamma \vdash expr \leadsto exp : con \\ \Gamma, var : con \vdash pat \Leftarrow var{:}con\ \mathsf{else}\ basis.\overline{\mathtt{Bind}}^{*}.\overline{\mathtt{Bind}} \leadsto sbnds : sdecs \end{array}}{\begin{array}{l} \Gamma \vdash \mathtt{val\ ()}\ pat = expr \leadsto \\ \quad 1 \triangleright var{=}\ exp, sbnds : \\ \quad 1 \triangleright var{:}con, sdecs \end{array}} \tag{105}$$

Rule 105: Monomorphic, non-recursive binding.

$$
\frac{\begin{array}{l}
sig = [\overline{tyvar_1}^*{:}[\overline{tyvar_1} : \Omega], \ldots, \overline{tyvar_n}^*{:}[\overline{tyvar_n} : \Omega], \\
\qquad 1^*{:}\Omega, \ldots, m^*{:}\Omega] \\
\Gamma, 1^* \rhd var : sig \vdash expr \rightsquigarrow exp : con \\
\Gamma, 1^* \rhd var : sig \vdash basis.\overline{\mathtt{Bind}}^*.\overline{\mathtt{Bind}} \\
\qquad\qquad\qquad \textsf{else}\ pat \Leftarrow exp : con \rightsquigarrow \\
\qquad\qquad lab_1{=}exp_1, \ldots, lab_n{=}exp_n : \\
\qquad\qquad lab_1{:}con_1, \ldots, lab_n{=}exp_n \\
\forall i \in 1..n : \\
\quad \Gamma, 1^* \rhd var : sig \vdash exp_i \downarrow con_i \\
\quad sbnd'_i := lab_i{=}(var : sig){\to}[\mathrm{it}{=}exp_i] \\
\quad sdec'_i := lab_i{:}(var : sig){\to}[\mathrm{it}{:}con_i]
\end{array}}{\begin{array}{l}
\Gamma \vdash \mathtt{val}\ (\, tyvar_1, \ldots,\ tyvar_n)\ \ pat = expr \rightsquigarrow \\
\qquad sbnd'_1, \ldots,\ sbnd'_n\ :\ sdec'_1, \ldots,\ sdec'_n
\end{array}} \tag{106}
$$

Rule 106: Polymorphic, non-recursive `val` bindings. (For space reasons, we show a simplified version of the full rule, which must take equality type variables into account.) This rule has the effect of only allowing polymorphism for irrefutable patterns. Note that type inference may introduce new type variables not mentioned in the source (as in `val f = fn x => x`).

$$
\frac{\begin{array}{c}
\Gamma \vdash strdec_1 \rightsquigarrow sbnds_1 : sdecs_1 \\
\Gamma, sdecs_1 \vdash strdec_2 \rightsquigarrow sbnds_2 : sdecs_2
\end{array}}{\begin{array}{l}
\Gamma \vdash strdec_1\ strdec_2 \rightsquigarrow \\
\qquad sbnds_1{+\!+}sbnds_2 : sdecs_1 {+\!+}\, sdecs_2
\end{array}} \tag{107}
$$

Rule 107: Sequential declarations are modelled with a syntactic append, except we must rename any labels (preserving the star convention) in $sbnds_1/sdecs_1$ appearing in $sbnds_2/sdecs_2$,

$$
\frac{\forall i \in 1..n : \quad \Gamma \vdash_{\mathrm{ctx}} \overline{longstrid_i} \rightsquigarrow path_i : sig_i}{\begin{array}{l}
\Gamma \vdash \mathtt{open}\ longstrid_1\ \cdots\ longstrid_n \rightsquigarrow \\
\qquad 1^*{=}path_1, \ldots, n^*{=}path_n : \\
\qquad 1^*{:}\, sig_1, \ldots, n^*{=}sig_n
\end{array}} \tag{108}
$$

$$
\frac{\Gamma \vdash ty \rightsquigarrow con : \Omega \qquad var \notin \mathrm{BV}(\Gamma)}{\begin{array}{l}
\Gamma \vdash \mathtt{exception}\ id\ \mathtt{of}\ ty \rightsquigarrow \\
\quad \overline{id}^*{=}[\mathrm{tag} \rhd var{=}\textsf{new\_tag}[con], \qquad\qquad : \\
\qquad\quad \overline{id}{=}\lambda(var'{:}con){:}\textsf{Tagged.tag}(var, var')] \\
\quad \overline{id}^*{:}[\mathrm{tag} \rhd var{:}con\ \textsf{Tag},\ \overline{id}{:}con{\to}\textsf{Tagged}]
\end{array}} \tag{109}
$$

$$\frac{\begin{array}{c}\Gamma \vdash_{\text{ctx}} \overline{\mathit{longid}} \rightsquigarrow \mathit{path.lab} : \mathit{con} \\ \Gamma \vdash \mathit{path}.\text{tag} : \mathit{con}'\end{array}}{\begin{array}{l}\Gamma \vdash \texttt{exception}\ \mathit{id} = \mathit{longid} \rightsquigarrow \\ \quad \overline{\mathit{id}}^{*} \text{=[tag=}\mathit{path}\text{.tag, } \overline{\mathit{id}}\text{=}\mathit{path.lab}\text{]} : \\ \quad \overline{\mathit{id}}^{*} \text{:[tag:}\mathit{con}'\text{, } \overline{\mathit{id}}\text{:}\mathit{con}\text{]}\end{array}} \tag{110}$$

Rule 110: We know that *longid* corresponds to an exception constructor because of the tag component.

$$\frac{\begin{array}{c}\mathit{var} \notin \mathrm{BV}(\Gamma) \\ \Gamma \vdash \mathit{strdec}_1 \rightsquigarrow \mathit{sbnds}_1 : \mathit{sdecs}_1 \\ \Gamma, 1^* \rhd \mathit{var}\text{:[}\mathit{sdecs}_1\text{]} \vdash \mathit{strdec}' \rightsquigarrow \mathit{sbnds}_2 : \mathit{sdecs}_2\end{array}}{\begin{array}{l}\Gamma \vdash \texttt{local}\ \mathit{strdec}\ \texttt{in}\ \mathit{strdec}'\ \texttt{end} \rightsquigarrow \\ \quad 1 \rhd \mathit{var}\text{=[}\mathit{sbnds}_1\text{]}, \mathit{sbnds}_2 : 1 \rhd \mathit{var}\text{:[}\mathit{sbnds}_2\text{]}, \mathit{sdecs}_2\end{array}} \tag{111}$$

Rule 111: We create a bindings for all of the declarations, but the local bindings are segregated into a substructure inaccessible from the EL.

$$\frac{\Gamma \vdash \mathit{tybind} \rightsquigarrow \mathit{sbnds} : \mathit{sdecs}}{\Gamma \vdash \texttt{type}\ \mathit{tybind} \rightsquigarrow \mathit{sbnds} : \mathit{sdecs}} \tag{112}$$

## D.6 Structure Expressions

$$\frac{\Gamma \vdash_{\text{ctx}} \overline{\mathit{longstrid}} \rightsquigarrow \mathit{path} : \mathit{sig}}{\Gamma \vdash \mathit{longstrid} \rightsquigarrow \mathit{path} : \mathit{sig}} \tag{113}$$

$$\frac{\Gamma \vdash \mathit{strdec} \rightsquigarrow \mathit{mod} : \mathit{sig}}{\Gamma \vdash \texttt{struct}\ \mathit{strdec}\ \texttt{end} \rightsquigarrow \mathit{mod} : \mathit{sig}} \tag{114}$$

$$\frac{\begin{array}{c}\Gamma \vdash_{\text{ctx}} \overline{\mathit{longfunid}} \rightsquigarrow \mathit{path}_f : (\mathit{var}_1 : \mathit{sig}_1) \rightharpoonup \mathit{sig}_2 \\ \Gamma \vdash_{\text{ctx}} \overline{\mathit{longstrid}} \rightsquigarrow \mathit{path} : \mathit{sig} \\ \Gamma \vdash_{\text{sub}} \mathit{path} : \mathit{sig} \preceq \mathit{sig}_1 \rightsquigarrow \mathit{mod} : \mathit{sig}' \\ \Gamma \vdash (\mathit{var}_1\text{:}\mathit{sig}) \rightharpoonup \mathit{sig}_2 \equiv \mathit{sig}' \rightharpoonup \mathit{sig}'' : \mathsf{Sig}\end{array}}{\Gamma \vdash \mathit{longfunid}\texttt{(}\ \mathit{longstrid}\texttt{)} \rightsquigarrow (\mathit{path}_f : \mathit{sig}' \rightharpoonup \mathit{sig}'')\ \mathit{mod} : \mathit{sig}''} \tag{115}$$

Rule 115: We insert an explicit coercion to drop and reorder components of the argument structure (which has signature *sig*), in order to match the domain signature of the functor

($sig_1$). The signature $sig'$ is the most-specific (and fully transparent) signature of the coerced structure, which may expose more types (is a sub-signature of) $sig_1$.

$$\frac{\begin{array}{c}\Gamma \vdash_{\mathrm{ctx}} longstrid \rightsquigarrow path : sig \\ \Gamma \vdash sigexp \rightsquigarrow sig' : \mathsf{Sig} \\ \Gamma \vdash_{\mathrm{sub}} path : sig \preceq sig' \rightsquigarrow mod : sig''\end{array}}{\Gamma \vdash longstrid : sigexp \rightsquigarrow mod : sig''} \quad (116)$$

Rule 116: Ascribing a signature to a structure using ":" hides components (this hiding being accomplished here via an explicit coercion), but allows the identity of the remaining type components to leak through. The rules for coercions ensure that $sig''$ will be fully transparent, maximizing propagation of type information.

$$\frac{\begin{array}{c}\Gamma \vdash_{\mathrm{ctx}} longstrid \rightsquigarrow path : sig \\ \Gamma \vdash sigexp \rightsquigarrow sig' : \mathsf{Sig} \\ \Gamma \vdash_{\mathrm{sub}} path : sig \preceq sig' \rightsquigarrow mod : sig''\end{array}}{\Gamma \vdash longstrid :> sigexp \rightsquigarrow (mod : sig') : sig'} \quad (117)$$

Rule 117: Ascribing a signature to a structure with $:>$ not only hides components, but restricts information about types to that which appears in the signature.

$$\frac{\begin{array}{c} var \notin \mathrm{BV}(\Gamma) \\ \Gamma \vdash strdec \rightsquigarrow sbnds : sdecs \\ \Gamma, 1^* \triangleright var{:}[sdecs] \vdash strexp \rightsquigarrow mod : sig\end{array}}{\begin{array}{l}\Gamma \vdash \texttt{let}\ strdec\ \texttt{in}\ strexp\ \texttt{end} \rightsquigarrow \\ \quad [1 \triangleright var{=}[sbnds], 2^*{=}mod] : \\ \quad [1 \triangleright var{:}[sdecs], 2^*{:}sig]\end{array}} \quad (118)$$

## D.7 Pattern Compilation

$$\frac{\begin{array}{c} lab \text{ fresh} \qquad \mathrm{type}(scon) = con \\ \Gamma \vdash exp : con\end{array}}{\begin{array}{l}\Gamma \vdash scon \Leftarrow exp : con \ \mathsf{else}\ exp' \rightsquigarrow \\ \quad lab{=}\mathsf{if}\ exp{=}_{con} scon\ \mathsf{then}\ \{\}\ \mathsf{else}\ \mathsf{raise}^{\mathsf{Unit}}\ exp' : \\ \quad lab{:}\mathsf{Unit}\end{array}} \quad (119)$$

Rule 119: Pattern match against a constant. We need primitive equality functions for constants which can appear in patterns.

$$\frac{\begin{array}{l} \quad \Gamma \vdash con \equiv \{lab'_1{:}con'_1, \ldots, lab'_k{:}con'_k\} : \Omega \\ \quad \{\overline{lab_1}, \ldots, \overline{lab_n}\} \subseteq \{lab'_1, \ldots, lab'_n\} \\ \forall i \in 1..n : \\ \quad \Gamma, lab \triangleright var{:}con \vdash pat_i \\ \qquad \Leftarrow \pi_{\overline{lab_i}}\ exp : con_i \ \mathsf{else}\ exp' \rightsquigarrow sbnds_i : sdecs_i \end{array}}{\begin{array}{l} \Gamma \vdash \{\, lab_1 = pat_1, \ldots, lab_n = pat_n \langle, \ldots \rangle \} \\ \qquad \mathsf{else}\ exp' \Leftarrow exp : con \rightsquigarrow \\ \quad sbnds_1, \ldots, sbnds_n : \\ \quad sdecs_1, \ldots, sdecs_n \end{array}} \quad (120)$$

Rule 120: Pattern match against a record of patterns. Because we disallow repeated variables in patterns, the syntactic concatenation of structure here is well-formed.

## References


[1] Andrew W. Appel. *Compiling with Continuations*. Cambridge University Press, 1992.

[2] Luca Cardelli. Typeful programming. In E. J. Neuhold and M. Paul, editors, *Formal Description of Programming Concepts*. Springer-Verlag, 1991.

[3] Luca Cardelli. Type systems. In Allen B. Tucker Jr., editor, *Handbook of Computer Science and Engineering*, pages 2208–2236. CRC Press, 1997.

[4] Jean-Yves Girard. Une extension de l'interprétation de Gödel à l'analyse, et son application à l'élimination des coupures dans l'analyse et la théorie des types. In Jens Erik Fenstad, editor, *Second Scandinavian Logic Symposium*, volume 63 of *Studies in Logic and the Foundations of Mathematics*, pages 63–92. North-Holland, 1971.

[5] Michael J. Gordon, Robin Milner, and Christopher P. Wadsworth. *Edinburgh LCF: a mechanised logic of computation*, volume LNCS 78. Springer-Verlag, 1979.

[6] Carl A. Gunter, Elsa L. Gunter, and David B. MacQueen. An abstract interpretation for ML equality kinds. *LNCS 526*, pages 112–130, 1991.

[7] Robert Harper. A simplified account of polymorphic references. Technical Report CMU-CS-93-169, School of Computer Science, Carnegie Mellon University, 1993.

[8] Robert Harper and Mark Lillibridge. A type-theoretic approach to higher-order modules with sharing. In *21st ACM Symposium on Principles of Programming Languages*, pages 123–137, 1994.

[9] Robert Harper and John C. Mitchell. On the type structure of Standard ML. *ACM Transactions on Programming Languages and Systems*, 15(2):211–252, 1993.

[10] Robert Harper and Greg Morrisett. Compiling polymorphism using intensional type analysis. In *22nd ACM Symposium on Principles of Programming Languages*, pages 130–141, 1995.

[11] Robert Harper and Christopher Stone. An interpretation of Standard ML in type theory. Technical Report CMU-CS-97-147, School of Computer Science, Carnegie Mellon University, 1997.

[12] Xavier Leroy. Polymorphism by name for references and continuations. In *20th ACM Symposium on Principles of Programming Languages*, pages 220–231, 1993.

[13] Xavier Leroy. Manifest types, modules, and separate compilation. In *21st ACM Symposium on Principles of Programming Languages*, pages 109–122, 1994.

[14] Xavier Leroy. A syntactic theory of type generativity and sharing. *Journal of Functional Programming*, 6(5):667–698, 1996.

[15] Mark Lillibridge. *Translucent Sums: A Foundation for Higher-Order Module Systems*. PhD thesis, School of Computer Science, Carnegie Mellon University, 1997.

[16] David MacQueen. Using dependent types to express modular structure. In *13th ACM Symposium on Principles of Programming Languages*, pages 277–286, 1986.

[17] Robin Milner. A proposal for Standard ML. In *1984 ACM Symposium on LISP and Functional Programming*, pages 184–197, 1984.

[18] Robin Milner, Mads Tofte, Robert Harper, and Dave MacQueen. *The Definition of Standard ML (Revised)*. MIT Press, 1997.

[19] John C. Mitchell and Gordon Plotkin. Abstract types have existential type. *ACM Transactions on Programming Languages and Systems*, 10(3):470–502, 1988.

[20] Eugenio Moggi. Notions of computation and monads. *Information and Computation*, 93(1):55–92, July 1991.

[21] Chris Okasaki. *Purely Functional Data Structures*. PhD thesis, School of Computer Science, Carnegie Mellon University, 1996.

[22] Andrew M. Pitts and Ian D. B. Stark. Observable properties of higher order functions that dynamically create local names, or: What's new? In *Mathematical Foundations of Computer Science, 18th International Symposium*, volume 711 of *LNCS*, pages 122–141. Springer-Verlag, Berlin, 1993.

[23] Gordon D. Plotkin. A structural approach to operational semantics. Technical Report DAIMI FN–19, Aarhus University, September 1981.

[24] John C. Reynolds. Towards a theory of type structure. In B. Robinet, editor, *Programming Symposium, Proceedings, Colloque sur la Programmation*, volume 19 of *LNCS*, pages 408–425, 1974.

[25] Dana S. Scott. Data types as lattices. *SIAM Journal on Computing*, 5:522–587, September 1976.

[26] Zhong Shao. An overview of the FLINT/ML compiler. In *1997 ACM SIGPLAN Workshop on Types in Compilation (TIC'97)*, June 1997.

[27] Zhong Shao and Andrew W. Appel. A type-based compiler for Standard ML. In *ACM SIGPLAN '95 Conference on Programming Language Design and Implementation*, pages 116–129, 1995.

[28] David Tarditi, Greg Morrisett, Perry Cheng, Chris Stone, Robert Harper, and Peter Lee. TIL: A type-directed optimizing compiler for ML. In *ACM SIGPLAN '96 Conference on Programming Language Design and Implementation*, pages 181–192, 1996.

[29] Mads Tofte. Type inference for polymorphic references. *Information and Computation*, 89(1):1–34, November 1990.

[30] Philip Wadler and Stephen Blott. How to make *ad-hoc* polymorphism less *ad-hoc*. In *16th ACM Symposium on Principles of Programming Languages*, pages 60–76, 1989.

[31] Andrew Wright. Simple imperative polymorphism. *Journal of Lisp and Symbolic Computation*, 8(4): 343–355, December 1995.

[32] Andrew Wright and Matthias Felleisen. A syntactic approach to type soundness. Technical Report TR91-160, Dept. of Computer Science, Rice University, 1991.

# 13 Unification and Polymorphism in Region Inference

**Mads Tofte and Lars Birkedal**

## 1 Introduction

Most programming languages provide some facility for dynamic allocation and de-allocation of memory cells. The reason for this is that the number of cells which the program wishes to allocate and use at some point during the computation often is much larger than the number of cells which have to exist at any one point of the computation.

The stack discipline which originated with Algol 60 [15] is a particularly elegant discipline for dynamic memory management. Restricted versions of the original stack discipline are used in many languages in current use, e.g., C and Pascal. In the stack discipline, every point of memory allocation is matched by a point of de-allocation, and these points are easy to identify from the program text. The evident connection between allocation and de-allocation makes it possible for programmers to reason about the lifetimes of storage cells. However, the stack discipline imposes rather severe restrictions on the programming language. For example, functions are not allowed to return lists or functions as results.

To overcome these limitations, many programming languages assume an additional memory area, the *heap*, which holds values whose final size or lifetime is not known when allocation of memory to hold the value takes place. In some languages, for example C, it is the responsibility of the programmer to allocate blocks of memory and to free them once they are no longer needed. While it is easy to allocate memory, it is in general extremely hard to know when it is safe to de-allocate memory. Intuitively, a memory cell can be reclaimed (it is "garbage"), if and only if its contents is not needed by the remainder of the computation. This is an undecidable property. To make matters worse, de-allocating memory too early can cause the program to crash, while de-allocating memory too late can cause "space leaks," i.e., programs that hold on to much more memory than is necessary. Moreover, unlike what is the case for the stack discipline, the programming language does not help the programmer in reasoning about lifetimes of storage cells.

The term "garbage collection" is traditionally used for a range of heap memory management techniques, including reference counting, copying collection and generational collection (see [25] for an excellent overview).[1] Common to all of these techniques is that there is a strict separation between the program which allocates memory, called the *mutator*, and the part of the runtime system, called the *garbage collector*, which manages recycling

MT's research supported in part by the Danish Research Council. LB's research supported in part by U.S. National Science Foundation Grant CCR-9409997.

[1] This use of language is arguably misleading: the stack discipline also collects garbage and it does so very efficiently, by popping the stack.

of memory. For some garbage collection schemes, it is hard for users to know when garbage collection takes place and how long it will take. Garbage collection was first used with Lisp; it is used both in implementations of functional and object oriented languages.

Garbage collection techniques have developed very significantly over the past decade and the time spent by garbage collection is often modest (say less than 5% of the total running time). However, the strict separation between allocation and de-allocation means that there is no language support for reasoning about the lifetimes of storage cells, and thus it is in general very difficult for programmers to reason about how much memory their programs will use.

Region-based memory management [23, 1, 2] is yet a form of automatic management of dynamic allocation. Conceptually, the store consists of a stack of *regions*. A region can be thought of as a heap which can grow dynamically depending on how many values it needs to hold. Regions are allocated and de-allocated in a stack-like manner, i.e., a region is not de-allocated unless it is the topmost region on the region stack. All values are put into regions, including for example lists and function closures. The only mechanism for freeing memory is to pop the region stack, which is a constant time operation, for a suitable choice of concrete representation of regions.

Rather than forcing the programmer to introduce and eliminate regions, we have taken the approach to use an existing language, Standard ML [11], as the source language. The region scheme, including the algorithms presented in this paper, are implemented in the ML Kit with Regions [21] which compiles Standard ML programs to C and HP PA-RISC code. The ML Kit subjects source programs to a particular static analysis, *region inference*. The analysis decides where regions should be allocated and de-allocated. Region inference also decides, for each value-producing expression in the program, into which region the value will be put. Region inference handles recursive datatypes and higher-order functions. Moreover, region inference preserves a close connection between program structure and lifetimes of values, making it possible for humans to reason about lifetimes and making it easy for profiling tools to report actual memory usage in terms of regions which can be related to the program text. Finally, the memory management directives which region inference inserts during compilation each use only constant time and space at runtime. Thus programs can be run as they are written, without hidden extra costs of unbounded size (in contrast to what is the case for other existing ML implementations).

Some programs are ill-suited for region inference. An example of such a program is an interpreter for S, K and I combinators. Here the region inference will not be able to distinguish lifetimes of different terms and memory usage will be linear in running time. However, even programs which were originally thought to require garbage collection (for instance Knuth-Bendix completion) have been made to run in much less space using regions than using traditional garbage collection; the region scheme is not magic, but it can often be used to obtain programs that have time and memory performance that is better than those reported for systems that use traditional garbage collection techniques. This is as one might expect, at a superficial level at least, for while most garbage collection techniques are general techniques which treat all programs equally, region inference specialises memory management to the particular program that is being compiled.

The relevance of region inference to this Festschrift is that Milner's work on type inference and type checking [10] has provided many of the technical insights which underlie region inference. (Other origins of region inference are listed in Section 3.) In particular, the idea of using unification in type checking and the notions of polymorphic type schemes and generic instance are heavily exploited in work on regions. As it happens, region inference is not restricted to languages that use ML-style type polymorphism. But as we describe below, there are close connections between region- and effect polymorphism and the ability to extend the stack discipline to cover language constructs found in SML, specifically recursive datatypes and higher-order functions.

The rest of this paper is organised as follows. We first introduce the region-annotated types that underlie region inference, illustrating the basic ideas by means of a well-known program: the towers of Hanoi. We then introduce a technical notion, *consistency*, which is required for the statement and proof of a key lemma. Informally speaking, this lemma (Lemma 6) says that Robinson's result [17] concerning most general unifiers of terms generalises to the case where terms are types which are annotated with regions and effects, provided the annotation is done consistently. We define operations corresponding to Milner's notions of generic instance and generalisation in the setting of region-annotated types and introduce a particular class of type schemes which is general enough to allow a limited form of polymorphic recursion in regions and yet restricted enough that one can prove that region inference always terminates.

## 2 Region-Annotated Programs

In this section we introduce the three kinds of region annotations which region inference inserts into source programs. Readers who are familiar with region inference may want to proceed directly to Section 3.

The Towers of Hanoi is the name of a game which involves one monk, three vertical pegs (A, B and C) an $n$ discs of different sizes. The discs have holes in them, so that the monk can stack them on top of each other on the pegs. Initially, there are $n$ discs on A, stacked in decreasing size (with the smallest disc at the top) while B and C contain no discs. The problem for the monk is to move the discs around between the pegs, one at the time, in such a way that at the end, C contains all the discs and A and B contain no discs. The moves have to be such that no disc is ever placed on top of a smaller disc.

```
fun hanoi(n, from, to, other, acc) =
   if n=0 then (from, to) :: acc
   else hanoi(n-1, from, other, to, (from, to) :: hanoi(n-1, other, to, from, acc))
val solution = hanoi(20,"a", "b", "c", nil)
```

**Figure 13.1**
The Towers of Hanoi (source program).

The Standard ML program in Figure 13.1 solves the problem. *hanoi*(*n*, *from*, *to*, *other*, *acc*) moves $n+1$ discs from the *from* peg to the *to* peg, using also the *other* peg, if necessary. Moves are accumulated onto the list *acc*.

Region inference translates this source program into the program shown below. Every value-producing expression has been decorated with an annotation of the form "at $\rho$", where $\rho$ is a *region variable*. The annotation indicates the region into which the value should be put. In line 18, for example, the constant 1 is put into region $\rho_{26}$.

```
1  fun hanoi at ρ5[ρ6,ρ7,ρ8,ρ9,ρ10,ρ11]( var6) =
2        let val n = #0 var6; val from = #1 var6;
3          val to = #2 var6; val other = #3 var6;
4          val acc = #4 var6
5        in letregion ρ13
6          in (case letregion ρ14 in (n = (0 at ρ14))at ρ13 end (*ρ14*)
7            of true => let val v170 = ((from, to) at ρ9, acc) at ρ8 in :: at ρ7 v170 end
8            | false =>
9              letregion ρ16, ρ18, ρ19 (* for region tuple, quintuple and n-1, respectively*)
10              in hanoi[ρ18,ρ7,ρ8,ρ9,ρ10,ρ19] at ρ16
11                (letregion ρ20 in ( n-1at ρ20) at ρ19 end (*ρ20*),
12                 from, other, to,
13                 let val v171 =
14                      ((from, to) at ρ9,
15                       letregion ρ22, ρ24, ρ25
16                         (* for region tuple, quintuple and n-1, respectively *)
17                       in hanoi[ρ24,ρ7,ρ8,ρ9,ρ10,ρ25] at ρ22
18                         (letregion ρ26 in (n-1at ρ26) at ρ25 end (*ρ26*),
19                          other, to, from, acc
20                         ) at ρ24
21                       end (*ρ22, ρ24, ρ25*)
22                      ) at ρ8
23                 in :: at ρ7 v171
24                 end
25                ) at ρ18
```

```
26              end (*ρ16, ρ18, ρ19*)
27            ) (*case*)
28          end (*ρ13*)
29        end;
30    val solution =
31      letregion ρ27, ρ29, ρ30
32      in hanoi[ρ29,ρ1,ρ2,ρ3,ρ4,ρ30] at ρ27
33        (20 at ρ30, "a" at ρ4, "b" at ρ4, "c" at ρ4, nil at ρ1) at ρ29
34      end (*ρ27, ρ29, ρ30*)
```

The construct "`letregion` $\rho$ `in` $e$ `end`" binds $\rho$ within $e$. At runtime, first a region is allocated and bound to $\rho$; then $e$ is evaluated, perhaps using the region for storing and fetching values; finally, upon reaching "`end`", the region is de-allocated. In line 18, for example, $\rho_{26}$ is only needed for the computation of $n - 1$. Regions can also contain tuples (see $\rho_{18}$ and $\rho_{24}$, for example) and closures (not illustrated by the example).

Notice that the region inference algorithm has given *hanoi* six additional formal region parameters: $\rho_6, \ldots, \rho_{11}$. These are enclosed in square brackets to distinguish them from parameters which the programmer writes. Correspondingly, the references to *hanoi* (lines 10, 17, and 32) each have six *actual region parameters*. The region parameters give the regions of the argument and result of the function. Result regions indicate where the function should put the result value, if it creates one. For example, $\rho_9$ is the region where the pairs which represent moves are put and $\rho_7$ holds the spine of the list of moves. $\rho_6$ is the region where the argument quintuple to *hanoi* is stored (we treat all tuples as boxed).

Notice that the three calls to *hanoi* have different actual region arguments. We refer to this feature as *region polymorphism*, a term that will be justified once we have introduced region-annotated types and type schemes. Note that even within the body of *hanoi*, the actual region arguments to *hanoi* differ from the formal region parameters. We refer to this feature of the system as *region-polymorphic recursion*; it is essential for obtaining good results.

By examining the region annotations one can determine that the maximal memory requirement for the computation will be $c + c_1 \times n + c_2 \times (2^{n+1} - 1)$ words, where $n$ is the first argument to *hanoi* (here 20), $c$ is a (small) constant, $c_1$ is the number of words it takes to represent the fixed size regions in lines 9 and 15 and $c_2$ is the number of words it takes to represent one move in the accumulating parameter. Here the third term clearly dominates. Indeed, for the ML Kit, $c_2$ is 4 (4 words = 16 bytes) and when running the program under the ML Kit one finds the expected maximal memory usage of approximately $c_2\text{words} \times 4\text{bytes/word} \times 2^{21} = 32$ Mb. The run takes 1.85 seconds of user time on an HP 9000s700 (C100). The corresponding numbers for the same program running under Standard ML of New Jersey, version 93, on the same machine are 75 Mb and 28.36 seconds, respectively. This difference in running times is particularly noteworthy when one considers that the ML Kit boxes all tuples, including the tuples of region variables that are passed to region-polymorphic functions; that is what regions $\rho_{16}$, $\rho_{22}$ and $\rho_{27}$ are used for.

## 3 Related Work

The basic ideas of the region inference scheme are described in [23]. An extended version, including a proof that the region inference rules are sound, may be found in [24]. Other analysis which have been combined with region inference are described in [1, 2].

The emphasis of this paper is on using unification to constrain region variables and arrow effects. (Arrow effects decorate function arrows in the region type system with information of how the function uses regions.) In the case of arrow effects, the difficulty is that the unification is of sets rather than terms. Similar forms of unification have been studied in record typing [16] and in type systems for polymorphic references [9].

The region inference algorithm that is currently used in the ML Kit is described and proved correct in [20]. It is a syntax-directed algorithm, similar to Milner's algorithm $W$, and it relies on the results about unification proved in the present paper.

A different approach to region inference is to use constraints. Constraints have been used in previous work on ML type inference [5], subtyping [12, 4] and effect systems [19, 18, 14, 13]. We are currently exploring using constraints for region inference. The relative merits of the two approaches to region inference (syntax-directed region inference versus constraint generation and constraint solving) are not clear at the time of writing. In both cases, however, termination of the algorithms depends crucially on the limitations on polymorphic recursion which we introduce in the present paper.

## 4 Region Inference Rules

In order to give an overview of the inference problem we are addressing, this section contains the inference rules which guide our region inference algorithms. (Presenting a full algorithm would require more space than is available.) Concepts and notation which will be defined in the subsequent sections of the paper are marked by forward references.

For the purpose of stating invariants about the region algorithms, it is useful to keep careful track of the sets of region and effect variables that are used by the algorithm. Thus we introduce (in Section 6) a notion of a *basis*, $B = (Q, \Phi)$ where $Q$ is a set of region variables and $\Phi$ is a set of *arrow effects*. Arrow effects decorate function arrows in derivations. An arrow effect takes the form $\epsilon.\varphi$, where $\epsilon$ is an effect variable and $\varphi$ is an effect. Amongst the invariants which are essential for obtaining the result about principal unifiers (Section 8), is that whenever $\epsilon_1.\varphi_1$ and $\epsilon_2.\varphi_2$ are both members of $\Phi$ and $\epsilon_1 = \epsilon_2$ then $\varphi_1 = \varphi_2$. The invariants about sets of region variables and arrow effects that turn out to be important are collected in the definition of *consistent bases* (Section 6). Section 6 also defines the *disjoint union* of bases ($B \uplus B'$) found in the rules.

The inference rules allow one to infer statements of the form $B, TE \vdash e : \mu, \varphi$, read: in basis $B$ and type environment $TE$, $e$ has type with place $\mu$ and effect $\varphi$. Effects and types with places are defined in Section 5. Given a consistent basis $B$, only some types with places make sense. This is captured by a definition (in Section 5) of what it means for a type with place $\mu$ to be *consistent in a basis, B*, written $B \vdash \mu$.

A *type environment*, $TE$, is a finite map from program variables to pairs of the form $(\sigma, \rho)$, where $\sigma$ is a region-annotated type scheme (Section 9) and $\rho$ is a region variable.

The expressions that appear in the rules are called "target expressions," since they are output from region inference. The terms contain enough type, region and effect information that the entire proof of the conclusion $B, TE \vdash e : \mu, \varphi$ is fully determined by $B$, $TE$ and $e$. Some of this information is not necessary at runtime. Therefore, in examples we often abbreviate `letregion` $B$ `in` $e$ `end` to `letregion` $\rho_1, \ldots, \rho_k$ `in` $e$ `end`, where $\{\rho_1, \ldots, \rho_k\} = Q\ of\ B$ (Section 6). Similarly, we often abbreviate

`letrec` $f : (\sigma, \rho_0)$ `(`$x$`)` $=$ $e_1$ `in` $e_2$ `end`

to `letrec` $f[\rho_1, \ldots, \rho_k]$ `at` $\rho_0$ `(x)` $=$ $e_1$ `in` $e_2$ `end`, where $\rho_1, \ldots, \rho_k$ are the bound region variables of $\sigma$.

In target expressions, every binding occurrence of a variable is decorated by a region type scheme (Section 9). Within the scope of the binding, each non-binding occurrence of the variable is annotated by its own *instantiation list* (Section 11) which defines an instance of the type scheme particular to that occurrence. Given a consistent basis $B$, only some instantiation lists are meaningful; Section 11 defines what it means for an instantiation list *il* to be *consistent in a basis, B*, written $B \vdash il$. In examples (and at runtime) we omit the first and third component of instantiation list triples, so that $x_{il}$ becomes simply $x[\rho_1, \ldots, \rho_k]$, where $(\_, [\rho_1, \ldots, \rho_k], \_) = il$.

Given a consistent basis $B$, only some region-annotated type schemes make sense: Section 10 defines what it means for a region-annotated type scheme $\sigma$ to be *consistent in a basis, B*, written $B \vdash \sigma$. Poitwise extension gives a relation $B \vdash TE$.

In the following, we write $B \vdash (TE,\ il, \mu)$ as a shorthand for $B \vdash TE$, $B \vdash\ il$ and $B \vdash \mu$. It turns out that $B, TE \vdash e : \mu, \varphi$ implies that $B$ is consistent and $B \vdash (TE, \mu, \varphi)$. In rule (6) we use the function *Observe* defined by $Observe(B, \varphi_1) = \varphi_1 \cap fv(B)$.

In the rules, $S$ denotes a *substitution*, as defined in Section 7.

$$\frac{\begin{array}{c} B \vdash (TE,\ il, \mu) \qquad TE(x) = (\sigma, \rho) \qquad \mu = (\tau, \rho) \\ \sigma = \forall \alpha_1 \cdots \alpha_n \epsilon_1 \cdots \epsilon_m . \tau_0 \qquad il = ([\tau_1, \ldots, \tau_n], [\,], [\epsilon'_1.\varphi'_1, \ldots, \epsilon'_m.\varphi'_m]) \\ S = (\{\alpha_1 \mapsto \tau_1, \ldots, \alpha_n \mapsto \tau_n\}, \{\}, \{\epsilon_1 \mapsto \epsilon'_1.\varphi'_1, \ldots, \epsilon_m \mapsto \epsilon'_m.\varphi'_m\}) \\ \tau = S(\tau_0) \end{array}}{B, TE \vdash x_{il} : \mu, \emptyset} \tag{1}$$

$$\frac{\begin{array}{c} B \vdash (TE,\ il, \mu) \qquad TE(x) = (\sigma, \rho) \qquad \mu = (\tau, \rho') \\ \sigma = \forall \alpha_1 \cdots \alpha_n \rho_1 \cdots \rho_k \epsilon_1 \cdots \epsilon_m . \tau_0 \qquad il = ([\tau_1, \ldots, \tau_n], [\rho'_1, \ldots, \rho'_k], [\epsilon'_1.\varphi'_1, \ldots, \epsilon'_m.\varphi'_m]) \\ S = (\{\alpha_1 \mapsto \tau_1, \ldots, \alpha_n \mapsto \tau_n\}, \{\rho_1 \mapsto \rho'_1, \ldots, \rho_k \mapsto \rho'_k\}, \{\epsilon_1 \mapsto \epsilon'_1.\varphi'_1, \ldots, \epsilon_m \mapsto \epsilon'_m.\varphi'_m\}) \\ \tau = S(\tau_0) \end{array}}{B, TE \vdash x_{il}\ \texttt{at}\ \rho' : \mu, \{\rho, \rho'\}} \tag{2}$$

$$\frac{B \vdash TE \qquad B, TE + \{x \mapsto \mu_x\} \vdash e_1 : \mu_1, \varphi_1 \qquad \varphi_0 \supseteq \varphi_1 \qquad (\{\rho\}, \{\epsilon.\varphi_0\}) \subseteq B}{B, TE \vdash \lambda x : \mu_x \cdot e_1 : (\mu_x \xrightarrow{\epsilon.\varphi_0} \mu_1, \rho), \{\rho\}} \tag{3}$$

$$\frac{B, TE \vdash e_1 : (\mu' \xrightarrow{\epsilon_0.\varphi_0} \mu, \rho_0), \varphi_1 \qquad B, TE \vdash e_2 : \mu', \varphi_2}{B, TE \vdash e_1\ e_2 : \mu, \varphi_1 \cup \varphi_2 \cup \{\epsilon_0, \rho_0\} \cup \varphi_0} \tag{4}$$

$$\frac{\begin{array}{c} B \vdash (TE, \varphi_1) \quad \sigma = \forall \alpha_1 \cdots \alpha_n \rho_1 \cdots \rho_k \epsilon_1 \cdots \epsilon_m . \tau_0 \quad \hat{\sigma} = \forall \rho_1 \cdots \rho_k \epsilon_1 \cdots \epsilon_m . \tau_0 \\ B_1 = \mathit{bound}(\sigma) \qquad B \uplus B_1 \text{ exists} \qquad \tau_0 = \mu_x \xrightarrow{\epsilon_0.\varphi_0} \mu_1 \qquad \mathit{btv}(\sigma) \cap \mathit{ftv}(TE) = \emptyset \\ B \uplus B_1, TE + \{f \mapsto (\hat{\sigma}, \rho_0)\} \vdash \lambda\, x : \mu_x \cdot e_1 : (\tau_0, \rho_0), \varphi_1 \\ B, TE + \{f \mapsto (\sigma, \rho_0)\} \vdash e_2 : \mu, \varphi_2 \end{array}}{B, TE \vdash \texttt{letrec}\ \ f : (\sigma, \rho_0)\,\texttt{(}x\texttt{)=}\ \ e_1\ \ \texttt{in}\ \ e_2\ \ \texttt{end} : \mu, \varphi_1 \cup \varphi_2} \tag{5}$$

$$\frac{B \uplus B_1 \text{ exists} \qquad B \uplus B_1, TE \vdash e_1 : \mu, \varphi_1 \qquad B \vdash (TE, \mu) \qquad \varphi = \mathit{Observe}(B, \varphi_1)}{B, TE \vdash \texttt{letregion}\ \ B_1\ \ \texttt{in}\ \ e_1\ \ \texttt{end} : \mu, \varphi} \tag{6}$$

## 5 Types and Effects

In this section we first motivate the region-annotated types and type schemes that are used in region inference and then define them formally.

### 5.1 Region Variables and Effects

The region scheme annotates every type constructor with a region variable. Also, type schemes can universally quantify region variables and (as in Milner's type discipline) type variables. The type scheme of *hanoi* (Section 2) is approximately the following:

$$\forall \rho_6\rho_7\rho_8\rho_9\rho_{10}\rho_{11}.\big((int, \rho_{11}) * (\alpha, \rho_{10}) * (\alpha, \rho_{10}) * (\alpha, \rho_{10}) * (((\alpha, \rho_{10}) * (\alpha, \rho_{10}), \rho_9)list_{\langle\rho_8\rangle}, \rho_7), \rho_6\big) \xrightarrow{\epsilon} (((\alpha, \rho_{10}) * (\alpha, \rho_{10}), \rho_9)list_{\langle\rho_8\rangle}, \rho_7)$$
$$\text{where } \epsilon = \{\rho_6, \rho_7, \rho_8, \rho_9, \rho_{11}\}$$

Here $\alpha$ is paired with $\rho_{10}$, *list* with $\rho_7$ and the tuple constructor $(\_ * \_ * \_ * \_ * \_)$ is paired with $\rho_6$. The datatype constructor *list* has an additional, so-called *auxiliary* region variable, here $\rho_8$. This is the region where the pairs to which cons $(::)$ is applied are put. The set $\epsilon$ which appears on the function arrow is an *effect*; it contains all the regions which the evaluation of the function body might access. *hanoi* reads from region $\rho_6$ (when it extracts the components of its argument quintuple), it reads *n* from region $\rho_{11}$ and it puts values into regions $\rho_7$, $\rho_8$ and $\rho_9$. The effect reveals that *hanoi* does not access $\rho_{10}$ at all.

In [23] there is a distinction between put and get effects; for example, the above effect would be written $\{\mathbf{get}(\rho_6), \mathbf{put}(\rho_7), \mathbf{put}(\rho_8), \mathbf{put}(\rho_9), \mathbf{get}(\rho_{11})\}$. This distinction is useful for other analyses and optimisations which can be combined with region inference [2]; however, for the purpose of this paper, the distinction between **put** and **get** is not important and is therefore omitted.

### 5.2 Effect Variables and Arrow Effects

In the type scheme for *hanoi* we use $\epsilon$ and "where" as meta-notation to make the type scheme easier to read. A crucial next step, invented in work on effect inference[18], is to make effect variables part of the language of types, on a par with type variables and region variables. Moreover, we represent "where $\epsilon = \{\rho_6, \rho_7, \rho_8, \rho_9, \rho_{11}\}$" by a formal object "$\epsilon.\{\rho_6, \rho_7, \rho_8, \rho_9, \rho_{11}\}$" which is called an *arrow effect*, because arrow effects appear on function arrows. Using an effect variable and an arrow effect, the type scheme for *hanoi* becomes:

$$\sigma_h = \forall \alpha\rho_6\rho_7\rho_8\rho_9\rho_{10}\rho_{11}\epsilon_{12}.\big((int, \rho_{11}) * (\alpha, \rho_{10}) * (\alpha, \rho_{10}) * (\alpha, \rho_{10}) * (((\alpha, \rho_{10}) * (\alpha, \rho_{10}), \rho_9)list_{\langle\rho_8\rangle}, \rho_7), \rho_6\big) \xrightarrow{\epsilon_{12}.\{\rho_6,\rho_7,\rho_8,\rho_9,\rho_{11}\}} (((\alpha, \rho_{10}) * (\alpha, \rho_{10}), \rho_9)list_{\langle\rho_8\rangle}, \rho_7)$$

As we shall see in Section 11 instantiation of type schemes allows universally quantified effects to increase; so one can equally think of $\epsilon.\varphi$ as meaning "$\epsilon$, where $\epsilon \supseteq \varphi$." Note that the scope of the effect variable is now given by $\forall$, which can bind type, region and effect variables. Capture-avoiding renaming of bound variables is permitted in the usual way.

In a first-order programming language, one could do region inference without effect variables. But for a higher-order language, effect variables are essential for representing the effects of (unknown) functions. To illustrate this, assume we continue our example program with the declarations:

```
fun app f x = f(x)
fun run n = app hanoi (n, "a", "b", "c", nil)
```

The function *app* has the type scheme

$$\sigma_{app} = \forall\alpha_1\alpha_2\rho_1\rho_2\rho_3\epsilon_1\epsilon_2\epsilon_3.\big((\alpha_1,\rho_1)\xrightarrow{\epsilon_1.\emptyset}(\alpha_2,\rho_2),\rho_3\big) \xrightarrow{\epsilon_2.\{\rho_4\}}\big((\alpha_1,\rho_1)\xrightarrow{\epsilon_3.\{\rho_3,\epsilon_1\}}(\alpha_2,\rho_2),\rho_4\big)$$

The arrow effect $\epsilon_3.\{\rho_3, \epsilon_1\}$ is justified as follows: $\rho_3$ has to be in the effect since the evaluation of $f(x)$ involves accessing $\rho_3$, the region holding the function $f$. Also, the effect of the expression $f(x)$ has to be at least the effect of the function $f$, irrespective of what actual arguments we pass in for $f$; this is represented by letting $\epsilon_1$ be in the arrow effect. In other words, *app* has an "effect dependent" type: the effect of *app* $f$ depends on the effect of $f$.

To see how this dependency comes into use, consider the application *app hanoi* in the declaration of *run*. Let $\alpha'$, $\rho'_6$, $\rho'_7$, $\rho'_8$, $\rho'_9$, $\rho'_{10}$, $\rho'_{11}$ and $\epsilon'_{12}$ be fresh variables. We can give the occurrence of *hanoi* in the declaration of *run* the following instance of $\sigma_h$:

$$\tau_h = \big((int,\rho'_{11}) * (\alpha',\rho'_{10}) * (\alpha',\rho'_{10}) * (\alpha',\rho'_{10}) * (((\alpha',\rho'_{10}) * (\alpha',\rho'_{10}),\rho'_9)list_{\langle\rho'_8\rangle},\rho'_7),\rho'_6\big) \xrightarrow{\epsilon'_{12}.\{\rho'_6,\rho'_7,\rho'_8,\rho'_9,\rho'_{11}\}}(((\alpha',\rho'_{10}) * (\alpha',\rho'_{10}),\rho'_9)list_{\langle\rho'_8\rangle},\rho'_7)$$

Similarly, the following type is an instance of $\sigma_{app}$:

$$\tau_0 = (\tau_h, \rho_{100}) \xrightarrow{\epsilon_{101}.\varphi'} (\tau_h, \rho_{102})$$

where $\rho_{100}$, $\epsilon_{101}$ and $\rho_{102}$ are fresh ($\varphi'$ will be determined shortly). Here we have instantiated the arrow effect $\epsilon_1.\emptyset$ of $\sigma_{app}$ to the arrow effect $\epsilon'_{12}.\{\rho'_6, \rho'_7, \rho'_8, \rho'_9, \rho'_{11}\}$ of $\tau_h$. But when we then instantiate the arrow effect $\epsilon_3.\{\rho_3, \epsilon_1\}$ from $\sigma_{app}$, the dependency of $\epsilon_3$ upon $\epsilon_1$ implies that the effect to which $\epsilon_3$ is instantiated must contain all that $\epsilon'_{12}$ stands for, i.e., the effect $\{\rho'_6, \rho'_7, \rho'_8, \rho'_9, \rho'_{11}\}$. In fact, the definition of generic instance presented in Section 11 will take $\varphi'$ to be $\{\rho_{100}, \epsilon'_{12}, \rho'_6, \rho'_7, \rho'_8, \rho'_9, \rho'_{11}\}$, where the presence of $\epsilon'_{12}$ keeps track of the fact that the result of evaluating *app hanoi*, when applied to ($n$, "*a*", "*b*", "*c*", *nil*), will call *hanoi*.

To sum up, effect variables are useful for tracking function applications in functional languages. Moreover, using effect polymorphism to represent function dependencies has two advantages:

1. The effect dependencies of *app* can be determined from its declaration alone, without looking at how the function is subsequently used;

2. In the scope of the declaration of *app*, if there are two applications, *app* $g$ and *app* $h$, say, then the arrow effects of $g$ and $h$ need not be the same;

Both advantages are inherited from Milner-style polymorphism.

### 5.3 Definitions

We assume a denumerably infinite set TyVar of *type variables*. We use $\alpha$ to range over type variables. Next, *ML types*, $\tau^{ML}$, and *ML type schemes*, $\sigma^{ML}$, are given by the grammar:

| | | |
|---|---|---|
| $\tau^{ML}$ | $::= \texttt{int} \mid \alpha \mid \tau^{ML} \to \tau^{ML}$ | ML type |
| $\sigma^{ML}$ | $::= \tau^{ML} \mid \forall\alpha.\sigma^{ML}$ | ML type scheme |

For the purpose of region inference, we assume two additional denumerably infinite sets:

| | |
|---|---|
| $\rho \in$ RegVar | region variables |
| $\epsilon \in$ EffVar | effect variables |

TyVar, RegVar and EffVar are assumed to be pairwise disjoint. An *atomic effect* is a region variable or an effect variable; an *effect* is a finite set of atomic effects:

| | |
|---|---|
| $\eta \in \text{AtEff} = \text{RegVar} \cup \text{EffVar}$ | atomic effect |
| $\varphi$ or $\{\eta_1, \ldots, \eta_k\} \in \text{Effect} = \mathit{Fin}(\text{AtEff})$ | effect |
| $\epsilon.\varphi \in \text{ArrEff} = \text{EffVar} \times \text{Effect}$ | arrow effect |

Annotated types are given by:

| | |
|---|---|
| $\tau ::= \texttt{int} \mid \alpha \mid \mu \xrightarrow{\epsilon.\varphi} \mu$ | annotated type |
| $\mu ::= (\tau, \rho)$ | annotated type with place |

The set of annotated types is denoted Type and the set of annotated types with places is denoted TypeWithPlace; "annotated type" is abbreviated to "type" when confusion with "ML type" is unlikely. In a function type $\mu \xrightarrow{\epsilon.\varphi} \mu'$ the object $\epsilon.\varphi$ is called an *arrow effect*. Formally, an arrow effect is a pair of an effect variable and an effect; we refer to $\epsilon$ and $\varphi$ as the *handle* and the *latent effect*, respectively.

Equality of types is defined by term equality, as usual, but up to set equality of latent effects. For example, the arrow effects $\epsilon.\{\rho, \rho'\}$ and $\epsilon.\{\rho', \rho\}$ are equal.

We refer to the above semantic objects (i.e., type variables, region variables, effect variables, atomic effects, effects, arrow effects, types and types with places) collectively as *basic* semantic objects and use $o$ to range over these. Erasure of region and effect information from annotated types yields ML types; it is defined recursively by:

$$\mathrm{ML}(\alpha) = \alpha; \quad \mathrm{ML}(\mathtt{int}) = \mathtt{int}; \quad \mathrm{ML}(\tau, \rho) = \mathrm{ML}(\tau)$$

$$\mathrm{ML}(\mu \xrightarrow{\epsilon.\varphi} \mu') = \mathrm{ML}(\mu) \rightarrow \mathrm{ML}(\mu')$$

Let $\tau$ or $\mu$ be a type or a type with place. The *arrow effects of* $\tau$ *(or* $\mu$*)*, written $\mathit{arreff}(\tau)$ (or $\mathit{arreff}(\mu)$) is the set of arrow effects defined by

$$\mathit{arreff}(\alpha) = \emptyset; \quad \mathit{arreff}(\mathtt{int}) = \emptyset; \quad \mathit{arreff}(\tau, \rho) = \mathit{arreff}(\tau)$$

$$\mathit{arreff}(\mu \xrightarrow{\epsilon.\varphi} \mu') = \{\epsilon.\varphi\} \cup \mathit{arreff}(\mu) \cup \mathit{arreff}(\mu')$$

The set of type variables, effect variables and region variables that occur free in a semantic object $A$ will be denoted $\mathit{ftv}(A)$, $\mathit{fev}(A)$ and $\mathit{frv}(A)$, respectively. For basic semantic objects, these functions are defined by:

$$\mathit{ftv}(\mathtt{int}) = \emptyset \quad \mathit{ftv}(\alpha) = \{\alpha\} \quad \mathit{ftv}(\mu \xrightarrow{\epsilon.\varphi} \mu') = \mathit{ftv}(\mu) \cup \mathit{ftv}(\mu') \quad \mathit{ftv}(\tau, \rho) = \mathit{ftv}(\tau)$$

$$\mathit{frv}(\rho) = \{\rho\} \qquad \mathit{frv}(\tau, \rho) = \{\rho\} \cup \mathit{frv}(\tau) \qquad \mathit{frv}(\mathtt{int}) = \mathit{frv}(\alpha) = \emptyset$$

$$\mathit{frv}(\mu \xrightarrow{\epsilon.\varphi} \mu') = \mathit{frv}(\mu) \cup \mathit{frv}(\epsilon.\varphi) \cup \mathit{frv}(\mu') \qquad \mathit{frv}(\epsilon.\varphi) = \varphi \cap \mathrm{RegVar}$$

$$\mathit{fev}(\rho) = \emptyset \qquad \mathit{fev}(\tau, \rho) = \mathit{fev}(\tau) \qquad \mathit{fev}(\mathtt{int}) = \mathit{fev}(\alpha) = \emptyset$$

$$\mathit{fev}(\mu \xrightarrow{\epsilon.\varphi} \mu') = \mathit{fev}(\mu) \cup \mathit{fev}(\epsilon.\varphi) \cup \mathit{fev}(\mu') \qquad \mathit{fev}(\epsilon.\varphi) = \{\epsilon\} \cup (\varphi \cap \mathrm{EffVar})$$

We denote the set of free variables of $A$ (of either kind) by $\mathit{fv}(A)$, i.e., $\mathit{fv}(A) = \mathit{frv}(A) \cup \mathit{ftv}(A) \cup \mathit{fev}(A)$.

A *finite map* is a function whose domain is finite. When $A$ and $B$ are sets, the set of finite maps from $A$ to $B$ is denoted $A \stackrel{\mathrm{fin}}{\rightarrow} B$. The domain and range of a finite map, $f$, are denoted $\mathrm{Dom}(f)$ and $\mathit{Rng}(f)$, respectively; the restriction of $f$ to a set, $A$, is written $f \downarrow A$. A finite map is often written explicitly in the form $\{a_1 \mapsto b_1, \ldots, a_k \mapsto b_k\}$, $k \geq 0$; in particular, the empty map is $\{\}$. For every $f : A \stackrel{\mathrm{fin}}{\rightarrow} B$ and $g : B \rightarrow C$ the finite map $g \bullet f : A \stackrel{\mathrm{fin}}{\rightarrow} C$ is defined by $\mathrm{Dom}(g \bullet f) = \mathrm{Dom}(f)$ and $(g \bullet f)(x) = g(f(x))$.

## 6 Consistent Bases

To obtain eager recycling of memory, regions should be kept distinct, unless they are forced to be equal. Although not all the concepts have been formally introduced yet, consider the region inference rules in Section 4. These rules specify which region annotations are permitted in a skeletal language. The region inference algorithm (not presented) will keep regions distinct, unless they are required by the rules to be equal. The only rule which forces regions to be equal is rule (4) which concerns function application. Since types are decorated with regions (and arrow effects) the two occurrences of $\mu'$ in the premises of the rule demand that function and argument agree not just on types but also on regions and effects. In order to satisfy the premises of the inference rule, the region inference algorithm needs to be able to unify types which contain region and effect information.

Hindley [6] and Milner [10] discovered that Robinson's unification algorithm can be used for unifying types. We assume that type inference has already been carried out by the time region inference is performed. Thus the problem we are faced with is to unify region-annotated types which have the same underlying ML types but which may have different region and effect annotations. This problem would be very simple, were it not for the fact that types can contain effects, which are sets. It is not the case that if a set unification problem has a solution (a substitution which when applied to the two sets makes them equal) then it has a most general solution.

However, the use of arrow effects suggests an alternative to using set unification. Assume we are given two arrow effects $\epsilon_1.\varphi_1$ and $\epsilon_2.\varphi_2$ which we want to "unify." (For simplicity, assume $\{\epsilon_1, \epsilon_2\} \cap (\varphi_1 \cup \varphi_2) = \emptyset$.) We now simply select one of the effect variables, say $\epsilon_1$, and let it stand for $\varphi_1 \cup \varphi_2$:

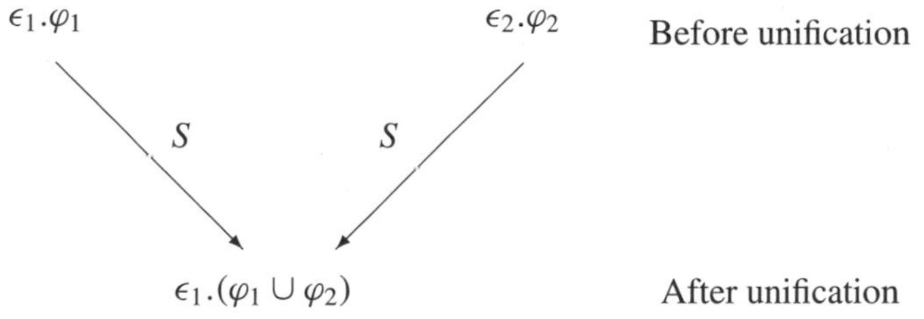


In the picture, $S$ is a substitution. (Substitutions will be defined in Section 7.)

Another way of thinking of $\epsilon_1.\varphi_1$ and $\epsilon_2.\varphi_2$ is as two constraints $\epsilon_1 \supseteq \varphi_1$ and $\epsilon_2 \supseteq \varphi_2$ [18]; then the "unification" of the two arrow effect corresponds to replacing $\epsilon_2$ by $\epsilon_1$ everywhere and replacing the two constraints by a single constraint $\epsilon_1 \supseteq (\varphi_1 \cup \varphi_2)$.

Although the region inference rules (1)–(6) can be expressed using constraints rather than arrow effects along the lines of [18], constraint sets complicate the definitions of type schemes, generic instance, generalisation and the *Observe* operation given later in this paper. The best approach seems to be to use arrow effects for presenting the region inference system and then either also use arrow effects in the algorithms (as we do in this paper) or relate the region rules presented in this paper to a separate inference system which uses constraints that are solved separately. We are currently also exploring the latter possibility.

It is convenient to be able to see what effect a given effect variable in a given type denotes without reference to a constraint set. Therefore, within the scope of a binding occurrence of an effect variable $\epsilon$, we want $\epsilon$ to be the handle of one and only one effect. There are other natural well-formedness conditions which we expect to hold. For example, in a type scheme of the form

$$\forall \epsilon_1 \epsilon_2.((\mu_1 \xrightarrow{\epsilon_1.\varphi_1} \mu_2), \rho_1) \xrightarrow{\epsilon_2.\varphi_2} \mu_3$$

if we have $\epsilon_1 \in \varphi_2$ then we should also have $\varphi_1 \subseteq \varphi_2$. These invariants are formalised by the notion of effect consistency defined below. As we shall see later, types which are decorated with arrow effects taken from an effect consistent set have most general unifiers, in a sense which will be made precise below.

DEFINITION 1 A set $\Phi$ of arrow effects is *effect consistent*, written $\vdash \Phi$, if

1. $\Phi$ is *functional*: for all $(\epsilon_1.\varphi_1) \in \Phi$ and $(\epsilon_2.\varphi_2) \in \Phi$ if $\epsilon_1 = \epsilon_2$ then $\varphi_1 = \varphi_2$;
2. $\Phi$ is *closed*: for all $(\epsilon.\varphi) \in \Phi$ and $\epsilon' \in \varphi$ there exists $\varphi'$ such that $(\epsilon'.\varphi') \in \Phi$;
3. $\Phi$ is *transitive*: for all $(\epsilon_1.\varphi_1) \in \Phi$ and $(\epsilon_2.\varphi_2) \in \Phi$ if $\epsilon_2 \in \varphi_1$ then $\varphi_2 \subseteq \varphi_1$; □

For any functional $\Phi$, the *effect map of* $\Phi$, written $\hat{\Phi}$, is the partial map from effect variables to effects defined by $\hat{\Phi}(\epsilon) = \varphi$, if $\epsilon.\varphi \in \Phi$. We define $frv(\Phi) = \cup\{frv(\epsilon.\varphi) \mid \epsilon.\varphi \in \Phi\}$ and $fev(\Phi) = \cup\{fev(\epsilon.\varphi) \mid \epsilon.\varphi \in \Phi\}$.

A *basis* is a pair $B = (Q, \Phi)$, where $Q$ is a set of region variables and $\Phi$ is a set of arrow effects. The set of bases is called Basis. We say that $B$ is *consistent*, written $\vdash B$, if $Q \supseteq frv(\Phi)$ and $\vdash \Phi$. We define $frv(B) = Q \cup frv(\Phi)$ and $fev(B) = fev(\Phi)$. Notice that if $B = (Q, \Phi)$ is consistent then $frv(B) = Q$ since $Q \supseteq frv(\Phi)$. Moreover, if $B = (Q, \Phi)$ is consistent then $fev(B) = \mathrm{Dom}(\hat{\Phi})$, since $\Phi$ is closed. The *domain* of a consistent basis $B = (Q, \Phi)$, written $\mathrm{Dom}(B)$, is the set $Q \cup fev(\Phi)$. A basis $B = (Q, \Phi)$ is *finite* if $Q$ and $\Phi$ are both finite sets. When $B$ is a basis we write $Q$ *of* $B$ and $\Phi$ *of* $B$ for the first and second component of $B$, respectively.

EXAMPLE 6.1 The basis $B_1 = (\{\rho_1\}, \{\epsilon_1.\emptyset, \epsilon_1.\{\rho_1\}\})$ is not consistent: $\epsilon_1$ cannot both denote the empty effect and the effect $\{\rho_1\}$. Formally, $B_1$ is not functional. However, $B_2 = (\{\rho_1\}, \{\epsilon_1.\emptyset, \epsilon_2.\{\rho_1\}\})$ is consistent. □

EXAMPLE 6.2 The basis $B_3 = (\{\rho_1, \rho_2\}, \{\epsilon_1.\{\rho_1\}, \epsilon_2.\{\epsilon_1, \rho_2\}\})$ is not consistent: the effect which $\epsilon_2$ denotes has $\epsilon_1$ as a member but is not a superset of the set which $\epsilon_1$ denotes. Formally: $B_3$ is not transitive. However, $B_4 = (\{\rho_1, \rho_2\}, \{\epsilon_1.\{\rho_1\}, \epsilon_2.\{\epsilon_1, \rho_1, \rho_2\}\}$ is consistent. □

Let $o$ range over basic semantic objects and let $B = (Q, \Phi)$ be a basis. We say that $o$ is *consistent in* $B$, if the sentence $B \vdash o$ can be inferred from the following rules:

$$\frac{\vdash B \quad \rho \in Q \textit{ of } B}{B \vdash \rho} \qquad \frac{\vdash B \quad \epsilon.\varphi \in \Phi \textit{ of } B}{B \vdash \epsilon.\varphi} \qquad \frac{\vdash B \quad \eta \in \mathit{fv}(B)}{B \vdash \eta}$$

$$\frac{\vdash B}{B \vdash \mathtt{int}} \qquad \frac{\vdash B}{B \vdash \alpha} \qquad \frac{B \vdash \tau \qquad B \vdash \rho}{B \vdash (\tau, \rho)} \qquad \frac{B \vdash \mu_1 \quad B \vdash \epsilon.\varphi \quad B \vdash \mu_2}{B \vdash \mu_1 \xrightarrow{\epsilon.\varphi} \mu_2}$$

$$\frac{\epsilon \notin \mathit{fev}(\Phi) \cup \varphi \qquad \vdash (Q, \Phi \cup \{\epsilon.\varphi\})}{(Q, \Phi) \vdash \varphi}$$

All these rules, except the last one, should be straightforward: they simply state that a semantic object is consistent in a basis $B = (Q, \Phi)$ only if (a) the basis is consistent by itself and (b) all the region and effect variables appearing in $o$ are free in $B$ and (c) if an arrow effect $\epsilon.\varphi$ occurs in $o$ then $\varphi$ is uniquely determined by the equation $\varphi = \hat{\Phi}(\epsilon)$. The last inference rule says that $\varphi$ is consistent in $B$ if, imagining that we pick a fresh effect variable $\epsilon'$, the extended basis $B \cup (\emptyset, \epsilon'.\varphi)$ would become consistent. Alternatively, this rule can be expressed as the conjunction of (a) $B = (Q, \Phi)$ is consistent, (b) $\varphi \subseteq \mathit{fv}(B)$ and (c) for all $\epsilon \in \varphi$ one has $\hat{\Phi}(\epsilon) \subseteq \varphi$.

EXAMPLE 6.3 Let $\mu = (\mathtt{int}, \rho_1)$. The types $\mu \xrightarrow{\epsilon_1.\emptyset} \mu$ and $\mu \xrightarrow{\epsilon_1.\{\rho_1\}} \mu$ cannot be consistent in the same basis. However, $\mu \xrightarrow{\epsilon_1.\emptyset} \mu$ and $\mu \xrightarrow{\epsilon_2.\{\rho_1\}} \mu$ are both consistent in the basis $B_2$ from Example 6.1. □

EXAMPLE 6.4 Consider the basis $B_4$ from Example 6.2. The effect $\{\rho_1\}$ is consistent in $B_4$; so is $\{\epsilon_1, \rho_1, \rho_2\}$, but not $\{\epsilon_2, \rho_1\}$. □

As usual, we often write "$B \vdash o$" to mean "there exists a proof tree with conclusion $B \vdash o$." It is easy to see that $B \vdash o$ implies that $B$ is consistent and that $\mathit{fv}(o) \subseteq \mathrm{Dom}(B)$.

Let $B_1 = (Q_1, \Phi_1)$ and $B_2 = (Q_2, \Phi_2)$ be bases. We define the *union* of $B_1$ and $B_2$, written $B_1 \cup B_2$ to be $(Q_1 \cup Q_2, \Phi_1 \cup \Phi_2)$. We define the *disjoint union* of $B_1$ and $B_2$, written $B_1 \uplus B_2$, to be $B_1 \cup B_2$ provided $B_1 \cup B_2$ is consistent and $\mathrm{Dom}(B_1) \cap \mathrm{Dom}(B_1) = \emptyset$, and undefined otherwise. Note that $B_1 \uplus B_2$ can be defined even in cases where $B_1$ and $B_2$ are not consistent by themselves. Typically, this concept is used for expressing disjointness of bound variables, for example in rule (5), where $B$ is consistent and $B \uplus B_1$ is consistent, but $B_1$ not necessarily is consistent, since it can contain occurrences of region and effect variables that are in $\mathrm{Dom}(B)$.

## 7 Substitution

Suppose for example that we want to unify the two types $\tau_1 = (\texttt{int}, \rho_1) \xrightarrow{\epsilon_1.\{\rho_1,\rho_2\}} (\texttt{int}, \rho_2)$ and $\tau_2 = (\texttt{int}, \rho_3) \xrightarrow{\epsilon_2.\emptyset} (\texttt{int}, \rho_3)$. These two types could arise during region inference, for example as the type of the `then` branch and the `else` branch, respectively, of the conditional:

```
if true then (fn x => x+1) else (fn y => y)
```

From the region variables that decorate `int` in $\tau_1$ and $\tau_2$ we see that a unifier for $\tau_1$ and $\tau_2$ has to map $\rho_1$, $\rho_2$ and $\rho_3$ to the same region variable, say $\rho_1$. But a unifier for $\tau_1$ and $\tau_2$ must also map the arrow effects in $\tau_1$ and $\tau_2$ to the same arrow effect, for example $\epsilon_1.\{\rho_1\}$. But how can a substitution map $\epsilon_2.\emptyset$ to $\epsilon_1.\{\rho_1\}$? Certainly it cannot, if substitutions simply map effect variables to effect variables. Letting substitutions map effect variables to effects and defining $S(\epsilon.\varphi)$ to be $S(\epsilon).S(\varphi)$ is not an option either for $S(\epsilon)$ would not be an effect variable and $S(\epsilon).S(\varphi)$ therefore not an arrow effect. The solution is to let substitutions map effect variables to arrow effects. For example, we allow $S_0^e = \{\epsilon_1 \mapsto \epsilon_1.\{\rho_1\}, \epsilon_2 \mapsto \epsilon_1.\{\rho_1\}\}$ as a substitution. The definition of substitution given below is such that $S_0^e(\epsilon_1.\{\rho_1\}) = \epsilon_1.\{\rho_1\} = S_0^e(\epsilon_2.\emptyset)$, i.e, that $S_0^e$ is a unifier for $\epsilon_1.\{\rho_1\}$ and $\epsilon_2.\emptyset$.

Formally, a *type substitution* is a map from type variables to types; a *region substitution* is a map from region variables to region variables; an *effect substitution* is a map from effect variables to arrow effects. We use $S^t$, $S^r$ and $S^e$ to range over type, region and effect substitutions, respectively. A *substitution* is a triple $(S^t, S^r, S^e)$; we use $S$ to range over substitutions. Substitution on basic semantic objects is defined as follows. Let $S = (S^t, S^r, S^e)$; then

**Effects**

$$S(\varphi) = \{S_r(\rho) \mid \rho \in \varphi\} \cup \{\eta \mid \exists \epsilon, \epsilon', \varphi'.\epsilon \in \varphi \wedge \epsilon'.\varphi' = S_e(\epsilon) \wedge \eta \in \{\epsilon'\} \cup \varphi'\}$$

**Arrow Effects**

$$S(\epsilon.\varphi) = \epsilon'.(\varphi' \cup S(\varphi)), \quad \text{where } \epsilon'.\varphi' = S_e(\epsilon)$$

**Types and Region Variables**

$$S(\texttt{int}) = \texttt{int} \quad S(\alpha) = S_t(\alpha) \quad S(\rho) = S_r(\rho)$$

$$S(\tau, \rho) = (S(\tau), S(\rho))$$

$$S(\mu \xrightarrow{\epsilon.\varphi} \mu') = S(\mu) \xrightarrow{S(\epsilon.\varphi)} S(\mu')$$

We write $S_2 \circ S_1$ for the composition of $S_2$ and $S_1$: $(S_2 \circ S_1)(x) = S_2(S_1(x))$. The *identity* substitution $\mathrm{Id} = (\mathrm{Id}^t, \mathrm{Id}^r, \mathrm{Id}^e)$, defined by $\mathrm{Id}^r(\rho)$ for all $\rho \in \mathrm{RegVar}$, $\mathrm{Id}^t(\alpha) = \alpha$ for all $\alpha \in \mathrm{TyVar}$, and $\mathrm{Id}^e(\epsilon) = \epsilon.\emptyset$ for all $\epsilon \in \mathrm{EffVar}$.

The *support* of a type substitution $S^t$, written $Supp(S^t)$, is the set $\{\alpha \in \mathrm{TyVar} \mid S^t(\alpha) \neq \alpha\}$. Similarly for region substitutions. The *support* of an effect substitution $S^e$, written $Supp(S^e)$, is the set $\{\epsilon \in \mathrm{EffVar} \mid S^e(\epsilon) \neq \epsilon.\emptyset\}$. The *support* of a substitution $S$, written $Supp(S)$, is the union of the supports of its three components. The *yield* of $S$, written $Yield(S)$, is $fv(Rng(S^t \downarrow (Supp(S^t))) \cup Rng(S^r \downarrow (Supp(S^r))) \cup Rng(S^e \downarrow (Supp(S^e))))$. The set of variables *involved in* $S$, written $Inv(S)$, is defined to be $Supp(S) \cup Yield(S)$.

A *finite substitution* is a triple $S = (S^t, S^r, S^e)$ where $S^t$, $S^r$ and $S^e$ are finite maps of the appropriate types. When $S'$ is a substitution and $S = (S^t, S^r, S^e)$ is a finite substitution, we write $S' \bullet S$ to mean the finite substitution $(S' \bullet S^t, S' \bullet S^r, S' \bullet S^e)$. The composition $S' \bullet S$ is useful when $S$ instantiates the bound variables of a type scheme and $S'$ is a substitution applied to the whole type scheme (see the proof of Lemma 7 for an example).

Every finite substitution can be extended a (total) substitution on basic semantic objects and we shall often tacitly assume that this extension has taken place before the substitution is applied.

Application of a substitution $S$ to a basis $B = (Q, \Phi)$ yields the basis $S(B) = (\{S(\rho) \mid \rho \in Q\}, \{S(\epsilon.\varphi) \mid \epsilon.\varphi \in \Phi\})$.

### 7.1 Contraction

It turns out, that unification always can be expressed as the composition of substitutions of a particularly simple kind, namely the so-called elementary contractions:

DEFINITION 2 Let $B = (Q, \Phi)$ be a consistent basis. A substitution $S$ is an *elementary contraction of $B$* if

1. $S = \mathrm{Id}$; or
2. $S = (\{\}, \{\rho_1 \mapsto \rho_2\}, \{\})$, for some $\rho_1, \rho_2 \in Q$; or
3. $S = (\{\}, \{\}, \{\epsilon_1 \mapsto \epsilon_2.\emptyset\})$, where $\{\epsilon_1, \epsilon_2\} \subseteq \mathrm{Dom}(\hat{\Phi})$ and $\hat{\Phi}(\epsilon_1) = \hat{\Phi}(\epsilon_2)$; or
4. $S = (\{\}, \{\}, \{\epsilon \mapsto \epsilon.\varphi\})$, for some $\epsilon$ and $\varphi$ with $\epsilon \in \mathrm{Dom}(\hat{\Phi})$ and $B \vdash \varphi$ and $\varphi \supseteq \hat{\Phi}(\epsilon)$; □

In terms of constraints, the third item allows us to collapse two constraints $\epsilon_1 \supseteq \varphi$ and $\epsilon_2 \supseteq \varphi$ into a single constraint $\epsilon_2 \supseteq \varphi'$ (where $\varphi'$ is $\varphi$ with any occurrence of $\epsilon_1$ replaced by $\epsilon_2$). Similarly, the fourth item corresponds to strengthening a constraint $\epsilon \supseteq \varphi_1$ to $\epsilon \supseteq \varphi_1 \cup \varphi'$, provided $\varphi \cup \varphi'$ is consistent in $B$. (In particular, one cannot introduce region and effect variables which are not already in $\mathrm{Dom}(B)$.)

Elementary contractions are idempotent. If $S$ is an elementary contraction of a consistent basis $B$, then $S(B)$ is consistent.

Let $B$ be a consistent basis. We say that a substitution $S$ is a *contraction* of $B$ if it can be written as a composition $S = S_n \circ \ldots \circ S_1$, $n \geq 1$, such that $S_1$ is an elementary contraction of $B$ and for all $i$ with $1 < i \leq n$, $S_i$ is an elementary contraction of $(S_{i-1} \circ \ldots \circ S_1)(B)$.

We say that $B_1$ is less than or equal to $B_2$, written $B_1 \leq B_2$, if there exists a contraction $S$ of $B_2$ such that $B_1 = S(B_2)$. Note that if $S$ is an elementary contraction of $B$ and $S(B) \neq B$ then there exists no contraction $S'$ of $S(B)$ such that $S'(S(B)) = B$. Thus $\leq$ is a partial order on consistent bases. We write $B_1 < B_2$ to mean $B_1 \leq B_2$ and $B_1 \neq B_2$.

LEMMA 3 Let $B_0$ be a finite, consistent basis. There exists no infinite descending chain:

$$B_0 > B_1 > B_2 > \cdots$$

A proof of the above lemma may be found in [20]. The lemma plays a crucial role in the proof that the region inference algorithm terminates. The region inference algorithm iterates over the program, contracting the basis and modifying the program annotations in the process. Things are arranged so that if the program has been traversed without making the basis smaller, then the annotated program is well-typed according to the region inference rules. Lemma 3 ensures that this will eventually happen.

LEMMA 4 Let $o$ be a basic semantic object and let $S$ be a contraction of a basis $B$. If $B \vdash o$ then $S(B) \vdash S(o)$.

In particular, if $B$ is consistent and $S$ is a contraction then $S(B)$ is consistent.

*Proof* By induction on the number of elementary contractions out of which $S$ is constructed, with an inner induction on the depth of $B \vdash o$. □

## 8 Unification

### 8.1 Unification of Arrow Effects

Let $B = (Q, \Phi)$ be a consistent basis and assume $\epsilon_1.\varphi_1 \in \Phi$ and $\epsilon_2.\varphi_2 \in \Phi$. A substitution $S$ is a *unifier for* $\epsilon_1.\varphi_1$ *and* $\epsilon_2.\varphi_2$ *in* $B$ if $S(B)$ is consistent and $S(\epsilon_1.\varphi_1) = S(\epsilon_2.\varphi_2)$. A substitution $S^*$ is a *most general unifier for* $\epsilon_1.\varphi_1$ *and* $\epsilon_2.\varphi_2$ *in* $B$, if $S^*$ is a unifier for $\epsilon_1.\varphi_1$ and $\epsilon_2.\varphi_2$ in $B$ and for every unifier $S$ for $\epsilon_1.\varphi_1$ and $\epsilon_2.\varphi_2$ in $B$ there exists a substitution $S'$ such that

1. $S(\rho) = S'(S^*(\rho))$, for all $\rho \in Q$;
2. $S(\epsilon.\varphi) = S'(S^*(\epsilon.\varphi))$, for all $\epsilon.\varphi \in \Phi$;

The following algorithm takes two arrow effects as arguments and returns an effect substitution which is a most general unifier for the two arrow effects:

*unifyArrEff*$(\epsilon_1.\varphi_1, \epsilon_2.\varphi_2) =$
let
  $S_1^e = \text{if } \varphi_2 \subseteq \varphi_1 \text{ then Id}^e \text{ else } \{\epsilon_1 \mapsto \epsilon_1.(\varphi_1 \cup \varphi_2)\}$
  $S_2^e = \text{if } \varphi_1 \subseteq \varphi_2 \text{ then Id}^e \text{ else } \{\epsilon_2 \mapsto \epsilon_2.(\varphi_1 \cup \varphi_2)\}$
  $S_3^e = \text{if } \epsilon_1 = \epsilon_2 \text{ then Id}^e \text{ else } \{\epsilon_2 \mapsto \epsilon_1.\emptyset\}$
in
  $S_3^e \circ S_2^e \circ S_1^e$
end

LEMMA 5 Let $B = (Q, \Phi)$ be a consistent basis and let $\epsilon_1.\varphi_1 \in \Phi$ and $\epsilon_2.\varphi_2 \in \Phi$. Then $S^e =$ *unifyArrEff*$(\epsilon_1.\varphi_1, \epsilon_2.\varphi_2)$ succeeds and

1. $S^e$ is a most general unifier for $\epsilon_1.\varphi_1$ and $\epsilon_2.\varphi_2$ in $B$;
2. $S^e$ is a contraction of $B$;
3. $S^e(B) = B$ implies $S^e = \text{Id}^e$;

*Proof* Let $(Q, \Phi) = B$. Since $B \vdash \varphi_1 \cup \varphi_2$ and $\varphi_1 \cup \varphi_2 \supseteq \varphi_1 = \hat{\Phi}(\epsilon_1)$, we have that $S_1^e$ is an elementary contraction, even if $\varphi_2 \not\subseteq \varphi_1$. Thus $S_1^e(B)$ is consistent. Next, $S_2^e$ is an elementary contraction of $S_1^e(B)$, since either $S_2^e = \text{Id}^e$ or $S_1^e(B) \vdash \varphi_1 \cup \varphi_2$ and $\varphi_1 \cup \varphi_2 \supseteq \widehat{S_1^e(\Phi)}(\epsilon_2) = \varphi_2$. Thus $S_2^e(S_1^e(B))$ is consistent. Next, $S_2^e(S_1^e(\epsilon_1.\varphi_1)) = S_2^e(\epsilon_1.(\varphi_1 \cup \varphi_2)) = \epsilon_1.(\varphi_1 \cup \varphi_2)$ and $S_2^e(S_1^e(\epsilon_2.\varphi_2)) = S_2^e(\epsilon_2.\varphi_2) = \epsilon_2.(\varphi_1 \cup \varphi_2)$. Thus $S_3^e$ is an elementary contraction of $S_2^e(S_1^e(B))$, even if $\epsilon_1 \neq \epsilon_2$. Thus $S^e$ is a contraction of $B$.

The following calculation shows that $S^e$ unifies $\epsilon_1.\varphi_1$ and $\epsilon_2.\varphi_2$: $S^e(\epsilon_1.\varphi_1) = S_3^e(S_2^e(S_1^e(\epsilon_1.\varphi_1))) = S_3^e(S_2^e(\epsilon_1.(\varphi_1 \cup \varphi_2))) = S_3^e(\epsilon_1.(\varphi_1 \cup \varphi_2)) = S_3^e(\epsilon_2.(\varphi_1 \cup \varphi_2)) = S_3^e(S_2^e(\epsilon_2.\varphi_2)) = S_3^e(S_2^e(S_1^e(\epsilon_2.\varphi_2)))$. Since $S^e$ is a contraction of $B$ we have that $S^e(B)$ is consistent, so $S^e$ really is a unifier for $\epsilon_1.\varphi_1$ and $\epsilon_2.\varphi_2$ in $B$.

Finally, we show that $S^e$ is a most general unifier. Let $S$ be any unifier for $\epsilon_1.\varphi_1$ and $\epsilon_2.\varphi_2$ in $B$. Let $\epsilon'.\varphi' = S(\epsilon_1.\varphi_1) = S(\epsilon_2.\varphi_2)$ and let $S' = \{\epsilon' \mapsto \epsilon'.\varphi'\} \circ S$. We now show that this $S'$ has the desired properties. Certainly, $S(\rho) = S'(S^e(\rho))$, for all $\rho \in Q$, since $S^e$ is an effect substitution. Next, take an arbitrary $\epsilon.\varphi \in \Phi$. We proceed by case analysis:

$\boxed{\epsilon \neq \epsilon_1 \wedge \epsilon \neq \epsilon_2 \wedge \epsilon_1 \notin \varphi \wedge \epsilon_2 \notin \varphi}$ Here $S'(S^e(\epsilon.\varphi)) = S'(\epsilon.\varphi) = \{\epsilon' \mapsto \epsilon'.\varphi'\}(S(\epsilon.\varphi)) = S(\epsilon.\varphi)$ since $S(\epsilon.\varphi)$ and $\epsilon'.\varphi'$ both are members of $S(\Phi)$, which, by assumption, is effect consistent.

$\boxed{\epsilon \neq \epsilon_1 \wedge \epsilon \neq \epsilon_2 \wedge (\epsilon_1 \in \varphi \vee \epsilon_2 \in \varphi)}$ Let $\epsilon''.\varphi'' = S(\epsilon)$. We first prove

$$S(\varphi) = S'(S^e(\varphi)) \tag{7}$$

We have $S(\varphi) = S(\varphi \cup \varphi_1 \cup \varphi_2)$ since $\{\epsilon_1, \epsilon_2\} \cap \varphi \neq \emptyset$ and therefore, by consistency, $\{\epsilon_1\} \cup \varphi_1 \subseteq \varphi$ or $\{\epsilon_2\} \cup \varphi_2 \subseteq \varphi$, so that $S(\{\epsilon_1\} \cup \varphi_1) = S(\{\epsilon_2\} \cup \varphi_2) \subseteq S(\varphi)$. Moreover, we have $S(\{\epsilon_2 \mapsto \epsilon_1.\emptyset\}(\varphi \cup \varphi_1 \cup \varphi_2)) \subseteq S(\varphi \cup \varphi_1 \cup \varphi_2)$, even if $\epsilon_1 \notin \varphi$; for in that case we must have $\epsilon_2 \in \varphi$ (by case assumption) and therefore $fv(S(\epsilon_1)) \subseteq \{\epsilon'\} \cup \varphi' \subseteq S(\varphi)$. We do not necessarily have $S(\{\epsilon_2 \mapsto \epsilon_1.\emptyset\}(\varphi \cup \varphi_1 \cup \varphi_2)) = S(\varphi \cup \varphi_1 \cup \varphi_2)$.[2] But $\varphi' \cup S(\{\epsilon_2 \mapsto \epsilon_1.\emptyset\}(\varphi \cup \varphi_1 \cup \varphi_2)) = S(\varphi \cup \varphi_1 \cup \varphi_2)$, since $S(\epsilon_1.\varphi_1) = S(\epsilon_2.\varphi_2) = \epsilon'.\varphi'$. Thus $S(\varphi) = S(\varphi \cup \varphi_1 \cup \varphi_2) = \varphi' \cup S(\{\epsilon_2 \mapsto \epsilon_1.\emptyset\}(\varphi \cup \varphi_1 \cup \varphi_2)) = S'(S^e(\varphi))$, proving (7). Now the following computation gives the desired result: $S'(S^e(\epsilon.\varphi)) = S'(\epsilon.S^e(\varphi)) = \{\epsilon' \mapsto \epsilon'.\varphi'\}(S(\epsilon.S^e(\varphi))) = \{\epsilon' \mapsto \epsilon'.\varphi'\}(\epsilon''.(\varphi'' \cup S(S^e(\varphi)))) = \epsilon''.(\varphi'' \cup \varphi' \cup S(S^e(\varphi))) = \epsilon''.(\varphi'' \cup S'(S^e(\varphi))) = \epsilon''.(\varphi'' \cup S(\varphi)) = S(\epsilon.\varphi)$.

$\boxed{\epsilon = \epsilon_1}$ Since $B$ is consistent we have $\epsilon.\varphi = \epsilon_1.\varphi_1$, so $S'(S^e(\epsilon.\varphi)) = \{\epsilon' \mapsto \epsilon'.\varphi'\}(S(S^e(\epsilon_1.\varphi_1))) = \{\epsilon' \mapsto \epsilon'.\varphi'\}(S(\epsilon_1.\{\epsilon_2 \mapsto \epsilon_1.\emptyset\}(\varphi_1 \cup \varphi_2))) = \epsilon'.\varphi' = S(\epsilon_1.\varphi_1) = S(\epsilon.\varphi)$.

$\boxed{\epsilon = \epsilon_2}$ Since $B$ is consistent we have $\epsilon.\varphi = \epsilon_2.\varphi_2$, so $S'(S^e(\epsilon.\varphi)) = \{\epsilon' \mapsto \epsilon'.\varphi'\}(S(S^e(\epsilon_2.\varphi_2))) = \{\epsilon' \mapsto \epsilon'.\varphi'\}(S(\epsilon_1.\{\epsilon_2 \mapsto \epsilon_1.\emptyset\}(\varphi_1 \cup \varphi_2))) = \epsilon'.\varphi' = S(\epsilon_2.\varphi_2) = S(\epsilon.\varphi)$.

□

## 8.2 Unification of Types

We now extend the above results about unification to cover annotated types. Let $B = (Q, \Phi)$ be a consistent basis and let $\tau_1$ and $\tau_2$ be types satisfying $B \vdash \tau_1$ and $B \vdash \tau_2$. A substitution $S$ is a *unifier of* $\tau_1$ *and* $\tau_2$ *in* $B$ if $S$ takes the form $(\{\}, S^r, S^e)$, $S(B)$ is consistent and $S(\tau_1) = S(\tau_2)$. Note that a unifier is not allowed to have type variables in its support (we do not attempt to do ML type inference and region inference simultaneously.) A substitution $S^*$ is a *most general unifier of* $\tau_1$ *and* $\tau_2$ *in* $B$, if $S^*$ is a unifier of $\tau_1$ and $\tau_2$ in $B$ and for every unifier $S$ of $\tau_1$ and $\tau_2$ in $B$ there exists a substitution $S'$ such that:

1. $S(\rho) = S'(S^*(\rho))$, for all $\rho \in Q$;
2. $S(\epsilon.\varphi) = S'(S^*(\epsilon.\varphi))$, for all $\epsilon.\varphi \in \Phi$;

[2] Example: Consider $\epsilon_1.\varphi_1 = \epsilon_1.\{\epsilon_2\}$, $\epsilon_2.\varphi_2 = \epsilon_2.\emptyset$; let $S(\epsilon_1) = \epsilon'.\emptyset$ and $S(\epsilon_2) = \epsilon'.\{\epsilon', \rho\}$. Then $S(\epsilon_1.\{\epsilon_2\}) = S(\epsilon_2.\emptyset) = \epsilon'.\{\epsilon', \rho\}$, $S^e(\epsilon_1) = S^e(\epsilon_2) = \epsilon_1.\{\epsilon_1\}$ but $S(\{\epsilon_1\}) = \{\epsilon'\} \subset \{\epsilon', \rho\} = S(\{\epsilon_1, \epsilon_2\})$.

Notice that the condition in item (1) is "for all $\rho \in Q$," not just "for all $\rho \in frv(\tau_1, \tau_2)$"; similarly, note that the condition in item (2) is "for all $\epsilon.\varphi \in \Phi$," not just "for all $\epsilon.\varphi \in arreff(\tau_1) \cup arreff(\tau_2)$." This stronger property of principal unifiers will be used several times in what follows. One can prove that if $S^*$ is a most general unifier for $\tau_1$ and $\tau_2$ in $B$ then $Inv(S^*) \subseteq fv(\tau_1, \tau_2)$.

The algorithm below computes most general unifiers in consistent bases:

```
unifyRho(ρ1, ρ2) =
  if ρ1 = ρ2 then Id
  else ({}, {ρ2 ↦ ρ1}, {})

unifyMu((τ1, ρ1), (τ2, ρ2)) =
  let
     S1 = unifyTy(τ1, τ2)
     S2 = unifyRho(S1ρ1, S1ρ2)
  in
     S2 ∘ S1
  end
```

```
unifyTy(τ1, τ2) = case (τ1, τ2) of
   (int, int) ⇒ Id
  | (α, β)       ⇒ if α = β then Id else FAIL
  | (μ1 --ϵ1.φ1--> μ2, μ1' --ϵ1'.φ1'--> μ2') ⇒
     let
        S1 = unifyMu(μ1, μ1')
        S2 = unifyArrEff(S1(ϵ1.φ1), S1(ϵ1'.φ1'))
        S3 = unifyMu(S2(S1(μ2)), S2(S1(μ2')))
     in
        S3 ∘ S2 ∘ S1
     end
  | (_, _) ⇒ FAIL
```

LEMMA 6 Let $B$ be a consistent basis and assume $B \vdash \tau_1$ and $B \vdash \tau_2$ and $\mathrm{ML}(\tau_1) = \mathrm{ML}(\tau_2)$. Then $S^* = unifyTy(\tau_1, \tau_2)$ succeeds and

1. $S^*$ is a most general unifier of $\tau_1$ and $\tau_2$ in $B$;
2. $S^*$ is a contraction of $B$;
3. $S^*(B) = B$ implies $S^* = \mathrm{Id}$;

Similarly for types with places ($\mu$) and region variables.

*Proof* By induction on the structure of $\mathrm{ML}(\tau_1)$. We show only the case $\tau_1 = \mu_1 \xrightarrow{\epsilon_1.\varphi_1} \mu_2$, in which case $\mathrm{ML}(\tau_1) = \mathrm{ML}(\tau_2)$ gives that $\tau_2$ must take the form $\mu_1' \xrightarrow{\epsilon_1'.\varphi_1'} \mu_2'$. We have $B \vdash \mu_1$, $B \vdash \mu_1'$ and $\mathrm{ML}(\mu_1) = \mathrm{ML}(\mu_1')$. Thus by induction

$$S_1 \text{ is a most general unifier for } \mu_1 \text{ and } \mu_1' \text{ in } B \tag{8}$$

$$S_1 \text{ is a contraction of } B \tag{9}$$

$$S_1(B) = B \text{ implies } S_1 = \mathrm{Id} \tag{10}$$

By (9) and Lemma 4 we have $S_1(B) \vdash S_1(\tau_1)$ and $S_1(B) \vdash S_1(\tau_2)$. Therefore, by Lemma 5, $S_2 = \mathit{unifyArrEff}(S_1(\epsilon_1.\varphi_1), S_1(\epsilon'_1.\varphi'_1))$ succeeds and

$$S_2 \text{ is a most general unifier for } S_1(\epsilon_1.\varphi_1) \text{ and } S_1(\epsilon'_1.\varphi'_1) \text{ in } S_1(B) \tag{11}$$

$$S_2 \text{ is a contraction of } S_1(B) \tag{12}$$

$$S_2(S_1(B)) = S_1(B) \text{ implies } S_2 = \text{Id} \tag{13}$$

By Lemma 4 on (12) we get $S_2(S_1(B)) \vdash S_2(S_1(\tau_1))$ and $S_2(S_1(B)) \vdash S_2(S_1(\tau_2))$. Also, $\text{ML}(S_2(S_1\mu_2)) = \text{ML}(\mu_2) = \text{ML}(\mu'_2) = \text{ML}(S_2(S_1\mu'_2))$, since $S_1$ and $S_2$ are contractions. By induction, $S_3 = \mathit{unifyMu}(S_2(S_1(\mu_2)), S_2(S_1(\mu'_2)))$ succeeds and

$$S_3 \text{ is a most general unifier for } S_2(S_1(\mu_2)) \text{ and } S_2(S_1(\mu'_2)) \text{ in } S_2(S_1(B)) \tag{14}$$

$$S_3 \text{ is a contraction of } S_2(S_1(B)) \tag{15}$$

$$S_3(S_2(S_1(B))) = S_2(S_1(B)) \text{ implies } S_3 = \text{Id} \tag{16}$$

Thus $\mathit{unifyTy}(\tau_1, \tau_2)$ succeeds with result $S^* = S_3 \circ S_2 \circ S_1$. From (8), (11) and (14) we get that $S^*$ is a unifier for $\tau_1$ and $\tau_2$ in $B$. From (9), (12) and (15) we get that $S^*$ is a contraction of $B$. From (9), (12) and (15) together with (10), (13) and (16) we get that $S^*(B) = B$ implies $S^* = \text{Id}$. It remains to prove that $S^*$ is a *most general* unifier for $\tau_1$ and $\tau_2$ in $B$. Let $S$ be any unifier for $\tau_1$ and $\tau_2$ in $B$ and let $(Q, \Phi) = B$. Now $S$ is a unifier for $\mu_1$ and $\mu'_1$ in $B$. Thus, by (8), there exists an $S'_1$ such that

$$\forall \rho \in Q.S(\rho) = S'_1(S_1(\rho)) \wedge \forall \epsilon.\varphi \in \Phi.S(\epsilon.\varphi) = S'_1(S_1(\epsilon.\varphi)) \tag{17}$$

Thus, since $S$ is a unifier for $\epsilon_1.\varphi_1$ and $\epsilon'_1.\varphi'_1$, $S'_1$ is a unifier for $S_1(\epsilon_1.\varphi_1)$ and $S_1(\epsilon'_1.\varphi'_1)$ in $S_1(B)$. Thus, by (11), there exists a $S'_2$ such that

$$\forall \rho \in S_1(Q).S'_1(\rho) = S'_2(S_2(\rho)) \wedge \forall \epsilon.\varphi \in S_1(\Phi).S'_1(\epsilon.\varphi) = S'_2(S_2(\epsilon.\varphi)) \tag{18}$$

Since $S$ is a unifier for $\mu_2$ and $\mu'_2$ in $B$ and (17) and (18) we have that $S'_2$ is a unifier for $S_2(S_1(\mu_2))$ and $S_2(S_1(\mu'_2))$ in $S_2(S_1(B))$. Thus, by (14), there exists an $S'_3$ such that

$$\forall \rho \in S_2(S_1(Q)).S'_2(\rho) = S'_3(S_3(\rho)) \wedge \forall \epsilon.\varphi \in S_2(S_1(\Phi)).S'_2(\epsilon.\varphi) = S'_3(S_3(\epsilon.\varphi)) \tag{19}$$

By (17), (18) and (19) we get the desired

$$\forall \rho \in Q.S(\rho) = S'_3(S^*(\rho)) \wedge \forall \epsilon.\varphi \in \Phi.S(\epsilon.\varphi) = S'_3(S^*(\epsilon.\varphi)) \tag{20}$$

□

It turns out that the premises of lemma 6 are always met in the region inference algorithm we use (this is proved in [20]). Therefore, unification never fails. Informally, the fact that the premise $\mathrm{ML}(\tau_1) = \mathrm{ML}(\tau_2)$ is satisfied is not surprising, for

1. region inference takes place after type inference; and

2. roughly, region inference simply re-typechecks the program using annotated versions of the types that were determined by type inference, so if two region-annotated types are unified, they will have the same underlying ML type.

EXAMPLE 8.1 The two types

$$\tau_1 = (\texttt{int}, \rho_1) \xrightarrow{\epsilon_2.\{\rho_1,\rho_3,\rho_4\}} (\texttt{int}, \rho_4)$$

and

$$\tau_2 = (\texttt{int}, \rho_5) \xrightarrow{\epsilon_6.\{\rho_5,\rho_7,\rho_8\}} (\texttt{int}, \rho_8)$$

are consistent in the basis $B = (\{\rho_1, \rho_3, \rho_4, \rho_5, \rho_7, \rho_8\}, \{\epsilon_2.\{\rho_1, \rho_3, \rho_4\}, \epsilon_6.\{\rho_5, \rho_7, \rho_8\}\}$. The result of $\mathit{unifyTy}(\tau_1, \tau_2)$ is the substitution $S = (S^t, S^r, S^e)$, where $S^t = \mathrm{Id}$, $S^r = \{\rho_5 \mapsto \rho_1, \rho_8 \mapsto \rho_4\}$ and $S^e = \{\epsilon_6 \mapsto \epsilon_2.\{\rho_1, \rho_3, \rho_4, \rho_7\}, \epsilon_2 \mapsto \epsilon_2.\{\rho_1, \rho_3, \rho_4, \rho_7\}\}$. By Lemma 6, $S$ is a contraction of $B$ and $S$ is a most general unifier for $\tau_1$ and $\tau_2$ in $B$. □

In Example 8.1, notice that $S$ does not map $\rho_3$ and $\rho_7$ to the same region variable: region and effect variables which occur in effects only in the types that are unified (i.e., they do not occur paired with a type constructor or as the handle of an arrow effect) are not affected by the unification algorithm. This distinction between different occurrences is important, also for the termination of region inference, so we define it formally. For basic semantic objects $o$, we define sets $\mathit{pfrv}(o)$ and $\mathit{pfev}(o)$ as follows:

$$\begin{aligned} \mathit{pfev}(\texttt{int}) &= \emptyset & \mathit{pfrv}(\texttt{int}) &= \emptyset \\ \mathit{pfev}(\alpha) &= \emptyset & \mathit{pfrv}(\alpha) &= \emptyset \\ \mathit{pfev}(\mu \xrightarrow{\epsilon.\varphi} \mu') &= \mathit{pfev}(\mu) \cup \mathit{pfev}(\mu') \cup \{\epsilon\} & \mathit{pfrv}(\mu \xrightarrow{\epsilon.\varphi} \mu') &= \mathit{pfrv}(\mu) \cup \mathit{pfrv}(\mu') \\ \mathit{pfev}(\tau, \rho) &= \mathit{pfev}(\tau) & \mathit{pfrv}(\tau, \rho) &= \mathit{pfrv}(\tau) \cup \{\rho\} \end{aligned}$$

The set $\mathit{pfev}(o)$ is called the set of *primary (free) effect variables of* $o$; the set $\mathit{pfrv}(o)$ is called the set of *primary (free) region variables of* $o$. We say that an effect variable $\epsilon$ is a *secondary effect variable* in $\tau$ if $\epsilon \in \mathit{fev}(\tau) \setminus \mathit{pfev}(\tau)$; similarly, we say that a region variable $\rho$ is *secondary* in $\tau$ if $\rho \in \mathit{frv}(\tau) \setminus \mathit{pfrv}(\tau)$.

Given types $\tau_1$ and $\tau_2$ with $\mathrm{ML}(\tau_1) = \mathrm{ML}(\tau_2)$, $\mathit{unifyTy}(\tau_1, \tau_2)$ returns a substitution which has only region and effect variables which are primary in $\tau_1$ or $\tau_2$ in its support. (In Example 8.1, $\rho_7$ and $\rho_3$ are secondary variables; all the other variables are primary.) This is as one would expect. For in order to obtain good separation of lifetimes, unification should only identify two region variables when they must denote the same region. Secondary occurrences of region variables do not force identification of regions. For example, amongst the less general unifiers for the two arrow effects $\epsilon.\{\rho_1, \rho_2\}$ and $\epsilon'.\{\rho_3, \rho_4\}$ we have $S = (\{\epsilon \mapsto \epsilon'.\emptyset\}, \{\rho_1 \mapsto \rho_3, \rho_2 \mapsto \rho_4\})$ and $S' = (\{\epsilon \mapsto \epsilon'.\emptyset\}, \{\rho_1 \mapsto \rho_4, \rho_2 \mapsto \rho_3\})$. These unifiers lead to smaller effects than the most general unifier, but they also lead to unnecessary identifications of regions and are therefore undesirable.

## 9 Type Schemes

Type schemes resemble the type schemes of Damas and Milner [3] but with additional quantification over region variables and effect variables:

$$\sigma ::= \forall\alpha_1 \cdots \alpha_n\rho_1 \cdots \rho_k\epsilon_1 \cdots \epsilon_m.\tau \qquad (n \geq 0, k \geq 0 \text{ and } m \geq 0)$$

Here $\tau$ is the *body* of $\sigma$, written *body*$(\sigma)$. The *bound variables of* $\sigma$, written $bv(\sigma)$, is the set $\{\alpha_1, \ldots, \alpha_n\} \cup \{\rho_1, \ldots, \rho_k\} \cup \{\epsilon_1, \ldots, \epsilon_m\}$; we define the set of *bound type variables of* $\sigma$, written $btv(\sigma)$, to be the set $\{\alpha_1, \ldots, \alpha_n\}$. The *free variables of* $\sigma$, written $fv(\sigma)$, is the set $fv(\tau)\setminus bv(\sigma)$. The bound variables of a type scheme must be distinct. The *arity* of $\sigma$ is the triple $(n, k, m)$.

The erase function, ML, of Section 5 is extended to type schemes by

$$\mathrm{ML}(\forall\alpha_1 \cdots \alpha_n\rho_1 \cdots \rho_k\epsilon_1 \cdots \epsilon_m.\tau) = \forall\alpha_1 \cdots \alpha_n.\,\mathrm{ML}(\tau)$$

We sometimes regard a type $\tau$ as the trivial type scheme $\forall.\tau$. Type schemes that arise from each other by renaming of bound variables are considered equal.

A type $\tau'$ is an *instance of* $\sigma = \forall\alpha_1 \cdots \alpha_n\rho_1 \cdots \rho_k\epsilon_1 \cdots \epsilon_m.\tau$, written $\sigma \geq \tau'$, if there exists a substitution $S$ such that $Supp(S) \subseteq bv(\sigma)$ and $S(\tau) = \tau'$. When we want to make a particular $S$ explicit, we say that $\tau'$ is an instance of $\sigma$ *via* $S$, written $\sigma \geq \tau'$ *via* $S$. Furthermore, we say that a type scheme $\sigma' = \forall\alpha'_1 \cdots \alpha'_{n'}\rho'_1 \cdots \rho'_{k'}\epsilon'_1 \cdots \epsilon'_{m'}.\tau'$ is an *instance of* $\sigma$ *(via* $S$*)*, written $\sigma \geq \sigma'$ (via $S$), if $\sigma \geq \tau'$ and $bv(\sigma') \cap fv(\sigma) = \emptyset$. As in Milner's type system one has:

LEMMA 7 Let $\sigma$ and $\sigma'$ be type schemes. Then $\sigma \geq \sigma'$ iff for every $\tau$, $\sigma' \geq \tau$ implies $\sigma \geq \tau$.

*Proof* Assume that for every $\tau$, $\sigma' \geq \tau$ implies $\sigma \geq \tau$. By renaming the bound variables of $\sigma'$, if necessary, achieve that $bv(\sigma') \cap fv(\sigma) = \emptyset$. Then $\sigma' \geq$ *body*$(\sigma')$ and thus, by assumption, $\sigma \geq$ *body*$(\sigma')$, showing $\sigma \geq \sigma'$. Conversely, assume $\sigma \geq \sigma'$ *via* $S$. Without loss of generality, we can assume that $S$ is finite and that $\mathrm{Dom}(S) = bv(\sigma)$. Assume

$\sigma' \geq \tau$ *via* $S'$. We then have $\sigma \geq \tau$ *via* $S' \bullet S$. To prove this, it suffices to prove

$$(S' \circ S)\tau_0 = (S' \bullet S)\tau_0 \tag{21}$$

where $\tau_0 = \mathit{body}(\sigma)$, for by assumption we have $(S' \circ S)\tau_0 = \tau$. We prove (21) by induction on the structure of $\tau_0$. We show only the case $\epsilon.\varphi \in \mathit{arreff}(\tau_0)$. Note that $(S' \bullet S)(\varphi) = (S' \circ S)(\varphi)$, since $\mathit{bv}(\sigma') \cap \mathit{fv}(\sigma) = \emptyset$. Now there are two cases. First, assume $\epsilon \in \mathrm{Dom}(S)$. Let $\epsilon'.\varphi' = S(\epsilon)$ and let $\epsilon''.\varphi'' = S'(\epsilon')$. Thus $(S' \bullet S)(\epsilon.\varphi) = \epsilon''.(\varphi'' \cup S'(\varphi') \cup (S' \bullet S)(\varphi)) = \epsilon''.(\varphi'' \cup S'(\varphi') \cup (S' \circ S)(\varphi)) = (S' \circ S)(\epsilon.\varphi)$, as desired. Second, assume $\epsilon \notin \mathrm{Dom}(S)$. Then $(S' \bullet S)(\epsilon.\varphi) = \epsilon.((S' \bullet S)(\varphi)) = \epsilon.((S' \circ S)(\varphi)) = (S' \circ S)(\epsilon.\varphi)$, since $\epsilon \in \mathit{fv}(\sigma)$ and $\mathit{bv}(\sigma') \cap \mathit{fv}(\sigma) = \emptyset$. □

As a consequence, $\geq$ is a transitive relation on type schemes. We say that $\sigma$ and $\sigma'$ are *equivalent*, written $\sigma \equiv \sigma'$, if $\sigma \geq \sigma'$ and $\sigma' \geq \sigma$. This relation is larger than just renaming of bound variables. For example, letting $\mu_0 = (\mathtt{int}, \rho_0)$ we have

$$\forall \epsilon\rho.\mu_0 \xrightarrow{\epsilon.\{\rho\}} \mu_0 \equiv \forall \epsilon\rho\rho'.\mu_0 \xrightarrow{\epsilon.\{\rho,\rho'\}} \mu_0 \tag{22}$$

Thus $\geq$ induces a partial order on equivalence classes of type schemes. This partial order is non-well-founded (just like the corresponding partial order on ML type schemes).

There are certain type schemes we want to reject as ill-formed, because they are in fundamental conflict with the idea of basing region inference on unification of consistent types.

DEFINITION 8 A type scheme $\sigma = \forall \alpha_1 \cdots \alpha_n \rho_1 \cdots \rho_k \epsilon_1 \cdots \epsilon_m.\tau$ is said to be *well-formed* if, for every arrow effect $\epsilon.\varphi$ occurring on a function arrow in $\tau$ if $\epsilon \notin \mathit{bv}(\sigma)$ then $\mathit{fv}(\varphi) \cap \mathit{bv}(\sigma) = \emptyset$. Otherwise, $\sigma$ is said to be *ill-formed*.

In other words, well-formedness requires that if the handle of an arrow effect in $\tau$ is free then the entire arrow effect is free.

We shall later impose a restriction which bans ill-formed type schemes. That this is to be expected is illustrated by the following example.

EXAMPLE 9.1 Consider the type scheme $\sigma = \forall \rho.(\mathtt{int}, \rho) \xrightarrow{\epsilon.\{\rho\}} (\mathtt{int}, \rho)$ which is ill-formed. The problem with $\sigma$ is that if it is instantiated twice, via different substitutions, say $S_1 = \{\rho \mapsto \rho_1\}$ and $S_2 = \{\rho \mapsto \rho_2\}$, then the two resulting types $(\mathtt{int}, \rho_1) \xrightarrow{\epsilon.\{\rho_1\}} (\mathtt{int}, \rho_1)$ and $(\mathtt{int}, \rho_2) \xrightarrow{\epsilon.\{\rho_2\}} (\mathtt{int}, \rho_2)$ are not consistent in any basis: $\epsilon$ cannot both "denote" the set $\{\rho_1\}$ and the set $\{\rho_2\}$. If, however, $\epsilon$ had been quantified as well, the type schemes would have been well-formed and one could pick fresh effect variables each time the type scheme were instantiated. □

## 10 Polymorphic Recursion

In practice, much of the ability of the region inference to reclaim memory comes from rule (5). The crucial point is that within $e_1$, the type environment associates $f$ with the region type scheme $\hat{\sigma}$, so that free occurrences of $f$ in $e_1$ potentially can be given types different from $\tau_0$. We refer to this feature as region-polymorphic recursion. (An example of region-polymorphic recursion at work was presented in Section 2.)

Notice that rule (5) does not allow polymorphic recursion in types: the type scheme for $f$ in $e_1$ is only $\hat{\sigma}$, not $\sigma$. Thus the region rules are faithful to the treatment of recursive functions in ML as far as type polymorphism is concerned [10]. The reason for this limitation is that type inference for (type-) polymorphic recursion is equivalent to semi-unification [5, 8], which is undecidable [7].

However, it can be proved that every well-typed source expression can be region-annotated in accordance with the region inference rules [24]. Moreover, in the absence of region-polymorphic recursion, Milner's notion of principal type schemes extends to region inference [22]. In the presence of polymorphic recursion, however, it is not known whether (in some sense) it is possible to infer a principal region type scheme for every ML-typable expression. There seems to be a tension between, on the one hand, the desire for obtaining region type schemes that are as general as possible and on the other hand the desire to know that region inference always terminates.

We have chosen to resolve this (alleged) tension in the favour of termination: the algorithm described in [20] always finds a region annotation which is legal according to the region inference rules, although in doing so, it may fail to give every recursive function in the program a region type scheme which is the most general one permitted by the region inference rules.

The algorithm in [20] handles polymorphic recursion using a two-phase approach. The first phase, called *spreading*, generates a (possibly large) basis by choosing fresh region and effect variables wherever a region or effect annotation is required in the target program. The second phase, called *fixed point resolution*, collapses region variables (and effect variables) by unifying region-annotated types. Unification of region-annotated types produces contractions of the basis (see Section 8), and a cornerstone of the termination proof is that no finite basis can be contracted indefinitely (Lemma 3). Thus a crucial idea in the algorithm is to separate the generation of fresh variables from the region inference proper. The same idea is used for ensuring termination in our constraint-based approach mentioned in Section 3.

But is it possible to know how many region and effect variables one needs for doing region inference for a given program without actually doing the region inference? This is where the distinction between secondary and primary region (and effect) variables in types becomes important. Given an ML type $\tau^{ML}$, let us consider the set of region annotated types $\tau$ for which $\mathrm{ML}(\tau) = \tau^{ML}$. For every such $\tau$, the number of region and effect variables that appear in primary positions in $\tau$ is bounded by the size of $\tau$: one at most needs one effect variable for each function arrow in $\tau^{ML}$ and one region variable for each occurrence of a type constructor or a type variable in $\tau^{ML}$. However, it is not clear how many secondary region and effect variables one might wish to have on function arrows that appear in $\tau^{ML}$. But in that case, how many bound region and effect variables does it take at most to make a region-annotated type scheme $\hat{\sigma}$ of the form found in rule (5)? Since there is no obvious bound on the number of secondary region and effect variables in $\tau_0$, and since there is in general nothing that prevents secondary region and effect variables from being universally quantified in $\hat{\sigma}$, there is no obvious bound on how many bound region and effect variables one will need for $\hat{\sigma}$.

Why does one need a bound on the arity of $\hat{\sigma}$? Because each free occurrence of $f$ within $e_1$ and $e_2$ potentially gives rise to generation of $k$ fresh region variables and $m$ fresh effect variables, where $(\_, k, m)$ is the arity of $\hat{\sigma}$. Without a bound on $k$ and $m$, how can we generate all the fresh region and effect variables we need in the initial phase?

To avoid an ever-expanding number of quantified secondary region and effect variables in region-annotated type schemes, our algorithm never produces type schemes which have quantified region or effect variables which occur in secondary positions of the body of the type scheme only (see Section 12). Formally, we define:

DEFINITION 9 A type scheme $\sigma = \forall \alpha_1 \cdots \alpha_n \rho_1 \cdots \rho_k \epsilon_1 \cdots \epsilon_m.\tau$ is said to have *structural quantification* if $\{\rho_1, \ldots, \rho_k\} \subseteq \mathit{pfrv}(\tau)$, $\{\epsilon_1, \ldots, \epsilon_m\} \subseteq \mathit{pfev}(\tau)$ and $\{\alpha_1, \ldots, \alpha_n\} \subseteq \mathit{ftv}(\tau)$.

The operation by which we form type schemes (see Section 12.2) only produces type schemes which have structural quantification.

EXAMPLE 10.1 The following expression has a type which contains a secondary region variable:

$$\begin{array}{l}\lambda z : (\alpha, \rho_0).\mathtt{let}\ x = 1\ \mathtt{at}\ \rho_1 \\ \qquad\qquad \mathtt{in}\ (\lambda y : (\mathtt{int}, \rho_2).(x + y)\ \mathtt{at}\ \rho_3)\ \mathtt{at}\ \rho_4 : \\ \qquad\qquad \underbrace{(\alpha, \rho_0) \xrightarrow{\epsilon_1.\{\rho_1,\rho_4\}} ((\mathtt{int}, \rho_2) \xrightarrow{\epsilon_2.\{\rho_1,\rho_2,\rho_3\}} (\mathtt{int}, \rho_3), \rho_4)}_{\tau_0}\end{array}$$

Here $\rho_1$ is a secondary region variable in $\tau_0$; it represents the region of a temporary value which is not necessarily in the same region as the argument or result of either of the two functions but which is captured in the function value (closure) of the function $\lambda y \cdots$. If the above function is used in a declaration of a region-polymorphic function

```
letrec f(z) = let x = 1···
```

then one might want to give $f$ the type scheme $\sigma = \forall \rho_0\rho_1\rho_2\rho_3\rho_4\epsilon_1\epsilon_2.\tau_0$ but this type scheme has non-structural quantification. Instead, the *RegEffClos* algorithm (Section 12.2) will construct the less general type scheme $\sigma = \forall \rho_0\rho_2\rho_3\rho_4\epsilon_1\epsilon_2.\tau_0$. □

We are now ready to extend the definition of consistency to cover type schemes. Let $\sigma = \forall \alpha_1 \cdots \alpha_n \rho_1 \cdots \rho_k \epsilon_1 \cdots \epsilon_m.\tau$ be a type scheme with structural quantification. The *bound basis of* $\sigma$, written *bound*$(\sigma)$, is the basis $(\{\rho_1, \ldots, \rho_k\}, \{\epsilon.\varphi \in \mathit{arreff}(\tau) \mid \epsilon \in \mathit{bv}(\sigma)\})$.

DEFINITION 10 Type scheme $\sigma = \forall \alpha_1 \cdots \alpha_n \rho_1 \cdots \rho_k \epsilon_1 \cdots \epsilon_m.\tau$ is *consistent in basis* $B$, written $B \vdash \sigma$, if $B$ is consistent, $\sigma$ has structural quantification and, letting $B' = \mathit{bound}(\sigma)$, the basis $B \uplus B'$ exists and is consistent and $B \uplus B' \vdash \tau$.

Notice that if $B \vdash \sigma$ and $\sigma = \forall \alpha_1 \cdots \alpha_n \rho_1 \cdots \rho_k \epsilon_1 \cdots \epsilon_m.\tau$ then, since $\sigma$ has structural quantification, we have $\mathrm{Dom}(\widehat{\Phi_\sigma}) = \{\epsilon_1, \ldots, \epsilon_m\}$, where $\Phi_\sigma = \Phi$ *of* *bound*$(\sigma)$.

LEMMA 11 If $B \vdash \sigma$ then $\sigma$ is well-formed.

*Proof* Assume $B \vdash \sigma$, where $\sigma = \forall \alpha_1 \cdots \alpha_n \rho_1 \cdots \rho_k \epsilon_1 \cdots \epsilon_m.\tau$. Let $B' = (Q', \Phi') = \mathit{bound}(\sigma)$. By $B \vdash \sigma$ we have that the basis $B \uplus B'$ exists, is consistent and $B \uplus B' \vdash \tau$. Take $\epsilon.\varphi \in \mathit{arreff}(\tau)$ and assume $\epsilon \notin \{\epsilon_1, \ldots, \epsilon_m\}$. Now $B \uplus B' \vdash \tau$ implies $\epsilon.\varphi \in \Phi\,\mathit{of}\,(B \uplus B')$. Since $B \uplus B'$ is consistent and $\epsilon \notin \mathit{bv}(\sigma)$ we have $\epsilon.\varphi \in B$. But then, since $B$ itself is consistent we have $\mathit{fv}(\epsilon.\varphi) \subseteq \mathit{fv}(B)$ and thus $\mathit{fv}(\epsilon.\varphi) \cap (Q', \mathrm{Dom}(\hat{\Phi}')) = \emptyset$. □

The definition of consistency does not depend on any particular choice of bound variables in $\sigma$, except that the bound variables must be chosen disjoint from $B$.

We emphasise that consistency of type schemes is introduced for algorithmic reasons only. Soundness of the region inference rules has been proved without assuming consistency[23, 24]. Also, we have not found the restriction to consistent type schemes (and the loss in polymorphism it entails) to be serious in practice.

DEFINITION 12 A type environment $TE$ is *consistent in* $B = (Q, \Phi)$, written $B \vdash TE$, if for all $x \in \mathrm{Dom}(TE)$, letting $(\sigma, \rho) = TE(x)$, one has $B \vdash \sigma$ and $\rho \in Q$.

This definition is used in the inference rules in Section 4.

## 11 Instantiation of Type Schemes

An *instantiation list* is a triple of the form

$$([\tau_1, \ldots, \tau_n], [\rho_1, \ldots, \rho_k], [\epsilon_1.\varphi_1, \ldots, \epsilon_m.\varphi_m]) \qquad n \geq 0, k \geq 0, m \geq 0$$

The triple $(n, k, m)$ is called the *arity* of the instantiation list. We use *il* to range over instantiation lists. Instantiation lists annotate program variables, see rules (1) and (2). We say that *il* is *consistent in basis* $B$, written $B \vdash il$, if $B \vdash \tau_i$, for all $i = 1 \ldots n$, $B \vdash \rho_i$, for all $i = 1 \ldots k$, and $B \vdash \epsilon_i.\varphi_i$, for all $i = 1 \ldots m$.

Let $\sigma$ be a type scheme $\forall \alpha_1 \cdots \alpha_n \rho_1 \cdots \rho_k \epsilon_1 \cdots \epsilon_m.\tau$ and let

$$il = ([\tau_1, \ldots, \tau_n], [\rho_1', \ldots, \rho_k'], [\epsilon_1'.\varphi_1', \ldots, \epsilon_m'.\varphi_m'])$$

be an instantiation list with the same arity as $\sigma$. Let $S = (\{\alpha_1 \mapsto \tau_1, \ldots, \alpha_n \mapsto \tau_n\}, \{\rho_1 \mapsto \rho_1', \ldots, \rho_k \mapsto \rho_k'\}, \{\epsilon_1 \mapsto \epsilon_1'.\varphi_1', \ldots, \epsilon_m \mapsto \epsilon_m'.\varphi_m'\})$. Then we refer to the type $\tau' = S(\tau)$ as the *instance of* $\sigma$ *given by il*; we write $\sigma \geq \tau'$ *via il* to mean that $\tau'$ is the instance of $\sigma$ given by *il*.

Consider the situation where $B$ is a basis, $\sigma$ a type scheme, *il* an instantiation list of the same arity as $\sigma$ and assume $B \vdash \sigma$ and $B \vdash il$. Surprisingly, perhaps, it is not necessarily the case that the instance of $\sigma$ via *il* is consistent in $B$. The reason is that the instantiation may produce arrow effects which are strictly larger than the arrow effects found in $B$.

EXAMPLE 11.1 Consider $B = (\{\rho_0\}, \{\epsilon_0.\emptyset\})$, $\sigma = \forall \epsilon \rho.(\texttt{int}, \rho_0) \xrightarrow{\epsilon.\{\rho\}} (\texttt{int}, \rho)$ and $S = (\{\rho \mapsto \rho_0\}, \{\epsilon \mapsto \epsilon_0.\emptyset\})$. The instance of $\sigma$ via $S$ is the type $\tau' = (\texttt{int}, \rho_0) \xrightarrow{\epsilon_0.\{\rho_0\}} (\texttt{int}, \rho_0)$, which is not consistent in $B$, since the arrow effect $\epsilon_0.\emptyset$ has "grown" to become $\epsilon_0.\{\rho_0\}$. Another way to explain this "growth" is as follows. Since $\epsilon$ and $\rho$ are quantified in $\sigma$, the arrow effect $\epsilon.\{\rho\}$ can be thought of a quantified constraint: $\forall \epsilon, \rho.(\epsilon \supseteq \{\rho\} \Rightarrow (\texttt{int}, \rho_0) \xrightarrow{\epsilon} (\texttt{int}, \rho))$. Thus instantiating $\epsilon$ and $\rho$ to $\epsilon_0$ and $\rho_0$, respectively, results in the constraint $\epsilon_0 \supseteq \{\rho_0\}$. We represent this "growth" of the set which $\epsilon_0$ denotes by application of the contraction $\{\epsilon_0 \mapsto \epsilon_0.\{\rho_0\}\}$ to $B$. □

In general, the operation of instantiating $\sigma$ using *il* in $B$ returns not just a type, $\tau'$, but also a contraction, which can be applied to $B$ to obtain a basis in which $\tau'$ is consistent.

The instantiation algorithm is defined by the mutually recursive function declarations shown below. All the functions return an effect substitution, which is a contraction of the basis; the main function is *inst*($\sigma$, *il*) which returns both an effect substitution and a type, the latter being the instance of $\sigma$ via *il*.

$$
\begin{array}{l}
\mathit{instArrEff}(S^e, \epsilon.\varphi) = \\
\quad \text{if } \epsilon \notin \mathrm{Dom}(S^e) \text{ then } \mathrm{Id}^e \\
\quad \text{else let } \epsilon_1.\varphi_1 = S^e(\epsilon) \\
\qquad\quad \text{in if } S^e(\varphi) \subseteq \varphi_1 \text{ then } \mathrm{Id}^e \\
\qquad\qquad \text{else } \{\epsilon_1 \mapsto \epsilon_1.(\varphi_1 \cup S^e(\varphi))\} \\
\qquad\quad \text{end}
\end{array}
$$

$$
\begin{array}{l}
\mathit{instTy}(S^e, \tau) = \text{case } \tau \text{ of} \\
\quad \alpha \Rightarrow \mathrm{Id}^e \\
\quad \mid \mathtt{int} \Rightarrow \mathrm{Id}^e \\
\quad \mid \mu_1 \xrightarrow{\epsilon.\varphi} \mu_2 \Rightarrow \\
\qquad \text{let } S_1^e = \mathit{instMu}(S^e, \mu_1) \\
\qquad\quad\;\; S_2^e = \mathit{instMu}\big(S_1^e \bullet S^e, S_1^e(\mu_2)\big) \\
\qquad\quad\;\; S_3^e = \mathit{instArrEff}\big(S_2^e \bullet \big(S_1^e \bullet S^e\big), \\
\qquad\qquad\qquad\qquad \big(S_2^e \circ S_1^e\big)(\epsilon.\varphi)\big) \\
\qquad \text{in } S_3^e \circ S_2^e \circ S_1^e \text{ end}
\end{array}
$$

$$
\mathit{instMu}(S^e, (\tau, \rho)) = \mathit{instTy}(S^e, \tau)
$$

$$
\begin{array}{l}
\mathit{inst}(\sigma, \; \mathit{il}) = \\
\quad \text{let } \forall \alpha_1 \cdots \alpha_n \rho_1 \cdots \rho_k \epsilon_1 \cdots \epsilon_m.\tau = \sigma \\
\qquad ([\tau_1, \ldots, \tau_n], [\rho'_1, \ldots, \rho'_k], [\epsilon'_1.\varphi'_1, \ldots, \\
\qquad \epsilon'_m.\varphi'_m]) = \mathit{il} \\
\qquad (\text{FAIL if } \sigma \text{ and } \mathit{il} \text{ have different arity}) \\
\qquad S = (S^t, S^r, S^e), \text{ where} \\
\qquad\quad S^t = \{\alpha_1 \mapsto \tau_1, \ldots, \alpha_n \mapsto \tau_n\} \\
\qquad\quad S^r = \{\rho_1 \mapsto \rho'_1, \ldots, \rho_k \mapsto \rho'_k\} \\
\qquad\quad S^e = \{\epsilon_1 \mapsto \epsilon'_1.\varphi'_1, \ldots, \epsilon_m \mapsto \epsilon'_m.\varphi'_m\} \\
\qquad S_1^e = \mathit{instTy}(S^e, S^r(S^t(\tau))) \\
\quad \text{in } \big(S_1^e, S_1^e(S^e(S^r(S^t\tau)))\big) \text{ end}
\end{array}
$$

LEMMA 13 Let $S^e$ be a finite effect substitution. Assume $\vdash B$, $B \uplus B'$ exists, $B \uplus B' \vdash \tau$, $B \vdash Rng(S^e)$ and $\mathrm{Dom}(S^e) = \mathrm{Dom}(\widehat{\Phi'})$, where $\Phi' = \Phi$ *of* $B'$. Then $S_1^e = \mathit{instTy}(S^e, \tau)$ succeeds and

1. $S_1^e$ is a contraction of $B$;
2. $S_1^e(B) \vdash (S_1^e \bullet S^e)(S_1^e(\tau))$;
3. $S_1^e(B) = B$ implies $S_1^e = \mathrm{Id}^e$.

Similarly with *instMu* and $\mu$ for *instTy* and $\tau$, and with *instArrEff* and $\epsilon.\varphi$ for *instTy* and $\tau$.

*Proof* Write $B$ in the form $(Q, \Phi)$ and write $B'$ in the form $(Q', \Phi')$. We first prove the result for *instArrEff* and $\epsilon.\varphi$ in place of *instTy* and $\tau$. As in the definition of *instArrEff*, make the following case analysis.

$\boxed{\epsilon \notin \mathrm{Dom}(S^e)}$ Here $S_1^e = \mathrm{Id}^e$, which is a contraction of $B$. Moreover, since $B \uplus B'$ exists and $B \uplus B' \vdash \epsilon.\varphi$ and $\epsilon \notin \mathrm{Dom}(S^e)$ and $\mathrm{Dom}(S^e) = \mathrm{Dom}(\hat{\Phi}')$ we have $B \vdash \epsilon.\varphi$. Thus $(S_1^e \bullet S^e)(S_1^e(\epsilon.\varphi)) = S^e(\epsilon.\varphi) = \epsilon.\varphi$. (In short, if the instantiation substitution $S^e$ does not have $\epsilon$ in its domain then it has no variable in $\varphi$ in its domain.) Thus (2) and (3) hold.

$\boxed{\epsilon \in \mathrm{Dom}(S^e) \wedge S^e(\varphi) \subseteq \varphi_1}$ Here $S^e_1 = \mathrm{Id}^e$, which is a contraction of $B$. Moreover, $(S^e_1 \bullet S^e)(S^e_1(\epsilon.\varphi)) = S^e(\epsilon.\varphi) = \epsilon_1.(\varphi_1 \cup S^e(\varphi)) = \epsilon_1.\varphi_1$. Since $\epsilon_1.\varphi_1 \in \mathit{Rng}(S^e)$ and $B \vdash \mathit{Rng}(S^e)$ we thus have (2) as desired. Also (3) holds.

$\boxed{\epsilon \in \mathrm{Dom}(S^e) \wedge S^e(\varphi) \not\subseteq \varphi_1}$ Here $S^e_1 = \{\epsilon_1 \mapsto \epsilon_1.(\varphi_1 \cup S^e(\varphi))\}$. Since $B \vdash \epsilon.\varphi$ and $B \vdash \mathit{Rng}(S^e)$ we have $B \vdash S^e(\varphi)$. Thus $S^e_1$ is a contraction of $B$ and since $S^e(\varphi) \not\subseteq \varphi_1$ we have $S^e_1(B) < B$. Thus (3) holds trivially. As for (2), we have

$$
\begin{aligned}
&\left(S^e_1 \bullet S^e\right)\left(S^e_1(\epsilon.\varphi)\right) && \\
&= S^e_1(S^e(\epsilon.\varphi)) && \text{since } \mathit{Inv}\left(S^e_1\right) \cap \mathrm{Dom}(S^e) = \emptyset \\
&= S^e_1(\epsilon_1.(\varphi_1 \cup S^e(\varphi))) && \\
&= \epsilon_1.(\varphi_1 \cup S^e(\varphi)) && \text{by the definition of } S^e_1
\end{aligned}
$$

Now $\epsilon_1.\varphi_1 \in \Phi$ so $S^e_1(\epsilon_1.\varphi_1) \in S^e_1(\Phi)$. Moreover, $S^e_1(\epsilon_1.\varphi_1) = \epsilon_1.(\varphi_1 \cup S^e(\varphi) \cup S^e_1(\varphi_1)) = \epsilon_1.(\varphi_1 \cup S^e(\varphi))$. Thus $S^e_1 B \vdash (S^e_1 \bullet S^e)(S^e_1(\epsilon.\varphi))$ as required.

We now proceed to the cases for *instTy* and *instMu*, which are done simultaneously, by structural induction on $\tau$ and $\mu$. The only interesting case is the following:

$\boxed{\tau \equiv \mu_1 \xrightarrow{\epsilon.\varphi} \mu_2}$ Since $B \uplus B' \vdash \tau$ we have $B \uplus B' \vdash \mu_1$, $B \uplus B' \vdash \mu_2$ and $B \uplus B' \vdash \epsilon.\varphi$. Following the definition of $\mathit{instTy}(S^e, \tau)$ we have by induction that $S^e_1 = \mathit{instMu}(S^e, \mu_1)$ succeeds and

$$S^e_1 \text{ is a contraction on } B \tag{23}$$

$$S^e_1(B) \vdash \left(S^e_1 \bullet S^e\right)\left(S^e_1 \mu_1\right) \tag{24}$$

$$S^e_1(B) = B \text{ implies } S^e_1 = \mathrm{Id}^e \tag{25}$$

By Lemma 4 on (23) and $B \uplus B' \vdash \mu_2$ we get $S^e_1(B \uplus B') \vdash S^e_1(\mu_2)$. Moreover, $S^e_1(B) \uplus S^e_1(B')$ exists and is equal to $S^e_1(B \uplus B')$. Moreover, $\mathrm{Dom}(S^e_1 \bullet S^e) = \mathrm{Dom}(S^e) = \mathrm{Dom}(\widehat{\Phi'_1})$ and $S^e_1(B) \vdash \mathit{Rng}(S^e_1 \bullet S^e)$, where $\Phi'_1 = \Phi \mathit{of}\, S^e_1(B')$. Thus by induction we have that $S^e_2 = \mathit{instMu}(S^e_1 \bullet S^e, S^e_1(\mu_2))$ succeeds and that

$$S^e_2 \text{ is a contraction on } S^e_1(B) \tag{26}$$

$$S^e_{21}(B) \vdash \left(S^e_{21} \bullet S^e\right)\left(S^e_{21} \mu_2\right) \tag{27}$$

$$S^e_{21}(B) = S^e_1(B) \text{ implies } S^e_2 = \mathrm{Id}^e \tag{28}$$

where $S^e_{21}$ is defined to be $S^e_2 \circ S^e_1$. (Here we use the general fact that for all substitutions $S_1$, $S_2$ and $S_3$, if $S_1$ is finite then $S_3 \bullet (S_2 \bullet S_1) = (S_3 \circ S_2) \bullet S_1$.) By (26) and (23) we get that $S^e_{21}(B)$

is consistent and that $S^e_{21}(B) \uplus S^e_{21}(B')$ exists and equals $S^e_{21}(B \uplus B')$. By Lemma 4 on $B \uplus B' \vdash \epsilon.\varphi$ and $B \vdash Rng(S^e)$ we have $S^e_{21}(B) \uplus S^e_{21}(B') \vdash S^e_{21}(\epsilon.\varphi)$ and $S^e_{21}(B) \vdash Rng(S^e_{21} \bullet S^e)$. Also $\mathrm{Dom}(S^e_{21} \bullet S^e) = \mathrm{Dom}(S^e) = \mathrm{Dom}(\widehat{\Phi'_2})$, where $\Phi'_2 = \Phi of\, S^e_{21}(B')$. Thus by the first part of the lemma we have that $S^e_3 = instArrEff(S^e_{21} \bullet S^e, S^e_{21}(\epsilon.\varphi))$ succeeds and that

$$S^e_3 \text{ is a contraction of } S^e_{21}(B) \tag{29}$$

$$S^e_{321}(B) \vdash \left(S^e_{321} \bullet S^e\right)\left(S^e_{321}(\epsilon.\varphi)\right) \tag{30}$$

$$S^e_{321}(B) = S^e_{21}(B) \text{ implies } S^e_3 = \mathrm{Id}^e \tag{31}$$

where $S^e_{321} = S^e_3 \circ S^e_{21}$. Thus $instTy(S^e, \tau)$ succeeds with result $S^e_{321}$. By (23), (26) and (29) we get that $S_{321}$ is a contraction of $B$, as required. Next, from (24) we get $S^e_{321}(B) \vdash (S^e_3 \circ S^e_2)((S^e_1 \bullet S^e)(S^e_1 \mu_1))$, i.e., since $Inv(S^e_{321}) \cap \mathrm{Dom}(S^e) = \emptyset$,

$$S^e_{321}(B) \vdash \left(S^e_{321} \bullet S^e\right)\left(S^e_{321}(\mu_1)\right) \tag{32}$$

Similarly, from (27) we get

$$S^e_{321}(B) \vdash \left(S^e_{321} \bullet S^e\right)\left(S^e_{321}(\mu_2)\right) \tag{33}$$

By (30), (32) and (33) we get the desired $S^e_{321}(B) \vdash (S^e_{321} \bullet S^e)(S^e_{321}(\tau))$. Finally, assume $S^e_{321}(B) = B$. Then $S^e_{321}(B) = S^e_{21}(B) = S^e_1(B) = B$, so $S^e_{321} = \mathrm{Id}^e$, by (25), (28) and (31). □

THEOREM 14 Assume $B \vdash \sigma$ and $B \vdash il$ (by which we mean that $B \vdash e$ for each list element $e$ of $il$). Also assume that $\sigma$ and $il$ have the same arity. Then $(S^e_1, \tau') = inst(\sigma, il)$ succeeds and

1. $S^e_1$ is a contraction of $B$;
2. $S^e_1(\sigma) \geq \tau'$ *via* $S^e_1(il)$ and $S^e_1(B) \vdash \tau'$;
3. $S^e_1(B) = B$ implies $S^e_1 = \mathrm{Id}^e$;

*Proof* Let $B' = (Q', \Phi') = bound(\sigma)$ and let $\tau$ be as in the definition of *inst*. Since $B \vdash \sigma$ we have $\vdash B$ and $B \uplus B' \vdash \tau$. Since $B \vdash il$ we have that $B \uplus (\emptyset, S^r(\Phi'))$ exists and that $B \uplus (\emptyset, S^r(\Phi')) \vdash S^r(S^t\tau)$, using the declarations in the definition of *inst*. Also, $\mathrm{Dom}(S^e) = \mathrm{Dom}(\widehat{S^r(\Phi')})$ and $B \uplus (\emptyset, S^r(\Phi')) \vdash Rng(S^e)$. Thus by Lemma 13 we have that $S^e_1 = inst(S^e, S^r(S^t(\tau)))$ succeeds and that

$$S^e_1 \text{ is a contraction of } B \tag{34}$$

$$S^e_1(B) \vdash \left(S^e_1 \bullet S^e\right)\left(S^e_1(S^r(S^t(\tau)))\right) \tag{35}$$

$$S^e_1(B) = B \text{ implies } S^e_1 = \mathrm{Id}^e \tag{36}$$

Thus $inst(\sigma, il)$ succeeds with result $(S_1^e, \tau') = (S_1^e, S_1^e(S^e(S^r(S^t(\tau)))))$. Moreover, (34) and (36) are two of the desired results. Also, by (34) and the fact that $B \uplus B'$ exists, we have $Inv(S_1^e) \cap Dom(S^e) = \emptyset$. Thus $(S_1^e \bullet S^e)(S_1^e(S^r(S^t(\tau)))) = S_1^e(S^e(S^r(S^t(\tau)))) = (S_1^e \bullet S^t, S_1^e \bullet S^r, S_1^e \bullet S^e)(S_1^e \tau)$. Furthermore, by (34) we have that $S^e(\sigma) = \forall \alpha_1 \cdots \alpha_n \rho_1 \cdots \rho_k \epsilon_1 \cdots \epsilon_m.S^e(\tau)$, without any renaming of bound variables being necessary. Thus $S_1^e(\sigma) \geq \tau'$ via $S_1^e(il)$ and $S_1^e(B) \vdash \tau'$ follow from (35). $\qquad \square$

## 12 Generalisation of Region and Effect Variables

In this section, we describe how to form type schemes from types. In order to ensure that the produced type schemes are consistent, an operation called *Below* is used.

### 12.1 The *Below* Operation

Let $B = (Q, \Phi)$ be a consistent basis and let $B_0 = (Q_0, \Phi_0)$ be a basis with $B_0 \subseteq B$—by which we mean $Q_0 \subseteq Q$ and $\Phi_0 \subseteq \Phi$. Clearly, $\Phi_0$ is functional and transitive, but it need not be closed. Also, we do not necessarily have $Q_0 \supseteq frv(\Phi_0)$. Thus $B_0$ is not necessarily consistent. However, there is a smallest basis (with respect to $\subseteq$), denoted $Below(B, B_0)$, which is consistent and satisfies $B \supseteq Below(B, B_0) \supseteq B_0$. It is defined thus: let $\Phi_1$ be the smallest closed subset of $\Phi$ satisfying $\Phi_1 \supseteq \Phi_0$. (This exists since $B$ is consistent and $B_0 \subseteq B$.) Further, let $Q_1$ be $Q_0 \cup frv(\Phi_1)$. Then $Below(B, B_0)$ is defined to be $(Q_1, \Phi_1)$.

### 12.2 The *RegEffClos* Operation

Damas and Milner [3] define a closure operation, let us write it $Clos_{TE}(\tau)$, which forms a type scheme from a type $\tau$ and a type environment $TE$. We now define the corresponding operation for forming region-annotated type schemes. Let $\tau$ be a type and let $\varphi_1$ be an effect. Further, let $B_0$ and $B$ be bases with $B \supseteq B_0$ and $B \vdash \tau$. (The basis $B_0$ contains region and effect variables that must not be quantified, for example because they occur free in the type environment.)

```
1    RegEffClos(B, B_0, φ)(τ) =
2        let
3            (Q, Φ) = B and (Q_0, Φ_0) = B_0
4            Q'_0 = Q_0 ∪ frv(φ) ∪ frv(τ) \ pfrv(τ)
5            Φ'_0 = Φ_0 ∪ {ε.φ' ∈ Φ | ε ∈ (φ ∪ (fev(τ) \ pfev(τ)))}
6            B_1 as (Q_1, Φ_1) = Below(B, (Q'_0, Φ'_0))
7            {ε_1.φ_1, ..., ε_m.φ_m} = Φ \ Φ_1
8            {ρ_1, ..., ρ_k} = Q \ Q_1
9            σ = ∀ρ_1 ··· ρ_k ε_1 ··· ε_m.τ
```

```
10  in
11      (B1, σ)
12  end
```

Here $Q'_0$ and $\Phi'_0$ contain the region and effect variables that must not be generalised. In addition to the variables in $B_0$, $Q'_0$ and $\Phi'_0$ include all region and effect variables in $\varphi$ and secondary region and effect variables in $\tau$ (see lines 4 and 5). In lines 7 and 8 we determine the set of region and effect variables that are generalised. The generalisation takes place in line 9.

For every type $\tau$ and basis $B$ with $B \vdash \tau$, we write $Below(B, (B_0, \tau))$ as a shorthand for $Below(B, (B_0 \cup (frv(\tau), arreff(\tau))))$.

LEMMA 15 Let $B \vdash \tau$, $B \vdash \varphi$, let $B_0$ be a basis and assume $B_0 \subseteq B$ and $B = Below(B, (B_0, \tau))$. Then $(B_1, \sigma) = RegEffClos(B, B_0, \varphi)(\tau)$ succeeds and $B_1 \vdash \sigma$ and $B_1 \vdash \varphi$ and $B \supseteq B_1 \supseteq B_0$.

*Proof* The call $(B_1, \sigma) = RegEffClos(B, B_0, \varphi)(\tau)$ clearly succeeds and $B \supseteq B_1 \supseteq B_0$ follows from the definition of *Below*. From $B = Below(B, (B_0, \tau))$ and the definition of $Q'_0$ and $\Phi'_0$ we get $\{\rho_1, \ldots, \rho_k\} \subseteq pfrv(\tau)$ and $\{\epsilon_1, \ldots, \epsilon_m\} \subseteq pfev(\tau)$. Let $B' = (Q \setminus Q_1, \Phi \setminus \Phi_1)$. Then $B' = bound(\sigma)$. Also, $B_1 \uplus B'$ exists and is equal to $B$, which is consistent. Also $B \vdash \tau$. Thus we have $B_1 \vdash \sigma$, according to Definition 10. Also, $B_1 \vdash \varphi$ holds by the definition of $Q'_0$ and $\Phi'_0$. □

An example of the use of *RegEffClos* was provided in Example 10.1.

## 13 Conclusion

A comparison between the type inference rules of Milner's polymorphic type discipline[3] and the region inference rules in Section 4 leads to the conclusion that upon something simple, something complicated will inevitably be erected. In our experience, however, Milner's type discipline carries even fairly heavy load well and we think that it is fascinating that it can be used for reasoning not just about the soundness of programs but also for reasoning about memory management.

## References


[1] A. Aiken, M. Fähndrich, and R. Levien. Better static memory management: Improving region-based analysis of higher-order languages. In *Proc. of the ACM SIGPLAN '95 Conference on Programming Languages and Implementation (PLDI)*, pages 174–185, La Jolla, CA, June 1995. ACM Press.

[2] L. Birkedal, M. Tofte, and M. Vejlstrup. From region inference to von Neumann machines via region representation inference. In *Proceedings of the 23rd ACM SIGPLAN-SIGACT Symposium on Principles of Programming Languages*, pages 171–183. ACM Press, January 1996. (accepted).

[3] L. Damas and R. Milner. Principal type schemes for functional programs. In *Proc. 9th Annual ACM Symp. on Principles of Programming Languages*, pages 207–212, Jan. 1982.

[4] Y. Fuh and P. Mishra. Type inference with subtypes. *Theoretical Computer Science (TCS)*, 73:155–175, 1990.

[5] F. Henglein. Type inference with polymorphic recursion. *ACM Transactions on Programming Languages and Systems*, 15(2):253, April 1993.

[6] R. Hindley. The principal type-scheme of an object in combinatory logic. *Trans. Amer. Math. Soc.*, 146:29–60, Dec. 1969.

[7] A. Kfoury, J. Tiuryn, and P. Urzyczyn. The undecidability of the semi-unification problem. *Information and Computation*, pages 83–101, 1993.

[8] A. J. Kfoury, J. Tiuryn, and P. Urzyczyn. Type reconstruction in the presence of polymorphic recursion. *ACM Transactions on Programming Languages and Systems*, 15(2):290–311, April 1993.

[9] X. Leroy. *Typage polymorphe d'un langage algorithmique*. PhD thesis, University Paris VII, 1992. English version: Polymorphic Typing of an Algorithmic Language, INRIA Research Report no. 1778, October 1992.

[10] R. Milner. A theory of type polymorphism in programming. *J. Computer and System Sciences*, 17:348–375, 1978.

[11] R. Milner, M. Tofte, R. Harper, and D. MacQueen. *The Definition of Standard ML (Revised)*. MIT Press, 1997.

[12] J. Mitchell. Coercion and type inference. In *Proc. 11th ACM Symp. on Principles of Programming Languages (POPL)*, 1984.

[13] F. Nielson, H. R. Nielson, and T. Amtoft. Polymorphic subtyping for effect analysis: the algorithm. Technical Report LOMAPS-DAIMI-16, Department of Computer Science, University of Aarhus (DAIMI), April 1996.

[14] H. R. Nielson and F. Nielson. Higher-order concurrent programs with finite communication topology. In *Conference Record of POPL'94: 21st ACM SIGPLAN-SIGACT Symposium on Principles of Programming Languages*, pages 84–97. ACM Press, January 1994.

[15] Peter Naur (ed.). Revised report on the algorithmic language Algol 60. *Comm. ACM*, 1:1–17, 1963.

[16] D. Rémy. Typechecking records and variants in a natural extension of ML. In *Proc. 16th Annual ACM Symp. on Principles of Programming Languages*, pages 77–88. ACM, Jan. 1989.

[17] J. Robinson. A machine-oriented logic based on the resolution principle. *J. Assoc. Comput. Mach.*, 12(1):23–41, 1965.

[18] J.-P. Talpin and P. Jouvelot. Polymorphic type, region and effect inference. *Journal of Functional Programming*, 2(3), 1992.

[19] J.-P. Talpin and P. Jouvelot. The type and effect discipline. In *Proceedings of the seventh IEEE Conference on Logic in Computer Science*, pages 162–173, June 1992. Also, (extended version) technical report EMP/CRI/A-206, Ecole des Mines de Paris, April 1992.

[20] M. Tofte and L. Birkedal. A region inference algorithm. Transactions on Programming Languages and Systems, 20(4): 734–767, July 1998.

[21] M. Tofte, L. Birkedal, M. Elsman, N. Hallenberg, T. H. Olesen, P. Sestoft, and P. Bertelsen. Programming with regions in the ML Kit. Technical Report DIKU-TR-98/25, Department of Computer Science, University of Copenhagen, 1998. (http://www.diku.dk/research-groups/topps/activities/topps/mlkit.html).

[22] M. Tofte and J.-P. Talpin. Data region inference for polymorphic functional languages (technical summary). Technical Report EMP/CRI/A-229, Ecole des Mines de Paris, 1992.

[23] M. Tofte and J.-P. Talpin. Implementing the call-by-value lambda-calculus using a stack of regions. In *Proceedings of the 21st ACM SIGPLAN-SIGACT Symposium on Principles of Programming Languages*, pages 188–201. ACM Press, January 1994.

[24] M. Tofte and J.-P. Talpin. Region-based memory management. *Information and Computation*, 132(2): 109–176, 1997.

[25] P. R. Wilson. Uniprocessor garbage collection techniques. In Y. Bekkers and J. Cohen, editors, *Memory Management, Proceedings, International Workshop IWMM92*, pages 1–42. Springer-Verlag, September 1992.

# 14 The Foundations of Esterel

**Gérard Berry**

## 1 Introduction

This paper informally presents the theoretical and practical foundations of synchronous programming of reactive systems, mostly focusing on the author's Esterel language. Synchronous languages are based on the perfectly synchronous concurrency model, in which concurrent processes are able to perform computation and exchange information in zero time, at least at a conceptual level. The synchronous model is well adapted to a very wide spectrum of computer applications, ranging from hardware circuit design to large-scale real-time process control, and including embedded systems, communication protocols, systems drivers, or user interfaces.

The synchronous model and languages are very different from models and languages well-known in the Computer Science community such as Petri Nets, CCS, CSP, or the $\pi$-calculus. Therefore, we find it useful to write a foundational paper explaining the application class, the model, the programming styles and languages based on it, their semantics, their implementation, and program verification. The development of synchronous languages was deeply influenced by the work of Robin Milner on process calculi and bisimulation. Since Robin Milner himself always expressed great interest in the subject, we find it natural to write that paper for a book dedicated to him. The paper is based on two invited lectures by the author: one at LICS'94, and the first Milner Lecture at Edinburgh University in 1996.

### 1.1 History

The perfectly synchronous model and languages appeared independently in the beginning of the 80's in different places. Esterel was defined by the author in Sophia-Antipolis [11, 10]. Lustre was defined by P. Caspi and N. Halbwachs in Grenoble [27]. Signal was developed by A. Benveniste and P. Le Guernic in Rennes [24]. In Israel, D. Harel introduced the Statecharts quasi-synchronous graphical formalism [30]. In Grenoble, F. Maraninchi defined the Argos formalism [38] that makes (restricted) Statecharts drawings fully synchronous. More recently, in Nice, C. Andre extended Argos into the SyncCharts formalism [2] that has the same expressive power as Esterel. Synchronous programming was also introduced in the framework of concurrent constraint programming by V. Saraswat *et al.* [46, 47]. See [26] for a joint presentation of Argos, Esterel, Lustre, and Signal.

R. Milner also introduced a form of synchrony primitive in his SCCS process calculus [40]; D. Austry and G. Boudol developed Milner's synchronous approach further in the Meije calculus [3]. The SCCS and Meije calculi are somewhat weaker than the aforementioned languages since they do not support negation, i.e. instantaneous test for signal absence. Nevertheless, they are useful to us for verification purposes.

The synchronous model and languages caught on quite easily in the automatic control community, where they did not fundamentally depart from models implicitly already in use in these areas. Esterel, Lustre, and Signal were actually designed and developed in mixed Control Theory and Computer Science teams.[1] The languages also entered the field of hardware design in the beginning of the 90's [5, 53], when it was realized that the synchronous model was identical to the zero-delay model of circuits.[2] Being somewhat unclassical compared to prevalent CSP or CCS based models, it took more time for the synchronous model to be accepted in the mainstream Computer Science community.

From the very beginning, the authors of synchronous languages developed or helped to develop software systems to support them and submitted them to industrial experimentation. The interest for synchronous languages in industry has grown steadily, and we think that their proper industrial career is about to start.

The development of synchronous languages has borrowed techniques from a number of usually disconnected fields. We already mentioned Control Theory. The semantics are given using Scott's fixpoint semantics and Plotkin's Structural Operational Semantics techniques [45]. The compilers are developed directly from the semantics, following the example of Robin Milner's ML language [42], itself in the line of Landin's viewpoint [35]. Automata theory techniques are used in the compilers [16, 12, 10]. Process calculi techniques such as bisimulation [41] or testing [31, 28] play a major role in program verification, as well as abstract interpretation techniques [25]. Synchronous hardware design, optimization, and verification techniques based on logic simplification techniques or on Binary Decision Diagrams [21, 14, 15] are now of prominent use in implementation and verification. Finally, constructive logic techniques as well as asynchronous hardware analysis techniques [17] turned out to be fundamental for solving the particularly important semantical causality problem for Esterel [52].

## 1.2 Overview of the Paper

Section 2 presents the application area, namely, deterministic reactive systems. Section 3 presents an analysis of models of concurrent computing, insisting on the synchronous model and its adequacy for reactive systems programming. Section 4 presents the linguistic

[1] The control-theory designers were Jean-Paul Rigault and Jean-Paul Marmorat for Esterel, Paul Caspi for Lustre, and Albert Benveniste for Signal.

[2] Thanks to Jean Vuillemin and Patrice Bertin at Digital Equipment Paris Research Laboratory; with them, the author also developed the 2z synchronous language based on 2-adic number theory [54], not presented here.

principles that underly synchronous languages, using the example of Esterel and Lustre. Section 5 presents the semantics and discusses the causality issues that are inherent in synchronous programming. In particular, we discuss the constructive semantics idea and its physical roots: the equivalence between propagation of electrical currents in circuits and proofs in constructive Boolean logic. Section 6 presents the techniques used to compile Esterel programs into automata, hardware circuits or conventional C programs, as well as optimization techniques. Finally, Section 7 discusses program verification.

## 2 Interactive and Reactive Systems

Instead of computing data outputs from data inputs, most modern computer-driven systems constantly interact with their environment and are themselves made of concurrent parts. Such systems fall into two distinct classes.

• In *interactive* systems, clients ask for access to resources that the system grants or allocates if and when possible. This class covers operating systems, data bases, networking, distributed algorithms, etc. The computer (network) is the leader of the interaction, and clients wait to be served. The main concerns are deadlock avoidance, fairness, and coherence of distributed information.

• In *reactive* or *reflex* systems, the computer rôle is to react to external stimuli by producing appropriate outputs in a timely way, the leader of the interaction being the environment. Reactive systems are prominent in industrial process control, airplane or automobile control, embedded systems, audio or video protocols, bus interfaces, systems or man-machine interfaces drivers, signal processing, etc. In reactive systems, the pace of the interaction is determined by the environment, not by the computers. Most often, clients cannot wait. The main concerns are correctness (safety) and timeliness.

The above terminology was introduced in [4] and we find it convenient to reuse it here, knowing of no better words. Of course, large scale systems can have components of both kinds. For instance, driving an airplane is mostly reactive, while communicating with the ground is mostly interactive. An automatic teller machine is reactive except for interactive communication with the bank.

Interactive and reactive systems deeply differ on the key issue of behavioral determinism. Interactive systems are naturally viewed as being non-deterministic. Being the master of the interaction, the system is allowed to make hidden internal choices about if and when requests are answered, and the answer to a sequence of inputs needs not be unique. On the other hand, behavioral determinism is a highly desirable and often mandatory property of slave reactive systems: the outputs of the system should be uniquely determined by its inputs and possibly by their timing. Think for example of airplane or automobile control, signal processing, or camera control.

Respecting either the non-deterministic or deterministic character of a system is mandatory for any formalism used to describe or program it. Since the behavior of a non-deterministic systems is far more complicated than that of a deterministic one (e.g., bugs may even be non-reproducible), the use of non-deterministic primitives should be reserved for interactive systems. In classical and well-studied concurrent formalisms such as Petri Nets or process calculi, non-determinism is built in. This makes the formalisms well-suited to interactive systems and not well-suited to reactive ones. The synchronous languages we study here are concurrent and deterministic. This makes them well suited to reactive systems and inadequate for interactive ones. No formalism is yet able to encompass both characteristics in a smoothly unified way.

Most reactive systems involve two kinds of activities, data handling and control handling, with a rather varied balance between them. At one extreme, signal processing applications are mostly data-oriented: the data flow is quite complex but the control is often reduced to pipelining of operators. At the other extreme, a bus interface is control-intensive and manipulates data in a trivial way, filling and emptying buffers. Data-intensive and control-intensive applications call for different specification and programming techniques. As far as synchronous languages are concerned, Lustre and Signal are tailored to data-intensive applications while Esterel, Statecharts, and its descendants are tailored to control-intensive applications. Large applications can have both data-intensive parts and control-intensive parts. Unifying the corresponding styles at the programming language level is an active area of research.

## 3 Models of Concurrent Computations

To deal with reactive or interactive systems, our first task is to look for an adequate concurrency model. Here, we mean a naive model that one can explain to non-computer scientists, not a 26-tuple of sets and relations. Such a model should have four characteristics. First, it should be simple and intuitive. Second, it should be physically meaningful with respect to its application class. Third, it should be compositional, in the sense that a group of agents can be viewed as a single agent and a sequence of communications can be viewed as a single communication. Last, it should be mathematically powerful to serve as a basis for semantics and verification. In our view, there are three fundamental and radically different models that can be described by analogy with elementary physics:

- **The Chemical Model.** Computing agents are viewed as molecules floating in a soup which is stirred by a magical mechanism called Brownian motion. Communication (computation) can occur when two or more molecules enter in contact, and it results in the destruction of some old molecules and the generation of some new ones.

- **The Newtonian Model.** Computing agents are viewed as planets moving in space. In each instant, planets move in function of their current speed, their acceleration being determined by the positions and weights of all other planets. In terms of information, everything is as if each planet communicates its weight and position to every other planet in zero time.
- **The Vibration Model.** Computing agents are viewed as molecules organized in a crystal. When a molecule is kicked, it pushes its neighbors, which generates a wave traveling at some predefined speed (e.g., the speed of sound).

The three models obey our four requirements in different ways. The main difference is the time $x$ it takes to establish a desired communication. Since sequencing communications sums up times, we can roughly express compositionality by the equation $x + x \sim x$ where $\sim$ is read as "homogeneous with." In the chemical model, $x$ is *arbitrary*, and *arbitrary* + *arbitrary* $\sim$ *arbitrary* implies compositionality. In the Newtonian model, $x$ is always 0, and $0 + 0 = 0$ holds trivially. In the vibration model, the communication time is fixed, or rather *bounded* if we allow for some non-determinism due to heat variations, and compositionality follows from *bounded* + *bounded* $\sim$ *bounded*. These are the three basic compositional models.

Chemistry is non-deterministic and asynchronous: there is no guarantee on the time it takes for two given molecules to interact, even if the interaction proper can be viewed as a synchronous act. The *Chemical Abstract Machine* or CHAM [9] is a mathematical version of chemistry that now routinely serves as a basis for the semantics of interactive process calculi or languages [43]. Being unable to express timeliness, the chemical model is obviously inappropriate for reactive systems.

In the Newtonian model, planets evolve in a deterministic and perfectly synchronous way. The Newtonian model will serve as a guideline for the definition and semantics of our synchronous languages, where we shall similarly assume that processes instantaneously exchange information in a deterministic way. For implementation, we shall use the more complex electrical vibration model, where information propagates with delay, where geometrical constraints may come in the picture, and where some (controllable) internal non-determinism may exist.

In physics, there is a well-known tension between the accuracy and the adequacy of a mathematical model. To compute planet or billiard ball trajectories, one can use either Einstein's generalized relativity theory or Newtonian mechanics. The former is more accurate but much harder, while the latter is less accurate but much easier and still adequate in most cases. The same happens in our field. The simplifying Newtonian assumption is adequate for programming, since it brings simplicity, determinism, and technology-independence at the language level. The more accurate vibration model that governs implementation is much harder, since actual response (propagation) times depend on implementation details and since a given system can be implemented in many different ways. To control how good the logical synchrony assumption is w.r.t. practical constraints, we have to estimate a bound on the actual reaction time for a given implementation. If the bound meets the specified timing constraints, we are happy. Otherwise, we either look for a better implementation or conclude that the intended system is infeasible with our technology. We would be satisfied to solve only 90% of the problems in this way and to leave the rest to more sophisticated or more manual techniques.

### 3.1 An Example: Synchronous Circuits

The simplest example of the joint use of Newtonian and vibration models is synchronous circuit design. An *acyclic combinational synchronous circuit* is pictured in Figure 14.1. In the *zero delay* (Newtonian) viewpoint, the circuit is viewed as a set of Boolean equations that has an acyclicity property: the equations can be ordered in such a way that any variable only depends on previously defined ones. Then, for any Boolean input, all the Boolean variables are uniquely defined by the equations. This view is used by the logic designer, who concentrates on the Boolean properties of the circuit, ignoring why and how the values are actually computed.

In the *electrical* vibration viewpoint, the circuit is viewed as an acyclic network of gates linked by wires. Boolean values are represented by voltages, say 0V and 5V, and wires and gates have bounded propagation delays. If the input voltages are kept stable to some Boolean voltages, then, after some predictable time, the output voltages stabilize at the right Boolean voltages. This is a physical fact, not a mathematical theorem. Since the number of input configurations is finite, it is possible to determine a maximum output stabilization time $\delta$

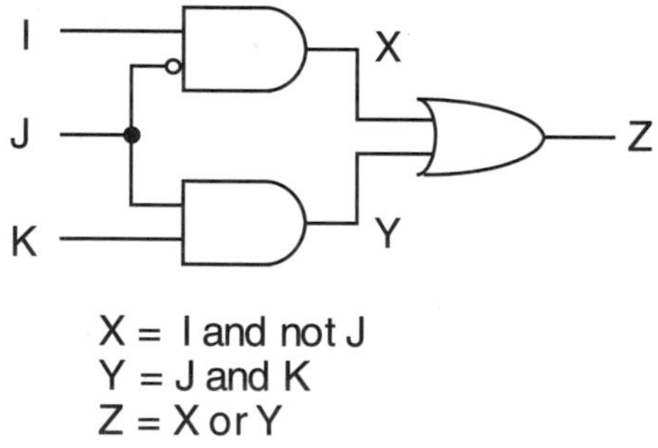


**Figure 14.1**
A synchronous circuit.

valid for all inputs. That view is taken by the electrical engineer, who does not care about what the circuit does and whose rôle is to minimize $\delta$ according to the current technology, using all possible tricks.

The technology-dependent value $\delta$ is the right and ideally the only interface between the logic designer the electrical engineer. Both know that waiting for $\delta$ time units ensures that the electrical circuit behaves as the zero-delay system of equations, which makes both of them happy.

An acyclic combinational circuit is memoryless. In *sequential circuits*, one adds elementary Boolean memories called *registers* to the combinational part to hold the state. A register is a delay element initialized to 0 and driven by a clock. The register input is an output of the combinational part, and the register output feeds back as an input to the combinational part. The output value of the register is initially 0, and then the value of its input at the previous clock tick. if $\delta$ is the stabilization time of the combinational part, a combinational reaction can be performed every $\delta$ time units. Changing the register output at clock tick consumes some additional time $\delta'$. If the clock period is bigger than $\delta+\delta'$ time units, the sequential circuit adequately performs a series of reactions both in the logical and in the electrical model.

### 3.2 Pure Synchrony in Software

The software analogue of synchronous circuits is *cycle-based reaction*, a very common model in software process control. The implementation cyclically repeats a sequence of three actions: reading the inputs, computing the reaction, and producing the corresponding outputs. Input events occurring during a reaction are queued for the next reaction, which makes the reaction atomic and deterministic. The Newtonian and vibration viewpoints are as for circuits. In the Newtonian viewpoint, we neglect the reaction time and we consider a reaction to be instantaneous. In the vibration viewpoint, we measure the maximum reaction time $\delta$ for a given platform and check how good the Newtonian approximation is with respect to the actual problem to be solved.

Focusing on time yields of course a simplified picture. In practice, space is equally important and one must explore different time / space implementation tradeoffs. This will be discussed in Section 6. Pipelining and distributed implementation can also be necessary. They will not be discussed here.

## 4 Synchronous Styles and Languages

This section is devoted to synchronous programming styles. We start with the data-flow styles of Lustre and Signal. Then, we introduce the imperative style used in Esterel and in graphical formalisms à la Statecharts.

### 4.1 The Data-Flow Style

The data-flow style is well-adapted to steady process-control applications and to signal processing. Consider a dynamical system of equations of the form:

$$X_{t+1} = U_{t+1} * sin(X_t + S_{t+1} - S_t)$$

$$S_{t+1} = cos(S_t + U_{t+1})$$

where $U$ is the input signal, $X$ is the output signal, with $X_0 = 0$, and $S$ is an internal state variable, with $S_0 = 1$. In such a system, there is already an implicit perfect synchrony assumption: the time taken by the arithmetical operations is 0. In Lustre [26, 27], the system is rewritten as follows:

```
node Control (U : float) returns (X : float);
var S : float;
let
   X = 0. -> (U*sin(pre(X)+S-pre(S)));
   S = 1. -> cos(pre(S)+U);
tel
```

or in an equivalent graphical form pictured in Figure 14.2.

The time indices are removed, and a variable such as $X$ denotes the sequence or *flow* of values $\{X_t \mid t \in N\}$ where $t$ is an integer discrete time index. Standard operators act

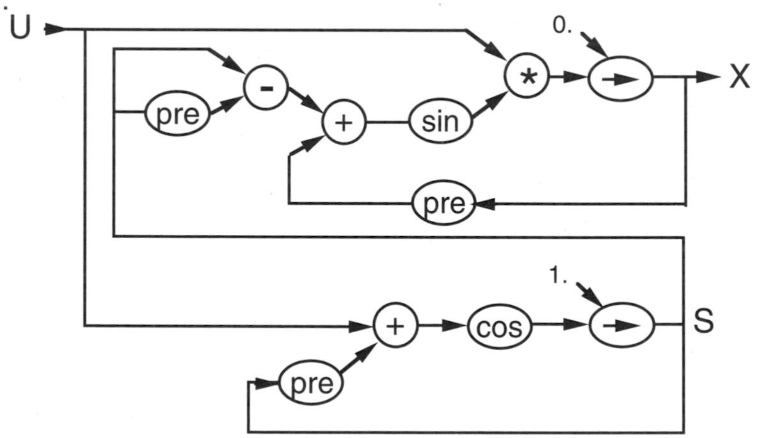


**Figure 14.2**
A graphical Lustre program.

synchronously: $X + Y = \{X_t + Y_t \mid t \in N\}$. The `pre` operator acts as an uninitialized delay: $\texttt{pre}(X)_{t+1} = X_t$ for $t > 0$ and $\texttt{pre}(X)_0 = nil$, where *nil* denotes uninitialization. Finally, the `->` operator provides flow initialization: $(X \texttt{ -> } Y)_0 = X_0$ and $(X \texttt{ -> } Y)_t = Y_t$ for $t > 0$.

Flows can be extracted from other flows using the `when` undersampling operator. If $B$ is a Boolean flow and $X$ is a flow of type $t$, then "$X$ `when` $B$" is a flow of type $t$ that contains only the values of $X$ whose indices $t$ are such that $B_t = true$, renumbered to form a proper flow. For instance, if $X = 0\ 1\ 2\ \ldots$ and $B = true\ false\ true\ \ldots$, then $(X \texttt{ when } B)_0 = 0$, $(X \texttt{ when } B)_1 = 2$, etc. In "$X$ `when` $B$," the Boolean flow $B$ is called the *clock* of the result. The constant flow `true` acts as the master clock. Flows can be computed at different rates according to their clock. An important restriction is that only flows having equal clocks can be combined by the operators. This ensures that any program can be computed with finite memory.

The Signal language [24] is similar, except that it also allows for *oversampling*, i.e., for creating flows that are faster than the inputs. Technically, Signal considers flow operators that define relations between flows instead of just functions in Lustre.

## 4.2 The Imperative Style

Consider now the following controller specification written in natural language:

> Emit the output `O` as soon as both the inputs `A` and `B` have been received. Reset the behavior whenever the input `R` is received.

As it stands, this simple specification is a little bit ambiguous. We additionally assume that nothing is to be done at initialization time and that the input signals can be simultaneous, as it is common in hardware. Furthermore, in the case where `R` occurs, the output should not be emitted and only the resetting should be performed.

A common way of making such a specification formal is to draw the picture of an automaton (also called a Mealy machine) as in Figure 14.3. The '.' operation in labels is the synchronous product of signals of SCCS [40] and Meije [3]. There are tools to analyze the behavior of such automata and to translate them into software programs or circuits. However, the direct specification of an automaton is not good programming style. In the automaton, the inputs and output names appear in many places, unlike in the specification. If we consider the same problem with $n$ basic inputs `A, B, C, ...`, the automaton explodes exponentially. Even for automata of manageable size, a little change to the specification may incur a major change to the automaton, which often ends with a full rewriting. These facts are well-known in Language Theory, where regular expressions are usually preferred to automata pictures.

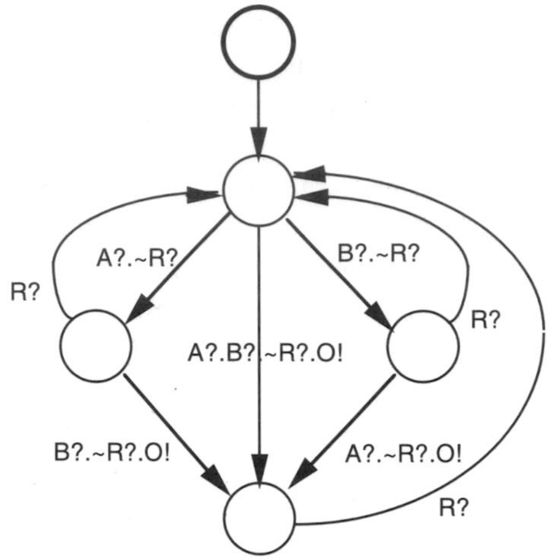


**Figure 14.3**
A Mealy machine.

Synchronous imperative formalisms aim at providing modular ways of describing control-intensive reactive behaviors. The basic principle is to help the user to write things only once. Although it is not always made explicit, the *Write Things Once* or *WTO* principle is clearly the basis for loops, procedures, higher-order functions, object-oriented programming and inheritance, concurrency vs. choice between interleavings, etc. Reactive programming will call for even more structure. In Esterel, the controller is written as follows:

```
module ABRO:
input A, B, R;
output O;
loop
   [ await A || await B ];
   emit O
each R
end module
```

with only one occurrence of `A`, `B`, `R`, and `O`.

In each reaction, each signal has a unique presence / absence status. For input signals, the status is given by the environment. For other signals, the status is absent by default, and it is set present by executing an `emit` statement. The "`await A`" instruction waits for `A` and terminates when `A` occurs. A parallel combination of two statements terminates instantaneously as soon as both statements are terminated. The time needed for synchronization is conceptually 0 (Newtonian). Therefore, "`await A || await B`" terminates instantaneously as soon as both `A` and `B` have occurred. The sequencing operator "$p$ ; $q$" instantaneously transfers control to $q$ when $p$ terminates. Therefore, `O` is emitted as soon as both `A` and `B` have been received. The "`loop` $p$ `each R`" operator is a *preemption* operator [6]. Its behavior is as follows: the body $p$ is immediately started and it runs freely until the next instant where `R` occurs. At that instant, $p$ is instantaneously killed, whatever its current state is, and $p$ is immediately restarted afresh. In "`loop...each`," preemption is called *strong* because it has priority over body execution: at preemption time, the body is *not* executed in the instant. Therefore, if `A`, `B`, and `R` are simultaneously present, then `O` is not emitted, as requested by the specification. The behavior is exactly that of the automaton, but the writing is much better. *Write Things Once* is achieved using the cooperation of sequencing, concurrency, and preemption constructs, each of them being indispensable.

Synchrony expresses that the internal bookkeeping necessary to execute statements takes no time, i.e. that it should be performed entirely within an input-output cycle in an implementation (see Section 3.2). The only constructs that take time are the ones explicitly required to do so, here "`await`" and "`loop...each`." Notice that synchrony of all other constructs is necessary to obtain the required behavior with no spurious silent move.

A graphical program for `ABRO` is pictured in Figure 14.4 States are hierarchically decomposed. Sourceless arrows indicate initial states. Bullets indicate termination, and the `R` arrow has a circle to indicate strong preemption. The SyncCharts formalism [2] is based on a similar graphical style and compiles into Esterel.

**4.2.1 Nested Preemptions and Exceptions** In Esterel, the essence of programming consists of controlling the life and death of activities by using preemption structures. The

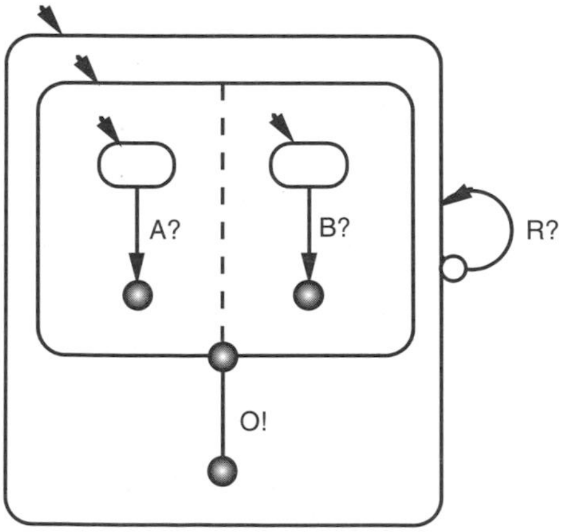


**Figure 14.4**
A chart for `ABRO`.

nesting of preemption structures expresses preemption priority in a natural way. Here is the basic training of an athlete:

```
module Runner:
input Second, Meter, Lap;
output ...; % not given here
every Morning do
   abort
      loop
         abort RunSlowly when 15 Second;
         abort
            every Step do
              Jump ||Breathe
            end every
         when 100 Meter;
         FullSpeed
      each Lap
   when 2 Lap
end every
end module
```

Here, the inputs are `Morning`, `Second`, `Step`, `Meter`, and `Lap`. The identifiers in italic represent statements not written here. In a lap, the full sequence is executed only if the lap is longer than `15 Second` plus `100 Meter`. If the lap is shorter than `15 Second`, one only runs slowly. If the lap is shorter than `15 Second` plus `100 Meter`, one never runs full speed. The same happens if mornings occurs very often.

Notice that any input can serve as a time unit in a preemption. In reactive programming, timing constraints should not be expressed only in seconds. When driving a car, if there is an obstacle at 30 meters, the timing constraint is "stop in less than 30 meters," no matter the time it takes to stop.

**4.2.2 Exceptions** Esterel supports an exception mechanism that is fully compatible with concurrency. When the athlete is getting older, he should worry about his heart during the most strenuous part of a lap:

```
trap HeartAttack in
   abort
      loop
         abort RunSlowly when 15 Second;
         abort
```

```
            every Step do
              Jump || Breathe || CheckHeart
            end every
         when 100 Meter;
         FullSpeed
      each Lap
   when 2 Lap
handle HeartAttack do
   GotoHospital
end trap
```

In *CheckHeart*, one should execute an exception raising statement of the form "`exit HeartAttack`" if there is any problem with the heart, which can be detected using the aforementioned preemption constructs. Then, the concurrent processes *Jump* and *Breathe* are immediately preempted,[3] and control immediately enters the `Goto Hospital` statement.

**4.2.3 Data Handling** Esterel programs can also manipulate data of arbitrary types. Here is a simple protocol:

```
module Sender :
input Message : Message; % from user
output Send : Message;   % to line
input Ack;               % from line
output Sent;             % to user
input Millisecond;       % from timer
loop
   await Message ;
   abort
      every 100 MilliSecond do
         emit Send(?Message)
      end every
   when Ack ;
   emit Sent
end loop
end module
```

[3] Technically, concurrent statements are *weakly preempted*, unlike with the `abort` statement: they are allowed to run for a last time in the reaction.

In addition to their presence / absence status which is as for pure signals, the signals `Message` and `Send` bear a value that belongs to an abstract type `Message`. In any reaction, a valued signal has exactly one value, which is determined by the environment for input signals and by the `emit` statements for other signals. The expression `?Message` yields the current value of `Message`. Esterel also supports non-shared variables that can be assigned to or passed to routines written in other languages.

By default, data-handling operations are assumed to be instantaneous, as in data-flow languages. However, Esterel also supports an `exec` primitive that makes it possible to call long external computations that do take time. This construct is very useful for computation tasks scheduling.

## 5 Semantics

The denotational semantics of data-flow languages is standard. Streams are modeled as infinite sequences, most often in Scott's classical cpo model, and sometimes using the $p$-adic metric $d(X, Y) = 2^{-n}$, where $n$ is the least integer such that $X_n \neq Y_n$ [54]. Equations are solved using fixpoint techniques based either on the Knaster-Tarski or on the Banach fixpoint theorems. Acyclic programs have well-defined unique solutions.

The semantics of imperative languages is more difficult. We give some clues for Esterel, referring to [7, 6] for more details. The first step is to define a *kernel calculus* from which the other statements are derived by macro-expansion. The Esterel kernel contains primitives for terminating, pausing for the instant, and exiting a trap, respectively written 0, 1 and $k$ with $k \geq 2$ (this numerical encoding follows an idea of Cousineau [22]). Signal emission is written $!s$, while $s\ ?\ p\ ,\ q$ instantaneously tests for the presence of a signal. Sequencing, looping, and synchronous concurrency are written $p\ ;\ q$, $p*$, and $p \mid q$. The preemption structures are suspension $s \supset p$, which freezes $p$ for the instant if $s$ is present, and trap declaration $\{p\}$. An auxiliary $\uparrow p$ operator is necessary for trap renumbering. Finally, local signals are declared using the classical hiding notation $p \backslash s$.

### 5.1 The Behavioral Semantics of Esterel

The primary semantics is the *behavioral semantics*. The reaction of a program $P$ to an input event $I$ is defined by a reaction $P \xrightarrow[I]{O} P'$ where $O$ is the output event and $P'$ is the derivative, i.e., the program that will perform the next reaction. The reaction is defined using an auxiliary inductive relation $p \xrightarrow[E]{E',\,k} p'$ where $p$ is a statement, $p'$ is its derivative, $E$ is the context event that tells which signals are present, $E'$ is the event made of the signals emitted by $p$ in $E$, and $k$ is a numerical completion code. Instantaneous signal broadcasting is obtained by imposing the invariant $E' \subset E$, which expresses that any statement hears what it is saying. Here are two of the rules:

$$\frac{p \xrightarrow[E]{E',0} p' \quad q \xrightarrow[E]{F',l} q'}{p\,;\,q \xrightarrow[E]{E' \cup F',\,l} q'} \quad (seq2)$$

$$\frac{p \xrightarrow[E]{E',k} p' \quad q \xrightarrow[E]{F',l} q'}{p \mid q \xrightarrow[E]{E' \cup F',\,max(k,l)} p' \mid q'} \quad (parallel)$$

Rule *(seq2)* is used for a sequence $p\,;\,q$ when $p$ terminates in the instant, i.e., returns code 0. Then $q$ is executed in the same rule premise, which models synchrony. Signal information flows from $p$ to $q$ because of the broadcasting invariant: one must have $E' \cup F' \subset E$, hence $E' \subset E$, which means that $q$ receives the signals emitted by $p$. Rule *(parallel)* defines the semantics of concurrency. The statements $p$ and $q$ are executed simultaneously in the same context $E$, and each of them receives the signals emitted by the other because of the broadcasting invariant. Control synchronization between the branches is performed by returning the maximum of their completion codes; this is the essence of the numerical encoding, see [7, 6].

### 5.2 Cyclic Instantaneous Dependencies and Paradoxes

For reactive programs, the two basic requirements are reactivity, i.e., existence of reaction for all inputs, and determinism, i.e., uniqueness of the reaction. Not all Esterel programs are reactive and deterministic. With output `X`, the program "`present X else emit X`" is non-reactive since `X` should be present if and only if it is not emitted, which contradicts instantaneous broadcasting. The program "`present X then emit X`" is non-deterministic since `X` should be present if and only if it is emitted, which does not determine its status. Such paradoxical programs must be rejected at compile-time. An easy way to reject them is to forbid static self-dependency of signals, in the same way one usually requires circuits to be acyclic. The above programs indeed corresponds to the nonsensical cyclic circuits "`X = not X`" and "`X = X`." However, requiring acyclicity turns out to be inadequate to Esterel practice. Users do write cyclic but sensible programs such as the following one:

```
module GoodCycle1 :
input I;
output X, Y;
```

```
present I then
   present X then emit Y end
else
   present Y then emit X end
end present
```

In GoodCycle1, X depends on Y and conversely, but it is immediately visible that any given status of I breaks the cycle. Assume for example I present. Then, the else branch of "present I" is not executed and X is not emitted. Therefore, X is absent, and Y is absent since it is not emitted either. The deduction is symmetrical if I is absent, with X and Y absent. Delays can also cut cycles:

```
module  GoodCycle2 :
output X, Y;
present X then emit Y end;
pause;
present Y then emit X end
```

In GoodCycle2, the dependency of X on Y is meaningful at first reaction only while the reverse dependency of Y on X is meaningful at second reaction only. The signals X and Y are both absent in any instant. As before, this is directly obvious on the source code.

Of course, these toy examples do not show why cycles are useful in practice. See [8] for the example of a naturally cyclic bus arbiter. In [36], it is shown that cyclic programs can be exponentially smaller than acyclic ones for the same behavior.

### 5.3 Logical Correctness and Further Paradoxes

An apparently simple way to deal with cycles is to require the programs to be reactive and deterministic, i.e., to have one and only one behavior for each input. This condition is also called *logical correctness*. It can be checked using BDD algorithms [29]. However, logical correctness also leads to somewhat paradoxical behavior. Consider the following Strange program:

```
module Strange:
output X, Y;
   present X then
      emit X
   end
||
```

```
present [X and not Y] then
   emit Y
end
```

An easy case inspection shows that there is only one logically consistent behavior, X and Y absent. That behavior is consistent since neither X nor Y is emitted. No other behavior is consistent. For instance, consider X present and Y absent. Then, "emit Y" is executed, which contradicts Y absent. Although Strange is logically correct, it is by no means understandable, which is more important to us. The reaction is not computed in a causal way.

The *constructive semantics* restricts the behavioral semantics by properly defining how information should causally propagate in programs, regardless of cycles. The foundations of the constructive semantics being much simpler to explain on circuits, let us first examine how Esterel programs are translated into Boolean circuits.

## 5.4 Translating Esterel Programs Into Circuits

The circuit semantics translates Esterel imperative programs into sequential circuits, see Section 3.1, or, equivalently, into Lustre data-flow programs. The basic idea is to associate a subcircuit with each statement, allocating gates and wires for control and signal propagation. Only the 1 or pause kernel unit-delay statement generates a register. All the other constructs only generate combinational logic. A first translation was presented in [5]. It rejected programs that can execute a given statement several times in different contexts in the same instant, which is possible (and useful) in Esterel. The translation has now been extended to cover that case as well, see [7].

If an Esterel program contains no cyclic instantaneous signal dependencies, then the circuit obtained by the translation has no combinational cycle. In that case, it is easy to see that both the Esterel program and the circuit are logically correct and that they have the same behavior. However, remember we also want to deal with dependency cycles in Esterel programs. Esterel cycles translate into combinational logic cycles, which implies that we also need to understand combinationally cyclic circuits. Consider first the circuit obtained by translating GoodCycle1 above:

```
X = (not I) and Y
Y = I and X
```

The circuit is also logically correct: I $= 0$ implies Y $= 0$ and then X $= 0$, while I $= 1$ implies X $= 0$ and then Y $= 0$. Notice that the correctness of the compiled equational circuit is much less directly visible than that of the imperative Esterel program. This is why cycles are usually rejected in data-flow languages and digital circuit design. The (simplified) circuit for `GoodCycle2` is

```
R = reg(1)
X = (not R) and Y
Y = R and X
```

where `reg` is the register construct (`reg(X) = 0->pre(X)` in Lustre). In the first instant, `R` $= 0$ implies `Y` $= 0$ and then `X` $= 0$. In all further instants, `R` $= 1$ implies `X` $= 0$ and then `Y` $= 0$. The circuit has no behavioral problem.

Consider now the circuit for `Strange`:

```
X = X
Y = X and not Y
```

As for Esterel, the only Boolean solution is `X` $= 0$, `Y` $= 0$, but that solution seems to come from nowhere.

### 5.5 Electrical Propagation in Cyclic Circuits

Let us now switch from the Newtonian Boolean model to the electrical vibration model. What happens if we implement `GoodCycle1`, `GoodCycle2`, and `Strange` with gates and wires? It is easy to see that `GoodCycle1` and `GoodCycle2` stabilize in bounded time for any input, exactly as if they were acyclic. On the contrary, `Strange` does not stabilize, since the `X` wire is not driven by a gate. Things become clearer by considering the following simpler `Hamlet` circuit:[4]

```
X = X or not X
```

Obviously, the only Boolean solution is `X` $= 1$ according to the law of excluded middle. Unfortunately, electrons never heard of excluded middle, and the electrical circuit does not stabilize for all gate and wire delays. For example, consider the delay assignment of Figure 14.5, where the bottom triangle represents an identity gate with delay 3 and where wires are delay-free (we are not precise about the delay model for lack of room, see [51, 52] for details). Then, assuming that all wires have initial value 0, the value of `X` oscillates forever between 0 and 1.

[4] To understand the name, interpret `X` as "to be."

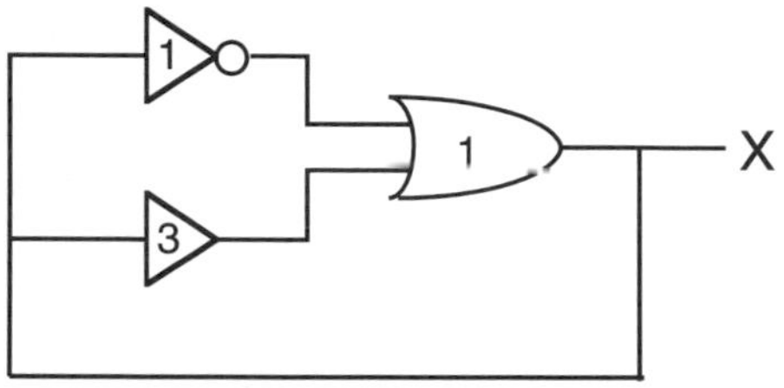


**Figure 14.5**
Delay assignment for unstable Hamlet.

## 5.6 The Constructive Boolean Logic

For `Hamlet`, the Boolean solution `X` $= 1$ is obtained by making a self-justifying guess and a proof by contradiction to reject `X` $= 0$. Electrons are unable of performing such fancy speculative reasoning, which we must therefore reject to model circuits. The solution is to use *constructive logic*, in which all values must be computed by explicit proofs. The constructive Boolean logic for combinational circuits is very simple. It can be presented in three equivalent ways: as a proof calculus, as a term rewriting system, or as the Scott semantics of Boolean equations.

The proof calculus deals with sequents of the form $\mathcal{C}, \mathcal{I} \vdash e \rightarrow b$, where $\mathcal{C}$ is the circuit presented as a system of equations, $\mathcal{I}$ is an input function that defines a Boolean value 0 or 1 for each input variable, $e$ is a Boolean expression written with the inputs and variables of $\mathcal{C}$, and $b$ is a Boolean value. The sequent is read "for the circuit $\mathcal{C}$, with input values $\mathcal{I}$, the expression $e$ evaluates to $b$." For expressions, we restrict ourselves to `not` and `or` operators; as usual, conjunction can be defined by $x$ `and` $y =$ `not` (`not` $x$ `or` `not` $y$). Let $\overline{0} = 1$ and $\overline{1} = 0$. The proof rules are as follows:

$$\frac{\mathcal{C}, \mathcal{I} \vdash e \rightarrow b}{\mathcal{C}, \mathcal{I} \vdash \texttt{not}\ e \rightarrow \overline{b}} \qquad (\textit{negation})$$

$$\frac{\mathcal{C}, \mathcal{I} \vdash e \rightarrow 1}{\mathcal{C}, \mathcal{I} \vdash e\ \texttt{or}\ e' \rightarrow 1} \qquad (\textit{left-or-1})$$

$$\frac{\mathcal{C}, \mathcal{I} \vdash e' \rightarrow 1}{\mathcal{C}, \mathcal{I} \vdash e\ \texttt{or}\ e' \rightarrow 1} \qquad (\textit{right-or-1})$$

$$\frac{\mathcal{C}, \mathcal{I} \vdash e \rightarrow 0 \quad \mathcal{C}, \mathcal{I} \vdash e' \rightarrow 0}{\mathcal{C}, \mathcal{I} \vdash e\ \texttt{or}\ e' \rightarrow 0} \qquad (\textit{or-0})$$

$$\frac{\mathcal{I}(\texttt{I}) = b}{\mathcal{C}, \mathcal{I} \vdash \texttt{I} \rightarrow b} \quad (input)$$

$$\frac{\texttt{X} = e \in \mathcal{C} \quad \mathcal{C}, \mathcal{I} \vdash e \rightarrow b}{\mathcal{C}, \mathcal{I} \vdash \texttt{X} \rightarrow b} \quad (variable)$$

A circuit $\mathcal{C}$ is said to be *constructive* for an input $\mathcal{I}$ if all variables can be evaluated to a Boolean value using the above rules. In this case, it is easy to see by induction on the length of the proof that the results form the unique solution of the Boolean system, establishing that constructiveness implies logical correctness and that the order of proof steps is immaterial.

It is easy to see that `GoodCycle1` and `GoodCycle2` are constructive for all inputs, while `Strange` and `Hamlet` are non-constructive. For `Hamlet`, there is no way to build a proof: a proof of $\texttt{X} \rightarrow b$ must end by rule (*variable*), but no proof of "`X or not X`" can be constructed without first proving $\texttt{X} \rightarrow b'$ for some $b'$.

In the term rewriting approach, the equations are oriented from right to left and the following constant-folding rules are added:

$\texttt{not}\ 0 \rightarrow 1$
$\texttt{not}\ 1 \rightarrow 0$
$1\ \texttt{or}\ x \rightarrow 1$
$x\ \texttt{or}\ 1 \rightarrow 1$
$0\ \texttt{or}\ 0 \rightarrow 0$

A circuit $\mathcal{C}$ is constructive for an input if each variable in $\mathcal{C}$ can be rewritten into a Boolean value using the input value assignment $\mathcal{I}$, the oriented equations and the above rules.

In the Scott denotational semantics view, variables are interpreted over the Scott Boolean domain $B_\perp = \{\perp, 0, 1\}$ and the Boolean operators are interpreted as the least monotonic functions that satisfy the above equations. Notice that `or` is interpreted by Plotkin's *parallel or*, a function that cannot be defined in software programming languages [44]. Then, for each input $\mathcal{I}$, the circuit $\mathcal{C}$ defines a monotonic function $\mathcal{C}_\mathcal{I}$ from variable values to variable values, and the circuit is said to be constructive if the value of any variable in the least fixpoint of $\mathcal{C}_\mathcal{I}$ has no $\perp$-component.

It is easy to see that the three definitions of constructiveness coincide. The fact that constructiveness is a variant of Scott semantics immediately implies compositionality. The main full abstraction theorem shows that constructive logic exactly matches electrical current propagation:

THEOREM 1 Let $\mathcal{C}$ be a circuit and $\mathcal{I}$ be an input event. Then $\mathcal{C}$ with input $\mathcal{I}$ electrically stabilizes in bounded time for all gate and wire delays if and only if it is constructive for $\mathcal{I}$.

In other words, a cyclic constructive circuit electrically stabilizes just as an acyclic one. It is natural to call constructive cyclic circuits combinational ones.

Notice that Theorem 1 is very much in the spirit of the Curry-Howard correspondence between computations and proofs [23]: an electrical computation performs a proof of a logical formula.

The proof of Theorem 1 is given by Shiple in [51]. For lack of room, we can only give a very brief proof sketch. The roots are in Brzozowski and Seger's analysis of asynchronous circuits [17]. Information propagation in the up-bounded inertial delay model is "asynchronous" because of gate and wire delays. Here, in the terminology of Section 3, asynchrony is vibrational rather than chemical since the delays are bounded from above. Given any circuit with delays, Brzozowski and Seger first show that, after a bounded time, only non-transient states of the circuit wires can be reached. Then, they present a technique called GWM (Global Multiple Winner) analysis that makes it possible to directly compute the reachable non-transient states, using a state transition system semantics that abstracts away delays. Next, they show that a ternary analysis using Scott's Booleans can be used to easily compute the least upper bound of the reachable non-transient states. Finally, Shiple shows that a circuit is constructive if and only if this least upper bound contains only the Booleans 0 and 1 identifying a unique stable state, i.e., if it stabilizes for all gate and wire delays.

Constructiveness is extended to sequential circuits by requiring the combinational part to be constructive for any input and any reachable state. There is no added difficulty, see [52] for details. The set of legal inputs can also be restricted using input relations, see [8, 7]. In that case, constructiveness is required only for the legal inputs.

Constructiveness for combinational and sequential circuits is decidable. The BDD-based algorithms presented in [36, 52] perform an efficient fixpoint computation in a symbolic version of Scott's semantics. They synthesize the set of inputs that make a circuit constructive and yield an equivalent acyclic version that may be better for practical implementation purposes since conventional synthesis tools do not handle cycles.

## 5.7 The Constructive Semantics of Esterel

The constructive semantics of Esterel lifts the basic constructiveness idea to the imperative constructs. The idea is to control the logical behavioral rules by means of two auxiliary constructive predicates that determine for each input what a program *must* do or *cannot* do in terms of control and signal propagation. In the reactive system terminology, proof steps are called microsteps and they are used to define fine-grain operational semantics. See [7] for the rules. As for circuits, the constructive semantics can be presented in an equivalent denotational form that is directly synchronous and compositional. The operational semantics is adequate for studying the execution of a reaction, while the denotational semantics directly defines the input/output function of a module, abstracting away all possible microstep orderings.

With respect to the circuit translation, the main result is as follows:

THEOREM 2 An Esterel program is constructive for an input if and only if the translated circuit is.

We are currently building a mechanically checked proof of that theorem using the COQ system [32].

Combining Theorem 1 and Theorem 2, we obtain the final result that an Esterel program is constructive if its circuit electrically stabilizes for all gate and wire delays. This final result shows that the constructive semantics is not only mathematical but also *physical*, which yields the most solid foundations to the language we can think of.

## 6 Implementation

Synchronous languages can be implemented on hardware or software centralized or distributed platforms. For simplicity, we concentrate on centralized software or hardware implementations. The reader interested in distributed implementation can refer to [18].

### 6.1 Control vs. Data

In imperative languages such as Esterel, the distinction between control and data is direct at source code level, see for instance the protocol in Section 4.2.3. A major property of Esterel is that control is *finite-state*. The implementation basically consists of building a deterministic control finite-state machine that schedules data-handling actions.

In data-flow languages, one can use the same implementation scheme by establishing a distinction between two kind of variables: actual data variables, to be computed at run-time, and control variables to be handled at compile-time using some kind of partial evaluation. Control variables are most often Boolean variables that express a property of the program state, e.g., some status is on or off; by extension, they can range over any finite set of values.

The control finite-state machine can be implemented in many different ways in software or hardware, with a variety of time-space tradeoffs. This gives us lots of freedom to meet application-dependent performance constraints. In the sequel, we detail the two main implementations, explicit automata and Boolean circuits, and we briefly discuss optimization issues. Implementation of data handling is comparatively easy provided one carefully analyzes the relationship between control dependencies and data dependencies.

### 6.2 Implementation by Explicit Automata

An explicit control automaton is given by a set of states and a transition from each state, which is a tree with unary or binary nodes. A unary node triggers a data action, a binary node is either an input signal presence test or a data test. The leaves of the transition are states. Reaction from a state follows the transition, executing the actions and performing the tests on the way, until reaching the state leaf from which the next reaction will start.

To compute the control automaton associated with an Esterel program, we adapt Brzozowski's *residual algorithm* originally introduced to translate regular expressions into automata [16, 12]. Given a program body $p$, we formally compute all derivatives $p'$ for all input event sequences as specified by the formal semantics, but leaving data values uninterpreted. Then, we construct a finite automaton having the derivatives as states. That automaton is often close to minimal, for yet largely unknown reasons. Automata can also be constructed from data-flow programs using partial evaluation techniques.

The main advantage of automata is speed. Executing a transition is very fast and independent of program size. Since executing the data actions at run-time is necessary for any implementation, automata are close to time-optimal amongst centralized implementations. Local signals used for internal communication between statements disappear in the automaton, exactly as intermediate non-terminals disappear in parser generation. Therefore, local signals are truly zero-delay at run-time. Further optimizations concerning the orders of tests in transitions are analyzed in [19].

The drawback of automata is of course size. Only relatively small applications can be handled. Automata are usually appropriate for protocols, drivers, or man-machine interface systems. Large process-control applications most often lead to size explosion.

### 6.3 Implementation Using Sequential Boolean Circuits

Sequential circuits were introduced in Section 3.1. Since $n$ Boolean registers can hold $2^n$ states, a sequential circuit can denote an exponentially bigger automaton, which makes the state space explosion vanish. Direct implementation of acyclic sequential circuits in hardware is performed by sequential logic synthesis systems [50]. Software implementation in the cycle-based model of Section 3.2 is easy: sort the equations according to the variable dependency relation, print the equations as C assignments in order, then print the assignments of new values to the registers. Other more efficient software implementations are discussed in [39].

The translation of a data-flow program into a synchronous Boolean circuit is a simple process. Roughly, for Lustre, each Boolean `pre` delay operator generates a register, and one additional register is generated for all initializations by the `->` operator. The translation of an Esterel program into a sequential circuit was already mentioned in Section 5.4. The circuit's worst-case size is the square of that of the source program, but the squaring factor rarely shows up in practice. The translation can yield cyclic circuits, which are analyzed for constructiveness and made acyclic using algorithms presented in [36, 52].

### 6.4 Circuit Optimization

The direct translation of high-level programs into circuits usually yields rather fat circuits that must be optimized before actual implementation. Fortunately, circuit optimization has been extensively studied in the hardware community. For Esterel, we borrowed many existing algorithms and we also developed specific algorithms that give good practical results. Optimization can be split into two subproblems: combinational optimization, and sequential optimization

In combinational optimization, the game is as follows: given a network of combinational gates, build another network optimized with respect to size or speed criteria. There is a wide variety of academic and industrial tools for that purpose, see [14]. In the previously described software implementation of circuits, the reaction time is roughly proportional to the number of equations and operators. Therefore, size optimization is the issue even for speed. Hardware-directed tools can be used as well, provided one pretends to optimize the "area of silicon."

The sequential optimization problem can also be called the *state assignment problem*. A sequential circuit obviously denotes a finite automaton, the states of which are the register Boolean configurations reachable from the initial state by some input sequence. The mapping from states to configurations is called the state assignment. Given a circuit, the goal is to denote the same automaton using more efficient state assignments and fewer registers.

If the automaton has $n$ states, it is clearly sufficient to use $log(n)$ registers. However, when changing the state assignment, one must change the combinational circuit accordingly. In the worst case, the new combinational size can be $2^{log(n)} = n$, which means that reducing the number of registers can make the combinational logic explode. The problem of finding the best $log(n)$ assignment is NP-complete and no good heuristics scale up for it. Furthermore, in many cases, adding a few registers can make the combinational logic much smaller. Therefore, the real problem is to find a good register / combinational logic tradeoff.

An Esterel program directly specifies such a tradeoff: a register is generated by each source Esterel temporal statement, and the combinational logic is generated by the other statements. Achieving *Write Things Once* ensures a good register assignment, which means that elegant programs have good implementation. However, there is often some unessential redundancy between the registers in the direct translation. In [48, 49], we present algorithms that reduce the number of registers without significantly changing the encoding, hence without making the logic explode.

For a simple example, consider the `ABRO` program of Section 4.2. Four registers are allocated: a boot register $b$, a register $A$ for "`await A`," a register $b$ for "`await B`," and a register $R$ for "`each R`." The boot register $b$ has initial value 0 and then value 1 at all cycles. The register $A$ (resp. $B$) has value 1 while waiting for `A` (resp. `B`), and the register $R$ has value 0 initially and 1 while waiting for $R$. Using BDD-based reachable states computation, one finds that $R$ is always 1 except at start time, which implies $R = b$. Therefore, one can remove $R$ and replace its output by that of $b$, without changing the logic. Combinational optimization then yields an optimal circuit. See [48] for more elaborate examples.

## 7 Verification

Since reactive software is often used for safety-critical applications, verification of program properties is fundamental. Here again, we directly benefit from work done in other areas such as process calculi and hardware circuit verification [34, 13, 20]. We are interested in safety properties of the kind "wrong things never happen" and in bounded-response properties of the kind "something useful will happen before some time" that are in fact safety properties. Liveness properties of the kind "something useful will happen some day" are usually much less important for reactive systems.

Many useful properties are data-insensitive and can be proved or disproved using only the finite-state control structure of a program. We present the two techniques we use most often for such pure control properties, bisimulation reduction and verification using observers. As a running example, we use a lift controller and we show how to verify that the lift cannot travel with the door open. Data-dependent properties are analyzed in [1, 25]. They are usually much harder and will not be considered here.

### 7.1 Bisimulation Reduction

Bisimulation has been originally introduced by David Park and Robin Milner to define equivalence between process calculi terms [41]. The variant we use here is *weak bisimulation.*

Consider the lift controller. For the door, there is an output signal `Open` sent by the controller to open the door and an input signal sent by a door sensor when the door is closed. For lift motion, there is an output signal `Start` sent by the controller to start the engine and an input signal `Stopped` sent by a sensor when the lift is stopped. There are of course many other signals such as call buttons, bells, and whistles, which are not relevant to the property we want to prove.

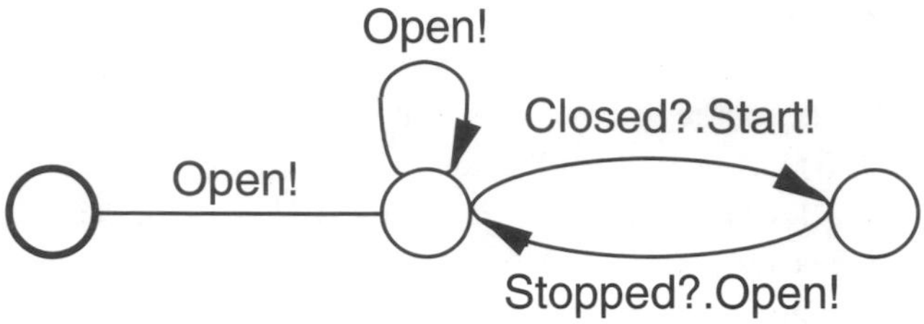


**Figure 14.6**
Bisimulation Reduction.

The first step is to erase the useless signals and to keep only the four relevant signals `Open`, `Closed`, `Start`, and `Stopped`. If none of these signals appears on a transition, the transition is called a silent transition $\tau$ as in CCS [41]. After this erasure process, the automaton has the same number of states, the same number of transitions, and fewer transition labels. It can also be non-deterministic.

The second verification step is to perform *weak bisimulation reduction*, which consists of computing the smallest weakly bisimilar transition system. This is a very intuitive operation that can be explained to any user without mathematics: the reduct has the *same behavior* w.r.t. the observed signals, no spurious path is introduced, and no path disappears. Figure 14.6 shows the result for the lift controller. On such a three-state automaton, the property we want to verify is immediate.

Bisimulation reduction is performed by various tools. For Esterel, we mostly use the FcTools system described in [13]. The implementation is very efficient for explicit automata, but as yet much less efficient for sequential circuits since bisimulation is expensive to compute with BDDs.

## 7.2 Verification by Observers

Verification by observers is probably a folk technique. It has been made systematic for synchronous languages by Halbwachs *et al.* [28]. A similar technique called *testing* has been extensively studied by M. Hennessy for process calculi [31].

The idea is described in Figure 14.7. The safety property to be verified for a program $P$ is expressed as another reactive program called the *observer* $O$, which is put in synchronous parallel with $P$. The observer takes as inputs the inputs and outputs of $P$. Its only output is a signal called `BUG`. Since not all input sequences may be meaningful for $P$, another reactive program $E$ called the *environment* can be put in synchronous parallel with $P$ and $O$ to only generate the useful input sequences. The outputs of $E$ are the inputs of $P$, and the inputs of $E$ are arbitrary signals acting as oracles. Notice that the synchronous observer $O$ is purely passive: it listens to $P$ without interfering with it, unlike in asynchronous formalisms

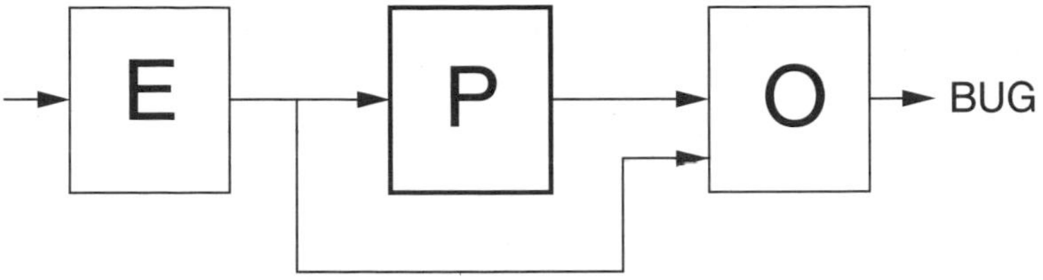


**Figure 14.7**
Verification by observers.

where the observer interacts with the observed process and can restrict its behavior, which is quite unnatural for verification purposes.

The verification consists of checking that the signal `BUG` is never emitted by the triple $E \mid\mid P \mid\mid O$ for any input sequence of $E$. This can be done using standard reachability analysis techniques for explicitly or implicitly encoded finite-state machines [21, 33]. If the property is false, one can build counter-examples, i.e., sequences of useful inputs of $P$ that violate the property.

Any synchronous language can be used to program the observer $O$ and the environment $E$. For the lift example, we can write the observer in Esterel as follows:

```
Module Doors:
input Start, Open, Closed;
output BUG;
loop
   await Open;
   abort
      await Start;
      emit BUG
   when Closed
end loop
```

Temporal logic is also a well-known way of expressing properties [37]. Lustre can easily encode a temporal logic of the past, sufficient for most safety properties [28]. The TempEst system described in [33] allows the user to specify the observer as a temporal logic property, which is compiled into an Esterel program.

## 8 Conclusion

In this overview paper, we have tried to cover all aspects of synchronous programming, from theory to implementation. The kernel is of course the synchronous model of deterministic concurrency. Languages were grouped in two categories: data-flow and imperative. Smoothly unifying both styles is one of the important remaining challenges (we cannot explain here why this is non-trivial). The semantics are now well-understood, and major progress has been made recently in understanding causality issues through a somewhat unexpected use of constructive logic. Efficient implementation uses techniques from automata theory and hardware. Program verification is based on process calculi and finite-state machine verification techniques.

For all the synchronous languages designers, what really matters is the *use* of the languages and compilers. A lot of emphasis has been put on developing techniques and tools that scale to real-size programs. We hope that the synchronous tools will make their users happy, both in academia and in industry, and that application will foster new ideas and new research directions.

## References

[1] R. Alur and D.L. Dill. A theory of timed automata. *Theoretical Computer Science*, 126:183–235, 1994.

[2] C. André. Representation and analysis of reactive behaviors: A synchronous approach. In *Proc. CESA'96, Lille, France*, July 1996.

[3] D. Austry and G. Boudol. Algèbre de processus et synchronisations. *Theoretical Computer Science*, 30(1): 91–131, 1984.

[4] G. Berry. Real-time programming: General purpose or special-purpose languages. In G. Ritter, editor, *Information Processing 89*, pages 11–17. Elsevier Science Publishers B.V. (North Holland), 1989.

[5] G. Berry. Esterel on hardware. *Philosophical Transactions Royal Society of London A*, 339:87–104, 1992.

[6] G. Berry. Preemption and concurrency. In *Proc. FSTTCS 93*, Lecture Notes in Computer Science 761, pages 72–93. Springer-Verlag, 1993.

[7] G. Berry. *The Constructive Semantics of Esterel*. Draft book, available at http://www.inria.fr/meije/esterel, 1996.

[8] G. Berry. *The Esterel Language Primer*. Draft book, available at http://www.inria.fr/meije/esterel, 1996.

[9] G. Berry and G. Boudol. The chemical abstract machine. *Theoretical Computer Science*, 96:217–248, 1992.

[10] G. Berry and G. Gonthier. The Esterel synchronous programming language: Design, semantics, implementation. *Science Of Computer Programming*, 19(2):87–152, 1992.

[11] G. Berry, S. Moisan, and J-P. Rigault. Esterel: Towards a synchronous and semantically sound high-level language for real-time applications. In *Proc. IEEE Real-Time Systems Symposium, Arlington, Virginia, IEEE Catalog 83CH1941-4*, pages 30–40, 1983.

[12] G. Berry and R. Sethi. From regular expressions to deterministic automata. *Theoretical Computer Science*, 48:117–126, 1986.

[13] A. Bouali, A. Ressouche, V. Roy, and R. de Simone. The fc2tools set. In *AMAST'96*, volume 1101 of *LNCS*, Munich, Germany, 1996.

[14] R.K. Brayton, G.D. Hachtel, and A.L. Sangiovanni-Vincentelli. Multilevel Logic Synthesis. *Proceedings of the IEEE*, 78(2):264–300, February 1990.

[15] R.E. Bryant. Symbolic Boolean Manipulation with Ordered Binary-Decision Diagrams. *ACM Computing Surveys*, 24(3):293–318, September 1992.

[16] J. Brzozowski. Derivatives of regular expressions. *Journal of the ACM*, 11(4), 1964.

[17] J. Brzozowski and C.-J. Seger. *Asynchronous Circuits*. Springer-Verlag, 1996.

[18] P. Caspi and A. Girault. Distributing reactive systems. In *Proc. Intnl. Conf. on Parallel and Distributed Computing Systems, Las Vegas*, 1994.

[19] C. Castelluccia, W. Dabbous, and S. O'Malley. Generating efficient protocol code from an abstract specification. In *Proc. ACM SIGCOMM, Stanford*, 1996.

[20] R. Cleaveland, J. Parrow, and B. Steffen. The concurrency workbench: A semantics based tool for the verification of concurrent systems. *ACM Transactions on Programming Languages and Systems*, 1(15):36–72, 1993.

[21] O. Coudert, C. Berthet, and J. C. Madre. Verification of Sequential Machines Based on Symbolic Execution. In *Proceedings of the Workshop on Automatic Verification Methods for Finite State Systems*, Grenoble, France, 1989.

[22] G. Cousineau. An algebraic definition for control structures. *Theoretical Computer Science*, 12:175–192, 1980.

[23] J.-Y. Girard, Yves Lafont, and Paul Taylor. *Proofs and Types*. Cambridge Univerity Press, 1989.

[24] P. Le Guernic, M. Le Borgne, T. Gauthier, and C. Le Maire. Programming real time applications with Signal. *Another Look at Real Time Programming, Proceedings of the IEEE, Special Issue*, Sept. 1991.

[25] N. Halbwachs. Delay analysis in synchronous programs. In *Proc. CAV'93*, pages 333–346, 1993.

[26] N. Halbwachs. *Synchronous Programming of Reactive Systems*. Kluwer, 1993.

[27] N. Halbwachs, P. Caspi, and D. Pilaud. The synchronous dataflow programming language Lustre. *Another Look at Real Time Programming, Proceedings of the IEEE, Special Issue*, Sept. 1991.

[28] N. Halbwachs, F. Lagnier, and P. Raymond. Synchronous observers and the verification of reactive systems. In *Proc. AMAST'93*, june 1993.

[29] N. Halbwachs and F. Maraninchi. On the symbolic analysis of combinational loops in circuits and synchronous programs. In *Euromicro'95*, Como (Italy), September 1995.

[30] D. Harel. Statecharts: a visual approach to complex systems. *Science of Computer Programming*, 8:231–274, 1987.

[31] M. Hennessy. *Algebraic Theory of Processes*. MIT Press, Cambridge, Massachusetts, 1988.

[32] Gérard Huet, Gilles Kahn, and Christine Paulin-Mohring. The Coq proof assistant : A tutorial : Version 6.1. Technical Report RT-204, INRIA, 1997.

[33] L. Jategaonkar Jagadeesan, C. Puchol, and J. E. Von Olnhausen. Safety property verification of Esterel programs and applications to telecommunications software. In *Proc. CAV'95, LNCS*. Springer-Verlag, July 1995.

[34] R.P. Kurshan. *Computer-Aided Verification of Coordinating Processes: The Automata-Theoretic Approach*. Princeton U. Press, Princeton, New Jersey, USA, 1995.

[35] P.J. Landin. The next 700 programming languages. *Comm. ACM*, 9:157–166, 1966.

[36] S. Malik. Analysis of cyclic combinational circuits. *IEEE Trans. Computer–Aided Design*, 13(7):950–956, 1994.

[37] Z. Manna and A. Pnueli. *The Temporal Logic of Reactive and Concurrent Systems: Specification*. Springer-Verlag, 1992.

[38] F. Maraninchi. The Argos language: graphical representation of automata and description of reactive systems. In *International Conference on Visual Languages, Kobe, Japan*, 1991.

[39] P.C. McGeer, K.L. Mcmillan, A. Saldanha, A. Sangiovanni-Vincentelli, and P. Scaglia. Fast discrete function evaluation using decision diagrams. In *Proc. International Conf. on Computer-Aided Design (ICCAD)*, 1995.

[40] R. Milner. Calculi for synchrony and asynchrony. *Theoretical Computer Science*, 25:267–310, 1983.

[41] R. Milner. *Communication and Concurrency*. Prentice-Hall International, Englewood Cliffs, 1989.

[42] R. Milner, M. Tofte, and R. Harper. *The definition of Standard ML*. MIT Press, 1991.

[43] Robin Milner. Functions as processes. *Journal of Mathematical Structures in Computer Science*, 2(2):119–141, 1992.

[44] G. Plotkin. LCF considered as a programming language. *Theoretical Computer Science*, 5(3):452–488, september 1976.

[45] G. Plotkin. A structural approach to operational semantics. Technical Report report DAIMI FN-19, University of Aarhus, 1981.

[46] V. A. Saraswat, R. Jagadeesan, and V. Gupta. Foundations of timed concurrent constrained programming. In S. Abramsky, editor, *Proc. 9th Ann. IEEE Symp. on Logic in Computer Science*. IEEE Computer Press, 1994.

[47] V. A. Saraswat, R. Jagadeesan, and V. Gupta. Default timed concurrent constraint programming. In *Proc. POPL'95, San Francisco, USA*, pages 272–285, 1995.

[48] E. Sentovich, H. Toma, and G. Berry. Latch optimization in circuits generated from high-level descriptions. In *Proc. ICCAD'96*, 1996.

[49] E. Sentovich, H. Toma, and G. Berry. Efficient latch optimization using exclusive sets. In *Proc. DAC'97, Anaheim*, 1997.

[50] E.M. Sentovich, K.J. Singh, C. Moon, H. Savoj, R.K. Brayton, and A Sangiovanni-Vincentelli. Sequential circuits design using synthesis and optimization. In *Proc. ICCD'92*, pages 328–333, 1992.

[51] T. Shiple. *Formal Analysis of Cyclic Circuits*. PhD thesis, University of California at Berkeley, 1996.

[52] T. Shiple, G. Berry, and H. Touati. Constructive analysis of cyclic circuits. In *Proc. International Design and Test Conference ITDC 96, Paris, France*, 1996.

[53] H. Touati and G. Berry. Optimized controller synthesis using Esterel. In *Proc. International Workshop on Logic Synthesis IWLS'93, Lake Tahoe*, 1993.

[54] J. Vuillemin. On circuits and numbers. *IEEE Transactions on Computers*, 43:8:868:27–79, 1994.

# 15 Pict: A Programming Language Based on the Pi-Calculus

**Benjamin C. Pierce and David N. Turner**

## 1 Introduction

Milner, Parrow, and Walker's $\pi$-calculus [MPW92, Mil91] generalizes the channel-based communication of CCS and its relatives by allowing channels to be passed as data along other channels. This extension introduces an element of *mobility*, enabling the specification and verification of concurrent systems with dynamically evolving communication topologies. Channel mobility leads to a surprising increase in expressive power, yielding a calculus capable of describing a wide variety of high-level concurrent features while retaining a simple semantics and tractable algebraic theory.

A similar combination of simplicity and expressiveness has made the $\lambda$-calculus both a popular object of theoretical investigation and an attractive basis for sequential programming language design. By analogy, one may wonder what kind of high-level programming language can be constructed from the $\pi$-calculus.

$$\frac{\text{Lisp, ML, Haskell, } \ldots}{\lambda\text{-calculus}} = \frac{?}{\pi\text{-calculus}}$$

A number of programming language designs have combined $\pi$-calculus-like communication with a functional core language, but none have gone so far as to take communication as the sole mechanism of computation. The primary motivation of the Pict project, begun at the University of Edinburgh in 1992, was to design and implement a high-level concurrent language purely in terms of the $\pi$-calculus primitives [PT97, Pie97].

Compiling a language based solely on communicating processes raises challenging code generation problems. To achieve acceptable performance for realistic applications, a $\pi$-calculus compiler must implement process creation, context switching, and communication on channels extremely efficiently, since these operations are the fundamental computational mechanism of the $\pi$-calculus and are therefore, for example, at least as pervasive as function calls in a functional language.

Another goal of the Pict project was to explore the practical applicability of our earlier theoretical work on type systems for the $\pi$-calculus [PS93, Tur96] and on $\lambda$-calculus type systems with subtyping [PT94, HP95, PS97b]. In particular, in [PT94] we proposed a powerful combination of subtyping and polymorphism as a basis for statically typed object-oriented programming in functional languages; equipping Pict with a similar type system provides a testbed for experiments with statically typed concurrent objects. Using such a powerful type system raises other important issues such as completeness of typechecking algorithms, efficiency of typechecking, and type inference.

The questions motivating the Pict project, then, can be summarized as follows: (1) What is it like to program in the $\pi$-calculus? What kind of high-level language can be built on it? (2) What kinds of concurrent objects arise in this setting? (3) Can the $\pi$-calculus be implemented efficiently? (4) Can we design a practical type system for the $\pi$-calculus combining subtyping and higher-order polymorphism?

In this paper, we offer our responses to these questions (concentrating on (1) and (4), since (2) has been addressed in detail in [PT95] and (3) in [Tur96]), and survey the current state of the Pict language. Section 2 defines the syntax and operational semantics of the core language and discusses some points where it differs from the theoretical $\pi$-calculus of Milner, Parrow, and Walker. Section 3 presents a type system for the core language, incorporating channel types, subtyping, record types, higher-order polymorphism, and simple recursive types. Section 4 constructs the full Pict language by means of translations into the core. Section 5 offers concluding remarks and directions for further research.

We shall not attempt to give a complete or definitive description of Pict here, since the language is experimental and subject to frequent change. (The formal Pict Language Definition [PT97] is kept up to date with the compiler.) Instead, our aim is to overview the important design decisions and to extract some of the lessons we learned from designing, implementing, and using Pict.

## 2 The Core Language

We now proceed to a formal definition of the syntax and semantics of the core language: an asynchronous, choice-free fragment of the $\pi$-calculus enriched with records and pattern matching.

### 2.1 The Pi-Calculus

To aid comparison, we begin with a brief review of the pure $\pi$-calculus of Milner, Parrow, and Walker. More details can be found in the original $\pi$-calculus papers [MPW92] and in Milner's tutorial [Mil91].

The computational world modeled by the $\pi$-calculus contains just two kinds of entities: processes and channels. Processes (sometimes called agents) are the active components of a system; they interact by synchronous rendezvous on channels, also called names or ports. When two processes synchronize, they exchange a single data value, which is itself a channel. The output process $\bar{x}y \cdot e_1$ sends $y$ along $x$ and then, after the output has completed, continues as $e_1$. Conversely, the input process $x(z) \cdot e_2$ waits until a value is received along $x$, substitutes it for the bound variable $z$, and continues as $e_2$. The parallel composition of these processes, written $\bar{x}y \cdot e_1 \mid x(z) \cdot e_2$, may thus synchronize on $x$, yielding the derivative $e_1 \mid \{z \mapsto y\}e_2$.

Fresh channels are introduced by the restriction operator $\nu$. The expression $(\nu x)e$ creates a fresh channel $x$ with lexical scope $e$. For example, writing $(\nu x)\ (\bar{x}y \cdot e_1 \mid x(z) \cdot e_2)$ localizes the channel $x$, ensuring that no other process can interfere with communication on $x$.

The expression $e_1 + e_2$ denotes an external choice between $e_1$ and $e_2$: either $e_1$ is allowed to proceed and $e_2$ is discarded, or vice versa. For example, the process $\bar{x}y \cdot e_1 \mid (x(z) \cdot e_2 + x(w) \cdot e_3)$ can reduce either to $e_1 \mid \{z \mapsto y\}e_2$ or to $e_1 \mid \{w \mapsto y\}e_3$. The nullary choice, written $\mathbf{0}$, is inert.

Infinite behavior in $\pi$-calculus is introduced by the replication operator $!e$, which informally denotes an arbitrary number of copies of $e$ running in parallel. This operator replaces the equivalent, but more complex, mechanism of mutually-recursive process definitions.

Some variants of the $\pi$-calculus include a matching operator $[x = y]e$, which allows $e$ to proceed if $x$ and $y$ are the same channel.

### 2.2 Core Language Design Issues

The core language of Pict differs from the $\pi$-calculus by some trivial extensions and some more important restrictions.

**2.2.1 Primitive Values** Like most high-level programming languages, Pict provides special syntax for a few built-in types: booleans, characters, strings, and integers. Adding such syntax does not change the fundamental character of the language at all, since all these types of data can easily be encoded as processes [Mil91]. To give the compiler maximum freedom to implement primitive values efficiently, the types `Bool`, `Char`, `String`, and `Int` are *abstract*: they reveal nothing about how values of these types are represented. Instead, built-in channels are provided for performing common operations. For example, `12` is a built-in value of type `Int` and the addition operation is represented as a built-in channel `+`. To add two numbers, we send them along the channel `+` together with a result channel `r` and then listen on `r` for the result of the calculation. Built-in channels are also provided for interacting with the environment; for example, the channel `print` is used to send strings to the standard output stream. The standard libraries provide built-in channels giving access to external libraries written in C and low-level operating system facilities such as file I/O, sockets, and UNIX signal handling.

**2.2.2 Records and Pattern Matching** A key choice in the design of Pict has been to define as much of the language as possible in terms of encodings. Section 4 describes many derived forms, including, for example, function abstraction and application. This style of definition means that we need only give operational semantics and typing rules for the core language; the rules for functions arise from the translation.

The pure $\pi$-calculus can easily encode "polyadic" communication, in which several channels are exchanged during a single communication [Mil91]. Similar encodings can be used for data structures such as records. However, such encodings do not always give rise to useful derived typing rules. In particular, when we started the Pict design, there were no type systems for the pure, monadic $\pi$-calculus (although more recent work on linear types [KPT96] may lead to such type systems). Therefore, we begin from a slightly more structured core language, which admits a simple, structural type system; in the same way, typed functional languages such as ML and Haskell are typically based on a $\lambda$-calculus extended with basic data constructors.

**2.2.3 Asynchrony** The fundamental communication primitive in $\pi$-calculus and most of its relatives is *synchronous rendezvous*, in which both sender and receiver are blocked until the communication occurs. For example, in the $\pi$-calculus expression $\bar{x}y \cdot e_1 \mid x(z) \cdot e_2$, the expression $e_1$ cannot proceed until the output on $x$ has completed; similarly, the expression $e_2$ cannot proceed until a value $z$ has been received along $x$.

The fact that output is synchronous enables a sending process to tell when its message has been received by another process. Unfortunately, depending on this information precludes a number of useful programming idioms involving buffering, delegation, and reordering of requests. For example, if a client and a server are sometimes run on separate machines, we may need to add a surrogate server process on the client's machine that forwards requests to the server's machine. Now a synchronization on the client's request channel indicates only that the surrogate, not the server, has received the request.

We allow only asynchronous output in Pict; this amounts to restricting the "continuation" of each output expression to the null process. The programmer must send an explicit acknowledgement or result to inform the client that its request has been processed, thereby eliminating any possible sensitivity to buffering or reordering of requests.

The investigation of asynchronous process calculi was initiated by Honda, Tokoro, and Yoshida [HT91, HY94] and Boudol [Bou92]. Amadio, Castellani, and Sangiorgi [ACS96] have more recently shown how several technical aspects of observational equivalence are simplified in the asynchronous case.

**2.2.4 No Choice** Early versions of the $\pi$-calculus used a completely unrestricted choice operator: in the expression $e_1 + e_2$, the branches $e_1$ and $e_2$ could be arbitrary processes. More recent presentations, for example [Mil91], use a more constrained operator called *guarded choice*, where $e_1$ and $e_2$ must be input expressions, output expressions, or choice expressions. Guarded choice is easier to formalize (especially in the context of a reduction semantics like the one we use here) and appears to capture all cases of practical interest.

In an asynchronous language, guarded choice should be restricted still further, since an asynchronous output in a choice is sensitive to buffering: $(\bar{w}y + e)$ can only discard $e$ if a process reads from $w$, while $(\bar{x}y + e) \mid x(z) \cdot \bar{w}z$ can reduce spontaneously to $\bar{w}y$.

In Pict we go a step further, dropping the choice operator altogether. This simplifies both formal semantics and implementation, and has little effect on the expressiveness of the language, since input-only choice is easy to implement as a library module [PT95, NP96]. (This has some cost in syntactic convenience, and some benefit in flexibility. Our library actually implements a subset of Reppy's *events* [Rep91], allowing the branches of a choice to be manipulated as data.) In fact, most Pict programs use simpler mechanisms such as locks and semaphores (cf. Section 4.6) for basic synchronisation tasks. For controlling concurrent execution of methods in objects, we have proposed a more specialized operator called *replicated* or *iterated choice* [PT95].

**2.2.5 Replicated Input, No Matching** The Pict core language makes two further simplifications of the pure $\pi$-calculus. First, we restrict replication to replicated input expressions. This variant has the same formal power as full replication, but has a simpler semantics and is closer to a realistic implementation. Second, we omit the matching operator, since its main functions (encoding conditional expressions and tracking side-conditions in axiomatizations of behavioral equivalences) are either subsumed by other features in Pict or irrelevant in the context of programming.

**2.2.6 Ascii Notation** Besides the more substantive changes discussed above, Pict substitutes a slightly more verbose ascii concrete syntax for the mathematical $\pi$-calculus notation:

| $\pi$-calculus | Pict | |
|---|---|---|
| $\bar{x}y \cdot \mathbf{0}$ | `x!y` | asynchronous output |
| $x(y) \cdot e$ | `x?y = e` | input prefix |
| $e_1 \mid e_2$ | `(e1 | e2)` | parallel composition |
| $(\nu x)e$ | `(new x e)` | channel creation |
| $!x(y) \cdot e$ | `x?*y = e` | replicated input |

## 2.3 Core Language Syntax

We now define the Pict core language syntax. Further details, such as lexical analysis rules, can be found in the Pict language definition [PT97]. The possible forms of each production are listed on successive lines. Keywords are set in typewriter font. An expression of the form $X \ldots X$ denotes a list of zero or more occurrences of $X$. The expression $\langle empty \rangle$ denotes an empty production.

The entities that can be communicated on channels are called *values*. They include variables, records of values, package values, rectype values, and constants.

| | | |
|---|---|---|
| *Val* | = *Id* | Variable |
| | [ *Label Val* . . . *Label Val* ] | Record |
| | { *Type* } *Val* | Polymorphic package |
| | ( rec : T *Val* ) | Rectype value |
| | *String* | String constant |
| | *Char* | Character constant |
| | *Int* | Integer constant |
| | *Bool* | Boolean constant |

| | | |
|---|---|---|
| *Label* | = ⟨*empty*⟩ | Anonymous label |
| | *Id* = | Explicit label |

There are no channel constants, only variables ranging over channels (note, however, that variables can range over any kind of value, not just channels). Record values generalise tuple values, since the labels in a record are optional.

Rectype values help the typechecker determine the types of recursive data structures; package values are part of the mechanism used to implement polymorphism in Pict. We defer the description of these to Sections 3.2 and 3.5.

Values can be decomposed by means of *patterns*. A variable pattern `x:T` binds the variable `x`. A package pattern `{X<T}p` binds the type variable `X` plus whatever variables are bound in `p`. A layered pattern `x:T@p` binds the variable `x` plus whatever variables are bound in `p`. All the variables bound by a pattern must be pairwise distinct.

| | | |
|---|---|---|
| *Pat* | = *Id* : *Type* | Variable pattern |
| | _ : *Type* | Wildcard pattern |
| | *Id* : *Type* @ *Pat* | Layered pattern |
| | [ *Label Pat* ... *Label Pat* ] | Record pattern |
| | { *Id* < *Type* } *Pat* | Package pattern |
| | ( rec : T *Pat* ) | Rectype pattern |

Note that all bound variables (and wildcards) are explicitly typed. In practice, many of these type annotations can be inferred automatically by the Pict compiler (cf. Section 3.7). A layered pattern can be used to bind a variable to a value at the same time as decomposing the value. For example, matching the pattern `x@[y z]` against the value `[33 true]` binds `x` to `[33 true]`, `y` to `33`, and `z` to `true`. We defer the description of rectype and package patterns to Sections 3.2 and 3.5.

A process prefixed by a pattern is called an *abstraction*. Introducing a separate syntactic class of abstractions leaves room for later expansion. We make use of this in the full language to allow higher-order functions to appear wherever process abstractions are allowed (cf. Section 4.5).

| | |
|---|---|
| *Abs* = *Pat* = *Proc* | Process abstraction |

In an abstraction `p = e`, variable occurrences in `p` are binders with scope `e`.

The basic forms of processes are output atoms, input prefixes, parallel compositions, processes prefixed by declarations, and conditional processes.

| | | |
|---|---|---|
| *Proc* = | *Val* `!` *Val* | Output atom |
| | *Val* `?` *Abs* | Input prefix |
| | *Val* `?*` *Abs* | Replicated input prefix |
| | `(` *Proc* `|` *Proc* `)` | Parallel composition |
| | `(` *Dec* *Proc* `)` | Local declaration |
| | `if` *Val* `then` *Proc* `else` *Proc* | Conditional |

Arbitrary values must be allowed to the left of `!` and `?` so that substitution is a total operation (cf. Section 2.6). Our type system guarantees that these values can only evaluate to channel names.

Finally, a `new` declaration introduces a new channel. Again, we make declarations a separate syntactic category to leave room for growth.

| | |
|---|---|
| *Dec* = `new` *Id* : *Type* | Channel creation |

The expression `(new x:T e)` binds `x` with scope `e`. Note that new channels are always annotated with explicit types.

## 2.4 Example

We now present some simple examples of Pict core language programs. In Section 3.2 we show how to annotate the examples with appropriate explicit type information. (Section 4.6 uses the additional features of the full language to express these examples much more concisely!)

The following process implements a "cons-cell server" that, when sent a triple `[hd tl r]`, constructs a process encoding a cons cell (with head `hd` and tail `tl`) and returns the address of the cons cell along the result channel `r`.

```
cons?*[hd tl r] = (new l (r!l | l?*[n c] = c![hd tl]))
```

Upon receiving a triple [hd tl r], we first create a new channel l (l can be thought of as the location of the cons cell). Then, in parallel, we return l along the result channel r and run the process l?*[n c] = c![hd tl]. This process responds to messages sent along l by sending hd and tl along c.

The following process behaves similarly, except that it constructs a nil, or empty, list. Upon receiving a tuple [r] containing just a result channel r, we create a new channel l. Then, in parallel, we return l along the result channel r and run the process l?*[n c] = n![]. This process responds to messages sent along l by sending the trivial value [] back along n.

```
nil?*[r] = (new l (r!l | l?*[n c] = n![]))
```

The following program fragment illustrates how we can interact with nil and cons to build a list containing the number 33. We first create a fresh result channel r1 and send it along the nil channel. In parallel, we wait for nil's reply to be sent along r1, binding the resulting value to e. We then create a second result channel r2 and send the tuple [33 e r2] to cons. This has the effect of building a cons cell whose head is 33 and tail is e. The location of the new cell is returned along r2.

```
(new r1 (nil![r1] |
         r1?e = (new r2 (cons![33 e r2] |
                         r2?l = ...))))
```

We can interrogate our list by sending a pair of channels [n c] along the channel l. By convention, an empty list will reply on n (by sending the trivial value []), while a cons cell will reply on c (by sending a pair of the head and tail of the list). The following process therefore executes the expression e if l is the empty list, and f if l is a cons cell (in which case hd and tl will be bound to the head and tail of l within f):

```
(new n (new c (l![n c] | n?[] = e | c?[hd tl] = f)))
```

## 2.5 Structural Congruence

In discussing these examples, we have appealed to an informal understanding of how Pict expressions behave. It is now time to make this understanding precise. Following [Mil91], the operational semantics of Pict programs is presented in two steps. First, we define a *structural congruence* relation $e_1 \equiv e_2$; this relation captures the fact that, for example, the order of the branches in a parallel composition has no effect on its behavior. Next, we define a *reduction relation* $e_1 \rightarrow e_2$, specifying how processes evolve by communication.

Structural congruence plays an important technical role as a device for simplifying the statement of the reduction relation. For example, we intend that the processes (x!v | x?y = e) and (x?y = e | x!v) both reduce to $\{y \mapsto v\}e$. Since these two are structurally congruent, it suffices to write the reduction rule only for the first case and to stipulate, in general, that if e contains some possibility of communication then any expression structurally congruent to e has the same possible behavior.

The first two structural congruence rules state that parallel composition is commutative and associative.

$$(e_1 \mid e_2) \equiv (e_2 \mid e_1) \qquad \text{(STR-COMM)}$$

$$((e_1 \mid e_2) \mid e_3) \equiv (e_1 \mid (e_2 \mid e_3)) \qquad \text{(STR-ASSOC)}$$

The third rule, called *scope extrusion* in the $\pi$-calculus literature, plays a crucial role in communication.

$$\frac{x \notin \mathit{freevars}(e_2)}{((\texttt{new } x{:}T\ e_1) \mid e_2) \equiv (\texttt{new } x{:}T\ (e_1 \mid e_2))} \qquad \text{(STR-EXTRUDE)}$$

Informally, it says that the scope of the channel x, which starts out private to the process $e_1$, can be extended to include $e_2$. The side-condition $x \notin \mathit{freevars}(e_2)$ ensures that $e_2$ does not already have a free channel named x. (This condition can always be satisifed by $\alpha$-converting the bound name x in the expression (new x:T $e_1$) before applying the scope extrusion rule.) For example, the process expression ((new x:T c!x) | e) may be transformed to (new x:T (c!x | e)), if e does not have x as a free variable. It is this rule that allows the new channel x to be communicated outside of its original scope to a process in e.

## 2.6 Substitution and Matching

To define reduction, we need some notation for matching values against patterns.

A *substitution* is a finite map associating variables with values and type variables with types. If $\sigma_1$ and $\sigma_2$ are substitutions with disjoint domains, then $\sigma_1 \cup \sigma_2$ is a substitution that combines the effects of $\sigma_1$ and $\sigma_2$. A substitution is extended to a function from values to values by applying it to variables that fall in its domain and leaving the rest unchanged. For example, applying the substitution $\sigma = \{x \mapsto a\} \cup \{y \mapsto []\}$ to the value [z [x] x y], written $\sigma$([z [x] x y]), yields [z [a] a []]. Substitution is extended in the usual way to an operation on processes, renaming bound variables as necessary to avoid capture.

When a value $\mathtt{v}$ is successfully matched by a pattern $\mathtt{p}$, the result is the substitution $\{\mathtt{p} \mapsto \mathtt{v}\}$ defined below. (If $\mathtt{v}$ and $\mathtt{p}$ do not have the same structure, then $\{\mathtt{p} \mapsto \mathtt{v}\}$ is undefined. The typing rules ensure that this cannot happen in well-typed programs.)

$$
\begin{aligned}
\{\mathtt{x:T} \mapsto \mathtt{v}\} &= \{\mathtt{x} \mapsto \mathtt{v}\} \\
\{\mathtt{\_:T} \mapsto \mathtt{v}\} &= \{\} \\
\{\mathtt{(x:T@p)} \mapsto \mathtt{v}\} &= \{\mathtt{x} \mapsto \mathtt{v}\} \cup \{\mathtt{p} \mapsto \mathtt{v}\} \\
\{\mathtt{(rec:T\ p)} \mapsto \mathtt{(rec:S\ v)}\} &= \{\mathtt{p} \mapsto \mathtt{v}\} \\
\{\mathtt{\{X<S\}p} \mapsto \mathtt{\{T\}v}\} &= \{\mathtt{X} \mapsto \mathtt{T}\} \cup \{\mathtt{p} \mapsto \mathtt{v}\} \\
\{\mathtt{[l_1p_1\ldots l_np_n]} \mapsto \mathtt{[l_1v_1\ldots l_nv_n\ldots]}\} &= \{\mathtt{p_1} \mapsto \mathtt{v_1}\} \cup \cdots \cup \{\mathtt{p_n} \mapsto \mathtt{v_n}\}
\end{aligned}
$$

This matching function traverses the structure of the pattern and the value in parallel, yielding bindings when variables are encountered in the pattern. (Note that the variables bound in a pattern are always distinct, so the $\cup$ operations in the definition are always well defined.)

The matching rule for records allows a record pattern to be matched by a record value with extra fields (at the end of the record). For example, the record pattern `[l=y]` matches the record value `[l=33 m=true]`. This gives rise to simple form of record subtyping that is particularly easy to implement. (It is common in theoretical calculi with records to permit extra fields to appear anywhere in a record during matching, but this significantly complicates the implementation of records, especially in the presence of separate compilation.)

## 2.7 Reduction

The reduction relation $\mathtt{e_1} \rightarrow \mathtt{e_2}$ may be read as "The process $\mathtt{e_1}$ *can evolve* to the process $\mathtt{e_2}$." That is, the semantics is nondeterministic, specifying only what *can* happen as the evaluation of a program proceeds, not what *must* happen. Any particular execution of a Pict program will follow just one of the possible paths.

The most basic rule of reduction is the one specifying what happens when an input prefix meets an output atom:

$$
\frac{\{\mathtt{p} \mapsto \mathtt{v}\} \text{ defined}}{\mathtt{(x!v\ |\ x?p\ =\ e)} \rightarrow \{\mathtt{p} \mapsto \mathtt{v}\}\mathtt{(e)}} \qquad \text{(RED-COMM)}
$$

In the case when the input expression is replicated, the communication rule is similar, except that the input expression is not consumed by the act of communication.

$$
\frac{\{\mathtt{p} \mapsto \mathtt{v}\} \text{ defined}}{\mathtt{(x!v\ |\ x?{*}p\ =\ e)} \rightarrow \mathtt{(}\{\mathtt{p} \mapsto \mathtt{v}\}\mathtt{(e)\ |\ x?{*}p\ =\ e)}} \qquad \text{(RED-RCOMM)}
$$

The next two rules allow reduction to proceed under declarations and parallel composition:

$$\frac{\mathtt{e}_1 \rightarrow \mathtt{e}_2}{(\mathtt{d}\ \mathtt{e}_1) \rightarrow (\mathtt{d}\ \mathtt{e}_2)} \qquad \text{(RED-DEC)}$$

$$\frac{\mathtt{e}_1 \rightarrow \mathtt{e}_3}{(\mathtt{e}_1 \mid \mathtt{e}_2) \rightarrow (\mathtt{e}_3 \mid \mathtt{e}_2)} \qquad \text{(RED-PRL)}$$

(The body of an input expression, on the other hand, *cannot* participate in reductions until after the input has been discharged. This fact is reflected in the absence of a "congruence rule" for input prefixes.) Reduction of conditional processes is straightforward. The typing rules ensure that the guard in a closed, well-typed conditional is either `true` or `false`.

$$\mathtt{if\ true\ then}\ \mathtt{e}_1\ \mathtt{else}\ \mathtt{e}_2 \rightarrow \mathtt{e}_1 \qquad \text{(RED-IF-T)}$$

$$\mathtt{if\ false\ then}\ \mathtt{e}_1\ \mathtt{else}\ \mathtt{e}_2 \rightarrow \mathtt{e}_2 \qquad \text{(RED-IF-F)}$$

The structural congruence relation captures the distributed nature of reduction. Any two subprocesses at the "top level" of a process expression (i.e. not guarded by any input prefixes) may be brought into proximity by structural manipulations and allowed to interact.

$$\frac{\mathtt{e}_1 \equiv \mathtt{e}_2 \rightarrow \mathtt{e}_3 \equiv \mathtt{e}_4}{\mathtt{e}_1 \rightarrow \mathtt{e}_4} \qquad \text{(RED-STR)}$$

Note that the reduction rules do not maintain any particular ordering among messages sent along the same channel. For example, in the process `(x!y | x!z | x?w = e)` either the value `y` or the value `z` may be communicated to the process `x?w = e`.

Strictly speaking, the semantics we have given is defined only for closed programs—we have been intentionally informal about the built in channels (such as `print`) which connect a Pict program to its environment. Sewell has proposed a more refined semantic framework explicitly incorporating interactions with the environment [Sew97].

## 2.8 Fairness

Even on closed programs, the reduction semantics of the previous section leaves one important issue unaddressed: it characterizes the set of possible behaviors of a process expression, but makes no commitment as to which of these behaviors will actually be observed when the expression is compiled and executed. For example, there is a valid execution of the process `(new x (x![] | x?*[] = x![] | x?[] = a![]))` in which the output `a![]` is never executed. A compiler that produced this behavior would be unsatisfactory, since it would fail to capture the programmer's intuitive expectation that the actions of subprocesses running in parallel will be interleaved *fairly*, so that the second input on `x` will eventually succeed.

We are unaware of any work explicitly formalizing fairness for $\pi$-calculus, but it seems likely that Costa and Stirling's work on fairness for CCS [CS87] can be generalized to the case of $\pi$-calculus. Costa and Stirling consider two kinds of fairness: *weak fairness* stipulates that if a process is continuously able to communicate on a channel then it must eventually be allowed to proceed; *strong fairness* insists that any process that is able to communicate on a channel infinitely often, even if not continuously, must eventually proceed. A weak fairness guarantee is sufficient to ensure that the output `a![]` in the above example will eventually be executed, since the input `x?[] = a![]` is continuously enabled. If, however, the process `x?*[] = x![]` is replaced by a process which does some other communication before sending `[]` along `x`, then a strong fairness guarantee would be required to ensure that the output `a![]` is eventually executed, since the input `x?[] = a![]` is not continuously able to communicate.

In practice, it is relatively easy to achieve a fair execution strategy by using FIFO channel queues and a round-robin policy for process scheduling. This guarantees that a process waiting to communicate on a channel will eventually succeed, assuming that enough partners become available. Our experience of writing applications in Pict has been that this execution strategy works well. For example, the FIFO queueing of the lock channel `l` in the reference cell of Section 4.6 ensures that competing `set` and `get` requests are handled fairly; the replicated choice construct of [PT95] exhibits similar good behavior.

## 3 Type System

The Pict type system has its roots in the theoretical literature on type systems for the $\pi$-calculus [Mil91, Gay93, VH93, PS93, Tur96] and for functional languages, among which its most immediate predecessors are Quest [Car91] and Amber [Car86]. The treatment of subtyping and higher-order polymorphism is based on recent work on static type systems for object-oriented languages [Car84, Bru94, CHC90, PT94, HP95, FM94, AC96, etc.] and the $\lambda$-calculus $F^{\omega}_{\leq}$ [Car90, CL91, PT94, PS97b, Com94]. The rules for channel types are taken from Pierce and Sangiorgi's type system for the pure $\pi$-calculus [PS93]. An early version of the Pict type system was presented in [PRT93].

Typed process calculi with related goals have been proposed by Nierstrasz [Nie95] and Vasconcelos [Vas94], among others. Further refinements to the channel typing discipline incorporating notions of linear channel usage have been studied by Honda [Hon93, Hon96], and more recently by Honda and Yoshida [HY94], Takeuchi, Honda, and Kubo [THK94],

Kobayashi and Yonezawa [KY94] and the present authors in collaboration with Kobayashi [KPT96].

### 3.1 Channel Types

Most type systems for process calculi and concurrent languages impose the constraint that each channel must be used throughout its lifetime to carry values of a single type. This restriction greatly simplifies the task of type analysis, since the well-typedness of a parallel composition `(e1 | e2)` is independent of the ordering of interactions between $e_1$ and $e_2$.

Since computation in Pict is based purely on communication over channels, the basic elements of its type system are the types of channels and of the values that they carry. For example, a process that outputs a value `v` along a channel `c` is well typed if `c` has type `^T` (read "channel carrying `T`") and `v` has type `T`.

### 3.2 Recursive Types

Like most programming languages, Pict offers the capability to build and manipulate recursive data structures like lists and trees. Such *recursive types* have received considerable attention in the literature [MPS86, CC91, AC93, etc.], and many different technical treatments have been proposed. Because the rest of the Pict type system is already somewhat complex and recursive types tend to be used only in small sections of code, we have chosen one of the simplest alternatives, where the "folding" and "unfolding" of the recursion must be managed explicitly by the programmer.

For example, suppose `R` is the recursive type `(rec X = ^X)`. A value of type `R` can be coerced, using a `rec` pattern, to a value of type `^R` (where the recursion in the type `R` has been unfolded once). Dually, a `rec` value construct can be used to coerce a value of type `^R` into a value of `R`.

We can use the recursive type `(rec L = ^[^[] ^[Int L]])` to represent the type of integer lists in our cons cell server from Section 2.4:

```
type IntList = (rec L = ^[^[] ^[Int L]])

cons?*[hd:Int tl:IntList r:^IntList] =
  (new l:^[^[] ^[Int IntList]]
   (r!(rec:IntList l) | l?*[n:^[] c:^[Int IntList]] = c![hd tl]))
```

The type annotations on `hd`, `tl` and `r` indicate that `cons` takes as arguments an integer and an integer list, and returns an integer list along the channel `r`. The type of the new channel `l` is an unfolding of the type `IntList`. The unfolded `IntList` type exposes the fact that a list is represented as a channel and enables us to use `l` in a replicated input operation. However, when we return `l` along the result channel `r`, we coerce the type of `l` to `IntList` (using a `rec` value construct).

Values of recursive type are "unfolded" during communication by patterns of the form `(rec:T p)`. For example, if `c` is a channel of type `^IntList`, then the bound variable `l` in the body of the process `c?(rec:IntList l) = ...` has type `^[^[] ^[Int IntList]]`, the unfolding of `IntList`.

### 3.3 Subtyping

Channel types serve a useful role in ensuring that all parts of a program use a given channel in a consistent way, eliminating the possibility of pattern matching failure (cf. Section 2.6) at run time. Of course, pattern matching failure is just one kind of bad behavior that programs may exhibit; especially in concurrent programs, the range of possible programming mistakes is vast: there may be unintended deadlocks, race conditions, and protocol violations of all kinds. Ultimately, one might hope to see static analysis tools capable of detecting many of these errors, but the technology required to do this is still far off. Fortunately, there are some simple ways in which channel types can be enriched so as to capture useful properties of programs while remaining within the bounds of current typechecking technology.

In Pict, it is relatively rare for a channel to be used for both input and output in the same region of the program; typically, some parts of a program use a given channel only for reading while in others it is used only for writing. For example, the cons-cell server in the example above only reads from the channel `cons`, while clients only write to `cons`. Similarly, given a request `[hd tl r]`, the server only writes to the result channel `r`, while the client only reads from it.

Pict exploits this observation by providing two refinements of the channel type `^T`: a type `!T` giving only the capability to write values of type `T` and, symmetrically, a type `?T` giving only the capability to read values of type `T`. For example, we can refine our type annotations for `cons` as follows:

```
type IntList = (rec L = ![![] ![Int L]])

cons?*[hd:Int tl:IntList r:!IntList] =
  (new l:^[![] ![Int IntList]]
   (r!(rec:IntList l) | l?*[n:![] c:![Int IntList]] = c![hd tl]))
```

The refined type annotations make it clear that `cons` only requires write capability on the channels `r`, `n`, and `c`. Note that the channel `l` is created with both read and write capabilities. The cons-cell server uses `l`'s read capability locally and gives the client the write capability.

The types `^T`, `?T`, and `!T` fall naturally into a *subtype relation* [PS93], since a channel of type `^T` may always be used in a context where one of type `?T` or `!T` is expected—for example, in an input or output expression.

### 3.4 Record Subtyping

One objective of the Pict project was to explore the applicability of our earlier theoretical work on type systems for object-oriented programming. In [PT94], we proposed a powerful combination of subtyping and polymorphism as a basis for statically-typed object-oriented programming in functional languages; equipping Pict with a similar type system makes it a useful testbed for experiments with statically typed concurrent objects.

We implement a simple form of record subtyping which allows record fields to be added to the end of a record. For example, the record type `[l=Int m=Bool]` is a subtype of `[l=Int]`. Unlike some record type systems, the order of the fields in a Pict record is significant. For example, `[m=Bool l=Int]` is *not* a subtype of `[l=Int m=Bool]`. Pict's simple record subtyping, in combination with the fact that the order of record fields is significant, significantly simplifies the compilation of record values, since the position of a field in a record can be determined from its type at compile time. (This is especially useful when separately compiling Pict programs.)

### 3.5 Polymorphism

The type system we have seen so far may readily be extended to include polymorphism, just as simply typed λ-calculus can be extended with polymorphism [Gir72, Rey74]. We support polymorphic communications by adding two new syntactic forms: package values `{T}v` and package patterns `{X}p`. For example, if `c` is a channel of type `^Int`, the output expression `z!{Int}[5 c]` sends along the channel `z` the type `Int` and the pair of values `5` and `c`. The type of `z` itself is `^{X}[X ^X]`, pronounced "channel carrying a type `X`, a value belonging to type `X`, and a channel carrying elements of `X`." In more familiar notation, this type might be written `^(∃X.[X !X])`. A process receiving from `z` has the form `z?{X}[v:X x:^X] = ...`, which binds the type variable `X` to the received type. The bound variables `v` and `x` have types `X` and `^X`. This effectively means that the only legal operation on `v` is to send it along `x`. This form of "parametric reasoning" in the polymorphic pi-calculus has been studied by Pierce and Sangiorgi [PS97a]. Other properties of the system are considered in Turner's thesis [Tur96].

We can now generalise our cons-cell server so that it is polymorphic in the list element type:

```
cons ?* X[hd:X tl:(List X) r:!(List X)] =
  (new l:^[![] ![X (List X)]]
   (r!(rec:(List X) l) | l?*[n:![] c:![X (List X)]] = c![hd tl]))
```

Clients of the polymorphic `cons` must now send an additional type argument along the `cons` channel. For example, the following process uses the polymorphic `cons` to build an integer cons cell (we assume the tail of the list, `tl`, has already been built and has type `(List Int)`):

```
(new r:^(List Int) (cons!Int[33 tl r] | r?l:(List Int) = ...))
```

Polymorphism and subtyping are combined by giving each bound type variable in a package value an *upper bound*, as in the polymorphic λ-calculus with bounded quantification, System $F_{\leq}$ [CW85, CMMS94]. For example, the type `^{X<T}[X ^X]` describes a channel that can be used to transmit a type `X` and two values of types `X` and `^X`, but also stipulates that the only legal values of `X` are subtypes of `T`.

Just as functions in Pict have no special status—being regarded as output channels on which clients can send tuples of arguments and a continuation channel where the function is to send the result—polymorphic functions are represented as output channels carrying package values. This "pun" entails that the primitive form of polymorphism in Pict is existential types, not universal types as in most typed λ-calculi.

### 3.6 Type Operators

Formally, the type `(List Int)` consists of an application of the type constructor `List` to the type `Int`. `List` itself is a function from types to types. To avoid nonsensical applications like `(List List)` or `(Int Int)`, we classify types and type operators according to their *kinds*, as in typed λ-calculi like System $F^{\omega}$ [Gir72, Bar92] and $F^{\omega}_{\leq}$ [Car90, CL91, PT94, PS97b, Com94]. Thus, the type system recognizes three distinct levels of expressions: values, types, and kinds. The level of values contains familiar entities like `5`, `true`, the tuple `[5 true]`, and channels. The level of types contains *proper types* like `Int`, `Bool`, `(List Int)`, `[Int Bool]`, and `^Int`, as well as *type operators* like `List`. The proper types classify values, in the sense that entities at the level of values may inhabit proper types: `5` inhabits `Int`, etc. In the same sense, kinds classify types: all the proper types inhabit the kind `Type`; type operators accepting one proper type parameter and yielding a proper type (like `List`) inhabit the kind `(Type→Type)`; type operators taking two proper type arguments and yielding a proper type inhabit the kind `(Type→(Type→Type))`; and so on.

### 3.7 Type Inference

Although Pict's core language is explicitly typed, it is important to allow at least some type annotations to be omitted from user programs. In some languages—for example, ML and Haskell, which are based on the Hindley-Milner type system—the compiler can automatically infer all necessary type annotations. Pict's type system, however, is significantly more powerful than the Hindley-Milner type system: in particular, it includes both polymorphism and subtyping. This means that we cannot expect to find an algorithm that can infer all the type annotations in a Pict program. Instead, we use a simple *partial* type inference algorithm—partial in the sense that it may sometimes have to ask the user to add more explicit type information rather than reconstructing in all annotations itself.

Pict's partial type inference algorithm exploits the fact that there are a number of common cases in which the type assigned to a bound variable is completely determined by the surrounding program context. For example, the variable `x` in the input expression `c?x=e` is known to have type `Int` if the channel `c` has type `^Int` in the surrounding context. Pict's type inference algorithm is local, in the sense that it only uses the immediately surrounding program context to try to fill in a missing annotation. This might at first seem rather restrictive, but our experience so far has been very favorable: our largest Pict programs are approximately 6000 lines long, and there are only a few cases where one feels that the type inference algorithm isn't inferring enough type annotations automatically. One of the reasons partial type inference works well in Pict is that many programs already contain explicit type annotations, for documentation purposes. In many cases, these explicit annotations are sufficient to uniquely determine the types that should be assigned to all other bound variables.

A simple type inference algorithm has two important benefits. Firstly, it makes it easy for Pict programmers to understand the process of type inference and thereby understand where type annotations are required and what type errors mean. Secondly, a simple type inference algorithm is easier to formalize: Pict's type inference algorithm forms part of the *specification* of the Pict language. Type systems for languages such as ML and Haskell are specified by means of a set of typing rules which non-deterministically pick the "correct" types for all bound variables. No details of the actual process of type inference are given (though it is necessary to prove that a sound and complete type inference algorithm does exist). By contrast, since we cannot infer all missing type annotations in Pict programs, it is necessary to specify exactly which type annotations can be inferred automatically. Because of the local nature of partial type inference in Pict, it is possible to describe the algorithm using rules that resemble Pict's typing rules but formalize how type information is propagated into and out of expressions.

In the rest of this paper, we concentrate on the explicitly typed language, omitting further discussion of type inference. See the Pict Language Definition for full details.

### 3.8 Notation

The syntax of type expressions is as follows:

| | | |
|---|---|---|
| *Type* = | `^` *Type* | Input/output channel |
| | `!` *Type* | Output-only channel |
| | `?` *Type* | Input-only channel |
| | `{` *Id* `<` *Type* `}` *Type* | Package type |
| | `[` *Label Type* . . . *Label Type* `]` | Record type |
| | *Id* | Type identifier |
| | `\` *Id* `:` *Kind* `=` *Type* | Type operator |
| | `(` *Type Type* `)` | Type application |
| | `(rec` *Id* `:` *Kind* `=` *Type* `)` | Recursive type |
| | `Top` `:` *Kind* | Maximal type |
| | `Int` | Integer type |
| | `Char` | Character type |
| | `Bool` | Boolean type |
| | `String` | String type |
| *Kind* = | `(` *Kind* $\rightarrow$ *Kind* `)` | Kind of type operators |
| | `Type` | Kind of types |

A *typing context* $\Gamma$ is a list of bindings associating variables with their types and type variables with their upper bounds. The metavariables $\Gamma$ and $\Delta$ range over contexts. The concatenation of $\Gamma$ and $\Delta$ is written $\Gamma, \Delta$.

The type system of Pict comprises axioms and inferences rules defining sets of derivable *statements* of the following forms:

| | |
|---|---|
| $\Gamma \vdash \mathtt{S} < \mathtt{T}$ | `S` is a subtype of `T` |
| $\Gamma \vdash \mathtt{v} \in \mathtt{T}$ | value `v` has type `T` under assumptions $\Gamma$ |
| $\Gamma \vdash \mathtt{d} \rhd \Delta$ | declaration `d` is well formed and yields bindings $\Delta$ |
| $\Gamma \vdash \mathtt{p} \in \mathtt{T} \rhd \Delta$ | pattern `p` requires type `T` and yields bindings $\Delta$ |
| $\Gamma \vdash \mathtt{a} \in \mathtt{T}$ | abstraction `a` is well formed and accepts type `T` |
| $\Gamma \vdash \mathtt{e}\ ok$ | process expression `e` is well formed |
| $\Gamma \vdash \mathtt{T} \in \mathtt{K}$ | type `T` has kind `K` |
| $\vdash \Gamma\ ok$ | context $\Gamma$ is well formed |

The first two kinds of statement are familiar from type systems for functional languages. The third is used for checking Pict declarations. Since a declaration cannot be sent over a channel, it does not itself have a type; however, it may give rise to a collection of variable bindings for some following scope, and we need to keep track of the types of these variables. The "type" of a declaration is therefore a typing context. Similarly, a pattern binds some variables and thus gives rise to a context; however, a pattern *also* has a type, since it can only match values of a certain form. An abstraction requires an argument of a certain form. A process expression yields neither bindings nor a value: it is simply either well formed or not. (A process is well formed in a given context if all its input- and output-subexpressions respect the typings of the channels over which communication occurs.) The last two forms of statements are the standard notions of well-formedness of types and typing contexts.

The rules for well-kinded types and well-formed contexts are familiar from the literature on higher-order typed λ-calculi (e.g. [HP95, PS97b]), and we do not discuss them here. The rest of this section presents a selection of the rules defining the remaining forms of typing statements. (A full description of the typing and kinding rules can be found in the Pict Language Definition.)

### 3.9 Subtyping

The subtype relation consists of two structural rules plus one or more rules for each type constructor or constant. The structural rules state that subtyping is reflexive and transitive and includes $\beta$-conversion on types so that, if `F` is the type operator `\X:Type = [X X]`, then `(F Int)` is equivalent to `[Int Int]`:

$$\frac{\mathtt{S} =_{\beta\mathtt{T}} \mathtt{T}}{\Gamma \vdash \mathtt{S} < \mathtt{T}} \qquad \text{(S-CONV)}$$

$$\frac{\Gamma \vdash \mathtt{S} \in \mathtt{K} \qquad \Gamma \vdash \mathtt{U} \in \mathtt{K} \qquad \Gamma \vdash \mathtt{T} \in \mathtt{K} \qquad \Gamma \vdash \mathtt{S} < \mathtt{U} \qquad \Gamma \vdash \mathtt{U} < \mathtt{T}}{\Gamma \vdash \mathtt{S} < \mathtt{T}} \qquad \text{(S-TRANS)}$$

Formally, the conversion relation $=_{\beta\mathtt{T}}$ contains both ordinary $\beta$-conversion ($\mathtt{((\backslash X:K=T)\ S} =_{\beta\mathtt{T}} \{\mathtt{X} \mapsto \mathtt{S}\}\mathtt{T}$) and a rule of "top-conversion" (cf. [PS97b]) that makes `Top` at operator kinds behave like a type operator ($\mathtt{Top:(K_1{\to}K_2)\ S} =_{\beta\mathtt{T}} \mathtt{Top:K_2}$).

Each type variable is a subtype of the upper bound declared for it in the context:

$$\Gamma_1, \mathtt{X{<}T}, \Gamma_2 \vdash \mathtt{X} < \mathtt{T} \qquad \text{(S-TVAR)}$$

$\texttt{Top:K}$ is a maximal type for each kind $\texttt{K}$. In particular, $\texttt{Top:Type}$, which may be written just $\texttt{Top}$, is the largest type.

$$\Gamma \vdash \texttt{S} < \texttt{Top:K} \qquad \text{(S-TOP)}$$

A record type $\texttt{S}$ is a subtype of another record type $\texttt{T}$ whenever $\texttt{S}$ contains more fields than $\texttt{T}$ (and the types of the corresponding field values are also subtypes). For example, if $\texttt{Char} < \texttt{Int}$ then $\texttt{[l=Char m=Bool]} < \texttt{[l=Int]}$.

$$\frac{\Gamma \vdash \texttt{T}_1 < \texttt{T}'_1 \quad \ldots \quad \Gamma \vdash \texttt{T}_n < \texttt{T}'_n}{\Gamma \vdash \texttt{[l}_1\texttt{T}_1 \ldots \texttt{l}_n\texttt{T}_n \ldots\texttt{]} < \texttt{[l}_1\texttt{T}'_1 \ldots \texttt{l}_n\texttt{T}'_n\texttt{]}} \qquad \text{(S-RECORD)}$$

The package type $\texttt{\{X<S}_1\texttt{\}S}_2$ is a subtype of $\texttt{\{X<T}_1\texttt{\}T}_2$ if the bounds $\texttt{S}_1$ and $\texttt{T}_1$ have the same kind, $\texttt{S}_1$ is a subtype of $\texttt{T}_1$, and $\texttt{S}_2$ is a subtype of $\texttt{T}_2$ under the assumption that $\texttt{X}$ is a subtype of $\texttt{S}_1$:

$$\frac{\Gamma \vdash \texttt{S}_1 \in \texttt{K} \qquad \Gamma \vdash \texttt{T}_1 \in \texttt{K} \qquad \Gamma \vdash \texttt{S}_1 < \texttt{T}_1 \qquad \Gamma, \texttt{X<S}_1 \vdash \texttt{S}_2 < \texttt{T}_2}{\Gamma \vdash \texttt{\{X<S}_1\texttt{\}S}_2 < \texttt{\{X<T}_1\texttt{\}T}_2} \qquad \text{(S-PACKAGE)}$$

The channel constructor $\texttt{?}$ is covariant in its argument and $\texttt{!}$ is contravariant. Operationally, this captures the observation that, for example, if a given channel $\texttt{x}$ is being used in a given context only to read elements of type $\texttt{T}$, then it is safe to replace $\texttt{x}$ by another channel $\texttt{y}$ carrying elements of type $\texttt{S}$ as long as any element that is read from $\texttt{y}$ may safely be regarded as an element of $\texttt{T}$—that is, as long as $\texttt{S}$ is a subtype of $\texttt{T}$.

$$\frac{\Gamma \vdash \texttt{S} < \texttt{T}}{\Gamma \vdash \texttt{?S} < \texttt{?T}} \qquad \text{(S-ICHAN)}$$

$$\frac{\Gamma \vdash \texttt{T} < \texttt{S}}{\Gamma \vdash \texttt{!S} < \texttt{!T}} \qquad \text{(S-OCHAN)}$$

Notice that the contravariance of $\texttt{!}$ gives rise to the usual rule of subtyping between types of functions. A function $\texttt{f} \in \texttt{S}_1 \rightarrow \texttt{S}_2$ is implemented in Pict as a server process reading requests of type $\texttt{[S}_1\ \texttt{!S}_2\texttt{]}$ from a channel $\texttt{f}$, performing the appropriate calculation, and returning its result on the channel provided as its second argument. From the point of view of a caller, the request channel $\texttt{f}$ has type $\texttt{![S}_1\ \texttt{!S}_2\texttt{]}$; this type is contravariant in $\texttt{S}_1$ and covariant in $\texttt{S}_2$, as expected:

$$\frac{\Gamma \vdash \texttt{T}_1 < \texttt{S}_1 \qquad \Gamma \vdash \texttt{S}_2 < \texttt{T}_2}{\Gamma \vdash \texttt{![S}_1\ \texttt{!S}_2\texttt{]} < \texttt{![T}_1\ \texttt{!T}_2\texttt{]}}$$

The constructor ^ is invariant in the subtype relation (i.e. ^S is a subtype of ^T only when S and T are equivalent). The type ^T is a subtype of both ?T and !T. That is, we are allowed to forget either the capability to write or the capability to read on a channel: a channel that can be used for both input and output may be used in a context where just one capability is needed.

$$\Gamma \vdash \texttt{\^{}T} < \texttt{?T} \qquad \text{(S-CHANICHAN)}$$

$$\Gamma \vdash \texttt{\^{}T} < \texttt{!T} \qquad \text{(S-CHANOCHAN)}$$

The subtype relation is extended pointwise from proper types to other kinds: if F and G are type operators, then we say F < G if (F T) < (G T) for all appropriately kinded argument types T.

$$\frac{\Gamma, \texttt{X<Top:K} \vdash \texttt{S} < \texttt{T}}{\Gamma \vdash \texttt{\textbackslash X:K=S} < \texttt{\textbackslash X:K=T}} \qquad \text{(S-ABS)}$$

$$\frac{\Gamma \vdash \texttt{S} < \texttt{T}}{\Gamma \vdash \texttt{(S U)} < \texttt{(T U)}} \qquad \text{(S-APP)}$$

For subtyping of recursive types, we use the familiar "Amber rule" [Car86, AC93], which states that (rec X=S) is a subtype of (rec Y=T) if we can show S < T under the assumption X < Y.

$$\frac{\Gamma, \texttt{Y<Top:K, X<Y} \vdash \texttt{S} < \texttt{T}}{\Gamma \vdash \texttt{(rec X:K=S)} < \texttt{(rec Y:K=T)}} \qquad \text{(S-REC)}$$

### 3.10 Values

If the current context contains the binding x:T for the variable x, then the type of x is T in this context (all bound variables are assumed to be unique, so there can be at most one binding for x in Γ):

$$\Gamma_1, \texttt{x:T}, \Gamma_2 \vdash \texttt{x} \in \texttt{T} \qquad \text{(V-VAR)}$$

If the values $\texttt{v}_1$ through $\texttt{v}_n$ have the types $\texttt{T}_1$ through $\texttt{T}_n$, then the record value $\texttt{[l}_1\texttt{v}_1 \ldots \texttt{l}_n\texttt{v}_n\texttt{]}$ has the record type $\texttt{[l}_1\texttt{T}_1 \ldots \texttt{l}_n\texttt{T}_n\texttt{]}$.

$$\frac{\Gamma \vdash \texttt{v}_1 \in \texttt{T}_1 \quad \ldots \quad \Gamma \vdash \texttt{v}_n \in \texttt{T}_n}{\Gamma \vdash \texttt{[l}_1\texttt{v}_1 \ldots \texttt{l}_n\texttt{v}_n\texttt{]} \in \texttt{[l}_1\texttt{T}_1 \ldots \texttt{l}_n\texttt{T}_n\texttt{]}} \qquad \text{(V-RECORD)}$$

A value v can be incorporated into an existential package of type {X<U}T if the "witness type" S is a subtype of U. The actual type of the value v must match the type T after the substitution of S for X.

$$\frac{\Gamma \vdash \mathtt{S} \in \mathtt{K} \qquad \Gamma \vdash \mathtt{U} \in \mathtt{K} \qquad \Gamma \vdash \mathtt{S} < \mathtt{U} \qquad \Gamma \vdash \mathtt{v} \in \{\mathtt{X} \mapsto \mathtt{S}\}\mathtt{T}}{\Gamma \vdash \mathtt{\{S\}v} \in \mathtt{\{X{<}U\}T}} \qquad \text{(V-PACKAGE)}$$

For example, if res has type ^Bool, then the value {Bool}[false res] has type {X}[X ^X], since false has type $\{\mathtt{X} \mapsto \mathtt{Bool}\}\mathtt{X} = \mathtt{Bool}$ and res has type $\{\mathtt{X} \mapsto \mathtt{Bool}\}\mathtt{\hat{}X} = \mathtt{\hat{}Bool}$. Readers familiar with typed $\lambda$-calculi will recognize the similarity of this rule to the standard introduction rule for existential types (e.g. [CW85, MP88]). The pattern typing rule P-PACKAGE in Section 3.12 plays the role of the standard elimination rule for existentials.

A value of a recursive type T can be formed from a value whose type matches the "unrolling" of T:

$$\frac{\Gamma \vdash \mathtt{T} \in \mathtt{Type} \qquad \mathtt{T} \rightsquigarrow \mathtt{U} \qquad \Gamma \vdash \mathtt{v} \in \mathtt{U}}{\Gamma \vdash \mathtt{(rec{:}T\ v)} \in \mathtt{T}} \qquad \text{(V-REC)}$$

where $\mathtt{T} \rightsquigarrow \mathtt{U}$ means that T is a recursive type and U is obtained from T by unrolling the recursion one step. For example, if R is the type (rec X:Type = ^X) and c is a channel of type ^R, then (rec:R c) has type R, since $\mathtt{R} \rightsquigarrow \mathtt{\hat{}R}$.

$$\frac{\mathtt{S} =_{\beta\mathtt{T}} \mathtt{(rec\ X{:}K\ =\ T)}}{\mathtt{S} \rightsquigarrow \{\mathtt{X} \mapsto \mathtt{(rec\ X{:}K\ =\ T)}\}\mathtt{T}} \qquad \text{(UNROLL-REC)}$$

In general, the unrolling operator $\rightsquigarrow$ must take into account the fact that the unrolling operation may be applied to a type expression formed by applying a recursively defined type operator to some arguments; in this case, the arguments are carried along unchanged to the result and the recursive type is unrolled "in-place":

$$\frac{\mathtt{S} =_{\beta\mathtt{T}} \mathtt{(T_1\ T_2)} \qquad \mathtt{T_1} \rightsquigarrow \mathtt{U}}{\mathtt{S} \rightsquigarrow \mathtt{(U\ T_2)}} \qquad \text{(UNROLL-APP)}$$

Finally, we allow types of values to be *promoted* in the subtype relation: if v is a value of type S and S is a subtype of T, then v also has type T.

$$\frac{\Gamma \vdash \mathtt{v} \in \mathtt{S} \qquad \Gamma \vdash \mathtt{S} < \mathtt{T}}{\Gamma \vdash \mathtt{v} \in \mathtt{T}} \qquad \text{(V-SUB)}$$

This rule embodies the principle of "safe substitutability" that underlies the subtype relation: the statement $\mathtt{S} < \mathtt{T}$ means that an element of S can always be used in a context where an element of T is required.

### 3.11 Declarations

A new declaration returns a binding for the new channel using the declared type (we check that the declared type is well kinded and equivalent to a channel type).

$$\frac{\Gamma \vdash \mathtt{T} \in \mathtt{Type} \qquad \Gamma \vdash \mathtt{T} =_{\beta\mathtt{T}} \mathtt{\hat{}U}}{\Gamma \vdash \mathtt{new\ x{:}T} \rhd \mathtt{x{:}T}} \quad \text{(D-NEW)}$$

### 3.12 Patterns

Pattern typing statements have the form $\Gamma \vdash \mathtt{p} \in \mathtt{T} \rhd \Delta$. That is, each pattern has a type, describing the shape of the values that it can match, and moreover gives rise to a set of type- and term-variable bindings.

A variable pattern x:T matches any value of type T and gives rise to a binding for the variable x.

$$\frac{\Gamma \vdash \mathtt{T} \in \mathtt{Type}}{\Gamma \vdash \mathtt{x{:}T} \in \mathtt{T} \rhd \mathtt{x{:}T}} \quad \text{(P-VAR)}$$

A wildcard pattern _:T matches any value of type T but does not give rise to any variable bindings.

$$\frac{\Gamma \vdash \mathtt{T} \in \mathtt{Type}}{\Gamma \vdash \mathtt{\_{:}T} \in \mathtt{T} \rhd \langle \textit{empty context} \rangle} \quad \text{(P-WILD)}$$

A layered pattern x:T@p matches a value of type T. We return whatever variables are bound in p, plus a binding for x.

$$\frac{\Gamma \vdash \mathtt{T} \in \mathtt{Type} \qquad \Gamma \vdash \mathtt{p} \in \mathtt{T} \rhd \Delta}{\Gamma \vdash \mathtt{x{:}T@p} \in \mathtt{T} \rhd \mathtt{x{:}T}, \Delta} \quad \text{(P-LAYERED)}$$

A rec pattern accepts a value of type T, but the subpattern p is matched against a value with the unfolded recursive type U.

$$\frac{\Gamma \vdash \mathtt{T} \in \mathtt{Type} \qquad \mathtt{T} \rightsquigarrow \mathtt{U} \qquad \Gamma \vdash \mathtt{p} \in \mathtt{U} \rhd \Delta}{\Gamma \vdash \mathtt{(rec{:}T\ p)} \in \mathtt{T} \rhd \Delta} \quad \text{(P-REC)}$$

A record pattern $\mathtt{[l_1p_1 \ldots l_np_n]}$ has the type $\mathtt{[l_1T_1 \ldots l_nT_n]}$, where the $\mathtt{T}_i$'s are the types of its elements, and gives rise to a set of bindings including all the bindings from its subpatterns.

$$\frac{\Gamma \vdash \mathtt{p_1} \in \mathtt{T_1} \rhd \Delta_1 \quad \ldots \quad \Gamma \vdash \mathtt{p}_n \in \mathtt{T}_n \rhd \Delta_n}{\Gamma \vdash \mathtt{[l_1p_1 \ldots l_np_n]} \in \mathtt{[l_1T_1 \ldots l_nT_n]} \rhd \Delta_1, \ldots, \Delta_n} \quad \text{(P-RECORD)}$$

A package pattern `{X<U}p` matches any value of type `{X<U}T`, where `T` is the type of the pattern `p` (under the assumption that `X` is a subtype of `U`). The pattern `{X<U}p` yields not only the bindings produced by `p`, but also the type binding `X<U`.

$$\frac{\Gamma \vdash \mathtt{U} \in \mathtt{K} \qquad \Gamma, \mathtt{X{<}U} \vdash \mathtt{p} \in \mathtt{T} \triangleright \Delta}{\Gamma \vdash \mathtt{\{X{<}U\}p} \in \mathtt{\{X{<}U\}T} \triangleright \mathtt{X{<}U}, \Delta} \qquad \text{(P-PACKAGE)}$$

### 3.13 Process Abstractions

A process abstraction `p=e` requires an argument of type `T`, where `T` is the type of the pattern `p`. The process `e` is typechecked in a context extended with the bindings $\Delta$ introduced by `p`.

$$\frac{\Gamma \vdash \mathtt{p} \in \mathtt{T} \triangleright \Delta \qquad \Gamma, \Delta \vdash \mathtt{e}\ \mathit{ok}}{\Gamma \vdash \mathtt{p{=}e} \in \mathtt{T}} \qquad \text{(A-ABS)}$$

### 3.14 Processes

The typing rules for processes are the simplest of all. The parallel composition of two processes is well formed in a given context if both parts are.

$$\frac{\Gamma \vdash \mathtt{e}_1\ \mathit{ok} \qquad \Gamma \vdash \mathtt{e}_2\ \mathit{ok}}{\Gamma \vdash \mathtt{(e_1 \mid e_2)}\ \mathit{ok}} \qquad \text{(E-PRL)}$$

An input expression `v?a` is well formed if `v` is a channel for which we have input permission, i.e., it has type `?T` for some `T`, and `a` is a well formed abstraction which accepts a value of type `T`.

$$\frac{\Gamma \vdash \mathtt{v} \in \mathtt{?T} \qquad \Gamma \vdash \mathtt{a} \in \mathtt{T}}{\Gamma \vdash \mathtt{v?a}\ \mathit{ok}} \qquad \text{(E-IN)}$$

Symmetrically, an output expression $\mathtt{v}_1\,!\,\mathtt{v}_2$ is well formed if $\mathtt{v}_1$ has an output channel type `!T`, for some `T`, and $\mathtt{v}_2$ has type `T`.

$$\frac{\Gamma \vdash \mathtt{v}_1 \in \mathtt{!T} \qquad \Gamma \vdash \mathtt{v}_2 \in \mathtt{T}}{\Gamma \vdash \mathtt{v}_1\,!\,\mathtt{v}_2\ \mathit{ok}} \qquad \text{(E-OUT)}$$

Finally, a local declaration provides a set of bindings $\Delta$ in which the process body is checked.

$$\frac{\Gamma \vdash \mathtt{d} \triangleright \Delta \qquad \Gamma, \Delta \vdash \mathtt{e}\ \mathit{ok}}{\Gamma \vdash \mathtt{(d\ e)}\ \mathit{ok}} \qquad \text{(E-DEC)}$$

A conditional expression is well formed if the guard expression has boolean type and the two branches of the conditional are well formed.

$$\frac{\Gamma \vdash \mathtt{b} \in \mathtt{Bool} \qquad \Gamma \vdash \mathtt{e}_1\ ok \qquad \Gamma \vdash \mathtt{e}_2\ ok}{\Gamma \vdash \mathtt{if\ b\ then\ e_1\ else\ e_2}\ ok} \tag{E-IF}$$

### 3.15 Type Safety

The relation between the type system and the operational semantics can be expressed in the form of two slogans: *evaluation cannot fail in well-typed processes*, and *reduction preserves typing*. We define runtime failure by means of a set of inference rule similar in form to Pict's reduction rules (for the sake of brevity, we only present the most important rules).

The most important type of failure we hope to prevent is pattern-matching failure during communication (this type of failure can also occur in a communication with a replicated input, but we elide that rule):

$$\frac{\{\mathtt{p} \mapsto \mathtt{v}\}\ \text{undefined}}{(\mathtt{x!v}\ \mid\ \mathtt{x?p} = \mathtt{e})\ fails} \tag{FAIL-COMM}$$

In addition, a process fails if it attempts to use any value other than a channel as the subject of a communication (recall that we do not have any syntax for channel constants, only variables which range over channels). For example, `[]!23` *fails*, since it attempts to use the record value `[]` as a channel. (We omit the rules for similar failures in input and replicated input prefixes.)

$$\frac{\mathtt{v}_1\ \text{is not a variable}}{\mathtt{v}_1\,!\,\mathtt{v}_2\ fails} \tag{FAIL-OUT}$$

Failures may also occur inside local declarations and parallel compositions of processes (the FAIL-STR rule, in combination with FAIL-PRL, captures the case when a failure occurs in the right-hand subterm of a parallel composition):

$$\frac{\mathtt{e}\ fails}{(\mathtt{d\ e})\ fails} \tag{FAIL-DEC}$$

$$\frac{\mathtt{e}_1\ fails}{(\mathtt{e}_1\ \mid\ \mathtt{e}_2)\ fails} \tag{FAIL-PRL}$$

We reuse the structural congruence relation (from Section 2.5) to capture the distributed nature of failures. A process is considered to have failed if any two subprocesses at the "top level" (i.e. not guarded by any input prefixes) may be brought into proximity by structural manipulations so that they fail.

$$\frac{\mathtt{e}_1 \equiv \mathtt{e}_2 \qquad \mathtt{e}_2\ \textit{fails}}{\mathtt{e}_1\ \textit{fails}} \qquad \text{(FAIL-STR)}$$

The key safety properties of the type system may now be stated formally:

**3.15.1 Conjecture [Type safety]:** If $\Gamma \vdash \mathtt{e}$ then $\mathtt{e}$ does not fail.

**3.15.2 Conjecture [Subject reduction]:** If $\Gamma \vdash \mathtt{e}_1$ and $\mathtt{e}_1 \rightarrow \mathtt{e}_2$ then $\Gamma \vdash \mathtt{e}_2$.

The metatheoretic foundations needed to carry out proofs of these properties are well established for the major components of the Pict type system—for channel types and subtyping by Pierce and Sangiorgi [PS93], for polymorphic channels by Turner [Tur96], and for higher-order polymorphism with subtyping by Pierce and Steffen [PS97b] and Compagnoni [Com94]. However, the properties for the full language remain conjectures, strictly speaking, since we have not checked the type system as a whole.

## 4 Derived Forms

The statically-typed core language of Pict is a powerful, safe, and unacceptably verbose programming notation. In this section, we show how more convenient high-level constructs are built up from the core by means of source-to-source translations—following in the tradition of numerous papers showing how various high-level features can be encoded in the $\pi$-calculus [San92, San94, San93, Mil90, Jon93, Wal95, Ama94, AP94, etc.]. We discuss only the more interesting translation rules; the complete list can be found in the Pict Language Definition.

### 4.1 Simple Translations

Large programs often contain long sequences of declarations like $\mathtt{(new\ x_1 \ldots (new\ x_n\ e))}$. To avoid proliferation of parentheses, we introduce the more compact syntactic form $\mathtt{(new\ x_1\ \ldots\ new\ x_n\ e)}$ in the high-level language. Formally, we extend the syntactic category of processes with $n$-ary declarations of the form $\mathtt{(d_1\ \ldots\ d_n\ e)}$ and introduce a translation rule

$$\mathtt{(d_1 \ldots d_n\ e)} \Rightarrow \mathtt{(d_1\ \ldots\ (d_n\ e))} \qquad \text{(TR-DECSEQ)}$$

that shows how $n$-ary declarations may be interpreted as expressions in the core language.

In sequences of declarations, it is often convenient to start some process running in parallel with the evaluation of the remainder of the declaration. We introduce the declaration keyword `run` for this purpose. After a declaration sequence has been translated into a nested collection of individual declarations, `run` declarations may be translated into simple parallel compositions:

(run $e_1$ $e_2$) $\Rightarrow$ ($e_1$ | $e_2$) (TR-RUN)

For example, the process

```
(run print!"twittering"
 run print!"rising"
 print!"overhead passing")
```

is transformed by TR-DECSEQ followed by two applications of TR-RUN into:

```
(print!"twittering" | (print!"rising" | print!"overhead passing"))
```

Many variants of the $\pi$-calculus allow *process abstractions* like $F(x, y) = \bar{x}y \mid \bar{x}y$. In Pict, such abstractions are introduced via the declaration keyword `def`, as in `def f [x y] = (x!y | x!y)`, and instances are created using the same syntax as output expressions, as in `f![a b]`. The coincidence between the notations for sending on a channel and instantiating a process abstraction is not accidental: we translate a process abstraction like the one above into a channel declaration `new f` and a replicated receiver `f?*[x y] = (x!y | x!y)`, so that instantiating an abstraction actually *is* just an output. Formally, this translation is captured by the following rule:

(def x p = $e_1$ $e_2$) $\Rightarrow$ (new x (x?*p = $e_1$ | $e_2$))

Recursive and mutually recursive definitions are also allowed. The first definition in a recursive group is introduced by `def`, the others with `and`.

```
def f [x y] = ... g![a b] ...
and g [z w] = ... f![a b] ...
```

The general translation rule, then, is:

(def $x_1 a_1$ ... and $x_n a_n$ e) $\Rightarrow$
(new $x_1$ ... (new $x_n$ ($x_1$?*$a_1$ | ... | $x_n$?*$a_n$ | e)) ... ) (TR-DEF)

Note that TR-DEF is a transformation on typed expressions. However, since the actual type of the channel $x_i$ is determined by the type of the pattern $p_i$, we omit the type annotation.

### 4.2 Complex Values

So far, all the value expressions we have encountered have been built up in an extremely simple way, using just variables, channels, basic values, tuples of values, and records of values. These *simple values* are important because they are exactly the entities that can be passed along channels and participate in pattern matching.

In real programs, it is very common to write an expression that computes a simple value and immediately sends it along some channel. For example, the process `(new n c!n)` creates a fresh channel `n` and sends it off along `c`. An alternative syntax for such expressions, which often makes them easier to understand, puts the whole value-expression *inside* the output: `c!(new n n)`. In general, it is useful to allow such expressions in any position where a simple value is expected. Formally, we extend the syntactic category of values with declaration values of the form `(d v)`. We use the term *complex value* for an expression in the extended syntax that does not fall within the core language.

When we write `c!(new n n)`, we do not mean to send the *expression* `(new n n)` along `c`. A complex value is always evaluated "strictly" to yield a simple value, which is substituted for the complex expression.

In introducing complex values, we have taken a fairly serious step: we must now define the meaning of a complex value occurring in any position where simple values were formerly allowed. For example, the nested expression `c![23 (new x x) (new y y)]` must be interpreted as a core language expression that creates two new channels, packages them into a simple tuple along with the integer `23` and sends the result along `c`.

We interpret arbitrary complex values using a general "continuation-passing" translation. Given a complex value `v` and a continuation channel `c`, the expression $[\![v \to c]\!]$ will denote a process that evaluates `v` and sends the resulting simple value along `c`. We then introduce translation rules for process expressions containing complex values. For example, the rule

$$v_1!v_2 \Rightarrow (\text{new } c\ ([\![v_1 \to c]\!] \mid c?x = [\![v_2 \to x]\!])) \qquad \text{(TR-OUT)}$$

translates an output $v_1!v_2$ into a process expression that first allocates a fresh continuation channel `c`, evaluates $v_1$, waits for its result to be sent along `c`, and then evaluates $v_2$, sending the result directly along the channel `x` that resulted from the evaluation of $v_1$. Input processes containing complex values are translated similarly:

$$v?a \Rightarrow (\text{new } c\ ([\![v \to c]\!] \mid c?x = x?a)) \qquad \text{(TR-IN)}$$

$$v?{*}a \Rightarrow (\text{new } c\ ([\![v \to c]\!] \mid c?x = x?{*}a)) \qquad \text{(TR-RIN)}$$

The continuation-passing translation itself is defined by induction on the syntax of value expressions:

$$
\begin{aligned}
[\![\mathtt{x} \rightarrow \mathtt{c}]\!] &= \mathtt{c!x} \\
[\![\mathtt{k} \rightarrow \mathtt{c}]\!] &= \mathtt{c!k} \\
[\![\mathtt{(d\ v)} \rightarrow \mathtt{c}]\!] &= \mathtt{(d}\ [\![\mathtt{v} \rightarrow \mathtt{c}]\!]\mathtt{)} \\
[\![\mathtt{(rec{:}T\ v)} \rightarrow \mathtt{c}]\!] &= \mathtt{(new\ c'}\ \ \mathtt{(}[\![\mathtt{v} \rightarrow \mathtt{c'}]\!]\ \mathtt{|}\ \mathtt{c'?x\ =\ c!(rec{:}T\ x)))} \\
[\![\mathtt{\{T\}v} \rightarrow \mathtt{c}]\!] &= \mathtt{(new\ c'}\ \ \mathtt{(}[\![\mathtt{v} \rightarrow \mathtt{c'}]\!]\ \mathtt{|}\ \mathtt{c'?x\ =\ c!\{T\}x))}
\end{aligned}
$$

Record values are evaluated left-to-right:

$$
\begin{aligned}
[\![\mathtt{[l_1v_1\ldots l_nv_n]} \rightarrow \mathtt{c}]\!] = \mathtt{(new\ c_1}\ \ &\mathtt{(}[\![\mathtt{v_1} \rightarrow \mathtt{c_1}]\!]\ \mathtt{|}\ \mathtt{c_1?x_1\ =\ \ldots} \\
&\mathtt{(new\ c_n}\ \ \mathtt{(}[\![\mathtt{v_n} \rightarrow \mathtt{c_n}]\!]\ \mathtt{|}\ \mathtt{c_n?x_n\ =} \\
&\quad \mathtt{c![l_1x_1\ldots l_nx_n]))\ \ \ldots\ \ ))}
\end{aligned}
$$

### 4.3 Value Declarations

Since complex value expressions may become long or involve expensive computations, it is convenient to introduce a new declaration form that evaluates a complex value and names its result. For example, `(val x = v e)` binds `x` to the result of evaluating `v` and then executes `e`. Formally, `val` declarations are translated using the continuation-passing translation:

$$
\mathtt{(val\ p{=}v\ e)} \;\Rightarrow\; \mathtt{(new\ c}\ \ \mathtt{(}[\![\mathtt{v} \rightarrow \mathtt{c}]\!]\ \mathtt{|}\ \mathtt{c?p\ =\ e))} \qquad \text{(TR-VAL)}
$$

Note that when a `val` declaration `(val p=v e)` is translated into the core language, the body `e` appears inside an input prefix. This fact implies that `val` declarations are *strict* or *blocking*: the body cannot proceed until the bindings introduced by the `val` have actually been established.

### 4.4 Application

Of course, allowing declarations inside values represents only a minor convenience; the usefulness of this extension by itself would not justify all of the foregoing machinery. But having established the basic pattern of simplifying complex value expressions by means of a continuation-passing transformation, we can apply it to a much more useful extension. In value expressions, we allow the *application* syntax $\mathtt{(v\ v_1\ \ldots\ v_n)}$. For example, if we define a `double` function by

```
def double [s:String r:!String] = concat![s s r]
```

(where `concat` is string concatenation), then, in the scope of the declaration, we can write `(double s)` as a value, dropping the explicit result channel `r`. For example, `print!(double "soothe")` causes `"soothesoothe"` to be sent along the built-in channel `print`.

In fact, we allow a slightly more general syntax for application which enables argument values to be labelled and witness types to be provided (in case the operation is polymorphic). We define the meaning of application by adding a clause to the definition of the continuation-passing translation:

$$
\begin{aligned}
&[\![(\mathtt{v}\ |\mathtt{T}_1 \ldots \mathtt{T}_n|\ \mathtt{l}_1\mathtt{v}_1 \ldots \mathtt{l}_n\mathtt{v}_n) \to \mathtt{c}]\!] \\
&\quad = (\mathtt{new}\ \mathtt{c}'\ \ ([\![\mathtt{v} \to \mathtt{c}']\!]\ |\ \mathtt{c}'?\mathtt{x} = \ldots \\
&\qquad (\mathtt{new}\ \mathtt{c}_1\ \ ([\![\mathtt{v}_1 \to \mathtt{c}_1]\!]\ |\ \mathtt{c}_1?\mathtt{x}_1 = \ldots \\
&\qquad\quad (\mathtt{new}\ \mathtt{c}_n\ \ ([\![\mathtt{v}_n \to \mathtt{c}_n]\!]\ |\ \mathtt{c}_n?\mathtt{x}_n = \\
&\qquad\qquad \mathtt{x!\{T_1\}\ldots\{T_n\}[l_1x_1\ldots l_nx_n\ c]))\ldots))))}
\end{aligned}
$$

The 'function' value `v` is evaluated first, followed by the argument values $\mathtt{v}_1$ to $\mathtt{v}_n$. Finally, the function is called and instructed to return its result along the application expression's continuation channel `c`.

## 4.5 Abstractions

Although Pict's core language and type system do not distinguish between "real functions" and processes that act like functions, it is nevertheless often useful to write parts of programs in a functional style. This is supported by a small extension to the syntactic class of abstractions, mirroring the ability to omit the names of result parameters in applications. For example, we replace a process definition of the form $\mathtt{def\ f\ [a_1\ a_2\ a_3\ r]\ =\ r!v}$, where the whole body of the definition consists of just an output of some (complex) value on the result channel `r`, by a "function definition" $\mathtt{def\ f\ (a_1\ a_2\ a_3)\ =\ v}$ that avoids explicitly giving a name to `r`. Formally, this is captured by the following translation rule for abstractions:

$$\mathtt{(|X_1{<}T_1\ldots X_n{<}T_n|\ \ l_1p_1\ldots l_np_n):T\ =\ v} \Rightarrow$$

$$\mathtt{\{X_1{<}T_1\}\ldots\{X_n{<}T_n\}[l_1p_1\ldots l_np_n\ \ r:!T]\ =\ r!v} \qquad \text{(TR-VABS)}$$

The derived form also allows for type arguments in a function definition, which are translated to package patterns. Note that the explicit result type annotation `T` becomes a type annotation `!T` on the result channel.

Since anonymous process declarations like `(def x [] = e x)` or `(def x () = v x)` are frequently useful for higher-order programming, we provide anonymous abstractions as a special form of value. We do not need an extra case in our continuation-passing translation to describe the meaning of this special form: we just add a local transformation on values:

`\a` ⇒ `(def x a  x)` (TR-ANONABS)

For example,

```
def applyTwice (f x) = (f (f x))
val y = (applyTwice \ (x) = (+ x 1)  3)
```

defines a function `applyTwice` and passes it an anonymous function that adds one to its argument.

### 4.6 Examples

To illustrate some of the high-level forms we have introduced, here is the list example from Section 2.4 rewritten using the full syntax:

```
type (List X) = (rec L = ![![] ![X L]])
def nil (|X|) : (List X) = (rec \ [n c] = n![])
def cons (|X| hd:X tl:(List X)) : (List X) = (rec \ [n c]
                                           = c![hd tl])
```

Uses of `nil` and `cons` can also be streamlined by using application syntax:

```
val l = (cons 22 (cons 33 (cons 44 (nil))))
```

Another example illustrates how we can build a simple reference cell object in Pict:

```
def newRef (|X| init:X) =
  (new l:^X
   run l!init
   [set = \ [v:X c:![]] = l?x = (l!v | c![])
    get = \ [r:!X]      = l?x = (l!x | r!x)])
```

Each message sent along `newRef` consists of a pair of values: `init`, the initial value of the reference cell that is to be created, and an implicit result channel that the server uses to return the newly created reference cell to the requesting client. After reading a request, the server creates a new channel `l` which acts as a "container" for the current value of the reference cell. Sending a value along `l` represents the action of placing a value in the container. Receiving a value from `l` empties the container; it is then the receiver's responsibility to refill the container by transmitting a new value along `l`. The container is initialized by sending `init` along `l`.

In parallel with initializing the container `l`, `newRef` returns a record containing `set` and `get` methods (process abstractions). Each method waits for a request on its service port; having received one, it reads `l` to obtain the current value of the cell, refills `l` as appropriate, and sends a result (or acknowledgement) to the client. It is possible that multiple copies of each method may be running in parallel at any given moment. But since there is never any more than one sender on `l`, all but one of them will be blocked waiting for an input on `l`.

## 5 Discussion

We now return to the motivating questions from the introduction and summarize what we have learned.

*What is it like to program in the $\pi$-calculus? What kind of high-level language can be built on it?*

The $\pi$-calculus is best thought of as a kind of concurrent machine code: it is simple, flexible, and efficiently implementable, and it offers a suitable target for compilation of higher-level linguistic features. Indeed, the variety of features whose semantics can be expressed in terms of message passing is so wide that many quite different language designs could have arisen from our experiment.

It is worth bearing in mind that choosing $\pi$-calculus as a semantic framework strongly discourages the use of some potentially useful language features, such as process priorities and exceptions, which cannot be easily formalized in this setting. A particularly important feature that is not addressed by $\pi$-calculus is physical distribution, since the semantic framework of the $\pi$-calculus lacks necessary concepts such as process location and failure. This shortcoming has been addressed in a recent language design project at Inria-Roquencourt, based on a variant of the $\pi$-calculus [FG96] extended with distribution primitives [FGL$^+$96]; a related project is underway at the University of Pennsylvania and Indiana. Cardelli's Obliq [Car95] achieves related aims by building on a primitive notion of network objects.

Pict belongs to a sizeable family of concurrent programming language designs inspired by theoretical calculi, including Vasconcelos's TyCo [Vas94], Kobayashi's HACL [Kob96], and numerous actor languages [Hew77, Agh86, etc.]. A particularly close relative is the language Oz [Smo95], which integrates functional, object-oriented, and concurrent constraint programming by translation into a common core calculus [Smo94]. Although this calculus uses concurrent constraints as its basic communication mechanism, the encoding of high-level features is strongly reminiscent of Pict.

Our choice of high-level language features leads to a programming style similar to that found in functional languages with channel-based concurrency such as PFL [Hol83], Amber [Car86], CML [Rep91, BMT92], Facile [GMP89], Poly/ML [Mat91], and Concurrent Haskell [JGF96]. The most significant difference lies in the type system: the impredicative polymorphism of Pict permits the encoding of polymorphic functions using polymorphic communication. This pun is not possible in languages whose type systems are based on ML polymorphism, where channels cannot carry messages of varying types. Also, the refined channel types provided by Pict (such as input-only and output-only channels) give the programmer useful extra control over channel usage in programs. Languages such as CML, Poly/ML, and Concurrent Haskell do not distinguish different modes of channel usage (and therefore also miss the opportunity to optimise the implementation of communication by exploiting explicit type information).

*What kinds of concurrent objects arise in this setting?*

We have found that a simple style of objects arises almost unavoidably in message-based concurrent programming: an object, in this view, is just a group of agents that cooperate to provide some collection of services to the "outside world," jointly maintaining the consistency of some shared data. It is convenient to group these services together as a record of named channels, allowing access to the whole collection of services to be passed around between clients as a single unit.

However, the more subtle mechanisms found in many concurrent object-oriented languages, such as dynamic method lookup and inheritance of synchronization policies, do not arise in the same "inevitable" way. Rather than commit to a particular high-level object model in Pict, we have chosen to provide a framework for experimenting with a variety of designs. Pict's type system incorporates a number of powerful constructs, such as higher-order subtyping, especially for this purpose. Preliminary experiments with concurrent objects in Pict are described in [PT95]. Some more sophisticated proposals are described in [NSL96].

*Can the $\pi$-calculus be implemented efficiently?*

Pict's high-level language is defined by means of a translation into a $\pi$-calculus core language. This is a very useful style of definition as far as the compilation of Pict is concerned, since it identifies a very small calculus that is sufficient to implement the whole of Pict. The operational semantics of $\pi$-calculus, plus a number well-known program equivalences, give rise a number of easy to implement (and provably correct) program optimizations, many of which generalise optimizations already commonly used in compilers for functional languages. Our Pict compiler does all of its static analysis of programs, optimization, and code generation using a $\pi$-calculus core language. Of course, encoding a high-level language into a low-level language such as $\pi$-calculus does run the risk of losing useful information about a program. Fortunately, we have so far been able to regain the information we need by exploiting explicit type information (in particular, we make heavy use of type information to optimize the implementation of communication).

Functional code, when compiled by our Pict compiler, comes out looking very like the code generated by a continuation-passing compiler. We compile to C for portability and easy inter-operability with existing program libraries, though this does have a significant cost in efficiency for the compiled code. (Tarditi, Acharya, and Lee [TAL90] report that, when they modified the New Jersey Standard ML compiler so that it generated C code, it produced code which ran approximately twice as slow as code produced by the native code generator.)

Preliminary comparisons of the code produced by Pict and New Jersey SML [Tur96] indicate that functional code compiled by Pict runs approximately six times slower than that produced by New Jersey SML. We find this quite encouraging, since the Pict compiler has had very little tuning and lacks a number of important optimisations; in particular, the representation of closures in Pict is not yet optimised in any way. Moreover, New Jersey SML has the advantage of compiling to native code. The code we generate is very similar to the code generated by Tarditi, Acharya, and Lee's `sml2c` compiler, so we might reasonably expect to gain a factor of two if we produced native code instead of C code, which would leave us within a factor of three of the performance of New Jersey SML.

To give an idea of how fast our channel-based communication primitives are, we compared the performance of the Pict `nqueens` program with an equivalent Concurrent ML program which uses CML's channel primitives to implement the result channels used in Pict [Tur96]. The CML program ran almost four times slower than Pict. This is not to say that CML programs in general run four times slower than Pict, since CML programs typically consist of large amounts of SML code, which runs faster. However, the comparison does give an idea of the raw performance of Pict's communication primitives (especially since the CML program had the advantage of being compiled to native code).

*Can we design a practical type system for the $\pi$-calculus combining subtyping and higher-order polymorphism?*

The Pict type system integrates a number of well-studied ideas: Milner's simple sorting discipline for channels [Mil91], polymorphic channels [Tur96], higher-order polymorphism [Gir72], input/output modalities [PS93], higher-order subtyping [Car90, CL91, PT94, PS97b, Com94], and recursive types [MPS86, AC93]. However, the key to obtaining a workable type system for Pict was the development of a practical type inference algorithm. Pict's partial type inference algorithm is surprisingly simple and easy to understand, but our experience has been that it gives very acceptable results. One of the reasons partial type inference works well in Pict is that many programs already contain explicit type annotations for the purposes of documentation. In many cases these explicit type annotations are sufficient to uniquely determine the types which should be assigned to all other bound variables.

In the design of Pict's type system we gave up the goal of complete type inference in preference for more powerful type-theoretic constructs. For example, Pict's impredicative polymorphism directly supports useful features such as first-class existential types, which are not expressible in simpler, predictive, polymorphic type systems. Thus, without any further extensions to the language, Pict programmers can structure programs using abstract datatypes, a facility that is used extensively in Pict's standard libraries. We are working on further extensions to Pict's type system which will enable better "programming in the large" but, unlike Standard ML, will not require a separate module-level language. In particular, we hope to extend Pict's treatment of existential types to account for type sharing, using techniques similar to those proposed by Leroy [Ler95] and Harper and Lillibridge [HL94].

## Acknowledgements

Robin Milner's past and present work on programming languages, concurrency, and the $\pi$-calculus in particular is very strongly in the background of this project, and conversations with Robin have contributed many specific insights. The idea of basing a programming language design on the $\pi$-calculus was planted by Bob Harper and developed into a research project in the summer of 1992 in discussions of concurrent object-oriented programming languages with the Edinburgh ML Club. From Davide Sangiorgi, we learned about the higher-order $\pi$-calculus and the many ways of encoding $\lambda$-calculi in the $\pi$-calculus. Didier Rémy helped build the original PIC compiler, on which the first version of the present Pict compiler was based [PRT93], and joined in many discussions about the integration of processes and functions. Uwe Nestmann's research on proof techniques for compilations between concurrent calculi sharpened our ideas about the formal foundations of Pict. Martin Steffen helped study the formal foundations of the subtyping algorithm. Dilip Sequeira contributed both code and ideas to an earlier implementation of type inference and record type checking. Kohei Honda, Nobuko Yoshida, and Peter Sewell helped us think about fairness in process calculi. Conversations with Luca Cardelli, Georges Gonthier, Sigbjorn Finne, Cliff Jones, Naoki Kobayashi, Martin Müller, Joachim Niehren, Oscar Nierstrasz, Simon Peyton Jones, John Reppy, Gert Smolka, and David Walker have deepened our understanding of the $\pi$-calculus and concurrent programming languages. Helpful comments from two anonymous referees improved this paper in many ways.

Pierce has been supported by fellowships from the U.K. Science and Engineering Research Council and Engineering and Physical Sciences Research Council, by the ESPRIT Basic Research Actions TYPES and CONFER and by the National Science Foundation under CAREER grant CCR-9701826. Turner has been supported by Harlequin Ltd. and a fellowship from the U.K. Engineering and Physical Sciences Research Council.

## References

[AC93] Roberto M. Amadio and Luca Cardelli. Subtyping recursive types. *ACM Transactions on Programming Languages and Systems*, 15(4):575–631, 1993. A preliminary version appeared in POPL '91 (pp. 104–118) and as DEC Systems Research Center Research Report number 62, August 1990.

[AC96] Martín Abadi and Luca Cardelli. *A Theory of Objects*. Springer-Verlag, 1996.

[ACS96] Roberto M. Amadio, Ilaria Castellani, and Davide Sangiorgi. On bisimulations for the asynchronous pi-calculus. In *Seventh International Conference on Concurrency Theory (CONCUR '96)*, August 1996.

[Agh86] Gul A. Agha. *Actors: a Model of Concurrent Computation in Distributed Systems*. MIT Press, Cambridge, MA, 1986.

[Ama94] Roberto M. Amadio. Translating core Facile. Technical Report ECRC-TR-3-94, European Computer-Industry Research Center, GmbH, Munich, 1994. Also available as a technical report from CRIN(CNRS)-Inria (Nancy).

[AP94] Amadio and Prasad. Localities and failures. *FSTTCS: Foundations of Software Technology and Theoretical Computer Science*, 14, 1994. Full version available as European Computer-Industry Research Center technical report ECRC-M2-R10, 1994.

[Bar92] Henk Barendregt. Lambda calculi with types. In Gabbay Abramsky and Maibaum, editors, *Handbook of Logic in Computer Science*, volume II. Oxford University Press, 1992.

[BMT92] Dave Berry, Robin Milner, and David N. Turner. A semantics for ML concurrency primitives. In *ACM Principles of Programming Languages*, January 1992.

[Bou92] Gérard Boudol. Asynchrony and the $\pi$-calculus (note). Rapporte de Recherche 1702, INRIA Sofia-Antipolis, May 1992.

[Bru94] Kim B. Bruce. A paradigmatic object-oriented programming language: Design, static typing and semantics. *Journal of Functional Programming*, 4(2), April 1994. A preliminary version appeared in POPL 1993 under the title "Safe Type Checking in a Statically Typed Object-Oriented Programming Language".

[Car84] Luca Cardelli. A semantics of multiple inheritance. In G. Kahn, D. MacQueen, and G. Plotkin, editors, *Semantics of Data Types*, volume 173 of *Lecture Notes in Computer Science*, pages 51–67. Springer-Verlag, 1984. Full version in *Information and Computation* 76(2/3):138–164, 1988.

[Car86] Luca Cardelli. Amber. In Guy Cousineau, Pierre-Louis Curien, and Bernard Robinet, editors, *Combinators and Functional Programming Languages*, pages 21–47. Springer-Verlag, 1986. Lecture Notes in Computer Science No. 242.

[Car90] Luca Cardelli. Notes about $F^{\omega}_{<:}$. Unpublished manuscript, October 1990.

[Car91] Luca Cardelli. Typeful programming. In E. J. Neuhold and M. Paul, editors, *Formal Description of Programming Concepts*. Springer-Verlag, 1991. An earlier version appeared as DEC Systems Research Center Research Report #45, February 1989.

[Car95] Luca Cardelli. A language with distributed scope. *Computing Systems*, 8(1):27–59, 1995. Short version in *Principles of Programming Languages (POPL)*, January 1995.

[CC91] Felice Cardone and Mario Coppo. Type inference with recursive types: Syntax and semantics. *Information and Computation*, 92(1):48–80, 1991.

[CHC90] William R. Cook, Walter L. Hill, and Peter S. Canning. Inheritance is not subtyping. In *Seventeenth Annual ACM Symposium on Principles of Programming Languages*, pages 125–135, San Francisco, CA, January 1990. Also in Carl A. Gunter and John C. Mitchell, editors, *Theoretical Aspects of Object-Oriented Programming: Types, Semantics, and Language Design* (MIT Press, 1994).

[CL91] Luca Cardelli and Giuseppe Longo. A semantic basis for Quest. *Journal of Functional Programming*, 1(4):417–458, October 1991. Preliminary version in ACM Conference on Lisp and Functional Programming, June 1990. Also available as DEC SRC Research Report 55, Feb. 1990.

[CMMS94] Luca Cardelli, Simone Martini, John C. Mitchell, and Andre Scedrov. An extension of system F with subtyping. *Information and Computation*, 109(1–2):4–56, 1994. A preliminary version appeared in TACS '91 (Sendai, Japan, pp. 750–770).

[Com94] Adriana B. Compagnoni. Decidability of higher-order subtyping with intersection types. In *Computer Science Logic*, September 1994. Kazimierz, Poland. Springer *Lecture Notes in Computer Science* 933, June 1995. Also available as University of Edinburgh, LFCS technical report ECS-LFCS-94-281, titled "Subtyping in $F^{\omega}_{\wedge}$ is decidable".

[CS87] G. Costa and C. Stirling. Weak and strong fairness in CCS. *Information and Computation*, 73(3):207–244, 1987.

[CW85] Luca Cardelli and Peter Wegner. On understanding types, data abstraction, and polymorphism. *Computing Surveys*, 17(4), December 1985.

[FG96] Cédric Fournet and Georges Gonthier. The reflexive chemical abstract machine and the join-calculus. In *Principles of Programming Languages*, January 1996.

[FGL+96] Cédric Fournet, Georges Gonthier, Jean-Jacques Lévy, Luc Maranget, and Didier Rémy. A calculus of mobile agents. In *7th International Conference on Concurrency Theory (CONCUR'96)*, pages 406–421, Pisa, Italy, August 1996. Springer-Verlag. LNCS 1119.

[FM94] Kathleen Fisher and John Mitchell. Notes on typed object-oriented programming. In *Proceedings of Theoretical Aspects of Computer Software, Sendai, Japan*, pages 844–885. Springer-Verlag, April 1994. LNCS 789.

[Gay93] Simon J. Gay. A sort inference algorithm for the polyadic $\pi$-calculus. In *Proceedings of the Twentieth ACM Symposium on Principles of Programming Languages*, January 1993.

[Gir72] Jean-Yves Girard. *Interprétation fonctionelle et élimination des coupures de l'arithmétique d'ordre supérieur*. PhD thesis, Université Paris VII, 1972.

[GMP89] Alessandro Giacalone, Prateek Mishra, and Sanjiva Prasad. Facile: A Symmetric Integration of Concurrent and Functional Programming. *International Journal of Parallel Programming*, 18(2):121–160, 1989.

[Hew77] C. Hewitt. Viewing control structures as patterns of passing messages. *Artificial Intelligence*, 8:323–364, 1977.

[HL94] Robert Harper and Mark Lillibridge. A type-theoretic approach to higher-order modules with sharing. In *Proceedings of the Twenty-First ACM Symposium on Principles of Programming Languages (POPL), Portland, Oregon*, pages 123–137, Portland, OR, January 1994.

[Hol83] Sören Holmström. PFL: A functional language for parallel programming, and its implementation. Programming Methodology Group, Report 7, University of Goteborg and Chalmers University of Technology, September 1983.

[Hon93] Kohei Honda. Types for dyadic interaction. In *CONCUR'93*, volume 715 of *Lecture Notes in Computer Science*, pages 509–523, 1993.

[Hon96] Kohei Honda. Composing processes. In *Principles of Programming Languages (POPL)*, pages 344–357, January 1996.

[HP95] Martin Hofmann and Benjamin Pierce. A unifying type-theoretic framework for objects. *Journal of Functional Programming*, 5(4):593–635, October 1995. Previous versions appeared in the Symposium on Theoretical Aspects of Computer Science, 1994, (pages 251–262) and, under the title "An Abstract View of Objects and Subtyping (Preliminary Report)," as University of Edinburgh, LFCS technical report ECS-LFCS-92-226, 1992.

[HT91] Kohei Honda and Mario Tokoro. An object calculus for asynchronous communication. In Pierre America, editor, *Proceedings of the European Conference on Object-Oriented Programming (ECOOP)*, volume 512 of *Lecture Notes in Computer Science*. Springer-Verlag, Berlin, Heidelberg, New York, Tokyo, 1991.

[HY94] Kohei Honda and Nobuko Yoshida. Combinatory representation of mobile processes. In *Principles of Programming Languages (POPL '94)*, pages 348–360, January 1994.

[JGF96] Simon Peyton Jones, Andrew Gordon, and Sigbjorn Finne. Concurrent Haskell. In *Conference Record of the 23rd ACM SIGPLAN-SIGACT Symposium on Principles of Programming Languages (POPL'96)*, pages 295–308, St. Petersburg, Florida, January 21–24, 1996. ACM Press.

[Jon93] Cliff B. Jones. A pi-calculus semantics for an object-based design notation. In E. Best, editor, *Proceedings of CONCUR'93*, LNCS 715, pages 158–172. Springer-Verlag, 1993.

[Kob96] Naoki Kobayashi. *Concurrent Linear Logic Programming*. PhD thesis, Department of Information Science, University of Tokyo, April 1996.

[KPT96] Naoki Kobayashi, Benjamin C. Pierce, and David N. Turner. Linearity and the pi-calculus. In *Principles of Programming Languages*, 1996.

[KY94] Naoki Kobayashi and Akinori Yonezawa. Type-theoretic foundations for concurrent object-oriented programming. In *Proceedings of ACM SIGPLAN Conference on Object-Oriented Programming Systems, Languages, and Applications (OOPSLA'94)*, pages 31–45, 1994.

[Ler95] Xavier Leroy. Applicative functors and fully transparent higher-order modules. In *Proceedings of the Twenty-Second ACM Symposium on Principles of Programming Languages (POPL), Portland, Oregon*, pages 142–153, San Francisco, California, January 1995.

[Mat91] David Matthews. A distributed concurrent implementation of Standard ML. Technical Report ECS-LFCS-91-174, University of Edinburgh, August 1991.

[Mil90] Robin Milner. Functions as processes. Research Report 1154, INRIA, Sofia Antipolis, 1990. Final version in *Journal of Mathematical Structures in Computer Science* 2(2):119–141, 1992.

[Mil91] Robin Milner. The polyadic $\pi$-calculus: a tutorial. Technical Report ECS–LFCS–91–180, Laboratory for Foundations of Computer Science, Department of Computer Science, University of Edinburgh, UK, October 1991. Appeared in *Proceedings of the International Summer School on Logic and Algebra of Specification*, Marktoberdorf, August 1991. Reprinted in *Logic and Algebra of Specification*, ed. F. L. Bauer, W. Brauer, and H. Schwichtenberg, Springer-Verlag, 1993.

[MP88] John Mitchell and Gordon Plotkin. Abstract types have existential type. *ACM Transactions on Programming Languages and Systems*, 10(3), July 1988.

[MPS86] David MacQueen, Gordon Plotkin, and Ravi Sethi. An ideal model for recursive polymorphic types. *Information and Control*, 71:95–130, 1986.

[MPW92] R. Milner, J. Parrow, and D. Walker. A calculus of mobile processes (Parts I and II). *Information and Computation*, 100:1–77, 1992.

[Nie95] Oscar Nierstrasz. Regular types for active objects. In O. Nierstrasz and D. Tsichritzis, editors, *Object-Oriented Software Composition*, pages 99–121. Prentice Hall, 1995. Earlier version in proceedings of *OOPSLA '93*, published in *ACM Sigplan Notices*, 28(10), October 1993, pp. 1–15.

[NP96] Uwe Nestmann and Benjamin C. Pierce. Decoding choice encodings. In *Proceedings of CONCUR '96*, August 1996.

[NSL96] Oscar Nierstrasz, Jean-Guy Schneider, and Markus Lumpe. Formalizing composable software systems—a research agenda. In *Formal Methods in Open, Object-Based Distributed Systems (FMOODS '96)*, February 1996.

[Pie97] Benjamin C. Pierce. Programming in the pi-calculus: A tutorial introduction to Pict. Available electronically, 1997.

[PRT93] Benjamin C. Pierce, Didier Rémy, and David N. Turner. A typed higher-order programming language based on the pi-calculus. In *Workshop on Type Theory and its Application to Computer Systems, Kyoto University*, July 1993.

[PS93] Benjamin Pierce and Davide Sangiorgi. Typing and subtyping for mobile processes. In *Logic in Computer Science*, 1993. Full version in *Mathematical Structures in Computer Science*, Vol. 6, No. 5, 1996.

[PS97a] Benjamin Pierce and Davide Sangiorgi. Behavioral equivalence in the polymorphic pi-calculus. In *Principles of Programming Languages (POPL)*, 1997. Full version to appear in *Journal of the ACM*.

[PS97b] Benjamin Pierce and Martin Steffen. Higher-order subtyping. *Theoretical Computer Science*, 176(1–2): 235–282, 1997. A preliminary version appeared in IFIP Working Conference on Programming Concepts, Methods and Calculi (PROCOMET), June 1994, and as University of Edinburgh technical report ECS-LFCS-94-280 and Universität Erlangen-Nürnberg Interner Bericht IMMD7-01/94, January 1994.

[PT94] Benjamin C. Pierce and David N. Turner. Simple type-theoretic foundations for object-oriented programming. *Journal of Functional Programming*, 4(2):207–247, April 1994. A preliminary version appeared in Principles of Programming Languages, 1993, and as University of Edinburgh technical report ECS-LFCS-92-225, under the title "Object-Oriented Programming Without Recursive Types".

[PT95] Benjamin C. Pierce and David N. Turner. Concurrent objects in a process calculus. In Takayasu Ito and Akinori Yonezawa, editors, *Theory and Practice of Parallel Programming (TPPP), Sendai, Japan (Nov. 1994)*, number 907 in Lecture Notes in Computer Science, pages 187–215. Springer-Verlag, April 1995.

[PT97] Benjamin C. Pierce and David N. Turner. Pict language definition. Available electronically, 1997.

[Rep91] John Reppy. CML: A higher-order concurrent language. In *Programming Language Design and Implementation*, pages 293–259. SIGPLAN, ACM, June 1991.

[Rey74] John Reynolds. Towards a theory of type structure. In *Proc. Colloque sur la Programmation*, pages 408–425, New York, 1974. Springer-Verlag LNCS 19.

[San92] Davide Sangiorgi. *Expressing Mobility in Process Algebras: First-Order and Higher-Order Paradigms*. PhD thesis, Department of Computer Science, University of Edinburgh, 1992.

[San93] Davide Sangiorgi. An investigation into functions as processes. In *Proc. Ninth International Conference on the Mathematical Foundations of Programming Semantics (MFPS'93)*, volume 802 of *Lecture Notes in Computer Science*, pages 143–159. Springer Verlag, 1993.

[San94] Davide Sangiorgi. The lazy lambda calculus in a concurrency scenario. *Information and Computation*, 111(1):120–153, 1994.

[Sew97] Peter Sewell. Observations on Pict, a nondeterministic programming language. Eighth International Conference on Concurrency Theory (CONCUR '97), 1997.

[Smo94] Gert Smolka. A Foundation for Concurrent Constraint Programming. In *Constraints in Computational Logics*, volume 845 of *Lecture Notes in Computer Science*, Munich, Germany, September 1994. Invited Talk.

[Smo95] Gert Smolka. The Oz programming model. In Jan van Leeuwen, editor, *Computer Science Today*, Lecture Notes in Computer Science, vol. 1000, pages 324–343. Springer-Verlag, Berlin, 1995.

[TAL90] David Tarditi, Anurag Acharya, and Peter Lee. No assembly required: Compiling Standard ML to C. Technical Report CMU-CS-90-187, School of Computer Science, Carnegie Mellon University, November 1990.

[THK94] Kaku Takeuchi, Kohei Honda, and Makoto Kubo. An interaction-based language and its typing system. In *Proceedings of PARLE'94*, pages 398–413. Springer-Verlag, 1994. Lecture Notes in Computer Science number 817.

[Tur96] David N. Turner. *The Polymorphic Pi-calulus: Theory and Implementation*. PhD thesis, University of Edinburgh, 1996.

[Vas94] Vasco T. Vasconcelos. Typed concurrent objects. In *Proceedings of the Eighth European Conference on Object-Oriented Programming (ECOOP)*, volume 821 of *Lecture Notes in Computer Science*, pages 100–117. Springer-Verlag, July 1994.

[VH93] Vasco T. Vasconcelos and Kohei Honda. Principal typing schemes in a polyadic pi-calculus. In *Proceedings of CONCUR '93*, July 1993. Also available as Keio University Report CS-92-004.

[Wal95] David Walker. Objects in the $\pi$-calculus. *Information and Computation*, 116:253–271, 1995.

# IV CONCURRENCY

# 16 On the Star Height of Unary Regular Behaviours

**Yoram Hirshfeld and Faron Moller**

## 1 Introduction

The *star height* of a regular expression is defined to be its maximum depth of nesting of the Kleene star closure operation. In this paper we are interested in the question as to whether or not the star height hierarchy of regular expressions is a genuine hierarchy when we interpret regular expressions as behaviours in the sense of Milner [1] and we restrict attention to a unary alphabet. That is, is it the case that for each integer $n$ there is a regular expression over the alphabet $\{a\}$ of star height $n$ such that no regular expression with star height less than $n$ is bisimilar to it?

The analogous question for regular languages is easily shown to be negative: it is an easy exercise in formal language theory to show that every regular language over a unary alphabet can be expressed by a regular expression with star height 1. However, Milner has conjectured in [1] that the answer for regular behaviours may well be positive. In this paper we demonstrate the validity of this conjecture. Note that if we allow our alphabet to contain (at least) two symbols, then as shown in [2] the star height hierarchy for regular languages does not collapse; a simple corollary of this, or of the result of this paper, is that this hierarchy also does not collapse for regular behaviours over alphabets of size greater than one.

The techniques that we introduce to demonstrate our result immediately give rise to Milner's *"loop derivative condition"* for infinite regular behaviours (Lemma 6.4 of [1]), giving a natural explanation for this phenomenon, and allow us to prove a further non-expressibility conjecture from [1], that a particular simple two-state automaton cannot be represented (up-to bisimilarity) by any regular expression. These applications of the techniques are presented as well in this paper as a precursor to the main result.

In Section 2 we provide a catalogue of basic definitions and results. In particular, we provide a "process algebraic" viewpoint of regular expressions and their associated finite automata. We end this section with a demonstration of Milner's *"loop derivative condition."* In Section 3 we present techniques which will prove useful for demonstrating our result, and end this section with a demonstration of the above-mentioned minor conjecture given by Milner [1]. Finally, in Section 4 we present the proof of Milner's star height conjecture.

## 2 Basic Definitions

In this section we briefly review some standard definitions from the theory of finite automata and regular expressions as well as present some basic notions of process theory. We end with an alternative proof of a result of Milner.

### 2.1 Automata, Languages, and Bisimulations

A *finite automaton* is a quintuple $M = \langle Q, \Sigma, \longrightarrow, s, F\rangle$, where: $Q$ is a finite set of *states*; $\Sigma$ is a finite *alphabet*; $\longrightarrow \;\subseteq\; Q \times \Sigma \times Q$ is a *transition relation*; $s \in Q$ is an *initial state*; and $F \subseteq Q$ is a set of *final (accepting) states*. We shall generally write the transition relation as $q \stackrel{a}{\longrightarrow} r$ for $\langle q, a, r\rangle \in \longrightarrow$, and we shall write $q \longrightarrow r$ whenever $q \stackrel{a}{\longrightarrow} r$ for some $a \in \Sigma$. We shall use $\longrightarrow^*$ and $\longrightarrow^+$ to represent, respectively, the reflexive transitive closure, and the transitive closure, of the relation $\longrightarrow$. We shall also write $q \stackrel{w}{\longrightarrow} r$ for $w = a_1 a_2 \cdots a_n \in \Sigma^*$ whenever there are states $q_1, q_2, \ldots, q_{n-1}$ such that $q \stackrel{a_1}{\longrightarrow} q_1 \stackrel{a_2}{\longrightarrow} \cdots q_{n-1} \stackrel{a_n}{\longrightarrow} r$. Inductively this relation is defined as: $q \stackrel{\lambda}{\longrightarrow} q$ for every state $q$ (where $\lambda$ represents the empty string, consisting of no symbols); and $q \stackrel{aw}{\longrightarrow} r$ whenever there is a state $q'$ such that $q \stackrel{a}{\longrightarrow} q' \stackrel{w}{\longrightarrow} r$. Note that care must be taken not to confuse $q \longrightarrow r$ and $q \stackrel{\lambda}{\longrightarrow} r$; we do not permit $\lambda$-transition in these automata, so whereas $q \longrightarrow r$ means that $q \stackrel{a}{\longrightarrow} r$ for some (unspecified) $a \in \Sigma$, $q \stackrel{\lambda}{\longrightarrow} r$ only holds when $q = r$.

The automaton is *deterministic* if the transition relation $\longrightarrow$ is deterministic, in the sense that for each state $q \in Q$ and each symbol $a \in \Sigma$ we have at most one state $r \in \Sigma$ such that $q \stackrel{a}{\longrightarrow} r$.

The *language* accepted by a state $q$ of an automaton, denoted $L(q)$, is defined to be the set of strings of symbols from $\Sigma^*$ which may lead from that state to a final state:

$$L(q) = \left\{w \in \Sigma^* : q \stackrel{w}{\longrightarrow} f \text{ for some } f \in F\right\}.$$

The language accepted by an automaton M, denoted $L(M)$, is then defined to be the language accepted by its initial state $s$: $L(M) = L(s)$.

The *norm* of a state $q \in Q$ of an automaton, denoted norm $(q)$, is defined to be the length of the shortest word accepted by that state:

$$\text{norm}\,(q) = \min\{\text{length}\,(w) : w \in L(q)\}.$$

By convention, we define norm $(q)$ to be infinite if $L(q) = \emptyset$. We say that the automaton is *normed* if all of its states have finite norm. Notice that if $q \longrightarrow r$ then norm $(q) \leq 1 +$ norm $(r)$; and if $0 <$ norm $(q) < \infty$ then $q \longrightarrow r$ for some $r$ with norm $(r) =$ norm $(q) - 1$.

A binary relation $\mathcal{R}$ between states of an automaton is a *bisimulation* if whenever $\langle q, r\rangle \in \mathcal{R}$ we have that

(i) If $q \stackrel{a}{\longrightarrow} q'$ then $r \stackrel{a}{\longrightarrow} r'$ with $\langle q', r'\rangle \in \mathcal{R}$;

(ii) If $r \stackrel{a}{\longrightarrow} r'$ then $q \stackrel{a}{\longrightarrow} q'$ with $\langle q', r'\rangle \in \mathcal{R}$;

(iii) $q \in F$ if and only if $r \in F$.

Two states $q$ and $r$ are *bisimilar*, or *bisimulation equivalent*, written $q \sim r$, if they are related by some bisimulation relation.

LEMMA 1

(i) If $q \sim r$ then $L(q) = L(r)$ and $\mathrm{norm}(q) = \mathrm{norm}(r)$.

(ii) Assuming that $q$ and $r$ are states of a normed and deterministic automaton, if $L(q) = L(r)$ then $q \sim r$.

*Proof*

(i) We can demonstrate by induction on the length of $w \in \Sigma^*$ that if $q \sim r$ and $q \xrightarrow{w} q'$ then $r \xrightarrow{w} r'$ with $q' \sim r'$. The result then easily follows.

(ii) Given a normed and deterministic automaton, it is straightforward to demonstrate that the binary relation $\{\langle q, r\rangle : L(q) = L(r)\}$ is a bisimulation. □

## 2.2 Regular Expressions and Their Automata

The language of *regular expressions* defined over the alphabet $\Sigma$ is given by the following syntax equation (where $a$ ranges over symbols of $\Sigma$):

$$e, f ::= \emptyset \mid \lambda \mid a \mid e + f \mid e \cdot f \mid e^*$$

The *star height* of a regular expression is defined to be its maximum depth of nesting of the Kleene star closure operation $e^*$, and is defined structurally as follows.

$$\begin{array}{ll} \mathrm{sh}(\emptyset) = 0 & \mathrm{sh}(e + f) = \max(\mathrm{sh}(e), \mathrm{sh}(f)) \\ \mathrm{sh}(\lambda) = 0 & \mathrm{sh}(e \cdot f) \;= \max(\mathrm{sh}(e), \mathrm{sh}(f)) \\ \mathrm{sh}(a) = 0 & \mathrm{sh}(e^*) \quad = 1 + \mathrm{sh}(e) \end{array}$$

Each regular expression $e$ gives rise to a *regular language* $L(e)$ defined structurally as follows.

$$\begin{array}{ll} L(\emptyset) = \emptyset & L(e + f) = L(e) \cup L(f) \\ L(\lambda) = \{\lambda\} & L(e \cdot f) \;= \{uv : u \in L(e) \text{ and } v \in L(f)\} \\ L(a) = \{a\} & L(e^*) \quad = \{u_1 \cdot u_2 \cdot \cdots \cdot u_n : n \geq 0 \text{ and each } u_i \in L(e)\} \end{array}$$

We can define the *norm* of an expression $e$ analogously to the norm of an automaton as the length of the shortest word in the language defined by the expression. This can be characterised structurally as follows.

$$\begin{array}{ll} \mathrm{norm}(\emptyset) = \infty & \mathrm{norm}(e + f) = \min(\mathrm{norm}(e), \mathrm{norm}(f)) \\ \mathrm{norm}(\lambda) = 0 & \mathrm{norm}(e \cdot f) \;= \mathrm{norm}(e) + \mathrm{norm}(f) \\ \mathrm{norm}(a) = 1 & \mathrm{norm}(e^*) \quad = 0 \end{array}$$

The language associated with a regular expression could alternatively be presented as the language accepted by the automaton associated with the expression as defined as follows. Firstly we define the following transition relation over regular expressions.

DEFINITION 2 The transition relation $\longrightarrow$ is defined to be the least relation satisfying the following inference rules: there is one axiom $(a)$ and five rules of inference which allow us to deduce a transition for a term (given below the line) if we can deduce a transition for a structurally simpler term (given above the line).

$$(a): \frac{}{a \xrightarrow{a} \lambda} \qquad (*): \frac{e \xrightarrow{a} e'}{e^* \xrightarrow{a} e' \cdot e^*}$$

$$(+_L): \frac{e \xrightarrow{a} e'}{e + f \xrightarrow{a} e'} \qquad (+_R): \frac{f \xrightarrow{a} f'}{e + f \xrightarrow{a} f'}$$

$$(\cdot_L): \frac{e \xrightarrow{a} e'}{e \cdot f \xrightarrow{a} e' \cdot f} \qquad (\cdot_R): \frac{f \xrightarrow{a} f'}{e \cdot f \xrightarrow{a} f'} (\mathrm{norm}\,(e) = 0)$$

Note that the side condition on the last rule ($\mathrm{norm}\,(e) = 0$) has just been characterized syntactically. Note further that $\mathrm{sh}\,(e) \geq \mathrm{sh}\,(f)$ whenever $e \longrightarrow f$ (and hence by induction whenever $e \longrightarrow^* f$).

The automaton associated with the regular expression $e$ defined over the alphabet $\Sigma$ is then given by $M_e = (Q, \Sigma, \longrightarrow, e, F)$, where $\longrightarrow$ is as given by Definition 2, $Q = \{f : e \longrightarrow^* f\}$ (which can easily be shown to be finite), and $F = \{f \in Q : \mathrm{norm}\,(f) = 0\}$.

We may now apply our automata-theoretic terms to regular expressions, and deduce for example that the language defined by a regular expression coincides with the language accepted by its associated automaton, as recorded by the following lemma.

LEMMA 3 For any regular expression $e$, $L(e) = L(M_e)$.

Although our construction of $M_e$ differs somewhat from that presented in the standard textbooks (as we translate regular expressions directly into $\lambda$-free automata rather than into automata with $\lambda$-transitions), the proof of Lemma 3 is still a straightforward exercise.

A further simple corollary of Lemma 3 is that the norm of an expression coincides with the norm of its associated automaton. Furthermore, we may adapt the definition of bisimilarity to hold between regular expressions—and between an expression and an automaton—and deduce the following important congruence property.

LEMMA 4 $\sim$ is a congruence relation over regular expressions. That is, if $e \sim f$ and $e' \sim f'$, then $e + e' \sim f + f'$, $e \cdot e' \sim f \cdot f'$, and $e^* \sim f^*$.

*Proof* Straightforward, by constructing appropriate bisimulation relations. For example, to demonstrate that $e^* \sim f^*$ whenever $e \sim f$, it suffices to demonstrate that the relation

$$\mathcal{R} = \{\langle e^*, f^* \rangle, \langle e' \cdot e^*, f' \cdot f^* \rangle : e \sim f \text{ and } e' \sim f'\}$$

is a bisimulation. □

## 2.3 Normal Forms and Milner's Loop Derivative Condition

In the sequel, we shall restrict ourselves in what constitutes a valid regular expression by not allowing any subexpression $e^*$ in which $\text{norm}(e) = 0$ or $\text{norm}(e) = \infty$ (which are syntactically-checkable conditions). The purpose of this restriction is to assure that the bodies of loops—that is, the terms appearing under star operations—must both contribute some behaviour when executed, and also be able to terminate in order to allow the loop to iterate. These restrictions are harmless in terms of expressivity and star height properties due to the following technical lemma.

LEMMA 5 Every regular expression is bisimilar to one of no greater star height having no subexpression $e^*$ for which $\text{norm}(e) = 0$ or $\text{norm}(e) = \infty$.

*Proof* We can demonstrate by induction on the structure of $e$ that if $\text{norm}(e) = 0$ then $e \sim \lambda + f$ for some $f$ of equal star height with $\text{norm}(f) \neq 0$. We may then replace any subexpression $e^*$ in which $\text{norm}(e) = 0$ with $f^*$, using the fact that $f^* \sim (\lambda + f)^*$. Finally, we may then replace any subexpression $e^*$ in which $\text{norm}(e) = \infty$ with $\lambda + e$, using the fact that $e^* \sim \lambda + e \cdot e^*$ and $e \cdot f \sim e$ whenever $\text{norm}(e) = \infty$. □

We shall henceforth assume that our expressions satisfy this restriction, that if $e^*$ ever appears as a subterm then $0 < \text{norm}(e) < \infty$. This restriction is clearly preserved through transitions: a transition cannot introduce a subterm $e^*$ which isn't already present.

We shall also read expressions modulo associativity and commutativity of $+$ and associativity of $\cdot$, as well as modulo the absorption of $\emptyset$ into $+$ and of $\lambda$ into $\cdot$. A moment's reflection on the transition rules will reveal that this will not affect the semantic interpretation of terms, as recorded by the following lemma.

LEMMA 6 Suppose that $q = r$ modulo associativity and commutativity of $+$, associativity of $\cdot$, and absorption of $\emptyset$ into $+$ and of $\lambda$ into $\cdot$. Then $\text{norm}(q) = \text{norm}(r)$; and if $q \xrightarrow{a} q'$ then $r \xrightarrow{a} r'$ for some $r'$ with $q' = r'$ modulo the above associativity, commutativity and absorption rules. Hence the automata of $q$ and $r$ are identical up to relabelling of states.

*Proof* By induction on the length of the derivation of $q = r$ modulo the given associativity, commutativity and absorption rules. □

The next lemma tells us that for an infinite expression—that is, one that has stars to unroll—we can burrow down through transitions to expose and unroll the most deeply nested star term which, not having any star subterms, must be finite. We first define the property of being infinite, both semantically and structurally.

DEFINITION 7 A regular expression is *infinite* if it can undergo an infinite sequence of transitions. This property is structurally definable as follows. $e^*$ is always infinite (given the above restrictions); $e + f$ is infinite if either $e$ is infinite or $f$ is infinite; and $e \cdot f$ is infinite if either $e$ is infinite, or $\text{norm}(e) < \infty$ and $f$ is infinite. All other terms are finite.

LEMMA 8 If $e$ is infinite, then $e \longrightarrow^+ f_0 \cdot f^* \cdot g$ for some finite $f$ and some $f_0$ where $f \longrightarrow^* f_0$ with $\text{norm}(f_0) = 0$.

*Proof* By induction on the structure of $e$, noting from Definition 7 that only terms of the form $e_1^*$, $e_1 + e_2$, and $e_1 \cdot e_2$ may be infinite.

(i) For $e \equiv e_1^*$, if $e_1$ is finite then (since $0 < \text{norm}(e_1) < \infty$) we have $e_1 \longrightarrow^+ e_1'$ with $\text{norm}\left(e_1'\right) = 0$, and so $e \longrightarrow^+ e_1' \cdot e_1^*$; otherwise if $e_1$ is infinite, our result follows by induction: $e_1 \longrightarrow^+ f_0 \cdot f^* \cdot g$, so $e \longrightarrow^+ f_0 \cdot f^* \cdot g \cdot e$.

(ii) If $e \equiv e_1 + e_2$ is infinite, then one of $e_1$ or $e_2$ must be infinite, from which our result follows by induction: $e_1 \longrightarrow^+ f_0 \cdot f^* \cdot g$ or $e_2 \longrightarrow^+ f_0 \cdot f^* \cdot g$, so $e \longrightarrow^+ f_0 \cdot f^* \cdot g$.

(iii) If $e \equiv e_1 \cdot e_2$ is infinite, then either $e_1$ is infinite, from which our result follows by induction: $e_1 \longrightarrow^+ f_0 \cdot f^* \cdot g$, so $e \longrightarrow^+ f_0 \cdot f^* \cdot g \cdot e_2$; or $\text{norm}(e_1) < \infty$ and $e_2$ is infinite, from which our result again follows by induction: $e_2 \longrightarrow^+ f_0 \cdot f^* \cdot g$, so $e \longrightarrow^+ f_0 \cdot f^* \cdot g$. □

In contrast to this, the following lemma demonstrates that finite expressions are indeed finite: that they can only perform a finite sequence of transitions.

LEMMA 9 Every sequence of transitions from a finite regular expression $e$ must eventually reach either the state $\emptyset$ or the state $\lambda$.

*Proof* By induction on the structure of $e$. □

The following is then a recasting in the present terminology of Milner's "loop derivative condition" (Lemma 6.4 from [1]).

LEMMA 10 If $e$ is infinite, then $e \longrightarrow^* e'$ for some $e' \sim h + k$ where $h$ is infinite and such that every transition sequence from $h$ has an initial segment

$$h \longrightarrow h_1 \longrightarrow \cdots \longrightarrow h_n \longrightarrow h' \quad (\text{for some } n \geq 0)$$

in which $\text{norm}(h_i) > 0$ for $1 \leq i \leq n$, and either $h' \sim \emptyset$ or $h' \sim h + h'$.

*Proof* Suppose that $e$ is infinite. By Lemma 8, $e \longrightarrow^* f_0{\cdot}f^*{\cdot}g$ for some finite $f$ and some $f_0$ with norm $(f_0) = 0$. Then $f_0 \cdot f^* \cdot g \sim f \cdot f^* \cdot g \;+\; f_0 \cdot f^* \cdot g$; and since norm $(f_0) < \infty$ we get that $f \cdot f^* \cdot g$ is infinite.

Since $f$ is finite with norm $(f) > 0$, Lemma 9 gives us that every transition sequence from $f \cdot f^* \cdot g$ must have an initial segment of the form

$$f \cdot f^* \cdot g \longrightarrow f_1 \cdot f^* \cdot g \longrightarrow \cdots \longrightarrow f_n \cdot f^* \cdot g \longrightarrow f' \cdot f^* \cdot g \quad (\text{for some } n \geq 0)$$

in which norm $(f_i) > 0$ (and hence norm $(f_i \cdot f^* \cdot g) > 0$) for $1 \leq i \leq n$, and either $f' \sim \emptyset$ (in which case $f' \cdot f^* \cdot g \sim \emptyset$) or norm $\left(f'\right) = 0$ (in which case $f' \sim \lambda + f'$, and hence $f' \cdot f^* \cdot g \sim f \cdot f^* \cdot g + f' \cdot f^* \cdot g$). □

## 3 Decorated Regular Expressions

The approach we take to attack the star height problem is based on a careful bookkeeping of the unrollings of star terms. In order to simplify our presentation, we shall introduce some decoration on expressions as they are derived through transitions. Specifically, we shall replace the transition rule $(*)$ in Definition 2 with the rule:

$$(*') : \quad \frac{e \stackrel{a}{\longrightarrow} e'}{e^* \stackrel{a}{\longrightarrow} [e']{\cdot}e^*}$$

We shall then need to define norm $([e]) = $ norm $(e)$, and to introduce one extra transition rule to Definition 2 to cater for the newly decorated syntax:

$$([\cdot]) : \quad \frac{e \stackrel{a}{\longrightarrow} e'}{[e] \stackrel{a}{\longrightarrow} [e']}$$

With this modification, it is evident (and can be easily demonstrated) that we have not altered the semantic meaning of terms. Specifically, norm $(e) = $ norm $\left(\widehat{e}\right)$, and $e \stackrel{a}{\longrightarrow} f$ is a transition in the new transition system exactly when $\widehat{e} \stackrel{a}{\longrightarrow} \widehat{f}$ is a transition in the original transition system, where $\widehat{e}$ and $\widehat{f}$ represent the terms $e$ and $f$, respectively, with their bracketting deleted.

The interpretation of bracketted terms is clear from how brackets may be introduced by the rules of inference defining the transitions: when a term $[f'] \cdot f^* \cdot g$ is encountered, this means that the term $f^*$ has been unrolled and the transition sequence is currently working its way through the transitions of $f$. The suffix $f^*{\cdot}g$ will not contain any bracketting—indeed it will be shown to be a suffix of the original expression—but $f'$ itself may be a bracketted term; this would imply that the execution of the body $f$ of the loop $f^*$ has itself unrolled a nested loop inside $f$. It is clear then (and can be verified inductively) that any term derived from an unbracketted term can have only opening brackets preceding any opening bracket;

and that if the innermost bracketted term is unfinished (that is, not in a final state with norm 0), then every transition must derive from this innermost term. We record these basic facts in the following lemma for future reference.

LEMMA 11 If $e \longrightarrow^* f$ where $e$ is an unbracketted term, then $f$ must be of the form

$$[[[\cdots[[[h]\cdot g_1]\cdot g_2]\cdot g_3\cdots]\cdot g_4]\cdot g_5]\cdot g_6$$

where $h$ and the $g_i$s are unbracketted terms. Furthermore, if norm $(h) > 0$ then any transition $f \longrightarrow f'$ must be of the form

$$[[[\cdots[[[h]\cdot g_1]\cdot g_2]\cdot g_3\cdots]\cdot g_4]\cdot g_5]\cdot g_6 \longrightarrow [[[\cdots[[[h']\cdot g_1]\cdot g_2]\cdot g_3\cdots]\cdot g_4]\cdot g_5]\cdot g_6$$

where $h \longrightarrow h'$.

Finally, as brackets are introduced when starred terms are unrolled, the nesting of brackets directly reflects the star height of the original term. To make this clear, we can extend the definition of the star height of regular expressions by defining $\mathrm{sh}([e]) = 1 + \mathrm{sh}(e)$, while maintaining the property that $\mathrm{sh}(e) \geq \mathrm{sh}(f)$ whenever $e \longrightarrow f$.

DEFINITION 12 We define here what it means for one expression $e$ to be a *suffix* of another expression $f$, which we write as $e \sqsubseteq f$:

(i) $f \sqsubseteq e\cdot f$ and $f \sqsubseteq e + f$; (in particular, $f \sqsubseteq f$ for every expression $f$;)

(ii) if $e \sqsubseteq f$ then $e\cdot g \sqsubseteq f\cdot g$;

(iii) if $e \sqsubseteq f$ and $f \sqsubseteq g$ then $e \sqsubseteq g$.

$e$ is a *proper suffix* of $f$ if $e \sqsubseteq f$ and $e \neq f$. Note that in this instance, the size of $e$ must be smaller than the size of $f$.

LEMMA 13

(i) If $e \longrightarrow f$ where $f$ contains no bracketting, then $f \sqsubseteq e$.

(ii) If $e \longrightarrow [f']\cdot f^*\cdot g$ then $f^*\cdot g \sqsubseteq e$.

(iii) If $e \longrightarrow^* [f']\cdot f^*\cdot g$ then $f^*\cdot g \sqsubseteq e$.

*Proof*

(i) The proof of (i) requires an induction on the depth of the derivation of the transition $e \longrightarrow f$. For example, for the rule

$$(\cdot_L): \frac{e_1 \stackrel{a}{\longrightarrow} e_1'}{e_1\cdot e_2 \stackrel{a}{\longrightarrow} e_1'\cdot e_2} \qquad \text{where } e_1'\cdot e_2 \text{ contains no bracketting,}$$

by induction we get that $e_1' \sqsubseteq e_1$, and hence $e_1' \cdot e_2 \sqsubseteq e_1 \cdot e_2$; and for the rule

$$(\cdot_R): \frac{e_2 \xrightarrow{a} e_2'}{e_1 \cdot e_2 \xrightarrow{a} e_2'} (\text{norm}(e_1) = 0) \qquad \text{where } e_2' \text{ contains no bracketting,}$$

by induction we get that $e_2' \sqsubseteq e_2$, and hence $e_2' \sqsubseteq e_1 \cdot e_2$. The remaining rules are equally straightforward.

(ii) Similarly, the proof of (ii) requires an induction on the depth of the derivation of the transition $e \longrightarrow [f'] \cdot f^* \cdot g$, with the only interesting case being that for the rule

$$(\cdot_L): \frac{e_1 \xrightarrow{a} e_1'}{e_1 \cdot e_2 \xrightarrow{a} e_1' \cdot e_2} \qquad \text{where} \quad e_1' \cdot e_2 = [f'] \cdot f^* \cdot g.$$

(a) If $e_1' = \lambda$ then $f^* \cdot g \sqsubseteq [f'] \cdot f^* \cdot g = e_2 \sqsubseteq e_1 \cdot e_2$.

(b) If $e_1' = [f']$ then $f^* \cdot g = e_2 \sqsubseteq e_1 \cdot e_2$.

(c) Finally, if $e_1' = [f'] \cdot f^* \cdot h$ (with $g = h \cdot e_2$) then by induction we get $f^* \cdot h \sqsubseteq e_1$, and hence $f^* \cdot g = f^* \cdot h \cdot e_2 \sqsubseteq e_1 \cdot e_2$.

(iii) Given (i) and (ii), the proof of (iii) requires a straightforward induction on the number of transitions in $e \longrightarrow^* [f'] \cdot f^* \cdot g$. □

We now arrive at the main technical lemma of the paper.

LEMMA 14

(i) Any infinite sequence of transitions must go through a term of the form $[f_0] \cdot f^* \cdot g$ where $f \longrightarrow^* f_0$.

(ii) If $e$ is infinite, then $e \longrightarrow^* [f_0] \cdot f^* \cdot g$ where $f \longrightarrow^* f_0$ with $\text{norm}(f_0) = 0$.

(iii) If $e$ in (ii) above is infinite and normed (that is, its associated automaton is normed), then $g$ can be assumed to be finite.

(iv) If $e$ in (ii) above is infinite and normed, and every state of its associated automaton is infinite, then $g$ can be assumed to be $\lambda$; that is, $e \longrightarrow^* [f_0] \cdot f^*$ where $f \longrightarrow^* f_0$ with $\text{norm}(f_0) = 0$.

*Proof*

(i) Any infinite sequence of transitions must include one whose derivation involves the rule $(*')$, as without this rule each expression in the transition sequence would be smaller than the previous one. It is then a simple induction on the depth of a derivation of a transition involving the rule $(*')$ that the resulting expression must be of the requisite form.

(ii) This is proven using a similar inductive argument as for Lemma 8 (without the requirement that $f$ be finite).

(iii) This is proven by induction on the size of the expression $e$. If the $g$ that we get from (ii) is finite then we are done; otherwise we can apply the argument inductively on $g$ (as it must be infinite and normed itself), since by Lemma 13(iii) $g$ must be a proper suffix—and hence smaller than—the expression $e$.

(iv) If $g \longrightarrow g'$ then some state of the automaton associated with $e$ must be bisimilar to the finite expression $g'$, which is impossible. Hence we must deduce that $g \sim \lambda$, from which we can show by a simple induction that $g = \lambda$. □

With this lemma in place, we may demonstrate the validity of the conjecture of Milner from Section 6 of [1] that the following normed two-state automaton is not expressible up-to bisimilarity by any regular expression.

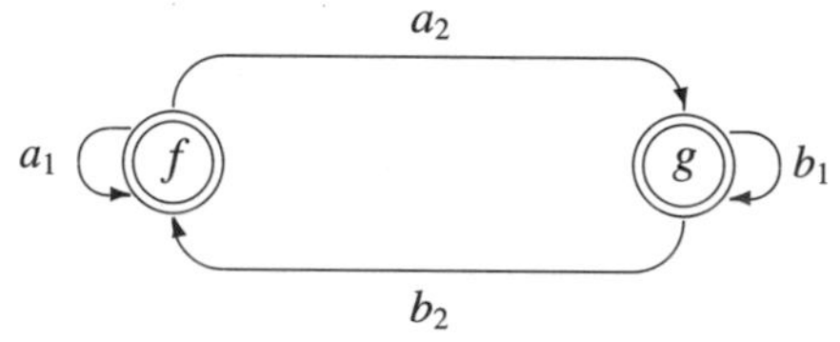


Here both states have infinite transition sequences originating from them, and both states are final states. Hence any regular expression which is bisimilar to either of these states must be infinite and have norm 0.

Suppose that $f$ and $g$ are regular expressions representing (up-to bisimilarity) the two states of the automaton as shown. Then from Lemma 14(iv) we would get that $f \longrightarrow^* [f_0] \cdot f_1^*$. this term must be bisimilar to either $f$ or $g$; without loss of generality say $f \sim [f_0] \cdot f_1^*$.

We must then deduce that $f_1 \stackrel{b_1}{\not\longrightarrow}$ and $f_1 \stackrel{b_2}{\not\longrightarrow}$. However we get $[f_0] \cdot f_1^* \stackrel{a_2}{\longrightarrow} [f_0'] \cdot f_1^* \sim g$ (either through a move of $f_0$ or by a new unrolling of $f_1$), from which we must then deduce that $f_1 \stackrel{a_1}{\not\longrightarrow}$ and $f_1 \stackrel{a_2}{\not\longrightarrow}$, thus leaving $f_1$ with no behaviour, contradicting our assumption that $0 < \text{norm}\,(f_1) < \infty$. We have thus demonstrated that the above automaton cannot in fact be represented up-to bisimilarity by any regular expression.

## 4 The Star Height Problem

In [1], Milner defined the regular expressions $e_1 = a^*$ and $e_{k+1} = (e_k \cdot a)^*$ for $k > 0$, and conjectured that for each $n > 0$, the regular expression $e_n$ with star height $n$ is not bisimilar to any regular expression $e$ with star height less than $n$. In this section, we prove the validity of this conjecture.

For each $n > 0$, define the following normed automaton over the singleton alphabet $\{a\}$ (where we omit the labelling of the transitions):

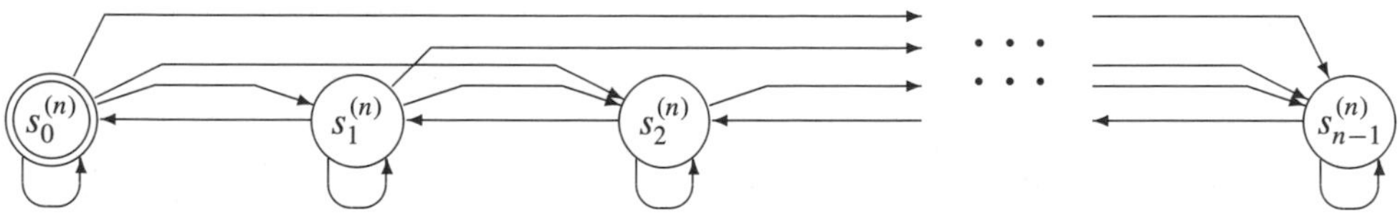


We can informally represent this automaton by the sequence of equations:

$$s_0^{(n)} = a \cdot s_0^{(n)} + a \cdot s_1^{(n)} + a \cdot s_2^{(n)} + \cdots + a \cdot s_{n-1}^{(n)} + \lambda; \quad \text{and}$$
$$s_k^{(n)} = a \cdot s_{k-1}^{(n)} + a \cdot s_k^{(n)} + a \cdot s_{k+1}^{(n)} + \cdots + a \cdot s_{n-1}^{(n)} \quad (0 < k < n).$$

LEMMA 15 $s_0^{(n)} \sim e_n$.

*Proof* For each $n > 0$, the relation

$$\begin{aligned}\mathcal{R} = \{ & \langle s_0^{(n)}, e_n \rangle, \\ & \langle s_1^{(n)}, e_{n-1} \cdot a \cdot e_n \rangle, \\ & \langle s_2^{(n)}, e_{n-2} \cdot a \cdot e_{n-1} \cdot a \cdot e_n \rangle, \\ & \quad \vdots \\ & \langle s_{n-1}^{(n)}, e_1 \cdot a \cdot e_2 \cdot a \cdot \cdots \cdot e_{n-1} \cdot a \cdot e_n \rangle \}\end{aligned}$$

is a bisimulation relating $s_0^{(n)}$ and $e_n$. □

Hence the automaton above—or more specifically the state $s_0^{(n)}$—can be expressed up-to bisimilarity by the regular expression $e_n$ of star height $n$. What we shall proceed to demonstrate is that *any* regular expression $e$ which is bisimilar to $s_0^{(n)}$ must have star height at least $n$.

Suppose then that $e$ is such a regular expression: $e \sim s_0^{(n)}$. By Lemma 14(iv) we must have that $e \longrightarrow^* [f_0] \cdot f^*$ where $f \longrightarrow^* f_0$ with norm $(f_0) = 0$. We must then have $[f_0] \cdot f^* \sim s_i^{(n)}$ for some $i$; and as bisimilar states must have equal norms (Lemma 1(i)), since norm $([f_0] \cdot f^*) = 0$ and norm $\left(s_i^{(n)}\right) = i$, we must in fact have that $[f_0] \cdot f^* \sim s_0^{(n)}$.

LEMMA 16 For each $i$ with $0 < i < n$, if $[\cdots [h] \cdots] \cdot f^* \sim s_i^{(n)}$ with norm $(h) = 1$ then $h \longrightarrow^* k = [\cdots [[g_0] \cdot g^* \cdot g'] \cdot k' \cdots] \cdot k''$ with $g' \sim a$ such that $[\cdots [k] \cdots] \cdot f^* \sim s_i^{(n)}$. (By this last term, we mean the term gotten by replacing $h$ with $k$ in the original term.)

*Proof* By simultaneous induction on the star height and the size of $h$.

With Lemma 11 in mind, we see that the infinite norm-preserving transition sequence

$$s_i^{(n)} \longrightarrow s_i^{(n)} \longrightarrow s_i^{(n)} \longrightarrow \cdots$$

must be matched up-to bisimilarity by a transition sequence

$$[\cdots[h]\cdots]\cdot f^* \longrightarrow [\cdots[h']\cdots]\cdot f^* \longrightarrow [\cdots[h'']\cdots]\cdot f^* \longrightarrow \cdots$$

given by a transition sequence

$$h \longrightarrow h' \longrightarrow h'' \longrightarrow \cdots$$

in which $1 = \text{norm}\,(h) = \text{norm}\,(h') = \text{norm}\,(h'') = \cdots$. By Lemma 14(i), some term in this last infinite transition sequence must be of the form $[g_0]\cdot g^*\cdot g'$ where $g \longrightarrow^* g_0$; we then have that $[\cdots[[g_0]\cdot g^*\cdot g']\cdots]\cdot f^* \sim s_i^{(n)}$, and that $1 = \text{norm}\,([g_0]\cdot g^*\cdot g') = \text{norm}\,(g_0) + \text{norm}\,(g')$.

(i) If $g' \sim a$ then we have our result.

(ii) If $\text{norm}\,(g_0) = 1$ then since $\text{sh}\,(g_0) \le \text{sh}\,(g) < \text{sh}\,(h)$ our result follows by induction.

(iii) If $\text{norm}\,(g') = 1$ but $g' \not\sim a$ then we must have that $g' \longrightarrow^+ g''$ with $\text{norm}\,(g'') = 1$. We then get that

$$[\cdots[[g_0]\cdot g^*\cdot g']\cdots]\cdot f^* \longrightarrow^+ [\cdots[g'']\cdots]\cdot f^* \sim s_i^{(n)}.$$

By Lemma 13(iii), $g''$ must be a proper suffix of $h$, and hence our result again follows by induction. □

LEMMA 17 For each $i$ with $0 < i < n$ we must have

$$[f_0]\cdot f^* \longrightarrow^* \underbrace{[\cdots[}_{\ge i}\,[g_0]\cdot g^*\cdot g']\cdots]\cdot f^* \sim s_i^{(n)}$$

such that $g' \sim a$ and $\text{norm}\,(g_0) = 0$.

*Proof* By induction on $i$.

For $i = 1 < n$, since $[f_0]\cdot f^* \sim s_0^{(n)}$, the transition $s_0^{(n)} \longrightarrow s_1^{(n)}$ must be matched by a transition $[f_0]\cdot f^* \longrightarrow [h]\cdot f^* \sim s_1^{(n)}$ (either from $f_0 \longrightarrow h$ or from $f \longrightarrow h$). The result then follows immediately from Lemma 16.

Suppose now that for some $i$ with $1 < i < n$, we have

$$[f_0] \cdot f^* \longrightarrow^* \underbrace{[\cdots[}_{\geq i-1} [g_0] \cdot g^* \cdot g'] \cdots] \cdot f^* \sim s_{i-1}^{(n)}$$

such that $g' \sim a$ and $\mathrm{norm}(g_0) = 0$. The norm-increasing transition $s_{i-1}^{(n)} \longrightarrow s_i^{(n)}$ must be matched by

$$\underbrace{[\cdots[}_{\geq i-1} [g_0] \cdot g^* \cdot g'] \cdots] \cdot f^* \longrightarrow \underbrace{[\cdots[}_{\geq i-1} [h] \cdot g^* \cdot g'] \cdots] \cdot f^* \sim s_i^{(n)}$$

(either from $g_0 \longrightarrow h$ or from $g \longrightarrow h$). The result then again follows immediately from Lemma 16. □

Finally, this then gives us our result: given a regular expression $e \sim s_0^{(n)}$, by Lemma 17 we must have:

$$e \longrightarrow^* [f_0] \cdot f^* \longrightarrow^* \underbrace{[\cdots[}_{\geq n-1} [g_0] \cdot g^* \cdot g'] \cdots] \cdot f^* \sim s_{n-1}^{(n)}$$

The star height of this derived term is thus at least $n$, and hence $\mathrm{sh}(e) \geq n$.

Thus, we have succeeded in demonstrating that for each $n > 0$, there is a regular expression $e_n$ over the alphabet $\{a\}$ with star height $n$ which is not bisimilar to any regular expression $e$ with star height less than $n$.

## References

[1] R. Milner. A complete inference system for a class of regular behaviours. *Journal of Computer and System Science* 28:439–466 (1984).

[2] A. Salomaa. *Jewels of Formal Language Theory*. Computer Science Press, Potomac, Md., 1981.

# 17 Combining the Typed λ-Calculus with CCS

**William Ferreira, Mathew Hennessy, and Alan S. A. Jeffrey**

## 1 Introduction

*CCS* is an abstract process description language whose study and understanding, [7], has been of great significance in the development of the theory of concurrency. An algebraic view is taken of processes in that their description is in terms of a small collection of primitive *constructors*, such as choice $+$, parallelism $\|$ and action prefixing $a?$, $a!$. These action prefixes designate the sending and receiving of a synchronisation impulse along a virtual channel $a$. Communication is deemed to be the simultaneous occurrence of these two events and is denoted by the special action $\tau$. So *CCS* expressions describe processes in terms of their synchronisation or communication potentials and the algebraic theory, expressed as equations over the constructors, is validated in terms of behavioural equivalences defined using these potentials.

Much research has been carried out on extending this elegant theory to more expressive process descriptive languages. Here we are concerned with languages in which the synchronisation is replaced by the exchange of data, where the abstract actions $a?$ and $a!$ are instantiated to $a?x$ and $a!v$, the reception and sending of data. In papers such as [5, 9], and even in [7], such extensions are considered but the domain of transmittable values is taken to have no computational significance. All data expressions denote a unique value and the computation of this value is not of concern. Here we are interested in situation in which the data space may be computationally complex and their evaluation may effect the behaviour of processes which use them.

A typed λ-calculus, based on some primitive set of data types, provides a non-trivial example of such a data space. It is also a very useful example as there are various existing programming languages, such as *CML* [10], *Facile* [3], which are based on different methods for combining the communication primitives of *CCS* with the typed λ-calculus.

In this paper we try, where possible, to unify *CCS* directly with the typed call-by-value λ-calculus, to find a *communicate-by-value* concurrent language. However, it is not possible to fully unify the process language with the functional language, due to the behaviour of *CCS* summation. The operational semantics for $\beta$-reduction includes:

$$(\lambda\, () \cdot e)\, () \xrightarrow{\tau} e$$

This work was partially supported by the EU EXPRESS Working Group, the Royal Society and the EPSRC research project GR/K60701.

If we were to allow function applications in $+$ contexts we would therefore have:

$$a!1 + (\lambda\,() \cdot b!1)\,() \xrightarrow{\tau} b!1 \qquad a!1 + b!1 \not\Rightarrow b!1$$

and so we would have:

$$(\lambda\,() \cdot e)\,() \neq e$$

We consider this to be an undesirable property of a functional language, and so we will distinguish between *processes* (which may be placed in $+$ contexts) and *expressions* (which may not). In this paper we distinguish syntactically between processes and expressions: in languages such as *CML* and *Facile* this distinction is made by the type system.

For the combined language, of expressions and processes, we define a variation of weak higher-order bisimulation equivalence, $\approx$. For expressions, $\approx$ is a congruence, and we have:

$$(\lambda\,() \cdot e)\,() \approx e$$

For processes, we have to modify $\approx$ slightly, in the standard manner [7], to take $+$ contexts into account. The resulting congruence is denoted $=^h$ and we have:

$$\tau \cdot p \neq^h p$$

In Section 2 we describe a language $\lambda_v^{con}$ which combines the call-by-value $\lambda$-calculus expressions with communicate-by-value *CCS* processes.

In Section 3 we then develop the variation of weak bisimulation equivalence, based on *higher-order bisimulations*, $\approx$, and show that the related *higher order bisimulation congruence* is preserved by all $\lambda_v^{con}$ contexts. We also show the resulting theory is both a generalization of the standard theory of *CCS* and call-by-value $\lambda$-calculus, and that all closed expressions can be converted to head normal form.

In Section 4 we discuss possible extensions, such as the use of symbolic techniques, and the call-by-name variant of the language.

## 2 The Language

This section is divided into three parts. The first outlines the syntax and operational semantics of a call-by-value $\lambda$-calculus, the second provides a communicate-by-value process language based on *CCS* [7], and the third combines the languages together as far as possible.

### 2.1 A Call-by-Value λ-Calculus

The language we use is typed, the types been given by the grammar:

$$A ::= \mathsf{unit} \mid \mathsf{bool} \mid \mathsf{int} \mid A \to A$$

Here int is used as an example of a *basic* type and we can easily incorporate others. For each type $A$ we assume an infinite set of variables, $Var_A$, ranged over by $x_A$, and some (indefinite) set of constants for manipulating values of the basic types, a typical example being succ the *successor* function over int. However, to increase readability we will omit the typing information from variables and constants unless absolutely necessary.

The syntax of the language is given by the following grammar:

$$e, f \ldots \in Exp ::= v \mid c\,e \mid \mathsf{if}\, e\, \mathsf{then}\, e\, \mathsf{else}\, e \mid \mathsf{let}\, x_A = e\, \mathsf{in}\, e \mid e\,e$$

$$v, w, \ldots \in Val ::= l \mid \mu x_{A \to B} \cdot (\lambda\, y_A \cdot e) \mid x_A$$

$$l \in Lit ::= \mathsf{true} \mid \mathsf{false} \mid () \mid 0 \mid 1 \mid \ldots$$

The main syntactic category is *Exp* but a sub-category of *value* expressions is also defined. The only non-trivial value expressions are function abstractions, or more accurately recursively defined function abstractions. Informally $\mu x \cdot (\lambda\, y \cdot e)$ denotes a recursively defined function whose definition could also be rendered as:

$$x \Longleftarrow \lambda\, y \cdot e$$

If $x$ does not occur in $e$ then we will often abbreviate $\mu x \cdot (\lambda\, y \cdot e)$ to $\lambda\, y \cdot e$.

Function abstraction and let are the only variable binding construct in the language. This leads to the standard definition of free and bound occurrences of variables, open and closed expressions, $\alpha$-equivalence, $=_\alpha$, and of substitution. However, we only ever require substitutions of the form $e[v/x]$, i.e., the substitution of a value $v$ for all free occurrences of a variable $x$ in an expression $e$.

We can associate with every expression at most one type. The typing judgements have a very simple form $\vdash e : A$ and the rules for inferring types are given in Figure 17.1. Of course we also need inference rules for the literals of any extra basic types used. We use $\lambda_v$, $(\lambda_v{}^\circ)$ to denote the set of all closed (open) well-typed expressions.

Intuitively every expression of type $A$ should denote a value of this type and the operational semantics describes, in an abstract form, a procedure for evaluating expressions to values in a call-by-value manner; of course because of the presence of recursion this evaluating procedure may never terminate. Formally the operational semantics is given in terms of two relations between closed expressions. The first, $e \xrightarrow{\tau}_e e'$, means that in one

$$\frac{}{\vdash \mathsf{true} : \mathsf{bool}} \qquad \frac{}{\vdash \mathsf{false} : \mathsf{bool}}$$

$$\frac{}{\vdash () : \mathsf{unit}} \qquad \frac{}{\vdash n : \mathsf{int}}[n \in \{0, 1, \ldots\}]$$

$$\frac{\vdash e : A \quad \vdash f : B}{\vdash \mathsf{let}\, x_A = e \,\mathsf{in}\, f : B} \qquad \frac{\vdash e : B}{\vdash \mu x_{A \to B} \cdot (\lambda\, y_A \cdot e) : A \to B}$$

$$\frac{\vdash e : A}{\vdash c\, e : B}[c : A \to B] \qquad \frac{\vdash e : A \to B \quad \vdash f : A}{\vdash e\, f : B}$$

$$\frac{\vdash e : \mathsf{bool} \quad \vdash f : A \quad \vdash g : A}{\vdash \mathsf{if}\, e \,\mathsf{then}\, f \,\mathsf{else}\, g : A} \qquad \frac{}{\vdash x_A : A}$$

**Figure 17.1**
Type Rules for λ expressions.

reduction step the evaluation of $e$ can be reduced to that of $e'$. For example to evaluate the expression $\mathsf{let}\, x = e \,\mathsf{in}\, f$ we first evaluate $e$, using the rule:

$$\frac{e \xrightarrow{\tau}_e e'}{\mathsf{let}\, x = e \,\mathsf{in}\, f \xrightarrow{\tau}_e \mathsf{let}\, x = e' \,\mathsf{in}\, f}$$

When $e$ produces a value $v$ then the evaluation proceeds evaluating the expression $f[v/e]$. In order to express this formally we need a second relation, $e \xrightarrow{\surd v}_e$ which tells when an expression $e$ has produced a value $v$ (the reason for the non-standard notation will become clear when we unify the expression and process languages in Section 2.3). The evaluation of $\mathsf{let}\, x = \ldots \,\mathsf{in} \ldots$ expressions is captured by the additional rule:

$$\frac{e \xrightarrow{\surd v}_e}{\mathsf{let}\, x = e \,\mathsf{in}\, f \xrightarrow{\tau}_e f[v/x]}$$

Similarly to evaluate an application $e\, f$, the expression $e$ is evaluated until we reach a value $e \xrightarrow{\tau}{}^{*}_{e} \xrightarrow{\surd v}_e$. Since $e$ is well-typed this value $v$ must be of the form $\mu x \cdot (\gamma\, y \cdot g)$ and the evaluation proceeds by evaluating $\mathsf{let}\, y = f \,\mathsf{in}\, g[v/x]$; this is captured by the rule:

$$\frac{e \xrightarrow{\surd \mu x \cdot (\gamma\, y \cdot g)}_e}{e\, f \xrightarrow{\tau}_e \mathsf{let}\, y = f \,\mathsf{in}\, g[\mu x \cdot (\lambda\, y \cdot g)/x]}$$

The application of constants $c\, e$ is handled in a similar manner; $e$ is evaluated to a value $v$ and then the value produced by $c\, v$ depends on the constant in question. The effect of constants can be expressed in terms of a function $\delta$, which given a constant and a value returns the corresponding expression. For example the behaviour of the constant $\mathsf{succ}$ is given by $\delta(\mathsf{succ}, n) = n + 1$.

Values:

$$\frac{}{v \xrightarrow{\surd v}_e}$$

Reductions:

$$\frac{e \xrightarrow{\surd \mu x\cdot(\lambda\, y\cdot g)}_e}{e\, f \xrightarrow{\tau}_e \mathsf{let}\, y = f\, \mathsf{in}\, g[\mu x \cdot (\lambda\, y \cdot g)/x]} \qquad \frac{e \xrightarrow{\surd v}_e}{\mathsf{let}\, x = e\, \mathsf{in}\, f \xrightarrow{\tau}_e f[v/x]}$$

$$\frac{e \xrightarrow{\surd \mathsf{true}}_e}{\mathsf{if}\, e\, \mathsf{then}\, f\, \mathsf{else}\, g \xrightarrow{\tau}_e f} \qquad \frac{e \xrightarrow{\surd \mathsf{false}}_e}{\mathsf{if}\, e\, \mathsf{then}\, f\, \mathsf{else}\, g \xrightarrow{\tau}_e g}$$

$$\frac{e \xrightarrow{\surd v}_e}{c\, e \xrightarrow{\tau}_e \delta(c, v)}$$

Context Rules:

$$\frac{e \xrightarrow{\tau}_e e'}{c\, e \xrightarrow{\tau}_e c\, e'} \qquad \frac{e \xrightarrow{\tau}_e e'}{e\, f \xrightarrow{\tau}_e e'\, f}$$

$$\frac{e \xrightarrow{\tau}_e e'}{\mathsf{if}\, e\, \mathsf{then}\, f\, \mathsf{else}\, g \xrightarrow{\tau}_e \mathsf{if}\, e'\, \mathsf{then}\, f\, \mathsf{else}\, g}$$

$$\frac{e \xrightarrow{\tau}_e e'}{\mathsf{let}\, x = e\, \mathsf{in}\, f \xrightarrow{\tau}_e \mathsf{let}\, x = e'\, \mathsf{in}\, f}$$

**Figure 17.2**
Operational Semantics for $\lambda_v$.

The two relations are defined to be the least ones which satisfy the rules given in Figure 17.2. The main properties of the operational semantics is captured in the following proposition, whose proof we leave to the reader:

PROPOSITION 2.1 (SUBJECT REDUCTION) For every closed expression $e$ in $\lambda_v$ such that $\vdash e : A$:

1. if $e \xrightarrow{\tau}_e e'$ then $\vdash e' : A$
2. if $e \xrightarrow{\surd v}_e$ then $\vdash v : A$ □

In addition, we can show that reduction of expressions is deterministic:

PROPOSITION 2.2 (DETERMINACY) For every closed expression $e$ in $\lambda_v$:

1. if $e \xrightarrow{\tau}_e e'$ and $e \xrightarrow{\tau}_e e''$ then $e' = e''$
2. if $e \xrightarrow{\surd v}_e$ and $e \xrightarrow{\surd v'}_e$ then $v = v'$ □

## 2.2 A Communicate-by-Value Process Calculus

In the previous section we presented a language $\lambda_v$ for sequential computation. We now present a language for concurrent computation, where the data communicated on channels are values taken from $\lambda_v$. In the next section we will show how these two languages can be combined to give a concurrent $\lambda$-calculus.

The syntax of the process language is given by the following grammar:

$$p, q \ldots \in Proc ::= p \nleftrightarrow p \mid p + p \mid \mathbf{0} \mid \tau \cdot p \mid k_A?x_A \cdot p \mid k_A!v \cdot p$$

The process $p \nleftrightarrow q$ represents two computation threads running concurrently—in this language $p$ and $q$ are treated symmetrically, but in the next section we introduce the notion of *main thread of computation*, so we use an asymmetric notation for parallel composition.

From *CCS* we adopt process *summation* $+$, the *deadlocked* process, $\tau$ prefix, and two constructs for the transmission and reception of values along channels, $k?x \cdot p$ and $k!v \cdot p$; we assume that for each type $A$, $k_A$ ranges over an infinite set of channels $Chan_A$. The input prefix is a variable binding operator in that in the expression $k?x \cdot p$ all free occurrences of $x$ in $p$ are bound.

Processes are typed with judgements $\vdash p : \pi$, given in Figure 17.3.

We now discuss the operational semantics of processes. We have three possible reductions for a process, based on the labeled transition system for *CCS*:

- $p \xrightarrow{\tau}_p p'$, meaning, as before, that one evaluation step reduces $p$ to $p'$. However here, $\xrightarrow{\tau}_p$ will model communication between independent evaluation threads. For example we will have $k!v \cdot e \nleftrightarrow k?x \cdot f \xrightarrow{\tau}_p e \nleftrightarrow f[v/x]$.
- We have the new relation $p \xrightarrow{k_A!v}_p p'$, meaning that a first possible step in the evaluation of the expression $p$ consists of the emission of a value $v$, along the channel $k_A$ and the computation can subsequently proceed by evaluating the expression $p'$. Communication between threads is *synchronous* and so this computation thread can only proceed if there is another concurrent thread which wishes to input a value along this channel.

$$\frac{}{\vdash \mathbf{0} : \pi} \qquad \frac{\vdash p : \pi}{\vdash \tau.p : \pi}$$

$$\frac{\vdash v : A, \ \vdash p : \pi}{\vdash k_A!v \cdot p : \pi} \qquad \frac{\vdash p : \pi}{\vdash k_B?x_B \cdot p : \pi}$$

$$\frac{\vdash p : \pi \quad \vdash q : \pi}{\vdash p + q : \pi} \qquad \frac{\vdash p : \pi \quad \vdash q : \pi}{\vdash p \nleftrightarrow q : \pi}$$

**Figure 17.3**
Type Rules for processes.

• The final relation is of the form $p \xrightarrow{k_A?}_p \lambda x_A \cdot p'$, meaning that the computation thread corresponding to $e$ can input a value along the channel $k_A$. This value is of type $A$ and is represented by the free variable $x_A$ in $p'$. In the terminology of [9] this represents a *late* operational semantics.

In fact the relation $\xrightarrow{k?_A}_p$ will be defined indirectly, in terms of more technically convenient relation $\xrightarrow{k_A?x_A}_p$, defined as $p \xrightarrow{k_A?x_A}_p p'$ iff $p \xrightarrow{k_A?}_p \lambda x_A \cdot p'$.

These relations are defined to be the least relations over closed processes that satisfy the rules given in Figure 17.4. In these rules we use:

$$a ::= k_A!v \mid k_A?x_A \qquad \mu ::= a \mid \tau$$

We have the following Subject Reduction property:

PROPOSITION 2.3 (SUBJECT REDUCTION) For every process $p$ such that $\vdash p : \pi$

1. $p \xrightarrow{\tau}_p p'$ implies $\vdash p' : \pi$
2. $p \xrightarrow{k_B!v} p'$ implies $\vdash v : B$ and $\vdash p' : \pi$
3. $p \xrightarrow{k_B?x_B} p'$ implies $\vdash p' : \pi$

*Proof* By rule induction on the relations involved. □

Communication Rules:

$$\frac{}{\tau \cdot p \xrightarrow{\tau}_p p}$$

$$\frac{}{k!v \cdot p \xrightarrow{k!v}_p p} \qquad \frac{}{k?x \cdot e \xrightarrow{k?x}_p e}$$

$$\frac{p \xrightarrow{k!v}_p p' \quad q \xrightarrow{k?x}_p q'}{p \mathbin{+\!\!\!\Vdash} q \xrightarrow{\tau}_p p' \mathbin{+\!\!\!\Vdash} q'[v/x]} \qquad \frac{p \xrightarrow{k?x}_p p' \quad q \xrightarrow{k!v}_p q'}{p \mathbin{+\!\!\!\Vdash} q \xrightarrow{\tau}_p p'[v/x] \mathbin{+\!\!\!\Vdash} q'}$$

Dynamic rules:

$$\frac{p \xrightarrow{\mu}_p p'}{p + q \xrightarrow{\mu}_p p'} \qquad \frac{q \xrightarrow{\mu}_p q'}{p + q \xrightarrow{\mu}_p q'}$$

Context Rules:

$$\frac{p \xrightarrow{\mu}_p p'}{p \mathbin{+\!\!\!\Vdash} q \xrightarrow{\mu}_p p' \mathbin{+\!\!\!\Vdash} q} \qquad \frac{q \xrightarrow{\mu}_p q'}{p \mathbin{+\!\!\!\Vdash} q \xrightarrow{\mu}_p p \mathbin{+\!\!\!\Vdash} q'}$$

**Figure 17.4**
Operational Semantics for processes.

### 2.3 Merging the λ and Process Calculi

In this section we unify the two languages considered in the previous sections. There are numerous ways in which one can conceive of such an unification. For example, as has been pointed out in [1], the language *Facile*, [3], may be considered as a call-by-value λ-calculus, such as $\lambda_v$, extended with an extra type $\mathsf{process}$. The syntax of expressions is then extended by various primitives for expressions of this new type, such as a parallel operator $\|$, operators for input and output on communication channels, and $\lambda_v$ is used to provide values which are transmitted and received by objects of this type. Thus in *Facile*, in particular in the abstract version studied in [1], there is a clear distinction between processes, expressions of type $\mathsf{process}$, and the expressions in the underlying λ-calculus. For example the parallel operator $\|$ can only be applied to processes, i.e., expressions of type $\mathsf{process}$.

By contrast, in *CML* [10] every expression is considered to be a *thread of computation*, and expressions can spawn concurrent threads. Our unification is based on this paradigm. At any one time there is a main thread of computation, whose result will be returned if that thread terminates. We represent this using the asynchronous parallel operator $p \mathrel{\#\!\!\triangleright} q$, which specifies that $q$ is the main thread of computation. For example $\mathsf{true} \mathrel{\#\!\!\triangleright} \mathsf{1}$ will return the result 1 and discard the result $\mathsf{true}$. This is reflected in the typing of our extended language; the type of $e \mathrel{\#\!\!\triangleright} f$ is given by that of $f$.

In *CML* there is still a distinction between processes (which can be placed in $+$ contexts) and expressions (which cannot). This is given by the $\mathsf{event}$ type constructor. In this paper for simplicity we will use a separate syntactic category for processes rather than a separate type—the full story is given in [2].

We extend the language of expressions by including all processes, and parallel composition of expressions:

$$e ::= v \mid c\,e \mid \mathsf{if}\, e\, \mathsf{then}\, e\, \mathsf{else}\, e \mid \mathsf{let}\, x_A = e\, \mathsf{in}\, e \mid e\,e \qquad \text{(as before)}$$

$$\mid\ p \mid e \mathrel{\#\!\!\triangleright} e \qquad \text{(new)}$$

We extend the language of processes by allowing any expression to be used as a process *as long as it is prefixed*:

$$p ::= p \mathrel{\#\!\!\triangleright} p \mid p + p \mid \mathbf{0} \qquad \text{(as before)}$$

$$\mid\ \tau \cdot e \mid k_A ? x_A \cdot e \mid k_A ! v \cdot e \qquad \text{(new)}$$

For example $\mathsf{true}$ is not a valid process, but $\tau \cdot \mathsf{true}$ is. The restriction on the use of expressions in processes is to ensure that weak bisimulation will be a congruence for expressions.

$$\frac{}{\vdash \mathbf{0} : A} \qquad \frac{\vdash p : A}{\vdash \tau \cdot p : A}$$

$$\frac{\vdash v : B,\ \vdash e : A}{\vdash k_B!v \cdot e : A} \qquad \frac{\vdash e : A}{\vdash k_B?x_B \cdot e : A}$$

$$\frac{\vdash p : A \quad \vdash q : A}{\vdash p + q : A} \qquad \frac{\vdash e : A \quad \vdash f : B}{\vdash e \,\#\!\!\!\!> f : B}$$

**Figure 17.5**
Type Rules for the merged language.

In this syntax output is restricted to being of values $k_A!v \cdot e$ rather than expressions $k_A!e \cdot f$. We can define an expression for arbitrary output as syntactic sugar:

$k!e \cdot f = \mathsf{let}\, x = e \,\mathsf{in}\, k!x \cdot f$

but note that this is an output *expression* rather than an output *process*, so cannot be placed in $+$ contexts.

The typing judgements for the new constructs are given in Figure 17.5. Note that the deadlocked process $\mathbf{0}$ can have any type. Also the types of processes such as $k_B?x_B \cdot e$, $k_B!v \cdot e$ are not dependent on the type of the channel, or the value communicated. Instead it is determined by the type of the potential value to which it can evaluate.

We use $\lambda_v^{con}$ to denote the set of well-typed closed expressions in the new syntax and as before use $(\lambda_v^{con})^\circ$ to denote the open expressions.

The operational semantics for $\lambda_v^{con}$ is given by unifying the previous operational semantics, and using a labeled transition system with labels:

$a ::= k_A!v \mid k_A?x_A \qquad \mu ::= a \mid \tau \qquad l ::= \mu \mid \surd v$

In particular, expressions can spawn subprocesses before returning a value, so $\xrightarrow{\surd v}$ transitions now have to have a residual, for example:

$p \,\#\!\!\!\!> \mathsf{true} \xrightarrow{\surd \mathsf{true}} p \,\#\!\!\!\!> \mathbf{0}$

These residuals have to be accommodated in other reductions, for example:

$\mathsf{if}\ p \,\#\!\!\!\!> \mathsf{true}\ \mathsf{then}\ e\ \mathsf{else}\ f \xrightarrow{\tau} p \,\#\!\!\!\!> \mathbf{0} \,\#\!\!\!\!> e$

We have the following Subject Reduction Theorem:

THEOREM 2.4 (SUBJECT REDUCTION) For every $e$ in $\lambda_v^{con}$ such that $\vdash e : A$

1. $e \xrightarrow{\tau} f$ implies $\vdash f : A$
2. $e \xrightarrow{\surd v} f$ implies $\vdash v : A$ and $\vdash f : A$

Values:

$$\frac{}{v \xrightarrow{\surd v} \mathbf{0}}$$

Communication Rules:

$$\frac{}{\tau.p \xrightarrow{\tau} p}$$

$$\frac{}{k!v \cdot e \xrightarrow{k!v} e} \qquad \frac{}{k?x \cdot e \xrightarrow{k?x} e}$$

$$\frac{e \xrightarrow{k!v} e' \quad f \xrightarrow{k?x} f'}{e \mathbin{\|\!\!>} f \xrightarrow{\tau} e' \mathbin{\|\!\!>} f'[v/x]} \quad \frac{e \xrightarrow{k?x} e' \quad f \xrightarrow{k!v} f'}{e \mathbin{\|\!\!>} f \xrightarrow{\tau} e'[v/x] \mathbin{\|\!\!>} f'}$$

Dynamic rules:

$$\frac{p \xrightarrow{\mu} p'}{p + q \xrightarrow{\mu} p'} \quad \frac{q \xrightarrow{\mu} q'}{p + q \xrightarrow{\mu} q'}$$

Reductions:

$$\frac{e \xrightarrow{\surd \mu x \cdot (\lambda y \cdot g)} e'}{e\, f \xrightarrow{\tau} e' \mathbin{\|\!\!>} \mathsf{let}\, y = f\, \mathsf{in}\, g[\mu x \cdot (\lambda y \cdot g)/x]} \quad \frac{e \xrightarrow{\surd v} e'}{\mathsf{let}\, x = e\, \mathsf{in}\, f \xrightarrow{\tau} e' \mathbin{\|\!\!>} f[v/x]}$$

$$\frac{e \xrightarrow{\surd \mathsf{true}} e'}{\mathsf{if}\, e\, \mathsf{then}\, f\, \mathsf{else}\, g \xrightarrow{\tau} e' \mathbin{\|\!\!>} f} \qquad \frac{e \xrightarrow{\surd \mathsf{false}} e'}{\mathsf{if}\, e\, \mathsf{then}\, f\, \mathsf{else}\, g \xrightarrow{\tau} e' \mathbin{\|\!\!>} g}$$

$$\frac{e \xrightarrow{\surd v} e'}{c\, e \xrightarrow{\tau} e' \mathbin{\|\!\!>} \delta(c, v)}$$

Context Rules:

$$\frac{e \xrightarrow{\mu} e'}{c\, e \xrightarrow{\mu} c\, e'} \qquad \frac{e \xrightarrow{\mu} e'}{\mathsf{if}\, e\, \mathsf{then}\, f\, \mathsf{else}\, g \xrightarrow{\mu} \mathsf{if}\, e'\, \mathsf{then}\, f\, \mathsf{else}\, g}$$

$$\frac{e \xrightarrow{\mu} e'}{\mathsf{let}\, x = e\, \mathsf{in}\, f \xrightarrow{\mu} \mathsf{let}\, x = e'\, \mathsf{in}\, f} \quad \frac{e \xrightarrow{\mu} e'}{e\, f \xrightarrow{\mu} e'\, f}$$

$$\frac{e \xrightarrow{\mu} e'}{e \mathbin{\|\!\!>} f \xrightarrow{\mu} e' \mathbin{\|\!\!>} f} \qquad \frac{f \xrightarrow{\mu} f'}{e \mathbin{\|\!\!>} f \xrightarrow{\mu} e \mathbin{\|\!\!>} f'}$$

$$\frac{f \xrightarrow{\surd v} f'}{e \mathbin{\|\!\!>} f \xrightarrow{\surd v} e \mathbin{\|\!\!>} f'}$$

**Figure 17.6**
Operational Semantics for $\lambda_v^{con}$.

3. $e \xrightarrow{k_B!v} f$ implies $\vdash v : B$ and $\vdash f : A$
4. $e \xrightarrow{k_B?} f$ implies $\vdash f : B \rightarrow A$

*Proof* By rule induction on the relations involved. □

We end this section by examining the properties of value production, the relation $\xrightarrow{\surd v}$.

PROPOSITION 2.5 The operational semantics of $\lambda_v^{con}$ satisfies the following properties:

- single-valuedness: If $e \xrightarrow{\surd v} e'$ then $e' \xrightarrow{\surd w}$ for no $w$.
- value-determinacy: $e \xrightarrow{\surd v} e'$ and $e \xrightarrow{\surd w} e''$ implies $e' = e''$ and $v = w$
- forward commutativity:

$$\begin{array}{ccc} e & \xrightarrow{\mu} & e_1 \\ {\scriptstyle \surd v}\downarrow & & \\ e_2 & & \end{array} \quad \textit{implies} \quad \begin{array}{ccc} e & \xrightarrow{\mu} & e_1 \\ {\scriptstyle \surd v}\downarrow & & \downarrow{\scriptstyle \surd v} \\ e_2 & \xrightarrow[\mu]{} & e_3 \end{array}$$

- backward commutativity:

$$\begin{array}{ccc} e & \xrightarrow{\surd v} & e_1 \\ & & \downarrow{\scriptstyle \mu} \\ & & e_2 \end{array} \quad \textit{implies} \quad \begin{array}{ccc} e & \xrightarrow{\surd v} & e_1 \\ {\scriptstyle \mu}\downarrow & & \downarrow{\scriptstyle \mu} \\ e_3 & \xrightarrow[\surd v]{} & e_2 \end{array}$$

*Proof* Routine induction on the syntax. □

These special properties of $\xrightarrow{\surd v}$ imply that in some sense the production of values is *asynchronous*; we will later show, using these properties, that if $e \xrightarrow{\surd v} e'$ then $e$ is semantically equivalent to the expression $e' \mathrel{+\!\!\!+\!\!\!>} v$. This latter term can produce the value $v$ but no subsequent behaviour can depend on its production.

## 3 A Semantic Theory

In this section we develop a semantic equivalence for $\lambda_v^{con}$ based on *bisimulations*. A typical semantic equivalence, $\sim$, is defined by abstracting in some manner from the operational semantics and is usually a relation over closed expressions, in our case over $\lambda_v^{con}$. This is extended in the standard way to a relation $\sim^\circ$ over open terms by letting $e \sim^\circ e'$ if $e\rho \sim e'\rho$ for all closed *substitutions* $\rho$, i.e. type-respecting functions from variables to closed values.

In this section, we will define two semantic equivalences $\approx^h$ and $=^h$ such that:

- $\approx^h$ is a congruence for $\lambda_v^{con}$ expressions, and $=^h$ is a congruence for $\lambda_v^{con}$ processes,
- $\approx^h$ generalises the standard theory of equality of the call-by-value $\lambda$-calculus,
- $=^h$ generalises Milner's observational congruence, [7], originally developed for *CCS*.

In the first subsection we explain the definition of *higher-order bisimulation equivalence* while some of its properties are investigated in the remainder.

### 3.1 Higher Order Bisimulations

Recall from [7] that that a relation $\mathcal{R}$ (over closed expressions from $\lambda_v^{con}$) is a (*strong*) *simulation* if the following diagram, representing a *transfer property*, can be completed:

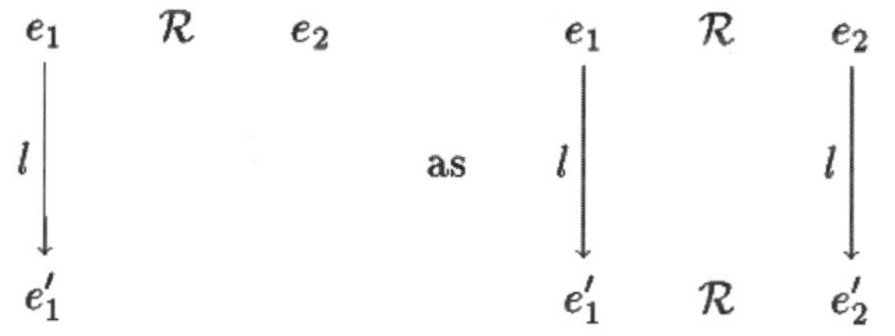

A semantic equivalence between expressions $\sim$ can then be defined as the largest symmetric simulation. There are many reasons why $\sim$ is inadequate as the basis of a semantic theory for $\lambda_v^{con}$; some of these are quite general while others are due to the nature of the language $\lambda_v^{con}$.

First in order to take into account the fact that $\xrightarrow{\tau}$ actions are unobservable we will require, as in [7], that the move $e_1 \xrightarrow{l} e_1'$ be matched by a *weak action* $e_2 \xRightarrow{\hat{l}} e_2'$, where

- $\xRightarrow{\varepsilon}$ is the reflexive transitive closure of $\xrightarrow{\tau}$
- $\xRightarrow{l}$ is $\xRightarrow{\varepsilon}\xrightarrow{l}$
- $\xRightarrow{\hat{l}}$ is $\xRightarrow{\varepsilon}$ if $l = \tau$ and $\xRightarrow{l}$ otherwise.

In order to ensure that only closed expressions of the same type are related we consider *typed-indexed* relations $\mathcal{R}$, i.e., families of relations $\mathcal{R}_A$ indexed by types $A$.

The requirement that an $l$-action be matched by one with exactly the same label is too strong. For example, the expressions $k_A!(\lambda x \cdot 1) \cdot \mathbf{0}$ and $k_A!(\lambda x \cdot \mathsf{succ}\,0) \cdot \mathbf{0}$ are differentiated although it would be difficult to conceive of a context which can distinguish them. The appropriate definition of simulation should compare not only expressions but also labels. To this end, for any type-indexed relation $\mathcal{R}$, define its *extension to labels* $\mathcal{R}^l$ by:

$$\frac{}{\tau\ \mathcal{R}^l_A\ \tau} \qquad \frac{v\ \mathcal{R}_A\ w}{\surd v\ \mathcal{R}^l_A\ \surd w} \qquad \frac{}{k?_B\ \mathcal{R}^l_A\ k?_B} \qquad \frac{v\ \mathcal{R}_B\ w}{k!_B v\ \mathcal{R}^l_A\ k!_B w}$$

We only require labels to be matched up to $\mathcal{R}^l$ rather than up to syntactic identity.

Unfortunately, the resulting equivalence now identifies all terms in normal form, since all a normal form can do is tick with its own value. We add the extra requirement that $\mathcal{R}$ be *structure preserving*, i.e.:

1. if $v_1\ \mathcal{R}_{A \to B}\ v_2$ then for all closed values $\vdash w : A$ we have $v_1\, w\ \mathcal{R}_B\ v_2\, w$
2. if $v_1\ \mathcal{R}_A\ v_2$ where $A$ is a base type then $v_1 = v_2$.

DEFINITION 3.1 (HIGHER-ORDER WEAK SIMULATION) A type-indexed relation $\mathcal{R}$ over extended $\lambda_v^{con}$ is a *higher-order weak simulation* if it is structure-preserving and the following diagram can be completed:

$$\begin{array}{ccc} e_1 & \mathcal{R} & e_2 \\ l_1 \downarrow & & \\ e_1' & & \end{array} \quad \text{as} \quad \begin{array}{ccc} e_1 & \mathcal{R} & e_2 \\ l_1 \downarrow & & \Downarrow \hat{l_2} \\ e_1' & \mathcal{R} & e_2' \end{array} \quad \text{where } l_1\ \mathcal{R}^l\ l_2$$

□

Let $\approx^h$ be the largest symmetric higher-order weak simulation. Since the identity relation $I$ is a higher-order simulation and $\mathcal{R}\,\mathcal{R}$ is whenever $\mathcal{R}$ is, it follows that $\approx^h$ is an equivalence relation.

However, as is usual for weak bisimulations and *CCS*, the choice construct $+$ is not preserved by $\approx^h$. For example $\tau \cdot \mathbf{0} \approx^h \mathbf{0}$ but $k_A!1 \cdot \mathbf{0} + \tau \cdot \mathbf{0} \not\approx^h k_A!1 \cdot \mathbf{0} + \mathbf{0}$. Fortunately we can adapt the usual remedy of Milner's observational equivalence, [7], to $\lambda_v^{con}$.

DEFINITION 3.2 (HIGHER-ORDER OBSERVATIONAL EQUIVALENCE) Let $=^h$ be the smallest symmetric relation such that the following diagram can be completed:

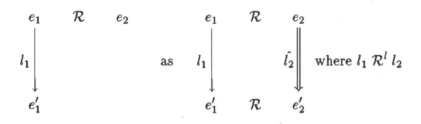

$$\begin{array}{ccc} e_1 & =^h & e_2 \\ {\scriptstyle l_1}\downarrow & & \\ e_1' & & \end{array} \quad \text{as} \quad \begin{array}{ccc} e_1 & =^h & e_2 \\ {\scriptstyle l_1}\downarrow & & \Downarrow{\scriptstyle l_2} \\ e_1' & \approx^h & e_2' \end{array} \quad \text{where } l_1 \approx^{h^l} l_2$$

□

THEOREM 3.3 $=^h$ is a congruence for $\lambda_v^{con}$ processes, and $\approx^h$ is a congruence for $\lambda_v^{con}$ expressions.

*Proof* It is easy to establish that $=^h$ is an equivalence relation and that it is preserved by operators such as $+$ and the various forms of action prefixing. However it is more difficult to prove that it, or indeed $\approx^h$, is preserved by the parallel construct, i.e. $e_i \approx^h f_i$ implies $e_1 \mathbin{+\!\!\!\!\!\!\Rightarrow} f_1 \approx^h e_2 \mathbin{+\!\!\!\!\!\!\Rightarrow} f_2$. For example if $e_i$ is $k_A?x \cdot g_i$ where $g_1 \approx^h g_2$ and $f_i$ are of the form $k_A!v_i \cdot \mathbf{0}$ where $v_1 \approx^h v_2$ then we need to establish $g_1[v_1/x] \approx^h g_2[v_2/x]$.

The proof uses Howe's technique, [6], and is relegated to the Appendix. □

THEOREM 3.4 $=^h$ is the largest congruence for $\lambda_v^{con}$ processes contained in $\approx^h$.

*Proof* Let $\approx$ be any congruence on $\lambda_v^{con}$ processes contained in $\approx^h$. To show $\approx$ is contained in $=^h$ it is sufficient to prove that if $p \approx q$ and $p \xrightarrow{\tau} p'$ then $q \xRightarrow{\tau} q'$ for some $q'$ such that $p' \approx^h q'$. Since $\approx$ is a congruence, we have $p + k!0 \approx q + k!0$ (for fresh $k$) and since $p + k!0 \xrightarrow{\tau} p'$ we have $q + k!0 \Longrightarrow q'$ and $p' \approx^h q'$. Since $p'$ cannot perform $k$, neither can $q'$, so we must have $q \xRightarrow{\tau} q'$. The result follows. □

It follows immediately that

COROLLARY 3.5 In $\lambda_v^{con}$:

- $e \approx^h f$ implies $\mu \cdot e =^h \mu \cdot f$
- $e \approx^h f$ implies $e =^h f$ or $\tau \cdot e =^h f$ or $e =^h \tau \cdot f$. □

### 3.2 Properties of $\lambda_v^{con}$ Expressions

We first examine $\lambda_v^{con}$ as a call-by-value $\lambda$-calculus, by considering $\lambda_v^{con}$ expressions up to weak bisimulation.

It is straightforward to show

$$(\lambda\, x \cdot e)\, v \approx^h e[v/x]$$
$$(\mu x \cdot (\gamma\ y \cdot e))\, v \approx^h e[\mu x \cdot (\gamma\ y \cdot e)/x][v/y]$$
$$\mathsf{let}\, x = v \,\mathsf{in}\, e \approx^h e[v/x]$$
$$\mathsf{let}\, y = (\mathsf{let}\, x = e \,\mathsf{in}\, f) \,\mathsf{in}\, g \approx^h \mathsf{let}\, x = e \,\mathsf{in}\, (\mathsf{let}\, y = f \,\mathsf{in}\, g) \quad \text{where } x \notin fv(g)$$

The last two are the left unit and associativity axioms of the monadic meta-language of [8]. The third unit equation:

$\mathsf{let}\, x = e \,\mathsf{in}\, x = e$

is more difficult to establish. Indeed as pointed out in [2] this is not true in arbitrary labeled transition systems, as can be seen from the following example:

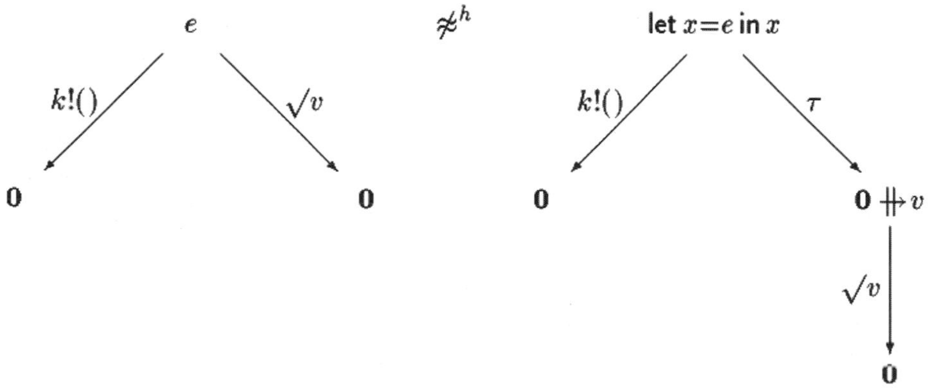


However in the labeled transition system generated by $\lambda_v^{con}$ we have:

PROPOSITION 3.6 If $e \xrightarrow{\sqrt{v}} e'$ then $e =^h e' \not\Vdash v$.

*Proof* The following is a higher-order bisimulation:

$\{(e, e' \not\Vdash v) \mid e \xrightarrow{\sqrt{v}} e'\} \cup \{(e', e' \not\Vdash \mathbf{0}) \mid e \xrightarrow{\sqrt{v}} e'\}$

Establishing this requires Proposition 2.5. □

COROLLARY 3.7 $e \approx^h \mathsf{let}\, x = e \,\mathsf{in}\, x$

*Proof* Using the previous Proposition one can show that

$\{(e, \mathsf{let}\, x = e \,\mathsf{in}\, x)\} \cup \approx^h$

is a higher-order bisimulation. □

These identities all involve the equivalence $\approx^h$ but using the first part of Corollary 3.5 they can be turned into identities for $=^h$. So for example we have

$$\tau \cdot e =^h \tau \cdot \mathsf{let}\, x = e\, \mathsf{in}\, x.$$

The second part of this Corollary indicates that by analysing the initial $\tau$ actions we can sometimes come up with slightly stronger identities. Examples of these are:

$$(\lambda x \cdot e)\, v =^h \tau \cdot e[v/x]$$
$$\mathsf{let}\, x = v\, \mathsf{in}\, e =^h \tau \cdot e[v/x]$$

We leave the reader to transform the other identities for $\approx^h$ given above to identities for $=^h$.

### 3.3 Properties of $\lambda_v^{con}$ Processes

We now turn our attention to the language viewed as a process algebra. The essential features of a process algebra such as *CCS* are a choice operator, a parallel operator and a notion of *action prefixing*. All of these appear in $\lambda_v^{con}$. We can take the syntactic expressions of the form $k_A!v\,\cdot$, $k_A?x\,\cdot$, $\tau\,\cdot$ to be action prefixes, ranged over by $\mu$. Note that even if $\mu \cdot e$ is a closed expression $e$ may be open. The following two $\tau$-law of CCS, [7], are valid:

$$p + \tau \cdot p =^h \tau \cdot p$$
$$\mu \cdot e =^h \mu \cdot \tau \cdot e$$

The third $\tau$-law

$$\mu \cdot (p + \tau \cdot q) = \mu \cdot q + \mu \cdot (p + \tau \cdot q)$$

is not in general true; but this is as expected as we have used a *late* operational semantics, [9], and this law does not hold in value-passing *CCS* for such a semantics. It is only satisfied for the $\tau$ prefix, and in this case it is derivable from the first law.

The choice operator satisfies the expected laws, those of a commutative monoid:

$$\mathbf{0} + p =^h p$$
$$p + p =^h p$$
$$(p_1 + p_2) + p_3 =^h p_1 + (p_2 + p_3)$$
$$p_1 + p_2 =^h p_2 + p_1$$

The parallel operator does not quite satisfy all the laws of *CCS*. It does satisfy:

$$
\begin{aligned}
\mathbf{0} \mathbin{\Vert\!\!\!\!\rightarrow} e &=^h e \\
(e_1 \mathbin{\Vert\!\!\!\!\rightarrow} e_2) \mathbin{\Vert\!\!\!\!\rightarrow} e_3 &=^h e_1 \mathbin{\Vert\!\!\!\!\rightarrow} (e_2 \mathbin{\Vert\!\!\!\!\rightarrow} e_3) \\
(e_1 \mathbin{\Vert\!\!\!\!\rightarrow} e_2) \mathbin{\Vert\!\!\!\!\rightarrow} e_3 &=^h (e_2 \mathbin{\Vert\!\!\!\!\rightarrow} e_1) \mathbin{\Vert\!\!\!\!\rightarrow} e_3
\end{aligned}
$$

It is not in general symmetric because of its interaction with the production of values; for example $1 \mathbin{\Vert\!\!\!\!\rightarrow} \mathbf{0} =^h \mathbf{0}$ but $\mathbf{0} \mathbin{\Vert\!\!\!\!\rightarrow} 1 =^h 1$.

In *CCS* every closed expression is semantically equivalent to a *sum-form*, i.e. an expression of the form

$$\sum_{i \in I} \mu_i \cdot e_i$$

In $\lambda_v^{con}$ we can also show that every expression (resp. process) is equivalent, up to $\approx^h$ (resp. $=^h$), to a such a form. This is the subject of the next subsection.

### 3.4 A Head Normal Form for Closed Finite Expressions

Here we outline a characterisation of $=^h$ in terms of equations and proof rules. The characterisation is restricted to *closed finite expressions* from the language $\lambda_v^{con}$, i.e. closed expressions in which for all occurrences of $\mu x \cdot (\lambda\, y \cdot e)$ $x$ does not occur free in $e$; as already explained in Section 2 such expressions will be denoted by $\lambda\, y \cdot e$.

The characterisation can be viewed as an extension of the equational characterisation of finite *CCS* expressions, [7]. These equations are given in Figure 17.7 although the third $\tau$-law from [7] is missing because we are dealing with a *late* behavioural equivalence, together with the usual structural rules for equational reasoning.

The syntax of $\lambda_v^{con}$ is larger than that of *CCS* and we need extra equations for each of the new syntactic constructs. These are given in Figure 17.8 and are of five kinds. The first gives the properties of parallelism as an associative operator with left units. The second gives the $\beta$-reduction rules for each of the operators. The others show how the process operators (parallelism, summation and prefixing) distribute through the functional operators (if, let and application).

Let $\vdash e = f$ denote that $e = f$ can be deduced in the resulting proof system. We leave the reader to check that this is sound, i.e. $\vdash e = f$ implies $e =^h f$. We will show that any closed finite expression can be converted into *head normal form*, that is:

$$\sum_i \mu_i \cdot e_i \quad \text{or} \quad \left(\sum_i \mu_i \cdot e_i \mathbin{\Vert\!\!\!\!\rightarrow}\right) v$$

Summation:

$$
\begin{aligned}
p + \mathbf{0} &= p \\
p + p &= p \\
p + q &= q + p \\
p + (q + r) &= (p + q) + r
\end{aligned}
$$

$$
\begin{aligned}
p + \tau \cdot p &= \tau \cdot p \\
\mu \cdot e &= \mu \cdot \tau \cdot e
\end{aligned}
$$

Interleaving law:

Let $p$, $q$ denote $\sum_i \mu_i \cdot e_i$, $\sum_j \nu_j \cdot f_j$, where $fv(\mu_i) \cap fv(\nu_j) = \emptyset$.

$$
\begin{aligned}
p \mathbin{+\!\!\!\!\!\!\rightarrow} q = &\sum_i \mu_i \cdot (e_i \mathbin{+\!\!\!\!\!\!\rightarrow} f) + \sum_j \nu_j \cdot (e \mathbin{+\!\!\!\!\!\!\rightarrow} f_j) \\
&+ \sum_{\mu_i = k!v, \nu_j = k?x} \tau \cdot (e_i \mathbin{+\!\!\!\!\!\!\rightarrow} f_j[v/x]) \\
&+ \sum_{\mu_i = k?x, \nu_j = k!v} \tau \cdot (e_i[v/x] \mathbin{+\!\!\!\!\!\!\rightarrow} f_j)
\end{aligned}
$$

**Figure 17.7**
Equations for *CCS*.

Note that we *cannot* use this directly to show completeness of the proof system, since the terms $e_i$ may be open, and we can only normalize closed terms. A complete proof system would require techniques taken from *symbolic bisimulation* [5], which is left for future work.

PROPOSITION 3.8 For every closed finite expression $e$ there is a head normal form $f$ such that $\vdash e = f$.

*Proof (Outline)* Show by induction on syntax that any process can be converted to the form $\sum_i \mu_i \cdot e_i$ and that any expression can be converted to the form $(\sum_i \mu_i \cdot e_i)$ $[\mathbin{+\!\!\!\!\!\!\rightarrow} v]$, where $[\mathbin{+\!\!\!\!\!\!\rightarrow} v]$ denotes an optional occurrence of $\mathbin{+\!\!\!\!\!\!\rightarrow} v$. The equational properties of $\mathbin{+\!\!\!\!\!\!\rightarrow}$ given by the "parallelism" and "process spawning" rules are needed only in the case of expressions whose head normal form is of the form $p \mathbin{+\!\!\!\!\!\!\rightarrow} v$. □

Concurrency:

$$\mathbf{0} \mathbin{+\!\!+\!\!>} e = e$$

$$v \mathbin{+\!\!+\!\!>} e = e$$

$$(e \mathbin{+\!\!+\!\!>} f) \mathbin{+\!\!+\!\!>} g = e \mathbin{+\!\!+\!\!>} (f \mathbin{+\!\!+\!\!>} g)$$

$$(e \mathbin{+\!\!+\!\!>} f) \mathbin{+\!\!+\!\!>} g = (q \mathbin{+\!\!+\!\!>} e) \mathbin{+\!\!+\!\!>} g$$

Reduction:

$$\textsf{if true then } e \textsf{ else } f = \tau \cdot e$$

$$\textsf{if false then } e \textsf{ else } f = \tau \cdot f$$

$$\textsf{let } x = v \textsf{ in } e = \tau \cdot e[v/x]$$

$$(\lambda\, x \cdot e)\, v = \tau \cdot e[v/x]$$

$$c\, v = \tau \cdot \delta(c, v)$$

Process spawning:

$$\textsf{if } (e \mathbin{+\!\!+\!\!>} e') \textsf{ then } f \textsf{ else } g = e \mathbin{+\!\!+\!\!>} (\textsf{if } e' \textsf{ then } f \textsf{ else } g)$$

$$\textsf{let } x = (e \mathbin{+\!\!+\!\!>} e') \textsf{ in } f = e \mathbin{+\!\!+\!\!>} (\textsf{let } x = e' \textsf{ in } f)$$

$$(e \mathbin{+\!\!+\!\!>} e')\, f = e \mathbin{+\!\!+\!\!>} (e'\, f)$$

$$c\, (e \mathbin{+\!\!+\!\!>} e') = e \mathbin{+\!\!+\!\!>} (c\, e')$$

Choice:

$$\textsf{if } (p + q) \textsf{ then } f \textsf{ else } g = (\textsf{if } p \textsf{ then } f \textsf{ else } g) + (\textsf{if } q \textsf{ then } f \textsf{ else } g)$$

$$\textsf{let } x = (p + q) \textsf{ in } f = (\textsf{let } x = p \textsf{ in } f) + (\textsf{let } x = q \textsf{ in } f)$$

$$(p + q)\, f = (p\, f) + (q\, f)$$

$$c\, (p + q) = (c\, p) + (c\, q)$$

Prefixing:

$$\textsf{if } \mu \cdot e \textsf{ then } f \textsf{ else } g = \mu \cdot (\textsf{if } e \textsf{ then } f \textsf{ else } g)$$

$$\textsf{let } x = \mu \cdot e \textsf{ in } f = \mu \cdot (\textsf{let } x = e \textsf{ in } f)$$

$$(\mu \cdot e)\, f = \mu \cdot (e\, f)$$

$$c\, (\mu \cdot e) = \mu \cdot (c\, e)$$

**Figure 17.8**
Extra equations.

## 4 Conclusions

In this paper we have described one method for combining the concurrency features of *CCS* with those of the typed $\lambda$-calculus. The resulting semantic theory can be viewed as an extension of the theory of bisimulation congruence of *CCS*, when restricted to the syntactic class of *processes*, and when applied to *expressions* as an extension of the theory of equality for call-by-value $\lambda$-calculus.

In section 3.4 we have briefly investigated a syntactic characterisation of this semantic theory using a combination of process algebra equations and those from the theory of equality for call-by-value $\lambda$-calculus. It is not surprising that these equations are incomplete even for expressions without recursion as the values being communicated may be higher-order abstractions. However even the introduction of rules such as

$$\frac{\text{for all } v,\ (\lambda\, x \cdot e_1)v = (\lambda\, y \cdot e_2)v}{\lambda\, x \cdot e_1 = \lambda\, y \cdot e_2} \qquad \frac{\text{for all } v,\ (\lambda\, x \cdot e_1)v = (\lambda\, y \cdot e_2)v}{k_A?x \cdot e_1 = k_A?y \cdot e_2}$$

will not lead to a complete characterisation. The problem is that the behaviour of a process such as $k_A?x \cdot e$ of type $B$ depends on the behaviour of $(\lambda\, x \cdot e)v$ where $v$ ranges over all values of type $B$. However $B$ may be any type, and in particular a type which has $A$ as a subtype, and therefore the proof rules above are not of great help in establishing judgements of the form $k_A?x \cdot e_1 = k_A?y \cdot e_2$. In order to obtain a complete syntactic characterisation the proof system needs to be generalised to *open expressions*, where the symbolic techniques of [5] may be applicable.

We have concentrated on a *communicate-by-value* paradigm because this is the approach taken in languages such as *CML* and *Facile*. However in *HO$\pi$*, [11], and *CHOCS*, [12], actual text or code is transmitted between processes, much in the same way as with standard $\beta$-reduction in the $\lambda$-calculus. In *CML* there is also a mechanism, using Event types, for this kind of data exchange and in *Facile* scripts are used in a similar manner. To study this form of communication an alternative to $\lambda_v^{con}$, say $\lambda_n^{con}$, could be designed with reductions such as:

$$(\lambda\, x \cdot e_1)e \xrightarrow{\tau} e_1[e/x], \qquad k_A!e \cdot e_1 \Vert\!\!\rightarrow k_A?x \cdot e_2 \xrightarrow{\tau} e_1 \Vert\!\!\rightarrow e_2[e/x]$$

We conjecture that in this language $\approx^h$ and $=^h$ are still congruences for *expressions* and *processes* respectively. Nevertheless it is known from [12] that higher-order bisimulation congruence is not preserved by all *CHOCS* contexts, the reason being that in *CHOCS* no distinction is made between *processes* and *expressions*. In $\lambda_v^{con}$, and the hypothetical $\lambda_n^{con}$, variables are *expressions* and may only be instantiated by expressions. If however $\lambda_n^{con}$ were further extended to allow variables to be instantiated by *processes*, and therefore the communication of *processes*, then $\approx^h$, $=^h$ would no longer be preserved by all contexts.

As a counterexample consider the two *processes* $p_1,\ p_2$ defined by $k_A!\mathbf{0}\cdot\mathbf{0},\ k_A!(\tau\cdot\mathbf{0})\cdot\mathbf{0}$ respectively. These two *processes* send the *processes* $\mathbf{0},\ \tau\cdot\mathbf{0}$, respectively, along the channel $k_A$ and it is straightforward to verify $p_1 =^h p_2$. However $C[p_1] \neq^h C[p_2]$ where $C$ is the context $k_A?x\cdot(x + l!0\cdot\mathbf{0}) \nrightarrow C[\ ]$.

This phenomenon also occurs in *CML* and is studied in [2]. A suitable modification of higher-order bisimulations equivalence called *hereditary* bisimulations is proposed and shown to be preserved by all *CML* contexts. This seems to be the most appropriate form of bisimulation for $\lambda_n^{con}$ extended with *process*-communication. However we leave this for further study.

## A Appendix: Congruence Proofs

We prove Theorem 3.3 using a variant of Howe's [6] technique, and following Gordon's [4] presentation. The proof follows closely that in Section 5 of [2] and here we merely state the required propositions.

*One-level deep* contexts are defined by

$$D ::= x \mid l \mid c\cdot_1 \mid \textsf{if}\cdot_1 \textsf{ then}\cdot_2 \textsf{ else}\cdot_3 \mid \textsf{let}\, x = \cdot_1 \textsf{ in}\cdot_2 \mid \cdot_1\cdot_2 \mid \mu x\cdot(\lambda\, y\cdot\cdot_1)$$
$$k_A?x\cdot\cdot_1 \mid k_A!\cdot_1\cdot\cdot_2 \mid \cdot_1 + \cdot_2 \mid \cdot_1 \nrightarrow \cdot_2$$

Let $D_n$ range over *restricted* one-level deep contexts: one-level deep contexts which do not use $+$.

For any pair of relations $\mathcal{R} = (\mathcal{R}^n, \mathcal{R}^s)$ with $\mathcal{R}^s \subseteq \mathcal{R}^n$, let its *compatible refinement*, $\widehat{\mathcal{R}}$ be defined by:

$$\widehat{\mathcal{R}}^n = \{(D_n[\vec{e}], D_n[\vec{f}]) \mid e_i\ \mathcal{R}^n\ f_i\} \cup \widehat{\mathcal{R}}^s$$
$$\widehat{\mathcal{R}}^s = \{(D[\vec{e}], D[\vec{f}]) \mid e_i\ \mathcal{R}^s\ f_i\}$$
$$\cup\, \{(\mu x\cdot(\lambda\, y\cdot e), \mu x\cdot(\lambda\, y\cdot f)) \mid e\ \mathcal{R}^n\ f\}$$
$$\cup\, \{(\tau\cdot e, \tau\cdot f) \mid e\ \mathcal{R}^n\ f\}$$
$$\cup\, \{(k?x\cdot e, k?x\cdot f) \mid e\ \mathcal{R}^n\ f\}$$
$$\cup\, \{(k!v\cdot e, k!w\cdot f) \mid e\ \mathcal{R}^n\ f,\ v\ \mathcal{R}^n\ w\}$$

The following proposition is easily established, using induction on contexts.

PROPOSITION A.1 If $\mathcal{R}$ is an equivalence and $\widehat{\mathcal{R}} \subseteq \mathcal{R}$, then $\mathcal{R}^s$ is a congruence on processes and $\mathcal{R}^n$ is a congruence on expressions. □

For any $\mathcal{R}$, its *compatible closure*, $\mathcal{R}^{\bullet}$, is given by:

$$\frac{e\ \widehat{\mathcal{R}^{\bullet}}\ e'\ \mathcal{R}^{\circ}\ e''}{e\ \mathcal{R}^{\bullet}\ e''}$$

where $\mathcal{R}^{\circ}$ is the natural extension of $\mathcal{R}$ to open terms. This definition of $\mathcal{R}^{\bullet}$ is specifically designed to facilitate simultaneous inductive proof on syntax (since the definition involves one-level deep contexts) and on reductions (since the definition involves inductive use of $\mathcal{R}^{\circ}$). This form of induction is precisely what is required to show the desired congruence results.

Its relevant properties are given in the three following Propositions. Their proofs are simple variants of the corresponding theorems in [4, 6] and are nearly identical to those in Section 5 of [2].

PROPOSITION A.2 If $\mathcal{R}^{\circ}$ is a preorder then $\mathcal{R}^{\bullet}$ is the smallest relation satisfying:

1. $\mathcal{R}^{\bullet}\mathcal{R}^{\circ} \subseteq \mathcal{R}^{\bullet}$,
2. $\widehat{\mathcal{R}^{\bullet}} \subseteq \mathcal{R}^{\bullet}$, and
3. $\mathcal{R}^{\circ} \subseteq \mathcal{R}^{\bullet}$. □

PROPOSITION A.3 If $\mathcal{R}$ is a preorder then for any $v\ \mathcal{R}^{\bullet s}\ w$:

1. if $e\ \mathcal{R}^{\bullet s}\ f$ then $e[v/x]\ \mathcal{R}^{\bullet s}\ f[w/x]$, and
2. if $e\ \mathcal{R}^{\bullet n}\ f$ then $e[v/x]\ \mathcal{R}^{\bullet n}\ f[w/x]$. □

PROPOSITION A.4 If $\mathcal{R}$ is an equivalence then $\mathcal{R}^{\bullet *}$ is symmetric. □

We need one specific property of the compatible closure of bisimulation:

PROPOSITION A.5 When restricted to closed expressions, $\approx^{h\bullet}$ is a simulation, and if $e =^{h\bullet} f$ and $e \xrightarrow{l_1} e'$ then $f \overset{l_2}{\Longrightarrow} f'$ where $l_1 \approx^{h\bullet} l_2$ and $e' \approx^{h\bullet} f'$.

*Proof* Very similar to the proof of Proposition 4.4 of [2]. □

We now have all the information we need to prove Theorem 3.3.

THEOREM A.6 $=^{h}$ is a congruence for $\lambda_v^{con}$ processes, and $\approx^{h}$ is a congruence for $\lambda_v^{con}$ expressions.

*Proof* Follows from Propositions A.2, A.5 and A.4. □

## References

[1] R. Amadio, L. Leth, and B. Thomsen. From a concurrent λ-calculus to the π-calculus. In *FCT'95*. Springer–Verlag, 1995.

[2] W. Ferreira, M. Hennessy, and A. Jeffrey. A Theory of Weak Bisimulation for Core CML. In *Proc. ACM SIGPLAN Int. Conf. Functional Programming*, pages 201–212. ACM Press, 1996.

[3] A. Giacalone, P. Mishra, and S. Prasad. A symmetric integration of concurrent and functional programming. *International Journal of Parallel Programming*, 18(2):121–160, 1989.

[4] A. Gordon. Bisimilarity as a theory of functional programming. In *Proceedings of MFPS95*, number 1 in Electronic Notes in Computer Science. Springer–Verlag, 1995.

[5] M. Hennessy and H. Lin. A proof system for value passing processes. *Formal Aspects of Computer Science*, pages 379–407,1996.

[6] D. Howe. Equality in lazy computation systems. In *Proceedings of LICS89*, pages 198–203, 1989.

[7] R. Milner. *Communication and Concurrency*. Prentice-Hall, 1989.

[8] Eugenio Moggi. Notions of computation and monad. *Information and Computation*, 93:55–92, 1991.

[9] J. Parrow and D. Sangiorgi. Algebraic theories for value-passing calculi. *Information and Computation*, 120:174–197, 1995.

[10] J. H. Reppy. A higher-order concurrent language. In *Proceedings of the ACM SIGPLAN 91 PLDI*, number 26 in SIGPLAN Notices, pages 294–305, 1991.

[11] D. Sangiorgi. *Expressing Mobility in Process Algebras: First-Order and Higher-Order Paradigms*. Phd thesis, Edinburgh University, Scotland, 1992.

[12] B. Thomsen. Higher order communicating systems theory. *Information and Computation*, 116:38–57, 1995.

# 18 Discrete Time Process Algebra with Silent Step

**J. C. M. Baeten, J. A. Bergstra, and M. A. Reniers**

## 1 Introduction

Process algebra was introduced by Milner in the form of CCS [18]. The original design of CCS and of subsequent versions of process algebra such as ACP [9] and TCSP [13] involves no explicit notion of time. Time is present in the interpretation of sequential composition: in $p \cdot q$ (ACP notation) the process $p$ should be executed before $q$. Process algebras can be introduced that support standardized features to incorporate a quantitative view on time. Time may be represented by means of non-negative reals, and actions can be given time stamps. This line is followed in [1] for ACP, in [20] for CCS and in [22] for CSP.

A second option is to divide time in slices indexed by natural numbers, to have an implicit or explicit time stamping mechanism that determines for each action the time slice in which it occurs and to have a time order within each slice only. This line has been followed in ATP [21], a process algebra that adds time slicing to a version of ACP based on action prefixing rather than sequential composition. Further, [15] has extended ACP with time slices whereas [20] have added these features to CCS. Following [5], we use the phrase *discrete time* process algebra if an enumeration of time slices is used.

The objective of this paper is to extend the discrete time process algebra of ACP as given in [5] with the silent step $\tau$. Silent steps have been a cornerstone of CCS since its introduction. Milner used weak bisimulation to model processes with silent step. Van Glabbeek and Weijland [14] introduced branching bisimulation which also deals with silent step, but is slightly less abstract. This will allow a notion of abstraction. We mention that [17] has extended $\mathrm{ACP}_\rho$, the real time ACP of [1], with silent steps. We present three views on discrete time process algebra with silent step: a version using relative timing (which we discuss extensively), a version using absolute timing, and a version using parametric timing, that integrates the relative and absolute timing versions.

There are many practical uses conceivable for timed process algebras. In particular, we mention the ToolBus (see [8]). This ToolBus contains a program notation called $T$ which is syntactically sugared discrete time process algebra. Programs in $T$ are called $T$-scripts. The runtime system is also described in terms of discrete time process algebra. By using randomized symbolic execution the ToolBus implementation enacts that the axioms of process algebra can be viewed as correctness preserving transformations of $T$-scripts. A comparable part of discrete time process algebra that is used to describe $T$-scripts has also been used for the description of $\phi$SDL, flat SDL, a subset of SDL that

Partial support received from ESPRIT Basic Research Action 7166, CONCUR2. This paper supersedes [3].

leaves out modularization and concentrates on timing aspects (see [11]). Discrete-time process algebra with relative timing has also been used for the formal specification of the $I^2C$-bus [12].

At this point we are happy to express our admiration for Milner's contributions. In process theory, but not just there, he has guided the work in such directions, that the perspective of relevance and application is almost self evident.

## 2 Discrete Time Process Algebra with Relative Timing

### 2.1 Basic Process Algebra with Time Free Actions

The signature of $\mathrm{BPA}^-_{\mathrm{drt}}$ has constants $cts(a)$ (for $a \in A$), denoting $a$ in the current time slice, and $cts(\delta)$ denoting a deadlock at the end of the current time slice. Also, we have the immediate deadlock constant $\dot{\delta}$ introduced in [5]. This constant denotes an immediate and catastrophic deadlock. Within a time slice, there is no explicit mention of the passage of time, we can see the passage to the next time slice as a clock tick. Thus, the $cts(a)$ can be called non-delayable actions: the action must occur before the next clock tick.

The operators are alternative and sequential composition, and the *relative discrete time unit delay* $\sigma_{\mathrm{rel}}$ (the notation $\sigma$ taken from [16]). The process $\sigma_{\mathrm{rel}}(x)$ will start $x$ after one clock tick, i.e., in the next time slice. In addition, we add the auxiliary operator $\nu_{\mathrm{rel}}$. This operator, called the *current slice time out* operator, or current slice operator in short, disallows an initial time step[1], it gives the part of a process that starts with an action in the current time slice. It is also used in [23, 12].

The axioms of $\mathrm{BPA}^-_{\mathrm{drt}}$ are A1-A5,A6ID,A7ID,DCS1-DCS4,DCSID,DRT1-DRT5, DRTSID, as given in Table 18.1. The axiom DRT1 is the time factorization axiom of ATP ([21]): it says that the passage of time by itself cannot determine a choice. The addition of a silent step in strong bisimulation semantics now just amounts to the presence of a new constant $cts(\tau)$ with the same axioms as the $cts(a)$ constants. We write $A_\tau = A \cup \{\tau\}$, $A_\delta = A \cup \{\delta\}$, etc. The axioms DRT3 and DRT5 are derivable from the other axioms (see [23]). Note that $x + cts(\delta) = x$ for all closed terms $x$ except those that are derivably equal to $\dot{\delta}$ (see Proposition 2.1.7), which implies that in a theory without immediate deadlock the law $x + cts(\delta) = x$ will hold.

The standard process algebra $\mathrm{BPA}_\delta$ can be considered as an SRM specification (Subalgebra of Reduced Model, in the terminology of [2]) of $\mathrm{BPA}^-_{\mathrm{drt}}$: consider the initial algebra of $\mathrm{BPA}^-_{\mathrm{drt}}$, reduce the signature by omitting $\dot{\delta}$, $\sigma_{\mathrm{rel}}$, $\nu_{\mathrm{rel}}$, then $\mathrm{BPA}_\delta$ is a complete axiomatization of the reduced model, under the interpretation of $a$, $\delta$ (from $\mathrm{BPA}_\delta$) by $cts(a)$, $cts(\delta)$.

[1] The Greek letter $\nu$ sounds like "now"; this correspondence is even stronger in Dutch.

**Table 18.1**
Axioms of $BPA_{drt}$ $(a \in A_{\tau\delta})$.

| | | | |
|---|---|---|---|
| $x + y = y + x$ | A1 | $x + \dot{\delta} = x$ | A6ID |
| $(x + y) + z = x + (y + z)$ | A2 | $\dot{\delta} \cdot x = \dot{\delta}$ | A7ID |
| $x + x = x$ | A3 | | |
| $(x + y) \cdot z = x \cdot z + y \cdot z$ | A4 | $\sigma_{rel}(x) + \sigma_{rel}(y) = \sigma_{rel}(x + y)$ | DRT1 |
| $(x \cdot y) \cdot z = x \cdot (y \cdot z)$ | A5 | $\sigma_{rel}(x) \cdot y = \sigma_{rel}(x \cdot y)$<br>$cts(\delta) \cdot x = cts(\delta)$ | DRT2<br>DRT3 |
| $\nu_{rel}(cts(a)) = cts(a)$ | DCS1 | $cts(a) + cts(\delta) = cts(a)$ | DRT4 |
| $\nu_{rel}(x + y) = \nu_{rel}(x) + \nu_{rel}(y)$ | DCS2 | $\sigma_{rel}(x) + cts(\delta) = \sigma_{rel}(x)$ | DRT5 |
| $\nu_{rel}(x \cdot y) = \nu_{rel}(x) \cdot y$ | DCS3 | $\sigma_{rel}(\dot{\delta}) = cts(\delta)$ | DRTSID |
| $\nu_{rel}(\sigma_{rel}(x)) = cts(\delta)$ | DCS4 | $\sigma^*_{rel}(x) = x + \sigma_{rel}(\sigma^*_{rel}(x))$ | DRTI1 |
| $\nu_{rel}(\dot{\delta}) = \dot{\delta}$ | DCSID | $ats(a) = \sigma^*_{rel}(cts(a))$ | ARTS |

**Table 18.2**
RSP(DRT).

| | |
|---|---|
| $y = x + \sigma_{rel}(y) \Longrightarrow y = \sigma^*_{rel}(x)$ | RSP(DRT) |

However, this is not the embedding of the time free theory into the discrete time theory that we prefer: it reduces the whole world to one time slice. Rather, we propose to view the time free actions as actions that can occur in any time slice. Following [5], we extend $BPA^-_{drt}$ to $BPA_{drt}$ by introducing constants $ats(a)$ (for $a \in A_{\tau\delta}$). The constant $ats(a)$ executes $a$ in an arbitrary time slice, followed by immediate termination. We define these constants in axiom ARTS (Any Relative Time Slice, see Table 18.1) using the operator $\sigma^*_{rel}$, the *time iteration* operator: $\sigma^*_{rel}(x)$ can start the execution of $x$ in the current time slice, and can always delay to the next time slice. The defining axiom for this operator takes the form of a recursive equation (see axiom DRTI1, Discrete Relative Time Iteration, in Table 18.1). The presentation using the time iteration operator here differs slightly from the presentation in [5]. There, we used the unbounded start delay operator $\lfloor\rfloor^\omega$ of [21] instead; the unbounded start delay operator can be simply expressed in terms of the time iteration operator as follows: $\lfloor x \rfloor^\omega = \sigma^*_{rel}(\nu_{rel}(x))$. In order to prove identities for the time iteration operator, we need a restricted form of the Recursive Specification Principle RSP (see, e.g. [6]). We call this principle RSP(DRT) (see Table 18.2).

We give a semantics for the theory $BPA_{drt}$ in terms of Plotkin-style operational rules. We have the following relations on the set of closed process expressions $T(BPA_{drt})$:

- action step $\subseteq T(BPA_{drt}) \times A_\tau \times T(BPA_{drt})$, notation $p \xrightarrow{a} p'$ (denotes action execution);
- action termination $\subseteq T(BPA_{drt}) \times A_\tau$, notation $p \xrightarrow{a} \surd$ (execution of a terminating action);

**Table 18.3**
Operational rules for $\text{BPA}_{\text{drt}}$ $(a \in A_\tau)$.

$$\text{ID}(\dot{\delta}) \qquad \frac{\text{ID}(x), \text{ID}(y)}{\text{ID}(x+y)} \qquad \frac{\text{ID}(x)}{\text{ID}(x \cdot y)} \qquad \frac{\text{ID}(x)}{\text{ID}(\nu_{\text{rel}}(x))}$$

$$cts(a) \xrightarrow{a} \surd \qquad ats(a) \xrightarrow{a} \surd \qquad ats(a) \xrightarrow{\sigma} ats(a) \qquad ats(\delta) \xrightarrow{\sigma} ats(\delta)$$

$$\frac{x \xrightarrow{a} x'}{x \cdot y \xrightarrow{a} x' \cdot y} \qquad \frac{x \xrightarrow{a} \surd}{x \cdot y \xrightarrow{a} y} \qquad \frac{x \xrightarrow{\sigma} x'}{x \cdot y \xrightarrow{\sigma} x' \cdot y}$$

$$\frac{x \xrightarrow{a} x'}{x + y \xrightarrow{a} x',\ y + x \xrightarrow{a} x'} \qquad \frac{x \xrightarrow{a} \surd}{x + y \xrightarrow{a} \surd,\ y + x \xrightarrow{a} \surd}$$

$$\frac{x \xrightarrow{\sigma} x',\ y \xrightarrow{\sigma} y'}{x + y \xrightarrow{\sigma} x' + y'} \qquad \frac{x \xrightarrow{\sigma} x',\ y \not\xrightarrow{\sigma}}{x + y \xrightarrow{\sigma} x',\ y + x \xrightarrow{\sigma} x'}$$

$$\frac{\neg\text{ID}(x)}{\sigma_{\text{rel}}(x) \xrightarrow{\sigma} x} \qquad \frac{x \xrightarrow{a} x'}{\nu_{\text{rel}}(x) \xrightarrow{a} x'} \qquad \frac{x \xrightarrow{a} \surd}{\nu_{\text{rel}}(x) \xrightarrow{a} \surd}$$

$$\frac{x \xrightarrow{a} x'}{\sigma^*_{\text{rel}}(x) \xrightarrow{a} x'} \qquad \frac{x \xrightarrow{a} \surd}{\sigma^*_{\text{rel}}(x) \xrightarrow{a} \surd} \qquad \frac{x \xrightarrow{\sigma} x'}{\sigma^*_{\text{rel}}(x) \xrightarrow{\sigma} x' + \sigma^*_{\text{rel}}(x)} \qquad \frac{x \not\xrightarrow{\sigma}}{\sigma^*_{\text{rel}}(x) \xrightarrow{\sigma} \sigma^*_{\text{rel}}(x)}$$

- time step $\subseteq T(\text{BPA}_{\text{drt}}) \times T(\text{BPA}_{\text{drt}})$, notation $p \xrightarrow{\sigma} p'$ (denotes passage to the next time slice);
- immediate deadlock $\subseteq T(\text{BPA}_{\text{drt}})$, notation $\text{ID}(p)$ (immediate deadlock, holds only for process expressions equal to $\dot{\delta}$).

We enforce the time factorization axiom DRT1 by phrasing the rules so that each process expression has at most one $\sigma$-step: in a transition system, each node has at most one outgoing $\sigma$-edge. The operational semantics in Table 18.3 uses predicates and negative premises. Still, using terminology and results of [24], the rules satisfy the *panth* format, and determine a unique transition relation on closed process expressions. Due to the presence of the immediate deadlock constant we have a notion of bisimulation which is slightly different from the usual *strong bisimulation.* This notion is called *strong tail bisimulation* in this paper. In the terminology of [24] this notion of strong tail bisimulation would be called a bisimulation anyway.

DEFINITION 2.1.1 (STRONG TAIL BISIMULATION) Two closed terms $p$ and $q$ are called *strongly tail bisimilar*, notation $p \leftrightarroweq q$, if there exists a symmetric binary relation $R$ on closed terms, called *strong tail bisimulation*, relating $p$ and $q$ such that for all $r, s$ with $R(r, s)$ we have:

1. if $r \xrightarrow{u} r'$ ($u \in A_{\tau\sigma}$), then there exists a node $s'$ such that $s \xrightarrow{u} s'$ and $R(r', s')$;
2. if $r \xrightarrow{a} \surd$ ($a \in A_\tau$), then $s \xrightarrow{a} \surd$;
3. if $\mathrm{ID}(r)$, then $\mathrm{ID}(s)$.

We state that strong tail bisimulation is a congruence with respect to the operators from the algebra $\mathrm{BPA_{drt}}$. Following [23] we can prove that $\mathrm{BPA_{drt}}$ is a sound and complete axiomatization of the model of closed process expressions modulo strong tail bisimulation equivalence.

Now, we want to define a notion of bisimulation that takes into account the special status of the immediate deadlock and the silent step. We start from the definition of branching bisimulation in the time free case, and adapt this to our timed setting. An immediate deadlock term can only be related to another immediate deadlock term. As a consequence, we can have no term that is related to $\surd$. This is different from the usual definition of branching bisimulation of [6, 14]. In order to emphasize this fact, we call the relations to be defined branching *tail* bisimulations. The following definition is easier to read if we use a couple of abbreviations: first, we write $p \xrightarrow{(u)} p'$ if either $p \xrightarrow{u} p'$ or $u \equiv \tau$ and $p = p'$. Further, we write $p \Longrightarrow q$ if it is possible to reach $q$ from $p$ by executing a number of $\tau$-steps (0 or more).

DEFINITION 2.1.2 (BRANCHING TAIL BISIMULATION) Two closed terms $p$ and $q$ are called *branching tail bisimilar*, notation $p \leftrightarrow_{\mathrm{bt}} q$, if there exists a symmetric binary relation $R$ on closed terms, called *branching tail bisimulation*, relating $p$ and $q$ such that for all $r, s$ with $R(r, s)$ we have:

1. if $r \xrightarrow{u} r'$ ($u \in A_{\tau\sigma}$), then there exist $s^*, s'$ such that $s \Longrightarrow s^* \xrightarrow{(u)} s'$ and $R(r, s^*)$ and $R(r', s')$;
2. if $r \xrightarrow{a} \surd$ ($a \in A_\tau$), then there exists $s^*$ such that $s \Longrightarrow s^* \xrightarrow{a} \surd$ and $R(r, s^*)$;
3. if $\mathrm{ID}(r)$, then $\mathrm{ID}(s)$.

Actually, we gave the definition of *semi*-branching bisimulation here, as optimized in [7]. The present definition is shorter and easier to work with than the original definition in [14], and induces the same equivalence relation (see [7]).

DEFINITION 2.1.3 (ROOTED BRANCHING TAIL BISIMULATION) If $R$ is a branching tail bisimulation, then we say that the related pair $(p, q)$ satisfies the *root condition* if:

1. if $p \xrightarrow{u} p'$ ($u \in A_{\tau\sigma}$), then there exists $q'$ such that $q \xrightarrow{u} q'$ and $R(p', q')$;
2. if $p \xrightarrow{a} \surd$ ($a \in A_\tau$), then $q \xrightarrow{a} \surd$.

A term $r$ is called *$\sigma$-reachable* from a term $p$ iff there exists a $k \in \mathbb{N}$ such that $p \equiv p_0 \xrightarrow{\sigma} p_1 \xrightarrow{\sigma} \cdots \xrightarrow{\sigma} p_k \equiv r$.

Two terms $p$ and $q$ are called *rooted branching tail bisimilar*, notation $p \underline{\leftrightarrow}_{\mathrm{rbt}}\, q$, if there is a branching tail bisimulation relation $R$ relating $p$ and $q$ such that whenever $R(r, s)$ and $r$ is $\sigma$-reachable from $p$, then the pair $(r, s)$ satisfies the root condition.

Thus the root condition amounts to the condition that the bisimulation is strong as long as no action is executed.

We can prove that rooted branching tail bisimulation is a congruence relation with respect to the operators from the algebra $\mathrm{BPA}_{\mathrm{drt}}$, thus obtaining the algebra $T(\mathrm{BPA}_{\mathrm{drt}})/\underline{\leftrightarrow}_{\mathrm{rbt}}$ of closed process expressions modulo rooted branching tail bisimulation. We can establish that the algebras $T(\mathrm{BPA}_{\mathrm{drt}})/\underline{\leftrightarrow}$, $T(\mathrm{BPA}_{\mathrm{drt}})/\underline{\leftrightarrow}_{\mathrm{bt}}$, and $T(\mathrm{BPA}_{\mathrm{drt}})/\underline{\leftrightarrow}_{\mathrm{rbt}}$ satisfy all laws of $\mathrm{BPA}_{\mathrm{drt}}$ + RSP(DRT).

THEOREM 2.1.4 (SOUNDNESS) The laws of $\mathrm{BPA}_{\mathrm{drt}}$ + RSP(DRT) are valid in $T(\mathrm{BPA}_{\mathrm{drt}})/\underline{\leftrightarrow}$, $T(\mathrm{BPA}_{\mathrm{drt}})/\underline{\leftrightarrow}_{\mathrm{bt}}$, and $T(\mathrm{BPA}_{\mathrm{drt}})/\underline{\leftrightarrow}_{\mathrm{rbt}}$.

Note that if we take the reduced model obtained by omitting the immediate deadlock constant, then we can define a notion of branching bisimulation without the tail condition, where a term can be related to $\surd$. Using the embedding of discrete time process algebra into real time process algebra given in [5] we find that our notion of silent step in time is in line with the notion of timed branching bisimulation of [17].

PROPOSITION 2.1.5 The following identities are derivable from $\mathrm{BPA}_{\mathrm{drt}}$ + RSP(DRT):

**Table 18.4**
Derivable equations.

| | |
|---|---|
| $\sigma^*_{\mathrm{rel}}(x + y) = \sigma^*_{\mathrm{rel}}(x) + \sigma^*_{\mathrm{rel}}(y)$ | DRTI2 |
| $\sigma^*_{\mathrm{rel}}(x \cdot y) = \sigma^*_{\mathrm{rel}}(x) \cdot y$ | DRTI3 |
| $\sigma^*_{\mathrm{rel}}(\sigma_{\mathrm{rel}}(x)) = \sigma_{\mathrm{rel}}(\sigma^*_{\mathrm{rel}}(x))$ | DRTI4 |
| $\sigma^*_{\mathrm{rel}}(\sigma^*_{\mathrm{rel}}(x)) = \sigma^*_{\mathrm{rel}}(x)$ | DRTI5 |
| $\sigma^*_{\mathrm{rel}}(\dot{\delta}) = ats(\delta)$ | DRTIID |
| $\nu_{\mathrm{rel}}(\sigma^*_{\mathrm{rel}}(x)) = \nu_{\mathrm{rel}}(x) + cts(\delta)$ | DCSTI |

As it turns out these identities are used in the proof of the completeness theorem. By using those, the principle RSP(DRT) does not have to be used directly, but only in the proof of these identities. As a matter of fact we prove completeness for the algebra $\mathrm{BPA}_{\mathrm{drt}}\tau$ + DRTI2-DRTI5, DRTIID, DCSTI. The most important place where those identities are used is the Elimination Theorem. This theorem expresses that every closed term can be rewritten into a *basic term*, i.e., a closed term with a more restricted syntax. We define basic terms over $\mathrm{BPA_{drt}}$ in such a way that they closely resemble the process graphs (see Section 3), in the sense that in every sum-context there is at most one summand ready to perform a time step, and that time iteration does not occur in any sum-context. To achieve this we define auxiliary sets of basic terms $\nu(\mathrm{BPA_{drt}})$, $\Sigma(\mathrm{BPA_{drt}})$, and $\Delta(\mathrm{BPA_{drt}})$.

DEFINITION 2.1.6 (BASIC TERMS) The set $B(\mathrm{BPA_{drt}})$ of *basic terms* over $\mathrm{BPA_{drt}}$ is defined inductively by:

1. $\dot{\delta} \in \nu(\mathrm{BPA_{drt}})$;
2. $a \in A_{\tau\delta} \Rightarrow cts(a) \in \nu(\mathrm{BPA_{drt}})$;
3. $a \in A_{\tau} \wedge p \in B(\mathrm{BPA_{drt}}) \Rightarrow cts(a) \cdot p \in \nu(\mathrm{BPA_{drt}})$;
4. $p, q \in \nu(\mathrm{BPA_{drt}}) \wedge p \not\equiv \dot{\delta} \wedge q \not\equiv \dot{\delta} \Rightarrow p + q \in \nu(\mathrm{BPA_{drt}})$;
5. $p \in B(\mathrm{BPA_{drt}}) \wedge p \not\equiv \dot{\delta} \Rightarrow \sigma_{\mathrm{rel}}(p) \in \Sigma(\mathrm{BPA_{drt}})$;
6. $p \in \nu(\mathrm{BPA_{drt}}) \wedge p \not\equiv \dot{\delta} \Rightarrow \sigma^{*}_{\mathrm{rel}}(p) \in \Delta(\mathrm{BPA_{drt}})$;
7. $\nu(\mathrm{BPA_{drt}}) \subseteq B(\mathrm{BPA_{drt}})$;
8. $\Sigma(\mathrm{BPA_{drt}}) \subseteq B(\mathrm{BPA_{drt}})$;
9. $\Delta(\mathrm{BPA_{drt}}) \subseteq B(\mathrm{BPA_{drt}})$;
10. $p \in \nu(\mathrm{BPA_{drt}}) \wedge p \not\equiv \dot{\delta} \wedge q \in \Sigma(\mathrm{BPA_{drt}}) \Rightarrow p + q, q + p \in B(\mathrm{BPA_{drt}})$.

With this definition of basic terms the normal form of $cts(b) + ats(a)$ is given by the term $(cts(b) + cts(a)) + \sigma_{\mathrm{rel}}(\sigma^{*}_{\mathrm{rel}}(cts(a)))$.

PROPOSITION 2.1.7 For closed $\mathrm{BPA_{drt}}$-terms $x$ such that $\mathrm{BPA_{drt}} \nvdash x = \dot{\delta}$ we have $\mathrm{BPA_{drt}} \vdash x + cts(\delta) = x$.

THEOREM 2.1.8 (ELIMINATION) For every closed $\mathrm{BPA_{drt}}$-term $p$ there exists a basic term $q$ such that

$$\begin{array}{l}\mathrm{A1,A2,A4,A5,A6ID,A7ID,DRT1\text{-}DRT3,DRTSID,DCS1\text{-}DCS4,DCSID,}\\ \mathrm{ARTS,DRTI1\text{-}DRTI5,DRTIID,DCSTI}\end{array} \vdash p = q.$$

Note that usually we are less careful with respect to the axioms used for the Elimination Theorem, we just write $\mathrm{BPA_{drt}} \vdash p = q$. However, with the upcoming proof of completeness in mind (see Section 4), we explicitly list the axioms used in the Elimination Theorem.

THEOREM 2.1.9 (COMPLETENESS) $\mathrm{BPA_{drt}}$ is a complete axiomatization of strong tail bisimulation on closed $\mathrm{BPA_{drt}}$ terms.

Now, the process algebra $\mathrm{BPA}_\delta$ can be considered as an SRM specification of $\mathrm{BPA}_{\mathrm{drt}}$: reduce the signature of the initial algebra of $\mathrm{BPA}_{\mathrm{drt}}$ by omitting $\dot{\delta}$, $\sigma_{\mathrm{rel}}$, $\nu_{\mathrm{rel}}$, $cts(a)$ (for $a \in A_{\tau\delta}$), and $\sigma^*_{\mathrm{rel}}$, then $\mathrm{BPA}_\delta$ is a complete axiomatization of the reduced model, with the interpretation of $a$ by $ats(a)$.

## 2.2 Axiomatization for Silent Step

Now we want to formulate algebraic laws for the silent step, that hold in the algebra $T(\mathrm{BPA}_{\mathrm{drt}})/\underline{\leftrightarrow}_{\mathrm{rbt}}$. We cannot just transpose the well-known laws, because of the special status of $\sigma$-steps. An example: $cts(a)\cdot(cts(\tau)\cdot(\sigma_{\mathrm{rel}}(cts(b)) + \sigma_{\mathrm{rel}}(cts(c))) + \sigma_{\mathrm{rel}}(cts(b)))$ is not rooted branching tail bisimulation equivalent to $cts(a)\cdot(\sigma_{\mathrm{rel}}(cts(b)) + \sigma_{\mathrm{rel}}(cts(c)))$, as in the first term, the choice for $b$ can be made by the execution of the $\sigma$-step, and in the second term, the choice must be made after the $\sigma$-step (however the second term is equal to $cts(a)\cdot\sigma_{\mathrm{rel}}(cts(b) + cts(c))$). In order to ensure that we do not split terms that both have an initial $\sigma$-step, we use the current slice operator $\nu_{\mathrm{rel}}$. In Table 18.5, DRTB1 and DRTB2 are variants of the branching law B2: $x\cdot(\tau\cdot(y+z)+y) = x\cdot(y+z)$. In DRTB1, we have the case where the 'loose' term ($y$ in B2) does not have an initial time step, in DRTB2 the other term ($z$ in B2) does not have an initial time step.

We add $cts(\delta)$ to ensure that the expression following $cts(\tau)$ does not equal $\dot{\delta}$. A simple instance is the identity $x\cdot cts(\tau)\cdot cts(\tau) = x\cdot cts(\tau)$. However, we do not have the law $x\cdot cts(\tau) = x$ (the counterpart of the branching law B1), as $cts(a)\cdot cts(\tau)\cdot\dot{\delta}$ must be distinguished from $cts(a)\cdot\dot{\delta}$ (this can be appreciated in a setting with parallel composition: the first term allows execution of actions in the current time slice from a parallel component after the execution of $a$, the second term does not).

In [3] the conditional axiom $cts(a)\cdot x = cts(a)\cdot y \;\Rightarrow\; cts(a)\cdot(\sigma_{\mathrm{rel}}(x) + \nu_{\mathrm{rel}}(z)) = cts(a)\cdot(\sigma_{\mathrm{rel}}(y) + \nu_{\mathrm{rel}}(z))$ was introduced to omit a $\tau$-step following one or more time steps. In this paper we replace this conditional axiom by DRTB3 (see Table 18.5). A simple instance is $cts(a)\cdot\sigma_{\mathrm{rel}}(cts(\tau)\cdot cts(b)) = cts(a)\cdot\sigma_{\mathrm{rel}}(cts(b))$.

**Table 18.5**
$\mathrm{BPA}_{\mathrm{drt}}\tau = \mathrm{BPA}_{\mathrm{drt}} + \mathrm{DRTB1\text{-}4}$.

| | |
|---|---|
| $x\cdot(cts(\tau)\cdot(\nu_{\mathrm{rel}}(y) + z + cts(\delta)) + \nu_{\mathrm{rel}}(y)) = x\cdot(\nu_{\mathrm{rel}}(y) + z + cts(\delta))$ | DRTB1 |
| $x\cdot(cts(\tau)\cdot(\nu_{\mathrm{rel}}(y) + z + cts(\delta)) + z) = x\cdot(\nu_{\mathrm{rel}}(y) + z + cts(\delta))$ | DRTB2 |
| $x\cdot(\sigma_{\mathrm{rel}}(cts(\tau)\cdot(y + cts(\delta))) + \nu_{\mathrm{rel}}(z)) = x\cdot(\sigma_{\mathrm{rel}}(y + cts(\delta)) + \nu_{\mathrm{rel}}(z))$ | DRTB3 |
| $x\cdot\sigma^*_{\mathrm{rel}}(cts(\tau)\cdot\sigma^*_{\mathrm{rel}}(\nu_{\mathrm{rel}}(y) + \nu_{\mathrm{rel}}(z) + cts(\delta)) + \nu_{\mathrm{rel}}(y))$ $= x\cdot\sigma^*_{\mathrm{rel}}(\nu_{\mathrm{rel}}(y) + \nu_{\mathrm{rel}}(z) + cts(\delta))$ | DRTB4 |

We have one additional axiom for the constant $ats(\tau)$. In axiom DRTB4 it appears as $\sigma^*_{\mathrm{rel}}(cts(\tau))$. Axiom DRTB4 can also be given as

$$x \cdot (ats(\tau) \cdot \sigma^*_{\mathrm{rel}}(\nu_{\mathrm{rel}}(y) + \nu_{\mathrm{rel}}(z) + cts(\delta)) + \sigma^*_{\mathrm{rel}}(\nu_{\mathrm{rel}}(y))) \\ = x \cdot \sigma^*_{\mathrm{rel}}(\nu_{\mathrm{rel}}(y) + \nu_{\mathrm{rel}}(z) + cts(\delta))$$

by replacing $\sigma^*_{\mathrm{rel}}(cts(\tau))$ by $ats(\tau)$ and using DRTI2, DRTI3, or as

$$x \cdot (ats(\tau) \cdot \lfloor y + z + cts(\delta) \rfloor^{\omega} + \lfloor y \rfloor^{\omega}) = x \cdot \lfloor y + z + cts(\delta) \rfloor^{\omega}$$

by also replacing $\sigma^*_{\mathrm{rel}}(\nu_{\mathrm{rel}}(y))$ by $\lfloor y \rfloor^{\omega}$, etc.

We find that rooted branching tail bisimulation is a congruence with respect to the operators from the algebra $\mathrm{BPA_{drt}}\tau$, and that the laws of $\mathrm{BPA_{drt}}\tau + \mathrm{RSP(DRT)}$ are valid in $T(\mathrm{BPA_{drt}}\tau)/\underline{\leftrightarrow}_{\mathrm{rbt}}$. Basic terms for $\mathrm{BPA_{drt}}\tau$ are defined in the same way as basic terms for $\mathrm{BPA_{drt}}$.

THEOREM 2.2.1 (SOUNDNESS) The laws of $\mathrm{BPA_{drt}}\tau + \mathrm{RSP(DRT)}$ are valid in $T(\mathrm{BPA_{drt}}\tau)/\underline{\leftrightarrow}_{\mathrm{rbt}}$.

Before we introduce a number of useful axioms for the silent step, we first define an auxiliary operator $\sigma^m_{\mathrm{rel}}$. The term $\sigma^m_{\mathrm{rel}}(x)$ represents the operator $\sigma_{\mathrm{rel}}$ applied to $x$ $m$ times, i.e., for $m \geq 0$:

$$\sigma^0_{\mathrm{rel}}(x) \quad = x$$

$$\sigma^{m+1}_{\mathrm{rel}}(x) = \sigma_{\mathrm{rel}}\left(\sigma^m_{\mathrm{rel}}(x)\right)$$

The generalizations of the axioms for silent step are useful in the completeness proof in Section 4.

PROPOSITION 2.2.2 (OTHER AXIOMS FOR ABSTRACTION) For closed $\mathrm{BPA_{drt}}\tau$-terms $p, x, y, z$, and $m \geq 0$, we have

1. $\mathrm{BPA_{drt}}\tau \vdash x \cdot \sigma^m_{\mathrm{rel}}(cts(\tau) \cdot (\nu_{\mathrm{rel}}(y) + z + cts(\delta)) + \nu_{\mathrm{rel}}(y))$
   $= x \cdot \sigma^m_{\mathrm{rel}}(\nu_{\mathrm{rel}}(y) + z + cts(\delta))$;
2. $\mathrm{BPA_{drt}}\tau \vdash x \cdot \sigma^m_{\mathrm{rel}}(cts(\tau) \cdot (\nu_{\mathrm{rel}}(y) + z + cts(\delta)) + z) = x \cdot \sigma^m_{\mathrm{rel}}(\nu_{\mathrm{rel}}(y) + z + cts(\delta))$;
3. $\mathrm{BPA_{drt}}\tau \vdash x \cdot \sigma^m_{\mathrm{rel}}(\sigma_{\mathrm{rel}}(cts(\tau) \cdot (\nu_{\mathrm{rel}}(y) + z + cts(\delta)) + \nu_{\mathrm{rel}}(y)) + \nu_{\mathrm{rel}}(p))$
   $= x \cdot \sigma^m_{\mathrm{rel}}(\sigma_{\mathrm{rel}}(\nu_{\mathrm{rel}}(y) + z + cts(\delta)) + \nu_{\mathrm{rel}}(p))$;
4. $\mathrm{BPA_{drt}}\tau \vdash x \cdot \sigma^m_{\mathrm{rel}}(\sigma_{\mathrm{rel}}(cts(\tau) \cdot (\nu_{\mathrm{rel}}(y) + z + cts(\delta)) + z) + \nu_{\mathrm{rel}}(p))$
   $= x \cdot \sigma^m_{\mathrm{rel}}(\sigma_{\mathrm{rel}}(\nu_{\mathrm{rel}}(y) + z + cts(\delta)) + \nu_{\mathrm{rel}}(p))$;
5. $\mathrm{BPA_{drt}}\tau \vdash x \cdot \sigma^m_{\mathrm{rel}}(\sigma_{\mathrm{rel}}(\sigma^*_{\mathrm{rel}}(cts(\tau) \cdot \sigma^*_{\mathrm{rel}}(\nu_{\mathrm{rel}}(y) + \nu_{\mathrm{rel}}(z) + cts(\delta)) + \nu_{\mathrm{rel}}(y))) + \nu_{\mathrm{rel}}(p))$
   $= x \cdot \sigma^m_{\mathrm{rel}}(\sigma_{\mathrm{rel}}(\sigma^*_{\mathrm{rel}}(\nu_{\mathrm{rel}}(y) + \nu_{\mathrm{rel}}(z) + cts(\delta))) + \nu_{\mathrm{rel}}(p))$.

Let us consider the embedding of the time free theory $\mathrm{BPA}_\delta^\tau$ in $\mathrm{BPA}_{\mathrm{drt}}\tau$. If we reduce the initial algebra of $\mathrm{BPA}_{\mathrm{drt}}\tau$ by reducing the signature by omitting $\dot{\delta}$, $ats(a)$ (for $a \in A_{\tau\delta}$), $\sigma_{\mathrm{rel}}$, $\nu_{\mathrm{rel}}$, $\sigma_{\mathrm{rel}}^*$, and interpret $a$ by $cts(a)$, we do not obtain $\mathrm{BPA}_\delta^\tau$ of [6, 14]. The first branching law $x \cdot \tau = x$ will not hold, but instead $x \cdot \tau \cdot y = x \cdot y$. We can nevertheless obtain $\mathrm{BPA}_\delta^\tau$ as an SRM specification as follows. First we add constants $ctstau(a)$ (for $a \in A_{\tau\delta}$) defined by $ctstau(a) = cts(a) \cdot cts(\tau)$. Then, by omitting $\dot{\delta}$, $cts(a)$, $ats(a)$, $\sigma_{\mathrm{rel}}$, $\nu_{\mathrm{rel}}$, $\sigma_{\mathrm{rel}}^*$ and interpreting $a$ as $ctstau(a)$, $\mathrm{BPA}_\delta^\tau$ becomes an SRM specification of $\mathrm{BPA}_{\mathrm{drt}}\tau$. The following proposition shows that analogues of DRTB1 and DRTB2 and in addition the first $\tau$-law are valid for the new constants.

PROPOSITION 2.2.3 The following laws are derivable from $\mathrm{BPA}_{\mathrm{drt}}\tau$:

1. $\mathrm{BPA}_{\mathrm{drt}}\tau \vdash ctstau(a) \cdot ctstau(\tau) = ctstau(a)$;
2. $\mathrm{BPA}_{\mathrm{drt}}\tau \vdash x \cdot (ctstau(\tau) \cdot (\nu_{\mathrm{rel}}(y) + z + cts(\delta)) + \nu_{\mathrm{rel}}(y)) = x \cdot (\nu_{\mathrm{rel}}(y) + z + cts(\delta))$;
3. $\mathrm{BPA}_{\mathrm{drt}}\tau \vdash x \cdot (ctstau(\tau) \cdot (\nu_{\mathrm{rel}}(y) + z + cts(\delta)) + z) = x \cdot (\nu_{\mathrm{rel}}(y) + z + cts(\delta))$.

As a consequence, we can prove $x \cdot ctstau(\tau) = x$ for all closed terms. Thus, we have embedded the time free theory into the relative discrete time theory. Again, this is not the embedding of the time free theory into the discrete time theory that we prefer: the whole world is reduced to one time slice.

We cannot obtain the time free theory $\mathrm{BPA}_\delta^\tau$ as an SRM specification by interpreting $a$ by $ats(a)$, since $ats(a) \cdot ats(\tau)$ is not branching tail bisimilar to $ats(a)$: the first term can still perform time steps after executing the action. Note that the second branching law is valid, as time iteration is the identity on all time free processes. In order to achieve an SRM specification, nonetheless, we will define a different interpretation of time free atoms in our timed setting. We define constants $atstau(a)$ as follows ($a \in A_{\tau\delta}$): $atstau(a) = ats(a) \cdot ats(\tau)$. If we reduce the initial algebra of $\mathrm{BPA}_{\mathrm{drt}}\tau$, with the additional constants $atstau(a)$, by omitting $\dot{\delta}$, $cts(a)$, $ats(a)$ (for $a \in A_{\tau\delta}$), $\sigma_{\mathrm{rel}}$, $\nu_{\mathrm{rel}}$, $\sigma_{\mathrm{rel}}^*$, and we interpret $a$ by $atstau(a)$, we do obtain $\mathrm{BPA}_\delta^\tau$ as an SRM specification. The following proposition shows that the analogue of DRTB4 and in addition the first $\tau$-law are valid for the new constants.

PROPOSITION 2.2.4 The following laws are derivable from $\mathrm{BPA}_{\mathrm{drt}}\tau$ for $a \in A_\tau$:

1. $atstau(a) \cdot atstau(\tau) = atstau(a)$;
2. $x \cdot (atstau(\tau) \cdot \sigma_{\mathrm{rel}}^*(\nu_{\mathrm{rel}}(y + z)) + \sigma_{\mathrm{rel}}^*(\nu_{\mathrm{rel}}(y))) = x \cdot \sigma_{\mathrm{rel}}^*(\nu_{\mathrm{rel}}(y + z))$.

## 3 A Graph Model for $\mathrm{BPA}_{\mathrm{drt}}\tau$

In Section 4, we will prove that the present axiomatization of silent step is complete for the model of closed terms modulo rooted branching tail bisimulation. We do this by showing completeness for a model that is isomorphic to $T(\mathrm{BPA}_{\mathrm{drt}})/\underline{\leftrightarrow}_{\mathrm{rbt}}$, namely a model consisting of process graphs.

In this section we proceed to define this graph model for $\mathrm{BPA}_{\mathrm{drt}}\tau$. An equivalence relation, called rooted branching tail bisimulation, is defined on the set of process graphs. Operators resembling the operators of the algebra both in name and in intention are defined on process graphs. Finally, we introduce an equivalent characterization of rooted branching tail bisimilarity in Section 3.4. This characterization of rooted branching tail bisimulation will be used in the completeness proof in Section 4.

### 3.1 Process Graphs

We define a set of process graphs as in [6] with labels from $A_{\tau\sigma}$ satisfying the extra condition that every node has *at most one* outgoing $\sigma$-labeled edge. End-nodes can be labeled with a label $\downarrow$ (for successful termination) or a label ID (for immediate deadlock). A $\sigma$-labeled edge may not lead to a successful termination node or an ID-labeled termination node.

DEFINITION 3.1.1 A *process graph* is a quintuple $\langle N, E, r, \downarrow, \mathrm{ID}\rangle$, where $N$ is a non-empty set of nodes, $E \subseteq N \times A_{\tau\sigma} \times N$ is a set of labeled edges, $r \in N$ is the root node, $\downarrow \subseteq N$ and $\mathrm{ID} \subseteq N$ are disjoint sets of successful termination nodes and immediate deadlock nodes respectively. The following criteria must hold for every process graph:

- every node can have at most one outgoing $\sigma$-edge (time factorization): for all $n \in N$, if there exist nodes $s$ and $t$ such that $n \xrightarrow{\sigma} s$ and $n \xrightarrow{\sigma} t$, then $s = t$;
- a successful termination or an immediate deadlock node cannot have an outgoing edge: for all $n \in \downarrow \cup \mathrm{ID}$: $\{n \xrightarrow{u} s \mid u \in A_{\tau\sigma} \wedge s \in N\} = \emptyset$;
- a successful termination or an immediate deadlock node cannot have an incoming $\sigma$-edge: for all $n \in \downarrow \cup \mathrm{ID}$, there does not exist a node $s \in N$ such that $s \xrightarrow{\sigma} n \in E$.

Actually, for our purposes we will only need graphs that are interpretations of closed terms. Such graphs always have finite node sets, and the only cycles that occur are of the form $s \xrightarrow{\sigma} s$. The class of all such process graphs is denoted by $\mathbf{G}$. We obtain the set of process graphs $\mathbf{G}^+$ by requiring in addition that the root node cannot have a successful termination label, i.e., $r \notin \downarrow$. For a process graph $g = \langle N, E, r, \downarrow, \mathrm{ID}\rangle$ and a node $s \in N$, the subgraph of $g$ with $s$ as its root node, notation $(g)_s$, is defined as follows: $(g)_s = \langle N, E, s, \downarrow, \mathrm{ID}\rangle$, where it is understood that only the nodes and edges that are reachable from $s$ are relevant. For a set $S$ and $E \subseteq N \times A_{\tau\sigma} \times N$, we define $S \otimes E = \{(s, n_1) \xrightarrow{u} (s, n_2) \mid s \in S \wedge n_1 \xrightarrow{u} n_2 \in E\}$. For a node $s \in N$ and $E \subseteq N \times A_{\tau\sigma} \times N$, we define $E[s \mapsto t]$ to be the set $E$ with all occurrences of $s$ replaced by node $t$. This notation is extended to replace nodes from a set $S$ simultaneously as follows: $E[s \in S \mapsto t]$. Note that $s$ can occur in $t$.

## 3.2 Tail Bisimulations

DEFINITION 3.2.1 Two graphs $g = \langle N_g, E_g, r_g, \downarrow_g, \mathrm{ID}_g\rangle$ and $h = \langle N_h, E_h, r_h, \downarrow_h, \mathrm{ID}_h\rangle$ are called *strongly tail bisimilar*, notation $g \leftrightarrow h$, if there exists a symmetric binary relation $R$, called *strong tail bisimulation*, on the nodes of $g$ and $h$ such that for all nodes $r, s$ with $R(r, s)$ we have:

1. the roots of $g$ and $h$ are related, i.e., $R(r_g, r_h)$;
2. if $r \xrightarrow{u} r' \in E_g \cup E_h$ $(u \in A_{\tau\sigma})$, then there exists a node $s'$ such that $s \xrightarrow{u} s' \in E_g \cup E_h$ and $R(r', s')$;
3. if $r \in \downarrow_g \cup \downarrow_h$, then $s \in \downarrow_g \cup \downarrow_h$;
4. if $r \in \mathrm{ID}_g \cup \mathrm{ID}_h$, then $s \in \mathrm{ID}_g \cup \mathrm{ID}_h$.

DEFINITION 3.2.2 Two graphs $g$ and $h$ are called *branching tail bisimilar*, notation $g \leftrightarrow_{\mathrm{bt}} h$, if there exists a symmetric binary relation $R$, called *branching tail bisimulation*, on the nodes of $g$ and $h$ such that for all nodes $r, s$ with $R(r, s)$ we have:

1. the roots of $g$ and $h$ are related;
2. if $r \xrightarrow{u} r' \in E_g \cup E_h$ $(u \in A_{\tau\sigma})$, then there exist nodes $s^*, s'$ such that $s \Longrightarrow s^* \xrightarrow{(u)} s' \in E_g \cup E_h$ and $R(r, s^*)$ and $R(r', s')$;
3. if $r \in \downarrow_g \cup \downarrow_h$, then $s \in \downarrow_g \cup \downarrow_h$;
4. if $r \in \mathrm{ID}_g \cup \mathrm{ID}_h$, then $s \in \mathrm{ID}_g \cup \mathrm{ID}_h$.

DEFINITION 3.2.3 If $R$ is a branching tail bisimulation, then we say that the related pair $(r, s)$ satisfies the *root condition* iff whenever $r \xrightarrow{u} r' \in E_g \cup E_h$ $(u \in A_{\tau\sigma})$, then there exists a node $s'$ such that $s \xrightarrow{u} s' \in E_g \cup E_h$ and $R(r', s')$.

Two graphs $g$ and $h$ are called *rooted branching tail bisimilar*, notation $g \leftrightarrow_{\mathrm{rbt}} h$, if there is a branching tail bisimulation relation $R$ between the nodes of $g$ and $h$ such that if $R(r, s)$ and $r$ is $\sigma$-reachable from the root of $g$ or $s$ is $\sigma$-reachable from the root of $h$, then the pair $(r, s)$ satisfies the root condition.

## 3.3 Isomorphy of the Term Model and the Graph Model

In this section we will define mappings *graph* and *term* which associate a process graph to a closed term and a closed term to a graph respectively. These mappings are such that they are each other's inverse modulo strong tail bisimulation. This results in a theorem that states that the term deduction model and the graph model are isomorphic. As a consequence the soundness result can be transfered from the term model to the graph model and the completeness result to come can be transformed from the graph model to the term model.

In the following definitions we define operators on the graph model which are both in appearance and in intention similar to the operators of the algebra. In these definitions we assume that the sets of nodes of the graphs to be composed are disjoint. This assumption is fair since we are only interested in process graphs modulo graph isomorphism (see Section 3.4 for a definition of graph isomorphism).

DEFINITION 3.3.1 The following constants are defined on the graph model, for $a \in A_\tau$:

$$\begin{aligned}
\dot{\delta} &= \langle \{r\}, \emptyset, r, \emptyset, \{r\} \rangle; \\
cts(\delta) &= \langle \{r\}, \emptyset, r, \emptyset, \emptyset \rangle; \\
cts(a) &= \langle \{r, s\}, \{r \xrightarrow{a} s\}, r, \{s\}, \emptyset \rangle; \\
ats(\delta) &= \langle \{r\}, \{r \xrightarrow{\sigma} r\}, r, \emptyset, \emptyset \rangle; \\
ats(a) &= \langle \{r, s\}, \{r \xrightarrow{\sigma} r, r \xrightarrow{a} s\}, r, \{s\}, \emptyset \rangle.
\end{aligned}$$

DEFINITION 3.3.2 Let $g = \langle N, E, r, \downarrow, \mathrm{ID} \rangle$. Assume that $\hat{r} \notin N$. Then $\sigma_{\mathrm{rel}}(g)$ is defined as follows:

1. if $r \in \mathrm{ID}$, then $\sigma_{\mathrm{rel}}(g) = \langle \{r\}, \emptyset, r, \emptyset, \emptyset \rangle$;
2. otherwise, $\sigma_{\mathrm{rel}}(g) = \langle N \cup \{\hat{r}\}, E \cup \{\hat{r} \xrightarrow{\sigma} r\}, \hat{r}, \downarrow, \mathrm{ID} \rangle$.

DEFINITION 3.3.3 Let $g = \langle N, E, r, \downarrow, \mathrm{ID} \rangle$. Then $\nu_{\mathrm{rel}}(g)$ is defined as follows:

$$\nu_{\mathrm{rel}}(g) = \langle N, E \backslash \{r \xrightarrow{\sigma} s \mid s \in N\}, r, \downarrow, \mathrm{ID} \rangle.$$

DEFINITION 3.3.4 Let $g = \langle N_g, E_g, r_g, \downarrow_g, \mathrm{ID}_g \rangle$ and $h = \langle N_h, E_h, r_h, \downarrow_h, \mathrm{ID}_h \rangle$. Then $g \cdot h$ is defined as follows:

$$\begin{aligned}
g \cdot h = \langle & (N_g \backslash \downarrow_g) \cup (\downarrow_g \times N_h) \\
, \ & E_g[f \in \downarrow_g \mapsto (f, r_h)] \cup \downarrow_g \otimes E_h \\
, \ & r_g \\
, \ & \downarrow_g \times \downarrow_h \\
, \ & \mathrm{ID}_g \cup (\downarrow_g \times \mathrm{ID}_h) \\
& \rangle.
\end{aligned}$$

Before we can define $+$ on the graph model, we first have to define a root unwinding map.

DEFINITION 3.3.5 The mapping $\rho$ is for all $g = \langle N, E, r, \downarrow, \mathrm{ID} \rangle$, defined as follows ($u \in A_{\tau\sigma}$):

$$\rho(g) = \langle N \cup \{\hat{r}\}, E \cup \{\hat{r} \xrightarrow{u} s \mid r \xrightarrow{u} s \in E\}, \hat{r}, \downarrow, \mathrm{ID} \cup \{\hat{r} \mid r \in \mathrm{ID}\} \rangle.$$

DEFINITION 3.3.6 Let $g = \langle N_g, E_g, r_g, \downarrow_g, \mathrm{ID}_g\rangle$ and $h = \langle N_h, E_h, r_h, \downarrow_h, \mathrm{ID}_h\rangle$. Then $g + h$ is defined as follows:

1. if $r_g \in \mathrm{ID}_g$, then $g + h = h$;
2. if $r_h \in \mathrm{ID}_h$, then $g + h = g$;
3. if $r_g \notin \mathrm{ID}_g$ and $r_h \notin \mathrm{ID}_h$, then

(a) if $r_g \xrightarrow{\sigma} r_g \in E_g$ and $r_h \xrightarrow{\sigma} r_h \in E_h$, then

$$\begin{aligned} g + h = \langle & (N_g \backslash \{r_g\}) \cup (N_h \backslash \{r_h\}) \cup \{r_{g+h}\} \\ , \ & E_g[r_g \mapsto r_{g+h}] \cup E_h[r_h \mapsto r_{g+h}] \\ , \ & r_{g+h} \\ , \ & \downarrow_g \cup \downarrow_h \\ , \ & \mathrm{ID}_g \cup \mathrm{ID}_h \\ \rangle & ; \end{aligned}$$

(b) if $r_g \xrightarrow{\sigma} s_g \in E_g$ and $r_h \xrightarrow{\sigma} s_h \in E_h$ for some $s_g \in N_g$ and $s_h \in N_h$ such that $s_g \not\equiv r_g$ or $s_h \not\equiv r_h$, then suppose that $\rho(g) = \langle N'_g, E'_g, r'_g, \downarrow'_g, \mathrm{ID}'_g\rangle$ and $\rho(h) = \langle N'_h, E'_h, r'_h, \downarrow'_h, \mathrm{ID}'_h\rangle$. Suppose that $r'_g \xrightarrow{\sigma} s'_g$ and $r'_h \xrightarrow{\sigma} s'_h$. Suppose that $(g)_{s'_g} + (h)_{s'_h} = \langle N, E, r, \downarrow, \mathrm{ID}\rangle$. Then,

$$\begin{aligned} g + h = \langle & N'_g \cup N'_h \cup N \cup \{r'_{g+h}\} \\ , \ & E'_g \backslash \{r'_g \xrightarrow{\sigma} s'_g\} \cup E'_h \backslash \{r'_h \xrightarrow{\sigma} s'_h\} \cup E \cup \{r'_{g+h} \xrightarrow{\sigma} r\} \\ , \ & r'_{g+h} \\ , \ & \downarrow'_g \cup \downarrow'_h \cup \downarrow \\ , \ & \mathrm{ID}'_g \cup \mathrm{ID}'_h \cup \mathrm{ID} \\ \rangle & ; \end{aligned}$$

(c) otherwise, suppose that $\rho(g) = \langle N'_g, E'_g, r'_g, \downarrow'_g, \mathrm{ID}'_g\rangle$ and $\rho(h) = \langle N'_h, E'_h, r'_h, \downarrow'_h, \mathrm{ID}'_h\rangle$. Then,

$$\begin{aligned} g + h = \langle & (N'_g \backslash \{r'_g\}) \cup (N'_h \backslash \{r'_h\}) \cup \{r'_{g+h}\} \\ , \ & E'_g[r'_g \mapsto r'_{g+h}] \cup E'_h[r'_h \mapsto r'_{g+h}] \\ , \ & r'_{g+h} \\ , \ & \downarrow'_g \cup \downarrow'_h \\ , \ & \mathrm{ID}'_g \cup \mathrm{ID}'_h \\ \rangle & . \end{aligned}$$

DEFINITION 3.3.7 Let $g = \langle N, E, r, \downarrow, \mathrm{ID}\rangle$. Then $\sigma^*_{\mathrm{rel}}$ is defined inductively as follows:

1. if $r \xrightarrow{\sigma} r$, then $\sigma^*_{\mathrm{rel}}(g) = g$;
2. if $r \xrightarrow{\sigma} s$ for some $s \neq r$, then define $\nu = \langle N, E\backslash\{r \xrightarrow{\sigma} s\}, r, \downarrow, \mathrm{ID}\rangle$ and $\psi = (g)_s$. Suppose $\sigma^*_{\mathrm{rel}}(\nu + \psi) = \langle N', E', r', \downarrow', \mathrm{ID}'\rangle$. Then,

$\sigma^*_{\mathrm{rel}}(g) = \langle N \cup N', E\backslash\{r \xrightarrow{\sigma} s\} \cup E' \cup \{r \xrightarrow{\sigma} r'\}, r, \downarrow \cup \downarrow', \mathrm{ID} \cup \mathrm{ID}'\rangle$;

3. otherwise, if $r \in \mathrm{ID}$, then $\sigma^*_{\mathrm{rel}}(g) = \langle\{r\}, \{r \xrightarrow{\sigma} r\}, r, \emptyset, \emptyset\rangle$, else $\sigma^*_{\mathrm{rel}}(g) = \langle N, E \cup \{r \xrightarrow{\sigma} r\}, r, \downarrow, \mathrm{ID}\rangle$.

This is a well-founded inductive definition since the length of the path from $r$ consisting of $\sigma$-steps only (not $\sigma$-loops) decreases.

The mapping *graph* which associates to a closed $\mathrm{BPA_{drt}}\tau$ term a process graph is defined inductively as can be expected by using the previously given operators on process graphs. Applying the mapping *graph* to an arbitrary closed $\mathrm{BPA_{drt}}\tau$ term always gives a graph without cycles other than $\sigma$-loops. Such graphs will be called root unwound process graphs on several occasions.

DEFINITION 3.3.8 The mapping $term$:$\mathbf{G}^+ \to T(\mathrm{BPA_{drt}}\tau)$ is for all process graphs $g = \langle N, E, r, \downarrow, \mathrm{ID}\rangle$ defined inductively by:

$$term(g) = \begin{cases} \sigma^*_{\mathrm{rel}}(term(\langle N, E\backslash\{r \xrightarrow{\sigma} r\}, r, \downarrow, \mathrm{ID}\rangle)) & \text{if } r \xrightarrow{\sigma} r \in E; \\ \dot{\delta} & \text{if } r \xrightarrow{\sigma} r \notin E \wedge r \in \mathrm{ID}; \\ cts(\delta) & \text{if } r \xrightarrow{\sigma} r \notin E \wedge r \notin \mathrm{ID} \wedge E = \emptyset; \\ \sum\limits_{r \xrightarrow{u} s \in E} term_g(r \xrightarrow{u} s) & \text{otherwise,} \end{cases}$$

where $term_g : E \to T(\mathrm{BPA_{drt}}\tau)$ is, for $a \in A_\tau$, defined by

$$term_g(r \xrightarrow{a} s) = \begin{cases} cts(a) & \text{if } s \in \downarrow; \\ cts(a) \cdot term((g)_s) & \text{otherwise;} \end{cases}$$

$$term_g(r \xrightarrow{\sigma} s) = \sigma_{\mathrm{rel}}(term((g)_s)).$$

THEOREM 3.3.9 (ISOMORPHY) $T(\mathrm{BPA_{drt}}\tau)/\underline{\leftrightarrow}$ and $\mathbf{G}/\underline{\leftrightarrow}$ are isomorphic.

### 3.4 Alternative Characterization of the Bisimulations

We proceed to find formulations for our bisimulation relations in terms of colourings, analogous to [14]. Let $\mathbf{C}$ be a given set, the set of colours. A *coloured graph* is a process graph with colours $C \in \mathbf{C}$ as labels attached at the nodes.

A *concrete coloured trace* of a coloured graph $g$ is a finite sequence $(C_0, a_1, C_1, \ldots, C_{k-1}, a_k, C_k)$ for which there exists a path $r_0 \xrightarrow{a_1} r_1 \xrightarrow{a_2} \cdots \xrightarrow{a_k} r_k$ from the root node $r_0$ of $g$ such that $r_i$ has colour $C_i$.

A *concrete consistent colouring* of a set of process graphs is a colouring of their nodes with the property that two nodes (also from the same graph) have the same colour only if they have the same concrete trace set and the same label. Two process graphs $g$ and $h$ are *concrete coloured trace equivalent*, notation $g \equiv_{cc} h$, if, for some concrete consistent colouring on $\{g, h\}$, they have the same concrete coloured trace set, or equivalently, the root nodes have the same colour. As in [14], we have the following theorem.

THEOREM 3.4.1 For process graphs $g, h \in \mathbf{G}$, we have $g \leftrightarrow h$ iff $g \equiv_{cc} h$.

An *abstract coloured trace* of a coloured graph is a sequence of the form $(C_0, a_1, C_1, a_2, \ldots, a_k, C_k)$ which is obtained from a concrete coloured trace of this graph by replacing all subsequences of the form $(C, \tau, C, \tau, \ldots, \tau, C)$ by $C$.

An *abstract consistent colouring* of a set of graphs is a colouring of their nodes with the property that two nodes have the same colour only if they have the same abstract coloured trace set and the same label. For two coloured graphs $g$ and $h$ we write $g \equiv_c h$, if, for some abstract consistent colouring on $\{g, h\}$, they have the same abstract coloured trace set. In the sequel, we leave out the adjectives 'abstract.'

THEOREM 3.4.2 For process graphs $g, h \in \mathbf{G}$, we have $g \leftrightarrow_{bt} h$ iff $g \equiv_c h$.

A *rooted coloured trace* of a coloured graph is a sequence of the form $(C_0, a_1, C_1, a_2, \ldots, a_k, C_k)$ which is obtained from a concrete coloured trace of this graph by replacing all non-$\sigma$-reachable subsequences $(C, \tau, C, \tau, \ldots, \tau, C)$ by $C$.

A *rooted consistent colouring* of a set of graphs is a colouring of their nodes with the property that two nodes have the same colour only if they have the same rooted coloured trace set and the same label. For two root unwound coloured graphs $g$ and $h$ we write $g \equiv_{rc} h$, if, for some rooted consistent colouring on $\{g, h\}$, they have the same rooted coloured trace set.

THEOREM 3.4.3 For process graphs $g, h \in \mathbf{G}$, we have $g \,\underline{\leftrightarrow}_{rbt}\, h$ iff $g \equiv_{rc} h$.

It is possible to colour the nodes of a root unwound process graph $g$ in such a way that two nodes have the same colour iff they can be related by a rooted branching tail autobisimulation on $g$. This colouring is rooted and consistent. The largest rooted branching tail autobisimulation relation of a graph is called its *canonical colouring*.

DEFINITION 3.4.4 Let $g$ be a root unwound process graph and consider its canonical colouring with colour set $\mathbf{C}$. Let $N(g)$, the *normal form* of $g$, be the graph which can be found by contracting all nodes with the same colour and removing $\tau$-loops. More precisely:

1. $N(g)$ has colours $C \in \mathbf{C}$ as its nodes;
2. $N(g)$ has an edge $C \xrightarrow{a} C'$ $(a \in A_\sigma)$ iff $g$ has an edge $r \xrightarrow{a} r'$ such that $r$ has colour $C$ and $r'$ has colour $C'$;
3. $N(g)$ has an edge $C \xrightarrow{\tau} C'$ iff $C \neq C'$ and $g$ has an edge $r \xrightarrow{\tau} r'$ and $r$ has colour $C$ and $r'$ has colour $C'$;
4. $C$ has a label $\downarrow$ iff $g$ has a node $r$ with label $\downarrow$ and $r$ has colour $C$;
5. $C$ has a label ID iff $g$ has a node $r$ with label ID and $r$ has colour $C$.

For all root unwound process graphs $g \in \mathbf{G}$, we have $g \leftrightarrow_{\text{rbt}} N(g)$.

DEFINITION 3.4.5 (GRAPH ISOMORPHISM) A *graph isomorphism* is a bijective relation $R$ between the nodes of two process graphs $g = \langle N_g, E_g, r_g, \downarrow_g, \text{ID}_g\rangle$ and $h = \langle N_h, E_h, r_h, \downarrow_h, \text{ID}_h\rangle$ such that:

1. the roots of $g$ and $h$ are related by $R$, i.e., $R(r_g, r_h)$;
2. if $R(r, s)$ and $R(r', s')$ then $r \xrightarrow{a} r' \in E_g$ iff $s \xrightarrow{a} s' \in E_h$;
3. if $R(r, s)$ then $r \in \downarrow_g$ iff $s \in \downarrow_h$ and $r \in \text{ID}_g$ iff $s \in \text{ID}_h$.

Two graphs are *isomorphic*, notation $g \simeq h$, iff there exists an isomorphism between them. Note that $\simeq$ is a congruence relation on process graphs. Note also that only the nodes which are reachable from the root nodes of $g$ and $h$ are taken into account. As a consequence we have that a process graph $g$ is graph isomorphic with the graph consisting of the edges and nodes of $g$ that are reachable from the root node of $g$.

As in [14] we have the following Normal Form Theorem.

THEOREM 3.4.6 (NORMAL FORM THEOREM) Let $g$ and $h$ be root unwound process graphs that are in normal form. Then $g \leftrightarrow_{\text{rbt}} h$ if and only if $g \simeq h$.

## 4 Completeness of the Axiomatization

### 4.1 Introduction

In this section we will prove, following the approach of [14], that $\text{BPA}_{\text{drt}}\tau$ is a complete axiomatization of rooted branching tail bisimulation on process graphs from $\mathbf{G}^+$. The basic idea in the completeness proof is to establish a graph rewriting system on process graphs, which is confluent and strongly normalizing (up to graph isomorphism), and for which every rewrite step preserves rooted branching tail bisimilarity. Confluence and strong normalization together are needed to ensure that for every process graph there is a unique normal form up to graph isomorphism. We want the rewrite steps of the graph rewriting system to preserve rooted branching tail bisimilarity since for every such rewrite step we can prove (rather easily) that the corresponding terms are derivably equal (see Theorem 4.4.3). Furthermore, we will show that the normal forms with respect to the graph rewriting system are normal forms in the sense of Section 3.4. As a consequence we have that the normal forms with respect to the graph rewriting system of two rooted branching tail bisimilar process graphs are isomorphic. All that remains is to show that for every term $p$, the mapping *term* $\circ$ *graph* is an identity modulo derivability. This is the sole subject of Section 4.3.

## 4.2 The Graph Rewriting System

The graph rewriting system will be such that it is capable of performing two transformations on process graphs. Firstly, it can contract two nodes which are essentially the same. Such nodes are called *double nodes*. Secondly, it can contract a $\tau$-edge that is redundant. Such $\tau$-edges are called *manifestly inert*.

DEFINITION 4.2.1 (DOUBLE NODES) A pair $(r, s)$, with $r \neq s$, of nodes in a process graph $g = \langle N, E, r, \downarrow, \mathrm{ID}\rangle$ is called a pair of *double nodes* if

- for all nodes $t \neq r, s$ and labels $u \in A_{\tau\sigma}$: $r \xrightarrow{u} t \in E$ iff $s \xrightarrow{u} t \in E$;
- $r \xrightarrow{\sigma} r \in E$ iff $s \xrightarrow{\sigma} s \in E$;
- $r \in \downarrow$ iff $s \in \downarrow$;
- $r \in \mathrm{ID}$ iff $s \in \mathrm{ID}$.

The following proposition formalizes the statement that double nodes are essentially the same: their subgraphs are isomorphic.

PROPOSITION 4.2.2 Let $g$ be a process graph. If $(r, s)$ is a pair of double nodes in $g$, then $(g)_r \simeq (g)_s$.

A $\tau$-edge between two nodes $r$ and $s$ is called manifestly inert if $r$ and $s$ agree with respect to the labels and $\sigma$-loops and if any other outgoing edge of $r$ is also an outgoing edge of $s$.

DEFINITION 4.2.3 (MANIFESTLY INERT $\tau$-EDGES) An edge $r \xrightarrow{\tau} s$ in a process graph $g$ is *manifestly inert* if $r$ is not $\sigma$-reachable from the root node of $g$, $r$ and $s$ have the same label (if any), and for all nodes $t$ and labels $a \in A_{\tau\sigma}$ such that $(a, t) \neq (\tau, s)$ and $(a, t) \neq (\sigma, r)$: $r \xrightarrow{a} t$ implies $s \xrightarrow{a} t$, and $r \xrightarrow{\sigma} r$ iff $s \xrightarrow{\sigma} s$.

Basically, for an edge to be manifestly inert means that it can be removed with one of the axioms for silent step. The next theorem states that in order to obtain a normal form for a process graph we only have to repeatedly unify a pair of double nodes or contract a manifestly inert $\tau$-edge.

THEOREM 4.2.4 A process graph $g \in \mathbf{G}$ without double nodes and without manifestly inert $\tau$-edges is in normal form.

*Proof* Let $g$ be a finite process graph which is not in normal form. Then it has at least one pair of different nodes with the same colour with respect to the canonical colouring. The *depth* of a node $s$ in $g$ is defined to be the number of edges in its longest path not counting $\sigma$-loops. Then, we define the *combined depth* of two nodes as the sum of their depths. We mention the following property of the depth of a node: if $r \xrightarrow{u} s$ $(r \neq s)$, then $d(s) < d(r)$. We will use it in the remainder of the proof.

Choose a pair $(r, s)$ of different, but equally coloured nodes in $g$ with minimal combined depth. Now we have the following trivial claim: if $r'$ and $s'$ are nodes in $g$ which have the same colour and moreover $d(r') + d(s') < d(r) + d(s)$, then $r' = s'$ (*). If this would not be the case then clearly $(r, s)$ is not a minimal pair.

Assume, without loss of generality, $d(s) \leq d(r)$. Now, we prove the following two properties:

1. if $r \xrightarrow{u} t$ and $(u, t) \neq (\tau, s)$, then $s \xrightarrow{u} t$, and
2. if $s \xrightarrow{u} t$, then $r \xrightarrow{\tau} s$ or $r \xrightarrow{u} t$.

Ad 1. Suppose that $r \xrightarrow{u} t$ and that $(u, t) \neq (\tau, s)$. Since $r$ and $s$ have the same colour we find that either (1) $u = \tau$ and $t$ has the same colour as $r$ and $s$, or (2) $s$ has the coloured trace $(C(r), u, C(t))$. For the first case we find $t = s$ from (*) and $d(t) < d(r)$. This is in contradiction with the assumption $(u, t) \neq (\tau, s)$. For the second case we reason as follows. Suppose that $s \xrightarrow{\tau} p$ with $C(p) = C(s)$. Then from $d(p) < d(s)$ we have $p = r$. Then we also have the following contradiction: $d(p) < d(s) \leq d(r)$. So clearly, $u \neq \tau$. Suppose that $s \xrightarrow{u} p$ for some node $p$ such that $C(p) = C(t)$. Since $d(p) < d(s)$ and $d(t) < d(r)$, we have $d(p) + d(t) < d(s) + d(r)$. We also have $C(p) = C(t)$ and $C(s) = C(r)$. But then we have by (*) that $t = p$. So clearly $s \xrightarrow{u} t$ is an edge in $g$.

Ad 2. Suppose that $s \xrightarrow{u} t$. Then we have $d(t) < d(s)$. But then also $d(t) + d(r) < d(s) + d(r)$. If $s$ and $t$ have the same colour, then by (*) we have $r = t$. This is in contradiction with $d(t) < d(s) \leq d(r)$. So clearly $s$ and $t$ do not have the same colour. Then $(C(s), u, C(t))$ is a coloured trace of $r$, since $s$ and $r$ have the same colour. Now two cases can be distinguished. First, suppose that $r \xrightarrow{\tau} p$ for some node $p$ such that $C(p) = C(r)$. Then $d(p) < d(r)$ and also $d(p) + d(s) < d(r) + d(s)$. Hence, from (*) we have $p = s$. So we have $r \xrightarrow{\tau} s$. Second, suppose that $r \xrightarrow{u} p$ ($u \neq \tau$) for some node $p$ with $C(p) = C(t)$. Since $d(p) < d(r)$ and $d(t) < d(s)$, we have $d(p) + d(t) < d(r) + d(s)$. From (*) we obtain $p = t$. So $r \xrightarrow{u} t$. Concluding, either $r \xrightarrow{\tau} s$ or $r \xrightarrow{u} t$.

From the two properties we just proved it follows that if $r \xrightarrow{\tau} s$ is an edge in $g$, then it is manifestly inert, and if $r \xrightarrow{\tau} s$ is not an edge in $g$, then $(r, s)$ is a pair of double nodes. □

The previous theorem can serve as a source of inspiration for defining the graph rewriting system.

DEFINITION 4.2.5 The rewriting relation $\rightarrow$ is defined by the following one-step reductions:

1. sharing a pair of double nodes $(r, s)$: replace all edges $t \xrightarrow{u} r$ by $t \xrightarrow{u} s$ (if not already there, otherwise just remove $t \xrightarrow{u} r$) and remove $r$ with all its outgoing edges from the graph.
2. contracting a manifestly inert $\tau$-edge $r \xrightarrow{\tau} s$: replace all edges $t \xrightarrow{a} r$ by $t \xrightarrow{a} s$ (if not already there, otherwise just remove $t \xrightarrow{a} r$) and remove $r$ with all its outgoing edges from the graph.

THEOREM 4.2.6 The graph rewrite relation $\rightarrow$ has the following properties:

1. if $g \in \mathbf{G}^+$ and $g \rightarrow h$, then $h \in \mathbf{G}^+$;
2. $\rightarrow$ preserves rooted branching tail bisimilarity, i.e., if $g \rightarrow h$, then $g \,\underline{\leftrightarrow}_{\mathrm{rbt}}\, h$;
3. the graph rewrite system is strongly normalizing;
4. the graph rewrite system is confluent (up to graph isomorphism).

*Proof* We will omit the proof for the first property. For the second property, we will show that rooted branching tail bisimilarity is preserved under the application of each of the two rewrite rules. (1) Sharing a pair of double nodes. Suppose that $(r, s)$ is a pair of double nodes in $g$. Then $\rightarrow$ identifies the nodes $r$ and $s$, i.e., it removes the node $r$. Then the relation $R = Id(h) \cup \{(r, s), (s, r)\}$ is clearly a rooted branching tail bisimulation between $g$ and $h$. (2) Contracting a manifestly inert $\tau$-edge. Suppose that $r \xrightarrow{\tau} s$ is a manifestly inert $\tau$-edge. The relation $R = Id(h) \cup \{(r, s), (s, r)\}$ is a rooted branching tail bisimulation between $g$ and $h$.

For the third property we reason as follows. Strong normalization of the graph rewrite system follows immediately from the following observations: (1) every finite process graph has only finitely many nodes, and (2) in every application of a rewrite rule the number of nodes decreases with one.

For the proof of the fourth property, suppose that $g$ has two normal forms $g_1$ and $g_2$. Then both $g_1$ and $g_2$ are without double nodes and without manifestly inert $\tau$-edges by Theorem 4.2.4. From the second item of this theorem and $g \rightarrow^* g_1$, $g \rightarrow^* g_2$, we have $g \underline{\leftrightarrow}_{\mathrm{rbt}} g_1$ and $g \underline{\leftrightarrow}_{\mathrm{rbt}} g_2$ and since rooted branching tail bisimilarity is an equivalence relation also $g_1 \underline{\leftrightarrow}_{\mathrm{rbt}} g_2$. From the Normal Form Theorem (Theorem 3.4.6) we obtain $g_1 \simeq g_2$. □

## 4.3 Correspondence between $\mathbf{G}^+$ and $\mathbf{BPA}_{\mathbf{drt}}\tau$

As already announced we need to show that the mapping *term* ∘ *graph* is an identity modulo derivability. For basic terms this turns out to be easy. The extension of this result to closed terms in general is based on the observation that for every axiom used in the Elimination Theorem the graphs corresponding to the left-hand side and the right-hand side are isomorphic, and hence the corresponding terms are derivably equal.

PROPOSITION 4.3.1 Let $g = \langle N, E, r, \downarrow, \mathrm{ID}\rangle$ and $s \in N$. Then $s \in \mathrm{ID}$ iff $term((g)_s) = \dot{\delta}$.

PROPOSITION 4.3.2 If $g, h \in \mathbf{G}^+$ and $g \simeq h$, then $A1, A2 \vdash term(g) = term(h)$.

PROPOSITION 4.3.3 For closed $\mathrm{BPA_{drt}}\tau$ terms $p$ and $q$, we have

1. if $p \in B(\mathrm{BPA_{drt}}\tau)$, then A1,A2,DRT4,DRT5 $\vdash term(graph(p)) = p$;
2. if A1,A2,A4,A5,A6ID,A7ID,DRT1-DRT3, DRTSID,DCS1-DCS4,DCSID,ARTS, DRTI1-DRTI5,DRTIID,DCSTI $\vdash p = q$, then $graph(p) \simeq graph(q)$.

THEOREM 4.3.4 For closed $\mathrm{BPA_{drt}}\tau$-terms $p$ we have

A1,A2,A4,A5,A6ID,A7ID,DRT1-DRT3,DRTSID,
DCS1-DCS4,DCSID,ARTS,DRTI1-DRTI5,DRTIID,DCSTI $\vdash term(graph(p)) = p$.

*Proof* By the Elimination Theorem we have the existence of a basic term $q$ such that

A1,A2,A4,A5,A6ID,A7ID,DRT1-DRT3,DRTSID,
DCS1-DCS4,DCSID,ARTS,DRTI1-DRTI5,DRTIID,DCSTI $\vdash p = q$.

Then we obtain from Proposition 4.3.3.2 that $graph(p) \simeq graph(q)$. Then, by Proposition 4.3.2, we have $A1, A2 \vdash term(graph(p)) = term(graph(q))$. By Proposition 4.3.3.1 we also have A1,A2,DRT4,DRT5 $\vdash term(graph(q)) = q$. So,

A1,A2,A4,A5,A6ID,A7ID,DRT1-DRT3,
DRTSID,DCS1-DCS4,DCSID,ARTS,
DRTI1-DRTI5,DRTIID,DCSTI $\vdash term(graph(p)) = term(graph(q)) = q = p$.

□

### 4.4 Every Rewrite Step Corresponds to a Proof Step

PROPOSITION 4.4.1 Let $(r, s)$ be a pair of double nodes in a process graph $g$. Then we have $A1, A2 \vdash term((g)_r) = term((g)_s)$.

*Proof* This proposition follows immediately from Proposition 4.2.2 and Proposition 4.3.2. □

PROPOSITION 4.4.2 Let $r \xrightarrow{\tau} s$ be a manifestly inert $\tau$-edge in a process graph $g$. Let $x$ be a closed $\mathrm{BPA}^-_{\mathrm{drt}}\tau$-term. Then

1. $\mathrm{BPA}^-_{\mathrm{drt}}\tau \vdash x \cdot \sigma^m_{\mathrm{rel}}(term((g)_r)) = x \cdot \sigma^m_{\mathrm{rel}}(term((g)_s))$;
2. $\mathrm{BPA}_{\mathrm{drt}}\tau \vdash x \cdot \sigma^m_{\mathrm{rel}}(\sigma_{\mathrm{rel}}(term((g)_r)) + \nu_{\mathrm{rel}}(y)) = x \cdot \sigma^m_{\mathrm{rel}}(\sigma_{\mathrm{rel}}(term((g)_s)) + \nu_{\mathrm{rel}}(y))$.

*Proof* We will only give the proof for the second property. The proof for the first property is similar (though easier). Since $r \xrightarrow{\tau} s$, we have $\neg\mathrm{ID}(r)$, and hence $\neg\mathrm{ID}(s)$. Then we have by Proposition 4.3.1 that $term((g)_s) \neq \dot{\delta}$ and therefore by Proposition 2.1.7, we have $term((g)_s) = term((g)_s) + cts(\delta)$. Two cases can be distinguished: (1) $r$ does not have a $\sigma$-loop, or (2) $r$ does have a $\sigma$-loop. We only show the derivation for the second case. Then $term((g)_r) = \sigma^*_{\mathrm{rel}}(cts(\tau) \cdot term((g)_s) + q)$ and $term((g)_s) = \sigma^*_{\mathrm{rel}}(p + q)$ for some basic terms $p$ and $q$ such that neither $p$ nor $q$ has a $\sigma$-summand. Then

$$
\begin{aligned}
\mathrm{BPA}_{\mathrm{drt}}\tau \vdash\ & x \cdot \sigma^m_{\mathrm{rel}}(\sigma_{\mathrm{rel}}(term((g)_r)) + \nu_{\mathrm{rel}}(y)) \\
&= x \cdot \sigma^m_{\mathrm{rel}}(\sigma_{\mathrm{rel}}(\sigma^*_{\mathrm{rel}}(cts(\tau) \cdot term((g)_s) + q)) + \nu_{\mathrm{rel}}(y)) \\
&= x \cdot \sigma^m_{\mathrm{rel}}(\sigma_{\mathrm{rel}}(\sigma^*_{\mathrm{rel}}(cts(\tau) \cdot \sigma^*_{\mathrm{rel}}(p + q) + q)) + \nu_{\mathrm{rel}}(y)) \\
&= x \cdot \sigma^m_{\mathrm{rel}}(\sigma_{\mathrm{rel}}(\sigma^*_{\mathrm{rel}}(cts(\tau) \cdot \sigma^*_{\mathrm{rel}}(p + q + cts(\delta)) + q)) + \nu_{\mathrm{rel}}(y)) \\
&= x \cdot \sigma^m_{\mathrm{rel}}(\sigma_{\mathrm{rel}}(\sigma^*_{\mathrm{rel}}(p + q + cts(\delta))) + \nu_{\mathrm{rel}}(y)) \\
&= x \cdot \sigma^m_{\mathrm{rel}}(\sigma_{\mathrm{rel}}(\sigma^*_{\mathrm{rel}}(p + q)) + \nu_{\mathrm{rel}}(y)) \\
&= x \cdot \sigma^m_{\mathrm{rel}}(\sigma_{\mathrm{rel}}(term((g)_s)) + \nu_{\mathrm{rel}}(y)).
\end{aligned}
$$

□

THEOREM 4.4.3 If $g \to h$, then $\mathrm{BPA}_{\mathrm{drt}}\tau \vdash term(g) = term(h)$.

*Proof* Suppose that $g \to h$. This must be due to either the sharing of a pair of double nodes, or the contraction of a manifestly inert $\tau$-edge. Each of these two rewritings in turn is built up from more elementary rewritings. These are the removal of an unreachable node, the replacement of an edge by another one, or the removal of an edge. With respect to the removal of unreachable parts of process graphs we have that the original graph and the resulting graph are isomorphic since unreachable nodes are not taken into account. For the sharing of a pair of double nodes $(r, s)$ or the contraction of a manifestly inert $\tau$-edge

$r \xrightarrow{\tau} s$ the following cases can be distinguished: (1) $r$ has no incoming edges, (2) $r$ does have an incoming edge $t \xrightarrow{u} r$ and $s$ does not have an incoming edge $t \xrightarrow{u} s$, or (3) $r$ has an incoming edge $t \xrightarrow{u} r$ and $s$ has an incoming edge $t \xrightarrow{u} s$. For double nodes we give the derivations for the second case and for manifestly inert $\tau$-edges we give the derivations for the third case:

• Let $(r, s)$ be a pair of double nodes in $g$ such that $r$ has an incoming edge $t \xrightarrow{u} r$ and such that $s$ does not have an incoming edge $t \xrightarrow{u} s$. In the case that $u \in A_\tau$, we have that for some basic term $p$: if $t$ does not have a $\sigma$-loop, then $term((g)_t) = cts(u) \cdot term((g)_r) + p$ and $term((h)_t) = cts(u) \cdot term((h)_s) + p$, or, if $t$ does have a $\sigma$-loop, then $term((g)_t) = \sigma^*_{\mathrm{rel}}(cts(u) \cdot term((g)_r) + p)$ and $term((h)_t) = \sigma^*_{\mathrm{rel}}(cts(u) \cdot term((h)_s) + p)$. Furthermore we have by construction that $(g)_s \simeq (h)_s$, and therefore by Proposition 4.3.2, $A1, A2 \vdash term((g)_s) = term((h)_s)$. Since $(r, s)$ is a pair of double nodes we have from Proposition 4.4.1 that $A1, A2 \vdash term((g)_r) = term((g)_s)$. Combining these gives us, in the case that $t$ does not have a $\sigma$-loop:

$$\begin{aligned}\mathrm{BPA_{drt}}\tau \vdash\ & term((g)_t)\\ &= cts(u) \cdot term((g)_r) + p\\ &= cts(u) \cdot term((g)_s) + p\\ &= cts(u) \cdot term((h)_s) + p\\ &= term((h)_t),\end{aligned}$$

and in the other case:

$$\begin{aligned}\mathrm{BPA_{drt}}\tau \vdash\ & term((g)_t)\\ &= \sigma^*_{\mathrm{rel}}(cts(u) \cdot term((g)_r) + p)\\ &= \sigma^*_{\mathrm{rel}}(cts(u) \cdot term((g)_s) + p)\\ &= \sigma^*_{\mathrm{rel}}(cts(u) \cdot term((h)_s) + p)\\ &= term((h)_t).\end{aligned}$$

If, on the other hand $u = \sigma$, then we have that for some basic term $p$: $term((g)_t) = \sigma_{\mathrm{rel}}(term((g)_r)) + p$ and $term((h)_t) = \sigma_{\mathrm{rel}}(term((h)_s)) + p$. Please note that $t$ cannot have a $\sigma$-loop since every node may have at most one outgoing $\sigma$-edge. We have, by construction, $(g)_s \simeq (h)_s$, and therefore by Proposition 4.3.2 also $A1, A2 \vdash term((g)_s) = term((h)_s)$. Finally, since $(r, s)$ is a pair of double nodes we have by Proposition 4.4.1 that $A1, A2 \vdash term((g)_r) = term((g)_s)$. Combining these gives us:

$$\begin{aligned}\mathrm{BPA_{drt}}\tau \vdash\ & term((g)_t)\\ &= \sigma_{\mathrm{rel}}(term((g)_r)) + p\\ &= \sigma_{\mathrm{rel}}(term((g)_s)) + p\\ &= \sigma_{\mathrm{rel}}(term((h)_s)) + p\\ &= term((h)_t).\end{aligned}$$

• Let $r \xrightarrow{\tau} s$ be a manifestly inert $\tau$-edge in $g$ such that $r$ has an incoming edge $t \xrightarrow{u} r$ and such that $s$ also has an incoming edge $t \xrightarrow{u} s$. Then, since $t$ cannot have two outgoing $\sigma$-edges, we have $u \in A_\tau$. Two cases are distinguished: $t$ does not have a $\sigma$-loop and $t$ does have a $\sigma$-loop. First, suppose that $t$ does not have a $\sigma$-loop. Then, we have that for some basic term $p$: $term((g)_t) = cts(u) \cdot term((g)_r) + cts(u) \cdot term((g)_s) + p$ and $term((h)_t) = cts(u) \cdot term((h)_s) + p$. Furthermore, we have by construction that $(g)_s \simeq (h)_s$, and therefore by Proposition 4.3.2 that $A1, A2 \vdash term((g)_s) = term((h)_s)$. Since $r \xrightarrow{\tau} s$ is a manifestly inert $\tau$-edge, we have by Proposition 4.4.2 that $\mathrm{BPA_{drt}}\tau \vdash cts(u) \cdot term((g)_r) = cts(u) \cdot term((g)_s)$. Combining these gives us:

$$\begin{aligned}\mathrm{BPA_{drt}}\tau \vdash\ & term((g)_t)\\ &= cts(u) \cdot term((g)_r) + cts(u) \cdot term((g)_s) + p\\ &= cts(u) \cdot term((g)_s) + cts(u) \cdot term((g)_s) + p\\ &= cts(u) \cdot term((g)_s) + p\\ &= cts(u) \cdot term((h)_s) + p\\ &= term((h)_t).\end{aligned}$$

Second, suppose that $t$ does have a $\sigma$-loop. Then, we have that for some basic term $p$: $term((g)_t) = \sigma^*_{\mathrm{rel}}(cts(u) \cdot term((g)_r) + cts(u) \cdot term((g)_s) + p)$ and $term((h)_t) = \sigma^*_{\mathrm{rel}}(cts(u) \cdot term((h)_s) + p)$. Furthermore, we have by construction that $(g)_s \simeq (h)_s$, and therefore by Proposition 4.3.2 that $A1, A2 \vdash term((g)_s) = term((h)_s)$. Since $r \xrightarrow{\tau} s$ is a manifestly inert $\tau$-edge, we have by Proposition 4.4.2 that $\mathrm{BPA_{drt}}\tau \vdash cts(u) \cdot term((g)_r) = cts(u) \cdot term((g)_s)$. Combining these gives us:

$$\begin{aligned}\mathrm{BPA_{drt}}\tau \vdash\ & term((g)_t)\\ &= \sigma^*_{\mathrm{rel}}(cts(u) \cdot term((g)_r) + cts(u) \cdot term((g)_s) + p)\\ &= \sigma^*_{\mathrm{rel}}(cts(u) \cdot term((g)_s) + cts(u) \cdot term((g)_s) + p)\\ &= \sigma^*_{\mathrm{rel}}(cts(u) \cdot term((g)_s) + p)\\ &= \sigma^*_{\mathrm{rel}}(cts(u) \cdot term((h)_s) + p)\\ &= term((h)_t).\end{aligned}$$

□

THEOREM 4.4.4 (COMPLETENESS) $\mathrm{BPA_{drt}}\tau$ is a complete axiomatization of rooted branching tail bisimilarity on process graphs.

*Proof* Let $p$ and $q$ be arbitrary closed $\mathrm{BPA_{drt}}\tau$ terms. Suppose that $graph(p) \underline{\leftrightarrow}_{\mathrm{rbt}}\, graph(q)$. Then we must prove that $\mathrm{BPA_{drt}}\tau \vdash p = q$. Let $g$ and $h$ be the unique normal forms with respect to $\rightarrow$ of $graph(p)$ and $graph(q)$ respectively. Then, by Theorem 4.2.6, we find $g \underline{\leftrightarrow}_{\mathrm{rbt}}\, graph(p) \underline{\leftrightarrow}_{\mathrm{rbt}}\, graph(q) \underline{\leftrightarrow}_{\mathrm{rbt}}\, h$. By Theorem 4.2.4 it follows that $g$ and $h$ must be in normal form in the sense of Section 3.4. Then, by

Theorem 3.4.6, we have $g \simeq h$. Thus, by Proposition 4.3.2, we have $\mathrm{BPA_{drt}}\tau \vdash \mathit{term}(g) = \mathit{term}(h)$. Also, by Theorem 4.3.4, we have $\mathrm{BPA_{drt}}\tau \vdash p = \mathit{term}(\mathit{graph}(p))$ and $\mathrm{BPA_{drt}}\tau \vdash \mathit{term}(\mathit{graph}(q)) = q$. By Theorem 4.4.3, we have $\mathrm{BPA_{drt}}\tau \vdash \mathit{term}(\mathit{graph}(p)) = \mathit{term}(g)$ and $\mathrm{BPA_{drt}}\tau \vdash \mathit{term}(h) = \mathit{term}(\mathit{graph}(q))$. Combining these gives us $\mathrm{BPA_{drt}}\tau \vdash p = \mathit{term}(\mathit{graph}(p)) = \mathit{term}(g) = \mathit{term}(h) = \mathit{term}(\mathit{graph}(q)) = q$. □

## 5 Additional Operators

In this section we will consider some extensions of $\mathrm{BPA_{drt}}\tau$. First a simple notion of time free projection will be introduced. This operator is useful when relating a specification without timing information to a specification with timing information. Also, an operator for parallel composition with communication is defined.

### 5.1 Time Abstraction

We have embedded the time free theory into the discrete time theory. We call a process *time free* if it can be generated from the constants $ats(a)$, $ats(\delta)$, $ats(\tau)$ and the operators $+, \cdot$. In this section, we define an operator that throws away all timing information, so that the image of a discrete time closed term will always be a time free term. This operator is called *time abstraction* or *time free projection*, and is denoted by $\pi_{\mathrm{tf}}$ (see [12]). We present axioms in Table 18.6, operational rules in Table 18.7. All axioms in Table 18.6 are sound

**Table 18.6**
Axioms for time abstraction ($a \in A_{\tau\delta}$).

| | |
|---|---|
| $\pi_{\mathrm{tf}}(\dot{\delta}) = ats(\delta)$ | $\pi_{\mathrm{tf}}(x + y) = \pi_{\mathrm{tf}}(x) + \pi_{\mathrm{tf}}(y)$ |
| $\pi_{\mathrm{tf}}(cts(a)) = ats(a)$ | $\pi_{\mathrm{tf}}(x \cdot y) = \pi_{\mathrm{tf}}(x) \cdot \pi_{\mathrm{tf}}(y)$ |
| $\pi_{\mathrm{tf}}(\sigma_{\mathrm{rel}}(x)) = \pi_{\mathrm{tf}}(x)$ | $\pi_{\mathrm{tf}}(\sigma^*_{\mathrm{rel}}(x)) = \pi_{\mathrm{tf}}(x)$ |

**Table 18.7**
Operational rules for time abstraction ($a \in A_\tau$).

$$\frac{x \xrightarrow{a} x'}{\pi_{\mathrm{tf}}(x) \xrightarrow{a} \pi_{\mathrm{tf}}(x')} \qquad \frac{x \xrightarrow{a} \surd}{\pi_{\mathrm{tf}}(x) \xrightarrow{a} \surd} \qquad \pi_{\mathrm{tf}}(x) \xrightarrow{\sigma} \pi_{\mathrm{tf}}(x)$$

$$\frac{x \xrightarrow{\sigma} x',\ \pi_{\mathrm{tf}}(x') \xrightarrow{a} x''}{\pi_{\mathrm{tf}}(x) \xrightarrow{a} x''} \qquad \frac{x \xrightarrow{\sigma} x',\ \pi_{\mathrm{tf}}(x') \xrightarrow{a} \surd}{\pi_{\mathrm{tf}}(x) \xrightarrow{a} \surd}$$

with respect to strong and rooted branching tail bisimulation on the term model. From these axioms one can easily derive $\pi_{\text{tf}}(ats(a)) = ats(a)$.

## 5.2 Merge with Communication

The extension of the theory $\text{BPA}_{\text{drt}}\tau$ with parallel composition, with or without communication, can be done along the lines of [3]. We present the extension with parallel composition with communication. In fact the axioms presented in this paper are almost identical to those presented in [3]. The only differences are that some minor mistakes are corrected (see [23]). The additional syntax has binary operators $\|$ (merge), $\lfloor\!\lfloor$ (left merge), and $|$ (communication merge) and unary operators $\partial_H$ (encapsulation, for $H \subseteq A$), and $\tau_I$ (abstraction, for $I \subseteq A$). We present axioms for $\text{ACP}_{\text{drt}}\tau$ in Table 18.8 and Table 18.9. The operational rules are exactly those given in [3] and are therefore omitted. We assume given a partial, commutative, and associative communication function $\gamma : A \times A \to A$.

**Table 18.8**
Axioms for parallel composition in $\text{ACP}_{\text{drt}}\tau$ $(a \in A_\tau)$.

| | |
|---|---|
| $x \parallel y = x \lfloor\!\lfloor y + y \lfloor\!\lfloor x + x \mid y$ | $cts(a) \mid cts(b) = cts(\gamma(a, b))$ if defined |
| $x \lfloor\!\lfloor \dot{\delta} = \dot{\delta}$ | $cts(a) \mid cts(b) = cts(\delta)$ otherwise |
| $\dot{\delta} \lfloor\!\lfloor x = \dot{\delta}$ | $cts(a) \mid cts(b) \cdot x = (cts(a) \mid cts(b)) \cdot x$ |
| $(x + y) \lfloor\!\lfloor z = x \lfloor\!\lfloor z + y \lfloor\!\lfloor z$ | $cts(a) \cdot x \mid cts(b) = (cts(a) \mid cts(b)) \cdot x$ |
| $cts(a) \lfloor\!\lfloor (x + cts(\delta)) = cts(a) \cdot (x + cts(\delta))$ | $cts(a) \cdot x \mid cts(b) \cdot y = (cts(a) \mid cts(b)) \cdot (x \parallel y)$ |
| $cts(a) \cdot x \lfloor\!\lfloor (y + cts(\delta)) = cts(a) \cdot (x \parallel (y + cts(\delta)))$ | $(x + y) \mid z = x \mid z + y \mid z$ |
| $\sigma_{\text{rel}}(x) \lfloor\!\lfloor (\sigma_{\text{rel}}(y) + \nu_{\text{rel}}(z)) = \sigma_{\text{rel}}(x \lfloor\!\lfloor y)$ | $x \mid (y + z) = x \mid y + x \mid z$ |
| $x \mid \dot{\delta} = \dot{\delta}$ | $\sigma_{\text{rel}}(x) \mid (\nu_{\text{rel}}(z) + cts(\delta)) = cts(\delta)$ |
| $\dot{\delta} \mid x = \dot{\delta}$ | $(\nu_{\text{rel}}(y) + cts(\delta)) \mid \sigma_{\text{rel}}(z) = cts(\delta)$ |
| | $\sigma_{\text{rel}}(x) \mid \sigma_{\text{rel}}(z) = \sigma_{\text{rel}}(x \mid y)$ |

**Table 18.9**
Axioms for renaming operators in $\text{ACP}_{\text{drt}}\tau$ $(a \in A_\tau)$.

| | | | |
|---|---|---|---|
| $\partial_H(\dot{\delta}) = \dot{\delta}$ | | $\tau_I(\dot{\delta}) = \dot{\delta}$ | |
| $\partial_H(cts(a)) = cts(a)$ | if $a \notin H$ | $\tau_I(cts(a)) = cts(a)$ | if $a \notin I$ |
| $\partial_H(cts(a)) = cts(\delta)$ | if $a \in H$ | $\tau_I(cts(a)) = cts(\tau)$ | if $a \in I$ |
| $\partial_H(x + y) = \partial_H(x) + \partial_H(y)$ | | $\tau_I(x + y) = \tau_I(x) + \tau_I(y)$ | |
| $\partial_H(x \cdot y) = \partial_H(x) \cdot \partial_H(y)$ | | $\tau_I(x \cdot y) = \tau_I(x) \cdot \tau_I(y)$ | |
| $\partial_H(\sigma_{\text{rel}}(x)) = \sigma_{\text{rel}}(\partial_H(x))$ | | $\tau_I(\sigma_{\text{rel}}(x)) = \sigma_{\text{rel}}(\tau_I(x))$ | |

PROPOSITION 5.2.1 We mention the following identities which are useful in the calculations to come:

1. $\sigma_{\text{rel}}(x) \parallel \sigma_{\text{rel}}(y) = \sigma_{\text{rel}}(x \parallel y)$;
2. $ats(a) \cdot x ⫫ \lfloor y \rfloor^{\omega} = ats(a) \cdot (x \parallel \lfloor y \rfloor^{\omega})$;
3. $cts(a) \cdot x ⫫ \sigma_{\text{rel}}(y) = cts(a) \cdot (x \parallel \sigma_{\text{rel}}(y))$;
4. $cts(a) \cdot x \parallel \sigma_{\text{rel}}(y) = cts(a) \cdot (x \parallel \sigma_{\text{rel}}(y))$;
5. $ats(a) \cdot x ⫫ cts(b) \cdot y = cts(a) \cdot (x \parallel cts(b) \cdot y)$;
6. $ats(a) \mid ats(b) = ats(c)$ if $\gamma(a, b) = c$, and $ats(a) \mid ats(b) = ats(\delta)$ otherwise;
7. $ats(a) \cdot x \mid ats(b) \cdot y = (ats(a) \mid ats(b)) \cdot (x \parallel y)$;
8. $ats(a) \cdot x \mid cts(b) \cdot y = (cts(a) \mid cts(b)) \cdot (x \parallel y)$;
9. $\partial_H(ats(a)) = ats(a)$ if $a \notin H$, and $\partial_H(ats(a)) = ats(\delta)$ if $a \in H$;
10. $\tau_I(ats(a)) = ats(a)$ if $a \notin I$, and $\tau_I(ats(a)) = ats(\tau)$ if $a \in I$.

PROPOSITION 5.2.2 The following identity, useful in verifications, can be proved for all closed terms $x, y$:

$$cts(a) \cdot (cts(\tau) \cdot (x + cts(\delta)) \parallel (y + cts(\delta))) = cts(a) \cdot ((x + cts(\delta)) \parallel (y + cts(\delta))).$$

## 5.3 Some Simple Calculations: Communicating Buffers

In this section, we give some simple calculations in order to illustrate the use of our discrete time theory. In the setting with unbounded start delay instead of time iteration these calculations can be found in [4]. We keep formulas compact by writing $\underline{\underline{a}}$ instead of $cts(a)$ and $a$ instead of $ats(a)$ (this is in line with notation used in [5, 12]).

The communication format follows the so-called *standard communication function.* Suppose we have given two finite sets, the set of messages or data $D$, and the set of ports $P$. For each $d \in D$ and $i \in P$, we have atomic actions $r_i(d)$, $s_i(d)$, $c_i(d)$ (denoting *receive, send* and *communicate* $d$ along $i$) and the only defined communications are $\gamma(r_i(d), s_i(d)) = \gamma(s_i(d), r_i(d)) = c_i(d)$. In time free process algebra, there is the following standard specification of a one-item buffer with input port $i$ and output port $j$:

$$B^{ij} = \sum_{d \in D} r_i(d) \cdot s_j(d) \cdot B^{ij}$$

A straightforward calculation (see e.g., [6], page 106) shows that the composition of two such buffers in sequence gives a two-item buffer. In the following, we consider three timed versions of this buffer. In each case, only one input per time slice is possible.

We can define a channel that allows one input in every time slice, and outputs with no delay, with input port $i$ and output port $j$ by the following recursive equation:

$$C^{ij} = \sum_{d \in D} r_i(d) \cdot \underline{\underline{s_j(d)}} \cdot \sigma_{\text{rel}}\left(C^{ij}\right)$$

We see $C^{ij} = \sigma^{*}_{\text{rel}}(\nu_{\text{rel}}(C^{ij})) = \lfloor C^{ij} \rfloor^{\omega}$. With $H = \{r_2(d), s_2(d) \mid d \in D\}$ we can derive:

$$\begin{aligned}
&\partial_H\left(C^{12} \parallel C^{23}\right)\\
&= \partial_H\left(C^{12} \mathbin{\|\!\lfloor} C^{23}\right) + \partial_H\left(C^{23} \mathbin{\|\!\lfloor} C^{12}\right) + \partial_H\left(C^{12} \mid C^{23}\right)\\
&= \sum_{d \in D} \partial_H\left(r_1(d) \cdot \underline{\underline{s_2(d)}} \cdot \sigma_{\text{rel}}\left(C^{12}\right) \mathbin{\|\!\lfloor} \lfloor C^{23} \rfloor^{\omega}\right)\\
&\quad + \sum_{d \in D} \partial_H\left(r_2(d) \cdot \underline{\underline{s_3(d)}} \cdot \sigma_{\text{rel}}\left(C^{23}\right) \mathbin{\|\!\lfloor} \lfloor C^{12} \rfloor^{\omega}\right)\\
&\quad + \sum_{d,e \in D} \partial_H\left(r_1(d) \cdot \underline{\underline{s_2(d)}} \cdot \sigma_{\text{rel}}\left(C^{12}\right) \mid r_2(e) \cdot \underline{\underline{s_3(e)}} \cdot \sigma_{\text{rel}}\left(C^{23}\right)\right)\\
&= \sum_{d \in D} r_1(d) \cdot \partial_H\left(\underline{\underline{s_2(d)}} \cdot \sigma_{\text{rel}}\left(C^{12}\right) \parallel C^{23}\right) + \sum_{d \in D} \delta \cdot \partial_H\left(\underline{\underline{s_3(d)}} \cdot \sigma_{\text{rel}}\left(C^{23}\right) \parallel C^{12}\right)\\
&\quad + \sum_{d,e \in D} \delta \cdot \partial_H\left(\underline{\underline{s_2(d)}} \cdot \sigma_{\text{rel}}\left(C^{12}\right) \parallel \underline{\underline{s_3(e)}} \cdot \sigma_{\text{rel}}\left(C^{23}\right)\right)\\
&= \sum_{d \in D} r_1(d) \cdot \left(\partial_H\left(\underline{\underline{s_2(d)}} \cdot \sigma_{\text{rel}}\left(C^{12}\right) \mathbin{\|\!\lfloor} C^{23}\right) + \partial_H\left(C^{23} \mathbin{\|\!\lfloor} \underline{\underline{s_2(d)}} \cdot \sigma_{\text{rel}}\left(C^{12}\right)\right)\right.\\
&\quad \left. + \partial_H\left(\underline{\underline{s_2(d)}} \cdot \sigma_{\text{rel}}\left(C^{12}\right) \mid C^{23}\right)\right) + \delta\\
&= \sum_{d \in D} r_1(d) \cdot \left(\underline{\underline{\delta}} + \sum_{e \in D} \partial_H\left(r_2(e) \cdot \underline{\underline{s_3(e)}} \cdot \sigma_{\text{rel}}\left(C^{23}\right)\right) \mathbin{\|\!\lfloor} \underline{\underline{s_2(d)}} \cdot \sigma_{\text{rel}}\left(C^{12}\right)\right.\\
&\quad \left. + \sum_{e \in D} \partial_H\left(\underline{\underline{s_2(d)}} \cdot \sigma_{\text{rel}}\left(C^{12}\right) \mid r_2(e) \cdot \underline{\underline{s_3(e)}} \cdot \sigma_{\text{rel}}\left(C^{23}\right)\right)\right)\\
&= \sum_{d \in D} r_1(d) \cdot \left(\underline{\underline{\delta}} + \underline{\underline{\delta}} + \underline{\underline{c_2(d)}} \cdot \partial_H\left(\sigma_{\text{rel}}\left(C^{12}\right) \parallel \underline{\underline{s_3(d)}} \cdot \sigma_{\text{rel}}\left(C^{23}\right)\right)\right)\\
&= \sum_{d \in D} r_1(d) \cdot \underline{\underline{c_2(d)}} \cdot \underline{\underline{s_3(d)}} \cdot \partial_H\left(\sigma_{\text{rel}}\left(C^{12}\right) \parallel \sigma_{\text{rel}}\left(C^{23}\right)\right)\\
&= \sum_{d \in D} r_1(d) \cdot \underline{\underline{c_2(d)}} \cdot \underline{\underline{s_3(d)}} \cdot \sigma_{\text{rel}}\left(\left(\partial_H\left(C^{12} \parallel C^{23}\right)\right)\right).
\end{aligned}$$

Next, we put $I = \{c_2(d) \mid d \in D\}$ and obtain the following recursive equation:

$$\tau_I \circ \partial_H\left(C^{12} \parallel C^{23}\right) = \sum_{d \in D} r_1(d) \cdot \underline{\underline{s_3(d)}} \cdot \sigma_{\text{rel}}\left(\tau_I \circ \partial_H\left(C^{12} \parallel C^{23}\right)\right).$$

We see that the composition behaves again as a no-delay channel, with input port 1 and output port 3.

It is interesting to see what happens if we change the previous specification slightly. Consider

$$D^{ij} = \sum_{d \in D} r_i(d) \cdot \sigma_{\mathrm{rel}}\left(\underline{\underline{s_j(d)}} \cdot D^{ij}\right).$$

This specification describes a buffer with capacity one and delay between input and output of one time unit. The composition $\partial_H(D^{12} \parallel D^{23})$ (with $H$ as above) satisfies the following recursive specification:

$$\begin{aligned}
X &= \sum_{d \in D} r_1(d) \cdot \sigma_{\mathrm{rel}}\left(\underline{\underline{c_2(d)}}\right) \cdot X_d, \\
X_d &= \sum_{e \in D} \underline{\underline{r_1(e)}} \cdot \sigma_{\mathrm{rel}}\left(\underline{\underline{s_3(d)}}\right) \cdot \underline{\underline{c_2(e)}} \cdot X_e \\
&\quad + \sigma_{\mathrm{rel}}\left(\underline{\underline{s_3(d)}} \cdot X + \sum_{e \in D} \underline{\underline{r_1(e)}} \cdot \underline{\underline{s_3(d)}} \cdot \sigma_{\mathrm{rel}}\left(\underline{\underline{c_2(e)}}\right) \cdot X_e\right) \qquad \text{(for } d \in D\text{)}.
\end{aligned}$$

Hiding the internal communications, we obtain

$$\begin{aligned}
\tau_I(X) &= \sum_{d \in D} r_1(d) \cdot \sigma_{\mathrm{rel}}(\tau_I(X_d)), \\
\tau_I(X_d) &= \sum_{e \in D} \underline{\underline{r_1(e)}} \cdot \sigma_{\mathrm{rel}}\left(\underline{\underline{s_3(d)}}\right) \cdot \tau_I(X_e) \\
&\quad + \sigma_{\mathrm{rel}}\left(\underline{\underline{s_3(d)}} \cdot \tau_I(X) + \sum_{e \in D} \underline{\underline{r_1(e)}} \cdot \underline{\underline{s_3(d)}} \cdot \sigma_{\mathrm{rel}}(\tau_I(X_e))\right).
\end{aligned}$$

The composition denotes a buffer with capacity two and delay of two time units. Now, we apply the time abstraction operator, and obtain the following specification:

$$\begin{aligned}
\pi_{\mathrm{tf}} \circ \tau_I(X) &= \sum_{d \in D} r_1(d) \cdot \pi_{\mathrm{tf}} \circ \tau_I(X_d), \\
\pi_{\mathrm{tf}} \circ \tau_I(X_d) &= s_3(d) \cdot \pi_{\mathrm{tf}} \circ \tau_I(X) + \sum_{e \in D} r_1(e) \cdot s_3(d) \cdot \pi_{\mathrm{tf}} \circ \tau_I(X_e).
\end{aligned}$$

This is exactly the result of the time free calculation on page 106 of [6] (after abstraction). We find that the following remarkable equation holds for the buffers $D^{ij}$, but not for the other variants of buffers we discuss:

$$\partial_H\left(\pi_{\mathrm{tf}}\left(D^{12}\right) \parallel \pi_{\mathrm{tf}}\left(D^{23}\right)\right) = \pi_{\mathrm{tf}} \circ \partial_H\left(D^{12} \parallel D^{23}\right).$$

Finally, we drop the restriction in the previous specification that output must occur before the next input. We obtain the following specification:

$$E^{ij} = \sum_{d \in D} r_i(d) \cdot \sigma_{\mathrm{rel}}\left(\underline{\underline{s_j(d)}} \parallel E^{ij}\right).$$

Now, the composition satisfies the following recursive specification:

$$
\begin{aligned}
Y^0 &= \sum_{d \in D} r_1(d) \cdot \sigma_{\mathrm{rel}}\left(Y^1_d\right), \\
Y^1_d &= \underline{\underline{c_2(d)}} \cdot Y^2_d + \sum_{e \in D} \underline{\underline{r_1(e)}} \cdot \underline{\underline{c_2(d)}} \cdot \sigma_{\mathrm{rel}}\left(Y^3_{de}\right) \quad (\text{for } d \in D), \\
Y^2_d &= \sigma_{\mathrm{rel}}\left(\underline{\underline{s_3(d)}} \cdot Y^0 + \sum_{e \in D} \underline{\underline{r_1(e)}} \cdot \underline{\underline{s_3(d)}} \cdot \sigma_{\mathrm{rel}}\left(Y^1_e\right)\right) + \sum_{e \in D} \underline{\underline{r_1(e)}} \cdot \sigma_{\mathrm{rel}}\left(Y^3_{de}\right) \quad (\text{for } d \in D), \\
Y^3_{de} &= \underline{\underline{s_3(d)}} \cdot Y^1_e + \underline{\underline{c_2(e)}} \cdot \left(\underline{\underline{s_3(d)}} \cdot Y^2_d + \sum_{f \in D} \underline{\underline{r_1(f)}} \cdot \underline{\underline{s_3(d)}} \cdot \sigma_{\mathrm{rel}}\left(Y^3_{ef}\right)\right) \\
&\quad + \sum_{f \in D} \underline{\underline{r_1(f)}} \cdot \left(\underline{\underline{c_2(e)}} \parallel \underline{\underline{s_3(d)}}\right) \cdot \sigma_{\mathrm{rel}}\left(Y^3_{ef}\right) \quad (\text{for } d, e \in D).
\end{aligned}
$$

After abstraction, we obtain the following specification for $Z^0 = \tau_I(Y^0)$:

$$
\begin{aligned}
Z^0 &= \sum_{d \in D} r_1(d) \cdot \sigma_{\mathrm{rel}}\left(Z^1_d\right), \\
Z^1_d &= \sigma_{\mathrm{rel}}\left(\underline{\underline{s_3(d)}} \cdot Z^0 + \sum_{e \in D} \underline{\underline{r_1(e)}} \cdot \underline{\underline{s_3(d)}} \cdot \sigma_{\mathrm{rel}}\left(Z^1_e\right)\right) + \sum_{e \in D} \underline{\underline{r_1(e)}} \cdot \sigma_{\mathrm{rel}}\left(Z^2_{de}\right) \quad (\text{for } d \in D), \\
Z^2_{de} &= \underline{\underline{s_3(d)}} \cdot Z^1_e + \sum_{f \in D} \underline{\underline{r_1(f)}} \cdot \underline{\underline{s_3(d)}} \cdot \sigma_{\mathrm{rel}}\left(Z^2_{ef}\right) \quad (\text{for } d, e \in D).
\end{aligned}
$$

Again, the delay between input and output is two time units, but now, it is possible that three data elements are present in the system at the same time.

## 6 Absolute and Parametric Timing

### 6.1 Discrete Time Process Algebra with Absolute Timing

We present a version of the theory in the previous section using absolute timing, where all timing is related to a global clock.

We start with constants $\mathit{fts}(a)$, denoting $a$ in the first time slice ($a \in A_{\delta\tau}$), followed by immediate termination. Besides, we have operators $+, \cdot$ as before. In addition, we have the *absolute discrete time unit delay* $\sigma_{\mathrm{abs}}$, that increments all timing in its scope. Thus, $\sigma_{\mathrm{abs}}(\mathit{fts}(a))$ denotes $a$ in the second time slice. In the axioms we use the absolute value operator $|\ |$. This operator turns out to be the identity for all processes using absolute timing only: it initializes a process in the first time slice. Note that in the term $\sigma_{\mathrm{abs}}(\mathit{fts}(a)) \cdot \mathit{fts}(\delta)$, after execution of the $a$ in slice 2, an immediate deadlock will occur. This term is different from $\sigma_{\mathrm{abs}}(\mathit{fts}(a) \cdot \mathit{fts}(\delta))$, where after the execution of $a$ in slice 2, further activity in this slice can take place (of a parallel process). We conclude that in the absolute time theory, the immediate deadlock constant $\dot{\delta}$ is necessary. The axiomatization of $\mathrm{BPA}_{\mathrm{dat}}$ adds the axioms of Table 18.10 to the axioms A1-5, A6ID, A7ID (see Table 18.1).

**Table 18.10**
Axioms of $\mathrm{BPA}_{\mathrm{dat}}$ ($a \in A_\tau$).

| | |
|---|---|
| $\sigma_{\mathrm{abs}}(x) + \sigma_{\mathrm{abs}}(y) = \sigma_{\mathrm{abs}}(x + y)$ | $\nu_{\mathrm{abs}}(\dot{\delta}) = \dot{\delta}$ |
| $\sigma_{\mathrm{abs}}(x) \cdot \dot{\delta} = \sigma_{\mathrm{abs}}(x \cdot \dot{\delta})$ | $\nu_{\mathrm{abs}}(\mathit{fts}(a)) = \mathit{fts}(a)$ |
| $\sigma_{\mathrm{abs}}(x) \cdot (\nu_{\mathrm{abs}}(y) + z) = \sigma_{\mathrm{abs}}(x) \cdot z$ | $\nu_{\mathrm{abs}}(x + y) = \nu_{\mathrm{abs}}(x) + \nu_{\mathrm{abs}}(y)$ |
| $\sigma_{\mathrm{abs}}(x) \cdot \sigma_{\mathrm{abs}}(y) = \sigma_{\mathrm{abs}}(x \cdot \lvert y \rvert)$ | $\nu_{\mathrm{abs}}(x \cdot y) = \nu_{\mathrm{abs}}(x) \cdot y$ |
| $\mathit{fts}(\delta) \cdot x = \mathit{fts}(\delta)$ | $\nu_{\mathrm{abs}}(\sigma_{\mathrm{abs}}(x)) = \mathit{fts}(\delta)$ |
| $\sigma_{\mathrm{abs}}(\dot{\delta}) = \mathit{fts}(\delta)$ | $\lvert \dot{\delta} \rvert = \dot{\delta}$ |
| $\mathit{fts}(a) + \mathit{fts}(\delta) = \mathit{fts}(a)$ | $\lvert \mathit{fts}(a) \rvert = \mathit{fts}(a)$ |
| $\sigma_{\mathrm{abs}}(x) + \mathit{fts}(\delta) = \sigma_{\mathrm{abs}}(x)$ | $\lvert x + y \rvert = \lvert x \rvert + \lvert y \rvert$ |
| $\sigma^*_{\mathrm{abs}}(x) = x + \sigma_{\mathrm{abs}}(\sigma^*_{\mathrm{abs}}(x))$ | $\lvert x \cdot y \rvert = \lvert x \rvert \cdot y$ |
| $\mathit{ats}(a) = \sigma^*_{\mathrm{abs}}(\mathit{fts}(a))$ | $\lvert \sigma_{\mathrm{abs}}(x) \rvert = \sigma_{\mathrm{abs}}(\lvert x \rvert)$ |

The extension with delayable actions is similar to the relative time case. Here, we see a large advantage of the time iteration operator over the unbounded start delay operator.

Again, we can find $\mathrm{BPA}^{\tau}_{\delta}$ as an SRM specification by using the interpretation of $a$ as $\mathit{atstau}(a)$. The extension with parallel composition can be found along the same lines as for the relative time case (see [5]). The principle RSP(DAT) can be used to prove identities for $\sigma^*_{\mathrm{abs}}$:

$$y = x + \sigma_{\mathrm{abs}}(y) \Longrightarrow y = \sigma^*_{\mathrm{abs}}(x) \qquad \text{RSP(DAT)}.$$

The operational rules are more complicated in this case, as we have to keep track of which time slice we are in, we have to keep track of the global clock. The pair $\langle x, n\rangle$ denotes $x$ in the $(n+1)$st time slice. The operational rules for the absolute value operator are trivial. For the operational rules for the constants $\mathit{fts}(a)$ ($a \in A_\tau$) and $\dot{\delta}$ and the operators $+$, $\cdot$, $\sigma_{\mathrm{abs}}$ we refer to [5]. Operational rules for $\nu_{\mathrm{abs}}$, $\sigma^*_{\mathrm{abs}}$, $\mathit{ats}(a)$ ($a \in A_\tau$) are presented in Table 18.11.

We also have to adapt the definition of bisimulation. A *strong bisimulation relation* is a symmetric binary relation $R$ on $P \times \mathbb{N}$ such that ($u \in A_{\tau\sigma}$, $a \in A_\tau$):

1. if $R(\langle s, n\rangle, \langle s', n'\rangle)$, then $n = n'$ and if $\mathrm{ID}(\langle s, n\rangle)$, then $\mathrm{ID}(\langle s', n'\rangle)$;
2. if $R(\langle s; n\rangle, \langle t, n\rangle)$ and $\langle s, n\rangle \xrightarrow{u} \langle s', n'\rangle$, then there is a term $t'$ such that $\langle t, n\rangle \xrightarrow{u} \langle t', n'\rangle$ and $R(\langle s', n'\rangle, \langle t', n'\rangle)$;
3. if $R(\langle s, n\rangle, \langle t, n\rangle)$ and $\langle s, n\rangle \xrightarrow{a} \langle \surd, n\rangle$, then $\langle t, n\rangle \xrightarrow{a} \langle \surd, n\rangle$.

We say process expressions $x$ and $y$ are *strongly (tail) bisimilar*, denoted $x \leftrightarrow y$, if there exists a strong bisimulation relation with $R(\langle x, 0\rangle, \langle y, 0\rangle)$. A *branching tail bisimulation relation* is a binary relation $R$ on $P \times \mathbb{N}$ such that ($u \in A_{\tau\sigma}$, $a \in A_\tau$):

**Table 18.11**
Operational rules for $\mathrm{BPA_{dat}}$ $(a \in A_\tau)$.

$$\frac{\langle x, 0\rangle \xrightarrow{a} \langle x', 0\rangle}{\langle \nu_{\mathrm{abs}}(x), 0\rangle \xrightarrow{a} \langle x', 0\rangle} \qquad \frac{\langle x, 0\rangle \xrightarrow{a} \langle \surd, 0\rangle}{\langle \nu_{\mathrm{abs}}(x), 0\rangle \xrightarrow{a} \langle \surd, 0\rangle} \qquad \frac{\mathrm{ID}(\langle x, 0\rangle)}{\mathrm{ID}(\langle \nu_{\mathrm{abs}}(x), 0\rangle)}$$

$$\mathrm{ID}(\langle \nu_{\mathrm{abs}}(x), n+1\rangle) \quad \langle ats(a), n\rangle \xrightarrow{a} \langle \surd, n\rangle \quad \langle ats(a), n\rangle \xrightarrow{\sigma} \langle ats(a), n+1\rangle \quad \langle ats(\delta), n\rangle \xrightarrow{\sigma} \langle ats(\delta), n+1\rangle$$

$$\frac{\langle x, n\rangle \xrightarrow{a} \langle x', n'\rangle}{\langle \sigma^*_{\mathrm{abs}}(x), n+k\rangle \xrightarrow{a} \langle x', n+k\rangle} \qquad \frac{\langle x, n\rangle \xrightarrow{a} \langle \surd, n'\rangle}{\langle \sigma^*_{\mathrm{abs}}(x), n+k\rangle \xrightarrow{a} \langle \surd, n+k\rangle} \qquad \langle \sigma^*_{\mathrm{abs}}(x), n\rangle \xrightarrow{\sigma} \langle \sigma^*_{\mathrm{abs}}(x), n+1\rangle$$

**Table 18.12**
Axioms for $\mathrm{BPA_{dat}}\tau$.

$$x \cdot (fts(\tau) \cdot (\nu_{\mathrm{abs}}(y) + z + fts(\delta)) + \nu_{\mathrm{abs}}(y)) = x \cdot (\nu_{\mathrm{abs}}(y) + z + fts(\delta))$$
$$x \cdot (fts(\tau) \cdot (\nu_{\mathrm{abs}}(y) + z + fts(\delta)) + z) = x \cdot (\nu_{\mathrm{abs}}(y) + z + fts(\delta))$$
$$x \cdot (\sigma_{\mathrm{abs}}(fts(\tau) \cdot (y + fts(\delta))) + \nu_{\mathrm{abs}}(z)) = x \cdot (\sigma_{\mathrm{abs}}(y + fts(\delta)) + \nu_{\mathrm{abs}}(z))$$
$$x \cdot \sigma^*_{\mathrm{abs}}(fts(\tau) \cdot \sigma^*_{\mathrm{abs}}(\nu_{\mathrm{abs}}(y) + \nu_{\mathrm{abs}}(z) + fts(\delta)) + \nu_{\mathrm{abs}}(y)) = x \cdot \sigma^*_{\mathrm{abs}}(\nu_{\mathrm{abs}}(y) + \nu_{\mathrm{abs}}(z) + fts(\delta))$$

1. if $R(\langle s, n\rangle, \langle s', n'\rangle)$, then $n = n'$ and if $\mathrm{ID}(\langle s, n\rangle)$, then $\mathrm{ID}(\langle s', n'\rangle)$;
2. if $R(\langle s, n\rangle, \langle t, n\rangle)$ and $\langle s, n\rangle \xrightarrow{u} \langle s', n'\rangle$, then there are terms $t^*, t'$ such that $\langle t, n\rangle \Longrightarrow \langle t^*, n\rangle \xrightarrow{(u)} \langle t', n'\rangle$ and $R(\langle s, n\rangle, \langle t^*, n\rangle)$, $R(\langle s', n'\rangle, \langle t', n'\rangle)$;
3. if $R(\langle s, n\rangle, \langle t, n\rangle)$ and $\langle s, n\rangle \xrightarrow{a} \langle \surd, n\rangle$, then there is a term $t'$ such that $\langle t, n\rangle \Longrightarrow \langle t', n\rangle \xrightarrow{a} \langle \surd, n\rangle$ and $R(\langle s, n\rangle, \langle t', n\rangle)$.

We say process expressions $x$ and $y$ are *branching tail bisimilar*, denoted $x \leftrightarrow_{\mathrm{bt}} y$, if there exists a branching tail bisimulation relation with $R(\langle x, 0\rangle, \langle y, 0\rangle)$. Process expressions $x$ and $y$ are *rooted branching tail bisimilar*, denoted $x \leftrightarrow_{\mathrm{rbt}} y$, if there exists a branching tail bisimulation relation with $R(\langle x, 0\rangle, \langle y, 0\rangle)$, that is strong for all pairs that can be reached from $\langle x, 0\rangle$, $\langle y, 0\rangle$ by just performing time steps.

Axioms for the silent step are comparable to the ones for relative time. The model of closed process expressions modulo rooted branching tail bisimilarity satisfies the axioms in Table 18.12.

## 6.2 Parametric Time

In this section we integrate the absolute time and the relative time approach. All axioms presented in the previous sections are still valid for all parametric time processes. We obtain a finite axiomatization, that allows an elimination theorem. As a consequence, we can expand expressions like $cts(a) \parallel fts(b)$, $cts(a) \parallel (fts(b) + ats(\delta))$.

We follow [5], where we introduced the operators $\odot$, the (relative) *time spectrum combinator*, and $\mu$, the *spectrum tail* operator. The absolute value operator can also be called the spectrum head operator. $P \odot Q$ is a process that, when initialized in the first time slice, behaves as $|P|$; when initialized in slice $n+1$ its behaviour is determined by $Q$ as follows: initialize in slice $n$ thereafter apply $\sigma_{\mathrm{abs}}$. The process $\mu(X)$ computes a process such that $X = |X| \odot \mu(X)$. For a parametric discrete time process we have the time spectrum sequence $|X|, |\mu(X)|, \left|\mu^2(X)\right|, \ldots$. For each infinite sequence $(P_n)_{n \in \mathbb{N}}$ one may imagine a process $P$ with $|\mu^n(P)| = P_n$ though not all such $P$ can be finitely expressed.

The theory $\mathrm{BPA_{dpt}}$ unites the theories $\mathrm{BPA_{drt}}$ and $\mathrm{BPA_{dat}}$ together with the additional axioms in Table 18.13. We extend with delayable actions, to $\mathrm{BPA_{dpt}}$, as indicated in [5]. We can define:

- $x$ is an absolute time process iff $\mathrm{BPA_{dpt}} \vdash x = |x|$;
- $x$ is an relative time process iff $\mathrm{BPA_{dpt}} \vdash x = \mu(x)$.

Each $\mathrm{BPA_{dpt}}$ process expression can be written in the form

$$X = |X| \odot |\mu(X)| \odot \ldots |\mu^n(X)| \odot \mu^{n+1}(X).$$

One can reduce each $|\mu^n(X)|$ to a $\mathrm{BPA_{dat}}$-term and if $n$ is sufficiently large, we can write $\mu^{n+1}(X)$ without any $\sigma_{\mathrm{abs}}$ or $fts(a)$, so it will be in the relative time signature. We call $(|X|, |\mu(X)|, |\mu^2(X)|, \ldots)$ the time spectrum expansion sequence (TSS) of $X$. Note that we obtain the following spectrum expansion for the $\nu_{\mathrm{rel}}$ operator:

$$\nu_{\mathrm{rel}}(x) = \nu_{\mathrm{abs}}(x) \odot \nu_{\mathrm{rel}}(\mu(x)).$$

**Table 18.13**
Additional axioms of $\mathrm{BPA_{dpt}}$ ($a \in A_\tau$).

| | |
|---|---|
| $\lvert cts(a)\rvert = fts(a)$ | $\mu(\dot{\delta}) = \dot{\delta}$ |
| $\lvert\sigma_{\mathrm{rel}}(x)\rvert = \sigma_{\mathrm{abs}}(\lvert\mu(x)\rvert)$ | $\mu(cts(a)) = cts(a)$ |
| $\lvert\nu_{\mathrm{rel}}(x)\rvert = \nu_{\mathrm{abs}}(\lvert x\rvert)$ | $\mu(x+y) = \mu(x) + \mu(y)$ |
| $\sigma_{\mathrm{abs}}(x) = \sigma_{\mathrm{abs}}(\lvert x\rvert)$ | $\mu(x \cdot y) = \mu(x) \cdot \mu(y)$ |
| $\nu_{\mathrm{abs}}(x) = \nu_{\mathrm{abs}}(\lvert x\rvert)$ | $\mu(\sigma_{\mathrm{rel}}(x)) = \sigma_{\mathrm{rel}}(\mu(x))$ |
| | $\mu(\nu_{\mathrm{rel}}(x)) = \nu_{\mathrm{rel}}(\mu(x))$ |
| | $\mu(fts(a)) = \dot{\delta}$ |
| $\lvert x \odot y\rvert = \lvert x\rvert$ | $\mu(\sigma_{\mathrm{abs}}(x)) = \lvert x\rvert$ |
| $\mu(x \odot y) = y$ | $\mu(\nu_{\mathrm{abs}}(x)) = \dot{\delta}$ |
| $x = \lvert x\rvert \odot \mu(x)$ | $\sigma_{\mathrm{abs}}(x) \cdot y = \sigma_{\mathrm{abs}}(x \cdot \mu(y))$ |

For further details, we refer to [5]. Now the axioms introduced for silent steps in relative and absolute time are valid in parametric time as well.

## 7 Concluding Remarks

We presented axioms for discrete time process algebra with silent step in branching bisimulation semantics. A small difference with previously published work is that we use time iteration instead of unbounded start delay and that the conditional axiom for silent step is replaced by an unconditional one. For the first version, relative discrete time process algebra, we have given soundness and completeness results with respect to the term model and the graph model (exploiting the isomorphy of those two structures). From this completeness result we can conclude that the principle RSP(DRT) that is used for deriving equalities concerning time iteration can be replaced by axioms.

We have given several embeddings of the time free theories $\text{BPA}_\delta$ and $\text{BPA}_\delta^\tau$ in the discrete time theories $\text{BPA}_{\text{drt}}$ and $\text{BPA}_{\text{drt}}\tau$ respectively.

The extension of the relative discrete time theories with additional operators such as time abstraction, merge with communication, encapsulation and abstraction follows along the same lines as in the time free theory. Some calculations regarding communicating buffers illustrate the use of the relative discrete time theory.

Finally, an outline is given for defining absolute and parametric time versions of discrete time process algebra.

An interesting topic for future research is obtaining soundness and completeness results for the absolute and parametric time process algebras as presented in this paper. The authors expect that, at least for the absolute time version, a similar approach should give these results. With respect to parametric time process algebra a lot of work has to be done. We have reasons to believe that the theory is sound, but a major open question is whether the theory is complete. Also issues relating to the applicability of the theory have to be investigated.

## References

[1] J. C. M. Baeten and J. A. Bergstra. Real time process algebra. *Formal Aspects of Computing*, 3(2):142–188, 1991.

[2] J. C. M. Baeten and J. A. Bergstra. On sequential composition, action prefixes and process prefix. *Formal Aspects of Computing*, 6(3):250–268, 1994.

[3] J. C. M. Baeten and J. A. Bergstra. Discrete time process algebra with abstraction. In H. Reichel, editor, *FCT'95, International Conference on Fundamentals of Computation Theory*, volume 965 of *Lecture Notes in Computer Science*, pages 1–15, Dresden, 1995. Springer-Verlag.

[4] J. C. M. Baeten and J. A. Bergstra. Some simple calculations in relative discrete time process algebra. In E. H. L. Aarts, H. M. M. ten Eikelder, C. Hemerik, and M. Rem, editors, *Simplex Sigillum Veri*, pages 67–74. Eindhoven University of Technology, 1995. Liber Amicorum dedicated to prof.dr. F. E. J. Kruseman Aretz.

[5] J. C. M. Baeten and J. A. Bergstra. Discrete time process algebra. *Formal Aspects of Computing*, 8(2): 188–208, 1996.

[6] J. C. M. Baeten and W. P. Weijland. *Process Algebra*, volume 18 of *Cambridge Tracts in Theoretical Computer Science*. Cambridge University Press, 1990.

[7] T. Basten. Branching bisimilarity is an equivalence indeed! *Information Processing Letters*, 58(3):141–147, 1996.

[8] J. A. Bergstra and P. Klint. The discrete time Toolbus. In M. Wirsing and M. Nivat, editors, *Algebraic Methodology and Software Technology (AMAST'96)*, volume 1101 of *Lecture Notes in Computer Science*, pages 286–305, Munich, 1996. Springer-Verlag.

[9] J. A. Bergstra and J. W. Klop. Process algebra for synchronous communication. *Information and Control*, 60(1/3):109–137, 1984.

[10] J. A. Bergstra and J. W. Klop. Algebra of communicating processes with abstraction. *Theoretical Computer Science*, 37(1):77–121, 1985.

[11] J. A. Bergstra and C. A. Middelburg. A process algebra semantics of $\phi$SDL. Technical Report LGPS 129, Utrecht University, Department of Philisophy, 1995.

[12] S. H. J. Bos and M. A. Reniers. The $I^2C$*-bus* in discrete-time process algebra. *Science of Computer Programming*, 29(1–2):235–258, 1997.

[13] S. D. Brookes, C. A. R. Hoare, and A. W. Roscoe. A theory of communicating sequential processes. *Journal of the ACM*, 31(3):560–599, 1984.

[14] R. J. van Glabbeek and W. P. Weijland. Branching time and abstraction in bisimulation semantics. *Journal of the ACM*, 43(3):555–600, 1996.

[15] J. F. Groote. Specification and verification of real time systems in ACP. In L. Logrippo, R. L. Probert, and H. Ural, editors, *Protocol Specification, Testing and Verification*, volume 10 of *Proc. IFIP WG 6.1 Tenth International Symposium*, pages 261–274, Ottawa, 1990. North-Holland.

[16] M. Hennessy and T. Regan. A process algebra for timed systems. *Information and Computation*, 177(2): 221–239, 1995.

[17] A. S. Klusener. *Models and Axioms for a Fragment of Real Time Process Algebra*. PhD thesis, Eindhoven University of Technology, 1993.

[18] R. Milner. *A Calculus of Communicating Systems*, volume 92 of *Lecture Notes in Computer Science*. Springer-Verlag, 1980.

[19] R. Milner. *Communication and Concurrency*. International Series in Computer Science. Prentice Hall International, 1989.

[20] F. Moller and C. Tofts. A temporal calculus of communicating systems. In J. C. M. Baeten and J. W. Klop, editors, *CONCUR'90—Theories of Concurrency: Unification and Extension*, volume 458 of *Lecture Notes in Computer Science*, pages 401–415, Amsterdam, 1990. Springer-Verlag.

[21] X. Nicollin and J. Sifakis. The algebra of timed processes, ATP: Theory and application. *Information and Computation*, 114(1):131–178, 1994.

[22] G. M. Reed and A. W. Roscoe. A timed model for communicating sequential processes. *Theoretical Computer Science*, 58(1–3):249–261, 1988.

[23] M. A. Reniers and J. J. Vereijken. Completeness in discrete-time process algebra. Technical Report CSR 96/15, Eindhoven University of Technology, Department of Computing Science, 1996.

[24] C. Verhoef. A congruence theorem for structured operational semantics with predicates and negative premises. *Nordic Journal of Computing*, 2(2):274–302, 1995.

# 19 A Complete Axiom System for Finite-State Probabilistic Processes

**Eugene W. Stark and Scott A. Smolka**

## 1 Introduction

In [Mil84], Robin Milner presented a sound and complete equational axiomatization of strong bisimulation for a regular subset of CCS formed from the null process $\mathbf{0}$, process variables, action prefixing, process summation, and (possibly unguarded) recursion. He exhibited a close connection between such expressions and finite-state *charts*, bisimulation classes of which he referred to as *behaviors*.

In this paper, we extend Milner's results to a setting in which binary summations are of the form $E\ {}_p{+}\ E'$—meaning intuitively that expression $E$ is chosen with probability $p$ and expression $E'$ with probability $1 - p$—and in which probabilistic bisimulation [LS92] replaces strong bisimulation. The inference system we obtain is nearly identical to Milner's, differing only in the following two ways: axioms mentioning summation are decorated with probabilities in the appropriate way, and the unit law $E\ {}_p{+}\ \mathbf{0} = E$, which is not sound for probabilistic bisimulation, is absent.

In obtaining our complete axiomatization of probabilistic bisimulation, the following main technical contributions can be identified:

- Our operational semantics for probabilistic processes maintains a clear separation between the *transitions* a process may perform and the *probabilities* assigned to transitions. This is especially important in the presence of unguarded recursion, as can be seen by considering a process such as $P \stackrel{def}{=} \mathbf{fix}\, X \cdot (a\mathbf{0}\ {}_{1/2}{+}\ X)$. Although $P$ has only a single transition (an $a$-transition to $\mathbf{0}$), there are infinitely many ways to infer this transition. Moreover, each such inference is associated with its own unique probability $(1/2, 1/4, 1/8, \ldots)$, and the probability of $P$'s $a$-transition is the (infinite) sum of these probabilities. Our recursive definition of transition probabilities formally captures each of the preceding intuitions.
- We present a direct generalization of Milner's *transition induction* proof technique, which we use to prove soundness of many of our axioms for probabilistic bisimulation. A similar technique was used in [GSS95] to show that probabilistic bisimulation is a congruence.
- We provide a succinct characterization of the consequences of the axioms for probabilistic summation, which allows us to check the provability of probabilistic summation

EWS's research supported in part by NSF grant CCR–9320846 and AFOSR grant F49620-96-1-0087.
SAS's research supported in part by NSF grant CCR–9505562 and AFOSR grants F49620-95-1-0508 and F49620-96-1-0087.

expressions (expressions built of variables and probabilistic summation only) "by inspection." That is, we show that two probabilistic summation expressions are provably equal if and only if the versions in which the probabilities are "erased" are provable in CCS, and the total probability assigned to a summand is the same in both expressions. (More general expressions, having probabilistic summation as the top-level operator, can also be accommodated through substitution.) Using this technique, we are able to avoid much of the tedious calculation of probabilities that would otherwise be necessary in a proof "from scratch" and, in the process, obtain a completeness proof whose structure closely mimics that of the corresponding proof in [Mil84].

The axiom system we study here was proposed in [JS90], where its soundness and completeness was also announced (for the class of probabilistic agents with *rational* probabilities labeling the summation operators). However, only a proof sketch of these results was provided. Jou, in his unpublished dissertation [Jou92], gave more detailed arguments in support of the soundness and completeness results, which showed that the assumption of rational probabilities was not required. Our work on the present paper began simply as an attempt to improve the presentation of the proofs in [Jou92], which seemed overly complicated. However, close scrutiny of these proofs revealed apparent subtle circularities in the proofs of soundness for the congruence laws. We were not able to untangle these circularities and maintain the overall structure of Jou's arguments, so we were forced to look for a new way of doing these proofs. The result was our discovery of the probabilistic generalization of Milner's transition induction technique, which made the soundness proofs much simpler. The presentation of this technique is one of the main contributions of the present paper. We have also improved upon Jou's completeness proof by avoiding the explicit calculation of probabilities in the construction of a characteristic system of equations for a probabilistic expression. As a result of these innovations, though we still use a few technical lemmas from [Jou92], most of the proof presented here is new.

In other related work, complete axiomatizations of probabilistic bisimulation were given by Baeten et al. in [BBS95] in the context of the process algebra ACP [BK84] but without recursion.

The structure of the rest of the paper is as follows. Section 2 presents the syntax and structural operational semantics of probabilistic expressions. Probabilistic bisimulation is defined in Section 3. Section 4 presents our axioms for probabilistic bisimulation and proves soundness. Section 5 gives our characterization of the consequences of the probabilistic summation laws. Section 6 establishes the completeness of our axiom system. Section 7 contains some concluding remarks.

## 2 Syntax and Semantics of Probabilistic Expressions

This section presents the syntax and operational semantics of probabilistic expressions, our probabilistic extension of the class of expressions Milner considered in [Mil84]. We begin by supposing an infinite set $\mathrm{Var} = \{X_1, X_2, \ldots\}$ of *agent variables*, and a set Act of *atomic actions*.

The syntax of *probabilistic expressions* (PE for short) is defined as follows:

$$E ::= X \mid aE \mid E \;{}_p{+}\; E' \mid \mathbf{fix}\, X \cdot E \qquad (X \in \mathrm{Var}, a \in \mathrm{Act}, 0 < p < 1).$$

The notions of free and bound variables are defined in the standard way, and a variable $X$ is *guarded* in expression $E$ if every free occurrence of $X$ in $E$ is contained in a subexpression of the form $aE'$. We regard two expressions as syntactically identical if they are equal up to change of bound variables, and we use $\equiv$ to denote this relationship. We use the term *(probabilistic) agent* to refer to a PE expression with no free variables. PA is the class of agents, with $P$ and $Q$ ranging over PA. We use $\mathbf{0}$ as an abbreviation for the agent $\mathbf{fix}\, X \cdot X$. In the sequel, if $p \in [0, 1]$, then $\overline{p}$ is used as an abbreviation for $1 - p$.

To define the operational semantics of PA, we first define, using standard structural operational semantics rules, the *transitions* of agents. These are given by the following axiom and inference rules:

$$aP \xrightarrow{a} P$$

$$\frac{P_1 \xrightarrow{a} Q}{P_1 \;{}_p{+}\; P_2 \xrightarrow{a} Q} \qquad \frac{P_2 \xrightarrow{a} Q}{P_1 \;{}_p{+}\; P_2 \xrightarrow{a} Q}$$

$$\frac{E\{\mathbf{fix}\, X \cdot E/X\} \xrightarrow{a} Q}{\mathbf{fix}\, X \cdot E \xrightarrow{a} Q}$$

where only $X$ is free in $E$.

Except for the probabilities decorating the $+$ signs, these are the same as Milner's rules for regular CCS agents.

We incorporate probability into the operational semantics by associating, with each triple $(P, a, Q)$ consisting of agents $P$ and $Q$ and action $a$, a *transition probability* $\mu(P, a, Q) \in [0, 1]$. That is, $\mu : \mathrm{PA} \times \mathrm{Act} \times \mathrm{PA} \to [0, 1]$. As a more suggestive notation, we shall write $\mu(P \xrightarrow{a} Q)$ instead of $\mu(P, a, Q)$. The function $\mu$ is defined to be the least fixed point of the recursive equation:

$$\mu = \mathcal{P}(\mu),$$

where $\mathcal{P}$ is defined as follows:

$$\mathcal{P}(\mu)(aP \xrightarrow{b} Q) = \begin{cases} 1, & \text{if } b = a \text{ and } P \equiv Q \\ 0, & \text{otherwise} \end{cases}$$

$$\mathcal{P}(\mu)(P_1 \ {}_p\!+ \ P_2 \xrightarrow{a} Q) = p \cdot \mu(P_1 \xrightarrow{a} Q) + \overline{p} \cdot \mu(P_2 \xrightarrow{a} Q)$$

$$\mathcal{P}(\mu)(\mathbf{fix}\, X \cdot E \xrightarrow{a} Q) = \mu(E\{\mathbf{fix}\, X \cdot E/X\} \xrightarrow{a} Q)$$

where, again, only $X$ is free in $E$.

It is easily verified that the interval [0, 1] is a CPO under the usual ordering on the real numbers. This ordering induces a pointwise ordering on the set of all functions $\mu$ taking triples $(P, a, Q)$ to [0, 1], so that this set also is a CPO. Moreover, the mapping $\mathcal{P}$ is a continuous mapping from this CPO to itself, so that the claimed least fixed point actually exists. Let $\mu^0$ be the identically zero function, and for $i \geq 0$ define $\mu^{i+1} = \mathcal{P}(\mu^i)$. We then have the usual characterization: $\mu = \sup_{i \geq 0} \mu^i$.

To illustrate the operational semantics of PA agents, consider once again the agent $P \stackrel{def}{=} \mathbf{fix}\, X \cdot (a\mathbf{0} \ {}_{1/2}\!+ \ X)$. As discussed in the Introduction, $P$ has a single inferable transition $P \xrightarrow{a} \mathbf{0}$, and there are infinitely many ways to infer it. By definition of $\mu$, the $(n+1)$st approximation of $\mu(t)$ is given by:

$$\begin{aligned}
\mu^{n+1}(\mathbf{fix}\, X \cdot (a\mathbf{0} \ {}_{1/2}\!+ \ X) \xrightarrow{a} \mathbf{0}) &= \mathcal{P}(\mu^n)(\mathbf{fix}\, X \cdot (a\mathbf{0} \ {}_{1/2}\!+ \ X) \xrightarrow{a} \mathbf{0}) \\
&= \mu^n(a\mathbf{0} \ {}_{1/2}\!+ \ \mathbf{fix}\, X \cdot (a\mathbf{0} \ {}_{1/2}\!+ \ X) \xrightarrow{a} \mathbf{0}) \\
&= \mathcal{P}(\mu^{n-1})(a\mathbf{0} \ {}_{1/2}\!+ \ \mathbf{fix}\, X \cdot (a\mathbf{0} \ {}_{1/2}\!+ \ X) \xrightarrow{a} \mathbf{0}) \\
&= 1/2 \cdot \mu^{n-1}(a\mathbf{0} \xrightarrow{a} \mathbf{0}) \\
&\quad + 1/2 \cdot \mu^{n-1}(\mathbf{fix}\, X \cdot (a\mathbf{0} \ {}_{1/2}\!+ \ X) \xrightarrow{a} \mathbf{0}) \\
&= 1/2 \cdot 1 + 1/2 \cdot \mathcal{P}(\mu^{n-2})(\mathbf{fix}\, X \cdot (a\mathbf{0} \ {}_{1/2}\!+ \ X) \xrightarrow{a} \mathbf{0}) \\
&\ \vdots \\
&= 1/2 + 1/4 + \cdots + 1/2^k \\
&\quad + 1/2 \cdot \mathcal{P}(\mu^{n-2k})(\mathbf{fix}\, X \cdot (a\mathbf{0} \ {}_{1/2}\!+ \ X) \xrightarrow{a} \mathbf{0})
\end{aligned}$$

if $n \geq 2k$. Thus, $\mu(t)$, the probability of $t$, is the infinite sum $1/2 + 1/4 + 1/8 + \cdots$, whose value is 1.

LEMMA 2.1 $\mu(P \xrightarrow{a} Q) > 0$ if and only if the transition $P \xrightarrow{a} Q$ is inferable from the SOS rules.

*Proof* A straightforward induction on $i$ establishes that $\mu^i(P \xrightarrow{a} Q) > 0$ if and only if transition $P \xrightarrow{a} Q$ is inferable from the SOS rules by a proof tree of depth at most $i$. Then, since every transition is inferable by a finite proof, it follows immediately that if $P \xrightarrow{a} Q$ is inferable then $\mu(P \xrightarrow{a} Q) > 0$. Conversely, if $\mu(P \xrightarrow{a} Q) > 0$, then since $\mu = \sup_{i \geq 0} \mu^i$, we must have $\mu^i(P \xrightarrow{a} Q) > 0$ for some $i \geq 0$, from which it follows that $P \xrightarrow{a} Q$ is inferable from the SOS rules by a proof tree of depth at most $i$. □

The next result shows that probabilistic agents $P$ are "sub-stochastic," in the sense that the total probability assigned to all transitions of $P$ is less than or equal to one. If the total probability is a value $p$ strictly less than one, then we regard the value $1 - p$ as a deadlock or stopping probability.

PROPOSITION 2.2 For any agent $P$ and $a \in \text{Act}$,

$$\sum_{Q \in \text{PA}} \mu(P \xrightarrow{a} Q) \leq 1.$$

*Proof* We claim that for all agents $P$ and all $i \geq 0$,

$$\sum_{Q \in \text{PA}} \mu^i(P \xrightarrow{a} Q) \leq 1.$$

The result then follows from the claim. For

$$\begin{aligned}
\sum_{P \in \text{PA}} \mu(P \xrightarrow{a} Q) &= \sup_{S \in \mathcal{F}(\text{PA})} \sum_{Q \in S} \sup_{i \geq 0} \mu^i(P \xrightarrow{a} Q) \\
&= \sup_{S \in \mathcal{F}(\text{PA})} \sup_{i \geq 0} \sum_{Q \in S} \mu^i(P \xrightarrow{a} Q) \\
&= \sup_{i \geq 0} \sup_{S \in \mathcal{F}(\text{PA})} \sum_{Q \in S} \mu^i(P \xrightarrow{a} Q) \\
&= \sup_{i \geq 0} \sum_{Q \in \text{PA}} \mu^i(P \xrightarrow{a} Q) \\
&\leq 1,
\end{aligned}$$

where $\mathcal{F}(\text{PA})$ denotes the collection of all finite sets of PA agents.

The proof of the claim is by induction on $i$, and it can be regarded as a variant of Milner's transition induction technique. We will be using this technique repeatedly throughout the paper.

1. In case $i = 0$, the result is trivial.

2. Suppose we have shown the result for some $i \geq 0$, and consider the case of $i + 1$. We consider the possible syntactic forms of $P$.

- If $P$ has the form $a\,Q$, then the only transition that can be inferred for $P$ is the transition $P \xrightarrow{a} Q$, and in this case $\mu^{i+1}(P \xrightarrow{a} Q) = 1$ by definition of $\mu$. Note that by Lemma 2.1, $\mu(P, a, Q') = 0$ for all $Q' \not\equiv Q$, since there is no inferable transition $P \xrightarrow{a} Q'$.
- If $P \equiv P_1\ {}_p{+}\ P_2$, then

$$\begin{aligned}\sum_{Q \in \mathrm{PA}} \mu^{i+1}(P \xrightarrow{a} Q) &= \sum_{Q \in \mathrm{PA}} p \cdot \mu^i(P_1 \xrightarrow{a} Q) + \bar{p} \cdot \mu^i(P_2 \xrightarrow{a} Q) \\ &= p \cdot \sum_{Q \in \mathrm{PA}} \mu^i(P_1 \xrightarrow{a} Q) + \bar{p} \cdot \sum_{Q \in \mathrm{PA}} \mu^i(P_2 \xrightarrow{a} Q) \\ &\leq p + \bar{p} \\ &= 1,\end{aligned}$$

where the induction hypothesis was used to obtain the inequality in the third line.

- Suppose $P \equiv \mathbf{fix}\, X \cdot E$. Then

$$\sum_{Q \in \mathrm{PA}} \mu^{i+1}(P \xrightarrow{a} Q) = \sum_{Q \in \mathrm{PA}} \mu^i(E\{P/X\} \xrightarrow{a} Q),$$

which is $\leq 1$ by induction hypothesis. □

In view of the previous result, for any set $\mathcal{S}$ of PA agents and any action $a$, the summation

$$\sum_{Q \in \mathcal{S}} \mu(P \xrightarrow{a} Q)$$

converges to a value $\leq 1$. We use the notation $\mu(P \xrightarrow{a} \mathcal{S})$ to denote this value.

## 3 Probabilistic Bisimulation

In this section, we define probabilistic bisimulation, Larsen and Skou's [LS92] probabilistic extension of strong bisimulation. We will subsequently completely axiomatize probabilistic bisimulation equivalence for probabilistic expressions.

A (strong) *bisimulation* is a binary relation $\mathcal{R}$ on agents that satisfies the following conditions:

1. Whenever $P\ \mathcal{R}\ P'$ and $P \xrightarrow{a} Q$, then there exists a transition $P' \xrightarrow{a} Q'$, such that $Q\ \mathcal{R}\ Q'$.
2. Whenever $P\ \mathcal{R}\ P'$ and $P' \xrightarrow{a} Q'$, then there exists a transition $P \xrightarrow{a} Q$, such that $Q\ \mathcal{R}\ Q'$.

A *probabilistic bisimulation* is an equivalence relation $\mathcal{R}$ on agents that satisfies the following condition:

- Whenever $P \mathcal{R} P'$, then for all actions $a$ and all equivalence classes $\mathcal{S}$ of $\mathcal{R}$ we have

$\mu(P \xrightarrow{a} \mathcal{S}) = \mu(P' \xrightarrow{a} \mathcal{S})$.

We call agents $P$ and $P'$ *bisimilar*, written $P \sim P'$, if there exists a bisimulation that relates them. Likewise, agents $P$ and $P'$ are *probabilistically bisimilar*, written $P \stackrel{\text{pr}}{\sim} P'$ if there exists a probabilistic bisimulation that relates them. We assume familiarity with the standard results about bisimulation and probabilistic bisimulation; in particular that bisimilarity is an equivalence relation which is the largest bisimulation, and that probabilistic bisimilarity is the largest probabilistic bisimulation.

Bisimilarity and probabilistic bisimilarity are extended to the relations *bisimulation equivalence* and *probabilistic bisimulation equivalence* on all PE expressions as follows:

- Let $E$ and $F$ be expressions whose free variables are contained in the set $\widetilde{X}$, and let $\# \in \{\sim, \stackrel{\text{pr}}{\sim}\}$. Then $E \# F$ if for all sets of agents $\widetilde{P}$, $E\{\widetilde{P}/\widetilde{X}\} \# F\{\widetilde{P}/\widetilde{X}\}$.

Unlike a bisimulation, a probabilistic bisimulation is required to be an equivalence relation on agents. Intuitively, the effect of this requirement is to ensure that agents $P$ and $Q$ are not distinguished from each other solely because $P$ and $Q$ have different sets of individual transitions to a set $\mathcal{S}$ of probabilistically indistinguishable agents. Rather, only the *total* probability of the sets of transitions from $P$ to $\mathcal{S}$ and from $Q$ to $\mathcal{S}$ should be used as a basis for distinguishing between $P$ and $Q$. Adopting this convention permits the identification of agents like $(a(b\mathbf{0}\ {}_{3/4}{+}\ c\mathbf{0})\ {}_{1/2}{+}\ a(c\mathbf{0}\ {}_{1/4}{+}\ b\mathbf{0}))\ {}_{2/3}{+}\ d\mathbf{0}$ and $a(b\mathbf{0}\ {}_{3/4}{+}\ c\mathbf{0})\ {}_{2/3}{+}\ d\mathbf{0}$, which would otherwise be distinguished unnecessarily. The next proposition shows that certain bisimulations are also definable starting from equivalence relations.

PROPOSITION 3.1 An equivalence relation $\mathcal{R}$ on agents is a bisimulation if and only if whenever $P \mathcal{R} P'$, then for all actions $a$ and all equivalence classes $\mathcal{S}$ of $\mathcal{R}$ we have

$P \xrightarrow{a} \mathcal{S}$ if and only if $P' \xrightarrow{a} \mathcal{S}$,

where by $P \xrightarrow{a} \mathcal{S}$ we mean that $P \xrightarrow{a} Q$ is inferable for some $Q \in \mathcal{S}$ (and similarly for $P' \xrightarrow{a} \mathcal{S}$).

*Proof* Straightforward from the definition of bisimulation. □

PROPOSITION 3.2 Suppose relation $\mathcal{R}$ is a probabilistic bisimulation. Then $\mathcal{R}$ is also a bisimulation. Thus, if $E \stackrel{\text{pr}}{\sim} F$ then $E \sim F$.

*Proof* Straightforward using Lemma 2.1 and Proposition 3.1. □

COROLLARY 3.3 If $E \overset{\text{pr}}{\sim} F$, then $E$ and $F$ have the same sets of free variables, and a free variable $X$ occurs guarded (unguarded) in $E$ if and only if it occurs guarded (unguarded) in $F$.

*Proof* If $E$ and $F$ are probabilistically equivalent, then they are bisimulation equivalent, and the stated properties hold for bisimulation equivalence. □

The following lemma about probabilistic bisimulation, which appeared originally in [Jou92], will be important for us:

LEMMA 3.4 Suppose $\mathcal{P}$ is a probabilistic bisimulation, and $\mathcal{R}$ is an arbitrary equivalence relation that contains $\mathcal{P}$. Then for all pairs of agents $(P, P') \in \mathcal{P}$, all actions $a$, and all equivalence classes $\mathcal{S}$ of $\mathcal{R}$:

$$\mu(P \xrightarrow{a} \mathcal{S}) = \mu(P' \xrightarrow{a} \mathcal{S}).$$

*Proof* The fact that $\mathcal{P}$ is a probabilistic bisimulation implies that

$$\mu(P \xrightarrow{a} \mathcal{S}') = \mu(P' \xrightarrow{a} \mathcal{S}')$$

whenever $(P, P') \in \mathcal{P}$ and $\mathcal{S}'$ is an equivalence class of $\mathcal{P}$. Since $\mathcal{R}$ is an equivalence relation that contains $\mathcal{P}$, every equivalence class $\mathcal{S}$ of $\mathcal{R}$ is a union of a pairwise disjoint collection of equivalence classes of $\mathcal{P}$. Thus,

$$\begin{aligned}\mu(P \xrightarrow{a} \mathcal{S}) &= \sum_{\mathcal{S}' \subseteq \mathcal{S}} \mu(P \xrightarrow{a} \mathcal{S}') \\ &= \sum_{\mathcal{S}' \subseteq \mathcal{S}} \mu(P' \xrightarrow{a} \mathcal{S}') \\ &= \mu(P' \xrightarrow{a} \mathcal{S}).\end{aligned}$$

□

Following [Jou92], we now give a probabilistic version of Milner's technique of "bisimulation up to bisimulation equivalence." This technique will be useful in proving the soundness of laws for recursion.

Formally, if $\mathcal{R}$ is an equivalence relation, then define $\overline{\mathcal{R}} = (\overset{\text{pr}}{\sim} \mathcal{R} \overset{\text{pr}}{\sim})^*$. The relation $\mathcal{R}$ is called a *probabilistic bisimulation up to* $\overset{\text{pr}}{\sim}$ if whenever $P \; \mathcal{R} \; P'$, then for all actions $a$ and all equivalence classes $\mathcal{S}$ of $\overline{\mathcal{R}}$ we have $\mu(P \xrightarrow{a} \mathcal{S}) = \mu(P' \xrightarrow{a} \mathcal{S})$.

LEMMA 3.5 If $\mathcal{R}$ is a probabilistic bisimulation up to $\overset{\text{pr}}{\sim}$, then $\overline{\mathcal{R}}$ is a probabilistic bisimulation. Moreover, $\mathcal{R} \subseteq \overset{\text{pr}}{\sim}$ and $\overline{\mathcal{R}}$ is $\overset{\text{pr}}{\sim}$.

*Proof* We have to show that whenever $P \; \overline{\mathcal{R}} \; P'$, then for all actions $a$ and all equivalence classes $\mathcal{S}$ of $\overline{\mathcal{R}}$ we have $\mu(P \xrightarrow{a} \mathcal{S}) = \mu(P' \xrightarrow{a} \mathcal{S})$. Now, $P \; \overline{\mathcal{R}} \; P'$ precisely when there exists a finite sequence of agents $P_0, P_1, \ldots, P_n$, with $P \equiv P_0$, $P_n \equiv P'$, and such that for all $i$ with $0 \leq i < n$ we have either $P_i \overset{\text{pr}}{\sim} P_{i+1}$ or else $P_i \; \mathcal{R} \; P_{i+1}$. But then $\mu(P_i \xrightarrow{a} \mathcal{S}) =$

$\mu(P'_{i+1} \xrightarrow{a} \mathcal{S})$ for all $i \geq 0$, because if $P_i \overset{\text{pr}}{\sim} P_{i+1}$ it follows from Lemma 3.4 using the definition of probabilistic bisimulation, and if $P_i \mathrel{\mathcal{R}} P_{i+1}$ it follows by hypothesis.

To prove the additional assertions, observe that $\overline{\mathcal{R}} \subseteq \overset{\text{pr}}{\sim}$ because $\overset{\text{pr}}{\sim}$ is the largest probabilistic bisimulation, and $\overset{\text{pr}}{\sim} \subseteq \overline{\mathcal{R}}$ by construction, so that $\overline{\mathcal{R}}$ is $\overset{\text{pr}}{\sim}$. It follows immediately that $\mathcal{R} \subseteq \overset{\text{pr}}{\sim}$. □

## 4 Axioms for Probabilistic Bisimulation Equivalence

In this section, we present our axiom system for probabilistic bisimulation equivalence and prove soundness. We will later show that our axioms constitute a complete equational axiomatization of probabilistic bisimulation equivalence; that is, the equation $E = F$ is deducible from the axiom system if and only if $E$ and $F$ are probabilistically bisimulation equivalent.

We consider the following axioms and rules for inferring assertions of the form $E = F$, where $E$ and $F$ are expressions:

**(E1)** $E = E$.

**(E2)** From $E = F$, infer $F = E$.

**(E3)** From $E = F$ and $F = G$, infer $E = G$.

**(C1a)** From $F = F'$ infer $F\{\widetilde{E}/\widetilde{X}\} = F'\{\widetilde{E}/\widetilde{X}\}$.

**(C1b)** From $\widetilde{E} = \widetilde{E}'$ infer $F\{\widetilde{E}/\widetilde{X}\} = F\{\widetilde{E}'/\widetilde{X}\}$.

**(C2)** From $E = E'$, infer $\textbf{fix}\, X \cdot E = \textbf{fix}\, X \cdot E'$.

**(S1)** $E\ {}_{p}{+}\ F = F\ {}_{\overline{p}}{+}\ E$.

**(S2)** $E\ {}_{p}{+}\ (F\ {}_{q}{+}\ G) = (E\ {}_{r}{+}\ F)\ {}_{s}{+}\ G$, whenever $p = rs$, $\overline{p}q = \overline{r}s$, and $\overline{s} = \overline{p}\,\overline{q}$.

**(S3)** $E\ {}_{p}{+}\ E = E$.

**(R1)** $\textbf{fix}\, X \cdot E = E\{\textbf{fix}\, X \cdot E/X\}$.

**(R2)** $\textbf{fix}\, X \cdot E\ {}_{p}{+}\ X = \textbf{fix}\, X \cdot E$.

**(R3)** From $E = F\{E/X\}$, where all occurrences of $X$ in $F$ are guarded, infer $E = \textbf{fix}\, X \cdot F$.

We write $\vdash E = F$ to assert that an equation $E = F$ is formally provable from the above axioms and rules.

Our goal is to show that the above axioms and inference rules are sound and complete for probabilistic bisimulation equivalence. In the remainder of this section, we consider soundness.

PROPOSITION 4.1 The following are sound for probabilistic bisimulation equivalence.

1. Laws (E1)–(E3).
2. Laws (S1)–(S3).
3. Law (C1a).

*Proof* 1. Obvious from the fact that probabilistic bisimulation equivalence is an equivalence relation.

2. The obvious construction of a probabilistic bisimulation works in each case to establish these laws in the special case that the left and right-hand sides are agents. A straightforward argument using the special case and the definition of probabilistic bisimulation equivalence on expressions with free variables extends the result to all expressions.

3. An immediate consequence of the definition of probabilistic bisimulation equivalence on expressions with free variables. □

PROPOSITION 4.2 Law (R1) is sound for probabilistic bisimulation equivalence.

*Proof* Consider the least equivalence relation $\mathcal{R}$ containing all pairs either of the form $(\mathbf{fix}\,X \cdot E, E\{\mathbf{fix}\,X \cdot E/X\})$ or of the form $(E\{\mathbf{fix}\,X \cdot E/X\}, \mathbf{fix}\,X \cdot E)$. By the definition of the operational semantics, a transition $\mathbf{fix}\,X \cdot E \xrightarrow{a} Q$ is inferable if and only if the transition $E\{\mathbf{fix}\,X \cdot E/X\} \xrightarrow{a} Q$ is inferable. Thus, applying Lemma 2.1, we have that

$$\mu(\mathbf{fix}\,X \cdot E \xrightarrow{a} Q) = 0 \text{ iff } \mu(E\{\mathbf{fix}\,X \cdot E/X\} \xrightarrow{a} Q) = 0,$$

Moreover, if $\mu(\mathbf{fix}\,X \cdot E \xrightarrow{a} Q) \neq 0$, then the fixed-point property of $\mu$ guarantees that the (inferable) transition $\mathbf{fix}\,X \cdot E \xrightarrow{a} Q$ is assigned the same probability as the corresponding (inferable) transition $E\{\mathbf{fix}\,X \cdot E/X\} \xrightarrow{a} Q$. From this, it is easily verified that the relation $\mathcal{R}$ is a probabilistic bisimulation. □

Our soundness proofs make use of the following technical substitution lemma, which is a variant of [Mil84], Lemma 5.6.

LEMMA 4.3 Suppose $G$ is an expression with free variables in $\langle \widetilde{X}, Z\rangle$, where $Z$ is not among the variables $\widetilde{X}$. Suppose $\widetilde{E}$ are expressions in which the variable $Z$ does not occur free. Then

$$G\{F/Z\}\{\widetilde{E}/\widetilde{X}\} \equiv G\{\widetilde{E}/\widetilde{X}\}\{F\{\widetilde{E}/\widetilde{X}\}/Z\}.$$

*Proof* By structural induction on $G$. □

In the next and subsequent results, we shall often have occasion to refer to a particular class of equivalence relations, for which some notation is convenient. If $\widetilde{E}$ and $\widetilde{F}$ are sets of expressions, and $\widetilde{X}$ is a set of variables, then define $\Omega(\widetilde{E}, \widetilde{F}, \widetilde{X})$ to be the reflexive, symmetric closure of the set of all pairs of expressions of the form $(G\{\widetilde{E}/\widetilde{X}\}, G\{\widetilde{F}/\widetilde{X}\})$, where $G$ is an expression with no free variables other than $\widetilde{X}$. Clearly, $\Omega(\widetilde{E}, \widetilde{F}, \widetilde{X})$ is an equivalence relation. We will use the notation $\Omega(E, F, X)$ when $\widetilde{E}$, $\widetilde{F}$, and $\widetilde{X}$ are singleton sets. Note that, in this case, taking $G$ to be $X$ shows that $\Omega(E, F, X)$ contains the pair $(E, F)$.

PROPOSITION 4.4 Law (C1b) is sound for probabilistic bisimulation equivalence.

*Proof* It suffices to prove the case in which the expressions $\widetilde{E}$ and $\widetilde{E}'$ are agents, and $F$ has no free variables other than $\widetilde{X}$. The general case follows easily from this special case, using the definition of probabilistic bisimulation equivalence for expressions with free variables.

To prove the special case, we show that the relation $\mathcal{R} = \Omega(\widetilde{E}, \widetilde{E}', \widetilde{X})$ is a probabilistic bisimulation up to $\overset{\text{pr}}{\sim}$. For this, it suffices to show that for all equivalence classes $\mathcal{S}$ of $\overline{\mathcal{R}}$, all actions $a$, and all expressions $G$ with no free variables other than $\widetilde{X}$, we have

$$\mu(G\{\widetilde{E}/\widetilde{X}\} \xrightarrow{a} \mathcal{S}) = \mu(G\{\widetilde{E}'/\widetilde{X}\} \xrightarrow{a} \mathcal{S})$$

We actually prove the following two assertions, whose conjunction implies the desired result:

1. For all $i \geq 0$, for all expressions $G$ with no free variables other than $\widetilde{X}$, for all equivalence classes $\mathcal{S}$ of $\overline{\mathcal{R}}$, and all actions $a$, we have
$$\mu^i(G\{\widetilde{E}/\widetilde{X}\} \xrightarrow{a} \mathcal{S}) \leq \mu(G\{\widetilde{E}'/\widetilde{X}\} \xrightarrow{a} \mathcal{S}).$$

2. The same statement with $\widetilde{E}$ and $\widetilde{E}'$ interchanged.

We consider only (1), as the proof of (2) is symmetric. We proceed by induction on $i$.

1. If $i = 0$, then we immediately have
$$\mu^i(G\{\widetilde{E}/\widetilde{X}\} \xrightarrow{a} \mathcal{S}) = 0 \leq \mu(G\{\widetilde{E}'/\widetilde{X}\} \xrightarrow{a} \mathcal{S}).$$

2. Suppose the result has been shown for some $i \geq 0$, and consider the case of $i + 1$. We consider the syntactic form of $G$:

- If $G$ is the variable $X_i$ in $\widetilde{X}$, then $G\{\widetilde{E}/\widetilde{X}\} = E_i$ and $G\{\widetilde{E}'/\widetilde{X}\} = E_i'$. Since by hypothesis $E_i$ and $E_i'$ are probabilistically equivalent, we have:

$$\begin{aligned}
\mu^{i+1}(G\{\widetilde{E}/\widetilde{X}\} \xrightarrow{a} \mathcal{S}') &= \mu^{i+1}(E_i \xrightarrow{a} \mathcal{S}) \\
&\leq \mu(E_i \xrightarrow{a} \mathcal{S}) \\
&= \mu(E_i' \xrightarrow{a} \mathcal{S}) \\
&= \mu(G\{\widetilde{E}'/\widetilde{X}\} \xrightarrow{a} \mathcal{S}),
\end{aligned}$$

where we have used Lemma 3.4 in replacing $E_i$ by $E_i'$.

• Suppose $G$ is $bG'$. Then $G\{\widetilde{E}/\widetilde{X}\}$ is $bG'\{\widetilde{E}/\widetilde{X}\}$ and $G\{\widetilde{E}'/\widetilde{X}\}$ is $bG'\{\widetilde{E}'/\widetilde{X}\}$. If $b \neq a$, then

$$\mu^{i+1}(G\{\widetilde{E}/\widetilde{X}\} \xrightarrow{a} \mathcal{S}) = 0 = \mu(G\{\widetilde{E}'/\widetilde{X}\} \xrightarrow{a} \mathcal{S}).$$

Suppose $b = a$. Then $G\{\widetilde{E}/\widetilde{X}\} \xrightarrow{b} H$ if and only if $H \equiv G'\{\widetilde{E}/\widetilde{X}\}$, and $G\{\widetilde{E}'/\widetilde{X}\} \xrightarrow{b} H$ if and only if $H \equiv G'\{\widetilde{E}'/\widetilde{X}\}$. By definition of $\overline{\mathcal{R}}$, either both $G'\{\widetilde{E}/\widetilde{X}\}$ and $G'\{\widetilde{E}'/\widetilde{X}\}$ are in $\mathcal{S}$ or both are not in $\mathcal{S}$. In the first case,

$$\mu^{i+1}(G\{\widetilde{E}/\widetilde{X}\} \xrightarrow{a} \mathcal{S}) = 1 = \mu(G\{\widetilde{E}'/\widetilde{X}\} \xrightarrow{a} \mathcal{S}),$$

and in the second case,

$$\mu^{i+1}(G\{\widetilde{E}/\widetilde{X}\} \xrightarrow{a} \mathcal{S}) = 0 = \mu(G\{\widetilde{E}'/\widetilde{X}\} \xrightarrow{a} \mathcal{S}).$$

• Suppose $G$ is $G_1 \;_p\!+ G_2$. Then $G\{\widetilde{E}/\widetilde{X}\}$ is $G_1\{\widetilde{E}/\widetilde{X}\} \;_p\!+ G_2\{\widetilde{E}/\widetilde{X}\}$ and $G\{\widetilde{E}'/\widetilde{X}\}$ is $G_1\{\widetilde{E}'/\widetilde{X}\} \;_p\!+ G_2\{\widetilde{E}'/\widetilde{X}\}$. Then

$$\mu^{i+1}(G\{\widetilde{E}/\widetilde{X}\} \xrightarrow{a} \mathcal{S}) = p \cdot \mu^i(G_1\{\widetilde{E}/\widetilde{X}\} \xrightarrow{a} \mathcal{S}) + \overline{p} \cdot \mu^i(G_2\{\widetilde{E}/\widetilde{X}\} \xrightarrow{a} \mathcal{S}),$$

and by the fixed-point property of $\mu$:

$$\mu(G\{\widetilde{E}'/\widetilde{X}\} \xrightarrow{a} \mathcal{S}) = p \cdot \mu(G_1\{\widetilde{E}'/\widetilde{X}\} \xrightarrow{a} \mathcal{S}) + \overline{p} \cdot \mu(G_2\{\widetilde{E}'/\widetilde{X}\} \xrightarrow{a} \mathcal{S}).$$

By induction,

$$\mu^i(G_1\{\widetilde{E}/\widetilde{X}\} \xrightarrow{a} \mathcal{S}) \leq \mu(G_1\{\widetilde{E}'/\widetilde{X}\} \xrightarrow{a} \mathcal{S}),$$

and similarly

$$\mu^i(G_2\{\widetilde{E}/\widetilde{X}\} \xrightarrow{a} \mathcal{S}) \leq \mu(G_2\{\widetilde{E}'/\widetilde{X}\} \xrightarrow{a} \mathcal{S}),$$

from which the result follows.

• Suppose $G$ is $\mathbf{fix}\, Z \cdot G'$. Then $G\{\widetilde{E}/\widetilde{X}\}$ is $\mathbf{fix}\, Z \cdot (G'\{\widetilde{E}/\widetilde{X}\})$ and $G\{\widetilde{E}'/\widetilde{X}\}$ is $\mathbf{fix}\, Z \cdot (G'\{\widetilde{E}'/\widetilde{X}\})$, because $\widetilde{E}$ and $\widetilde{E}'$ are agents. Then

$$\begin{aligned}\mu^{i+1}(G\{\widetilde{E}/\widetilde{X}\} \xrightarrow{a} \mathcal{S}) &= \mu^i(G'\{\widetilde{E}/\widetilde{X}\}\{G\{\widetilde{E}/\widetilde{X}\}/Z\} \xrightarrow{a} \mathcal{S}) \\ &= \mu^i(G'\{G/Z\}\{\widetilde{E}/\widetilde{X}\} \xrightarrow{a} \mathcal{S}),\end{aligned}$$

and by the fixed-point property of $\mu$:

$$\begin{aligned}\mu(G\{\widetilde{E}'/\widetilde{X}\} \xrightarrow{a} \mathcal{S}) &= \mu(G'\{\widetilde{E}'/\widetilde{X}\}\{G\{\widetilde{E}'/\widetilde{X}\}/Z\} \xrightarrow{a} \mathcal{S}) \\ &= \mu(G'\{G/Z\}\{\widetilde{E}'/\widetilde{X}\} \xrightarrow{a} \mathcal{S}),\end{aligned}$$

where we have used Lemma 4.3 in each case. By induction

$$\mu^i(G'\{G/Z\}\{\widetilde{E}/\widetilde{X}\} \stackrel{a}{\longrightarrow} \mathcal{S}) \leq \mu(G'\{G/Z\}\{\widetilde{E}'/\widetilde{X}\} \stackrel{a}{\longrightarrow} \mathcal{S}),$$

from which the result follows. □

PROPOSITION 4.5 Law (C2) is sound for probabilistic bisimulation equivalence.

*Proof* It suffices to establish the result for the special case in which $E$ and $E'$ have no free variables other than $X$, as the general case follows easily from the special case using properties of substitution.

Suppose $E$ and $E'$ are probabilistically equivalent. We claim that the relation $\mathcal{R} = \Omega(\mathbf{fix}\, X \cdot E, \mathbf{fix}\, X \cdot E', X)$ is a probabilistic bisimulation up to $\stackrel{\text{pr}}{\sim}$. To prove this, it suffices to show that for all expressions $G$ with no free variables other than $X$, all actions $a$, and all equivalence classes $\mathcal{S}$ of $(\stackrel{\text{pr}}{\sim} \mathcal{R} \stackrel{\text{pr}}{\sim})^*$ we have:

$$\mu(G\{\mathbf{fix}\, X \cdot E/X\} \stackrel{a}{\longrightarrow} \mathcal{S}) = \mu(G\{\mathbf{fix}\, X \cdot E'/X\} \stackrel{a}{\longrightarrow} \mathcal{S}).$$

As in the proof of Proposition 4.4, we prove a stronger result consisting of the conjunction of the following two properties:

1. For all $i \geq 0$, all expressions $G$ with no free variables other than $X$, all actions $a$, and all equivalence classes $\mathcal{S}$ of $(\stackrel{\text{pr}}{\sim} \mathcal{R} \stackrel{\text{pr}}{\sim})^*$ we have:

$$\mu^i(G\{\mathbf{fix}\, X \cdot E/X\} \stackrel{a}{\longrightarrow} \mathcal{S}) \leq \mu(G\{\mathbf{fix}\, X \cdot E'/X\} \stackrel{a}{\longrightarrow} \mathcal{S}).$$

2. The same statement with $E$ and $E'$ interchanged.

The proof proceeds in a fashion similar to that of Proposition 4.4. The case in which $G$ is the variable $X$ requires an application of (C1a) and Lemma 3.4. The case in which $G$ is $\mathbf{fix}\, Z \cdot G'$ uses Lemma 4.3. We omit the details. □

PROPOSITION 4.6 Law (R2) is sound for probabilistic bisimulation equivalence.

*Proof* It suffices to establish the result for the special case in which $E$ and $E'$ have no free variables other than $X$, as the general case follows easily from the special case using properties of substitution.

Suppose $E$ and $E'$ are probabilistically equivalent. We claim that the relation $\mathcal{R} = \Omega(\mathbf{fix}\, X \cdot E\ {}_p{+}\ X, \mathbf{fix}\, X \cdot E, X)$ is a probabilistic bisimulation. To prove this, it suffices to show that for all expressions $G$ with no free variables other than $X$, all actions $a$, and all equivalence classes $\mathcal{S}$ of $\mathcal{R}$ we have:

$$\mu(G\{\mathbf{fix}\, X \cdot E\ {}_p{+}\ X/X\} \stackrel{a}{\longrightarrow} \mathcal{S}) = \mu(G\{\mathbf{fix}\, X \cdot E/X\} \stackrel{a}{\longrightarrow} \mathcal{S}).$$

As in the previous soundness proofs, we prove a stronger result consisting of the conjunction of the following two properties:

1. For all $i \geq 0$, all expressions $G$ with no free variables other than $X$, all actions $a$, and all equivalence classes $\mathcal{S}$ of $\mathcal{R}$ we have:

$$\mu^i(G\{\mathbf{fix}\, X \cdot E \;{}_p{+}\; X/X\} \xrightarrow{a} \mathcal{S}) \leq \mu(G\{\mathbf{fix}\, X \cdot E/X\} \xrightarrow{a} \mathcal{S}).$$

2. The same statement with $\mathbf{fix}\, X \cdot E \;{}_p{+}\; X$ and $\mathbf{fix}\, X \cdot E$ interchanged.

Since the statements to be proved are not symmetric as in the previous cases, we consider both (1) and (2). As usual, both are proved by induction on $i$.

We first consider (1):

1. If $i = 0$, then

$$\mu^i(G\{\mathbf{fix}\, X \cdot E \;{}_p{+}\; X/X\} \xrightarrow{a} \mathcal{S}) = 0 \leq \mu(G\{\mathbf{fix}\, X \cdot E/X\} \xrightarrow{a} \mathcal{S}),$$

and the result is immediate.

2. Suppose we have shown the result for some $i \geq 0$, and consider the case of $i+1$. Again, the only interesting cases are when $G$ is the variable $X$ and when $G$ is $\mathbf{fix}\, Z \cdot G'$.

- If $G$ is the variable $X$, then $G\{\mathbf{fix}\, X \cdot E \;{}_p{+}\; X/X\} = \mathbf{fix}\, X \cdot E \;{}_p{+}\; X$ and $G\{\mathbf{fix}\, X \cdot E/X\} = \mathbf{fix}\, X \cdot E$. Now,

$$\mu^{i+1}(\mathbf{fix}\, X \cdot E \;{}_p{+}\; X \xrightarrow{a} \mathcal{S}) = \mu^i((E \;{}_p{+}\; X)\{\mathbf{fix}\, X \cdot E \;{}_p{+}\; X/X\} \xrightarrow{a} \mathcal{S}).$$

By induction hypothesis

$$\mu^i((E \;{}_p{+}\; X)\{\mathbf{fix}\, X \cdot E \;{}_p{+}\; X/X\} \xrightarrow{a} \mathcal{S}) \leq \mu((E \;{}_p{+}\; X)\{\mathbf{fix}\, X \cdot E/X\} \xrightarrow{a} \mathcal{S}),$$

which is just

$$\mu(E\{\mathbf{fix}\, X \cdot E/X\} \;{}_p{+}\; \mathbf{fix}\, X \cdot E \xrightarrow{a} \mathcal{S}).$$

By the fixed point property of $\mu$:

$$\begin{aligned}
\mu(E\{\mathbf{fix}\, X \cdot E/X\} \;{}_p{+}\; \mathbf{fix}\, X \cdot E \xrightarrow{a} \mathcal{S}) &= p \cdot \mu(E\{\mathbf{fix}\, X \cdot E/X\} \xrightarrow{a} \mathcal{S}) \\
&\quad + \overline{p} \cdot \mu(\mathbf{fix}\, X \cdot E \xrightarrow{a} \mathcal{S}) \\
&= p \cdot \mu(\mathbf{fix}\, X \cdot E \xrightarrow{a} \mathcal{S}) \\
&\quad + \overline{p} \cdot \mu(\mathbf{fix}\, X \cdot E \xrightarrow{a} \mathcal{S}) \\
&= \mu(\mathbf{fix}\, X \cdot E \xrightarrow{a} \mathcal{S}),
\end{aligned}$$

completing the proof.

- Suppose $G$ is $\mathbf{fix}\, Z \cdot G'$. Then

$$G\{\mathbf{fix}\, X \cdot E \;_p\!+ X/X\} \equiv \mathbf{fix}\, Z \cdot (G'\{\mathbf{fix}\, X \cdot E \;_p\!+ X/X\})$$

and

$$G\{\mathbf{fix}\, X \cdot E/X\} \equiv \mathbf{fix}\, Z \cdot (G'\{\mathbf{fix}\, X \cdot E/X\}),$$

because $E$ has no free variables other than $X$. Thus

$$\begin{aligned}\mu^{i+1}(G\{\mathbf{fix}\, X \cdot E \;_p\!+ X/X\} \xrightarrow{a} \mathcal{S}) &= \mu^{i}(G'\{\mathbf{fix}\, X \cdot E \;_p\!+ X/X\} \\ &\qquad \{G\{\mathbf{fix}\, X \cdot E \;_p\!+ X/X\}/Z\} \xrightarrow{a} \mathcal{S}) \\ &= \mu^{i}(G'\{G/Z\}\{\mathbf{fix}\, X \cdot E \;_p\!+ X/X\} \xrightarrow{a} \mathcal{S}),\end{aligned}$$

and by the fixed-point property of $\mu$:

$$\begin{aligned}\mu(G\{\mathbf{fix}\, X \cdot E/X\} \xrightarrow{a} \mathcal{S}) &= \mu(G'\{\mathbf{fix}\, X \cdot E/X\}\{G\{\mathbf{fix}\, X \cdot E/X\}/Z\} \xrightarrow{a} \mathcal{S}) \\ &= \mu(G'\{G/Z\}\{\mathbf{fix}\, X \cdot E/X\} \xrightarrow{a} \mathcal{S}),\end{aligned}$$

where Lemma 4.3 has been applied as usual. By induction

$$\mu^{i}(G'\{G/Z\}\{\mathbf{fix}\, X \cdot E \;_p\!+ X/X\} \xrightarrow{a} \mathcal{S}) \leq \mu(G'\{G/Z\}\{\mathbf{fix}\, X \cdot E/X\} \xrightarrow{a} \mathcal{S}),$$

from which the result follows.

Finally, we consider (2). The proof is essentially the same as for (1), except the case in which $G$ is the variable $X$. In this case $G\{\mathbf{fix}\, X \cdot E \;_p\!+ X/X\} = \mathbf{fix}\, X \cdot E \;_p\!+ X$ and $G\{\mathbf{fix}\, X \cdot E/X\} = \mathbf{fix}\, X \cdot E$. Now,

$$\mu^{i+1}(\mathbf{fix}\, X \cdot E \xrightarrow{a} \mathcal{S}) = \mu^{i}(E\{\mathbf{fix}\, X \cdot E/X\} \xrightarrow{a} \mathcal{S}).$$

By induction hypothesis

$$\mu^{i}(E\{\mathbf{fix}\, X \cdot E/X\} \xrightarrow{a} \mathcal{S}) \leq \mu(E\{\mathbf{fix}\, X \cdot E \;_p\!+ X/X\} \xrightarrow{a} \mathcal{S}).$$

By the fixed point property of $\mu$:

$$\begin{aligned}\mu(E\{\mathbf{fix}\, X \cdot E \;_p\!+ X/X\} \xrightarrow{a} \mathcal{S}) &= p \cdot \mu(E\{\mathbf{fix}\, X \cdot E \;_p\!+ X/X\} \xrightarrow{a} \mathcal{S}) \\ &\quad + \overline{p} \cdot \mu(E\{\mathbf{fix}\, X \cdot E \;_p\!+ X/X\} \xrightarrow{a} \mathcal{S}) \\ &= \mu((E \;_p\!+ X)\{\mathbf{fix}\, X \cdot E \;_p\!+ X/X\} \xrightarrow{a} \mathcal{S}) \\ &= \mu(\mathbf{fix}\, X \cdot E \;_p\!+ X \xrightarrow{a} \mathcal{S}),\end{aligned}$$

completing the proof. □

The following result, which extends a result of Milner ([Mil89b], Lemma 13 p. 102), is needed to establish the soundness of (R3).

LEMMA 4.7 Suppose $E$ is an expression containing no free variables other than $X$, such that all free occurrences of $X$ are guarded. If $E\{P/X\} \xrightarrow{a} P'$, then $P'$ takes the form $E'\{P/X\}$ (for some expression $E'$), and in addition $E\{Q/X\} \xrightarrow{a} E'\{Q/X\}$ for any $Q$. Moreover, for all $i \geq 0$ we have

$$\mu(E\{P/X\} \xrightarrow{a} E'\{P/X\}) = \mu(E\{Q/X\} \xrightarrow{a} E'\{Q/X\}).$$

*Proof* The proof of the first part is by transition induction, exactly as in Milner. To prove the second part, we use an induction technique similar to that used for the previous results, to prove the following assertion:

- For all $i \geq 0$ and for all expressions $E$ with no free variables other than $X$, such that all free occurrences of $X$ are guarded,

$$\mu^i(E\{P/X\} \xrightarrow{a} E'\{P/X\}) = \mu^i(E\{Q/X\} \xrightarrow{a} E'\{Q/X\}).$$

The details are straightforward, and are omitted. □

PROPOSITION 4.8 Law (R3) is sound for probabilistic bisimulation equivalence.

*Proof* Suppose $E \overset{\text{pr}}{\sim} F\{E/X\}$, where $X$ is guarded in $F$. Let $\mathcal{R}$ be the relation $\Omega(E, \textbf{fix}\, X \cdot F, X)$. We claim that $\mathcal{R}$ is a probabilistic bisimulation. We have to show that

$$\mu(G\{E/X\} \xrightarrow{a} \mathcal{S}) = \mu(G\{\textbf{fix}\, X \cdot F/X\} \xrightarrow{a} \mathcal{S})$$

for all expressions $G$ with no free variables other than $X$, all actions $a$, and all equivalence classes $\mathcal{S}$ of $\mathcal{R}$. Once again we prove the following two statements:

1. For all $i \geq 0$, all expressions $G$ with no free variables other than $X$, all actions $a$, and all equivalence classes $\mathcal{S}$ of $\mathcal{R}$ we have:

$$\mu^i(G\{E/X\} \xrightarrow{a} \mathcal{S}) \leq \mu(G\{\textbf{fix}\, X \cdot F/X\} \xrightarrow{a} \mathcal{S}).$$

2. The same statement with $E$ and $\textbf{fix}\, X \cdot F$ interchanged.

Since the statements to be proved are not symmetric, we must consider both (1) and (2). These are proved, as usual, by induction on $i$, with the induction step containing a case analysis on the syntactic form of $G$. For (1), when $G$ is the variable $X$, we need to use Lemma 4.7 together with the hypothesis that $X$ is guarded in $F$. For (2), no new ideas are involved. The remaining details are omitted. □

## 5 Probabilistic Summation

In this section, we establish a general theorem about probabilistic summation, which will allow us to check the provability of a certain class of expressions "by inspection." That is, we show that an equation between expressions formed using only variables and probabilistic summation is provable from (S1)–(S3) if and only if the same equation, with the probabilities "erased," is provable in CCS, and the left- and right-hand sides assign the same total probabilities to variables. This result, in conjunction with law (C1a), will prove particularly useful in the completeness proof of Section 6.

Formally, to each PE expression $E$, we associate an *unguardedness function*

$\text{ung}_E : \text{Var} \to [0, 1]$,

defined to be the least solution of the following recursive conditions:

1. If $E$ is $X$, then $\text{ung}_E(X) = 1$ and $\text{ung}_E(Y) = 0$ for all $Y \not\equiv X$.
2. If $E$ is $aF$, then $\text{ung}_E(X) = 0$ for all $X$.
3. If $E$ is $E\ {}_p{+}\ F$, then $\text{ung}_E(G) = p \cdot \text{ung}_E(G) + \overline{p} \cdot \text{ung}_F(G)$.
4. If $E$ is $\textbf{fix}\, X \cdot F$, then $\text{ung}_E(X) = 0$, and $\text{ung}_E(Y) = \text{ung}_F(Y)$ for all $Y \not\equiv X$.

Intuitively, $\text{ung}_E(X)$ gives the total probability assigned to unguarded occurrences of variable $X$ in expression $E$. We may regard $\text{ung}_E(X)$ as the "degree of unguardedness" of variable $X$ in expression $E$.

LEMMA 5.1 $\text{ung}_E(X) = 0$ if and only if $X$ is guarded in $E$.

*Proof* Easy structural induction on $E$. □

Call a PE expression $E$ a *summation expression* if it is formed using variables and probabilistic summation only. The laws (S1)–(S3) allow us to prove a normal-form lemma for summation expressions. For this, it is convenient to have a notation for probabilistic $n$-ary summation.

We define the notation $\sum_{i=1}^{n}\{(p_i, E_i) : 1 \le i \le n\}$, where $\{(p_i, E_i) : 1 \le i \le n\}$ is a nonempty set of pairs, the $E_i$ are probabilistic expressions, and the $p_i \in (0, 1)$ have the property that $\sum_{i=1}^{n} p_i = 1$, recursively as follows:

1. $\sum\{(1, E)\} = E$.
2. If $n > 1$, then

$$\sum\{(p_i, E_i) : 1 \le i \le n\} = \sum\{(p_i/\overline{p}_n, E_i) : 1 \le i \le n-1\}\ {}_{\overline{p}_n}{+}\ E_n.$$

When no confusion can arise about the meaning, we often write

$$\sum_{i=1}^{n} p_i \cdot E_i$$

instead of

$$\sum\{(p_i, E_i) : 1 \leq i \leq n\}.$$

LEMMA 5.2 Suppose $E$ is a summation expression. Then $\vdash E = E'$, where $E'$ has the form $\sum_{i \in I} p_i \cdot X_i$, with the $X_i$ distinct variables in lexicographic order.

*Proof* Easy structural induction on $E$, using (S1)–(S3). In essence, one simply proves the corresponding result about ordinary summation without the probability labels, and then fills in the probabilities in the only way permitted by (S1)–(S3). □

The following proposition allows us to check the provability of probabilistic summation expressions "by inspection." To state this result, define the *erasing* of a PE expression $E$ to be the CCS expression $\text{erase}(E)$ obtained by removing all the probabilities annotating the $+$ operators.

PROPOSITION 5.3 Suppose $E$ and $E'$ are PE summation expressions. Then $\vdash E = E'$ if and only if the following two conditions hold:

1. $\vdash \text{erase}(E) = \text{erase}(E')$ is provable using the erasings of laws (S1)–(S3).
2. $\text{ung}_E = \text{ung}_{E'}$.

*Proof* Clearly, if $\vdash E_1 = E_2$ is provable using (S1)–(S3), then $\vdash \text{erase}(E_1) = \text{erase}(E_2)$ is provable using the erasings of (S1)–(S3). It is also easy to check that for each of the laws (S1)–(S3), if $L$ denotes the left-hand side and $R$ denotes the right-hand side, then $\text{ung}_L = \text{ung}_R$.

Conversely, suppose conditions (1) and (2) hold. By Lemma 5.2, we can use (S1)–(S3) to prove $\vdash E = \sum_{i=1}^{n} p_i \cdot X_i$, where the $X_i$ are distinct variables in lexicographic order, and $\vdash E' = \sum_{i=1}^{n'} p'_i \cdot X'_i$, where the $X'_i$ are distinct variables in lexicographic order. Erasing the probabilities from these proofs, and using (1), we conclude that the erasings of (S1)–(S3) suffice to prove $\vdash E = \sum_{i=1}^{n} X_i$ and $\vdash E = \sum_{i=1}^{n'} X'_i$. It follows (standard results about the erasings of laws (S1)–(S3)) that $n = n'$ and $X_i \equiv X'_i$ for $1 \leq i \leq n$. Using (2), we conclude that $p_i = p'_i$ for $1 \leq i \leq n$, hence $\sum_{i=1}^{n} p_i \cdot X_i$ and $\sum_{i=1}^{n'} p'_i \cdot X'_i$ are identical, thus showing $\vdash E = E'$ is provable using (S1)–(S3). □

## 6 Completeness

In this section, we adapt the completeness proof of Milner for bisimulation equivalence of regular CCS expressions to a completeness proof for probabilistic bisimulation equivalence of PE expressions. The proof follows Milner in its main ideas; however some variation is required because: (1) the unit law $E\ {}_p{+}\ \mathbf{0} = E$ is not sound for probabilistic bisimulation equivalence, and (2) the construction of the characteristic set of equations for $E = E'$ has to take probabilities into account.

We first restate Milner's "Unique Solution of Equations" theorem. The theorem and its proof carry over without change to the probabilistic setting.

THEOREM 1 (UNIQUE SOLUTION OF EQUATIONS) Let $\widetilde{X} = \langle X_1, \ldots, X_m \rangle$ and $\widetilde{Y} = \langle Y_1, \ldots, Y_n \rangle$ be distinct variables, and $\widetilde{F} = \langle F_1, \ldots, F_m \rangle$ expressions with free variables in $\langle \widetilde{X}, \widetilde{Y} \rangle$ in which each $X_i$ is guarded. Then there exist expressions $\widetilde{E} = \langle E_1, \ldots, E_m \rangle$ with free variables in $\widetilde{Y}$ such that

$$\vdash E_i = F_i\{\widetilde{E}/\widetilde{X}\} \qquad (i \le m).$$

Moreover, if the same property may be proved when $\widetilde{E}$ are replaced by expressions $\widetilde{E}' = \langle E'_1, \ldots, E'_m \rangle$ with free variables in $\widetilde{Y}$, then

$$\vdash E'_i = E_i \qquad (i \le m).$$

*Proof* By induction on $m$, exactly as in Milner. □

The next result is a version of Milner's "Equational Characterization" theorem. The statement is complicated somewhat by the presence of probabilities on the summations and the fact that we do not have the unit law for $\mathbf{0}$.

THEOREM 2 (EQUATIONAL CHARACTERIZATION) For any expression $E$, with free variables in $\widetilde{Y}$, there exist expressions $E_1, \ldots, E_p$ $(p \ge 1)$, with free variables in $\widetilde{Y}$, satisfying $p$ equations, each of which has one of the following three forms, where $1 \le i \le p$:

1. $\vdash E_i = \sum_{j=1}^{m(i)} p_{ij} \cdot E'_{ij}$

where each expression $E'_{ij}$ is either $\mathbf{0}$ or has the form $a_{ij} E_{f(i,j)}$.

2. $\vdash E_i = \sum_{j=1}^{n(i)} q_{ij} \cdot Y_{g(i,j)}$

where the variables $Y_{g(i,j)}$ are enumerated without repetition.

3. $\vdash E_i = \sum_{j=1}^{m(i)} p_{ij} \cdot E'_{ij}\ {}_r{+}\ \sum_{j=1}^{n(i)} q_{ij} \cdot Y_{g(i,j)}$

where the first term satisfies the conditions in (1), and the second term satisfies the conditions in (2).

Moreover, $\vdash E = E_1$.

*Proof* As in [Mil84], the proof is by induction on the structure of $E$. The only nontrivial case is $E \equiv \mathbf{fix}\, X \cdot F$. In this case, by induction we have expressions $F_1, \ldots, F_p$ satisfying $p$ equations, each of which has one of the three forms shown above, moreover $\vdash F = F_1$. Using (C2) we have $\vdash E = \mathbf{fix}\, X \cdot F_1$.

In each of the $p$ equations, the variable $X$ might or might not appear as one of the $Y_{g(i,j)}$. We consider whether $X$ appears in this way in the first equation; that is, as one of the $Y_{g(1,j)}$. If $X$ is not one of the $Y_{g(1,j)}$, then from $\vdash E = \mathbf{fix}\, X \cdot F_1$, using (R1) we have $\vdash E = F_1\{E/X\}$. Suppose $X$ is one of the $Y_{g(1,j)}$. If $F_1$ has form (2) above with $n(1) = 1$, then we have immediately $\vdash E = \mathbf{fix}\, X \cdot F_1 \equiv \mathbf{0}$. Otherwise, we can use (R2) and Proposition 5.3, in conjunction with (C1a), to eliminate the unguarded occurrence of $X$, and then use (R1) to show $\vdash E = F_1'\{E/X\}$, where $F_1'$ takes one of the forms (1)–(3), and $X$ does not occur free in $F_1'$.

Thus, whether or not $X$ appears in the first equation, we have

$$\vdash E = F_1'\{E/X\},$$

where either $\vdash F = F_1'$ or $\vdash F = F_1' \,{}_s\!+ X$, where $F_1'$ takes one of the forms (1)–(3), and $X$ does not occur free in $F_1'$.

We now proceed as in Milner, setting

$$E_i \equiv F_i\{E/X\} \qquad (1 \le i \le p),$$

and observing that by rearranging terms using Proposition 5.3 in conjunction with (C1a), we obtain equations of the desired form. Moreover, $\vdash E = E_1$ follows from $\vdash F = F_1$, and the expressions $E_i$ are easily seen to have free variables in $\widetilde{Y}$. □

We now present a lemma that is useful for the completeness proof. It basically says that variables appear unguarded with equal probability in probabilistically bisimilar expressions. We first need the following cancellation rule ([Jou92], Proposition 7.5), which is not sound in the non-probabilistic case. It may be viewed as a "unique fixed point" result for a limited form of unguarded recursion. The proof given below is essentially that of Jou.

LEMMA 6.1 If $E \overset{\text{pr}}{\sim} E \,{}_p\!+ F$, then $E \overset{\text{pr}}{\sim} F$.

*Proof* Suppose $\widetilde{X}$ contains all the free variables of $E$ and $F$. If $E \overset{\text{pr}}{\not\sim} F$, then there exist agents $\widetilde{P}$, and action $a$, and a probabilistic bisimulation equivalence class $\mathcal{S}$, such that

$$\mu(E\{\widetilde{P}/\widetilde{X}\} \xrightarrow{a} \mathcal{S}) \neq \mu(F\{\widetilde{P}/\widetilde{X}\} \xrightarrow{a} \mathcal{S}).$$

But then, letting $E'$ and $F'$ abbreviate $E\{\widetilde{P}/\widetilde{X}\}$ and $F\{\widetilde{P}/\widetilde{X}\}$, respectively, we have:

$$\begin{aligned}\mu((E' \;{}_p{+}\; F') \xrightarrow{a} \mathcal{S}) - \mu(E' \xrightarrow{a} \mathcal{S}) &= p \cdot \mu(E' \xrightarrow{a} \mathcal{S}) + \overline{p} \cdot \mu(F' \xrightarrow{a} \mathcal{S}) \\ &\quad - \mu(E' \xrightarrow{a} \mathcal{S}) \\ &= \overline{p} \cdot (\mu(F' \xrightarrow{a} \mathcal{S}) - \mu(E' \xrightarrow{a} \mathcal{S})) \\ &\neq 0.\end{aligned}$$

It follows that $E' \stackrel{\mathrm{pr}}{\not\sim} E' \;{}_p{+}\; F'$, hence $E \stackrel{\mathrm{pr}}{\not\sim} E \;{}_p{+}\; F$. □

The following result is [Jou92], Proposition 7.10, only with a simpler proof.

LEMMA 6.2 Suppose $E' \;{}_p{+}\; X \stackrel{\mathrm{pr}}{\sim} F' \;{}_q{+}\; X$, where $E'$ and $F'$ contain no unguarded occurrences of $X$. Then $E' \stackrel{\mathrm{pr}}{\sim} F'$ and $p = q$.

*Proof* If $E' \;{}_p{+}\; X \stackrel{\mathrm{pr}}{\sim} F' \;{}_q{+}\; X$, then by (C1a) we have $E' \;{}_p{+}\; E' \stackrel{\mathrm{pr}}{\sim} F' \;{}_q{+}\; E'$, and hence $E' \stackrel{\mathrm{pr}}{\sim} F' \;{}_q{+}\; E'$ by (S3). It follows by Lemma 6.1 that $E' \stackrel{\mathrm{pr}}{\sim} F'$.

To show $p = q$, let $a$ be an action not occurring in $E'$ or $F'$. Since $E' \;{}_p{+}\; X \stackrel{\mathrm{pr}}{\sim} F' \;{}_q{+}\; X$, by (C1a) we have $E'\{a\mathbf{0}/X\} \;{}_p{+}\; a\mathbf{0} \stackrel{\mathrm{pr}}{\sim} F'\{a\mathbf{0}/X\} \;{}_q{+}\; a\mathbf{0} \stackrel{\mathrm{pr}}{\sim} E'\{a\mathbf{0}/X\} \;{}_q{+}\; a\mathbf{0}$. Then

$$\mu((E'\{a\mathbf{0}/X\} \;{}_p{+}\; a\mathbf{0}) \xrightarrow{a} \mathbf{0}) = p \cdot \mu(E'\{a\mathbf{0}/X\} \xrightarrow{a} \mathbf{0}) + \overline{p},$$

and

$$\mu((E'\{a\mathbf{0}/X\} \;{}_q{+}\; a\mathbf{0}) \xrightarrow{a} \mathbf{0}) = q \cdot \mu(E'\{a\mathbf{0}/X\} \xrightarrow{a} \mathbf{0}) + \overline{q}.$$

Since these two quantities must be equal, we have:

$$(p - q) \cdot \mu(E'\{a\mathbf{0}/X\} \xrightarrow{a} \mathbf{0}) = (p - q).$$

Since $E'$ contains no unguarded occurrences of $X$ and action $a$ does not occur in $E'$, we have

$$\mu(E'\{a\mathbf{0}/X\} \xrightarrow{a} \mathbf{0}) = 0.$$

It follows that $p = q$. □

The following completeness proof follows much the same lines as the one in [Mil84]. Given probabilistically bisimilar $E$ and $E'$, a "product" equational system is constructed from their respective equational characterizations. $E$ and $E'$ are then both shown to be solutions of this system; by uniqueness of solutions to guarded equations, completeness is established. The main technical consideration in moving to the probabilistic setting is the calculation of the probabilities for the product equational system.

THEOREM 3 (COMPLETENESS) If $E \stackrel{\mathrm{pr}}{\sim} E'$ then $\vdash E = E'$.

*Proof* Let $E$ and $E'$ have free variables in $\widetilde{Y}$. By Theorem 2 there are: expressions $E_1, \ldots, E_p$ satisfying $p$ equations, each of which has one of the three forms in Theorem 2; expressions $E'_1, \ldots, E'_{p'}$ satisfying $p'$ equations, each one of which has one of the three forms in Theorem 2; and moreover $\vdash E = E_1$ and $\vdash E' = E'_1$. For simplicity in what follows, we assume that all equations are of form (3). The argument differs only in inessential details for equations of forms (1) or (2). Thus, we suppose that

$$\vdash E_i = \sum_{j=1}^{m(i)} p_{ij} \cdot E_{ij} \;{}_{r_i}\!+ \sum_{j=1}^{n(i)} q_{ij} \cdot Y_{g(i,j)} \qquad (i \leq p)$$

where each $E_{ij}$ is either $\mathbf{0}$ or of the form $a_{ij} E_{f(i,j)}$, and

$$\vdash E'_{i'} = \sum_{j'=1}^{m'(i')} p'_{i'j'} \cdot E'_{i'j'} \;{}_{r'_{i'}}\!+ \sum_{j'=1}^{n'(i')} q'_{i'j'} \cdot Y_{g'(i',j')} \qquad (i' \leq p').$$

where each $E'_{i'j'}$ is either $\mathbf{0}$ or of the form $a'_{i'j'} E'_{f'(i',j')}$.

Now let $I = \{\langle i, i' \rangle \mid E_i \overset{\text{pr}}{\sim} E'_{i'}\}$. Since $E \overset{\text{pr}}{\sim} E'$ by hypothesis, and in addition $\vdash E = E_1$ and $\vdash E' = E'_1$ imply by soundness that $E \overset{\text{pr}}{\sim} E_1$ and $E' \overset{\text{pr}}{\sim} E'_1$, we have $E_1 \overset{\text{pr}}{\sim} E'_1$, so that $\langle 1, 1 \rangle \in I$. Moreover, the following hold for each $\langle i, i' \rangle \in I$:

1. There exists a total surjective relation $J_{ii'}$ between $\{1, \ldots, m(i)\}$ and $\{1, \ldots, m'(i')\}$, given by

$$J_{ii'} = \{\langle j, j' \rangle \mid \text{either } E_{ij} \equiv \mathbf{0} \equiv E'_{i'j'} \text{ or else } a_{ij} = a'_{i'j'} \text{ and } \langle f(i,j), f'(i',j') \rangle \in I\}.$$

2. $r_i = r'_{i'}$.
3. $\sum\{p_{ij} \mid E_{ij} \equiv \mathbf{0}\} = \sum\{p'_{i'j'} \mid E'_{i'j'} \equiv \mathbf{0}\}$.
4. $\vdash \sum_{j=1}^{n(i)} q_{ij} \cdot Y_{g(i,j)} = \sum_{j'=1}^{n'(i')} q'_{i'j'} \cdot Y'_{g'(i',j')}$.

To prove assertion (4), observe that $E_i \overset{\text{pr}}{\sim} E'_{i'}$, in conjunction with Corollary 3.3, implies that $E_i$ and $E'_{i'}$ have the same sets of unguarded variables, and the fact that these variables occur with the same probabilities follows from Lemma 6.2. The provability of (4) then follows from Proposition 5.3. Using Lemma 6.2 with $E_i \overset{\text{pr}}{\sim} E'_{i'}$ also yields assertion (2) and the following relation:

$$\sum_{j=1}^{m(i)} p_{ij} \cdot E_{ij} \overset{\text{pr}}{\sim} \sum_{j'=1}^{m'(i')} p'_{i'j'} \cdot E'_{i'j'}. \qquad (5)$$

By the relation (5) and the definition of probabilistic bisimulation, for any given action $a$, the total probability associated with all summands prefixed by $a$ on the left-hand side of relation (5) is the same as the total probability associated with all the $a$-prefixed summands on the right-hand side. Since the sum of all the probabilities in a summation expression must equal one, assertion (3) now follows immediately.

To prove assertion (1), let $J_{ii'}$ be defined as stated. To show that $J_{ii'}$ is total, consider an arbitrary $i \leq p$. For each $j \leq m(i)$, the term $E_{ij}$ is either $\mathbf{0}$ or else has the form $a_{ij} E_{f(i,j)}$. In the former case, since the term $E_{ij}$ occurs with positive probability, the total probability associated with summands in $E_i$ of the form $a_{ij} E_{f(i,j)}$ must be less than one. Using $E_i \overset{\text{pr}}{\sim} E'_{i'}$ together with Lemma 2.1, we conclude that the total probability associated with summands in $E'_{i'}$ of the form $a_{i'j'} E_{f'(i',j')}$ must also be less than one. This, in turn, implies that the total probability associated with summands in $E'_{i'}$ of the form $\mathbf{0}$ must be positive, thus establishing the existence of a $j'$ such that $\langle j, j' \rangle \in J_{ii'}$ and $E_{ij} \equiv \mathbf{0} \equiv E'_{i'j'}$. In the latter case, we have $\mu(E_i \xrightarrow{a_{ij}} E_{f(i,j)}) > 0$, hence using $E_i \overset{\text{pr}}{\sim} E'_{i'}$ together with Lemma 2.1 we conclude the existence of $j'$ such that $\mu(E'_{i'} \xrightarrow{a} E'_{f'(i',j')}) > 0$ and $E_{f(i,j)} \overset{\text{pr}}{\sim} E'_{f'(i',j')}$, so that $\langle f(i,j), f'(i',j') \rangle \in I$, thus completing the proof that $J_{ii'}$ is total. Symmetric reasoning establishes its surjectivity.

Now, let $J_{ii'}(j)$ denote the image of $j \in \{1, \ldots, m(i)\}$ under $J_{ii'}$ and $J_{ii'}^{-1}(j')$ the preimage of $j' \in \{1, \ldots, m'(i')\}$ under $J_{ii'}$. Let $[j]_{ii'}$ denote the set $J_{ii'}^{-1}(J_{ii'}(j))$ and let $[j']_{ii'}$ denote the set $J_{ii'}(J_{ii'}^{-1}(j'))$. It follows easily from the definitions that

1. If $\langle i, i'_1 \rangle \in I$ and $\langle i, i'_2 \rangle \in I$, then $[j]_{ii'_1} = [j]_{ii'_2}$ for $1 \leq j \leq m(i)$. Similarly, if $\langle i_1, i' \rangle \in I$ and $\langle i_2, i' \rangle \in I$, then $[j']_{i_1 i'} = [j']_{i_2 i'}$ for $1 \leq j \leq m'(i')$.
2. Note that if $k_1 \in [j]_{ii'}$ and $k_2 \in [j]_{ii'}$, then either $E_{ik_1} \equiv \mathbf{0} \equiv E_{ik_2}$ or else $E_{ik_1} \equiv a_{ik_1} E_{f(i,k_1)}$ and $E_{ik_2} \equiv a_{ik_2} E_{f(i,k_2)}$, where $a_{ik_1} = a_{ik_2}$. Similarly, if $k'_1 \in [j']_{ii'}$ and $k'_2 \in [j']_{ii'}$, then either $E'_{i'k'_1} \equiv \mathbf{0} \equiv E'_{i'k'_2}$ or else $E'_{i'k'_1} \equiv a_{i'k'_1} E'_{f'(i',k'_1)}$ and $E'_{i'k'_2} \equiv a_{i'k'_2} E'_{f'(i',k'_2)}$, where $a_{i'k'_1} = a_{i'k'_2}$.

Define

$$\nu_{ij} = \sum_{k \in [j]_{ii'}} p_{ik} \qquad \text{(any } i', \ \langle i, i' \rangle \in I)$$

and

$$\nu'_{i'j'} = \sum_{k' \in [j']_{ii'}} p'_{i'k'} \qquad \text{(any } i, \ \langle i, i' \rangle \in I)$$

From the hypothesis that $E$ and $E'$ are probabilistically bisimulation equivalent, it is easily seen that $\nu_{ij} = \nu'_{i'j'}$ whenever $\langle i, i' \rangle \in I$ and $\langle j, j' \rangle \in J_{ii'}$.

We now consider the formal equations, one for each $\langle i, i' \rangle \in I$:

$$X_{ii'} = \sum_{\langle j,j' \rangle \in J_{ii'}} \left( \frac{p_{ij} p'_{i'j'}}{\nu_{ij}} \right) \cdot F_{iji'j'} \;{}_{r_i}\!\!+ \sum_{j=1}^{n(i)} q_{ij} \cdot Y_{g(i,j)}$$

where $F_{iji'j'} \equiv \mathbf{0}$ if $E_{ij} \equiv \mathbf{0} \equiv E_{i'j'}$, and otherwise $F_{iji'j'} \equiv a_{ij} X_{f(i,j),f'(i',j')}$.

First we assert that these equations are provably satisfied when each $X_{ii'}$ is instantiated to $E_i$. To see this, note that the typical equation becomes

$$E_i = \sum_{\langle j,j' \rangle \in J_{ii'}} \left( \frac{p_{ij} p'_{i'j'}}{\nu_{ij}} \right) \cdot F_{ij}\{E_i / X_{ii'}\} \;{}_{r_i}\!\!+ \sum_{j=1}^{n(i)} q_{ij} \cdot Y_{g(i,j)} \qquad (*)$$

and is provable, since—as $J_{ii'}$ is total—its right-hand side differs at most by repeated summands from that of the already proved equation for $E_i$. Moreover, the total probability of a repeated summand is the same as the probability associated with that summand in the already proved equation. That is, the total probability, in the first term of the equation for $X_{ii'}$, associated with all summands identical to $E_{f(i,j)}$ is

$$\frac{1}{\nu_{ij}} \cdot p_{ij} \cdot \sum_{k' \in [j']_{ii'}} p'_{i'k'} = p_{ij}.$$

Proposition 5.3 in conjunction with (C1a) thus suffice to prove $(*)$. A completely symmetric argument, relying on the surjectivity of the $J_{ii'}$, suffices to show the equations are provably satisfied when each $X_{ii'}$ is instantiated to $E'_i$.

Finally, we note that each $X_{ii'}$ is guarded in the right-hand sides of the formal equations. It immediately follows from Theorem 1 that $\vdash E_i = E'_{i'}$ for each $\langle i, i' \rangle \in I$, and hence $\vdash E = E'$. □

## 7 Conclusions

We have presented a complete equational axiomatization of probabilistic bisimulation for finite-state probabilistic processes. Probabilistic extensions of the transition-induction and bisimulation-up-to proof techniques [Mil89a] figured prominently in our soundness proof. Although our axiom system can be seen as a relatively minor variation of the one obtained by Milner [Mil84] for strong bisimulation, new insights and a careful accounting of probability were required to obtain the end result.

Though in the nonprobabilistic case one cannot delete the guardedness hypothesis in rule (R3), it is interesting to note that in the probabilistic case a stronger version of (R3) is in fact sound. Define variable $X$ to be *probabilistically guarded* in expression $E$ if $\text{ung}_E(X) < 1$. By Lemma 5.1, if $X$ is guarded, then it is probabilistically guarded. Then it can be shown that (R3) is sound for probabilistic bisimulation equivalence, even if the hypothesis that $X$ is guarded in $F$ is weakened to the hypothesis that $X$ is probabilistically guarded in $F$. This is because, in essence, the only way that an unguarded, but probabilistically guarded variable $X$ can appear in an expression is as a "top-level" summand with probability $< 1$. In the context of a recursion on $X$, such summands can always be eliminated using (R2).

A compelling open problem is the extension of our results to a weaker notion of probabilistic bisimulation that takes silent $\tau$-transitions into account, such as that proposed in [BH97]. Previous work by Milner [Mil89b] is again likely to guide the choice of axioms and inference rules.

## References


[BBS95] J. C. M. Baeten, J. A. Bergstra, and S. A. Smolka. Axiomatizing probabilistic processes: ACP with generative probabilities. *Information and Computation*, 121(2):234–255, September 1995. Preliminary version appeared in *Proceedings of CONCUR '92 — Third International Conference on Concurrency Theory*, Lecture Notes in Computer Science, Vol. 630, pp. 472–485, Springer-Verlag (1992).

[BH97] C. Baier and H. Hermanns. Weak bisimulation for fully probabilistic processes. *Proceedings of Computer Aided Verification (CAV'97)*, Vol. 1254 of *Lecture Notes in Computer Science*, pp. 119–130, Springer-Verlag (1997).

[BK84] J. A. Bergstra and J. W. Klop. Process algebra for synchronous communication. *Information and Computation*, 60:109–137, 1984.

[GSS95] R. J. van Glabbeek, S. A. Smolka, and B. Steffen. Reactive, generative, and stratified models of probabilistic processes. *Information and Computation*, 121(1):59–80, August 1995.

[Jou92] C.-C. Jou. *Aspects of Probabilistic Process Algebra*. PhD thesis, SUNY at Stony Brook, Stony Brook, New York, 1992.

[JS90] C.-C. Jou and S. A. Smolka. Equivalences, congruences, and complete axiomatizations for probabilistic processes. In J. C. M. Baeten and J. W. Klop, editors, *Proceedings of the First International Conference on Concurrency Theory (CONCUR '90)*, Vol. 458 of *Lecture Notes in Computer Science*, pages 367–383, Berlin, 1990. Springer-Verlag.

[LS92] K. G. Larsen and A. Skou. Bisimulation through probabilistic testing. *Information and Computation*, 94(1):1–28, September 1992.

[Mil84] R. Milner. A complete inference system for a class of regular behaviours. *J. Comput. System Sci.*, 28: 439–466, 1984.

[Mil89a] R. Milner. *Communication and Concurrency*. International Series in Computer Science. Prentice Hall, 1989.

[Mil89b] R. Milner. A complete axiomatisation for observational congruence of finite-state behaviours. *Information and Computation*, 81:227–247, 1989.

# V MOBILITY

# 20 A Calculus of Communicating Systems with Label Passing—Ten Years After

**Uffe H. Engberg and Mogens Nielsen**

## 1 Preface

This note is dedicated to Robin Milner on his 60th birthday. On this occasion we have taken the opportunity of commenting on a report of ours from 1986 on an extension of Milner's CCS with label passing [EN86],—a piece of work that was directly inspired by Milner's work on proces calculi, and indeed had its beginnings in joint work with Milner.

The challenging problem of extending CCS with a notion of label (or channel) passing was motivated and formulated by Milner already in 1979, before CCS was published. At the time Milner was spending his sabbatical at the University of Aarhus, and in discussions with one of us (Nielsen) we looked upon various ideas for such extensions of CCS, but did not manage to get any of these to work properly. In 1985 Engberg was looking for a subject for his MSc thesis, and we decided to make another attempt at the six year old problem and ideas. At that time, a few attempts had already been made towards calculi with notions of mobility (as it was later called by Milner *et al.* in [MPW89]), notably the parametric channels by Astesiano and Zucca [AZ84] and the LNET formalism by Kennaway and Sleep [KS83], which was a form of hybrid between CCS and the actor model of Hewitt. However, no attempt had been made toward a calculus with a proper algebraic theory, and following the ideas of Milner, we took it as our main challenge to develop such a calculus, which would enhance the expressibility of CCS by introducing a notion of channel passing, and at the same time preserve as much as possible of the algebraic theory of CCS. As we put it at the time: "With all the thought behind the elegance of CCS this is a sound principle to apply in any attempt to extend CCS."

So our goals were reasonably concrete. The theory of CCS was there, and we designed our own small set of examples, which we used as "expressiveness benchmarks" (Eratosthenes' sieve, a pushdown store, and an extension of Milner's translation of an imperative programming language into CCS, [Mil80]). We tried out several approaches but most of them failed in one or more respects, and we never managed to get quite the calculus we were after. However, a particularly promising approach was presented and studied in the MSc thesis of Engberg, finished at the turn of the year 1985–86. Engberg's thesis introduced an extension of CCS, called ECCS, with an operational semantics, some suggestions for behavioural equivalences, and our benchmark examples of modelling and reasoning using the calculus. The essential contents of the thesis was reported only in a preliminary form in an Technical Report from the University of Aarhus, [EN86], which was accompanied in Engberg's MSc thesis by 112 pages of handwritten proofs. We never produced a version of the report suitable for publication.

In the conclusion of [EN86], we pointed out that ECCS was not "quite right," in several respects. But we also expressed confidence "that ECCS represents a step on the right track." We may have taken some steps in the right direction, but Milner himself and his co-workers Joachim Parrow and David Walker took the main step when they introduced the $\pi$-calculus. In their seminal paper [MPW89] Milner *et al.* comment in their conclusion:

> Engberg and Nielsen (1986) did not publish their report, and it has not received due attention, probably because its treatment of constants, variables, and names is somewhat difficult. Many features of the $\pi$-calculus are due to them, in particular the replacement of the CCS relabelling by syntactic substitution (crucial for the formulation of the semantic rules); the semantic treatment of scope extrusion; the extension of the definition of bisimulation to account for name parameters; the definition of strong bisimilarity (which they call simply 'strong equivalence'); and the soundness of most algebraic laws. We made many failed attempts to depart from their formulation. Our contribution has been to remove all discrimination among constant names, variable names, and values, yielding a more basic calculus; to discriminate between ground and non-ground equivalence (needed to replace the constant-variable discrimination); to strengthen the algebraic laws—in particular the expansion law—in order to achieve complete equational theories; to encode value-computation in the calculus in a tractable way (with the help of a new match construct); and to provide rather simple encodings of functional calculi—the $\lambda$-calculus and combinatory algebra.

One of our aims here is to point out that the gap between [EN86] and the $\pi$-calculus was bigger than indicated by the quote above. The paper [MPW89] actually not only provided a much simpler and more elegant calculus with a proper theory, but also corrected a number of our conceptual and technical mistakes, as we will point out. We can see the step from ECCS to the $\pi$-calculus as an example of Milner famous use of Occam's razor.

We would like to recall here some of the ideas from [EN86] which seem to have survived in the development of calculi with mobility, those summarised by our goal "to extend CCS to allow passing of individual channels, viewing restriction as a formal binder, and to allow dynamic change of scope of such binders in connection with communication." Our modest aim is to add a commentary on the background and the development of these early calculi of mobile processes seen from our own perspective. We have no ambition of covering the wide range of further developments of Milner and many other researchers over the past ten years; Victor and Nestmann maintain a Web based bibliography of works on the $\pi$-calculus [VN].

We have chosen to start by quoting the entire Introduction from [EN86]. The reason is not that the text is particularly interesting reading today from a technical point of view, but we think it gives an account of the kind of reasoning we went through at the time, and hence some of the motivation for ECCS. Next, we present some of the contents of [EN86], and elaborate on the similarities and differences between ECCS and the $\pi$-calculus with respect to syntax, derivation rules, behavioural equivalence, and expressiveness. We finish off by quoting and commenting on the entire Conclusion from [EN86].

## 2 Introduction from 1986

In the original version of CCS, as presented in [Mil80], *structured* dynamically evolving configurations such as the pushdown store can be obtained by means of recursion and the chaining combinator.

It is less clear that the same can be obtained for *unstructured* dynamically evolving configurations like the example studied in [Mil80, chapter 9], translating a concurrent programming language with unboundedly many concurrent activations of a single procedure into CCS. There it was pointed out that a solution would be to allow the passage of communication links as values between one agent and another, but that CCS was probably defective in this respect. It was also noted that the usefulness of such a solution was not limited to language translations.

In [DG83] it is mentioned that in general, the exchange of ports (communication links) between agents, would be a natural way to model the exchange of communication capabilities.

In later versions of CCS (see [Mil83, Mil84]) a more basic calculus, which allows infinite summation but not direct value communication, was introduced. It was shown how the original version—a richer calculus—could be encoded. Value communication and manipulation was encoded essentially by indexing the labels and the agent identifiers. Labels or communication links could also be encoded (as special cases of values). A similar approach has been made by [AZ84] which conceptually only differs a little from Milner's approach. A very different approach called LNET is presented in [KS83]. LNET might be described as a hybrid of actor languages and CCS.

We have made a different approach for several reasons.

Although the later basic calculus in a sense allows the passage of communication links as values between one agent and another, Milner himself notices in [Mil84]: "It is quite certain that the slender syntax of our basic calculus and even the derived notations which we have considered, are not sufficient always to present such applications [with passage of communication links] in a *lucid* way." Most of the problems are left for the "programmer."

Our approach will be more in keeping with the original version of CCS, at the same time widening the connection to the lambda-calculus and reducing the number of primitive operators (no relabelling) without loss of expressiveness. In [Mil80] Milner asks the question whether CCS's primitive constructs are the smallest possible set and says that they need a re-examination. Since we have not got the relabelling operator we to some extent deal with this question. It is our belief that the parts of our approach which concern this could be done for the basic calculus too.

We will now discuss what requirements the new calculus allowing passage of communication links should meet. It will be referred to as ECCS (Extended CCS).

In what follows there is a slight syntactical difference to CCS. $\alpha?x.B$ is written for $\alpha x.B$, where $x$ is *bound by*? and its scope is $B$ meaning that a value can be received at $\alpha$. Similarly we write $\alpha!v.B$ for sending a value.

To get a first idea of what we mean by allowing passage of communication links (labels) consider the example:

$$B_0 \mid B_1 \equiv \alpha!8.\beta?x.\delta!x.\text{nil} \mid \alpha?y.\beta!y.\text{nil}$$

which is a CCS program. According to CCS it can develop like this:

$B_0 \mid B_1$
$\downarrow\tau$
$\beta?x.\delta!x.\text{nil} \mid \beta!8.\text{nil}$
$\downarrow\tau$
$\delta!8.\text{nil} \mid \text{nil}$

If we replace 8 by $\lambda$ it is no longer a CCS program, but we wish such communications of labels to be possible in ECCS. If $x$ and $y$ are replaced by $\mathsf{x}$ and $\mathsf{y}$—variables qualifying over labels—we expect the program to be able to develop in the same way:

$\alpha!\lambda.\beta?\mathsf{x}.\delta!\mathsf{x}.\text{nil} \mid \alpha?\mathsf{y}.\beta!\mathsf{y}.\text{nil}$
$\downarrow\tau$
$\beta?\mathsf{x}.\delta!\mathsf{x}.\text{nil} \mid \beta!\lambda.\text{nil}$
$\downarrow\tau$
$\delta!\lambda.\text{nil} \mid \text{nil}$

*Communication of labels* would be of no use if it was not *possible to use a received label for later communication*, so the following modification of the example,

$$B_0 \mid B_1 \equiv \alpha!\lambda.\lambda?x.\delta!x.\text{nil} \mid \alpha?\mathsf{y}.\mathsf{y}!5.\text{nil}$$

should be possible so that a development could be:

$B_0 \mid B_1$
$\downarrow\tau$
$\lambda?x.\delta!x.\text{nil} \mid \lambda!5.\text{nil}$
$\downarrow\tau$
$\delta!5 \cdot \text{nil} \mid \text{nil}$

Up till now there has probably not been any problem in understanding these basic requirements. This is due to the simplicity of the examples. In [DG83], the following more complicated example is studied:

$$(B_0 \mid B_1) \setminus \alpha \mid B_2 \equiv (\lambda?y.y!.\text{nil} \mid \lambda!\alpha.\alpha?.\text{nil}) \setminus \alpha \mid \lambda!\alpha.\alpha?.\text{nil}$$

The agent $B_0$ can receive a label at $\lambda$ and the label is bound to the variable $y$. If the received label $\alpha$ comes from the agent $B_1$ it agrees with our intuition if the system upon the communication results in:

$$(\alpha!.\text{nil} \mid \alpha?.\text{nil}) \setminus \alpha \mid \lambda!\alpha.\alpha?.\text{nil}.$$

But what should the result look like if the label received originates from the outside agent $B_2$? Should it be possible to pass $\alpha$ from $B_2$ to $B_0$? If the system instead looked like

$$(B_0 \mid B_3) \setminus \beta \mid B_2 \equiv (\lambda?y.y!.\text{nil} \mid \lambda!\beta.\beta?.\text{nil}) \setminus \beta \mid \lambda!\alpha.\alpha?.\text{nil}, \alpha \neq \beta$$

it would seem natural if the result was $(\alpha!.\text{nil} \mid B_3) \setminus \beta \mid \alpha?.\text{nil}$. The labels visible for agent $B_2$ are the same in both cases. From the viewpoint of $B_2$ there seems no reason why $(B_0 \mid B_1) \setminus \alpha$ and $(B_0 \mid B_3)\setminus\beta$ should behave differently. It will therefore be a *central requirement to ECCS, that the name of a label restricted should be of no importance to the behaviour* in the same way as change of bound variable in $\lambda?x.$—does not influence the behaviour in CCS. This also seems natural if one takes up the attitude that one is communicating via links and that the communications via a certain link should be the same no matter what name is chosen for that link. In terms of experiments on machines as sketched in [Mil80]: the buttons are the same no matter what names are printed on them.

The same question arises in a different situation and the problems seem closely connected. Let $\lambda?y.B \equiv \lambda?y.(\alpha!5.\text{nil} \mid \alpha?x.y!x.\text{nil}) \setminus \alpha$. What should the result look like after a label (say $\alpha$) is received at $\lambda$ and substituted for $y$ in $B$? The situation is very similar to the one above, except that dependence of the names of the restricted labels is displaced to the substitution. We therefore *demand the same independence of actual names used for restriction when substituting a label.*

We will now study one further requirement to ECCS through an example mentioned in [Mil84]. Consider the agent **A** managing some resources $\mathbf{R}_i$ $(1 \leq i \leq n)$ which signal to **A** via $\lambda$ when they are available. Other agents make requests for resources to **A** via $\gamma$. Let **Q** be such a potentially requesting agent. The situation can be pictured as:

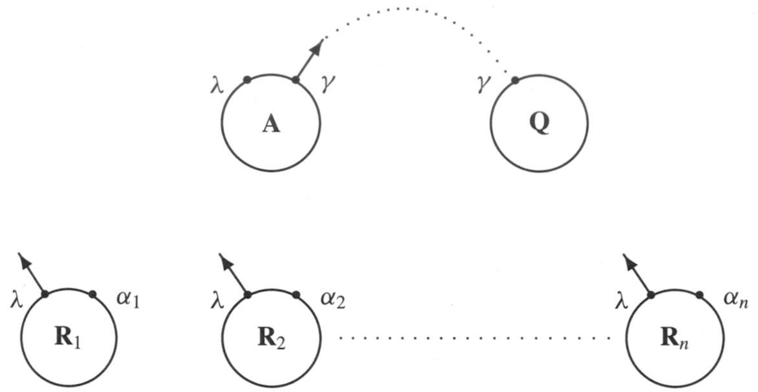


where the resource $\mathbf{R}_i$ is accessed through $\alpha_i$. A common solution is to write the system as

$(\mathbf{Q} \mid \mathbf{A} \mid \mathbf{R}_1 \mid \ldots \mid \mathbf{R}_n) \setminus A$, where $A = \{\alpha_i;\ 1 \leq i \leq n\}$

and to let **A** somewhere contain a subexpression like $\gamma!i.B$ meaning that **A** communicates the index of an available resource via $\gamma$; and let **Q** contain a subexpression like $\gamma?x.(\ldots\alpha_x!\ldots\alpha_x?\ldots)$ where $\gamma?k$ means receiving the index and using it for communication with resource $\mathbf{R}_x$ via $\alpha_x$. The problem of such solutions passing indexes as a kind of identification is that all potential resources must be known at the time when the administrator **A** and the system is written in order not to mix up indexes. Furthermore the family of indexed labels $\{\alpha_i\}$ must be known in advance.To illustrate this we consider a very simple system with a requesting agent and two resources.

$\mathbf{Q} \ \equiv \gamma?x.\alpha_x!8.\alpha_x?y.\delta!y.\text{nil}$

$\mathbf{R}_1 \equiv \text{fix}\, X\langle\lambda!1.\alpha_1?x.\alpha_1!2 * x.X\rangle$

$\mathbf{R}_2 \equiv \text{fix}\, X\langle\lambda!2.\alpha_2?x.\alpha_2!x + x.X\rangle$

We leave out the details of **A**. $A$ would in this example be $\{\alpha_1, \alpha_2\}$.

If one wants to add a new resource $\mathbf{R}_3$ to the system one must inspect the system to see that communications between requesting agents is done via labels of type $\alpha_x$ and that $\alpha_1$, $\alpha_2$ already is used. It is not enough to know the way they communicate (the communication protocol they use) and that requests for resources are done to **A** via $\gamma$ and resource availability is reported via $\lambda$. Furthermore **A** must be extended with $\{\alpha_3\}$ if '3' is used to identify $\mathbf{R}_3$.

This shows a certain *lack of modularity which we want to avoid.*

Therefore it should be possible to write the different agents independently of each other only knowing the interface to **A**, i.e., $\mathbf{R}_i$ knows $\lambda$ of **A** and **Q** knows $\gamma$ of **A**. As a consequence it must be possible for $\mathbf{R}_i$ to have a label which in a certain sense is unique in all contexts and which later can be used as communication link between $\mathbf{R}_i$ and **Q**. In addition the label shall remain unique or private to $\mathbf{R}_i$ and **Q** after it is communicated through **A** via $\lambda$ and $\gamma$, (except of course if it is communicated further from either **Q** or $\mathbf{R}_i$).

Last but not least we impose the restriction to keep as close as possible to Milner's CCS—e.g. *preserving as many as possible of the algebraic properties of CCS*. This requirement is actually quite independent of the extension we seek. With all the thought behind the elegancy of CCS this is a sound principle to apply in any attempt to extend CCS.

We will now give an idea of how ECCS can be made in order to meet these requirements.

Milner has already drawn attention to the connection between the binder "?" in $\alpha?x.$— of CCS and the binder "$\lambda$" in the lambda-calculus ([Mil80, p.49]). He also introduced a textual substitution postfix which has similar characteristics as the substitution prefix of the lambda-calculus (see [Mil80, p.67]) namely: when applied, change of bound variables is done as necessary to avoid clashes. It is clear that the substitution postfix formally can be handled along the lines of the substitution prefix of the lambda-calculus as long as we are only concerning the binding construct $\alpha?x.$—. But it is less clear that the binding construct fix $\tilde{X}$ introduced for recursion in [Mil83, Mil84] can be handled formally within the same framework, especially when $\tilde{X} = \langle X_i; i \in I\rangle$ an $I$-indexed family of distinct variables where $I$ is a uncountable set. One of our aims will therefore be to lift the results for the extension where fix appears as binder too (though only for finite $\tilde{X}$).

In order to meet the requirement of independence of actual names used for restriction we will furthermore widen the idea of bound and free occurrences to include labels as well, with "\" as the binding symbol for labels. In the lambda-calculus a central notion is $\alpha$-convertibility between functions with respect to bound variables. The idea is that functions which are equal "up to bound variables" denote the same function when applied to the same arguments. With our requirement that behaviour expressions which are equal "up to bound labels" should behave equally, it seems natural to extend the notion of $\alpha$-convertibility to include labels bound by "\."

The close relationship between substitution of variables and $\alpha$-convertibility (in the following just convertibility) will therefore also be generalised to substitution of labels. At the same time we thereby obtain the possibility to change unbound labels of a behaviour expression (i.e., the sort) and can therefore omit the postfixed relabelling operator. For the third requirement (possibility to have a unique or private label, to communicate it and for it to remain unique) notice that the label $\alpha$ in some sense is unique to $B$ in $B \setminus \alpha$ since $\alpha$ can be used only for internal communication and cannot interfere with other $\alpha$'s appearing in any contexts $B \setminus \alpha$ could be in. So in order to communicate $\alpha$ it must be possible to extend

$\alpha$'s scope to include the recipient. This and the remaining uniqueness is obtained through a (minor) extension of the inference rules.

To put the comments above differently, we want to extend CCS to allow passing of individual channels, viewing restriction as a formal binder, and to allow dynamic change of scope of such binders in connection with communication.

In order to get an idea of the possibilities of ECCS we turn back to the example of an administrator **A** and some agents $\mathbf{Q}_i$ requesting some resources $\mathbf{R}_j$ via the administrator.

We will make the simplifying assumption that it does not matter what resource a requesting agent gets, though the resources may be implemented differently as long as they obey the same communication protocol. If the administrator uses the "first-come-first-served" policy, it can be implemented as a FIFO-queue where a requesting agent enters the queue at the rear and leaves it at the front when a resource is available:

$$\mathbf{A} \equiv (\gamma?\mathit{newreq}.\mathbf{T}(\mathit{newreq}, \sigma) \mid \sigma!.\mathrm{nil}) \setminus \sigma,$$

$$\mathbf{T} \equiv \mathrm{fix}\, X\langle \mathit{oldreq}, x\rangle\langle(\gamma?\mathit{newreq}.X(\mathit{newreq}, \sigma)| \\ x?.\lambda?\mathit{freeres}.\mathit{oldreq}!\mathit{freeres}.\sigma!.\mathrm{nil}) \setminus \sigma\rangle$$

Each slanted name denotes a label variable ($\lambda, \gamma \neq \sigma$).

The administrator can be viewed as consisting of a series of elements each containing a waiting agent (*oldreq*). At the rear new requests are received ($\gamma?\mathit{newreq}$) and a new element created. The front element receives the name of an available resource ($\lambda?\mathit{freeres}$) and passes it on to the waiting agent ($\mathit{oldreq}!\mathit{freeres}$). After doing this it signals to the next ($\sigma!$) that it is the new front element now. Notice that the elements at the front and rear can serve the agents and resources concurrently.

We now turn to the parts of the resources and requesting agents which concern the communication between them and the administrator. A resource could look something like:

$$\mathbf{R}_j \equiv \mathrm{fix}\, X\, \tilde{p}\langle(\lambda!\alpha.\underline{\alpha?x}.\ldots\underline{\alpha!e}.X(\ldots)) \setminus \alpha\rangle, \alpha \neq \lambda$$

and a requesting agent:

$$\mathbf{Q}_i \equiv \ldots(\gamma!\beta.\beta?x.\underline{x!e'}.\ldots\underline{x?y}.\ldots) \setminus \beta \ldots, \beta \neq \gamma$$

The underlined actions correspond to the communication protocol between requesting agents and resources for this special example. The other shown actions concern the communication with the administrator. The label $\alpha$ in the resource is restricted and therefore unique or private for $\mathbf{R}_j$. Upon sending it to the administrator, its scope is extended to include the administrator (in accordance with Com→(3) and Res→(2) in section 3.3). A new name is possibly chosen in order not to interfere with other labels within the new scope such that it remains private to the resource. Afterwards it is passed on to the requesting agent at the front of the queue and the scope includes the agent in the same manner as before. The same happens when the requesting agent sends its private label—which acts like an identification—to the administrator. Notice that, after it has served an agent, a resource restores itself such that it sends a new private label when reporting that it is available.

## 3 ECCS and the $\pi$-Calculus

In the following we would like to present our original calculus ECCS, and to elaborate a little on its relationship to the $\pi$-calculus of Milner *et al.* [MPW89]. Let us start by the syntax.

### 3.1 Syntax

We chose to base our calculus on three types of expressions: behaviour expressions, label expressions and ordinary data expressions. Accordingly, we assumed the following disjoint sets of variables and labels: label variables (ranged over by $\mathsf{x}, \mathsf{y}, \ldots$), process variables $(X, Y, \ldots)$ and labels $(\alpha, \beta, \ldots)$.

In order to present the syntax and semantics of ECCS, we introduced the following rather clumsy conventions of associating symbols with domains of values and variables:

$a$: label or label variable,

$b, c$: variable or label (bindable elements),

$e$: label, label variable (label expressions) or a data expression built from constant and function symbols as usual (e.g., used as actual parameters to recursive process definitions),

$f$: data expression alone,

$p, x, y$: label variables or data variables (e.g., used for formal parameters to recursive process definitions),

$v$: label or data,

$M, N$: label, label variable, data expression, process variable or a indexed recursive process definition,

$B, E$: behaviour expressions.

Based on this, the complete syntax of ECCS is listed in Table 20.1. As you see, our syntax followed closely that of CCS from [Mil80]. Besides minor points, like our use of the ? and ! notation for input and output actions respectively, the main difference is, of course, the introduction of label variables on top of the other data variables from CCS, and the correspondingly more complex definitions of free variables, FV, free labels (sort), L, and bound variables and labels, $\mathcal{B}$. Table 20.1 was based on conventions and assumptions like the following.

**Table 20.1**
Syntax table for ECCS behaviour expressions.

| Form | $B''$ | $\mathrm{FV}(B'')$ | $\mathrm{L}(B'')$ | $\mathcal{B}(B'')$ |
|---|---|---|---|---|
| Inaction | nil | $\emptyset$ | $\emptyset$ | $\emptyset$ |
| Action | $\lambda?y.B$ | $\mathrm{FV}(B) - \{y\}$ | $\mathrm{L}(B) \cup \{\lambda\}$ | $\mathcal{B}(B) \cup \{y\}$ |
| | $\mathbf{x}?y.B$ | $(\mathrm{FV}(B) - \{y\}) \cup \{\mathbf{x}\}$ | $\mathrm{L}(B)$ | $\mathcal{B}(B) \cup \{y\}$ |
| | $\lambda!e.B$ | $\mathrm{FV}(B) \cup \{e\}$ | $\mathrm{L}(B) \cup \mathrm{L}(e)$ | $\mathcal{B}(B) \cup \mathcal{B}(e)$ |
| | $\mathbf{x}!e.B$ | $\mathrm{FV}(B) \cup \{e\} \cup \{\mathbf{x}\}$ | $\mathrm{L}(B) \cup \mathrm{L}(e)$ | $\mathcal{B}(B) \cup \mathcal{B}(e)$ |
| | $\tau.B$ | $\mathrm{FV}(B)$ | $\mathrm{L}(B)$ | $\mathcal{B}(B)$ |
| Summation | $B + B'$ | $\mathrm{FV}(B) \cup \mathrm{FV}(B')$ | $\mathrm{L}(B) \cup \mathrm{L}(B')$ | $\mathcal{B}(B) \cup \mathcal{B}(B')$ |
| Composition | $B \mid B'$ | $\mathrm{FV}(B) \cup \mathrm{FV}(B')$ | $\mathrm{L}(B) \cup \mathrm{L}(B')$ | $\mathcal{B}(B) \cup \mathcal{B}(B')$ |
| Restriction | $B \setminus \alpha$ | $\mathrm{FV}(B)$ | $\mathrm{L}(B) - \{\alpha\}$ | $\mathcal{B}(B) \cup \{\alpha\}$ |
| Recursion | $\mathrm{fix}_i\ \tilde{X}\,\tilde{p}\,\tilde{E}(\tilde{e})$ | $(\mathrm{FV}(\tilde{E}) - \{\tilde{X},\ \tilde{p}\}) \cup \{\tilde{e}\}$ | $\mathrm{L}(\tilde{E}) \cup \mathrm{L}(\tilde{e})$ | $\mathcal{B}(\tilde{E}) \cup \{\tilde{X},\ \tilde{p}\} \cup \mathcal{B}(\tilde{e})$ |
| | $X(\tilde{e})$ | $\{X\} \cup \{\tilde{e}\}$ | $\mathrm{L}(\tilde{e})$ | $\mathcal{B}(\tilde{e})$ |
| Conditional | **if** $f$ **then** $B$ **else** $B'$ | $\{f\} \cup \mathrm{FV}(B) \cup \mathrm{FV}(B')$ | $\mathrm{L}(B) \cup \mathrm{L}(B')$ | $\mathcal{B}(f) \cup \mathcal{B}(B) \cup \mathcal{B}(B')$ |

i) $\{e\}$ denotes the set of (free) variables occurring in expression $e$.

ii) Vectors of variables are allowed in recursive process definitions (only!), where $\langle X_1, \ldots, X_n \rangle$ is abbreviated $\tilde{X}$.

iii) Labels and label variables are also allowed as actual parameters to a recursion expression.

iv) Two elements of the syntax are said to be *comparable* if they are the same type like e.g., a label $\alpha$ and a label variable $\mathbf{x}$, a behaviour expression $E$ and a process variable $X$, etc.

v) *Formal parameters*, $\tilde{p}$, and *actual parameters*, $\tilde{e}$, of a recursion definition are tacitly assumed to be of the same dimension and corresponding elements to be comparable.

vi) In a conditional expression no label or label variable may be contained in $f$ to form a boolean expression.

For comparison we recapitulate the syntax of the $\pi$-calculus of Milner *et al.* Agents or process expressions of the $\pi$-calculus are defined as follows:

$$P ::= \mathbf{0} \mid x(y).P \mid \bar{x}y.P \mid \tau.P \mid P + Q \mid P \mid Q \mid (x)P \mid [x = y]P \mid A(y_1, \ldots, y_n),$$

where $w, x, y, z$ range over (link) names, $P$ and $Q$ range over agents and $A$ over agent identifiers. Here $\mathbf{0}$ represents inaction. The action prefixes $x(y).$, $\bar{x}y.$ and $\tau.$ corresponds to input-, (free) output- and silent-prefix respectively. The restriction of $x$ to $P$ is denoted

**Table 20.2**
The $\pi$-calculus actions.

| $\alpha$ | Kind | fn($\alpha$) | bn($\alpha$) |
|---|---|---|---|
| $\tau$ | Silent | $\emptyset$ | $\emptyset$ |
| $\bar{x}y$ | Free Output | $\{x, y\}$ | $\emptyset$ |
| $x(y)$ | Input | $\{x\}$ | $\{y\}$ |
| $\bar{x}(y)$ | Bound Output | $\{x\}$ | $\{y\}$ |

$(x)P$ to stress that it is regarded as a name-binding operator. $[x = y]P$ represents matching of names and behaves like $P$ if $x$ equals $y$ and otherwise like $\mathbf{0}$.

Each agent identifier $A$ must be associated a unique defining equation $A(y_1, \ldots, y_n) \stackrel{\text{def}}{=} P$ with $\text{fn}(P) \subseteq \{y_1, \ldots, y_n\}$, where Milner *et al.* use $\text{fn}(P)$ to denote the free names of $P$. $\text{fn}(P)$ is defined structurally on $P$ similarly as FV for ECCS in Table 20.1. In the same way $\text{bn}(P)$ denotes the bound names of $P$ and $\text{n}(P)$ is just the names of $P$ whether free or bound. The free and bound names of the action prefixes can be seen in the first three lines of Table 20.2.

The simplifications of Milner *et al.* are particularly striking on the syntactical level. They removed non-label expressions, blurred the distinction between labels and label variables, and replaced the fix recursion construct with defining equations. Consequently the number of binders and syntactic categories was diminished considerably and a much more elegant language was obtained.

The only possible label expressions of ECCS were labels and label variables. In contrast Milner *et al.* allowed a matching construct (which in our setup would correspond to testing labels for equality), and used it to give tractable encodings of data computations and a powerful form of expansion law.

Following [Mil80] we did not state any language of data expressions (non-label expressions) in the presentation of the calculus, and as such the calculus can be regarded as parametrised in the language of data expressions. However, given the data encodings of Milner *et al.* and successors, it should be clear that ECCS can be simulated in the $\pi$-calculus.

Though we deliberately chose the fix construct to handle recursion we could have used a system of defining equations. For a defining equation $A(\tilde{p}) \stackrel{\text{def}}{=} E$ we would as Milner *et al.* have to demand $\text{FV}(E) \subseteq \{\tilde{p}\}$. However, we would also have to demand $E$ to have no free labels, i.e., $\text{L}(E) = \emptyset$, since different occurrences of $A$ can be in the scope of restrictions and so possibly subject to different $\alpha$-conversions. This somewhat unpleasant condition is avoided with the fix recursion construct. In follow up papers [Mil90, Mil91], Milner obtained an even more basic calculus using the replication operator "!."

### 3.2 Substitution, Conversion

As indicated earlier we relied heavely on notions of substitution and convertability. Not only were these notions from the λ-calculus generalised to behaviour expressions regarding input and fix as variable binders, but more importantly restricton was viewed as a proper (label) binder as in λ-calculus. This crucial idea was suggested to us by Matthew Hennessy in discussions on the development of ECCS.

In ECCS $[M/b]B$ is defined provided $M$ is comparable to $b$ and denotes the result of syntactically substituting $M$ for all (free) occurrences of the bindable element $b$ in the expression $B$, with change of comparable bound elements as necessary to avoid clashes. The substitution prefix is defined not only for behaviour expressions but also for atomic elements such as labels, data-values and variables.

Having generalised substitution, we generalised $\alpha$-conversion to handle the three forms of binders, and defined a convertibility relation, cnv, over behaviour expressions accordingly. Substitution and conversion were shown to satisfy the expected properties such as preservation of convertability under substitution.

In the $\pi$-calculus a substitution is simply a function $\sigma$ from names to names which is the identity except on a finite set of names. $P\sigma$ denotes the simultaneous substitution of $z\sigma$ for $z$ in $P$ with change of bound names to avoid captures. Milner *et al.* writes $\{y/x\}$ for $\sigma$ in the special case where $\sigma$ is $y$ on $x$ and the identity elsewhere. $\equiv_\alpha$ denotes the $\alpha$-convertibility relation on agents. Also these $\pi$-calculus notions of substitution and $\alpha$-conversion were shown by Milner *et al.* to satisfy the expected properties.

However, even if essentially the same kinds of results were obtained for the ECCS and the $\pi$-calculus notions of substitution and $\alpha$-conversion, the removal of the fix recursion construct, non-label expressions and the distinction between labels and label variables in the $\pi$-calculus, simplified the formal treatment of these notions considerably in the $\pi$-calculus.

### 3.3 Derivations

The operational rules of ECCS are shown in Table 20.3. Before relating them to those of the $\pi$-calculus a few comments are needed.

First of all, we were looking for a definition of an action relation $B \xrightarrow{\Gamma} B'$ over *programs*, i.e. for $B$ and $B'$ such that $\mathrm{FV}(B) = \mathrm{FV}(B') = \emptyset$, much in the spirit of CCS, where for a program $B$, the resulting behaviour expression $B'$ is also a program. This is not the case with ECCS, which we considered a drawback! So, we thought of $B \xrightarrow{\lambda?x} B'$ as "$B$ becomes $[v/x]B'$ under $\lambda?v$ where $v$ is any value $x$ can assume, i.e. $v$ is a value comparable to $x$," and our definition of behavioural equivalence was deliberately defined only in terms of derivation rules $B \xrightarrow{\Gamma} B'$ for which $B$ is a program—see later.

**Table 20.3**
The ECCS transition rules. Each L-rule has a symmetric R-rule.

| | | | | |
|---|---|---|---|---|
| Ina→ | | nil has no atomic actions | | |
| Act→ | (1) | $\lambda?x.B \xrightarrow{\lambda?y} [y/x]B$ | | |
| | (2) | $\lambda!v.B \xrightarrow{\lambda!v} B$ | | |
| | (3) | $\tau.B \xrightarrow{\tau} B$ | | |
| Sum→ | L: | $\dfrac{B_0 \xrightarrow{\Gamma} B_0'}{B_0 + B_1 \xrightarrow{\Gamma} B_0'}$ | | |
| Com→ | (1)L: | $\dfrac{B_0 \xrightarrow{\Gamma} B_0'}{B_0 \mid B_1 \xrightarrow{\Gamma} B_0' \mid B_1}$ | (2)L: | $\dfrac{B_0 \xrightarrow{\lambda!v} B_0',\ B_1 \xrightarrow{\lambda?x} B_1'}{B_0 \mid B_1 \xrightarrow{\tau} B_0' \mid [v/x]B_1'}$ |
| | (3)L: | $\dfrac{B_0 \xrightarrow{\lambda!\mathsf{X}} B_0',\ B_1 \xrightarrow{\lambda?\mathsf{X}} B_1',\ \alpha \notin \mathrm{L}(B_i)}{B_0 \mid B_1 \xrightarrow{\tau} [\alpha/\mathsf{X}](B_0' \mid B_1') \setminus \alpha}$ | | |
| Res→ | (1) | $\dfrac{B \xrightarrow{\Gamma} B',\ \alpha \notin \mathrm{L}(\Gamma)}{B \setminus \alpha \xrightarrow{\Gamma} B' \setminus \alpha}$ | (2) | $\dfrac{B \xrightarrow{\lambda!\alpha} B',\ \lambda \neq \alpha}{B \setminus \alpha \xrightarrow{\lambda!\mathsf{X}} [\mathsf{X}/\alpha]B'}$ |
| Rec→ | | $\dfrac{[\mathrm{fix}\ \tilde{X}\,\tilde{p}\,\tilde{E}/\tilde{X}][\tilde{v}/\tilde{p}]E_i \xrightarrow{\Gamma} B}{\mathrm{fix}_i\ \tilde{X}\,\tilde{p}\,\tilde{E}(\tilde{v}) \xrightarrow{\Gamma} B}$ | | |
| Con→ | L: | $\dfrac{B_0 \xrightarrow{\Gamma} B_0'}{\textbf{if}\ \mathsf{true}\ \textbf{then}\ B_0\ \textbf{else}\ B_1 \xrightarrow{\Gamma} B_0'}$ | | |

When looking at the axioms and inference rules in Table 20.3 defining the atomic action relation please recall that we only write $[M/b]$ when $M$ and $b$ are comparable. So for instance the inference rules Com→(2) are only defined when $v$ and $x$ are comparable. Similarly the axiom Act→(1) is only defined for $y$ and $x$ comparable.

Finally, let us quote one technical proposition and four of our original notes on the action relation:

PROPOSITION 1 If $B \xrightarrow{\Gamma} B'$ is a part of an inference which ensures $C \xrightarrow{\Gamma} C'$ then $\mathrm{FV}(C) = \emptyset$ implies $\mathrm{FV}(B) = \emptyset$.

i) By Proposition 1 it is clear that if Act→(1) is the basis of an inference which ensures an action of a program then $\mathrm{FV}(\lambda?x.B) = \emptyset$ and an arbitrarily chosen $y$ will therefore be just as good as $x$. Furthermore it will not interfere with variables in another part of the program since, also by Proposition 1, any other part of the program which can form an action cannot have free variables. For instance if $D = C \mid \lambda?x.B$ is a program and $D \xrightarrow{\lambda?x} C \mid B'$ then $x$ cannot be free in $C$. Therefore it is ensured in Com→(2) that $v$ is substituted in the "right" place. Com→(1), Com→(2) correspond to those of CCS.

ii) The reason for letting $(\lambda?x.B, [y/x]B)$ be in the relation $\stackrel{\lambda?y}{\longrightarrow}$ is that we wish $\alpha$-convertible programs to be behaviourally equivalent. This could have been obtained through a modification of the definition of strong equivalence, but we have found it more convenient here.

iii) Two inference rules are added to CCS: Com$\rightarrow$(3) and Res$\rightarrow$(2). They make it possible to extend the scope of a label. Res$\rightarrow$(2) cancels the restriction and for the reasons mentioned in i) it does not matter which variable is chosen (as long as it is a label variable of course). In Com$\rightarrow$(3) the restriction is reintroduced and the label made available to the recipient. The actual name of the label is chosen such that it does not interfere with other names in the new scope by the condition $\alpha \notin \mathrm{L}(B_i)$. Notice that the original name can be chosen if it does not appear in the environment outside the old and inside the new scope.

iv) The definition depends heavily on the substitution prefix and its properties as seen in Act$\rightarrow$(1), Com$\rightarrow$(2), Com$\rightarrow$(3) and Res$\rightarrow$(2). Most of all it depends on the property that a label or variable which "passes through" a bound occurrence by substitution changes the names of the bound occurrence and "passes" on, thereby avoiding any conflict.

So much for the derivation rules of ECCS. The corresponding rules of the $\pi$-calculus are shown in Table 20.4

Comparing the transition rules of Table 20.3 and Table 20.4 the interesting parts are the treatments of "scope extension," as we called it, or "scope extrusion" as it was later called by Milner *et al.*

Notice the close correspondence between the action symbols, $\Gamma$, used in the action relation and the prefix constructs of ECCS, also following the spirit of CCS. Not having the ECCS possibility of distinguishing between $\stackrel{\lambda!v}{\longrightarrow}$ and $\stackrel{\lambda!\boldsymbol{X}}{\longrightarrow}$ in defining the transition relations of the $\pi$-calculus, Milner *et al.* introduced a fourth kind of action, bounded output $\bar{x}(y)$, which has no corresponding prefix form in the syntax of the calculus, but captures the idea that a private name $y$ is output on the port $\bar{x}$. With this notation the OPEN and CLOSE rules of Table 20.4 correspond closely to the Res$\rightarrow$(2) and Com$\rightarrow$(2) rules of Table 20.3, essentially using different syntax for making the same semantic distinction between "normal" output and output carrying a restricted name out of its scope. The actions of the $\pi$-calculus are summarised in Table 20.2.

Also notice that both sets of transition rules follow the late instantiation scheme, i.e. instantiation (by a label or data-value) of a variable bound by an input prefix is deferred to the time of inferring internal communication (Com$\rightarrow$(2) and Com$\rightarrow$(3)). At first glance

**Table 20.4**
The $\pi$-calculus Rules of Actions. Rules involving the binary operators $+$ and $|$ additionally have symmetric forms.

$$\text{TAU-ACT: } \frac{-}{\tau.P \xrightarrow{\tau} P} \qquad \text{OUTPUT-ACT: } \frac{-}{\bar{x}y.P \xrightarrow{\bar{x}y} P}$$

$$\text{INPUT-ACT: } \frac{-}{x(z).P \xrightarrow{x(w)} P\{w/z\}} \quad w \notin \mathrm{fn}((z)P)$$

$$\text{SUM: } \frac{P \xrightarrow{\alpha} P'}{P + Q \xrightarrow{\alpha} P'} \qquad \text{MATCH: } \frac{P \xrightarrow{\alpha} P'}{[x = x]P \xrightarrow{\alpha} P'}$$

$$\text{IDE: } \frac{P\{\tilde{y}/\tilde{x}\} \xrightarrow{\alpha} P'}{A(\tilde{y}) \xrightarrow{\alpha} P'} \quad A(\tilde{x}) \stackrel{\mathrm{def}}{=} P$$

$$\text{PAR: } \frac{P \xrightarrow{\alpha} P'}{P \mid Q \xrightarrow{\alpha} P' \mid Q} \quad \mathrm{bn}(\alpha) \cap \mathrm{fn}(Q) = \emptyset$$

$$\text{COM: } \frac{P \xrightarrow{\bar{x}y} P' \quad Q \xrightarrow{x(z)} Q'}{P \mid Q \xrightarrow{\tau} P' \mid Q'\{y/z\}} \qquad \text{CLOSE: } \frac{P \xrightarrow{\bar{x}(w)} P' \quad Q \xrightarrow{x(w)} Q'}{P \mid Q \xrightarrow{\tau} (w)(P' \mid Q')}$$

$$\text{RES: } \frac{P \xrightarrow{\alpha} P'}{(y)P \xrightarrow{\alpha} (y)P'} \; y \notin \mathrm{n}(\alpha) \qquad \text{OPEN: } \frac{P \xrightarrow{\bar{x}y} P'}{(y)P \xrightarrow{\bar{x}(w)} P'\{w/y\}} \; \begin{array}{l} y \neq x \\ w \notin \mathrm{fn}((y)P') \end{array}$$

CLOSE appears to be relatively different from Com$\rightarrow$(3) and less late. However, Milner *et al.* actually define the transition relations using the following rule:

$$\frac{P \xrightarrow{\bar{x}(w)} P' \quad Q \xrightarrow{x(z)} Q'}{P \mid Q \xrightarrow{\tau} (w)(P' \mid, Q'\{w/z\})} \quad w = z \text{ or } w \notin \mathrm{fn}(Q').$$

Due to the elegancy of their formulation of the system of transition rules, they are able to replace the rule with CLOSE. The issue of early versus late instantiation was introduced in [MPW89, MPW91].

Also, many of our concerns on interference of variables were avoided in the $\pi$-calculus by dropping the distinction between labels and variables and by introducing the explicit side condition in PAR rule of Table 20.4, ensuring that free variables are not accidentally bound in the COM or CLOSE rule. Since we worked on programs (with no free variables) we did not need a similar condition in Com$\rightarrow$(1) as explained in note i) to the action relation.

The following theorem from [EN86] establishes an important connection between substitution, conversion and the action relations in ECCS:

THEOREM 2

(a) $C \xrightarrow{\Gamma} C' \Rightarrow [\delta/\gamma]C \xrightarrow{[\delta/\gamma]\Gamma} C''$ cnv $[\delta/\gamma]C'$

(b) The following diagram commutes in the sense that if $B_0$ cnv $B_1 \xrightarrow{\Gamma} B_1'$ then $B_0'$ exists such that $B_0 \xrightarrow{\Gamma} B_0'$ cnv $B_1'$ and vice versa:

$$\begin{array}{ccc} B_0 & \text{cnv} & B_1 \\ \downarrow\Gamma & & \downarrow\Gamma \\ B_0' & \text{cnv} & B_1' \end{array}$$

(c) $[\delta/\gamma]C \xrightarrow{\Gamma} D$ implies that there exist $\Gamma'$ and $D'$ such that

$C \xrightarrow{\Gamma'} D'$ and $[\delta/\gamma]D'$ cnv $D$, $[\delta/\gamma]\Gamma' = \Gamma$.

As later pointed out to us by David Walker, there was a mistake in our formulation of Theorem 2 (c) which is not correct as stated in the case where $\Gamma = \tau$. As a counterexample consider

$$[\delta/\gamma](\gamma? \mid \delta!) \xrightarrow{\tau} \text{nil}.$$

However, the statement holds provided $\delta$ is not in the sort of $C$ as correctly formulated for the $\pi$-calculus in Lemma 4 from Part II [MPW89] where also the rest of Theorem 2 is shown for the $\pi$-calculus.

### 3.4 Behavioural Equivalences

Since our overall goal was a generalisation of the algebraic theory of CCS, our search for an appropriate operational semantics for ECCS was done in parallel with a corresponding search for appropriate generalisations of Milner's notions of strong and observational equivalences from [Mil80]. However, whereas our operational semantics changed several times, our generalisations of the behavioural equivalences were actually quite stable. The notions we adopted just seemed the most natural generalisations to us, but looking back, it is obvious that there were several alternatives which we did not even think of, some of them already pointed out in [MPW89]. If we focus on the strong equivalence, our generalisation looked as given in Table 20.5. To get a nicer formulation of the equivalence, the last two lines were originally joined in a single line (relying on a notation for the union of input and output actions). For clarity and the sake of a later comment, it is here presented with two separate cases.

Our definition was accompanied in [EN86] by claims of a number of properties expected for a proper lifting of the algebraic theory of CCS, e.g., the following three theorems.

**Table 20.5**
The ECCS definition of strong equivalence between programs.

$B_0 \sim B_1$ iff $\forall k \geq 0 : B_0 \sim_k B_1$, where $B_0 \sim_k B_1$ is defined:

$B_0 \sim_0 B_1$ is always true
$B_0 \sim_{k+1} B_1$ iff for all $\Gamma (i = 0, 1)$:

$$\begin{array}{ll} \text{i) } B_i \xrightarrow{\Gamma} B'_i \Rightarrow \exists B'_{i\oplus 1} : B_{i\oplus 1} \xrightarrow{\Gamma} B'_{i\oplus 1} \text{ and} & \\ \quad B'_i \sim_k B'_{i\oplus 1}, & \text{if } \Gamma = \tau, \lambda!v \\ \quad \forall v : [v/x]B'_i \sim_k [v/x]B'_{i\oplus 1}, & \text{if } \Gamma = \lambda?x \\ \quad \forall \alpha : [\alpha/\mathsf{x}]B'_i \sim_k [\alpha/\mathsf{x}]B'_{i\oplus 1}, & \text{if } \Gamma = \lambda!\mathsf{x} \end{array}$$

THEOREM 3

(a) $\sim$ is an equivalence relation (b) $B_0 \sim_{k+1} B_1$ implies $B_0 \sim_k B_1$

(c) $B_0 \sim B_1$ implies $B_0 \sim_k B_1$ for all $k$ (d) $B_0$ $\mathsf{cnv}$ $B_1$ implies $B_0 \sim B_1$

Also, we claimed that we almost had a congruence in the following formal sense, with closure under general substitution, Theorem 4, as "perhaps the hardest to accept":

THEOREM 4 $B_0 \sim B_1$ implies $[\delta/\gamma]B_0 \sim [\delta/\gamma]B_1$.

THEOREM 5 $[v/x]B_0 \sim [v/x]B_1$ for all $v$ implies $\lambda?x.B_0 \sim \lambda?x.B_1$

$$\begin{array}{lll} B_0 \sim B_1 \text{ implies} & \lambda!v.B_0 \sim \lambda!v.B_1 & \tau.B_0 \sim \tau.B_1 \\ & B_0 + C \sim B_1 + C & C + B_0 \sim C + B_1 \\ & B_0 \mid C \sim B_1 \mid C & C \mid B_0 \sim C \mid B_1 \\ & B_0 \setminus \alpha \sim B_1 \setminus \alpha & \end{array}$$

The corresponding definition of strong ground bisimilarity adopted by Milner *et al.* is given in Table 20.6.

Apart from the fact that the two definitions refer to two different syntactic languages, there are a few more interesting differences worth commenting. In retrospect it is clear that our definition of strong equivalence was unsatisfactory for several reasons.

First of all, our definition was presented along the lines of the definition in the original version of CCS, i.e., in terms of a decreasing sequence of equivalence relations, and not in the more elegant Park and Milner style of strong bisimulation [Par81, Mil83]. The reason was not that we were unaware of this style of definition, but our proof skills were simply insufficient to see how to carry through the proofs for a bisimulation version of our definition. What we failed to see was how to define suitable bisimulation relations in the cases involving restriction. Milner *et al.* elegantly solved this by using inductively defined

**Table 20.6**
The $\pi$-calculus definition of strong simulation, strong ground bisimilarity and strong bisimilarity.

$\mathcal{S}$ is a strong simulation if $P \; \mathcal{S} \; Q$ implies

1. If $P \xrightarrow{\alpha} P'$ and $\alpha$ is a free action,
then for some $Q'$, $Q \xrightarrow{\alpha} Q'$ and $P' \; \mathcal{S} \; Q'$
2. If $P \xrightarrow{x(y)} P'$ and $y \notin n(P, Q)$,
then for some $Q'$, $Q \xrightarrow{x(y)} Q'$ and for all $w$, $P'\{w/y\} \; \mathcal{S} \; Q'\{w/y\}$
3. If $P \xrightarrow{\bar{x}(y)} P'$ and $y \notin n(P, Q)$,
then for some $Q'$, $Q \xrightarrow{\bar{x}(y)} Q'$ and $P' \; \mathcal{S} \; Q'$

A binary relation $\mathcal{S}$ is a strong bisimulation if both $\mathcal{S}$ and its inverse are strong simulations.

Two agents $P$ and $Q$ are strongly ground bisimilar, written $P \dot{\sim} Q$ iff there exists a strong bisimulation $\mathcal{S}$ such that $P \; \mathcal{S} \; Q$.

$P$ and $Q$ are strongly bisimilar, written $P \sim Q$, iff $P\sigma \dot{\sim} Q\sigma$ for all substitutions $\sigma$.

bisimulation relations essentially allowing proof techniques which we only found possible with the given definition. Their insight also led to the introduction of an auxiliary definition of strong bisimulation up to restriction.

Another reason is a consequence of the previously mentioned problem in Theorem 2. As we shall see shortly, our strong equivalence does not in general preserve substitution of labels and consequently it cannot, with the present formulation, be a congruence w.r.t. restriction. The definition should be modified in the case of output actions with variables, following the corresponding case in the definition of strong ground bisimilarity above, i.e. such that substitution only quantifies over labels not in the sort of $B_0$ and $B_1$. A more correct version of the definition of Table 20.5 would have the last line replaced by:

$$\forall \alpha \notin \mathrm{L}(B_0, B_1) : [\alpha/\mathbf{x}]B_i' \sim_k [\alpha/\mathbf{x}]B_{i\oplus 1}', \text{ if } \Gamma = \lambda!\mathbf{x}$$

Consequences of the problem in Theorem 2 can also be detected in Theorem 4 as the following counter example shows.

$$B_0 \equiv \gamma? \mid \delta!, \quad B_1 \equiv \gamma?.\delta! + \delta!.\gamma?$$

So not only was our original Theorem 4 hard to accept—it was false as stated!

However, the theorem holds under the proviso that $\delta$ is not in the sort of $B_0$ and $B_1$, as correctly formulated for the $\pi$-calculus in [MPW89]. And with the modified definition of strong equivalence this is all what is needed for it to be a congruence w.r.t. restriction, as correctly noticed by and proved by Milner *et al.*

Notice that both definitions are late, in the sense that for input actions, the behaviour expressions $B_0'$ and $B_1'$ are required to be equivalent for all (program) instantiations of the bound variable. However, Milner *et al.* soon started looking at alternatives, see e.g., [MPW91] for definitions and characterisations of early and late bisimulations.

The next theorem collects some algebraic properties proved in the thesis accompanying [EN86] for ECCS. In the theorem $g$ stands for a guard, i.e. $\tau$, $a!e$, $a?x$ or $a!x$.

THEOREM 6 (FOR PROGRAMS)

Sum$\sim$

(1) $B_0 + B_1 \sim B_1 + B_0$ (2) $B_0 + (B_1 + B_2) \sim (B_0 + B_1) + B_2$

(3) $B + \text{nil} \sim \text{nil}$ (4) $B + B \sim B$

Com$\sim$

(1) $B_0 \mid B_1 \sim B_1 \mid B_0$ (2) $B_0 \mid (B_1 \mid B_2) \sim (B_0 \mid B_1) \mid B_2$

(3) $B \mid \text{nil} \sim B$ (4) If $B_0$, $B_1$ are sums of guards then $B_0 \mid B_1 \sim$

$$\begin{aligned}&\textstyle\sum\{g.(B_0' \mid B_1);\ g.B_0' \text{ a summand of } B_0\}+\\&\textstyle\sum\{g.(B_0 \mid B_1');\ g.B_1' \text{ a summand of } B_1\}+\\&\textstyle\sum\{\tau.(B_0' \mid [v/x]B_1');\ \lambda!v.B_0' \text{ a s. of } B_0,\ \lambda?x.B_1' \text{ a s. of } B_1\}+\\&\textstyle\sum\{\tau.([v/x]B_0' \mid B_1');\ \lambda?x.B_0' \text{ a s. of } B_0,\ \lambda!v.B_1' \text{ a s. of } B_1\}\end{aligned}$$

Res$\sim$

(1) $(g.B) \setminus \alpha \sim \begin{cases} \text{nil} & \text{if } g = \alpha!v \\ g.B \setminus \alpha & \text{if } \alpha \notin \mathrm{L}(g) \end{cases}$

(2) $B \setminus \alpha \sim B$, provided $\alpha \notin \mathrm{L}(B)$ (3) $B \setminus \alpha \setminus \beta \sim B \setminus \beta \setminus \alpha$

(4) $(B_0 + B_1) \setminus \alpha \sim B_0 \setminus \alpha + B_1 \setminus \alpha$ (5) $(B_0 \mid B_1) \setminus \alpha \sim B_0 \setminus \alpha \mid B_1 \setminus \alpha$, provided $\alpha \notin \mathrm{L}(B_0) \cap \mathrm{L}(B_1)$

Rec$\sim$ $\text{fix}_i\ \tilde{X}\,\tilde{p}\,\tilde{E}(\tilde{v}) \sim [\text{fix}\ \tilde{X}\,\tilde{p}\,\tilde{E}/\tilde{X}][\tilde{v}/\tilde{p}]E_i$

Con$\sim$

$L$: **if** true **then** $B_0$ **else** $B_1 \sim B_0$ $R$: **if** false **then** $B_0$ **else** $B_1 \sim B_1$

Again a few comments are in place. First of all, our rationale at the time was to make sure that we had appropriately generalised versions of the laws from Milner's axiomatisation of CCS, and we did not even consider the issue of completeness. Given that ECCS is parametrised in the language of data expressions, completeness would anyway be relative to the completeness of a proof system for data expressions in case such one would exist. However, Milner *et al.* had the superiority and insight to abandon the features of CCS irrelevant for mobility. With the simplifications they were able to give an equational theory for strong ground bisimulation complete for finite agents, based on versions of the laws from the Theorem above for ECCS, with one notable strengthening: Com$\sim$(4) of Theorem 6 ("small" Expansion Theorem). Compared with the expansion theorem adopted by Milner *et al.* it lacks cases for guards like $(\lambda!\alpha.B') \setminus \alpha$ corresponding to bound output actions in their terminology.

Furthermore, [EN86] also lifted strong equivalence to open expressions much in the same way as when Milner *et al.* introduced nonground bisimilarity. However, we could not lift our expansion theorem smoothly, a problem which was solved by Milner *et al.* by introducing the matching construct. More importantly, we only introduced our notion to allow ourselves to reason algebraically on our benchmark examples. Milner *et al.* initiated the study of nonground strong bisimilarity in its own right, e.g., proving that it forms a proper congruence for the $\pi$-calculus.

In addition an observational equivalence was suggested in [EN86], but the equivalence was only studied to the extent that certain desired properties of one of the benchmark examples (in particular the pushdown store) could be proven.

### 3.5 Expressiveness

As mentioned in the Preface, we had developed our own small set of benchmark examples to test expressiveness. One of them was based on some problems concerning CCS identified in chapter 9 of [Mil80], providing a phrase-by-phrase translation of an imperative programming language $P$ into CCS. In this test of the expressiveness of CCS, Milner observed difficulties in handling certain programming language constructs, e.g., procedure call mechanisms with call-by-reference, and procedures admitting several concurrent activations. In the following we recall how these problems were overcome by ECCS, mainly because this part of [EN86] at least to some extent could explain some of the complications of ECCS, certainly motivated originally by this particular benchmark.

Let us briefly repeat parts of the translation scheme of $P$ into CCS from [Mil80]. The values of variables from $P$ are kept in CCS registers:

$$\mathrm{LOC} \equiv \alpha?x.\,\mathrm{fix}\, X\langle y\rangle\langle \alpha?x.X(x) + \gamma!y.X(y)\rangle(x)$$

$\mathrm{LOC}_Z$ is the register specially devoted to variable $Z$ by defining:

$$\mathrm{LOC}_Z \equiv [\alpha_Z/\alpha][\gamma_Z/\gamma]\,\mathrm{LOC}$$

A value for $Z$ is stored via $\alpha_Z$ and read via $\gamma_Z$, and the scope of a variable is limited by restricting with $L_Z = \{\alpha_Z, \gamma_Z\}$.

$\pi$-calculus The translation of $P$-expressions $E$ ($[\![E]\!]$) is such that it delivers the result via $\varrho$, introducing the notation:

$$B_0 \text{ result } B_1 \text{ denoting } (B_0 \mid B_1) \setminus \varrho$$

And finally, a translated program $[\![C]\!]$ signals its completion via $\delta$ whereupon it "dies." It is therefore convenient to define

$$\mathrm{done} \equiv \delta!.\mathrm{nil}$$

and

$B_0$ before $B_1 \equiv ([\beta/\delta]B_0 \mid \beta?.B_1) \setminus \beta$

for a $\beta \notin L(B_0) \cup L(B_1)$.

Now we suggested in [EN86] to translate a procedure declaration with call-by-value and call-by-result parameters into ECCS as follows

$$[\![\text{ PROC } G(\text{VALUE } X, \text{RESULT } Y) \text{ is } C_G]\!] = \\ \text{fix } X_G\langle(\alpha_G!\lambda.(X_G \mid (LOC_X \mid LOC_Y \mid \lambda?x.\alpha_X!x.[\![C_G]\!]) \\ \text{before } \gamma_Y?y.\lambda!y.\text{nil})) \setminus L_X \setminus L_Y)) \setminus \lambda\rangle$$

and to translate a corresponding call as

$$[\![\text{ CALL } G(E, Z)]\!] = [\![E]\!] \text{ result } (\varrho?x.\alpha_G?y.y!x.y?z.\alpha_Z!z.\text{done})$$

The problem identified by Milner in handling concurrent activations was in this translation solved by letting the activated procedure return a communication link private to the caller and that particular activation. Our solution to the problem of procedures with call-by-reference parameters consisted of translating procedure declarations as

$$[\![\text{ PROC } G(\text{REF } Z) \text{ is } C_G]\!] = \text{fix } X_G\langle(\alpha_G!\lambda.(X_G \mid (\lambda?z_\alpha.\lambda?z_\gamma.[z_\alpha/\alpha_Z][z_\gamma/\gamma_Z][\![C_G]\!]) \\ \text{before } \lambda!.\text{nil})) \setminus \lambda\rangle$$

and corresponding calls as

$$[\![\text{ CALL } G(Y)]\!] = \alpha_G?y.y!\alpha_Y.y!\gamma_Y.y?.\text{done}.$$

The issue of expressiveness of the $\pi$-calculus was addressed much more seriously Milner *et al.* They showed how the effect of process-passing could be achieved by link-passing and gave encodings of values and various data structures. More notably they devised encodings of combinator calculi and the lazy $\lambda$-calculus.

Given the data encodings of Milner *et al.*, they would be able to deal with all of our benchmark examples and in particular the problems of the translation could be solved in the $\pi$-calculus exactly as in ECCS.

## 4 Conclusion from 1986

ECCS as presented here is one attempt at a smooth extension of CCS satisfying the goals outlined in the introduction. In the process of defining ECCS we have considered a great number of alternatives—slowly converging to ECCS in its present form. We feel, and we hope the reader feels the same, that ECCS is reasonably in line with the elegancy of Milner's CCS—at least this has been one of our main guidelines in the process. We also feel there are some sound ideas underlying the calculus of ECCS, but we certainly do not claim that ECCS is the end product. There are still aspects with which we feel uneasy, and let us just mention a few.

One has to do with the fact that in ECCS, as presented here, only one value may be communicated at a time. As long as we are only concerned with normal data-values, it is obvious how to extend the calculus to allow tuples of values (as in CCS). But for label values the situation is not quite so clear. At least, it requires some thought how to formulate "multi-change of scope in connection with single communication." We have chosen to present ECCS without going into these problems. Also, we have deliberately chosen not to consider the problems involved in generalising CCS to allow passing of processes.

Another slightly displeasing thing about ECCS is the fact that labels are somehow considered both as variables (bound by restriction) and values (to be substituted for label variables bound by input commands).

Furthermore, ECCS obviously needs to be tried out on more challenging examples than the small toy problems we have considered in this paper.

Despite considerations like the above, which indicate that ECCS is maybe not yet "quite right," we are confident that ECCS represents a step on the right track in the process of solving the problems we set out to solve.

## 5 Final Remarks

Looking back at our Conclusion from 1986, the problem of sending multiple links or channels was successfully solved by Milner in a paper on the polyadic $\pi$-calculus [Mil91] through the use of structural congruence. Essentially the notion of $\alpha$-convertibility is built into the definition of the action relations by adding a rule ensuring that a behaviour expression can do whatever action an $\alpha$-equivalent expression can do, where we had this as a derived property of strong equivalence, i.e., that $\alpha$-convertable programs are strong equivalent. After the appearance of the chemical abstract machine [BB90] Milner presented the semantics of the $\pi$-calculus via structural congruence in the paper "Functions as Process" [Mil90] (where the main issue was the encoding possibilities w.r.t. the $\lambda$-calculus) and showed that the new and by far much simpler formulation of the semantics was consistent with the original operational semantics. The idea was soon to find footing in the community, see e.g., Crasemann [Cra92] for an extensive use.

Regarding our comments on the dual role of labels, Milner *et al.* took (as commented in section 3.1) it to its logical conclusion and identified labels and label variables.

And finally, on the issue of challenging examples, Milner *et al.* considered a number additional examples most notably encodings of $\lambda$-calculi. Later additional "natural" mobility examples came up—cf. [Mil91, Wal91, OP92, Jon93]

But all this is just a small part of the impressive amount of research which has been done over the years on the $\pi$-calculus by Milner and many other researchers, and which is beyond the scope of this note.

## Acknowledgment

We would like to thank Glynn Winskel, Paola Quaglia, the editors, and two anonymous referees for valuable comments.

## References

[AZ84] Egidio Astesiano and Elena Zucca. Parametric channels via label expressions in CCS. *Theoretical Computer Science*, 33:45–64, 1984.

[BB90] Gerard Berry and Gerard Boudol. The chemical abstract machine. In *Seventeenth Annual ACM Symposium onn Principles of Programming Languages*, pages 81–94, San Francisco, California, January 17–19, 1990. ACM Press, New York. Appears also in *Theoretical Computer Science*, 92:217–248, 1992.

[Cra92] Christoph Crasemann. *$\pi\lambda$-Kalküle für Prozesse und Funktionen*. PhD thesis, Christian-Albrechts-Universität Kiel, February 1992. Insitut für Informatik und Praktische Mathematik, Bericht Nr. 9302.

[DG83] Thomas W. Doeppner, Jr. and Alessandro Giacalone. A formal description of the UNIX operating system. In *Proceedings of the Second Annual ACM Symposium on Principles of Distributed Computing*, pages 241–253. Montreal, Quebec, Canada, August 1983.

[EN86] Uffe H. Engberg and Mogens Nielsen. A calculus of communicating systems with label passing. Technical Report DAIMI PB-208, Department of Computer Science, University of Aarhus, May 1986. 38 pp. URL: `http://www.daimi.au.dk/PB/208/`.

[Jon93] Cliff B. Jones. A pi-calculus semantics for an object based design notation. In E. Best, editor, *CONCUR'93, 4$^{th}$ Intl. Conference on Concurrency Theory*, volume 715 of *Lecture Notes in Computer Science*, pages 158–172. Springer-Verlag, 1993.

[KS83] J. Richard Kennaway and M. Ronan Sleep. LNET: syntax and semantics of a language for parallel processes. Internal report, University of East Anglia, UK, February 1983.

[Mil80] Robin Milner. *A Calculus of Communicating Systems*, volume 92 of *Lecture Notes in Computer Science*. Springer-Verlag, 1980.

[Mil83] Robin Milner. Calculi for Synchrony and Asynchrony. *Theoretical Computer Science*, 25:267–310, 1983.

[Mil84] Robin Milner. Lectures on a calculus for communicating systems. In S. D. Brookes, A. W. Roscoe, and G. Winskel, editors, *Seminar on Concurrency*, volume 197 of *Lecture Notes in Computer Science*, pages 197–220. Springer-Verlag, 1984.

[Mil90] Robin Milner. Functions as processes. Research Report 1154, INRIA, Sofia Antipolis, 1990. Appears also in *Automata, Languages and Programming 17th Int. Coll.*, volume 443 of *Lecture Notes in Computer Science*, pages 167–180, July 1990, and in *Journal of Mathematical Structures in Computer Science*, 2(2):119–141, 1992.

[Mil91] Robin Milner. The polyadic $\pi$-calculus: a tutorial. Technical Report ECS-LFCS-91-180, Laboratory for Foundations of Computer Science, Department of Computer Science, University of Edinburgh, UK, October 1991. Also in *Logic and Algebra of Specification*, ed. F. L. Bauer, W. Brauer and H. Schwichtenberg, Springer-Verlag, 1993.

[MPW89] Robin Milner, Joachim Parrow, and David Walker. A Calculus of Mobile Processes, Part I & II. Technical Report LFCS-89-85 & LFCS-89-86, University of Edinburgh, June 1989. Appears also in *Information and Computation*, 100(1):1–77, September 1992.

[MPW91] Robin Milner, Joachim Parrow, and David Walker. Modal logics for mobile processes. LFCS Report Series ECS-LFCS-91-136, University of Edinburgh, April 1991. Appears also in Jos C. M. Baeten and Jan Frisco Groote, editors, *Proceedings on Concurrency Theory (CONCUR '91)*, volume 527 of *Lecture Notes in Computer Science*, pages 45–60, August 1991, and in *Theoretical Computer Science*, 114(1):149–171, 1993.

[OP92] Fredrik Orava and Joachim Parrow. An algebraic verification of a mobile network. *Journal of Formal Aspects of Computing*, 4:497–543, 1992.

[Par81] David Park. Concurrency and Automata on Infinite Sequences. In *Theoretical Computer Science, 5th GI-Conference, Karlsruhe, March 1981*, volume 104 of *Lecture Notes in Computer Science*, pages 167–183. Springer-Verlag, March 1981.

[VN] Björn Victor and Uwe Nestmann. Bibliography on Mobile Processes and the pi-Calculus. URL: `http://liinwww.ira.uka.de/bibliography/Theory/pi.html`.

[Wal91] David Walker. $\pi$-calculus semantics of object-oriented programming languages. In Takayasu Ito and Albert Meyer, editors, *Theoretical Aspects of Computer Software*, volume 526 of *Lecture Notes in Computer Science*, pages 532–547. Springer-Verlag, 1991. Available as Report ECS-LFCS-90-122, University of Edinburgh.

# 21 Trios in Concert

**Joachim Parrow**

## 1 Introduction

The $\pi$-calculus [MPW92, Mil91] is a basic calculus for describing reactive processes, i.e., processes that continually interact with an environment. Although there is yet no definite measure on its expressiveness there is strong evidence that its primitives are enough for a wide variety of purposes. Within the $\pi$-calculus it is possible to naturally encode the functional paradigms of the $\lambda$-calculus [Mil92] and of object oriented formalisms [Wal95]. The ability to directly represent mobility, in the sense of processes that reconfigure their interconnection structure when they execute, makes it easy to model systems where processes move between different locations and where resources are allocated dynamically [OP92, Ora94]. It can also naturally encode higher-order communication where processes are transmitted in communications [San93] and in this way lays the foundation for many programming languages.

The expressive power of the $\pi$-calculus over other process algebras such as CCS [Mil89] or ACP [BW90] has been debated. All such algebras have a construct $P \mid Q$ which represents $P$ and $Q$ executing in parallel. One feature which distinguishes the $\pi$-calculus from other formalisms is the ability of a process to invent a new port name and send that name to other processes. This is achieved with the restriction operator, $(\nu x)P$ (akin to CCS restriction, $P \backslash x$) together with the output prefix $\bar{a}x$; when these are combined into $(\nu x)\bar{a}x.P$ we have a process emitting a newly invented name. Since that process may itself be under the scope of an iterative construct such as replication, written "!," we can formulate processes such as $!\,(\nu x)\bar{a}x.P$ which provide an unlimited supply of new names.

The $\pi$-calculus is an algebra in the sense that terms are built as arbitrary combinations of such constructs. For example, replication can operate on terms of any size and new names can be generated at several places, so terms can be quite complex. It is then natural to ask how much of this complexity is necessary in order to attain the full expressive power. In this paper I shall present a fragment of the calculus, in the form of a subset of its terms, such that any $\pi$-calculus term is weakly equivalent to a term in the fragment. This throws light on exactly what it is that makes the $\pi$-calculus so powerful. Another consequence is that all interesting decision problems for that fragment are undecidable.

The fragment is formed as follows. Prefix operators are limited to occur in *trios*, terms of the form $\alpha.\beta.\gamma.\mathbf{0}$. A trio is thus capable of at most three interactions. Replication only operates on such trios. The possibly replicated trios are combined through the parallel operator, together with a term $!\,(\nu x)\bar{a}x$ which invents new names. The main idea is that in order to emulate an arbitrary $\pi$-calculus term $P$ it is enough to have one trio for each subterm of $P$, controlling the activities of that subterm. These trios work in concert to ensure that the right subterms execute at the right time.

There appears to be little work directly aimed at finding such fully expressible fragments of process algebras. Related efforts within the $\pi$-calculus are Sangiorgi's result that guarded replication can replace all instances of unguarded replication while preserving strong equivalence [San94] and Honda and Tokoro's work on asynchronous communication [HT92], although neither of these attempt to reduce terms to the simplest possible parallel components. Such a reduction is easier to accomplish with a synchronous parallel operator, allowing multiway rendezvous, because then one component can interact with several other simultaneously. Examples of results in this direction are my investigation of a synchronous process algebra [Par90] where three basic terms combined in parallel generate all finite-control terms, and Gonthier's normal forms for MEIJE [Gon85]. Vaandrager [Vaa93] gives a general account of expressiveness in process algebras, where much effort has focussed on operators rather than terms following the pioneering work of de Simone [dS85]. In other models of computation this kind of result is more common, for example within the $\lambda$-calculus a small set of combinators is enough to express any closed $\lambda$-term [Bar84].

The following three sections contain our notational conventions, an explanation of the translation into trios, and the proof of the main result. This amounts to a rather technical exercise; a concluding more general section points out the main implications and variants of the construction.

## 2 Notation

To appreciate the following sections the reader should have some previous experience with the $\pi$-calculus. This section points out the particular notation and conventions used here.

We will work with the polyadic $\pi$-calculus without summation and without matching, and with replication rather than recursion. So assume a countable set of names ranged over by $a, b, \ldots, x, y, \ldots$ and let $\tilde{u}, \tilde{v}, \ldots$ range over sequences of names. The syntax of $\pi$-calculus terms, ranged over by $P, Q, \ldots$ is given by

$$
\begin{array}{lll}
P ::= & \mathbf{0} & \text{(inaction)} \\
 & \tau.Q & \text{(silent prefix)} \\
 & \bar{a}\tilde{v}.Q & \text{(output prefix)} \\
 & a(\tilde{v}).Q & \text{(input prefix)} \\
 & (\nu x)Q & \text{(restriction)} \\
 & Q \mid R & \text{(parallel composition)} \\
 & !\,Q & \text{(replication)}
\end{array}
$$

In the input prefix the members of $\tilde{v}$ must be pairwise distinct. Restriction and input bind names, and the notions of free and bound names are standard as is the notion of substitution of the name $x$ for the free occurrences of $y$ in $P$, written $P\{^x\!/y\}$, generalized to substitutions of sequences of equal length $P\{^{\tilde{w}}\!/\tilde{u}\}$ (where the members of $\tilde{u}$ are pairwise distinct). We will also use substitutions on prefixes and names with the obvious interpretation. The empty sequence is written $\epsilon$ and can be omitted in the prefix forms (so, e.g., $\bar{a}\epsilon$ can be written $\bar{a}$) and the length of $\tilde{u}$ is $|\tilde{u}|$. The abbreviation $(\nu z_1 \ldots z_n)P$ means $(\nu z_1) \ldots (\nu z_n)P$, in particular $(\nu\epsilon)P$ means just $P$.

We will not distinguish between alpha-equivalent terms, and therefore whenever convenient assume that in each term every bound name is distinct from all other names in the term.

The semantics of terms is given in a family of transition relations $\xrightarrow{\alpha}$ where $\alpha$ is an action, i.e., either $\tau$, the silent action, or $\bar{a}(\nu\tilde{x})\tilde{v}$, where all elements in $\tilde{x}$ are also in $\tilde{v}$, an output action, or $a(\tilde{v})$, an input action, where elements of $\tilde{v}$ are pairwise distinct. The *subject* of the input and output action above is $a$, and the *object* is the rest of the action. Note that the object of the output action contains not only a sequence of names ($\tilde{v}$) but also a binding of a subset of them ($\nu\tilde{x}$). If $\tilde{x} = \epsilon$ we omit $\nu$ and the brackets and write the output action simply $\bar{a}\tilde{v}$.

The transition relations are defined in the way which is now standard in the literature on the $\pi$-calculus, see Table 21.1. We use the "late" version of the semantics, where the rule for input prefix does not instantiate the bound names. There is a scope opening rule for restriction which adds a binding in the object of an output action. There is also a rule for inferring communication between parallel components which outputs respectively inputs objects of equal length on the same subject. This entails a substitution of the output object for the input object and adds a restriction for each name bound in the output object. The rule for replication simply says that $!\,P$ has the same transitions as $(!\,P) \mid P$.

**Table 21.1**
Transition relations of agents. We assume that all involved bound names are distinct. Alpha-variants of agents are considered identical and so have the same transitions. The rules for parallel composition have symmetric forms.

$$\alpha.P \xrightarrow{\alpha} P \qquad\qquad \frac{!\,P \mid P \xrightarrow{\alpha} P'}{!\,P \xrightarrow{\alpha} P'}$$

$$\frac{P \xrightarrow{\bar{a}(\nu\tilde{x})\tilde{z}} P', \quad Q \xrightarrow{a(\tilde{v})} Q', \quad |\tilde{z}| = |\tilde{v}|}{P|Q \xrightarrow{\tau} (\nu\tilde{x})(P' \mid Q'\{\tilde{z}/\tilde{v}\})} \qquad\qquad \frac{P \xrightarrow{\alpha} P'}{P|Q \xrightarrow{\alpha} P'|Q}$$

$$\frac{P \xrightarrow{\bar{a}(\nu\tilde{x})\tilde{z}} P', \quad y \in \tilde{z}}{(\nu y)P \xrightarrow{\bar{a}(\nu y\tilde{x})\tilde{z}} P'} \qquad\qquad \frac{P \xrightarrow{\alpha} P', \quad y \notin \alpha}{(\nu y)P \xrightarrow{\alpha} (\nu y)P'}$$

We will use the *open* bisimulation equivalences originally proposed by Sangiorgi [San96]. A *strong* open bisimulation $\mathcal{S}$ is a binary relation on agents such that if $P\mathcal{S}Q$ then for every transition $P \xrightarrow{\alpha} P'$ (where the names bound in $\alpha$ do not occur free in $P$ or $Q$) there is a simulating transition $Q \xrightarrow{\alpha} Q'$ with $P'\mathcal{S}Q'$ and vice versa; moreover it must also hold that $P\{^x/_y\}\mathcal{S}Q\{^x/_y\}$ for all $x$, $y$, i.e., the relation is closed under arbitrary substitution.[1] Two agents $P$ and $Q$ are *strongly equivalent*, written $P \sim Q$, if $P\mathcal{S}Q$ for some strong open bisimulation.

As usual we let $\stackrel{\hat{\tau}}{\Longrightarrow}$, or sometimes $\Longrightarrow$, mean $(\xrightarrow{\tau})^n$ for some $n \geq 0$ and, for $\alpha \neq \tau$, we let $\stackrel{\hat{\alpha}}{\Longrightarrow}$ or $\stackrel{\alpha}{\Longrightarrow}$ mean $\Longrightarrow\xrightarrow{\alpha}\Longrightarrow$. The *weak* (open) equivalence, $\approx$, is defined in terms of weak open bisimulations where the simulating transition for $P \xrightarrow{\alpha} P'$ is $Q \stackrel{\hat{\alpha}}{\Longrightarrow} Q'$. Both $\sim$ and $\approx$ are congruences in this version of the $\pi$-calculus, and they are strictly finer than the "early" and "late" congruences.

## 3 Trios and Concerts

A *trio* is a $\pi$-calculus term consisting of exactly three nested prefixes, i.e., of the form $\alpha.\beta.\gamma.\mathbf{0}$. We will in trios also admit a derived form of output prefix $\bar{a}(\nu x)x.P$, defined to mean $(\nu x)\bar{a}x.P$, outputting a single bound name along $a$. A trio containing such a derived prefix is called an *inventive* trio (it invents a new name $x$ and makes that available to its environment). A *degenerate* trio contains less than three prefixes. A degenerate trio is of course weakly equivalent to the proper trio formed by filling the missing prefixes with $\tau$, so we will include the degenerate trios among the trios. A trailing $\mathbf{0}$ will be omitted. Therefore, e.g., $\alpha$ is also a (degenerate) trio, corresponding to the proper trio $\alpha.\tau.\tau.\mathbf{0}$.

A *concert* of trios is a restriction of a parallel composition of possibly replicated trios, i.e., an agent of type

$$(\nu\tilde{z})((!)T_1 \mid \cdots \mid (!)T_n)$$

where each $T_i$ is a trio, and at most one of the $T_i$ is inventive. The main result in this paper is that for each agent there is a weakly equivalent concert. The idea is that the concert for $P$ will have one trio for each subterm of $P$. This trio is responsible for "enacting" that subterm when appropriate. Since this may involve enacting further subterms—for example, enacting $P_1|P_2$ entails enacting $P_1$ and $P_2$—the trio may call on other trios to do this. Furthermore, the only inventive trio will be a general "name provider" which sends new names to other trios at need.

[1] Sangiorgi's original formulation was slightly different but the present definition yields the same equivalence and is easier in the context of this paper.

To make this work we must assume a unique set of names through which the trios can call each other. We do this as follows. To each term $P$ we associate a new unique *trigger* name $z_P$. The intuition is that transmitting something along $z_P$ will invoke the trio responsible for the execution of $P$. We further introduce one new name $z_\nu$. It is along this name that the name provider will send its new names to other trios. These trigger names are all distinct. Formally this means that we extend the calculus by introducing these names; at the end of this section we shall see that this extension, although convenient, is not strictly necessary for the main result.

DEFINITION 1 Let $P$ be an agent where we assume that all bound names are unique, and let $\tilde{u}$ be a sequence of pairwise distinct names. The *$\tilde{u}$-breakdown* of $P$, written $\mathcal{B}_{\tilde{u}}(P)$ is an agent defined inductively as follows.

| $P$ | $\mathcal{B}_{\tilde{u}}(P)$ | |
|---|---|---|
| $\mathbf{0}$ | $z_{\mathbf{0}}(\tilde{u})$ | |
| $\tau.Q$ | $z_P(\tilde{u}).\tau.\overline{z_Q}\tilde{u}$ | $\mid \mathcal{B}_{\tilde{u}}(Q)$ |
| $\overline{a}\tilde{v}.Q$ | $z_P(\tilde{u}).\overline{a}\tilde{v}.\overline{z_Q}\tilde{u}$ | $\mid \mathcal{B}_{\tilde{u}}(Q)$ |
| $a(\tilde{v}).Q$ | $z_P(\tilde{u}).a(\tilde{v}).\overline{z_Q}\tilde{u}\tilde{v}$ | $\mid \mathcal{B}_{\tilde{u}\tilde{v}}(Q)$ |
| $(\nu x)Q$ | $z_P(\tilde{u}).z_\nu(x).\overline{z_Q}\tilde{u}x$ | $\mid \mathcal{B}_{\tilde{u}x}(Q)$ |
| $Q \mid R$ | $z_P(\tilde{u}).\overline{z_Q}\tilde{u}.\overline{z_R}\tilde{u}$ | $\mid \mathcal{B}_{\tilde{u}}(Q) \mid \mathcal{B}_{\tilde{u}}(R)$ |
| $!Q$ | $!z_P(\tilde{u}).\overline{z_P}\tilde{u}.\overline{z_Q}\tilde{u}$ | $\mid !\mathcal{B}_{\tilde{u}}(Q)$ |

Notice that $\mathcal{B}_{\tilde{u}}$ binds the names $\tilde{u}$. The breakdown of $P$ consists of a (possibly replicated) leading trio, in parallel with the breakdown of the subterms of $P$. The leading trio is called a *prefix* trio if $P$ is a prefix form, otherwise it is called a *control* trio. So, using $!(P|Q) \sim\, !P|!Q$ and $!!P \sim\, !P$, we can push all replication inwards in $\mathcal{B}_{\tilde{u}}(P)$ until it becomes a parallel composition of possibly replicated trios, one for each subterm of $P$. There will be one prefix trio for each prefix in $P$, and one control trio for each other subterm in $P$. Each of these has a unique trigger.

The object $\tilde{u}$ corresponds to the name instantiations which are needed when executing a subterm. These names are bound outside the subterm, in other words they are placeholders for something which will be determined outside the subterm. The intention is that $\mathcal{B}_{\tilde{u}}(P)$ in parallel with a trigger $\overline{z_P}\tilde{w}$ will enact $P\{\tilde{w}/\tilde{u}\}$. If we start with $\mathcal{B}_\epsilon(P)$ then each subterm $Q$ in $P$ will be broken down to $\mathcal{B}_{\tilde{u}}(Q)$, where $\tilde{u}$ is the sequence of bindings outside $Q$ whose scope extend into $Q$. It may appear strange that $\tilde{u}$ are bound in $\mathcal{B}_{\tilde{u}}(Q)$ whereas they are free in $Q$. But in the definition of $\mathcal{B}$ we are interested in $Q$ *as a subterm of* $P$ (it may be clearer to think of it as $\mathcal{B}_{P,\tilde{u}}(Q)$, even though the definition turns out to be independent of $P$) and although $\tilde{u}$ are free in $Q$ they are bound in $P$. Of course, using alpha-conversion they can be renamed so the definition of $\mathcal{B}_{\tilde{u}}(Q)$ really only depends on the length of $\tilde{u}$. But note that $a$ in the clauses for output and input (and also $\tilde{v}$ in the clause for output) may be among $\tilde{u}$.

The leading trio corresponding to $\mathcal{B}_{\tilde{u}}(P)$ begins by awaiting, on its trigger $z_P$, the reception of the names which shall instantiate the bound names $\tilde{u}$. When those have been received the trio takes different actions depending on the form of $P$. If $P$ is a prefix $\alpha.Q$ the trio will enact $\alpha$ and then activate $Q$ through its trigger, forwarding $\tilde{u}$. If $\alpha$ is an input prefix then the sequence of bound names will grow (bound names are unique so $\tilde{u}$ and $\tilde{v}$ will be disjoint), and therefore the new names received in the input ($\tilde{v}$) will be appended to the names transferred into $Q$. For $\alpha = \tau$ we could actually have simplified the definition to $\mathcal{B}_{\tilde{u}}(\tau.Q) = \mathcal{B}_{\tilde{u}}(Q)$ (since $Q \approx \tau.Q$) at the expense of the symmetric treatment of the prefixes.

If $P$ is a restriction $(\nu x)Q$, then it proceeds to collect along $z_\nu$ a new name, which it appends to the names transferred into $Q$. The intention is that $\mathcal{B}_{\tilde{u}}(P)$ is executed in parallel with a name provider sending new names along $z_\nu$.

If $P$ is a parallel composition then its control trio simply activates the factors of $P$. For this to work it is important that each trio begins with a reception along its trigger. If for example the breakdown of $\mathbf{0}$ would be $\mathbf{0}$ (rather than $z_{\mathbf{0}}(\tilde{u})$) then $\mathcal{B}_{\tilde{u}}(\mathbf{0} \mid R)$ would never reach the point where $R$ is activated.

Finally, if $P$ is a replication $!\,Q$, its replicated control trio does two things: first it activates a new incarnation of itself and then it activates (an incarnation of) $Q$. Because of the replications this means that arbitrarily many copies of $Q$ can be started. It would not be enough to define $\mathcal{B}_{\tilde{u}}(!\,Q) = \,!\,\mathcal{B}_{\tilde{u}}(Q)$; in that case one activation of $\mathcal{B}_{\tilde{u}}(!\,Q)$ would only result in one activation of $Q$.

It is worth explaining a possible controversy here when $P$ has a subterm occurring in several positions, as in $(\bar{a}.\bar{b}) \mid \bar{b}$. In the breakdown of that term there will be two trios triggered by $z_{\bar{b}}$, one for each occurrence of $\bar{b}$. As it turns out this is harmless, since whenever someone signals on $z_{\bar{b}}$, the execution of $\bar{b}$ will be started in one of the trios—it does not matter which one (see the proof of Lemma 6 in the next section)! Note that our assumption about unique bound names forbids agents like $a(x).\bar{x}y \mid a(y).\bar{x}y$ where a subterm $\bar{x}y$ occurs in different places with different bound names (in that case it would really matter which trio was activated).

The translation of an agent into a concert now goes as follows.

DEFINITION 2 Let the *name inventor* $N$ be defined by

$$N = \,!\,\overline{z_\nu}(\nu x)x$$

and let $Z(P)$, the triggers of $P$, be defined by

$$Z(P) = \{z_\nu\} \cup \{z_Q : Q \text{ is a subterm of } P\}.$$

The *translation* $\mathcal{T}(P)$ of an agent $P$ is defined to be

$$\mathcal{T}(P) = (\nu Z(P))(\mathcal{B}_\epsilon(P) \mid \overline{z_P} \mid N)$$

Restriction is commutative so restricting on a set of names is a well defined operation, up to strong equivalence. Note that $\mathcal{T}(P)$ is equivalent (using the laws $!(P|Q) \sim !P|!Q$ and $!!P \sim !P$) to a restricted parallel composition of possibly replicated trios where only $N$ is inventive, i.e., $\mathcal{T}(P)$ is equivalent to a concert.

THEOREM 3 $\quad P \approx \mathcal{T}(P)$.

The idea behind the proof is that $(\nu Z(P))(\mathcal{B}_{\tilde{u}}(P) \mid \overline{z_P}\tilde{w} \mid N)$ is bisimilar to $P\{\tilde{w}/\tilde{u}\}$ for all $\tilde{u}$, $\tilde{w}$ of equal length. The proof is simply to establish a bisimulation relating these agents, by showing how their transitions correspond to each other. The details are contained in the next section.

The definition of $\mathcal{T}(P)$ uses the trigger names only in bound positions. Since the set of names is infinite and each $\mathcal{T}(P)$ only contains a finite set of names, there is an alpha-variant of $\mathcal{T}(P)$ which does not use the trigger names. So the extension of the calculus to include these names is not strictly necessary, although it simplifies the proof.

A variant of the same result is to redefine $\mathcal{B}_{\tilde{u}}$ so that *all* trios in $\mathcal{B}_{\tilde{u}}(P)$ are replicated. Since a trio only starts executing when signalled to do so it is harmless to replicate it. The concert will then be more uniform, consisting of replicated trios plus only one non-replicated trio (the trigger $\overline{z_P}$ in $\mathcal{T}(P)$).

## 4 Proof

To prove the theorem we establish a weak (open) bisimulation including $(P, \mathcal{T}(P))$. To do this, we begin by defining the agents *correlated* to $P\{\tilde{w}/\tilde{u}\}$ in this bisimulation. These are essentially the agents obtained by starting $\mathcal{B}_{\tilde{u}}(P)$ by sending $\tilde{w}$ along the trigger for $P$.

DEFINITION 4 $\quad$ Assume $\tilde{w}$ and $\tilde{u}$ have equal length, and $\tilde{u}$ are pairwise distinct. The set of agents $\mathcal{C}_{\tilde{u}}^{\tilde{w}}(P)$ is defined to be

$$\mathcal{C}_{\tilde{u}}^{\tilde{w}}(P) = \{\overline{z_P}\tilde{w} \mid \mathcal{B}_{\tilde{u}}(P)\} \cup \mathcal{D}_{\tilde{u}}^{\tilde{w}}(P)$$

where $\mathcal{D}_{\tilde{u}}^{\tilde{w}}(P)$ is defined inductively as follows:

| $P$ | $\mathcal{D}_{\tilde{u}}^{\tilde{w}}(P)$ | |
|---|---|---|
| $\mathbf{0}$ | $\{\mathbf{0}\}$ | |
| $\tau.Q$ | $\{\tau.\overline{z_Q}\tilde{w} \mid \mathcal{B}_{\tilde{u}}(Q)\}$ | |
| $\overline{a}\tilde{v}.Q$ | $\{\overline{a}\tilde{v}\{\tilde{w}/\tilde{u}\}.\overline{z_Q}\tilde{w} \mid \mathcal{B}_{\tilde{u}}(Q)\}$ | |
| $a(\tilde{v}).Q$ | $\{a(\tilde{v})\{\tilde{w}/\tilde{u}\}.\overline{z_Q}\tilde{w}\tilde{v} \mid \mathcal{B}_{\tilde{u}\tilde{v}}(Q)\}$ | |
| $(\nu x)Q$ | $\{z_\nu(x).\overline{z_Q}\tilde{w}x \mid \mathcal{B}_{\tilde{u}x}(Q)\}$ | |
| | $\cup\{(\nu x')C_Q : C_Q \in \mathcal{C}_{\tilde{u}x}^{\tilde{w}x'}(Q)\}$ | ($x'$ fresh) |
| $Q \mid R$ | $\{\overline{z_Q}\tilde{w}.\overline{z_R}\tilde{w} \mid \mathcal{B}_{\tilde{u}}(Q) \mid \mathcal{B}_{\tilde{u}}(R)\}$ | |
| | $\cup\{(C_Q \mid C_R) : C_Q \in \mathcal{C}_{\tilde{u}}^{\tilde{w}}(Q),\ C_R \in \mathcal{C}_{\tilde{u}}^{\tilde{w}}(R)\}$ | |
| $!\,Q$ | $\{(!\,z_P(\tilde{u}).\overline{z_P}\tilde{u}.\overline{z_Q}\tilde{u} \mid \overline{z_P}\tilde{w}.\overline{z_Q}\tilde{w} \mid (\overline{z_Q}\tilde{w} \mid)^n$ | |
| | $!\,\mathcal{B}_{\tilde{u}}(Q) \mid C_1 \mid \cdots \mid C_m) : n, m \geq 0, C_i \in \mathcal{C}_{\tilde{u}}^{\tilde{w}}(Q)\}$ | |

Now define the relation $\mathcal{S}$ by

$$\mathcal{S} = \{(P\{\tilde{w}/\tilde{u}\},\ R) : R \in \{(\nu\tilde{z})(N \mid C_P) : C_P \in \mathcal{C}_{\tilde{u}}^{\tilde{w}}(P)\},\ |\tilde{w}| = |\tilde{u}|,\ \tilde{z} = Z(P)\}$$

It is then clear that $(P, \mathcal{T}(P))$ is in $\mathcal{S}$. The significant properties are the following:

LEMMA 5 $\mathcal{S}$ is closed under substitution of names (up to strong equivalence).

*Proof* A straightforward and tedious examination of the definitions. Consider a pair $(P\{\tilde{w}/\tilde{u}\},\ R)$ where $R = (\nu\tilde{z})(N \mid C_P)$ and $C_P \in \mathcal{C}_{\tilde{u}}^{\tilde{w}}(P)$. For a substitution $\{x/y\}$ we can assume without loss of generality that $x, y \notin \tilde{z}$ (otherwise we have to alpha-convert $R$ to satisfy this). So $R\{x/y\}$ is $(\nu\tilde{z})(N \mid C_P\{x/y\})$. The important fact is that if $C_P \in \mathcal{C}_{\tilde{u}}^{\tilde{w}}(P)$ then $C_P\{x/y\} \in \mathcal{C}_{\tilde{u}'}^{\tilde{w}'}(P)$, where $\{\tilde{w}'/\tilde{u}'\} = \{\tilde{w}/\tilde{u}\}\{x/y\}$. To be precise this holds only up to a strong version of strong equivalence, which requires the inference of actions to have equal lengths (i.e., two agents are related if they have related derivatives inferred through proofs of equal length). However, that is enough for the purpose of the proofs below. □

LEMMA 6 Assume $P\{\tilde{w}/\tilde{u}\}\mathcal{S}R$. If $P\{\tilde{w}/\tilde{u}\} \xrightarrow{\alpha} P'$, then $R \Longrightarrow \xrightarrow{\alpha} R'$ and for some $\tilde{x}$, $P' \sim (\nu\tilde{x})P''$ and $R' \sim (\nu\tilde{x})R''$ and $P''\mathcal{S}R''$.

*Proof* The proof is an induction over the length of the inference of the transition in the antecedent. It consists of a rather long case analysis and only a few of the cases are shown here.

Consider the case where the antecedent is inferred through the rule for input prefix. Then $\alpha = a\{\tilde{w}/\tilde{u}\}(\tilde{v})$ and $P = a(\tilde{v}).Q$, where we without loss of generality assume that

$\tilde{v}$ has no element in common with $\tilde{w}$ or $\tilde{u}$ (otherwise we have to first alpha-convert $P$). Therefore $P' = Q\{\tilde{w}/\tilde{u}\}$. Now consider $R$. There are two possibilities, because $\mathcal{C}^{\tilde{w}}_{\tilde{u}}(P)$ has two elements: $C_1 = \overline{z_P}\tilde{w} \mid \mathcal{B}_{\tilde{u}}(P)$ and $C_2 = a\{\tilde{w}/\tilde{u}\}(\tilde{v}).\overline{z_Q}\tilde{w}\tilde{v} \mid \mathcal{B}_{\tilde{u}\tilde{v}}(Q)$ (the latter comes from $\mathcal{D}^{\tilde{w}}_{\tilde{u}}(P)$ which here is a singleton). Put $R_i = (\nu\tilde{z})(N \mid C_i)$. Clearly $R_1 \xrightarrow{\tau} R_2$. Also $R_2 \xrightarrow{\alpha} R'$ where $R' = (\nu\tilde{z})(N \mid C')$ where $C' = \overline{z_Q}\tilde{w}\tilde{v} \mid \mathcal{B}_{\tilde{u}\tilde{v}}(Q)$. So $C' \in \mathcal{C}^{\tilde{w}\tilde{v}}_{\tilde{u}\tilde{v}}(Q)$. So $R'$ is related in $\mathcal{S}$ to $Q\{\tilde{w}\tilde{v}/\tilde{u}\tilde{v}\} = Q\{\tilde{w}/\tilde{u}\}$, fulfilling the lemma (with $\tilde{x} = \epsilon$).

Consider next the case where the antecedent is inferred through the rule for scope opening and $P = (\nu x)Q$. So we have $\alpha = \bar{a}(\nu x\tilde{y})\tilde{v}$, and in a shorter inference $Q\{\tilde{w}/\tilde{u}\} \xrightarrow{\alpha'} P'$ with $\alpha' = \bar{a}(\nu\tilde{y})\tilde{v}$, i.e., $\alpha$ extends $\alpha'$ by one additional binding in the object. There are several possibilities for $R$, but as in the previous case all of them can evolve (through one or two $\tau$ actions) to $(\nu\tilde{z})(N \mid (\nu x')C')$ where $C' \in \mathcal{C}^{\tilde{w}x'}_{\tilde{u}x}(Q)$. Because bound names can be assumed to be distinct we can choose $x' = x$ and assume that $x$ is not in $\tilde{w}, \tilde{u}$. So, $C' \in \mathcal{C}^{\tilde{w}x}_{\tilde{u}x}(Q)$. Therefore $R'$ is related in $\mathcal{S}$ to $Q\{\tilde{w}x/\tilde{u}x\} = Q\{\tilde{w}/\tilde{u}\}$. Therefore, by induction and $Q\{\tilde{w}/\tilde{u}\} \xrightarrow{\alpha'} P'$ it holds that $(\nu\tilde{z})(N \mid C')$ simulates $Q$ as stated by the lemma. But then $R$ also simulates $P$, through the scope opening rule.

The case where the antecedent is inferred through the rule for communication is notationally heavy so we will just go through the main ideas. If $P = P_1 | P_2$ and $P \xrightarrow{\alpha} P'$ with $\alpha = \tau$ is inferred from $P$ as a communication between $P_1$ and $P_2$, then we consider the output and input actions from $P_1$ and $P_2$ respectively; by induction they must be simulated by $(\nu\tilde{z})(N \mid C_1)$ and $(\nu\tilde{z})(N \mid C_2)$ where $C_1$ and $C_2$ belong to the proper $\mathcal{C}$-sets. We therefore have that $(\nu\tilde{z})(N \mid C_1) \mid (\nu\tilde{z})(N \mid C_2)$ can simulate the communication. The case is completed by showing that this agent is strongly equivalent with $(\nu\tilde{z})(N \mid C_1 \mid C_2)$, which is in the $\mathcal{C}$-set for $P$ itself. When the communication carries bound names restriction operators may appear in the derivatives. This explains the necessity of the "$(\nu\tilde{x})$" in the statement of the lemma.

To show the strong equivalence needed for this case we establish that pairs

$$((\nu\tilde{z})(N \mid C_1) \mid (\nu\tilde{z})(N \mid C_2), \quad (\nu\tilde{z})(N \mid C_1 \mid C_2))$$

form a strong bisimulation. Clearly, the only difficulty in finding simulating transitions is for the left hand side to simulate a transition in the right hand side $(\nu\tilde{z})(N \mid C_1 \mid C_2)$ where $C_1$ and $C_2$ communicate along a trigger in $\tilde{z}$. Perhaps disappointingly, $C_1$ and $C_2$ may actually share such a trigger since the parallel composition may have been created by replication in an earlier part of the induction. Assume without loss of generality that the transition involves a trio in $C_1$ activating, along $z \in \tilde{z}$, a trio $z(\tilde{u}).D$ in $C_2$. Then in $C_1$ there must also be a trio activated by $z$ (since a trigger is only introduced in $\mathcal{B}$ along with a trio activated by it); moreover by the assumption about the uniqueness of the triggers and the fact that replication creates syntactically identical copies this trio must also be $z(\tilde{u}).D$.

So the transition then is of the kind

$$(\nu\tilde{z})(N \mid C_1' \mid z(\tilde{u}).D \mid C_2' \mid z(\tilde{u}).D) \xrightarrow{\tau}$$
$$\quad (\nu\tilde{z})(N \mid C_1'' \mid z(\tilde{u}).D \mid C_2' \mid D\{\tilde{w}/\tilde{u}\})$$

But then of course there is also another transition where $C_1$ activates its own trio rather than the one in $C_2$:

$$(\nu\tilde{z})(N \mid C_1' \mid z(\tilde{u}).D \mid C_2' \mid z(\tilde{u}).D) \xrightarrow{\tau}$$
$$\quad (\nu\tilde{z})(N \mid C_1'' \mid D\{\tilde{w}/\tilde{u}\} \mid C_2' \mid z(\tilde{u}).D)$$

The derivatives of these two transitions are strongly equivalent (since parallel composition is associative). The latter transition involves a communication within $C_1$ and can therefore be simulated by $(\nu\tilde{z})(N \mid C_1) \mid (\nu\tilde{z})(N \mid C_2)$, which therefore also simulates the former transition, up to strong equivalence.

Finally, consider the case where the antecedent is inferred through the rule for replication. Again we just provide a sketch. If $P = !\,Q$ and $P\{\tilde{w}/\tilde{u}\} \xrightarrow{\alpha} P'$, then through a shorter inference $(P|Q)\{\tilde{w}/\tilde{u}\} \xrightarrow{\alpha} P'$. Then we know by induction that this is simulated by $R = (\nu\tilde{z})(N|C)$ where $C \in \mathcal{C}_{\tilde{u}}^{\tilde{w}}(P|Q)$. Consider this $C$; it is (possibly after one or two $\tau$-actions) a parallel composition $C_P|C_Q$ where the factors belong to the $\mathcal{C}$-sets of $P$ and $Q$ respectively. It then follows (by definition of $\mathcal{D}$ for replication: just increase $m$ by one!) that this parallel composition is itself a member of $\mathcal{C}_{\tilde{u}}^{\tilde{w}}(P)$. Therefore the simulation of $R$ for $P|Q$ also is an adequate simulation for $P$. □

LEMMA 7 Assume $P\{\tilde{w}/\tilde{u}\}\mathcal{S}R$. If $R \xrightarrow{\alpha} R'$, then either (i) $\alpha = \tau$ and $P\{\tilde{w}/\tilde{u}\}\mathcal{S} \sim R'$, or (ii) $P\{\tilde{w}/\tilde{u}\} \xrightarrow{\alpha} P'$ and for some $\tilde{x}$, $P' \sim (\nu\tilde{x})P''$ and $R' \sim (\nu\tilde{x})R''$ and $P''\mathcal{S}R''$.

*Proof* In $R$ we say that the *essential* prefixes are the ones with subject $a$, and also the $\tau$-prefix, in the definitions of $\mathcal{B}$, $\mathcal{C}$ and $\mathcal{D}$. Thus these correspond directly to the prefixes in $P$. We distinguish the cases when $R \xrightarrow{\alpha} R'$ is inferred from the action from at least one essential prefix, and when it is inferred without any such actions.

Assume $R \xrightarrow{\alpha} R'$ is inferred without any actions from essential prefixes. Then it must be an internal communication within $R = (\nu\tilde{z})(N \mid C)$ for $C \in \mathcal{C}_{\tilde{u}}^{\tilde{w}}(P)$, so $\alpha = \tau$. We can then show that also $P\{\tilde{w}/\tilde{u}\}\mathcal{S} \sim R'$. The proof is through a tedious inspection of the definitions, by showing that if $C \in \mathcal{C}_{\tilde{u}}^{\tilde{w}}(P)$ and $C \xrightarrow{\alpha} C'$ does not involve an essential prefix, then in this case also $C'$ is strongly equivalent to a member of $\mathcal{C}_{\tilde{u}}^{\tilde{w}}(P)$. In other words, $\mathcal{C}_{\tilde{u}}^{\tilde{w}}(P)$ is closed under transitions not involving essential prefixes. This satisfies part (i) of the consequent of the lemma.

Then assume $R \xrightarrow{\alpha} R'$ involves an essential prefix. In this case we can show part (ii) of the consequent of the lemma. The proof is mainly a converse of the proof of Lemma 6, noting that when $R$ has an unguarded essential prefix then the corresponding prefix in $P$ also is unguarded. We omit the details which are long but routine given the proof of Lemma 6. □

We can now easily complete the proof of Theorem 3. From the three lemmata above it follows that $\mathcal{S}$ is a weak open bisimulation up to restriction and strong equivalence. Bisimulations up to restriction and equivalence have been treated extensively in previous work on the $\pi$-calculus [MPW92] and in a similar manner we conclude that agents related by $\mathcal{S}$ are weak open equivalent. In particular, $P \approx \mathcal{T}(P)$.

## 5 Conclusion

We have seen that concerts inherit all the expressive power of the full $\pi$-calculus, up to weak equivalence. The concerts are limited in that prefixes are nested to the depth of at most three, that parallel composition does not occur under prefix, that replication is only applied to trios, and that there is only one occurrence of restriction under replication. This type of "minimal parallel components" is to our knowledge the only of its kind for the $\pi$-calculus or indeed for any process algebra with an asynchronous parallel operator (disallowing multiway rendezvous).

The consequences of this result are significant in the theory of the $\pi$-calculus. We still have no good measure on the expressiveness of the full calculus. Obtaining such a measure may involve demonstrating that other basic formalisms can encode the $\pi$-calculus and here it may be useful to know that it suffices to encode a limited form of the calculus, for example where parallel composition occurs only at a top level. Also, when designing implementation strategies for the calculus it may help to know that it suffices to implement limited forms, for example that one central name provider is enough.

The result can also be seen as a negative result in the quest for decidable subcalculi. It is known that in the full $\pi$-calculus it is possible to constructively encode arbitrary Turing machines. Therefore problems such as equivalence and model checking and termination of $\pi$-calculus terms are undecidable. The expressive power and hence undecidability can be seen as emanating from the replication operator, which is the only operator through which the size of a term can increase in a transition. Without replication the sets of transition sequences from terms are finite (up to alpha-conversion) and hence the problems mentioned above are decidable. But there are decidable subcalculi which admit terms with infinite sets of transition sequences; a prime example is the so called "finite-control" fragment investigated by Dam [Dam95] formed by using recursion rather than replication and requiring that parallel composition does not occur in recursive definitions. It may have been hoped that a similar decidable subcalculus can be found with replication rather than recursion, but this appears now not to be the case: even if replication is limited to trios the calculus is fully expressive and hence undecidable (since our translation into concerts is constructive). Since recursion and replication are interdefinable ($!\,P$ can be defined recursively as $!\,P \stackrel{\text{def}}{=} !\,P \mid P$, note that this is *not* finite-control) the result also puts a limit on the complexity of recursive definitions required for full expressiveness.

An obvious question is whether a similar result holds for *duos*, two nested prefixes, of kind $\alpha.\beta.\mathbf{0}$, in place of trios. The answer is negative: when replication is limited to duos, even some finite-control agents are not expressible! To see this consider the agent $P \stackrel{\text{def}}{=} a.b.P$ where for simplicity the prefixes $a, b$ have empty objects. (Using replication instead of recursion we would write $P = (\nu z)(\bar{z} \mid !\,z.a.b.\bar{z})$). Let $D$ be an agent where replication only operates on duos and assume $D \approx P$. We shall derive a contradiction. For $D \approx P$ to hold there must be an infinite transition sequence

$$D \Longrightarrow D_0 \stackrel{a}{\longrightarrow} D_1 \stackrel{b}{\Longrightarrow} D_2 \stackrel{a}{\longrightarrow} D_3 \stackrel{b}{\Longrightarrow} \cdots$$

where $D_n \approx D_{n+2}$ and $D \approx D_0$. Each of the actions $a$ in this sequence must emanate from some prefix in $D$. But $D$ is syntactically finite so some prefix in $D$ must give rise to infinitely many $a$. That prefix therefore must lie under a replication and hence in a duo in $D$. Consider some $D_{2n} \stackrel{a}{\longrightarrow} D_{2n+1}$ where such a prefix gives rise to the $a$ action. There are two cases depending on where in the duo the prefix resides. Either the prefix is the first in the duo in $D$, as in $!\,a.\gamma.\mathbf{0}$. Then the same duo is present in $D_{2n}$ (the operands of replication do not change as a result of transitions) and since it is replicated and can yield one $a$ transition it can yield several, i.e., $D_{2n} \stackrel{a}{\longrightarrow} D' \stackrel{a}{\longrightarrow} \cdots$, contradicting $D_{2n} \approx D$. Or the prefix is the last in the duo in $D$, then $D_{2n}$ must have formed from $D$ by executing the first prefix in that duo leaving a parallel factor $a.\mathbf{0}$. In $D_{2n} \stackrel{a}{\longrightarrow} D_{2n+1}$ we then have that $D_{2n+1}$ is formed by replacing the factor $a.\mathbf{0}$ by $\mathbf{0}$. Since $D_{2n+1} \stackrel{b}{\Longrightarrow}$ it then follows $D_{2n} \stackrel{b}{\Longrightarrow}$ because the addition of a parallel factor cannot decrease the possible transitions. But $D_{2n} \stackrel{b}{\Longrightarrow}$ contradicts $D_{2n} \approx D$. The conclusion is that no such $D$ can exist.

Limiting replication to duos we can still define some non-finite-control processes (e.g., $!\,a.b.\mathbf{0}$ is not finite-control) so the decidability of equivalence in this situation is open. If we restrict attention to concerts of possibly replicated duos (forbidding agents like $a.!\,b.c.\mathbf{0}$) then there are even finite agents which are not expressible. For example, $a.b.a.\mathbf{0}$ is not expressible as a concert of duos; an argument similar to the above shows that $b$ here can occur neither at the head nor at the tail of a duo. Combining such arguments we get the picture in Figure 21.1 exhibiting relative expressive power of some classes of agents.

If replication is limited to solos (one prefix) then agents are finite-control and equivalence is therefore decidable (the agent $!\,\alpha.\mathbf{0}$ is equivalent to the finite-control recursive definition $P \stackrel{\text{def}}{=} \alpha.P$).

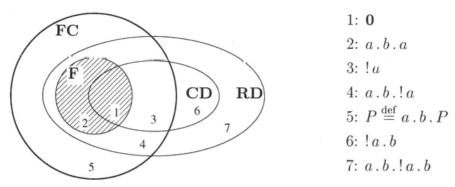

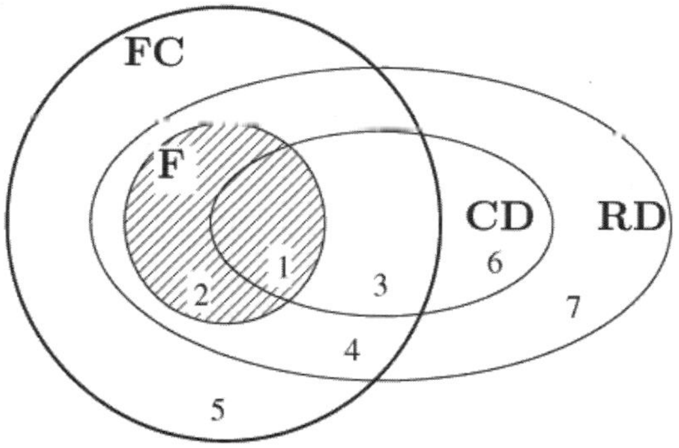


1: $\mathbf{0}$

2: $a \,.\, b \,.\, a$

3: $!\,a$

4: $a \,.\, b \,.\, !\,a$

5: $P \stackrel{\text{def}}{=} a \,.\, b \,.\, P$

6: $!\,a \,.\, b$

7: $a \,.\, b \,.\, !\,a \,.\, b$

**Figure 21.1**
Relative expressiveness of the classes **FC** (finite-control), **F** (finite), **RD** (replication restricted to duos) and **CD** (concerts of possibly replicated duos). All regions are nonempty, the numbers show examples of inhabitants.

In this paper we have used the polyadic $\pi$-calculus. A corresponding result appears impossible in the monadic $\pi$-calculus, where the objects in input and output actions must have length one, i.e., exactly one name is transferred in each communication. For consider the agent

$$a(x_1).\cdots.a(x_n).\bar{b}x_1.\cdots.\bar{b}x_n$$

If we want to translate this with a similar strategy where each subagent is enacted by starting a designated agent, then the designated agent for the subterm $\bar{b}x_1.\cdots.\bar{b}x_n$ must receive $n$ names, and in the monadic calculus this requires a string of $n$ input prefixes. However, by generalizing the notion of concert so that arbitrary strings of prefixes (rather than just trios) are allowed we can obtain a similar construction. This of course leaves open the question of expressiveness and decidability of concerts of trios in the monadic calculus.

Also, the construction is impossible for CCS, which can be thought of as the zero-ary $\pi$-calculus in that no objects are allowed in actions. The reason has here to do with the restriction operator. If restriction occurs under a replication operator then that entails a mechanism for creating new names. In the $\pi$-calculus concerts this mechanism is localized to a single name provider which sends those names, as objects in communications, to the places where they are needed. In CCS this is not possible so a similar strategy for encoding restriction will not work. Even relaxing the requirement that there can only be one inventive trio will not help; for example when encoding $!\,(\nu x)(P \mid Q)$ the encodings of $P$ and $Q$ must somehow learn of their new common private name $x$. For this reason it appears that parallel compositions under replication is necessary in CCS, though again the question is open.

Finally, the result is not applicable in the presence of summation. Using unguarded summation, $P + Q$, means that weak equivalence is not a congruence and it is difficult to see how the translation could be extended. However with guarded summation, of the form

$$\alpha_1.P_1 + \cdots + \alpha_n.P_n$$

I conjecture an extension which requires the use of *branch trios* of the kind $\alpha.(\beta + \gamma.\delta)$ (these contain four prefixes and only earn the attribute "trio" in that prefix is still nested to depth three). The translation of the guarded summation above is a parallel composition of one branch trio

$$z_i(\tilde{u}).(\overline{z_{i+1}}\tilde{u} + \alpha_i.\overline{z_{P_i}}\tilde{u})$$

for each summand $\alpha_i.P_i$ where addition in the index of $z$ is modulo $n$. The parallel composition of the branch trios works like a round-robin protocol in a ring through the triggers $z_i$; the "token" $\tilde{u}$ is passed around the ring until one of the trios decides on its leading action $\alpha_i$. For finitely branching agents unguarded summation can be encoded with guarded summation so this device is quite powerful. Of course, using only proper concerts it is impossible to encode any kind of summation since $\alpha + \beta$ is not weakly equivalent to any summation-free agent. Similarly, instances of the *matching* operator $[x = y]P$ (read "if $x = y$ then $P$") from many version of the $\pi$-calculus cannot be encoded because $[x = y]\alpha$ is not equivalent to any matching-free agent.

## References


[Bar84] H. Barendregt. *The Lambda Calculus*. North Holland, 1984.

[BW90] J. Baeten and W. Weijland. *Process Algebra*. Cambridge Tracts in Theoretical Computer Science 18. Cambridge University Press, 1990.

[Dam95] M. Dam. On the decidability of process equivalences for the $\pi$-calculus. In V. S. Alagar and M. Nivat, editors, *4th International Conference on Algebraic Methodology and Software Technology, AMAST'95*, volume 936 of *Lecture Notes in Computer Science*, pages 169–183. Springer-Verlag, 1995.

[dS85] R. de Simone. Higher-level synchronising devices in MEIJE-SCCS. *Theoretical Computer Science*, 37(3):245–267, 1985.

[Gon85] G. Gonthier. Algebraic calculi of processes and net expressions. *Theoretical Computer Science*, 40: 329–337, 1985.

[HT92] K. Honda and M. Tokoro. On asynchronous communication semantics. In M. Tokoro, O. Nierstrasz, and P. Wegner, editors, *Object-Based Concurrent Computing*, volume 612 of *Lecture Notes in Computer Science*, pages 21–51. Springer-Verlag, 1992.

[Mil89] R. Milner. *Communication and Concurrency*. Prentice Hall, 1989.

[Mil91] R. Milner. The polyadic $\pi$-calculus: a tutorial. Technical Report ECS-LFCS-91-180, Laboratory for Foundations of Computer Science, Department of Computer Science, University of Edinburgh, UK, October 1991. Also in *Logic and Algebra of Specification*, ed. F. L. Bauer, W. Brauer and H. Schwichtenberg, Springer-Verlag, 1993.

[Mil92] R. Milner. Functions as processes. *Journal of Mathematical Structures in Computer Science*, 2(2): 119–141, 1992.

[MPW92] R. Milner, J. Parrow, and D. Walker. A calculus of mobile processes, Parts I and II. *Journal of Information and Computation*, 100:1–77, September 1992.

[OP92] F. Orava and J. Parrow. An algebraic verification of a mobile network. *Journal of Formal Aspects of Computing*, 4:497–543, 1992.

[Ora94] F. Orava. *On the Formal Analysis of Telecommunication Protocols*. PhD thesis, Department of Computer Systems, Uppsala University, Sweden, May 1994.

[Par90] J. Parrow. The expressive power of parallelism. *Future Generation Computer Systems*, 6:271–285, 1990.

[San93] D. Sangiorgi. From $\pi$-calculus to Higher-Order $\pi$-calculus—and back. In *Proceedings of TAPSOFT'93*, volume 668 of *Lecture Notes in Computer Science*, pages 151–166. Springer-Verlag, 1993.

[San94] D. Sangiorgi. On the bisimulation proof method. Revised version of Technical Report ECS-LFCS-94-299, University of Edinburgh, 1994. An extended abstract can be found in Proc. of MFCS'95, LNCS 969, 1994. Available electronically as `ftp://ftp.dcs.ed.ac.uk/pub/sad/bis-proof.ps.Z`.

[San96] D. Sangiorgi. A theory of bisimulation for the $\pi$-calculus. *Acta Informatica*, 33:69–97, 1996. Earlier version published as Report ECS-LFCS-93-270, University of Edinburgh. An extended abstract appeared in LNCS 715 (Proc. CONCUR'93).

[Vaa93] F. Vaandrager. Expressiveness results for process algebras. In J. W. de Bakker, W. P. de Roever, and G. Rozenberg, editors, *Proceedings REX Workshop on Semantics: Foundations and Applications,* Beekbergen, The Netherlands, June 1992, volume 666 of *Lecture Notes in Computer Science*, pages 609–638. Springer-Verlag, 1993.

[Wal95] D. Walker. Objects in the $\pi$-calculus. *Journal of Information and Computation*, 116(2):253–271, 1995.

# 22 Concurrent Objects as Mobile Processes

**Xinxin Liu and David Walker**

## 1 Introduction

When asked in the interview to accompany the publication of his Turing Award lecture [15] to "comment on the strong trend toward object-oriented programming in the U.S.," Robin Milner began his reply with a characteristically carefully constructed assertion:

> Object-oriented programming is a wonderful example of how fruitful things don't happen very precisely.

He continued:

> Different computer science theories are needed to explain object-oriented programming because it is partly about concurrency.... One theory that is contributing a lot to object-oriented programming is the development of a type structure. That part does not primarily have to do with concurrency. On the other hand, the dynamic part, or the behavioural aspect of object-oriented programming, particularly concurrent object-oriented programming, is precisely what we should try to understand from the point of view of concurrency because concurrency is about independent objects.

This paper is intended as a contribution to the development of that understanding. Its viewpoint is that the general models of concurrent systems with changing structure provided by calculi of mobile processes based on the $\pi$-calculus [16] can play a valuable role. From this viewpoint, systems prescribed by concurrent object-oriented programs *are* mobile processes, and a semantic definition of a concurrent object-oriented language can be given by a structural translation of its phrases into the language of a calculus (which has a well-established semantic theory). It is our view that this method of definition can give very natural and direct semantic accounts and that in addition to these important qualities it has two further, related, benefits. First, the process-calculus theory may be used to reason rigorously about the behaviours of systems prescribed by concurrent object-oriented programs; and attempts to do this stimulate further fruitful development of the theory—see e.g. [10, 19] where notions of *partial confluence* of processes are introduced and used to establish the correctness of program transformation rules. Secondly, the general models act as an accessible unifying and simplifying framework, a single arena for the definition of different languages, within which concepts and techniques arising in various domains can be generalized and transferred to others.

The idea of using a process calculus to give a semantic definition of a concurrent programming language was first explored by Milner [12, 13]. There a semantic account of a

XL's research supported by a grant from the U.K. Engineering and Physical Sciences Research Council.

concurrent imperative language with shared variables was given by translation to the process calculus CCS. The use of CCS as a semantic basis for sequential object-oriented languages was studied in [18]. The $\pi$-calculus is a descendant of CCS via the calculus ECCS [5]. Its primitive notion is *naming*. Processes interact by using names; and by mentioning names in interactions, processes may pass to one another the ability to interact with other processes. Within this framework one has a direct, rigorous account of reference-passing. In [25] a semantic definition for a simple concurrent object-oriented language was given by translation to the monadic $\pi$-calculus. That work was developed in [27] using the polyadic $\pi$-calculus as semantic basis. In particular, the usefulness of the kind of simple sorting system introduced in [14] in capturing some linguistic structure was shown, and a close correspondence was established between a semantics by translation and a reformulation of the operational semantics of [3] for a variant of a language in the POOL family [2]. A semantics by translation to the $\pi$-calculus was also given in [7], while [6] introduced a calculus very closely related to a fragment of the $\pi$-calculus motivated directly by study of concurrent objects.

In definitions such as these, data (Booleans, integers, etc.), stores, expressions, commands, objects, classes, and systems are all represented as name-passing processes. So flexible is the idea of name-passing that evaluation of expressions, control flow within commands, interaction between objects, and creation of objects can all be expressed using it. However, these descriptions are at a low level of abstraction: it is difficult to formulate and prove properties of interest about systems or their components. In [28] the usefulness of the process abstractions and richer type system of the Higher-Order $\pi$-calculus [23] in retaining more linguistic structure in translation were studied, while in [26] the utility of a definition based on an amalgamation of the $\pi$-calculus and value-passing CCS was shown in reasoning about simple systems. The work on the design and implementation of the Pict programming language [21], an interesting experimental language based on the $\pi$-calculus, has yielded many insights concerning the expression of behaviour in mobile-process calculi and enrichments of them; it has also advanced understanding of type-theoretic aspects of concurrent programming. A further development is [24] in which an interpretation of the first-order (sequential) functional object calculus of [1] in a typed version of $\pi$-calculus is given which validates the subtyping relation and the typing judgments of the object calculus and is computationally adequate. Other closely-related work on concurrent objects includes [17, 9].

In this paper we describe an extension of the $\pi$-calculus which is particularly suitable for the purpose of semantic definition and illustrate how a translation technique involving *process continuations* makes it possible to give very natural and direct semantic accounts of languages; see also [11]. This calculus includes process abstractions as in the Higher-Order $\pi$-calculus and data other than names, while excluding higher-order interaction. This combination allows very succinct and direct definition without the need to employ the relatively complex theory of higher-order interaction. Indeed the definition we will give has the feature that an object is interpreted as a process whose only actions represent interactions between objects, creations of objects, and interactions of objects with the system's environment. This, it is argued, captures well the pre-theoretic notion of object, at least in its behavioural aspects.

The language we use to illustrate the ideas is derived from the POOL family incorporating a construct of a language in [7] which allows one object to delegate to another the responsibility for returning to a third object the result of a method invocation. Before the development of process-calculus semantics, the POOL family had been the subject of extensive semantic study. For example as mentioned earlier an operational semantics was given in [3], while [4] offered a denotational semantics based on metric spaces. Also as remarked before, a close correspondence between a reformulation of the semantics of [3] and that by translation to the polyadic $\pi$-calculus was established in [27]. The metric-space semantics, which was in turn related in [22] to the operational semantics, is complicated, as one would expect given the nature of the kind of language under consideration. Correspondence results such as these relating different semantic models are important, not only in helping to clarify concepts in concurrent object-oriented programming, but also in making it possible to bring to bear a variety of reasoning tools for different purposes. In our view, valuable characteristics of the process-calculus semantics are its succinctness, directness and relative simplicity.

The programming language is introduced together with an informal account of its semantics in the next section. Section 3 contains some illustrative examples concerning it. In section 4 the mobile-process calculus is described. The semantic definition occupies section 5. Remarks on it are collected in the final section.

## 2 A concurrent Object-Oriented Language

In this section we introduce the programming language and give an informal account of its semantics. The language is statically typed with types $\mathsf{bool}$ (Booleans), $\mathsf{int}$ (integers), $\mathsf{unit}$ (the one-element type) and $\mathsf{ref}(A)$ for $A$ a class name from the set $\mathsf{C}$. The language has Boolean and integer constants and a constant $\mathsf{nil}$ which is overloaded and is used to represent a reference to no object, the 'undefined' value of types $\mathsf{bool}$ and $\mathsf{int}$, and the value of type $\mathsf{unit}$. In the abstract syntax definitions below we use $K$ to range over constants, $m$ over method names from the set $\mathsf{M}$, $A$ over class names, $X$ over variable names from the set $\mathsf{V}$, $E$ over expressions, and $V$ over sets of method names, and we write $\tilde{Z}$ for a tuple $Z_1, \ldots, Z_n$ of syntactic entities. The abstract syntax of expressions is as follows:

$$
\begin{aligned}
E \ ::= \ & K \mid X \mid \mathsf{new}(A) \mid \mathsf{op}(\tilde{E}) \\
\mid \ & X := E \mid E_1;\ E_2 \mid \mathsf{if}\ E\ \mathsf{then}\ E_1\ \mathsf{else}\ E_2 \mid \mathsf{while}\ E_1\ \mathsf{do}\ E_2 \\
\mid \ & \mathsf{synch}\ E!m(\tilde{E}) \mid \mathsf{asynch}\ E!m(\tilde{E}) \mid \mathsf{commit}\ E!m(\tilde{E}) \\
\mid \ & \mathsf{answer}\ V \mid \mathsf{output}(E) \mid \mathsf{input}\,.
\end{aligned}
$$

Declarations are given as follows. First, variable declarations are given by

$$Vdec \ ::= \ \mathsf{var}\ X_1 : T_1, \ldots, X_p : T_p$$

where $T$ ranges over types. Then method declarations are given by

$$Mdec \ ::= \ \mathsf{method}\, m(\tilde{X} : \tilde{T}) : T,\ Vdec,\ E$$

with $m$ the method name, $\tilde{X}$ of types $\tilde{T}$ its formal parameters, $T$ its result type, and $E$ its body with *Vdec* declaring variables local to it. Sequences of method declarations are given by

$$Mdecs \ ::= \ Mdec_1, \ldots, Mdec_q$$

and class declarations by

$$Cdec \ ::= \ \mathsf{class}\ A,\ Vdec,\ Mdecs,\ E$$

where $A$ is the name of the class, *Vdec* declares its instance variables, *Mdecs* declares its methods, and $E$ is its body which prescribes the behaviour of each its instances. Finally, program declarations are given by

$$Pdec \ ::= \ Cdec_1, \ldots, Cdec_r.$$

Execution of *Pdec* begins with the creation of a *root object*, an instance of the last class declared in it. Each object has a private store in which are held values of the Boolean, integer and ref-types. A value of type ref($A$) is a reference to an object of class $A$. When an object is created, all its variables have the value nil and evaluation of its body begins. An informal account of the evaluation of expressions follows; typing is explained below.

The evaluation of $X$ involves reading the value of the variable $X$ from the store. Evaluation of new($A$) results in the creation of an object of class $A$; the value of the expression is a reference to that object. op ranges over simple arithmetic and Boolean operators. The assignment, sequence, conditional and loop expressions are standard. The evaluation of synch $E!m(\tilde{E})$, of asynch $E!m(\tilde{E})$ and of commit $E!m(\tilde{E})$ all involve the evaluation of $E$ and then of the expressions in the tuple $\tilde{E}$, followed by the invocation of method $m$ with parameters the values of $\tilde{E}$ in the object to which the value of $E$ is a reference; in each case the invocation involves a synchronization between the two objects concerned. The evaluation of synch $E!m(\tilde{E})$ is then blocked until a value is returned as the result of the method invocation; the returned value is the value of the synch expression. In contrast, the evaluation of asynch $E!m(\tilde{E})$ is completed by the invocation; the value of the asynch expression is nil. A result may be implicitly returned to an object as the value of a synch expression when the evaluation of a method body is completed; the value returned is the value of the expression comprising the method body. However, the object which returns a result to an object $\gamma$ may not be the one in which $\gamma$ invoked a method in evaluating the synch expression. When, in evaluating a method body, an object $\alpha$ evaluates an expression commit $E!m(\tilde{E})$ by invoking method $m$ in the object $\beta$ to which the value of $E$ is a reference with parameters the values of $\tilde{E}$, it is implicit that: either (i) the value of the body of the method of $\alpha$ in which the commit expression occurs is not to be returned to any object, in which case the value of the body of method $m$ in object $\beta$ is not to be returned to any object; or (ii) by invoking method $m$ in $\beta$, $\alpha$ delegates to $\beta$ the task of returning a result to an object $\gamma$, thereby freeing itself from the responsibility of returning a result to $\gamma$. The evaluation of answer $V$ by an object $\beta$ begins when an object $\alpha$ invokes one of the methods named in the set $V$. It is completed when the body of the method is evaluated. The value of an answer expression is nil of type unit. Evaluation of output($E$) involves evaluation of $E$ and the emission of its integer value to the environment; the value of the output expression is nil of type unit. Evaluation of input consumes an integer from the environment, that being the expression's value.

As a simple example, one might define a class the sole function of whose instances is to interact with the environment:

```
class IO,
method in():int,
    input,
method out(X:int):unit,
    output(X),
while true do answer [in, out]
```

In giving a semantic definition of the language in a later section, information about types of expressions will play an important role. We give an outline of the typing discipline. Consider *Pdec* as above. *Pdec* is well-typed if for each occurrence of an expression $E$ in it, for some type $T$ a judgment $\vdash E : T$ may be inferred within the system of rules below. An inference is carried out in the appropriate context. If $E$ is a subexpression of a class body, that is determined by the types of the instance variables of the class; if $E$ is a subexpression of a method body, the context is determined by the types of the instance variables of the appropriate class and of the formal parameters and local variables of the method. We require that the names of the instance variables, formal parameters and local variables within a class are distinct from one another. We require also that a commit expression may occur only in a method body (not in the body of a class definition), and that no answer expression may occur in a method body. It is not difficult to modify the definition to account for the relaxation of the latter requirement. The type inference rules are as follows.

1. $\vdash K : T$ if $T$ is the type of $K$,
2. $\vdash X : T$ if $X$ is of type $T$ in the appropriate context,
3. $\vdash \mathsf{new}(B) : \mathsf{ref}(B)$,
4. $\vdash \mathsf{op}(\tilde{F}) : T$ if $\vdash \tilde{F} : \tilde{T}$ and op has argument type $\tilde{T}$ and result type $T$,
5. $\vdash X := F : \mathsf{unit}$ if for some $T$, $\vdash F : T$ and $X$ is of type $T$ in the appropriate context,
6. $\vdash F_1; F_2 : T$ if $\vdash F_2 : T$ and $\vdash F_1 : T_1$ for some $T_1$,
7. $\vdash \mathsf{if}\ F\ \mathsf{then}\ F_1\ \mathsf{else}\ F_2 : T$ if $\vdash F : \mathsf{bool}$, $\vdash F_1 : T$ and $\vdash F_2 : T$,
8. $\vdash \mathsf{while}\ F_1\ \mathsf{do}\ F_2 : \mathsf{unit}$ if $\vdash F_1 : \mathsf{bool}$ and $\vdash F_2 : \mathsf{unit}$,
9. $\vdash \mathsf{synch}\ F!m'(\tilde{F}) : T$ if $\vdash F : \mathsf{ref}(B)$, in class $B$ the declaration of $m'$ is of the form method $m'(\tilde{X}{:}\,\tilde{T}){:}\,T,\ Vdec',\ E'$, and $\vdash \tilde{F} : \tilde{T}$,
10. $\vdash \mathsf{asynch}\ F!m'(\tilde{F}) : \mathsf{unit}$ if $\vdash F : \mathsf{ref}(B)$, in class $B$ the declaration of $m'$ is of the form method $m'(\tilde{X}{:}\,\tilde{T}){:}\,T,\ Vdec',\ E'$, and $\vdash \tilde{F} : \tilde{T}$,
11. $\vdash \mathsf{commit}\ F!m'(\tilde{F}) : \mathsf{unit}$ if $\vdash F : \mathsf{ref}(B)$, in class $B$ the declaration of $m'$ is of the form method $m'(\tilde{X}{:}\,\tilde{T}){:}\,T,\ Vdec',\ E'$, $\vdash \tilde{F} : \tilde{T}$, and the result type of the method in which the commit expression occurs is $T$ (i.e. is the same as that of the method $m'$ in class $B$),
12. $\vdash \mathsf{answer}\ V : \mathsf{unit}$ if each name in $V$ is the name of a method declared in the class in which the answer expression occurs,
13. $\vdash \mathsf{output}(E) : \mathsf{unit}$ if $\vdash E : \mathsf{int}$,
14. $\vdash \mathsf{input} : \mathsf{int}$.

Finally, it is required that for each method declaration method $m(\tilde{X} : \tilde{T}) : T,\ Vdec,\ E$, we have $\vdash E : T$, i.e., that the type of the method body be the result type of the method.

## 3 Examples

In this section we illustrate aspects of the language through some simple examples.

The instances of the following class declaration may be used to construct binary tree-structured symbol tables.

```
class T,
var K:int, V:ref(A), L:ref(T), R:ref(T),
method insert(X:int, W:ref(A)):unit,
   if K=nil then (K:=X ; V:=W ; L:=new(T) ; R:=new(T))
   else if X=K then V:=W
```

```
        else if X<K then asynch L!insert(X,W)
             else asynch R!insert(X,W),
method search(Y:int):ref(A),
    if K=nil then nil
    else if Y=K then V
        else if Y<K then (commit L!search(Y) ; nil)
             else (commit R!search(Y) ; nil),
while true do answer [insert, search]
```

An object of this class represents a node which stores in its variables `K`, `V`, `L`, `R` an integer key, a value (a reference to an object of some class `A`), and references to two instances of the class (its left and right children in the tree structure of which it is a component). It has two actions: the method `insert` which allows a key-value pair to be inserted, and the method `search` which returns the value associated with its key parameter (or **nil** if there is none). Note how the use of **asynch** and **commit** expressions in the method bodies allow objects of class `T` to enjoy concurrent behaviour. In particular, if the `search` method is invoked in a node with a key smaller (resp. larger) than that stored there, the node will commit that search to its left (resp. right) child, thereby delegating to the child object the responsibility for returning the result of the search. Note that the '`; nil`' following the **commit** expressions in method `search` give the method body the correct type, **ref**$(A)$.

The instances of the following class may be used to build integer priority queues.

```
class Q,
var V:int, P:ref(Q),
method add(X:int):unit,
    if V=nil then (V:=X ; P:=new(Q))
    else if V<X then asynch P!add(X)
        else (asynch P!add(V) ; V:=X),
method rem():int,
    commit new(C)!return(V) ;
    if V=nil then P:=nil else V:=synch P!rem() ;
    nil,
while true do answer [add, rem]
class C,
method return(V:int):int,
    V,
answer [return]
```

Each instance of Q represents a cell which stores an integer in the variable V and a pointer to another cell in the variable P. A priority queue is composed of a chain of cells in which integers are stored in ascending order. New cells are created and appended to the chain as integers are added via the method add. The smallest integer held in the queue (or nil if the queue is empty) is returned and removed by the rem method. When the rem method is invoked, a new object of class C is created and the task of returning the smallest integer in the queue (or nil if there is none) is delegated to that object. This allows more concurrent activity within a queue than would otherwise be possible. The final '; nil' in the method rem gives the method body the correct type, int.

Next we illustrate how the *Cbox* construct of some object-oriented languages [8] may be expressed in the language. An example of the use of CBoxes is outlined in the following fragment of a class declaration.

(a)
```
Cbox V1:ref(A), V2:ref(A) ;     % declaration of Cboxes
...
asynch X!m(V1,V2) ;             % Cboxes passed as parameters
...
Y1:=V1 ;                        % proceed only when a value is in V1
...
Y2:=V2;                         % proceed only when a value is in V2
```

A value may be given to a Cbox by the object to which it is passed as a parameter or by an object to which it is committed. For instance:

(b)
```
method m(V1:ref(A),V2:ref(A)):unit,    % declaration of method m
    ...
    V1:=value ;                        % give value to Cbox V1
    ...
    commit Z!m'(V2) ;                  % commit responsibility
                                       % for giving value to V2
```

In the language we can express this as follows. We first define

```
class C,
var V:ref(A),
method put(X:ref(A)):unit,
   V:=X,
method get():ref(A),
   V,
answer [put] ; answer[get]
```

and then replace (a) by (c) and (b) by (d) where

(c)
```
V1:=new(C) ; V2:=new(C) ;     % create Cbox objects
asynch X!m(V1,V2) ;           % Cboxes passed as parameters
...
Y1:=synch V1!get() ;
...
Y2:=synch V2!get() ;
```

(d)
```
method m(V1:ref(C),V2:ref(C)):unit,   % declaration of m
    ...
    asynch V1!put(value) ;            % give value to Cbox V1
    ...
    commit Z!m'(V2) ;                 % commit responsibility for
                                      % giving value to V2.
```

## 4 A Mobile-Process Calculus

In this section we describe an extension of the $\pi$-calculus which has data values other than names and includes higher-order process abstractions as in the Higher-Order $\pi$-calculus while excluding higher-order communication. This calculus will be used to give a semantic definition for the programming language. The other data types and higher-order process abstractions of the calculus are used extensively in the semantic definition. The exclusion of higher-order communication allows the calculus to employ the relatively simple bisimilarity theory of the $\pi$-calculus.

Assume a set $\mathcal{N}$ of *names*, a set of *values* including $\mathcal{N} \cup \{\mathsf{true}, \mathsf{false}\}$, and a set of *first-order terms* including the values. These terms describe the data part of the calculus. Assume also a partial evaluation function $\twoheadrightarrow$ from first-order terms to values.

The *higher-order terms* are the *process expressions* $P$, $Q$ and *abstractions* $F$ defined as follows where we assume sets of agent constants $D$ and agent variables $X$:

$$P \ ::= \ \Sigma_{j \in J} \pi_j \cdot P_j \mid P \mid Q \mid (\nu x)P \mid \mathsf{if}(t \rhd P, Q) \mid F\langle \tilde{H} \rangle$$

$$F \ ::= \ (\tilde{u})P \mid D \mid X$$

where the prefixes $\pi$ are given by

$$\pi \ ::= \ \bar{t}\langle \tilde{t} \rangle \mid t(\tilde{y}) \mid \tau$$

and $x$, $y$ range over names, $t$ over first-order terms, $u$ over names and agent variables, $D$ over agent constants, $X$ over agent variables, and $H$ over first-order and higher-order terms. Note that all prefixes are first-order. Further, the indexing set $J$ in the guarded summation is finite. We assume that each agent constant $D$ has a defining equation $D \stackrel{\text{def}}{=} (\tilde{u})P$ where $\tilde{u}$ contains all names and agent variables occurring free in $P$ (binding is explained below).

We write $\mathbf{0}$ for the empty summation and $\pi$ for $\pi \cdot \mathbf{0}$. In $t(\tilde{y}) \cdot P$, $(\nu x)P$ and $D \stackrel{\text{def}}{=} (\tilde{u})P$, the occurrences of $\tilde{y}$, $x$ and $\tilde{u}$ are binding with scope $P$. We assume the standard notions of free names and variables, substitution, alpha-conversion etc., and identify process expressions which differ only by change of bound names and variables. Briefly, $\Sigma_{j \in J}\pi_j \cdot P_j$ is a guarded choice, $P|Q$ a concurrent composition and $\mathsf{if}(t \triangleright P, Q)$ a conditional, while in $(\nu x)P$ the scope of the name $x$ is restricted to P. This will be made precise by the transition rules given below.

Before describing these we present a typing system for the calculus. In addition to being essential for avoiding confusion between entities of different kinds appearing in the calculus, such a system is helpful in organizing the semantic definition of the programming language and in using it to reason about programs. Assume a set of types which contains the Boolean type $\mathsf{bool}$ with values $\mathsf{true}$, $\mathsf{false}$ and each of a set of atomic types called *link sorts* whose values are the names of $\mathcal{N}$. Assume that each first-order term $t$ has a unique type $\iota$, written $t\colon \iota$. Assume that the partial evaluation function $\twoheadrightarrow$ has the property that if $t\colon \iota$ and $t \twoheadrightarrow v$ then $v\colon \iota$.

The type discipline of the calculus is an extension of the type system for the first-order terms. The first component of the extension is a partial function $\lambda$ (a *sorting*) from link sorts to tuples of first-order types. The intention is that if $\lambda(\mathsf{L}) = (\tilde{\iota})$ then a name of sort $\mathsf{L}$ may be used to communicate tuples of values of the types $\tilde{\iota}$. For example if $\lambda(\mathsf{L}) = (\mathsf{bool}, \mathsf{L})$ then a name of type $\mathsf{L}$ may be used to pass pairs whose first component is a Boolean and whose second component is a name of the same type. The second component of the extension is the introduction of higher-order types. A *higher-order type* is of the form $\mathsf{abs}(\xi_1, \ldots, \xi_n)$ where $\xi_1, \ldots, \xi_n$ are first-order or higher-order types. These are types for processes and process abstractions. For example, if $P$ is a process expression with free names $x$, $y$ of types $\mathsf{L}_1, \mathsf{L}_2$ respectively, then $(x\ y)P$ is of type $\mathsf{abs}(\mathsf{L}_1, \mathsf{L}_2)$. We will use $\xi$ to range over types. Formally, we assume a type system for the first-order terms as above, and suppose that each agent variable and agent constant is assigned a higher-order type. Then each well-typed process expression and abstraction acquires a unique type as follows.

1. $\Sigma_{j \in J}\pi_j \cdot P_j\colon \mathsf{abs}()$ if for each $j \in J$ one of the following holds:

(a) $\pi_j$ is of form $\bar{t}\langle\tilde{t}\rangle$ where $t\colon \mathsf{L}$, $\lambda(\mathsf{L}) = (\tilde{\iota})$, $\tilde{t}\colon \tilde{\iota}$ and $P_j\colon \mathsf{abs}()$,

(b) $\pi_j$ is of form $t(\tilde{y})$ where $t\colon \mathsf{L}$, $\lambda(\mathsf{L}) = (\tilde{\iota})$, $\tilde{y}\colon \tilde{\iota}$ and $P_j\colon \mathsf{abs}()$,

(c) $\pi_j$ is $\tau$ and $P_j\colon \mathsf{abs}()$.

2. $P \mid Q$: $\mathsf{abs}()$ if $P$: $\mathsf{abs}()$ and $Q$: $\mathsf{abs}()$.
3. $(\nu x)P$: $\mathsf{abs}()$ if $P$: $\mathsf{abs}()$ and $x$: $\mathsf{L}$ for some link sort $\mathsf{L}$.
4. $\mathsf{if}(t \rhd P, Q)$: $\mathsf{abs}()$ if $P$: $\mathsf{abs}()$, $Q$: $\mathsf{abs}()$ and $t$: $\mathsf{bool}$.
5. $F\langle \tilde{H} \rangle$: $\mathsf{abs}()$ if $F$: $\mathsf{abs}(\tilde{\xi})$ and $\tilde{H}$: $\tilde{\xi}$.
6. $(\tilde{u})P$: $\mathsf{abs}(\tilde{\xi})$ if $P$: $\mathsf{abs}()$ and $\tilde{u}$: $\tilde{\xi}$.

A defining equation $D \stackrel{\text{def}}{=} F$ is *well-typed* if $F$ has the same type as $D$. As explained earlier, the calculus includes higher-order abstractions—in the last two rules, the types in $\tilde{\xi}$ may be higher-order—while excluding higher-order interaction: recall, in the first rule, that the sorting $\lambda$ maps link sorts to tuples of first-order types.

In giving the transition rules of the calculus, we restrict attention to *processes*, i.e. those $P$: $\mathsf{abs}()$ closed in the sense that no agent variable occurs free in $P$. The rules are obtained from those of the $\pi$-calculus by incorporating an appropriate treatment of first-order terms. The relations are labelled by actions $\alpha$ of which there are three kinds: the silent action $\tau$, output actions $(\nu\tilde{z})\overline{x}\langle\tilde{v}\rangle$, and input actions $x\langle\tilde{v}\rangle$. Here $x$ is a name, $\tilde{v}$ is a tuple of values and $\tilde{z}$ is the set $\text{bn}(\alpha)$ of bound names of the action $\alpha$; also $\text{bn}(\tau) = \emptyset$ and $\text{bn}(x\langle\tilde{v}\rangle) = \emptyset$. We write $\text{fn}(Q)$ for the set of names occurring free in $Q$. The relations are defined by the following rules from which the symmetric forms of 4 and 5 are elided.

1. $\ldots + t(\tilde{y}) \cdot P + \ldots \xrightarrow{x\langle\tilde{v}\rangle} P\{\tilde{v}/\tilde{y}\}$ provided $t \twoheadrightarrow x$, $t$: $\mathsf{L}$ and $\tilde{v}$: $\lambda(\mathsf{L})$; here $P\{\tilde{v}/\tilde{y}\}$ is the result of substituting the components of $\tilde{v}$ for the corresponding components of $\tilde{y}$ in $P$.
2. $\ldots + \overline{t}\langle\tilde{t}\rangle \cdot P + \ldots \xrightarrow{\overline{x}\langle\tilde{v}\rangle} P$ provided $t \twoheadrightarrow x$ and $\tilde{t} \twoheadrightarrow \tilde{v}$.
3. $\ldots + \tau \cdot P + \ldots \xrightarrow{\tau} P$.
4. If $P \xrightarrow{\alpha} P'$ then $P \mid Q \xrightarrow{\alpha} P' \mid Q$ provided $\text{bn}(\alpha) \cap \text{fn}(Q) = \emptyset$.
5. If $P \xrightarrow{(\nu\tilde{z})\overline{x}\langle\tilde{v}\rangle} P'$ and $Q \xrightarrow{x\langle\tilde{v}\rangle} Q'$ then $P \mid Q \xrightarrow{\tau} (\nu\tilde{z})(P' \mid Q')$ provided $\tilde{z} \cap \text{fn}(Q) = \emptyset$.
6. If $P \xrightarrow{\alpha} P'$ then $(\nu x)P \xrightarrow{\alpha} (\nu x)P'$ provided $x$ does not occur in $\alpha$.
7. If $P \xrightarrow{(\nu\tilde{z})\overline{x}\langle\tilde{v}\rangle} P'$ then $(\nu y)P \xrightarrow{(\nu\tilde{z}y)\overline{x}\langle\tilde{v}\rangle} P'$ provided $y$ occurs in $\tilde{v} - (\tilde{z} \cup \{x\})$.
8. If $P\{\tilde{H}/\tilde{u}\} \xrightarrow{\alpha} P'$ then $((\tilde{u})P)\langle\tilde{H}\rangle \xrightarrow{\alpha} P'$.
9. If $F\langle\tilde{H}\rangle \xrightarrow{\alpha} P'$ and $D \stackrel{\text{def}}{=} F$ then $D\langle\tilde{H}\rangle \xrightarrow{\alpha} P'$.
10. If $P \xrightarrow{\alpha} P'$ then $\mathsf{if}(t \rhd P, Q) \xrightarrow{\alpha} P'$ provided $t \twoheadrightarrow \mathsf{true}$.
11. If $Q \xrightarrow{\alpha} Q'$ then $\mathsf{if}(t \rhd P, Q) \xrightarrow{\alpha} Q'$ provided $t \twoheadrightarrow \mathsf{false}$.

A convenient derived form is the *replication* $!\,(\nu\tilde{x})\pi \cdot P$ defined by

$$!\,(\nu\tilde{x})\pi \cdot P \stackrel{\text{def}}{=} (\nu\tilde{x})\pi \cdot (P \mid !\,(\nu\tilde{x})\pi \cdot P)$$

which may repeatedly interact via $\pi$ to activate new instances of $P$.

It can be proved that the type system has the following property: if $P$: $\mathsf{abs}()$ and $P \xrightarrow{\alpha} P'$ then $P'$: $\mathsf{abs}()$.

## 5 The Semantic Definition

In this section we give a semantic definition of the programming language by translation to the calculus. As mentioned earlier the type system plays an important rôle in organizing the definition. Fix a program declaration *Pdec* whose meaning is to be defined. First we stipulate that the basic types of the calculus are as follows.

1. The link sorts (we treat "sort" and "type" as synonyms):

| | |
|---|---|
| $\mathsf{M}_A^m$ | for $A \in \mathsf{C}$ and $m \in \mathsf{M}$, invocation links |
| $\mathsf{R}_T$ | for $T$ a type, result links |
| $\mathsf{C}_A$ | for $A \in \mathsf{C}$, creation links |
| $\mathsf{E}$ | external links. |

The use of link sorts will be explained below.

2. The non-reference types of the programming language, i.e., $\mathsf{bool}$, $\mathsf{int}$ and $\mathsf{unit}$. Each constant $K$ and each operator $\mathsf{op}$ of the programming language is present in the calculus.

3. For each class $A$ appearing in *Pdec*, a record type $\{m_1 : \mathsf{M}_A^{m_1}, \ldots, m_q : \mathsf{M}_A^{m_q}\}$ where $m_1, \ldots, m_q$ are the names of the methods of $A$. For notational simplicity we abbreviate this calculus record type to $\mathsf{ref}(A)$. We refer to terms of type $\mathsf{ref}(A)$ as *object names* of class $A$. Such terms will be the process-calculus representations of 'object identifiers.' If $\alpha$ is an object name of class $A$ and $m \in \{m_1, \ldots, m_q\}$ then $\alpha : m$ is a field-selection term. (We use ':' rather than '.' to avoid possible confusion with prefixing operators.)

4. Finally, suppose that in *Pdec* class $A$ has instance variables $\tilde{X} : \tilde{T}$ and methods $m_1, \ldots, m_q$ with $m_i$ of result type $T_i$ taking parameters $\tilde{Y}_i : \tilde{T}_i$ and having local variables $\tilde{Z}_i : \tilde{U}_i$ where the $\tilde{X}, \tilde{Y}, \tilde{Z}$ are all distinct. Then we abbreviate to $\mathsf{S}_A$ the record type

$$\{\tilde{X} : \tilde{T},\ \tilde{Y}_i : \tilde{T}_i,\ \tilde{Z}_i : \tilde{U}_i,\ R_{m_i} : \mathsf{R}_{T_i},\ \rho : \mathsf{bool},\ \iota : \mathsf{ref}(A)\}_{1 \le i \le q}$$

and we refer to terms of this type as *A-stores* (or simply *stores*). The $\tilde{X}, \tilde{Y}, \tilde{Z}$-fields contain the process-calculus representations of the values held in an object's store; the $\tilde{R}$-fields are used to hold the names of links which should be used for returning the results of method invocations; the $\rho$-field indicates whether or not a result is to be returned in the currently active method invocation, if there is one; and in the $\iota$-field is stored the object name of the object. In addition to field-selection terms as above we have field-update terms: if $\sigma$ is a store, $\tilde{\ell}$ are distinct indices of some of its fields and $\tilde{t}$ terms of the appropriate types then $\sigma[\tilde{t}/\tilde{\ell}]$ is the term representing update of the $\tilde{\ell}$-fields of $\sigma$ to $\tilde{t}$.

The values of the basic types are as follows: of the link sorts, the names; of the non-reference types of the programming language, true, false, 0, 1, ... and nil; and of the record types, the terms $\{\tilde{\ell} = \tilde{v}\}$ where $\tilde{v}$ are values. The partial evaluation function $\twoheadrightarrow$ is defined in the obvious way.

The sorting $\lambda$ is the following partial function on link sorts. First

$$\lambda(\mathsf{C}_A) = (\mathsf{ref}(A))$$
$$\lambda(\mathsf{E}) = (\mathsf{int})$$

and if in the definition of class $A$ in *Pdec* we have method $m(Y_1\colon T_1, \ldots, Y_n\colon T_n)\colon T$, *Vdec*, $E$, then

$$\lambda(\mathsf{M}_A^m) = (T_1, \ldots, T_n, \mathsf{R}_T, \mathsf{bool})$$
$$\lambda(\mathsf{R}_T) = (T).$$

The significance of the sorting will become clear when the semantic mapping is given. Briefly, it is based on the following ideas:

1. A name of sort $\mathsf{C}_A$ may be used to communicate object names of class $A$. Names of sort $\mathsf{C}_A$ will be used in representing creation of objects.
2. A name of sort $\mathsf{E}$ may be used to communicate integers. Such names will be used in representing the interaction of a program with its environment.
3. A name of sort $\mathsf{M}_A^m$ will represent a link via which method $m$ may be invoked in an object of class $A$. In an invocation are sent parameters, represented by values of types $T_1, \ldots, T_n$, a name of link sort $\mathsf{R}_T$ along which a result may be returned, and a Boolean value indicating whether or not a result is to be returned.
4. A name of sort $\mathsf{R}_T$ will represent a link via which a result of sort $T$ may be returned.

The main higher-order type we use in the translation is $\mathsf{abs}(\mathsf{abs}(T, \mathsf{S}_A), \mathsf{S}_A)$; it is the type of process abstractions representing expressions of type $T$ occurring in class $A$.

A program prescribes the possible evolutions of a system of objects. Although objects may enjoy concurrent activity, computation within each object is sequential. This clear division, common to many but not all concurrent object-oriented languages, allows us to employ at the object level semantic techniques developed to treat sequential programming languages and at the system level techniques of process calculus which give a good account of interaction between objects. Thus, briefly, objects will be represented as sequential processes and systems as restricted compositions of such processes together with processes representing class definitions. The latter will be replicator processes capable of generating processes representing new objects. The main task is thus to give for each class definition a process representing a newly-created object of the class.

To begin to do this we remark first that in modelling the local state of an object one might use an environment, associating locations with variables names, and a store, associating values with locations. Since here we wish to focus on other aspects of the semantic definition which interact only mildly with the modelling of the state, we represent it using simply a store, a finite association of values with variable names. This is the reason for the assumption made earlier that within a class definition all instance variables, local variables and parameters have distinct names.

The most complicated part of the semantic definition is the representation of expressions. The evaluation of an expression in a given store yields a value and a possibly altered store. The meaning of an expression $E$ of type $T$ can also be considered in a context where it is the 'initial part' of a larger expression $E'$. More specifically, suppose that (i) we know for an arbitrary store $s$ the resulting value $v$ and possibly altered store $s'$ on evaluating $E$ in $s$, and (ii) the meaning of the rest of the expression $E'$ is given as an agent abstraction of type $\mathsf{abs}(T, \mathsf{S}_A)$, i.e. a *continuation* $k$ which when applied to the $v$ and $s'$ in (i) gives a process $k\langle v, s'\rangle$ representing the behaviour of $E'$ after evaluation of $E$. Then the semantics of $E$ is completely specified by describing how it transforms a $(k, s)$-pair into a process. The definition interprets an expression $E$ of type $T$ as a second-order agent abstraction $[\![E]\!]$ which when applied to an abstraction $k$ of type $\mathsf{abs}(T, \mathsf{S}_A)$, representing a continuation, and a store $s$ of type $\mathsf{S}_A$ yields a process $[\![E]\!]\langle k, s\rangle$ representing the combined behaviour of $E$ and $k$ on $s$. The definition is given in Figure 22.1 where $k$ is a variable of the second-order type $\mathsf{abs}(T, \mathsf{S}_A)$, $s$, $s_1$ etc. names of type $\mathsf{S}_A$, and $v$, $v_1$ etc. names of the appropriate types. Note that we give the definitions of $\mathsf{op}(\tilde{E})$, $\mathsf{synch}\ E!m(\tilde{E})$, $\mathsf{asynch}\ E!m(\tilde{E})$ and $\mathsf{commit}\ E!m(\tilde{E})$ only in sample cases; the others are similar. The name $n_A : \mathsf{C}_A$ occurs free in the $\mathsf{new}(A)$-clause of the definition. This appears to violate the requirement that in a defining equation $D \stackrel{\text{def}}{=} (\tilde{u})P$, $\tilde{u}$ should contain all names occurring free in $P$. However as explained in [16] the $\pi$-calculus has a conventional way of treating constant names and this carries over to the present calculus. In fact as we will see below, these constant names are abstracted in the representation of a program.

To grasp the definition consider first $[\![X]\!]$. Suppose that $k$ is a continuation of type $\mathsf{abs}(T', \mathsf{S}_A)$, where $X$ is of type $T'$, which when applied to a value and a store yields a process. Since the evaluation of $X$ with store $s$ just produces the value $s : X$ with store unchanged, $[\![X]\!]\langle k, s\rangle$, the total effect of evaluating $X$ with continuation $k$ and store $s$, is $k\langle s : X, s\rangle$ which enacts $k$ with the value $s : X$ using the unchanged store $s$. Contrast this with $[\![X := E]\!]\langle k, s\rangle$ which evaluates $E$ in store $s$ yielding a value $v$ and store $s'$ and then applies $k$ to $\mathsf{nil}$, the value of type $\mathsf{unit}$ of the assignment, and the updated store $s'[v/X]$. In $[\![\mathsf{synch}\ E_1!m(E_2)]\!]\langle k, s\rangle$ first $E_1$ is evaluated in $s$ yielding $v_1, s_1$ and then $E_2$

$$
\begin{aligned}
[\![K]\!] &\stackrel{\text{def}}{=} (k\,s)\,k\langle K, s\rangle\\
[\![X]\!] &\stackrel{\text{def}}{=} (k\,s)\,k\langle s : X, s\rangle\\
[\![\mathsf{new}(A)]\!] &\stackrel{\text{def}}{=} (k\,s)\,n_A(v)\cdot k\langle v, s\rangle\\
[\![\mathsf{op}(E_1, E_2)]\!] &\stackrel{\text{def}}{=} (k\,s)\,[\![E_1]\!]\langle (v_1\,s_1)[\![E_2]\!]\langle (v_2\,s_2)k\langle \mathsf{op}\,v_1 v_2, s_2\rangle, s_1\rangle, s\rangle\\
[\![X := E]\!] &\stackrel{\text{def}}{=} (k\,s)\,[\![E]\!]\langle (v\,s')k\langle \mathsf{nil}, s'[v/X]\rangle, s\rangle\\
[\![E_1; E_2]\!] &\stackrel{\text{def}}{=} (k\,s)\,[\![E_1]\!]\langle (v\,s')[\![E_2]\!]\langle k, s'\rangle, s\rangle\\
[\![\mathsf{if}\ E\ \mathsf{then}\ E_1\ \mathsf{else}\ E_2]\!] &\stackrel{\text{def}}{=} (k\,s)[\![E]\!]\langle (v\,s')\mathsf{if}(v \triangleright [\![E_1]\!]\langle k, s'\rangle, [\![E_2]\!]\langle k, s'\rangle), s\rangle\\
[\![\mathsf{while}\ E_1\ \mathsf{do}\ E_2]\!] &\stackrel{\text{def}}{=} W \qquad \text{a constant defined by}\\
W &\stackrel{\text{def}}{=} (k\,s)\,[\![E_1]\!]\langle (v\,s')\mathsf{if}(v \triangleright [\![E_2]\!]\langle (v_0\,s_0)W\langle k, s_0\rangle, s'\rangle, k\langle \mathsf{nil}, s'\rangle), s\rangle\\
[\![\mathsf{synch}\ E_1!m(E_2)]\!] &\stackrel{\text{def}}{=} (k\,s)\,[\![E_1]\!]\langle (v_1\,s_1)[\![E_2]\!]\langle (v_2\,s_2)\,(\nu r)\,\overline{v_1 : m}\langle v_2, r, \mathsf{true}\rangle\cdot r(v).\\
&\qquad k\langle v, s_2\rangle, s_1\rangle, s\rangle\\
[\![\mathsf{asynch}\ E_1!m(E_2)]\!] &\stackrel{\text{def}}{=} (k\,s)\,[\![E_1]\!]\langle (v_1\,s_1)[\![E_2]\!]\langle (v_2\,s_2)\,\overline{v_1 : m}\langle v_2, \mathsf{nil}, \mathsf{false}\rangle.\\
&\qquad k\langle \mathsf{nil}, s_2\rangle, s_1\rangle, s\rangle\\
[\![\mathsf{commit}\ E_1!m(E_2)]\!] &\stackrel{\text{def}}{=} (k\,s)\,[\![E_1]\!]\langle (v_1\,s_1)[\![E_2]\!]\langle (v_2\,s_2)\,\overline{v_1 : m}\langle v_2, s_2 : R_{m'}, s_2 : \rho\rangle.\\
&\qquad k\langle \mathsf{nil}, s_2[\mathsf{nil}/R_{m'}, \mathsf{false}/\rho]\rangle, s_1\rangle, s\rangle\\
[\![\mathsf{answer}\ V]\!] &\stackrel{\text{def}}{=} (k\,s)\,\Sigma\{A_m\langle k, s\rangle \mid m \in V\}\\
[\![\mathsf{output}(E)]\!] &\stackrel{\text{def}}{=} (k\,s)\,[\![E]\!]\langle (v\,s')\overline{\mathsf{out}}\langle v\rangle.\,k\langle \mathsf{nil}, s'\rangle, s\rangle\\
[\![\mathsf{input}]\!] &\stackrel{\text{def}}{=} (k\,s)\,\mathsf{in}(v)\cdot k\langle v, s\rangle
\end{aligned}
$$

**Figure 22.1**
The translation of expressions.

is evaluated in $s_1$ yielding $v_2, s_2$. Then the name $v_1 : m$ is used to invoke method $m$ in the object-agent of which $v_1$ is the object name with parameter $v_2$; also sent are a new name $r$ of the apropriate $\mathsf{R}_T$ sort, and the Boolean true indicating that a result should be returned via $r$. The agent then waits to receive a result $v$ on $r$ before continuing as $k\langle v, s_2\rangle$. Contrast this with $[\![\mathsf{asynch}\ E_1!m(E_2)]\!]\langle k, s\rangle$ whose behaviour is similar except that on $v_1 : m$ are sent the distinguished nil return link and the Boolean false indicating no result is to be returned, and that the agent proceeds immediately as $k\langle \mathsf{nil}, s_2\rangle$. In the translation of $[\![\mathsf{commit}\ E_1!m(E_2)]\!]\langle k, s\rangle$, on $v_1 : m$ are sent the name $s_2 : R_{m'}$ (where $m'$ is the name of the method in which the commit expression occurs) and the Boolean $s_2 : \rho$. If that Boolean is true, the name $s_2 : R_{m'}$ is to be used by the process representing the object to which the value of $E_1$ is a reference to return the value of the body of its method $m$; if the Boolean is false, no value is to be returned. The subsequent behaviour is $k\langle \mathsf{nil}, s_2[\mathsf{nil}/R_{m'}, \mathsf{false}/\rho]\rangle$, capturing that the process is freed from any responsibility it had for returning a result, that it relinquishes the return link it had, and that the value of the commit expression is nil.

A method declaration $Mdec \equiv \mathsf{method}\, m(\tilde{Y} : \tilde{T}),\ \mathsf{var}\, \tilde{Z} : \tilde{U},\ E$ is translated as the following constant definition; in it note that $s:\iota:m$ is a name of sort $\mathsf{M}_A^m$ where $A$ is the name of the class in which $Mdec$ occurs.

$$A_m \stackrel{\text{def}}{=} (k\, s)\, s:\iota:m(\tilde{v}, r, b) \cdot [\![E]\!]\langle (v\, s')\, \mathsf{if}(s':\rho \ \triangleright \bar{r}\langle v\rangle \cdot k\langle \mathsf{nil}, s'\rangle, k\langle \mathsf{nil}, s'\rangle),$$
$$s[\tilde{v}/\tilde{Y}, \mathsf{nil}/\tilde{Z}, r/R_m, b/\rho]\rangle\,.$$

To explain the prefix $n_A(v)$ in $[\![\mathsf{new}(A)]\!]$ we first give the representation of a class declaration. Suppose $Cdec$ is $class\ A,\ Vdec,\ Mdecs,\ E$ where $Vdec$ is $\mathsf{var}\ \tilde{X} : \tilde{T}$ and $Mdecs$ is $Mdec_1, \ldots, Mdec_q$ with formal parameters $\tilde{Y}$ and local variables $\tilde{Z}$. Then

$$[\![Cdec]\!] \stackrel{\text{def}}{=} !\,(\nu h_1 \ldots h_q)\, \overline{n_A}\langle \alpha\rangle \cdot [\![E]\!]\langle (v\, s)\mathbf{0}, \sigma_0\rangle$$

where $\alpha = \{m_1 = h_1, \ldots, m_q = h_q\}$, $\sigma_0 = \{\tilde{X} = \mathsf{nil}, \tilde{Y} = \mathsf{nil}, \tilde{Z} = \mathsf{nil}, \tilde{R} = \mathsf{nil}, \rho = \mathsf{nil}, \iota = \alpha\}$. The replicator $[\![Cdec]\!]$ may repeatedly emit on the link name $n_A$ of sort $\mathsf{C}_A$ a fresh object name $\alpha$ of type $\mathsf{ref}(A)$ and thereby activate a new instance of the class with initial store $\sigma_0$ in which all variables have $\mathsf{nil}$ values. The prefix $n_A(v)$ in $[\![\mathsf{new}(A)]\!]$ complements that in the representation of the class declaration so $[\![\mathsf{new}(A)]\!]\langle k, s\rangle$ receives a fresh object name $\alpha$ via $n_A$ and then continues as $k\langle \alpha, s\rangle$.

Finally we have the representation of a program. If $Pdec$ is $Cdec_1, \ldots, Cdec_r$ where $Cdec_i$ defines $A_i$ then

$$[\![Pdec]\!] \stackrel{\text{def}}{=} (\nu n_{A_1} \ldots n_{A_r})\,([\![Cdec_1]\!] \mid \ldots \mid [\![Cdec_r]\!] \mid n_{A_r}(x) \cdot \mathbf{0})$$

where $n_{A_r}(x) \cdot \mathbf{0}$ activates an instance of $Cdec_r$ as the root object. Note that the only free names of $[\![Pdec]\!]$ are $\mathsf{in}$ and $\mathsf{out}$ of link sort $\mathsf{E}$.

To illustrate the definition we apply the translation to the class T from section 3. It yields

$$[\![\mathrm{T}]\!] \stackrel{\text{def}}{=} !\,(\nu ins, srch)\, \overline{n_{\mathrm{T}}}\langle \{\mathtt{insert} = ins,\ \mathtt{search} = srch\}\rangle .\ D\langle (v\, s)\mathbf{0}, \sigma_0\rangle$$

with

$$D \stackrel{\text{def}}{=} (k\, s)(A_I\langle (v_0\, s_0) D\langle k, s_0\rangle, s\rangle + A_S\langle (v_0\, s_0) D\langle k, s_0\rangle, s\rangle)$$
$$A_I \stackrel{\text{def}}{=} (k\, s)\, s:\iota:\mathtt{insert}\,(x, w, r, b) \cdot [\![E_I]\!]\langle k, s[x/X, w/W, r/\mathsf{R}_I, b/\rho]\rangle$$
$$A_S \stackrel{\text{def}}{=} (k\, s)\, s:\iota:\mathtt{search}\,(y, r, b) \cdot [\![E_S]\!]\langle k, s[y/Y, r/\mathsf{R}_S, b/\rho]\rangle$$

where "$I$" abbreviates `insert` and "$S$" abbreviates `search`,

$$\sigma_0 = \{K = \mathsf{nil},\ V = \mathsf{nil},\ L = \mathsf{nil},\ R = \mathsf{nil},\ X = \mathsf{nil},\ W = \mathsf{nil},\ Y = \mathsf{nil},$$
$$\mathsf{R}_I = \mathsf{nil},\ \mathsf{R}_S = \mathsf{nil},\ \rho = \mathsf{nil},\ \iota = \{\mathtt{insert} = ins,\ \mathtt{search} = srch\}\}$$

and $E_I$, $E_S$ are the bodies of the insert and search methods respectively. From the definition we have, where cond abbreviates a nested conditional, for the body of the insert method

$$
\begin{aligned}
[\![E_I]\!] \stackrel{\text{def}}{=} (k\,s)\mathsf{cond}(s:K = \mathsf{nil} \;&\rhd\; n_{\mathrm{T}}(t_1)\cdot n_{\mathrm{T}}(t_2)\cdot k\langle \mathsf{nil}, s[x/K, w/V, t_1/L, t_2/R]\rangle,\\
s:X = s:K \;&\rhd\; k\langle \mathsf{nil}, s[w/V]\rangle,\\
s:X < s:K \;&\rhd\; \overline{s:L:\mathtt{insert}}\,\langle s:X, s:W, \mathsf{nil}, \mathsf{false}\rangle\cdot k\langle \mathsf{nil}, s\rangle,\\
s:X > s:K \;&\rhd\; \overline{s:R:\mathtt{insert}}\,\langle s:X, s:W, \mathsf{nil}, \mathsf{false}\rangle\cdot k\langle \mathsf{nil}, s\rangle)
\end{aligned}
$$

and for the body of the search method

$$
\begin{aligned}
[\![E_S]\!] \stackrel{\text{def}}{=} (k\,s)\mathsf{cond}(s:K = \mathsf{nil} \;&\rhd\; \overline{s:\mathsf{R}_S}\langle \mathsf{nil}\rangle\cdot k\langle \mathsf{nil}, s\rangle,\\
s:Y = s:K \;&\rhd\; \overline{s:\mathsf{R}_S}\langle s:V\rangle\cdot k\langle \mathsf{nil}, s\rangle,\\
s:Y < s:K \;&\rhd\; \overline{s:L:\mathtt{search}}\,\langle s:Y, s:\mathsf{R}_S, s:\rho\rangle\cdot k\langle \mathsf{nil}, s\rangle,\\
s:Y > s:K \;&\rhd\; \overline{s:R:\mathtt{search}}\,\langle s:Y, s:\mathsf{R}_S, s:\rho\rangle\cdot k\langle \mathsf{nil}, s\rangle).
\end{aligned}
$$

## 6 Remarks

A semantic definition for a concurrent object-oriented programming language with a simple type system has been given by a structural translation to a mobile-process calculus. Distinctive features of the definition are the effective use of the type system, first-order data and higher-order abstractions of the calculus. The higher-order abstractions are central to the process-continuation technique. That is analogous to uses of continuations in denotational semantics for sequential languages and allows a compositional semantic definition. The restriction to first-order interaction makes it possible to use the relatively simple and powerful analytical techniques developed for first-order processes to reason about the process-calculus representations of (fragments of) programs. The programming language, though small, contains several interesting synchronization mechanisms found in a variety of object-oriented languages. The succinctness of the semantic definition is evidence of the suitability of the combination of features present in the calculus for giving semantic definitions for such languages.

Here we have not studied in detail the relationship between this form of semantic definition and others mentioned in the introduction. Roughly, its relationship to an operational semantics in the style of [3] is as follows. In each case a program is represented as a transition system. A computation in the translational semantics can be mirrored by a corresponding computation in the operational semantics which, because of the latter's finer grain of action, typically involves more computation steps. A computation in the operational semantics will typically involve configurations having no direct correlates in the translational semantics. However, any finite computation in the operational semantics can be continued so as to reflect a computation in the translational semantics. See [27] for a detailed account of a relationship of this kind between an operational semantics and a finer-grained semantics by translation to the $\pi$-calculus.

The data part of the calculus can be tailored to allow succinct definition of other language features. Consider, for instance, the effect of relaxing the requirement that no answer expression occur in a method body. Then instead of a single store, it would be appropriate to use a list (stack) of stores to record the values of the parameters and local variables of the unfinished method invocations of an object. In a similar vein, if objects were to be considered as having queues in which requests for method invocations were to be stored, suitable enrichment of the data part would again be appropriate.

Although the calculus has higher-order process abstractions as in the Higher-Order $\pi$-calculus, it has only first-order interaction. This is appropriate here since in the language considered, as in many other concurrent object-oriented languages, objects interact by passing references (and simple data) to one another. Systems prescribed by them are thus susceptible of analysis using reasoning techniques of first-order process calculi; these are relatively tractable compared to their analogues in higher-order calculi as in for instance [23]. Examples of such analysis are [10, 19] where the theory of bisimilarity is used to underpin proofs of the correctness of syntactic transformation rules whose application increases the scope for concurrent activity within systems of objects prescribed by concurrent object-oriented programs without altering their observable behaviours. A further example is the use of algebraic properties in the proof in [24] of the computational adequacy of an interpretation of the functional object calculus of [1] in a typed $\pi$-calculus. In the study of concurrent object-oriented programming languages with higher-order communication, fragments of the Higher-Order $\pi$-calculus with an enriched data part should be helpful.

The process-calculus sorting regime used in the semantic definition takes the simple form of [14]: a name of a given link sort may be used to send or to receive a tuple of values having the first-order types prescribed by the sorting. In [20] a refinement was introduced in which distinction is made among the abilities to use a name for sending, for receiving, or for both. This allows a form of subtyping: see also [21]. It is also very useful in reasoning about systems: see for instance [24]. The proofs of [19] also make use of this more informative discipline in a setting with name matching of sorts rather than the structural matching of [20]. The study of typing disciplines for mobile processes both receives impetus from the practice of concurrent object-oriented programming and contributes usefully to its clarification and development.

Although in this paper we have considered only one small language with a simple type system, we strongly believe that ideas presented here can be used to give useful semantic definitions for a wide variety of languages. The discovery that this belief were mistaken would provide a valuable stimulus to the further development of the theory of mobile processes.

## References

[1] M. Abadi and L. Cardelli. A theory of primitive objects: untyped and first-order systems. In *Proceedings of TACS'94*, pages 296–320. Springer, 1994.

[2] P. America. Issues in the design of a parallel object-oriented language. *Formal Aspects of Computing*, 1: 366–411, 1989.

[3] P. America, J. de Bakker, J. Kok, and J. Rutten. Operational semantics of a parallel object-oriented language. In *Proceedings of POPL'86*, pages 194–208. ACM Press, 1986.

[4] P. America, J. de Bakker, J. Kok, and J. Rutten. Denotational semantics of a parallel object-oriented language. *Information and Computation*, 83:152–205, 1989.

[5] U. Engberg and M. Nielsen. A calculus of communicating systems with label passing. Technical report, University of Aarhus, 1986.

[6] K. Honda and M. Tokoro. An object calculus for asynchronous communication. In *Proceedings of ECOOP'91*, pages 133–147. Springer, 1991.

[7] C. Jones. Constraining interference in an object-based design method. In *Proceedings of TAPSOFT'93*, pages 136–150. Springer, 1993.

[8] D. Kafura and R. G. Lavender. Concurrent object-oriented languages and the inheritance anomoly. In T. Casavant, editor, *Parallel Computers: Theory and Practice*. Computer Society Press, 1995.

[9] N. Kobayashi and A. Yonezawa. Type-theoretic foundations for concurrent object-oriented programming. In *Proceedings of OOPSLA'94*. ACM Press, 1994.

[10] X. Liu and D. Walker. Confluence of processes and systems of objects. In *Proceedings of CAAP'95*, pages 217–231. Springer, 1995.

[11] X. Liu and D. Walker. Partial confluence of processes and systems of objects. Technical report, University of Warwick, 1995.

[12] R. Milner. *A Calculus of Communicating Systems*. Springer, 1980.

[13] R. Milner. *Communication and Concurrency*. Prentice-Hall, 1989.

[14] R. Milner. The polyadic $\pi$-calculus: a tutorial. In *Logic and Algebra of Specification*. Springer, 1992.

[15] R. Milner. Elements of interaction. *Communications of the ACM*, 36:78–97, 1993.

[16] R. Milner, J. Parrow, and D. Walker. A calculus of mobile processes, parts 1 and 2. *Information and Computation*, 100:1–77, 1992.

[17] O. Nierstrasz and M. Papathomas. Towards a type theory for active objects. Technical report, University of Geneva, 1990.

[18] M. Papathomas. *Language design rationale and semantic framework for concurrent object-oriented programming*. PhD thesis, University of Geneva, 1992.

[19] A. Philippou and D. Walker. On transformations of concurrent object programs. In *Proceedings of CONCUR'96*, pages 131–146. Springer, 1996.

[20] B. Pierce and D. Sangiorgi. Typing and subtyping for mobile processes. In *Proceedings of LICS'93*, pages 376–385. Computer Society Press, 1993.

[21] B. Pierce and D. Turner. Concurrent objects in a process calculus. In *Theory and Practice of Parallel Programming, Sendai, Japan*, pages 187–215. Springer, 1994.

[22] J. Rutten. Semantic correctnes for a parallel object-oriented language. *SIAM Journal on Computing*, 19(2):341–383, 1990.

[23] D. Sangiorgi. *Expressing mobility in process algebras: first-order and higher-order paradigms*. PhD thesis, University of Edinburgh, 1992.

[24] D. Sangiorgi. An interpretation of typed objects into typed $\pi$-calculus. Technical report, INRIA, 1996.

[25] D. Walker. $\pi$-calculus semantics for object-oriented programming languages. In *Proceedings of TACS'91*, pages 532–547. Springer, 1991.

[26] D. Walker. Algebraic proofs of properties of objects. In *Proceedings of ESOP'94*, pages 501–516. Springer, 1994.

[27] D. Walker. Objects in the $\pi$-calculus. *Information and Computation*, 116:253–271, 1995.

[28] D. Walker. Process calculus and parallel object-oriented programming languages. In T. Casavant, editor, *Parallel Computers: Theory and Practice*, pages 369–390. Computer Society Press, 1995.

# 23 λ-Calculus, Multiplicities, and the π-Calculus

**Gérard Boudol and Cosimo Laneve**

## 1 Introduction

A few years ago, Milner, Parrow, and Walker introduced a calculus of mobile processes [20], now called the $\pi$-calculus, which is a name passing extension of Milner's CCS [17]. A version of this calculus was first discovered by Engberg and Nielsen [10], following early discussions between Nielsen and Milner (see the conclusion of [20], Part I). The paper [20] nicely demonstrated the usefulness of the name passing discipline, by a series of examples showing clearly its expressiveness. Milner quickly realized that one can encode the $\lambda$-calculus into the $\pi$-calculus [18], a remarkable achievement, showing the universality of the $\pi$-calculus in some sense. This result was further studied and extended, most notably by Sangiorgi [23], who established that the $\pi$-calculus is powerful enough to encode a very general form of agent passing.

Milner actually gave two encodings in [18], one for the *lazy* $\lambda$-calculus of Abramsky and Ong [3], and another for the weak call-by-value $\lambda$-calculus of Plotkin [22]. It turns out that, in both cases, the $\pi$-calculus is strictly more expressive than the $\lambda$-calculus, in the sense that some $\lambda$-terms that are equated using $\lambda$-calculus means can be distinguished in the $\pi$-calculus. Milner then raised the question: "*Exactly what is the* semantics *induced upon $\lambda$-terms by encoding them into the $\pi$-calculus*?" In more concrete terms, one could ask: how does a functional language survive when integrated within concurrent features? For instance, which program transformations or optimization techniques remain valid? The purpose of this paper is to investigate Milner's question, for the "lazy encoding."

To introduce our contribution, let us first formulate the question more precisely. In CCS-like calculi, there is a natural notion of *immediate observability*: a process $P$ is immediately observable, in notation $P\downarrow$, if $P$ exhibits, without any internal computation, a capability of communicating with its environment. That is, $P$ is able to perform an action (input or output). Now a process $P$ is *observable*, in notation $P\Downarrow$, if it may become immediately observable, possibly after some internal computations, that is $\exists P',\ P \stackrel{*}{\rightarrow} P' \ \&\ P'\downarrow$. The semantic preorder on the $\pi$-calculus that Milner considered in [18] is defined as follows:

$$P \sqsubseteq Q \ \Leftrightarrow\ \text{for all contexts } C,\ C[P]\Downarrow \Rightarrow C[Q]\Downarrow$$

This is known as the *may testing* semantics, also used when dealing with the denotational semantics of the $\lambda$-calculus, see [26] for instance. Now, denoting by $\mathcal{E}[\![M]\!]u$ the encoding of a $\lambda$-term $M$ in the $\pi$-calculus (this involves a name parameter $u$, the actual value of

Research was partially supported by the ESPRIT Basic Research Project 6454-CONFER.

which is immaterial), the question is to determine exactly what is the preorder on λ-terms given by

$$M \sqsubseteq_\pi N \;\Leftrightarrow\; \mathcal{E}[\![M]\!]u \sqsubseteq \mathcal{E}[\![M]\!]u$$

Sangiorgi studied a similar question, where the may testing $\sqsubseteq$ is replaced by *weak bisimulation*, denoted here $\approx$. He showed—see [23, 24], and especially [25], from which we shall borrow some results—that this "$\pi$-semantics" $M \approx_\pi N$ on λ-terms coincides with equality in a semantics given by Lévy in [13] for the λ-calculus. In [15], Longo gave a suggestive presentation of Lévy's interpretation, by means of what are now called *Lévy-Longo trees*, a refinement of the well-known Böhm trees (see [4]), suited for the weak λ-calculus where any divergent term such as $\Omega = (\lambda x\, xx)(\lambda x\, xx)$ is different from $\lambda x\, \Omega$. Lévy's interpretation provides a rather intensional semantics for λ-terms, which may be regarded as the finest reasonable semantics one can imagine. This was established by Longo in [15], who showed that any "reasonable" λ-model induces a semantics which is weaker than Lévy's one. Then the $\pi$-semantics on λ-terms is at the same time very sharp and still "reasonable."

In [25], Sangiorgi indicates that one may suspect that may testing equivalence $M \simeq_\pi N$ (that is $M \sqsubseteq_\pi N$ and $N \sqsubseteq_\pi N$) and bisimulation $M \approx_\pi N$ coincide—a reason should be that λ-terms are "deterministic processes." This is indeed a consequence of a result of this paper: we show, thus answering Milner's question, that $M \sqsubseteq_\pi N$ coincides with $M \sqsubseteq_{\mathcal{L}} N$, the preorder induced by Lévy's interpretation, that is the inclusion of Lévy-Longo trees. Considering Sangiorgi's work, the fact that $\pi$-calculus semantics of λ-terms is again related to Lévy's semantics should not be too surprising. In particular, the fact that Lévy's semantics is stronger than $\pi$-may testing is a direct consequence of results of [25]. However, the proof method we use for showing

$$M \sqsubseteq_\pi N \Rightarrow M \sqsubseteq_{\mathcal{L}} N$$

is completely different from that of [25] for the similar implication involving bisimulation $\approx_\pi$ in place of may testing. In fact, the way we prove it is the main contribution of this paper.

To prove this implication, we use a refinement of the λ-calculus introduced in [6], namely the *λ-calculus with multiplicities*. To motivate this refinement, let us point out one typical reason why the $\pi$-calculus is more discriminating than the λ-calculus. Milner's encoding translates $\beta$-reduction as follows:

$$\mathcal{E}[\![(\lambda x M)N]\!]u \;\rightarrow\; (\nu x)(\mathcal{E}[\![M]\!]u \mid\, !x(w)\mathcal{E}[\![N]\!]w) \;\approx\; \mathcal{E}[\![[N/x]M]\!]u$$

where $!P$ represents an infinite parallel composition $(P \mid \cdots \mid P \cdots)$, see [19] for instance (the version of the $\pi$-calculus we use is presented in Section 2 below). This is needed to adequately model the fact that, in an application $RN$, the argument $N$ is *infinitely available* for the function $R$. Indeed, if $R = \lambda x M$, this term reduces to $[N/x]M$ where the argument is copied within $M$ as many times as there are free occurrences of $x$. One cannot predict the "multiplicity" of $x$ in $M$, because $M$ could be reduced to another term where this variable is duplicated. This is the case for instance if $M = (\mathbf{2}x)$ where $\mathbf{2} = \lambda fy.f(fy)$.

Now, in the $\pi$-calculus, one is not compelled to use infinitely available resources. For instance, one could write something like a λ-term where the argument is available at most $m$ times, namely:

$$(\nu x)(\mathcal{E}[\![M]\!]u \mid \underbrace{x(w)\mathcal{E}[\![N]\!]w \mid \cdots \mid x(w)\mathcal{E}[\![N]\!]w}_{m})$$

Our purpose is to show that the limited availability of a resource is precisely the reason why the $\pi$-calculus is more discriminating than the λ-calculus. Firstly, we note that this provides us with extra discriminating power. For instance, the two terms $xx$ and $x(\lambda y.xy)$ are equated in the canonical denotational semantics of the lazy λ-calculus (see [3]), while, in the $\pi$-calculus, one may distinguish them by providing just one sample of the identity $\mathbf{I} = \lambda zz$ for $x$. More precisely, the term

$$(\nu x)(\mathcal{E}[\![xx]\!]u \mid x(w)\mathcal{E}[\![\mathbf{I}]\!]w)$$

is not observable—it reduces to a deadlock—, whereas

$$(\nu x)(\mathcal{E}[\![x(\lambda y\,.\,xy)]\!]u \mid x(w)\mathcal{E}[\![\mathbf{I}]\!]w)$$

converges.

This led us to introduce a λ-calculus with explicit (finite or infinite) *multiplicities*, writing $MN^m$ where $m \in \mathsf{N} \cup \{\infty\}$ to mean that $N$ is available at most $m$ times for $M$. As a particular case, we get the usual λ-terms, where all the multiplicities are infinite—in which case we may omit them, to keep the standard notation. We call this new calculus the $\lambda_{\mathsf{m}}$-calculus. Obviously, as in the $\pi$-calculus, evaluating a $\lambda_{\mathsf{m}}$-term may end up with a *deadlock*. This is the case of $(\lambda x\,.\,xx)\mathbf{I}^1$, for instance, where one needs two values for $x$ but has just one.

Actually, the $\pi$-calculus suggests an even more liberal extension of the λ-calculus. After all, one is not compelled to use copies of the same argument as resources. One could write in the $\pi$-calculus:

$$(\nu x)(\mathcal{E}[\![M]\!]u \mid x(w)\mathcal{E}[\![N_1]\!]w \mid \cdots \mid x(w)\mathcal{E}[\![N_m]\!]w)$$

For example, it is possible to encode in this way a non-deterministic *internal choice*:

$$\mathcal{E}[\![M \oplus N]\!]u = (\nu x)(\mathcal{E}[\![x]\!]u \mid x(w)\mathcal{E}[\![M]\!]w \mid x(w)\mathcal{E}[\![N]\!]w)$$

The further extension of the $\lambda$-calculus where the arguments, that is $P$ in $MP$ are *bags* of terms was introduced in [6]. The syntax for bags follows that of the $\pi$-calculus: $\mathsf{0}$ is the empty bag and $(P \mid Q)$ is the (multiset) union of $P$ and $Q$. However, we write $M^\infty$ for a bag consisting of $M$ with an infinite multiplicity, rather than $!M$. We call this the *$\lambda$-calculus with resources*, or $\lambda_\mathsf{r}$-calculus. Obviously, it contains the $\lambda$-calculus with multiplicities, since one may let $N^m = (N \mid \cdots \mid N)$, $m$ times.

The $\lambda_\mathsf{m}$ and $\lambda_\mathsf{r}$-calculi are similar in spirit to the $\lambda$-calculus. They are all based on the idea of a function applied to arguments, or more generally to bags of arguments. They could be "implemented" by variants of the same abstract machine where the value of a variable in the environment may be something more complex than $M^\infty$. However, the evaluation mechanisms exhibit different features. In the lazy $\lambda$-calculus, the evaluation is deterministic, that is, at most one reduction is possible at each step, and may either diverge or terminate on a value, i.e., an abstraction. In the $\lambda_\mathsf{m}$-calculus, evaluation is still deterministic, but in addition it may deadlock. The $\lambda_\mathsf{r}$-calculus further adds possible *non determinism* in the evaluation, because one may choose any of the resources that a bag contains to instantiate a variable. Therefore, it is natural to refine not only the syntax and evaluation, but also the semantics.

In this paper we take the view that divergence, deadlock and convergence are distinguished by the observer. More precisely, divergence is not observed, while deadlock and convergence are observed differently. Then the may testing semantics for $\lambda_\mathsf{m}$ and $\lambda_\mathsf{r}$ is defined as follows:

$M$ is observationally less than $N$ if and only if for all contexts $C$, if $C[M]$ may deadlock then $C[N]$ may deadlock, and if $C[M]$ may converge to a value, then $C[N]$ may converge to a value.

By taking the contexts to be $\lambda_\mathsf{m}$-contexts or $\lambda_\mathsf{r}$-contexts we get two preorders $\sqsubseteq_\mathsf{m}$ and $\sqsubseteq_\mathsf{r}$, the second one being obviously stronger. Our main result is that, as far as $\lambda$-terms are concerned, explicit multiplicities—that is, potential deadlocks—are enough to distinguish as much as the $\pi$-calculus and Lévy's interpretation. In particular, non-deterministic features like internal choice are not needed for testing $\lambda$-terms. That is, for $M, N \in \Lambda$:

$$M \sqsubseteq_\mathcal{L} N \;\Leftrightarrow\; M \sqsubseteq_\mathsf{r} N \;\Leftrightarrow\; M \sqsubseteq_\mathsf{m} N \;\Leftrightarrow\; M \sqsubseteq_\pi N$$

We should also mention that, if we are interested in equivalences, not preorders, then a weaker observational semantics, where deadlocks are not observed, is enough to ensure a similar result, see [9, 8]. These results may be surprising, because the $\lambda$-calculus with multiplicities is purely deterministic, with no parallel facility. This contrasts with a previous result by Sangiorgi showing that "*non-determinism is exactly what is necessary to add to the $\lambda$-calculus to make it as discriminating as the $\pi$-calculus*"—in fact, the unary non-deterministic operator given by $\uplus M = (M \oplus \Omega)$ is enough, see [24]. Remember, however, that Sangiorgi uses a bisimulation semantics, for which non-determinism has some flavour of introducing potential deadlocks. For instance $\uplus M \rightarrow \Omega$ means that $M$, regarded as a resource, may vanish. Here we may have a different conclusion, regarding Milner's question: *the possibility of deadlocks is essentially what the π-calculus adds to the lazy λ-calculus.*

The paper is organized as follows: the first two sections give a brief account of the π-calculus and the weak λ-calculus. Then we introduce the λ-calculus with resources and the λ-calculus with multiplicities, their syntax and evaluation mechanism. Next we define the observational semantics and show the context lemma. The last two sections are devoted to the proof of our main result: we first show, establishing the approximation lemma and the separation lemma, that Lévy's semantics coincides with that induced by the $\lambda_{\mathsf{r}}$ and $\lambda_{\mathsf{m}}$-calculi. Then we show that these are weaker than the π-calculus semantics. The converse is proved using Sangiorgi's results in [25]. Finally we conclude by comparing our results with related work.

## 2 The π-Calculus

In this paper we adopt the same asynchronous "mini" π-calculus as in [25], built upon a given denumerable set $\mathcal{N}$ of *names*, ranged over by $u, v, w \ldots$ The differences with other versions, e.g., in [20, 18, 19], are the following: firstly, we do not use the sum and matching constructs $P + Q$ and $[u = v]P$. The *input* construct $u(v_1, \ldots, v_k)P$ allows $P$ to receive on the channel $u$ several names simultaneously, as in the polyadic π-calculus of [19]. Correspondingly, an output sends several names simultaneously. However, it is not a guard. That is, it takes the form of an asynchronous *message* $\bar{u}v_1 \cdots v_k$. Besides the "empty" process $\mathsf{0}$, the remaining constructs are *parallel composition* $(P \mid Q)$, *replication* $!P$ and *restriction*, or scoping $(\nu u)P$. The syntax of this (mini) π-calculus is thus:

$$P ::= \mathsf{0} \mid \bar{u}v_1 \cdots v_k \mid u(v_1, \ldots, v_k)P \mid (P \mid P) \mid !P \mid (\nu u)P$$

where $k \geq 0$ and $u, v_1, \ldots, v_k$ are names. We let $\Pi$ denote the set of π-terms, ranged over by $P, Q, \ldots$ The names $v_1, \ldots, v_k$ in an input prefix $u(v_1, \ldots, v_k)$ are assumed to be pairwise distinct. They are bound by this construct, and similarly $u$ is bound by a restriction $(\nu u)$. We denote by $\mathsf{fn}(P)$ and $\mathsf{bn}(P)$ the set of names occurring respectively free and bound in $P$, and $\mathsf{nm}(P)$ denotes the union of these two sets. We denote by $[^u/_v]P$ the operation of substituting the name $u$ for $v$ in $P$. This may require some renaming, to avoid binding $u$, as in the λ-calculus. More generally, we denote by $[^{u_1, \ldots, u_n}/_{v_1, \ldots, v_n}]P$ the simultaneous substitution of $u_1, \ldots, u_n$ for $v_1, \ldots, v_n$ respectively in $P$. We denote by

$P =_\alpha Q$ the $\alpha$-conversion, that is the least congruence satisfying

$$u(v_1, \ldots, v_k)P =_\alpha u(w_1, \ldots, w_k)[w_1/v_1] \cdots [w_k/v_k]P$$

where $w_1, \ldots, w_k$ are distinct names not in $\mathsf{nm}(P)$, and

$$(\nu u)P =_\alpha (\nu v)[v/u]P$$

where $v \notin \mathsf{nm}(P)$. We shall sometimes write $\bar{u}\tilde{v}$ for $\bar{u}v_1 \cdots v_k$, and similarly for the input prefix $u(\tilde{v})P$, for the substitution $[\tilde{w}/\tilde{v}]P$, and for a sequence of restrictions $(\nu\tilde{u})P$.

The *structural equivalence* $P \equiv Q$ over $\pi$-terms is the least congruence containing $=_\alpha$, and satisfying the following equations:

$$(P \mid (Q \mid R)) \equiv ((P \mid Q) \mid R) \qquad ((\nu u)P \mid Q) \equiv (\nu u)(P \mid Q) \quad (u \notin \mathsf{fn}(Q))$$

$$(P \mid Q) \equiv (Q \mid P) \qquad (\nu u)(\nu v)P \equiv (\nu v)(\nu u)P$$

$$(P \mid \mathsf{0}) \equiv P \qquad (\nu u)\mathsf{0} \equiv \mathsf{0}$$

$$!P \equiv (P \mid !P)$$

The *reduction* relation $P \rightarrow P'$ is given by the following rules:

$$(\bar{u}w_1 \cdots w_k \mid u(v_1, \ldots, v_k)P) \rightarrow [w_1, \ldots, w_k/v_1, \ldots, v_k]P \qquad \frac{Q \equiv P\ ,\ P \rightarrow P'}{Q \rightarrow P'}$$

$$\frac{P \rightarrow P'}{(P \mid Q) \rightarrow (P' \mid Q)} \qquad \frac{P \rightarrow P'}{(\nu u)P \rightarrow (\nu u)P'}$$

We may simply write the basic reduction step as

$$(\bar{u}\tilde{w} \mid u(\tilde{v})P) \;\rightarrow\; [\tilde{w}/\tilde{v}]P$$

provided that the sequences of names $\tilde{w}$ and $\tilde{v}$ have the same length. To distinguish $\pi$-reduction from other notions of reduction we shall consider, we sometimes use the notation $P \rightarrow_\pi P'$. The reflexive and transitive closure of this relation is denoted $\stackrel{*}{\rightarrow}$, as usual. The predicate $P\!\downarrow$ of *immediate observability* is defined by

$$P\!\downarrow \;\Leftrightarrow\; \exists u.\ P \downarrow u$$

where $P \downarrow u$ is the least relation satisfying

$$\bar{u}v_1 \cdots v_k \downarrow u \qquad \& \qquad u(v_1, \ldots, v_k)P \downarrow u$$

$$P \downarrow u \Rightarrow (P \mid Q) \downarrow u \quad \& \quad (Q \mid P) \downarrow u \quad \& \quad !P \downarrow u$$

$$P \downarrow u \;\&\; u \neq v \Rightarrow (\nu v)P \downarrow u$$

The following is easy to check:

*Remark 2.1* $P \downarrow u$ if and only if either

(i) $P \equiv (\nu\tilde{w})(\bar{u}\tilde{v} \mid Q)$ with $u$ not in $\tilde{w}$, or

(ii) $P \equiv (\nu\tilde{w})(u(\tilde{v})R \mid Q)$ with $u$ not in $\tilde{w}$.

The predicate $P\Downarrow$ of *observability* is given by

$$P\Downarrow \;\Leftrightarrow\; \exists P' \cdot P \stackrel{*}{\rightarrow} P' \;\&\; P'\downarrow$$

Like for reduction, we shall sometimes use the notations $P\downarrow_\pi$ and $P\Downarrow_\pi$. A context, or more accurately a $\pi$-context is a term $C$ written using the syntax of the $\pi$-calculus enriched with a constant [], the hole. We denote by $C[P]$ the term obtained by filling the hole with $P$ in $C$. Note that some free names of $P$ may be bound by the context.

DEFINITION 2.2 (OBSERVATIONAL SEMANTICS) The *observational semantics* of the $\pi$-calculus is the preorder defined as follows:

$$P \sqsubseteq_\pi Q \;\Leftrightarrow\; \text{for all } \pi\text{-contexts } C,\; C[P]\Downarrow \;\Rightarrow\; C[Q]\Downarrow$$

This preorder is clearly a precongruence, that is

$$P \sqsubseteq_\pi Q \Rightarrow C[P] \sqsubseteq_\pi C[Q]$$

We denote by $\simeq_\pi$ the equivalence associated with the observational semantics, that is

$$P \simeq_\pi Q \;\Leftrightarrow\; P \sqsubseteq_\pi Q \quad \& \quad Q \sqsubseteq_\pi P$$

For instance, we have $\mathsf{0} \simeq_\pi (\nu u)\bar{u}$, therefore $\mathsf{0}$ need not be a primitive of the calculus. However, it is convenient to include this constant, and more specifically to have the law $(P \mid \mathsf{0}) \equiv P$.

In the following we shall use a result which is proved by Sangiorgi in [25]. He defines an equivalence on the $\pi$-calculus based on labelled transitions between $\pi$-terms. These transitions may be defined as follows: the labels are either input actions, that is $a = u(v_1, \ldots, v_k)$, or output actions $a = (\nu w_1) \cdots (\nu w_n)\bar{u}v_1 \cdots v_k$, and:

(i) $P \stackrel{a}{\rightarrow} P'$ where $a = u(v_1, \ldots, v_k)$ if and only if $P \equiv (\nu u_1) \cdots (\nu u_n)(u(v_1, \ldots, v_k)R \mid Q)$ with $u \notin \{u_1, \ldots, u_n\}$ and $v_i \notin \mathsf{fn}(Q)$, and $P' = (\nu u_1) \cdots (\nu u_n)(R \mid Q)$

(ii) $P \stackrel{a}{\rightarrow} P'$ where $a = (\nu w_1) \cdots (\nu w_m)\bar{u}v_1 \cdots v_k$ if and only if $P \equiv (\nu u_1) \cdots (\nu u_n)(\bar{u}v_1 \cdots v_k \mid Q)$ with $u \notin \{u_1, \ldots, u_n\}$, $\{w_1, \ldots, w_m\} = \{u_1, \ldots, u_n\} \cap \{v_1, \ldots, v_k\}$ and $P' = (\nu s_1) \cdots (\nu s_h)Q$ where $\{s_1, \ldots, s_h\} = \{u_1, \ldots, u_n\} - \{w_1, \ldots, w_m\}$.

Clearly $P\downarrow$ if and only if $P \xrightarrow{a} P'$ for some $a$ and $P'$. Now by just removing the *symmetry* requirement from Sangiorgi's Definition 2.2 of "weak ground bisimilarity," one may define:

DEFINITION 2.3 (SIMULATION) A relation $\mathcal{S}$ on $\pi$-terms is a *simulation* if it satisfies:

(i) if $P\,\mathcal{S}\,Q$ and $P \rightarrow P'$ then there exists $Q'$ such that $Q \xrightarrow{*} Q'$ and $P'\,\mathcal{S}\,Q'$,

(ii) if $P\,\mathcal{S}\,Q$ and $P \xrightarrow{a} P'$ then there exists $Q'$ such that $Q \xrightarrow{*}\xrightarrow{a}\xrightarrow{*} Q'$ and $P'\,\mathcal{S}\,Q'$.

*$P$ simulates $Q$*, written $P \preceq_\pi Q$, if $P\,\mathcal{S}\,Q$ for some simulation $\mathcal{S}$.

Then we have:

LEMMA 2.4 The relation $\preceq_\pi$ is a precongruence.

This is essentially Sangiorgi's Corollary 3.6 [25], once one remarks that symmetry does not play any role in the proof.

COROLLARY 2.5 $P \preceq_\pi Q \Rightarrow P \sqsubseteq_\pi Q$

This is obvious since

$P\Downarrow \;\&\; P \preceq_\pi Q \Rightarrow Q\Downarrow$

## 3 The Weak λ-Calculus

The denumerable set $\mathcal{X}$ of variables used to build λ-terms is assumed to be a subset of $\mathcal{N}$, such that $\mathcal{N} - \mathcal{X}$ is infinite. When we write $u,\ v,\ w \ldots$ we usually mean names that are not variables, and we use $x,\ y,\ z \ldots$ to range over $\mathcal{X}$. We recall that λ-terms are given by the following grammar:

$M ::= x \mid \lambda x M \mid (MM)$

We assume the reader is familiar with the notions of free and bound variables, $\alpha$-conversion $M =_\alpha N$, substitution $[N/x]M$, and $\beta$-conversion $M =_\beta N$, that is the congruence generated by $(\lambda x M)N = [N/x]M$, see [4]. We use the standard notations: $\Lambda$ is the set of λ-terms, $\Lambda^\circ$ is the subset of closed terms, $\lambda x_1 \ldots x_n.M$ stands for $\lambda x_1 \ldots \lambda x_n M$, and $MN_1 \cdots N_n$ abbreviates $(\cdots (MN_1) \cdots N_n)$.

In the λ-calculus literature, the word *weak* refers to the failure or disregarding of the $\xi$-rule of $\beta$-conversion, that is $M = N \Rightarrow \lambda x M = \lambda x N$ (see Howard's weak λ-equality in [11]). In particular, if $\xi$ is not considered as a computation rule, then a closed normal form is a "weak head normal form," that is simply an abstraction $\lambda x M$—this is the notion of value adopted in the operational semantics of programming languages, see [22] for instance. From the point of view of observational semantics, this amounts to identifying all the strongly unsolvable terms, but not necessarily the unsolvable ones. Typically, one has $\lambda x\Omega \neq \Omega$ in the weak λ-calculus, while these two terms must be equated in *sensible* λ-theories (see [4]).

The weak λ-calculus was studied in depth by Abramsky and Ong (see [2, 3]), who call it the *lazy* λ-calculus. One may observe that, for $M$ closed, $M =_\beta \lambda xN$ if and only if $M$ has a normal form with respect to the "lazy" reduction relation $\rightarrow_\ell$ over λ-terms, given by the following two rules:

$$(\lambda xM)N \rightarrow_\ell [N/x]M \qquad \frac{M \rightarrow_\ell M'}{MN \rightarrow_\ell M'N}$$

Then, defining the observability predicate by

$$M{\Downarrow_\ell} \Leftrightarrow \exists M'.\ M \stackrel{*}{\rightarrow}_\ell M' \ \&\ M'{\downarrow_\ell}$$

where $M{\downarrow_\ell}$ simply means that $M$ is an abstraction $\lambda xN$, one defines the (*weak*, or *lazy*) *observational semantics* for the λ-calculus exactly as we did for the π-calculus:

$$M \sqsubseteq_\ell N \ \Leftrightarrow\ \text{for all contexts } C,\ C[M]{\Downarrow_\ell} \Rightarrow C[N]{\Downarrow_\ell}$$

This was shown in [3] to be equivalent to the coinductively defined "applicative bisimulation" introduced by Abramsky in [2]. One should note that, although $\xi$ is not taken as a computation rule, it is semantically valid. More generally, one has:

$$M =_\beta N \Rightarrow M \simeq_\ell N$$

In [13], Lévy defined an interpretation of the weak λ-calculus, based on a refinement of Wadsworth's notion of syntactic approximant [26], as follows:

DEFINITION 3.1 (LÉVY'S INTERPRETATION) The set $\mathcal{L}$ of (lazy) approximants, ranged over by $A, B, \ldots$, is the least subset of $\Lambda$ containing $\lambda x_1 \ldots x_n.\Omega$, and $\lambda x_1 \ldots x_n.xA_1 \cdots A_m$ whenever $A_i \in \mathcal{L}$. For $M \in \Lambda$, the *direct approximation* of $M$ is the term $\varpi(M)$ of $\mathcal{L}$ inductively defined by:

$$\varpi(\lambda x_1 \ldots x_n.\,(\lambda y.\,M)NM_1 \cdots M_k) = \lambda x_1 \ldots x_n.\,\Omega$$
$$\varpi(\lambda x_1 \ldots x_n.\,yM_1 \cdots M_k) = \lambda x_1 \ldots x_n.\,y\,\varpi(M_1) \cdots \varpi(M_k)$$

The *interpretation* of $M \in \Lambda$ is $\mathcal{A}(M) = \{\varpi(N) \mid M =_\beta N\}$. *Lévy's preorder* on λ-terms, denoted $M \sqsubseteq_\mathcal{L} N$, is the inclusion of sets of approximants $\mathcal{A}(M) \subseteq \mathcal{A}(N)$. The equality $M =_\mathcal{L} N$ is $\mathcal{A}(M) = \mathcal{A}(N)$.

Lévy's main result is that his preorder is a precongruence. An immediate consequence is

$$M \sqsubseteq_\mathcal{L} N \Rightarrow M \sqsubseteq_\ell N$$

One may characterize Lévy's preorder on approximants: $A \sqsubseteq_{\mathcal{L}} B$ if and only if $A$ is a *prefix* of $B$, where the prefix ordering is the precongruence $\preceq$ on approximants generated by $\Omega \preceq A$. The Church-Rosser property has the following consequence (see [13]):

LEMMA 3.2 For any $M \in \Lambda$, the set $\mathcal{A}(M)$ is directed with respect to the prefix preorder, that is

$$\forall A', A'' \in \mathcal{A}(M)\ \exists A \in \mathcal{A}(M).\ A' \preceq A\ \&\ A'' \preceq A$$

Moreover, it is easy to see that $\mathcal{A}(M)$ is in fact an *ideal*, that is it is downward-closed with respect to the prefix ordering:

$$A \in \mathcal{A}(M)\ \&\ B \preceq A \Rightarrow B \in \mathcal{A}(M)$$

This is because any term $M$ is $\beta$-convertible to a redex, namely $(\mathbf{I}\, M)$ where $\mathbf{I}$ is the identity $\lambda xx$, whose direct approximation is $\Omega$. In particular, we have $\Omega \in \mathcal{A}(M)$ for any $M$.

In [15], Longo gave a suggestive presentation of Lévy's interpretation, by means of what are now called Lévy-Longo trees, which were further studied by Ong in [21]. These are refinements of the well-known Böhm trees (see [4]), adapted to the lazy regime. The Lévy-Longo trees are possibly infinite, node-labelled trees, where the labels are either $\Upsilon$, representing terms of infinite order as $\Xi = (\lambda fx.\, ff)(\lambda fx.\, ff)$, or $\lambda x_1 \ldots x_n.\bot$, representing terms as $\lambda x_1 \cdots x_n.\, \Omega$, or $\lambda x_1 \ldots x_n.\, x$, representing the "head" of a solvable term, as in Böhm trees. To define these trees, let us first recall the notion of a $\lambda$-term of *proper order* $n$, with $n \in \mathsf{N} \cup \{\infty\}$:

1. $M \in \mathsf{PO}_0 \Leftrightarrow \forall M'.\ M \xrightarrow{*}_{\ell} M' \Rightarrow \exists M''.\ M' \rightarrow_{\ell} M''$
2. $M \in \mathsf{PO}_{n+1} \Leftrightarrow \exists x\ \exists M' \in \mathsf{PO}_n.\ M \xrightarrow{*}_{\ell} \lambda x M'$
3. $M \in \mathsf{PO}_{\infty} \Leftrightarrow \forall n\ \exists x_1, \ldots, x_n\ \exists M'.\ M \xrightarrow{*}_{\ell} \lambda x_1 \cdots x_n.\, M'$

A term has some proper order if and only if it is unsolvable, or in other words, it has no head variable. The *Lévy-Longo tree* of a $\lambda$-term $M$, $\mathsf{LT}(M)$, is defined—rather informally—as follows:

1. $\mathsf{LT}(M) = \Upsilon$ if $M \in \mathsf{PO}_{\infty}$;
2. $\mathsf{LT}(M) = \lambda x_1 \cdots x_n.\bot$ if $M \in \mathsf{PO}_n$;
3. $\mathsf{LT}(M) =$ $\lambda x_1 \ldots x_n.\, x$ if $M =_{\beta} \lambda x_1 \ldots x_n.\, x M_1 \cdots M_k$.

   $\mathsf{LT}(M_1)$ $\cdots$ $\mathsf{LT}(M_k)$

To recover Lévy's ordering $M \sqsubseteq_{\mathcal{L}} N$ on the tree representation, one defines an operation $\lambda x T$ on trees, consisting in prefixing the label of the root of $T$ by $\lambda x$, with the rule that $\lambda x \Upsilon = \Upsilon$. Then a tree $T$ is less than $T'$ whenever $T'$ is obtained from $T$ by replacing some leaves labelled $\lambda x_1 \ldots x_n.\bot$ in $T$ by trees $\lambda x_1 \ldots x_n.T''$. An example of an infinite Lévy-Longo tree is provided by Wadsworth's combinator $\mathbf{J}$, satisfying $\mathbf{J} =_\beta \lambda xy.\, x(\mathbf{J}y)$, which may be defined by $\mathbf{J} = (\lambda f \lambda xy.\, x(ffy))(\lambda f \lambda xy.\, x(ffy))$. The tree for this term is:

$$\begin{array}{rcl} \mathsf{LT}(\mathbf{J}) & = & \lambda x y_0.x \\ & & \quad | \\ & & \lambda y_1.y_0 \\ & & \quad | \\ & & \lambda y_2.y_1 \\ & & \quad \vdots \end{array}$$

In the rest of this section we start relating the λ-calculus with the π-calculus. The main result here, which we prove using Sangiorgi's results in [25], is that Lévy's interpretation is *adequate* with respect to the "π-semantics." Let us first recall the encoding of the λ-calculus into the π-calculus given by Milner [18], written in the "asynchronous" and polyadic style. It is the mapping

$$\mathcal{E}[\![\cdot]\!]\colon \Lambda \times (\mathcal{N} - \mathcal{X}) \to \Pi$$

defined as follows:

$$\begin{aligned} \mathcal{E}[\![x]\!]u &= \bar{x}u \\ \mathcal{E}[\![\lambda x M]\!]u &= u(x, v)\mathcal{E}[\![M]\!]v \\ \mathcal{E}[\![MN]\!]u &= (\nu v)(\mathcal{E}[\![M]\!]v \mid (\nu x)(\bar{v}xu \mid \mathcal{E}[\![x := N]\!])) \qquad \text{where } x \notin \mathsf{fv}(N) \text{ and} \\ \mathcal{E}[\![x := N]\!] &= {!x(w)}\mathcal{E}[\![N]\!]w \end{aligned}$$

In this encoding, the name $u$ represents a "continuation," standing for the evaluation context of the λ-term, that is pointing to the argument sequence for that term. In the case where the term is an application, the first argument is pushed on the top of this sequence (the resulting evaluation context is now $v$). More precisely, a pointer $x$ to the first argument is stacked, since the encoding models an environment machine for the lazy λ-calculus, where the operation of substitution is replaced by access to environment entries $[\![x := N]\!]$ binding names to terms. In the case of an abstraction $\lambda x M$, the first item $x$ of the argument sequence is popped from the current continuation $u$, and the rest $v$ is passed to the body $M$. In the case of a variable $x$, the encoding represents the application of this name to the current argument sequence. The encoding establishes a close correspondence between the reduction relations of the two calculi, see [18, 25]. For instance we have:

$$\mathcal{E}[\![(\lambda x M)N]\!]u \;\rightarrow\; (\nu x)(\mathcal{E}[\![M]\!]u \mid \mathcal{E}[\![x := N]\!])$$

Note however that $\mathcal{E}[\![(\lambda x M)N]\!]u$ reduces to something "similar to" the encoding of $[N/x]M$, though not exactly to $\mathcal{E}[\![[N/x]M]\!]u$.

We shall abusively denote by $M \sqsubseteq_\pi N$ the relation $\mathcal{E}[\![M]\!]u \sqsubseteq_\pi \mathcal{E}[\![N]\!]u$, which does not depend on the name $u$. This is the preorder on λ-terms we are interested in. In [25], Sangiorgi gives a characterization of the equality of λ-terms in Lévy's interpretation. By removing the symmetry requirement from his Definition 7.7, one can characterize the preorder $\sqsubseteq_\mathcal{L}$ as follows: $M \sqsubseteq_\mathcal{L} N$ if and only if

(i) either $M$ diverges, that is $M \in \mathsf{PO}_0$,

(ii) or $M \xrightarrow{*}_\ell \lambda x M'$, and there exists $N'$ such that $N \xrightarrow{*}_\ell \lambda x N'$ and $M' \sqsubseteq_\mathcal{L} N'$,

(iii) or $M \xrightarrow{*}_\ell x M_1 \cdots M_n$ and $N \xrightarrow{*}_\ell x N_1 \cdots N_n$ for some $N_1, \ldots, N_n$ such that $M_i \sqsubseteq_\mathcal{L} N_i$.

Then Sangiorgi shows

$$M \sqsubseteq_\mathcal{L} N \Rightarrow M \preceq_\pi N$$

This is his Theorem 7.15 [25], once one remarks that the symmetry requirement is inessential. Then an immediate consequence of this result and Corollary 2.5 is the following:

THEOREM 3.3 (ADEQUACY OF LÉVY'S INTERPRETATION)

$$M \sqsubseteq_\mathcal{L} N \Rightarrow M \sqsubseteq_\pi N$$

It is possible to give a direct proof of this theorem, by showing that for any $\pi$-context $C$, if $C[\mathcal{E}[\![M]\!]u]\Downarrow$ then there is only a finite amount of information about $M$ that needs to be known to ensure the observability of $C[\mathcal{E}[\![M]\!]u]$. That is:

$$C[\mathcal{E}[\![M]\!]u]\Downarrow \;\Leftrightarrow\; \exists A \in \mathcal{A}(M) \;\; C[\mathcal{E}[\![A]\!]u]\Downarrow$$

This may be proved by induction on the length of the reduction of $C[\mathcal{E}[\![M]\!]u]$ into an immediately observable term, and by induction on the context $C$. However, since a "redex"—that is, a subterm performing a reduction step—is "distributed" in a $\pi$-term, we have to analyze the contribution of $M$ to the reduction. This may be done using the labelled transitions of $\mathcal{E}[\![M]\!]u$. Moreover, when $M \rightarrow M'$, the $\pi$-term $\mathcal{E}[\![M]\!]u$ does not directly reduce to $\mathcal{E}[\![M']\!]u$, but rather it reduces to a term which is equivalent, in a very strong sense, to $\mathcal{E}[\![M']\!]u$. Therefore, a direct proof of the theorem would not be very different from the proof of Sangiorgi's result, which relies on a thorough analysis of the labelled transitions of encodings of λ-terms.

## 4   The λ-Calculus with Resources

As we said in the introduction, to prove the converse of Theorem 3.3 we shall use a refinement of the λ-calculus introduced in [6], where the argument $R$ in an application $(MR)$ is a bag of terms. To define the evaluation in this calculus, it is convenient to use the notion of *explicit substitution* of Curien et al. [1] (though with a different operational meaning), written $M\langle R/x\rangle$. Then the syntax of our λ-calculus with resources, or $\lambda_r$-calculus, is as follows:

$$E ::= x \mid \lambda x E \mid (ER) \mid E\langle R/x\rangle$$
$$R ::= \bigcirc \mid E \mid (R \mid R) \mid E^\infty$$

To avoid any confusion with usual λ-terms, denoted $M$, $N$, ... we use $E$, $F$, ... to range over terms of our calculus. The set of terms is $\Lambda_r$. The bags of terms will be denoted $P$, $Q$, ... when no confusion with π-terms may arise.

  We denote by $\mathsf{fv}(E)$ and $\mathsf{bv}(E)$ the sets of free and bound variables of $E$. This is defined as usual, except that $x$ is bound in $E$ by the construct $\langle R/x\rangle$, that is

$$\mathsf{fv}(E\langle R/x\rangle) = (\mathsf{fv}(E) - \{x\}) \cup \mathsf{fv}(R)$$

where $\mathsf{fv}(R)$ is defined in the obvious way: $\mathsf{fv}(P \mid Q) = \mathsf{fv}(P) \cup \mathsf{fv}(Q)$, and so on. The set of closed terms is denoted $\Lambda_r^\circ$. We shall consider $\lambda_r$-terms up to α-conversion. This is defined as usual, with the additional clause that $([z/x]E)\langle R/z\rangle =_\alpha E\langle R/x\rangle$, where $z$ is neither free nor bound in $E$. The *structural equivalence* over $\Lambda_r$ is the least congruence containing α-conversion and satisfying:

$$(P \mid (Q \mid R)) \equiv ((P \mid Q) \mid R) \qquad\qquad EP\langle Q/x\rangle \equiv E\langle Q/x\rangle P \quad (*)$$
$$(P \mid Q) \equiv (Q \mid P) \qquad\qquad E\langle P/x\rangle\langle Q/z\rangle \equiv E\langle Q/z\rangle\langle P/x\rangle \quad (**)$$
$$(P \mid \bigcirc) \equiv P$$
$$E^\infty \equiv (E \mid E^\infty)$$

$(*)$ where $x \notin \mathsf{fv}(P)$
$(**)$ where $x \neq z$, $x \notin \mathsf{fv}(Q)$ and $z \notin \mathsf{fv}(P)$.

  Note that the substitution items may always be pushed on the right of a term. That is, $E\langle Q/x\rangle P$ may always be regarded, by possibly renaming $x$, as $EP\langle Q/x\rangle$. Therefore, any term $E$ is, up to structural equivalence, of the form $HP_1 \cdots P_n\langle Q_1/x_1\rangle \cdots \langle Q_k/x_k\rangle$ where $H$ is either a variable or an abstraction.

  The reduction relation on $\Lambda_r$ is split into two parts: one is the usual (weak) β-reduction, written with explicit substitutions. The second part deals with the management of substitution. Since in our calculus, the resources may be of limited availability, we will not "perform" the substitutions $\langle P/x\rangle$ by distributing them over the subterms. We will rather use them in a delayed manner, waiting for a resource to be actually needed for $x$. Assuming that any term $E$ has the shape $H P_1 \cdots P_n \langle Q_1/x_1\rangle \cdots \langle Q_k/x_k\rangle$ where $H = \lambda x F$ or $H = x$, we may describe intuitively the reduction relation as follows:

(1) if $H$ is an abstraction $\lambda x F$, there are two cases: either $n = 0$, in which case $E$ is a normal form (a *closure*, that is an abstraction within the environment $\langle Q_1/x_1\rangle \cdots \langle Q_k/x_k\rangle$), or there is an argument, i.e. $n \neq 0$, in which case the following reduction takes place:

$$E \;\rightarrow\; F\langle P_1/x\rangle P_2 \cdots P_n \langle Q_1/x_1\rangle \cdots \langle Q_k/x_k\rangle$$

This is formalized by saying that the reduction rules include the $\beta$-rule, written with explicit substitutions, and allow to perform computations in the left subterm of $ER$ and $E\langle R/x\rangle$. Moreover, one should be able to first transform $E$ into a term having the appropriate shape. Then our first rules for reduction are:

$$(\lambda x E)R \rightarrow E\langle R/x\rangle \qquad\qquad \frac{F \equiv E\ ,\ E \rightarrow E'}{F \rightarrow E'}$$

$$\frac{E \rightarrow E'}{ER \rightarrow E'R} \qquad\qquad \frac{E \rightarrow E'}{E\langle R/x\rangle \rightarrow E'\langle R/x\rangle}$$

(2) if $H$ is a variable $x$ (the *head* variable), one looks for the first substitution for it, if any, in the environment $\langle Q_1/x_1\rangle \cdots \langle Q_k/x_k\rangle$. Assume that $i$ is the first index such that $x_i = x$. Then one fetches for $x$ a resource out of $Q_i$, that is a term $F \in \Lambda_{\mathsf{r}}$ such that $Q_i \equiv (F \mid R)$, if any. The rest $R$ is left for future use. Roughly, the following reduction takes place in this case:

$$E \;\rightarrow\; F P_1 \cdots P_n \langle Q_1/x_1\rangle \cdots \langle R/x_i\rangle \cdots \langle Q_k/x_k\rangle$$

Notice that $F$ is a term, not a bag, and therefore such a reduction cannot be performed if the bag $Q_i$ is empty, that is $Q_i \equiv \mathsf{O}$. One should be careful not to bind any free variable of $F$. That is, one should first rename the variables $x_1, \ldots, x_i$, so that they do not occur in $F$. To state the "fetch" rule, which is the last rule for reduction, it is convenient to introduce an auxiliary relation $E\langle F/x\rangle \rightsquigarrow E'$, meaning that $x$ is the head variable of $E$, and that $E'$ is obtained by placing $F$ in the head position in $E$. The rules are as follows:

$$\frac{E\langle F/x\rangle \rightsquigarrow E'}{E\langle (F \mid R)/x\rangle \rightarrow E'\langle R/x\rangle}\ (*) \qquad\qquad x\langle E/x\rangle \rightsquigarrow E$$

$$\frac{E\langle F/x\rangle \rightsquigarrow E'}{ER\langle F/x\rangle \rightsquigarrow E'R} \qquad\qquad \frac{E\langle F/x\rangle \rightsquigarrow E'}{E\langle R/z\rangle\langle F/x\rangle \rightsquigarrow E'\langle R/z\rangle}\ (**)$$

($*$) the *fetch* rule, where $x \notin \mathsf{fv}(F)$.
($**$) where $x \neq z$ and $z \notin \mathsf{fv}(F)$.

To distinguish the $\lambda_{\mathsf{r}}$-reduction from the one of the $\pi$ and $\lambda$-calculi, we shall use the notation $E \rightarrow_{\mathsf{r}} F$. It is not difficult to check that the rules for reduction appropriately formalize the computation steps we intuitively described above, that is:

LEMMA 4.1 $E \rightarrow_{\mathsf{r}} E'$ if and only if

(i) either $E \equiv (\lambda x F) P_1 \cdots P_n \langle Q_1/x_1 \rangle \cdots \langle Q_k/x_k \rangle$ with $n > 0$, and $E' = F\langle P_1/x \rangle P_2 \cdots P_n \langle Q_1/x_1 \rangle \cdots \langle Q_k/x_k \rangle$,

(ii) or $E \equiv x_i P_1 \cdots P_n \langle Q_1/x_1 \rangle \cdots \langle F \mid R/x_i \rangle \cdots \langle Q_k/x_k \rangle$ where $j \leq i \Rightarrow x_j \notin \mathsf{fv}(F)$ and $j < i \Rightarrow x_j \neq x_i$, and $E' = F P_1 \cdots P_n \langle Q_1/x_1 \rangle \cdots \langle R/x_i \rangle \cdots \langle Q_k/x_k \rangle$.

This reduction process is more like evaluation in an abstract machine setting, where the states have the form $(E, P_1 \cdots P_n, \langle Q_1/x_1 \rangle \cdots \langle Q_k/x_k \rangle)$, than a preorder associated with an equational theory, as $\beta$-reduction, possibly with explicit substitutions, is usually presented (see [1, 4] for instance). It is possible to define a notion of reduction in this broader sense for the $\lambda_{\mathsf{r}}$-calculus, but this is not relevant for the purpose of this paper. One may immediately observe that $\lambda_{\mathsf{r}}$-reduction exhibits some features that make it very different from $\beta$-reduction, namely:

(1) *non-determinism*. Since the composition $(P \mid Q)$ of bags of resources is commutative, the fetch rule is non deterministic: one may fetch any of the resources that a bag contains. This is best exemplified by defining a non deterministic *internal choice*:

$$(E \oplus F) =_{\mathrm{def}} x\langle E \mid F/x \rangle \qquad x \notin \mathsf{fv}(E) \cup \mathsf{fv}(F)$$

Clearly

$$(E \oplus F) \rightarrow_{\mathsf{r}} E\langle F/x \rangle \qquad \text{and} \qquad (E \oplus F) \rightarrow_{\mathsf{r}} F\langle E/x \rangle$$

Now any reasonable semantics should equate $E\langle P/x \rangle$ and $E$ whenever $x \notin \mathsf{fv}(E)$, therefore $(E \oplus F)$ adequately represents the choice between $E$ and $F$.

(2) *deadlocks*. A deadlock arises whenever a resource is both needed and absent. Typically, a term like $x\, P_1 \cdots P_n \langle \mathsf{O}/x \rangle$ cannot perform any reduction. Therefore, besides the usual normal forms—abstractions calling for an argument—there is a new kind of irreducible term: variables waiting in vain for a resource.

One may identify which construct of $\Lambda_{\mathsf{r}}$ is responsible for a particular feature of the evaluation process. In other words, one may define various sub-calculi of $\Lambda_{\mathsf{r}}$ where evaluation is constrained in some way. Clearly, non-determinism comes from the fact that a bag may contain two different terms—and from the commutativity of the bag union operation. Then a natural restriction to consider is to deal with bags made of copies of the same term. Such a bag is just a term with an explicit finite or infinite *multiplicity*, defined as follows:

$$\begin{aligned} E^0 &= \mathsf{O} \\ E^{m+1} &= (E \mid E^m) \end{aligned}$$

The $\lambda$-*calculus with multiplicities* is the sub-calculus $\Lambda_{\mathsf{m}}$ of $\Lambda_{\mathsf{r}}$ given by the grammar:

$$E ::= x \mid \lambda x E \mid (E E^m) \mid E\langle E^m/x\rangle$$

where $m \in \mathsf{N} \cup \{\infty\}$. This is the calculus we considered in [9, 8]. In particular, we showed in [9] that this sub-calculus is *deterministic* in the sense that, up to structural equivalence, a $\lambda_{\mathsf{m}}$-term may perform at most one reduction in one step:

LEMMA 4.2 For any $E, F \in \Lambda_{\mathsf{m}}$, if $E \equiv F$ then

$$E \rightarrow_{\mathsf{r}} E' \ \& \ F \rightarrow_{\mathsf{r}} F' \Rightarrow E' \equiv F'$$

As a matter of fact, the reduction relation in $\Lambda_{\mathsf{m}}$ may be described in a slightly more precise way than as the restriction of the $\lambda_{\mathsf{r}}$-reduction to $\lambda_{\mathsf{m}}$-terms. Indeed, one can see that the laws for structural equivalence regarding the bags are useless when considering $\lambda_{\mathsf{m}}$-terms. Namely, the structural equivalence $\equiv_{\mathsf{m}}$ on $\Lambda_{\mathsf{m}}$ is the least congruence containing $\alpha$-conversion and satisfying

$$E G^n \langle F^m/x\rangle \equiv_{\mathsf{m}} E\langle F^m/x\rangle G^n \qquad \text{and} \qquad E\langle G^n/x\rangle\langle F^m/z\rangle \equiv_{\mathsf{m}} E\langle F^m/z\rangle\langle G^n/x\rangle$$

with the same side conditions as above. Then the $\lambda_{\mathsf{m}}$-reduction $\rightarrow_{\mathsf{m}}$ is given as $\lambda_{\mathsf{r}}$-reduction, replacing $R$ by $F^m$ and $\equiv$ by $\equiv_{\mathsf{m}}$ in the rules for $\rightarrow_{\mathsf{r}}$, and modifying the fetch rule as follows:

$$\frac{E\langle F/x\rangle \rightsquigarrow E'}{E\langle F^{m+1}/x\rangle \rightarrow E'\langle F^m/x\rangle}$$

(again, with the same side condition as for the fetch rule).

Obviously, deadlocks are still possible when evaluating $\lambda_{\mathsf{m}}$-terms. On the other hand, this would be avoided if any resource from a bag were available at will. Then another sub-calculus of $\Lambda_{\mathsf{r}}$ that naturally arises is the $\lambda$-calculus with "infinite resources" $\Lambda_{\infty\mathsf{r}}$, given by the grammar:

$$\begin{aligned} E &::= x \mid \lambda x E \mid (E R) \mid E\langle R/x\rangle \\ R &::= E^\infty \mid (R \mid R) \end{aligned}$$

Internal choice is obviously definable in this calculus:

$$(E \oplus F) \;=\; x\langle E^{\infty} \mid F^{\infty}/x\rangle \qquad x \notin \mathsf{fv}(E) \cup \mathsf{fv}(F)$$

Indeed, $\Lambda_{\infty\mathsf{r}}$ is essentially the same as $\Lambda_{\oplus}$, the usual λ-calculus enriched with internal choice (see [5]). Therefore, while evaluation in $\Lambda_{\mathsf{m}}$ is deterministic with potential deadlocks, in $\Lambda_{\infty\mathsf{r}}$ it is non deterministic, without deadlocks. The intersection of the two sub-calculi, denoted $\Lambda_{\infty}$, is given by the grammar

$$E ::= x \mid \lambda x E \mid (E E^{\infty}) \mid E\langle E^{\infty}/x\rangle$$

This last sub-calculus may be regarded as "the λ-calculus," with explicit resources. Indeed, there is an obvious translation from $\Lambda$ to $\Lambda_{\infty}$, namely:

$$\begin{aligned} \mathcal{G}[\![x]\!] &= x \\ \mathcal{G}[\![\lambda x M]\!] &= \lambda x \mathcal{G}[\![M]\!] \\ \mathcal{G}[\![M N]\!] &= (\mathcal{G}[\![M]\!]\, \mathcal{G}[\![N]\!]^{\infty}) \end{aligned}$$

In [6] we showed that this translation is fully abstract. To see what this means, we first have to define the observational semantics.

## 5 The Observational Semantics

We have seen that the evaluation of a given $\lambda_{\mathsf{r}}$-term may diverge, deadlock or terminate properly, and that these possibilities are not mutually exclusive. Then the notion of observability may be richer than in the λ-calculus, and this gives us some freedom in defining the observational semantics of our calculus.

Since we are dealing with "may testing" for the π-calculus, we shall keep this kind of semantics for our λ-calculus with resources. This is much weaker than the bisimulation semantics usually adopted when dealing with a non deterministic calculus (see [24], for instance), though we shall see that, as far as the λ-calculus is concerned, may testing is as fine as bisimulation. As we suggested, computations in $\Lambda_{\mathsf{r}}$ may be observed in several ways. To formalize this point, let us introduce a domain of *observations* $\mathsf{D} = \{\bot, \delta, \gamma\}$, the elements of which respectively represent divergence, deadlock and proper termination, that is convergence to a value. In our calculus, a *value* is a closure, that is a term given by the grammar:

$$V ::= \lambda x E \mid V\langle P/x\rangle$$

Let $\mathcal{V}$ denote the set of values. A *deadlock* is a closed term $F$ which is a normal form, but not a value, that is $\{F' \mid F \rightarrow F'\} = \emptyset$ and $F \notin \mathcal{V}$. We denote by $\mathcal{W}$ the set of deadlocks.

Then we define the observation function $\mathsf{obs}(E)$, associating a set of observations with any closed term $E$, as follows:

1. $\bot \in \mathsf{obs}(E)$ if and only if $E$ may diverge, that is there exists an infinite sequence $(E_n)_{n \in \mathsf{N}}$ of terms such that $E_0 = E$ and $E_n \rightarrow_{\mathsf{r}} E_{n+1}$ for any $n \in \mathsf{N}$,
2. $\delta \in \mathsf{obs}(E)$ if and only if $E$ may deadlock, that is $\exists F \in \mathcal{W}. E \stackrel{*}{\rightarrow}_{\mathsf{r}} F$,
3. $\gamma \in \mathsf{obs}(E)$ if and only if $E$ may converge, that is $\exists V \in \mathcal{V}. E \stackrel{*}{\rightarrow}_{\mathsf{r}} V$.

For instance, if $E \in \Lambda_{\mathsf{m}}$ then $\mathsf{obs}(E)$ is a singleton, and if $E \in \Lambda_{\infty\mathsf{r}}$ then $\mathsf{obs}(E) \subseteq \{\bot, \gamma\}$. To define the observational semantics, we must have some means to compare the elements of $\mathsf{D}$. Given a preorder on $\mathsf{D}$, we say that $E$ is observationally better than $F$ if, for any $\lambda_{\mathsf{r}}$-context $C$ closing both $E$ and $F$, and for any observation $o \in \mathsf{obs}(C[F])$, there exists an observation $o' \in \mathsf{obs}(C[E])$ which is better than $o$.

Several observation scenarios, that is preorders on $\mathsf{D}$, are possible—taking Scott's view that divergence provides no information, that is any observation is better than $\bot$. In the "standard" scenario, deadlock is not distinguished from divergence. The corresponding observational semantics has the usual definition in this case, based on the observability predicate $E{\Downarrow}$ meaning that $E$ may have a value. This is the semantics we adopted in [6, 9] for the $\lambda$-calculus with multiplicities $\Lambda_{\mathsf{m}}$. We showed that, for this calculus, this semantics is the same as the one we would get by adopting a different scenario, where $\delta$ is strictly in between $\bot$ and $\gamma$, see [8].

In [9] we characterized the standard semantics induced by $\lambda_{\mathsf{m}}$-contexts over $\lambda$-terms, showing that it is strictly weaker than Lévy's semantics. Since here we are dealing with the relationships between the $\lambda$ and $\pi$ calculi, it is appropriate to consider another observation scenario, called the "flat" scenario in [8]. This is given by the *flat ordering* $\leq$ on $\mathsf{D}$, that is:

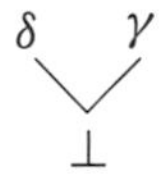


DEFINITION 5.1 (OBSERVATIONAL SEMANTICS) The *observational semantics* of the $\lambda_{\mathsf{r}}$-calculus is the preorder defined as follows:

$$E \sqsubseteq_{\mathsf{r}} F \Leftrightarrow \text{for all } \lambda_{\mathsf{r}}\text{-contexts } C,\ \forall o \in \mathsf{obs}(C[E])\ \exists o' \in \mathsf{obs}(C[F]) \quad o \leq o'$$

It is implicitly assumed in this definition that $C[E]$ and $C[F]$ are both closed, since $\mathsf{obs}$ is only defined on closed terms. By restricting the contexts to be $\lambda_{\mathsf{m}}$, or $\lambda_{\infty\mathsf{r}}$, or $\lambda_{\infty}$-contexts in the definition, we get corresponding preorders $\sqsubseteq_{\mathsf{m}}$, $\sqsubseteq_{\infty\mathsf{r}}$ and $\sqsubseteq_{\infty}$ respectively. Note that in the two latter cases, the observational semantics has the standard definition: $E$ is less than $F$ if, for all contexts $C$, if $C[E]$ may converge then $C[F]$ may converge. We denote by $\simeq_{\mathsf{r}}$, $\simeq_{\mathsf{m}}$,

$\simeq_{\infty r}$ and $\simeq_{\infty}$ the respective associated equivalences. There is an obvious ordering relation between these semantics: a broader class of contexts determines a stronger semantics. In [6] we showed:

$$\forall M, N \in \Lambda \cdot M \sqsubseteq_{\ell} N \;\Leftrightarrow\; \mathcal{G}[\![M]\!] \sqsubseteq_{\infty} \mathcal{G}[\![N]\!]$$

This justifies our claim that $\Lambda_{\infty}$ is "the (weak) λ-calculus". Therefore, we shall omit the translation $\mathcal{G}$, and regard λ-terms as terms of $\Lambda_{\mathsf{r}}$, with implicit infinite multiplicities. This allows us to write $M \sqsubseteq_{\mathsf{r}} N$, $M \sqsubseteq_{\mathsf{m}} N$ and $M \sqsubseteq_{\infty\mathsf{r}} N$ for $M$ and $N$ in $\Lambda$.

Let us see some examples. One can see that $\eta$-expansion on λ-terms is neither increasing nor decreasing in general with respect to the observational semantics. For instance, $x \not\sqsubseteq_{\mathsf{r}} \lambda y(xy)$ and $\lambda y(xy) \not\sqsubseteq_{\mathsf{r}} x$ because if we let $C = [\,]\langle {}^{\mathsf{O}}/x\rangle$ then $\mathsf{obs}(C[x]) = \{\delta\}$ while $\mathsf{obs}(C[\lambda y(xy)]) = \{\gamma\}$. Similarly, let $\Xi = (\lambda f x \cdot f f)(\lambda f x \cdot f f)$. Then $\Xi$ is not comparable with the identity $\mathbf{I}$, since $\mathsf{obs}(\mathbf{I}\,\mathsf{O}) = \{\delta\}$ while $\mathsf{obs}(\Xi\;\mathsf{O}) = \{\gamma\}$. These examples show that $\sqsubseteq_{\mathsf{m}}$ is strictly stronger than $\sqsubseteq_{\ell}$ on λ-terms.

Due to the universal quantification over contexts, the definition of the observational semantics is not very manageable: it is usually quite difficult to prove an inequation $E \sqsubseteq_{\mathsf{r}} F$. In [16], Milner stated and proved a property of the typed λ-calculus called the *context lemma*, which was then generalized to the λ-calculus by Lévy [14], establishing that, in order to "test" a (closed) λ-term, it is enough to apply it. The context lemma also holds in the λ-calculus with resources. To prove this fact, we first introduce a restricted kind of contexts, the *applicative contexts*, ranged over by $K, L \ldots$ These are given by the grammar:

$$K ::= [\,] \mid (K\,P) \mid K\langle P/x\rangle$$

where $P$ is any bag. Note that $E \rightarrow_{\mathsf{r}} F \Rightarrow K[E] \rightarrow_{\mathsf{r}} K[F]$. Now we define the *applicative testing* preorder, which is the observational preorder restricted to applicative contexts, that is:

$$E \sqsubseteq_{\mathsf{r}}^{\mathcal{A}} F \overset{\text{def}}{\iff} \forall K \cdot \forall o \in \mathsf{obs}(K[E])\ \exists o' \in \mathsf{obs}(K[F]) \quad o \leq o'$$

In [9], we proved the following:

LEMMA 5.2 Let $E, F \in \Lambda_{\mathsf{r}}$, and let $z \notin \mathsf{fv}(E) \cup \mathsf{fv}(F)$. Then

$$E \sqsubseteq_{\mathsf{r}}^{\mathcal{A}} F \Rightarrow [z/x]E \sqsubseteq_{\mathsf{r}}^{\mathcal{A}} [z/x]F$$

Now we prove the context lemma.

LEMMA 5.3 (THE CONTEXT LEMMA)

$$E \sqsubseteq_{\mathsf{r}} F \Leftrightarrow E \sqsubseteq_{\mathsf{r}}^{\mathcal{A}} F$$

*Proof* The direction "⇒" is obvious. To establish "⇐," we use the notion of a *multiple context*, that is the notion of a context where there may be several kinds of holes, indexed by positive integers, i.e. $[]_i$. For any such context involving only holes whose indexes are less than $k$, we define $C[E_1, \ldots, E_k]$ in the obvious way, that is by filling the hole $[]_i$ by the corresponding term $E_i$. We shall also use the notation $C[\tilde{E}]$ for $C[E_1, \ldots, E_k]$. Let $\mathcal{S}$ be the relation consisting of the pairs of closed terms of the form $(C[E_1, \ldots, E_k], C[F_1, \ldots, F_k])$ where $E_i \sqsubseteq_{\mathrm{r}}^{\mathcal{A}} F_i$ for any $i$. We show the following:

1. if $E \, \mathcal{S} \, F$ and $E \xrightarrow{l} E' \in \mathcal{V}$ then $F \xrightarrow{*} F'$ for some $F' \in \mathcal{V}$,
2. if $E \, \mathcal{S} \, F$ and $E \xrightarrow{l} E' \in \mathcal{W}$ then $F \xrightarrow{*} F'$ for some $F' \in \mathcal{W}$.

where $E \xrightarrow{l} E'$ means that $E$ reduces in $l$ steps to $E'$. We proceed by induction on $(l, h)$, w.r.t. the lexicographic ordering, where $h$ is the number of occurrences of holes in $C$. We may write $C = C_0 C_1 \cdots C_m$ where $C_0$ is either a hole $[]_i$, or a variable $x$, or an abstraction context $\lambda x\, B$, and the $C_j$'s, for $j > 0$, are bags or substitution contexts. We examine the possible cases (this proof technique is directly adapted from Lévy's one [14], with the notable difference that we are dealing with open terms).

(1) if $C_0 = \lambda x B$, we have, by pushing the substitutions on the right while possibly renaming the variables that are bound by these substitutions:

$$C[\tilde{E}] \equiv (\lambda x B[\tilde{G}]) B_1[\tilde{G}] \cdots B_p[\tilde{G}] \langle D_1[\tilde{G}]/x_1 \rangle \cdots \langle D_q[\tilde{G}]/x_q \rangle$$

where $\tilde{G} = G_1, \ldots, G_s$ and the $G_j$'s are obtained from the $E_i$'s by renaming some free variables by fresh ones (note that in performing this transformation on $C[\tilde{E}]$ we may have replaced some holes $[]_i$ of $C$ by new holes $[]_j$, in which a particular renaming of $E_i$ will be put). There are two subcases. If $p = 0$ then $C[\tilde{E}]$ is a value, for any $\tilde{E}$. Otherwise ($p > 0$), we have $l > 0$ since $C[\tilde{E}]$ is neither a value nor a deadlock. Let

$$C' = B\langle B_1/x \rangle B_2 \cdots B_p \langle D_1/x_1 \rangle \cdots \langle D_q/x_q \rangle$$

Then

$$C[\tilde{E}] \rightarrow C'[\tilde{G}] \xrightarrow{l-1} E'$$

and

$$C[\tilde{F}] \rightarrow C'[\tilde{H}]$$

where $H_1, \ldots, H_s$ are obtained from the $F_i$'s by the same renamings as the one we used to get the $G_j$'s from the $E_i$'s. Then one uses the previous lemma, and the induction hypothesis to conclude.

(2) if $C_0 = x$, we have, as in the previous case

$$C[\tilde{E}] \equiv zB_1[\tilde{G}]\cdots B_p[\tilde{G}]\langle D_1[\tilde{G}]/x_1\rangle\cdots\langle D_q[\tilde{G}]/x_q\rangle$$

Let $i$ be the first index such that $x_i = z$ (such an $i$ exists since $C[\tilde{E}]$ is closed). There are again two subcases. If $D_i[\tilde{G}] \equiv \mathsf{0}$ then $C[\tilde{E}]$ is a deadlock. Since $\mathsf{0}$ is not a $\lambda_{\mathsf{r}}$-term, we have $D_i[\tilde{H}] \equiv \mathsf{0}$ for any $\tilde{H}$, therefore $C[\tilde{F}]$ is a deadlock too. Otherwise, $D_i[\tilde{G}] \equiv (B[\tilde{G}] \mid D_i'[\tilde{G}])$ where $B[\tilde{G}] \in \Lambda_{\mathsf{r}}$, so that if we let

$$C' = B\,B_1\cdots B_p\langle D_1/x_1\rangle\cdots\langle D_i'/x_i\rangle\cdots\langle D_q/x_q\rangle$$

we have

$$C[\tilde{E}] \to C'[\tilde{G}] \xrightarrow{l-1} E'$$

Since

$$C[\tilde{F}] \to C'[\tilde{H}]$$

we may conclude as in the previous case.

(3) if $C_0 = [\,]_i$, let $C' = E_i C_1 \cdots C_m$. This context has $h-1$ holes, and obviously $C'[\tilde{E}] = C[\tilde{E}]$, therefore by induction hypothesis if $C[\tilde{E}] \xrightarrow{l} E'$ with $E' \in \mathcal{V}$ or $E' \in \mathcal{W}$, then there exists $F''$ such that $F'' \in \mathcal{V}$ or $F'' \in \mathcal{W}$ respectively, and $C'[\tilde{F}] \xrightarrow{*} F''$. Since $C'[\tilde{F}] = E_i\, C_1[\tilde{F}]\cdots C_m[\tilde{F}]$ and $E_i \sqsubseteq_{\mathsf{r}}^{A} F_i$, we conclude that $C[\tilde{F}] \xrightarrow{*} F'$ for some $F'$ such that $F' \in \mathcal{V}$ or $F' \in \mathcal{W}$ respectively. □

*Remark 5.4* Using the Context Lemma it is easy to verify that $\Omega \sqsubseteq_{\mathsf{r}} E$ for any $E$. Then for instance

$$m \leq n \Rightarrow \lambda x_1 \cdots x_m \cdot \Omega \sqsubseteq_{\mathsf{r}} \lambda x_1 \cdots x_n \cdot \Omega$$

Another consequence of the Context Lemma we shall use is the following:

LEMMA 5.5

(i) For any $E, F \in \Lambda_{\mathsf{r}}$, $E \to_{\mathsf{r}} F \Rightarrow F \sqsubseteq_{\mathsf{r}} E$. Moreover, $(\lambda x E)P \simeq_{\mathsf{r}} E\langle P/x\rangle$.

(ii) For any $E, F \in \Lambda_{\mathsf{m}}$, $E \to_{\mathsf{m}} F \Rightarrow F \simeq_{\mathsf{r}} E$.

*Proof* The first point should be obvious, since $E \to_{\mathsf{r}} F \Rightarrow K[E] \to_{\mathsf{r}} K[F]$ for any applicative context $K$, therefore $o \in \mathsf{obs}(K[F]) \Rightarrow o \in \mathsf{obs}(K[E])$. For the second point, note that if $o \in \mathsf{obs}(K[(\lambda x E)P])$ then also $o \in \mathsf{obs}(K[E\langle P/x\rangle])$ since any non-empty reduction sequence originating in $K[(\lambda x E)P]$ must start with $K[(\lambda x E)P] \to_{\mathsf{r}} K[E\langle P/x\rangle]$. The last point is shown in a similar way, that is, using the fact that $\lambda_{\mathsf{m}}$-reduction is deterministic. □

Note that the first implication cannot be reversed in general, because $\lambda_r$-reduction is non deterministic. It is an easy exercise to show, using the Context Lemma, that internal choice is a *join*:

$$(E_0 \oplus E_1) \sqsubseteq_r E \;\Leftrightarrow\; E_0 \sqsubseteq_r E \quad \& \quad E_1 \sqsubseteq_r E$$

COROLLARY 5.6

(i) For any $M, N \in \Lambda \quad M =_\beta N \Rightarrow M \simeq_r N$.

(ii) Moreover, if $A \in \mathcal{A}(M)$ then $A \sqsubseteq_r M$.

*Proof* The first point is an immediate consequence of the previous lemma. Regarding the second, if $A \in \mathcal{A}(M)$ then by definition there is $N =_\beta M$ such that $A = \varpi(N)$. We have $N \simeq_r M$, and $A \sqsubseteq_r N$ since $\sqsubseteq_r$ is a precongruence such that $\Omega \sqsubseteq_r X$ for any $X$ (see the previous remark). □

## 6 The Discriminating Power of Multiplicities

In this section we characterize the semantics induced *over* $\lambda$*-terms* by the $\lambda$-calculi with resources and multiplicities. We show that, for $M, N \in \Lambda$, $M \sqsubseteq_r N$ and $M \sqsubseteq_m N$ both coincide with Lévy's ordering $M \sqsubseteq_{\mathcal{L}} N$.

As a first step towards these results, we establish a property that we call the *approximation lemma* (*cf.* [14]). It states that, to observe $C[M]$ in some way (where $M$ is a $\lambda$-term and $C$ a $\lambda_r$-context), only a finite amount of information about $M$ needs to be known. Intuitively, this should be clear, because $M$ can only participate by a finite number of reduction steps in a computation of $C[M]$. Moreover, it is only when $M$ shows up in the head position, as a function applied to a series of arguments, that it has to exhibit some specific finite intensional content, like beginning with a series of abstractions. Then any term having at least the same intensional content is as good as $M$, as far as the observability within the context $C$ is concerned. The appropriate formalization of "finite intensional content" is given by approximants.

LEMMA 6.1 (THE APPROXIMATION LEMMA) For any $\lambda_r$-context $C$ and for every $M \in \Lambda$ with $C[M]$ closed:

$$o \in \mathsf{obs}(C[M]) \;\Rightarrow\; \exists A \in \mathcal{A}(M)\, \exists o' \geq o. \quad o' \in \mathsf{obs}(C[A])$$

*Proof* We use multiple contexts, as in the context lemma (again, the explicit substitution construct is very convenient for this proof). That is, we deal with terms of the form $C[M_1, \ldots, M_k]$ rather than $C[M]$. Firstly, we note that if $o = \bot$ then one can take $\Omega$ as the appropriate approximant for any $M_i$ (recall that $\Omega \in \mathcal{A}(M)$ for any $M$). Then we show the following:

1. if $C[M_1, \ldots, M_k] \xrightarrow{l} V \in \mathcal{V}$ then there exist $A_1, \ldots, A_k$ such that $A_i \in \mathcal{A}(M_i)$ for any $i$ and $C[A_1, \ldots, A_k] \xrightarrow{*} V'$ for some $V' \in \mathcal{V}$,
2. if $C[M_1, \ldots, M_k] \xrightarrow{l} W \in \mathcal{W}$ then there exist $A_1, \ldots, A_k$ such that $A_i \in \mathcal{A}(M_i)$ for any $i$ and $C[A_1, \ldots, A_k] \xrightarrow{*} W'$ for some $W' \in \mathcal{W}$.

The proof is entirely similar to the one of the Context Lemma 5.3. The details are left to the reader. You should use the following facts:

1. $A \in \mathcal{A}(M) \Rightarrow [z/x]A \in \mathcal{A}([z/x]M)$. This is needed because some of the $M_i$'s may have to be duplicated and renamed.
2. $\mathcal{A}(M)$ is directed (with respect to the prefix ordering $\preceq$, see the Lemma 3.2). This is needed because some of the $M_i$'s may occur in different positions in $C[\tilde{M}]$, where different approximants may be used.
3. $A \preceq B \Rightarrow A \sqsubseteq_{\mathsf{r}} B$ (see the Corollary 5.6).

A complete proof of a similar result, for the $\lambda_{\mathsf{m}}$-calculus with the standard observation scenario, may be found in [9]. □

A consequence of this lemma, together with the Corollary 5.6(ii) is that $M \sqsubseteq_{\mathcal{L}} N$ implies $M \sqsubseteq_{\mathsf{r}} N$ (see the Theorem 6.3 below). To prove the converse, the key result is a *separation lemma*, showing that if $M$ and $N$ differ in Lévy's interpretation, then there is a context with multiplicities $C$ *separating* these two terms, in the sense that $\mathsf{obs}(C[M]) \not\leq \mathsf{obs}(C[N])$ (this makes sense since both $\mathsf{obs}(C[M])$ and $\mathsf{obs}(C[N])$ are singletons in this case). The proof uses a refinement of the classical "Böhm-out technique" (see [4]). As such, it uses the *tupling* combinators

$$\mathbf{P}_n = \lambda x_1 \cdots x_{n+1}.\, x_{n+1} x_1 \cdots x_n$$

and the *projections*

$$\mathbf{U}_i^n = \lambda x_1 \cdots x_n . x_i$$

LEMMA 6.2 (THE SEPARATION LEMMA) Let $M, N \in \Lambda$ and $\mathsf{fv}(M) \cup \mathsf{fv}(N) \subseteq \{x_1, \ldots, x_n\}$. If $M \not\sqsubseteq_{\mathcal{L}} N$ then there exist $p_1, \ldots, p_n$ and $m_1, \ldots, m_n$ in $\mathsf{N}$ such that for any $q_1, \ldots, q_n$ with $q_i \geq p_i$ there exist closed bags $P_1, \ldots, P_r$ which are either $\mathbf{P}_q{}^m$ with $m \in \mathsf{N}$, or $(\mathbf{U}_i^n)^\infty$, or else $\Omega^\infty$, such that

$$\mathsf{obs}\big(M\langle \mathbf{P}_{q_1}^{m_1}/x_1\rangle \cdots \langle \mathbf{P}_{q_n}^{m_n}/x_n\rangle P_1 \cdots P_r\big) \not\leq \mathsf{obs}\big(N\langle \mathbf{P}_{q_1}^{m_1}/x_1\rangle \cdots \langle \mathbf{P}_{q_n}^{m_n}/x_n\rangle P_1 \cdots P_r\big).$$

For lack of space, we omit the proof, and just give a sketch (again, a proof of a similar result for the standard observation scenario is given in full details in [9]. The situation here is simpler, because the semantics $\sqsubseteq_{\mathsf{r}}$ is much more discriminating than the standard one, therefore it is easier to separate terms by distinguishing deadlock from divergence). To apply Böhm's technique, it is convenient to use an alternative characterization of Lévy's preorder, as the "limit" of a decreasing sequence of preorders:

$$M \sqsubseteq_{\mathcal{L}} N \;\Leftrightarrow\; \forall k \in \mathsf{N}. M \leq_k N$$

where $\leq_k$, the intensional preorder at order $k$, is given by

1. $M \leq_0 N$ for any $M$ and $N$;
2. $M \leq_{k+1} N$ if and only if

(a) $M \in \mathsf{PO}_n$ and $N =_\beta \lambda x_1 \cdots x_m \cdot N'$ with $m \geq n$, or

(b) $M =_\beta \lambda x_1 \ldots x_n . x M_1 \cdots M_s$ and $N =_\beta \lambda x_1 \ldots x_n . x N_1 \cdots N_s$ with $M_i \leq_k N_i$ for $1 \leq i \leq s$.

Then the separation lemma is established by induction on the least integer $k$ such that $M \not\leq_k N$, and by a systematic inspection of the possible cases. It must be noted that the easiest proof of such a separation lemma would be obtained using a version of the $\lambda_{\mathsf{r}}$-calculus where the commutativity law $(P \mid Q) \equiv (Q \mid P)$ is disallowed (except for $Q = \mathsf{0}$). In this case, for any resource term we have either $R \equiv \mathsf{0}$, or $R \equiv (E \mid P)$ for a unique $E$. Such a calculus, where the resources are arranged not as bags, but in a stack-like manner, is deterministic (in the sense of the Lemma 4.2), but it allows to use different values for the various occurrences of a given variable in the head position. This is exactly what we need to apply the "Böhm-out" technique. However, we may prove the finer result involving only terms with multiplicities, using the tupling combinators as Böhm did for the $\lambda$-calculus. □

Now we can prove the main result of this section:

THEOREM 6.3 For any $M, N \in \Lambda$

$$M \sqsubseteq_{\mathcal{L}} N \;\Leftrightarrow\; M \sqsubseteq_{\mathsf{r}} N \;\Leftrightarrow\; M \sqsubseteq_{\mathsf{m}} N$$

*Proof* Assume that $M \sqsubseteq_{\mathcal{L}} N$, and let $C$ be a $\lambda_{\mathsf{r}}$-context such that $o \in \mathsf{obs}(C[M])$. By the Approximation Lemma 6.1, there exist $A \in \mathcal{A}(M)$ and $o' \geq o$ such that $o' \in \mathsf{obs}(C[A])$. We have $A \in \mathcal{A}(N)$, therefore by the Corollary 5.6 there exists $o'' \geq o'$ such that $o'' \in \mathsf{obs}(C[N])$. This shows $M \sqsubseteq_{\mathcal{L}} N \Rightarrow M \sqsubseteq_{\mathsf{r}} N$. The implication $M \sqsubseteq_{\mathsf{r}} N \Rightarrow M \sqsubseteq_{\mathsf{m}} N$ is trivial. Finally the implication $M \sqsubseteq_{\mathsf{m}} N \Rightarrow M \sqsubseteq_{\mathcal{L}} N$ is the Separation Lemma. □

## 7 Relating the Calculi

In this section we show that, as far as λ-terms are concerned, the $\pi$, $\lambda_{\mathsf{r}}$ and $\lambda_{\mathsf{m}}$-semantics all coincide with Lévy's interpretation. This is our main result. In order to prove it, we relate the $\pi$, $\lambda_{\mathsf{r}}$ and $\lambda_{\mathsf{m}}$-calculi. Let us first see how the $\lambda_{\mathsf{r}}$-calculus may be encoded into the $\pi$-calculus.

The idea of the encoding is quite simple: we have seen that $\mathcal{E}[\![(\lambda x M)N]\!]u$ reduces to $(\nu x)(\mathcal{E}[\![M]\!]u \mid \mathcal{E}[\![x := N]\!])$, a term that might be taken as representing $[{}^{N}/{}_{x}]M$. This gives us the way we shall encode explicit substitutions $E\langle {}^{P}/{}_{x}\rangle$. It just remains to encode the bags, or more precisely the substitution items $\langle {}^{P}/{}_{x}\rangle$. The syntax we chose for bags should indicate how to proceed. Here is the encoding:

$$\begin{aligned}
\mathcal{B}[\![x]\!]u &= \bar{x}u \\
\mathcal{B}[\![\lambda x E]\!]u &= u(x, v)\mathcal{B}[\![E]\!]v \\
\mathcal{B}[\![E R]\!]u &= (\nu v)(\mathcal{B}[\![E]\!]v \mid (\nu x)(\bar{v}xu \mid \mathcal{B}[\![x := R]\!])) \\
\mathcal{B}[\![E\langle {}^{R}/{}_{x}\rangle]\!]u &= (\nu x)(\mathcal{B}[\![E]\!]u \mid \mathcal{B}[\![x := R]\!]) \\
\mathcal{B}[\![x := \mathsf{1}]\!] &= \mathsf{0} \\
\mathcal{B}[\![x := E]\!] &= x(w)\mathcal{B}[\![E]\!]w \\
\mathcal{B}[\![x := (P \mid Q)]\!] &= (\mathcal{B}[\![x := P]\!] \mid \mathcal{B}[\![x := Q]\!]) \\
\mathcal{B}[\![x := E^{\infty}]\!] &= !\mathcal{B}[\![x := E]\!]
\end{aligned}$$

Clearly, Milner's encoding from $\Lambda$ to $\Pi$ factorizes into the translation from $\Lambda$ to $\Lambda_{\infty}$ composed with the previous encoding:

$$\forall M \in \Lambda \cdot \mathcal{E}[\![M]\!]u \;=\; \mathcal{B}[\![\mathcal{G}[\![M]\!]]\!]u$$

Note also that the encoding of internal choice is exactly the one we would expect:

$$\mathcal{B}[\![E \oplus F]\!]u \;=\; (\nu x)(\bar{x}u \mid x(w)\mathcal{B}[\![E]\!]w \mid x(w)\mathcal{B}[\![F]\!]w)$$

Regarding the correspondence between the notions of reduction, the situation is now better than in the case of $\lambda$ versus $\pi$: we can show that the reduction steps are exactly mimicked in both directions. Actually, the $\lambda_{\mathsf{r}}$-calculus was designed exactly for this purpose. In particular, we can show the following:

LEMMA 7.1 For any closed $\lambda_{\mathsf{r}}$-term $E$

$$\mathcal{B}[\![E]\!]u\Downarrow_{\pi} \;\Leftrightarrow\; \gamma \in \mathsf{obs}(E)$$

That is, one can test in the $\pi$-calculus whether a closed $\lambda_{\mathsf{r}}$-term has a value or not. This shows that this encoding is adequate with respect to the "standard" observational semantics, where deadlocks are not observed.

However, this is not enough for our purpose, since we want to be able to detect also the potential deadlocks using $\pi$-calculus means. To this end, we could modify the observational semantics of the $\pi$-calculus, allowing deadlocks to be observable in this calculus (in the $\pi$-calculus, a deadlock is a term that does not perform any transition, labelled or unlabelled). This is not the way we shall follow here, since we are interested in the observational semantics as it was given by Milner in [18].

We shall instead establish that it is possible to detect deadlocks arising in the $\lambda$-calculus with multiplicities $\Lambda_{\mathsf{m}}$, using the $\pi$-calculus as it is. Intuitively, the reason is this: in the $\lambda_{\mathsf{m}}$-calculus, since the resources are always copies of a given term, one may assume that they are consumed sequentially, that is, without using the commutativity of bag composition. Then one may modify the previous encoding accordingly: a substitution item $\langle E^m/x\rangle$ (where $m \in \mathsf{N}$) is not encoded as a parallel composition of $m$ identical items $\langle E^1/x\rangle$, but as a "stack" of resources, and a specific signal is emitted when no resource is available anymore, that is when there is a potential deadlock. Let us assume that $\delta$ and $\gamma$ are names, belonging to $\mathcal{N}$. Immediate observability on these names will represent respectively deadlock and divergence of the encoded terms. We define the encoding $\mathcal{B}_\delta$ from $\Lambda_{\mathsf{m}}$ into $\Pi$, as follows:

$$\begin{aligned}
\mathcal{B}_\delta[\![x]\!]u &= \bar{x}u \\
\mathcal{B}_\delta[\![\lambda x E]\!]u &= u(x,v)\mathcal{B}_\delta[\![E]\!]v && v \neq \delta \\
\mathcal{B}_\delta[\![EF^m]\!]u &= (\nu v)(\mathcal{B}_\delta[\![E]\!]v \mid (\nu x)(\bar{v}xu \mid \mathcal{B}_\delta[\![x := F^m]\!])) && v \neq \delta \\
\mathcal{B}_\delta[\![E\langle F^m/x\rangle]\!]u &= (\nu x)(\mathcal{B}_\delta[\![E]\!]u \mid \mathcal{B}_\delta[\![x := F^m]\!])
\end{aligned}$$

$$\begin{aligned}
\mathcal{B}_\delta[\![x := E^0]\!] &= x(w)\bar{\delta} && w \neq \delta \\
\mathcal{B}_\delta[\![x := E^{m+1}]\!] &= x(w)(\mathcal{B}_\delta[\![E]\!]w \mid \mathcal{B}_\delta[\![x := E^m]\!]) && w \neq \delta \\
\mathcal{B}_\delta[\![x := E^\infty]\!] &= !x(w)\mathcal{B}_\delta[\![E]\!]w && w \neq \delta
\end{aligned}$$

where $m \in \mathsf{N}$. Obviously, we have, for $M \in \Lambda$

$$\mathcal{E}[\![M]\!]u \;=\; \mathcal{B}_\delta[\![\mathcal{G}[\![M]\!]]\!]u$$

The operational correspondence established by this encoding is shown by the following lemma.

LEMMA 7.2 Let $E$ be a closed $\lambda_{\mathsf{m}}$-term, and $u \neq \delta$. Then

(i) if $E \equiv_{\mathsf{m}} F$ then $\mathcal{B}_\delta[\![E]\!]u \equiv_\pi \mathcal{B}_\delta[\![F]\!]u$,

(ii) if $E \rightarrow_{\mathsf{m}} E'$ then $\mathcal{B}_\delta[\![E]\!]u \rightarrow_\pi P$ for some $P$ such that $P \equiv_\pi \mathcal{B}_\delta[\![E']\!]u$,

(iii) if $\mathcal{B}_\delta[\![E]\!]u \rightarrow_\pi P$ then either $E$ is a deadlock and $P \downarrow \delta$, or $E \rightarrow_{\mathsf{m}} E'$ for some $E'$ such that $P \equiv_\pi \mathcal{B}_\delta[\![E']\!]u$.

*Proof* The first point is easily proved, by induction on the definition of $E \equiv_{\mathsf{m}} F$. For the second point, we use the Lemma 4.1. We have

$$E \equiv_{\mathsf{m}} H F_1^{m_1} \cdots P_n^{m_n} \langle G_1^{r_1}/x_1 \rangle \cdots \langle G_k^{r_k}/x_k \rangle$$

where $H = \lambda x F$ or $H = x$, the variables $x_i$ are pairwise distinct, and $i < j \Rightarrow x_i \notin \mathsf{fv}(Q_j)$. Then

$$\begin{aligned}\mathcal{B}_\delta[\![E]\!]u \equiv_\pi (\nu \tilde{u})(\nu \tilde{z})(\nu \tilde{x})\big(\mathcal{B}_\delta[\![H]\!]u_1 \mid \bar{u}_1 z_1 u_2 \mid \mathcal{B}_\delta\big[\!\big[z_1 := F_1^{m_1}\big]\!\big] \mid \\ \vdots \\ \bar{u}_n z_n u \mid \mathcal{B}_\delta\big[\!\big[z_n := F_n^{m_n}\big]\!\big] \mid \\ \mathcal{B}_\delta\big[\!\big[x_1 := G_1^{r_1}\big]\!\big] \mid \cdots \mid \mathcal{B}_\delta\big[\!\big[x_k := G_k^{r_k}\big]\!\big]\big)\end{aligned}$$

If $H = \lambda x F$ we have $\mathcal{B}_\delta[\![H]\!]u_1 = u_1(x, v)\mathcal{B}_\delta[\![F]\!]v$, therefore, in this case where

$$E' = F\langle F_1^{m_1} x\rangle F_2^{m_2} \cdots F_n^{m_n} \langle G_1^{r_1} x_1 \rangle \cdots \langle G_k^{r_k} x_k \rangle$$

we have

$$\begin{aligned}\mathcal{B}_\delta[\![E]\!]u \rightarrow_\pi (\nu \tilde{u})(\nu \tilde{z})(\nu \tilde{x})\big(\mathcal{B}_\delta[\![[z_1/x]F]\!]u_2 \mid \mathcal{B}_\delta\big[\!\big[z_1 := F_1^{m_1}\big]\!\big] \mid \\ \bar{u}_2 z_2 u_3 \mid \mathcal{B}_\delta\big[\!\big[z_2 := F_2^{m_2}\big]\!\big] \mid \\ \vdots \\ \bar{u}_n z_n u \mid \mathcal{B}_\delta\big[\!\big[z_n := F_n^{m_n}\big]\!\big] \mid \\ \mathcal{B}_\delta\big[\!\big[x_1 := G_1^{r_1}\big]\!\big] \mid \cdots \mid \mathcal{B}_\delta\big[\!\big[x_k := G_k^{r_k}\big]\!\big]\big)\end{aligned}$$

that is $\mathcal{B}_\delta[\![E]\!]u \rightarrow_\pi P$ with $P \equiv_\pi \mathcal{B}_\delta[\![E']\!]u$.

If $H = x_i$, then $r_i > 0$ and $E' = G_i F_1^{m_1} \cdots F_n^{m_n} \langle G_1^{r_1}/x_1 \rangle \cdots \langle G_i^{r_i - 1}/x_i \rangle \cdots \langle G_k^{r_k}/x_k \rangle$, we have, since $\mathcal{B}_\delta[\![x_i]\!]u_1 = \bar{x}_i u_1$ and $\mathcal{B}_\delta[\![x_i := G_i^{r_i}]\!] = x_i(w)(\mathcal{B}_\delta[\![G_i]\!]w \mid \mathcal{B}_\delta[\![x_i := G_i^{r_i - 1}]\!])$

$$\begin{aligned}\mathcal{B}_\delta[\![E]\!]u \rightarrow_\pi (\nu \tilde{u})(\nu \tilde{z})(\nu \tilde{x})\big(\mathcal{B}_\delta[\![G_i]\!]u_1 \mid \bar{u}_1 z_1 u_2 \mid \mathcal{B}_\delta\big[\!\big[z_1 := F_1^{m_1}\big]\!\big] \mid \\ \vdots \\ \bar{u}_n z_n u \mid \mathcal{B}_\delta\big[\!\big[z_n := F_n^{m_n}\big]\!\big] \mid \\ \mathcal{B}_\delta\big[\!\big[x_1 := G_1^{r_1}\big]\!\big] \mid \cdots \mid \mathcal{B}_\delta\big[\!\big[x_i := G_i^{r_i - 1}\big]\!\big] \mid \cdots \mid \mathcal{B}_\delta\big[\!\big[x_k := G_k^{r_k}\big]\!\big]\big)\end{aligned}$$

that is, again, $\mathcal{B}_\delta[\![E]\!]u \rightarrow_\pi P$ with $P \equiv_\pi \mathcal{B}_\delta[\![E']\!]u$.

Regarding the last point, we may assume, as in for the previous point, that $E$ has the following shape:

$$E \equiv_{\mathsf{m}} H F_1^{m_1} \cdots P_n^{m_n} \langle G_1^{r_1}/x_1 \rangle \cdots \langle G_k^{r_k}/x_k \rangle$$

where $H = \lambda x F$ or $H = x$, the variables $x_i$'s are pairwise distinct, and $i < j \Rightarrow x_i \notin \mathsf{fv}(Q_j)$. If $\mathcal{B}_\delta[\![E]\!]u \rightarrow_\pi P$ then either $H$ is an abstraction, or a variable $x_i$ with $r_i > 0$, in which cases it is easy to see that there exists $E'$ such that $E \rightarrow_{\mathsf{m}} E'$ and $P \equiv_\pi \mathcal{B}_\delta[\![E']\!]u$, or $H = x_i$ with $r_i = 0$, that is, $E$ is a deadlock, and

$$\begin{aligned} P \;=\; (\nu\,\tilde{u})(\nu\,\tilde{z})(\nu\,\tilde{x})\big(\bar{\delta} \mid\ & \bar{u}_1 z_1 u_2 \mid \mathcal{B}_\delta\left[\!\left[z_1 := F_1^{m_1}\right]\!\right] \mid \\ & \vdots \\ & \bar{u}_n z_n u \mid \mathcal{B}_\delta\left[\!\left[z_n := F_n^{m_n}\right]\!\right] \mid \\ & \mathcal{B}_\delta\left[\!\left[x_1 := G_1^{r_1}\right]\!\right] \mid \cdots \mid \mathcal{B}_\delta\left[\!\left[x_{i-1} := G_{i-1}^{r_{i-1}}\right]\!\right] \mid \\ & \mathcal{B}_\delta\left[\!\left[x_{i+1} := G_{i+1}^{r_{i+1}}\right]\!\right] \mid \cdots \mid \mathcal{B}_\delta\left[\!\left[x_k := G_k^{r_k}\right]\!\right]\big) \end{aligned}$$

and clearly $P \downarrow \delta$. □

One can now see that if $\mathcal{B}_\delta[\![E]\!]u \xrightarrow{*}_\pi P\!\downarrow$ then either $E$ has a value and $P \downarrow u$, or $E$ reduces into a deadlock and $P \downarrow \delta$. Therefore we have:

COROLLARY 7.3 For any closed $\lambda_{\mathsf{m}}$-term $E$

$$(\nu\delta)\mathcal{B}_\delta[\![E]\!]\gamma \Downarrow_\pi \;\Leftrightarrow\; \gamma \in \mathsf{obs}(E) \qquad \text{and} \qquad (\nu\gamma)\mathcal{B}_\delta[\![E]\!]\gamma \Downarrow_\pi \;\Leftrightarrow\; \delta \in \mathsf{obs}(E)$$

For $E, F \in \Lambda_{\mathsf{m}}$, let us write $E \sqsubseteq_\pi F$ for $\mathcal{B}_\delta[\![E]\!] \sqsubseteq_\pi \mathcal{B}_\delta[\![F]\!]$. Note that for $\lambda$-terms $M, N \in \Lambda$, this coincides, up to the identification of $M$ with $\mathcal{G}[\![M]\!]$, with our previous definition of $M \sqsubseteq_\pi N$, that is $\mathcal{E}[\![M]\!]u \sqsubseteq_\pi \mathcal{E}[\![N]\!]u$.

PROPOSITION 7.4 For any $E, F \in \Lambda_{\mathsf{m}}$

$$E \sqsubseteq_\pi F \Rightarrow E \sqsubseteq_{\mathsf{m}} F$$

*Proof* Let $C$ be a $\lambda_{\mathsf{m}}$-context, and $o \in \mathsf{obs}(C[E])$. We have to show that there exists $o' \in \mathsf{D}$ such that $o \le o'$ and $o' \in \mathsf{obs}(C[F])$. This is obvious if $o = \bot$. If $o = \gamma$, then by the Corollary 7.3 we have $(\nu\delta)\mathcal{B}_\delta[\![C[E]]\!]\gamma \Downarrow_\pi$. Since the encoding $\mathcal{B}_\delta$ is defined in a compositional way, there is a multiple $\pi$-context $D$ and names $u_1, \ldots, u_k$ such that

$$\mathcal{B}_\delta[\![C[G]]\!]\gamma = D[\mathcal{B}_\delta[\![G]\!]u_1, \ldots, \mathcal{B}_\delta[\![G]\!]u_k]$$

for any $G \in \Lambda_{\mathsf{m}}$, therefore $(\nu\delta)\mathcal{B}_\delta[\![C[F]]\!]\gamma \Downarrow_\pi$ since $E \sqsubseteq_\pi F$, hence $\gamma \in \mathsf{obs}(C[F])$ by the Corollary 7.3. The case $o = \delta$ is similar. □
We can now prove the announced result:

THEOREM 7.5 For any $M, N \in \Lambda$

$$M \sqsubseteq_{\mathcal{L}} N \Leftrightarrow M \sqsubseteq_{\mathsf{r}} N \Leftrightarrow M \sqsubseteq_{\mathsf{m}} N \Leftrightarrow M \sqsubseteq_\pi N$$

*Proof* The first two equivalences are given by the Theorem 6.3, $M \sqsubseteq_\pi N \Rightarrow M \sqsubseteq_{\mathsf{m}} N$ is given by the previous proposition, while $M \sqsubseteq_{\mathcal{L}} N \Rightarrow M \sqsubseteq_\pi N$ is given by the Theorem 3.3. □

## 8 Conclusion

To conclude this paper, let us briefly comment on our result, with respect to related work. Firstly, we note that the π-may testing equivalence $M \simeq_\pi N$ on λ-terms coincides with the π-bisimulation $M \approx_\pi N$ considered by Sangiorgi (see [24, 25]), since he showed that the latter coincides with equality $M =_{\mathcal{L}} N$ in Lévy's interpretation. It is worth recalling here that the π-bisimulation $M \approx_\pi N$ also coincides with the bisimulation $M \approx_\oplus N$ induced by the λ-calculus enriched with internal choice $(M \oplus N)$, as shown by Sangiorgi in [24].

The reasons why we preferred to deal with may testing—besides the fact that this is the semantics considered by Milner in [18]—are the following. Firstly, bisimulation does not preserve the interpretation we would like to have for some constructs, and especially for internal choice. Moreover, given an encoding of a calculus into another, a bisimulation semantics, being based on the interaction capabilities of the encoded terms, does not leave any room to play with the target calculus. On the other hand, in the may testing approach, one has the possibility to identify sub-calculi of the target, and see what is the resulting semantics on the source calculus. Let us explain these two points in more detail.

In investigating the full abstraction problem for the lazy λ-calculus, Abramsky found out that this calculus is too weak. To make it "complete" with respect to the canonical denotational semantics, one must enrich it with a convergence testing facility, and some parallel feature, see [2, 3]. Milner discovered that one can encode the *convergence testing combinator* $\mathsf{C}$ of Abramsky in the π-calculus, namely:

$$\mathcal{E}[\![\mathsf{C}]\!]u =_{\text{def}} u(x, v)(\nu w)(\bar{x}w \mid \bar{w}xw.\mathcal{E}[\![\mathbf{I}]\!]v)$$

(note that one uses an output guard). This combinator is such that $(\mathsf{C}M)$ converges, to the identity $\mathbf{I}$, if and only if $M$ converges. As for the parallel convergence testing combinator $\mathsf{P}$, such that $\mathsf{P}MN$ converges, to the identity $\mathbf{I}$, if and only if $M$ converges or $N$ converges, one could encode it as follows, using output guards:

$$\mathcal{E}[\![\mathsf{P}]\!]u =_{\text{def}} u(x, v)v(y, w)(\nu r)(\nu s)\bar{x}r.\bar{y}s.(\nu o)(\bar{r}xr.\bar{o} \mid \bar{s}ys.\bar{o} \mid o()\mathcal{E}[\![\mathbf{I}]\!]w)$$

However, parallel convergence testing is not the most general way to deal with parallel functions. In [5, 7] we have shown that parallel composition of functions is simply the *join* in the denotational semantics, which may be represented in the syntax by internal choice. For instance, $\mathsf{P} = (\lambda xy.\mathsf{C}x) \oplus (\lambda xy.\mathsf{C}y)$. Obviously, to preserve some properties of the interpretation of internal choice as a join, like for instance $\mathbf{I} \oplus \Omega = \mathbf{I}$, one should replace the bisimulation by a weaker notion, e.g. a simulation semantics, as given by the Definition 2.3. But then it is not clear that adding internal choice to the $\lambda$-calculus makes it as powerful as the $\pi$-calculus.

Clearly, the may testing semantics is far less sensitive than bisimulation to the specific way we describe the operational behaviour of the constructs of a calculus. It is closer to the denotational approach, whose purpose is precisely to abstract away from this operational description. Moreover, the may testing scenario leaves some room for questions that could not be asked using a bisimulation semantics. For instance, one may ask whether it is possible to identify interesting sub-calculi of the $\pi$-calculus, making it closer to the "complete" lazy $\lambda$-calculus, enriched with convergence testing and some parallel facility. As Lavatelli shows in [12], such a calculus may be adequately encoded into the $\pi$-calculus, though the encoding is not fully abstract—and we have seen why: the $\pi$-calculus adds the possibility of creating and detecting deadlocks. Now, provided that we adopt the may testing semantics, the encoding of the $\lambda$-calculus is not very much affected by modifying the translation of abstractions, as follows:

$$\mathcal{E}[\![\lambda x M]\!]u \;=\; !u(x, v)\mathcal{E}[\![M]\!]v$$

The encoding then goes into a sub-calculus where any input prefix takes the form $!u(v_1, \ldots, v_k)P$. Actually, since the law $!P \equiv (P \mid !P)$ is still useful, it would be more convenient to adopt a different notion of reduction, namely

$$(\bar{u}\tilde{w} \mid u(\tilde{v})P) \;\rightarrow\; ([\tilde{w}/\tilde{v}]P \mid u(\tilde{v})P)$$

rather than modifying the syntax. Then one could interpret $u(v_1, \ldots, v_k)P$ as providing the "service" $P$ under the name $u$, which does not disappear once requested, while a message $\bar{u}w_1 \cdots w_k$ is a call to this service, or an application of it, with parameters $w_1, \ldots, w_k$. In this "$\pi!$-calculus" internal choice is still definable—more generally, $\pi!$ may be used as a target to encode the $\lambda$-calculus with "infinite resources" $\Lambda_{\infty r}$. Therefore one may conjecture that the bisimulation semantics induced by this encoding on $\lambda$-terms is still the equality of Lévy-Longo trees. On the other hand, one may wonder whether the may testing semantics induced on $\lambda$-terms by this kind of restricted $\pi$-calculus (we should also allow output guards, to be able to define convergence testing) differs from the canonical denotational semantics.

## References

[1] M. Abadi, L. Cardelli, P. L. Curien, and J. J. Lévy. Explicit substitutions. *Journal of Functional Programming*, 1:375–416, 1991.

[2] S. Abramsky. The Lazy Lambda Calculus. In D. Turner, editor, *Research Topics in Functional Programming*, pages 65–116. Addison-Wesley, 1989.

[3] S. Abramsky and C.-H. Luke Ong. Full abstraction in the lazy lambda calculus. *Information and Computation*, 105(2):159–267, 1993.

[4] H. P. Barendregt. *The Lambda Calculus*. North-Holland, 1985.

[5] G. Boudol. A Lambda Calculus for Parallel Functions. Technical Report 1231, INRIA Sophia-Antipolis, May 1990.

[6] G. Boudol. The lambda calculus with multiplicities. Technical Report 2025, INRIA Sophia-Antipolis, September 1993.

[7] G. Boudol. Lambda-calculi for (strict) parallel functions. *Information and Computation*, 108(1):51–127, 1994.

[8] G. Boudol and C. Laneve. Termination, deadlock and divergence in the λ-calculus with multiplicities. *Electronic Notes in Computer Science*, 1, 1995. Proceedings of the 11th Mathematical Foundations of Programming Semantics Conference.

[9] G. Boudol and C. Laneve. The discriminating power of multiplicities in the λ-calculus. *Information and Computation*, 126(1):83–102, 1996.

[10] U. Engberg and M. Nielsen. A calculus of communicating systems with label passing. Technical report, Daimi PB-208, Aarhus University, 1986.

[11] R. Hindley and G. Longo. Lambda-calculus models and extensionality. *Zeitschr. f. Math. Logik und Grundlagen d. Math.*, 26:289–310, 1980.

[12] C. Lavatelli. Non-deterministic lazy λ-calculus vs π-calculus. Technical report, LIENS-93-15, Ecole Normale Supérieure, Paris, 1993.

[13] J. J. Lévy. An algebraic interpretation of the $\lambda\beta K$-calculus; and an application of a labelled λ-calculus. *Theoretical Computer Science*, 2(1):97–114, 1976.

[14] J. J. Lévy. *Réductions Correctes et Optimales dans le Lambda Calcul*. PhD thesis, Université Paris VII, 1978.

[15] G. Longo. Set theoretical models of lambda calculus: Theories, expansions and isomorphisms. *Annals of Pure and Applied Logic*, 24:153–188, 1983.

[16] R. Milner. Fully abstract models of typed λ-calculi. *Theoretical Computer Science*, 4:1–22, 1977.

[17] R. Milner. *Communication and Concurrency*. Prentice Hall, 1989.

[18] R. Milner. Functions as processes. *Mathematical Structures in Computer Science*, 2:119–141, 1992.

[19] R. Milner. The Polyadic π-Calculus: A Tutorial. In F. Bauer, W. Brauer, and H. Schwichtenberg, editors, *Logic and Algebra of Specification*, pages 203–246. Springer Verlag, 1993.

[20] R. Milner, J. Parrow, and D. Walker. A calculus of mobile processes. *Information and Computation*, 100(1): 1–77, 1992.

[21] C.-H. Luke Ong. *The Lazy Lambda Calculus: an Investigation into the Foundations of Functional Programming*. PhD thesis, Imperial College of Science and Technology, University of London, 1988.

[22] G. Plotkin. Call-by-name, call-by-value and the λ-calculus. *Theoretical Computer Science*, 1:125–159, 1975.

[23] D. Sangiorgi. *Expressing Mobility in Process Algebras: First-Order and Higher-Order Paradigms*. PhD thesis, University of Edinburgh, 1993.

[24] D. Sangiorgi. The lazy lambda calculus in a concurrency scenario. *Information and Computation*, 120(1): 120–153, 1994.

[25] D. Sangiorgi. Lazy functions and mobile processes. This Volume, 1999.

[26] C. Wadsworth. The relation between computational and denotational properties for Scott $D_\infty$-model of the lambda-calculus. *SIAM Journal on Computing*, 5:488–521, 1976.

# 24 Lazy Functions and Mobile Processes

**Davide Sangiorgi**

## 1 Introduction

In [20] Milner examines the encoding of the $\lambda$-calculus into the $\pi$-calculus [22]; the former is the universally accepted basis for computations with *functions*, the latter aims at being its counterpart for computations with *processes*. More precisely, Milner shows how the evaluation strategies of the *lazy $\lambda$-calculus* and of (a weak form of) *call-by-value $\lambda$-calculus* [1, 25] can be faithfully mimicked. The characterisation of the equivalence induced on $\lambda$-terms by the encodings is left as an open problem. It also remains to be studied which kind of $\lambda$-calculus model—if any—can be constructed from the process terms. These are the main questions tackled in this paper.

A deep comparison between a process calculus and the $\lambda$-calculus is interesting for several reasons; indeed, virtually all proposals for process calculi with the capability of treating—directly or indirectly—processes as first class objects have incorporated attempts at embedding the $\lambda$-calculus. From the process calculus point of view, it is a significant test of expressiveness, and helps in getting deeper insight into its theory. From the $\lambda$-calculus point of view, it provides the means to study $\lambda$-terms in contexts other than purely sequential ones, and with the instruments available in the process calculus. For example, an important behavioural equivalence upon process terms gives rise to an interesting equivalence upon $\lambda$-terms. Moreover, the relevance of those $\lambda$-calculus evaluation strategies which can be efficiently encoded is strengthened. More practical motivations for describing functions as processes are to provide a semantic foundation for languages which combine concurrent and functional programming and to develop parallel implementations of functional languages.

We shall focus on Milner's lazy $\lambda$-calculus encoding. This is the simplest encoding of the $\lambda$-calculus into the $\pi$-calculus we are aware of. It also seems "canonical" in the sense of being the "natural" encoding of the lazy strategy. (By contrast, a few variants of the call-by-value strategy have been considered—two of them in Milner's original paper [20]—and it is not clear which one should be preferred.) Below, Milner's encoding of the lazy $\lambda$-calculus is simply called "Milner's encoding".

The lazy $\lambda$-calculus was proposed by Abramsky[1] and motivated by the practice of functional programming implementations; thus, for instance, reductions inside abstractions are forbidden. Abramsky also equipped the lazy $\lambda$-terms with a notion of operational equivalence, called *applicative bisimulation*, which follows the bisimulation idea originally formulated by Park and Milner in concurrency theory.

[1] On closed $\lambda$-terms, Abramsky's lazy strategy coincides with Plotkin's *call-by-name* strategy [25].

Briefly, our programme is the following. We begin by examining the operational correspondence between source and target terms of Milner's encoding. We then use the encoding to construct a $\lambda$-*model* from the $\pi$-calculus processes. The equality on $\lambda$-terms induced by the model is the same as that induced, via the encoding, by the behavioural equality adopted on the $\pi$-calculus. In accordance with the theory of the lazy $\lambda$-calculus, the model validates a conditional form of extensionality. However, the model is not fully abstract. Not surprisingly so: $\pi$-calculus is richer — and hence more discriminating—than the $\lambda$-calculus; the latter is purely sequential, whereas the former can also express parallelism and non-determinism. To obtain *full abstraction*[2], we strengthen the operational equivalence on $\lambda$-terms. This is achieved using a refinement of applicative bisimulation. The resulting relation, called *open applicative bisimulation*, is perhaps the simplest extension of applicative bisimulation to open terms; it can be easily shown to coincide with the equality determined by *Lévy-Longo Trees*, the lazy variant of *Böhm Trees*.

Open applicative bisimulation has also been studied in [29]; the results in [29] show how to achieve the same discrimination by remaining with closed terms but enriching the $\lambda$-calculus with operators, that is symbols equipped with reduction rules describing their behaviour.

This paper is an improved version of part of the author's PhD thesis [27] (from which we extracted the extended abstract [28]). The proofs are different: In [27], Milner's encoding was factorised through an encoding into the *Higher-Order $\pi$-calculus* (HO$\pi$), an extension of the $\pi$-calculus with higher-order features like term-passing, and then all work was carried out from within HO$\pi$. The advantage of HO$\pi$ is that the encoding of the $\lambda$-calculus is easier. In this paper, however, we work within the $\pi$-calculus, because it is a more primitive calculus and because recent results about its theory allow us to have tractable proofs, indeed similar to those one would need in HO$\pi$. Some of the theory of the $\pi$-calculus is further developed in this paper: For instance, we prove that *ground bisimulation*, a form of bisimulation where no name instantiation on input actions is required, is a congruence relation on a $\pi$-calculus sublanguage similar to those proposed by Boudol [5], Honda and Tokoro [14]. An immediate consequence is that various $\pi$-calculus bisimilarity equivalences (ground, late, early, open) coincide on this sublanguage. (Similar results have been independently obtained by Hansen, Hüttel and Kleist [10].)

Another difference with [27] is that, there, the $\lambda$-calculus had to be enriched with symbols called *constants* in order to prove full abstraction for the $\lambda$-model. In this paper, we shall be able to avoid constants; thus the statement of the results is simpler and the correspondence with the Lévy-Longo Tree equality more direct.

[2] The term "full abstraction" is due to Milner [19] and Plotkin [26].

The paper is self-contained, but some familiarity with the $\pi$-calculus would be useful. We introduce the part of $\pi$-calculus sufficient for the encoding of the lazy $\lambda$-calculus in Section 2. The theory of this calculus we shall need is introduced in Section 3. In Section 4 we review the lazy $\lambda$-calculus and Milner's encoding. In Section 5 we examine the operational correspondence between source and target terms of the encoding. In Section 6 we define the $\lambda$-model and present some properties of it. In Section 7 we study full abstraction of the model.

## 2 The Mini $\pi$-Calculus

Throughout the paper, $\mathcal{R}$ ranges over relations. The composition of two relations $\mathcal{R}$ and $\mathcal{R}'$ is written $\mathcal{R}\,\mathcal{R}'$. We often use infix notation for relations; thus $P\mathcal{R}Q$ means $(P, Q) \in \mathcal{R}$. A tilde represents a tuple. The $i$-th elements of a tuple $\tilde{E}$ is referred to as $E_i$. Our notations are extended to tuples componentwise. Thus $\tilde{P}\mathcal{R}\tilde{Q}$ means $P_i\mathcal{R}Q_i$ for all components.

### 2.1 Syntax

Small letters $a, b, \ldots, x, y, \ldots$ range over the infinite set of names, and $P, Q, R, \ldots$ over the set $\mathcal{P}r$ of processes. The part of the polyadic $\pi$-calculus [21] we shall use, which we shall refer to as the *mini $\pi$-calculus*, is built from the operators of inaction, input prefix, output, parallel composition, restriction, and replication:

$$P := \mathbf{0} \mid a(\tilde{b}).\, P \mid \bar{a}\langle\tilde{b}\rangle \mid P_1 \mid P_2 \mid \nu\, a\, P \mid\ !\, P.$$

When the tilde is empty, the surrounding brackets () and $\langle\rangle$ will be omitted. $\mathbf{0}$ is the inactive process. An input-prefixed process $a(\tilde{b}).\, P$, where $\tilde{b}$ has pairwise distinct components, waits for a tuple of names $\tilde{c}$ to be sent along $a$ and then behaves like $P\{\tilde{c}/\tilde{b}\}$, where $\{\tilde{c}/\tilde{b}\}$ is the simultaneous substitution of names $\tilde{b}$ with names $\tilde{c}$. An output particle $\bar{a}\langle\tilde{b}\rangle$ emits names $\tilde{b}$ at $a$. Parallel composition is to run two processes in parallel. The restriction $\nu\, a\, P$ makes name $a$ local, or private, to $P$. A replication $!\, P$ stands for a countable infinite number of copies of $P$ in parallel. If $I = \{i_1, \ldots, i_n\}$, then $\Pi_{i\in I} P_i$ abbreviates $P_{i_1} \mid \ldots \mid P_{i_n}$. We assign parallel composition the lowest precedence among the operators.

The most notable features of this language w.r.t. other formulations of the polyadic $\pi$-calculus are the absence of the sum and of the match operators (usually written $P + Q$ and $[a = b]P$, respectively), and the limited form of output guarding available, with a null continuation. We chose this language because it has some useful algebraic properties, some of which are reported in Section 3. Similar languages have been studied by Honda and Tokoro [14], who call the language *$\nu$-calculus*, and Boudol [5], who calls it *asynchronous*

$\pi$*-calculus*—appropriately so, since the emission of a message does not impose any sequencing constraints. The languages in [14] and [5], however, only allow *monadic* communications.

## 2.2 Terminologies and Notations

In prefixes $a(\tilde{b})$ and $\bar{a}\langle\tilde{b}\rangle$, we call $a$ the *subject* and $\tilde{b}$ the *object*. We use $\alpha$ to range over prefixes. We often abbreviate $\alpha.\mathbf{0}$ as $\alpha$, and $\boldsymbol{\nu}\, a\, \boldsymbol{\nu}\, b\, P$ as $\boldsymbol{\nu}\, a, b\, P$. An input prefix $a(\tilde{b}).P$ and a restriction $\boldsymbol{\nu}\, b\, P$ are binders for names $\tilde{b}$ and $b$, respectively, and give rise in the expected way to the definition of *free names* (fn), *bound names* (bn) and *names* (n) of a term or a prefix, and *alpha conversion*. Substitutions are of the form $\{\tilde{b}/\tilde{c}\}$, and are finite assignments of names to names. We use $\sigma$ and $\rho$ to range over substitutions. If $\sigma = \{\tilde{b}/\tilde{c}\}$, then $\sigma(a)$ is $b_i$ if $a = c_i$, and $a$ if $a \notin \tilde{c}$. The application of a substitution $\sigma$ to an expression $E$ is written $E\sigma$. Substitutions have precedence over the operators of the language; $\sigma\rho$ is the composition of substitutions where $\sigma$ is performed first, therefore $P\sigma\rho$ is $(P\sigma)\rho$.

A context is a process expression with holes. There can be an arbitrary, but finite, number of different holes $[\cdot]_1, \ldots, [\cdot]_n$ in a context, and each of these holes may appear more than once. If $C$ contains at most holes $[\cdot]_1, \ldots, [\cdot]_n$, then we say that $C$ is an $n$-ary context, and if $\tilde{P}$ is a vector of $n$ processes, then $C[\tilde{P}]$ is the process obtained by replacing each occurrence of the hole $[\cdot]_i$ with the $i$-th component of $\tilde{P}$.

Throughout the paper, we allow ourselves some freedom in the use of alpha conversion on names; thus we assume that the application of a substitution does not affected bound names of expressions (so, for all $\sigma$, we have $(\boldsymbol{\nu}\, b\, P)\sigma = \boldsymbol{\nu}\, b\,(P\sigma)$ and, if $\sigma(a) = c$, $(a(\tilde{b}).\, P)\sigma = c(\tilde{b}).\,(P\sigma)$); similarly when comparing the transitions of two processes we assume that the bound names of the transitions do not occur free in the processes. In a statement, we say that a name is *fresh* to mean that it is different from any other name which occurs in the statement or in objects of the statement like processes and substitutions.

## 2.3 Sorting

Following Milner [21], we only admit *well-sorted agents*, that is agents which obey a predefined *sorting* discipline in their manipulation of names. The sorting prevents arity mismatching in communications, like in $\bar{a}\langle b, c\rangle \mid a(x).Q$. A sorting is an assignment of *sorts* to names, which specifies the arity of each name and, recursively, of the names carried by that name. We write $a : s$ if name $a$ has sort $s$. We do not present the formal system of sorting because it is not essential in the exposition of the topics in the present paper.

**Table 24.1**
The transition system for the mini-$\pi$-calculus

$$\texttt{inp}: a(\tilde b)\cdot P \xrightarrow{a(\tilde b)} P \qquad \texttt{out}: \bar a\langle\tilde b\rangle \xrightarrow{a\langle\tilde b\rangle} \mathbf{0}$$

$$\texttt{rep}: \frac{P|!P \xrightarrow{\mu} P'}{!P \xrightarrow{\mu} P'} \qquad \texttt{par}: \frac{P \xrightarrow{\mu} P'}{P|Q \xrightarrow{\mu} P'|Q} \text{ if } \mathrm{bn}(\mu)\cap\mathrm{fn}(Q)=\emptyset$$

$$\texttt{com}: \frac{P \xrightarrow{a(\tilde c)} P' \qquad Q \xrightarrow{(\nu\tilde d)\bar a\langle\tilde b\rangle} Q'}{P|Q \xrightarrow{\tau} \nu\tilde d(P'\{\tilde b/\tilde c\}|Q')} \text{ if } \tilde d\cap\mathrm{fn}(P)=\emptyset$$

$$\texttt{res}: \frac{P \xrightarrow{\mu} P'}{\nu a P \xrightarrow{\mu} \nu a P'} a\notin \mathrm{n}(\mu) \qquad \texttt{open}: \frac{P \xrightarrow{(\nu\tilde d)\bar a\langle\tilde b\rangle} P'}{\nu c P \xrightarrow{(\nu c,\tilde d)\bar a\langle\tilde b\rangle} P'} c\in\tilde b-\tilde d,\ a\neq c.$$

## 2.4 Transition System and Bisimulation

The transition system of the calculus is presented in Table 24.1. We have omitted the symmetric versions of rules `par` and `com`. Alpha convertible processes have deemed to have the same transitions. We use $\mu$ to range over actions. Bound names, free names and names of an action $\mu$ are written $\mathrm{bn}(\mu)$, $\mathrm{fn}(\mu)$ and $\mathrm{n}(\mu)$, respectively. An output action without bound names is a *free output*. We often abbreviate $P \xrightarrow{\tau} Q$ with $P \longrightarrow Q$, and write $P \xrightarrow{\hat\mu} Q$ to mean $P \xrightarrow{\mu} Q$ if $\mu\neq\tau$, and $P = Q$ or $P \xrightarrow{\tau} Q$ if $\mu=\tau$. The 'weak' arrow $\Longrightarrow$ is the reflexive and transitive closure of $\longrightarrow$, and $\xRightarrow{\mu}$ is $\Longrightarrow\xrightarrow{\mu}\Longrightarrow$; moreover, $P \xRightarrow{\hat\mu} Q$ means $P \xRightarrow{\mu} Q$ if $\mu\neq\tau$, and $P \Longrightarrow Q$ if $\mu=\tau$.

DEFINITION 2.1 (STRONG AND WEAK GROUND BISIMILARITY) A symmetric relation $\mathcal{R}\subseteq \mathcal{P}r\times\mathcal{P}r$ is a *strong ground bisimulation* if $P\mathcal{R}Q$ and $P \xrightarrow{\mu} P'$ imply that there exists $Q'$ s.t. $Q \xrightarrow{\mu} Q'$ and $P'\mathcal{R}Q'$. Two processes $P$ and $Q$ are *strongly ground bisimilar*, written $P\sim Q$, if $P\mathcal{R}Q$ for some strong bisimulation $\mathcal{R}$. The weak versions of the relations (*weak ground bisimulation, weak ground bisimilarity*) are defined in the usual way—just replace $Q \xrightarrow{\mu} Q'$ with $Q \xRightarrow{\hat\mu} Q'$. We indicate weak ground bisimilarity as $\approx$, and sometime we call it *observational equivalence*.

In the definition above[3], no name instantiation is required in the clause for input actions. Therefore, for instance, to check whether two processes $a(\tilde b).\ P$ and $a(\tilde b).\ Q$ are equivalent, we do not have to examine all possible instantiations of names $\tilde b$ in $P$ and $Q$, but it suffices to check that $P$ and $Q$ alone are equivalent. Surprisingly enough, in the mini $\pi$-calculus these forms of bisimilarity are preserved by name instantiations and are congruence relations

[3] We use the adjective ground to emphasize the absence of name instantiations. The terminology ground equivalence was used in [22], pp 28, with quite a different meaning.

(Section 3). The fact that the meaning of agents can be captured without considering more than one instance of an input is an important and useful property in equivalence and model checking, sometimes is called *data-independence* [15].

Observational equivalence is the semantic equality on the $\pi$-calculus we are mainly interested in; other relations, like strong bisimilarity and expansion, will serve as auxiliary to it.

## 3 Some Properties of Bisimilarity on the Mini $\pi$-Calculus

### 3.1 Congruence

In this section, $\sim_{\rm L}$ denotes the original bisimilarity of the $\pi$-calculus [22], defined as ground bisimilarity but with the following clause for input actions:

"$P \stackrel{a(\tilde{b})}{\longrightarrow} P'$ imply that there exists $Q'$ s.t. $Q \stackrel{a(\tilde{b})}{\longrightarrow} Q'$ and for all $\tilde{c}$, $P'\{\tilde{c}/\tilde{b}\}\mathcal{R}Q'\{\tilde{c}/\tilde{b}\}$."

Both strong and weak ground bisimilarity (Definition 2.1) are preserved by all operators of the language. We only show the argument for weak bisimilarity, whose case is more delicate. Our proof refines, and is inspired by, an idea by Honda, who proved a similar congruence result for the $\nu$-calculus [13]. However, Honda's definition of bisimilarity is not purely ground, since name instantiation is contemplated in the input clause (technically speaking, Honda allows *free input* actions); this makes the congruence w.r.t. parallel composition straightforward. Indeed, Honda's bisimilarity is a variant of the standard bisimilarity $\sim_{\rm L}$. Moreover, Honda's transition system incorporates certain structural laws, which can then be applied in all contexts independently of the behavioural equivalence adopted.

The crux of the congruence argument is to show that ground bisimilarity is preserved by name instantiation. (Proposition 3.5).

LEMMA 3.1 If $P \stackrel{(\nu \tilde{d})\, \bar{a}\langle\tilde{b}\rangle}{\longrightarrow} P'$, then $P \sim_{\rm L} \nu\, \tilde{d}\, (\bar{a}\langle\tilde{b}\rangle \mid P')$.

*Proof* By transition induction. We only need simple algebraic laws for $\sim_{\rm L}$, like congruence w.r.t. parallel composition. □

LEMMA 3.2 If $P \stackrel{(\nu \tilde{d})\, \bar{a}\langle\tilde{b}\rangle}{\Longrightarrow} P_1 \stackrel{a(\tilde{e})}{\Longrightarrow} P_2$, then $P \Longrightarrow\sim_{\rm L} \nu\, \tilde{d}\, (P_2\{\tilde{b}/\tilde{e}\})$.

*Proof* If $P \stackrel{(\nu \tilde{d})\, \bar{a}\langle\tilde{b}\rangle}{\Longrightarrow} P_1$, then there are $P_1'$ and $P_1''$ s.t. $P \Longrightarrow P_1' \stackrel{(\nu \tilde{d})\, \bar{a}\langle\tilde{b}\rangle}{\longrightarrow} P_1'' \Longrightarrow P_1$. By Lemma 3.1,

$$P_1' \sim_{\rm L} \nu\, \tilde{d}\, (\bar{a}\langle\tilde{b}\rangle \mid P_1'') \,. \qquad (1)$$

Since $P_1'' \stackrel{a(\tilde{e})}{\Longrightarrow} P_2$, we have $\nu\,\tilde{d}\,(\bar{a}\langle\tilde{b}\rangle \mid P_1'') \Longrightarrow \nu\,\tilde{d}\,(P_2\{\tilde{b}/\tilde{e}\})$; hence, by (1), also $P_1' \Longrightarrow\sim_{\mathrm{L}} \nu\,\tilde{d}\,(P_2\{\tilde{b}/\tilde{e}\})$. From this and $P \Longrightarrow P_1'$, we get $P \Longrightarrow\sim_{\mathrm{L}} \nu\,\tilde{d}\,(P_2\{\tilde{b}/\tilde{e}\})$. □

LEMMA 3.3

1. If $P \stackrel{\mu}{\longrightarrow} P'$, then $P\sigma \stackrel{\mu\sigma}{\longrightarrow} P'\sigma$;
2. If $P \stackrel{\mu}{\Longrightarrow} P'$, then $P\sigma \stackrel{\mu\sigma}{\Longrightarrow} P'\sigma$.

LEMMA 3.4

1. If $P\sigma \stackrel{\mu'}{\longrightarrow} P'$ with $\mu' \neq \tau$, then $P \stackrel{\mu}{\longrightarrow} P''$ with $\mu' = \mu\sigma$ and $P' = P''\sigma$.
2. If $P\sigma \longrightarrow P'$ then either
   (a) $P \longrightarrow P''$ and $P' = P''\sigma$, or
   (b) $P \stackrel{(\nu\,\tilde{d})\,\bar{a}\langle\tilde{b}\rangle}{\longrightarrow} \stackrel{c(\tilde{e})}{\longrightarrow} P''$ with $\sigma(a) = \sigma(c)$ and $P' \sim_{\mathrm{L}} \nu\,\tilde{d}\,(P''\{\tilde{b}/\tilde{e}\}\sigma)$.

*Proof* Another transition induction. We only show the details for assertion (2), in the case when the last rule used is com. Then $P = P_1 \mid P_2$ and $P\sigma = P_1\sigma \mid P_2\sigma$. Moreover, the last step in the derivation of $P\sigma \longrightarrow P'$ is of the form

$$\frac{P_1\sigma \stackrel{x(\tilde{e})}{\longrightarrow} P_1' \qquad P_2\sigma \stackrel{(\nu\,\tilde{d})\,\bar{x}\langle\tilde{z}\rangle}{\longrightarrow} P_2'}{P_1\sigma \mid P_2\sigma \longrightarrow \nu\,\tilde{d}\,(P_1'\{\tilde{z}/\tilde{e}\} \mid P_2')}.$$

By assertion (1), there are $a, c, \tilde{b}, P_1''$ and $P_2''$ s.t.

$$P_1 \stackrel{c(\tilde{e})}{\longrightarrow} P_1'' \qquad \text{and} \qquad P_2 \stackrel{(\nu\,\tilde{d})\,\bar{a}\langle\tilde{b}\rangle}{\longrightarrow} P_2''$$

with $\sigma(a) = \sigma(c) = x$, $\sigma(\tilde{b}) = \tilde{z}$, $P_1''\sigma = P_1'$ and $P_2''\sigma = P_2'$. If $a = c$, then we can infer

$$P_1 \mid P_2 \longrightarrow \nu\,\tilde{d}\,(P_1''\{\tilde{b}/\tilde{e}\} \mid P_2'') \stackrel{\mathrm{def}}{=} P''$$

and we have $P''\sigma = P'$, as by assertion (2.a). If $a \neq c$, then we have

$$P_1 \mid P_2 \stackrel{(\nu\,\tilde{d})\,\bar{a}\langle\tilde{b}\rangle}{\longrightarrow} P_1 \mid P_2'' \stackrel{c(\tilde{e})}{\longrightarrow} P_1'' \mid P_2'' \stackrel{\mathrm{def}}{=} P''$$

and $\nu\,\tilde{d}\,(P''\{\tilde{b}/\tilde{e}\}\sigma) = \nu\,\tilde{d}\,(P_1''\{\tilde{b}/\tilde{e}\}\sigma \mid P_2''\sigma) = P'\sigma$, as by assertion (2.b). □

In the two proofs below, a symmetric relation $\mathcal{R}$ is a *weak ground bisimulation up to restriction and up to* $\sim$ if $P\mathcal{R}Q$ and $P \stackrel{\mu}{\longrightarrow} P''$ imply that there exist $\tilde{d}$, $P'$ and $Q'$ s.t. $P'' \sim \nu\,\tilde{d}\,P'$, $Q \stackrel{\hat{\mu}}{\Longrightarrow}\sim \nu\,\tilde{d}\,Q'$ and $P'\mathcal{R}Q'$. A standard argument shows that if $\mathcal{R}$ is a weak ground bisimulation up to restriction and up to $\sim$ then $\mathcal{R} \subseteq \approx$.

PROPOSITION 3.5 (INSENSITIVITY OF $\approx$ TO NAME INSTANTIATIONS) $P \approx Q$ implies $P\sigma \approx Q\sigma$.

*Proof* We show that

$$\mathcal{R} = \{(P\sigma, Q\sigma) \ : \ P \approx Q\}$$

is a weak ground bisimulation up to restriction and up to $\sim$. Suppose $P\sigma \stackrel{\mu'}{\longrightarrow} P''$. We have to find $\tilde{d}$, $P'$ and $Q'$ s.t.

$$P'' \sim \nu\, \tilde{d}\, P', \qquad Q\sigma \stackrel{\widehat{\mu'}}{\Longrightarrow}\sim \nu\, \tilde{d}\, Q' \qquad \text{and} \qquad P' \mathcal{R} Q'. \tag{2}$$

We distinguish the case when $\mu' \neq \tau$ and $\mu' = \tau$. If $\mu' \neq \tau$, then, by Lemma 3.4(1), $P \stackrel{\mu}{\longrightarrow} P_1$ with $\mu' = \mu\sigma$ and $P'' = P_1\sigma$. Since $P \approx Q$, we have $Q \stackrel{\mu}{\Longrightarrow} Q_1$ with $P_1 \approx Q_1$. Now, by Lemma 3.3, we have $Q\sigma \stackrel{\mu\sigma}{\Longrightarrow} Q_1\sigma$; for $\tilde{d} = \emptyset$, $P' \stackrel{\text{def}}{=} P''$ and $Q' \stackrel{\text{def}}{=} Q_1\sigma$ this proves (2).

Now, suppose $\mu' = \tau$. According to Lemma 3.4(2), there are two subcases to consider. In the first, we have $P \longrightarrow P_1$ and $P'' = P_1\sigma$; this can be handled as the case $\mu' \neq \tau$ above. In the other subcase, we have $P \stackrel{(\nu\, \tilde{d})\, \bar{a}\langle \tilde{b}\rangle}{\longrightarrow} P_1 \stackrel{c(\tilde{e})}{\longrightarrow} P_2$ with $\sigma(a) = \sigma(c)$ and $P'' \sim_{\mathrm{L}} \nu\, \tilde{d}\, (P_2\{^{\tilde{b}}/_{\tilde{e}}\}\sigma)$; since $\sim_{\mathrm{L}} \subseteq \sim$, also $P'' \sim \nu\, \tilde{d}\, (P_2\{^{\tilde{b}}/_{\tilde{e}}\}\sigma)$. Since $P \approx Q$, we have $Q \stackrel{(\nu\, \tilde{d})\, \bar{a}\langle \tilde{b}\rangle}{\Longrightarrow} Q_1 \stackrel{c(\tilde{e})}{\Longrightarrow} Q_2$ with $P_2 \approx Q_2$. Let $x = \sigma(a)$ and $\tilde{z} = \sigma(\tilde{b})$; by Lemma 3.3, we also have $Q\sigma \stackrel{(\nu\, \tilde{d})\, \bar{x}\langle \tilde{z}\rangle}{\Longrightarrow} Q_1\sigma \stackrel{x(\tilde{e})}{\Longrightarrow} Q_2\sigma$. Finally, by Lemmas 3.2 and the inclusion $\sim_{\mathrm{L}} \subseteq \sim$, $Q\sigma \Longrightarrow\sim \nu\, \tilde{d}\, (Q_2\sigma\{^{\tilde{z}}/_{\tilde{e}}\}) = \nu\, \tilde{d}\, (Q_2\{^{\tilde{b}}/_{\tilde{e}}\}\sigma)$. For $P' \stackrel{\text{def}}{=} P_2\{^{\tilde{b}}/_{\tilde{e}}\}\sigma$ and $Q' \stackrel{\text{def}}{=} Q_2\{^{\tilde{b}}/_{\tilde{e}}\}\sigma$, this proves (2). □

COROLLARY 3.6 (CONGRUENCE OF $\approx$) $P \approx Q$ implies:

1. $P \mid R \approx Q \mid R$;
2. $a(\tilde{b}).\, P \approx a(\tilde{b}).\, Q$;
3. $!\, P \approx\, !\, Q$;
4. $\nu\, b\, P \approx \nu\, b\, Q$.

*Proof* By exhibiting the appropriate bisimulation relations. We only sketch the argument for assertion (1). We take the set of all pairs of the form $(P \mid R, Q \mid R)$, with $P \approx Q$, and prove that this is a weak ground bisimulation up to restriction. The most interesting case to look at is how $Q \mid R$ can match an interaction between $P$ and $R$ where $P$ performs the input. Thus, suppose $P \mid R \longrightarrow \nu\, \tilde{d}\, (P'\{^{\tilde{b}}/_{\tilde{e}}\} \mid R')$, for some $P'$ and $R'$ s.t. $P \stackrel{a(\tilde{e})}{\longrightarrow} P'$ and $R \stackrel{(\nu\, \tilde{d})\, \bar{a}\langle \tilde{b}\rangle}{\longrightarrow} R'$. Since $P \approx Q$, there is $Q'$ s.t. $Q \stackrel{a(\tilde{e})}{\Longrightarrow} Q' \approx P'$. Hence $Q \mid R \Longrightarrow \nu\, \tilde{d}\, (Q'\{^{\tilde{b}}/_{\tilde{e}}\} \mid R')$. Since, by Proposition 3.5, $\approx$ is preserved by substitutions, we have $P'\{^{\tilde{b}}/_{\tilde{e}}\} \approx Q'\{^{\tilde{b}}/_{\tilde{e}}\}$. This is enough, because $\mathcal{R}$ is a bisimulation up to restriction. □

Let $\approx_{\rm L}$ be the weak version of $\sim_{\rm L}$, defined using the weak arrow $\stackrel{\hat{\mu}}{\Longrightarrow}$ in the usual way. This is the weak bisimilarity proposed in [22].

COROLLARY 3.7 The relations $\approx_{\rm L}$ and $\approx$ coincide.

*Proof* For the containment $\approx_{\rm L} \subseteq \approx$, one shows that $\approx_{\rm L}$ is a weak ground bisimulation; the opposite containment can be established similarly, if one uses the fact that $\approx$ is closed under substitutions. □

In $\pi$-calculus literature, the relations $\sim_{\rm L}$ and $\approx_{\rm L}$ are sometimes called *late* bisimilarities, to distinguish them from other formulations of bisimilarity like the *early* and *open* ones (see [9]); these differ from the former because name instantiation is used in a different position in the bisimilarity clauses. An argument similar to that in Corollary 3.7 shows that *in the mini $\pi$-calculus ground bisimilarity also coincides with early and open bisimilarities.* In view of these results, in the remainder of the paper ground bisimulation will be simply called *bisimulation*. These results stand in contrast with what happens in the full $\pi$-calculus, where ground bisimulation, open bisimulation, late bisimulation and congruence, early bisimulation and congruence are all different relations. (In the full $\pi$-calculus, the congruence induced by ground bisimulation coincides with early congruence; this because ground bisimulation is in between barbed bisimulation [23, 27] and early bisimulation, whose induced congruence coincide [27].)

## 3.2 Proof Techniques

For the proof of one of the main results in the paper, namely Theorem 7.14, we shall use a proof technique for bisimulation in order to reduce the size of the relation to exhibit. In the bisimilarity clause, this technique allows us to manipulate the derivatives of two processes with the *expansion relation* and to cancel a common context. It extends a technique in [30] where contexts can only be monadic and static (i.e., they can only be of the form $\boldsymbol{\nu}\,\tilde{b}\,(P \mid [\cdot])$). The expansion relation [3, 31], written $\lesssim$, is an asymmetric variant of $\approx$ which takes into account the number of $\tau$-actions performed by processes. Thus, $P \lesssim Q$ holds if $P \approx Q$ and $Q$ has at least as many $\tau$-moves as $P$.

DEFINITION 3.8 (EXPANSION) A relation $\mathcal{R} \subseteq \mathcal{P}r \times \mathcal{P}r$ is an *expansion* if $P \mathcal{R} Q$ implies:

1. Whenever $P \stackrel{\mu}{\longrightarrow} P'$, there exists $Q'$ s.t. $Q \stackrel{\mu}{\Longrightarrow} Q'$ and $P' \mathcal{R} Q'$;
2. whenever $Q \stackrel{\mu}{\longrightarrow} Q'$, there exists $P'$ s.t. $P \stackrel{\hat{\mu}}{\longrightarrow} P'$ and $P' \mathcal{R} Q'$.

We say that $Q$ *expands* $P$, written $P \lesssim Q$, if $P \mathcal{R} Q$, for some expansion $\mathcal{R}$.

The relation $\lesssim$ is a preorder and enjoys the same congruence properties as $\approx$, including the closure w.r.t. substitutions. The following is a chain of strict inclusions: $\sim \subset \lesssim \subset \approx$.

DEFINITION 3.9 A symmetric relation $\mathcal{R}$ is a *weak bisimulation up-to context and up-to* $\gtrsim$ if $P \mathcal{R} Q$ and $P \xrightarrow{\mu} P''$ imply that there are a context $C$ and processes $\tilde{P}'$ and $\tilde{Q}'$ s.t. $P'' \gtrsim C[\tilde{P}']$, $Q \stackrel{\hat{\mu}}{\Longrightarrow} \gtrsim C[\tilde{Q}']$ and $\tilde{P}' \mathcal{R} \tilde{Q}'$. A relation $\mathcal{R}$ is *closed under substitutions* if $(P, Q) \in \mathcal{R}$ implies $(P\sigma, Q\sigma) \in \mathcal{R}$, for all substitution $\sigma$.

LEMMA 3.10 Suppose that $\mathcal{R}$ is is closed under substitutions and is a weak bisimulation up-to context and up-to $\gtrsim$. If $(\tilde{P}, \tilde{Q}) \in \mathcal{R}$ and $C[\tilde{P}] \xrightarrow{\mu} P'$, then there are a context $C'$ and processes $\tilde{P}'$ and $\tilde{Q}'$ s.t. $P' \gtrsim C'[\tilde{P}']$, $C[Q] \stackrel{\hat{\mu}}{\Longrightarrow} \gtrsim C'[\tilde{Q}']$ and $\tilde{P}' \mathcal{R} \tilde{Q}'$.

*Proof* Proceeding by induction on the structure of $C$. □

THEOREM 3.11 If $\mathcal{R}$ is is closed under substitutions and is a weak bisimulation up-to context and up-to $\gtrsim$, then $\mathcal{R} \subseteq \approx$.

*Proof* We use the previous lemma to show that this relation is a weak bisimulation:

$$\{(P, Q) : \text{ for some context } C \text{ and processes } \tilde{P}, \tilde{Q} \text{ it holds that } P \gtrsim C[\tilde{P}],\ Q \gtrsim C[\tilde{Q}] \text{ and } \tilde{P} \mathcal{R} \tilde{Q}\ \}$$ □

It is possible that, in the mini $\pi$-calculus, the closure-under-substitutions hypothesis of Theorem 3.11 is not necessary. With this hypothesis, the proof of the theorem is similar to that of Theorem 3.8 in [30].

### 3.3 Some Laws for Bisimilarity

For ease of reference, in this section we have collected some simple laws for bisimilarity which we shall apply several times in the paper. First, two laws for restriction and parallel composition:

**L1:** $\nu a\, (P \mid Q) \sim P \mid \nu a\, Q$, if $a \notin \mathrm{fn}(P)$;

**L2:** $\nu a\, (a(\tilde{e}).\, P \mid \bar{a}\langle \tilde{b} \rangle.\, Q) \gtrsim \nu a\, (P\{\tilde{b}/\tilde{e}\} \mid Q)$.

Next, we report some distributivity laws for private replications, i.e., for systems of the form

$$\nu y\, (P \mid\ !\, y(\tilde{q}).\, Q)$$

in which $y$ may occur free in $P$ and $Q$ only in output subject position. One should think of $Q$ as a private resource of $P$, for $P$ is the only process who can access $Q$; indeed $P$ can activate as many copies of $Q$ as needed.

LEMMA 3.12 Suppose $a$ occurs free in $P$, $R$, $Q$ only in output subject position. Then:

1. $\nu a\,(P \mid R \mid\, !a(\tilde{b}).\,Q) \sim \nu a\,(P \mid\, !a(\tilde{b}).\,Q) \mid \nu a\,(R \mid\, !a(\tilde{b}).\,Q)$;
2. $\nu a\,((!\,P) \mid\, !a(\tilde{b}).\,Q) \sim\ !\nu a\,(P \mid\, !a(\tilde{b}).\,Q)$;
3. $\nu a\,(\alpha.\,P \mid\, !a(\tilde{b}).\,Q) \sim \alpha.\,\nu a\,(P \mid\, !a(\tilde{b}).\,Q)$, if $\mathrm{bn}(\alpha) \cap \mathrm{fn}(a(\tilde{b}).\,Q) = \emptyset$ and $a \notin \mathrm{n}(\alpha)$;
4. $\nu a\,((\nu c\, P) \mid\, !a(\tilde{b}).\,Q) \sim \nu c\,\nu a\,(P \mid\, !a(\tilde{b}).\,Q)$ if $c \notin \mathrm{fn}(a(\tilde{b}).\,Q)$;
5. $\nu a\,(P \mid\, !a(\tilde{b}).\,Q) \sim P$, if $a \notin \mathrm{fn}(P)$;
6. $\nu a\,(\bar{a}\langle\tilde{d}\rangle \mid\, !a(\tilde{b}).\,Q) \gtrsim Q\{^{\tilde{d}}/_{\tilde{b}}\}$, if $a \notin \mathrm{fn}(Q\{^{\tilde{d}}/_{\tilde{b}}\})$.

*Proof* Assertions (3–6) are easy. Assertions (1) and (2) have been first proved by Milner (see [21]) by exhibiting appropriate strong bisimulations (Milner proved the result for $\sim_{\mathrm{L}}$ that, in the mini $\pi$-calculus, coincides with $\sim$). □

### 3.4 Abstractions

In Milner's encoding of the lazy $\lambda$-calculus into the $\pi$-calculus, described in the next section, the encoding of a $\lambda$-term is parametric on a name, that is, is a function from names to $\pi$-calculus processes. We call such expressions *abstractions*. For the purposes of this paper unary abstractions, i.e., with only one parameter, suffice. An abstraction with parameter $a$ and body $P$ is written $(a)\,P$, and is a binder for $a$ of the same nature as the input prefix binder $b(a).\,P$. If $F \stackrel{\mathrm{def}}{=} (a)\,P$, then $F\langle b\rangle$, called *application*, abbreviates $P\{^b/_a\}$—the actual parameter $b$ substitutes the formal parameter $a$ in the body of $F$. Application has the same syntactic precedence as substitution (i.e., the highest), whereas abstraction has the lowest precedence; thus $(a)\,\alpha_1.\,(F_1\langle q\rangle\sigma \mid \alpha_2.\,F_2\langle r\rangle)$ means $(a)\,((\alpha_1.\,((F\langle q\rangle)\sigma)) \mid \alpha_2.\,(F_2\langle r\rangle))$.

Processes and abstractions form the class $\mathcal{P}r^*$ of *agents*. $F$ and $G$ range over abstractions; $A$ over agents. To distinguish logically different agents, we assign them a sort: A process takes the sort (); and, if name $a$ has sort $s$, then an abstraction $(a)\,P$ takes sort $(s)$. We extend bisimulation to abstractions and set $(a)\,P \sim (a)\,Q$ (resp. $(a)\,P \approx (a)\,Q$) if $P \sim Q$ (resp. $P \approx Q$); note that, as for input prefixes, so for abstractions instantiations of the bound name are not not needed. The congruence of $\sim$ and $\approx$ is preserved by the abstraction and application constructs; the latter because both bisimulations are preserved by name instantiation.

## 4 Milner's Encoding of the Lazy Lambda Calculus

### 4.1 The Lazy λ-Calculus

We let $x$ and $y$ range over the set of λ-calculus variables. The set $\Lambda^{\mathrm{o}}$ of λ-terms is defined by the grammar

$$M := x \;\Big|\; \lambda x.\, M \;\Big|\; M_1 M_2 \,.$$

Free variables, closed terms, substitution, alpha-conversion etc. are defined as usual [4, 12]. We maintain the freedom on alpha conversion that we used in the $\pi$-calculus, so to assume freshness of bound variables whenever needed. The set of free variables in the term $M$ is $\mathrm{fv}(M)$, and the subclass of $\Lambda^{\mathrm{o}}$ only containing the closed terms is $\Lambda$. We group brackets on the left; therefore $MNL$ is $(MN)L$. We abbreviate $\lambda x_1. \cdots .\lambda x_n.M$ as $\lambda x_1 \cdots x_n.M$, or $\lambda \tilde{x}.M$ if the length of $\tilde{x}$ is not important. Symbol $\Omega$ is the always-divergent term $(\lambda x.xx)(\lambda x.xx)$.

In Abramsky's *lazy lambda calculus* [1], the redex is always at the extreme left of a term. The reduction relation $\longrightarrow \subseteq \Lambda^{\mathrm{o}} \times \Lambda^{\mathrm{o}}$ (for our purposes we need it defined on open terms) is determined by the two rules:

$$\texttt{Beta} : (\lambda x.M)N \longrightarrow M\{^{N}\!/x\}, \qquad \texttt{App} : \frac{M \longrightarrow M'}{MN \longrightarrow M'N}.$$

The reflexive and transitive closure of $\longrightarrow$ is $\Longrightarrow$. We write $M \Downarrow$ if $M$ is convergent, i.e., it can reduce to an abstraction. In the remainder of the paper, unless otherwise specified, $M, N, L$ are from $\Lambda^{\mathrm{o}}$.

### 4.2 Milner's Encoding

We informally explain Milner's encoding $\mathcal{E}$ of the lazy λ-calculus into the $\pi$-calculus. The core of any encoding of the λ-calculus into a process calculus is the translation of function application. This becomes a particular form of parallel combination of two agents, the function and its argument; beta-reduction is then modeled as process interaction. Since the syntax of the $\pi$-calculus only allows for the transmission of names along channels, the communication of a term is simulated by the communication of a *trigger* for it.

In the λ-calculus, λ is, crudely, the only port; a λ-terms receives its argument at λ. In the $\pi$-calculus, there are infinitely-many ports, so the encoding of a λ-term $M$ is parametric over a port $p$. This can be thought of as the *location* of $M$, for $p$ represents the unique port along which $M$ interacts with its environment. $M$ receives two names along $p$: The first is a trigger for its argument and the second is the location to be used for the next interaction. The encoding is presented in Table 24.2. It is slightly different from Milner's original encoding [20] in the rule for application: In Milner's encoding, the particle $\bar{r}\langle x, q\rangle$ guards the process

**Table 24.2**
The encoding of the lazy λ-calculus

$$\mathcal{E}[\![\lambda x.M]\!] \stackrel{\text{def}}{=} (p)p(x,q).\mathcal{E}[\![M]\!]\langle q\rangle$$
$$\mathcal{E}[\![x]\!] \stackrel{\text{def}}{=} (p)(\bar{x})\langle p\rangle$$
$$\mathcal{E}[\![MN]\!] \stackrel{\text{def}}{=} (p)\nu r, x(\mathcal{E}[\![M]\!]\langle r\rangle|\bar{r}\langle x, p\rangle|!x(q).\mathcal{E}[\![N]\!]\langle q\rangle),\ x \text{ fresh.}$$

$!\,x(q).\,\mathcal{E}[\![N]\!]\langle q\rangle$. We modified the guard into a parallel composition, so to use only the operators of the mini $\pi$-calculus, because $x$ is restricted and hence $\bar{r}\langle x, q\rangle$ is blocking for $!\,x(q).\,\mathcal{E}[\![N]\!]\langle q\rangle$.

Two sorts of names are used in the encoding: *Location names* like by $p, q$ and $r$, and *trigger names* like by $x$, $y$ and $z$. For simplicity, we have assumed that the set of trigger names is the same as the set of λ-variables. If $s_{\text{loc}}$ denotes the sort of the location names, then the encoding of a λ-term is an abstraction of sort $(s_{\text{loc}})$. In the remainder of the paper, all abstractions we write have sort $(s_{\text{loc}})$, names $p, q, r, \ldots$ are location names, and $x, y, z, \ldots$ are trigger names.

## 5 Operational Correspondence for the Encoding

In this section, we carefully examine the operational correspondence between source and target terms of the encoding. This will also be the basis for the study of full abstraction in Section 7. First, we introduce a process notation which allows us to give a simpler description of encodings of λ-terms with a variable in head position. We recall that $\sim$ is strong bisimilarity and $\lesssim$ is the expansion relation.

DEFINITION 5.1 For $n > 0$, we define:

$$\mathcal{O}_n\langle r_o, r_n, F_1, \ldots, F_n\rangle \stackrel{\text{def}}{=} \nu\, r_1, \ldots, r_{n-1}, x_1, \ldots, x_n$$
$$(\bar{r}_o\langle x_1, r_1\rangle \mid \ldots \mid \bar{r}_{n-1}\langle x_n, r_n\rangle \mid !\,x_1(q).\,F_1\langle q\rangle \mid \ldots \mid !\,x_n(q_n).\,F_n\langle q_n\rangle)$$

where names $r_1, \ldots, r_{n-1}, x_1 \ldots, x_n, q$ are fresh.

The $i$-th output of $\mathcal{O}_n\langle r_o, r_n, F_1, \ldots, F_n\rangle$, namely $\bar{r}_i\langle x_i, r_{i+1}\rangle$, liberates the agent $!\,x_i(q).\,F_i\langle q\rangle$ and the successive output at $r_{i+1}$.

LEMMA 5.2

1. If $n > 1$ and $\mathcal{O}_n\langle r_o, r_n, F_1, \ldots, F_n\rangle \xrightarrow{\mu} P$, then $\mu = (\nu\, x_1, r_1)\bar{r}_o\langle x_1, r_1\rangle$ and $P \sim \mathcal{O}_{n-1}\langle r_1, r_n, F_2, \ldots, F_n\rangle \mid !\,x_1(q).\,F_1\langle q\rangle$.
2. If $n > 0$, then $\mathcal{E}[\![x M_1 \ldots M_n]\!]\langle r_n\rangle \sim \nu\, r_o\,(\bar{x}\langle r_o\rangle \mid \mathcal{O}_n\langle r_o, r_n, \mathcal{E}[\![M_1]\!], \ldots, \mathcal{E}[\![M_n]\!]\rangle)$.

*Proof* Proceed by induction on $n$. □

LEMMA 5.3

1. If $M \longrightarrow N$, then $\mathcal{E}[\![M]\!]\langle p\rangle \longrightarrow\gtrsim \mathcal{E}[\![N]\!]\langle p\rangle$.
2. If $M = \lambda x.\, N$, then $\mathcal{E}[\![M]\!]\langle p\rangle \stackrel{p(x,q)}{\longrightarrow} \mathcal{E}[\![N]\!]\langle q\rangle$.
3. If $M = x$ then $\mathcal{E}[\![M]\!]\langle p\rangle \stackrel{\bar{x}\langle p\rangle}{\longrightarrow} \mathbf{0}$.
4. If $M = xM_1 \ldots M_n$, $n > 0$, then $\mathcal{E}[\![M]\!]\langle p\rangle \stackrel{(\nu q)\bar{x}\langle q\rangle}{\longrightarrow}\sim \mathcal{O}_n\langle q, p, \mathcal{E}[\![M_1]\!], \ldots, \mathcal{E}[\![M_n]\!]\rangle$.

*Proof* Assertions (2) and (3) are immediate from the definition of the encoding. Assertion (4) follows from Lemma 5.2(2). Assertion (1) is proved by induction on the structure of $M$. The most interesting case is when $M = (\lambda x.\, M_1)M_2$ and $N = M_1\{^{M_2}/x\}$. We have

$$\mathcal{E}[\![(\lambda x.M)N]\!]\langle p\rangle \longrightarrow\sim \boldsymbol{\nu} x\, (\mathcal{E}[\![M]\!]\langle p\rangle \mid\, !x(r).\, \mathcal{E}[\![N]\!]\langle r\rangle)\,.$$

Then

$$\boldsymbol{\nu} x\, (\mathcal{E}[\![M]\!]\langle p\rangle \mid\, !x(r).\, \mathcal{E}[\![N]\!]\langle r\rangle) \gtrsim \mathcal{E}[\![M\{^N/x\}]\!]\langle p\rangle \qquad (3)$$

can be proved proceeding by induction on the structure of $M$, and using the distributivity properties of private replications in Lemma 3.12; alternatively, (3) can be inferred as an instance of Lemma 6.3. □

PROPOSITION 5.4 (OPERATIONAL CORRESPONDENCE ON THE REDUCTIONS OF $M$)

1. If $M \Longrightarrow N$, then $\mathcal{E}[\![M]\!]\langle p\rangle \Longrightarrow\gtrsim \mathcal{E}[\![N]\!]\langle p\rangle$.
2. If $M \Longrightarrow \lambda x.\, N$, then $\mathcal{E}[\![M]\!]\langle p\rangle \stackrel{p(x,q)}{\Longrightarrow} \gtrsim \mathcal{E}[\![N]\!]\langle q\rangle$.
3. If $M \Longrightarrow x$ then $\mathcal{E}[\![M]\!]\langle p\rangle \stackrel{\bar{x}\langle q\rangle}{\Longrightarrow} \gtrsim \mathbf{0}$.
4. If $M \Longrightarrow xM_1 \ldots M_n, n > 0$, then $\mathcal{E}[\![M]\!]\langle p\rangle \stackrel{(\nu q)\bar{x}\langle q\rangle}{\Longrightarrow} \gtrsim \mathcal{O}_n\langle q, p, \mathcal{E}[\![M]\!]_1, \ldots, \mathcal{E}[\![M_n]\!]\rangle$.

*Proof* Assertion (1) is proved using induction on the number of steps made by $M$ and Lemma 5.3(1). The other assertions are consequences of assertion (1) and of Lemma 5.3(2-4). □

PROPOSITION 5.5 (OPERATIONAL CORRESPONDENCE ON THE WEAK TRANSITIONS OF $\mathcal{E}[\![M]\!]\langle p\rangle$)

1. If $\mathcal{E}[\![M]\!]\langle p\rangle \Longrightarrow P$, then there is $N$ s.t. $M \Longrightarrow N$ and $P \gtrsim \mathcal{E}[\![N]\!]\langle p\rangle$.
2. If $\mathcal{E}[\![M]\!]\langle p\rangle \Longrightarrow\stackrel{\mu}{\longrightarrow} P$ and $\mu$ is an input action, then $\mu = p(x, q)$ and there is $N$ s.t. $M \Longrightarrow \lambda x.\, N$, $P \gtrsim \mathcal{E}[\![N]\!]\langle q\rangle$.
3. If $\mathcal{E}[\![M]\!]\langle p\rangle \stackrel{\mu}{\Longrightarrow} P$ and $\mu$ is a free output, then there is $x$ s.t. $\mu = \bar{x}\langle p\rangle$ and $P \gtrsim \mathbf{0}$.

4. If $\mathcal{E}[\![M]\!]\langle p\rangle \stackrel{\mu}{\Longrightarrow} P$ and $\mu$ is a non-free output, then there are $x$ and $M_1, \ldots, M_n, n > 0$, s.t. $\mu = (\nu\, q)\, \bar{x}\langle q\rangle$, $M \Longrightarrow x M_1 \ldots M_n$, and $P \gtrsim \mathcal{O}_n\langle q, p, \mathcal{E}[\![M]\!]_1, \ldots, \mathcal{E}[\![M_n]\!]\rangle$.

*Proof* By induction on the length of the transition of $\mathcal{E}[\![M]\!]\langle p\rangle$. For the basic case, note that for each $M$ and $p$, process $\mathcal{E}[\![M]\!]\langle p\rangle$ has only one possible transition, hence the thesis follows by Lemma 5.3. □

## 6 A λ-Model from the Process Terms

The results of operational correspondence in the previous section, although enlightening, do not settle the issue of the correctness of the encoding. We complement these results with the construction of a λ-model. This shows that the encoding yields a λ-theory and, therefore, that the $\pi$-calculus representation of functions validates the basic axioms and inference rules of the λ-calculus.

A *partial function* $\varphi$ from a set $D_1$ to a set $D_2$ can be undefined on some elements of $D_1$; the subset of $D_1$ on which $\varphi$ is defined is dom($\varphi$). If dom($\varphi$) is finite, then $\varphi$ is *finite*. We write $\varphi[\, d_2/d_1\,]$ for the function which maps $d_1$ to $d_2$ and which behaves like $\varphi$ on the remaining elements of $D_1$. To ease readability, we sometimes abbreviate $\varphi(d)$ as $\varphi_d$.

Excellent discussions on λ-models can be found in [18, 4, 12], where other definitions, equivalent to the one below, are presented. A *finite valuation in a set D* is a finite function from the set of λ-variables to $D$. Below, *finite* evaluations are enough because the set of free variables of a λ-term is finite.

DEFINITION 6.1 (λ-MODEL, [12]) A λ-*model* is a triple $< D, \cdot, \mathcal{M} >$, where $D$ is a set with at least two elements, '·' is a mapping from $D \times D$ to $D$ and $\mathcal{M}$ is a mapping which assigns, to each λ-term $M$ and finite valuation $\rho$ in $D$ with fv($M$) $\subseteq$ dom($\rho$), a member $\mathcal{M}[\![M]\!]_\rho \in D$ such that:

1. $\mathcal{M}[\![x]\!]_\rho = \rho(x)$
2. $\mathcal{M}[\![MN]\!]_\rho = \mathcal{M}[\![M]\!]_\rho \cdot \mathcal{M}[\![N]\!]_\rho$
3. $\mathcal{M}[\![\lambda x.M]\!]_\rho \cdot \boldsymbol{d} = \mathcal{M}[\![M]\!]_{\rho[\boldsymbol{d}/x]}$ for all $\boldsymbol{d} \in D$
4. $\mathcal{M}[\![M]\!]_\rho = \mathcal{M}[\![M]\!]_\sigma$ if $\rho(x) = \sigma(x)$ for all $x$ free in $M$
5. $\mathcal{M}[\![\lambda x.M]\!]_\rho = \mathcal{M}[\![\lambda y.M\{y/x\}]\!]_\rho$, $y$ not free in $M$
6. if $\mathcal{M}[\![M]\!]_{\rho[\boldsymbol{d}/x]} = \mathcal{M}[\![N]\!]_{\rho[\boldsymbol{d}/x]}$ for all $\boldsymbol{d} \in D$, then $\mathcal{M}[\![\lambda x.M]\!]_\rho = \mathcal{M}[\![\lambda x.N]\!]_\rho$.

We wish to construct a λ-model using $\pi$-calculus agents and the encoding $\mathcal{E}$ of the λ-calculus into the $\pi$-calculus. It is reasonable that the model should respect observation equivalence ($\approx$), which is the semantic equality adopted in the $\pi$-calculus. So, for a

$\pi$-calculus agent $A$, let $[A]_{\approx}$ be the equivalence class of $A$, namely

$$[A]_{\approx} \stackrel{\text{def}}{=} \{A' \ : \ A' \in \mathcal{P}r^* \text{ and } A \approx A'\}.$$

The elements of the domain $D$ of the model will be the equivalence classes of the $\pi$-calculus agents with the same sort $(s_{\text{loc}})$ as the agents encoding $\lambda$-terms:

$$D \stackrel{\text{def}}{=} \{[F]_{\approx} \ : \ F \in \mathcal{P}r^* \text{ and } F \text{ has sort } (s_{\text{loc}})\}. \tag{4}$$

The definition of application on these elements follows the translation of $\lambda$-application in $\mathcal{E}$:

$$\begin{array}{l}[G]_{\approx} \cdot [F]_{\approx} \stackrel{\text{def}}{=} [(p)\boldsymbol{\nu}\, r, x\, (G\langle r\rangle \mid \bar{r}\langle x, p\rangle \mid\ !\, x(q).\, F\langle q\rangle)]_{\approx} \\ \quad \text{for} \quad p, x, r, q \text{ not free in } F, G.\end{array} \tag{5}$$

The definition of application is consistent since, by the congruence properties of $\approx$, the result of the application does not depend upon the representatives $G$ and $F$ chosen from the equivalence classes. We are left with the definition of $\mathcal{M}[\![M]\!]_{\rho}$. The valuation $\rho$ maps a $\lambda$-variable $x$ to $\rho(x)$, which is a set of bisimilar $\pi$-calculus agents. Given a valuation $\rho$, we denote by $\hat{\rho}$ a "conversion" of $\rho$ which operates on a $\pi$-calculus name $x$ and selects a representative out of the equivalence class of $\rho(x)$; that is, $\hat{\rho}(x) \in \rho(x)$ if $x \in \text{dom}(\rho)$, and $\hat{\rho}(x)$ is undefined if $x \notin \text{dom}(\rho)$. Now, the mapping $\mathcal{M}$ of the $\lambda$-model is defined in terms of $\mathcal{E}$ as follows:

$$\mathcal{M}[\![M]\!]_{\rho} \stackrel{\text{def}}{=} \left[(p)\,\boldsymbol{\nu}\,\tilde{y}\,\Big(\mathcal{E}[\![M]\!]\langle p\rangle\{\tilde{y}/\tilde{x}\}\Big|\prod_i !\, y_i(q).\,\hat{\rho}_{x_i}\langle q\rangle\Big)\right]_{\approx} \tag{6}$$

where $\tilde{y}$ and $q$ are fresh names, $\tilde{x} = \text{dom}(\rho)$, and $x_i$ (resp. $y_i$) is the $i$-th component of $\tilde{x}$ (resp. $\tilde{y}$). The use of fresh names $\tilde{y}$ in the outermost restriction—and hence the substitution $\{\tilde{y}/\tilde{x}\}$—is needed to avoid that free names of $\hat{\rho}_{x_i}$ become bound, for names $\tilde{x}$ might occur free in $\hat{\rho}_{x_i}$. Definition (6) is independent of the representatives of the equivalence classes selected by $\hat{\rho}$, since $\approx$ is a congruence.

Agent $\hat{\rho}_{x_i}$ is used in (6) as a private resource for $\mathcal{E}[\![M]\!]\langle p\rangle\{\tilde{y}/\tilde{x}\}$, accessible through name $y_i$. Behaviourally, this amounts to replacing the translation of the $\lambda$-calculus variable $x_i$ with the agent $\hat{\rho}_{x_i}$. This idea is formalised in Lemma 6.3 using the encoding $\hat{\mathcal{E}}$ below.

DEFINITION 6.2 Let $\varphi$ be a finite function from trigger names to abstractions of sort $(s_{\text{loc}})$. The mapping $\hat{\mathcal{E}}[\![-]\!]_{\varphi}$, from $\lambda$-terms to $\pi$-calculus abstractions of sort $(s_{\text{loc}})$, is defined inductively thus:

$$\hat{\mathcal{E}}[\![\lambda x.M]\!]_\varphi \stackrel{\text{def}}{=} (p)\, p(x,q).\,\hat{\mathcal{E}}[\![M]\!]_\varphi\,\langle q\rangle$$

$$\hat{\mathcal{E}}[\![x]\!]_\varphi \stackrel{\text{def}}{=} \begin{cases} \varphi_x & \text{if } x \in \text{dom}(\varphi) \\ (p)\,\bar{x}\langle p\rangle & \text{if } x \notin \text{dom}(\varphi) \end{cases}$$

$$\hat{\mathcal{E}}[\![MN]\!]_\varphi \stackrel{\text{def}}{=} (p)\,\boldsymbol{\nu}\, r, x\,\Big(\hat{\mathcal{E}}[\![M]\!]_\varphi\,\langle r\rangle \mid \bar{r}\langle x, p\rangle \mid\, !\,x(q).\,\hat{\mathcal{E}}[\![N]\!]_\varphi\,\langle q\rangle\Big)$$

where $p, q, r$ and $x$ are fresh.

Note that, since $x$ is fresh w.r.t. $\varphi$, in $p(x,q).\,\hat{\mathcal{E}}[\![M]\!]_\varphi\,\langle q\rangle$ we have $x \neq a$ and $x \notin \text{fn}(\varphi_a)$, for all $a \in \text{dom}(\varphi)$.

LEMMA 6.3 If $\rho$ is a finite evaluation with $\tilde{x} = \text{dom}(\rho)$, and $\tilde{y}, q$ are fresh, then

$$\boldsymbol{\nu}\,\tilde{y}\left(\mathcal{E}[\![M]\!]\langle p\rangle\{\tilde{y}/\tilde{x}\}\,\middle|\, \prod_i !\,y_i(q).\,\hat{\rho}_{x_i}\langle q\rangle\right) \gtrsim \hat{\mathcal{E}}[\![M]\!]_{\hat{\rho}}\,\langle p\rangle$$

*Proof* By induction on the structure of $M$. We consider two cases and abbreviate $\prod_i !\,y_i(q).\,\hat{\rho}_{x_i}\langle q\rangle$ as $P_{\tilde{y}}$.

**(1)** $M = y$ and $y \in \text{dom}(\rho)$. We have:

$$\begin{aligned}
&\boldsymbol{\nu}\,\tilde{y}\,(\mathcal{E}[\![M]\!]\langle p\rangle\{\tilde{y}/\tilde{x}\} \mid P_{\tilde{y}}) && = \text{(definition of } \mathcal{E})\\
&\boldsymbol{\nu}\,\tilde{y}\,(\bar{y}\langle p\rangle \mid P_{\tilde{y}}) && \sim \text{(Lemma 3.12(5))}\\
&\boldsymbol{\nu}\,y\,(\bar{y}\langle p\rangle \mid\, !\,y(q).\,\hat{\rho}_x\langle q\rangle) && \gtrsim \text{(Lemma 3.12(6))}\\
&\hat{\rho}_x\langle p\rangle && = \hat{\mathcal{E}}[\![M]\!]_{\hat{\rho}}\,\langle p\rangle
\end{aligned}$$

**(2)** $M = NL$. We have:

$$\begin{aligned}
&\boldsymbol{\nu}\,\tilde{y}\,(\mathcal{E}[\![M]\!]\langle p\rangle\{\tilde{y}/\tilde{x}\} \mid P_{\tilde{y}}) && = \text{(definition of } \mathcal{E})\\
&\boldsymbol{\nu}\,\tilde{y}\,\Big(\boldsymbol{\nu}\,r,z\,\Big(\mathcal{E}[\![N]\!]\langle r\rangle\{\tilde{y}/\tilde{x}\} \mid \bar{r}\langle z,p\rangle \mid\, !\,z(q).\,(\mathcal{E}[\![L]\!]\langle q\rangle\{\tilde{y}/\tilde{x}\})\Big) \mid P_{\tilde{y}}\Big) && \sim \text{(law } \mathbf{L1})\\
&\boldsymbol{\nu}\,r,z,\tilde{y}\,\Big(\mathcal{E}[\![N]\!]\langle r\rangle\{\tilde{y}/\tilde{x}\} \mid \bar{r}\langle z,p\rangle \mid\, !\,z(q).\,(\mathcal{E}[\![L]\!]\langle q\rangle\{\tilde{y}/\tilde{x}\}) \mid P_{\tilde{y}}\Big) && \sim (*)\\
&\boldsymbol{\nu}\,r,z\,\Big(\boldsymbol{\nu}\,\tilde{y}\,\Big(\mathcal{E}[\![N]\!]\langle r\rangle\{\tilde{y}/\tilde{x}\} \mid P_{\tilde{y}}\Big) \mid \bar{r}\langle z,p\rangle \mid\, !\,z(q).\,\boldsymbol{\nu}\,\tilde{y}\,\Big(\mathcal{E}[\![L]\!]\langle q\rangle\{\tilde{y}/\tilde{x}\} \mid P_{\tilde{y}}\Big)\Big) && \gtrsim \text{(induction)}\\
&\boldsymbol{\nu}\,r,z\,\Big(\hat{\mathcal{E}}[\![M]\!]_{\hat{\rho}}\,\langle r\rangle \mid \bar{r}\langle z,p\rangle \mid\, !\,z(q).\,\hat{\mathcal{E}}[\![L]\!]_{\hat{\rho}}\,\langle q\rangle\Big) && = \hat{\mathcal{E}}[\![NL]\!]_{\hat{\rho}}\,\langle p\rangle
\end{aligned}$$

where $(*)$ is derived from the distributivity laws for private replications in Lemma 3.12. □

Corollary 6.4 shows the relationship between mapping $\mathcal{M}$ and encoding $\hat{\mathcal{E}}$.

COROLLARY 6.4 $\mathcal{M}[\![M]\!]_\rho = [\,\hat{\mathcal{E}}[\![M]\!]_{\hat{\rho}}]_\approx$

*Proof* From the definitions of $\hat{\mathcal{E}}$ and $\mathcal{M}$, and Lemma 6.3. □

We can now define the λ-model.

DEFINITION 6.5 (MODEL $\mathcal{D}$) We set $\mathcal{D} \stackrel{\text{def}}{=} < D, \cdot, \mathcal{M} >$, for $D$, $\cdot$, and $\mathcal{M}$ as given in (4), (5) and (6).

LEMMA 6.6 If $\mathcal{M}[\![M]\!]_{\rho[\tilde{\boldsymbol{d}}/\tilde{x}]} = \mathcal{M}[\![N]\!]_{\rho[\tilde{\boldsymbol{d}}/\tilde{x}]}$ for all $\tilde{\boldsymbol{d}}$, then $\hat{\mathcal{E}}[\![M]\!]_{\hat{\rho}} \approx \hat{\mathcal{E}}[\![N]\!]_{\hat{\rho}}$.

*Proof* Take $F_x \stackrel{\text{def}}{=} (p)\,\bar{x}\langle p\rangle$ and $\boldsymbol{d}_x \stackrel{\text{def}}{=} [\,F_x]_{\approx}$. By Corollary 6.4, $\mathcal{M}[\![M]\!]_{\rho[\tilde{\boldsymbol{d}}_x/\tilde{x}]} = \mathcal{M}[\![N]\!]_{\rho[\tilde{\boldsymbol{d}}_x/\tilde{x}]}$ implies

$$\hat{\mathcal{E}}[\![M]\!]_{\hat{\rho}[\tilde{F}_x/\tilde{x}]} \approx \hat{\mathcal{E}}[\![N]\!]_{\hat{\rho}[\tilde{F}_x/\tilde{x}]}\,. \tag{7}$$

Moreover, by definitions of $\hat{\mathcal{E}}$ and $\tilde{F}_x$,

$$\text{for all } L \quad \hat{\mathcal{E}}[\![L]\!]_{\hat{\rho}[\tilde{F}_x/\tilde{x}]} = \hat{\mathcal{E}}[\![L]\!]_{\hat{\rho}}\,. \tag{8}$$

Now, (7) and (8) prove that $\hat{\mathcal{E}}[\![M]\!]_{\hat{\rho}} \approx \hat{\mathcal{E}}[\![N]\!]_{\hat{\rho}}$. □

COROLLARY 6.7 $\mathcal{E}[\![M]\!] \approx \mathcal{E}[\![N]\!]$ iff, for all $\rho$, $\mathcal{M}[\![M]\!]_\rho = \mathcal{M}[\![N]\!]_\rho$.

*Proof* The implication from left to right follows from the definition of $\mathcal{M}$ and congruence of $\approx$. Now, the implication from right to left. By Lemma 6.6, $\mathcal{M}[\![M]\!]_\rho = \mathcal{M}[\![N]\!]_\rho$ for all $\rho$ implies $\hat{\mathcal{E}}[\![M]\!]_\emptyset \approx \hat{\mathcal{E}}[\![N]\!]_\emptyset$. This proves the result since, for all $L$, $\hat{\mathcal{E}}[\![L]\!]_\emptyset = \mathcal{E}[\![L]\!]$. □

THEOREM 6.8 $\mathcal{D}$ is a λ-model.

*Proof* We look at the main clauses of Definition 6.1.

**(Clause 2)** We have:

$$\begin{aligned}
&\mathcal{M}[\![MN]\!]_\rho && = \text{(Corollary 6.4)}\\
&[\,\hat{\mathcal{E}}[\![MN]\!]_{\hat{\rho}}]_{\approx} && = \text{(definition of } \hat{\mathcal{E}})\\
&[\,(p)\nu\, r, x \left(\hat{\mathcal{E}}[\![M]\!]_{\hat{\rho}}\,\langle r\rangle \mid \bar{r}\langle x, p\rangle \mid\, !\,x(q).\,\hat{\mathcal{E}}[\![N]\!]_{\hat{\rho}}\,\langle q\rangle\right)]_{\approx} && = \text{(definition of application in the model)}\\
&[\,\hat{\mathcal{E}}[\![M]\!]_{\hat{\rho}}]_{\approx} \cdot [\,\hat{\mathcal{E}}[\![N]\!]_{\hat{\rho}}]_{\approx} && = \text{(Corollary 6.4)}\\
&\mathcal{M}[\![M]\!]_\rho \cdot \mathcal{M}[\![N]\!]_\rho &&
\end{aligned}$$

**(Clause 3)** Let $\boldsymbol{d} = [\,F]_{\approx}$. By Corollary 6.4,

$$\mathcal{M}[\![\lambda x.M]\!]_\rho \cdot \boldsymbol{d} = \left[(p)\nu\, r, z\left(\hat{\mathcal{E}}[\![\lambda x.\,M]\!]_{\hat{\rho}}\,\langle r\rangle \mid \bar{r}\langle z, p\rangle \mid\, !\,z(q).\,F\langle q\rangle\right)\right]_{\approx},$$

and $\quad \mathcal{M}[\![M]\!]_{\rho[\boldsymbol{d}/x]} = [\,\hat{\mathcal{E}}[\![M]\!]_{\hat{\rho}[F/x]}]_{\approx}\,.$

We have

$$\begin{array}{ll}
\nu r, z \left(\hat{\mathcal{E}}[\![\lambda x.\, M]\!]_{\hat{\rho}} \langle r\rangle \mid \bar{r}\langle z, p\rangle \mid\ !\, z(q).\, F\langle q\rangle\right) & = \\
\nu r, z \left(r(x, q).\, \hat{\mathcal{E}}[\![M]\!]_{\hat{\rho}} \langle q\rangle \mid \bar{r}\langle z, p\rangle \mid\ !\, z(q).\, F\langle q\rangle\right) & \approx \text{(laws } \mathbf{L1,L2}) \\
\nu z \left(\hat{\mathcal{E}}[\![M]\!]_{\rho} \langle p\rangle\{z/x\} \mid\ !\, z(q).\, F\langle q\rangle\right) & \approx (*) \\
\hat{\mathcal{E}}[\![M]\!]_{\hat{\rho}[\,F/x\,]} \langle p\rangle &
\end{array}$$

where $(*)$ is obtained using Lemma 6.3 to expand the definition of $\hat{\mathcal{E}}$.

**(Clause 6)** By Lemma 6.6, if $\mathcal{M}[\![M]\!]_{\rho[\boldsymbol{d}/x]} = \mathcal{M}[\![N]\!]_{\rho[\boldsymbol{d}/x]}$ for all $\boldsymbol{d}$, then $\hat{\mathcal{E}}[\![M]\!]_{\hat{\rho}} \approx \hat{\mathcal{E}}[\![N]\!]_{\hat{\rho}}$. Since $\approx$ is a congruence, we get

$$(p)\ p(x, q).\, \hat{\mathcal{E}}[\![M]\!]_{\hat{\rho}} \langle q\rangle \approx (p)\ p(x, q).\, \hat{\mathcal{E}}[\![N]\!]_{\hat{\rho}} \langle q\rangle.$$

By Corollary 6.4 and the definition of $\hat{\mathcal{E}}$, this means $\mathcal{M}[\![\lambda x.M]\!]_{\rho} = \mathcal{M}[\![\lambda x.N]\!]_{\rho}$. □

We could have tried to be more selective in the definition of model $\mathcal{D}$, and take $D^* = \{[\,\mathcal{E}[\![M]\!]]_{\approx} : M \in \Lambda\}$ as its domain; then $\mathcal{D}^* = < D^*, \cdot, \mathcal{M} >$ represents the *interior* of $\mathcal{D}$ [12]. But it turns out that $\mathcal{D}^*$ is *not* a $\lambda$-model. Clause (6) in Definition 6.1 fails. As counterexample, take the terms $\lambda x.\, xx$ and $\lambda x.\, (x\lambda y.\, (xy))$. Their encodings into $\pi$-calculus are not behaviourally equivalent (see Lemma 7.5). Hence $\mathcal{M}[\![\lambda x.\, xx]\!]_{\emptyset} \neq \mathcal{M}[\![\lambda x.\, (x\lambda y.\, (xy))]\!]_{\emptyset}$ However, for all closed $N$, if $\boldsymbol{d} = [\,\mathcal{E}[\![N]\!]]_{\approx}$, we have

$$\mathcal{M}[\![xx]\!]_{[\boldsymbol{d}/x]} = [\,\mathcal{E}[\![NN]\!]]_{\approx} = [\,\mathcal{E}[\![N(\lambda y.\, (Ny))]\!]]_{\approx} = \mathcal{M}[\![x(\lambda y.\, (xy))]\!]_{[\boldsymbol{d}/x]}.$$

Therefore $\mathcal{D}$ is an example of a $\lambda$-model whose interior is not a $\lambda$-model; see [11] for more examples.

Since $\mathcal{D}$ is a $\lambda$-model, we can infer all properties of $\lambda$-models for it and, hence, the two corollaries below (for the proof of the first, one also needs Corollary 6.7). We write $\lambda\beta \vdash M = N$ if $M = N$ is an equation in the formal theory given by the alpha and beta axioms plus the rules of inference for equivalence and congruence.

COROLLARY 6.9 (VALIDITY OF BETA EQUALITY FOR $\mathcal{E}$) If $\lambda\beta \vdash M = N$, then $\mathcal{E}[\![M]\!] \approx \mathcal{E}[\![N]\!]$. □

COROLLARY 6.10 $< D, \cdot >$ is a combinatory algebra where the two distinguished elements $\boldsymbol{k}$ and $\boldsymbol{s}$ can be defined as $\boldsymbol{k} = [\,\mathcal{E}[\![\lambda xy.x]\!]]_{\approx}$, and $\boldsymbol{s} = [\,\mathcal{E}[\![\lambda xyz.(xz(yz))]\!]]_{\approx}$. □

However model $\mathcal{D}$ is *not* extensional, i.e., it is not a $\lambda\eta$ model. As counterexample, take $\Omega$ and $\lambda x.(\Omega x)$. Then $\mathcal{E}[\![\Omega]\!]\langle p\rangle \not\approx \mathcal{E}[\![\lambda x.(\Omega x)]\!]\langle p\rangle$, since $\mathcal{E}[\![\Omega]\!]\langle p\rangle \approx \mathbf{0}$, whereas $\mathcal{E}[\![\lambda x.(\Omega x)]\!]\langle p\rangle$ can perform a visible action at $p$. This failure is not too surprising, since our encoding mimics the lazy λ-calculus, in which the $\eta$ rule is not valid. However, as in the lazy λ-calculus, the $\eta$ rule holds if $M$ is convergent:

THEOREM 6.11 (CONDITIONAL EXTENSIONALITY) If $x \notin \mathrm{fv}(M)$, then $M \Downarrow$ implies $\mathcal{E}[\![\lambda x.\,(Mx)]\!] \approx \mathcal{E}[\![M]\!]$.

*Proof* If $M \Downarrow$, then $M \Longrightarrow \lambda z.\,N$, for some $z$ and $N$. Therefore also $Mx \Longrightarrow N\{^x/_z\}$. By validity of beta equality for $\mathcal{E}$ (Corollary 6.9)

$$\mathcal{E}[\![M]\!] \approx \mathcal{E}[\![\lambda z.\,N]\!] \tag{9}$$

and $\mathcal{E}[\![Mx]\!] \approx \mathcal{E}[\![N\{^x/_z\}]\!]$. Applying the latter equality in $\mathcal{E}[\![\lambda x.\,(Mx)]\!]$ one gets

$$\mathcal{E}[\![\lambda x.\,(Mx)]\!] \approx \mathcal{E}[\![\lambda x.\,N\{^x/_z\}]\!] \approx \mathcal{E}[\![\lambda z.\,N]\!]\,. \tag{10}$$

Equalities (9) and (10) prove the theorem. □

## 7 Full Abstraction

Full abstraction, first studied by Milner [19] and Plotkin [26], is the problem of finding a denotational interpretation for a programming language such that the resulting semantic equality coincides with a notion of operational indistinguishability.

Inspired by the work of Milner and Park in concurrency, Abramsky [1] introduced an operational equivalence on closed lazy λ-terms called *applicative bisimulation*.

DEFINITION 7.1 A symmetric relation $\mathcal{R} \subseteq \Lambda \times \Lambda$ is an *applicative bisimulation* if $M\mathcal{R}N$ and $M \Longrightarrow \lambda x.\,M'$ imply that there is an $N'$ such that $N \Longrightarrow \lambda x.\,N'$ and $M'\{^L/_x\}\ \mathcal{R}N'\{^L/_x\}$, for all $L \in \Lambda$. Two terms $M, N \in \Lambda \times \Lambda$ are *applicative bisimilar*, written $M \simeq N$, if $M\mathcal{R}N$ holds, for some applicative bisimulation $\mathcal{R}$.

Applicative bisimulation can then be extended to open terms: If $M, N \in \Lambda^{\mathrm{o}}$ with $\mathrm{fv}(M, N) \subseteq \{\tilde{x}\}$, then $M \simeq N$ if for all $\tilde{L} \subseteq \Lambda$, we have $M\{^{\tilde{L}}/_{\tilde{x}}\} \simeq N\{^{\tilde{L}}/_{\tilde{x}}\}$.

Applicative bisimulation has been extensively studied by Abramsky and Ong [2]; in particular, they have showed that it is a congruence relation.

The classical setting in which the full abstraction problem has been developed is the simply typed λ-calculus. With the introduction of the operational equivalence resulting from applicative bisimulation, it can be neatly transferred to the untyped λ-calculus and it has motivated elegant works by Abramsky, Ong and Boudol ([2, 6]). A denotational interpretation is said to be *sound* if it only equates operationally equivalent terms, *complete* if it equates all operationally equivalent terms, and *fully abstract* if it is sound and complete.

We call the equality on $\lambda$-terms induced by model $\mathcal{D}$ of the previous section *$\lambda$-observation equivalence*.

DEFINITION 7.2 ($\lambda$-OBSERVATION EQUIVALENCE) For $M, N \in \Lambda^{o}$, we say that $M$ and $N$ are *$\lambda$-observationally equivalent*, written $M \approx_\lambda N$, if for all valuation $\rho$ with $\mathrm{dom}(\rho) = \mathrm{fv}(M, N)$, it holds that $\mathcal{M}[\![M]\!]_\rho = \mathcal{M}[\![N]\!]_\rho$.

By Corollary 6.7, $\lambda$-observation equivalence coincides with the equivalence induced, via encoding $\mathcal{E}$, by $\pi$-calculus observation equivalence:

PROPOSITION 7.3 For all $M, N \in \Lambda^{o}$, it holds that $M \approx_\lambda N$ iff $\mathcal{E}[\![M]\!] \approx \mathcal{E}[\![N]\!]$. □

Model $\mathcal{D}$ of Definition 6.5 is sound but not complete w.r.t. applicative bisimulation. To show this, we prove that bisimilarity between the encoding of two $\lambda$-terms implies (applicative) bisimilarity between the two original $\lambda$-terms, whereas the opposite implication fails. (Similar results on a comparison between behavioural equivalence on $\lambda$-terms and on their $\pi$-calculus encodings are also proved by Milner [20], using different proofs and counterexamples.)

PROPOSITION 7.4 (SOUNDNESS OF $\mathcal{D}$ W.R.T. $\simeq$) $M \approx_\lambda N$ implies $M \simeq N$.

*Proof* It suffices to show that for all $M, N \in \Lambda$, $\mathcal{E}[\![M]\!] \approx \mathcal{E}[\![N]\!]$ implies $M \simeq N$.

Abramsky and Ong [2] have proved that applicative bisimulation can be described in terms of the convergence predicate $M \Downarrow$: For terms $M, N \in \Lambda$, the property

"in all closed $\lambda$-context $C$, $C[M] \Downarrow$ iff $C[N] \Downarrow$"

holds if and only if $M \simeq N$.

Let us first extend the convergence predicate to $\pi$-calculus processes: We set $P \Downarrow$ if $P$ can perform a visible action, i.e., there is $\mu \neq \tau$ and $P'$ s.t. $P \stackrel{\mu}{\Longrightarrow} P'$. Propositions 5.4 and 5.5 show that for all closed $\lambda$-terms and names $p$,

$$M \Downarrow \quad \text{iff} \quad \mathcal{E}[\![M]\!]\langle p\rangle \Downarrow. \tag{11}$$

Now, $\mathcal{E}[\![M]\!]\langle p\rangle \approx \mathcal{E}[\![N]\!]\langle p\rangle$ implies that $\mathcal{E}[\![M]\!]\langle p\rangle \Downarrow$ iff $\mathcal{E}[\![N]\!]\langle p\rangle \Downarrow$. Therefore, since $\mathcal{E}$ is compositional and $\approx$ is a congruence, $\mathcal{E}[\![M]\!]\langle p\rangle \approx \mathcal{E}[\![N]\!]\langle p\rangle$ also implies that for all closed $\lambda$-calculus contexts $C$, $\mathcal{E}[\![C[M]]\!]\langle p\rangle \Downarrow$ iff $\mathcal{E}[\![C[N]]\!]\langle p\rangle \Downarrow$. This and (11) give $M \simeq N$. □

PROPOSITION 7.5 (NON-COMPLETENESS OF $\mathcal{D}$ W.R.T. $\simeq$) There are $M_1, M_2 \in \Lambda$ s.t. $M_1 \simeq M_2$ but $M_1 \not\approx_\lambda M_2$.

*Proof* It is, roughly, a consequence of the fact that the interior of $\mathcal{D}$ is not a model, hence we can reuse the terms $M_1 \stackrel{\text{def}}{=} \lambda x.\, xx$ and $M_2 \stackrel{\text{def}}{=} \lambda x.\, (x\lambda y.\, (xy))$. We have $M_1 \simeq M_2$ if for all $N \in \Lambda$, $NN \simeq N\lambda y.\, (Ny)$. If $N$ is convergent, then, by conditional extensionality, $N \simeq \lambda y.\, (Ny)$ and hence, since $\simeq$ is a congruence relation, $NN \simeq N\lambda y.\, (Ny)$. If $N$ is not convergent, then $NN \simeq \Omega \simeq N\lambda y.\, (Ny)$.

On the other hand, we have $\mathcal{E}[\![M_1]\!] \not\approx_\lambda \mathcal{E}[\![M_2]\!]$; the difference between the two processes can be detected by an external observer after 5 interactions. □

Given a denotational interpretation which is not fully abstract, there are two natural directions to achieve full abstraction:

- to cut down the existing "over-generous" semantic domain (*restrictive approach*);
- to enrich the language (*expansive approach*).

The two approaches are exemplified by the solutions to the full abstraction problem for PCF (a typed $\lambda$-calculus extended with fixed points, boolean and arithmetic features) proposed by Milner [19] and Plotkin [26]; in the latter, PCF is augmented with a 'parallel or' operator.

Also in the case of our model $\mathcal{D}$ we can attempt both directions. In this paper we examine the expansive approach. We first summarise the study of the restrictive approach, reported in [27] (but the process calculus used is the Higher-Order $\pi$-calculus rather than $\pi$-calculus). Two constraints are imposed, resulting in a different model: Only the interior of the model is used; the behavioural equivalence on process terms is weakened. Intuitively, the latter is achieved by restricting the class of contexts in which two terms can be tested: As $\lambda$-terms are *only* used in $\lambda$-calculus contexts, so we require that their encodings be used only in encodings of $\lambda$-calculus contexts. Technically, this is expressed using *barbed bisimulation* [23], a bisimilarity equivalence which can be relativised on a class of contexts. Barbed bisimulation coincides with $\approx$ if powerful enough contexts are allowed, but it is coarser otherwise. The model finally obtained is not only fully abstract, but also *fully expressive*, in the sense that all objects of the domain of interpretation are $\lambda$-definable.

### 7.1 Expansive Approach

In the expansive approach, we study $\lambda$-observation equivalence, i.e., the equivalence induced on $\lambda$-terms by model $\mathcal{D}$ and, hence, by the $\pi$-calculus encoding. The goal is to derive a *direct* characterisation of $\lambda$-observation equivalence, i.e., a characterisation not mentioning the encoding.

Propositions 7.4 and 7.5 show that applicative bisimulation is strictly coarser than $\lambda$-observation equivalence. The counterexample in Proposition 7.5 indicates that there is structure in a $\lambda$-term which is observable in a concurrency setting but not in a purely-functional setting. In particular, in concurrency we can observe *when* the input of a function is used in its body. To achieve the same discrimination, we refine applicative bisimulation. The new relation, called *open applicative bisimulation*, represents perhaps the simplest way to extend applicative bisimulation to open terms.

DEFINITION 7.6 A symmetric relation $\mathcal{R} \subseteq \Lambda^{\mathrm{o}} \times \Lambda^{\mathrm{o}}$ is an *open applicative bisimulation* if $M\mathcal{R}N$ implies:

1. if $M \Longrightarrow \lambda x.\, M'$, then there exists $N'$ s.t. $N \Longrightarrow \lambda x.\, N'$ and $M'\mathcal{R}N'$;
2. if $M \Longrightarrow xM_1 \ldots M_n$, for some $n \geq 0$, then then there exist $N_1, \ldots, N_n$ s.t. $N \Longrightarrow xN_1 \ldots N_n$ and $M_i\mathcal{R}N_i$, for all $1 \leq i \leq n$.

Two terms $M, N \in \Lambda^{\mathrm{o}}$ are *open applicative bisimilar*, written $M \simeq^{\mathrm{o}} N$, if $M\mathcal{R}N$, for some open applicative bisimulation $\mathcal{R}$.

Clause (2), which takes care of terms with a variable in head position, was not present in the definition of applicative bisimulation, where all terms are closed. Moreover, by contrast with applicative bisimulation, in clause (1) no term instantiation on $\lambda$-abstractions is required. This simplification is possible because we work on open terms and can be justified with the congruence of $\simeq^{\mathrm{o}}$. (A straightforward proof of the congruence of $\simeq^{\mathrm{o}}$ utilises the full abstraction Theorems 7.13 and 7.14 and the congruence of $\pi$-calculus bisimilarity $\approx$.) Two useful facts to know are:

LEMMA 7.7 If $M \Longrightarrow N$, then $M \simeq^{\mathrm{o}} N$.

LEMMA 7.8 Let $\rho$ be a substitution from $\lambda$-variables to $\lambda$-variables. If $M \simeq^{\mathrm{o}} N$, then $M\rho \simeq^{\mathrm{o}} N\rho$.

Open applicative bisimulation is reminiscent of a tree representation of $\lambda$-terms. Indeed, it is easy to prove that it coincides with the Lévy-Longo Tree equality, which equates two terms $M, N \in \Lambda^{\mathrm{o}}$ if they have the same Lévy-Longo Tree; see [29] or [24].[4]

Lévy-Longo Trees (briefly LT) are the lazy variant of *Böhm Trees* (briefly BT), the most popular tree structure in the $\lambda$-calculus. BT's only correctly express the computational content of $\lambda$-terms in a "strict" regime, while they fail to do so in a lazy regime. For instance, in a lazy scheme, the terms $\lambda x.\Omega$ and $\Omega$ are distinguished, but since *unsolvable* [4], they have identical BT's. These terms have different LT's, because LT's take into account the order of unsolvability of a term, i.e., the maximal number of $\lambda$-abstractions which the term can exhibit. LT's were introduced in [17]—where they were simply called trees—developing an

[4] Open applicative bisimulation coincides with the equivalence induced by Ong's *lazy PSE ordering* [24]; however, a conceptual difference between the two is the emphasis that Ong's preorder places on $\eta$-expansion.

original idea by Lévy [16]; see [8], in this volume, for their definition, or else [17, 24, 29]. We write $LT(M)$ for the Lévy-Longo Tree of $M$.

THEOREM 7.9 (CORRESPONDENCE WITH LÉVY-LONGO TREES, [24, 29]) For all $M, N \in \Lambda^{\mathrm{o}}$, we have $M \simeq^{\mathrm{o}} N$ iff $LT(M) = LT(N)$. □

## 7.2 The Full Abstraction Theorems

We need a few lemmas before tackling the full abstraction theorems. Lemma 7.10 shows a decomposition property for weak bisimulation; Lemmas 7.11 and 7.12 show properties of the processes $\mathcal{O}_n\langle r_o, r_n, F_1, \ldots, F_n\rangle$, introduced in Section 5 to represent the encoding of $\lambda$-terms with a variable in head position.

For a process $P$, we let $\mathcal{N}_P$ be the set of names along which $P$ can perform an action, i.e.,

$$\mathcal{N}_P = \{a \ : \ \text{for some and } P' \text{ and } \mu \text{ with subject } a,\ P \stackrel{\mu}{\Longrightarrow} P'\}\,.$$

LEMMA 7.10

1. Suppose $fn(P_1, P_2) \cap \left(\mathcal{N}_{Q_1} \cup \mathcal{N}_{Q_2}\right) = \emptyset$. Then $P_1 \mid Q_1 \approx P_2 \mid Q_2$ implies $P_1 \approx P_2$.
2. Let $x, q \notin \mathrm{fn}(F, G)$. Then $!\,x(q).\,F\langle q\rangle \approx\ !\,x(q).\,G\langle q\rangle$ implies $F \approx G$.

*Proof* We first prove (1). Relation

$$\mathcal{R} = \{(P_1, P_2) \ : \ P_1 \mid Q_1 \approx P_2 \mid Q_2 \quad \text{for some } Q_1, Q_2 \text{ with } fn(P_1, P_2) \cap \left(\mathcal{N}_{Q_1} \cup \mathcal{N}_{Q_2}\right) = \emptyset\}$$

is a weak bisimulation. The proof is straightforward: Since $\mathrm{fn}(P_1, P_2) \cap (\mathcal{N}_{Q_1} \cup \mathcal{N}_{Q_1}) = \emptyset$, no interaction between $P_i$ and $Q_i$ is possible, $i = 1, 2$. Moreover, if all bound names of actions of $P_1$ and $P_2$ are fresh, then the side condition of $\mathcal{R}$ is preserved.

Now assertion (2). We have to show that $F\langle q\rangle \approx G\langle q\rangle$. We can assume, without loss of generality, that $q$ is different from $x$. Since $!\,x(q).F\langle q\rangle \approx\ !\,x(q).G\langle q\rangle$ and $!\,x(q).F\langle q\rangle \xrightarrow{x(q)} F\langle q\rangle \mid\ !\,x(q).F\langle q\rangle$, we have, for some $P$,

$$!\,x(q).G\langle q\rangle \stackrel{x(q)}{\Longrightarrow} P \approx F\langle q\rangle \mid\ !\,x(q).F\langle q\rangle. \tag{12}$$

Since $x$ does not occur in $G\langle q\rangle$, no interaction between $G\langle q\rangle$ and $!\,x(q).G\langle q\rangle$ may have occurred; therefore $P$ is of the form $P_G \mid\ !\,x(q).G\langle q\rangle$, for some $P_G$ s.t.

$$G\langle q\rangle \Longrightarrow P_G. \tag{13}$$

Thus (12) can be written as $P_G \mid\ !x(q).G\langle q\rangle \approx F\langle q\rangle \mid\ !x(q).F\langle q\rangle$. From this, we get

$$P_G \approx F\langle q\rangle \tag{14}$$

using the assertion (1) of the lemma, since $\mathcal{N}_{!x(q).G\langle q\rangle} = \mathcal{N}_{!x(q).F\langle q\rangle} = \{x\}$ and $x$ is not free in $F\langle q\rangle$ and $P_G$. In a symmetric way (just exchange $F$ and $G$), we can derive, for some $P_F$,

$$F\langle q\rangle \Longrightarrow P_F, \qquad \text{and} \qquad P_F \approx G\langle q\rangle. \tag{15}$$

Now, we exploit (13-15) to show that $F\langle q\rangle \approx G\langle q\rangle$: For this, we take

$$\mathcal{R} = \{(F\langle q\rangle, G\langle q\rangle), (G\langle q\rangle, F\langle q\rangle)\} \cup \approx$$

and show that it is a weak bisimulation. Suppose $F\langle q\rangle \xrightarrow{\mu} Q_F$. We show how $G\langle q\rangle$ can match this move: Since $F\langle q\rangle \approx P_G$, we have $P_G \stackrel{\hat{\mu}}{\Longrightarrow} Q_G \approx Q_F$; therefore, using (13), $G\langle q\rangle \Longrightarrow P_G \stackrel{\hat{\mu}}{\Longrightarrow} Q_G \approx Q_F$, which closes the bisimulation. The case in which $G\langle q\rangle$ moves first is analogous. □

LEMMA 7.11 If $\mathcal{O}_n\langle r_o, r_n, F_1, \ldots, F_n\rangle \approx \mathcal{O}_m\langle r_o, r_m, G_1, \ldots, G_m\rangle$, then $n = m$.

*Proof* If $n \neq m$, then one of the two processes can perform more consecutive output actions than the other. □

LEMMA 7.12 It holds that

$$\mathcal{O}_n\langle r_o, r_n, F_1, \ldots, F_n\rangle \approx \mathcal{O}_n\langle r_o, r_n, G_1, \ldots, G_n\rangle \text{ iff } F_i \approx G_i \text{ for all } 1 \le i \le n.$$

*Proof* The implication from right to left can be inferred from the congruence properties of $\approx$. Thus, we only have to consider the implication from left to right. We proceed by induction on $n$. We only consider the inductive case. Let

$$P \stackrel{\text{def}}{=} \mathcal{O}_n\langle r_o, r_n, F_1, \ldots, F_n\rangle, \qquad Q \stackrel{\text{def}}{=} \mathcal{O}_n\langle r_o, r_n, G_1, \ldots, G_n\rangle.$$

By Lemma 5.2(1), the only transitions they can perform are

$$P \xrightarrow{(\nu\, x_1, r_1)\bar{r}_o\langle x_1, r_1\rangle} \sim \mathcal{O}_{n-1}\langle r_1, r_n, F_2, \ldots, F_n\rangle \mid\ !x_1(q).\, F_1\langle q\rangle,$$

$$Q \xrightarrow{(\nu\, x_1, r_1)\bar{r}_o\langle x_1, r_1\rangle} \sim \mathcal{O}_{n-1}\langle r_1, r_n, G_2, \ldots, G_n\rangle \mid\ !x_1(q).\, G_1\langle q\rangle.$$

Let $P_1 \stackrel{\text{def}}{=} \mathcal{O}_{n-1}\langle r_1, r_n, F_2, \ldots, F_n\rangle$, and $Q_1 \stackrel{\text{def}}{=} \mathcal{O}_{n-1}\langle r_1, r_n, G_2, \ldots, G_n\rangle$. The only actions that $!x_1(q).\, F_1\langle q\rangle$ and $!x_1(q).\, G_1\langle q\rangle$ can perform are at $x_1$ and, by Lemma 5.2(1), the only actions that $P_1$ and $Q_1$ can perform are at $r_1$. Since $r_1$ is not free in $!x_1(q).\, F_1\langle q\rangle$ and $!x_1(q).\, G_1\langle q\rangle$, and $x_1$ is not free in $P_1$ and $Q_1$, using Lemma 7.10(1) twice we infer

$$!x_1(q).F_1\langle q\rangle \approx\ !x_1(q).G_1\langle q\rangle \quad \text{and} \quad P_1 \approx Q_1$$

Now from the former we get $F_1 \approx G_1$ using Lemma 7.10(2); from the latter we get $F_i \approx G_i$, $2 \le i \le n$ using the inductive assumption. □

We are now ready to prove that open applicative bisimilarity coincides with λ-observation equivalence.

THEOREM 7.13 (SOUNDNESS OF $\mathcal{D}$ W.R.T. $\simeq^{\rm o}$) $M \approx_\lambda N$ implies $M \simeq^{\rm o} N$.

*Proof* By Proposition 7.3, it suffices to prove that $\mathcal{E}[\![M]\!] \approx \mathcal{E}[\![N]\!]$ implies $M \simeq^{\rm o} N$. If $\mathcal{E}[\![M]\!] \approx \mathcal{E}[\![N]\!]$ then, for any $p$, $\mathcal{E}[\![M]\!]\langle p\rangle \approx \mathcal{E}[\![N]\!]\langle p\rangle$. We prove that

$$\mathcal{R} = \{(M, N) \;:\; \mathcal{E}[\![M]\!]\langle p\rangle \approx \mathcal{E}[\![N]\!]\langle p\rangle, \quad \text{for some } p\}$$

is an open applicative bisimulation. First, suppose $M \Longrightarrow \lambda x.M'$. We have to find $N'$ s.t. $N \Longrightarrow \lambda x.N'$ and $(M', N') \in \mathcal{R}$. From $M \Longrightarrow \lambda x.M'$ and Proposition 5.4(2), we get

$$\mathcal{E}[\![M]\!]\langle p\rangle \stackrel{p(x,q)}{\Longrightarrow} \gtrsim \mathcal{E}[\![M']\!]\langle q\rangle.$$

Since $\mathcal{E}[\![M]\!]\langle p\rangle \approx \mathcal{E}[\![N]\!]\langle p\rangle$, there is $P''$ s.t.

$$\mathcal{E}[\![N]\!]\langle p\rangle \stackrel{p(x,q)}{\Longrightarrow} P'' \approx \mathcal{E}[\![M']\!]\langle q\rangle. \tag{16}$$

We can decompose $\mathcal{E}[\![N]\!]\langle p\rangle \stackrel{p(x,q)}{\Longrightarrow} P''$ into $\mathcal{E}[\![N]\!]\langle p\rangle \Longrightarrow\stackrel{p(x,q)}{\longrightarrow} P' \Longrightarrow P''$, for some $P'$. Then, using Proposition 5.5(1-2), we infer that there are $N'$ and $N''$ s.t. $N \Longrightarrow \lambda x.\, N'$ and $N' \Longrightarrow N''$ with $P' \gtrsim \mathcal{E}[\![N']\!]\langle q\rangle$ and

$$P'' \gtrsim \mathcal{E}[\![N'']\!]\langle q\rangle. \tag{17}$$

Moreover, by validity of beta equality (Corollary 6.9),

$$\mathcal{E}[\![N']\!]\langle p\rangle \approx \mathcal{E}[\![N'']\!]\langle p\rangle. \tag{18}$$

Since $\lesssim \subseteq \approx$, we can combine (16), (17) and (18) and derive $\mathcal{E}[\![M']\!]\langle q\rangle \approx \mathcal{E}[\![N']\!]\langle q\rangle$; hence $(M', N') \in \mathcal{R}$, which concludes the case.

Now, suppose $M \Longrightarrow xM_1 \ldots M_n$, for some $x$ and $M_1, \ldots, M_n$. We suppose $n > 0$; the case $n = 0$ is simpler. We have to find $N_1, \ldots, N_n$ s.t. $N \Longrightarrow xN_1 \ldots N_n$ and $M_i \mathcal{R} N_i$, for all $i$.

From Proposition 5.4(4), we get

$$\mathcal{E}[\![M]\!]\langle p\rangle \stackrel{(\nu q)\tilde{x}\langle q\rangle}{\Longrightarrow} \gtrsim \mathcal{O}_n\langle q, p, \mathcal{E}[\![M_1]\!], \ldots, \mathcal{E}[\![M_n]\!]\rangle$$

and, from $\mathcal{E}[\![M]\!]\langle p\rangle \approx \mathcal{E}[\![N]\!]\langle p\rangle$ and Proposition 5.5(4), for some $m$ and $N_1, \ldots, N_m$,

$$\mathcal{E}[\![N]\!]\langle p\rangle \stackrel{(\nu q)\tilde{x}\langle q\rangle}{\Longrightarrow} \gtrsim \mathcal{O}_m\langle q, p, \mathcal{E}[\![N_1]\!], \ldots, \mathcal{E}[\![N_m]\!]\rangle \tag{19}$$

with $\mathcal{O}_n\langle q, p, \mathcal{E}[\![M_1]\!], \ldots, \mathcal{E}[\![M_n]\!]\rangle \approx \mathcal{O}_m\langle q, p, \mathcal{E}[\![N_1]\!], \ldots, \mathcal{E}[\![N_m]\!]\rangle$. From this and Lemmas 7.11 and 7.12 we infer that $m = n$ and that $\mathcal{E}[\![M_i]\!] \approx \mathcal{E}[\![N_i]\!]$, for all $i$. Moreover, from (19) and Proposition 5.5(4) we infer that

$$N \Longrightarrow xN_1 \ldots N_n.$$

Since $\mathcal{E}[\![M_i]\!] \approx \mathcal{E}[\![N_i]\!]$, for any $p$, $\mathcal{E}[\![M_i]\!]\langle p\rangle \approx \mathcal{E}[\![N_i]\!]\langle p\rangle$; hence $(M_i, N_i) \in \mathcal{R}$. □

THEOREM 7.14 (COMPLETENESS OF $\mathcal{D}$ W.R.T. $\simeq^{\mathrm{o}}$) $M \simeq^{\mathrm{o}} N$ implies $M \approx_\lambda N$.

*Proof* We show that

$$\mathcal{R} = \bigcup_p \{(\mathcal{E}[\![M]\!]\langle p\rangle, \mathcal{E}[\![N]\!]\langle p\rangle) \ : \ M \simeq^{\mathrm{o}} N\}.$$

is closed under substitutions and is a weak bisimulation up-to context and up-to $\gtrsim$. By Theorem 3.11, this implies $\mathcal{R} \subseteq \approx$.

First, we show that $\mathcal{R}$ is closed under substitutions. The free names of a process $\mathcal{E}[\![M]\!]\langle p\rangle$ are $\{p\} \cup \{x : x \in \mathrm{fv}(M)\}$. Therefore, for all name substitution $\sigma$ there is a variable substitution $\rho$ s.t.

$$\mathcal{E}[\![M]\!]\langle p\rangle\sigma = \mathcal{E}[\![M\rho]\!]\langle \sigma(p)\rangle.$$

Lemma 7.8 shows that $\simeq^{\mathrm{o}}$ is closed under variable substitutions; hence $\mathcal{R}$ is closed under name substitutions.

Now we show that $\mathcal{R}$ is a weak bisimulation up-to context and up-to $\gtrsim$. Let $(\mathcal{E}[\![M]\!]\langle p\rangle, \mathcal{E}[\![N]\!]\langle p\rangle) \in \mathcal{R}$, and suppose that $\mathcal{E}[\![M]\!]\langle p\rangle \xrightarrow{\mu} P$; there are four cases to consider, according to whether $\mu$ is a silent, an input, a free output or a non-free output. The first three cases are simpler, so we only show the argument for the last case (to handle the last case we shall need both up-to context and up-to $\gtrsim$, whereas for the first three cases up-to $\gtrsim$ is enough).

Thus, suppose $\mu$ is a non-free output. By Proposition 5.5(4), $\mu = (\nu q)\,\bar{x}\langle q\rangle$, and there are $x$ and $M_1, \ldots, M_n$ s.t. $M = xM_1 \ldots M_n$ and $P \gtrsim \mathcal{O}_n\langle q, p, \mathcal{E}[\![M_1]\!], \ldots, \mathcal{E}[\![M_n]\!]\rangle$. Since $M \simeq^{\mathrm{o}} N$, there are $N_1, \ldots, N_n$ s.t.

$$N \Longrightarrow xN_1 \ldots N_n \tag{20}$$

and

$$M_i \simeq^{\mathrm{o}} N_i, \qquad \text{for all } 1 \leq i \leq n. \tag{21}$$

Now, from (20), by Proposition 5.4 we get

$$\mathcal{E}[\![N]\!]\langle p\rangle \overset{(\nu q)\,\bar{x}\langle q\rangle}{\Longrightarrow} \gtrsim \mathcal{O}_n\langle q, p, \mathcal{E}[\![N_1]\!], \ldots, \mathcal{E}[\![N_n]\!]\rangle$$

and from (21) we get

$$(\mathcal{E}[\![M_i]\!]\langle r\rangle, \mathcal{E}[\![N_i]\!]\langle r\rangle) \in \mathcal{R},$$

for all $r$. Summarising, we have obtained that

$$\begin{array}{ll} \mathcal{E}[\![M]\!]\langle p\rangle \stackrel{(\nu q)\bar{x}\langle q\rangle}{\Longrightarrow} & \gtrsim \mathcal{O}_n\langle q, p, \mathcal{E}[\![M_1]\!], \ldots, \mathcal{E}[\![M_n]\!]\rangle, \\ \mathcal{E}[\![N]\!]\langle p\rangle \stackrel{(\nu q)\bar{x}\langle q\rangle}{\Longrightarrow} & \gtrsim \mathcal{O}_n\langle q, p, \mathcal{E}[\![N_1]\!], \ldots, \mathcal{E}[\![N_n]\!]\rangle, \text{ and} \\ (\mathcal{E}[\![M_i]\!]\langle r\rangle, \mathcal{E}[\![N_i]\!]\langle r\rangle) \in \mathcal{R}, & \text{for all } r \text{ and } 1 \le i \le n. \end{array}$$

This is enough, because $\mathcal{R}$ is a bisimulation up-to context and up-to $\gtrsim$. □

It is worth stressing that the "up-to context and up-to $\gtrsim$" technique allows us a substantial simplification of the proof of Theorem 7.14.

## 8 Conclusions

We summarise the results of Proposition 7.3, Theorems 7.9, 7.13 and 7.14:

COROLLARY 8.1 For all $M, N \in \Lambda^o$ it holds that

$$M \approx_\lambda N \text{ iff } \mathcal{E}[\![M]\!] \approx \mathcal{E}[\![N]\!] \text{ iff } M \simeq^o N \text{ iff } LT(M) = LT(N).$$ □

In words, on $\lambda$-terms all these equalities coincide: Equality in the model, equality induced by $\pi$-calculus observational equivalence via the encoding, open applicative bisimilarity, and equality of the Lévy-Longo trees.

In the case of the *affine* $\lambda$-calculus, which collects those $\lambda$-terms in which a variable may occur free at most once in any subterm, we can also add the original applicative bisimulation ($\simeq$) to these equalities (Boudol and Laneve have proved that on the affine $\lambda$-calculus applicative bisimulation coincides with the Lévy-Longo Tree equality [7]).

In this paper, as behavioural equivalence for $\pi$-calculus we have used (weak) bisimulation. However, the main results presented (construction of the $\lambda$-model, full abstraction) should be largely independent of the choice of behavioral equivalence. Bisimulation is widely accepted as the finest extensional behavioural equivalence one would like to impose on processes; on the opposite extreme, as the coarsest equivalence, one normally places *trace equivalence*. We believe that, on processes encoding $\lambda$-terms, bisimulation and trace equivalence coincide. This is suggested by the determinism of the encoded lazy $\lambda$-terms. It also confirmed by our results and results by Boudol and Laneve [7]. We have related bisimulation on these processes to the Lévy-Longo Tree equality; Boudol and Laneve have related the Lévy-Longo Tree equality to *Morris's context-equivalence* of the *lambda calculus with multiplicities*, a form of enriched lazy $\lambda$-calculus. Roughly, Morris's context-equivalence equates two terms if they have the same convergence properties in all contexts; in process algebras, it usually coincides with trace equivalence. (On this topic, see also [8].)

## Acknowledgements

A series of discussions with Robin Milner has inspired the work reported in the paper. I also benefited from comments by Matthew Hennessy and Gordon Plotkin, and from suggestions by Mads Tofte and the two anonymous referees. This paper is dedicated to Robin Milner. Working in his group has been a great fortune for me, and it is my greatest pleasure to acknowledge my debt to him with a paper in this book.

## References

[1] S. Abramsky. The lazy lambda calculus. In D. Turner, editor, *Research Topics in Functional Programming*, pages 65–116. Addison-Wesley, 1989.

[2] S. Abramsky and L. Ong. Full abstraction in the lazy lambda calculus. *Information and Computation*, 105:159–267, 1993.

[3] S. Arun-Kumar and M. Hennessy. An efficiency preorder for processes. *Acta Informatica*, 29:737–760, 1992.

[4] H. Barendregt. *The Lambda Calculus: Its Syntax and Semantics*, volume 103 of *Studies in Logic*. North Holland, 1984. Revised edition.

[5] G. Boudol. Asynchrony and the $\pi$-calculus. Technical Report 1702, INRIA Sophia Antipolis, 1992.

[6] G. Boudol. A lambda calculus for (strict) parallel functions. *Information and Computation*, 108(1):51–127, 1994.

[7] G. Boudol and C. Laneve. The discriminanting power of multiplicities in the $\lambda$-calculus. *Information and Computation*, 126(1):83–102, 1996.

[8] G. Boudol and C. Laneve. $\lambda$-calculus, Multiplicities and the $\pi$-calculus. In this volume.

[9] G. Ferrari, U. Montanari, and P. Quaglia. A $\pi$-calculus with explicit substitutions: the late semantics. *Proc. MFCS'94*, LNCS 841. Springer Verlag, 1994.

[10] M. Hansen, H. Hüttel, and J. Kleist. Bisimulations for asynchronous mobile processes. In *Proc. Tbilisi Symposium on Language, Logic, and Computation*, 1996. Also available as BRICS Report No. EP-95-HHK, Aalborg University, Denmark 1996.

[11] J. R. Hindley and G. Longo. Lambda calculus models and extensionality. *Zeitschr. f. math. Logik und Grundlagen d. Math.*, 26:289–310, 1980.

[12] J. R. Hindley and J. P. Seldin. *Introduction to Combinators and $\lambda$-calculus*. Cambridge University Press, 1986.

[13] K. Honda. Two bisimilarities for the $\nu$-calculus. Technical Report 92-002, Keio University, 1992.

[14] K. Honda and M. Tokoro. On asynchronous communication semantics. *Proc. ECOOP '91*, LNCS 612, pages 21–51. Springer Verlag, 1992.

[15] B. Jonsson and J. Parrow. Deciding bisimulation equivalences for a class of non-finite-state programs. *Information and Computation*, 107:272–302, 1993.

[16] J.-J. Lévy. An algebraic interpretation of equality in some models of the lambda calculus. In *Lambda Calculus and Computer Science Theory*, LNCS 37, pages 147–165. Springer Verlag, 1975.

[17] G. Longo. Set theoretical models of lambda calculus: Theory, expansions and isomorphisms. *Annales of Pure and Applied Logic*, 24:153–188, 1983.

[18] A. Meyer. What is a model of the lambda calculus? *Information and Control*, 52:87–122, 1982.

[19] R. Milner. Fully abstract models of typed lambda calculus. *Theoretical Computer Science*, 4:1–22, 1977.

[20] R. Milner. Functions as processes. Research Report 1154, INRIA, Sophia Antipolis, 1990. Final version in *Journal of Mathem. Structures in Computer Science* 2(2):119–141, 1992.

[21] R. Milner. The polyadic $\pi$-calculus: a tutorial. Technical Report ECS–LFCS–91–180, LFCS, Dept. of Comp. Sci., Edinburgh Univ., October 1991.

[22] R. Milner, J. Parrow, and D. Walker. A calculus of mobile processes, (Parts I and II). *Information and Computation*, 100:1–77, 1992.

[23] R. Milner and D. Sangiorgi. Barbed bisimulation. *Proc. 19th ICALP*, LNCS 623, pages 685–695. Springer Verlag, 1992.

[24] L. Ong. *The Lazy Lambda Calculus: an Investigation into the Foundations of Functional Programming*. PhD thesis, University of London, 1988. Also Prize Fellowship Dissertation, Trinity College, Cambridge, 256 pp.

[25] G. D. Plotkin. Call by name, call by value and the $\lambda$-calculus. *Theoretical Computer Science*, 1:125–159, 1975.

[26] G. D. Plotkin. LCF as a programming language. *Theoretical Computer Science*, 5:223–255, 1977.

[27] D. Sangiorgi. *Expressing Mobility in Process Algebras: First-Order and Higher-Order Paradigms*. PhD thesis CST–99–93, Department of Computer Science, University of Edinburgh, 1992.

[28] D. Sangiorgi. An investigation into functions as processes. In *Proc. MFPS'93*, LNCS 802, pages 143–159. Springer Verlag, 1993.

[29] D. Sangiorgi. The lazy lambda calculus in a concurrency scenario. *Information and Computation*, 111(1): 120–153, 1994.

[30] D. Sangiorgi. Locality and non-interleaving semantics in calculi for mobile processes. *Theoretical Computer Science*, 155:39–83, 1996.

[31] D. Sangiorgi and R. Milner. The problem of "Weak Bisimulation up to". *Proc. CONCUR '92*, LNCS 630, pages 32–46. Springer Verlag, 1992.

## Contributors

**Samson Abramsky**
University of Edinburgh

**J. C. M. Baeten**
Eindhoven University of Technology

**Sergey Berezin**
Carnegie Mellon University

**J. A. Bergstra**
Utrecht University

**Gérard Berry**
Centre de Mathimatiques Appliquies
Ecole des Mines de Paris

**Lars Birkedal**
Carnegie Mellon University

**Gérard Boudol**
INRIA, Sophia-Antipolis

**Edmund Clarke**
Carnegie Mellon University

**Pierre Collete**
University of Manchester

**Robert L. Constable**
Cornell University

**Pierre-Louis Curien**
CNRS, University Paris

**Jaco de Bakker**
CWI, Amsterdam

**Uffe H. Engberg**
University of Aarhus

**William Ferreira**
University of Sussex

**Fabio Gadducci**
University of Pisa

**Mike Gordon**
University of Cambridge

**Robert Harper**
Carnegie Mellon University

**Matthew Hennessy**
University of Sussex

**Yoram Hirshfeld**
Tel Aviv University

**Tony Hoare**
University of Oxford

**Gérard Huet**
INRIA, Rocquencourt

**Paul B. Jackson**
University of Edinburgh

**Alan S. A. Jeffrey**
University of Sussex

**Somesh Jha**
Carnegie Mellon University

**He Jifeng**
University of Oxford

**Cliff B. Jones**
University of Newcastle

**Cosimo Laneve**
University of Bologna

**Xinxin Liu**
State University of New York at Stony Brook

**Will Marrero**
Carnegie Mellon University

**Faron Moller**
Uppsala University

**Ugo Montanari**
University of Pisa

**Pavel Naumov**
Cornell University

**Mogens Nielsen**
Aarhus University

**Joachim Parrow**
Royal Institute of Technology (KTH), Stockholm

**Lawrence C. Paulson**
University of Cambridge

**Benjamin C. Pierce**
University of Pennsylvania

**Gordon Plotkin**
University of Edinburgh

**M. A. Reniers**
Eindhoven University of Technology

**Amokrane Saïbi**
INRIA, Rocquencourt

**Augusto Sampaio**
Federal University of Pernambuco

**Davide Sangiorgi**
INRIA, Sophia Amtipolis

**Scott A. Smolka**
State University of New York at Stony Brook

**Eugene W. Stark**
State University of New York at Stony Brook

**Christopher Stone**
Carnegie Mellon University

**Mads Tofte**
IT University in Copenhagen

**David N. Turner**
An Teallach, Ltd.

**Juan Uribe**
Cornell University

**Franck van Breugel**
York University

**David Walker**
Oxford University

**Glynn Winskel**
University of Aarhus